ALASKA, a bibliography

1570-1970

with subject index

Compiled by

ELSIE A. TOURVILLE

G. K. HALL & CO., 70 LINCOLN STREET, BOSTON, MASS. 1974

Library of Congress Cataloging in Publication Data

Tourville, Elsie A
    Alaska: a bibliography, 1570-1970.

    1. Alaska--Bibliography. I. Title.
Z1255.T67   016.91798   74-8468
ISBN 0-8161-1063-8

ISBN 0-8161-1063-8

CONTENTS

PREFACE

The present-day need for a reference work devoted solely to Alaska and Alaska-related subjects inspired compilation of this bibliography.

The time span covered is 1570 to 1970. Books and pamphlets are recorded. Among the classifications to be found are children's books, photograph albums, fiction, and cook books. There are translations in many languages, including Alaskan Indian and Eskimo dialects.

Printings in which Alaska is represented by chapters or sections as opposed to entire content are included. Geographic factors influenced inclusion of material which is not directly Alaskan in content. Tentative attempts to define the limits of the northern land mass were made in the year 1570 by Abraham Ortelius [no.3420]; and, in the year 1597 by Cornelius Wytfliet [no.4984]. Printings in the early and mid-eighteenth century revealed continuing cartographic disparities. In the late eighteenth century and throughout the nineteenth, when explorers, fur traders, gold-seekers, missionaries and tourists began to make their way North, boundaries were yet vaguely known. Therefore, those printings which chronicle exploration along the northwest coast of North America, Arctic exploration, and the gold rush of '98 in the Yukon Territory of neighboring Canada were recorded when some portion of content was considered to be important in relation to the geographic region that is now Alaska.

The evolution of Alaska as a Territory, and in 1959, as a State is reflected in two distinctive kinds of printings. Both are well-represented in this bibliography. One is promotional material encompassing commercial brochures, prospectuses and travel guides. The other is Alaskan imprints. The Alaskan imprint frequently provides insight into an Alaskan's personal philosophy. His comment can be pertinent, practical and often-times pungent.

Publications of the United States government and those of the State (or Territory) of Alaska have been omitted, with the exception of the occasional federal printing that has been reprinted in a trade edition. Serial publications were also omitted, as were unpublished works in the form of manuscripts, diaries, and theses.

Entries are alphabetized and numbered. There is extensive cross-referencing. The index is by subject. Items in the index are by author, abbreviated title, date and bibliography number. To indicate general geographic setting, a coded number in parenthes accompanies the bibliography number.

PREFACE

Information used to form entries derives from a wide variety of sources. These were carefully noted in the compiler's files for every entry.

Of the total effort expended to compile the bibliography, many aspects of research were carried out during visits of varying length and at various times to the following libraries:

North Star Borough Library, Fairbanks, Alaska.
  (Formerly George Thomas Memorial Library and
  Fairbanks Public Library).
Elmer E. Rasmuson Library, University of Alaska,
  College, Alaska.
Seattle Public Library, Seattle, Washington.
Summer Institute of Linguistics Library,
  Fairbanks, Alaska. (Wycliffe Bible Translators).
U. S. Library of Congress, Washington, D. C.

In addition to opportunities for research provided by the libaries listed above, access to several small private collections in Fairbanks, Alaska also proved to be extremely helpful. The compiler's own catalogued collection of Alaskana, which now numbers close to fifteen hundred volumes, was another source of great usefulness.

In discussion of sources, it should not be overlooked that individuals opened doors to research. Appreciation is expressed to persons who generously responded to written requests for information, to library staff members who graciously made facilities available, to private collectors who shared their libraries, and to those in the book field who through the years diligently searched out and quoted Alaskana.

The list of references which were used in compilation of this work is divided into two general categories. The first consists of bibliographies, selected reference works, and selected texts. The second contains other written sources of a miscellaneous nature. The number in brackets indicates a volume to be found in the bibliography.

REFERENCES

Bibliographies, Selected Reference Works, Selected Texts.

ADDICOTT, WARREN O.   Neogene marine mollusks of the Pacific Coast of North America;   an annotated bibliography, 1797-1969. Washington, D. C., 1973.   201p.   graph, map, index.   (U. S. Geological Survey Bull. 1362)   [Miocene and Pliocene age]

ALASKA MUNICIPAL LEAGUE 1972 DIRECTORY. Juneau, 1972. (20)p. wrps.

ALASKA PRESS CLUB. Alaska blue book. Anchorage, 1963. [no. 103]

ALASKA RESOURCE DEVELOPMENT DIRECTORY.   Fairbanks, Cooperative Extension Service, University of Alaska, 1971.   rev. 52p.   wrps.

ALASKA STATE DIVISION OF STATE LIBRARIES, Juneau.   Bibliography of Alaska native organizations and selected references on Alaska native land claims.   July 1971.   22p.   wrps.

ALASKA STATE DIVISION OF STATE LIBRARIES, Juneau.   Some books about Alaska received in 1970.   n. d.   9p.

ALASKA STATE LIBRARY ASSOC., Bibliographic Committee.   A cache of Alaska reading currently in print.   Fiction-Non-fiction.   Jan. 1967.   folder.

ALASKA, State (Territory).   SEE ALSO
      Fritts, C. E.;   Wickersham, James.

ALASKAN BOUNDARY TRIBUNAL.   Volume 2 (0f 7).   pp.511-520. *Geographical and topographical information relative to southeastern Alaska.   Maps and charts.*   [also atlases and books containing maps] Washington, D. C., 1904. (Doc. 162. 58th Congress. 2d Sess.)

ALASKAN BOUNDARY TRIBUNAL.   Volume 4 (0f 7).   pp.243-250. *Maps and charts.*   [continued from vol. 2] Washington, D. C., 1903. (Doc. 162.   58th Congress.   2d Sess.)

ALASKAN SCIENCE CONFERENCE of the National Academy of Sciences, Washington, Nov. 9-11, 1950.   Proceedings.   Washington, D. C., 1951.   ix,216p.   map.   (National Research Council Bull. 122)

ALASKAN SCIENCE CONFERENCE of the National Academy of Sciences, Washington, Nov. 9-11, 1950.   Selected papers.   Washington, D.C., 1952.   vi,305p.   illus. diagrs. tables, maps.   (Arctic Institute of N. A. Spec. Pub. no. 1)

ANDREWS, CLARENCE LEROY.   *Some Russian books on Alaskan history, by C. L. Andrews.*   pp.75-87, Pacific Northwest Quarterly, vol. 28, no. 1.   January 1937.   ftntes.

ALASKAN BIBLIOGRAPHY

REFERENCES

Bibliographies, Selected Reference Works, Selected Texts.

ANDREWS, CLARENCE LEROY. *The historical Russian library of Alaska.* pp.201-204, Pacific Northwest Quarterly, vol. 29, no. 2. April 1938.

ARCTIC BIBLIOGRAPHY.
Vols. 1-12. Washington, D. C., 1953-65.
Vol. 13. Montreal, McGill Univ. Press, 1967.
Vols. 14-15. Montreal, McGill-Queen's Univ. Press, 1969 and 1971.

BALCOM, MARY G. The Catholic Church in Alaska. Chicago, Adams Press, [c1970] 149p. illus. bibliog.[p.143], index.

BARBEAU, C. M. Totem poles. Ottawa, 1964. Vol. 2(of 2 vols.) [bibliog. pp.845-848] [no. 394]

BARTSCH, PAUL and others. A bibliography and short biographical sketch of William Healey Dall (with one plate). Washington, D.C., 1946. pl. (Smithsonian Misc. Coll. vol. 104, no. 15. (Pub. 3810) January 30, 1946)

BEAN, TARLETON H. *Bibliography of the Salmon of Alaska and adjacent regions. (Issued March 9, 1893).* pp.39-49, Bulletin of U. S. Fish Commission, Washington, D. C., 1894. Vol. 12 for 1892.

BENSIN, B. M. Russian Orthodox Church in Alaska 1794-1967. Toms River, N. J., n. d. [1966 ?] [no bibliog.] [no. 506]

BERTON, P. Klondike fever. N. Y., 1958. [pp.439-445, note on sources. pp.446-457, bibliog.] [no. 547]

BOOKS IN PRINT. N. Y., Bowker, var. dates. Author, Title, Subject Guides.

BRINSMADE, E. M. Books on Alaska for young people. Sitka, 1961. [no. 662]

BRINSMADE, E. M. Children's books on Alaska. Sitka, 1956. [no. 663]

CHURCH MISSIONS PUBLISHING CO. Indian tribes and missions. A hand book ... [c1926] [no. 931]

COOK, DOROTHY E. and ESTELLE A. FIDELL, comps. Fiction catalog 1942-1946. Supplement to the 1941 edition. A subject, author and title list of 1451 works of fiction in the English language with annotations. N. Y., Wilson, 1947. 205p.

CUMULATIVE BOOK INDEX. N. Y., Wilson, 1965-1969.

REFERENCES

Bibliographies, Selected Reference Works, Selected Texts.

DARTMOUTH COLLEGE LIBRARY. Dictionary catalog of Stefansson collection on polar regions. Boston, 1967. [no. 1187]

DOLPHIN, GEORGE R., comp. Marine atlases in the Dartmouth College Library; a descriptive list presented to Nathaniel L. Goodrich, Librarian. Hanover, N. H., 1950. 29p. illus. facsims. wrps. (Bull. Extra no. 1)

FAIRBANKS PUBLIC LIBRARY, Children's Department. Alaska and the northern lands. Books added to the Children's Room in 1964-65. Feb. 1966. 2p. [later to become North Star Borough Library]

FAIRBANKS PUBLIC LIBRARY. Alaska non-fiction acquisitions list. var. dates [1964-1967] [later to become North Star Borough Library]

FARQUHAR, P. and M. P. ASHLEY. A list of publications relating to the mountains of Alaska. N. Y., 1934. [no. 1528]

FOOTE, D. C. and S. K. MacBAIN. Selected regional bibliography for human geographical studies of native populations in Central Alaska. Montreal, 1964. [no. 1594]

FORTUINE, ROBERT. Health of Eskimos; bibliography 1857-1967. Hanover, N. H., 1968. [no. 1615]

FREDERICK, ROBERT A. *Caches of Alaskana, library and archival sources of Alaskan history.* pp.39-79, Alaska Review, Fall and Winter, 1966-67. Vol. 2, no. 3.

FRITTS, CRAWFORD E. and MILDRED E. BROWN. Bibliography of Alaskan geology 1831-1918. College, Alaska State Division of Geological Survey, Dept. of Natural Resources, 1971. 88p. map, index, wrps.
    ... 1919-1949. College, 1971. 92p.
    ... 1950-1959. College, 1971. 83p.
    ... 1960-1964. College, 1971. 81p.
    ... 1965-1968. College, 1972. 112p. [by C. E. Fritts and
          Ellen J. Tuell]

FULLER, GRACE HADLEY. Alaska, a selected list of recent references. Washington, D. C., 1943. 181p. index. (U. S. Library of Congress, Division of Bibliography) [authorized facsim. edition by University Microfilms, Ann Arbor, Mich., 1968]

FULLER, GRACE HADLEY. Aleutian Islands; a list of references. Washington, D. C., 1943. 41p. index. (U. S. Library of Congress, Division of Bibliography) [authorized facsim. edition by University Microfilms, Ann Arbor, Mich., 1968]

ALASKAN BIBLIOGRAPHY

REFERENCES

Bibliographies, Selected Reference Works, Selected Texts.

GABRIELSON, I. N. and F. C. LINCOLN. The birds of Alaska. Harrisburg, Penna., 1959. [pp.854-908, bibliog.] [no. 1668]

GARFIELD, BRIAN. The thousand-mile war. World War II in Alaska and the Aleutians. N. Y., Ballantine Books, 1971. (Ballantine no. 02152-5-125) 405p. front.(dble. map), illus. bibliog. index. [pp.376-378, bibliographic remarks. pp.379-394, bibliog.]

GILL, THEODORE. Bibliography of the fishes of the Pacific Coast of the United States to the end of the year 1879. Washington, D. C., 1882. 73p. index, wrps. (Bull. of U. S. National Museum no. II)

GREAT BRITAIN NATIONAL MARITIME MUSEUM. Catalogue of the Library. Volume 1. Voyages and travels. London, H. M. S. O., 1968. 403p. illus. maps(2 fold.), indexes. [has chronology of voyages, index of ships]

GREAT BRITAIN NATIONAL MARITIME MUSEUM. Catalogue of the Library. Volume 2. Part 1. Biography. General index. Volume 2. Part 2. Biography. Reference index. London, H. M. S. O., 1969. 2 vols. 501p. and pp.503-977.

GREAT BRITAIN NATIONAL MARITIME MUSEUM. Catalogue of the Library. Volume 3. Parts 1 and 2. Atlases and cartography. London, H. M. S. O., 1971. 2 vols. 654p. and pp.655-1166. illus. facsims. index.

GRIER, MARY C. Oceanography of the North Pacific Ocean, Bering Sea and Bering Strait; a contribution toward a bibliography. N. Y., 1969. [no. 1855]

HINCKLEY, TED C. *William Henry Seward and his Sitka address of August 12, 1869; notes on the heretofore unpublished and probably correct version.* pp.49-61, Alaska Review, no. 16. 1972. ftntes.

HOWES, WRIGHT, comp. U.S.iana (1650-1950) Revised and enlarged edition. N. Y., Bowker, 1962. (Newberry Library) 652p.

HULTÉN, ERIC. Flora of Alaska. Stanford, Calif., 1968.[pp.987-994, bibliog.] [no. 2227]

KLEIN, B. and D. ICOLARI. Reference encyclopedia of the American Indian. N. Y., B. Klein and Co., 1967. [pp.189-329, bibliog.]

LADA-MOCARSKI, VALERIAN. Bibliography of books on Alaska published before 1868. New Haven, 1969. [no. 2579]

ALASKAN BIBLIOGRAPHY

REFERENCES

Bibliographies, Selected Reference Works, Selected Texts.

MAAKESTAD, J. L., edit. The Lutheran Church in Alaska. Brief histories of the Lutheran Churches in Alaska in chronological order of their founding. Anchorage, Ken Wray's Print Shop, 1967. 54p. illus. front. wrps. [has no bibliog.]

MARSHALL, GEORGE. *Bibliography of Robert Marshall; a supplement.* pp.31-35, Living Wilderness, vol. 19, no. 49. Summer 1954. illus.

MARSHALL, GEORGE. *Robert Marshall as a writer. Bibliography of Robert Marshall, 1901-1939. With reviews of his published works and biographical appreciations.* pp.14-23, Living Wilderness, vol. 16, no. 38. Autumn 1951.

MATTHEWS, Wm., comp. Canadian diaries and autobiographies. Berkeley, University of Calif. Press, 1950. 130p. index(6p.)

MEEKER, RUTH ESTHER. Six decades of service 1880-1940. A history of the Woman's Home Missionary Society of the Methodist Episcopal Church. no pl., [c1969] 405p. index. [pp.291-304, history of Alaskan missions, no bibliog.]

MOORE, TERRIS. Mt. McKinley; pioneer climbs. College, Alaska, 1967. [pp.173-175, explanation of ftntes. pp.177-195, literature references] [no. 3166]

MORGAN, MURRAY. Bridge to Russia; those amazing Aleutians. N.Y., 1947. [pp.205-213, bibliog.] [no. 3181]

MURDOCK, G. P. Ethnographic bibliography of N. A. New Haven, 1960. [no. 3246]

NEW SOUTH WALES PUBLIC LIBRARY, Sydney. Bibliography of Capt. James Cook. Sydney, 1970. [no. 3294]

OLSEN, MICHAEL L. A preliminary list of references for the history of agriculture in Pacific Northwest and Alaska. Davis, Calif., 1968. [no. 3404]

ORTH, DONALD J. Dictionary of Alaska place names. Washington, D. C., 1967. 1084p. maps. (U. S. Geological Survey Prof. Paper no. 567) [pp.6-44, sources of names. pp.1072-1084, selected bibliography]

OSWALT, WENDELL. Alaskan Eskimos. S. F., 1967. [pp.261-279, bibliog.] [no. 3436]

ALASKAN BIBLIOGRAPHY

REFERENCES

Bibliographies, Selected Reference Works, Selected Texts.

OSWALT, WENDELL. Mission of change in Alaska. Eskimos and Moravians on the Kuskokwim. San Marino, Calif., 1963. [has bibliographic ftntes.] [no. 3437]

OSWALT, WENDELL. The Kuskokwim River drainage, Alaska; an annotated bibliography. College, Alaska, 1965. 73p. wrps. (Univ. of Alaska Anthropological Papers, vol. 13, no. 1)

PILLING, JAMES CONSTANTINE. Bibliography of the Eskimo language. Washington, D. C., 1887. 116p. index, wrps. (U. S. Bureau of Ethnology, Smithsonian Institution)

POTTER, LOUISE. Old times on Upper Cook's Inlet. Anchorage, 1967. [p.43, source materials] [no. 3663]

RESEARCH INSTITUTE OF ALASKA. Alaska survey and report. Anchorage, 1970. 2 vols. [nos. 3784-5]

SABIN, JOSEPH. Dictionary of books relating to America. N. Y., 1868-1936.

SMITH, CHARLES W. Pacific Northwest Americana. Portland, Ore., 1950. [no. 4193]

STATON, FRANCES M. and MARIE TREMAINE. Bibliography of Canadiana. Toronto, 1965. Supplement, 1959. [no. 4289]

[STEFANSSON, VILHJALMUR] Bibliography of articles Vilhjalmur Stefansson January 1960. [Hanover, Dartmouth College Library, n. d. (The Stefansson Collection)] 18p.

[STEFANSSON, VILHJALMUR] *Stefansson Collection news.* pp.44-48, Polar Notes, no. 6, June 1955.

[STREETER, THOMAS WINTHROP] The celebrated collection of Americana formed by the late Thomas Winthrop Streeter. Index. A dictionary check-list of the seven sale catalogues October 1966-October 1969. Compiled by Edward J. Lazare. N. Y., Parke-Bernet Galleries, 1970. 352p. index.

[STREETER, THOMAS WINTHROP] The Thomas Winthrop Streeter collection of Americana. Volume 6. The Pacific west, Oregon, British Columbia, Alaska, Canada, Hawaii, maps. N. Y., Parke-Bernet Galleries, 1969. pp.2284-2766. index.

SUNDBORG, GEORGE. Bibliography and abstracts on the subject of agriculture in Alaska, 1867-1942. Juneau, U. S. National Resources Planning Board, Region X, 1942. 139p.

ALASKAN BIBLIOGRAPHY

REFERENCES

Bibliographies, Selected Reference Works, Selected Texts.

TEWKESBURY'S WHO'S WHO IN ALASKA. Seattle, 1947. [no. 4482]

THOMAS, TAY. Cry in the wilderness. Anchorage, [c1967] [pp.123-124, bibliog.] [no. 4500] [churches]

TORONTO PUBLIC LIBRARY. Canadian northwest; bibliographic sources ... Hudson's Bay Co., fur trade and early history Canadian northwest. Toronto, 1931. [no. 4557]

TRANSPORT REQUIREMENTS FOR THE GROWTH OF NORTHWEST NORTH AMERICA. Letter from the Chairman, Alaska International Rail and Highway Commission. Volume 2 (of 3 vols.) Research report by Battelle Memorial Institute. May 25, 1961. Washington, D. C., 1961. var. p. tables, maps(fold.), reference lists, wrps. (House Doc. no. 176, vol. 2. 87th Congress, 1st Session)

ULLOM, JUDITH C. Folklore of the North American Indians; an annotated bibliography. Washington, D. C., 1969. 126p. index. (U. S. Library of Congress, Children's Book Section, General Reference and Bibliog. Division)

U. S. BUREAU OF INDIAN AFFAIRS, Department of the Interior. Economic development of American Indians and Eskimos; 1930 through 1967; a bibliography. Compiled by Departmental Library. Washington, Sept. 1968. 263p. (Bibliography Series no. 10)

U. S. BUREAU OF OUTDOOR RECREATION, Dept. of the Interior. Index of selected outdoor recreation literature. Washington, D. C., 1967-1969. vols. 1-4.

U. S. FEDERAL FIELD COMMITTEE FOR DEVEOPMENT PLANNING IN ALASKA, Anchorage, Alaska. Alaska natives and the land. Washington, D. C., Oct. 1968. 565p. illus. figs. maps(some col., 1 loose fold.), bibliog. wrps. [bibliog. pp.556-565]

U. S. FOREST SERVICE, Dept. of Agriculture. Selected references on forest and related natural resources. Washington, D. C., 1963. rev. May 1963. 16p.

U. S. LIBRARY OF CONGRESS. A guide to the study of the United States of America. Representative books reflecting the development of American life and thought. Prepared under the direction of Roy P. Basler by Donald H. Mugridge and Blanche P. McCrum. Washington, D. C., 1960. iii-xv,193p. index. (General Reference and Bibliography Division. Reference Dept.)

U. S. LIBRARY OF CONGRESS. Catalog of book subjects. var. years. ... Catalog of printed cards. var. years. ... National union catalog. var. years.

REFERENCES

Bibliographies, Selected Reference Works, Selected Texts.

U. S. LIBRARY OF CONGRESS, Law Library. Russian administration of Alaska and the status of the Alaskan natives. By Vladimir Gsovski, Chief of the Foreign Law Section. Washington, D. C., 1950. 99p. ftntes. appendixes, bibliographic survey, index. (Senate Doc. 152. 181st Congress. 2d Session)

U. S. SEE ALSO
   Addicott, W. O.   Lamson-Scribner, F.
   Alaska Resource Develop. Dir.   Orth, D. J.
   Alaskan Boundary Tribunal   Pilling, J. C.
   Arctic bibliography   Sundborg, Geo.
   Bartsch, P.   Transport requirements ...
   Bean, T. H.   [Battelle report]
   Fuller, J. C.

WALKER, ERNEST P. and others. Mammals of the world. Volume III. A classified bibliography. By orders, geographically and general. Selected list of periodicals. Baltimore, Johns Hopkins Press, 1964. 769p.

WASHBURN, H. B. Mt. McKinley and Alaska Range in literature. Descriptive bibliography. Boston, 1951. [no. 4748]

WICKERSHAM, JAMES. A bibliography of Alaskan literature 1724–1924. Cordova, Cordova Daily Times Print, 1927. 635p. (Misc. Pub. Alaska Agricultural College and School of Mines, vol. 1)

WOODBRIDGE, H. C., JOHN LONDON and GEORGE H. TWENEY. Jack London; a bibliography. Georgetown, Calif., 1966. [no. 4955]

WORKMAN, W. B. and K. W. WORKMAN. *Some perspectives in the anthropology of the North Pacific rim.* pp.62–80, Alaska Review, no. 16, 1972. [pp.74–80, bibliog.]

YARMOLINSKY, AVRAHM. Aleutian manuscript collections. N. Y., 1944. [no. 4988]

YARMOLINSKY, AVRAHM. Kamchadal and Asiatic manuscript collections. N. Y., 1947. [no. 4989]

Other Sources. [Bracketed notes indicate extent of compiler's survey of periodicals]

ALASKA CONSTRUCTION AND OIL, Seattle, Wash. Monthly periodical, published since 1959. [var. single issues]

ALASKA INDUSTRY, Anchorage, Alaska. Monthly periodical, published since 1969. [var. single issues]

ALASKAN BIBLIOGRAPHY

REFERENCES

Other Sources. [Bracketed notes indicate extent of compiler's survey of periodicals]

ALASKA JOURNAL, Anchorage, Alaska. Quarterly periodical, published since 1970. [all issues to current]

ALASKA LIFE, Seattle, Wash. Monthly periodical, founded in 1937. No longer published. [var. issues, 1946-1947]

ALASKA MAGAZINE, Anchorage, Alaska. Monthly periodical. (formerly Alaska Sportsman, founded in 1935) [all issues to current]

ALASKA REVIEW, Anchorage, Alaska. Periodical published irregularly since 1963. (Alaska Methodist University) [all issues to current]

ALASKA SPORTSMAN. SEE ALASKA MAGAZINE.

ALASKA STATE HISTORICAL LIBRARY. *Correspondence*.

BEAVER, Winnipeg, Manitoba, Canada. Quarterly periodical. (The Hudson's Bay Co.) [issues 1969 to current, var. earlier single issues]

FAIRBANKS DAILY NEWS-MINER, Fairbanks, Alaska. Periodical, daily newspaper. [issues 1963 to 1973, also var. yearly special issues, see also OIL AND RESOURCE DEVELOPMENT]

HERITAGE OF ALASKA. nos. 1-9. Written and produced by Herb Hilscher. [Anchorage, Alaska, National Bank of Alaska, 1968] series of folders.

[McDONALD, ROBERT] *Photocopies* of several title pages of translations in Takudh (Tukudh) Indian dialect by *Archdeacon* McDonald. Original volumes in Rare Book Collection, Elmer E. Rasmuson Library, University of Alaska, College, Alaska.

A MAGYAR ALASZKA-IRODALOM./Bibliográfiai vázlat./I. Alaszkáról szóló magyar Kiadványok. n. d. [ca 1960 ?] *Typewritten list*. [one and a half pages (total of 3) Second part general works on U. S. for Hungarian immigrants]

OIL AND RESOURCE DEVELOPMENT. Weekly supplement to Fairbanks Daily News-Miner. [var. issues 1969-1973]

PATHFINDER, Valdez, Alaska. Monthly periodical first published in 1920. (Pioneers of Alaska) [var. single issues, 1920, 1921 and 1923]

REFERENCES

Other Sources. [Bracketed notes indicate extent of compiler's
    survey of periodicals]

PEABODY MUSEUM OF ARCHAEOLOGY AND ETHNOLOGY, Harvard University,
Cambridge, Mass. *Photocopies* of cards for Alaskan subjects in
card catalog.

SITKA PRINTING CO., Sitka, Alaska. *Correspondence.*

SPIRIT OF MISSIONS, N. Y. Monthly periodical. [Episcipal
Church] [bound volumes 1896-99, 1900, 1903-06 and 1909. Single
issues 1920-22]

TONGASS PUBLISHING CO. *Correspondence.*

TUNDRA TIMES, Fairbanks, Alaska. Weekly periodical, published
from 1962. [all issues to current]

U. S. SMITHSONIAN INSTITUTION, Washington, D. C. *Photocopies*
of cards for Alaskan subjects in card catalog. (Office of Anthropology and Archaeology, Reference Library)

UNIVERSITY OF WASHINGTON LIBRARIES, Pacific Northwest Collection,
Seattle, Washington. *Correspondence.*

WRANGELL SENTINEL PRESS, Wrangell, Alaska. *Correspondence.*

ABBREVIATIONS

adverts. advertisements
annot. annotated
anr. another
append. appendix
Ausg. Ausgabe
auth. author

bd. band (Swedish)
Bd. Band (German)
bibliog. bibliography
bull. bulletin

c copyright
ca circa
chapt. chapter
co-auth. co-author
co-edit. co-editor
col. colored
comp. compiled, compiler
cont. continued, continuously
contemp. contemporary

dble. double
dblep. doubledpage
diagr. diagram
dupl. duplicated

ed. edition
edit. edited, editor
enl. enlarged

facsim. facsimile
fict. fiction
fig. figure
fold. folded, folding
front. frontispiece
ftnte. footnote

gloss. glossary

hrsg. herausgegeben

illus illustrated, illustrator
impr. impression
incls. includes
introd. introduction

juv. juvenile

ℓ leaf, leaves

mimeo. mimeographed
misc. miscellaneous
mod. modern
mtd. mounted

n.d. no date of publication
n.s. new series
no. number
no pl. no place (of pub.)
nr. near

occas. occasional

p., pp. page, pages
photo photograph
pl. plate
poet. poetry
port. portrait
[pseud.] [pseudonym]
predisl. predisloviem
print. printer, printing
pt. part
pub. publication, publisher

red. redakt͡sei
rept. report
rev. revised
ringb. ringbound

sect. section
sep. separate
suppl. supplement

T., Th. Teil, Theil
t.p. title page
tipografii͡a
tr. translation, translator
trad. traduit

var. dates various dates
var. ed. variant editions,
          various editions
var. p. various paylngs
vocab. vocabulary
vol. volume

USE OF BRACKETS [   ]
    to enclose information
        not on title page
    to enclose annotation at
        end of entry

BIBLIOGRAPHY

A

Abbott, A. SEE no. 1847, Green, P.

Abridgment voyage ... 1784. SEE no. 1919, [Cook, Jas.]

Abridgment voyage ... 1789. SEE no. 3650, [Portlock, N.]

According to Grandfather ... 1965. SEE no. 2748, Loftus, A.

According to Mama ... 1956. SEE no. 249, Anderson, L. D.

According to Papa ... 1957. SEE no. 3506, Paul, D.

Account of *California* ... 1748. SEE no. 1344, [Drage, T. A.]

ACKERMAN, ROBERT E. Archaeological survey, Glacier Bay National Monument, southeastern Alaska. Pullman, Washington, 1964 and 1965. (Washington State University, Laboratory of Anthropology, Report of Investigations, pt. 1, no. 28 and pt. 2, no. 36)   1

ACKERMAN, ROBERT E. Prehistory in the Kuskokwim-Bristol Bay region, southwestern Alaska. Pullman, Washington, 1964. (Washington State University, Laboratory of Anthropology, Report of Investigations, pt. 1, no. 26)   2

Across continent ... [1890 ?] SEE no. 3352, Northern Pac. R.R.

Acts ... in Haida. 1898. SEE no.664, British & For. Bible Soc.

ADAM, LEONHARD. Nordwestamerikanische Indianerkunst. [TITLE TR. Northwest American Indian art] Berlin, E. Wasmuth, [1923] 44p. pls. bibliog. (Orbus Pictus, Bd. 17)   3

ADAMOV, ARKADIĬ GRIGOR'EVICH. G. I. Shelekhov; pod red M. S. Bodnarskogo. [TITLE TR. G. I. Shelekhov; edited by M. S. Bodnarskiĭ] Moskva, Gosudarstvenooe Izdatel'stvo Geograficheskoĭ Literatury, 1952. 43p. illus. port. map.[SEE ALSO no. 5]   4

ADAMOV, ARKADIĬ GRIGOR'EVICH. G. I. Shelekhov, zamechatel'nyi russkiĭ moreplavatel' i issledovatel'. Stenogramma publichnoĭ lekt͡sii, prochitannoĭ v Moskve. [TITLE TR. G. I. Shelekhov, a remarkable Russian seaman and explorer. Stenograph of a public lecture delivered in Moscow] Moskva, Pravda, 1951. 30p. port. map. [cf no. 4]   5

ADAMOV, ARKADIĬ GRIGOR'EVICH. Pervye russkie issledovateli Ali͡aski. Posobie dli͡a uchiteleĭ srednei shkoly. [TITLE TR. The first Russian explorers of Alaska. A manual for high school teachers] Moskva, Gosudarstvennoe Uchebno-pedagogicheskoe izd-vo Ministerstva prosveshchenii͡a RSFSR, 1950. 124p. illus. maps (incl. 1 fold.), bibliog.   6

ALASKAN BIBLIOGRAPHY

ADAMOV, ARKADIĬ GRIGOR'EVICH. Po neizvedannym putīam. [TITLE TR. On unknown roads] Leningrad, Goskul'tprosvetizdat, 1950. 136p. illus. map(fold.) [Russian America] 7

ADAMS, ANDY. Alaska ghost glacier mystery. N. Y., Grosset and Dunlap, [c1961] 175p. front. (A Biff Brewster Mystery Adventure, no. 6) 8

ADAMS, BEN. Alaska; the big land. N.Y., Hill and Wang, [c1959] 213p. photos, sketches by George Ahgupuk, maps, bibliog. index. 9

ADAMS, BEN. The last frontier; a short history of Alaska. N.Y., Hill and Wang, [c1961] 181p. photos, sketches by George Ahgupuk, map(dble.), glossary, bibliog. index. 10

Adams, Glen. SEE no. 2354, Jewitt, J. R. Narrative ... 1815.

ADAMS, JOHN and OTHERS. A bibliography of Canadian plant geography. Toronto, University of Toronto Press, 1928-47 and Ottawa, King's Printer, 1951-. In progress. 9 pts. [pts. 1-5 incl. Alaska] 11

Address ... Alaska-Yukon-Pacific Exposition ... 1909.
    SEE no. 145, Alaska-Yukon-Pacific Exposition.

ADELUNG, JOHANN CHRISTOPH and JOHANN SEVERIN VATER. Mithridates oder allgemeine Sprachenkunde mit dem Vater Unser als Sprachprobe in bey nahe fünf hundert Sprachen und Mundarten, von Johann Christoph Adelung. Churfürstle, Sächsischem Hofrath und Ober-Bibliothekar. Erster[-Vierter] Theil. Berlin, in der Vossischen Buchhandlung, 1806[-1817] 4 vols. [vol. 3 in 3 pts.] ANR. Hildesheim and N. Y., G. Olms, 1970. reprint. 12

ADLER, BRUNO WILHELM KARL ADOLPH. Der nordasiatische Pfeil; ein Beitrag sur Kenntnis der Antropogeographie des asiatischen Nordens. [TITLE TR. The northern Asiatic arrow] Leiden, E. J. Brill, 1901. 40p. illus. map. [also issued as supplement to Internationales Archiv für Ethnographie, vol. 14, 1901. Author's Ph.D. thesis] 13

ADNEY, TAPPAN. The Klondike stampede. N. Y., Harper, 1900. [c1899] 471p. pls.(some fold.), facsims.(some fold.), maps(incl. 1 dble.), append. ANR. Seattle, Shorey Book Store, 1968. (Shorey Photocopy no. 111) ANR. Fairfield, Wash., Ye Galleon Press, 1968. ltd. ed. [1900 ed. HAS COVER TITLE The Klondike stampede of 1897-1898] 14

ADRIAN, CHARLES R. Governing our fifty states and their communities. N. Y., McGraw-Hill, 1963. 130p. ftntes. bibliog. (Foundations of American Government and Political Science) 15

Adventures of Yankee ... 1831. SEE no. 2664, [Ledyard, John]

AGNEW, EDITH J. Leo of Alaska. N. Y., Friendship Press, 1958.
114p. illus. 16

AGNEW, EDITH J. My Alaska picture story book. N. Y., Friendship
Press, 1948. 56p. illus. photos. 17

AGRANAT, GRIGORIĬ ABRAMOVICH and V. F. PUZANOVA. Energetika,
sel'skoe i promyslovoe khozĭaistvo Amerikanskogo Severa. [TITLE
TR. Energetics, agriculture, fishing and hunting economy of the
American North] Moskva, Izd-vo Akademii nauk SSSR, 1962. 184p.
tables, maps(fold.), bibliog. (Akademiĭa Nauk SSSR Gosĕkonomsovet SSSR. Sovet po izucheniĭu proizvoditel'nykh sil, Komissiĭa
po problemam Severa) [Alaska and northern Canada] 18

AGRANAT, GRIGORIĬ ABRAMOVICH, A. B. KUPRIĬANOV and V. F. PUZANO-
VA. Naselenie i resursey Amerikanskogo Severa. [TITLE TR. The
population and resources of the American North] Moskva, Izd-vo
Akademii nauk SSSR, 1963. 230p. tables, maps, bibliog. 19

AGRANAT, GRIGORIĬ ABRAMOVICH. Novaĭa tekhnika i osvoenie zaru-
bezhnogo Severa. [TITLE TR. New technology and development of
the foreign North] Moskva, Izd-vo Akademii nauk SSSR, 1960. 126p.
map(fold.), bibliog. (Akademiĭa Nauk SSSR. Sovet po izucheniĭu
proizvoditel'nykh sil. Komissiĭa po problemam Severa) 20

AGRANAT, GRIGORIĬ ABRAMOVICH, A. B. KUPRIĬANOV and V. F. PUZANO-
VA. Promyshlennost' i transport Amerikanskogo Severa. Otv. re-
daktor S. V. Slavin. [TITLE TR. Industry and transportation in
the American North] Moskva, Izd-vo Akademii nauk SSSR, 1962.
271p. tables, maps(some fold.), bibliog. (Gosĕkonomsovet SSSR,
Sovet po izucheniĭu proizvoditel'nykh sil. Komissiĭa po problemam Severa) [Alaskan and Canadian Arctic] 21

Agranat, Grigoriĭ Abramovich. SEE ALSO no. 5020,
    Zagoskin, L. A. Puteshestviĭa ... 1956.

Ahgupuk, George Aden. SEE nos.
    9, Adams, Ben. Alaska ... [c1959];
    10, Adams, Ben. Last frontier ... [c1961];
    1847, Green, P. I am Eskimo ... 1959;
    2429, Keithahn, E. L. Alaskan igloo tales. 1958;
    2429, Keithahn, E. L. Igloo tales. 1944.

AHMAOGAK, ROY and DONALD H. WEBSTER. Iñupiam ukaluŋi; Eskimo
reader, No. 1, No. 2, and No. 3. Fairbanks, Summer Institute of
Linguistics, [1963 ?] 3 vols. 16p., 20p., and 24p. illus. (Wycliffe Bible Translators) 22

Ahmaogak, Roy. SEE ALSO nos.
    4445, Tagarook, P. Jesus kamanaḳtuat ... n. d.;
    4746, Wartes, Wm. C. Utḳiaġvik Iñupiat ... 1959;
    4772, Webster, D. H. Iñupiat Suuvat ? [c1968]

3

Ahsoak, Russell. SEE no. 2382, Jones, L. B. Tundra tales.1959.

Aichinger, Gerhard. SEE no. 23, Aick, Gerhard [pseud.]

AICK, GERHARD [pseud.] Schweres Eis voraus ! Der Kampf um die
Nordwest-Passage. [TITLE TR. Heavy ice ahead ! The struggle
for the Northwest Passage] Wien-Heidelberg, Carl Ueberreuter,
1953. 239p. pls. endmaps. [Author is Gerhard Aichinger]   23

Akademiia nauk. SEE nos. 4615-17, U. S. S. R.

AKASOFU, SYUN-ICHI. Polar and magnetospheric substorms. Dor-
drecht, Holland, D. Reidel, [c1968] xviii, 280p. illus. maps,
bibliogs. (Astrophysics and Space Science Library, vol. 11)
[based, in part, on research conducted at Geophysical Institute,
University of Alaska, College, Alaska]   24

AKERS, FLOYD [pseud.] The Boy Fortune Hunters in Alaska. Chicago,
Reilly and Britton, [1908] 271p. [author is Lyman Frank Baum]25

AKIF'EV, IVAN NIKOLAEVICH. Na dalekii Siever za zolotom; iz
dnevnika krugosvietnago puteshestviia 1900 goda. [TITLE TR. To
the far North for gold; from a diary of a round-the-world voyage
in 1900] Saint Petersburg, Kommerch. Skoropech. E. Tile, 1902.
200p. illus. [brief visit to Alaska]   26

Aknik, SEE no. 1847, Green, P. I am Eskimo ... 1959.

Akugluk. SEE nos. 5026-31, Zibell, Wilfried.

ALASKA. no pl., n. d. [Anchorage, 1967 ?] 22p. illus. maps.
[highway sketches]   27

Alaska. 1915. SEE no. 35, Alaska Bur., Seattle Chamber of Com-
    merce.

Alaska. [19__ ?] SEE no. 3353, Northern Pacific RR. Co.

Alaska. 1930. SEE no. 3486, Pan Pacific Progress.

Alaska. [1909]-1910. SEE no. 4203, Smith, Maude P.

Alaska; a sketch ... 1883. SEE no. 1478, [Episcopal Church]

Alaska; a spectacular ... 1868. SEE no. 5015, Z., Q.

Alaska ahead. 1939. SEE no. 112, Alaska Steamship Co.

ALASKA ALMANAC. Seattle, 1905 through 1907. [compiled by W. M.
Sheffield] Seattle, 1908 through 1909. [compiled by E. S. Har-
rison] var. p. illus. maps.   28

Alaska, along ... [191_ ?] SEE no. 4830, White Pass & Yukon Ry.

ALASKA AMALGAMATED COPPER CO. Reports on properties. Spokane, 1906. 24p.   29

Alaska - America's ... 1954. SEE no. 96, Alaska Opportunist.

Alaska and Alaska Highway. 1949. SEE no. 192, American Automobile Assoc.

Alaska and the gold fields of the Yukon. 1898. SEE no. 1834, Great Northern Ry.

Alaska and the gold fields of the Yukon ... [1899 ?] SEE no. 3343, North-American Transportation & Trading Co.

Alaska and the scenic Yukon ... [19__ ?] SEE no. 4831, White Pass & Yukon Ry.

Alaska and the Yukon and the triangle tour ... 1930. SEE no. 820, Canadian National Railroad.

ALASKA AND THE YUKON, general information. no pl., 1937.   30

Alaska and the Yukon Terr. 1916. SEE no. 4832, White Pass & Yukon Ry.

Alaska and the Yukon Terr. [19__ ?] SEE no. 4610, Union Book & Pub. Co.

Alaska, Atlin ... [1928 ?] SEE no. 4833, White Pass & Yukon Ry.

ALASKA BAR ASSOC., Juneau. Alaska Bar Association and sketch of judiciary, Anno Domini 1901. Compiled by Arthur K. Delaney. S. F., Sanborn, Vail & Co., Printers and Binders, 1901. 79p. 31

ALASKA BAR ASSOC., Juneau. Proceedings at its annual meeting held in the city of Juneau, November 25, 1898. Constitution, officers and roll of members included for the year 1899. Douglas City, Douglas Island News Pub. House, 1899. 16p.   32

Alaska blue book. 1963. SEE no. 103, Alaska Press Club.

THE ALASKA BOOK; story of our northern treasureland. Chicago, J. C. Ferguson, pub., 1960. 320p. photos(some col.), maps. 33

ALASKA BUREAU, Great Falls, Montana. Alaska, direct route, highway log to Fairbanks. [ca 1949] map.   34

ALASKA BUREAU, Seattle Chamber of Commerce. Alaska. Seattle, 1915. 16p.   35

ALASKA BUREAU, Seattle Chamber of Commerce. Alaska, "our frontier wonderland." Seattle, 1913. 92p. illus. maps. ANR. 1913. 2d ed. rev. 93p. illus. maps. OTHERS 1914-1921, var. ed. var.p. 36

ALASKA BUREAU, Seattle Chamber of Commerce. Alaska tour 1913.
Published by Oregon-Washington Railroad and Navigation Company.
Seattle, 1913.   37

ALASKA BUREAU, Seattle Chamber of Commerce. Develop Alaska dinner, auspices of Alaska Bureau and Arctic Club, November 27, 1911.
Seattle, A. A. Sherman, 1911. 16p. [program]   38

ALASKA BUREAU, Seattle Chamber of Commerce. The nation needs
coal. Permit the coal of Alaska to be used. Seattle, 1917.
17p.   39

ALASKA BUREAU, Seattle Chamber of Commerce. The origin, activities and supporters of the Bureau. Seattle, 1915. 20p.   40

Alaska business directory ... [c1948] SEE
    no. 4480, Tewkesbury, Wm.

ALASKA BUYERS' GUIDE: a classified business directory for Alaskans, with listings from Seattle, Tacoma, Portland, San Francisco. Seattle, 1957. 64p. illus.   41

Alaska, Calif., Yellowstone ... 1925. SEE
    no. 3757, Raymond & Whitcomb Co.

ALASKA CENTENNIAL; as told in one thousand pictures ... featuring
Anchorage; "air crossroads of the world." Edited by Marjorie
Roberts. [Anchorage, Alaska Publications, 1967] 432p. illus.
photos.   42

ALASKA CENTRAL RAILROAD CO. Map of surveyed route; statement
by George W. Dickinson, President. Seattle, 1903. 51p.   43

ALASKA CENTRAL RAILROAD CO. Official prospectus. Seattle,
Yerkes Printing Co., 1902. 16p. illus. map.   44

ALASKA CENTRAL RAILROAD CO. Through the Alaska gateway to the
world's richest store-house of mineral wealth. Seattle, 1906.
26p.   45

Alaska citizen band radio directory. 1968. SEE
    no. 3626, Polar Bear Citizen Band Club.

ALASKA COAL CO. Prospectus. S. F., Women's Cooperative Printing Union, 1871. 18p.   46

ALASKA COAST CO. Southwestern Alaska route. Seattle, 1907.
16p.   47

ALASKA COAST EXPLORATION CO. Six months prospecting along the
coast of Alaska for $300. Seattle, 1898. 8p.   48

ALASKA COMMERCIAL CO. Alaska fur seals. Letter addressed to Hon. Nathan F. Dixon, Chairman, Committee on Commerce, House of Representatives. [no pl., 1870] 20p.   49

ALASKA COMMERCIAL CO. Alaska seal fisheries. [no pl., 1870] 4p.   50

ALASKA COMMERCIAL CO. By-laws. S. F., 1870.   51

ALASKA COMMERCIAL CO. Reply of the Alaska Commercial Company to the charges of Governor Alfred P. Swineford of Alaska against the company in his annual report for the year 1887. [S. F., 1887 ?] 107p. maps(fold.), appends.   52

ALASKA COMMERCIAL CO. The seal and seal islands. By N. L. Jeffries, attorney for the company. [Washington, D. C. ?], 1870. 25p.   53

ALASKA COMMERCIAL CO. To the Klondike gold fields and other points of interest in Alaska. [S. F., H. S. Crocker Co., 1898] 73p. photos, map(fold.) EARLIER ED. ? HAS COVER TITLE   To the Klondike and Alaska gold fields. S. F., 1897]   54

Alaska Commercial Co. SEE ALSO nos.
    760, Buynitzky, S. M. English-Aleut. vocab. 1871;
    2168, Honcharenko, A. Pervonachaljnoe ... 1871;
    2302, Is the trade of Alaska Terr. ... 1871;
    2375, Johnston, S. P. Alaska Commercial Co. ... 1940;
    2475, Kitchener, L. D. Flag over North. 1954.

ALASKA COPPER CO. Alaska Copper Company office, Seattle, Washington: mines, Copper Mountain, Alaska. Seattle, [1902 ?] 35p. illus. map(dble.), diagrs.   55

Alaska Copper Co. SEE ALSO no. 2496, Knight's island ...[1905?]

ALASKA COPPER CORP. Report of Alfred B. Iles. April 3, 1913. N. Y., 1913. 7p.   56

ALASKA CRIPPLED CHILDREN'S ASSOC. and SHISHMAREF DAY SCHOOL. Eskimo cook book; prepared by students of Shishmaref Day School, Shishmaref, Alaska. no pl., n. d. [2d ed., pre1952] 36p. illus. index, wrps. mimeo. [four inches by five and three-quarters inches in size] ANR. Anchorage, Alaska Crippled Children's Assoc., [c1952] [four inches by five inches in size]   57

ALASKA CRIPPLED CHILDREN'S ASSOC. Out of Alaska's kitchens. Ketchikan, Ketchikan Alaska Chronicle, 1958. 4th print. 241p. illus. photos(col.)   58

Alaska cruises ... [1912 ?] SEE no. 3444, Pacific Coast Steamship Co.

Alaska Day Festival, Inc. SEE no. 1946, Hardcastle, R.

Alaska Development and Mining Co. SEE
    no. 2440, Kennecott Copper Corp.

ALASKA DEVELOPMENT CO. Coal and oil. Seattle, Homer M. Hill
Pub. Co., 1898. 16p.   59

Alaska, direct route ... [ca 1949] SEE
    no. 34, Alaska Bureau, Great Falls.

ALASKA DIRECTORY AND GAZETTEER, 1934-35·. Seattle, 1935. 422p. 60

ALASKA EARTHQUAKE; a photo story of that disaster. Edited by
Marjorie Roberts. Anchorage, Alaska Publications, 1964. (48)p.
illus.   61

Alaska earthquake, March 27, 1964. SEE
    no. 3273, National Bd. of Fire Underwriters.

Alaska earthquake pictorial. 1964. SEE
    no. 2949, Mac's Photo Service.

Alaska excursion. Season of 1915. SEE
    no. 3445, Pacific Coast Steamship Co.

Alaska excursion tours. n. d. SEE
    no. 113, Alaska Steamship Co.

Alaska excursions. SEE no. 3446, Pacific Coast Steamship Co.

Alaska; facts about Cordova. 1914. SEE
    no. 1080, Cordova, Town of.

ALASKA FACTS; what Alaska is today, a word picture of America's
last frontier and what it offers to those interested in this vast
territory. Seattle, 1945. 62p. illus. maps.   62

Alaska fisherman's almanac ... 1946. SEE
    no. 1152, Daily Alaska Fishing News.

Alaska förr och nu ... 1897. SEE
    no. 4409, Svenska Missionsförbundet i Amerika.

Alaska; frontier fur ... 1954. SEE
    no. 3456, Pacific Northwest Industries.

ALASKA FUR AND SILVER FOX CO. The story of the silver fox.
Seattle, Ivey Press, 1909. 32p. [cf no. 109]   63

Alaska fur-seal bill. 1869. SEE
    no. 209, American-Russian Commercial Co.

Alaska fur seals. [1870] SEE no. 49, Alaska Commercial Co.

Alaska glaciers ... 1906. SEE no. 114, Alaska Steamship Co.

Alaska gold fields. n. d. SEE no. 3351, Northern Navigation Co.

ALASKA HANDY GOLD MINING COMPANY of Chichagof Island, Alaska.
no pl., n. d. 4p.   64

ALASKA HERALD-FREE PRESS. Saratoga, Calif., R & E Research Associates, 1967. 4 vols. [offset reprint of Russian-American
newspaper first published in S. F., 1868-72]   65

THE ALASKA HIGHWAY. [pl. ?, ca 1944] 40p. illus. map.   66

Alaska Highway. 1955. SEE no. 802, Canada.

Alaska highway and travel guide ... [c1950] SEE no. 4481.
   Tewkesbury, Wm.

ALASKA HIGHWAY GUIDE WITH MAPS. Just published. Restrictions
removed to publish details of the Alcan. Dawson Creek, [ca 1947]
ANR. North Battleford, Saskatchewan, [ca 1949]   67

Alaska highway poems. [c1944] SEE no. 2667, Lee, Frank C.

Alaska Highway Research Co. SEE no. 3114, Milepost.

Alaska Highway sketches ... [1963 ?] SEE no. 4152, Silvers,
   Connie.

ALASKA HISTORICAL ASSOC., Juneau. Descriptive booklet on the
Alaska Historical Museum, issued by the Alaska Historical Association ... edited by Rev. A. P. Kashevaroff. Juneau, 1922. 61p.
illus. pls. OTHERS [1923 ?], 1927, 1928, 1929, [1933 ?] var. p.
                                                                     68

ALASKA HISTORICAL ASSOC., Juneau. Native Alaskan art in the
State Historical Museum, Juneau, Alaska. Photos and text by Edward L. Keithahn, Librarian and Curator. Juneau, 1959. (78)p.
pls. index. (Published jointly with Alaska Historical Library
and Museum, Juneau)   69

ALASKA HUNTING AND FISHING GUIDE. Edited by E. Fortier. Anchorage, Rhodes & Fortier, pub., 1960 1st ed. 69p. illus.
maps. ANR. 1961-62. 70p.   70

Alaska Indian basketry. 1904. SEE no. 115, Alaska Steamship Co.

Alaska Indian mythology ... 1915. SEE no. 3552, Pacific Coast
   Steamship Co.

ALASKAN BIBLIOGRAPHY

Alaska - information ... 1953. SEE no. 97, Alaska Opportunities and Highway.

Alaska information. 1916. SEE no. 4990, Young, C. Y., Co.

Alaska insurance quiz. 1969. SEE no. 3617, Piver, Jack.

Alaska interlude. [1939 ?] SEE no. 116, Alaska Steamship Co.

Alaska, its gold ... [1897 ?] SEE no. 5011, Yukon Trading, Mining & Exploration Co.

Alaska; its resources. n. d. SEE no. 4623, United States-British Columbia Corp.

ALASKA JUNEAU GOLD MINING CO. Annual reports for the years ending December 31, 1915 through 1923. no pl., n. d. 9 vols. [each year separate]   71

Alaska - Land of gold ... n. d. SEE no. 1835, Great Northern Ry.

ALASKA, LAND OF PROMISE, highway section included. Featuring the new land-sea route to Alaska. Anchorage, Armed Forces Publications, 1963. 96p. illus. ANR. Anchorage, Holiday Publications, 1963. rev. ed. 103p. illus. maps. ANR. Anchorage, Alaska Publications, [c1964] (26)27-69(11)p. photos, ports. maps, index, wrps. [editor-publisher is Marjorie Roberts]   72

ALASKA LEAGUE OF WESTERN WRITERS. Anthology of contemporary Alaskan poetry. Anchorage, Karen's Services, 1956. 1st ed. ANR. ANTHOLOGY WITH TITLE The second anthology of contemporary Alaskan poetry. Anchorage, Poets' Committee, Alaska League of Western Writers, 1957. 45p.   73

[ALASKA LIFE, Seattle] Anchorage - nerve center of Alaska. By Louis Jacobin. no pl.,[1945 ?] 22p. photos, wrps.   74

[ALASKA LIFE, Seattle] Fairbanks - the golden heart of Alaska. Bt Louis Jacobin. no pl., [1945 ?] 20p. photos, wrps.   75

[ALASKA LIFE, Seattle] Juneau - the capitol of Alaska and Douglas - city of homes. no pl., [1945 ?] 26p. photos, wrps. [Juneau ... written by Louis Jacobin: Douglas ... by Val A. Poor]
                                                            76

[ALASKA LIFE, Seattle] Ketchikan "first city in Alaska." no pl., [1945 ?] 20p. photos, wrps.   77

[ALASKA LIFE, Seattle] Nome and northwestern Alaska. There's no place like Nome. By Louis Jacobin. no pl., [1945 ?] 20p. photos, wrps. ANR. WITH TITLE Nome and the Seward Peninsula. no pl., [1945 ?]   78

[ALASKA LIFE, Seattle]   Seward - gateway to the Kenai empire.
By H. Everett Hoy. no pl., [1945 ?] 20p. photos, wrps.   79

Alaska literary directory. 1964. SEE no. 628, Bowen, R. O.

ALASKA MAGAZINE PUBLISHING CO. Book of animals and birds. With
cartoons and Alaska oddities by Weil. Ketchikan, 1940. 1st
print. (56)p. OTHERS 1942. 2d ed.: 1943. 3rd ed.: and 1944.
4th ed.   80

ALASKA MAGAZINE PUBLISHING CO. Book of pictures of "the last
frontier." With cartoons and Alaska oddities by Weil. Ketchikan, 1941. 1st print. (56)p. ANR. 1944. 3rd print.   81

ALASKA MAGAZINE PUBLISHING CO. Book of totems and Indians. With
cartoons and Alaska oddities by Weil. Ketchikan, 1942. (58)p.
ANR. 1943. (60)p.   82

ALASKA MAGAZINE PUBLISHING CO. One hundred events that built
Alaska. An Alaska Sportsman Book. With 50 pictures of scenic
Alaska. Compiled by Louis R. Huber, edited by Ethel Dassow.
Ketchikan, 1944. (52)p. photos.   83

ALASKA MAGAZINE PUBLISHING CO. The mountain wonderland, a guide
to beautiful Revilla Island in southeastern Alaska. Ketchikan,
[ca 1945] photos.   84

Alaska Magazine Publishing Co. SEE ALSO nos.
     92-93, Alaska Northwest Pub. Co.
        775, Caldwell, J. B. What to expect in Alaska ...1945.

ALASKA MEXICAN GOLD MINING CO. Annual statement, Superintendent's report, balance sheet and profit and loss account. With
statement of receipts and disbursements. For the years ending
December 31, 1893 through 1916. London, Crowther & Goodman,
1894-1917. [24 separate years in 24 vols.]   85

Alaska Mexican Gold Mining Co. SEE ALSO no. 1506,
     Exploration Co. Annual reports. 1920-24.

ALASKA MINING AND ENGINEERING SOC. Constitution and by-laws.
Juneau, n. d. 8p.   86

ALASKA MINING AND ENGINEERING SOC. Perseverance Mine meeting,
March, 1917; papers by G. T. Jackson, R. R. Van Valkenburg, and
others. Part 1. Mining industries and societies. Part 2. Gold
mines and mining. Juneau, Juneau Empire Print, 1918.   87

ALASKA MINING AND ENGINEERING SOC. Thane meeting, November 16,
1917; papers by E. V. Daveler, R. Hatch, and others. Juneau,
Juneau Empire Print, 1918.   88

Alaska mining law, Fed. ... 1950. SEE no. 3861, Roden, Henry.

Alaska mining law manual. [ca 1966] SEE no. 2075, Herbert, C. F.

Alaska mining law, with explan. ... 1913. SEE no. 3863,
    Röden, Henry.

Alaska mining laws passed ... 1915. SEE no. 3940, Saint George
    & Cathcart.

Alaska Moving Picture Co. SEE no. 1313, Dobbs' Alaska Moving
    Picture Co.

ALASKA NATIONAL BANK. New state of Alaska. [Fairbanks, 1959 ?]
36p. illus. maps.   89

ALASKA NATIVE BROTHERHOOD. Constitutions of Grand and Subordinate Camps, 1920-22. Juneau, Alaska Sunday Capitol Press, 1922.
19p.   90

"Alaska Nellie." SEE no. 2648, Lawing, Nellie (Trosper) Neal.

ALASKA NEWS AGENCY. Quake. [Anchorage ? 1964 ?] photos.   91

ALASKA NORTHWEST PUBLISHING CO. The Alaska traveler's geography. Limited edition, maps and photos Alaska Highway system, as
published in Alaska Sportsman and Milepost. Juneau, 1963. illus. maps.   92

ALASKA NORTHWEST PUBLISHING CO. The Alaskan camp cook. Trail
and kitchen tested recipes of Alaska's guides (and their wives!)
collected by the Territorial Sportsmen's Association. As seri-
ally run in Alaska Sportsman. Juneau, 1962. 1st ed. 88p. illustrated by Rie Muñoz.   93

Alaska Northwest Publishing Co. SEE ALSO nos.
        80-84, Alaska Magazine Pub. Co.;
        3114, Milepost.

ALASKA-NORTHWESTERN RAILROAD. Prospectus. N. Y., n. d. 15p. 94

Alaska Nurses' Assoc. SEE no. 3243, Muñoz, Rie.
    Nursing in North ... [c1967]

Alaska oddities ... 1958. SEE no. 4867, Wikstrom, Robert.

Alaska oil and gas handbook. 1958. SEE no. 4580, Troutman, A.

ALASKA OIL AND GUANO CO. Statement in relation to the Alaska
fisheries, by Carl Spuhn, President. no pl., 1910. 23p.   95

ALASKA OPPORTUNIST. Alaska - the last frontier. Hollywood,
Calif., 1947. ANR. WITH TITLE Alaska - America's last frontier.
Directory. 1954.   96

ALASKA OPPORTUNITIES AND HIGHWAY; Alaska - information and opportunities, highway information including new John Hart Highway.
Seattle, 1953. [Hart Highway is in Canada]   97

Alaska opportunities; register. 1947. SEE no. 3485,
     Pan Americana Pub. Co.

Alaska, "our frontier ..." 1913. SEE no. 36, Alaska Bur.

Alaska, Pacific Coast ... 1924. SEE no. 1058, Cook Co., Thos.

ALASKA-PACIFIC CONSOLIDATED MINING CO. Sixth report to stockholders. Period from January 1, 1940 to December 31, 1940. no
pl., 1940. 22p. illus. map(fold.)   98

ALASKA PACKERS ASSOC. Argo red salmon cookbook; how to eat
canned salmon. S. F., 1911. 36p.   99

ALASKA PACKERS ASSOC. influenza epidemic of 1919. Report on activities of the company on Bristol Bay. S. F., 1919. 48p. 100

ALASKA PACKERS ASSOC. Influenza epidemic of 1919. "Service,"
the true measure of any institution lies in the service it ren-
ders. S. F., 1919. 36p.   101

ALASKA PETROLEUM AND COAL CO. Prospectus. Seattle, n. d. 12p.
                                                              102

Alaska petroleum directory. SEE no. 316, Atkinson, Thos. H., jr.

Alaska; pocket edition ... 1916. SEE no. 4947, Woman's
     Amer. Baptist Home Mission Soc.

Alaska poetry 1964. SEE no. 141, Alaska Writers Workshop.

ALASKA PRESS CLUB. The Alaska blue book. Book of Alaskan facts.
Anchorage, 1963. 1st ed. 208p. illus. maps, bibliog. indexes.
                                                              103

ALASKA PROSPECTOR'S SERVICE. Gold panning, Alaska. Anchorage,
[ca 1958] maps.   104

ALASKA PUBLICITY AND TRADE AGENCY. Two hundred questions and
answers on Alaska. Seattle, 1914. 31p.   105

Alaska Railroad. SEE no. 129, Alaska, the newest homeland.

ALASKA RANGE GUIDES ASSOC. Shoot 'em in Alaska ! Fairbanks,
[19__] 24p. illus.   106

Alaska Research Co. SEE no. 3114, Milepost.

ALASKA REVIEW. Three artists of Alaska. Fred and Sara Machetanz by Joseph Lawton. William Kimura by Frank Buske. Anchorage, Alaska Methodist University, 1965. illus. (Alaskana Series, no. 1. Reprinted from: Alaska Review, pp.55-78)   107

Alaska Review. SEE ALSO no. 1645, Frederick, Robert A.

Alaska salmon recipe book. 1961. SEE no. 2712, Lind Print. Co.

Alaska's Capitol City cook book ... 1962. SEE no. 755, Business & Prof. Women's Club.

Alaska schedules ... 1939. SEE no. 117, Alaska Steamship Co.

Alaska's cooking. 1959. SEE no. 240, Anchorage Woman's Club.

Alaska seal fisheries. [1870] SEE no. 50, Alaska Commercial Co.

THE ALASKA SHORT LINE RAILWAY AND NAVIGATION CO., INC. under the laws of the State of Washington, December 1, 1903. [Seattle, 1903 ?] 36p. front.(fold. map)   108

ALASKA SILVER FOX AND FUR FARMS CO. The story of a fox. Fairbanks, n. d. 11p. [cf no. 63]   109

Alaska Sled Dog and Racing Assoc. (or) Alaskan Sled Dog and Racing Assoc. SEE no. 2705, Life in Anchorage ... 1958.

ALASKA SMELTING AND DEVELOPMENT CO. Prospectus. Seward, n. d. 16p. ANR. January 20, 1907. 20p.   110

Alaska sourdough stories. 1956. SEE no. 2511, Kosmos, Geo.

Alaska Specialties Co. SEE no. 4241, Soldier's souvenir handy book ... [1944 ?]

Alaska Sportsman. SEE nos.
     83, Alaska Magazine Pub. Co.;
     92, Alaska Northwest Pub. Co.

Alaska's struggle for self government ... [1950] SEE no. 237, Anchorage Daily Times.

ALASKA STATE FAIR, Inc., Palmer. Premiums list and directory. Second annual fair, Sept. 2-5, 1960. Palmer, 1960. 120p. illus. wrps.   111

Alaska Statehood Assoc. SEE no. 4398, Sundborg, Geo. Statehood for Alaska. 1946.

ALASKA STEAMSHIP CO. Alaska ahead. Seattle, 1939. 31p. illus. map.   112

14

ALASKA STEAMSHIP CO. Alaska excursion tours. no pl., n. d. 24p. illus. map. 113

ALASKA STEAMSHIP CO. Alaska glaciers and ice fields. By Lloyd W. MacDowell. Seattle, 1906. 18p. illus. ANR. Seattle, Shorey Book Store, 1965. facsim. reprint. 114

ALASKA STEAMSHIP CO. Alaska Indian basketry. By Lloyd W. Mac-Dowell. Seattle, 1904. (14)p. illus.(some col.) ANR. Seattle, Shorey Book Store, 1964. facsim. reprint. 115

ALASKA STEAMSHIP CO. Alaska interlude. [Seattle, 1939 ?] 24p. illus. 116

ALASKA STEAMSHIP CO. Alaska schedules, the Alaskan Line. Seattle, Frank McCafferty, 1939. illus. 117

ALASKA STEAMSHIP CO. Copper River and Northwestern Railway, April-October, 1914. Seattle, 1914. 30p. illus. maps, wrps. ANR. Seattle, 1916. 54p. illus. maps, wrps. 118

ALASKA STEAMSHIP CO. Let's go sailing sheltered seas. [c1948] 22p. 119

ALASKA STEAMSHIP CO. My Alaska cruise. Seattle, [19__ ?] 11p. illus. 120

ALASKA STEAMSHIP CO. Sailing sheltered seas to the land of the midnight sun. Seattle, Frank McCafferty, 1933. (40)p. photos, sketches, map(in pocket) 121

ALASKA STEAMSHIP CO. Scenery ahead in Alaska, the good-natured map of Alaska. Seattle, Frank McCafferty, n. d. 8p. illus. (col.) 122

ALASKA STEAMSHIP CO. Sportsman's guide to Alaska. Seattle [ca 1952] illus. 123

ALASKA STEAMSHIP CO. Statement by Alaska Steamship Company concerning the through rates and divisions with the government railroad in Alaska. Seattle, 1923. 39p. 124

ALASKA STEAMSHIP CO. This is Alaska; sailing sheltered seas. [c1948] illus. map(col.) 125

ALASKA STEAMSHIP CO. Totem poles of Alaska and Indian mythology. By Lloyd W. MacDowell. Seattle, 1905. 16p. illus. ANR. 1906. 18p. ANR. Seattle, Shorey Book Store, 1964. facsim. of 1906 ed. (Shorey Photocopy no. 62) 126

ALASKA STEAMSHIP CO. Trip to wonderful Alaska. By Lloyd W. Mac-
dowell. Seattle, 1905. 24p. illus. ANR. 1906. 32p. ANR.
Seattle, Shorey Book Store, 1964. facsim. of 1906 ed. (Shorey
Photocopy no. 63)   127

Alaska Steamship Co. SEE ALSO no. 2440, Kennecott Copper Corp.
    First annual report ... 1915.

THE ALASKA STORY. Seattle, Gothic Press, 1951. illus.   128

Alaska survey & report. [c1970] SEE no. 3785, Research Institute
    of Alaska.

Alaska tax reporter. 1963. SEE no. 998, Commerce Clearing
    House.

Alaska, the Eldorado ... 1897. SEE no. 1903, [Hall, Edw. H.]

Alaska - the 49th ... [c1958] SEE no. 4339, Sterling Pub. Co.

Alaska, "the Great Land." n. d. SEE no. 3678, Presbyterian
    Church.

Alaska - the last frontier. 1947. SEE no. 96, Alaska Opportu-
    nist.

Alaska, the marvelous ... 1899. SEE no. 3447, Pacific Coast
    Steamship Co.

ALASKA, THE NEWEST HOMELAND. Anchorage, 1930. 15p. illus.
maps. ANR. no pl., 1931. 15p. illus. maps. ANR. 1935. (issued by Alaska Railroad)   129

Alaska, the Richardson Road ... 1922. SEE no. 4634, Valdez
    Miner.

Alaska, "the treasure ... " n. d. SEE no. 3679, Presbyterian
    Church.

ALASKA TIN MINES CO. A few facts about the tin mining industry
in the United States. Providence, n. d. 4p.   130

Alaska; top o' the world tours. 1924. SEE no. 3464, Pacific
    Steamship Co.

Alaska; totem poles ... 1911. SEE no. 4948, Woman's Amer.
    Baptist Home Mission Soc.

Alaska tour 1913. SEE no. 37, Alaska Bur.

Alaska tours ... 1898. SEE no. 1836, Great Northern Ry.

ALASKA TRADE COMMITTEE. Are you going to the Klondike or Alaska gold fields ? San Francisco is the best place to start from. S. F., 1898. 12p.   131

ALASKA TRANSPORTATION, TRADING AND MINING CO. The great Klondike gold fields; an exhaustive description and full information for prospectors. N. Y., 1897. 30p.   132

ALASKA TRAVEL GUIDE. Salt Lake City, Lake Advertising Agency, 1965. 5th Northwest edition. 178p. photos, maps, index. ANR. 1967. Centennial edition. 306p. illus.(some col.), maps. [yearly]   133

Alaska Travel Research Co. SEE no. 3114, Milepost.

Alaska traveler's geography. 1963. SEE no. 92, Alaska Northwest
    Pub. Co.

ALASKA TREADWELL GOLD MINING CO. Annual statement. Superinten- dent's report, balance sheet and profit and loss account ... for the years ... 1891 through 1916. London, Crowther & Goodman, 1892-1917. [26 separate years in separate vols.]   134

Alaska Treadwell Gold Mining Co. SEE ALSO no. 1506,
    Exploration Co. Annual reports ... 1920-24.

ALASKA UNITED COPPER EXPLORATION CO. Annual reports submitted to the stockholders by the Board of Directors. Seattle, Ivy Press, January 12, 1912. 27p. ANR. 1913. 8p.   135

ALASKA UNITED COPPER EXPLORATION CO. Expert opinions, together with statistics of dividend paying copper mines of the United States and valuable articles on the manifold uses of copper; it is put out to show the possibilities of Alaska in the production of copper in the near future. no pl., 1910. 40p. illus.   136

ALASKA UNITED COPPER EXPLORATION CO. Report on properties of the company, 1906-07. Chicago, George E. Renneker, 1907. 40p.
                                                                      137

ALASKA UNITED GOLD MINING CO. Annual statement. Superinten- dent's report, Secretary's balance sheet, and profit and loss account with detailed statement of receipts and disbursements for the years ending December 31, 1896 through 1916. London, Crowther & Goodman, 1897-1917. [21 separate years in 21 sepa- rate vols.]   138

Alaska United Gold Mining Co. SEE ALSO No. 1506,
    Exploration Co. Annual reports ... 1920-24.

ALASKA UTILITIES DEVELOPMENT CO., Valdez. Will you hear the knock of opportunity ? Chicago, 1914. 16p.   139

ALASKAN BIBLIOGRAPHY

Alaska via ... Inside Passage ... 1958. SEE no. 821,
    Canadian National Steamship Lines.

Alaska via Totem Pole route. 1906. SEE no. 3448,
    Pacific Coast Steamship Co.

ALASKA WEEKLY. Alaska year book. Seattle, 1926. var. p., illus. [annual]   140

 Alaska whaling ... n. d. SEE no. 525,
    Bering Sea Commercial Co.

Alaska; who's here ... 1955. SEE no. 2335, Jeffery, Edmond C.

ALASKA WRITERS WORKSHOP. Alaska poetry 1964. The poems included in this chapbook were selected from the 1964 production of
the fifty members of the Alaska Writers Workshop by Dr. Edmund
Skellings ... Fairbanks, Commercial Printing Co., n. d. 25p.141

Alaska year book. 1926. SEE no. 140, Alaska Weekly.

Alaska, Yukon and ... [1939] SEE no. 4834,
    White Pass & Yukon Ry.

Alaska-Yukon gazetteer ... 1901. SEE no. 3628,
    Polk, R. L., & Co.

Alaska-Yukon gold book ... 1930. SEE no. 319, Atwood, Fred.

ALASKA-YUKON-KLONDIKE GOLD SYNDICATE. Klondike gold. Portland,
Maine, 1897. 10p.   142

ALASKA-YUKON-KLONDIKE GOLD SYNDICATE. Klondike gold miners.
Portland, Maine, 1897. 32p.   143

ALASKA-YUKON-KLONDIKE GOLD SYNDICATE. The story of Klondike.
Portland, Maine, 1898. 3rd ed. 32p.   144

ALASKA-YUKON-PACIFIC EXPOSITION. Address delivered at the
opening of the Alaska-Yukon-Pacific Exposition by James J. Hill.
Seattle, June 1, 1909. 26p.   145

ALASKA-YUKON-PACIFIC EXPOSITION. ... 1909; an international
fair, June 1 to October 15 [sic], showing the products, resources
advantages and scenic beauty of the Alaska-Yukon country. By
Henry Martz. Seattle, 1908. 110p. illus.   146

ALASKA-YUKON-PACIFIC EXPOSITION. ... Seattle, June 1-October 16,
1909. St. Paul, Northern Pacific Railroad, General Passenger
Dept., 1909. 45p. illus. map.   147

ALASKA-YUKON-PACIFIC EXPOSITION. General history, Alaska-Yukon-Pacific Exposition, fully illustrated, compliments of Hotel Butler Annex, Seattle, Washington. [Seattle], 1909. illus. ports.
148

ALASKA-YUKON-PACIFIC EXPOSITION. Glimpses of the Alaska-Yukon-Pacific Exposition; Seattle, Washington and the great northwest, original photographic gems depicting ... exhibit palaces ... scenery ... growth and resources of the great western America. Chicago, Laird & Lee, [c1909 by William H. Lee] (120)p. [photo album]
149

ALASKA-YUKON-PACIFIC EXPOSITION. Industrial progress in Alaska. Alaska exhibit, Department of the Interior, Alaska-Yukon-Pacific Exposition, Seattle, 1909. Seattle, Gateway Print. Co., 1909. 32p.
150

ALASKA-YUKON-PACIFIC EXPOSITION. Official catalogue, Department of Fine Arts. Seattle, 1909. 78p. illus.
151

ALASKA-YUKON-PACIFIC EXPOSITION. Official daily program. September 18, 1909.
152

ALASKA-YUKON-PACIFIC EXPOSITION. Official guide to the Alaska-Yukon-Pacific Exposition ... Seattle, Washington, June 1 to October 16, 1909. Seattle, Alaska-Pacific Pub. Co., 1909. 96p. illus.
153

ALASKA-YUKON-PACIFIC EXPOSITION. One hundred and fifty latest views of the Alaska-Yukon-Pacific Exposition and the Puget Sound country; official Exposition photographs. Seattle, 1909. 128p. illus. by Robert Allan Reid.
154

ALASKA-YUKON-PACIFIC EXPOSITION. Proceedings at the temporary unveiling of the statue of the late Secretary Seward, and at the luncheon and banquet in honor of General William H. Seward and William H. Seward, Jr., Friday, September 10, 1909, at the Alaska-Yukon-Pacific Exposition. Albany, J. B. Lyon, Print., 1909. 55p. [Seward Day]
155

ALASKA-YUKON-PACIFIC EXPOSITION. Report of the Alaska-Yukon-Pacific Exposition Committee of the State of Washington, L. P. Hornberger, Commissioner. Seattle, Pacific Press, 1910. 157p.
156

ALASKA-YUKON-PACIFIC EXPOSITION. Report of the Legislative Committee from the State of New York to the Alaska-Yukon-Pacific Exposition, 1909. Transmitted to the Legislature, January 25, 1910, B. M. Wilcox, Chairman. Albany, J. B. Lyon, Print., 1910. 197p. [incls. address by General Wm. H. Seward]
157

ALASKAN BIBLIOGRAPHY

ALASKA-YUKON-PACIFIC EXPOSITION. Report to the 25th Legislative
Assembly, January 10, 1909, W. H. Wehrung, President. Salem,
Oregon Committee for the Alaska-Yukon-Pacific Exposition, 1909.
7p.   158

ALASKA-YUKON-PACIFIC EXPOSITION. Seattle, the gateway to Alaska
and the Orient ... Official publication. Portland Postcard Co.,
1909. illus. pls.   159

ALASKA-YUKON-PACIFIC EXPOSITION. Souvenir guide ... held at Seattle, Washington, June 1 to October 16, 1909. By Seattle Electric Co. [Seattle, 1909] 64p. illus.   160

ALASKA-YUKON-PACIFIC EXPOSITION. The world's most beautiful exposition ... Issued by Department of Publicity. Seattle, Ivy
Press, 1909. 22p. illus. map.   161

Alaska-Yukon-Pacific Exposition. SEE ALSO nos.
     912, Chicago & Northwestern Ry. A-Y-P ... [1909 ?];
     1411, Edgren, Adolph. Jubel kantat ... 1909;
     3467, Pacific Univ. Souvenir ... [1909]

Alaskan Agriculturist. SEE no. 238, Anchorage Garden Club.

Alaskan and Yukon R. Gold Fields Bur. of Information. SEE
     no. 3140, Miner's guide ... [1898]

Alaskan Boundary Tribunal. Protocols ... 1903. SEE
     no. 1815, Great Britain. Foreign Office.

Alaskan camp cook. 1962. SEE no. 93, Alaska Northwest Pub. Co.

Alaskan earthquake pictorial. 1964. SEE no. 992, Color Art Print.

Alaskan market ... 1958. SEE no. 4507, J. Walter Thompson Co.

Alaskan opportunities ... [ca 1946] SEE no. 166, Alcan Pub. Co.

ALASKAN PUB. CO. Great Alaska earthquake. no pl., [1965 ?]
illus.   162

Alaskan Sled Dog and Racing Assoc. (or) Alaska Sled Dog and Ra-
     cing Assoc. SEE no. 2705, Life in Anchorage ... 1958.

ALASKANS UNITED, PUB. Destination Juneau. no pl., [1964]   163

ALBEE, WILLIAM and RUTH ALBEE. Alaska challenge. By Ruth and
Bill Albee with Lyman Anson. Illustrated. N. Y., Dodd Mead,
1940. 366p. illus. pls. ports. endmaps. [teaching school,
Cape Prince of Wales, in 1930']   164

Albee, William. SEE ALSO no. 2409, Kangkuk.

20

ALBRIGHT, HORACE M. and FRANK J. TAYLOR. "Oh Ranger !" A book about the national parks. Stanford, Calif., Stanford University Press, 1928. 178p. illus. by Ruth Taylor White, endmaps, index. [only brief references to Alaska]   165

ALCAN PUB. CO. Alaskan opportunities register. Hollywood, Calif., [ca 1946]   166

ALDRICH, HERBERT L. Arctic Alaska and Siberia; or, eight months with the Arctic whalemen by Herbert L. Aldrich who made the cruise with the fleet of 1887. Chicago, Rand McNally, 1889. 234p. front.(fold. map), pls. sketches, map. ANR. New Bedford, Mass., Reynolds Print. Co., 1937. 48p. illus. reprint.   167

ALEKSEEV, ALEKSANDR IVANOVICH. Okhotsk kolybel' russkogo tik-hookeanskogo flota. [TITLE TR. Okhotsk, the cradle of the Russian Pacific fleet] Khabarovsk, Khabarovskoe knizhnoe izd-vo, 1958. 158p. illus. ports. maps, bibliog. [base for exploration and Russian-American Co.]   168

Aleutskiĭ bukvar'. [ca 1839] SEE no. 4600, [Tyzhnov, Il'ias ?]

ALEXANDER, CHARLES PAUL. The crane flies of Alaska and the Canadian northwest; Tipulidae, Diptera; the genus *Erioptera* Meigen. Ann Arbor, University of Michigan, April 22, 1955. 33p. illus. bibliog. (Museum of Zoology)   169

Alexander, W. D. SEE no. 1083, Corney, P. Voyages ... 1896.

ALFTHAN, A. E. Hafsutterns och pelssälens geografiske utbred-ning. [TITLE TR. The geographic distribution of the sea otter and the fur seal] Helsingfors, 1903. 32p. table, ftntes. (Geografiska föreningen i Finland, Meddelanden, 6:12)   170

All about Alaska. 1887. SEE
    no. 3449, Pacific Coast Steamship Co.

All about Klondike. 1897. SEE no. 476, Belcher, H. A.

ALL ABOUT THE KLONDIKE gold mines by J. A. Knox and J. G. Pratt. N. Y., The Miners' News Pub. Co., [1897] 59p. map.   171

All-Alaska review ... 1928-30. SEE
    nos. 1076-77, Cordova Daily Times.

ALL ALASKA SWEEPSTAKES, Nome. Souvenir of second annual all Alaska Sweepstakes. Nome Daily Nugget [for Nome Kennel Club], 1909. (20)p. illus. ANR. Knik, Iditarod Trail Committee, 1969. facsim. reprint [by Ken Wray's Print Shop, Anchorage] 172

ALLAN, ALEXANDER. Hunting the sea otter. London, H. Cox, 1910. 188p. front. pls.   173

ALLAN, ALLAN ALEXANDER "SCOTTY." Gold, men and dogs. N. Y., Putnam, 1931. 337p. front.(port.)   174

Allan, Allan Alexander "Scotty." SEE ALSO nos.
    1175, Darling, E. B. Baldy of Nome. 191];
    1692, Garst, S. Scotty Allan ... 1946;
    4895, Willoughby, B. Gentlemen unafraid. 1928;
    4904, Willoughby, B. Trail eater. 1929.

Allen, A. S. SEE no. 3453, Pacific Coast Steamship Co.

ALLEN, C. C. The platinum metals. Ottawa, Queen's Printer, 1961. 68p. illus. diagrs. graphs, tables, maps, bibliog. (Canada. Department of Mines and Technical Surveys, Mineral Resources Division, Mineral Report no. 3)   175

Allen, C. F. SEE no. 3666, Poulter, Thos. C.

Allen, Courtney, illus. SEE no. 4130, Shore, E. B.

ALLEN, DURWARD LEON. Our wildlife legacy. N. Y., Funk & Wagnall, 1954. 422p. illus. bibliog. [incls. Alaskan]   176

ALLEN, EDWARD WEBER. Jean François Galaup de Lapérouse, a check list. S. F., [printed by L. R. Kennedy], 1941. 18p. port. reprint [from California Historical Society Quarterly, vol. XX, no. 1, March, 1941]   177

ALLEN, EDWARD WEBER. North Pacific; Japan, Siberia, Alaska, Canada. N. Y., Professional and Technical Press, 1936. 282p. front.(col.), pls. maps, endmaps.   178

ALLEN, EDWARD WEBER. The Halibut Commission, its legal powers and functions. Seattle, 1936. (International Fisheries Commission Circular no. 1)   179

ALLEN, EDWARD WEBER. The vanishing Frenchman, the mysterious disappearance of Lapérouse. Rutland, Vt., Charles E. Tuttle Co., 1959. 1st ed. 321p. illus. facsim. endmaps, bibliog. index.180

Allen, Eugene C. SEE no. 386, Bankson, Russell Arden.

Allen, Eugene T., co-auth. SEE no. 3275, National Geog. Soc.

Allen, Jerry, co-auth. SEE no. 720, Buchan, Laura.

ALLEN, JOEL ASAPH. Description of a new caribou from Kenai Peninsula, Alaska. [N. Y., The Knickerbocker Press, 1901] extract [from Bulletin of the American Museum of Natural History, vol. XIV, art. X, May 28, 1901, pp.143-48]   181

ALLEN, JOEL ASAPH. On the eared seals, (Otoriadae), with detailed descriptions of the North Pacific species. Together with an account of the habits of northern fur seals, (*Callorhinus urinus*), by Charles Bryant. Cambridge, Mass., Harvard University, 1870. 108p. pls. figs. (Museum of Comparative Zoology, Bulletin, vol. 2, no. 1)   182

Allen, Joseph C., co-auth. SEE no. 591, Bodfish, H. H.

ALLEN, L. H. Alaska's Kenai Peninsula. Hope, Alaska, [by author, ca 1947]   183

Allen, M. W., co-auth. SEE no. 4561, Townley, S. D.

Allen, O. W., tr. SEE no. 3901, Rouquette, L.-F.

ALLEN, T. D. Prisoners of the polar ice. Phila., Westminster Press, 1959.   184

ALLEN, WILLIS BOYD. The gold-hunters of Alaska. N. Y., H. M. Caldwell, 1889. 348p. illus. pls. ANR. Boston, Dana Estes, 1889. [With running title: The red mountain of Alaska. cf no. 187]   185

ALLEN, WILLIS BOYD. Gulf and glacier; or, the Percivals in Alaska. Boston, D. Lothrop, 1892. 243p. pls.   186

ALLEN, WILLIS BOYD. The red mountain of Alaska. Boston, Estes and Lauriat, 1889. 1st ed. 348p. pls. ANR. London, n. d. 320p. [see also no. 185]   187

ALMANAC PUBLISHING CO. Farmer's almanac for the year of our Lord 1967. Edited by Ray Geiger. no pl., 1966. (45)p. illus. (Alaska Purchase Centennial edition)   188

ALMQUIST, ARDEN Covenant missions in Alaska. Chicago, Covenant Press, 1962.   189

Alsop, Richard, edit. SEE no. 2354, Jewitt, J. R.

ALTSHELER, WILLIAM B. Maladministration through the Alaska syndicate; extract from the official record. Five years "Conservation" as set forth in the Congressional investigation of the Interior Department and Forestry Service. The Ballinger-Pinchot controversy. Louisville, Ky., [by author], 1910. 25p.   190

Amadeo di Savoia, Luigi, Duke of the Abruzzi. SEE nos. 1226-28, deFilippi, Filippo.

Amadeus, Rev. Mother. SEE no. 2709, Life of ...
     Ursuline Missions Montana and Alaska ... 1923.

AMEIGH, GEORGE, jr. and YULE M. CHAFFIN. Alaska's Kodiak Island; a camera report of life at Kodiak. [Anchorage, Anchorage Print. Co.], 1962. 163p. illus. photos, map.   191

AMERICAN AUTOMOBILE ASSOC. Alaska and the Alaska Highway. Washington, D. C., 1949. 23p. illus. maps.   192

AMERICAN BIBLE SOC. God-im uḳaluṇi. John, Ephesians, James, 1 John. no pl., 1946. ANR. 1964. Rev. Standard Version. 146p. (Division of Christian Education, National Council of Churches) [in Iñupiat Eskimo and English]   193

AMERICAN BIBLE SOC. Kanegriarat ashilret, Matthewm, Markim, Lukam, Johnamtlu igatlgit, Tamat tselli igatlgitnik ilankgtsoagluting. Mumigtsimalret Yugstun, Kuskokwigmiut Awatetnilinguttlu kanlautsetstun. N. Y., 1929. 270p. [Kuskokwim Eskimo gospels and selections]   194

AMERICAN BIBLE SOC. Kanereakakgtak. Agaiutim Akkute Nutarak Atinimtgun Jesus Christusakun, Mumigtsimalret Yugstun Kuskorfagamuit Awatetnilingutdlo kanlautsetstun. no pl., 1967. Corrected Edition. 500 copies. 627p. (New Testament no. 263) [in Kuskokwim Eskimo dialect]   195

AMERICAN BIBLE SOC. Tuyurtiṇi Paulum. Tilizam Zuummiunun. Romans in Eskimo. Printed in Mexico, 1948. 62p.   196

American Can Co. SEE no. 625, Boutwell, W. D.

AMERICAN COMMITTEE FOR INTERNATIONAL WILDLIFE PROTECTION. The present status of the musk-ox in Arctic North America and Greenland, with notes on distribution, extirpation, transplantation, protection, habits and life history. Prepared by Elisabeth Hone. Cambridge, Mass., 1934. 87p. pls. maps(sketch) (Special Pub. no. 5)   197

AMERICAN EXPRESS, Travel Department. Summer tours to Alaska. Escorted tours, Alaska, Summer 1927. no pl., 1927. 21p. illus. photos(col.)   198

American Game Protective Assoc. SEE no. 797,
   Camp Fire Club of America.

AMERICAN GEOGRAPHICAL SOC. Geography in the making; the American Geographical Society, 1851-1951. Edited by John Kirtland Wright. N. Y., 1952. 437p. pls. ports. diagrs. endmaps, list of officers and personnel, publications and index.   199

AMERICAN GEOGRAPHICAL SOC. Nine glacier maps, northwestern North America; to accompany nine separate map sheets on scale of 1:10,000. N. Y., 1960. 22p. illus. index map, maps(fold. col.), bibliog. appends. (Special Pub. no. 34) [eight glaciers in Alaska, one in Washington]   200

AMERICAN GEOGRAPHICAL SOC. Physical map of the Arctic. N. Y.,
1930.   201

AMERICAN GEOGRAPHICAL SOC. Pioneer settlement, cooperative studies by twenty-six authors. Edited by W. L. G. Joerg. N. Y.,
1932. 473p. diagrs. figs. tables, maps. (Special Publication
no. 14) [has article on Alaskan agriculture by C. C. George-
son]   202

AMERICAN GEOGRAPHICAL SOC. Problems of polar research; a se-
ries of papers by thirty-one authors. Edited by W. L. G. Joerg.
N. Y., 1928. 479p. illus. diagrs. maps(incl. 1 fold.) (Spe-
cial Publication no. 7) [papers by Lincoln Ellsworth, Diamond
Jenness, Umberto Nobile, Knud Rasmussen, L. H. Stejneger, Sir
Hubert Wilkins, others]   203

AMERICAN GEOGRAPHICAL SOC. Readings in the geography of North
America; a selection of articles from the Geographical Review.
N. Y., 1952. 466p. illus. pls. maps. (Reprint Series no. 5)
[papers by W. O. Field, D. Jenness, others]   204

American Geographical Soc. SEE ALSO nos.
     2360, Joerg, W. L. G. Brief hist. polar ... 1930;
     2360, Joerg, W. L. G. Two polar maps ... 1930;
     3339, Nordenskiöld, N. O. G. Geog. polar ... 1928.

American Insurance Assoc. SEE
     no. 3273, National Bd. Fire Underwriters.

American Jubilee Co. SEE no. 2489, Klondyke and gold ... 1897.

AMERICAN LIBRARY ASSOC. The A. L. A. in Alaska, July 1925.
Itinerary and members of party. Seattle, 1925. 12p.   205

American Library Assoc. SEE ALSO no. 1171, Dana, J. C.

American Mining Congress. SEE nos.
     2391, Joslin, Falcon. Alaska ... 1912;
     2392, Joslin, Falcon. Needs ... [1921]

AMERICAN MUSEUM OF NATURAL HISTORY. The Andrew J. Stone explorations in arctic and subarctic America. N. Y., 1905. 38p.   206

AMERICAN ORNITHOLOGISTS' UNION. Check-list of North American
birds, prepared by a Committee of ... constituting the "Systema
avium" for North America north of Mexico. Lancaster, Penna.,
1931. 4th ed. 526p. index [earlier editions 1886, 1895, 1910
with 18 supplements issued between, prior to 4th]   207

American Orthodox Messenger. SEE
     no. 211, Amerikanskiĭ Pravoslavnyi Viestnik.

American panorama ... 1960. SEE no. 2149, Holiday Magazine.

AMERICAN PRESS. One hundred pictures of little known Alaska.
N. Y., 1935. 73p. [photos from collection of Father Bernard
Hubbard]   208

AMERICAN-RUSSIAN COMMERCIAL CO. The Alaska fur-seal bill.
S. F., 1869. 12p.   209

AMERICAN-RUSSIAN COMMERCIAL CO. By-laws. Organized May, 1853.
S. F., O'Meara & Painter, Printers, 1855.   210

American-Russian frontiers. 1944. SEE no. 4403, Survey Assoc.

America's wonderlands. 1966. SEE no. 3274, National Geog. Soc.

AMERIKANSKIĬ PRAVOSLAVNYI VIESTNIK. Dieĩaniĩa svĩatykh apostol,
na Aleutsko-lis'ev. narĩechiĩ. [TITLE TR. Acts of the Holy
Apostles in the Aleutian-Fox dialect] N. Y., 1902. 118p.   211

Amerika's Nordwest-Küste. 1883. SEE nos. 534 and 536, Berlin,
    Königlichen Museen.

AMES, ROBERT ANDREW. The cheechako. A novel of the Alaska-
Yukon gold rush. N. Y., Lothrop, Lee & Shepard, 1958. 242p.212

Amichin, D. N., edit. SEE no. 3338, Nordenskiöld, N. O. G.

Amoretti, Carlo, tr. SEE no. 1548, Ferrer Maldonado, L.

Amundsen, Gustav S. SEE nos. 219-22, Amundsen, R. E. G.

Amundsen, Roald Engelbregt Gravning. [Alphabetical title guide
    to chronological entries]

        Air pioneering ... 213.   My life ... 224.
        Amund.-Ells. polar ... 215. My polar flight ... 217.
        Amund.-Ells. polfly. ... 214. Nordostpass. ... 225.
        Den forste flukt. 219.   "Northwest Pass." 227.
        Der erste Flug. 220.   Nordvestpass. 226.
        En avion ... 216.   Norwestpass. 228.
        First crossing ... 222.   Our polar ... 218.
        First flight ... 221.   Sci. results ... *Gjøa*. 229.
        Mitt liv ... 223.

AMUNDSEN, ROALD ENGELBREGT GRAVNING. Air pioneering in the Arctic; the two polar flights of Roald Amundsen and Lincoln Ellsworth. Pt. 1: The 1925 flight from Spitzbergen to 88° North;
Pt. 2: The first crossing of the Polar Sea, 1926. Edited by
Lincoln Ellsworth. N. Y., National Americana Society, 1929.
126p. pls. ports. facsims. maps.   213

AMUNDSEN, ROALD ENGELBREGT GRAVNING and others. Amundsen-Ellsworth polflyoning 1925. Gjennem luften til 88° nord. [TITLE TR. The Amundsen-Ellsworth polar flight 1925. Through the air to 88° N.] Gyldendal, Norsk Forlag, 1925. 278p. pls. ports. maps.
214

TRANSLATIONS - Amundsen-Ellsworth polflyoning ... 1925, CHRONOLOGICALLY.

Amundsen-Ellsworth polar flight. N. Y., 1925.   215

En avion vers le Pole Nord. Paris, 1925.   216

My polar flight. London, Hutchinson, 1925. 292p. illus. charts.   217

Our polar flight; the Amundsen-Ellsworth polar flight, by Roald Amundsen, Lincoln Ellsworth and other members of the expedition; illustrated from photos taken on the expedition. N. Y., Dodd Mead, 1925. 373p. front. ports. maps. [with added chapt. by L. Ellsworth]   218

AMUNDSEN, ROALD ENGELBREGT GRAVNING. Den forste flukt over Polhavet, med bidrag av Gustav S. Amundsen, B. L. Gottwaldt, Joh. Hover, Finn Malmgren, Hj. Riiser-Larsen. [TITLE TR. The first flight over the Polar Sea] Oslo, Gyldendal, Norsk Forlag, 1926. pls. ports. diagrs. map(fold. at back)   219

TRANSLATIONS - Den forste flukt ... 1926, CHRONOLOGICALLY.

Der erste Flug über das Polarmeer, mit Beitragen von Gustav S. Amundsen, B. L. Gottwaldt, Joh. Hover, Finn Malmgren, Hj. Riiser-Larsen. Einzig autorisierte übersetzung von Walter J. Briggs. Leipzig, Grethlein, [1927] 261p. pls. ports. map(fold.)   220

The first flight across the Polar Sea, with additional chapters by Joh. Hover, Hj. Riiser-Larsen, Gustav Amundsen, Finn Malmgren, B. L. Gottwaldt. London, Hutchinson, 1927. 274p. illus. chart.   221

First crossing of the Polar Sea, with additional chapters by other members of the expedition. Garden City, N. Y., Doubleday Doran, 1928 [c1927] 324p. pls. ports. facsim. map, index.   222

AMUNDSEN, ROALD ENGELBREGT GRAVNING. Mitt liv som polarforster. [TITLE TR. My life as a polar explorer] Oslo, Gyldendal, Norsk Forlag, 1927. 256p. pls. ports. [see no. 224 for tr.]   223

AMUNDSEN, ROALD ENGELBREGT GRAVNING. My life as an explorer. Garden City, N. Y., Doubleday Doran, 1928 [c1927] 282p. front. illus. facsims. diagrs. maps, append. index. [tr. of no. 223] 224

AMUNDSEN, ROALD ENGELBREGT GRAVNING. Nordostpassagen. Maudfaerden langs Asiens kyst 1918-20. H. U. Sverdrups ophold blandt Tsjuktsjerne. Godfred Hansens depotekspedition 1919-20. [TITLE TR. The Northeast Passage. The voyage of the "Maud" along the coast of Asia, 1918-20. H. U. Sverdrup's sojourn among the Chukchis. Godfred Hansen's Depot Expedition, 1919-20] Kristiana, Gyldendal, 1921. 467p. pls. ports. facsim. maps(fold.) 225

AMUNDSEN, ROALD ENGELBREGT GRAVNING. Nordvestpassagen; beretning om Gjøa-ekspeditionen 1903-07. Med et tillaeg av premierløitnent Godfred Hansen. [TITLE TR. The Northwest Passage; report of the *Gjøa* Expedition, 1903-07. With a supplement by First Lieutenant Godfred Hansen] Kristiana, H. Aschehoug, 1907. 511p. illus. maps(incl. 2 fold.) 226

TRANSLATIONS - Nordvestpassagen ... 1907, CHRONOLOGICALLY.

"The Northwest Passage;" being the record of a voyage of exploration of the ship "Gjøa" 1903-07, by Roald Amundsen, with a supplement by First Lieutenant Hansen, vice-commander of the expedition; with about one hundred and thirty-nine illustrations and three maps. London, Constable, 1908. 2 vols. 335p. and 379p. fronts. ports. pls. maps (incl. 2 fold. in pocket) [has added index] 227

Norwestpassagen. Halasz Gyula, Vilàgikodalom Kiad, 1922. 175p. illus. maps. 228

AMUNDSEN, ROALD ENGELBREGT GRAVNING. The scientific results of the Norwegian Arctic Expedition in the *Gjøa,* 1903-06, under the conduct of Roald Amundsen. [Oslo, Cammermeyer, 1930-33] 3 vols. illus. tables, diagrs. map(dble.) (Geofysiske publikasjoner, vol. 6-8) 229

Amundsen, Roald Engelbregt Gravning. SEE ALSO nos.
    309, Arneson, Odd. Roald Amundsen som har var. 1929;
    607, Boni, Armand. Roald Amundsen. 1946;
    940, Clark, H. T. Episodes Amundsen-Ellsworth flights. 1928.
    1944, Hanssen, H. J. Gjennem Isbaksen ... 1941;
    1945, Hanssen, H. J. Voyages of modern viking. 1936;
    2188, Houdenak, G. Roald Amundsens Siste Ferde ... 1934;
    2569, Kugelmass, J. A. Roald Amundsen; saga ... 1955;
    2711, Lind, J. V. A. Fungi ... *Gjøa* ... 1910;
    2818, L'vov, V. E. Zavoevanie poliarnykh pustyn'. 1928;
    2821, Lynge, B. Lichens *Gjøa* expedition. 1921;
    3311, Nilsson, G. A. Sjöfarare; Kåserier ... 1957;
    3313, Nobile, U. Gli Italiana al Polo Nord. 1945;
    3314, Nobile, U. In volo alla conquista ... 1928;

Amundsen, Roald Engelbregt Gravning. SEE ALSO nos.
    3315, Nobile, U. My polar flights ... 1961;
    3342, "Norge" al Polo Nord ... 1926;
    3497, Partridge, B. Amundsen ... 1929;
    3527, Peisson, E. Pôles ... aventure ... 1952;
    3950, Samoilovich, R. L. Putik poliusu. 2. izd. 1933;
    4410, Sverdrup, H. U. Dynamics tides ... *Maud* ... 1926;
    4411, Sverdrup, H. U. General report ... 1933;
    4412, Sverdrup, H. U. Meteorology ... 1930;
    4413, Sverdrup, H. U. Tre aar ... 1926;
    4544, Toland, J. Ships in sky ... dirigibles. 1957;
    4627, Vaeth, J. G. To ends of earth ... [c1962];
    4937, Wisting, Oscar. 16 år med Roald Amundsen ... 1930.

ANATOLIĬ, *Arkhimandrit*. Indiane Aliaski; byt i religiia ikh.
[TITLE TR. The Indians of Alaska; their life and religion]
Odessa, Tip. E. I. Fesenko, [1907 ?] 139p. illus.   230

ANATOLIĬ, *Arkhimandrit*. Indianskoe plemia Tlingit. [TITLE TR.
The Tlingit Indian tribe] N. Y., Press of Orthodox Messenger,
1899. 88p.   231

Anchorage, all-America city. 1957. SEE no. 317, Atwood, E.

ANCHORAGE CHAMBER OF COMMERCE. Anchorage; the metropolis of
Alaska. Compiled by Anchorage Chamber of Commerce. Anchorage,
May 1918. 24p. map.   232

ANCHORAGE CHAMBER OF COMMERCE. Today's facts about Anchorage –
"Crossroads of the world." Anchorage, 1944. 10p. illus. (Chamber of Commerce Bulletin no. 2)   233

ANCHORAGE, CROSSROADS OF THE WORLD. A guide and map to Anchorage, Palmer and the Matanuska Valley. East Anchorage, [ca 1945]
72p. illus. maps.   234

Anchorage; crossroads to adventure ... 1962. SEE no. 2150.

ANCHORAGE DAILY NEWS. Flood. Anchorage, 1967. (28)p. illus.
[photos taken from issues of Anchorage Daily News, of flood in
Fairbanks, August 14, 1967]   235

ANCHORAGE DAILY NEWS. The village people. Anchorage, 1966.
53p. illus. photos, maps.   236

ANCHORAGE DAILY TIMES. Alaska's struggle for self government.
Eighty-three years of neglect. A summary of the colorful cir-
cumstances under which throttling controls have been allowed to
retard, delay and obstruct Alaska's development. Drawn principally from a manuscript prepared in 1945 by Mrs. Robert B. Atwood of Anchorage. Anchorage, 1950. 19p. reprint [from editorial pages March 24-April 19, 1950]   237

Anchorage fun book. 1967. SEE no. 1207, Davis, P. E.

ANCHORAGE GARDEN CLUB. So you think you will have a flower garden in Alaska ? no pl., n. d. [Anchorage ? 1953] (12)p. illus.
[published courtesy of Alaskan Agriculturist magazine]   238

ANCHORAGE GUIDE PUBLISHING CO. What's doing in Anchorage.
Anchorage, 1955. 32p. illus. [annual]   239

Anchorage - nerve center ... [1945 ?] SEE no. 74, Alaska Life.

Anchorage; the metropolis ... 1918. SEE
     no. 232, Anchorage Chamber of Commerce.

ANCHORAGE WOMAN'S CLUB. Alaska's cooking. Anchorage, Dec.1959.
1st print. ANR. Dec. 1964. enl. 4th print. ANR. Nov. 1965.
5th print. [printed by Color Art Print. Co.] 282p. front.
photos, sketches, indexes of recipes and contributors.   240

Andersen, J. C. SEE no. 5037, Zimmermann, H.

ANDERSON, ALEXANDER CAULFIELD. Notes on north-western America.
Montreal, Mitchell & Wilson, Printers, 1876. 22p. [natural
history Alaska and northwestern Canada]   241

Anderson, Bern. The life and voyages Capt. Geo. Vancouver ...
     1966. SEE no. 242.

ANDERSON, BERN. Surveyor of the sea; the life and voyages of
Captain George Vancouver. Seattle, University of Washington
Press, 1960. xii,274p. illus. ports. engrs. maps, bibliog.
index. ANR. WITH TITLE The life and voyages of Captain George
Vancouver, surveyor of the sea. Seattle, University of Washing-
ton Press, 1966. 1st paperback edition. 274p. front.(dble.
map), illus. maps, append. notes, bibliog. index. (Washington
Paperbacks WP-17)   242

ANDERSON, EVA GREENSLIT. Dog-team doctor; the story of Dr.
Romig. Caldwell, Idaho, Caxton, 1940. 298p. front. pls.
ports. facsims. endmaps.   243

Anderson, G. S., co-auth. SEE no. 2241, Hussey, K. M.

ANDERSON, HOBSON DEWEY and WALTER CROSBY EELLS. Alaska natives;
a survey of their sociological and educational status. Stanford, Calif., Stanford University Press, 1935. 472p. front.
(fold. map), pls. ports. plans, tables, diagrs. maps, append.
bibliog. index. (School of Education, Stanford University)
[pub. simult. London, Oxford University Press]   244

ANDERSON, ISABEL W. P. Odd corners. N. Y., Dodd Mead, 1917.
[has chapt. on Alaska, pp.110-24]   245

ANDERSON, J. P.   Alaska-grown plants,   grown and for sale by Juneau florists. Juneau, February 12, 1918. 8p.   246

ANDERSON, JACOB PETER.   Flora of Alaska and adjacent parts of Canada,   an illustrated descriptive text of all vascular plants known to occur within the region covered.   Integrated and indexed at the Anderson Herbarium,   by Richard W. Pohl,   Curator. Ames, Iowa State University Press, 1959. 543p. illus. [offset reprint of nine fascicles with corrections,   integrated paging and index to Taxa]   247

ANDERSON, JIM. Boating on the Yukon River ... collated, translated and related by Jim Anderson. Juneau, 1930. 48p.   248

Anderson, K. A., co-auth. SEE no. 1468, Enemark, D. C.

ANDERSON, LAURA DAVID. According to Mama, by Laura David Anderson as told to Audrey Loftus. Fairbanks, St. Matthews's Episcopal Guild, 1956. 1st print. 38p. illus. [Athabascan Indians of Upper Tanana River]   249

Anderson, R. C., co-edit. SEE no. 3533, [Penrose, C. V.]

ANDERSON, R. M. and B. B. ROSWIG. Planning, zoning and subdivision. A summary of statutory law in fifty states. Albany, New York State Federation of Official Planning Organizations, 1966. 231p. tables, maps.   250

Anderson, Rudolph Martin.   SEE nos.
    4307, Stefansson, V. My life with Eskimo. 1913;
    4323-24, Stefansson, V. Stefansson-Anderson Arctic
            exped. ... 1919 and 1914.

ANDERSON, WILLIAM R. First under the North Pole; the voyage of the *Nautilus*. Cleveland, World Publishing Co., 1959.   64p. illus. maps.   251

ANDERSON, WILLIAM R. and CLAY BLAIR, jr. *Nautilus:*90° North. Cleveland, World Publishing Co., 1959. 251p. illus. photos, endmaps. ANR. N. Y., New American Library of World Literature, 1959. paperback. (no. KDS 11)   252

Andreev, A. I. SEE nos. 263 and 264, Andreyev, A. I.

Andrew J. Stone explorations ... 1905. SEE
    no. 206, American Museum of Natural History.

ANDREWS, CLARENCE LEROY. Nuggets of northland verse, panned from the gravels of the past. Seattle, 1935. 46p.   253

ANDREWS, CLARENCE LEROY. The Eskimo and his reindeer in Alaska. Caldwell, Idaho, Caxton, 1939. 253p. front. pls. ports. map, notes, glossary, bibliog. index.   254

ANDREWS, CLARENCE LEROY. The pioneers and the nuggets of verse they panned from the gravels of the past. Seattle, Luke Tinker, Commercial Printer, 1935. ANR. Eugene, Ore., [by author], 1937. 55p. illus. [sketches and verse by eye-witnesses]   255

ANDREWS, CLARENCE LEROY. The story of Alaska. By C. L. Andrews. Seattle, Lowman and Hanford, 1931. 1st ed. 258p. pls. ports. map, notes, index. OTHERS Caldwell, Idaho, Caxton, 1932 AND 1938. rev. and enl. ANR. 1953 [8th print. of 1938 ed.] 332p. front.(port.), pls. ports. maps(incl. 1 fold. at back), endmaps, bibliog. index.   256

ANDREWS, CLARENCE LEROY. The story of Sitka; the historic out-post of the northwest coast. The chief factory of the Russian American Company. Seattle, Lowman and Hanford, 1922. 108p. illus. photos, map(fold. at back), ftntes. ANR. Caldwell, Ida-ho, Caxton, 1945. 3rd rev. ed. 144p. front. pls. ports. end-maps. ANR. Seattle, Shorey Book Store, 1965. (Shorey Photo-copy no. 94) [facsim. of 1922 ed.]   257

ANDREWS, CLARENCE LEROY. Wrangell and the gold of the Cassiar; a tale of fur and gold in Alaska. By Clarence L. Andrews. Se-attle, Luke Tinker, Commercial Printer, [c1937] 60p. front. illus. facsim. engrs. ftntes. maps, wrps.   258

ANDREWS, RALPH WARREN. Curtis' western Indians. Seattle, Superior Pub. Co., 1962. 1st ed. 176p. illus.   259

ANDREWS, RALPH WARREN and A. K. LARSSEN. Fish and ships; this was fishing from the Columbia to Bristol Bay. Seattle, Superior Pub. Co., 1959. 173p. illus. photos, index. ANR. N. Y., Bo-nanza Books, n. d.   260

ANDREWS, RALPH WARREN. Indian primitive, Northwest Coast Indi-ans of the former days. Seattle, Superior Pub. Co., 1960. 175p. illus. photos, bibliog. index. ANR. N. Y., Bonanza Books, n. d.261

ANDREWS, RALPH WARREN and HARRY A. KIRWAN. This was seafaring, a sea chest of salty memories. Seattle, Superior Pub. Co., 1955. 1st ed. 108p. illus.   262

ANDREYEV, ALEKSANDR IGNAT'EVICH. Russian discoveries in the Pa-cific and in North America in the 18th and 19th centuries; a collection of materials. Translated from Russian by Carl Gins-burg. Ann Arbor, Mich., J. W. Edwards, 1952. 214p. (Russian Translations Project Series of American Council of Learned Soci-eties, no. 13) [tr. of no. 264]   263

ANDREYEV, ALEKSANDR IGNAT'EVICH. Russkie otkrytiïa v Tikhom okeane i Severnoĭ Amerika v XVIII veke. Moskva, OGIZ Gosudarst-vennoe izd-vo geograficheskoĭ literatury, 1948. 382p. illus. port. maps(fold.), bibliog.(ftntes.) [see no. 263 for tr.]   264

Andreyev, Aleksandr Ignat'evich. SEE ALSO no. 4760, Waxell, S. L.

Angell, C., illus. SEE no. 434, Baxter, D. V.

Angiolini, tr. SEE no. 2563, Krusenstern, A. J. von.

ANGUS, H. F., edit. British Columbia and the U. S., the North Pacific slope from fur trade to aviation. By F. W. Howay, W. N. Sage and H. F. Angus. Toronto, Ryerson Press, 1942. 408p. illus. maps. (Carnegie Endowment for International Peace, Division of Economics and History)   265

ANNABEL, RUSSELL. Alaskan tales. N. Y., A. S. Barnes, 1953. 137p.   266

ANNABEL, RUSSELL. Hunting and fishing in Alaska. N. Y., Knopf, 1948. 341p. front.(col.), pls. (Borzoi Books for Sportsmen) 267

ANNABEL, RUSSELL. Tales of a big game guide. N. Y., Derrydale Press, 1938. ltd. ed. of 950 copies. 198p.   268

Anson, Lyman, co-auth. SEE nos.
    164, Albee, Wm. Alaska challenge. 1940;
    691, Brower, Chas. D. Fifty years below zero. 1942.

Anthony, H. E., co-edit. SEE no. 612, Boone and Crockett Club.

ANTI-MONOPOLY ASSOCIATION OF THE PACIFIC COAST. A history of the wrongs of Alaska; an appeal to the people and press of America, printed by order of ... February 1875. S. F., 1875. 43p.   269

ANTI-MONOPOLY ASSOCIATION OF THE PACIFIC COAST. Resolutions ... S. F., 1874. 4p.   270

ANZER, RICHARD C. "DIXIE." Klondike gold rush, as recalled by a participant. N. Y., Pageant Press, 1959. 236p.   271

APPEAL OF YUKON MINERS to the Dominion of Canada and incidently some account of the mines and mining of Alaska and the Provisional District of Yukon. Ottawa, The Portimer Co. Print, [1898] 128p.   272

APPEL, BENJAMIN. We were there in the Klondike gold rush. N. Y., Grosset and Dunlap, 1956. 175p. illus. by Irv Docktor.
                                                                       273

Appendix a shimalgiagum ... n. d. SEE no. 1381, [Duncan, Wm.]

APPLETON, LeROY H. Indian art of the Americas. N. Y., Scribners, 1950. 279p. pls.(col.) [Indians and Eskimos of Alaska and northwestern Canada]   274

Appleton's guide-book ... 1893. SEE no. 4025, Scidmore, E. R.

Arbuthnot. SEE no. 1824, Great Britain.

ARCHER, F. A., comp. A heroine of the North; the memoirs of
Charlotte Selina Bompas (1830-1917), wife of the first Bishop of
Selkirk. With extracts from her journal and letters. London,
Society for Promoting Christian Knowledge, 1929. 187p. front.
port. map.   275

ARCTANDER, JOHN WILLIAM. The apostle of Alaska; the story of
William Duncan of Metlakahtla. N. Y., Revell, [c1909] 395p.
front.(port.), pls. map(fold.), index. ANR. N. Y., Revell,
1909. 2d ed.   276

ARCTANDER, JOHN WILLIAM. The lady in blue, a Sitka romance.
Seattle, Lowman and Hanford, 1911. 59p. photos by W. H. Case.
                                                                277

ARCTIC BROTHERHOOD. The Arctic Brotherhood; a souvenir history
of the order, setting forth its aims, its ambitions and the good
it has accomplished from its incipiency, its relations to Alaska
and the great northland, supplemented by individual histories of
its various subordinate camps; richly illuminated with graphic
scenes of the northland, embellished with portraits and interspersed with business announcements, etc., pub. ... Executive
Building Board. By Godfrey Chealander and Richard White. Seattle, I. N. Davidson, Acme Pub. Co., 1909. 104p. illus. ports.
                                                                278

ARCTIC BROTHERHOOD. Constitution of the Grand Camp of the Arctic Brotherhood and constitution and by-laws of Subordinate
Camps. As adopted by the Provisional Grand Camp, 1899, 1900,
with amendments adopted by the Grand Camp 1901, 1902, 1903,
1904, 1905, 1906, 1907, 1910. no pl., n. d. 60p. index.   279

ARCTIC BROTHERHOOD. Convention, convened at Douglas, Alaska,
under the auspices of Camp Treadwell No. 14, Arctic Brotherhood,
March 12-14, 1913. Temporary and permanent organization of convention. Proceedings of convention. Submitted to Arctic Brotherhood Camps for ratification. Organization of Grand Camp.
Camps represented. Names of delegates. Place to hold first
Grand Camp. Officers elected. Record of sessions. Appointment
of executive officers. Adjourned "sine die." no pl., n. d.
11p.   280

Arctic Brotherhood. Proceedings ... [chronologically] SEE
     nos. 281-96.

ARCTIC BROTHERHOOD. Proceedings of the Grand Camp of the Arctic
Brotherhood, Skagway, Sept. 4-6, 1901. Skagway, Daily News
Print, 1901. 14p.   281

ARCTIC BROTHERHOOD. Proceedings of the Grand Camp. Second Session. Dawson, Yukon Territory, Aug. 6-8, 1902. Dawson, Daily News Print, 1902. 16p.   282

ARCTIC BROTHERHOOD. Proceedings of the Grand Camp. Third Session. Skagway, Alaska, Aug. 17-19, 1903. Skagway, Daily Alaskan Print, 1903. 19p.   283

ARCTIC BROTHERHOOD. Proceedings of the Grand Camp. Fourth Session. Seattle, Washington, Nov. 1-6, 1904. Skagway, Daily Alaskan Print, 1904. 32p.   284

ARCTIC BROTHERHOOD. Proceedings of the Grand Camp. Fifth Session. Seattle, Washington, Nov. 6-10, 1905. Seattle, Trade Register Print, 1905. 62p.   285

ARCTIC BROTHERHOOD. Proceedings of the Grand Camp. Sixth Session, Vancouver, B. C., Nov. 7 & 8, 1906. Seattle, Trade Register Print, 1906. 52p.   286

ARCTIC BROTHERHOOD. Proceedings of the Grand Camp. Seventh Session. Tacoma, Washington, Nov. 7-9, 1907. Seattle, Trade Register Print, 1907. 66p.   287

ARCTIC BROTHERHOOD. Proceedings of the Grand Camp. Eighth Session. Victoria, B. C., Nov. 4-7, 1908. Seattle, Gateway Print Co., 1908. 79p.   288

ARCTIC BROTHERHOOD. Proceedings of the Grand Camp. Ninth Session. Seattle, Washington, Nov. 2-4, 1909. Skagway, Daily Alaskan Print, 1909. 55p.   289

ARCTIC BROTHERHOOD. Proceedings of the Grand Camp. Tenth Session. Vancouver, B. C., Nov. 1-3, 1910. Skagway, Daily Alaskan Print, 1910. 70p.   290

ARCTIC BROTHERHOOD. Eleventh annual proceedings of the Grand Camp. Portland, Ore., Nov. 14-16, 1911. Skagway, Daily Alaskan Print, 1911. 41p.   291

ARCTIC BROTHERHOOD. Twelfth annual proceedings of the Grand Camp. North Vancouver, B. C., Nov. 12-14, 1912. Skagway, Daily Alaskan Print, 1912. 45p.   292

ARCTIC BROTHERHOOD. Proceedings of the thirteenth annual Session of the Grand Camp, convened at Juneau, Alaska, July 8-11, 1913. Juneau, Alaska Daily Empire Print, 1913. 20p.   293

ARCTIC BROTHERHOOD. Thirteenth annual proceedings of the Grand Camp, at Seattle, Washington, Nov. 11-13, 1913. no pl., n. d. 32p.   294

ARCTIC BROTHERHOOD. Proceedings of the fourteenth Session of the Grand Camp at Juneau, Alaska, March 14-18, 1915. Juneau, 1915. 21p.   295

ARCTIC BROTHERHOOD. Proceedings of the fifteenth Session of the Grand Camp held at Juneau, Alaska, March 13-19, 1917. Juneau, 1917. 24p.   296

ARCTIC BROTHERHOOD. Ritualistic ceremony adopted by the Provisional Grand Camp of the Arctic Brotherhood. no pl., Jan. 1900. 34p. ANR. ? Ritualistic ceremony adopted ... Aug. 17, 18 and 19, 1900. Skagway, Daily News Print, Jan. 1900. 19p.   297

ARCTIC CLUB, Seattle. Arctic Club, 1908-58; fiftieth anniversary. Seattle, Evergreen Co., [1958 ?] 47p. illus. ports. 298

ARCTIC CLUB, Seattle. Officers, committees, members, by-laws and rules. Seattle, 1901. front. illus. ANR. 1913.   299

Arctic Club, Seattle. SEE ALSO no. 38, Alaska Bureau.

Arctic geography and ethnology. 1875. SEE
    no. 3907, Royal Geographic Soc.

ARCTIC INSTITUTE OF NORTH AMERICA, Montreal. Catalogue of the Library of the Arctic Institute of North America. Montreal, 1968. 4 vols. 3,174p.   300

Arctic Institute of North America, Montreal. SEE ALSO
    no. 3905, Rowley, Diana, edit.

ARCTIC MISCELLANIES; a souvenir of the late polar search by the officers and seamen of the expedition. London, Colburn & Co., 1852. 2d ed. 347p.(plus 16p. of pls.) front.(col.), illus. [1st ed. in 1851. Extracts from newspaper "Aurora Borealis" edited by Dr. Donnett, surgeon on ship *Assistance*, Austin-Ommaney expedition 1850-51 in search for Sir John Franklin]   301

Arctic oil ... 1969. SEE no. 2636, Lathrop High School,

Arctic regions ... search Franklin ... 1853. SEE
    no. 4156, [Simmonds, P. L.]

Arctic research ... 1955. SEE no. 3905, Rowley, Diana.

Arctic world ... 1873. SEE no. 3961, Sargent, Epes.

Arctic zoology, 1784-87. SEE no. 3531, [Pennant, Thos.]

Are you going to Klondike or Alaska ... 1898. SEE
    no. 131, Alaska Trade Committee.

Are you going to Klondike. Take ... 1897. SEE
    no. 4265, Spokane Chamber of Commerce.

Argo red salmon cookbook ... 1911. SEE
    no. 99, Alaska Packers Assoc.

Argonaut [pseud.] SEE no. 1497, [Etches, J. C.]

ARGUMENT UPON THE JUSTICE AND EXPEDIENCY of the order issued by
the government for the detaining all ships bound to the ports of
Spain, freighted with treasures or warlike stores.   London,
Stockdale, 1805. 63p.   302

Armed Forces Pub. SEE no. 4034, Seattle, Century 21
    Exposition 1962.

ARMSBY, J. K., Co. The position of San Francisco in the canned
salmon trade. S. F., 1904.   303

ARMSTRONG, ALEXANDER. A personal narrative of the discovery of
the Northwest Passage; with numerous incidents of travel and
adventure during nearly five years' continuous service in the
Arctic regions while in search of the expedition under Sir John
Franklin, by late surgeon and naturalist of H.M.S. "Investigator".
London, Hurst and Blackett, 1857. 616p. illus. front.(col.),
map(fold.)   304

ARMSTRONG, NEVILL ALEXANDER DRUMMOND. After big game in the Upper Yukon. London, John Long, 1937. 287p. front. illus. pls.
maps.   305

ARMSTRONG, NEVILL ALEXANDER DRUMMOND. Yukon yesterdays; thirty
years of adventure in the Klondike; personal memories of the famous Klondike gold rush, first-hand accounts of lucky strikes,
stories of Dawson in the wild "Nineties, together with adventure
in mining, exploring and big game hunting in the unknown sub-
Arctic. London, John Long, 1936. 287p. front.(port.), illus.
pls. facsims. endmaps, index.   306

ARMSTRONG, TERENCE R. Russian settlement in the north. London,
Cambridge University Press, 1965.   307

ARNELL, HAMPUS WILHELM. Die mosse der Vega-expedition. [TITLE
TR. The mosses from the *Vega* expedition] Stockholm, Almqvist &
Wiksell, 1917. 111p. (Arkiv für Botanik. Bd. 15, no. 5, 1910-19,
pub. 1917) [incls. St. Lawrence Island, other Alaskan]   308

ARNESON, ODD. Roald Amundsen som har var. [TITLE TR. Roald A-
mundsen as he was] Oslo, Gyldendal, Norsk forlag, 1929. 205p.
pls. ports.   309

Arnold, G., auth. SEE no. 3417, Oregon. Dept. Educ.

Arnold, Leslie. SEE no. 4497, Thomas, Lowell.

Arnott, G. A. W., co-auth. SEE no. 2173, Hooker, Wm. J.

ARON, WILLIAM. The distribution of animals in the eastern North Pacific and its relationship to physical and chemical conditions. Seattle, University of Washington, 1960. 220p. tables, diagrs. maps, bibliog. (Department of Oceanography Technical Report no. 63)   310

ART INSTITUTE OF CHICAGO. Yakutat south. Indian art of the northwest coast. Catalogue by Allen Wardwell. Chicago, 1964. 82p. illus.(some col.), map(on cover). [exhibit Mar. 13 to Apr. 26, 1964]   311

ART WORK OF SEATTLE AND ALASKA. Racine, Wisconsin, W. D. Harney Photogravure Co., 1907. 9 vols. wrps. var.p. [some of the photos by Frank Nowell, article on Alaska written by Thomas Nowell]   312

Ashley, M. P., co-edit. SEE no. 1528, Farquhar, F. P.

Ashmead, W. H. SEE no. 1950, Harriman Alaska Exped.

[ASSHER, BEN] A nomad in North America. Pen pictures by a sojourner in the new world. By "Ben Assher." London, R. Holder, 1927. 293p. front. pls.   313

Association on American Indian Affairs. SEE nos.
    729, Burge, M. S. Indians of Upper Tanana ...1938;
    1595, Foote, D. C. Human geog. studies ... Pt. Hope ...1966;
    1596, Foote, D. C. Human geog. studies ... Upper Kobuk. 1966.

Astor, John Jacob. SEE no. 3645, Porter, K. W.

Athearn, R. G., co-auth. SEE no. 3819, Riegel, R. E.

ATHERTON, GERTRUDE. Rezanov. N. Y., Authors & Newspapers Assoc., 1906. 320p. front. illus.(col.), pls. facsim. ANR. N. Y., Boni & Liveright, 1906. 255p. ANR. N. Y., Modern Library, 1906. 255p.   314

ATKINS, BARTON. Modern antiquities; comprising sketches of early Buffalo and the Great Lakes; also sketches of Alaska. Buffalo, The Courier Co., 1898. 190p. illus.   315

ATKINSON, THOMAS H., jr., edit. Alaska petroleum directory. Volume 4, 1962-63. The 49th State's oil and gas industry guide. Revised. Anchorage, Petroleum Publications, 1962. 130p. illus. maps.   316

Atlas geograficheskikh otkrytiĭ ... 1964. SEE no. 4615,
    U. S. S. R. Akademiia nauk.

ATWOOD, EVANGELINE. Anchorage, all-America city. Portland, Ore., Binfords & Mort, 1957. 118p. illus. pls. endmaps, append. 317

ATWOOD, EVANGELINE. We shall be remembered. Anchorage, Alaska Methodist University Press, 1966. 1st ed. 191p. front.(photo), photos, endmaps, bibliog.(note), appends. index. [homesteading Matanuska Valley] 318

Atwood, Evangeline. SEE ALSO no. 237, Anchorage Daily Times.

ATWOOD, FRED, edit. The Alaska-Yukon gold book; a roster of the progressive men and women who were the argonauts of the Klondike gold stampede and those who are identified with the pioneer days and subsequent development of Alaska and the Yukon Territory. Seattle, Sourdough Stampede Association, 1930. 147p. pls. ports. map. 319

ATWOOD, GEORGE H. Along the Alcan. N. Y., Pageant Press, 1960. 1st ed. 212p. illus. maps, endmaps. 320

Atwood, Mrs. Robert B. SEE no. 237, Anchorage Daily Times.

Atwood, W. W. SEE no. 4971, Wright, Hamilton.

AUBERT, FREDERIC. L'Ouest Canadien et le Jukon. Chartres, Imp. M. Laffray, 1907. 87p. 321

AUER, HARRY ANTON. Camp fires in the Yukon. Concinnati, Stewart & Kidd, 1916. 204p. illus. pls. maps. ANR. London, 1917, ANR. N. Y., Appleton, 1926[c1916] 322

Auf unbekannten Meeren; Jas. Cook's Tagebuch ... n. d. SEE no. 1052, [Cook, James]

AUGUR, HELEN. Passage to glory; John Ledyard's America. Garden City, N. Y., Doubleday, 1946. 310p. pls. ports. bibliog. 323

AUMACK, THOMAS M. Rivers of rain; being a fictional accounting of the adventures and misadventures of John Rodgers Jewitt, captive of the Indians at Friendly Cove on Nootka Island in northwest America. Portland, Ore., Binfords & Mort, 1948. 216p. 324

Ausherman, B. M., co-comp. SEE no. 2108, Hills, W. J. Klondike ... 1897.

AUSTIN, BASIL. The diary of a ninety-eighter. Mt. Pleasant, Mich., [printed by John Cumming], 1968. 191p. illus. maps (incl. front.map) 325

AUSTIN, H. T. and WILLIAM PERRY. A review of the proceedings of
the Arctic searching expeditions under command of Captain H. T.
Austin, C.B. and Captain Perry. London, J. D. Potter, 1851.
30p.,23p.,22p. map(fold.) (Arctic papers, no. 1-3. Also a
separate issue of vol. 20, Nautical Magazine, Oct.-Dec. 1851.
pp.529-58, pp.569-91 and pp.667-73)   326

Austin, H. T. SEE ALSO no. 301, Arctic misc. ... 1852.

Authentic Alaska information. [1896 ?] SEE no. 1620,
     Fowler, Frank S., & Co.

Authentic narrative ... 1783. SEE no. 1017, [Cook, Jas.]

Authentic statement ... 1790. SEE no. 1498, [Etches, J. C.]

AUZIAS de TURENNE, RAYMOND. Le dernier mamouth. Paris, Colmann-
Levy, 1904. 286p.   327

AUZIAS de TURENNE, RAYMOND. Le roi du Klondike. Paris, Levy,
[18__ ?] 288p.   328

AUZIAS de TURENNE, RAYMOND. Voyage au pays des mines d'or; le
Klondike. Paris, Levy, 1898. 318p. illus. ports. maps. OTHERS
in 1899. 2d and 3rd eds.   329

AVERKIEVA, Ĩu. P. Rabstvo u Indieĩsev Severnoĭ Ameriki. Moscow,
1941. 100p.   330

AVERKIEVA, Ĩu. P. Razlozhenie rodovoĭ obshchiny i formirovanie
ranneklassovykh otnosheniĭ v obshchestve Indeiĩsev severo-
zapadnogo poberezh'ĩa Svernoĭ Ameriki. [TITLE TR. Decline of the
clan community and formation of early class relations in the society of the Northwest coast Indians of North America] Moskva,
Izd-vo Akademii nauk SSSR, 1961. 272p. illus. maps, bibliog.
(Akademiĩa nauk SSSR. Institut étnografiĭ. Trudy t. 70)   331

                              B

B., W. SEE no. 1308, Dixon, George.

BABCOCK, JOHN PEASE and OTHERS. Investigations of the International Fisheries Commission to December 1930, and their bearing
on regulations of the Pacific halibut fishery. Seattle, 1930.
29p. charts(incl. 1 fold.), diagrs. (International Fisheries
Commission Report, no. 7) [other authors, W. A. Found, Miller
Freeman and Henry O'Malley]   332

BACK, H. S. Something about Alaska and the Arctic region,
especially the Yukon Plateau. Caldwell, Idaho, Caxton, 1927.
32p. front.(port.)   333

BADÉ, WILLIAM FREDERIC. The life and letters of John Muir. Boston, Houghton Mifflin, 1924. 2 vols. fronts.(ports.), illus. [also in "The writings of John Muir," vols. 9 and 10 of Sierra Edition and Manuscript Edition. SEE ALSO nos. 3226 and 3229]334

BADLAM, ALEXANDER. The wonders of Alaska. S. F., Bancroft, 1890. 152p. front. pls. maps. ANR. 1890. 2d ed. rev. 148p. ANR. 1891. 3rd ed. rev. 154p.   335

BAEDEKER, KARL. The Dominion of Canada, with Newfoundland and an excursion to Alaska; handbook for travellers. Leipsic,[sic] 1894. 1st ed. 254p. plans, maps, index. ANR. 1900. 2d ed. 268p. plans, maps. ANR. Leipzig, Karl Baedeker and N. Y., Scribner, 1907. 3rd ed. 331p. plans, maps. ANR. 1922. 4th ed. rev. 420p. plans, maps.   336

BAEDEKER, KARL. The United States, with excursions to Mexico, Cuba, Porto Rico, and Alaska; handbook for travellers. Leipzig, Karl Baedeker and N. Y., Scribner, 1909. 4th ed. rev. 724p. plans, maps.   337

BAER, KARL ERNST von. Avtobiografiīa; red. E. N. Pavlovskogo; perevod i kommentariī B. E. Raĭkova. [TITLE TR. Autobiography; E. N. Pavlovskiĭ, editor; translation and annotations by B. E. Raĭkov] Leningrad, Izd-vo Akademii nauk SSSR, 1950. 544p. illus. ports. bibliog. index. (Akademiīa nauk SSSR. Nauchno-populīarnaīa seriīa; memuary) [tr. of no. 341]   338

BAER, KARL ERNST von. Eine Selbstbiographie, gekürzt herausgegeben von Paul Conradi. Leipzig, Verlag von E. Bruhns, 1912. 220p. port. [abridged ed. of no. 341]   339

BAER, KARL ERNST von. Feier der 50-jahrigen Dienstzeit des Vice-Admirals von Krusenstern. Saint Petersburg, 1839.   340

BAER, KARL ERNST von. Nachrichten über Leben und Schriften, mitgeteit von ihm selbst. Saint Petersburg, 1865. 674p. OTHERS 1866 and 1886. reprinted. [see no. 338 for tr. and no. 339 for aBr. ed.]   341

BAER, KARL ERNST von. Statistische und ethnographische Nachrichten über die Russischen Besitzungen an der Nordwestküste von Amerika. Gesammelt von dem ehemaligen Oberverwalter dieser Besitzungen, contre admiral v. Wrangell. Mit den Berechnungen aus Wrangell's Witterungsbeobachtungen und andern Zusätzen vermehrt von K. E. v. Baer. [TITLE TR. Statistical and ethnographic information on the Russian possession on the northwest coast of America, collected by the administrator of these possessions, Vice-Admiral v. Wrangell ... with computations from Wrangell's weather observations and other additions made by K. E. v. Baer] Saint Petersburg, Akademie der Wissenschaften, 1839. 332p. map(fold.), table(fold.) (Beiträge zur Kenntniss des Russischen Reiches. Bd. 1)   342

Baerg, Harry, illus. SEE no. 618, Booth, E. S.

BAGLEY, CLARENCE BOOTH. Indian myths of the Northwest Coast.
Seattle, Loman & Hanford, 1930. 145p. front.(port.), illus. 343

BAIDUKOV, GEORGIĬ FILIPOVICH. Nash polet v Ameriku;   zapiski
letchika-shturmana.   [TITLE TR. Our flight to America;   notes
of the navigator]   Moskva, Partizdat TSK VKP(6), 1937.   34p.
illus.   344

     TRANSLATION - Nash polet ... 1937.

     Over the North Pole. Translated by Jessica Smith. N. Y.,
          Harcourt Brace, 1938. 99p. pls. ports. endmaps.   345

BAIDUKOV, GEORGIĬ FILIPOVICH.   O Chkalove. [TITLE TR.   About
Chkalov]   Moskva, Gos. izd-vo "Khudozhestvennaĭā literatura,"
1939. 201p. port.   346

Baidukov, Georgiĭ Filipovich. SEE ALSO nos.
     922, Chkalov, V. P. Shturmanskiĭ ... [1939 ?];
     923, Chkalov, V. P. Navigator's ... 1939;
     4279, Stalinskiĭ Marshrut Prodolzhen ... 1937.

BAILEY, ALFRED MARSHALL. Birds of Arctic Alaska. Denver, Colorado Museum of Natural History, 1948. 317p. front.(port.), illus. photos, map(sketch), bibliog. index.   (Popular Series,
no. 8)   347

BAILEY, ALFRED MARSHALL.   The birds of Cape Prince of Wales,
Alaska.   Denver, Colorado Museum of Natural History, 1943.
113p. illus. map, bibliog. index. (Proceedings, vol. 18, no.1)
                                                              348

BAILEY, BERNADINE.   Picture book of Alaska.   Chicago, Albert
Whitman, 1959.   (14)p. front. map, illus. ANR. 1963. rev.
illus.   349

Bailey, J. L., jr. SEE no. 2423, Keep, J.

BAILEY, THOMAS A. A diplomatic history of the American people.
N. Y., 1950. ANR. N. Y., Appleton-Century-Crofts, 1958. 6th
ed. ix,896p. [references to Bering Sea controversy]   350

BAILEY, THOMAS A. America faces Russia; Russian-American relations from early times to our day. Ithaca, Cornell University
Press, 1950. xi,375p. ANR. Gloucester, Mass., Peter Smith,
1964. reprint.   351

BAILLIE-GROHMAN, WILLIAM ADOLPH. Fifteen years' sport and life in the hunting grounds of western America and British Columbia with a chapter by Mrs. Baillie-Grohman. Illustrated by seventy-seven photographs, including the best trophies of North American big game killed by English and American sportsmen, with table of measurements and notes, with three specially prepared maps of the northwest coast of the United States, British Columbia and the Kootenay district. London, H. Cox, 1900. 403p. port. pls. maps(fold.), index. ANR. 1907. 2d ed.   352

BAINES, THOMAS. Northern goldfield diaries. Edited by J. P. R. Wallis. N. Y., Humanities Press, 1965. 3 vols.   353

BAIRD, ANDREW. Sixty years on the Klondike. Vancouver, B. C., Gordon Black, 1965. 111p. illus. [series of articles in Western Miner magazine]   354

BAIRD, PATRICK D. and D. J. SALT. Report on expedition Snow Cornice. Ottawa, National Research Council of Canada, 1949. 13p. graphs, diagrs. (Associate Committee on Soil and Snow Mechanics. Technical Memorandum no. 14)   355

Baird, Spencer Fullerton. SEE no. 1166. Dall, Wm. H.

BAITY, ELIZABETH CHESLEY. Americans before Columbus; with drawing and maps by C. B. Falls. N. Y., Viking, 1951. 256p. illus. drawings, photos, maps. ANR. 1961. rev. ed. 224p. illus.
                                                            356

Baker, Geo. E., edit. SEE no. 4079, Seward, Wm. H.

BAKER, J. N. L. A history of geographical discovery and exploration. London, G. G. Harrap, 1931.   357

BAKER, JOHN. Southeastern opportunity bulletin. Ketchikan, n.d. [ca 1953]   358

BAKER, JOHN CLAPP. Baptist history of the north Pacific Coast, with special reference to western Washington, British Columbia and Alaska. Philadelphia, American Baptist Pub. Soc., [1912] 472p. front.(port.), illus. ports.   359

Baker, Milford, co-edit. SEE nos.
    614-16, Boone and Crockett Club.

BALBI, A. Atlas ethnog. du globe on classification des peuples anciens et modernes d'apres leur langues. Paris, Rey and Gravelier, 1826. pls.   360

Balch, Edwin Swift. Der Nordpol ... 1914. SEE no. 364.

BALCH, EDWIN SWIFT, edit. Letters and papers relating to the
Alaska frontier. Philadelphia, Press of Allen, Lane and Scott,
1904. 134p. maps.   361

BALCH, EDWIN SWIFT. Mount McKinley and mountain climbers'
proofs. Philadelphia, Campion and Co., 1914. 142p. illus. 362

BALCH, EDWIN SWIFT. The North Pole and Bradley Land. Philadelphia, Campion and Co., 1913. 91p. map.   363

    TRANSLATION - North Pole and ... 1913.

    Der Nordpol und Bradley Land ... autorisierte deutsche uber-
        setzung von Erwin Volckmann; mit einer kartenskizze.
        Hamburg, A. Janssen, 1914. 62p. map.   364

BALCH, THOMAS WILLING. Die Alaska-Grenze; eine geschichtliche,
politische und staatsrechtliche Abhandlung. Alleinberechtigte
deutsche Ausg. von Erwin Volckmann. Würzburg, Gebr. Memminger,
1922. 145p. maps. [tr. of no. 366]   365

BALCH, THOMAS WILLING. The Alaska frontier. Philadelphia, Allen, Lane & Scott, 1903. 198p. front. maps [for tr. see no.
365]   366

BALCH, THOMAS WILLING. The Alasko-Canadian frontier. Philadelphia, Press of Allen, Lane and Scott, 1902. 45p. maps. [re-
printed from: Franklin Institute Journal, vol. 153, pp.161-192.
March 1902]   367

BALCHEN, BERNT. Come north with me; an autobiography. N. Y.,
Dutton, 1958. 318p. illus. maps, index. ANR. London, 1959.
318p. photos, maps, index.   368

Balchen, Bernt. SEE ALSO no. 2494, Knight, C.

BALCOM, MARY G. Creek Street. Chicago, Adams Press, 1963.
115p. illus.   369

BALCOM, MARY G. Ghost towns of Alaska. Chicago, Adams Press,
1965. 80p. illus. maps, bibliog.   370

BALCOM, MARY G. Ketchikan, Alaska's totem land. The Tlingit,
the Tsimshian, the white man. Totems in Saxman Totem Park.
Chicago, Adams Press, [c1961] 127p. illus. bibliog. wrps.
ANR. 1968. 2d ed. 137p. illus. bibliog. wrps.   371

Baldwin, A. C. SEE no. 2249, Hyde, Alexander.

BALDWIN, ED. The Alaska gardener. no pl., n. d. [Anchorage, ca
1958] 38p. (The Northlander)   372

BALDWIN, GORDON C. America's buried past. N. Y., Putnam, 1962.
192p.   373

BALL, JOHN DUDLEY, jr. Arctic showdown; an Alaskan adventure.
N. Y., Duell, Sloan & Pearce, 1966. 147p. illus.   374

BALLAINE, JOHN EDMUND. Strangling of the Alaska Railroad, government owned project built at cost of over $462,000,000, devel-
opments suppressed, millions wasted, victim of intrigue cen-
tering in New York, confidential contracts in evidence; the
simple remedy, a constructive program of developments honestly
applied. [Seattle ?, 1923 ?] 42p.   375

Ballinger, Richard H. SEE no. 4211, Smyth, Nathan A.

BALLOU, MATURIN MURRAY. The new Eldorado; a summer journey to
Alaska. Boston, Houghton Mifflin, 1889. 352p. OTHER EDITIONS
to 1899.   376

BANCROFT, FREDERIC. The life of William H. Seward ... N. Y.,
Harper, 1900. 2 vols. illus. fronts. ports.   377

BANCROFT, HUBERT HOWE. Chronicles of the builders of the Commonwealth. S. F., 1891-92. 7 vols.   378

BANCROFT, HUBERT HOWE. History of Alaska, 1730-1885. S. F.,
A. L. Bancroft & Co., 1886. 775p. illus. maps(incl. some fold.)
bibliog. index. ANR. S. F., The History Co., 1890. 775p. ANR.
N. Y., Antiquarian Press, 1959. reprint ed. ltd. to 750 copies.
ANR. N. Y., McGraw-Hill, 1967. reprint ed. ANR. N. Y., Hafner
Pub. Co., 1970. reprint ed. [also in "Works ..." vol. 33] 379

BANCROFT, HUBERT HOWE. History of the northwest coast, 1543-
1846. S. F., A. L. Bancroft & Co., 1884. 2 vols. 793p. and
768p. illus. maps, bibliog. index. ANR. S. F., 1890. 2 vols.
ANR. N. Y., Bancroft Co., n. d. 2 vols. ANR. N. Y., McGraw-
Hill, 1967. 2 vols. reprint. [also in "Works ... " vols.
27-28]   380

BANCROFT, HUBERT HOWE. The native races of the Pacific States
of North America. S. F., A. L. Bancroft & Co., 1874-75. 5 vols.
illus. maps, bibliog. index. ANR. N. Y., D. Appleton, 1874-75.
5 vols. OTHERS 1882, 1883-86 AND 1890. ANR. N. Y., 1967. reprint. [also in "Works ... " vols. 1-5]   381

BANDI, HANS-GEORG. Alaska, Urgeschichte Geschichte, Gegenwart.
Stuttgart, Berlin, Köln, Main, Kohlhammer, 1967. 148p. illus.
maps, bibliog. (Urban Bücher, 104)   382

Bandi, Hans-Georg. Eskimo prehistory. SEE no. 383.

BANDI, HANS-GEORG. Urgeschichte der Eskimo. Stuttgart, G. Fischer, 1965. 171p. illus. maps, bibliog. ANR. IN ENGLISH: Eskimo prehistory. Translated by Ann E. Keep. College, University of Alaska Press, [c1969] 1st print. xii,226p. illus. figs. maps, endmaps, bibliog. append. index. (University of Alaska Dept. of Anthropology and Geography, Studies of Northern Peoples, no. 2. Edward H. Hosley, editor)   383

Bandi, Hans-Georg. SEE ALSO no. 4006, Schmitz, C. A.

BANFIELD, ALEXANDER WILLIAM FRANCIS. A revision of the reindeer and caribou genus *Rangifer*. Ottawa, 1961. 137p. illus. diagrs. tables, maps, bibliog. (Canada. Dept. of Northern Affairs and National Resources. National Museum Bulletin no. 177, Biol. Ser. no. 66) [covers Eurasian and North American with summary in Russian]   384

BANK, TED. Birthplace of the winds. N. Y., Thos. Y. Crowell Co., 1956. 274p. photos, sketches. [Aleutian Islands]   385

BANKSON, RUSSELL ARDEN. The Klondike Nugget. Caldwell, Idaho, Caxton, 1935. 349p. illus. front. ports. pls. [biog. Eugene C. Allen, newspaper publisher]   386

Bankson, Russell. SEE ALSO no. 4499, Thomas, Lowell, jr.

Bannister, Henry M. SEE no. 2326, James, Jas. Alton.

BANOW, EDWARD MAGAWLY. The diary of Edward Magawly Banow. Newport, R. I., [privately printed], 1948. [Klondike gold rush]387

Baranov, Aleksandr Andreevich. SEE nos.
      907, Cheney, W. Way of north ... 1905;
      909, Chevigny, H. Lord of Alaska ... 1942;
      2455, Khlĭebnikov, K. T. Zhizneopisanie... 1835;
      3814, Ricks, M. B. Earliest hist. Alaska ... 1970;
      4840, White, S. E. Pole star. 1953.

BARANSKIĬ, N. N., edit. Amerikanskiĭ Sever; sbornik perevodnykh stateĭ, so vstup, stat'eĭ I. I. Ermasheva, pod obshcheĭ red. N. N. Baranskogo. [TITLE TR. The American North; a collection of translated articles, with an introduction by I. I. Ermashev, under the editorship of N. N. Baranskiĭ] Moskva, Izd-vo inostrannoĭ lit-ry, 1950. 290p. maps(some fold.)   388

BARBEAU, CHARLES MARIUS. Alaska beckons. By Marius Barbeau. Illustrated by Arthur Price. Caldwell, Idaho, Caxton, 1947. 343p. front. illus. bibliog. ANR. Toronto, Macmillan of Canada, 1947.   389

46

BARBEAU, CHARLES MARIUS.   Haida myths illustrated in argillite.
Ottawa, Queen's Printer, 1953. 417p. illus. (Canada. National
Museum Bulletin no. 127, Anthropological Ser. no. 32)   390

BARBEAU, CHARLES MARIUS.   Medicine men on the north Pacific
coast.   Ottawa, Queen's Printer, 1958. 95p. illus. photos.
(Canada. National Museum Bulletin no. 42)   391

BARBEAU, CHARLES MARIUS. Pathfinders in the north Pacific.
Drawings by Arthur Price. Caldwell, Idaho, Caxton, 1958. 235p.
illus. bibliog. index. ANR. Toronto, Ryerson Press, 1958.   392

BARBEAU, CHARLES MARIUS and G. MELVIN. The Indian speaks. Caldwell, Idaho, Caxton, 1943. 117p. illus. ANR. Toronto, 1943. 393

BARBEAU, CHARLES MARIUS.   Totem poles. Ottawa, Queen's Printer,
1964. 2 vols. [vol. 1: *Totem poles according to crests and
topics*. vol. 2: *Totem poles according to location*] 433p. and
pp.435-880. illus. pls. endmaps, bibliog. (Canada. National
Museum Bulletin no. 119, Anthropological Ser. no. 30) ANR. 1950.
1st ed. [incls. southeastern Alaska]   394

BARBEAU, CHARLES MARIUS.   Tsimsyan myths, illustrated. Ottawa,
1961. 97p. illus. endmaps.   (Canada. Dept. Northern Affairs
and Natural Resources.   National Museum Bulletin no. 174, Anthropological Ser. no. 51)   395

Barbeau, Charles Marius. SEE ALSO nos.
     4202, Smith, M. W. Tsimshian ... 1951;
     4427, Swayze, Nansi. Man hunters ... 1960.

BARBER, J. W. Alaskan gold fields;   a few facts regarding the
Copper River country. L. A., 1897. 8p.   396

BARBER, OLIVE. Meet me in Juneau. Portland, Binfords and Mort,
1960. 1st ed. 175p. illus. photos. ANR. 1963. 258p.   397

Barcelo, N. Y., co-auth.   SEE no. 4229, Sobreviela, M.

BARFUS, E. von. Die goldsucher am Klondyke.   Stuttgart, [ca
1880] illus.(col. pls.)   398

Bark, L. D., co-auth. SEE no. 1551, Feyerherm, A. M.

BARKER, ELIZA B.   Alaska, a historical impersonation.   N. Y.,
Woman's Board of Home Missions of the Presbyterian Church, 1912.
14p.   399

BARLOW, ROGER.   Secret mission to Alaska.   N. Y., Grosset and
Dunlap, 1966. 158p. (Sandy Steele Adventures.   Tempo Books)
ANR. N. Y., Grosset and Dunlap, 1959.   400

Barnard, John. SEE no. 1826. Great Britain.

BARNES, CLIFFORD A. and THOMAS G. THOMPSON. Physical and chemical investigations in Bering Sea and portions of the north Pacific Ocean. Seattle, University of Washington, 1938. 208p.
charts. (Publications in Oceanography, vol. 3, no. 2)   401

Barnes, Clifford A., co-auth. SEE ALSO nos.
     962, Coachman, L. K. Contrib. Bering Sea water ... 1961;
     4510, Thompson, Thos. G. Distrib. dissolved oxygen ... 1934.

Barnes, Kathleen. SEE no. 1853, Gregory, H. E.

BARNUM, FRANCIS. Grammatical fundamentals of the Innuit language
as spoken by the Eskimo of the western coast of Alaska. Boston,
Ginn & Co., 1901. 384p. tables, diagrs.   402

BARNUM, FRANCIS. Life on the Alaska Mission, with an account of
the foundation of the Mission and the work performed. Woodstock,
Md., Woodstock College Press, 1893. 39p.   403

BARNUM, FRANCIS. To the Yukon River by way of Chilkoot Pass.
[Woodstock, Md. ?, 1896 ?] 18p. (Woodstock Letters)   404

BARRELL, GEORGE. Notes of voyages and incidents ... in a career
of thirty years at sea (1823-54). Springfield, Illinois, 1890.
[Alaska, Hawaii and California in 1824-25]   405

BARRETT-HAMILTON, GERALD E. H. Report of his mission to the
Russian seal islands in 1897. London, 1898. 67p.   406

BARRINGTON, DAINES. Miscellanies of the Honourable Daines Barrington. London, 1781. 557p. ports. maps, charts. [incls.
Maurelle, F. A. "Journal voyage in 1775 ... " 1781]   407

Barrington, Daines. SEE ALSO nos.
     3036, Maurelle, F. A. Journal ... 1781;
     4570, [Travers, de Val ?] Summary observations ...1776.

BARROW, HENRY D. Paradise North; an Alaskan year. With thirty-
five line drawings by Susan Barrow. N. Y., Dial Press, 1956.
242p. illus. map, bibliog. [tide pool studies]   408

BARROW, JOHN, edit. A chronological history of voyages into the
Arctic regions; undertaken chiefly for the purpose of discovering
a north-east, north-west, or polar passage between the Atlantic
and Pacific ... London, J. Murray, 1818. 379p. +48p. illus. map
(fold.), append.   409

     TRANSLATION - Chronological history ... 1818.

     Storia cronologica del viaggi al polo artico, recata in lin-
       gua Italiana da N. N. Milan, 1820. 2 vols.   410

BARROW, JOHN. Cook's voyages of discovery. Edited by John Barrow ... with eight illustrations in colour by John Williamson. London, A. & C. Black, 1904. 417p. ANR. 1925. 411

BARROW, JOHN. Cook's voyages, 1768-80. New edition, edited by J. Barrow, and letters of Captain Cook hitherto unpublished, and a facsimile of log book. Edinburgh, 1860. illustrated by C. A. Doyle. 412

Barrow, John. Storia cronologica ... 1820. SEE no. 410.

BARROW, JOHN. Voyages of discovery and research within the arctic regions, from the year 1818 to the present time ... abridged and arranged from official narratives, with occasional remarks. London, J. Murray, 1846. 530p. ANR. N. Y., 1846. 359p. 413

Barrow, Susan. SEE no. 408, Barrow, Henry D.

Barruel, P., co-auth. SEE no. 1694, Gaussen, H.

[BARSUKOV, IVAN PLATOVICH] Innokentiĭa, mitropolit moskovskiĭ i kolomenskiĭ, po ego sochineniĭa, pis'ma i rozskazam sovremennikov. [TITLE TR. Innocent, Metropolitan of Moscow and Kolomena, in his writings, letters, and reports of his contemporaries] Moscow, Synodic Printery, 1883. 769p. pls. [biog. of I. E. P. Veniaminov, first Bishop of Alaska] 414

[BARSUKOV, IVAN PLATOVICH] Life and work of Innocent, the Archbishop of Kamchatka, the Kuriles and the Aleutian Islands, and later the Metropolitan of Moscow. S. F., Cubery & Co.,Printers, 1897. 23p. [based upon "Pis'ma Innokentiĭa ... " 1897-1901, "printed for distribution among the people by request of the Most Reverend Bishop Nicholas."] 415

[BARSUKOV, IVAN PLATOVICH] Pis'ma Innokentiĭa, metropolit moskovskiĭ i kolomenskiĭ, 1828-1878. [TITLE TR. Letters of Innocent, Metropolitan of Moscow and Kolomena, 1828-1878] St. Petersburg, 1897-1901. 3 vols. 416

[BARSUKOV, IVAN PLATOVICH] Tvoreniĭa Innokentiĭa, metropolit moskovskiĭ. [TITLE TR. The works of Innocent, Metropolitan of Moscow] Moscow, Synodic Printery, 1887. 3 vols. 1407p. 417

Barsukov, Ivan Platovich. SEE ALSO no. 3934, S., Z.

BARTELS TIN MINING CO. Tin in the United States of America, richest mines in the world discovered in Alaska. N. Y., 1904. 14p. 418

BARTLETT, ROBERT ABRAM. Sails over ice, by Captain "Bob" Bartlett. N. Y., Scribner, 1934. 301p. illus. front. endmaps. [ship *Effie M. Morrissey*] 419

BARTLETT, ROBERT ABRAM and RALPH T. HALE. The last voyage of the
Karluk, as related by her master, Robert A. Bartlett, and here
set down by Ralph T. Hale. Boston, Small, Maynard, 1916. 1st
ed. 329p. front. pls. ports. maps, plans, facsims. ANR. Boston,
Hale, Cushman and Flint, 1928. ANR. WITH TITLE Northward Ho !
The last voyage of the *Karluk*. Boston, Small, Maynard, 1919. 2d
print. [flagship of Canadian Arctic Expedition of 1813-16]   420

BARTLETT, ROBERT ABRAM. The log of "Bob" Bartlett, the true
story of forty years of seafaring and exploration. N. Y., Putnam,
1928. 352p. front.(port.), pls. ANR. N. Y., Blue Ribbon Books,
1932. 6th impr.   421

Bartlett, Robert Abram. SEE ALSO nos.
    1844, Green, F. Bob Bartlett ... 1929;
    3705, Putnam, G. P. Mariner ... [c1947];
    3962, Sarnoff, P. Ice pilot ... 1966;
    4573, Treadwell, A. L. Polychaetus annelids ... 1926.

BARTLEY, DEANE C., edit. Cachets of the U. S. Frigate *Constitution*, Pacific coast cruise, 1933-34. Seattle, 1934. 128p. illus. ports. facsims.   422

BARTZ, FRITZ. Alaska. Stuttgart, K. F. Koehler, 1950. 384p.
illus. pls. maps(incl. some fold.), bibliog. (Geographisce Hand-
bücher; hrsg. von Hermann Lautensach)   423

BARTZ, FRITZ. Fischgründe und Fischereiwirtschaft an der Westküste Nordamerikas; Werdegang, Lebens und Sidelungsformen eines
jungen Wirtschaftsraumes. [TITLE TR. Fishing grounds and
fisheries economy on the west coast of North America; the genesis, forms of life and settlement of a young economic area]
Kiel, Buchdruckerei Schmidt & Kaunig, 1942. 174p. illus. text-
figs. maps(text), bibliog. (Kiel Universität, Geographisces Institut. Schriften, Bd. 12)   424

Bashutski, A., tr. SEE no. 1375, Dumont d'Urville, J. S. C.

BASKINE, GERTRUDE. Hitch-hiking the Alaska Highway. Toronto,
Macmillan of Canada, 1944. 317p.   425

BATCHELOR, GEORGE. Unification of North America. A law, a busi-
ness, a duty, a plan of continental construction. N. Y., August
Brentano, Jan. 1, 1867. 16p. [incls. reference to purchase of
Russian America]   426

BATES, EMILY KATHARINE. Kaleidoscope; shifting scenes from
east to west. London, Ward & Downey, 1889. 275p. [some reference to Alaska]   427

BATES, RUSSELL S. The man on the dump, his songs and adventures,
a booklet of verse; with decorations by the author. Seattle,
O. Patten & Co., 1909. 67p. illus. (A-Y-P Souvenir Edition) 428

BATH, MARKUS. Ultra-long-period motions from the Alaska earthquake of July 10, 1958. Uppsala, 1958. 12p. graphs, tables,
bibliog. (Uppsala Universitet Meteorologiska Institutichen,
Meddelande no. 61) [reprinted from: Geofisica para e applicata.
Milano, 1958, vol. 41, pp.91-100]   429

BATTEN, E. STANLEY. The summertime reversal of winds in the
lower stratosphere. Santa Monica, Calif., Rand Corporation,
June 17, 1959. 18 ℓ maps, graphs, references. (Presented at
National Conference on Stratospheric Meteorology, Minneapolis,
Minnesota, Aug. 31-Sept. 3, 1959) [Naknek, Alaska: Seattle,
Washington: Thule, Greenland]   430

BAUER, H. Ein Leben für die Eskimo; das Schichsal des For-
schens Knud Rasmussen. [TITLE TR. A life for the Eskimos; the
fate of the explorer, Knud Rasmussen] Leipzig, Brockhaus, 1960.
209p. illus. map, bibliog.   431

Baum, Lyman Frank. SEE no. 25, [Akers, Floyd, pseud.]

BAXTER, DOW VAWTER and F. H. WADSWORTH. Forest and fungus suc-
cession in the lower Yukon Valley. Ann Arbor, University of
Michigan, 1939. 52p. illus. pls. tables, diagrs. (School of
Forestry and Conservation Bulletin no. 9)   432

BAXTER, DOW VAWTER and REED W. VARNER. Importance of fungi and
defects in handling Alaskan airplane spruce. Ann Arbor, University of Michigan, 1942. 35p. pls. (School of Forestry and Conservation Circular no. 6)   433

BAXTER, DOW VAWTER, B. LABARCE and W. HILDEBRAND. On and off
Alaskan trails. Drawings by Carleton Angell. no pl., 1937.
184p. pls. endmaps.   434

Bayard, Thos. F. SEE no. 4453, Tansill, Chas.

BAYLISS, CLARA K. A treasury of Eskimo tales. N. Y., Thomas Y.
Crowell, 1922. 135p. illus.(col.) by George Carlson.   435

BAYLY, GEORGE. Sea-life sixty years ago. A record of adventures which led up to the discovery of the relics of the long-
missing expedition commanded by the Comte de La Pérouse. N. Y.,
Harper, 1886. 191p.   436

[BAYLY, WILLIAM] The original astronomical observations made in
the course of a voyage to the northern Pacific Ocean for the discovery of a north east or north west passage, wherein the north
west coast of America and north east coast of Asia were explored
in His Majesty's ships, the *Resolution* and *Discovery* in the
years 1776, 1777, 1778, 1779 and 1780, by Captain James Cooke and
Lt. James King and Mr. William Bayly ... London, W. Richardson,
1782. 351p. diagr. [also attributed to John Rickman]   437

BEACH, REX. Alaskan adventures; three thrilling novels of the far north in one volume: The Spoilers, The Barrier, The Silver Horde. N. Y., A. L. Burt, n. d. (c1909] 313p., 309p., 389p. 438

BEACH, REX. Oh, shoot ! Confessions of an agitated sportsman. With illustrations from photographs taken by the author. N. Y., Harper, 1921. 281p. illus. ANR. WITH TITLE Confessions of a sportsman (Oh shoot ! Confessions of an agitated sportsman) Garden City, N. Y., Garden City Pub. Co., 1927 [c1921] front. (pl.), pls. (The Star Series) 439

BEACH, REX. Pardners. N. Y., McClure, Phillips, 1905. 278p. front. pls. ANR. N. Y., A. L. Burt, n. d. [short stories] 440

BEACH, REX. Personal exposures. N. Y., Harper, [c1940] 1st. ed. 303p. [biog.] 441

BEACH, REX. The barrier, a novel. N. Y., Harper, [c1908] 1st ed. 309p. front.(pl.), pls. ANR. N. Y., A. L. Burt, n. d. [c1908] [also in no. 438] 442

BEACH, REX. The crimson gardenia and other tales of adventure. N. Y., Harper, [1916] 377p. 443

BEACH, REX. The goose woman and other stories. N. Y., Harper, 1925 [c1925] 1st ed. 266p. [of five short stories, two have Alaskan settings, *Cave Stuff* and *The Michigan Kid*] 444

BEACH, REX. The iron trail; an Alaskan romance. N. Y., Harper, 1913. 391p. front.(pl.), pls. ANR. N. Y., A. L. Burt, n. d. ANR. N. Y., Doubleday, 1965. 305p. (Dolphin Books C459) 445

BEACH, REX. The silver horde. N. Y., Harper, [c1909] 390p. front.(pl.), pls. illus. by Harvey T. Dunn. ANR. N. Y., A. L. Burt, n. d. ANR. N. Y., P. F. Collier, n. d. (Yukon Edition) [also in no. 438] 446

BEACH, REX. The spoilers. By Rex E. Beach. N. Y., Harper, 1906 [c1905] 314p. front.(pl.), pls. illus. by Clarence F. Underwood. [also in no. 438] ANR. N. Y., A. L. Burt, n. d. ANR. WITH TITLE The spoilers, a play in four acts. By Rex Beach and James McArthur. no pl., n. d. 177p. 447

BEACH, REX. The winds of chance. N. Y., Harper, [c1918] 522p. front.(pl.), pls. ANR. N. Y., P. F. Collier, 1918. (Yukon Edition) 448

BEACH, REX. Valley of thunder. N. Y., Farrar and Rinehart, 1939. 326p. 449

BEACH, REX. World in his arms. N. Y., Putnam, 1945. 214p. 450

Beach, Rex.   SEE ALSO nos.
   3202, Morrow, Wm. W.   "The spoilers." 1916;
   4499, Thomas, Lowell, jr.   Trail of '98. [c1962]

BEACH, W. W., edit.   The Indian miscellany; containing papers
on the history, antiquities, arts, languages, religion, traditions and superstitions of the American aborigines; travels and
adventures in the Indian country; incidents of border warfare
... Albany, J. Munsell, 1877. 490p. illus. [incls. *Alaskan
mummies* by W. H. Dall, pp.344-51, reprinted from: American
Naturalist, Aug. 1875 issue]   451

BEACH, WILLIAM NICHOLAS.   In the shadow of Mount McKinley.
N. Y., Derrydale Press, 1931. 289p. front.(col.), pls. ports.
paintings by Carl Rungius, photos by author, map(fold.), endmaps.
                                                                452

BEAGLEHOLE, JOHN CAWTE, edit.   The exploration of the Pacific.
London, A. & C. Black, 1934. [incls. voyages of Capt. James
Cook]   453

BEAGLEHOLE, JOHN CAWTE, edit.   The journals of Captain James
Cook on his voyages of discovery. Cambridge, Cambridge University Press, 1955-56. 3 vols. (Published for the Hakluyt Society) [vol. 3 contains voyages of *Resolution* and *Discovery*]   454

BEATTIE, KIM.   Brother, here's a man ! The saga of Klondike
Boyle. N. Y., Macmillan, 1940. 1st print. 309p. front. pls.
ports.   455

BEATTIE, WILLIAM GILBERT.   Marsden of Alaska, a modern Indian,
minister, missionary, musician, engineer, pilot, boat builder,
and church builder. N. Y., Vantage Press, 1955. 246p.   456

BEATY, JOHN Y.   Sharp ears, the baby whale. Philadelphia, Lippincott, 1938.   457

BEAUTIES OF CAPTAIN COOK'S VOYAGES ... containing ... the manners
and customs of the inhabitants of Nootka Sound ... London, G.
Lister, 1785. 129p. pl.   458

BEAVER, C. MASTEN.   Fort Yukon trader; three years in an Alaskan wilderness. N. Y., Exposition Press, [c1955] 1st ed.
185p. front.(port.), pls. [Northern Commercial Co. trading
post]   459

Beaver Club of Oregon.   SEE no. 874, Cavana, Violet V.

[BECHERVAISE, JOHN?]   Thirty-six years of a seafaring life.
Portsea, 1864. 336p. [with Capt. F. W. Beechey in 1826 and
1827]   460

Bechtel-Price-Callahan.   SEE no. 1562, Finnie R.

BECK, GEORGE J. Soncth-Shan (The old hat). N. Y. Womans' Board of Home Missions of the Presbyterian Church, 1909. 7p.   461

Beck, Larry. SEE nos. 4048, 4057, Service, Robert W.

BECKER, ETHEL ANDERSON. A treasury of Alaskana. Seattle, Superior Pub. Co., 1969. 1st ed. 183p. photos, index. [photos by gold rush photographers]   462

BECKER, ETHEL ANDERSON. Klondike '98. Hegg's album of the 1898 Alaska gold rush. Portland, Ore., Binfords & Mort, 1949. 1st ed. 127p. illus. photos by Eric A. Hegg, maps. ANR. WITH TITLE Klondike '98; E. A. Hegg's gold rush album. Portland, Ore., Binfords & Mort, 1967. rev. ed. 96p.   463

Beddie, M. K., edit. SEE no. 3294, New South Wales, Library.

BEE, JAMES W. and E. RAYMOND HALL. Mammals of northern Alaska on the Arctic Slope. Lawrence, University of Kansas, 1956. 309p. front.(col.), figs.(incl. maps), tables, bibliog. (Museum of Natural History Misc. Pub. no. 8, pt. 1. Mammals, Alaska. pt. 2. Mammals, Arctic regions)   464

BEEBE, BURDETTA FAYE and JAMES RALPH JOHNSON. American bears. N. Y., David McKay, 1965. illus.   465

BEEBE, IOLA. The true life story of Swiftwater Bill Gates by his mother-in-law. no pl., 1908. 139p. illus. ports. ANR. Seattle, Lumberman's Printing Co., 1915. 139p. illus. ports. 466

BEECHEY, FREDERICK WILLIAM. Narrative of a voyage to the Pacific and Beering's Strait to co-operate with the Polar Expeditions; performed in His Majesty's ship *Blossom*, under the command of Captain F. W. Beechey, R. N. ... in the years 1825, 26, 27, 28. Published by authority of the Lords Commissioners of the Admiralty. In two parts. London, Henry Colburn & Richard Bentley, 1831. 2 vols. 392p. and pp.393-742. illus. pls. maps(incl. 2 fold.) ANR. London, Henry Colburn & Richard Bentley, 1831. 2 vols. enl. ed. 472p. and 452p. illus. pls. maps(fold.), append. ANR. Philadelphia, Carey & Lea, 1832. 493p. [1832 ed. has no pls. maps or append., has added ftntes.] [see no. 468 for tr.] 467

BEECHEY, FREDERICK WILLIAM. Reise nach dem Stillen Ocean und der Beeringstrasze zur Mitwirkung bei den Polarexpeditionen, ausgefuhrt in Konigl. Engl. Schiffe *Blossom* unter dem Commando des Capitain F. W. Beechey in den Jahren 1825, 26, 27, und 28; hrsg. im Auftrage der Lords-Commissare der Admiralitat, aus dem Englischen ubersetzt. Weimer, Verlage des Landes-industrie, 1832. 2 vols. pl.(fold.), map, table. (Neue Bibliothek der wichtigsten Reisebeschreibungen der Erd- und Volkerkunde. Bd. 59, and 61) [tr. of no. 467]   468

BEECHEY, FREDERICK WILLIAM and others. The zoology of Captain Beechey's voyage; compiled from the collections and notes made by Captain Beechey, the officers and naturalist of the expedition, during a voyage to the Pacific and Behrings' Straits performed in His Majesty's ship *Blossom*, under the command of Captain F. W. Beechey ... in the years 1825, 26, 27, 28. London, H. G. Bohn, 1839. 180p. illus. pls.(col.) maps(incl. 1 fold.)
469

Beechey, Frederick William. SEE ALSO nos.
  460, [Bechervaise, John ?] Thirty-six years ... 1864;
  2173, Hooker, Wm. J. Botany ... 1841;
  2219, Huish, R. Narrat. voyages ... 1836.

BEGG, ALEXANDER. Report relative to the Alaskan Boundary question. Victoria, B. C., R. Wolfendon, 1896. 17p.   470

BEGG, ALEXANDER. Review of the Alaskan Boundary question. Victoria, B. C., T. R. Cusack, 1900. 32p. reprint (from British Columbia Misc. Records, vol. 7, June, July and Aug. 1900]   471

Bering Sea arbitration ... 1893. SEE no. 581, [Blowitz, H.]

Beim, Jerrold. SEE no. 472.

BEIM, LORRAINE and JERROLD BEIM. The little igloo. N. Y., Harcourt, 1941. (72)p. illus.(col.) by Howard Simon.   472

BEKLEMISHEV, K. V. and E. A. LUBNY-GERTSYK. Distribution of zooplankton in the northeastern Pacific during the winter of 1958-59. Nanaimo, British Columbia, Biological Station, 1959. map, bibliog. (Canada. Fisheries Research Board Translation Series no. 261. Tr. of *Raspredelenie zooplantona v severovostochnoĭ chasti Tikhogo okeana zimoĭ 1958-59 gg.* from Akademiia nauk SSSR. Doklady 1959. t. 128, no. 6, pp.1271-73)   473

BEL, JEAN-MARC. Gites auriferes du Klondike (Yukon, Canada). Communication donnee a la seance du District de Paris de la Societe de l'industrie minerale, le 10 Decembre 1903, par J.-M. Bel ... St. Etienne, Soc. de l'imp. Theolier, J. Thomas et cie, 1905. 43p. (Extrait du Bull. de la Soc. de l'industrie minerale. Quart. ser., tome 4, 1905)   474

BELCHER, EDWARD. Narrative of a voyage round the world, performed in Her Majesty's ship *Sulphur*, during the years 1836-42, including details of the naval operations in China, from December 1840 to November 1841 ... By Sir Edward Belcher ... Commander of the expedition. London, Henry Colburn, 1843. 2 vols. xxxviii,387p. and vi,474p. pls. maps(fold.), index. [California, Columbia River, and northwest coast]   475

Belcher, Edward. SEE ALSO nos. 2116, 2117,
  Hinds, R. B.

BELCHER, H. A., edit. All about Klondike. Full particulars by a returned miner. Gold fields described. London, Simpkins, 1897.   476

BELDEN, A. L. The fur trade of America and some of the men who made and maintain it, together with furs and fur-bearers of other continents and countries and islands of the sea. N. Y., The Peltries Pub. Co., 1917. 591p.   477

BELIAKOV, ALEKSANDR VASIL'EVICH.   Iz Moskvy v Ameriku Cherez Severnyĭ poliũs. [TITLE TR. From Moscow to America across the North Pole] [Moskva], Izd-vo TSK VLKSM Molodaiĩa Gvardiĩa,1938. 214p.   478

Beliakov, Alexandr Vasil'evich. SEE ALSO nos.
     922, Chkalov, V. P. Shturmanskiĭ ... [1939 ?];
     923, Chkalov, V. P. Navigator's ... 1939;
     4279, Stalinskiĭ Marshrut Prodolzhen ... 1937.

BELL, BAILEY E. Alaska snowtrapped.   N. Y., Vantage Press, 1960. 1st ed. 194p.   479

BELL, E. MOBERLY. Flora Shaw. London,Constable, 1947. [biog. of news reporter for "The Times" of London, covering Klondike gold rush]   480

Bell, F. H., co-auth. SEE nos.
     4513, Thompson, Wm. F. Biol. ... halibut ... no. 1. 1931;
     4514, Thompson, Wm. F. Biol. ... halibut ... no. 2. 1934.

Bell, John. SEE no. 2948, McPherson, M.

BELL, MARGARET ELIZABETH. Danger on Old Baldy. N. Y., William Morrow, 1944. 224p. front.(col.), illustrated by Hamilton Greene.   481

BELL, MARGARET ELIZABETH. Daughter of Wolf House. N. Y., William Morrow, 1957. 218p.   482

BELL, MARGARET ELIZABETH. Enemies in Icy Strait. N. Y., William Morrow, 1945. 206p.   front.(col.), illustrated by George M. Richards, map.   483

BELL, MARGARET ELIZABETH. Love is forever. N. Y., William Morrow, 1954. 218p.   484

BELL, MARGARET ELIZABETH. Ride out the storm. N. Y., William Morrow, 1951. 256p. front.(col.), illus.   485

BELL, MARGARET ELIZABETH. The pirates of Icy Strait. N. Y., William Morrow, 1943. 224p. illustrated by Harvey Kidder. ANR. 1944. (Victory Edition)   486

BELL, MARGARET ELIZABETH. The totem casts a shadow. N. Y., William Morrow, 1949. 224p. front.(col.) by Louis Darling. 487

BELL, MARGARET ELIZABETH. Touched with fire; Alaska's George William Steller. N. Y., William Morrow, 1960. 189p. 488

BELL, MARGARET ELIZABETH. Watch for a tall white sail. N. Y., William Morrow, 1948. 222p. front.(col.) by Louis Darling. (Morrow Junior Book) 489

BELL, WILLIAM HEMPHILL. The quiddities of an Alaskan trip. Illustrated by W. H. Bell, Capt. C. S. U. S. A. Portland, Ore., G. A. Steel & Co., 1873. (67)p. illus. 61 numbered lithographs on 31 rectos. 490

BELLARD, WALTER, comp. The Klondyke mines and the golden valley of the Yukon. Jersey City, A. Datz, 1897. 16p. 491

BELLESSORT, ANDRE. La Pérouse, avec un portrait et une carte. Paris, Plon-Nourrit et cie, 1926. 126p. front.(port.), illus. map(fold.) (Nobles vies, grande oeuvres, 8) 492

BELLIN, JACQUES NICOLAS. Carte Reduite de l'Ocean Septentrional compris entre l'Asie et l'Amérique. Suivant las Découvertes qui one été faites par les Russes Dressée au Dépôt des Cartes et Plans de la Marine, Pour le Service des Vaisseaux du Roy. Par Ordre de M. le Duc de Praslin, Ministre de la Marine Par le Sr. Bellin Ingénieur de Marine Censeur Royal de l'Académie de Marine et de la Société Royale de Londres. Cette Carte est Dressée sur les Journaux des Navigateurs Russes sur la Carte et les Memoires de l'Académie Imperiale de Petersbourg et autres Memoires publiés en Allemand par Mr. le Professeur Muller. [Paris], 1766. [map no. 89 in Bellin's "Hydrographie Francoise," 1802] 493

BELLIN, JACQUES NICOLAS. Remarques sur la Carte Reduite de l'Ocean Septentrional, Compris entre l'Asie et l'Amérique, suivant Les Découvertes qui ont été faites par les Russes; Dressée au Dépôt des Cartes & Plans de la Marine, pour le service des Vaisseaux du Roi, par ordre de M. le Duc de Praslin, Ministre d'Etat, ayant le Department de la Marine; Par le Sieur Bellin, Ingénieur de la Marine & du Dépôt, Censeur Royal, de l'Academie de Marine, & de la Société Royale de Londres, 1766. Paris, de l'Imp. de Didot, Chez le St. Bellin, [1766] 9p. 494

BELOV, MIKHAIL. Semên Dezhnev. Moskva, Izd-vo "Morskoi transport," 1955. 155p. illus. facsims. maps(incl. 2 fold.), bibliog. indexes. 495

Below zero; songs ... 1903. SEE no. 3382, Officers, U. S. Revenue Cutter Service.

Belshaw, C. S., co-auth. SEE no. 1999, Hawthorn, H. B.

Belyavin, Vasili Ivanovich. SEE nos. 4538-39, Tikhon, *Bishop*.

BENDEL, BERNHARD. Aus Alaska. Von Sitka nach dem Chilkcat-
Fluss, 1868. Weser Ztg. 10 Ort. 1872.   496

BENEDICT, NEAL D. The Valdez and Copper River Trail, Alaska,
with 158 photographic views. Hasting, Fla., 1899. 10p. [copy-
right filed, book not printed]   497

BENHAM, DANIEL. Sketches of the life of Jan August Miert, acting
interpreter of the Esquimeaux language to the Arctic expedition
on board H. M. S. "Investigator," Capt. M'Clure 1850, 1, 2, 3.
London, Mallalieu, 1853. 34p. front.(port.)   498

BENIOWSKI, MORIZ AUGUST. The memoirs and travels of Mauritius
Augustus, Count de Benyowsky, in Siberia, Kamchatka, Japan, the
Liukiu Islands and Formosa; from the translation of his origi-
nal manuscript (1741-1771), by William Nicholson, F.R.S., 1790.
Edited by Captain Pasfield Oliver. London, T. F. Unwin, 1898.
399p. front.(port.), pls. map(fold.) ANR. London, Kegan,
Paul, Trench, Trubner & Co., 1904. 636p. front.(port.), pl.499

Beniowski, Moriz August. SEE ALSO nos.
    2514, Kotzebue, A. F. F., von. Count Benyowsky ... 1798;
    3543, Pertek, J. Polacy na szlakach ... 1957.

BENNETT, MRS. FRED S. A people without a country. N. Y., Woman's Board Home Missions of the Presbyterian Church, n. d. 16p.
(Publication no. 443)   500

BENNETT, JOHN E. Alaska, its waters, land and life; an illustrated lecture. S. F., Mysell-Rollins Co., 1899. 32p.   501

BENSIN, BASIL M. Arctic cold frames for northern climates.
Fairbanks, 1952. 5p. illus. diagrs.   502

BENSIN, BASIL M. Arctic garden solar reflectors and radiators
for northern climates. Fairbanks, 1952. 7p. illus. diagrs. 503

BENSIN, BASIL M. Coal dust for Alaskan gardens. College, Alaska, 1952. 9p. illus. diagrs. table, map(in text), bibliog. 504

BENSIN, BASIL M. History of the Greek Orthodox Catholic Church
in North America. N. Y., 1941.   505

BENSIN, BASIL M. Russian Orthodox Church in Alaska 1794-1967.
Special publication for the Centennial Celebration of the purchase of Alaska by the United States from the Russian empire in
1867. Toms River, N. J., Ocean County Sun, n. d. [1966 ?] 80p.
illus. front. maps, lists of churches, priests, chapels, Sunday
Schools and parishes, errata note. [printed for Russian Orthodox Greek Church of North America, Diocese of Alaska, Sitka] 506

Benson, Benny. SEE no. 2537, Krasilovsky, P.

BENT, SILAS. An address before the St. Louis Historical Society, December 10, 1868, & repeated by request before the Mercantile Library Association, January 21, 1869, upon the thermometric gateways to the Pole; surface currents of the ocean and the influence of the latter upon the climate of the world. St. Louis, R. F. Studley & Co., 1869. 29p. front.(fold. map)   507

BENT, SILAS. An address delivered before the St. Louis Mercantile Library Association, January 6th, 1872, upon the thermal paths to the Pole, the currents of the ocean and the influence of the latter upon the climates of the world. St. Louis, 1872. 40p. maps(2 fold. incl. front.)   508

Bentham, G. SEE no. 2116, Hinds, R. B.

BENTON, BELL. A B C for Alaska. no pl., 1967. (15)p. illus. wrps.   509

BENTON AND BOWLES, INC. Our 49th State ... an adventure in marketing. N. Y., 1959.   510

Benyowski, Moriz August. SEE no. 499, Beniowski, Moriz August.

Beresford, Wm. SEE no. 1308, Dixon, George.

BERG, BEN. Guide to your choice of hunting grounds. Madison, Wisc., B. J. Berg Co., [ca 1962] 228p. maps. [incls. Alaskan]   511

BERG, LEV SEMENOVICH. Ocherki po istorii russkikh geograficheskikh otkrytii. [TITLE TR. Sketches on the history of Russian geographical discoveries] Moskva, Leningrad, Izd-vo Akademii nauk SSSR, 1946. 358p. illus. ports. maps, bibliogs. [Published by the Academy of Sciences, U. S. S. R., in its popular scientific series] ANR. Moskva, Leningrad, Izd-vo Akademii nauk SSSR, 1949. 2d ed. corrected and enl. 465p. ports. maps (2 fold.), bibliog.   512

BERG, LEV SEMENOVICH. Otkrytie Kamchatki i ekspeditsii Beringa, 1725-42. [TITLE TR. The discovery of Kamchatka and the Bering expeditions, 1725-42] Leningrad, Izd-vo Glavsevmorputi, 1935. 411p. illus. pls. maps(some fold.), bibliog. (Poliarnaia biblioteka) [see no. 515, 1st ed.]   513

BERG, LEV SEMENOVICH. Otkrytie Kamchatki i ekspeditsii Beringa, 1725-42. [TITLE TR. The discovery of Kamchatka and the Bering expeditions, 1725-42] Moskva, Izd-vo Akademii nauk SSSR, 1946. 3rd ed. 379p. illus. maps(some fold.), bibliog. [see no. 515 for 1st ed.]   514

BERG, LEV SEMENOVICH. Otkrytie Kamchatki i kamchatskie ékspedi-
t̆sii Beringa. [TITLE TR. The discovery of Kamchatka and the
Kamchatka expeditions of Bering] Petrograd, Gos. izd-vo, 1924.
246p. illus. maps(incl. some fold.), bibliog. (Biblioteka puteshestviĭ, 4) [for 2d and 3rd eds. see nos. 513 and 514]   515

BERG, LEV SEMENOVICH. Velikie russkie puteshestvenniki. [TITLE
TR. Account of lives and exploits of ten Russian explorers, 15th
to 19th centuries] Moskva, Gos izd-vo detskoĭ literatury, 1950.
295p. illus. maps(incl. 1 fold.)[incls. Chirikov and Golovnin]
516

Berg, Lev Semenovich. SEE ALSO nos.
    2531, Krasheninnikov, S. P. Opisanie ... 1755;
    2546, Kruber, A. A., edit. Biblioteka ... 1924.

BERGEN, HANS von. Jagdfahrten in Kanada und Alaska. [TITLE TR.
Hunting trips in Canada and Alaska] Neudam, J. Neumann, 1928.
264p. pls. maps(incl. 1 fold.)   517

BERGENDAHL, ERLING. Alaskadage, en tre tusen mils faerd gjennem
"The top of the world." Oslo, Some & Co.'s Forlag, 1926. 211p.
illus. facsim.   518

BERGER, ANDRE. Dan les Neiges de l'Alaska. Paris, Bernardin-
Bechet, 1930. 140p. (Collection "Les Grande Chasses")   519

BERGER, CHARLES J. How to raise and train an Alaskan malemute.
Jersey City, TFH Publications, 1963. 64p. illus. bibliog. 520

BERGMAN, STEN. Beröm da upptöcktsfärder, efter svenska och üt-
landska källor skildrade av Sten Bergman. [TITLE TR. Famous
voyages of discovery described by Sten Bergman, according to
Swedish and foreign sources] Stockholm, A. Bonnier, 1939. 190p.
illus. front. pls. maps.   521

BERGSLAND, KNUT. A grammatical outline of the Eskimo language
of West Greenland. Oslo, Skrivemaskinstua, 1955. 160p. [from
Greenland to Norton Sound, Alaska]   522

BERGSLAND, KNUT. Aleut dialects of Atka and Attu. Philadelphia,
American Philosophical Society, 1959. 128p. illus. maps, bibliog. ftntes. (Transactions, New Series, vol. 49, pt. 3, 1959)
523

BERGSLAND, KNUT. The Eskimo-Uralic hypothesis. Helsinki,
Suomalais-ugrilainen seura, 1959. 29p. bibliog. (Aikakauskir-
ja, vol. 61, no. 2)   524

Bering, Vitus Jonassen. SEE nos.
    531, Berkh, V. N. Pervoe ... 1823;
    721, Büchner, Eug. Die Abbildungen ... 1891;
    927, Chukovskiĭ, N. K. Bering [in Russ.] 1961.

Bering, Vitus Jonassen.   SEE ALSO nos.
   1193, Davidson, Geo.   Tracks ... 1741;
   1272, Denton, V. L.   Far west coast. 1924;
   1369, DuHalde, J. B.   Descript. geog. ... 1735;
   1599, Ford, Corey.   Where sea breaks its back. 1966;
   1755, Golder, F. A.   Bering's voyages ... 1922;
   1773, Goodhue, C.   Journey into fog ... 1944;
   1796, Granberg, W. J.   Voyage into darkness. 1960;
   2546, Kruber, A. A., edit.   Biblioteka ... 1924;
   2642, Lauridsen, P.   Vitus Bering ... [in Eng.] 1889;
   2643, Lauridsen, P.   Vitus J. Bering og de russ. ... 1885;
   2744, Lobanov-Rostovskiĭ, A. Ĭà.   Kratkaĭà ... 1824;
   3023, Masterson, J.   Bering's successors. 1948;
   3233, Müller, G. F.   Nachrichten ... 1758;
   3254, Murphy, R.   Haunted voyage. 1961;
   3435, Ostrovskiĭ, B. G.   Velikaĭà ... 1937;
   3475, Pallas, P. S.   Neue nordische Beyträge ... 1781-96;
   3499, Pasetskiĭ, V. M.   Vitus Bering [in Russ.] 1958;
   3526, Pedersen, H. H. S.   Vitus Berings minde. 1943;
   3528, Pekarskiĭ, P. P.   Arkhivnyĭà ... 1869;
   3625, Pokrovskiĭ, A. A., edit.   Éksped. Beringa ... 1941;
   3735, Rasmussen, K. J. V.   Dansk udlaengsel ... 1931;
   3881, Rørdam, V.   Dansk liv. 1938;
   4238, Sokolov, A. P.   Sievernaĭà ... 1851;
   4276, Staehlin, J. v. S.   Das von den Russen ... 1774;
   4331, Steller, G. W. ... ausfuhrliche Beschreibung ... 1753;
   4332, Steller, G. W. ... Beschreibung ... 1774;
   4333, Steller, G. W. ... Reise von Kamtschatka ... 1793;
   4390, Sumner, B. H.   Short hist. Russia. 1944;
   4758, Waxell, S. L.   American expedition. [1952];
   4759, Waxell, S. L.   Vitus Berings eventyrlige ... 1948;
   4760, Waxell, S. L.   Vtoraĭà Kamchatskaĭà ... 1940;
   4794, Wendt, H.   Entdeckungsfahrt ... 1952;
   4946, Wolff, O.   Levnetsefterretninger ... 1822.

Bering River Coal Co.   SEE no. 2440, Kennecott Copper Corp.

BERING SEA COMMERCIAL CO.   Alaska whaling as an investment under modern methods. Chicago, n. d. 23p. front.   525

BERING SEA CO.   Report of the Board of Directors to the stock-holders of the Bering Sea Company, October 16, 1913. [N. Y. ?, 1913] 8p.   526

Berkh, Vasiliĭ Nikolaevich.   Chronological history ... 1938.
   SEE no. 528.

BERKH, VASILIĬ NIKOLAEVICH.   Khronologicheskaĭà istoriĭà otkry-tiĭà Aleutskikh ostrovov; ili, Podvigi rossiĭskago kupechestva. S. Prisovokupleniem istoricheskago izviestiĭà o miekhovoi tor-govliē. Sanktpeterburg, N. Grecha, 1823. 169p. tables(fold.), map(fold.)   527

BERKH, VASILIĬ NIKOLAEVICH.
    TRANSLATION - Khronolog. istoriĭa ... Aleutskikh ostrovov ...
    1823.

    The chronological history of the discovery of the Aleutian
        islands; or, The exploits of the Russian merchants, with
        the supplement of historical data on fur trade. Seattle,
        U. S. Works Progress Administration, 1938. 127p. [trans-
        lated by D. Krenov and reproduced from typed copy. For
        anr. tr. see no. 2414]   528

BERKH, VASILIĬ NIKOLAEVICH. Khronologischeskaĭa istoriĭa vsiekh
puteshestviĭa v siev, polĭarnyĭa strany s prisovokupleniem
obozrennia fizicheskikh sovisto togo kraĭa. [TITLE TR. Chronological history of all voyages to northern polar lands, with survey of the physical nature of the country] St. Petersburg, 1821-
23. 2 vols. in 1. 356p. pls. maps.   529

BERKH, VASILIĬ NIKOLAEVICH. Opisanie neschastnago korablekru-
sheniĭa fregata R.-A. K-1 *Nevy* ... [TITLE TR. Account of the
disastrous wreck of the R.-A. Company's frigate *Neva* near New
Archangel] St. Petersburg, 1817. 46p.   530

BERKH, VASILIĬ NIKOLAEVICH. Pervoe morskoe puteshestvie Rossiĭan
predpriniatoe dlia riesheniĭa geograficheskoĭ zadachi: Soedin-
iaeĭsia li Aziĭa s Amerikoiu ? i sovershennoe v 1727-29 godakh
pod nachaljstvom Flota Kap. I-go ranga Vitusa Beringa. [TITLE
TR. First sea voyage of the Russians undertaken to solve the
geographical problem: Are Asia and America united ? and performed in 1727-29 under Captain Bering] St. Petersburg, Imperial Academy of Science, 1823. 126p. table(fold.), map.   531

BERKH, VASILIĬ NIKOLAEVICH. Puteshestvie, po sievernoĭ Amerikie
k Ledovitomu moriu i Tikhomu okeanu, sovershennyia g. Khernom i
Miakenziem s prisovokupleniem opisaniĭa, miekhovoĭ torgovli v
Kanadia proizvodimoi, sviekh zvĭerei v Amerikie obrietaiush-
chikhsia, nravov, obyknovienem vnutrennykh dikikh. s. angl. na
ostrovie Kadiakie. [TITLE TR. Voyage through North America to
the Frozen Sea and Pacific Ocean, made by Messrs. Hearne and Mac-
Kenzie with description of the fur trade in Canada, wild animals
found in America, and characters and customs of the Interior natives. Tr. from the Eng. at Kadiak Island. Dedicated to the
Russian-American Co.] St. Petersburg, 1808. 196p. map [taken
from the writings of Samuel Hearne and Alexander MacKenzie] 532

BERKH, VASILIĬ NIKOLAEVICH. Zhizneopisaniĭa pervykh Ross. admiralov ili opyt istoriĭ Ross. flota. [TITLE TR. Biographies
of the first Russian admirals, or an attempt toward a history of
the Russian Navy] St. Petersburg, Morsk. Tip., 1831-36. 4 vols.
1162p.   533

Berkh, Vasilii Nikolaevich. SEE ALSO no. 3814, Ricks, M. B.

BERLIN KÖNIGLICHEN MUSEEN. Museum Für Völkerkunde, Ethnologische
Abteilung. Amerika's Nordwest-Küste. Neuste Ergebnisse ethnologischer Reisen. Aus den Sammlungen der Königlichen Museen zu
Berlin. [TITLE TR. The northwest coast of America. Latest results of ethnological travels. From the collections of the Royal
Museum at Berlin] Berlin, A. Asher & Co., 1883. 13p. pls.
(some col.) [incls. Tlingits, Haidas and Tsimshians. See also
no. 536]   534

TRANSLATION - Amerika's Nordwest-Küste. 1883.

The north-west coast of America; being results of recent
    ethnological researches, from the collections of the Royal
    Museum at Berlin, published by the directors of the Eth-
    nological Department, translated from the German. London,
    Asher & Co., [1883] 12p. 14 ℓ pls.(incl. some col.)
    ANR. N. Y., Dodd Mead, [1883]   535

BERLIN KÖNIGLICHEN MUSEEN. Museum Für Völkerkunde, Ethnologische
Abteilung. Amerika's Nordwest-Küste ... Herausgegeben von der
Direction der Ethnologischen Abteilung. Neue Folge. [TITLE TR.
The northwest coast of America ... Published by the directors of
Ethnological Department. New Series] Berlin, A. Asher & Co.,
1884. 6p. pls. map(col.) [incls. Eskimos of Kotzebue and Nor-
ton Sounds]   536

BERNHARDI, CHARLOTTE. Memoir of the celebrated Admiral Adam John
de Krusenstern, the first Russian circumnavigator. Translated by
his daughter Madame Charlotte Bernhardi and edited by Rear-Admiral Sir John Ross. London, Longmans, Green, Brown & Longmans,
1856. 75p. illus. port. ANR. Seattle, Shorey Book Store,
1965. 77p. illus. [photocopy]   537

BERRILL, JACQUELYN. Wonders of the Arctic. N. Y., Dodd Mead,
1959. 94p. drawings by author, map, index.   538

Berry, Eric, illus. SEE no. 2109, Hillyer, Wm. H.

BERRY, ERICK. Mr. Arctic; an account of Vilhjalmur Stefansson.
N. Y., David McKay, 1966. illus.   539

BERRY, WILLIAM D. Deneki, an Alaskan moose. Written and illustrated by William D. Berry. N. Y., Macmillan and London, Col-
lier-Macmillan Ltd., 1965. 1st print. (45)p. illus. map, bibliog.   540

Berry, William D., illus. SEE ALSO no. 3701, Pruitt, Wm. O.,jr.

Berson, A., co-edit. SEE no. 2287, International Soc. Explorat.
    Arctic regions by means of aircraft.

Bertholf, E. P. SEE no. 1755, Golder, F. A.

BERTO, HAZEL DUNAWAY. North to Alaska's shining river. Indianapolis, Bobbs-Merrill, 1959. 224p. map. [B.I.A. teacher, 1925-
28, Norton Sound]   541

BERTON, LAURA BEATRICE. I married the Klondike. Boston, Little
Brown, [c1954] 269p. pls. ANR. London, Hutchinson, 1955.
231p. pls. ANR. Toronto, McClelland & Stewart, 1961. 231p.
(front.(port.), pls. endmaps.   542

BERTON, PIERRE. A Klondike bibliography. Kleinsburg, Ontario,
1958. 23p. mimeographed. [used in writing "The Klondike fever," nos. 546 and 547]   543

BERTON, PIERRE. Stampede for gold; the story of the Klondike.
N. Y., Knopf, 1955. 176p. illus. by Duncan Macpherson, maps
(in text). ANR. WITH TITLE The golden trail, no. 545.   544

BERTON, PIERRE. The golden trail. Toronto, Macmillan, 1957.
147p. illus. by Duncan Macpherson. (Great stories of Canada)
ANR. WITH TITLE Stampede for gold, see no. 544.   545

BERTON, PIERRE. The Klondike. Toronto, McClelland & Stewart,
1958. ANR. WITH TITLE The Klondike fever, see no. 547.   546

BERTON, PIERRE. The Klondike fever. The life and death of the
last great gold rush. N. Y., Knopf, 1958. 1st ed. 457p. illus. maps, bibliog. ALSO WITH TITLE The Klondike,(no. 546) 547

BERTON, PIERRE. The mysterious north. N. Y., Knopf, 1956.
345p. illus. index. ANR. London, 1956. 345p. illus. index.
                                                                 548

BESANT, WALTER. Captain Cook. London and N. Y., Macmillan,
1890. 191p.   549

BEST, EVA. Alaska Christmas candles. Chicago, Educational Pub.
Co., n. d.   550

BETHUNE, W. C. and others. Canada's western northland; its
history, resources, population and administration. Assembled by
W. C. Bethune. Ottawa, King's Printer, 1937. 162p. illus.
tables, maps(sketch). (Canada. Department of Mines and Resources. Lands, Parks and Forests Branch) [incls. Alaska-Yukon
boundary references]   551

Bibliography of Captain James Cook ... 1928. SEE
    no. 3294, New South Wales Pub. Library.

BICKNELL, EDWARD. The territorial acquisition of the United
States. Boston, Small, Maynard, 1899. ANR. 1904.   552

BIDENKAP, OLAF. Fortegnelse over de arktiske bryozoer. [TITLE TR. Catalog of Arctic bryozoans] Bergen, J. Grieg, 1906. 79p. tables, bibliog. (Museum. Aarbok, no. 9, Bergen, Norway) 553

BIELKOV, Z. and I. NETSVIETOV. Molitvy i piesnopieniia na kvikhpakskokuskikvimskom nariechii. [TITLE TR. Prayers and canticles in the Yukon-Kuskokwim dialect] N. Y., Brooks Bros., 1896. 88p. 554

BIGELOW, MARVYN JAY. Urdag, the Aleut. N. Y., Vantage Press, 1955. 167p. 555

Billecocq, J. B. L. J., tr. SEE no. 3058, Meares, J.

Billings, J. SEE nos.
    3965, Sarychev, G. A. Puteshestvie flota ... 1802;
    3970, Sarychev, G. A. Puteshestvie Kapitana ... 1811;
    3973, Sauer, M. Account Geog. ...1802.

BINGHAM, JOSEPH W. Report on the international law of Pacific coastal fisheries. Stanford, Stanford University Press, 1938. 75p. 556

BIOGRAPHIE DU DOCTEUR MERTENS, naturaliste et medicin de l'expedition autor du monde executee en 1827-28 sur la corvette la *Seniavine*. no pl., n. d. [with F. P. Litke] 557

Bird-finding along interior Alaska's highways. [1965] SEE
    no. 1512, Fairbanks Bird Club.

Bird-finding in Interior and Southcentral ... 1967. SEE
    no. 2449, Kessel, B.

BIRKELAND, KNUT B. The whalers of Akutan. An account of modern whaling in the Aleutian Islands. New Haven, Yale University Press and London, Oxford University Press, 1926. 171p. front. (pl.), pls. 558

Birket-Smith, Kaj. [Alphabetical title guide to chronological entries]

Chugach Eskimo ... 565.   Menneskets ... 562.
Eskimoerne. 559.   Moeurs ... 563.
Eskimos. 560-61.   Naturmennesker. 564.
Eyak Indians ... 566.

BIRKET-SMITH, KAJ. Eskimoerne, med forord av Knud Rasmussen. København, Nordisk Forlag, 1927. 239p. illus. map(fold.), append. bibliog. ANR. Rhodos, 1961. 301p. illus. map, bibliog. (Grønlanske selskab) 559

BIRKET-SMITH, KAJ. TRANSLATIONS - Eskimoerne. 1927.

    The Eskimos. Translated by W. E. Calvert, revised by Profes-
        sor C. D. Forde, foreword by D. Jenness. London, Methuen,
        1936. 250p. pls. endmap, bibliog. ANR. N. Y., 1936.
        250p.   560

    The Eskimos. London, Methuen, 1959. 2d ed. rev. and ex-
        tended. 262p. photos, endmap, append. bibliog. index.
        561

BIRKET-SMITH, KAJ. Menneskets mangfoldighet. København, 1958.
pls.   562

BIRKET-SMITH, KAJ. Moeurs et coutumes des Eskimo. Préf. de
Diamond Jennes. Nouv. éd. rev. [TITLE TR. Mores and customs of
the Eskimos. Introduction by Diamond Jenness. New rev. ed.]
Paris,Payot, 1955. 292p. illus. map, bibliog. [prepared in
collaboration with Claude Desgoffe]   563

BIRKET-SMITH, KAJ. Naturmennesker. [TITLE TR. Primitive
peoples. København, Chr. Erichsen, 1934. 2 pts. 199p. and
184p. pls.(col.)   564

BIRKET-SMITH, KAJ. The Chugach Eskimo. København, Nationalmu-
seets Publikationsfond, 1953. 261p. front. illus. map, tables.
(Copenhagen. Nationalmuseet. Skrifter. Etnografisk Raekke,
VI)   565

BIRKET-SMITH, KAJ and F. de Laguna. The Eyak Indians of the
Copper River Delta, Alaska, Copenhagen, Levin & Munksgaard, 1938.
591p. illus. ports. maps, bibliog. (Det. Kgl. Danske Vidensk.
Selskab.)   566

Birket-Smith, Kaj, edit. SEE ALSO no. 3746,
    Rasmussen, K. Mindeudgave ... 1934-35.

BISHOP, ERNEST FRANKLIN. The timber wolf of the Yukon. no pl.,
Digest Press, 1923. [printed by W. B. Conkey, Co., Chicago, The
Hammond Press] 278p. front.(col.), port. [novel from play con-
cerning Canadian Royal Northwest Mounted Police]   567

Bishop of Caledonia. SEE nos. 3816 and 3817, Ridley, Wm.

BIXBY, WILLIAM. Track of the *Bear*. N. Y., McKay, 1965. 309p.
illus. endmaps, bibliog. index.   568

Black Beaver (James Conrad Lewis) SEE nos.
    770, Caldwell, E. N. Alaska Trail dogs. 1945;
    2697, Lewis, James Conrad. Black Beaver ...1911.

BLACK, D. JAN and N. A. OSTENSO. Gravity observations from Ice
Island Arlis-II, 6 Oct. 1961 to 8 Apr. 1962. Madison, Wisconsin,
University of Wisconsin, 1962. 26p. maps, graphs, tables, bibliog. (Geophysical and Polar Research Center Contrib. no. 91)
569

Black Luk (George Edward Lewis) SEE no. 770, Caldwell, E. N.
    Alaska trail dogs. 1945.

BLACK, MARTHA LOUISE PURDY. My seventy years as told to Elizabeth Bailey Price. London, T. Nelson & Sons, 1938. 1st ed.
317p. front. pls. ports. facsim. ANR. 1939. 570

BLACK, MARTHA LOUISE PURDY. Yukon wild flowers. Vancouver,
Price, Templeton Syndicate, [1940 ?] 95p. illus. from photos
by Hon. George Black. 571

BLACKERBY, ALVA W. and LINN A. FORREST. Tale of an Alaska whale.
Portland, Ore., Binfords and Mort, 1955. 31p. illus. drawings.
[Thlinget totem legend] 572

BLACKLOCK, ALASKA [pseud.] Nick of the woods. Portland, Ore.,
Jensen Pub. Co., 1916. 222p. illus. port. [locale is not Alaskan: one brief mention only of Alaska] 573

Blacklock, Alaska [pseud.] SEE ALSO no. 2696, Lewis, G. E.

Blaine, Jas. G. SEE no. 4595, Tyler, Alice (Felt)

Blair, Clay, jr., co-auth. SEE no. 252, Anderson, Wm. R.

BLASCHKE, EDUARD LEONTJEVICH. Topographia medica portus Novi-
Archangelscensis, sedis principalis coloniarium Rossicarum in
Septentrionali America. St. Petersburg, K. Weinhober & Son,
1842. 84p. front. pl.(fold.), map(fold.), tables(fold.) ANR.
Dissertatio inauguralis sistens topographiam medicam portus Novi-
Archangelscensis ... 1842. 574

BLEEKER, SONIA. The Eskimo; Arctic hunters and trappers. N.Y.,
William Morrow, 1959. 160p. illus. Patricia Boodell. 575

BLEEKER, SONIA. The sea hunters; Indians of the northwest
coast. By Sonia Bleeker, illustrated by Althea Karr. N. Y.,
William Morrow, 1951. [c1951] 159p. illus. index. [incls. those
of southeastern Alaska] 576

BLOCH, IVAN. Alaska's power resources in relation to mineral development. Portland, Ore., Ivan Bloch and Assoc., 1956. reprint
(from J. Electrochemical Soc., vol. 12, no. 10) 577

BLOCK, BISKOP. Rimelig formodning at de oprindelige Amerikanere nedstamme fra en mongolisk Aet, som i en meget tidlig Verdenalder er kommen over fra det Nordösllige Asia til det nortvestlige Amerika. Copenhagen, 1804. 37p. 578

Blomkvist, E. E., co-edit. SEE no. 5020, Zagoskin, L. A.

BLOND, GEORGES. The plunderers. Translated by Frances Frenaye. N. Y., Macmillan, 1951. 1st print. 243p. front. map. [fictional account Pribilof Island fur seals] 579

BLOUNT, ELLEN S. North of 53; an Alaskan journey. London, Percy Lund Humphries, n. d. [1925] 128p. photos by author, pls. map. 580

[BLOWITZ, HENRI GEORGES STEPHANE ADOLPHE OPPER de] The Bering Sea arbitration, letters to the Times by its special correspondent, together with the award. Reprinted by permission of the proprietors. London, W. Clowes & Son and Toronto, Carswell Co., 1893. 87p. 581

Blunt, Harry L. SEE no. 4286, Stark, Chas. R., jr.

BOAS ANNIVERSARY VOLUME: anthropological papers written in honor of Franz Boas ... presented to him on the twenty-fifth anniversary of his doctorate, 9th of Aug., 1906. N. Y., G. E. Stechert & Co., 1906. xix,559p. front. illus. pls.(incl. 1 fold.), ports. tables(some fold.), diagrs.(some fold.), bibliog. 582

BOAS, FRANZ. Contributions to the ethnology of the Kwakiutl. N. Y., Columbia University Press, 1925. 357p. (Contributions to Anthropology, vol. 3) [references also to Tsimshian and Tlingits] 583

BOAS, FRANZ. Facial paintings of the Indians of the north Pacific coast. N. Y., American Museum of Natural History, 1898. (Memoirs, no. 2, pt. 1) 584

BOAS, FRANZ. Grammatical notes on the language of the Tlingit Indians. Philadelphia, University Museum, 1917. 179p. pl. (fold.) (Pennsylvania University Museum Anthropological Papers, vol. 8, no. 1) 585

BOAS, FRANZ. Indianische Sagen von der nord-Pacifischen Küste Amerikas. [TITLE TR. Indian legends from the north Pacific coast of America] Berlin, A. Asher, 1895. 363p. map. reprint (from Proc. Berlin Society for Anthropology, Ethnology, and Prehistory, 1891-95) [southeastern Alaskan included] 586

BOAS, FRANZ. Primitive art. Oslo, H. Ashehoug and Cambridge, Harvard University Press, 1927. 376p. illus. pls. (Instituttet for sammenlignende kulturforskning, ser. B, Skrifter, 13) ANR. N. Y., 1955. ANR. Magnolia, Mass., Peter Smith, 1962. 587

BOAS, FRANZ. Race, language and culture. N. Y., 1940. illus.
588

BOAS, FRANZ. The use of masks and head-ornaments on the northwest coast of America. no pl., 1890. 9p. pls.   589

Boas, Franz. SEE ALSO nos.
    1460, Emmons, Geo. T. Chilkat blanket ... 1907;
    1759, Goldschmidt, W. Anthrop. Franz Boas 1959;
    2109, Hillyer, Wm. h. Box of daylight . 1931;
    2357, Jochelson, W. Aleut folklore ... n. d.;
    4416, Swanton, John R. Haida songs ... 1912;
    4710, Voegelin, C. F. Index Franz Boas collection ... 1945.

BOBROV, NIKOLAI NIKOLAEVICH. Chkalov. Moskva, Gos. izd-vo
"Khudozhestvennaia literatura," 1940. 318p. pls. ports.(some
col.), map(fold. col.), facsims. [Arctic flights of V. P.
Chkalov]   590

BODFISH, HARTSON HARTLETT. Chasing the bowhead, as told to
Joseph C. Allen. Cambridge, Mass., Harvard University Press,
1936. illus. pls. ports(incl. front.) [whaling north of Bering
Strait]   591

BODNARSKIĬ, MITROFAN STEPANOVICH. Ocherki po istorii russkogo
zemlevedeniia, I. [TITLE TR. Essay on the history of Russian
geography, I] Moskva, Izd-vo Akademii nauk SSSR, 1947. 290p.
maps(fold.), append. bibliog. (Akademiia nauk SSSR. Nauchnopopu-
liarnaia seriia)   592

Bodnarskiĭ, Mitrofan Stepanovich. SEE ALSO nos.
    4, Adamov, A. G. G. I. Shelikhov ... 1952;
    1303, Divin, V. A. V. M. Golovnin ... 1951;
    2814, Lupach, V. S. I. F. Kruzenshtern ... 1953.

BOGDANOVICH, KARL IVANOVICH. Ocherki Chukotskogo poluostrova.
[TITLE TR. Sketches of the Chukotsk Peninsula] S.-Peterburg,
Tip. A. S. Suvorina, 1901. 239p. illus. pls. diagrs.(fold.),
plans(fold.), map(fold.), bibliog. index. [note made of purchase
of reindeer for Alaska]   593

BOGDANOVICH, KARL IVANOVICH. Ocherki Nome. [TITLE TR. Sketches
of Nome] S.-Peterburg, Tip. A. S. Suvorina,1901. 116p. pls.
map(fold.)   594

BOHN, DAVID. Glacier Bay; the land and the silence. Edited by
David Brower. S. F., Sierra Club, 1967. 168p. photos(some
col.)   595

BOHN, DAVID. The Juneau Ice Field research project. no pl.,
n. d. 7p. illus. maps, bibliog. reprint (from Mazama, Dec. 1958.
vol. 40, no. 13)   596

BOILLOT, LEON. Aux mines d'or du Klondike. Du Lac Bennett a
Dawson City. Paris, Hachette & C'ie, 1899. Levallois-Perret,
Imp. 1st ed. 255p. front. pls. map(fold.) ANR. Paris, 1909.
                                                              597

BOITSOV, LEONTIĬ VASIL'EVICH. Kotikovoe Khoziaĭstvo. [TITLE TR.
Sealing industry] Moskva, Vneshtorgizdat, 1934. 195p. illus.
tables, diagrs. bibliog. [incl. Pribilof Islands]   598

BOJESEN, HJALMAR HJORTH. Az Alaskai Indianusok Között. Tarka
Könyvek. Utleiras, 1921. (Tábori Piroska I. sor. S. Kolliga-
tum 8)   599

BOLANZ, MARIA [pseud.] So Hago. N. Y., Vantage Press, 1963.
1st ed. 94p. bibliog. [author is Mrs. Marilyn B. Williams -
fictional study of Tlingit Indians]   600

BOLOTOV, IVANOF. Kratkoe opisanie ob Amer. ostrovie Kadjiakie,
sobrannoe iz dostoviernykh zapisok i raspolozhennoe na topogr.,
klimat., statist., i esteticheskoe otdieleniia. [TITLE TR.
Short description of the American island Kodiak, collected from
authentic reports and arranged in topographic, climatic, statistical, and esthetic sections] Moskva, 1805. 18p.   601

Bolton, Herbert E., co-edit. SEE no. 4335, Stephens, H. M.

Bolyan, Helen. SEE nos. 3008 and 3009, Martin, Martha [pseud.]

Bomback, R. H., photog. SEE no. 2176, Hooper, Jas. T.

Bompas, Charlotte Selina. SEE no. 275, Archer, F. A.

BOMPAS, WILLIAM CARPENTER. Diocese of MacKenzie River. London,
Society for Promoting Christian Knowledge, 1888. 108p. front.
(map) (Colonial Church Histories)   602

BOMPAS, WILLIAM CARPENTER. Lessons and prayers in the Tenni or
Slavi language of the Indians of MacKenzie River in the northwest territory of Canada. London, Society for Promoting Christian Knowledge, 1892. 126p. front. illus.   603

BOMPAS, WILLIAM CARPENTER. Northern lights on the Bible; drawn
from a bishop's experience during twenty-five years in the great
northwest. London, J. Nisbet, [18__ ?] 211p. front.(fold. map)
                                                              604

BOMPAS, WILLIAM CARPENTER. Western Esquimaux primer. London,
Gilbert and Rivington, n. d. 23p.   605

Bompas, William Carpenter. SEE ALSO nos.
     275, Archer, F. A. Heroine of north ... 1929;
     966, Cody, Hiram Alfred. Apostle of north ... 1908;

Bompas, William Carpenter. SEE ALSO nos.
   1794, Grahame, N. Bishop Bompas ... 1925;
   3253, Murphy, E. F. Bishop Bompas. n. d.

BONE, SCOTT CARDELLA. Chechahco and sourdough; a story of Alaska. Atascadero, Calif., Western Pub., 1926. 281p. front. pls. map. [author a former territorial governor of Alaska]   606

Bone, Scott Cardella. SEE ALSO no. 3486, Pan Pacific Progress.

BONI, ARMAND. Roald Amundsen. Tilburg, Nederland's Boskhuis, 1946. 222p. illus.   607

Book of animals and birds. 1940. SEE
   no. 80, Alaska Mag. Pub. Co.

Book of common prayer ... in Haida. 1899. SEE
   no. 1479, [Episcopal Church]

Book of pictures "Last Frontier." 1941. SEE
   no. 81, Alaska Mag. Pub. Co.

Book of totems ... 1942. SEE
   no. 82, Alaska Mag. Pub. Co.

BOONE AND CROCKETT CLUB. American big game in its haunts. The book of the Boone and Crockett Club. N. Y., Forest and Stream Pub. Co., 1904. 1st ed. 497p. Edited by George Bird Grinnell.
                                                                    608

BOONE AND CROCKETT CLUB. American game mammals and birds. Edited by John C. Phillips. A catalog of books 1582-1925 on sports, natural history and conservation. Boston, Houghton Mifflin, 1930.   609

BOONE AND CROCKETT CLUB. Hunting and conservation; the book of the Boone and Crockett Club. Edited by George Bird Grinnell and Charles Sheldon. New Haven, Yale University Press, 1925. 548p. illus. [incls. establishment of McKinley National Park]   610

BOONE AND CROCKETT CLUB. Hunting at high altitudes. The book of the Boone and Crockett Club. Edited by George Bird Grinnell. N. Y., Harper, 1913. 511p. front.(port.), pls.   611

BOONE AND CROCKETT CLUB. North American big game. Edited by Alfred Ely, Harold E. Anthony and R. R. M. Carpenter. N. Y., Scribner, 1939. 533p. illus. photos and drawings.   612

BOONE AND CROCKETT CLUB. Records of North American big game. Edited by Prentiss N. Gray. N. Y., Derrydale Press, 1932. ltd. ed. of 500 copies.   613

BOONE AND CROCKETT CLUB. Records of North American big game. Edited by Samuel B. Webb, Grancel Fitz and Milford Baker. N. Y., Scribner, 1952. 174p. illus. 614

BOONE AND CROCKETT CLUB. Records of North American big game. Edited by Samuel B. Webb, Grancel Fitz and Milford Baker. N. Y., Henry Holt, 1958. OTHERS 1959 and 1960. 615

BOONE AND CROCKETT CLUB. Records of North American big game. Edited by Milford Baker. N. Y., Holt, Rinehart & Winston, 1964. ANR. 1965. 398p. front.(col. photo), illus. charts, tables, maps. 616

Boone and Crockett Club. SEE ALSO no. 797, Camp Fire Club.

BOONE, LALLA ROOKH. Captain George Vancouver and his work on the northwest coast. no pl., 1934. 114p. 617

BOOTH, ERNEST SHELDON. Birds of the west. Illustrated by Harry Baerg and Carl Petterson. College Place, Wash., 1948. 397p.618

BOOTH, ERNEST SHELDON. Birds of the west, including Alaska, western Canada and Hawaii. Illustrated by Harry Baerg, Carl Petterson and Jocelyn Cass. Escondido, Calif., Outdoor Pictures, 1960. 3rd ed. 413p. illus.(some col.), append. bibliog. 619

BORDEN, CHARLES A. He sailed with Captain Cook. Illustrated by Ralph Ray. N. Y., Thomas Y. Crowell, 1952. 620

BORDEN, COURTNEY LOUISE. The cruise of the *Northern Light*; explorations and hunting in the Alaskan and Siberian Arctic; in which the sea-scouts have a great adventure. By Mrs. John Borden. N. Y., Macmillan, 1928. 317p. front.(port.), illus. endmaps, glossary, appends. bibliog. [Borden-Field Museum 1927 Alaska Arctic Expedition] 621

Borden, Mrs. John. SEE Borden, Courtney Louise.

Borden, R. L. SEE no. 4145, Siem, Conrad.

BORDMAN, PAUL, comp. Captain Paul Bordman's Klondike and Yukon guide; facts for Klondikers, authentic accounts of different trails, boat building and other useful information of the "land of gold." L. A., McBride Press, 1897. 36p. 622

Borisov, A., tr. SEE no. 3690, Price, E. V.

BOSCO, ANTOINETTE. Charles John Seghers, pioneer in Alaska. N. Y., P. J. Kenedy, 1960. illus. 623

Bossi, L., tr. SEE no. 3978, Sauer, M.

BOSTOCK, HUGH SAMUEL. Physiography of the Canadian Cordillera, with special reference to the area north of the 55th parallel. Ottawa, King's Printer, 1948. 106p. front. pls. map(fold.) (Canada. Geological Survey, Memoir no. 247) [incls. aerial photos of Yukon Plateau and St. Elias Mtns.] 624

Bostock, Hugh Samuel, co-auth. SEE ALSO no. 3774, Reed, J. C.

BOUTWELL, W. D., comp. Teacher's guide to "Alaska Silver Millions." [pl. ?], American Can Co., 1936. 8p. illus. bibliog.625

BOVET, LOUIS A., jr. Moose hunting in Alaska, Wyoming and Yukon Territory. Philadelphia, Dorrance, 1933. 143p. pls. maps. 626

BOVILLE, BYRON W., M. A. MacFARLANE and H. A. STEINER. An atlas of stratospheric circulation, Oct. 1958-Mar. 1959. Montreal, McGill University, 1959. 10p. maps(col.), sections, tables, bibliog. (Arctic Meteorological Research Group Pub. in Meteorology no. 37) [also issued as: Canada. Defense Research Board, DPhy. R(G) Misc. G4] 627

BOWEN, ROBERT O. and R. A. CHARLES, comp. Alaska literary directory. Anchorage, Alaska Methodist University, 1964. 628

BOWEN, ROBERT O. An Alaskan dictionary. Spenard, Alaska, Nooshnik Press, 1965. 35p. 629

BOWEN, ROBERT SIDNEY. Red Randall in the Aleutians. N. Y., Grosset and Dunlap, 1945. 214p. 630

BOWEN, VERNON. The lazy beaver. N. Y., David McKay, 1948. illus. 631

BOWMAN, WALDO G. and others. Bulldozers come first. The story of U. S. war construction in foreign lands. By Waldo G. Bowman, Harold W. Richardson, Nathan A. Bowers, Edward J. Cleary and Archie N. Carter. N. Y., McGraw-Hill, 1944. 1st ed. 278p. front. illus. endmaps. [Alaska and the Aleutians, pp.75-145] 632

BOYCE, WILLIAM DICKSON. Alaska and the Panama Canal. Chicago, Rand McNally, 1914. 163p. illus. ports. reprint (from author's U. S. Colonies and Dependencies, see no. 635) 633

BOYCE, WILLIAM DICKSON. Alaska, present and future; its railroads, mines, fisheries, agriculture, people, and laws. What Alaska wants and needs. no pl., 1913. 48p. 634

BOYCE, WILLIAM DICKSON. United States colonies and dependencies, illustrated; the travels and investigations of a Chicago publisher in the colonial possessions and dependencies of the United States, with 600 photographs of interesting people and scenes. Chicago, Rand McNally, 1914. 1st ed. xvi,638(3)p. illus. map, endmaps, index. [section reprinted: see no. 633] 635

BOYD, AUBREY. Smoky Pass. N. Y., Dutton, 1932. 313p.   636

BOYD, EUNICE MAYS. Doom in the midnight sun. N. Y., Farrar and Rinehart, [c1944] 274p,   637

BOYD, EUNICE MAYS. Murderer wears mukluks. N. Y., Farrar and Rinehart, 1945. 248p.   638

Boye, A. E., tr. SEE no. 2562, Krusenstern, A. J., von.

Boyle, Gertrude M., co-edit. SEE no. 4289, Station, F. M.

Boyle, "Klondike" SEE no. 455, Beattie, Kim.

Brackstad, H. L., tr. SEE no. 3325, Nordenskiöld, N. A. E.

BRADNER, ENOS. Northwest angling. Portland, Ore., Binfords and Mort, 1950. illus. ANR. 2d ed. rev. 1966.   639

BRADY, ELIZABETH P. Sheldon Jackson; a progressive missionary. N. Y., Woman's Board of Home Missions of the Presbyterian Church, 1911. 8p.   640

Brady, John G. SEE no. 3794, Reynolds-Alaska Development Co.

BRADY, MRS. JOHN G. The first missionary in Alaska: Mrs. A. R. McFarland. A sketch. N. Y., Woman's Board of Home Missions of the Presbyterian Church, 1912. 8p.   641

BRAMBLE, CHARLES A. Klondike; a manual for goldseekers. N. Y., R. F. Fenno & Co., 1897. 313p. pls. map(fold.)   642

BRAND, DONALD DILWORTH and FRED E. HARVEY, edits. So live the works of men; seventieth anniversary volume honoring Edgar Lee Hewett. Albuquerque, N. M., 1939. 366p. illus. bibliog. [includes contribution by Aleš Hrdlička, *Anthropological and archaeological riches in the far northwest*, pp.215-220]   643

Brande, R. A., tr. SEE no. 4319, Stefansson, V.

BRANDT, HERBERT. Alaska bird trails; adventures of an expedition by dog sled to the delta of the Yukon River at Hooper Bay. Cleveland, Bird Research Foundation, 1943. 464p. front.(col.), pls.(some col.), from paintings by Major Allen Brooks and Edward R. Kalmbach; photos by Frank Dufresne, Olaus J. Murie and the author; pen sketches by C. C. Mitchell, J. R. Moody and L. B. Towle.   644

BRANDT, J. F. Prodromus descriptionis animalium ab H. Mertansio in orbis terrarum circumnavigatione observatorum. Pt. 1. St. Petersburg, 1835. [voyage of F. P. Litke]   645

BRANDT, KARL. Whale oil, an economic analysis. Stanford, Calif., Stanford University, 1940. 264p. illus. graphs, tables, maps, append. bibliog. (Food Research Institute. Fats and Oils Studies, no. 7, June 1940)   646

BRANDT, KARL. Whaling and whale oil during and after World War II. Stanford, Calif., Stanford University, 1948. 48p. graphs, tables. (Food Research Institute, War-Peace Pamphlets, no. 11)
                                                                647

Bransom, Paul, illus. SEE nos.
    2100, Hibben, F. C. Hunting American bears . 1945;
    2852, McCracken, H. Biggest bear ... 1943;
    2854, McCracken, H. Flaming bear. 1951;
    2855, McCracken, H. Last of sea otters. 1942.

BRATRUD, OTTO. Beating to windward; afloat and ashore with Captain Otto M. Bratrud, Ret. Seattle, printed by L. & H. Printing Co., 1961. 243p. illus.   648

Brasher, R. I., illus. SEE no. 3770, Reed, Chas. K.

Brass serpent and other stories. n. d. SEE no. 4979. Wycliffe Bible Translators.

BRECKENRIDGE, GERALD. The Radio Boys rescue the lost Alaskan expedition. N. Y., A. L. Burt, [1922 ?] 227p. illus. front.
                                                                649

BREETVELD, JIM. Getting to know Alaska. N. Y., Coward-McCann, 1958. 64p. illus. by Don Lambo.   650

BREITFUS, LEONID L'VOVICH. Arktis, der derzeitige Stand unserer Kenntnisse über die Erforschung der Nordpolargebiete. Text sur historischen und physikalischen Karte. [TITLE TR. The Arctic. Text for the historical and physical maps] Berlin, Verlag von Dietrich Reimer (Andrew and Steiner), 1939. 195p. illus. maps (2 fold. in pocket), index. [in German and English]   651

BREITFUS, LEONID L'VOVICH. Das Nordpolargebist, seine Natur, Bedeutung uns Erforschung. [TITLE TR. The north polar region, its nature, significance and exploration] Berlin, Springer-Verlag, 1943. 179p. illus. maps(incl. 1 fold.) (Verständlich Wissenschaft, 18. Bd.)   652

BREITFUS, LEONID L'VOVICH. Die Erforschung der Polargebiete in den Jahren 1932 bis 1947. [TITLE TR. Exploration of the polar regions in the years 1932 to 1947] Gotha, Justus Perthes, 1950. 320p. index. (Geographisches Jahrbuch, Bd. 60) [bibliog. of 4,518 items]   653

Breitfus, Leonid L'vovich. SEE nos.
    2287, International Soc. Explorat. Arctic Regions ... 1929;
    5024, Zeidler, P. G. Polarfahrten ... 1927.

Bremner, John. SEE no. 4068, Seton-Karr, H. W.

Brent, S. M., edit. SEE no. 3784, Research Institute of Alaska.

Bressett, K. SEE no. 1787, Gould, M. M.

Breton, J. B. J., tr. SEE no. 1037, [Cook, James]

Brevig, T. L. SEE no. 2367, Johnshoy, W.

BREWER, CHARLES. Reminiscences ... [Boston], 1884. 67p.   654

BREWSTER, BENJAMIN. The first book of Eskimos. N. Y., Franklin
Watts, 1952. 45p. illus.(col. and sepia) by Ursula Koering.655

BREWSTER, BENJAMIN. The first book of Indians. N. Y., Franklin
Watts, 1950. 65p. illus. by Ursula Koering. ANR. 1963. 72p. 656

BRIDGES, WILLIAM. Walt Disney's animal adventures in lands of
ice and snow. Racine, Wisc., Whitman Pub. Co., 1963. 92p. illus. photos. (A Badger Book)   657

Brief introduction Eskimo with useful phrases. n. d. SEE
    no. 4767, [Webster, D. H.]

BRIGGS, HORACE. Letters from Alaska and the Pacific Coast. Buffalo, Press of E. H. Hutchinson, 1889. 87p.   658

Briggs, Walter J., tr. SEE no. 220, Amundsen, R. E. G.

BRIGHT, ELIZABETH. Alaska, treasure trove of tomorrow; the
story of the discovery, exploration, settlement, geography,
people and towns, wildlife, industry and future of America's
frozen asset. N. Y., Exposition Press, 1956. 1st ed. 203p.
(Banner Book)   659

BRINDZE, RUTH. The story of gold. N. Y., Vanguard, 1954. illus.   660

BRINDZE, RUTH. The story of the totem pole. N. Y., Vanguard,
1951. 64p. illus.(some col.) by Jeffe Kimball.   661

BRINSMADE, ELLEN MARTIN. Books on Alaska, for young people, annotated bibliography. Sitka, Sitka Print. Co., 1961. 24p. index, wrps.   662

BRINSMADE, ELLEN MARTIN. Children's books on Alaska. An annotated list. Sitka, Sitka Print. Co., 1956. 32p. index, wrps.
                                                             663

BRITISH AND FOREIGN BIBLE SOCIETY. The acts of the Apostles, in Haida. no pl., 1898. 145p.   664

BRITISH AND FOREIGN BIBLE SOCIETY. The gospel according to St. John, in Haida. no pl., 1899. 116p.   665

BRITISH AND FOREIGN BIBLE SOCIETY. The gospel according to St. Luke, in Haida. no pl., 1899. 156p.   666

BRITISH AND FOREIGN BIBLE SOCIETY. The gospel according to St. Mark. Evangelistib Markusib Aġlaugit. London, [Printer Billings and Sons, Guildford], 1916. 68p. [has cover title "St. Mark, English-Eskimo"]   667

BRITISH AND FOREIGN BIBLE SOCIETY. St. Mark's kloosh yiem, kopa nesika. Saviour Jesus Christ. London, 1912. 111p. [Chinook Jargon]   668

BRITISH COLUMBIA DISTRICT TELEGRAPH AND DELIVERY CO., 1891-1941, fifty years of service. Vancouver, 1941. (16)p. illus. pls. 669

BRITISH COLUMBIA MINING JOURNAL. Overland to Klondike through Cariboo, Omineca, Cassiar and Lake Teslin; the poor man's route. Peoria, Illinois, Franks, 1898. 34(30)p. illus. map. 670

BRITISH COLUMBIA NATURAL RESOURCES CONFERENCE, 12th, Harrison Hot Springs, B. C., Nov. 18-20, 1959. Transactions, resources of the northern Cordilleran. no pl., 1959. 206p. tables, maps, bibliogs.   671

British Columbia pilot. 1954. SEE no. 4995, Young, R. B.

BRITISH COLUMBIA-YUKON-ALASKA HIGHWAY COMMISSION. Report on proposed highway through British Columbia and Yukon Territory to Alaska. Ottawa, 1941. 2 vols. paged cont. 382p. photos, maps (fold.), tables, append. ANR. Ottawa, 1942. 46p. maps(fold.) [contains pt. 1, vol. 1 and pt. 4, vol. 1, plus append.]   672

BRITTON, MAX E. Vegetation of the Arctic tundra. Corvallis, Oregon State University Press, 1966. 64p. illus. maps, bibliog. (Biological Colloquium Pub.) [in no. 4865, "Arctic Biology," 1st ed. A revised print. separate and in no. 1936]   673

Britton, Max E. SEE ALSO nos.
    1936, Hansen, H. P., edit. Arctic biology. 1967;
    4865, Wiggins, Ira L., edit. Arctic biology. 1957.

BROADUS, ELEANOR HAMMOND. John Jewitt, the captive of Nootka. Toronto, Ryerson, 1928. 32p. illus. (Ryerson Canadian History Readers)   674

BROCH, HJALMAR. Oktokorallen des nördlichsten pazifischen Ozeans, und ihre Bezichung zur atlantischen Fauna. [TITLE TR. Octocorals from the northermost Pacific Ocean and their relation to the fauna of the Atlantic Ocean] Oslo, Jacob Dybwad, 1936. 53p. illus.(incl. sketch maps), bibliog. (Norske videnskaps-akademi. Avhandlinger 1. Matemisk-naturvidenskapelig klasse, 1935, no. 1) [Sea of Japan to Bering Sea]   675

BROCH, HJALMAR. Untersuchungen an Stylasteriden (Hydrokorallen), Teil 1. [TITLE TR. Investigations on Stylasteridae (Hydroco-rals), Pt. 1] Oslo, Jacob Dybwad, 1936. 103p. illus. pls. (Norske videnskaps-akademi, Oslo, 1, Matematisk-naturvidenska-pelig klasse, Skrifter, 1936, no. 8)   676

BROCH, HJALMAR. Untersuchungen an Stylasteriden (Hydrokorallen). [TITLE TR. Investigations on Stylasteridae (Hydrocorals)] Oslo, Jacob Dybwad, 1942. 113p. illus. pls. bibliog. (Norske viden-skaps-akademi, Oslo, 1, Matematisk-naturvidenskapelig klasse, Skrifter, 1942, no. 3) [incls. Bering Sea and Gulf of Alaska]
677

BROKE, HORATIO GEORGE. With sack and stock in Alaska. London, Longmans Green, 1891. 158p. front.(fold. map) and map(fold.) [diary of Mt. St. Elias climb in 1888]   678

Bronshtein, ĨŪ. I., tr. SEE no. 4760, Waxell, S. L.

Bronson, Clark, illus. SEE no. 1367, Dugdale, Vera.

[BROOKE, ROBERT ?] Remarks and conjectures on the voyage of the ships *Resolution* and *Discovery*, in search of a northerly passage from Kampschacka to England after the death of Captain Cook. London, 1780. 48p. [also sometimes ascribed to Samuel Engel]
679

Brookes, Richard, tr. SEE no. 1370, DuHalde, J. B.

BROOKS, ALFRED HULSE. Blazing Alaska's trails. Edited by Burton Fryxell. Caldwell, Idaho, Caxton, 1953. 528p. illus. maps, endmaps, tables, bibliog. [edited from posthumous notes]   680

BROOKS, ALFRED HULSE. The future of Alaska coal. no pl., 1911. 10p. reprint [from Proceedings of American Mining Congress, 14th Session]   681

BROOKS, ALFRED HULSE. Mountain exploration in Alaska. Phila-delphia, American Alpine Club, 1914. 22p. illus. maps. (Alpina Americana, no. 3)   682

Brooks, Alfred Hulse. SEE ALSO no. 1012, Cook, F. A.

BROOKS, ALICE M. and WILLIETTA E. KUPPLER. The clenched fist. Philadelphia, Dorrance, 1948. 206p. [teachers, Kenai Pen.] 683

BROOKS, ALLAN and H. S. SWARTH. A distributional list of the
birds of British Columbia. Berkeley, Calif., Cooper Ornithological Club, 1925. 158p. front.(col.), illus. map(fold.) (Pacific Coast Avifauna, no. 17)   684

Brooks, Allan, illus. SEE ALSO nos.
     644, Brandt, H. Alaska bird trails. 1943;
     2261, Ingersoll, E. Alaskan bird-life. 1914.

BROOKS, CHARLES WOLCOTT. Japanese wrecks, stranded and picked
up adrift in the north Pacific Ocean, ethnologically considered,
as furnishing evidence of a constant infusion of Japanese blood
among the coast tribes of northwestern Indians. Read before the
California Academy of Sciences, March 1, 1875. S.F., 1876. 23p.
map. reprint (in: Proceedings, California Academy of Sciences)
ANR. Fairfield, Wash., Ye Galleon Press, 1964. ltd. ed. of
400 copies. 23p. map, wrps. [facsim. of 1876 ed.]   685

BROOKS, PAUL.   Roadless area; from the Alaskan tundra to the
game reserves of East Africa.   N. Y., Knopf, 1964. 1st ed.
260p.   illus. sketches by author(incl. front.) [has chapter on
McKinley National Park, pp.110-132]   686

BROOKS-VINCENT, LA BELLE.   The scarlet life of Dawson and the
roseate dawn of Nome.   Illustrated.   Personal experiences and
observations of the author La Belle Brooks-Vincent.   S. F.,
Brown, Meese & Craddock, [1900]   205p.   illus. photos, pls.
half-tones by William Brown   687

BROSIUS, SAMUEL M.   A menace to the reindeer industry. Philadelphia, Indian Rights Association, 1906. 7p. (Indian Rights Association Pub. no. 75, 2d ser.)   688

BROSTROM, IVAN.   The new gold fields at Cape Nome.   Their history, location and output.   Written from personal observation.
By Ivan Brostrom. S. F., Phillips & Smyth, 1899. 1st ed. 39p.
map(fold.)   689

BROUGH, CLAYTON. The thrill of seeing Alaska.   Toledo, Ohio,
[ca 1951] illus.   690

Broughton, William Robert. SEE nos.
     4637, [Vancouver, Geo.] Voyage ... 1789;
     4643, [Vancouver, Geo.] Narrative ... 1802.

BROWER, CHARLES DeWITT. Fifty years below zero; a lifetime of
adventure in the far North, by Charles D. Brower in collaboration
with Philip J. Farrelly and Lyman Anson. N. Y., Dodd Mead, 1942.
310p. front. pls. ports. ANR. 1954. ANR. N. Y., Grosset &
Dunlap, n. d. (Great Adventure Library)   691

BROWER, CHARLES DeWITT. King of the Arctic.   London, Robert
Hale, 1958.   692

Brower, David, edit.   SEE no. 595, Bohn, David.

Brower, Helen, co-auth.   SEE no. 3023, Masterson, James R.

Brown, Alec, tr.   SEE no. 4717, Voyage of *Chelyuskin*.

BROWN, ANGELINE M.   How to know and select furs.   World fur
guide.   Sew your own garments.   Make all kinds of things !
Sketches, patterns.   Tok, Alaska, Golden Mammoth Enterprises.
[printed by Instant Cash and Carry Printing, Anchorage], 1966.
1st ed.   64p.   illus.   693

BROWN, DAZIE M.   Metlakahtla.   Seattle, H. M. Hill Pub. Co.,
1907.   19p.   694

Brown, Emily Ivanoff.   SEE nos.
     4534, [Tickasook] Eskimo legend ... [c1959];
     4535, Tickasook Inupiut homes. 1956.

BROWN, GUS, Co.   The gold fields of Alaska.   What to take and
how to get there.   Seattle, 1897.   11p.   695

BROWN, JOHN W.   An abridged history of Alaska.   Seattle, Gateway
Printing Co., 1909.   96p.   illus. maps.   696

BROWN, LLOYD A.   The story of maps.   Boston, Little Brown, 1949.
                                                                 697

Brown, Robert, edit.   SEE no. 2354, Jewitt, J. R.

BROWN, ROBERT NEAL RUDMOSE.   The polar regions;   a physical and
economic geography of the Arctic and Antarctic.   London, Methu-
en, 1927.   245p.   maps(some fold.), bibliog.   698

Brown, Roderick Haig.   SEE nos. 1893 and 1894. Haig-Brown,
     Roderick.

Brown, William, illus.   SEE no. 687, Brooks-Vincent, La Belle.

BROWNE, BELMORE.   The conquest of Mount McKinley;   the story of
three expeditions through the Alaskan wilderness to Mount McKinley, North America's highest and most inaccessible mountain.
Appendix by Herschel C. Parker.   With 100 illustrations from original drawings by the author and from photographs and maps.
N. Y., Putnam, 1913.   381p.   front.(col.), pls.(some col.), map
(fold.), endmaps, append. index.   ANR. Boston, Houghton Mifflin,
1956.   381p.   illus. [some illus. by Bradford Washburn]   699

BROWNE, BELMORE.   The frozen barrier;   a story of adventure on
the coast of Behring Sea, with illustrations from original drawings by the author.   N. Y., Putnam, 1921.   267p.   front. (pl.),
pls.   700

BROWNE, BELMORE. The quest of the golden valley; a story of adventure on the Yukon. With eight illustrations from original drawings by the author. N. Y., Putnam, 1916. 279p. front.pls.
701

BROWNE, BELMORE. The white blanket; the story of an Alaskan winter. With illustrations from original drawings by the author. N. Y., Putnam, 1917. 137p. front. pls.
702

Browne, Belmore, co-auth. SEE ALSO no. 797, Camp Fire Club of America.

Browne, G. W., co-edit. SEE no. 1328, [Dole, Nathan Haskell]

BROWNE, WILLIAM HENRY JAMES. Ten coloured views taken during the Arctic expedition of Her Majesty's ships "Enterprise" and "Investigator" under the command of Capt. James C. Ross, drawn by W. H. Browne, with a summary of the expedition in search of Capt. Sir John Franklin. London, Ackermann & Co., 1850. 8p. pls.(col.)
703

BRUCE, H. ADDINGTON. The romance of American expansion. N. Y., Moffat, Yard & Co., 1909. 264p. [incls. Alaskan purchase] 704

BRUCE, MINER WAIT. Alaska; its history and resources, goldfields, routes and scenery. Seattle, Lowman & Hanford, 1895. 1st ed. 128p. front. pls. maps, map(fold. in pocket) ANR. N. Y., Putnam, 1899. rev. and enl. 237p. front. pls. maps (fold. incl. 1 in pocket), index.
705

BRUET, EDMOND. L'Alaska; géographie, exploration, géologie, minéralogie, faune, peuplement, flore, ressources naturelles. Paris, Payot, 1945. 451p. illus. pls. maps(incl. numbered dble.), tables, bibliog.
706

BRUHL, GUSTAV. Zwischen Alaska und Feuerland. Bilder aus den neuen welt. Berlin, Verlag von A. Asher & Co., 1896. 722p. 707

Bryan, Wm. S. SEE no. 1102, Cox, Jas.

Bryant, C., co-auth. SEE no. 182, Allen, Joel A.

BRYANT, CHARLOTTE KRUGER. The Terry twins in Alaska. L. A., Cowman Pub., 1957. 76p.
708

BRYANT, CHARLOTTE KRUGER. The Terry twins in Alaska find a treasure. L. A., Cowman Pub., 1961. 91p.
709

BRYANT, CHARLOTTE KRUGER. Top o' the world. Grand Rapids, Zondervan, 1951. 137p.
710

BRYCE, GEORGE. The siege and conquest of the North Pole. London, Gibbings & Co., 1910. 334p. maps.
711

BUACHE, JEAN NICOLAS and CIRIACO de ZEVALLOS. Disertaciones sobre la navegacion a las Indias Orientales por el Norte de la Europa. Escritas. La Primera: por M. Bauche, de la Academia de Ciencias de Paris, y la segunda; por el Capitan de Fragata de la Real Armada D. Ciriaco de Zevallos. Isla de Leon, Y.D.C.G.M. Año de 1798. (vi)I-XXII,41p. [notes by Buache and Zevallos on Ferrer Maldonado claim]   712

BUACHE, JEAN NICOLAS. Mémoire sur les pays de l'Asie et de l'Amérique, situes au nord de la Mer du Sud. Accompagne d'une carte de comparaison des plans de M. M. Engel and De Vaugondy, avec le plan des cartes modernes. Paris, L'Auteur, 1775. 22p. map(fold.)   713

Buache, Jean Nicolas. SEE ALSO nos.
    1471, Engel, Samuel. Mémoires et observations ... 1765;
    4661, Vaugondy, Robert, de. Mémoire sur les pays ...1774.

BUACHE, PHILIP. Carte des nouvelles découvertes au nord de la Mer du Sud, tant a l'est de la Siberie et du Kamtchatka qu'a l'ouest de la nouvelle France, dressée sur les mémoires de M. de l'Isle ... par Phillippe Buache ... et presentée a l'Academie ... du 8 Avril 1750, par M. de l"Isle. [accompanies [Buache, Philip] "Explication de la carte ..." 1752. SEE no. 716]   714

BUACHE, PHILIP. Considerations géographiques et physiques sur les nouvelles découvertes au nord de la Grande Mer, appellé'e vulgairement la Mer du Sud; avec des cartes qui y sont relatives. Par Philippe Buache, Premier géographe de Sa Majeste & de l'Académie Royale de Sciences. Paris, sous la Privilege de l'Académie Royale des Sciences [de l'Imprimerie de Ballard], 1753[-55] 3 pts. in 1. 160p. pls.(fold.), maps.   715

Buache, Philip. Erklarung ... 1753. SEE no. 717.

[BUACHE, PHILIP] Explication de la carte des nouvelles découvertes au nord de la Mer du Sud. Paris, Desaint & Saillant, 1752. 18p. [accompanied by author's "Carte des nouvelles ..." no. 714]   716

    TRANSLATION - Explication ... 1752.

    Erklarung der Charte von der neuen Entdeckungen welchegegen
        Norden des Sudmeers gemacht worden sind. A. de. Franz v.
        J. V. Krause. Berlin, 1753. 48p.   717

BUACHE, PHILIP. Expose des découvertes au nord de la Grande Mer, soit dans le nord-est de l'Asie, soit dans le nord-ouest de l'Amérique, entre le 160. degre de longitude & le 287. & depuis le 43. de latitude Septentrionale jusqu'au 80. Découvertes des Russes ... Découvertes des François ... Resultat de diverses recherches faites par seu Guillaume Delisle & Philippe Buache ...

BUACHE, PHILIP. Expose ... [continued]
... Découvertes de l'Amiral de Fonte ... Presente au Roy Le 2.
Septembre 1753. Avec les considérations géographiques & physiques sur ces découvertes, & les 6. cartes qui y sont relatives, par Philippe Buache, Premier Géographe de Sa Majeste, &
de l'Académie des Sciences. [Paris, 1753] maps(fold.)   718

BUACHE, PHILIP. Liste des cartes concernant les nouvelles découvertes au nord de la Grande Mer, appellée vulgairement la Mer
du Sud; et indication des articles qui composent les considérations géographiques & physiques, publiées en differentes portions, pour servir d'explication auxdites cartes; avec l'ap-
probation & sous le privilege de l'Académie des Sciences, depuis
1752, jusqu'en 1755. Par Philippe Buache, Premier Géographe du
Roi & de l'Académie. [Paris, 1755] maps(fold.), views(fold.)719

Buache, Philip. SEE ALSO no. 2693, Lettre d'un officier ...1753.

BUCHAN, LAURA and JERRY ALLEN. Hearth in the snow. N. Y., Wilfred Funk, 1952. 306p. pls.   720

Buchanan, G. E. SEE no. 4190, Smith, A. M.

BÜCHNER, EUG. Die Abbildungen der nordischen Seekuh (*Rhytina
gigas*, Zimm.) mit besonderer Berucksichtigung neu aufgefundener
handschriftlicher material in Seiner Majestät Höchst Eigenen
Bibliothek zu Zarskoje Sselo. [TITLE TR. The illustrations of
the northern seacow (*Rhytina gigas*, Zimm.) with special consi-
deration of the newly found manuscripts in his Majesty's own
library at Tsarskoye S'elo] St. Petersburg, Akademiia nauk SSSR,
1891. 24p. pl. (Mémoires, Ser. 7, t. 38, no. 7) [from Bering
second expedition, 1734-43]   721

BUDDINGTON, ARTHUR F. Alaskan nickel minerals. N. J., Princeton, 1924.   722

BUDELER, W. Vortoss ins Unbekannte; das grosse Abenteuer der
Forschung im Internationalen Geophysikalischen Jahr. [TITLE TR.
Advance into the unknown; the great adventure of research during
the International Geophysical Year] Munchen, Ehrenwirth, 1960.
342p. illus. maps, graphs, bibliog. [drifting stations and
general account of IGY]   723

"Buffalo" Jones. SEE no. 2370, Jones, Charles J.

BUGBEE, JOHN S., HENRY E. HAYDON and ORVILLE T. PORTER. Poems on
Alaska, the land of the midnight sun. Descriptive, personal, hu-
merous. By authors residing in the Territory. Sitka, Alaska
Print., 1891. 62p. index.   724

Bühler, Alfred. SEE no. 4006, Schmitz, C. A.

BUHRO, HARRY. Rough-stuff and moonlight. Of deeper love hath none. Philadelphia, Dorrance, 1948. 217p. front. pls. by author.   725

Bull, Charles Livingston, illus. SEE nos.
     1299, Diven, R. J. Rowdy. 1927;
     2771, London, Jack. Call of wild. 1903.

BUNDY, HALLOCK C. The Valdez-Fairbanks Trail; the story of a great highway. The Tanana Valley-Valdez, the gateway to an empire - a guide for the Alaska traveller. Seattle, The Alaska Pub. Co., 1910. 88p.   726

BUNN, IOLA FINCH. Growing up in Alaska. A story for children about today's Eskimos. N. Y., Exposition Press, 1965. 1st ed. 126p. front. illus. by Frederic Salzman.   727

Bunnell, Chas. E., edit. SEE no. 2102, Hick, Geo.

Burcham, M., edit. SEE no. 3417, Oregon. Dept. Educ.

BURFORD, VIRGIL and WALT MOREY. North to danger, by Virgil Burford as told to Walt Morey. N. Y., John Day, 1954. 254p. illus. map. ANR. London, Hale, 1955. 190p. illus. map. ANR. Caldwell, Idaho, Caxton, [c1969] 267p. photos by Charles J. Ott, map.   728

Burg, Amos, co-edit. SEE no. 3198, Morris, F. L.

BURGE, M. S. Indians of the upper Tanana region of Alaska. N. Y., Association on American Indian Affairs, 1938. 19p.   729

Burger, Carl. SEE no. 2857, McCracken, H.

[BURGES, JAMES B.] A narrative of the negotiations occasioned by the dispute between England and Spain in the year 1790. London, privately printed, 1791. 307p. ANR. [no pl., 1791 ?] [Nootka Sound controversy]   730

[Burges, James B. ?] SEE no. 4762, [Webb, Francis ?]

BURGESS, THORNTON W. The Christmas reindeer. N. Y., 1926. 139p.   731

BURGLON, NORA. Lost Island. Chicago, J. C. Winston Co., 1939. 261p. illus. by James Reid. ANR. Chicago, J. C. Winston Co., 1949. 261p. front.(col.), illus.   732

BURK, CREIGHTON A. Geology of the Alaska Peninsula; island arc and continental margin. Geologic map supplement. Tectonic map supplement. N. Y., Geologic Society of America, 1965. 250p. illus. pls. maps(3 fold. col. in portfolio) (Geologic Society of America Memoir no. 99)   733

BURKE, CLARA HEINTZ and ADELE COMANDINI. Doctor Hap. N. Y.,
Coward-McCann, 1961. 319p. [biog. of Dr. Grafton Burke]   734

Burke, Margaret Knudsen. SEE no. 4270, Springer, John.

BURKHOLDER, MABEL. Captain Cook. Toronto, Ryerson, 1928. 32p.
(Canadian History Readers)   735

Burland, Cottie A., co-auth. SEE no. 2176, Hooper, Jas. T.

Burlington and Missouri River Railroad Co. SEE
     no. 1722, Gillette, Edw.

Burnett, Ruth. SEE no. 3265, Myers, H.

BURNETT, W. R. The goldseekers. Garden City, N. Y., Doubleday,
1962. 1st ed. 283p. endmaps.   736

BURNETTE, O. LAWRENCE, jr. and W. C. HAYGOOD. Soviet view of
the American past. Glenview, Illinois, Scott, Foresman & Co.,
1964.   737

BURNEY, JAMES. A chronological history of north-eastern voyages
of discovery; and of the early eastern navigations of the Russians. By Captain James Burney, F.R.S. London, Printed by Luke
Hansard & Sons, for Payne and Foss, and John Murray, 1819. 1st
ed. 310p. maps(fold.)   738

BURNEY, JAMES. A memoir on the voyage of D'Entrecasteaux, in
search of La Perouse. London, Luke Hansard, 1820. 21p.   739

Burney, James. SEE ALSO nos.
     1273, D'Entrecasteaux, A. R. J. B. Voyage ... 1808;
     2963, Manwaring, G. E. My friend the Admiral ... 1931.

BURNS, WALTER NOBLE. A year with a whaler. N. Y., Outing Pub.
Co., 1913. 250p. pls. [Bering and Chukchi Seas]   740

BURPEE, LAWRENCE J. On the old Athabaska Trail. Toronto, Ryerson, 1926. ANR. N. Y., Frederick A. Stokes, 1927. 259p.
front. pls.   741

BURPEE, LAWRENCE J. The search for the western sea; the story
of the exploration of northwestern America. Toronto, Musson
Book Co., 1908. 2 vols. 651p. front. pls. ports. maps, index.
ANR. N. Y., Appleton, 1908. ANR. London, A. Rivers, 1908. ANR.
Toronto, Macmillan of Canada, 1935. 2 vols. 609p. illus. maps,
index. ANR. N. Y., Macmillan, 1936. 2 vols.   742

Burpee, Lawrence J. SEE ALSO no. 3256, Murray, A. H.
     Journal of Yukon. 1910.

BURR, AGNES RUSH. Alaska, our beautiful northland of opportunity; a description of its rivers, mountains, glaciers, volcanoes,
and other beautiful and unusual scenic features and of the rare
delights it offers travellers, big game hunters, mountain climbers, explorers; its towns and pioneer settlements; the government railroad and Mount McKinley National Park; its rich resources; its openings for new business enterprises; its Indians, their primitive customs and present development; its romantic early history when Russian, Spanish, and other nations sought
its wealth; the gold rush days; its present progress and bright
future. With a map and fifty-four plates of which six are in
color. Boston, Page Co., 1919. 428p. pls.(incl. front. and 5
in col.), map(fold.), bibliog. index. (See America First Series)
743

BURRALL, W. T. A trip to the far west of British Columbia.
Wisbech, 1891. 26p.   744

Burriel, Andres Marcos. SEE no. 4669, Venegas, Miguel.

BURROUGHS, JOHN. Far and near. Boston, Houghton, 1904. 287p.
front.(port.)   745

Burroughs, John. SEE ALSO nos.
    1950, Harriman Alaska Exped.1899;
    4431, Swift, H. (H.) Edge of April...1957.

BURROWS, E. G. The Arctic tern and other poems. N. Y., Grove
Press, 1957. 1st. ed. of 100 numbered, signed copies. 60p.
(Evergreen Book of Poetry E-56)   746

BURROWS, ELIZABETH. Irene of Tundra Towers. Garden City, N. Y.,
Doubleday, 1928. 311p. front.)col.), illus. by James Daugherty.
747

BURROWS, ELIZABETH. Judy of the Whale Gates; the strange hap-
penings that followed the stranding of the yacht *Aphoon* among
the volcanic islands of Alaska. Garden City, N. Y., Doubleday,
1930. 1st ed. 296p. illus. by James Daugherty.(Junior Books)
748

BURTON, JOHN E. Twenty-three opinions on Alaska tin, both placer and vein tin; what three years has proved and what the
probable future will be. Other mineral resources of Alaska.
Issued in the interest of the United States Alaska Tin Mining
Co. Milwaukee, Fowler Print. Co., 1908. 24p.   749

BUSCHMANN, JOHANN CARL EDUARD. Die Pima-Sprache und die Sprache
der Koloschen dargestellt von Joh. Carl Ed. Buschmann. Berlin,
F. Dümmler's Verlags-Buchhandlung, 1857. 1,1,321-432p. [also
sep. in: Königliche Adademie der Wissenschaften zu Berlin, Abhandlungen, aus dem Jahre 1856. pt. 3, pp.321-432]   750

BUSCHMANN, JOHANN CARL EDUARD. Die Spuren der aztekischen Sprache im nördlichen Mexico und höheren amerikanischen Norden. Zugleich eine Musterung der Völker und Sprachen des nördlichen Mexico's und der Westseite Nordamerika's von Guadalaxara an bis zum Eis- meer. Von Joh. Carl Ed. Buschmann. [TITLE TR. Traces of the Aztec language in northern Mexico and the higher American North. Simultaneously a review of the peoples and languages of northern Mexico and the west side of North America from Guadalaxara to the Arctic Ocean] Berlin, Gedruckt in der Wissenschaften, 1859. (vi)vii-xii,819p. index. [also separate in: Königliche Aka- demie der Wissenschaften zu Berlin. Abhandlungen, aus dem Jahre 1859, Berlin, 1859, Zweiter Supplement-Band, pp.1-819]   751

BUSCHMANN, JOHANN CARL EDUARD. Die Völker und Sprachen Neu-Mexi- ko's und der Westseite des britischen Nordamerika's dargestellt von Joh. Carl Ed. Buschmann. Berlin, E. Dümmler's Verlags-Buch- handlung, 1858. 1,1,pp.209-414. [reprinted from: Königliche Akademie der Wissenschaften zu Berlin, Abhandlungen aus dem Jahre 1857, pp.209-414, Berlin, 1858]   752

BUSCHMANN, JOHANN CARL EDUARD. Systematische Worttafel des athapaskischen Sprachstamms, aufgestellt und erläutert von Joh. Carl Ed. Buschmann. Dritte Abtheilung des Apache. Berlin, F. Dümmler's Verlags-Buchhandlung, 1860. 1,1,pp.501-586. [also in: Königliche Akademie der Wissenschaften zu Berlin, Abhandlungen aus dem Jahre 1859. pt. 3, pp.501-586, Berlin, 1860]   753

Bush, K. J. SEE no. 1950, Harriman Alaska Expedition.

BUSH, RICHARD J. Reindeer, dogs and snow-shoes; a journal of Siberian travel and explorations in the years 1865, 1866 and 1867. N. Y., 1871. 529p. illus. ANR. London, 1872. [some mention of St. Michael]   754

BUSINESS AND PROFESSIONAL WOMEN'S CLUB, Juneau. Alaska's Capi- tol City cook book; compiled and illustrated by Edith Johnson. no pl., 1962. 1st ed. 129p. illus.   755

Buske, Frank, co-auth. SEE no. 107, Alaska Review.

Busse, J. H., tr. SEE nos. 3966 and 3969, Sarychev, G. A.

BUTCHER, DEVEREUX. Exploring our national parks and monuments; prepared under the auspices of the National Parks Association. Boston, 1949. 2d ed. 224p. illus. ANR. Boston, Houghton, 1954. 4th ed. 288p. illus.(incl. come col.), maps, bibliog. ANR. 1960. 5th ed. 2d rev. print. 288p. [incls. Mt. McKinley, Glacier Bay and Katmai]   756

BUTCHER, DEVEREUX. Exploring our national wildlife refuges. Boston, Houghton, 1963. 2d ed. rev. 340p. illus. map, index.   757

BUTCHER, DEVEREUX. Seeing America's wildlife, in our national refuges. Prepared under the auspices of Defenders of Furbearers. N. Y., Devin-Adair, 1955. 338p. photos, map, bibliog. index. PP.225-51, Aleutian Islands National Wildlife Refuge and Kenai National Moose Range: pp.263-67, Mt. McKinley National Park: scattered Alaskan photos and references throughout]   758

BUTLER, EVELYN I. and GEORGE A. DALE. Alaska; the land and the people. Illustrated with photographs. N. Y., Viking Press, 1957. 159p. front. photos, maps.   759

BUYNITZKY, STEPHEN NESTOR. English-Aleutian vocabulary. Prepared by Stephen N. Buynitzky. Published by The Alaska Commercial Co. S. F., Alta California Book & Job Printing House, 1871. i-iv,5-13p. [vocab. in parallel columns]   760

BYHAN, ARTHUR. Die Polarvölker ... Leipzig, Quelle & Meyer, 1909. 148p. pls. maps (Wissenschaft und Bildung ... 63)   761

BYRD, ERNESTINE N. Black wolf of Savage River. Berkeley, Calif., Parnassus Press, 1959. illus.   762

BYRD, ERNESTINE N. Ice king. N. Y., Scribner, 1965. 142p. 763

Byrns, Richard H., edit. SEE no. 4944, Wolff, E.

C

CADWALLADER, CHARLES LEE. Reminiscences of the Iditarod Trail; placer mining days in Alaska. By Charles Lee Cadwallader, dedicated to his daughters Mary Bergman and Jane Browne. Mainly my experiences mushing in and out over the Iditarod Trail in 1917 and in 1919 and my two years' work in the Iditarod-Flat area. no pl., n. d. [1966 ?] 26p. append. names of roadhouses and owners in 1917, index, persons in narrative, wrps.   764

CADZOW, DONALD A. Native copper objects of the Copper Eskimos. N. Y., Museum of American Indians, 1920. 22p. pls. (Heye Foundation, Indian Notes and Monographs, Misc. Contrib. no. 8)   765

CAIRNES, DeLORME DONALDSON. The Yukon-Alaska International Boundary, between Porcupine and Yukon Rivers. Ottawa, Government Printing Bureau, 1914. 161p. front. pls. tables(fold.), maps(2 fold. in pocket). (Canada. Geological Survey, Memoir no. 67, Geol. Ser. 49)   766

[CALASANCTIUS, SISTER MARY JOSEPH] The voice of Alaska; a missioner's memories. Translated from the French. Lachin, Quebec, Sisters of St. Anne Press, 1935. 349p. pls. ports. map(fold.) [tr. of no. 768]   767

[CALASANCTIUS, SISTER MARY JOSEPH] Voix de'Alaska; fondation de la mission Ste. Croix. Memoires de Soeur Marie Joseph Calasanz religeuse missionaire de la Congregation des soeurs de Sainte Anne. [TITLE TR. Voice of Alaska; a missioner's memories] Lachin, Quebec, Procure des Missions des Soeurs de Sainte Anne, 1930. 209p. illus. ports. [Holy Cross Mission, Yukon Valley: for tr. see no. 767]   768

Calasanz, Soeur Marie Joseph. SEE [Calasanctius, Sister Mary Joseph]

CALDER-MARSHALL, ARTHUR. Lone wolf; the story of Jack London. London, Methuen, 1961. 188p. (Children Everywhere Series) ANR. N. Y., Duell, Sloan & Pearce, 1962. 168p.   769

Calder-Marshall, Arthur. SEE ALSO no. 2770, London, Jack.

CALDWELL, ELSIE NOBLE. Alaska trail dogs. N. Y., Richard R. Smith, 1945 [c1945] 150p. illus. front.(map), pls. ports. facsims.   770

Caldwell, Erskine, edit. SEE no. 4888, Williamson, Thames Ross.

CALDWELL, FRANK. Wolf the storm leader. N. Y., Dodd,Mead, 1929. 160p. illus. by Edward A. Poucher. ANR. N. Y., Dodd, Mead, 1930. 183p. front. pls.   771

CALDWELL, HOWARD W. Alaska and Hawaii. Chicago, Ainsworth & Co., 1900.   772

CALDWELL, J. B. Calgary route to the Klondike gold fields; description of routes; miners' and prospectors' outfitting guide. no pl., n. d. 10p.   773

CALDWELL, J. B. Introducing Alaska. N. Y., Putnam, 1947. 202p. illus. pls. endmaps, append.   774

CALDWELL, J. B. What to expect in Alaska; a series of six articles ... originally published in the Alaska Sportsman. Ketchikan, Alaska Magazine Publishing Co., 1945. 28p. illus. photos. ANR. 1946. reprinted and rev. 28p. illus. wrps.   775

CALKINS, R. H. High tide. Seattle, The Marine Digest Pub. Co., 1952.   776

California, B. C., Wash., Alaska, Mexico. 1904. SEE no. 3450, Pacific Coast Steamship Co.

CALLAHAN, JAMES MORTON. American foreign policy in Canadian relations. N. Y., Cooper Square Pub., 1967. 576p. maps, bibliog. reprint of 1937 ed.   777

CALLAHAN, JAMES MORTON. American relations in the Pacific and the far east, 1784-1900. Baltimore, Johns Hopkins Press, 1901. 177p. (Studies in History and Political Science, Ser. 19, nos. 1-3)   778

CALLAHAN, JAMES MORTON. Russo-American relations during the American Civil War. Morgantown, West Virginia, West Virginia University, 1908. 18p. (Dept. of History and Political Science Studies in American History, Ser. 1, Diplomatic History, nos. 2 and 3)   779

CALLAHAN, JAMES MORTON. The Alaska purchase and Americo-Canadian relations. Morgantown, West Virginia, West Virginia University, 1908. 44p. (Dept. History and Political Science Studies in American History, Ser. 1, Diplomatic History, nos. 2 and 3)   780

CALLISON, J. P. Wolf predation in the north country. Seattle, privately printed, 1948. 89p. illus. ftntes.   781

Calvert, W. E., tr. SEE nos.
    560, Birket-Smith, Kaj. Eskimos. 1936;
    3027, Mathiassen, T. Archaeol. ...1930;
    3749, Rasmussen, K. J. V. Alaskan Eskimos ... 1952.

CALVIN, JACK. Fisherman 28. Boston, Little Brown, 1930. 325p. front.(col.), pls. illus. by Mahlon Blaine.   782

CALVIN, JACK. Sitka, a history of the town. Sitka, Arrowhead Press, 1936. 40p. illus. photos, sketches. ANR. WITH TITLE Sitka, past and present. Sitka, Sitka Printing Co., 1950. rev. ANR. 1959. rev. 40p. illus. photos, sketches. ANR. 1966. 40p. illus. photos, sketches. ANR. 1968. rev. 39p. illus.   783

CALVIN, JACK. Square-rigged. Boston, Little Brown, 1929. 334p. front.(col.), pls. illus. by Mahlon Blaine.   784

Calvin, Jack. SEE ALSO no. 3812, Ricketts, Edw. F.

CAMERON, CHARLOTTE. A cheechako in Alaska and the Yukon. London, T. F. Unwin, 1920. 291p. pls. map(fold.) ANR. London, F. A. Stokes, 1920. 291p. front.(port.), pls. map(col. fold.)   785

CAMERON, EDNA M. Children of the tundra. Philadelphia, Lippincott, 1963. illus. [Eskimo, Aleut, Athabascan]   786

CAMP, FRANK B. Alaska nuggets; written and published in Alaska by an Alaskan. Anchorage, Alaska Pub. Co., 1921. 45p. ANR. Anchorage, Alaska Pub. Co., 1922. 2d print. 66p. illus. [poetry]   787

CAMPBELL, ARCHIBALD. The restless voyage; being an account by Archibald Campbell, seaman, of his wanderings in five oceans from 1806 to 1812. Written and published in Edinburgh in 1816 and supplemented and re-edited in 1948 from documents dealing with his further history in Scotland and America by Stanley D. Porteus. London, Harrap, 1949. 280p.   788

CAMPBELL, ARCHIBALD. Voyage round the world, from 1806 to 1812, in which Japan, Kamschatka, the Aleutian Islands and the Sandwich Islands were visited ... Edinburgh, A. Constable & Co., 1816. 288p. map. OTHERS Jena, 1817 (in German) 162p.: Amsterdam, 1818 (in Dutch): 1817, 1819, 1822 and 1825.(var. Eng. eds. var. pub.) ANR. Amsterdam, N. Isreal and N. Y., Da Capo Press, 1969. (Bibliotheca Australiana, no. 50)   facsim of 1816 ed. 789

CAMPBELL, COLIN, comp. The White Pass and Yukon route to the golden north. Seattle, Press of Trade Register, 1901. 104p. illus. ANR. WITH COVER TITLE Official hand-book, 1902. Golden north. The White Pass and Yukon route to the golden north. Seattle, Press of Trade Register, 1902. 78p. illus. map.   790

CAMPBELL, EDGAR O. Pĕ nēl´ lŭ ´ghā- Ŏong wĕ´ĕ pŭk. Ō kōōt- ŏ kōōz ē tĭt- Kē yŏ ghŭ nŭ ghum- ē yŏ´ŏ nŭng. Edgar O. Campbell, M. D. Philadelphia, The Westminster Press and N. Y., Women's Board of Home Missions of the Presbyterian Church in the U. S. A. 1910 [c1910] 27p. illus. wrps. [Eskimo reader, Gambell, St. Lawrence Island]   791

CAMPBELL, JOHN MARTIN, edit. Prehistoric cultural relations between the Arctic and temperate zones of North America. Montreal, 1962. 181p. pls. maps, bibliog. (Arctic Institute of North America Tech. Paper no. 11, Symposium 25th annual meeting, Society for American Archaeology)   792

CAMPBELL, LUTHER EUGENE. The age of gold, being a collection of northland tales, song, sketch and narrative, miner legend and campfire reflections all gleaned at firsthand and done in faithful metre by an eager listener. [COVER TITLE A travail of the Eldorado. A. Y. P. Souvenir Edition] S. F., Whittaker and Ray Wiggin Co., 1909. 1st ed. 115p. front.(port.)   793

CAMPBELL, ROBERT. The discovery and exploration of the Youcon (Pelly) River, by the discoverer, Robert Campbell, F. R. G. S., lately a chief factor in the Hudson's Bay Co. Winnipeg, Manitoba Free Press, 1885. 18p.   794

CAMPBELL, ROBERT. Two journals of Robert Campbell, 1808-51 and 1850-53. Seattle, Shorey Book Store, 1958. 1st facsim. ed. 151p. ANR. June 1967. 2d facsim. ed. [reprinted from typed copies]   795

Campbell, Robert. SEE ALSO no. 805, Canada. Fifth book ...

CAMPBELL, WILLIAM. Arctic patrols; stories of the Royal Canadian Mounted Police. Milwaukee, Bruce Pub. Co., 1936. 335p. front.(port.), pls. maps. [Northwest Territory and Yukon]   796

CAMP FIRE CLUB OF AMERICA. A plea for Mount McKinley National Park; Mount McKinley National Park an economic asset; by Belmore Browne and Robert Sterling Yard. N. Y., 1916. 10p. (Published and circulated by the Camp Fire Club of America, The Boone and Crockett Club and American Game Protective Association)
797

CAMP FIRE CLUB OF AMERICA. A square deal for the fur seal. An open letter and exhibits from the Camp Fire Club of America to the American people, July 6, 1910. N. Y., 1910. 23p.   798

CAMPION MINING AND TRADING CO. Facts from Alaska gold fields. Mines located at Nome, Alaska. Chicago, 1903. 45p.   799

CAMSELL, CHARLES and M. W. MAXWELL. Canada's new northwest; a study of the present and future development of MacKenzie District of the Northwest Territories, Yukon Territory, and the northern parts of Alberta and British Columbia. Ottawa, King's Print., 1947. 155p. diagrs.(1 fold.), maps(some fold.) (North Pacific Planning Project, Joint Economic Committee of Canada and U. S.) [incls. Canol Project, also Alaska Highway]   800

CAMSELL, CHARLES. Son of the North. Toronto, Ryerson Press, 1954. 244p. illus. port. maps(text) [autobiog.]   801

CANADA. Alaska Highway. Ottawa, Queen's Print., 1955. 16p. illus. table. (Dept. Northern Affairs and National Resources, Travel Bureau, Canadian Section) ANR. 1959. 24p. illus. ANR. 1960. 31p. illus. map, table. [HAS TITLE Alaska Highway; road to Yukon adventure. Compiled in co-operation with Travel Bureau, Northern Administration and Land Branch of Department of Northern Affairs and National Resources; and Customs Division of Department of National Revenue]   802

CANADA. Canada's reindeer herd. Ottawa, 1938. 9p. illus. map. (Dept. Mines and Resources, Lands, Parks and Forests Branch) [from Kotzebue Sd., Alaska to east of MacKenzie Delta, Canada]803

CANADA. Data record, current measurements Hecate Project, 1954. Queen Charlotte Sound, Hecate Strait, Dixon Entrance. Nanaimo, B. C., March 1955. 74p. chart(text), bibliog. (Joint Commission on Oceanography, Pacific Oceanography Group)   804

CANADA. Fifth book of reading lessons. Toronto, 1883. (Royal Readers, Special Canadian Series) [incls. Robert Campbell's account of discovery of Yukon River]   805

CANADA. Physical and chemical data record, Hecate Project, 1954. Queen Charlotte Sound, Hecate Strait, Dixon Entrance, Nanaimo, B. C., January 1955. 99p. charts(text), tables, bibliog. (Fisheries Research Board, Pacific Oceanography Group)   806

CANADA. Physical and chemical data record, Hecate Project, with Appendix I, current observations, 1955. Queen Charlotte Sound, Hecate Strait, Dixon Entrance. Nanaimo, B. C., August 1955. 107p. charts(text), tables, bibliog. (Fisheries Research Board, Pacific Oceanography Group)   807

CANADA. Physical and chemical data record, North Pacific surveys, Continental Shelf and Gulf of Alaska, July 22 to Aug. 16, 1958. Ottawa, Queen's Print., Sept. 22, 1958. 107p. illus. map, graphs, tables, bibliog. (Fisheries Research Board, Ms Report Series, Oceanography and Limnology, no. 29)   808

CANADA. Physical and chemical data record, North Pacific surveys, Western Aleutians and Bering Sea, June 27 to Aug. 14, 1958. Ottawa, Queen's Print., Sept. 22, 1958. 104p. illus. map, graphs, tables, bibliog. (Fisheries Research Board, Ms Report Series, Oceanography and Limnology, no. 28)   809

CANADA. Proceedings of the Special Committee on sealing and fisheries in Pacific waters. H. H. Hersey, Chairman. Ottawa, King's Print., 1934. 7 vols. paged cont. (Senate, 5th Session, 17th Parliament)   810

CANADA. Regulations for placer mining along the Yukon River and its tributaries; North West Territory. Approved by order in Council, no. 1189, of 21st May, 1897, as amended. no pl., 1897. 6p. (Department of the Interior)   811

CANADA. Report as to the rights of the Hudson's Bay Company under their charter, the renewal of the license of occupation, the character of the soil and climate of the territory, and its fitness for settlement. T. L. Terrill, Chairman. Toronto, 1857. 25p. (Parliament. Legislative Assembly. Select Committee on rights of the Hudson's Bay Company)   812

CANADA. Report of the Royal Commission appointed by Order in Council of date May 20th, 1919, to investigate the possibilities of the reindeer and musk-ox industries in the Arctic and sub-Arctic regions of Canada. John Gunion Rutherford, Chairman. Ottawa, [1921 ?] 116 ℓ , plus 546 ℓ of appendixes in 3 vols. photos(mounted) (Royal Commission on possibilities of reindeer and musk-ox industries in the Arctic and sub-Arctic regions) [appendix II contains U. S. Dept. of Interior reports on Alaskan reindeer] ANR. (without appendixes) Ottawa, King's Print., 1922. 99p.   813

CANADA. Reports of North West Mounted Police of Canada, 1896-1901.   814

CANADA. Surface water supply of Canada. Pacific drainage, B.C.
and Yukon Territory, climatic years 1950-51 and 1951-52. Ottawa,
Queen's Print., 1955. 435p. map(text), tables. (Department of
Northern Affairs and National Resources, Water Resources Paper,
no. 114)   815

CANADA. The Yukon Territory; a brief description of its administration, resources, development. Ottawa, 1938. 13p. map
(Department of Mines and Resources, Lands, Parks and Forests
Branch) OTHERS 1943, 1944, 1946. rev. and enl. ANR. 1947,
by W. F. Lothian. 52p. map(dble.), appends. bibliog.   816

CANADA. The Yukon Territory; its history and resources. Ottawa, Government Print. Bur., 1909. 140p. (Issued by direction
of Hon. Frank Oliver, Minister of the Interior, Ottawa) ANR.
1909. 181p. rev. and enl. pls.(incl. 1 fold.), tables, diagrs.
ANR. 1916. rev. and enl. 233p. pls.(incl. 3 fold.) ANR. 1926.
100p. ports. tables, facsims. map(fold.) (Issued by North West
Territory and Yukon Branch of Department of the Interior)[first
printed in 1907, 140p.]   817

Canada. SEE ALSO nos.
      175, Allen, C. C. Platinum metals. 1961;
      355, Baird, P. D. Report exped. Snow Cornice. 1949;
      384, Banfield, A. W. F. Revision reindeer and caribou.1961;
      390, Barbeau, C. M. Haida myths ...1953;
      391, Barbeau, C. M. Medicine men on No. Pac. coast ...1958;
      394, Barbeau, C. M. Totem poles. 1950;
      395, Barbeau, C. M. Tsimsyan myths ... 1961;
      627, Boville, B. W. Atlas stratospheric circul. ...1959;
      766, Cairnes, DeL. D. Yukon-Alaska Int'l. Boundary ...1914;
      800, Camsell, Chas. Canada's new northwest ...1947;
      952, Clemens, W. A. Fishes of Pac. coast ...1946;
      1100, Cowan, P. R. Visit to no. substations and Alaska.1946;
      1216, Dawson, Geo. M. Report explorat. Yukon ... 1898;
      1320, Dodimead, A. J. Atlas oceanog. ...1960;
      1321, Dodimead, A. J. Oceanog. atlas ...1961;
      1322-24, Dodimead, A. J. Oceanog. data record ...1960-62;
      1325, Dodimead, A. J. Report oceanog. investigations ...1958;
      1343, Dozois, L. O. R. Precise leveling B. C. ...1951;
      1377, Dunbar, M. J. Prelim. rpt. Bering Strait scheme.1960;
      1378, Dunbar, M. J. Second report Bering Strait dam. 1962;
      1590-92, Fofonoff, N. P. Transport computations ...1960-63;
      1597, Forbes, H. A. Gaxetteer No. Canada ...1948;
      1721, Gillett, J. M. Gentians ...1963;
      1848, Greenaway, K. R. Aerial reconn. ...1948;
      1892, Hagglund, M. G. Formation ... sea ice. 1955;
      1995, Hawkes, E. W. "Inviting-in"feast ...1913;
      2238, Hunter, Joseph. Report on boundary line. 1878;
      2268, Innes, M. J. S. Gravity measurements ...1957;
      2274, International Boundary Commission. Jt. report ...1952;
      2277, International Geol. Cong. Guidebook ...1913;
      2346, Jenness, D. Indians of Canada. 1932;

CANADA. SEE ALSO nos.
    2348, Jennings, W. T. Report ... routes to Yukon ... 1898;
    2460, King, W. F. Joint rpt. .:. boundary ... 1901;
    2481, Kitto, F. H. Yukon ... 1929;
    2583, Laing, H. M. Birds ... *Thiepval* 1925;
    2628, La Rocque, J. A. A. Catalogue mollusca ... 1953;
    2656, Leahey, A. H. Prelim. soil survey ... 1943;
    2657, Leahey, A. H. Rpt. Exper. Substa. Whitehorse...[1946?];
    2668, Leechman, D. Vanta Kutchin. 1954;
    2795, Lord, C. S. Geol. Alaska Highway ... 1944;
    2826, McAllister, D. E. List marine fishes ... 1960;
    2827, McAllister, D. E. Placement of prowfishes ... 1961;
    2837, McConnell, R. G. Prelim. Klondike gold fields...1900;
    2838, McConnell, R. G. Rpt. explor. Yukon ... 1890;
    2839, McConnell, R. G. Rpt. gold values ... 1907;
    2840, McConnell, R. G. Rpt. Klondike gold fields. 1901;
    2930, MacLean, T. A. Lode mining in Yukon ... 1914;
    2946, Macoun, John. Catalogue Canadian birds. 1900;
    2947, Macoun, John. Climate and soil of Yukon. 1903;
    3135, Mills, David. Canadian view Alaskan boundary ... 1899;
    3341, Norford, B. S. Illus. Canadian fossils ... 1962;
    3359, Northwood, T. D. Depth measurements ... 1948;
    3388, Ogilvie, Wm. Copy further rpt. ... 1899;
    3390, Ogilvie, Wm. Evidence ... alleged malfeasance...1899;
    3391, Ogilvie, Wm. Information ... Yukon District. 1897;
    3394, Ogilvie, Wm. Klondike official guide ... 1898;
    3395, Ogilvie, Wm. Truths about Klondike ... 1897;
    3401, Oliver, E. H. Canadian northwest ... 1914;
    3458, Pacific Science Congress. Trade of Canada ... 1933;
    3586, Pike, G. C. Guide to whales, porpoises ... 1954;
    3643, Porsild, A. E. Reindeer grazing ... 1929;
    3697, Pritchard, A. L. Pacific salmon ... 1930;
    3730, Rand, A. L. Mammals of Yukon. 1945;
    3753, Ravenhill, A. Cornerstone Canadian culture ... 1944;
    3904, [Rowatt, H. H.] Rpt. respect Yukon Terr. 1907;
    3992, Scarth, W. H. Report trip to Yukon. 1897;
    4134, Shortt, T. M. Summer birds Yakutat Bay ... 1939;
    4312, Stefansson, V. Prehist. ... commerce Arctic ... 1914;
    4434, Swithinbank, C. W. M. Ice atlas ... 1960;
    4463, Taverner, P. A. Birds of Canada. 1934;
    4464, Taverner, P. A. Birds of western Canada. 1926;
    4462, Taverner, P. A. Study ... red-tailed hawk ... 1927;
    4547, Tolmie, W. F. Comparative vocabs. Indian ... 1884;
    4587, Tully, J. P. Assessment temp. structure ... 1961;
    4651, van Steensel, M. People of light and dark ... 1966;
    4868, Wiley, S. C. Colonization ... 1960;
    4911, Wilson, H. P. Comparison ... wind date. 1961;
    5010, Yukon Territory, Commissioner. Interim report ... 1906.

CANADA'S ALASKAN DISMEMBERMENT; an analytical examination of the
fallacies underlying the Tribunal award. Niagara-on-the-Lake,
Ontario, C. Thonger, 1904. 76p. [Anglo-Russian treaty, 1825,
and Alaska Boundary Commission, 1903]   818

Canada's new northwest ... 1947. SEE no. 800, Camsell, Chas.

Canada's reindeer herd. 1938. SEE no. 803, Canada.

CANADA STEAMSHIP LINES, Ltd. The far west; catalogue of a selection of early views, maps, charts and plans of the Great Lakes, the far west, the Arctic and Pacific Oceans from the William H. Cloverdale Collection of historical Canadiana at the Manoir Richelieu, Murray Bay, P. Q., exhibited by the Thunder Bay Historical Society, Ft. William, Ontario, Port Arthur, Ontario; March 13 to April 30, 1943. Montreal, 1943. 22p. illus. maps.   819

Canada's western northland ... 1937. SEE no. 551, Bethune, W.C.

Canadian catalogue of books ... 1959. SEE no. 4556, Toronto Public Library.

Canadian Clubs, Assoc. of. SEE no. 4720, Wade, F. C.

CANADIAN NATIONAL RAILROAD AND STEAMSHIP LINES. Alaska and the Yukon and the triangle tour of British Columbia. no pl., 1930. 20p. photos.   820

CANADIAN NATIONAL STEAMSHIP LINES. Alaska via the historic Inside Passage. S. S. *Prince George*. no pl., 1958. illus. map.
                                                                     821

Canadian North West; a bibliog. ... 1931. SEE no. 4557, Toronto Public Library.

CANADIAN PACIFIC RAILWAY CO. One thousand miles of cruising through the fiords of British Columbia via Canadian Pacific "Princess Line." Vancouver, 1936. 6p. illus. map.   822

CANADIAN PACIFIC RAILWAY CO. Roads of adventure through the Canadian Rockies, Alaska and the evergreen playground. no pl., 1932. (32)p. illus. map(fold.)   823

Canadian Pacific Railway Co. SEE ALSO no. 1554, Finck, Henry T.

Canadian Railway development. 1933. SEE no. 1410, Edgar, J. H.

CANE, CLAUDE RICHARD JOHN. Summer and Fall in western Alaska; the record of a trip to Cook's Inlet after big game. London, H. Cox, 1903. 191p. front. pls.   824

Canham, T. H. SEE no. 3687, Prevost, Jules L.

CANTON, FRANK M. Frontier trails; the autobiography of Frank M. Canton. Edited by E. E. Dale. Boston, Houghton, 1930. 1st ed. 236p. front. pls. ports. [Alaska and Oklahoma]   825

CANTWELL, GEORGE G.   The Klondike; a souvenir.   Seattle, pub. by Rufus Buck, general agent B. T. Carr, [1900 ?]   74 pls. on 37𝓁 , no text.   ANR.   S. F., Rufus Buck, 1901.   186 illus.   826

Cantwell, George G., illus.   SEE ALSO no. 1914, Hallock, Chas.

Cape Nome Steamers.   SEE no. 2935, McMicken, E. G.

Capitain Jàkob Cook dritte Entdeckungs-Reise ... 1787.   SEE
    no. 1030, [Cook, James]

"Captain Bob"   SEE nos. 419-21, Bartlett, Robert Abram.

CAPTAIN COOK, BI-CENTENARY, 1928;   souvenir of the bicentenary celebrations arranged in the Cleveland district.   Middlesbrough, Hood, 1928.   24p.   front. pls. ports. facsims.   827

Captain Cook's third and last voyage ... [1785 ?], 1786, 1795, 1809.   SEE nos. 1023, 1026, 1033, 1038, [Cook, James]

Captain Cook's three voyages ... 1792, 1797, 1814.   SEE
    nos. 1031, 1036, 1040, [Cook, James]

Captain Cook's voyages ... 1811, 1897.   SEE nos. 1039 and 1051,
    [Cook, James]

CAPTAIN COOK's VOYAGES OF DISCOVERY.   London, J. M. Dent, 1906.   479p.   pl.   ANR.   1915.   (Everyman's Library.   Travel and Topography)   828

CAPTAIN COOK'S VOYAGES OF DISCOVERY.   London, Cassell, 1908.   446p.   (The People's Library)   829

Captain James Cook, for ages 12 to 14 years.   n. d.   SEE
    no. 4813, Whitcombe & Tombs, Ltd.

CAPTAIN LILLIE'S BRITISH COLUMBIA, Puget Sound and South East Alaska coast guide.   Vancouver, B. C., Progress Pub. Co., 1947.
          830

CARAS, ROGER A.   Monarch of Deadman Bay;   the life and death of a Kodiak bear.   Boston, Little Brown, 1969.   185p.   illus.   831

Cardot, J.   SEE no. 1950, Harriman Alaska Expedition.

[CAREY, T. J.]   Klondike ... and all about it, by a practical mining engineer.   [WRAPPER TITLE: A mine of knowledge;   Klondike and all about it ... Alaska and its hoarded treasures ...]   N. Y. Excelsior Pub. House, T. J. Carey, Prop., 1897.   1st ed.   144p. map(fold.), diagr. wrps.   (Excelsior Library of Popular Handbooks no. 48, Aug. 1897)   832

Carleton, Will.   SEE no. 4816.   White (E. W.) Pub. Co.

Carlson, Geo., illus. SEE no. 435, Bayliss, Clara K.

CARLSON, GERALD F. Two on the rocks, the adventures of a young American school teacher and his wife among the Eskimos on Little Diomede Island in Bering Strait. N. Y., David McKay, 1967.
193p. photos.   833

CARLSON, LELAND. An Alaskan gold mine; the story of No. 9 Above. Evanston, Illinois, Northwestern University Press, 1951.
178p. illus. ports. maps. (Northwestern University Studies, Social Sciences Ser. no. 7)   834

CARLSON, S. W. and LEONID SOROKA. Faith of our fathers, the Eastern Orthodox religion. Minneapolis, Olympic Press, 1954.
ANR. 1962. 3rd ed. rev. 176p.   835

CARLSON, WILLIAM. Opportunities in southeastern Alaska. Ketchi-kan, [ca 1939] 24p.   836

CARLSON, WILLIAM S. Lifelines through the Arctic. N. Y., Duell, Sloan and Pearce, 1962. 1st ed. 271p. pls. photos, endmaps, bibliog. [air transportation]   837

CARMACK, GEORGE WASHINGTON. My experiences in the Yukon. Pri-vately printed by Marguerite Carmack. Seattle, Trade Printery, 1933. 16p. illus. port.   838

Carnarvon, Fourth Earl of. SEE no. 1809, Great Britain.

Carothers, Grady, photog. SEE no. 3373, O'Brien, E. F.

CARPENTER, ALLAN. Alaska; from its glorious past to the pre-sent. Chicago, Children's Press, 1965.   839

CARPENTER, EDMUND SNOW, edit. Anerca. Toronto, J. M. Dent, (44)p. illus. [English tr. poems and prose passages, Eskimos Greenland to Alaska]   840

CARPENTER, FRANCES. Canada and her northern neighbors. N. Y., American Book Co., 1946. 438p. illus. ports. maps.   841

CARPENTER, FRANCES. Our little friends of Eskimo Land, Papik and Natsek. N. Y., American Book Co., 1931. 239p. illus. by Curtiss Sprague. front.(col.), endmaps, glossary.   842

CARPENTER, FRANK GEORGE. Alaska; our northern wonderland. Gar-den City, N. Y., Doubleday Page, 1923. 319p. front. pls. ports. maps(col. fold.), bibliog. index. (Carpenter's World Travels)843

CARPENTER, FRANK GEORGE. North America. N. Y., American Book Co., 1910. 410p. (Carpenter's Geographical Reader) [section on Alaska and seal islands]   844

CARPENTER, HERMAN M. Three years in Alaska. Philadelphia, The
Howard Co., 1901. 105p. pls. port.   845

CARPENTER, ROBERT RALPH MORGAN. Games trails from Alaska to
Africa. Philadelphia, 1938. 180p. front. pls. ports. maps.
ANR. 1944. privately printed. 236p. [southeastern Alaska] 846

CARPENTER, ROBERT RALPH MORGAN. Games trails in Idaho and Alaska.
no pl., 1940. 43p. pls. [Wood River, east central Alaska] 847

Carpenter, Robert Ralph Morgan. SEE ALSO no. 612,
    Boone and Crockett Club. North American big game. 1939.

CARPENTER, STANLEY J. and W. J. La CASSE. Mosquitoes of North
America, north of Mexico. Berkeley, University of California
Press, 1955. 360p. figs. pls. bibliog. [incls. Alaska and
northern Canada]   848

CARRIGHAR, SALLY. Icebound summer. N. Y., Knopf, 1953. 1st ed.
262p. illus. by Henry B. Kane, map. ANR. London, Travel Book
Club, 1955. 269p. [Seward Peninsula]   849

CARRIGHAR, SALLY. Moonlight at midday. N. Y., Knopf, 1958. 1st
ed. 392p. illus. photos, map, bibliog. index. [Nome and Unalakleet, Seward Peninsula]   850

CARRIGHAR, SALLY. Wild voice of the north; the chronicle of an
Eskimo dog. Illustrated with photographs. Garden City, N. Y.,
Doubleday, 1959. 191p. illus. photos. [Nome]   851

CARRINGTON, HUGH. Life of Captain Cook. London, Sidgwick &
Jackson, 1939.   852

Carrington, T. S., co-auth. SEE no. 4223, Sniffen, M. K.

CARROLL, JAMES A. The first ten years in Alaska; memoirs of a
Fort Yukon trapper; 1911-22. N. Y., Exposition Press, 1957.
1st ed. 120p. illus.   853

CARROTHERS, WILLIAM ALEXANDER. The British Columbia fisheries.
Toronto, University of Toronto Press, 1941. 136p. tables. 854

Carruth, J. H. SEE no. 3583, Pierce, W. H.

CARRUTHERS, JOSEPH. Captain James Cook, R.N., one hundred and
fifty years after. N. Y., Dutton, 1930.   855

CARSTENSEN, VERNON, edit. The public lands; studies in the
history of the public domain. Madison, University of Wisconsin
Press, 1968. 548p.   856

CARTER, JAMES C. Fur-seal arbitration; oral argument of James C. Carter on behalf of the United States before the Tribunal of Arbitration convened at Paris under the provisions of the treaty between the United States of America and Great Britain, concluded February 29, 1892. Paris, Chamerot & Renouard, Printers, 1893. 379p. wrps.   857

CARTER, NICHOLAS [pseud.] A Klondike claim; or, Won by sheer nerve. N. Y., Street & Smith, 1897. 218p. [author is John Russell Coryell]   858

CARTER, W. R. "TED" Home gardening for southeastern Alaska and coastal regions. no pl., [ca 1944]   859

Cartwright, B., jr., edit. SEE no. 3953, Samwell, D.

CASAGRANDE, JOSEPH B., edit. In the company of man. N. Y., Harper & Row, 1960. [anthropological studies]   860

CASE, ROBERT ORMOND. The Yukon drive. Garden City, N. Y., Doubleday Doran, 1929. 1st ed. 359p.   861

CASE, ROBERT ORMOND. West of Barter River. Garden City, N.Y., Doubleday Doran, 1941. 272p. (A Double D Western)   862

Case, W. H., photog. SEE no. 277, Arctander, J. Wm.

Cass, Jocelyn, illus. SEE no. 619, Booth, E. S.

CASSIN, JOHN. Illustrations of the birds of California, Texas, Oregon, British and Russian America; containing descriptions and figures of all the North American birds not given by former American authors and a general synopsis of North American ornithology. Philadelphia, Lippincott, 1856. pls.(col.) ANR. 1862.   863

CASSIN, JOHN. Mammalogy and ornithology. Philadelphia, 1859. 466p. pls. and atlas. (U. S. Exploring Expedition during years 1838-42, under command of Charles Wilkes)   864

Castéra, J., tr. SEE no. 3974, Sauer, M.

CASTLE, N. H. Treatise on searches and seizures under prohibition laws in force in Alaska. Juneau, Empire Print., Jan. 1, 1922. 55p.   865

CASWELL, JOHN EDWARDS. Arctic frontiers: United States explorations in the far north. Norman, University of Oklahoma Press, 1956. 1st ed. 232p. illus. bibliog. index.   866

CASWELL, JOHN EDWARDS. The utilization of the scientific reports of U. S. Arctic expeditions 1850-1909. Stanford, Stanford University, 1951. 304p. bibliog. (Tech. Rpt. no. 2, 1951)   867

Cathcart. SEE no. 3940, St. George.

CATHERALL, ARTHUR. Arctic sealer. N. Y., Criterion, 1960. 868

CATHERALL, ARTHUR. Lone seal pup. N. Y., Dutton, 1965. illus.
869

Catholic Church. Liturgy and ritual in Tinne language. 1904.
SEE no. 2352, Jette, Julius.

CATHOLIC DAUGHTERS OF AMERICA, Court of the Little Flower no.
1243, Juneau. Juneau's gold mine of Alaskan recipes. Compiled
by Court of the Little Flower no. 1243, C. D. A., Juneau. Kansas City, Mo., Bev-Ron Pub. Co., 1960. 98p. illus. index. 870

Catholic manual of prayers in Innuit. [ca 1950 ?] SEE
no. 2790, Lonneux, M. J.

Catholic prayers and hymns in Innuit. 1899. SEE
no. 3830, Robau, Father.

Catholic prayers and hymns in Tinneh language. 1897. SEE
no. 2259, Indian Boys' Press.

CATTO, WILLIAM. The Yukon administration. Dawson, King St. Job
Office, 1902. 43p. 871

CAUGHEY, JOHN WALTON. History of the Pacific coast. L. A.,
privately printed, 1933. 429p. front. pls. ports. maps. ANR.
N. Y., Prentice-Hall, 1938. 429p. front. pls. ports. maps. 872

CAUGHEY, JOHN WALTON. Hubert Howe Bancroft, historian of the
west. Berkeley, University of California Press, 1946. 422p.
front. pls. ports. facsims. 873

CAVANA, VIOLET V. Alaska basketry. Portland, Oregon, privately
printed by Beaver Club of Oregon, 1917. 50p. illus. watercolor
drawings mounted on 10p. incl. front. ltd. ed. of 102 copies.874

CAWSTON, VEE. Matuk, the Eskimo boy. N. Y., Lantern Press,
1965. (28)p. illus. by Haris Petie, glossary. 875

CENTINAIRE DE LA MORT DE LaPÉROUSE. Paris, Société de Geographie, 1888. bibliog. 876

CENTKIEWICZ, CZESLAW JACEK and A. CENTKIEWICZ. Czeluskin; wy-
danie piąte, poprawione i uzupelnione. [TITLE TR. Cheluskin;
5th edition, revised and enlarged] Warszawa, Czytelnik, 1953.
103p. illus. 877

Century 21 Exposition, 1962. SEE no. 4034, Seattle.

Cevallos, Ciriaco de. SEE no. 5025, Zevallos, Ciriaco de.

CHAFFEE, ALLEN. Sitka, the snow baby. Illustrated by Peter Da-
Ru. Springfield, Mass., Milton Bradley Co., 1923. 116p. front.
pls. glossary, ftntes. ANR. 1929.   878

CHAFFIN, YULE M. Koniag to king crab. Kodiak, Chaffin, Inc.,
1967. 247p. illus. maps, bibliog.   879

Chaffin, Yule M. SEE ALSO no. 191, Ameigh, Geo. C., jr.

CHALMERS, J. W. Fur trade governor; George Simpson, 1820-60.
Edmonton, Alberta, Institute of Applied Art, 1960. 190p. illus.
maps, bibliog. [incls. visit to Sitka in 1841]   880

CHAMBERLIN, J. L. and F. STEARNS. A geographic study of the
clam, *Spisula polynyma* (Stimpson). N. Y., American Geographical
Society, 1963. 12p. maps, graphs, table, bibliog. (Serial Atlas of the Marine Environment, folio 3)   881

CHAMBERLIN, RALPH VARY and W. IVIE. The spiders of Alaska.
Salt Lake City, University of Utah, 1947. 103p. pls. index.
(Bulletin, vol. 37, no. 10. Biol. Ser. vol. 10, no. 3)   882

CHAMBERS, ERNEST JOHN. The Royal North-West Mounted Police, a
corps history. Montreal-Ottawa, Mortimer Press, 1906. front.
ports.   883

CHAMISSO, LOUIS C. A., von. Bemerkungen u. Ansichten auf einer
Entdeckungs-reise in d. jahren 1815-18 auf dem Schiffe *Rurik*
unter dem Befehls des Lt. O. von Kotzebue. Weimar, 1821. 240p.
pls. table(fold.), maps. [reprinted: see no. 886]   884

CHAMISSO, LOUIS C. A., von. and C. GUIL. De animalibus quibus-
dam e classe vermium Linnaeana in circumnavigatione terrae
auspicante comite N. Romanzoff duce O. de Kotzebue annis 1815-
18 peracta observatis. no pl., Espenhardt, n. d. Fasc. 2.
[Fasc. 1 published in Berlin, 1819]   885

CHAMISSO, LOUIS C. A., von. Reise um die Welt mit der Romanz-
offischen Entdeckungs Expedition in den jahren 1815-18, auf der
Brig *Rurik*, Capt. Otto von Kotzebue. Leipzig, 1836. 2 vols.
[reprint of no. 884. Also in author's "Werke." Berlin, 1864.
6 vols. in 3]   886

Chamisso, Louis C. A., von. Werke. 1864. SEE no. 886.

Chamisso, Louis C. A., von. SEE ALSO nos.
    925, Choris, L. Voyage pittoresque ... 1822;
    2418, Kaulfuss, G. F. Enum. filicum ... 1824;
    2516-29, Kotzebue, Otto, von.

CHANCE, NORMAN A. The Eskimo of north Alaska. N. Y., Holt,
1967. 107p. front.(map), illus. (Case studies in cultural anthropology) [Barrow, Kaktovik and Wainwright]   887

CHANDLER, EDNA WALKER and BARRETT WILLOUGHBY. Pioneer of Alaska skies; the story of Ben Eielson. Boston, Ginn, 1959. 179p. illus.   888

CHANEY, RALPH WORKS and HERBERT L. MASON. A Pleistocene flora from Fairbanks, Alaska. N. Y., American Museum of Natural History, 1936. 17p. illus. (Novitates no. 887)   889

Chanimum, illus. SEE nos.
     1723, Gillham, Chas. E. Byond Clapping Mtns. 1943;
     1724, Gillham, Chas. E. Medicine men Hooper Bay ... 1955.

Channing, E., co-edit. SEE no. 1972, Hart, A. B.

CHAPELLE, HOWARD I. American small sailing craft. N. Y., W. W. Norton, 1951. illus. plans.   890

CHAPMAN, JOHN WIGHT. A camp on the Yukon. Cornwall-on-Hudson, N. Y., Idlewild Press, 1948. 214p. illus. map.   891

CHAPMAN, JOHN WIGHT. Alaska's great highway. By Rev. J. W. Chapman, D.D. [Hartford ?], Church Missions Pub. Co., 1909. 15p. front. pls. (A Round Robin to the Older Juniors. Pub. no. 71)   892

CHAPMAN, JOHN WIGHT. Our missions in Alaska. Hartford, Feb. 1894. 15p. illus. map. [Episcopalian]   893

CHAPMAN, JOHN WIGHT. Ten'a texts and tales from Anvik, Alaska; with vocabulary by Pliny Earle Goddard. Leyden, E. J. Brill and N. Y., G. E. Stechert, 1914. 230p. (American Ethnological Society Pubs. vol. 6)   894

CHAPMAN, MAY NEELY. The animistic beliefs of the Ten'a of the lower Yukon, Alaska. Hartford, Church Missions Pub. Co., 1939. 15p. (Church in Story and Pageant Pub. 65)   895

Chapman, R. H., co-auth. SEE no. 2446, Kerr, M. B.

CHAPMAN, SYDNEY. IGY: the year of discovery, the story of the International Geophysical Year. Ann Arbor, University of Michigan Press, 1959. 111p. illus.   896

Charles, R. A. SEE no. 628, Bowen, R. O.

CHARLES, SIDNEY DEAN and ROYAL GRATTAN SOUTHWORTH. U. S. mining laws, on discovery, staking and recording; general information useful to miners. Charlton vs Kelly. Fairbanks, Charles & Southworth, 1906. 29p.   897

Chase, William Henry. Alaska, the trail blazers ... 1951. SEE no. 899.

CHASE, WILLIAM HENRY. Alaska's mammoth brown bears. By Will
Chase. Kansas City, Mo., Burton Pub. Co., 1947. rev. ed. 129p.
drawings, photos, append. notes.   898

CHASE, WILLIAM HENRY, comp. Pioneers of Alaska; the trail blazers of bygone days. Compiled by Will H. Chase. Illustrations
from photographs and old prints. Kansas City, Mo., Burton Pub.
Co., 1951. 203p. illus. index to illus., lists of Pioneers of
Alaska Igloos. (Sponsored by Grand Igloo, Pioneers of Alaska)
[has cover title: Alaska. The trail blazers of bygone days]899

CHASE, WILLIAM HENRY. Reminiscences of Captain Billie Moore.
By Will H. Chase. Kansas City, Mo., Burton Pub. Co., 1947.
236p. front.(port.) [owner & captain of steamships freighting
to gold fields, 1870s]   900

CHASE, WILLIAM HENRY. The sourdough pot. Kansas City, Mo.,
Burton Pub. Co., 1923. ANR. 1943. 206p. front.   901

Chateaubriand, François A. R. Recollections ... SEE no. 902.

CHATEAUBRIAND, FRANÇOIS A. R., Vicomte de. Souvenire d'Italie,
d'Angleterre et de l'Amérique ... London, 1815. 2 vols. 262p.
and 298p. ANR. WITH TITLE Recollections ... London, 1815.
2 vols. 258p. and 314p. ANR. London, 1816. 2 vols. ANR.
Philadelphia, 1816. ANR. Dresden, 1816. [in German] [sketches
voyages of Bering, Vancouver, others in preface]   902

CHAVANNE, JOSEF, A. KARPF and FRANZ Le MONNIER. Die Literateur
über die Polar-Regionen der Erde. [TITLE TR. The literature on
the polar regions of the earth] Wien, E. Hölzel, 1878. 335p.
index. [Hrsg. von der K. K. Geographischen Gesellschaft in
Wien]   903

Chealander, G. SEE no. 278, Arctic Brotherhood.

CHEESMAN, EVELYN. Sealskins for silk. N. Y., Abelard-Schuman,
1956. 237p. illus.   904

Chellson, H. C. SEE no. 4715, von Bernewitz, M. W.

Chemin de fer trans-Alaska-Sibérien ... [1902 ?] SEE
    no. 4436, Syndicat Français du Trans-Alaska Sibérien.

CHENEY, WARREN. His wife. Indianapolis, Bobbs Merrill, 1907.
395p. front.   905

CHENEY, WARREN. The challenge. Illustrated by N. C. Wyeth.
Indianapolis, Bobbs Merrill, 1906. 386p. illus.   906

CHENEY, WARREN. The way of the north; a romance of the days of
Baranof. N. Y., Doubleday Page, 1905. 320p. ANR. 1906. (Historical Series)   907

Chernenko, M. B., edit. SEE no. 5020, Zagoskin, L. A.

Cherneysheva, M. D., auth. SEE no. 2967, Marich, M. [pseud.]

CHERRINGTON, B. M. Theatres of war; Alaska and the Arctic. Denver, University of Denver, 1943. 9p. bibliog. (Social Science Foundation, Journeys Behind the News, no. 17)   908

CHEVIGNY, HECTOR. Lord of Alaska; Baranov and the Russian adventure. N. Y., Viking, 1942. 1st ed. 320p. bibliog. index. ANR. London, R. Hale, 1946. 255p. endmaps, bibliog. ANR. Portland, Ore., Binfords and Mort, 1950. 320p. bibliog. index.   909

CHEVIGNY, HECTOR. Lost empire; the life and adventures of Nikolai Petrovich Rezanov. N. Y., Macmillan, 1937. 356p. front.(port.), bibliog. index.   910

CHEVIGNY, HECTOR. Russian America; the great Alaskan venture 1741-1867. N. Y., Viking, 1965. 1st ed. 274p. maps, endmaps, bibliog. index.   911

CHICAGO AND NORTHWESTERN RY. CO. Alaska-Yukon-Pacific Exposition, June 1-Oct. 16, 1909. [no pl., 1909 ?] 20p. illus.   912

Chicago and Northwestern Ry. Co. SEE ALSO no. 3455,
    Pacific northwest and Alaska ... [1915 ?]

Chicago, Milwaukee and St. Paul Ry. SEE nos.
    3344, North Pacific country. 1907;
    4294, Steele, Jas. Wm. A golden era. 1897.

Chicago, Milwaukee, St. Paul and Pacific Railroad Co. SEE nos.
    3344, North Pacific coast country. 1907;
    3455, Pacific northwest and Alaska ... [1915 ?]

CHICAGO RECORD. Klondike; the Chicago Record's book for gold seekers. [TITLE ON SPINE The Chicago Record's book for gold seekers] Chicago, Chicago Record, 1897. 413p. front. pls. maps(incl. some dble.), index. ANR. Chicago, 1897. 413p. (Souvenir Edition) ANR. Chicago, 1897. enl. ed. 555p. OTHERS Boston, Desmond Pub. Co., 1897. Chicago, Monroe Book Co., 1897. Philadelphia, Colonial Pub. Co., 1897. Toronto, Briggs, 1897. Tucson, Ariz., Tombstone Nugget Pub. Co., [1966 ?] [reprint of Chicago Record ed.] 100p. front,(map), sketches, diagrs. maps(incl. 1 dble.), wrps. ANR. WITH TITLE Klondike; a book for gold seekers. Philadelphia, Globe Bible Co., 1897. 555p.   913

CHICHAGOF KING MINING CO. The great lesson of the great depression. Tacoma, Washington, 1934. 32p.   914

Chichagov, Vasili Yakov. SEE nos.
    2753, Lomonosov, M. V. Razsuzhdenie ... 1759;

3232, Müller, G. F. Herrn v. Tschitschagow ... 1793;
4236, Sokolov, A. P. Proekt Lomonosova ... 1854.

CHICKERING, WILLIAM H. Within the sound of these waves. N. Y.,
Harcourt, 1956.   915

Chief Wholecheeze Alaskan coloring book. [c1966] SEE
    no. 4246, Southwest Operating Co.

Childe, Rheta Louise. SEE no. 2493, Knapp, Frances.

[Chimmo, Wm.] SEE no. 1499, Euryalus ... 1860.

Chinard, Gilbert. SEE no. 2620, La Perouse, J. F. G. de.

CHIPPERFIELD, JOSEPH E. Boru; dog of the O'Malley. Illustrated by C. Gifford Ambler. N. Y., David McKay, 1966. 180p.
front. map.   916

Chips and sticks ... 1886. SEE no. 4816, White, E. W., Pub. Co.

Chirikov, Alexei Ilich. SEE nos.
    516, Berg, L. S. Velikiĭ russkiĭ ... 1950;
    1193, Davidson, Geo. Tracks and landfalls ... [1901];
    1301, Divin, V. A. A. I. Chirikov ... 1950;
    1302, Divin, V. A. Velikiĭ russkiĭ ... 1953;
    2658, Lebedev, D. M. Plavanie A. I. Chirikova ... 1951;
    4238, Sokolov, A. P. Sievernaĩa Eksped. 1733-43. 1851;
    4276, Staehlin, Jacob v. S. Das von den Russen ... 1774.

Chisam, M. M., co-auth. SEE no. 3951, Samson, Sam.

CHITTENDEN, NEWTON H. Travels in British Columbia and Alaska;
circular 10 of the World's Guide for home, health and pleasure
seekers, containing new and valuable information concerning this
comparatively unknown region, its physical features, climate,
resources and inhabitants. Victoria, B. C., 1882. 84p.   917

CHITTY, ARTHUR BEN. Hudson Stuck of Alaska. N. Y., National
Council of Churches, 1962. (Pioneer Builders for Christ Ser.)918

Chkalov, Valeriĭ Pavlovich. [Alphabetical title guide to
    chronological entries]

    Dva pereleta. 919.   Shturmanskiĭ. 922.
    Nash transpolĩarnyĭ. 920.   Unser Transpolarflug. 921.
    Navigator's. 923.

CHKALOV, VALERIĬ PAVLOVICH, G. F. BAIDUKOV and A. V. BELIAKOV.
Dva pereleta. [TITLE TR. Two flights] Moskva, Gos. voen. izd-
vo Narkomata oborony Sciuze SSR, 1938. 275p. pls. maps(sketch,
some fold.), diagrs.(some fold.)   919

CHKALOV, VALERIĬ PAVLOVICH. Nash transpoliârnyĭ reis; Moskva-Severnyĭ poliûs-Svernaîâ Amerika. [TITLE TR. Our trans-polar flight; Moscow-North Pole-America] Moskva, Gos. izd-vo polit. lit-ry, 1938. 63p. front. 920

    TRANSLATION - Nash transpoliârnyĭ reis ... 1938.

    Unser Transpolarflug. Moskau, Verlag für fremdsprachige Literatur, 1939. 118p. illus. pls. ports. 921

CHKALOV, VALERIĬ PAVLOVICH and others. Shturmanskiĭ bortovoĭ zhurnal samoleta NO-25. Moskva, Leningrad, [1939 ?] facsim. ed. 16p. photos, map, diagrs. 922

    TRANSLATION - Shturmanskiĭ ... [1939 ?]

    Navigator's log book, airplane NO-25; first non-stop flight Moscow-North Pole-United States of America. Moscow, Leningrad, State Art Publishers, 1939. 30(20)p. pl.(col., mtd.), port. facsims. diagrs. map(fold.) [incls. also *Via the North Pole to America*, by A. V. Beliakov] 923

Chkalov, Valeriĭ Pavlovich. SEE ALSO nos.
    344, Baidukov, G. F. Nash polet ... 1937;
    345, Baidukov, G. F. Over North Pole. 1938;
    346, Baidukov, G. F. O Chkalove. 1939;
    478, Beliakov, A. V. Iz Moskvy v Ameriku ... 1938;
    590, Bobrov, N. N. Chkalov. 1940;
    2584, Laktionev, A. F. Severnyĭ poliûs. 1955;
    3416, Ordin, A. Velikiĭ lëtchik ... 1949;
    4279, Stalinskiĭ Marshrut Prodolzhen ... 1937.

CHOLNOKY, JENO. Amerika. 231 keppel es terkeppel. Franklin, 1936. 602p. [scattered references to Alaska on pp.79, 152, 154-6, 217-8, 226-7, 236] 924

CHORIS, LOUIS. Voyage pittoresque autour du monde, avec des portraits de sauvages d'Amérique, d'Asia, d'Afrique, et des iles du Grand Ocean; des paysages, des vues maritimes, et plusieurs objets d'histoire naturelle; accompagne de descriptions par M. le baron Cuvier, et M. A. d'Chamisso, et d'observations sur les cranes humains, par M. le Docteur Gall. Par M. Louis Choris, peintre. [TITLE TR. Picturesque voyage around the world, with portraits of savages of America, Asia, Africa, and the islands of the Great Ocean; landscapes, seascapes, and several objects of natural history; together with descriptions by Baron Cuvier and Mr. A. de Chamisso, and with observations on human crania by Dr. Gall. By Mr. Louis Choris, painter] Paris, Impr. de Firmin Didot, 1822. illus. pls. [with addenda, Paris, 1821-23. port. pls. maps] 925

CHRISTOE, ALICE HENSEN. Treadwell, an Alaskan fulfillment. Drawings by Adelaide Hanscom Leeson. [Seattle, 1909 ?] 27p. 926

CHUKOVSKIĬ, NIKOLAI KORNEEVICH. Bering. Moskva, Izd-vo "Molo-daiā Guardiiā" 1961. 128p. illus. map, bibliog. (Zhizn' zame-chatel'nykh liudeĭ. Seriiā biografiĭ, no. 19) [in Russian]   927

CHUKOVSKIĬ, NIKOLAI KORNEEVICH. Voditeli fregatov. [TITLE TR. Commanders of warships] Moskva, Voennoe Izd-vo Ministerstva Vooruzhennykh sil Soiūza SSR, 1947. 275p. pls. ports. map (fold.) [Krusenstern on *Nadezhda* and Lisianskiĭ on *Neva*, 1803-06]   928

CHURCH OF ENGLAND. Selections. Tsimshian, Wila Yelth. Mor-ning prayer in Tsimshian. no pl., n. d. 21p.   929

CHURCH MISSIONARY SOCIETY. Deputation of Metlakatla. Report. no pl., n. d. 44p.   930

CHURCH MISSIONS PUBLISHING CO. Indian tribes and missions. A handbook of general history of the North American Indians, early missionary efforts and missions of the Episcopal Church. Hart-ford, [c1926] var. pagings, in 5 pts. front.(port.), pls. fac-sim. map, appends. bibliog. index. (The Church in Story and Pageant) [pt. 5, "Missions to the natives of Alaska."] ANR. WITH TITLE A handbook of the Church's mission to the Indians. 1914.   931

CHURCHILL, AWNSHAM, JOHN CHURCHILL and THOMAS OSBORNE. A col-lection of voyages and travels, some now first printed from original manuscripts, others now first published in English, with a general preface giving an account of the progress of navigation, from its first beginning. London, 1732. 6 vols. and London, 1747. 2 vols. pls. maps. (A collection of voyages and travels, consisting of authentic writers ... compiled from the Library of the late Earl of Oxford. Harleian Voyages, nos. 7 and 8)   932

CHURCHILL, AWNSHAM, JOHN CHURCHILL and THOMAS OSBORNE. A col-lection of voyages and travels ... 1745. 2 vols. folio. pls. (some dble.), maps(some dble.) by Herman Moll. [a separate issue of no. 932 - incls. those of Capt. James Cook]   933

Churchill, John. SEE nos. 932-33, Churchill, Awnsham.

CIPOLLA, ARNALDO. Norte America y los Norte Americanos; viaje por Alaska, Canada ye Estados Unidos; traduccion del Italiano de Ramon Mondria. Santiago, Concepcion, Chile, Nascimento, 1929. 264p.   934

CLAIRMONT, D. H. J. Deviance among Indians and Eskimos in Akla-vik, N. W. T. Ottawa, 1963. 84p. table, map, bibliog. (Cana-da. Northern Co-ordination and Research Centre, NCRC-63-9) [in-cluding references to Alaskan Eskimos]   935

CLARK, ARTHUR H., jr. Arctic archibenthal and abyssal mollusks from drifting station Alpha. Cambridge, Mass., 1960. 19p. illus. tables, bibliog. (Harvard University Museum of Comparative Zoology. Breviora no. 119. March 8, 1960) 936

CLARK, ELLA E. Indian legends of the Pacific northwest. Berkeley, University of California, 1953. illus. 937

CLARK, ERNEST D. and RAY W. CLOUGH. The salmon canning industry. [Seattle, Blyth & Co., 1927 ?] 26p. 938

CLARK, FLORENCE MATILDA. Roadhouse tales; or, Nome in 1900. By M. Clark. Girard, Kansas, Appeal Pub. Co., 1902. 260p. front. pls. 939

CLARK, HAROLD T. Episodes of the Amundsen-Ellsworth Arctic flights. Cleveland, Museum of Natural History, 1928. 940

CLARK, HENRY W. Alaska, the last frontier. N. Y., Grosset and Dunlap, n. d. [c1930, c1939] 246p. front.(dble. map), pls. maps, index. [rev. and enl. from no. 942] 941

CLARK, HENRY W. History of Alaska. N. Y., Macmillan, 1930. 208p. front.(dble. map), pls. maps, index. [for later ed. see no. 941] 942

CLARK, HORACE FLETCHER and others. Miner's manual, United States, Alaska, the Klondike. Containing annotated manual of procedure; statues and regulations; mining regulations of Northwest Territory, British Columbia and Yukon district; glossary on mining terms, and information regarding Alaska and the Klondike. By Horace F. Clark, Charles C. Heltman and Charles F. Consul. Chicago, Callaghan & Co., 1898. 943

Clark, Lois, co-auth. SEE no. 1664, Frye, T. C.

Clark, M. SEE no. 939, Clark, Florence Matilda.

CLARK, SUSIE C. Lorita; an Alaskan maiden. Boston, Lee and Shepard, 1892. 171p. 944

Clark, W. G. SEE no. 3208, Mother Lode Copper Mines Co.

Clark, Walter Eli. SEE nos.
1328, Dole, N. H. Alaska. 1910;
1329, [Dole, N. H.] Our northern domain ... 1910.

CLARKE, TOM E. Alaska challenge. N. Y., Lothrop, Lee and Shepard, 1959. 222p. 945

CLARKE, TOM E. Back to Anchorage. N. Y., Lothrop, Lee and Shepard, 1961. 946

CLARKE, TOM E. No furs for the Czar. N. Y., Lothrop, Lee and Shepard, 1962. 191p.   947

CLARKE, TOM E. The puddle jumper; the adventures of a young flier in Alaska. N. Y., Lothrop, Lee and Shepard, 1960. 191p.
                                                                         948

CLAWSON, MARIAN and BURNELL HELD. The Federal lands, their use and management. Baltimore, Johns Hopkins Press, 1957. 501p. ANR. Lincoln, University of Nebraska, 1965.   949

CLAY, CASSIUS MARCELLUS. Oration on Alaska annexation before students and historical class of Berea College, Berea, Kentucky, October 16, 1895. Richmond, Ky., Pantagraph Job Works, 1896. 10p.   950

Clay, Cassius Marcellus. SEE ALSO no. 3838, Robertson, Jas. R.

CLEMENS, W. A. A check list of the marine fauna and flora of the Canadian Pacific coast. Ottawa, 1933. 88p.   951

CLEMENS, W. A. and G. V. WILBY. Fishes of the Pacific coast of Canada. Ottawa, Fisheries Research Board, 1946. photos. ANR. 1949. photos. ANR. Ottawa, Fisheries Research Board, 1961. 443p. illus.(some col.), append. glossary, bibliog. index. (Bulletin no. 68, 2d ed.) [Puget Sound to Bering Sea]   952

CLEMENTS, JAMES I. The Klondyke by J. I. Clements, discoverer of El Dorado and owner with Clarence Berry and Frank Keller of the celebrated El Dorado claims Four and Five. How the brakeman gained his thousands in four months. A complete guide to the gold fields. Illustrated, honest, reliable, accurate. Edited by G. Wharton James. L. A., B. R. Baumgardt & Co., 1897. 98p. pls. map.   953

CLEVELAND, BESS A. Alaskan cookbook, for homesteader or gourmet. Game preparation, sourdough secrets, Salmon Derby recipes, frontier formulas. Sketches by Richard E. Meyer. Photographs by J. Malcolm Greany. Berkeley, Howell-North, 1960. 164p. illus. index.   954

CLEVELAND, BESS A. Frontier formulas; an Alaskan cook book. Juneau, by author, 1952. 212p. photos by J. Malcolm Greany.955

Cleveland, H. W. S., comp. SEE no. 958, Cleveland, R. J.

CLEVELAND, LIBRA JAN. Pacific shores; the Pacific states, Alaska, California, Hawaii, Oregon, Washington. Chicago, Children's Press, 1962. 93p. illus. by Tom Dunnington. (Enchantment of America Series)   956

CLEVELAND, RICHARD JEFFRY. A narrative of voyages and commercial enterprises. Cambridge, Mass., J. Owen, 1842. 2 vols. 249p. and 240p. ANR. 1843. 2d ed. 2 vols. in 1. 249p. and 244p. ANR. Boston, C. H. Pierce, 1850. 3rd ed. 407p. pls. ANR. N.Y., Leavitt & Allen, 1855. 4th ed. 407p. OTHERS London, N. Bruce, 1842 and 1843. 144p.   957

CLEVELAND, RICHARD JEFFRY. Voyages of a merchant navigator of the days that are past. Compiled from the journals and letters of the late Richard J. Cleveland, by H. W. S. Cleveland. N. Y., Harper, 1886. 245p.   958

Clifton, Talbot. SEE no. 959, Clifton, Violet.

CLIFTON, VIOLET. The book of Talbot. N. Y., Harcourt Brace, 1933. 439p. illus. front.(port.), ports. maps, notes. ANR. London, 1933. 439p. illus. [diary of Talbot Clifton in Alaska, Klondike, Barren Grounds and the Lena River area of Russia] 959

CLOWES, WILLIAM LAIRD, edit. The Royal Navy - a history. Boston, Little Brown, 1899-1903. 7 vols.   960

CLUM, JOHN P. A trip to the Klondike through the stereoscope. From Chicago, Illinois, to St. Michaels, Alaska, during the ... crusade of 1897-8 to the gold fields of Alaska. Meadville, Penna. and St. Louis, Mo., The Keystone View Co., 1899. 56p.
                                                                        961

COACHMAN, LAWRENCE K. and C. A. BARNES. The contribution of Bering Sea water to the Arctic Ocean. Seattle, University of Washington Press, 1961. 14p. tables, graphs, maps, bibliog. (Contribution no. 249, Department of Oceanography. ALSO IN Arctic, pp.147-61, vol. 14, no. 3, Sept. 1961)   962

Coal and oil. 1898. SEE no. 59, Alaska Development Co.

COBB, JOHN N. The canning of fishery products; showing the history of the art of canning; the methods followed with each species, and suggestions for canning unutilized species; where, when, and how they are obtained; together with other information of much value to canners. Seattle, M. Freeman, 1919. 217p.   963

COCHRAN, GEORGE M. Indian portraits of the Pacific northwest. Portland, Ore., Binfords and Mort, 1959. 65p. illus. ports.964

COCHRANE, JOHN D. Narrative of a pedestrian journey through Russia and Siberian Tartary ... to the Frozen Sea and Kamtchatka, 1820-23. By Captain John D. Cochrane. London, 1824. 564p. maps(fold.) ANR. London, 1824. 2d impr. enl. 2 vols. 428p. and 344p. pls.(incl. 2 col.), maps, append. ANR. Philadelphia, H. C. Carey & I. Lea, 1824. ANR. N. Y., Collins and Hannay, 1824. ANR. Edinburgh, 1829. 2 vols. [also coast isles n.w. Amer.] 965

CODY, HIRAM ALFRED. An apostle of the north, memoirs of the
Right Reverend William Carpenter Bompas, D. D., first Bishop of
Athabaska, 1874-84; first Bishop of MacKenzie River, 1884-91;
first Bishop of Selkirk (Yukon), 1891-1906, with an introduction
by the Most Reverend S. P. Matheson. London, Seeley, 1908.
385p. front.(port.), pls. ports. ANR. N. Y., Dutton, 1908.
ANR. Toronto, Musson, 1908. ANR. London, Seeley, 1910. 2d ed.
386p. illus. index. ANR. N. Y., Dutton, 1913. 3rd ed.   966

BOMPAS, HIRAM ALFRED. On trail and rapid by dog-sled and canoe.
Philadelphia, Lippincott, 1911. (13)203p. front. pls. ANR.
London, Seeley, 1919. 4th ed. 202p. pls.   967

Coe, Douglas.   [Alphabetical title guide to chronological
      entries]
                        La route de l'Alaska. 969.
                        Road to Alaska. 968.
                        Vägen till Alaska. 970.

COE, DOUGLAS, [pseud.] Road to Alaska; the story of the Alaska
Highway. Story by Douglas Coe. Pictures by Winfield Scott Hos-
kins. N. Y., Julian Messner, [c1943] 175p. front.(dble. map),
sketches, maps. [co-authors are Samuel Epstein and Beryl Wil-
liams]   968

      TRANSLATIONS - Road to Alaska ... 1943, chronologically.

      La route de l'Alaska. Paris, Le Sillage, 1946. 137p.
         illus.   969

      Vägen till Alaska; en bok om en väg och om de män som
         byggde den med illustrationer av Winfield Scott Hoskins.
         Oversattning av P. E. Virgin. [TITLE TR. The road to
         Alaska; the story of the road and the men who built it.
         With illustrations by Winfield Scott Hoskins. Translated
         by P. E. Virgin] Stockholm, Kooperativa förbundets bok
         förlag, 1946. illus. map.   970

Coe, W. R. SEE no. 1950, Harriman Alaska Exped.

COFFEY, LEORA STEPHENSON. Wilds of Alaska big-game hunting.
N. Y., Vantage Press, 1963. 1st ed. 172p. illus. photos,
line drawings.   971

COFFIN, CHARLES C. The seat of empire. pl.?, pub.?, 1870.
[advocate of railroad connecting Asia and America]   972

Coffin, G., co-auth. SEE no. 4754, Waterman, T. F.

COLBY, MERLE ESTES. Alaska; a guide to Alaska, last American
frontier. N. Y., Macmillan, 1939. 427p. illus. photos,
sketches, maps(incl. fold. in pocket), endmaps, append. bibliog.
index. (American Guide Series, Federal Writers' Project)   973

COLBY, MERLE ESTES. Alaska; a profile with pictures, with an invitation from the Governor, Ernest Gruening. N. Y., Duell, Sloan and Pearce, 1940. 58p. illus. photos with captions. 974

COLE, A. B. Yankee surveyors in the Shogun's seas; records of the U. S. Surveying Expedition to the North Pacific Ocean, 1853-56. Princeton, N. J., Princeton University Press, 1947. 161p.
975

COLE, CORNELIUS. Memoirs of Cornelius Cole, ex-senator of the United States from California. N. Y., McLoughlin Bros., 1908. 1st ed. 354p. port. [material on purchase of Alaska] 976

Collection of prayers, hymns ... Catholic Eskimos Seward Peninsula ... 1916. SEE no. 2582, Lafortune, B.

Collier, D. SEE no. 3010, Martin, Paul S.

COLLIER, WILLIAM ROSS and EDWIN VICTOR WESTRATE. The reign of Soapy Smith; monarch of misrule in the last days of the old West, and the Klondike gold rush. Garden City, N. Y., Doubleday, 1935. 299p. front. port., pls. ANR. Garden City, N. Y., Sundial Press, 1937. 977

COLLIERY ENGINEER CO. Placer mining. A hand-book for Klondike and other miners and prospectors with introductory chapters regarding the recent gold discoveries in the Yukon Valley, the routes to the gold fields, outfit required, and mining regulations of Alaska and the Canadian Yukon. Also map of the Yukon Valley, embracing all the information obtainable from reliable sources up to December 1st, 1897. Scranton, Penna., The Colliery Engineer Co., 1897. 1st ed. 146p. illus. front.(fold. map), maps, diagrs. ANR. Seattle, Shorey Book Store, 1966. (Shorey Reprint no. 106) [facsim. of 1897 ed.] 978

COLLINS, ARCHIE FREDERICK. Jack Heaton, gold seeker. N. Y., Frederick A. Stokes, 1921. 238p. illus. by Morgan Dennis. 979

COLLINS, FRANCIS A. Mountain climbing. N. Y., The Century Co., 1923. [Alaskan ranges, others] 980

COLLINS, HENRY BASCOM. An Okvik artifact from southwest Alaska and stylistic resemblances between early Eskimo and paleolithic art. Hanover, N. H., Dartmouth College Library, 1959. (Occasional Publication of Stefansson Collection, no. 1) 981

COLLINS, HENRY BASCOM. Arctic area, indigenous period. Mexico City, Instituto Panamericano de Geografia e Historia, 1954. 152p. bibligg. (Comision de Historia, Program of the History of America, no. 68) 982

COLLINS, HENRY BASCOM. Prehistoric Eskimo harpoon heads from Bering Strait. [Washington ?, 1941 ?] [reprinted from Journal of Washington Academy of Science, vol. 31, no. 7, July 15, 1941. pp.318-24. illus.]   983

COLLINS, RAYMOND and SALLY JO COLLINS. Dinak'i. [TITLE TR. Upper Kuskokwim Athabaskan dictionary] Fairbanks, Summer Institute of Linguistics, 1966. 74p. illus. [Nikolai, Alaska]984

COLLINS, RAYMOND and SALLY JO COLLINS. Dinak'i Ch'its'utozre. [TITLE TR. Upper Kuskokwim Athabaskan reader, 1] Nikolai via McGrath, Summer Institute of Linguistics, 1966. ltd. ed. of 50 copies. 20p. illus. word list.   985

COLLINSON, RICHARD. Journal of H. M. S. *Enterprise* on the expedition in search of Sir John Franklin's ships by Behring Strait, 1850-55. By Captain Richard Collinson, commander of the expedition. With a memoir of his other services. Edited by his brother, Major-General T. B. Collinson. London, S. Low, Marston, Searle & Rivington, 1889. 531p. front.(col.), illus. ports. maps(fold.), append. [through Bering Strait east and return, Camden Bay, Alaska]   986

Collinson, Richard. SEE ALSO nos.
    1823, 1824, 1826, 1829 and 1832, Great Britain. Parl.
        House of Commons (Franklin search);
    3907, Royal Geographic Soc. Arctic geog. ... 1875.

Collinson, T. B., edit. SEE no. 986, Collinson, Richard.

COLLIS, SEPTIMA MARIA. A woman's trip to Alaska; being an account of a voyage through the inland seas of the Sitkan archipelago, in 1890. By Septima M. Collis (Mrs. General C. H. T. Collis). N. Y., Cassell Pub. Co., 1890. 194p. illus.(some col.), pl.(fold.), ports. map.   987

COLLISON, WILLIAM HENRY. In the wake of the war canoe; a stirring record of forty years' successful labour, peril and adventure amongst the savage Indian tribes of the Pacific coast and the piratical headhunting Haidas of the Queen Charlotte Islands, British Columbia. London, Seeley, 1915. 351p. front. pls. map. ANR. N. Y., Dutton, 1916. 351p. pls. map. ANR. Toronto, Musson, n. d. 351p. front. pls. map. [missionary to Haida and Tsimshean Indians, B. C. and southeast Alaska]   988

Collyer, Bert E. SEE no. 1703, Gibbons, Chas. H.

COLNETT, JAMES. The journal of Captain James Colnett aboard the "Argonaut" from April 26th, 1789 to November 3, 1791. Edited with introduction and notes by F. W. Howay. Toronto, Champlain Society, 1940. ed. of 550 copies. 328p. pls. maps (Champlain Society Publication no. 26)   989

COLNETT, JAMES. Voyage to the south Atlantic and round Cape Horn into the Pacific Ocean, for the purpose of extending the spermaceti whale fisheries, and other objects of commerce, by ascertaining the ports, bays, harbours, and anchoring berths in certain islands and coasts in those seas at which the ships of the British merchants might be refitted. Undertaken and performed ... in the ship *Rattler*. London, W. Bennett, 1798. 179p. illus. pls. maps. [this ed. pissibly written by William Combe ?] EARLIER EDS. Trenton, 1787. 16p. AND Philadelphia, 1797. 27p.　　　　　　　　　　　　　　　　　　990

COLONIAL CHURCH CHRONICLE AND MISSIONARY JOURNAL. Mission of the Russian Church to the Aleoutine Islands. no pl., 1849 and 1851. [in 2 pts.]　　　　　　　　　　　　　　　　　991

COLOR ART PRINTING CO. Alaskan earthquake pictorial. Anchorage, Color Art Printing Co., 1964. 48p. illus.　　　　　　　　992

COLP, HARRY D. The strangest story ever told. N. Y., Exposition Press, 1953. 1st ed. 46p. ANR. Petersburg, Petersburg Press, 1966. 2d ed. 32p. map [Thomas Bay near Wrangell]　　　993

COLQUHOUN, A. R. Greater America; maps of Pacific expansion. N. Y., Harper, 1904.　　　　　　　　　　　　　　　994

Colson, Pedro de Novo y. SEE nos. 3361-2, Novo y Colson, Pedro de.

Colthorpe, S. E., co-auth. SEE no. 1848, Greenaway, K. E.

COLYER, VINCENT. Bombardment of Wrangel, Alaska. Washington, D. C., 1870. (33)p. illus.　　　　　　　　　　　　995

Comandini, Adele, co-auth. SEE no. 734, Burke, Clara Heintz.

[Combe, Wm. ?] SEE no. 990, Colnett, Jas.

Combe, Wm., edit. SEE no. 3056, Meares, J.

Come into my kitchen. [1967] SEE no. 4949, Woman's Soc. of Christian Service.

COMFORT, MILDRED H. Peter and Nancy in the United States and Alaska. Chicago, Beckley-Cardy Co., 1940. 368p.　　　996

Coming copper port of world. 1916. SEE no. 1078, Cordova Daily Times.

Comments; Alaska, Atlin ... [19_ ?] SEE no. 4835, White Pass and Yukon Ry.

COMMENTS ON THE CONVENTION WITH SPAIN relating largely to the Pacific Ocean, northwest coast of America, and especially to Nootka Sound. London, Axtell, 1790. 28p.   997

COMMERCE CLEARING HOUSE. Alaska tax reporter. Chicago, 1963. 104 looseleaf pages.   998

Compendious history ... 1784. SEE no. 1020, [Cook, Jas.]

Compiled laws of Alaska, 1933 ... [1934 ?]   SEE
    no. 3862, Roden, Henry.

Comstock, Enos B., illus. SEE no. 2849, McCracken, H.

CONANT, MELVIN. The long polar watch; Canada and the defense of North America. N. Y., Harper, 1962. 204p. map, ftnte. references. (Council on Foreign Relations)   999

Conchological Club of So. Calif. SEE no. 1932, Hanna, G. Dallas..

Concrete statement of facts ... 1904. SEE no. 3794,
    Reynolds-Alaska Development Co.

Condliffe, J. B., edit. SEE no. 2271, Institute of Pac.
    Relations, 2d Conf., Honolulu.

CONE, EDWARD. Beyond the sky-line; short poems pertaining to the northland, by the "bard of the Kuskokwim," dedicated to Igloo no. 15, Pioneers of Alaska. N. Y., Bouillion-Briggs, 1923. 90p.   1000

CONKEY CO., W. B. The official guide to the Klondyke country and the gold fields of Alaska with the official maps. Profusely illustrated. Vivid descriptions and thrilling experiences. The most complete and thoroughly exhaustive collection of every known information necessary to a full realization of the immense resources of the gold fields of Alaska, and replete with authentic instructions regarding how to get there, when to go, and what to do when the new Eldorado of the great northwest is reached. Chicago, W. B. Conkey Co., 1897 [c1897] 296p. front. pls. maps.
                                                                        1001

CONKLE, EARL JUDSON. Alaska gold. N. Y., Pageant, 1953. [poetry]   1002

CONKLE, ELLSWORTH PROUTY. Two hundred were chosen; a play in three acts. N. Y., French, 1937. 49p. front. [settlers in Matanuska Valley]   1003

CONNOLLY, J. B. Master mariner; life and voyages of Amasa Delano. Garden City, N. Y., Doubleday, 1943.   1004

CONNOR, RALPH [pseud.] Corporal Cameron of the Northwest Mounted Police; a tale of the MacLeod Trail. Toronto, Westminster,
1906. ANR. N. Y., Doran, 1912. 454p. [author is Charles
William Gordon]   1005

CONRAD, EARL. The governor and his lady; the story of William
Henry Seward and his wife Frances. N. Y., Putnam, 1960. 433p.
ANR. Toronto, Longmans Green, 1960. [chapt. 60, pp.404-23,
Baron De Stoeckl and purchase of Alaska]   1006

Conradi, Paul. SEE no. 339, Baer, Karl Ernst von.

Consul, Chas. F., co-auth. SEE no. 943, Clark, H. F.

Continuation authentic statement ... 1790. SEE
    no. 1497, [Etches, John Cadman]

CONVENTION BETWEEN THE UNITED STATES AND THE EMPIRE OF JAPAN,
and treaty concerning the cession of the Russian possessions in
North America to the United States. Carefully collated with the
originals at Washington. Boston, Little Brown, 1868. 8p. 1007

COOK FOUNDATION, DAVID C. Ḳuliaḳtuaḳ Iñuusiagun Jesus. Matthew-
millu, Mark-millu, Luke-millu, John-millu. no pl., n. d. (16)p.
illus.(col. in comic strip form) [Kobuk River Eskimos]   1008

COOK, FREDERICK ALBERT. Finding the North Pole; Dr. Cook's own
story of his discovery, April 21, 1908; the story of Commander
Peary's discovery, April 6, 1909; together with the marvelous
record of former Arctic expeditions. Introduction by George W.
Melville. Edited by Charles Morris. [Philadelphia ? c1909]
448p. front. pls. ports. [refs. McKinley climb]   1009

COOK, FREDERICK ALBERT. My attainment of the Pole; being the
record of the expedition that first reached the boreal center,
1907-09. N. Y., Polar Pub. Co., 1911. 1st ed. 604p. front.
pls, ports. facsims. diagrs. append. index. ANR. ... with the
final summary of the polar controversy. N. Y., Mitchell Kennerly, 1912. 610p. ANR. N. Y. Mitchell Kennerly, 1913. Press ed.
3rd print. "By special arrangements this edition is marketed by
The Polar Publishing Co. 601 Steinway Hall, Chicago." 610p. +
8p. index. front.(port.), pls. sketches, append. [much about
McKinley climbs]   1010

COOK, FREDERICK ALBERT. Return from the Pole; edited, with an
introduction by Frederick J. Pohl. N. Y., Pellegrini & Cudahy,
1951. 335p. illus. port. map, bibliog. ftntes. ANR. London,
1953. 254p. illus. photos, endmap, bibliog. ANR. Wo Norden
Süden ist. 1954.   1011

COOK, FREDERICK ALBERT. To the top of the continent; discovery, exploration and adventure in sub-arctic Alaska. The first ascent of Mount McKinley, 1903-06. N. Y., Doubleday Page, 1908. 321p. illus. photos by author, front.(col.), pls. sketches, maps(incl. 1 dble.), appends. by A. H. Brooks, W. H. Osgood and Charles Sheldon. ANR. London, Hodder & Stoughton, 1908. 321p. front.(col.), drawings, photos by author, maps.   1012

Cook, Frederick Albert. SEE ALSO nos.
    362, Balch, E. S. Mt. McKinley ... proofs. 1914;
    363, Balch, E. S. No. Pole and Bradley Land. 1913;
    699, Browne, B. Conquest Mt. McKinley ... 1913;
    711, Bryce, Geo. Seige ... North Pole. 1910;
  1389, Dunn, R. Shameless diary explorer. 1907;
  1391, Dunn, R. World alive. 1956;
  1646, Freeman, A. A. Case for Dr. Cook. 1961;
  1704, Gibbons, R. W. Hist. eval. Cook-Peary ... 1954;
  1705, Gibbons, R. W. F. A. Cook, pioneer ... 1965;
  1909, Hall, T. F. Has No. Pole been discovered ? 1917;
  3121, Miller, Jas. M. Discovery No. Pole ... [c1909];
  3896, Rost, E. C. Mt. McKinley and bearing polar...1914;
  4972, Wright, H. S. Great white north ... 1910;
  4975, Wright, Theon. Big nail. 1970.

Cook, James. [Alphabetical title guide to chronological entries]

Abridgment. 1019.
Auf unbekannten. 1052.
Authentic narr. 1017.
Capitain Jakob. 1028, 1030.
Capt. Cook's third. 1023,
   1026, 1033, 1038.
Capt. Cook's three. 1031,
   1036, 1040.
Capt. Cook's voy. 1039, 1051.
Compendious hist. 1020.
Dritte Entdeckungs. 1028.
Dritte und letzt. 1029.
Histoire. 1034.
Histoire abregee. 1032.

Journal. 1014.
Navigazioni. 1043, 1045.
Nueste Reis. 1027.
Reise nach. 1024.
Storia de'viaggi. 1022.
Tagebuch. 1015.
Three. 1042, 1050, 1053.
Troisieme. 1016, 1025, 1037.
Voyage. 1013, 1021, 1035,
   1041, 1046.
Voyages. 1044, 1047, 1048,
   1049.
Voyages round. 1054.
Zuverlassige. 1018.

COOK, JAMES and JAMES KING. A voyage to the Pacific Ocean, undertaken by the command of His Majesty, for making discoveries in the northern hemisphere, to determine the position and extent of the west side of North America; its distance from Asia; and the practicability of a northern passage to Europe. Performed under the direction of Captains Cook, Clerke, and Gore, in His Majesty's ships the *Resolution* and *Discovery*, in the years 1776, 1777, 1778, 1779, and 1780. London, G. Nicol and T. Cadell, 1784. 1st ed. 3 vols. + atlas. 421p. 549p. and 558p. pls.(some fold.), maps(some fold.) ANR. London, G. Nicol, 1785. 3 vols. + atlas.   1013

[COOK, JAMES and JAMES KING] ABRIDGMENTS, TRANSLATIONS, OTHER
ACCOUNTS - A voyage to Pacific ... 1784, chronologically.
[1781-1783]

Journal of Captain Cook's last voyage to the Pacific Ocean on
Discovery, performed in the years 1776, 1777, 1778, 1779;
illustrated with cuts and a chart showing the tracts of the
ships employed in this expedition, faithfully narrated from
the original ms. Dublin, Price, Whitestone, Chamberlaine,
1781. 396p. front. pls. map(fold.) ANR. London, Newbery,
1781. 388p. front. (fold. pl.), pls.(incl. 1 fold.), map
(fold.) ANR. 1785. new ed. 376p. pls. map(fold.) ANR.
Ann Arbor, Mich., University Microfilms, 1966. facsim.
reprint. ANR. Amsterdam, N. Israel and N. Y., Da Capo Press,
1967. (Bibliotheca Australiana, 2d ser. no. 16) facsim. reprint of London 1781 ed. [ascribed to John Rickman] 1014

Tagebuch eine entdekkungs-reise nach der Sud-see in den jahren
1776 bis 1780 unter anfuhrung der Captains Cook, Clerke, Gore
und King. Mit einer neuen verbesserten Karte und Kupfer
nach der origihellin handsschrift getreulich beschrieben.
Eine uebersetzung nebst anmerkungen von Johan Reinhold
Forster. Berlin, Bey, Haude & Spener, 1781. 1015

Troisième voyage de Cook; ou, Journal d'une expédition faite
dans la Mer Pacifique du sud & du nord, en 1776, 1777, 1778,
1779 & 1780. Traduit l'Anglois. Paris, Pissot, 1782.
x,508p. illus. map. ANR. Paris, Belin, Volant, 1782. 2d
ed. front. map. ANR. Paris, Belin, 1783. 376p. pls. ANR.
Versailles, Poinçot, et Paris, Belin, 1783. 3rd ed. lxiv,
454p. front. map. [ascribed to John Rickman, translated by
Jean Nicolas Demeunier] 1016

An authentic narrative of a voyage to the Pacific Ocean, performed by Captain Cook and Captain Clerke in His Brittanic
Majesty's ships the *Resolution* and *Discovery*, in the years
1776, 1777, 1778, 1779, and 1780 ... Also a large introduction, exhibiting an account of the several voyages round
the globe, with an abstract of the principal expeditions to
Hudson's Bay, for the discovery of a northwest passage. By
an officer on board the *Discovery*. Philadelphia, Printed
and sold by Robert Bell, 1783. 2 vols. in 1. 230p.
[ascribed to John Rickman, also to Wm. Ellis] 1017

Zuverlassige Nachricht von der dritten und letzen Reise der
Capitains Cook und Clerke in den koniglichen Schiffen, die
Resolution and *Discovery*, in den Jahren von 1776 bis 1780,
besonders in der Absicht, eine Nordwestliche Durchfahrt
zwischen Asia und Amerika ausfindig zu machen. Aus dem Englischen ubersetz. Frankfurt, Kosten der Verlags Kasse,
1783. 324p. map. 1018

[COOK, JAMES and JAMES KING] ABRIDGMENTS, TRANSLATIONS, OTHER
    ACCOUNTS - A voyage to Pacific ... 1784, chronologically.
    [1784-1785 ?]

An abridgment of Captain Cook's last voyage performed in the
    years 1776, 1777, 1778, 1779, and 1780, for making disco-
    veries in the northern hemisphere, by order of His Majesty.
    Extracted from the 4th ed. in 3 volumes, containing a rela-
    tion of all interesting transactions, particularly those
    relative to the unfortunate death of Captain Cook; with his
    life, by Captain King. London, Kearsley, 1784. 441p.
    front. map(fold.)   1019

A compendious history of Captain Cook's last voyage performed
    in the years 1776, 1777, 1778, 1779 and 1780; in which all
    the interesting transactions are recorded, particularly
    those relative to his unfortunate death, with a map of the
    new discoveries and the tract of the ships. London, Kear-
    ley, 1784. new ed. maps. ANR. 1787. 5th ed. 442p.   1020

A voyage to the Pacific Ocean; undertaken by the command of
    His Majesty for making discoveries in the northern hemi-
    sphere; performed under the direction of Captains Cook,
    Clerke, and Gore in the years 1776, 1777, 1778, 1779, and
    1780; being a copious, comprehensive, and satisfactory
    abridgment of the Voyage, written by Captain James Cook and
    Captain James King, illustrated with cuts. London, Printed
    for J. Stockdale, Scatcherd & Whitaker, C. Fielding & J.
    Hardy, 1784. 4 vols. pls.(some fold.), maps(some fold.)
    ANR. Dublin, 1784. 3 vols. 421p., 549p., 559p. port. pls.
    maps, table(fold.) ANR. Perth, R. Morison & Son, 1785. 4
    vols. front. pls. maps. ANR. London, Printed for C. Stal-
    ker, 1788.   1021

Storia de'viaggi intrapresi per ordine di S. M. Brittanica dal
    Capitano G. C., ricavata dalle autentiche relazioni del me-
    desimo, e dalle osservazioni di varj filosofi Ingesi, com-
    pagni di tali spedizioni, con una introduzione generale con-
    tenente la notizia de'pui celebri viaggi precedenti ... il
    tutto arricchito di note ... Napoli, 1784-85. 13 vols. 1022

Captain Cook's third and last voyage to the Pacific Ocean in
    the years 1776, 1777, 1778, 1779 and 1780, faithfully a-
    bridged from the quarto edition published by order of His
    Majesty. London, Fielding & Stockdale, [1785 ?] 372p.
    front.(port.), pls.   1023

Reise nach dem Stillen Ocean, auf Befehl der Konigs von Gros-
    brittanien unternommen. Entdeckungen en der Nordlichen Halb-
    kugel zu machen, die Lage und Ausdehnung der Westseite von
    Nordamerika, ihre entfernung von Asien; unde die Moglich-
    keit einer Nordlichen Durchfahrt nach Europa zu bestimmen.
    Unter der anfuhrung der Kapitaine Cook, Clerke und Gore in

[COOK, JAMES and JAMES KING] ABRIDGMENTS, TRANSLATIONS, OTHER
    ACCOUNTS - A voyage to Pacific ... 1784, chronologically.
    [1785-1787]

    den Schiffen *Resolution* und *Discovery*, in den jahren 1776,
    7, 8, 9, 80. In einigen auszugen aus dem Englischen uber-
    setzt. Mit einer Reisekarte und Kupfern. Frankfurt, Carl
    Gottlieb Strauss, 1785. 208p. pls. map.   1024

    Troisième voyage de Cook; ou, Voyage à l'Océan Pacifique, or-
    donné par le Roi d'Angleterre, pour faire des découvertes
    dans l'hémisphère nord, pour déterminer la position & l'é-
    tendue de la côte ouest de l'Amérique septentrionale, sa
    distance de l'Asie, & résoudre la question du passage au
    nord. Exécuté sous la direction des Capitaines Cook, Clerke
    & Gore, sur les vaisseaux la *Resolution* & la *Découverte*, en
    1776, 1777, 1778, 1779 & 1780. Traduit de l'Anglois par
    M. D. Ouvrage enrich de cartes & de plans, d'après las re-
    lèvemens pris par le Lieutenant Henri Roberts, sous l'in-
    spection du Capitaine Cook, & d'une multitude de planches
    ... dessinés ... par M. Webber. Les deux premiers volumes
    de l'original ont été composes par le Capitaine Jacques Cook,
    & le troisième par le Capitaine Jacques King. Paris, Hotel
    de Thou, 1785. 4 vols. ANR. Paris, Raymond, 1819. 4 vols.
          1025

    Captain Cook's third and last voyage to the Pacific Ocean, in
    the years 1776-80. Together with an account of his death.
    Faithfully abridged from the quarto edition. London, J.
    Fielding, 1786.   1026

    Neuste Reisbeschreibungen oder Jakob Cook's dritte und letze
    Reise, welche auf Befehl des Konigs von England nach den
    Sudinseln der stillen Meeres und dann weiter nach den Nord-
    amerikanischen und Asiatischen Kusten, um die Moglichkeit
    einer nordlichen Durchfahrt nach Europa zu entscheiden, en
    dem jahren 1776 bis 1780 unternommen worden. Mit Kupfern.
    Nurnberg und Leipzig, C. Weigel und Schneider, 1786. 2 vols.
    pls. map.   1027

    Dritte Entdeckungs-Reise nach dem Nordpol hinauf unternommen
    und mit den Schiffen *Resolution* und *Discovery*, wahrend der
    Jahre 1776 bis 1780 ausgefuhrt; aus dem Englischen ubersetzt
    von Georg Forster. Berlin, Haude, 1787 ? vols, pls. port.
    table, maps. [Variant title ? Des Capitan James Cook's
    dritte Entdeckungs-reise ... in das stille Meer und nach dem
    Nordpol hinauf unternommen ...wahrend der jahre 1776 bis
    1780 ... Aus den Tagbuchern des Captain Cook, unter der ...
    Befehlshaber Clerke, Gore und King. Aus dem Englischen
    ubersetzt von C. Forster. cf no. 1030]   1028

[COOK, JAMES and JAMES KING] ABRIDGMENTS, TRANSLATIONS, OTHER
    ACCOUNTS - A voyage to Pacific ... 1784, chronologically.
    [1787-1796]

    Dritte und letzte Reise oder Geschichte einer Entdeckungsreise
        nach dem Stillen Ocean unter der Anfuhrung der Captains Cook,
        Clerke, und Gore in Sr. Majestat Schiffen, der *Resolution*
        und der *Discovery*, wahrend den Jahren 1776, 1777, 1778, 1779
        und 1780, aus den Tagbuchern der Capitaine James Cook und
        James King, eine Uebersetzers nach der zwoten grossen En-
        glischen Ausgabe, von Johann Ludwig Wetzel. Anspach, Kosten
        des Uebersetzers gedruckt mit Messererischen Schriften, 1787.
        4 vols. front.(port.), pls. maps.   1029

    Des Capitain Jacob Cook dritte Entdeckungs-Reise in die Sudsee
        und nach dem Nordpol. Auf Befehl Sr. Grosbritten. Majest.
        George des Dritten unternommen und in den Schiffen *Resolution*
        und *Discovery* wahrend der jahre 1776 bis 1780 ausgefuhrt.
        Aus den Tagebuchern der Schiffsbefehlshaber Herren Cook,
        Clerke, Gore und King imgleichen des Schiffswundarztes Herrn
        Anderson vollstandig beschrieben. Aus dem englischen uber-
        setzt ... von Herrn Georg Forster. Berlin, Bey, Haude und
        Spener, 1789. 4 vols. and atlas. port., pls. maps(fold.),
        table(fold.) [See also no. 1028]   1030

    Captain Cook's three voyages to the Pacific Ocean. Faithfully
        abridged from the quarto edition. Containing a particular
        relation of all the interesting transactions during the
        several voyages. Boston, 1792. 2 vols. pls.   1031

    Histoire abregee des premier, secund et troisième voyages atour
        du monde par Cook. Basilo, Thurneysen, 1795. 3 vols. 1032

    Captain Cook's third and last voyage to the Pacific Ocean, in
        the years 1776-80. Together with an account of his death.
        Faithfully abridged from the quarto edition. Worcester,
        Mass., Isaiah Thomas, 1795. 216p.   1033

    Histoire des premier, secund et troisième voyages atour du
        monde, par Cook; mise a la partee du tout le monde, par
        Beranger. Avec figares et une grande mappe monde en deux
        hemispheres, ou sont marquees les découvertes les plus re-
        centes et les routes des trois voyages ce Cook, dressee par
        Henisson. Paris, Chez Fr. Dufart, Imprimeur-Librair, 1796.
                                                                     1034

    A voyage to the Pacific Ocean for making discoveries in the
        northern hemisphere; performed under the direction of Cap-
        tain James Cook, and Captain James King, illus. with elegant
        plates and a large chart. N. Y., Printed by Tiebout and
        O'Brien for Benjamin Gomez, 1796. 4 vols. pls. ANR. Edin-
        burgh, 1798. 4 vols. ANR. London, n. d. 4 vols.   1035

[COOK, JAMES and JAMES KING] ABRIDGMENTS, TRANSLATIONS, OTHER
    ACCOUNTS - A voyage to Pacific ... 1784, chronologically.
    [1797-1830]

   Captain Cook's three voyages to the Pacific Ocean ... Faith-
      fully abridged from the quarto editions ... To which is pre-
      fixed the life of Captain Cook. Boston, Printed by Manning
      & Loring, for Thomas & Andrews, and D. West, 1797.   1036

   Troisième voyage de James Cook, autour du monde, sur la côte
      nord-ouest d'Amérique, la côte nord-est d'Asie, et dans les
      regions du pole boreal; fait en 1776, 1777, 1778, 1779 et
      1780, tr. nouv. par J. B. J. Breton. Paris, Lepetit, 1804.
      4 vols. in 2 (Bibliotheque portative des voyages, t. 26-29)
                                                              1037

   Captain Cook's third and last voyage to the Pacific Ocean, in
      the years 1776, 7, 8, 9 and 80. Extracts from the life and
      public services of Captain James Cook, written by Captain
      King. Faithfully abridged from the quarto edition. Hudson,
      A. Stoddard, 1809. 96p.   1038

   Captain Cook's voyages around the world for making discoveries
      toward the North and South Poles. With an appendix. Man-
      chester, 1811. 566p. pls.   1039

   Captain Cook's three voyages to the Pacific Ocean, the first
      performed in the years 1768, 9, 70 and 71; the second in
      1772, 3, 4 and 75; the third and last in 1776, 7, 8, 9 and
      80. Faithfully abridged from the quarto editions, etc. to
      which is prefixed the life of Captain Cook. N. Y.,
      Duyckinck, 1814. 2 vols.   1040

   A voyage to the Pacific Ocean; undertaken by the command of
      His Majesty, for making discoveries in the northern hemi-
      sphere, performed under the direction of Captains Cook,
      Clerke, and Gore in the years ... Compiled from the various
      accounts of that voyage hitherto unpublished. Embellished
      with 40 elegant engravings. Philadelphia, 1818. 2 vols.1041

   The three voyages of Captain James Cook round the world. Lon-
      don, Longmans, 1821. 7 vols.   1042

   Navigazioni de Cook del grande oceano ed intorno al globo.
      Livorno, Tipografia Vignozzi, 1826.   1043

   The voyages of Captain James Cook round the world, comprehen-
      ding a history of the South Sea Islands, etc. London,
      Jacques & Wright, 1826. 2 vols. pls.   1044

   Navigazioni de Cook. Del grande oceano ed intorno al globo par
      servire d'introduzione alla raccolta de viaggi. Torino,
      Dalla Stamperia Alleana, 1830. 15 vols.   1045

[COOK, JAMES and JAMES KING] ABRIDGMENTS, TRANSLATIONS, OTHER
     ACCOUNTS - A voyage to Pacific ... 1784, chronologically.
     [1831-n. d.]

A voyage to the Pacific Ocean for making discoveries in the
     northern hemisphere under the direction of Captains Cook,
     Clerke, and Gore in the years 1776, 7, 8, 9, and 80, with an
     introductory review of maritime discovery down to the time
     of Captain Cook; with the copperplate engravings. Leith,
     Printed by and for William Reid & Son and Henry Constable,
     Edinburgh, 1831. 1 vol. pls.   1046

The voyages of Captain James Cook. Illustrated with maps and
     numerous engravings on wood. With an appendix, giving an
     account of the present condition of the South Sea Islands,
     etc. ... London, Wm. Smith, 1842. 2 vols. ANR. 1846. 1047

The voyages of Captain James Cook round the world. N. Y.,
     J. Tallis & Co., 1853-54. 2 vols. illus.   1048

The voyages of Captain James Cook round the world, illustrated
     with maps and numerous engravings on wood and steel. Lon-
     don, The London Printing & Publishing Co., 1853-54. 2 vols.
                                                            1049

Three voyages to the Pacific Ocean. The first performed in
     the years 1766-70; the second in 1772-75; the third in
     1776-80. Abridged from the original editions. Prefixed,
     the life of Captain Cook. Boston, Thomas & Andrews & D.
     West, 1897.   1050

Captain Cook's voyages round the world, with an introduction
     by M. P. Synge. London, Nelson, 1897. 512p. illus. maps.
                                                            1051

Auf unbekannten Meeren; James Cooks Tagebuch seiner dritten
     Entdeckungsfahrt in die Sudsee und das Nordliche Eismeer,
     ausgewahlt von Paul Schneider. Hrsg. von der freien Lehrer
     Vereinigung fur Kunstpfege zu Berlin. Leipzig, R. Voigt-
     landers Verlag, n. d. 235p. front. pls.   1052

The three voyages of Captain Cook round the world. With ...
     portrait, and memoir ... engravings. London, J. Limbird,
     n. d. new ed.   1053

Voyages round the world; undertaken and performed by royal
     authority; ... first, second, third and last voyage. Lon-
     don, Alex Hogg, n. d. 6 vols.   1054

[Cook, James and James King] SEE ALSO nos.
     323, Augur, H. Passage to glory, Ledyard ... 1946;
     411, Barrow, J. Cook's voyages ... 1904;
     412, Barrow, J. Cook's voyages ... 1860;

437, [Bayly, Wm.]   Orig. astronom. observations ... 1782;
453, Beaglehole, J. C.   Exploration Pacific. 1934;
454, Beaglehole, J. C.   Journals Capt. Cook ... 1955-56;
458, Beauties Cooks' voyages ... 1785;
549, Besant, W.   Capt. Cook. 1890;
735, Burkholder, M. Capt. Cook. 1928;
827, Capt. Cook, bi-centenary ... 1928;
828, Capt. Cook's voyages ... 1906;
829, Capt. Cook's voyages ... 1908;
852, Carrington, H. Life of ... 1939;
855, Carruthers, J. Capt. Jas. Cook 150 years after. 1930;
915, Chickering, Wm. H. Within sound waves. 1956;
932-3, Churchill, A. Collect. voyages ... 1732 and 1745;
1105, Coxe, Wm. Comparative view Russ. disc. ... 1787;
1170, Damm, H. Jas. Cook; die suche nach dem sudland. 1922;
1250, DeLeeuw, A. Jas. Cook, world explorer. 1963;
1272, Denton, V. L. Far west coast. 1924;
1443, Ellis, Wm. Authentic narrative ... 1782;
1469, Engel, S. Anmerkungen ... 1780;
1605, Forster, G. Cook, der Entdecker. 1789;
1606-7, Forster, G. Geschichte der Reisen ... 1791 and 1792;
1613, Forster, J. R. Observations ... 1778;
1702, Gianetti, M. Elegy ... [1785];
1712, Gilbert, G. Death of Capt. Jas. Cook. 1926;
1762, Golenishchev-Kutuzov, L. I. Puteshestvie ... 1805-10;
1789, Gould, R. T. Capt. Cook. 1935;
1997, Hawkesworth, J. Voyages disc. ... [189_ ?]
2076, Heritage Press. Explorations ... 1948;
2160, Holmes, M. Introd. to bibliog ...1936;
2161, Holmes, M. Capt. Jas. Cook ... bibliographic ... 1952;
2204, Howay, F. W. Zimmermann's Capt. Cook. 1930;
2272, Interesting acct. ... Dr. Kippis. 1790;
2385, Jones, M. Story three voyages ... 1870;
2461, Kingston, Wm. H. G. Capt. Cook; life ... n. d.;
2464, Kippis, A. Narrat. voyages ... [1812 ?];
2465, Kippis, A. Capt. Cook's voyages ... 1924;
2466, Kippis, A. Life of ... 1788;
2467-8, Kippis, A. Vie du Capitaine Cook ... 1789;
2469, Kippis, A. Voyages ... 1826;
2471, Kirchof, N. A. J. Auszug aus Cook ... 1794;
2476, Kitson, A. Capt. Jas. Cook ... 1907;
2477, Kitson, A. Life of ... 1911;
2495, Knight, F. Young Capt. Cook. 1966;
2595, Lang, J. Story of Capt. Cook. 1906;
2663, Ledyard, J. Journal ... 1783;
2664, [Ledyard, J.] Adventures Yankee ... 1831;
2706-8, Life of Capt. Cook. n. d., 1824, 1831;
2710, Life, voyages and discoveries ... 1859;
2741, Lloyd C. Voyages ... round world. 1949;
2802, Low, C. R. Capt. Cook's three voyages ... n. d.;
2963, Manwaring, G. E. My friend the Admiral ... James
        Burney. 1931;
2992, Marshall, J. B. Capt. Cook's voyages ... n. d.;

3086, Merrett, J. Capt. Jas. Cook. 1957;
3087, Merrill, E. D. Botany Cook's voyages. 1954;
3231, Muir, J. R. Life and achievements ... 1939;
3237, Munford, J. K. John Ledyard ... 1939;
3238, Munford, J. K. John Ledyard's journal ... [c1963];
3294, New South Wales, Public Lib. Bibliog. ... 1928;
3500, Pasteur, J. D. Reizen rondom de waerld ... 1795-1809;
3533, [Penrose, C. V.] Memoir Jas. Trevenen ... 1959;
3575, Phillips, Richard. General collection. ... 1809-10;
3603, Pinkerton, J. General collection ... 1808-14;
3688, Price, A. G. Explorations ... journals ... 1957;
3821, Rienits, R. Voyages Capt. Cook. 1968;
3851, Robolsky, M. Life ... Englisches Lesebuch ... 1864;
3953-4, Samwell, D. Narrative death ... 1916 and 1786;
3955, [Samwell, D.] Details ... mort du Kapit. Cook. 1786;
4032, Seaman, J. V. New general atlas ... 1821;
4046, Selsam, M. E. Quest Capt. Cook. 1962;
4168, Skelton, R. A. Capt. Jas. Cook after 200 yrs. 1969;
4169, Skelton, R. A. Capt. Jas. Cook hydrographer ... 1954;
4170, Skelton, R. A. Charts and views ... 1955;
4171, Skelton, R. A. Explorers' maps ... 1958;
4172, Skelton, R. A. Marine surveys Jas. Cook ... 1967;
4253, [Sparks, J.] Travels John Ledyard ... 1834;
4257, Spence, S. A. Capt. Jas. Cook ... bibliog. 1960;
4260, Sperry, Armstrong. All about ... 1960;
4261, Sperry, Armstrong. Le Capitaine Cook ... 1965;
4414, Svet, Ia. M. Moreplavatel' ... 1963;
4435, Syme, R. Capt. Cook, Pacific explorer. 1960;
4437, Synge, M. B. Book of discovery. 1962;
4438, Synge, M. B. Captain Cook's voyages ... 1897;
4439, Synge, M. B. Cook's voyages ... 1894;
4484, Thiery, M. Vie et voyages ... 1929;
4485, Thiery, M. Life & voyages ... 1929;
4486, Thiery, M. Capt. Cook ... 1930;
4529, Three famous voyages Capt. Jas. Cook ... [189_ ?];
4645, Vandercook, J. W. Great sailor; life ... 1951;
4703, Villiers, A. J. Capt. Cook ... 1967;
4704, Villiers, A. J. Capt. Jas. Cook ... [c1967];
4705, Villiers, A. J. Pioneers of seven seas. 1956;
4735, Walton, J. Six explorers. 1942;
4743, Warner, O. M. W. English maritime writing. 1958;
4744, Warner, O. M. W. Great seamen. 1961;
4813, Whitcombe & Tombs, Ltd. Capt. Jas. Cook ... n. d.;
4814, Whitcombe & Tombs, Ltd. Under Cook's flag ... [19_?];
4878, Williams, G. British search for n. w. passage. 1962;
4886, Williamson, Jas. A. Builders of empire. 1925;
4887, Williamson, Jas. A. Cook and opening of Pacific. 1948;
5033, Zimmermann, H. ... Reise um die welt mit Capt.
          Cook. 1781.

COOK, JOHN ATKINS. Pursuing the whale; a quarter-century of
whaling in the Arctic. Boston, Houghton Mifflin, 1926. 344p.
front. pls. ports. [Bering, Chukchi and Beaufort Seas]   1055

COOK, JOSEPH J. and WILLIAM L. WISNER. Killer whale ! N. Y.,
Dodd Mead, 1963.   1056

COOK, JOSEPH J. and WILLIAM L. WISNER. Warrior whale. N. Y.,
Dodd Mead, 1966. illus. [giant sperm whale off coast of
Alaska]   1057

COOK CO., THOMAS. Alaska, Pacific Coast and national parks,
summer tours. N. Y., 1924. 44p. illus.   1058

COOKE, CECIL and "DOC" NORRIS. Fascinating Alaska. Seattle,
Reed and Reed, 1947. 4p.(text), 26p.(illus.)   1059

Cooking favorites of Fairbanks. [ca 1965 ?]   SEE
     no. 2969, Marian Society.

COOLEY, RICHARD A. Alaska; a challenge in conservation. By
Richard A. Cooley. Madison, University of Wisconsin Press, 1966.
186p. pls. figs. tables, maps, append. bibliog. index. ANR.
1967. 2d print. 170p. wrps. (University of Wisconsin Press no.
W-70)   1060

COOLEY, RICHARD A. Politics and conservation; the decline of
the Alaska salmon. N. Y., Harper & Row, 1963. 230p. illus.
graphs, tables, map, bibliog. index. [doctoral thesis]   1061

COOLIDGE, LOUIS ARTHUR. Klondike and the Yukon country; a
description of our Alaskan land of gold, from the latest official and scientific sources and personal observations, with a
chapter by John F. Pratt, Chief of the Alaskan Boundary Expedition of 1894. Philadelphia, H. Altemus, 1897. 213p. pls. maps
(incl. 1 fold.) ANR. Philadelphia, H. Altemus, 1897. 251p.
front. pls. maps(incl. 1 fold.)   1062

COOMBS, CHARLES J. Alaska bush pilot. Evanston, Illinois, Harper & Row, 1963. 256p. illus. maps. [biog. of Carl Ben Eiel-
son]   1063

COOMBS, CHARLES J. Bush flying in Alaska. N. Y., Morrow, 1961.
95p. front.(map), drawings by Morgan Henninger.   1064

COONEY, EDITH. Alaskamo (I love Alaska) Yakima, Wash., Franklin Press, 1966. 149p. front. [salmon gill-netting, southeast
Alaska]   1065

Cooper, G. A., co-auth. SEE no. 4607, Ulrich E. O.

COOPER, JOHN M. Snares, deadfalls and other traps of the northern Algonquians and northern Athapaskans. Washington, D. C.,
Catholic University of America, 1938. 144p. pls. diagrs. bibliog. (America Anthropology Series no. 5)   1066

COOPER, WILLIAM SKINNER. A contribution to the history of the Glacier Bay National Monument. Minneapolis, University of Minnesota, March 1956. 36p. bibliog. [botany, ecology]   1067

COOPER, WILLIAM SKINNER. Vegetation of the Prince William Sound region, Alaska; with a brief excursion into post-pleistocene climatic history. Durham, N. C., 1942. 22p. illus. maps(sketch), bibliog. (Ecological Monographs, vol. 12, no. 1, Jan. 1942)1068

COPELAND, DONALD A. True book of little Eskimos. Chicago, Children's Press, 1953. illus. by Mary Gehr.   1069

Copper and gold mines ... 1903. SEE
    no. 1862, Grindall Mining & Smelting Co.

COPPER RIVER AND NORTHWESTERN RAILWAY. The finding of an empire. [Seattle, White Advertising Bureau, 1909 ?] 19p. front. photos.   1070

Copper River and Northwestern Railway. SEE ALSO nos.
    118, Alaska Steamship Co. Copper R. and Northwestern Ry....
        1914;
    2440, Kennecott Copper Corp. Annual report. 1915 and 1918.

Copper River and Northwestern Railway, Apr.-Oct. ... 1914. SEE
    no. 118, Alaska Steamship Co.

COPPER RIVER JOE [pseud.] A golden cross (?) on trails from the Valdez Glacier. L. A., White-Thompson, 1939. 200p. illus. by N. G. Thompson, front.(col.), pls. [author is Charles Henry Remington]   1071

COPPER RIVER MINING, TRADING AND DEVELOPMENT CO., Valdez. A guide for Alaskan miners, settlers and tourists. Seattle, Trade Register Print, 1902. 93p. illus. ports. map.   1072

CORBEL, JEAN. Neiges et glaciers. [TITLE TR. Snows and glaciers] Paris, Libr. Armand Colin, 1962. 224p. graphs, tables, maps, bibliog.   1073

CORBETT, JOHN. The lake country. Rochester, N. Y., 1898. 161p. [has reference to mining town of Sunrise, on Cook Inlet]   1074

CORDIER, ALBERT H. Some big game hunts ... illustrated from photographs made by the author unless otherwise specified. Kansas City, Mo., Union Bank Note Co., 1911. 317p. illus.   1075

Cordier, E. J. SEE no. 1749, Goepp, E.

CORDOVA DAILY TIMES. All-Alaska review for 1928. Cordova, Dec. 15, 1928. 64p. illus.   1076

CORDOVA DAILY TIMES. All-Alaska review for 1930. Cordova, 1930. 64p. illus.   1077

CORDOVA DAILY TIMES. Coming copper port of the world. Cordova, 1916. (32)p. pls.   1078

CORDOVA DAILY TIMES. Cordova, Alaska; coming port of the world. no pl., April 1914. 32p.   1079

CORDOVA, COMMON COUNCIL. Alaska; facts about Cordova. no pl., April 1914. 16p.   1080

CORDOVA, COMMON COUNCIL. Rules, by-laws and ordinances adopted by the Common Council of the town of Cordova, Alaska, up to Sept. 1914. Cordova, Cordova Daily Alaskan Print, 1914. 80p.
1081

COREY, AUDREY LEONA. White angel of the trails. N. Y., Carlton Press, 1968.   1082

CORNEY, PETER. Puteshestvie G. P. Kornea k siev.-zapadynm beregam Ameriki i v Kitai v 1813-18, a prisovokupleniem izviestiia o Ross, poseleniakh na sem berego Ameriki. no pl., Sievernyi Arkhiv, 1822, 23. 18p. and 19p. [tr. of London Literary Gazette printing, 1821, see no. 1084]   1083

CORNEY, PETER. Voyages in the Northern Pacific; narrative of several trading voyages from 1813 to 1818, between the northwest coast of America, the Hawaiian Islands and China, with a description of the Russian establishments on the northwest coast; interesting early account of Kamehameha's realm; manners and customs of the people, etc. and sketch of a cruise in the service of the independents of South America in 1819. With preface and appendix of valuable confirmatory letters prepared by Prof. W. D. Alexander. Honolulu, Thos. G. Thrum, Pub., 1896. 138p. [reprinted from The London Literary Gazette, 1821] ANR. WITH TITLE Early voyages in the north Pacific 1813-1818. Fairfield, Wash., Ye Galleon Press, 1965. ltd. ed. 914 copies [facsim. of 1896 ed. with added material and photos] 238p. front. ports. facsims. index. [for tr. of 1821 print. see no. 1083]   1084

CORRESPONDENCE RELATIVE TO THE SEIZURE of British American vessels in Behrings Sea by the United States authorities in 1886. Ottawa, McLean, Roger, Printers, 1887. 47p. ANR. WITH TITLE Correspondence relative to the seizure of British American vessels in Behrings Sea by the United States authorities in 1886-87. Ottawa, Brown, Chamberlin, Printers, 1888. 103p.   1085

Corry, Trevor, edit. SEE no. 4837, White Pass & Yukon Ry.

CORSER, HARRY PROSPER. Legendary lore of the Alaska totems. Juneau, Purity Pharmacy, 1910. pls. ANR. Juneau, Purity Pharmacy, 1911. (50)p. pls.(mtd.)   1086

CORSER, HARRY PROSPER. Mere man; or, doing as they do in Alaska. A playette. Ketchikan, Ketchikan Press, 1915. 8p. [bound with *Richard Kemper's Christmas*]   1087

CORSER, HARRY PROSPER. Seventy-six page history of Alaska. By H. P. Corser, M. S., author of "Totem lore." no pl., 1927. 76p. front.(port.), photos.   1088

CORSER, HARRY PROSPER. Totem lore and the land of the totem; including Totem lore, sixth edition and Through the ten thousand islands of Alaska, second edition. By H. P. Corser, M. S. Juneau, Nugget Shop, n. d. 97(3)p. photos, append. [HAS COVER TITLE Totem lore of the Alaska Indians and the land of the totem] ANR. WITH TITLE Totem lore and the land of the totem; including Totem lore, seventh edition and Through the ten thousand islands of Alaska, third edition. Juneau, 1933. 102p. illus. ANR. WITH TITLE Totem lore and the land of the totem; including Totem lore, eighth edition and Through the ten thousand islands of Alaska, fourth edition. Juneau, Nugget Shop, n. d. [1934 ?] 110p. illus.   1089

CORSER, HARRY PROSPER. Totem lore of the Alaska Indians. no pl., n. d. (48)p. illus. OTHERS WITH SAME TITLE:
2d. ed. no pl., n. d. [printed by Williamson-Haffner Co., Denver] 48p. photos;
3rd ed. Ketchikan, Ryus Drug, [1916] 60p. illus.;
4th ed. Juneau, Nugget Shop, Simpson & Wright, n. d. (3)4-64(1)p. front. photos, append. wrps.;
5th ed. Juneau, Nugget Shop, n. d. [1923] 59p. illus.
OTHERS WITH TITLE Totem lore of the Alaska Indian and the land of the totem:
8th rev. ed. Wrangell, Bear Totem Store, 1932. 83p. illus. ports.;
9th rev. ed. Wrangell, W. C. Waters, 1940. 116p. illus. ports. map.   1090

CORSON, JOHN W. Home rule for Alaska. Speech of John W. Corson at Juneau Convention, November 14, 1907. Forty years of Congressional indifference. Is the Ordinance of 1787 to apply to Alaska ? Seward, Published by Republican Territorial Committee, June 1, 1908. 15p.   1091

CORSON, JOHN W. Is the Ordinance of 1787 to apply to Alaska ? The story of forty years of Congressional indifference. Valdez, Published by Republican Territorial Committee, 1907. 21p. 1092

Cory, Vivian, auth. SEE no. 1133, Cross, Victoria [pseud.]

CORYELL, HUBERT VANSANT. Klondike gold. N. Y., Macmillan, 1938. 319p. illustrated by Armstrong Sperry.   1093

Coryell, John Russell. SEE no. 858, Carter, Nicholas [pseud.]

COSTELLO, JOSEPH A.   The Siwash, their life, legends and tales;
Puget Sound and Pacific Northwest ... Seattle, The Calvert Co.,
1895.   169p.   front. pls. ports.   1094

COTTEN, BRUCE.   An adventure in Alaska during the gold excitement of 1897-98.   A personal experience.   Baltimore, Sun Printing Office, 1922.   107p.   1095

Cotter, Frank J.   SEE no. 3379, O'Cotter, Pat [pseud.]

COUCH, JAMES S.   Philately below zero, a postal history of
Alaska.   State College, Penna., American Philatelic Society,
1957.   81p.   photos, facsims. bibliog.   1096

Coues, Elliott.   SEE no. 1975, Harting, Jas. E.

COUNCIL CITY AND SOLOMON RIVER RAILROAD.   U. S. mail route,
freight and passenger traffic.   Issued January 25, 1907.   N. Y.,
1907.   12p.   1097

Coutousove, L. G., tr.   SEE no. 3968, Sarychev, G. A.

COUZENS, F. S.   The sayings of Dr. Bushwacker;   describes Sitka
and Alaska.   N. Y., 1867.   1098

COVARRUBIAS, MIGUEL.   The eagle, the jaguar, and the serpent;
Indian art of the Americas;   vol. 1, North America;   Alaska,
Canada, the United States.   N. Y., Knopf, 1954.   311(11)p.   pls.
line drawings, photos.   [includes Amerind and Eskimo]   1099

COWAN, P. R.   Visit to northern Substations and Alaska.   Ottawa,
Canadian Experimental Farms Service, 1946.   4p.   1100

COWLES, B. K.   Alaska; interesting and reliable information relating thereto;   containing also the Organic Act of the Territory.   Madison, Wisc., Democrat Co., 1885.   16p.   1101

COX, JAMES.   Our own country;   representing our native land and
its splendid natural scenery, etc., constituting a complete historic and geographic picturesque America.   Revised by William S.
Bryan.   St. Louis, Mo., Jno. W. Corley Pub. & Promotion Co.,
1913.   336p.   1102

COX, MARY.   John Driggs among the Eskimos.   N. Y., National
Council of Churches, 1956.   (Builders for Christ Series) [Point
Hope]   1103

COX, MARY.   Peter Trimble Rowe.   N. Y., National Council of
Churches, 1959.   (Pioneer Builders for Christ Series)   1104

Coxe, William. [Alphabetical title guide to chronological en-
tries]

Account Russ. disc. ... 1106.   Die neuen Entdeckung. ... 1108.
Comparative view ... 1105.   Nouvelles découvertes ... 1107.

COXE, WILLIAM. A comparative view of the Russian discoveries with
those made by Captains Cook and Clerke; and a sketch of what remains to be ascertained by future navigators. London, Printed by
J. Nichols, for T. Cadell, 1787. 1st ed. 31p. [issued separate,
also as supplement to 3rd ed. SEE no. 1106]   1105

COXE, WILLIAM. Account of the Russian discoveries between Asia
and America. To which are added, the conquest of Siberia, and
the history of the transactions and commerce between Russia and
China. London, Printed by J. Nichols, for T. Cadell, 1780. 1st
ed. 344p. pl.(fold.), maps(fold.) ANR. London, T. Cadell, 1787.
3rd ed. with supplement. [SEE no. 1105] 454p. front. (fold.
map), maps(fold.), errata, appends. bibliog. indexes. ANR. London, Cadell & Davies, 1803. 4th ed. enl. 500p. pl.(fold.),
front.(fold. map), maps(some fold.) ANR. London, Cadell &
Davies, 1804. 4th ed. enl. ltd. to 60 copies. 380p. pl.
front.(map), maps(some fold.)   1106

TRANSLATIONS - Account ... 1780, CHRONOLOGICALLY.

Nouvelles découvertes des Russes entre l'Asie et l'Amérique,
avec l'histoire de la conquete de la Sibérie et du commerce
des Russes et des Chinois. Trad. de l'Anglois de M. Coxe.
Neuchatel et Paris, Impr. Soc. Typ., 1781. 320p. pl. maps.
ANR. Paris, 1781. 314p. pl. map.   1107

Die neuen Entdeckungen der Russen zwischen Asien und Amerika
nebst der geschichte der eroberung Siberiens und des handels
der Russen und Chineser, aus dem Eng. des Herrn Coxe ubersetzt. Frankfurt und Leipzig, J. G. Fleischner, 1783. 409p.
pls. maps.   1108

Coxe, William. SEE ALSO nos. 1606-7, Forster, J. G. A.
Geschichte der Reisen ... 1791 and 1792.

CRAIG, JAMES. On the Yukon Trail. By James Craig. Chicago,
The Reilly & Lee Co., [c1922] 223p. front.(pl.) (The Radio-
Phone Boys Stories)   1109

CRAIG, LULU ALICE. Glimpses of sunshine and shade in the far
North, or, my travels in the land of the midnight sun. Cincinnati, The Editor Pub. Co., 1900. 123p. front.(col.), port. pls.
(incl. 1 col.)   1110

CRAIG, MORTE H. In the shadow of the Pole. Seattle, Acme Pub. Co., 1909. 2d ed. 34p. illus. [poetry]   1111

CRANDELL, JULIE V. The story of the Pacific salmon. Portland, Binfords & Mort, 1946. 59p. pls.   1112

CRANE, ALICE ROLLINS. Smiles and tears from the Klondyke. A collection of stories and sketches with eight illustrations. N. Y., Doxey's at the Sign of the Lark, 1901. 203p. front. (port.), ports. photos. [writings of Wm. Ogilvie, Wm. Galpin, Ella Cunningham, A. F. George, Alice Rollins Crane]   1113

Crane, Alice Rollins. SEE ALSO no. 3871,
    Rollins, Alice M. W. [same author ?]

CRANE, WALTER R. Gold and silver, comprising an economic history of mining in the United States. N. Y., John Wiley, 1908.
                                                                1114

CRANE, WARREN EUGENE. Totem tales. N. Y., Revell, 1932. 95p. front.(pl.), pls. ANR. Seattle Shorey Book Store, 1966. facsim. of 1932 ed. (Shorey Photocopy, no. SJS119)   1115

Crawford, Allan. SEE nos.
    4226, Snyder, L. L. Birds of Wrangell Isl. ... 1926;
    4314, Stefansson, V. Adventure Wrangel Isl. 1925.

CRAWFORD, JOHN W., "Capt. Jack" Souvenir of song and story. Happy New Year, 1898. N. Y., 1898. 30p.   1116

CREEKMORE, RAYMOND. Lokoshi learns to hunt seals. N. Y., Macmillan, 1946. illus.   1117

CRESSMAN, LUTHER SHEELEIGH and D. E. DUMOND. Research on Northwest prehistory; prehistory in the Naknek drainage, Southwestern Alaska. Eugene, University of Oregon, 1962. 54p. pls. maps. (Department of Anthropology)   1118

Creswell, S. G., illus. SEE no. 2835, M'Clure, R. J. LeM.

CREWE, E. O. Gold fields of the Yukon and how to get there. Chicago, Cole, 1897. 61p. illus. maps.   1119

CREWE, FRED. Camp Hades #23. Suggested by Alfred T. Costlett, and dedicated to Royal G. Southworth, Camp Cleary #22, Arctic Brotherhood. Fairbanks, 1910. 8p. ANR. 1925.   1120

CREWE, FRED. Log of the sloop "North" or, two seasons in the gold fields of Cook's Inlet, Alaska. Seattle, 1896. 4p.   1121

CREWE, FRED. Poems of Klondyke's early days and Alaska's long white trail; photos of the Klondyke stampede taken in 1897-98. Milwaukee, North American Press, 1921. 60p. pls.(1 col.)   1122

CRICHTON, CLARKE, jr. Frozen-in ! Adventures of the "Nanuk's" cabin boy north of Siberia. London, 1930. 148p. [attempted rescue of *Nanuk* by fliers Eielson and Borland]   1123

Crimont, Joseph. SEE no. 3979, Savage, A. H.

CRISLER, LOIS. Arctic wild. N. Y., Harper, 1958. 301p. illus. photos. ANR. London, 1959. 274p. photos. ANR. N. Y., Harper & Row, 1964. 1st paperback edition (Perennial Library) [wolves, Brooks Range]   1124

CRISWELL TRAVEL SERVICE, Los Angeles. Summer journeys to Alaska and the Yukon, "Land of the Midnight Sun," season 1931. L. A., 1931. 71p. illus.   1125

CROFT, ANDREW. Polar exploration. London, A. & C. Black, 1939. 268p. pls. maps, diagr. (Epics of the 20th Century) ANR. London, 1947. 2d ed. rev. and enl. 268p. pls. maps. ANR. N. Y., Macmillan, 1947.   1126

CROMWELL, GEORGE R., edit. America scenic and descriptive, from Alaska to the Gulf of Mexico. Series of panoramic pictures. N. Y., [1894] illus.   1127

CROSBY, THOMAS. Up and down the North Pacific coast by canoe and mission ship. Toronto, Missionary Society of Methodist Church, [1914] 403p. front.(port.), pls. ports. (The Young People's Forward Movement Department) [mainly coastal B. C., but also Wrangell, Alaska]   1128

CROSS, AUSTIN F. Cross roads. Montreal, Southam Press, 1936. 301p.   1129

CROSS, JAMES F. Eskimo adoption. N. Y., American Missionary Association, n. d. 7p.   1130

CROSS, JAMES F. Eskimo children. N. Y., American Missionary Association, n. d. 8p.   1131

CROSS, JAMES F. Eskimo women. N. Y., American Missionary Association, n. d. 4p.   1132

CROSS, VICTORIA [pseud.] A girl of the Klondike. N. Y., Geo. Munro's Sons, 1898. 133p. [author is Vivian Cory]   1133

Crosson, Joe. SEE no. 3658, Potter, Jean.

Cruising world's smoothest waterway ... 1929. SEE no. 3465, Pacific Steamship Co.

CROUSE, NELLIS MAYNARD. The search for the Northwest Passage. N. Y., Columbia University Press, 1934. 533p. front. pls. map (fold.)   1134

CROWE, GEORGE R. and DELORIS DEE CROWE. Plan-A-Flight to Alaska. A complete flight guide to the Alaska Highway. Anchorage, Plan-A-Flight Publications, 1968. 120p. illus. maps(1 fold.)   1135

CRUMP, IRVING. The boy's book of Arctic exploration. N. Y., Dodd Mead, 1925. 310p. illus. photos.   1136

Csermak, G. de Rohan. SEE no. 3868, Rohan-Csermak, G. de.

CULLUM, RIDGWELL. The bull moose. Philadelphia, Lippincott, 1931. 384p.   1137

CUMMINGS, HENRY, comp. A synopsis of the cruise of the U.S.S. "Tuscarora" from the date of her commission to her arrival in San Francisco, California, September 2, 1874. S. F., Cosmopolitan Steam Printing Co., 1874. 61p.   1138

CUNNINGHAM, CAROLINE. The talking stone, being early American stories told before the white man's day on this continent by the Indians and Eskimos. Selected and retold by Caroline Cunningham. N. Y., Knopf, 1939. 1st ed. 118p. illus. by Richard Floethe, map.   1139

Cunningham, Ella. SEE no. 1113, Crane, Alice Rollins.

CUNYNGHAME, FRANCIS. Lost trail. London, Faber & Faber, 1953.   1140

CURLE, JAMES HERBERT. The gold mines of the world. London, Simpkin, 1902. 2d ed. 319p. ANR. London, Routledge, 1905. 3rd ed.   1141

CURTIN, WALTER R. Yukon voyage; unofficial log of the steamer *Yukoner*. Caldwell, Idaho, Caxton, 1938. 299p. front.(map), photos, facsims. append. (list of Yukon River steamboats) [diary of Pat Galvin expedition to Dawson, 1897-98]   1142

CURTIS, CLAUDE H. The gospel in Alaska. S. F., Gospel Missions Press, 1946. 91p. front. pls.   1143

CURTIS, EDWARD S. The North American Indian; being a series of volumes picturing and describing the Indians of the United States and Alaska, written, illustrated and published by Edward S. Curtis; edited by Frederick W. Hodge ... Seattle, E. S. Curtis, 1907-15. 10 vols. ANR. N. Y., 1907-30, printed by Plimpton Press, Norwood, Mass. 20 vols. (text) 20 vols. (portfolios of pls.) ltd. to 500 sets. ANR. N. Y., Johnson Reprint Corp., 1970. 20 vols. plus 4 vols.(supplement)   1144

Curtis, Edward S. SEE ALSO no. 259, Andrews, R. W.

CURTIS, JACK. The kloochman, a novel. N. Y., Simon & Schuster, 1966. 1st print. 286p.   1145

CURWOOD, JAMES OLIVER. The Alaskan; a novel of the north.
N. Y., Cosmopolitan Book Corp., 1922. 326p. front. pls. ANR.
Toronto, Copp, 1923.   1146

CUSHMAN, DAN. The great north trail; America's route of the
ages. N. Y., McGraw-Hill, 1966. 383p. illus. maps, bibliog.
(American Trail Series) [from Texas to Klondike]   1147

Cuvier, Baron le. SEE no. 925, Choris, Louis.

CYRIAX, RICHARD J. Sir John Franklin's last Arctic expedition.
The Franklin expedition. A chapter in the history of the Royal
Navy. London, 1939. 222p. maps(fold.), index.   1148

D

DABOVICH, S. The Holy Orthodox Church; or, the ritual services
and sacraments of the Eastern Apostolic Church. Wilkes-Barre,
Penna., 1898.   1149

DABOVICH, S. The lives of the Saints, and several lectures and
sermons. S. F., Murdock Press, 1898. 127p.   1150

DAFOE, JOHN W. Clifford Sifton in relation to his times. Toronto, Macmillan of Canada, 1931. 552p. ports. [Sifton was British agent in Alaskan boundary dispute]   1151

DAILY ALASKA FISHING NEWS. Alaska fisherman's almanac for 1946.
Edited by Ballard Hadman. Ketchikan, 1946. 1st annual. 200p.
illus. OTHERS 1947, 1948.   1152

DALBY, MILTON A. The sea saga of Dynamite Johnny O'Brien;
American master mariner for fifty-three years; a seaman for
sixty-five years; whose shipmates and friends called him the
"Nestor of the Pacific," who feared God but defied His storms;
who fought the good fight, whose fists were as hard as his
spirit was stout. Seattle, Lowman & Hanford, 1933. 249p.
front. pls. ports.   1153

Dale, Edw. Everett, edit. SEE no. 825, Canton, Frank M.

Dale, Geo. A., co-auth. SEE no. 759, Butler, E. I.

DALE, JOHN. Round the world by Doctor's orders. Being a narra-
tive of a year's travel in Japan, Ceylon, Australia, China,
New Zealand, Canada, the United States, etc. etc. London, E.
Stock, 1894. 350p. front. pls. [has one chapt. on Alaska's
Glacier Bay, pp.273-93]   1154

DALL, WILLIAM HEALEY. Alaska and its resources. Boston, Lee & Shepherd, 1870. 627p. front.(pl.), pls. map(fold. in back), appends. glossary, vocabs. bibliog. index. ANR. London, Sampson Low, 1870. 627p. ANR. N. Y., Arno Press, 1970. facsim. ed. (American Environmental Studies)   1155

DALL, WILLIAM HEALEY. Catalogue of shells from Bering Strait and the adjacent portions of the Arctic Ocean, with descriptions of three new species. no pl., Feb. 26, 1874. (also in: Proceedings, California Academy of Sciences, April 1874. vol. 5, pp.246-53)   1156

DALL, WILLIAM HEALEY. Descriptions of new species of Mollusca from the coast of Alaska, with notes on some rare forms. no pl., Apr. 9, 1873. (also in: Proceedings, California Academy of Sciences, May 1873. vol. 5, pp.57-62. illus.)   1157

DALL, WILLIAM HEALEY. Descriptions of new species of Mollusca from the northwest coast of America. no pl., Dec. 17, 1872. (also in: Proceedings, California Academy of Sciences, January 1873. vol. 4, pt. 5, pp.302-3, illus.)   1158

DALL, WILLIAM HEALEY. Descriptions of three new species of Crustacea, parasitic on the Cetacea of the northwest coast of America. no pl., Nov. 9, 1872. (also in: Proceedings, California Academy of Sciences, January 1873. vol. 4, pt. 5, pp.281-3)   1159

DALL, WILLIAM HEALEY. Notes on the avifauna of the Aleutian Islands, especially those west of Unalashka. no pl., Mar. 14, 1874. (also in: Proceedings, California Academy of Sciences, April 1874. vol. 5, pp.270-81)   1160

DALL, WILLIAM HEALEY. Notes on the avi-fauna of the Aleutian Islands, from Unalaska eastward. no pl., Feb. 8, 1873. (also in: Proceedings, California Academy of Sciences, April 1873. vol. 5, pp.12-15)   1161

DALL, WILLIAM HEALEY. On new parasitic Crustacea from the northwest coast of America. no pl., Mar. 3, 1874. (also in: Proceedings, California Academy of Sciences, April 1874. vol. 5, pp.254-55)   1162

DALL, WILLIAM HEALEY. On the parasites of the cetaceans of the northwest coast of America, with descriptions of new forms. no pl., Dec. 17, 1872. (also in: Proceedings, California Academy of Sciences, January 1873. vol. 4, pt. 5, pp.299-302)   1163

DALL, WILLIAM HEALEY. Preliminary descriptions of new species of mollusks from the northwest coast of America. no pl., Oct.8, 1872. (also in: Proceedings, California Academy of Sciences, January 1873. vol. 4, pt. 5, pp.27-271. pl.)   1164

DALL, WILLIAM HEALEY. Preliminary descriptions of new species of mollusks from the northwest coast of America. no pl., March 19, 1877. (from: Proceedings, California Academy of Sciences, vol. 7, pp.1-6) [vol. 7 never published] 1165

DALL, WILLIAM HEALEY. Spencer Fullerton Baird; a biography, including selections from his correspondence with Audubon, Agassiz, Dana, and others ... Philadelphia, Lippincott, 1915. 462p. illus. 1166

DALL, WILLIAM HEALEY. The native tribes of Alaska. An address before the Section of Anthropology of the A. A. A. S. at Ann Arbor, August 1885. Salem, Mass., Printed at Salem Press, 1885. 19p. (also in: Proceedings, A. A. A.S, 1885. vol. 34) 1167

DALL, WILLIAM HEALEY and others. The Yukon territory; the narrative of W. H. Dall, leader of the expedition to Alaska in 1866-68; the narrative of an exploration made in 1887 in the Yukon district, by George M. Dawson. Extracts from the report of an exploration made in 1896-97 by Wm. Ogilvie ... introduction by F. Mortimer Trimmer ... London, Downey & Co., 1898. 438p. front. pls. tables, map(fold.) 1168

Dall, William Healey. SEE ALSO nos.
    451, Beach, W. W., edit. Indian misc. 1877;
    1950, Harriman Alaska Exped. 1899. vols. 2 and 13;
    2082, Herron, E. A. First scientist of Alaska. 1958;
    3269, Nadaillac, Marquis de. Prehistoric America. 1884.

DALLAS, ALEXANDER GRANT. San Juan, Alaska, and the north-west boundary. London, Henry S. King, 1873. 11p. 1169

DAMM, HANS, edit. James Cook; die suche nach dem sudland. Nach den aufzeichnungen Georg Forsters bearbeitet von dr. Hans Damm. Leipzig, F. A. Brockhaus, 1922. 157p. 1170

DANA, JOHN COTTON and others. The far north-west; being the record, with pictures of a journey over the Canadian Pacific to Alaska, to California, to the Yellowstone, and home by the Northern Pacific, in July, 1905. Newark, N. J., Published for the Travelers by Baker Printing Co., 1906. 40p. plus 62p. of photos, front. sketches, map. [over 400 copies printed as record of trip to American Library Assoc. conference in Portland, Ore.]1171

DANA, MARVIN. The shooting of Dan McGrew; a novel by Marvin Dana based on the famous poem of Robert W. Service; profusely illustrated with scenes from the photo play. N. Y., Grosset & Dunlap, [c1915] 317p. front. pls. 1172

DANENHOWER, JOHN WILSON. Lt. Danenhower's narrative of the "Jeannette." Boston, J. R. Osgood, 1882. 102p. front.(port.), pl. map(dble.) 1173

Danenhower, John Wilson. SEE ALSO no. 2129,
    History ... "Jeannette" ... 1882.

DANIEL, HAWTHORNE. Bare hands; being the story of the extraordinary steamboat that was built on Devil's Island off the coast
of Alaska by four shipwrecked men. By Hawthorne Daniel. Illus-
strated by Arthur A. Jansson. N. Y., Coward-McCann, [c1929]
244p. front.(col.), pls. ANR. N. Y. Grosset & Dunlap, n. d.
reprint.   1174

Dankoler, Harry. SEE no. 1225, Dee, Harry [pseud.]

DARLING, ESTHER BIRDSALL. Baldy of Nome; an immortal of the
trail. S. F., A. M. Robertson, 1912. 75p. front. pls. ANR.
Philadelphia, Penn Pub. Co., 1917. 301p. front.(col.), pls.
ANR. N. Y. Knopf, 1947.   1175

DARLING, ESTHER BIRDSALL. Boris, grandson of Baldy. Philadelphia, Penn Pub. Co., 1936. 317p. illus. ANR. N. Y., 1950.
317p.   1176

DARLING, ESTHER BIRDSALL. For the honor and glory of France.
Reprinted through courtesy Vanity Fair, N. Y. and Le Gaulois,
Paris. Translated into French by Leon de Tinseau. no pl., n.d.
18p. [sled dogs sent to France for use in World War 1]   1177

DARLING, ESTHER BIRDSALL. Luck of the trail. Garden City,
Doubleday Doran, 1933. 309p. front.(col.)   1178

DARLING, ESTHER BIRDSALL. Navarre of the north; a thrilling
story of the grandson of Baldy of Nome. Garden City, Doubleday
Doran, 1930. 268p. front. ANR. Garden City, Sun Dial Press,
1937. 268p. (Young Moderns Bookshelf)   1179

DARLING, ESTHER BIRDSALL. No boundary line. N. Y., Wm. Penn
Pub. Co., 1942. 288p.   1180

DARLING, ESTHER BIRDSALL. The break-up. Philadelphia, 1928.
320p. ANR. N. Y., 1928. 320p.   1181

DARLING, ESTHER BIRDSALL. The great dog races of Nome, held under
the auspices of the Nome Kennel Club, Nome, Alaska. Official
souvenir history. Esther Birdsall Darling (President, 1916).
Photographs by Lomen Brothers, Nome. no pl., n. d. (28)p. illus. front. pls. ANR. facsim. ed. Knik, Iditarod Trail Committee, 1969. [printed by Ken Wray's Print Shop, Anchorage]   1182

DARLING, ESTHER BIRDSALL. Up in Alaska; illustrated by Mary
Crete Crouch. Sacramento, Jo Anderson Press, 1912. 59p. illus.
[poetry]   1183

DARLING, FRANK FRASER. Pelican in the wilderness; a naturalist's
odyssey in North America. N. Y., Random House, 1956.   1184

Darling, Frank Fraser, co-auth. SEE ALSO no. 2682,
    Leopold, A. S.

Darling, Lois, illus. SEE no. 1599, Ford, Corey.

DARLING, LOUIS. Seals and walruses. N. Y., Morrow, 1955. 63p.
illus. map.   1185

DARSIE, RICHARD FLOYD. Notes on American mosquito pupae, 1.
description of *Aedes riparius* and *A. pionips:* Diptera, Culici-
dae. Dover, Delaware Agricultural Experiment Station, Misc.
Paper 200, Publication 263, and Department of Entomology, Scientific Article no. 183, February 15, 1954. illus. (also in:
Transactions, Entomological Society of Washington, vol. 57, no.1,
pp.23-29. illus.) [incls. Alaska, Yukon and Northwest Terri-
tory]   1186

DARTMOUTH COLLEGE LIBRARY, Hanover, N. H. Dictionary catalog of
the Stefansson collection on the Polar regions. Boston, G. K.
Hall & Co., 1967. 8 vols.   1187

DASHKEVICH, ANTHONY. Arkhanqels-Mikhailovskiĭ pravoslavnyi sobor
v Sitkhie. [TITLE TR. The Russian Orthodox cathedral of Archang-
gel Michael at Sitka] N. Y., 1899. 71p. [in Russian and English on opposite pages]   1188

Dassow, Ethel, edit. SEE no. 83, Alaska Magazine Pub. Co.

Daubrée, M., edit. SEE no. 3323, Nordenskiöld, N. A. E.

Daveler, E. V. SEE no. 88, Alaska Mining & Eng. Soc.

DAVIDSON, D. S. Family hunting territories in northwestern
North America. Edited by F. W. Hodge. N. Y., Heye Foundation,
Museum of the Americn Indian, 1928. 34p. map(fold. inside back
cover), ftntes. (Indian Notes & Monographs, Misc. Contrib.
no. 46)   1189

DAVIDSON, DONALD THOMAS and others. The geology and engineering
characteristics of some Alaskan soils. Ames, Iowa State University, 1959. 149p. illus. maps, graphs, diagrs. tables, bibliog.
(Bulletin, vol. 58, no. 29, Dec. 16, 1959. Also issued as:
Iowa Engineering Experimental Station Bulletin, no. 186)   1190

DAVIDSON, GEORGE. The Alaska boundary. S. F., Alaska Packer's
Association, 1903. 235p. port. maps(2 fold.) [issued in a
small edition]   1191

DAVIDSON, GEORGE. The glaciers of Alaska that are shown on Russian charts or mentioned in older narratives. S. F., Geographical Society of the Pacific, 1904. 98p. (Transactions and Proceedings, ser. 2, vol. 3)   1192

DAVIDSON, GEORGE. The tracks and landfalls of Bering and Chiri-
kof on the northwest coast of America, from the point of their
separation in latitude 49°10', longitude 176°40' west, to their
return to the same meridian, June, July, August, Sept., Oct.,
1741. S. F., Geographical Society of the Pacific [printed by
J. F. Partridge], 1901. front.(port.), chart(fold.) (Transactions and Proceedings, ser. 2, vol. 1, 1902. pp.1-44)   1193

DAVIDSON, GORDON CHARLES. The northwest company. Berkeley,
University of California, 1918. 349p. pls. maps, bibliog. index. (Publications in History, vol. 7)   1194

Davidson, I. N. SEE no. 278, Arctic Brotherhood.

DAVIES, GRIFFITH. The complete Chinook jargon or Indian trade
language of Oregon, Washington, British Columbia, Alaska, Idaho
and other parts of the north Pacific coast. Seattle,   1888.
40p.   1195

DAVIES, RAYMOND ARTHUR. Arctic Eldorado; a dramatic report on
Canada's northland, the greatest unexploited region in the world,
with a workable four year plan. Toronto, Ryerson Press, 1944.
97p. [references to Alaska Highway, Canol Project, others] 1196

DAVIS, CAROL BEERY. Alaska driftwood. Denver, 1953. 80p.
illus. [poetry]   1197

DAVIS, CAROL BEERY. Songs of the totem. Juneau, Empire Printing Co., 1939. 48p. front. illus. music [words of songs in
English and Tlingit]   1198

DAVIS, ELLIS A. Davis' standard encyclopedia: Montana, Idaho,
Alaska, Washington and Oregon; the Pacific northwest. Berkeley,
1910. 216p. illus. maps(3 fold.)   1199

DAVIS, GEORGE THOMPSON BROWN. An Indian Arcadia in Alaska. An
account of the town of Metlakahtla and the mission work of W.
Duncan among the Tsimshian Indians. N. Y., 1904.   1200

DAVIS, GEORGE THOMPSON BROWN. Metlahahtla; a true narrative of
the redman. Chicago, Ram's Horn Co., 1904. 128p. illus. ANR.
Seattle, Shorey Book Store, 1964. 128p. photocopy facsim. of
1904 ed.   1201

DAVIS, HORACE. Record of Japanese vessels driven upon the northwest coast of America and its outlying islands, read before American Antiquarian Society at April meeting, 1872. Worcester,
Mass., Charles Hamilton, 1872. 22p. pls.   1202

Davis, Jefferson C. SEE no. 2864, McDonald, Jos. L.

DAVIS, MARY LEE. Alaska; the great bear's cub. Boston, W. A. Wilde Co., 1930. 314p. front.(port.), pls. endmaps, photos by author, sketches by Olaus J. Murie. 1203

DAVIS, MARY LEE. Sourdough gold, the log of a Yukon adventure. With maps by the author and illustrated by photographs. Boston, W. A. Wilde Co., 1933. 351p. front.(pl.), pls. maps(incl. 1 fold. in back) [gold rush diaries of "Dun Scotus," (Dr. James Foster Scott)] 1204

DAVIS, MARY LEE. Uncle Sam's attic; the intimate story of Alaska. Boston, W. A. Wilde Co., [c1930] 402p. front.(photo), pls. map, endmaps, photos by author. 1205

DAVIS, MARY LEE. We are Alaskans. Boston, W. A. Wilde Co., 1931. 335p. front. pls. ports. photos by author, sketches by Olaus J. Murie. 1206

DAVIS, PHYLLIS EILEEN and CYNTHIA ROE SMITH. Anchorage fun book. Anchorage, 1967. 1207

DAVIS, ROBERT H. Let's go with Bob Davis to India, Ceylon, Venezuela; the Caribbean, Puerto Rico, Alaska and the Yukon, Gaspe, Chesapeake Bay. N. Y., 1940. 452p. photos, index. 1208

DAVIS, ROBERT TYLER, edit. Native arts of the Pacific northwest; from the Rasmussen collection of the Portland Art Museum. Introductory text by Robert Tyler Davis. Stanford, Stanford University Press, 1949. 165p. pls.(some col.), map. 1209

DAVY, GEORGES. La foi jurée; étude sociologique du problème du contract; la formation du lien contractuel. [TITLE TR. The sworn faith; a sociological study of the problem of contract; the formation of contractual bonds] Paris, Alcan, 1922. 379p. (Travaux de l'année sociologique) [incls. Tlingit, Haida, Tsimshian and Kwakiutl] 1210

DAVYDOV, GAVRILLA IVANOVICH. Dvukratnoe Puteshestvie V Ameriku Morskikh Ofitserov Khvostova i Davydova, Pisannoe sim Poslyednim. Chast Pervaya[-Vtoraya] [TITLE TR. Account of two voyages to America of the Naval Officers Khvostov and Davydov, written by the latter] Volume one [-two] 2 vols. in one. St. Petersburg, Pechatan v Morskoi Tipografii, 1810-12. 287p. and 224p. [see no. 1212 for tr.] 1211

DAVYDOV, GAVRILLA IVANOVICH. Reise der russisch-kaiserlichen Flott-Officere Chwostow und Dawydow von St. Petersburgh durch Siberien nach Amerika und zurück in den Jahren 1802, 1803 und 1804. Beschreiben von Dawydow und aus dem Russischen ubersetzt von D. Carl Joh. Schultz. Berlin, bei Friedrich Maurer, 1816. 253p. [tr. of no. 1211] 1212

DAVYDOV, ÍÛRIÍ VLADIMIROVICH. Dzhon Franklin. [TITLE TR. John Franklin] Moskva, Gos. izd-vo geograf. lit-ry, 1956. 47p. illus. port. map. (Zamechatel'nye geografy i puteshestvenniki)
1213

DAWES, LENORE. I reached for a star; poems. N. Y., Exposition Press, 1951. 63p. port.
1214

DAWSON, CARL ADDINGTON. The new northwest. Toronto, University of Toronto Press, 1947. 341p. pls. maps(sketch) (Canada. Social Sciences Research Council) [incls. Alaska Railroad, Alaska Highway and Matanuska Valley]
1215

DAWSON, GEORGE M. and R. G. McCONNELL. Report on an exploration in the Yukon district, N. W. T., and adjacent northern portion of British Columbia, 1887, with extracts relating to the Yukon district from report on an exploration in the Yukon and Mackenzie basins, 1887-88, by R. G. McConnell. Ottawa, S. E. Dawson, 1898. 244p. (Canada. Geological Survey Pub.)
1216

Dawson, George M. SEE ALSO nos.
    1168, Dall, Wm. H. Yukon Terr. ... 1898;
    4547, Tolmie, W. F. Comparative vocab. Indian ... 1884.

DAWSON, WILL. Coastal cruising; an authoritative guide to British Columbian, Puget Sound-San Juan Islands waters, and the water-ways of south-east Alaska. Vancouver, Mitchell Press, 1965. new enl. ed. 243p. illus. ports. maps.
1217

DAY, BETH. Glacier pilot; the story of Bob Reeve and the flyers who pushed back Alaska's air frontiers. N. Y., Henry Holt, 1957. 1st ed. 348p. photos, map.
1218

Day, Beth. SEE ALSO no. 2484, Klaben, H. Hey, I'm alive ! 1964.

DAY, LUELLA. The tragedy of the Klondike; this book of travels gives the true facts of what took place in the gold-fields under British rule. N. Y., privately printed, 1906. 181p. front. (port.), pls.
1219

Days forever flown. 1892. SEE no. 1982, [Haselhurst, May A.]

DEANS, JAMES. Tales from the totems of the Hidery; collected by James Deans, edited by Oscar Lovell Triggs. Chicago, International Folk-Lore Association, 1899. 96p. front. pls. (Archives, vol. 2)
1220

D'Anvers, N., tr. SEE no. 3269, Nadaillac, Marquis de.

d'Anville, J. J. B., cartog. SEE no. 1369, DuHalde, J. B.

De Armond, Dale, illus. SEE nos.
    1671, Gaines, R. Chilkoot Charlie. 1951;
    1673, Gaines, R. Second book Chilkoot ... 1955;
    1791, Graber, A. H. East to Alaska. 1960.

De ARMOND, ROBERT NEIL. The founding of Juneau. By R. N. De Armond. Juneau, Gastineau Channel Centennial Association, 1967. 214p. illus. photos, ports, map, bibliog. index. (Centennial Edition)   1221

De ARMOND, ROBERT NEIL. Some names around Juneau. Sitka, Sitka Printing Co., 1957. 48p.   1222

Dease, P. W. SEE no. 4160, Simpson, A.

deBAETS, MAURICE. Monseigneur Seghers, l'apotre de l'Alaska. Paris, H. Oudin, 1896. 237p. port. facsim. maps(2 fold.) ANR. Ghent, 1896. 237p. ANR. Ghent, 1897. 283p. [see no. 1224 for tr.]   1223

deBAETS, MAURICE. The apostle of Alaska; life of the Most Reverend Charles John Seghers, a translation of Maurice deBaet's "Vie de Monseigneur Seghers." Translated by Sister Mary Mildred, S. S. A. Foreword by the Most Rev. John C. Cody. Paterson, N. J., St. Anthony Guild Press, 1943. 292p. front.(port.), illus. index. [tr. of no. 1223]   1224

Decline and fall of Samuel Sawbones, M.D. on Klondike ... 1900.
    SEE no. 2675, [Leisher, J. J.]

DEE, HARRY [pseud.] James Griffin's adventures in Alaska. Milwaukee, J. H. Yewdale, 1903. 276p. front. pls. (Adventure Series) [author is Harry E. Dankoler]   1225

Defenders of Furbearers. SEE no. 758, Butcher, D.

deFilippi, Filippo. Ascent of Mt. St. Elias ... 1900. SEE
    no. 1227.

deFilippi, Filippo. Forschungsreise ... 1900. SEE no. 1228.

deFILIPPI, FILIPPO. La spedizione di Sua Altezza reale, il principe Luigi Amedeo di Savoia, duca degli Abruzzi, al Monte Sant' Elia (Alaska) 1897, illustrata da Vittorio Sella. A beneficio delle guide alpine italiane. [TITLE TR. The expedition of His Royal Highness, Prince Luigi Amadeo di Savoia, Duke of the Abruzzi to Mount Saint Elias (Alaska) 1897, illustrated by Vittorio Sella] Milano, U. Hoepli, 1900. 284p. pls.(incl. 4 fold.panoramic), maps(fold.), appends. bibliog.   1226

deFILIPPI, FILIPPO. TRANSLATIONS - Laspedizione ... 1900,
    chronologically.

  The ascent of Mt. St. Elias (Alaska) by H. R. H. Prince Luigi
    Amadeo di Savoia, Duke of the Abruzzi, narrated by Filippo
    de Filippi, illustrated by Vittorio Sella and translated by
    Signora Linda Villari with the author's supervision. N. Y.,
    F. A. Stokes, 1900. 241p. front. pls.(incl. 4 fold. pano-
    ramic), maps(fold.) ANR. Westminster, Archibald Constable
    Co., 1900. 241p.   1227

  Die Forschungsreise S. K. H. des Prinzen Ludwig Amadeus von
    Savoyen, Herzogs der Abruzzen, nach dem Eliasberge in Alaska
    im Jahre 1897 ... Aus dem Italianischen übersetzt von Pro-
    fessor Baron G. Locella. Mit 127 in den text gedruckten und
    34 Tafeln Abbildengen, 4 Panoramen und 2 Karten. Leipzig,
    Verlagsbuchhandlung, von J. J. Weber, 1900. 257p. illus.
    maps.   1228

de Fonte, Bartolome. SEE cross-references listed under
    de la Fuente, Bartolome.

deFONVIELLE, WILFRID. Aventures d'un chercheur d'or au Klondike.
Paris, A. L. Guyot, 1900. 2 vols.   1229

deFONVIELLE, WILFRID. Aventures d'un Français au Klondyke. Paris, Société Francaise d'Éditions d'Art, 1901. 268p.illus. 1230

DeGARMO, MARGARET. Alaska, questions and answers for Mission
Circles and hands. Chicago, The Woman's American Baptist Home
Missionary Society, 1912. 22p.   1231

d'HARCOURT, RAOUL. Arts de l'Amerique. Paris, Éditions de
Chene, 1948. 199p. illus. photos by Emmanuel Sougez, maps.
[for tr. see no. 1233]   1232

d'HARCOURT, RAOUL. Primitive art of the Americas. Translated
by Arnold Rosin. N. Y., Tudor Pub. Co., 1950. 199p. illus.
photos by Emmanuel Sougez, maps. [tr. of no. 1232]   1233

d'Harnoncourt, Rene, co-auth. SEE no. 1334, Douglas, F. H.

deLabillardiere, Jacques Julian Houten. Account of voyage ...
    1800. SEE no. 1235.

deLABILLARDIERE, JACQUES JULIAN HOUTEN. Relation du voyage à la
recherche de La Pérouse, fait par ordre de l'Assemblée Consti-
tuante, pendant les années 1791, 1792, et pendant la premiere et
la secunde année de la Republique Française. Paris, H. J. Jan-
sen, 1799. 2 vols. and atlas. pls. table, map(fold.) ANR.
Paris [1800] 2 vols. and atlas. pls. by Dien.   1234

deLABILLARDIERE, JACQUES JULIAN HOUTEN. TRANSLATIONS - Relation du voyage ... 1799, chronologically.

An account of a voyage in search of La Pérouse undertaken by order of the Constituent Assembly in the years 1791, 1792, and 1793 in the *Recherche* and *Esperance,* ships of war under the command of Bruni D'Entrecasteaux, translated from the French. London, J. Debrett, 1800. 2 vols. pls. map(fold.)

1235

Voyage in search of La Pérouse, performed by order of the Constituent Assembly, during the years 1791, 92, 93, and 94, and drawn up by M. Labillardiere, one of the naturalists attached to the expedition. Translated from the French. London, J. Stockdale, 1800. 2 vols. pls. map(fold.), tables.

1236

de LaCoeur, Louis. SEE no. 3986, Savvage, Jehan.

DELACOUR, JEAN THEODORE. Preliminary note on the taxonomy of Canada geese, *Branta canadensis.* N. Y., American Museum of Natural History, 1951. 10p. (Novitates, no. 1537)   1237

de La CROIX, ROBERT. Mysteries of the North Pole. Translated from the French by Edward Fitzgerald. London, F. Muller, 1954. 216p. illus. maps(text), bibliog. ANR. N. Y., J. Day Co., 1956. 251p. [tr. of: Les disparus du pôle]   1238

de la Fuente, Bartolome. SEE nos.
    1257, Delisle, J. N. Nouvelles cartes ... 1753;
    1312, Dobbs, A. Account ... Hudson's Bay ... 1744;
    1760, Goldson, Wm. Observations ... Straits of Anian ...
          1793;
    2336, [Jefferys, Thos. ?] Great probability ... 1768;
    3194, Mornas, Buy de. Cosmographie ... 1770;
    4662, Vaugondy, R. D. de. Observations ... 1753.

de La GRASSERIE, RAOUL. Cinq langues de la Colombie brittanique; haida, tsimshian, kwagiutl, nootka et tlinkit, grammaires, vocabulaires, textes, traduits et analyses. Paris, J. Maisonneuve, 1902. 530p. (Bibliotheque linguistique americaine, t. 24)   1239

de LAGUNA, FREDERICA. An anthropological survey of the northern Tlingit, 1949. [Bryn Mawr, Penna., 1924] 26p.   1240

de LAGUNA, FREDERICA. An anthropological survey of the Tlingit of Chatham Strait. [Bryn Mawr, Penna., 1950]   1241

de LAGUNA, FREDERICA. An archaeological survey in northern Tlingit territory, 1949. [Bryn Mawr, Penna., 1949 ?] 11p. 1342

de LAGUNA, FREDERICA. Chugach prehistory, the archaeology of
Prince William Sound, Alaska. Seattle, University of Washington
Press, 1956. 289p. front. maps, plans, tables, diagrs. bibliog.
index. (University of Washington Publication in Anthropology,
vol. 13)   1243

de LAGUNA, FREDERICA. Fog on the mountain. Garden City, Doubleday Doran, 1938. 275p. front., map (Crime Club)   1244

de LAGUNA, FREDERICA, edit. Selected papers from the American
Anthropologist, 1888-1920. Edited by Frederica de Laguna; with
an essay on the beginnings of anthropology in America, by A. Irving Hallowell. Evanston, Illinois, Row, Peterson, 1960. 930p.
illus. ports. facsims. bibliogs.   1245

de LAGUNA, FREDERICA. Some dynamic forces in Tlingit society.
Albuquerque, University of New Mexico Press, 1952. 12p. bibliog. ftntes.   1246

de LAGUNA, FREDERICA. The archaeology of Cook Inlet, Alaska;
by Frederica de Laguna ... with a chapter on skeletal material
by Bruno Oetteking ... Philadelphia, Published for the University Museum by University of Pennsylvania Press, 1934. 263p.
plans, diagr. pls.(some fold.), tables, bibliog.   1247

de LAGUNA, FREDERICA. The prehistory of northern North America
as seen from the Yukon. Menasha, Wisc., 1947. 360p. pls.
illus. appends. bibliog. (Memoirs of Society for American Archaeology, no. 3. Supplement to: American Antiquity, vol. 12,
no. 3, pt. 2, 1947)   1248

de Laguna, Frederica. SEE ALSO no. 566, Birket-Smith, K.
    Eyak Indians Copper River delta. 1938.

[Delaney, Arthur K.] SEE no. 31, Alaska Bar Assoc. and
    sketch of judiciary ... 1901.

DELANO, AMASA. A narrative of voyages in the northern and southern hemispheres ... Boston, 1817. 598p. ports. map. ANR.
Boston, 1818. 2d ed.   1249

Delano, Amasa. SEE ALSO no. 1004, Connolly, J. B. Master
    mariner ... 1943.

de la Pijardiere, Louis de LaCoeur. SEE no. 3986, Savvage, J.

de Launay, Cordier. SEE no. 2641, Launay de Valery, Cordier de.

DeLEEUW, ADELE. James Cook; a world explorer. Champaign, Illinois, Garrard Pub., 1963.   1250

deLesseps, Jean Baptiste Barthelemy.   [Alphabetical title guide
    to chronological entries]

Des Herrn von Lesseps. 1253.   Journal historique. 1251.
Herrn von Lesseps. 1254.   Travels Kamtschatka. 1252.
Hist. dagverhaal. 1255.   Voyage de. 1256.

deLESSEPS, JEAN BAPTISTE BARTHÉLEMY.   Journal historique du voyage de M. deLesseps ... employé dans l'éxpedition de M. le comte
de La Pérouse ... depuis l'instant où il a quitte les frégatees
francoises au port Saint-Pierre et Saint-Paul du Kamtschatka.
jusqu'a son arrivée en France, le 17 Octobre 1788 ... Paris, Imprimerie Royale, 1790.   2 vols. 280p. and 380p.   pl. maps.   1251

    TRANSLATIONS - Journal historique du voyage ... 1790,
    chronologically.

    Travels in Kamtschatka during the years 1787 and 1788.   Trans-
    lated from the French of M. deLesseps ... interpreter to the
    Count de La Pérouse, now engaged in a voyage round the world,
    by command of his most Christian Majesty.   London, J. John-
    son, 1790.   2 vols. 238p. and 408p. map.   1252

    Des Herrn von Lesseps ... reise von Kamtschatka, nach Frank-
    reich.   Aus dem franzosischen von Herrn Professor Villaume
    ... Riga und Leipzig, J. F. Hartknoch, 1791.   2 vols. in 1.
    map(fold.)   1253

    Herrn von Lesseps, gefahrten des grafen de La Pérouse, reise
    durch Kamtschatka und Siberien nach Frankreich.   Aus dem
    franzosischen ubersetzt.   Mit anmerikungen von Johann Rein-
    hold Forster.   Berlin, Vossiche Buchhandlung, 1791.   304p.
                                                                 1254

    Historische dagverhaal zijner reize, zeder thet verlaten van
    de Laperouse in de haven van St. Pieter naar het fr. ...
    Utrecht, 1792.   2 vols.   1255

    Voyage de M. De Lesseps du Kamtschatka en France.   Paris,
    Maurice Dreyfours, n. d. 248p.   1256

deLesseps, Jean Baptiste Barthélemy.   SEE ALSO nos.
    2613, La Pérouse, J. F. G. de.   Voyage ... 1798;
    2619, La Pérouse, J. F. G. de.   Voyage ... 1831.

DELISLE, JOSEPH NICOLAS.   Nouvelles cartes des découvertes de
l'Amiral de Fonte, et autres navigateurs Espagnols, Portugais,
Anglois, Hollandois, Francois & Russes, dans les Mers Septentrionales, avec leur explication;   qui comprend, l'histoire des
voyages, tant par terre que par mer, dans la partie Septentrionale de la terre, les routes de navigation, les extraits des
journaux de marine, les observations astronomiques, & tout ce
qui peut contribuer au progrès de la navigation, avec la

description des pays, l'histoire & les moeurs des habitans, le commerce que l'on y peut faire, &c. Par M. de l'Isle, Professeur de Mathematiques au College Royal ... Paris, 1753. 60p. (76p. in some copies) maps(incl. 2 fold.) ANR. Paris, 1754.1257

Delisle, Joseph Nicolas. SEE ALSO nos.
   714, Buache, P.   Cartes des nouvelles ... 1750;
   716, [Buache, P.   Explication ... 1752;
  1311, [Dobbs, A.] Letter from Russ. sea-officer ... 1754;
  2693, Lettre d'un officier de la marine russ. ... 1752.

DeLOACH, DANIEL BARTON. The salmon canning industry. Corvallis, Oregon State College Press, 1939. 118p. tables, graphs, diagrs. ftntes. (Monographs, Economic Studies, no. 1)   1258

DeLONG, EMMA. Explorer's wife. Introduction by Vilhjalmur Stefansson. N. Y., 1938. 252p.   1259

DeLong, Emma, edit. SEE ALSO no. 1260, DeLong, Geo. W.

DeLONG, GEORGE W. The voyage of the *Jeannette*; the ship and ice journals of George W. DeLong, Lieutenant-Commander, U. S. N. and Commander of the polar expedition of 1879-1881. Edited by his wife, Emma DeLong. Boston, Houghton Mifflin, 1883. 2 vols. 911p. fronts. ports. pls. maps(some fold.), append. index. ANR. London, K. Paul, 1883. 2 vols. illus. ANR. Boston, 1884. 1260

DeLong, George W. SEE ALSO nos.
  1173, Danenhower, J. W. Narrative ... "Jeannette." 1882;
  1259, DeLong, Emma. Explorer's wife. 1938;
  1444, Ellsberg, Edw. Cruise of *Jeannette*. 1949;
  1445, Ellsberg, Edw. Hell on ice ... 1938;
  1715, Gilder, W. H. Ice-pack ... *Jeannette* ... 1883;
  1716, Gilder, W. H. In Eis und Schnee ... 1884;
  1717, Gilder, W. H. Der Untergang ... 1922;
  1718, Gilder, W. H. Gibel' ėkspeditsiĭ *Zhanetty*. 1923;
  2129, History ... "Jeannette" ... 1882;
  3075, Melville, Geo. W. In Lena Delta ... 1885;
  3226, Muir, John. Cruise of *Corwin*. 1917;
  3295, Newcomb, R. L. Our lost explorers ... 1882;
  3540, Perry, R. *Jeannette* ... 1882;
  3677, Prentiss, H. M. Great polar current ... 1897;
  3950, Samoĭlovich, R. L. Put'k poliŭsu ... 1933;
  4880, Williams, H. L. History ... shipwreck ... 1882.

del Perugia, Paul. SEE no. 3544, Perugia, Paul del.

[de MARBAULT, M. ?] Essai sur le commerce de Russie, avec l'histoire de ses découvertes. Amsterdam, 1777. 300p. map (fold.)   1261

DeMENTE, BOYE. Once a fool. Phoenix, Arizona, by author, 1965. [Japan to Alaska in amphibious jeep]   1262

[Demeunier, Jean Nicolas, tr.]   SEE no. 1016, [Cook, Jas.]

Demeunier, Jean Nicolas, tr.   SEE no. 4640, Vancouver, Geo.

de Mirabeau, M.   SEE no. 3383, Official papers ... 1790.

de Navarette, Martin Fernandez.   SEE no. 3279,
     Navarette, Martin Fernandez de.

DENIS, FERDINAND JEAN.   Les Californies, l'Oregon et l'Amérique
russe.   Paris, Didot, 1849.   108p.   1263

DENISON, B. WEBSTER.   Alaska today.   Caldwell, Idaho, Caxton,
1949.   374p.   illus.   ports.   maps.   ANR. 1950.   2d ed.   374p.
illus. photos, maps, index.   1264

DENISON, MERRILL.   Klondike Mike;   an Alaskan odyssey.   N. Y.,
Wm. Morrow, 1943.   393p.   pls. endmaps.   ANR. Cleveland, World
Pub., 1945.   ANR. Seattle, L. O. Johnson, 1948.   393p.   illus.
ANR. Toronto, McClelland & Stewart, 1965.   1st paperback print.
393p.   no illus. (Canadian Best-Seller Library, no. 12)   ANR.
London, Jarrolds, n. d. 326p.   front. port. photos, facsims.
endmaps.   1265

DENISON, MURIEL.   Susannah, a little girl with the Mounties.
N. Y., Dodd Mead, 1941.   illus.   1266

DENISON, MURIEL.   Susannah of the Mounties.   N. Y., Random House,
1959.   1267

DENISON, MURIEL.   Susannah of the Yukon.   N. Y., Dodd Mead, 1937.
[c1937]   343p.   front. pls. illus. by Marguerite Bryan.   ANR.
N. Y., 1943.   1268

DENISON, MURIEL.   Susannah rides again.   N. Y., 1941.   1269

DENKSCHRIFTEN der russischen geographischen gessellschaft zu
St. Petersburg.   Weimar, 1849.   vol. 1 [only vol. pub.]   652p.
maps.   [Zagoskin and island off northwest coast]   1270

DENNIS, JAMES TEACKLE.   On the shores of an inland sea;   travels
in Alaska.   Philadelphia, Lippincott, 1895.   79p.   front. illus.
[Sitka by Inland Passage]   1271

Dennis, LaR. J., co-auth.   SEE no. 4342, Steward, A. N.

Dennis, Morgan, illus.   SEE no. 979, Collins, A. F.

de Novo y Colson, Pedro   SEE 3361-2, Novo y Colson, Pedro de.

Densmore, Frances.   SEE no. 2139, Hofmann, Chas.

DENTON, VERNON LLEWELLYN. The far west coast. Toronto, J. M.
Dent, 1924. 297p. illus. maps, bibliog. [reference to James
Cook, George Vancouver, Vitus Bering]   1272

D'ENTRECASTEAUX, A. R. J. B. Voyage de Entrecasteaux, envoye a
la récherche de La Perouse. Pub. par ordre de Sa Majeste l'empereur et roi, sous le ministere de S. E. le vice-admiral De-
cres, comte de l'empire. Rédigé par M. de Rossel ... Paris, Imprimerie imperiale, 1808. 2 vols. and atlas.   1273

D'Entrecasteaux, A. R. J. B. SEE ALSO nos.
     739, Burney, Jas. Memoir ... 1820;
     1234-6, deLabillardiere, J. J. H. Relation ... 1799.

de Poncins, Gontran. SEE no. 3638, Poncins, Gontran de Mon-
     taigne, Vicomte de.

Deputation of Metlakatla. n. d. SEE no. 930,
     Church Missionary Soc.

Derby day in Yukon ... [1910] SEE no. 5004, Yukon Bill.

de Rohan-Csermak, G. SEE Rohan-Csermak, G. de.

deROQUEFEUIL, CAMILLE. Journal d'un voyage autor du monde, pendant les années 1816, 1817, 1818 et 1819, par M. Camille deRoquefeuil. Paris, 1823. 2 vols. 344p. and 407p. maps. [for tr.
see nos. 1275-6]   1274

deROQUEFEUIL, CAMILLE. Reise um die welt in den jahren 1816 bis
1819. Aus dem franzosischen des Herrn Camille de Roquefeuil.
Jena, Bransche buchhandlung, 1823. 396p. [a tr. of no. 1274]
                                                           1275

deROQUEFEUIL, CAMILLE. Voyage round the world, between the
years 1816-19. London, Sir R. Phillips & Co., 1823. 112p. [a
tr. of no. 1274]   1276

DESCRIPTION OF CRUISE along Alaska coastline aboard the "Westward." no pl., n. d. illus. map.   1277

Descriptive booklet on Alaska Hist. Museum ... 1922. SEE
     no. 68, Alaska Historical Soc.

Descriptive of Fairbanks ... 1916. SEE
     no. 1515, Fairbanks Commercial Club.

Desgoffe, Claude, tr. SEE no. 563, Birket-Smith, K.

de Silva, Antonio Carlos Simoens. SEE no. 4158,
     Simoens de Silva, Antonio Carlos.

DESJARDINS, JOSEPH-ALPHONSE. En Alaska; deux mois sous la tente. Montreal, Imprimerie du Messager, 1930.   293p.   illus. ports. wrps.   1278

DESMOND, ALICE CURTIS.   The sea cats.   N. Y., Macmillan, 1944. 216p.   illus. endmaps.   [fict. acct. sealing and Pribilof Islands]   1279

DESMOND, ALICE CURTIS.   The talking tree.   N. Y., Macmillan, 1949. 177p. illus. by Ralph Ray.   1280

Destination Juneau. 1964. SEE no. 163, Alaskans United.

Dethridge, K. SEE no. 1788, Gould, M. M.

de Tinseau, Leon, tr. SEE no. 1177, Darling, E. B.

deVaugondy, Robert. SEE nos. 4660-2, Vaugondy, Robert de.

Develop Alaska dinner...1911. SEE no. 38, Alaska Bur., Seattle.

Development and resources southeast Alaska. 1923. SEE
    no. 2399, Juneau Empire Print.

De VIGNE, HARRY CARLOS. The time of my life; a frontier doctor in Alaska. Philadelphia, Lippincott, 1942. 336p. ANR. London, R. Hale, 1943. 243p. [autobiog.]   1281

De Vighne, Harry Carlos. SEE ALSO no. 4840,
    White, S. E. Pole star. 1935.

DEVINE, EDWARD JAMES.   A travers l'Amérique de terre-neuve a l'Alaska (impressions de deux ans de sejour sur la cote de Bering). Premiere traduction française. Abbeville, F. Paillart, Imprimeur, [1905 ?] 267p. pls. map(dble.) [mining, Nome and Kotzebue. SEE no. 1283 for tr.]   1282

DEVINE, EDWARD JAMES.   Across widest America; Newfoundland to Alaska with the impression of two years' sojourn on the Bering Coast. Montreal, The Canadian Messenger, 1905.   307p. front. (port.), pls. maps(fold.)   ANR. N. Y., Benziger Bros., 1906. [tr. of no. 1282]   1283

De WINDT, HARRY. From Paris to New York by land. N. Y., Frederick Warne & Co., 1901. ANR. London, G. Newnes, 1904. 311p. photos, maps. [via Russia, Siberia, Bering Strait, Alaska] 1284

De WINDT, HARRY. My restless life. London, Grant Richards, 1909.   1285

De WINDT, HARRY. Through the gold-fields of Alaska to Bering
Straits. N. Y., Harper, 1898. 314p. front. photos, paintings
by George E. Lyon, map(fold.), appends. errata slip, index. ANR.
London, Chatto & Windus, 1898. 312p. pls. ports. maps. ANR.
London, Chatto & Windus, 1899. new ed.   1286

D'WOLF, JOHN. A voyage to the North Pacific and a journey
through Siberia, more than half a century ago. By Captain John
D'Wolf. Cambridge, Mass., Welch, Bigelow & Co., Printers to the
University, 1861. 147p. ed. ltd. to 100 copies. ANR. Fairfield, Washington, Ye Galleon Press, 1968. ltd. numbered ed. of
600 copies. illus. port. map. [facsim. of 1861 ed. enl. format]
                                                             1287
D'Wolf, John. SEE ALSO no. 3243, Munro, W. H.

de YBARRA Y BERGE, JAVIER. De California a Alaska; historia de
un descubrimiento. Madrid, Graficas Uguinal, 1945. 188p. maps
(incl. 1 fold.) (Instituto de Estudios Politicos. Coleccion
Espana, ante el mundo)   1288

Dezhnev, Semen. SEE nos.
    495, Belov, Mikhail. Semen Dezhnev. 1955;
    3949, Samoĭlov, V. A. Semen Dezhnev i ego vremiĩa. 1945.

Dhu, Oscar. SEE no. 2912, Mackay, Angus.

D'ĩakonov, M. A., edit. SEE no. 3744, Rasmussen, K.

DICE, LEE RAYMOND. The land vertebrate associations of interior
Alaska. Ann Arbor, University of Michigan, 1920. 24p. pls.
map(sketch) (Museum of Zoology Occasional Papers no. 85)   1289

DICK, J. W. Down North. Alberta, Canada, by author, 1944. 2d
enl. ed. [poetry about Alaska Highway]   1290

Dickinson, Geo. W. SEE no. 43, Alaska Central Ry.

DICKINSON, JACOB McG. The Alaskan Boundary case; a paper read
before the American Bar Association at the 27th annual meeting,
St. Louis, Missouri, September 26, 1904. St. Louis, 1904. 32p.
[also in: Transactions American Bar Assoc. 1904. pp.335-66]1291

Didier Robert de Vaugondy. SEE no. 4660, Vaugondy, Didier
    Robert de.

DIECK, HERMAN, edit. The marvellous wonders of the Polar world.
Being a complete and authentic history of voyages and discoveries in the Polar regions, including the expeditions of Sir
John Franklin, Lieut. DeHaven, Dr. Kane, Dr. Hayes, Admiral Rogers ... cruise and loss of the *Jeannette* ... from the narratives
of Lieut. Greely, Commander Schley, Lieut. Danenhower, and the
other gallant heroes ... The whole carefully edited by Herman
Dieck ... profusely illustrated ... original sketches and photo-

graphs. Dayton, Ohio, Goodwyn & Worman, 1885. 527p.(200)p.
illus. maps. ANR. Philadelphia, National Pub. Co., 1885. 527p.
(200)p. illus. maps.   1292

Die glaubwürdigkeit von Maldonados ... 1712. SEE no. 2577,
     L., B. V.

Dieīaniīa sviātykh apostol ... 1902. SEE no. 211,
     Amerikanskiī Pravoslavnyi Viestnik.

DIETZ, ARTHUR ARNOLD. Mad rush for gold in the frozen north.
L. A., Times-Mirror Printing & Binding House, 1914. 281p. front.
(ports.), photos by W. A. Sharp, pls. ports.   1293

Diezmann, A., tr. SEE no. 1373, Dumont d'Urville, J. S. C.

DIGBY, GEORGE BASSETT. The mammoth and mammoth hunting in
northeast Siberia. London, H. F. & G. Witherby, 1926. photos,
map.   1294

Dill, R. F., co-auth. SEE no. 4110, Shepard, F. P.

DILL, W. S. The lond day; reminiscences of the Yukon. Ottawa,
Graphic, 1926., 232p. illus.   1295

DILLON, PETER. Narrative and successful results of a voyage in
the South Seas performed by order of the government of British
India, to ascertain the actual fate of La Perouse's expedition.
By Chevalier Captain P. Dillon. London, Hurst, Chance & Co.,
1829. 2 vols. front. pl. map(fold.)   1296

DILLON, PETER. Voyage aux îles de la mer du Sud, en 1827 et
1828, et relation de la découverte du sort de La Pérouse. Dédie
au Roi par le Capitaine Peter Dillon, ex-commandant du vaisseau
de la compagnie anglaise des Indes-Orientales, *La Résearche*.
Paris, Pillet Aîne, 1830. 2 vols. 294p. 361p. plus. 18p. 1297

DILLON, WALLACE. Salmon. Chicago, Follett Pub. Co., 1962. 1298

Dimond, Anthony. SEE no. 2080, Herron, E. A.

di Savoia, H. R. H. Prince Luigi Amadeo, Duke of the Abruzzi.
     SEE no. 1226, deFillippi, Filippo.

Disney, Walt. SEE nos.
     657, Bridges, Wm. ... animal adventures ... ice ... 1963;
     2800, Louvain, R. White wilderness ... 1958;
     4756, Watson, J. W. ... Seal Island. 1958.

DIVEN, ROBERT JOSEPH. Rowdy. N. Y., Century, 1927. 220p.
front. pls. illus. by Charles Livingston Bull.   1299

DIVIN, V. A. A. I. Chirikov, vydaiūshchiĭsīa russkiĭ moreplava-tel' i uchenyĭ; k 250-letiūi so dnīā rozhdeniīā. [TITLE TR. A. I. Chirikov, an outstanding Russian navigator and scientist; on the 250th anniversary of his birthday.] Moskva, Izd-vo "Znanie", 1953. 32p. map, bibliog. (Vsesoiūznoe obshchestvo po raznaniĭ, ser. 3, no. 64) [rev. ed. of no. 1301]   1300

DIVIN, V. A. A. I. Chirikov, zamechatel'nyĭ russkiĭ moreplava-tel' i uchenyĭ. Stenogramma publichnoĭ lektsiĭ prochitanoĭ v tsentral'nom lektorii obshchestva v Moskve. [TITLE TR. A. I. Chirikov, a remarkable Russian navigator and scientist. Steno-graph of a public lecture, delivered in the Central Hall of the Society in Moscow] Moskva, Izd-vo "Pravda", 1950. 30p. map, bibliog. ftntes. [Society for Dissemination of Political and Sci-entific Knowledge] ANR. See no. 1300.   1301

DIVIN, V. A. Velikiĭ russkiĭ moreplavatel' A. I. Chirikov. [TITLE TR. A great Russian navigator, A. I. Chirikov] Moskva, Gos. izd-vo Geogr. lit-ry, 1953. 277p. maps(6 fold.), bibliog.   1302

DIVIN, V. A. V. M. Golovnin. Pod red. M. S. Bodnarskogo. [TITLE TR. V. M. Golovnin. M. S. Bodnarskiĭ, editor] Moskva, Gos. izd-vo geogr. literatury, 1951. 39p. illus.port.map. 1303

DIXON, FRANKLIN W. Mystery at Devil's Paw. N. Y., Grosset & Dunlap, 1959. illus.   1304

DIXON, FRANKLIN W. Through the air to Alaska; or, Ted Scott's search in Nugget Valley. N. Y., Grosset & Dunlap, 1930. 216p.   1305

Dixon, George. [Alphabetical title guide to chronological entries]

Der Kapitaine Portlock's. 1310.   Voyage autour. 1309.
Further remarks. 1306.   Voyage round. 1308.
Remarks. 1307.

DIXON, GEORGE. Further remarks on the voyages of John Mears, Esq., in which several important facts misrepresented in the said voyages relative to geography and commerce are fully sub-stantiated, to which is added a letter from Captain Duncan con-taining a decisive refutation of several unfounded assertions of Mr. Mears and a final reply to his answer. London, Stockdale, 1791. 80p.   1306

DIXON, GEORGE. Remarks on the voyages of John Meares, Esq. in a letter to that gentleman. London, Stockdale, 1790. 37p.   1307

DIXON, GEORGE. A voyage round the world; but more particularly to the north west coast of America; performed in 1785, 1786, 1787, and 1788, in the *King George* and *Queen Charlotte*, Captains Portlock and Dixon. Dedicated, by permission, to Sir Joseph Banks, Bart. By Captain George Dixon. London, Geo. Goulding, 1789. i-xxix,1-352,353-360,1-47p. pls.(some fold.), maps(some fold.), appends. ANR. London, Geo. Goulding, 1789. 2d ed. ANR. Amsterdam, N. Israel and N. Y., Da Capo Press, 1968. (Bibliotheca Australiana, no.37) facsim. ed. [contains a series of letters written by "W. B." i.e. William Beresford, supercargo on *Queen Charlotte*, edited by Dixon]   1308

TRANSLATIONS - Voyage round world ... 1789, chronologically.

Voyage autour du monde, et principalement a la cote nord-
   ouest de l'Amerique, Fait en 1785, 1786, 1787, et 1788; A
   bord du *King-George* et de la *Queen-Charlotte*, par les Capi-
   taines Portlock et Dixon. Dedie, par permission, a Sir Joseph Banks ... Traduit de l'Anglois, par M. Le Bas. Paris,
   Chez Maradon, 1789. 2 vols. 581p. 292p. plus. 46p. pls.
   (some fold.), maps(fold.), append.   1309

Der Kapitaine Portlock's und Dixon's Reise um die Welt besonders nach der Nordwestlichen Küste von Amerika währends der
   Jahre 1785 bis 1788 in den Schiffen *King George* and *Queen
   Charlotte*, Herausgegeben von dem Kapitaine Georg Dixon. Aus
   dem Englischen übersetzt und mit Anmerkungen erläutert von
   Johann Reinhold Forster, der Rechte, Medicin, und Weltweish-
   eit Doktor, Professor der Naturgeschichte und Mineralogie auf
   der Königl. Preusz, Frederichs-Universität, Mitglied der Königl. Akademie der höheren und schönen Wissenschaften zu
   Berlin. Mit vielen Kupfern und einer Landkarte. Berlin,
   Christian Friedrich Bosz und Sohn, 1790. 4,11,i-xxii,1-314p.
   pls. map.   1310

Dixon, George. SEE ALSO nos.
   1606-07, Forster, J. G. A. Geschichte ... 1791 and 1792;
   2202, Howay, F. W., edit. Dixon-Mears controversy. 1929;
   3052, Mears, J. Answer to Mr. Geo. Dixon ... 1791;
   3648, Portlock, N. Voyage ... majesty. [1789];
   3649, [Portlock, N.] Voyage ... Soc. Fur Trade. 1789;
   3650, [Portlock, N.] Abridgement ... 1789;
   3651, [Portlock, N.] Nathaniel Portlock's ... 1796;
   3652, [Portlock, N.] Reis naar de nord-west kust ... 1795;
   3653, [Portlock, N.] Voyage ... 1803;
   3780 Reisen nach nordwestlichen Kuste ... 1795.

[DOBBS, ARTHUR] A letter from a Russian sea-officer, to a per-
son of distinction at the court of St. Petersburgh; containing
his remarks upon Mr. de l'Isle's chart and memoir, relative to
the new discoveries northward and eastward from Kamtschatka. By
N. N. Together with some observations on that letter ... to
which is added Mr. de l'Isles's explanatory memoir on his chart

published at Paris, and now translated from the original French.
London, Printed for A. Linde and sold by J. Robinson, 1754. 83p.
1311

DOBBS, ARTHUR. An account of the countries adjoining to Hudson's
Bay, in the north-west part of America; containing a description of their lakes and rivers, the nature of the soil and climates, and their methods of commerce, &c. shewing the benefit to
be made by settling colonies, and opening a trade in these parts;
whereby the French will be deprived in a great measure of their
traffick in furs, and the communication between Canada and Mississippi be cut off. With an abstract of Captain Middleton's
journal, and observations upon his behaviour during his voyage,
and since his return. To which are added, 1. A letter from
Bartholomew de Fonte, giving an account of his voyage from Lima
to Peru, to prevent, or seize upon any ships that should attempt
to find a north-west passage to the South Sea. 11. An abstract
of all the discoveries which have been publish'd of the islands
and countries in and adjoining to the great western ocean between America, India, and China, &c 111. The Hudson's Bay Company's charter. IV. The standard of trade in those parts of
America; with an account of the exports and profits made annually by the Hudson's Bay Company. V. Vocabularies of the languages of several Indian nations adjoining to Hudson's Bay. The
whole intended to show the great probability of a northwest passage. London, J. Robinson, 1744. front. (fold. map) ANR. N.Y.,
Johnson Reprint Corp., and Yorkshire, Eng., S. R. Publishers
Ltd., 1967. (3)211(3)p. front.(fold. map), errata. [facsim.
of 1744 ed.] 1312

Dobbs, Arthur. SEE ALSO no. 2693, Lettre d'un officier de
la marine russienne ... 1752.

DOBBS' ALASKA MOVING PICTURE CO., INC. Initial Performance,
R. C. Button, Manager. Friday, Dec. 4, at the Auditorium. Mo-
ving pictures, vaudeville and sketches from "San Toy" Musical
Director, Mr. Claude H. Myrick. Stage Director, J. B. M'Keon.
Fairbanks, Press of Fairbanks Daily News, n. d. 16p. 1313

DOBROVOL'SKIĬ, A. D. Plavaniia F. P. Litke; pod red N. N. Zubova. [TITLE TR. The voyage of F. P. Litke; edited by N. N.
Zubov] Moskva, Gos. izd-vo geogr. lit-ry, 1948. 1314

Dobson, F. W., co-auth. SEE no. 1590, Fofonoff, N. P.

DOCKSTADER, FREDERICK J. Indian art in America; the arts and
crafts of the North American Indian. London, Studio Books,
1960. ANR. Greenwich, Conn. and N. Y., Graphic Society, 1961.
224p. pls.(incl. some col.), map, bibliog. index. ANR. 1966.
2d ed. rev. 1315

DODGE, ERNEST STANLEY and GERARD WARD, edits. American activities in the Central Pacific, 1790-1890; a history, geography
and ethnography of the Pacific Islands. Introduction by Ernest
S. Dodge. Ridgewood, N. J., Gregg Press, 1966. 8 vols. illus.
maps, index.   1316

DODGE, ERNEST STANLEY. Northwest by sea. N. Y. and Cambridge,
Oxford University Press, 1961. 348p. illus. maps, bibliog. 1317

Dodge, Ernest Stanley, co-edit. SEE ALSO nos.
     1900, Hale, H. E. Ethnog. ... 1966;
     2561, Krusenstern, A. J. von. Voyage ... 1967;
     2600, Langsdorff, G. H. von. Voyages ... 1967;
     2724, Lisianskiĭ, I. F. Voyage ... 1967.

DODGE, HOWARD LEWIS. Attraction of the compass; or, the blonde
Eskimo, a romance of the north based upon facts of a personal
experience. Long Beach, California, Seaside Printing Co., 1916.
243p. front.(port.), pls.   1318

Dodge, Norman L., edit. SEE no. 2353, Jewitt, J. R.

DODGE, WILLIAM SUMNER. Oration by Honorable William Sumner
Dodge delivered at Sitka, Alaska, Saturday, July 4th, 1868.
"Liberty, her struggles, perils and triumphs." S. F., Alta
California Printing House, 1868. 30p.   1319

DODIMEAD, ALLAN J. Atlas of oceanographic data, North Pacific
survey, Jan. 12-Feb. 10, 1960. Nanaimo, B. C., Fisheries Research Board of Canada, 1960. 4p.(text), 45p.(maps, diagrs.),
bibliog. (Ms. Rpt. Ser., Oceanographic and Limnological, no.
69, June 7, 1960) [Gulf of Alaska]   1320

DODIMEAD, ALLAN J. and F. FAVORITE. Oceanographic atlas of the
Pacific subarctic region, 1958. Ottawa, Fisheries Research Board
of Canada, 1961. 6p. charts, graphs, table, bibliog. (Ms. Rpt.
Ser., Oceanographic and Limnological, no. 92, April 10, 1961)
                                                                1321

DODIMEAD, ALLAN J. and others. Oceanographic data record, North
Pacific surveys, July 10 to Sept. 6, 1960. Ottawa, Fisheries
Research Board of Canada, 1960. 329p. illus. map, graphs,
tables, bibliog. (Ms. Rpt. Ser., Oceanographic and Limnological,
no. 82, October 12, 1960)   1322

DODIMEAD, ALLAN J. and others. Oceanographic data record, North
Pacific surveys, May 16 to July 1, 1961. Ottawa, Fisheries Research Board of Canada, 1961. 337p. illus. maps, graphs, tables, bibliog. (Ms. Rpt. Ser., Oceanographic and Limnological,
no. 101, Sept. 20, 1961)   1323

DODIMEAD, ALLAN J. and others.   Oceanographic data record, North
Pacific survey, May 23 to July 5, 1962.   Ottawa, Fisheries Research Board of Canada, 1962.   384p.   illus. map, graphs, tables,
bibliog.   (Ms. Rpt. Ser., Oceanographic and Limnological, no.
138)   1324

DODIMEAD, ALLAN J.   Report on oceanographic investigations in
the northeast Pacific Ocean during Aug. 1956, Feb. 1957, and
Aug. 1957.   Ottawa, Fisheries Research Board of Canada, 1958.
14p. plus 35p. maps and graphs, bibliog.   (Ms. Rpt. Ser., Oceanographic and Limnological, no. 20, July 31, 1958)   1325

Doklad komiteta ... russkikh amerikanskikh koloniĭ.   1863-64.
    SEE no. 4619, U. S. S. R. Komitet ob Ustroistvie ...

DOLAN, EDWARD F., r.   White battleground;   the conquest of the
Arctic, with maps by James MacDonald.   N. Y., Dodd Mead, 1961.
303p.   maps.   1326

DOLCH, EDWARD W.   Stories from Alaska.   Champaign, Illinois,
Dolch Books, Garrard Pub., 1961.   (Folklore of the World Series)
                                                                   1327

DOLE, NATHAN HASKELL and G. WALDO BROWNE, edits.   Alaska; by the
Honorable Walter E. Clarke [sic]   Boston, Marshall Jones Co.,
1910.   pls.(incl. front., some col.), photos, map(fold.col.)
(Vol. 9 of: The new America and the far east, pp.1477-1684)1328

[DOLE, NATHAN HASKELL]   Our northern domain;   Alaska, picturesque, historic and commercial.   Boston, Dana Estes & Co.,
237p.   front. pls.   1329

DONAHUE, RALPH J.   Ready on the right.   Kansas City, 1946.
194p.   illus. [autobiog. Seabee in Aleutian Island]   1330

Donan, Patrick.   SEE no. 3447, Pacific Coast Steamship Co.

DONNELLY, ELEANOR CECILIA.   A Klondike picnic;   the story of a
day, with genuine letters from two gold-seekers in Alaska. N.Y.,
Benziger Bros., 1898.   160p.   1331

[Donnett, Jas. J. L., edit.]   SEE no. 301, Arctic Misc. ...1851.

DONSKOI, VLADIMIR.   Ekuiatle shkaljtnyk chaku ka lsa alvuskuu,
Tlingit-khenakh ka Anushi-khenakh kakhavuzukh ka chuchjiaiuta-
kakhou.   Evusyny Shitka Inkhuatliaatych Vladimir Donskoi ka
Tlingit Kakhuakhchi-tyn Mikhail Sinkiellj.   [TITLE TR.   Short
history of the Old and New Testaments by questions and answers,
in the Russian and Tlingit languages, compiled by Sitka priest
Vladimir Donskoi with the assistance of Tlingit interpretator,
Michael Sinkiel]   N. Y., Tip. Amerikanskiĭ Pravda Viestnik,
1901.   215p.   1332

Donskoi, Vladimir, tr. SEE ALSO no. 3309,
   Nikolai, Bishop (of the Aleutians and Alaska)

Dorr, R. L. (Childe). SEE no. 2493, Knapp, F. and R. L. Childe.

DORRANCE, JAMES FRENCH. The golden Alaskan. N. Y., Macaulay
Co., 1931. 311p.   1333

Douglas, David. SEE no. 2171, Hooker, Wm. J.

Douglas, Dick, jr. SEE nos. 1337-8, Douglas, Robert D.

DOUGLAS, FREDERIC HUNTINGTON and RÉNE D'HARNONCOURT. Indian art
of the United States. N. Y., Museum of Modern Art, 1941. 1st
ed. 219p. illus. bibliog. ANR. 1948. 2d rev. ed. 204p.
illus. pls.(some col.), bibliog.   1334

Douglas, Frederic Huntington, co-auth. SEE ALSO Jeancon, J. A.

DOUGLAS, MARY. The frozen north; the story of north polar expeditions with Nordenskiöld, Nares, Greely, DeLong, Nansen and
Jackson-Harmsworth. Boston, DeWolfe, Fiske, n. d. 176p. pls.
(col.), maps. (The Favorite Library)   1335

DOUGLAS, ROBERT D. A boy scout in the grizzly country. By Dick
Douglas, jr. N. Y., Putnam, 1929. 181p. front. pls. photos,
ports.   1336

DOUGLAS, ROBERT D. In the land of the thunder mountains; adventures with Father Hubbard among the volcanoes of Alaska.
N. Y., Brewer, Warren and Putnam, 1932. 160p. pls. ports.
map. [Boy Scouts, Alaska Peninsula]   1337

Douglas, Wm. SEE no. 3057, Meares, J.

DOVE, WALTER E. A progress report on studies of the parasites
of reindeer. [Golovnin, Alaska, 1929 ?] 18 ℓ 50 photos. 1338

DOW, PETER. Alaska; America's northern wonderland. Hot
Springs, Arkansas, by author, 1927. 128p. front. pls.(incl. 1
col.), port.   1339

DOWNES, ANNE MILLER. Natalia, a novel of old Alaska. Philadelphia, Lippincott, 1960. 1st ed. 286p.   1340

Downey, R. A., edit. SEE no. 1639, Frazer, Jas. G.

DOWNIE, WILLIAM. Hunting for gold; reminiscences of personal
experience and research in the early days of the Pacific coast
from Alaska to Panama. S. F., Press of California Pub. Co.,
1893. 407p. front.   1341

DOWNING AND CLARKE, Pub. Pocket dictionary of the Chinook jargon, the Indian trading language of Alaska, the Northwest Territory, and the northern Pacific coast. S. F., 1898. 32p.
1342

DOZOIS, L. O. R. Precise leveling in British Columbia and Yukon Territory. Ottawa, King's Printer, 1951. rev. and enl. ed. 238p. diagrs. table. (Canada. Geodetic Survey Pub. no. 24) [incls. 24 miles of Alaska Highway in Alaska, as well as 820 miles in Yukon Territory]
1343

[DRAGE, THEODORE SWAINE] An account of a voyage for the disco- very of a north-west passage by Hudson's Streights, to the wes- tern and southern ocean of America. Performed in the year 1746 and 1747 in the ship *California*, Capt. Francis Smith, Commander. By the clerk of the *California*. Adorned with cuts and maps. London, Printed; And Sold by Mr. Jolliffe, in St. James's-street; Mr. Corbett, in Fleet-street; and Mr. Clarke, under the Royal Exchange, [1748] 2 vols. vii,237p.(vol. 1); var. p.(vol.2) pls. facsims. maps(fold.) [author sometimes known as Charles Swaine, or Theodore Swindrage]
1344

[Drage, Theodore Swaine ?] SEE ALSO no. 2336, [Jefferys, Thos.?] Great probability n. w. passage ... 1768.

DRAKE, MARIE. Alaskana; our last frontier, glimpses of its co- lorful yesterdays and highlights of today. Juneau, by author, printed by Alaska Daily Empire, 1938. 48p. illus. photos, map, bibliog.
1345

DREANY, E. JOSEPH. A Maxton book about Alaska. N. Y., Maxton, 1959. n.p. illus. (Maxton Books for Young People, no. 49) 1346

DREANY, E. JOSEPH. Life in the Arctic. N. Y., Maxton, 1960. 25p. illus.(some col.)
1347

Dreany, E. Joseph, illus. SEE ALSO nos.
    2830, McBride, Jas. L. Smoky Valley claim. 1948;
    4739, Ware, K. Let's read ... 1960.

DREBERT, FERDINAND. A brief history of Bethel, Alaska. Bethel, [ca 1942] ANR. L. A., University of California, 1963. (Depart- ment of Anthropology) [reproduced from original]
1348

DREBERT, FERDINAND. Alaska missionary, a testimony to God's faithfulness, and to the power of the Gospel. Bethlehem, Pen- sylvania, Moravian Book Shop, Distributor, 1959. 165p. pls. [Moravian missionary to Eskimos of lower Kuskokwim River, 1912 to 1954]
1349

Dredging for gold ... [1897 ?]   SEE no. 5012, [Yukon Trading, Mining & Exploration Co.]

DRIGGS, JOHN BEACH. Short sketches from oldest America. Philadelphia, Geo. W. Jacobs, 1905. 163p. front. pls. [Pt. Hope Eskimos]   1350

Driggs, John Beach. SEE ALSO no. 1103, Cox, Mary. John Driggs among Eskimos. 1956.

DRISCOLL, JOSEPH. War discovers Alaska. Philadelphia, Lippincott, 1943. 1st ed. 351p. front. pls. endmaps.   1351

Dritte Entdeckungs-Reise ... 1787. SEE no. 1028, [Cook, Jas.]

Dritte und letzte Reise ... 1787. SEE no. 1029, [Cook, Jas.]

DRIVER, HAROLD E. Indians of North America. Chicago, University of Chicago Press, 1961. 685p. illus. drawings, photos, maps, bibliog. [Arctic to Panama]   1352

DRIVER, HAROLD E. The contribution of A. L. Kroeber to culture area theory and practice. Baltimore, Waverly Press, 1962. 28p. bibliog. (Indiana University Pub. in Anthropology and Linguistics, Memoir no. 18)   1353

DROONBERG, EMIL. Das Siwash-madchen; Erzahlungen aus dem Kanadischen Felsengebirge und von der Kuste des Stillen Ozeans. Leipzig, Wilhelm Goldmann Verlag, 1925. 119p. (4.Aufl.)   1354

DROONBERG, EMIL. Die Goldwascher am Klondike; Roman aus der Zeit der grossen Goldfunde in Kanada und Alaska. Leipzig, Wilhelm Goldmann Verlag, 1925. 284p. (13.-14.Aufl.)   1355

DRUCKER, PHILIP. Cultures of the north Pacific coast. S. F., Chandler Pub. Co., 1965. 243p. illus.(some col.), maps, bibliog. (Chandler Pub. in Anthropology and Sociology)   1356

DRUCKER, PHILIP. Indians of the northwest coast. N. Y., McGraw-Hill, 1955. 208p. illus. map, bibliog. (American Museum of Natural History Anthropology Handbook no. 10) ANR. Garden City, N. Y., Doubleday, 1963. 224p. photos, drawings, maps, bibliog. index. (American Museum Science Books, the Natural History Press)   1357

DRUMHELLER, EHRLICHMAN CO., Seattle. A review of the salmon industry with particular reference to Pacific American fisheries. Seattle, Drumheller, Ehrlichman and White, 1935. 27p. illus. tables, diagrs.   1358

DRURY, W. H., jr. Bog flats and physiographic processes in the upper Kuskokwim River region, Alaska. Cambridge, Harvard University Press, 1956. 130p. (Contrib. Gray Herbarium, no. 178)1359

DUANE, RUSSELL. The case of the "Sayward," being the law oration delivered at the Commencement exercises of the University of Pennsylvania, in the Academy of Music, Philadelphia, June 11, 1891. Philadelphia, T. & J. W. Johnson, 1891. 14p. [Bering Sea arbitration]   1360

DUDLEY, BRONSON. The story of Alaska. Pictures by Charles Waterhouse. N. Y., Grosset & Dunlap, [1968] 61p. illus.(col.), index. (The American Nation Series)   1361

DUFLOT de MOFRAS, EUGENE. Duflot de Mofras's travels on the Pacific Coast, translated, edited and annotated by Marguerite Eyer Wilbur; foreword by Dr. Frederick Webb Hodge. Santa Ana, Calif., Fine Arts Press, 1937. 2 vols. 273p. and 352p. illus. pls. maps(incl. 1 fold.), facsim. bibliog. index. [tr. of no. 1363]   1362

DUFLOT de MOFRAS, EUGENE. Exploration du Territoire de l'Orégon, des Californies et de la Mer Vermeille, éxecutée pendant les années 1840, 1841 et 1842, par M. Duflot de Mofras, Attaché a la Légation de France à Mexico; ouvrage publié par ordre du Roi, sous les auspices de M. le Maréchal Soult, Duc de Dalmatie, Président du Conseil, et de M. le Ministre des Affaires Étrangères. Paris, Arthur Bertrand, Editeur. Typographie de Firmin Didot Frères, Imprimeurs, 1844. 1st ed. 4 vols. plus atlas. paged cont. fronts. pls. maps(incl. 1 fold. at back of atlas) ANR. 1844. 2 vols. with atlas. pls. maps, tables. ANR. 2 vols. in 4 without atlas. ANR. 3 vols. [for edited, annotated tr. see no. 1362]   1363

DUFRESNE, FRANK. Alaska's animals and fishes. Illustrated by Bob Hines. W. Hartford, Vt., Countryman Press, 1946. ed. ltd. to 475 copies signed by author and artist. 297p. front.(col.), pls.(col.), endmaps. ANR. N. Y., A. S. Barnes, 1946. trade ed. 297p. pls.(col.), drawings, endmaps. illus. by Bob Hines. [by former Director of Alaska Game Commission]   1364

DUFRESNE, FRANK. My way was north, an Alaskan autobiography. Introduction by Corey Ford. With drawings by Rachel S. Horne. N. Y., Holt, Rinehart & Winston, 1966. 1st ed. 274p. illus.
                                                              1365

DUFRESNE, FRANK. No room for bears. With drawings by Rachel S. Horne. N. Y., Holt, Rinehart & Winston, 1965. 252p. illus.
                                                              1366

Dufresne, Frank. SEE ALSO nos.
     644, Brandt, H. Alaska bird trails. 1943;
     3288, Nelson, K. and C. Ford. Daughter of gold rush. 1958.

DUGDALE, VERA. Album of North American animals. Illustrated by Clark Bronson. Chicago, Rand McNally, 1966. 1st print. 112p. drawings(col.), sketches, range maps, index.   1367

DUGRE, ADELARD. Les Oblates dans l'extreme Nord. [TITLE TR.
The Oblates in the far North] Montreal, 1922. 16p. (Oeuvre
des Tracts, no. 41) [Yukon and MacKenzie districts]   1368

DUHALDE, JEAN-BAPTISTE. Description géographique, historique,
chronologique, politique, et physique de la Chine et de la Tar-
tarie Chinoise. Paris, Lemercier, 1735. 4 vols. 592p., 726p.,
567p. and 520p. pls. maps. ANR. La Hague, 1736. 4 vols. 488p.,
834p., 652p. and 606p. pls. maps. [with atlas entitled "Nouvel
atlas de la Chine de la Tarterie chinoise, et du Thibet," by
J. J. B. d'Anville. La Hague, 1737] [Bering's first voyage and
map. For tr. see no. 1370]   1369

DUHALDE, JEAN-BAPTISTE. The general history of China. Con-
taining a geographical, historical, chronological, political,
and physical description of the empire of China, Chinese-Tartary,
Corea, and Thibet. Including an exact and particular account of
their customs, manners, ceremonies, religion, arts, and sciences.
Done from the French of J. DuHalde by Richard Brookes. London,
J. Watts, 1736. 4 vols. ANR. London, J. Watts, 1741. 4 vols.
ANR. [in German] Rostock, 1747-56. 5 vols. [tr. of no. 1369]
                                                                1370

Duhalde, Jean-Baptiste. Nouvel atlas ... 1737. SEE no. 1369.

Dumas, C. F. G., tr. SEE no. 3235, Müller, G. F.

Dumitrashko, N. V., co-edit. SEE no. 2531, Krasheninnikov, S.P.

Dumond, D. E., co-auth. SEE no. 1118, Cressman, L. S.

Dumont d'Urville, Jules Sébastien César. [Alphabetical title
     guide to chronological entries]

     Malerische. 1373.   Voyage de découverte. 1371.
     Puteshestvie. 1375.   Voyage pittoresque. 1372.
     Viaggio. 1374.

DUMONT d'URVILLE, JULES SÉBASTIEN CÉSAR. Voyage de découvertes
autour du monde et la recherche de La Pérouse par M. J. Dumont
d'Urville, Capitaine de vaisseau, éxecute ... sur la corvette
L'Astrolabe, pendant les années 1826, 1827, 1828 et 1829. Histoire du voyage. Paris, Roret, 1832. 5 vols. 528p., 632p.,
746p., 760p. and 716p. [separate atlas. Paris, Tastin, 1833.
charts, pls.]   1371

DUMONT d'URVILLE, JULES SÉBASTIEN CÉSAR. Voyage pittoresque
autour du monde. Resume general des voyages de découvertes de
... Cook, Krusenstern, Kotzebue, La Pérouse, Lutke, &c. Paris,
L. Tenre, 1834-5. 2 vols. 576p., 584p. pls. maps. ANR.
Paris, 1848. 2 vols.   1372

DUMONT d'URVILLE, JULES SÉBASTIEN CÉSAR. TRANSLATIONS - Voyage
   pittoresque ... 1834-35, chronologically.

   Malerische Reise um die Welt. Eine geordnate zusammenstellung
   des Wissenwerthesten von dem Entdeckungsreisen eines ...
   Krusenstern, &c. In's Deutsche ubertragen von A. Diezmann.
   Leipzig, 1835-37. 2 vols.   1373

   Viaggio pittoresco intorno al mondo ossia riassunto generale
   de'viaggi e scoperte di ... Krusenstern ... Tr. italiana del
   sig. L. L. Venice, 1841. 2 vols.   1374

   Puteshestvie vokrug svieta, sostavlennoe iz puteshestviĭ Ma-
   gellana ... Kruzensterna, Golovnina, Kotsebu, i dr. Izdanno
   pod rukovodstvom Diumont Diurvilia. Perevedena A. Bashut-
   skim. [TITLE TR. A voyage round the world, founded on the
   voyages of Magellan and others, under the direction of Dumont d'Urville. Tr. by A. Bashutski] St. Petersburg, 1843.
   4 vols. 1265p.   1375

Dun Scotus. SEE no. 1204, Davis, M. L.

DUNBAR, C. O. Parafusulina from the Permian of Alaska. N. Y.,
American Museum of Natural History, 1946. 4p. pl. (Novitates,
no. 1325. Sept. 16, 1946)   1376

DUNBAR, M. J. Preliminary report on the Bering Strait scheme.
Ottawa, Northern Coordination and Research Centre, Department of
Northern Affairs and Natural Resources, 1960. 17p. maps.
(NCRC-60-1)   1377

DUNBAR, M. J. Second report on the Bering Strait dam. Ottawa,
Northern Coordination and Research Centre, Department of Northern
Affairs and Natural Resources, 1962. 23 ℓ maps, table.
(NCRC-62-6)   1378

DUNCAN, SINCLAIR THOMSON. From Shetland to British Columbia,
Alaska and the United States; being a journal of travels, with
narrative of return journey after three years' exploration.
Lerwick, Scotland, Charles J. Duncan, 1911. 282p. front.(port.)
                                                               1379

DUNCAN, WILLIAM. Appeal by William Duncan to the United States
Commissioner of Indian Affairs for lands and liberty for the
Metlakahtla Indians of British Columbia. Washington, D. C.,
Dec. 10, 1886. 6p. ["Old" Metlakatla, B. C., Canada, up to
1887. Church moved to "New" Metlakatla, Annette Island, Alaska
in 1887]   1380

DUNCAN, WILLIAM. Appendix a shimalgiagum liami, hymns in Zimshian for the use of the Church at Metlakahtla. Metlakahtla,
B. C., n. d. (9)p. [prior to 1887]   1381

[DUNCAN, WILLIAM] Metlahkatlah; ten years' work among the Tsim-
sheean Indians. London, Church Missionary House, 1869. 135p.
map. (The Gospel in the Far West) ANR. 1871. 4th ed. 119p.
map(fold.) (The Missions of the Church Missionary Society, no.
2) [in British Columbia]   1382

DUNCAN, WILLIAM and ROBERT TOMLINSON. Metlakahtla and the Church
Missionary Society. Defense of the position taken by the native
Christians and their teachers and an answer to the charges
brought against them, most of which are written by William Duncan and Robert Tomlinson. Victoria, B. C., Munroe Miller, 1887.
44p.   1383

Duncan, William. SEE ALSO nos.
    276, Arctander, J. Wm. Apostle of Alaska ... [c1909];
    1200, Davis, Geo. T. B. Indian arcadia ... 1904;
    1897, Halcombe, J. J. Stranger than fiction. 1872;
    2503, Kohlstedt, Edw. D. Wm. Duncan ... 1957;
    4785, Wellcome, H. S. Story of Metlakahtla. 1887;
    4795, Wentworth, E. Mission to Metlakatla. 1968.

DUNHAM, SAMUEL CLARKE. The goldsmith of Nome, and other verse.
By Sam C. Dunham. Washington, D. C., The Neale Pub. Co., 1901.
80p.   1384

DUNHAM, SAMUEL CLARKE. The men who blaze the trail, and other
poems, with an introduction by Joaquin Miller. By Sam C. Dunham.
N. Y., Barse & Hopkins, 1913. 126p.   1385

Dunlop, H. A., co-auth. SEE no. 4513, Thompson, Wm. F.

DUNN, JOHN. History of the Oregon Territory and British North
American fur trade with an account of the habits and customs of
the principal native tribes on the northern continent. London,
Edwards, 1844. 359p. ANR. London, 1846. reprint. [history of
Hudson's Bay Co.]   1386

DUNN, JOHN. The Oregon Territory and the British North American
fur trade. With an account of the habits and customs of the
principal native tribes on the northern continents. Philadelphia, Zieber, 1845. 236p. (The Home and Travellers Library,
Semimonthly, no. 8)   1387

DUNN, ROBERT. Santa Claus on the beach. Chicago, Brown &
Howell Co., 1914. 63p.   1388

DUNN, ROBERT. The shameless diary of an explorer. N. Y., Outing
Pub. Co., 1907. 297p. illus. photos by author. front. pls.
maps(fold.) [member of F. A. Cook expedition to climb Mt.
McKinley]   1389

DUNN, ROBERT. The youngest world; a novel of the frontier.
N. Y., Dodd Mead, 1914. 492p.   1390

DUNN, ROBERT. World alive; a personal story. N. Y., Crown
Pub. Co., 1956. 480p. [autobiog., mountaineering, Klondike
gold prospecting]   1391

Dunnan, C. D. SEE no. 3552, Pacific Coast Steamship Co.

DUNNING, WILLIAM A. Paying for Alaska, some unfamiliar incidents in the process. N. Y., Ginn & Co., 1912. 13p.   1392

Du Petit-Thouars, Abel Aubert. SEE nos. 3555-56, Petit-Thouars,
    Abel Aubert Du.

Durham, R. C., co-auth. SEE no. 2494, Knight, C.

DURHAM, WILLIAM. Canoes and kayaks of western America. Seattle,
Copper Canoe Press, 1960. 104p. illus. bibliog.   1393

DURLACH, THERESA M. The relationship systems of the Tlingit,
Haidas and Tsimshian. N. Y., G. E. Stechert, 1928. 177p. table
(fold.), bibliog. (Pub. American Ethnological Society, vol. 11)
                                                                   1394

Duro, C. F. SEE no. 3361, Novo y Colson, P. de.

DUTCHER, RUSSELL R., C. L. TROTTER and W. SPACKMAN, jr. Petrography and palynology of certain coals of the Arctic Slope of
Alaska. University Park, Pennsylvania State University, [1958?]
56p. pls. maps, tables, bibliog.   1395

DUTILLY, ARTHEME A. Bibliography of bibliographies on the Arctic.
Washington, D. C., Catholic University of America, 1945. 47p.
diagr. map(sketch) (Pub. no. 1B)   1396

DYER, E. JEROME. The gold fields of Canada and how to reach
them; being an account of the routes and mineral resources of
northwestern Canada. London, G. Philip & Son, 1898. 268p.
front. maps(incl. 1 fold.)   1397

DYER, E. JEROME. The routes and mineral resources of northwestern Canada. Published under the auspices of the Incorporated
London Chamber of Mines. London, F. Philip & Son, 1898. 268p.
front. maps.   1398

Dynamite Johnny O'Brien. SEE nos.
    1153, Dalby, M. A. Sea saga ... 1933;
    2801, Herron, E. A. Dynamite Johnny ... 1962;
    4958, Woods, H. T. God's loaded dice. 1948.

DYNES, W. M. Dynes' Alaska directory and buyers guide. Ketchikan, June, 1920.   1399

DYNES, W. M., comp. Dynes' tours of Alaska and directory of southeastern Alaska. Juneau, 1921. (vol. 1, no. 1) 144p. ANR. Juneau, n. d. 84p. illus. map(fold.) 1400

DYSON, JAMES LINDSAY. The world of ice. By James L. Dyson. N. Y., Knopf, 1962. 292p. photos, charts, maps, glossary, bibliog. index. (A Borzoi Book) ANR. 3rd print. 305p. photos, charts, maps by Rafael Palacios, glossary, bibliog. index. 1401

E

EASTERN STAR, ORDER OF. By-laws adopted October 11, 1913. Midnight Sun Chapter 6, Fairbanks. Fairbanks, Citizen Print. Co., 1914. 16p. 1402

EASTMAN, FRED. Unfinished business of the Presbyterian Church in America; prepared under the direction of the Board of Home Missions of the Presbyterian Church in the U. S. A., and the Woman's Board of Home Missions, the Board of Publication and Sabbath School Work, the Board of Missions for Freedmen. Philadelphia, The Westminster Press, 1921. 176p. [pp.127-41 about Alaska] 1403

Eastman Oil Well Survey Co. SEE no. 3125, Miller, Maynard M.

Eastwood, A. SEE no. 4909, Wilson, C. G.

Eaton, C. M. SEE no. 3208, Mother Lode Copper Mines Co.

EATON, JOHN. Sheldon Jackson, a pioneer in the new West. Condensed from an article by General John Eaton in "The Review of Reviews." N. Y., Woman's Board of Home Missions of the Presbyterian Church, 1898. 15p. 1404

Eben, Isaac, illus. SEE no. 4534, [Tickasook]

EBERHART, BETH. A crew of two. Garden City, Doubleday, 1961. 1st ed. 286p. drawings by author, endmaps. 1405

EDDY, JOHN WHITTEMORE. Hunting on Kenai Peninsula and observations on the increase of big game in North America. Seattle, Lowman & Hanford, 1924. 90p. front. pls. 1406

EDDY, JOHN WHITTEMORE. Hunting the Alaska brown bear; the story of a sportsman's adventure in an unknown valley after the largest carnivorous animal in the world. N. Y., Putnam, 1930. 253p. front. pls. ports. maps(fold.), endmaps. 1407

EDELSTEIN, JULIUS C. Alaska comes of age. N. Y., Putnam, 1942. 62p. illus. maps(incl. 1 dble.) (American Council, Institute Pacific Relations, Far Eastern Pamphlets, no. 8) 1408

EDERER, BERNARD FRANCIS. Through Alaska's back door. N. Y.,
Vantage Press, 1954. 162p. illus. endmaps. [canoe trip on
interior rivers]   1409

EDGAR, J. H. and N. THOMPSON. Canadian Railway development.
Toronto, Macmillan of Canada, 1933.   1410

EDGREN, ADOLPH. Jubel kantat for solo, kvartett och kor utford-
pa Svenska dagen den 31 juli 1909 a Alaska-Yukon-Pacific exposition; libretto of Emanuel Schmidt och musik of Adolph Edgren.
Seattle, Edgren School of Music, 1909. 60p. illus. ports. 1411

Edington, A. C. SEE no. 1934, Hansen, A. H.

EDMONDS, H. M. W. The Eskimo of St. Michael and vicinity as related by H. M. W. Edmonds. Edited by Dorothy Jean Ray. College,
University of Alaska Press, 1966. 143p. front. illus. map,
ftntes. bibliog. index. (Anthropological Papers, vol. 13, no. 2,
Dec. 1966)   1412

EDMONSON, MUNRO S. Status terminology and social structure of
the North American Indians. Seattle, University of Washington
Press, 1958. 84p. tables, bibliog. append. (American Ethnological Society) [incls. Eskimo along with such Indian societies
as Kwakiutl and Yakut]   1413

EDWARDS, DELTUS MALIN. The toll of the Arctic seas. By Deltus
M. Edwards. Illustrated by G. A. Coffin. N. Y., H. Holt, 1910.
449p. front.(pl.), pls. ports. maps(incl. 1 fold.), bibliog.
index. ANR. London, Chapman & Hall, 1910. [17 explorers from
Barendz to Peary, incl. Bering, Franklin, Amundsen, others] 1414

EDWARDS, WILLIAM SEYMOUR. In to the Yukon. N. Y., Robert
Clarke Co., 1904. 319p. front. pls. maps. ANR. Cincinnati,
Robert Clarke Co., 1905. 2d ed. 335p. front. pls. maps [via
Inside Passage and Skagway]   1415

Eells, W. C., co-auth. SEE no. 244, Anderson, H. D.

EFIMOV, ALEKSEĬ VLADIMIROVICH. Iz istoriĭ russkikh ėkspediĭsiĭ
na Tikhon okeane. [TITLE TR. From the history of Russian expeditions to the Pacific Ocean] Moskva, Voennoe izd-vo Minister-
stvavooruzhennykh sil Soĭuza SSR, 1948. 341p. maps(incl. some
fold.), appends. bibliog.(titles.)   1416

EFIMOV, ALEKSEĬ VLADIMIROVICH. Iz istoriĭ velikikh russkikh
geograficheskikh otkrytiĭ. [TITLE TR. From the history of the
great Russian geographical discoveries] Moskva, Gosudarstvennoe
Uchebno-pedagogicheskoe izd-vo ministra prosveshcheniĭa RSFSR,
1949. abr. ed. 149p. illus. maps(incl. some fold.)   1417

EFIMOV, ALEKSEĬ VLADIMIROVICH. Iz istoriĭ velikikh russkikh geograficheskikh otkrytiĭ v Severnom Ledovitom i tikhom okeanakh; XVII-pervaĭa polovina XVIII. [TITLE TR. From the history of the great Russian geographic discoveries in Arctic and Pacific Oceans in the 17th and first half of the 18th century] Moskva, Gos. Izd. geogr. liter., 1950. 317p. illus. ports. maps, appends. indexes. 1418

EFIMOV, ALEKSEĬ VLADIMIROVICH and SERGEI ALEKSANDROVICH TOKAREV, edits. Narody Ameriki. [TITLE TR. The peoples of America. Edited by A. V. Efimov and S. A. Tokarev] Moskva, Izd-vo Akademii nauk SSSR, 1959. 2 vols. illus. pls.(col.), maps(some fold.), bibliog. (Narody mira; ètnograficheskie ocherki) [vol. 1. 672p. North America and Greenland. vol. 2. Latin America] 1419

EFIMOV, ALEKSEĬ VLADIMIROVICH and N. S. ORLOVA. Otkrytiĭa russkikh zemleprokhodtsev i poliarnykh morekhodov XVII veka na Severo-Vostoke Aziĭ, sbornik dokumentov. Sostavlen N. S. Orlovoi, pod red. A. V. Efimov. [TITLE TR. Discoveries of Russian travelers and polar seafarers in northeastern Asia during the 17th century; a collection of documents, assembled by N. S. Orlova under the editorship of A. F. Efimov] Moskva, Gos. Izd-vo geogr. lit-ry, 1951. 619p. facsims. maps(incl. some fold. and 1 facsim. in pocket), indexes. 1420

EFIMOV, ALEKSEĬ VLADIMIROVICH. Velikie russkie geografisheskie otkrytiĭa (v XVII i pervoi polovine XVIII v.) stenogramma publichnoĭ lektsii prochitannoĭ v tsentral'nom lektoriĭ obshchestva v Moskve. [TITLE TR. Great Russian geographic discoveries (in 17th and first half of the 18th centuries); stenograph of a public lecture delivered in Central Lecture Hall of the Society in Moscow] Moskva, Vsesoĭuznoe obshchestvo po rasprostraneniĭu politicheskikh i nauchnykh znani. Izd-vo "Pravda," 1949. 23p. 1421

EFIMOVA, ALEKSANDRA AFANAS'EVNA. Otechestvennye puteshestvenniki v kurse geografiĭ v-vii klassa. [TITLE TR. Russian travelers in the geography course for classes 5-7] Moskva, Opyt peredovago uchiteliĭa. Gosud. uchebno-pedagogicheskoe izd-vo, 1954. 74p. bibliog. 1422

Efremov, P., edit. SEE no. 3932, Ryleev, K. F.

EGGLESTON, EDWARD. Stories of American life and adventure; third grade reader. N. Y., American Book Co., 1895. 214p. [section on Alaska, pp.207-14] 1423

EICHWALD, CARL EDUARD VON. Geognostisch-paleontologische Bemerkungen über die Halbinsel Mangischlak und die aleutischen Inseln. [TITLE TR. Geognostic-paleontological remarks on the Mangishlak Peninsula and the Aleutian Islands] St. Petersburg, Akademie der Wissenschaften, 1871. 200p. pls. [marine mollusks] 1424

EIDE, ARTHUR HANSIN. Drums of Diomede; transformation of the
Alaska Eskimo. Hollywood, Calif., House-Warven, 1952. 242p.
pls. [Little Diomede Island]   1425

Eielson, Carl Ben. SEE nos.
      888, Chandler, E. W. Pioneer of Alaska skies ... 1959;
      1063, Coombs, C. J. Alaska bush pilot. 1963;
      2085, Herron, E. A. Wings over Alaska. 1959;
      3658, Potter, J. Flying frontiersmen. [c1956];
      3870, Rolfsrud, E. N. Brother to eagle ... 1952;
      4493, Thomas, L. Famous first flights. 1968;
      4496, Thomas, L. Sir Hubert Wilkins ... [c1961];
      4871, Wilkins, G. H. Flying the Arctic. 1928;
      4894, Willoughby, B. Alaskans all. 1933.

EINARSEN, ARTHUR SKOGMAN. Black brant, sea goose of the Pacific
Coast. Seattle, University of Washington Press, 1965. 142p.
photos, sketches by Harold Cramer Smith, maps, charts, tables,
bibliog. index.   1426

Eisen, G. SEE no. 1950, Harriman Alaska Exped. 1899. vol. 12.

EISENLOHR, LOUIS HENRY and RILEY WILSON. Memories from Philadelphia to Charlestown, Maryland via Nome, Alaska. By Louis H.
Eisenlohr and Riley Wilson. Salutations: compiled for compli-
mentary distribution by ... to their friends. [Philadelphia,
The Keystone Pub. Co.], 1918. 96p. illus. front. photos,
sketches, facsims.   1427

EL DORADO PUBLISHING CO. The modern El Dorado. An account of
the gold fields of Alaska and the neighboring placer mines in
British Columbia ... together with a brief account of Alaska's
resources and scenic features, copiously illustrated. Des
Moines, The El Dorado Pub. Co., George A. Miller Printing Co.,
1897. 96p. pls. maps.   1428

ELBERT, PAUL A. I love the land. Verses by an Alaskan. N. Y.,
Carlton Press, 1963. 152p. (A Lyceum Book)   1429

ELBERT, PAUL A. Josephine, the friendly moose. Fairbanks,
printed by Commercial Printing Co. for Anni Dolney, Happy Acres,
1966. 20p. photos(some col.), wrps.   1430

ELEONSKAĬA, ELENA NIKOLAEVNA. Aleuty. [TITLE TR. Aleuts]
Moskva, Izd. Gos. t͡sentr. muzei͡a narodovedeni͡a, 1929. 16p.
illus. bibliog.   1431

Elford, C. R., co-auth. SEE no. 3820, Riehl, H.

ELIADE, MIRCEA. Le chamanisme et les techniques archaiques de
l'extase. Paris, Payot, 1951. 447p. bibliog. [incl. Alaskan
Eskimo. For tr. see no. 1433]   1432

ELIADE, MIRCEA. Shamanism; archaic techniques of ecstasy.
Translated by Willard R. Trask. N. Y., Pantheon Books, 1964.
[tr. of no. 1432]   1433

ELIOT, WILLARD AYRES. Birds of the Pacific coast, including a
brief account of the distribution and habitat of one hundred and
eighteen birds that are more or less common to the Pacific coast
states and British Columbia, many of which are found eastward to
the Rocky Mountains and beyond; with fifty-six colorplates, by
R. Bruce Horsfall. N. Y., Putnam, 1923. 211p. front.(col.),
pls.(col.)   1434

ELIOT, WILLARD AYRES. Forest trees of the Pacific coast; including a brief account of the outstanding characters, distribution and habitat of the trees native to Alaska, British Columbia, Washington, and Oregon; most of which are also found in
Idaho and northern California and eastward to the western slopes
of the Rocky Mountains, by Willard Ayres Eliot assisted by G. B.
McLean, illustrated principally from original photographs by
George C. Stephenson. N. Y., Putnam, 1938. 565p. front. pls.
bibliog. index. ANR. Portland, Binfords and Mort, 1948. rev.
ed. photos, line drawings, index.   1435

Elliot, D. G., co-auth. SEE no. 3879, Roosevelt, T.

ELLIOTT, HENRY WOOD. Alaska og Salorne; af Overstat fra Eng-
lisk, ved O Strom, Cammerymer. Kristiana, 1888. illus. maps.
                                                             1436

ELLIOTT, HENRY WOOD. Our Arctic province; Alaska and the seal
islands. N. Y., Scribner, 1886. 473p. pls. maps. SAME 1887.
ANR. London, Sampson, Low, Marsten, 1886. illus. by many drawings from nature and maps. 473p. front. pls. ports. maps.
ANR. N. Y., Scribner, 1897. drawings, maps (Library of Contemporary Exploration and Adventure)   1437

Elliott, Henry Wood. SEE ALSO nos.
    1975, Harting, Jas. E. Fauna Prybilov Islands ... 1875;
    2264, Ingersoll, E. In richest Alaska ... 1897.

Elliott, L. SEE no. 2240, Huntington, Jas.

Elliott, M. SEE no. 3486, Pan Pacific Progress.

ELLIS, CLYDE R. Field guide for Alaska prospectors and miners.
pl. ?, pub. ?, 1939. 21p.   1438

ELLIS, EDWARD S. Klondike nuggets; and how two boys secured
them. Illustrated by O. Lowell. N. Y., Doubleday and McClure,
1898. 255p.   1439

ELLIS, EDWARD S. The young gold seekers of the Klondike. Illustrated by F. A. Carter. Philadelphia, Penn Pub. Co., 1912. 311p.
                                                             1440

ELLIS, FRANK H. Canada's flying heritage. Toronto, University of Toronto Press, 1954. 388p. illus. diagrs. [incls. 1st Alaskan Air Expedition, 1920]   1441

ELLIS, T. MULLETT. Tales of the Klondike. London, Bliss Sands & Co., 1898. 164p. ANR. Toronto, Copp Clark Co., 1898.   1442

ELLIS, WILLIAM. An authentic narrative of a voyage performed by Captain Cook and Captain Clerke, in His Majesty's ships *Resolution* and *Discovery* during the years 1776-80. In search of a north-west passage between the continents of Asia and America. Including a faithful account of all their discoveries, and the unfortunate death of Captain Cook. Illustrated with a chart and a variety of cuts. By W. Ellis, assistant surgeon to both vessels. London, Printed for G. Robinson, J. Sewell, J. Debrett, 1782. 2 vols. 358p. (vol. 1) 347p. (vol. 2) pls. map(fold.) ANR. (in Eng.) Altenburg, C. E. Richter, 1788. 2 vols. maps (fold.) [cf nos. 1017-18]   1443

ELLSBERG, EDWARD. Cruise of the *Jeannette*. By Captain Edward Ellsberg, U. S. N. R. Illustrated by Gerald Foster. N. Y., Dodd Mead, 1949. 275p. sketches. [version of no. 1445 for children]   1444

ELLSBERG, EDWARD. Hell on ice; the saga of the "Jeannette." N. Y., Dodd Mead, 1938. 421p. endmap.   1445

ELLSWORTH, LINCOLN. Beyond horizons. By Lincoln Ellsworth, Lieutenant Commander, United States Naval Reserve. Garden City, N. Y., Doubleday Doran, 1938. 1st ed. 403p. front.(pl.), ports. maps, appends. [autobiog.]   1446

Ellsworth, Lincoln. SEE ALSO nos.
    203, American Geog. Soc. Problems polar research ... 1928;
    213, Amundsen, R. E. G. Air pioneering ... 1929;
    214, Amundsen, R. E. G. Amundsen-Ellsworth polflyoning.1925;
    215, Amundsen, R. E. G. Amundsen-Ellsworth polar ... 1925;
    220, Amundsen, R. E. G. First flight ... 1927;
    940, Clark, H. T. Episodes Amundsen-Ellsworth ... 1928;
    4627, Vaeth, J. G. To ends earth ... [c1962]

ELLSWORTH, LYMAN R. Guys on ice. N. Y., David McKay, 1952. 277p. [World War II, Pribilof Islands]   1447

ELLSWORTH, LYMAN R. Halibut schooner. N. Y., David McKay, 1953. 242p. illus. endmaps. ANR. London, 1954. [Gulf of Alaska] 1448

ELTON, CHARLES. Voles, mice and lemmings. London, 1942.   1449

Ely, A., co-edit. SEE no. 612, Boone and Crockett Club.

EMERSON, A. B. Ruth Fielding in Alaska; or, The girl miners of Snow Mountain. N. Y., 1926. 209p. illus.   1450

Emerson, B. K. SEE no. 1950, Harriman Alaska Exped. 1899. vol.4.

EMERSON, HARRINGTON. Alaska; the Pacific Coast power of the future, and Alaskan railroad projects. no pl., 1904. 10p.   1451

EMERSON, HARRINGTON. The Alaskan railway problem.   N. Y., The Emerson Co., n. d.   3p.   1452

Emerson, R., photog. SEE no. 4730, Walford, L. A.

EMERSON, WILLIAM CANFIELD.   The land of the midnight sun;   the story in words and pictures of the Alaska Highway, Alaska,   the Alaska Indians, and the Alaska Eskimos.   By Dr. William Canfield Emerson. Photos by author. Philadelphia, Dorrance, 1956. 179p. illus.   1453

EMERY, GEORGE D.   The new mining law of Alaska,   with forms, 1913.   Seattle, Pioneer Print. Co., 1913.   25p.   1454

EMERY, RUSSELL GUY.   Adventure north.   Illustrated by Manning deV. Lee. Philadelphia, McRae-Smith, 1947. 246p. illus.   1455

EMMANUEL, MARTHE.   La France et l'exploration polaire;   de Verrazano a La Pérouse, 1523-1778.   [TITLE TR.   France and polar exploration from Verrazano to La Perouse, 1523-1778]   Paris, Nouvelles Editions Latines, 1959.   397p.   illus. maps.   1456

EMMONS, GEORGE THORNTON.   Jade in British Columbia and Alaska, and its use by the natives.   N. Y., Museum of the American Indian, Heye Foundation, 1923.   53p.   illus. pls.(some col.)   (Indian Notes and Monographs, Misc. ser. no. 35)   1457

EMMONS, GEORGE THORNTON.   Slate mirrors of the Tsimshian. N. Y., Museum of the American Indian, Heye Foundation, 1921. 21p. front. pls.   (Indian Notes and Monographs, Misc. Pub. no. 15)   1458

EMMONS, GEORGE THORNTON.   The basketry of the Tlingit.   N. Y., Knickerbocker Press, 1903.   (Memoir, American Museum of Natural History, vol. 3, pt. 2, pp.229-277)   1459

EMMONS, GEORGE THORNTON.   The Chilkat blanket, with notes on the blanket designs, by Franz Boas.   N. Y., American Museum of Natural History, 1907.   (Memoir, Whole Ser., vol. 3.   Anthropol., vol. 2, no. 3, pp.329-400)   1460

EMMONS, GEORGE THORNTON.   The Emmons journal.   Eugene, Oregon, Koke-Tiffany Co., n. d.   11p.   illus. diagr.   1461

EMMONS, GEORGE THORNTON.   The Tahltan Indians,   illustrated by specimens in the George G. Heye collection. Philadelphia, University of Pennsylvania, 1911.   120p.   illus. pls. map.   (Museum of Anthropology Pub., vol. 4, no. 1)   1462

EMMONS, GEORGE THORNTON. The whale house of the Chilkat. N. Y., American Museum of Natural History, 1916. 33p. illus. pls. (some col.) (Anthropological Papers, vol. 19, pt. 1)   1463

EMMONS, L. A. A prophetic abstract from the proceedings of the Trojan Society for the retardation of science, for the year of our Lord 1870. Reported by L. Emmons, under spirit influence. Respectfully dedicated to the A. A. A. S. Troy, N. Y., W. H. Young and Blake, 1870. 20p. [incls. references to Alaska and Wm. Healey Dall]   1464

Emory, Wm. H. SEE no. 1737, Gleaves, A.

ENDERS-SCHICHANOWSKY, AUGUSTA. Im Wunderland Alaska; erleb-nisse und eindrucke einer deutschen frau in der Arktis. Leipzig, Dieterich, 1926. 208p. front.(port.), pls. maps.   1465

ENDICOTT, WENDELL. Adventures in Alaska, and along the trail; with one hundred and fifty-eight illustrations from photographs. N. Y., Frederick A. Stokes, 1928. 344p. front. pls. endmaps.1466

ENDRESEN, FRIDTJOF. Alaska Kaller; nordmanns live og eventyr i Alaska. Oslo, Bergendahl, 1956. 267p. illus.   1467

ENEMARK, D. C. and K. A. ANDERSON. Instrumentation for auroral zone balloon experiments and summary of field operations. Iowa City, Iowa State University, 1959. 11, 17   tables, diagrs. bibliog. (Tech. Report, no. 59-17)   1468

Engel, Samuel. [Alphabetical title guide to chronological entries]

Anmerkungen. 1469.	Mémoires. 1471.
Extraites raisonnes. 1473.	Remarques. 1470.
Geographische. 1472.	

ENGEL, SAMUEL. Anmerkungen über den Theil von Cap. Cook's Reise-Relation, so die Meerenge Zwischen Asia und Amerika an-siehet; in einem brief durch herrn S. Engel. no pl., 1780. 1st ed. 30p. [for tr. see no. 1470]   1469

ENGEL, SAMUEL. Remarques sur la Partie de la Relation du Voyage du Capitaine Cook, qui Concerne le Détroit entre l'Asie et l'Amérique. Dans une lettre adressee a' M. D. ... par Mr. le Baillif Engel. Traduite de l'allemand & augmentée, pouvant ser-vir de suite au Mémoire du même auteur de 1779. Avec une carte dressée avec soin. Berne, Imprimé chez F. Samuel Fetscherin, 1781. 26p. maps. ANR. Geneva, 1781. [tr. of 1469, which has no map]   1470

[ENGEL, SAMUEL] Mémoires et Observations Geographiques et Critiques sur la Situation des Pays Septentrionaux de l'Asie et de l'Amérique, d'apres les Relations les Plus Recentes. Auxquelles on a joint un Essai sur la route aux Indes par le Nord, & sur un Commerce trés riche à établir dans la mer du Sud. Avec deux nouvelles Cartes dressees conformement à ce systeme. Par Mr. ***. Lausanne, Chez Antoine Chapuis, Imprimeur, 1765. 268p. 2 maps(fold.)   1471

ENGEL, SAMUEL. TRANSLATIONS AND REISSUES Memoires et Observations ... 1765, chronologically.

   Geographische und Kritische nachrichten und Anmerkungen über die lage der nordlichen gegenden von Asien und Amerika ... welchen noch ein versuch über einen weg durch norden nach Indien, und über die errichtung eines ... handels in die Sudsee beygefuget ist ... Nebst zwo ... karten. Aus dem franzosichen ubersetzet, von dem herrn verfasser ... durch geschen, verb. und mit vielen neuen zusatzen berichert ... Mietau, Hasenpoth und Leipzig, bei Jacob Friedrich Hinz, 1772. 268p. 2 maps. ANR. Basel, 1777. 5 maps.   1472

   Extraites raisonnes des voyages faits dans les parties septentrionales de l'Asie et de l'Amèrique, ou nouvelles preuves de la possibilite d'un passage aux Indes par le Nord; demontrees par Mr. Engel. Lausanne, Jules Henri Pott et Co., 1779. 268p. 2 maps.   1473

[Engel, Samuel ?] SEE ALSO no. 679, [Brooke, Robert ?] Remarks and conjectures ... 1780.

ENGLE, ELOISE. Earthquake; the story of Alaska's Good Friday disaster. N. Y., John Day, 1966. illus. photos, bibliog. 1474

ENGLUND, JOH. FR. På äventyr i vilda västern och Alaska; verklighetsskildringar. [TITLE TR. Adventures in the wild west and Alaska; tales of actual happenings] Oskarshamn, Oskarshamns-Bladets Boktryckeri, 1924. 160p. illus.   1475

ENGSTROM, EMIL. John Engstrom, the last frontiersman. By Emil Engstrom. N. Y., Vantage Press, [c1956] 1st ed. (6)7-156p. [Tanana Camp and Fox, near Fairbanks in Interior, ca 1907] 1476

ENOCK, CHARLES REGINALD. The great Pacific Coast, twelve thousand miles in the golden west, being an account of life and travel in the western states of North and South America, from California, British Columbia, and Alaska; to Mexico, Panama, Peru and Chile; and a study of their physical and political conditions, by C. Reginald Enock ... with sixty-four full-page illustrations and a map. London, G. Richards, 1909. 356p. front. illus. map. ANR. N. Y., Scribner, 1910. [chapt. on Alaska and Yukon, pp.242-55]   1477

Entrecasteaux, A. R. J. B. de.   SEE no. 1273, D'Entrecasteaux, A. R. J. B.

[EPISCOPAL CHURCH] Alaska; a sketch of the country and its people. Domestic Committee of the Protestant Episcopal Church in the United States. no pl., 1883. 20p.   1478

[EPISCOPAL CHURCH] Book of common prayer. Selections. Haida. Book of common prayer; portions of the book of common prayer in Haida. London, 1899. 29p.   1479

[EPISCOPAL CHURCH] Morning and evening prayer and the Holy Communion together with selections of the Psalms translated into the Eskimo language of the Tigara tribe of Arctic Alaska. N.Y., Fisher and Thul, 1923. 91p.   1480

[EPISCOPAL CHURCH] Service book; being parts of the Book of Common Prayer set forth for use in the dialect of the Qliyuku-whutana Indians at the Mission of Our Savior, Tanana, Alaska. Denatla Cughalyo Grunit Buyi Knutsukhudidayi, Whukoneltuni Cun, Culic Yulh, Qliyukuwhutana Kunaji Yit, Mission of Our Savior, Tanana, Alaska. Translated by Rev. Jules L. Prevost. N. Y., Bible and Common Prayer Book Society, 1908. 109p.   1481

[EPISCOPAL CHURCH] Tukudh primer for the Tinne Indians. London, Gilbert & Rivington, n. d. 55p.   1482

EPSTEIN, SAMUEL and BERYL WILLIAMS. The real book about Alaska. By Samuel Epstein and Beryl Williams. Illustrated by Mary Stevens. Garden City, N. Y., Garden City Books, 1952. 1st ed. 191p. illus. map, append. index. ANR. N. Y., Doubleday, 1961. rev. ed. 192p. illus.   1483

Epstein, Samuel, co-auth. SEE ALSO no. 968,
    Coe, Douglas [pseud.] Road to Alaska ... [c1943]

ERDMANN, HUGO. Alaska; ein Beitrag zur Geschichte nordischer Kolonisation; Bericht, dem Herrn Minister der Geistlichen, Unterrichts und Medizinal-Angelegenheiten erstattet; mit 68 Abbildungen und Karten-skizzen im text und einer Karte von Alaska. [TITLE TR. Alaska; a contribution to the history of northern colonization; report to the Minister of Religion, Education and Health ...] Berlin, D. Reimer (Ernst Vohsen), 1909. 223p. illus. front. pls. maps(incl. 1 fold.)   1484

ERICKSON, JOHN. Report of John Erickson on the Mineral Creek claims in Alaska. no pl., 1915. 4p.   1485

Erman, A., tr. SEE no. 2728, Litke, F. P.

Erman, E., edit. SEE no. 3335, Nordenskiöld, N. A. E.

ERMAN, GEORG ADOLF. Reise um die Erde durch Nord-Asien und die beiden Oceane in den Jahren 1828, 1829 und 1830 ausgeführt von Adolf Erman. [TITLE TR. Journey around the world through northern Asia and both oceans in the years 1828, 1829 and 1830] Berlin, G. Reimer, 1833-48. 2 vols. in 5. 2793p. pls.(fold.), maps(fold.), 2 atlases in 1 vol. [brief mention of Sitka]   1486

ERMASHEV, I. I. "Poliãrna strategica" i poliãrna ėkspanziiã. [TITLE TR. "Polar strategy" and polar expansion] Sofiiã, Izd-vo na Bulg. rabotnicheska partiiã (komunisti), 1947. 37p. [U.S. military bases after World War II]   1487

ERNST, ALICE H. Wolf ritual of the northwest coast. Eugene, University of Oregon, 1952.   1488

ERSKINE, WILSON FISKE. Katmai; a true narrative. London, Abelard-Schuman, 1962. 223p. line drawings by author, photos, map. [eruption of Katmai volcano in 1912]   1489

ERSKINE, WILSON FISKE. Trap pirates in Alaska. London, Abelard-Schuman, 1964. [fict.account of salmon cannery]   1490

ERSKINE, WILSON FISKE. White water; an Alaskan adventure. London, Abelard-Schuman, 1960. 256p. front. line drawings by author, photos, charts. [autobiog. commercial fishing, shipping, whaling along Alaskan coast]   1491

ERSPAMER, ALICE McGILL. Klondike widow. N. Y., Pageant Press, 1953. 239p.   1492

ESCHSCHOLTZ, JOHANN FRIEDRICH. Zoologischer atlas, enthaltend Abbildungen und Beschreibungen neuer Thierarten, wahrend des Flott-capitains von Kotzebue zweiter Reise um die Welt, auf der Russisch-Kaiserlichen Kriegsschlupp *Predpriatie* in den Jahren 1823 bis 1826 beobachtet von Dr. Friedr. Eschscholtz, Professor und Director des Zoologischen Museum an der Universität zu Dorpat, Mitglied mehrerer gelehrten Gesellschaften, Russ. Kais. Hofrathe und Ritter des Ordens des theil-Wladimir. Erstes Heft. Berlin, Gedruckt und verlegt Bei G. Reimer, 1829. 5 pts. 17(18), 13(14), 18,19(2), and 28p. pls. in each pt.(col.), front.(port.) bibliog.   1493

Eskimo cook book ... n. d. SEE no. 57, Alaska Crippled
    Children's Assoc.

Eskimo legend of Kotzebue. [c1959] SEE no. 4534, [Tickasook]

ESKIMO LIFE IN ALASKA, a photo story of these Arctic people. Anchorage, Alaska Publications, 1964. (46)p. [Marjorie Roberts, Publisher]   1494

Eskimos ... 1962. SEE no. 1753, Golden Press.

ESPINOSA y TELLO, JOSE de. Appendix to "Relacion del viage ...
Sutil y *Mexicana* ..." Madrid, 1806. 20p. [for "Relacion ..."
1802. See no. 1676]   1495

ESPINOSA y TELLO, JOSE de. Memorias sobre las observaciones
astronomicas, hechas por los navegantes Españoles en distintos
lugares del globo; las guales han servido para la formacion de
las cartas de marear publicadas por la direction de trabajos
hidrograficos de Madrid; ordenadas por don Josef Espinosa y
Tello. Madrid, En la Imprenta Real, 1809. 2 vols. in 5 pts.
170p., 184p., 224p., 199p. and 320p. pls.(5 fold.)   1496

Essai sur le commerce de Russie ... 1777. SEE no. 1261,
     [De Marbault, M. ?]

[ETCHES, JOHN CADMAN] A continuation of an authentic statement
of all the facts relative to Nootka Sound, its discovery, history, settlement, commerce, and the public advantages to be derived from it, with observations on a libel, which has been
traced to a foreign ambassador; in a second letter by Argonaut.
London, W. S. Fores, 1790. 34p. [see no. 1498]   1497

[ETCHES, JOHN CADMAN] An authentic statement of all the facts
relative to Nootka Sound; its discovery, history, settlement,
trade and the probable advantages to be derived from it; in an
address to the King. London, printed for J. Debrett, 1790. 1st
ed. 26p. [Etches as supercargo with J. Meares. See also no.
1497]   1498

Etches, John Cadman. SEE ALSO NO. 3052, Meares, J.

EURYALUS; tales of the sea, a few leaves from the diary of a
midshipman. London, J. D. Potter, 1860. 332p. pls.(col.)
[author is Capt. William Chimmo, R. N., midshipman on H. M. S.
Herald, Franklin searches in Alaskan waters]   1499

[EURYALUS ?] Midshipman's diary; a few notes extracted from the
cockpit journal of a man-of-war ... London, J. D. Potter, 1862.
332p. pls.(col.) [a later version of no. 1499 ?]   1500

EVANS, ALLEN ROY. Meat; a tale of the reindeer trek, 1929-35.
London, Hurst & Blackett, [1935] 288p. front. pls. map. ANR.
Toronto, McClelland & Stewart, 1935. no illus. ANR. WITH TITLE
Reindeer trek. N. Y., Coward McCann, 1935. 269p. pls.   1501

EVANS, ALLEN ROY. Northward Ho ! London, 1947. 220p. endmaps.
[Alaska Highway]   1502

Evans, Allen Roy. Reindeer trek. SEE no. 1501.

Evans, Edward Ratcliffe Garth Russell. SEE nos. 3212-4,
     Mountevans, Edw. Ratcliffe Garth Russell Evans.

EVANS, ROBLEY D. A sailor's log. Recollections of forty years of naval life. N. Y., D. Appleton, 1902. 466p. front.(port.), illus. index. [chapters 24 through 28 on sealing violations, Alaska coastal waters]   1503

EVERETTE, OLIVER P. God has been Northward always. Alaska poems by Oliver Everette. Seattle, Bradley Printing & Litho-graph Co., 1965. 96p. sketches, wrps.   1504

EWART, JOHN S. The Kingdom of Canada, imperial federation, the colonial conferences, the Alaska boundary and other essays. To-ronto, Morang, 1908. 370p.   1505

Experiences of Chilcat George. 1911. SEE no. 3681,
    Presbyterian Church.

Expert opinions ... 1910. SEE no. 136, Alaska United Copper
    Exploration Co.

Explication de la carte des nouvelles decouvertes ... 1752.
    SEE no. 716, [Buache, P.]

EXPLORATION COMPANY, LIMITED. Annual reports to the shareholders of the Alaska Treadwell Gold Mining Co., Alaska Mexican Gold Mining Co., and the Alaska United Gold Mining Co., for 1919 through 1923. London, Crowther & Goodman, 1920 through 1924. [in separate years]   1506

EXPLORATION ET LE MYSTERIEUX NAUFRAGE de Laperouse. Arvengas, Albi, 1945.   1507

EXPLORERS CLUB. Through hell and high water. N. Y., Robert M. McBride, 1941. 1st ed. 385p. front. port. map, decorative end-papers by Frederick Machetanz. [special edition for members of Explorers Club, each inscribed - has several articles on Alaska]
                                                           1508

Extraits raisonnes ... 1779. SEE no. 1473, [Engel, Samuel]

Eyries, J. B. B., tr. SEE no. 2565, Krusenstern, A. J. von.

F

Faas, R. W., co-auth. SEE no. 2242, Hussey, R. M.

FABER, KURT. Unter Eskimos und Walfischfängern; eismeerfahrten eines jungen Deutschen, von Kurt Faber. Stuttgart, Robert Lutz, 1916. 369p. front. pls. map. ANR. 1942. abr. by author's brother. 272p. front.(col.), pls.(col.), map(fold.)   1509

Facts about Alaska ... 1932. SEE no. 2450,
    Ketchikan Alaska Chronicle.   1510

Facts and conditions ... n. d. SEE no. 2195,
    Houston Dredging & Hydraulic Co.

Facts and history ... 1904. SEE no. 4622,
    United States Alaska Tin Mining Co.

Facts ... finds and figures. 1897. SEE no. 5013,
    Yukon Trading, Mining & Exploration Co.

Facts for Klondikers ... 1898. SEE no. 5008, Yukon Pub. Co.

Facts from Alaska gold fields. 1903. SEE no. 790,
    Campion Mining & Trading Co.

FACTS ON ALASKA. no pl., [1902 ?] 30p. [cf nos. 1722 and
4036]   1510

Facts on Alaska. [1904 ?] SEE no. 4036,
    Seattle Post-Intelligencer.

Facts on Alaska. Report made to Pacific Construction ...
    1904. SEE no. 1722, Gillette, Edw.

Fainberg, L. A., edit. SEE no. 3744, Rasmussen, K. J. V.

FAIR, AGNES THECLA. Sourdough's bible. Seattle, Trustee Print.
Co., 1910. [c1910] 57p. [partly in verse]   1511

FAIRBANKS BIRD CLUB. Bird-finding along interior Alaska's highways. By Brina Kessel and Robert B. Weeden. Fairbanks, [1965]
21p. map.   1512

FAIRBANKS CHAMBER OF COMMERCE: Fairbanks, Alaska; Tanana Valley, Alaska. [Seattle ?], Metropolitan Press Print. Co., 1908.
24p.   1513

FAIRBANKS CHRISTIAN SCIENCE SOCIETY. By-laws and rules of the
Fairbanks Christian Science Society, April 18, 1913. 13p.   1514

FAIRBANKS COMMERCIAL CLUB. Descriptive of Fairbanks, "Alaska's
golden heart." Published for those seeking information regarding conditions in interior Alaska. Fairbanks, 1916. 63p.
illus. pls.(fold.)   1515

FAIRBANKS COMMERCIAL CLUB. Interior Alaska, the home of opportunity, the golden heart of Alaska. From Fairbanks, issued for
the Fairbanks Commercial Club by W. F. Thompson. [Fairbanks,
Fairbanks Daily News-Miner Print., 1914] 24p.   1516

FAIRBANKS COMMERCIAL CLUB. What Fairbanks, Alaska's golden
heart, has to offer in the way of inducements to the miner, the
capitalist, and the home seeker. Fairbanks, Press of Fairbanks
Times, Sept. 1911. 12p.   1517

FAIRBANKS COMMUNITY HOSPITAL ASSOCIATION. A survey of community
health resources and needs; by Gerhard Hartmann, Ph.D., Hospital Consultant, October 1961. no pl., 1961. 198p. charts,
bibliog.   1518

FAIRBANKS COOK BOOK of tested recipes. Compiled by the Ladies
of the Presbyterian Church. Fairbanks, 1913. 132p.   1519

FAIRBANKS DAILY NEWS-MINER. The low-down truth of Alaska. Constituting the 1923 annual of the Fairbanks Daily News-Miner.
Fairbanks, 1923. 48p. illus. photos.   1520

FAIRBANKS FOURTH OF JULY CELEBRATION, official program. 1909.
16p. ANR. 1910. 20p. [incls. Caspar Fischer's three shows.
Auditorium, July 2, 3, 7, 1910] ANR. [Fairbanks ?], Times
Print., 1912. 32p. ANR. [Fairbanks ?], Citizen's Print. & Sta-
tionery Co., 1913. 32p. ANR. Fairbanks, Press of Fairbanks
Times, 1915. 36p. [for July 5 and 6]   1521

Fairbanks - golden heart ... [1945?] SEE no. 75, [Alaska Life]

Fairbanks, golden heart city. 1968. SEE no. 2655,
    League of Women Voters.

FAIRBANKS HARMONIE SOCIETY. Souvenir, February 13, 1909. Fairbanks, Times Pub. Co., 1909. 32p. illus.   1522

FAIRBANKS, TOWN OF. Ordinances, 1907. City of Fairbanks, Alaska. Fairbanks, Daily Times Press, 1907. 115p.   1523

FAIRBANKS, TOWN OF. Revised ordinances of the town of Fairbanks,
Alaska, enacted December 13, 1912. Ordinance no. 177. Fairbanks, 1912. 83p.   1524

Fairbridge, R. W., co-auth. SEE no. 3803, Richards, H. G.

Family favorites. [ca 1955] SEE no. 1526,
    Farmers Loop Homemakers Club.

Far north-west ... 1906. SEE no. 1171, Dana, J. C.

Far west ... 1943. SEE no. 819, Canada Steamship Lines.

FARIS, JOHN T. The Alaskan pathfinder; the story of Sheldon
Jackson for boys with an introduction by John A. Marquis. N. Y.,
Fleming H. Revell, 1913. 221p. front.(port.), pls. ANR.
1926.   1525

Farmers' almanac ... 1967. 1966. SEE no. 188, Almanac Pub. Co.

Farmers Loop Homemakers Club, Fairbanks. Family favorites.
[Fairbanks, ca 1955] [cook book, approx. 300 copies]   1526

FARQUHAR, FRANCIS PELOUBET. A brief chronology of discovery in the Pacific Ocean from Balboa to Captain Cook's first voyage, 1513-1770. S. F., Grabhorn Press, 1943. 14p. illus.   1527

FARQUHAR, FRANCIS PELOUBET and MILDRED P. ASHLEY. A list of publications relating to the mountains of Alaska. N. Y., American Alpine club, 1934. 37p.   1528

FARRAR, FREDERICK SLEIGH. Arctic assignment; the story of the *St. Roch*. By F. S. Farrar. Edited by Barrett Bonnezen. Illustrated by Vernon Mould. Toronto, Macmillan. 1955. 180p. illus. endmaps. (Great Stories of Canada) [traverse of northwest passage, 1930-42, by Royal Canadian Mounted Police]   1529

FARRAR, VICTOR JOHN. An elementary syllabus of Alaskan history. By Victor J. Farrar. [Seattle ?], March 15, 1924. 19p. bibliog.
                                                                  1530

FARRAR, VICTOR JOHN. The annexation of Russian America to the United States. By Victor J. Farrar. Washington, D. C., W. F. Roberts, 1937. 142p. bibliog. ANR. N. Y., Russell and Russell, 1966.   1531

FARRAR, VICTOR JOHN. The purchase of Alaska. By Victor J. Farrar. Washington, D. C., W. F. Roberts, 1934. 50p. bibliog. ANR. 1935. enl. ed. 118p. bibliog.   1532

Farrelly, P. J., collab. SEE no. 691, Brower, Chas. D.

Farwell, R. F. SEE nos.
    1938, Hansen, S. E. Capt. Farwell's ... piloting ... 1951;
    1939, Hansen, S. E. Hansen handbook ... piloting ... 1931.

FAST, EDWARD G. Catalogue of antiquities and curiosities collected in the Territory of Alaska by Edward G. Fast, consisting of more than two thousand most valuable and unique specimens of antiquity ... Also a collection of fire arms, a large geological collection, &c. Now on exhibition at the Clinton Hall Art Galleries. [N. Y.], Leavitt, Strebeigh & Co., [1869 ?] 32p. front. illus. [HAS COVER TITLE Catalogue of Alaskan antiquities and curiosities ...]   1533

Father Herman. SEE nos.
    1534, *Father* Herman ... n. d.;
    1756, Golder, F. A. *Father* Herman ... [191_ ?];
    2413, Kashevaroff, A. P. *Father* Herman. [1916 ?];
    4122, Shiels, A. W. Work of Veniaminov ... 1947;
    4632, [Valaam Monastery] Zhiznj Valaamskago ... 1894.

Father Herman, Russian missionary to Alaska. no pl., n. d. 12p. port. [cf no. 2413]   1534

Favorite, F., co-auth. SEE no. 1321, Dodimead, A. J.

Favorite recipes. 1944. SEE no. 3942,
   Saint Matthew's Episcopal Church.

FAY, SPOFFORD & THORNDIKE and TRYCK, NYMAN & ASSOCIATES. Preliminary evaluation of air terminal facilities and requirements
at Anchorage International Airport, Anchorage, Alaska. Anchorage, 1960. 36p.,46p. tables, maps, illus. [has appended report by Kimball, Eastburn & Associates, *Future air traffic at
the Anchorage International Airport, Alaska, November 1960*] 1535

FAY, SPOFFORD & THORNDIKE and TRYCK, NYMAN & ASSOCIATES. Preliminary evaluation of air terminal facilities and requirements
at Fairbanks International Airport, Fairbanks, Alaska. Anchorage, 1960. 33p., 44p. illus. tables, maps. [has appended report by Kimball, Eastburn & Associates, *Future air traffic at
the Fairbanks International Airport, Alaska, November 1960*] 1536

Federoff, Geo., illus. SEE no. 1682, Garfield, V. E.

FEJES, CLAIRE. People of the Noatak. Illustrated by the author.
N. Y., Knopf, 1966. 1st ed. 368p. illus. map. [a study of
Eskimos of northwest coastal Alaska] 1537

FEJES, CLAIRE. Primeval land and other poems. Illustrated by
the author. Fairbanks, published by Joseph Fejes, 1959. 45p.
illus. 1538

FELL, SARAH. Threads of Alaskan gold. no pl., n. d. 35p. illus. pls. ports. 1539

FELPS, JETTIE I. Such a folly. Boston, Meador Pub. Co., 1956.
207p. front. port. 1540

FENN, G. M. To win or to die. London, [ca 1900] 408p. illus.
[Klondike] 1541

Fenner, C. N., co-auth. SEE no. 3275, National Geographic Soc.
   ... Katmai ... 1923.

FENWICK, GEORGE. An Athabascan princess. N. Y. and Seattle,
Alice Harriman Co., 1910. 156p. illus. 1542

FERBER, EDNA. Great son. Garden City, N. Y., Doubleday, 1944.
281p. [hist.fict. with Seattle locale, some mention of Alaska]
1543

FERBER, EDNA. Ice palace. Garden City, N. Y., Doubleday, 1958.
[c1958] 1st ed. 411p. ANR. N. Y., Macfadden-Bertell Corp.,
1964. 343p. paperback. (A Macfadden Book, no. 95-104MB) [fict.
account of modern Alaska] 1544

Ferguson, Archie. SEE no. 3658, Potter, Jean.

Ferguson, J. G., pub. SEE no. 33, Alaska book ... 1960.

Ferguson, R. J., edit. SEE no. 1575, Fitzgerald, E. M.

Fergusson, B., edit. SEE no. 2777, London, J.

FERNALD, KAY and KAY McDOWELL. Rubles to statehood. Anchorage, K & K Enterprises, 1965. 132p. illus. bibliog. [catalog of numismatic items; trade tokens, medals, coins]   1545

FERNANDEZ, JUSTINO. Tomas de Suria y su Viaje con Malaspina. Mexico, 1939.   1546

FERRER MALDONADO, LORENZO. Appendix to Viaggio dal mare ... 1810. By Carlo Amoretti; Lettera apologetica di C. A. al Sig. B. di L. Milan, 1813. 19p.   1547

FERRER MALDONADO, LORENZO. Viaggio dal mare Atlantico al Pacifico per la via del nordouest fatto dal Capitano Lorenzo Ferrer Maldonado l'anno MDLXXXVIII. Tradotto da un Manoscritto Spagnuolo inedito della Biblioteca Ambrosiana di Milano da Carlo Amoretti ... Inserito nella Parte II, del Vol. I, della Cl. di Sc. Mor. e Pol. e di Letterat. dell' Istituto nazionale italiano. [Milano], 1810. 72p. pls.(fold.) ANR. Milano, Dalla Tipografia di Giovanni Silvestri, 1811. 98p. pls. maps(fold.), index, errata. (Agli Scalini del Duomo, num. 994) ANR. Bologna, 1812. 96p. maps. [for tr. see no. 1549]   1548

FERRER MALDONADO, LORENZO. Voyage de la mer Atlantique a l'ocean Pacifique par le nord-ouest dans la mer glaciale par le capitaine Laurent Ferrer Maldonado, l'an 1588. Nouvellement traduit d'un manuscrit Espagnol et suivi d'un discours qui endemontre l'authenticite et la veracité, par Charles Amoretti. Plaisance, de l'Imprimerie del Magno, 1812. 84p. pls.(fold.), maps. [tr. of no. 1548]   1549

Ferrer Maldonado, Lorenzo. SEE ALSO nos.
      712, Buache, J. N. Disertaciones sobre ... 1798;
      2577, L., B. V. Die glaubwürdigkeit ... 1712;
      3362, Novo y Colson, Pedro de. Sobre los viajes ... 1881;
      5025, Zevallos, Ciriaco de. Memorias sobre ... 1798.

FERRY TO ALASKA. no pl., [1967] Centennial Edition. 96p. illus.(come col.), map(fold. col.)   1550

A few facts about tin mining ... n. d. SEE no. 130,
      Alaska Tin Mines Co.

A few facts about tin mining ... n. d. SEE no. 3466,
      Pacific Tin Mines Co.

A few facts concerning Valdez railroad terminus. 1914. SEE
      no. 1567, Fish, J.

FEYERHERM, A. M., L. DEAN BARK and W. C. Burrows. Probabilities of sequences of wet and dry days in Alaska. Manhattan, Kansas State University, n. d. 55p. (Kansas Agricultural Experimental Station, Tech. Bull. no. 139c)   1551

FIELD, HENRY MARTYN. Our western archipelago. By Henry M. Field. With illustrations. N. Y., Scribner, 1895. 250p. front. pls. map.   1552

Field, W. O. SEE no. 204, American Geog. Soc.

FIELDHOUSE, FELICE. Yukon holiday. N. Y., Longmans Green, 1940. 230p.   1553

Filippi, Filippo de. SEE nos. 1226-8, deFilippi, Filippo.

FINCK, HENRY THEOPHILUS. The Pacific Coast scenic tour, from southern California to Alaska, the Canadian Pacific Railway, Yellowstone Park, and the Grand Canyon. By Henry T. Finck. N. Y., Scribner, 1890. 309p. pls. map. OTHERS London, Low, 1891 AND N. Y., Scribner, 1907.   1554

FINDEISEN, HANS. Das Tier als Gott, Dämon und Ahne; eine Untersuchung über das Erleben des Tieres in der Altmenschheit. [TITLE TR. The animal as god, demon, and ancestor; a study of the animal's position in primitive man's spiritual life] Stuttgart, Kosmos, Gesellschaft der Naturfreunde, 1956. 80p. illus. bibliog. [incls. North American Eskimos and Indians]   1555

Finding of an empire. [1909 ?] SEE no. 1070, Copper River and Northwestern Ry.

FINDLAY, ALEXANDER G. A directory for the navigation of the Pacific Ocean with descriptions of its coasts, islands, etc. ... London, R. H. Laurie, 1851. 2 vols. [mention of George Vancouver and James Cook]   1556

FINK, ALBERT. "As to Wickersham; reasons why Wickersham should not be returned to Congress." Fairbanks, 1910.   1557

FINK, ALBERT. The Alaska situation. no pl., Press of Shaw Bros., n. d. 12p.   1558

FINK, BRUCE. The lichen flora of the United States. Ann Arbor, University of Michigan Press, 1935. 426p. ANR. 1960. illus.
                                                                     1559

FINNEY, GERTRUDE E. To survive we must be clever. Illustrated by Carl Kidwell. N. Y., David McKay, 1966. 179p. glossary of Aleut language, illus.   1560

FINNIE, RICHARD. Canada moves north. N. Y., Macmillan, 1942. 227p. pls. ports. map. ANR. 1948. rev. ed. 239p.   1561

FINNIE, RICHARD. Canol. The sub-arctic pipeline and refinery project constructed by Bechtel-Price-Callahan for the Corps of Engineers, U. S. Army, 1942-44. Text and documentary photographs. S. F., Ryder & Ingram, 1945. 210p. front.(col.), pls. (some col.), maps, append. 1562

FINTON, W. L. Alaskan bear adventures, the story of a sportsman—naturalist's hunt for the world's largest bear on the bleak Bering Sea shores of the Alaska Peninsula. N. Y., Daniel Ryerson, 1937. 167p. front. illus. endmaps, bibliog. 1563

Fire Underwriters' Assoc. of Northwest. SEE no. 2118, Hine, Chas. C.

First city, Ketchikan ... 1916. SEE no. 2452, Ketchikan, Citizens of.

Fischer, F., co-auth. SEE no. 2603, Langsdorff, G. H. von.

FISCHER, J. E. Sibirische geschichte von der entdeckung Sibiriens bis auf die eroberung dieses landes durch die russ. waffen. St. Petersburg, 1768. 2 vols. [see no. 1565 for tr.] 1564

FISCHER, J. E. Sibirskaîa istoriîa s samago otkrytiîa Sibiri do zavoevaniîa sei zemli rossiiskim oruzhiem. Translated from the German by I. Golubtsev. St. Petersburg, Imp. Acad. Sci., 1774. 631p. maps. [tr. of no. 1564] 1565

FISH, BYRON. Alaska. Photos by Bob and Ira Spring, text by Byron Fish. Seattle, Superior Pub. Co., 1965. 1st ed. 157p. photos(some col.), endmaps. ANR. 1970. rev. ed. 1566

FISH, J. A few facts concerning Valdez railroad terminus. By J. Fish. Valdez, Valdez Commercial Assoc., 1914. 16p. 1567

FISHER ASSOCIATES, Inc., L. State of Alaska; air trade study and master plan, Anchorage International Airport. S. F., L. Fisher Associates, Inc., 1962. 35 ℓ maps, bibliog. 1568

FISHER ASSOCIATES, Inc., L. State of Alaska; air trade study and master plan, Fairbanks International Airport. S. F., L. Fisher Associates, Inc., 1962. 28 ℓ illus. bibliog. 1569

FISHER, JAMES. The fulmar. With a painting by Peter Scott. London, Collins, 1952. 496p. illus. appends. bibliog. (The New Naturalist Series, no. 6) [incls. Pacific, Aleutians and Pribilofs] 1570

Fisher, James, co-auth. SEE ALSO no. 3553, Peterson, R. T. Wild America ... 1955.

FISHER, PHYLLIS.   The Alaskan wild game cookbook.   Illustrated
by Jane Hafling.   Special mushroom section by M. Elizabeth
Deisher.   Anchorage, Alaska Color Art Print. Co., 1961.   104p.
1571

FISHER, RAYMOND H.   The Russian fur trade 1500-1700.   Berkeley,
University of California Press, 1943.   (Publications in History,
vol. 31)
1572

Fisher, R. C., co-edit.   SEE no. 1589, Fodor, E., edit.

FITCH, EDWIN M.   The Alaska Railroad.   N. Y., Frederick A. Praeger, 1967.   326p.   photos, maps, bibliog. index.   (Praeger Library of U. S. Government Departments and Agencies)
1573

FITZ, FRANCES ELLA.   Lady sourdough.   By Frances Ella Fitz as
told to Jerome Odlum.   N. Y., Macmillan, 1941.   319p.   front.
pls. ports. facsims.   [Nome]
1574

FITZGERALD, EMILY McCORKLE.   An Army doctor's wife on the frontier;   letters from Alaska and the far west, 1874-78.   Edited by
Abe Laufe.   Preliminary editing by Russell J. Ferguson.   Pittsburgh, University of Pittsburgh Press, 1962.   352p.   illus. pls.
ports. endmaps.
1575

Fitzgerald, Dr. Jenkins (John) A.   SEE no. 1575,
    Fitzgerald, Emily McC.

Flack, M., co-auth.   SEE no. 2751, Lomen, H.

FLEISCHMANN, MAX C.   After big game in Arctic and Tropic;   a
sportsman's notebook of the chase off Greenland and Alaska;   in
Africa, Norway, Spitzbergen and the Cassiar.   Cincinnati, Jennings & Graham, 1909.   248p.   front. illus.
1576

FLETCHER, A. L.   Boy scouts in Alaska; or, camp on the glaciers.
Bt Major A. L. Fletcher.   Chicago, 1913.   153p.   front.
1577

FLETCHER, INGLIS.   Vilhjalmur Stefansson.   N. Y., Nomad Pub. Co.,
1925.
1578

Fleurieu, Charles Pierre Claret de.   Die neuste ... n. d.
    SEE no. 1581.

FLEURIEU, CHARLES PIERRE CLARET de.   Voyage autour du monde, pendant les années 1790, 1791, et 1792, par Etienne Marchand, pré-
cedé d'une   introduction historique ... avec cartes et figures;
Par C. P. Claret Fleurieu ... Paris, de l'Imprimerie de la Republique, An VI, An VII, An VIII, An VIII. 4 vols. [1798-1800]
628p., 676p., 432p. and 159p. pl. table, maps(fold.)   ANR. Paris,
[1798-1800]   5 vols.   294p., 530p., 475p., 560p. and atlas of
maps, pl.
1579

FLEURIEU, CHARLES PIERRE CLARET de. TRANSLATIONS - Voyage ...
[1798-1800], chronologically.

A voyage round the world, performed during the years 1790, 91
and 92. By Etienne Marchand, preceded by a historical introduction and illustrated by charts, &c. Translated from
the French of C. P. Claret Fleurieu. London, T. N. Longman
and O. Rees, 1801. 2 vols. plus atlas. 361p., 503p., 105p.
maps. ANR. 1801. 2 vols. and atlas. 536p., 663p., 105p.
maps. ANR. Amsterdam, N. Israel and N. Y., Da Capo Press,
1969. 2 vols. map (Bibliotheca Australiana, 3d ser., nos.
23, 24) [facsim. ed.]   1580

Die neuste Reise um die Welt ... Leipzig, n. d. 2 vols. pl.
map.   1581

FLINT, STAMFORD RAFFLES. Mudge memoirs; being a record of
Zachariah Mudge and some members of his family. Truro, England,
Netherton, 1883. 258p. ports. [Zachariah Mudge on *Discovery*
at Nootka Sound]   1582

FLODERUS, BJÖRN GUSTAV OSKAR. A strange species of *Salix* from
Alaska. Stockholm, Almquist & Wiksell, 1935. 3p. (Arkiv för
Botanik, Bd. 27A, no. 2)   1583

FLODERUS, BJÖRN GUSTAV OSKAR. Two Linnean species of *Salix* and
their allies. Stockholm, Almquist & Wiksell, 1940. 54p. pls.
(Arkiv för Botanik, Bd. 29A, no. 18) [incl. Alaskan species]1584

Floeth, R., illus. SEE no. 1139, Cunningham, C.

Flood. 1967. SEE no. 235, Anchorage Daily News.

FLOOD, MILFORD. Arctic journal, and other works, including Ruall
Dwelly [and] Of prairie rapparees. L. A., Wetzel Pub. Co.,
1950. 459p. illus. endmaps. [incls. journal Oct. 1943-July
1944. Canol Project]   1585

FLORA, CHARLES and EUGENE FAIRBANKS. The sound and the sea.
Bellingham, Washington, Pioneer Print. Co., 1968. [marine invertebrates, northwest Pacific coast]   1586

FLOWER, ROUSSEAU HAYNER. Cephalopods from the Seward Peninsula
of Alaska. N. Y., Paleontological Research Institution, 1941.
22p. illus. pls. (Bulletins of American Paleontology, vol. 27,
no. 102)   1587

FLUKE, CHARLES LEWIS. The *Metasyrphus* species of North America
(Diptera, Syrphidae). N. Y., American Museum of Natural History,
1952. 27p. illus. figs. (Novitates, no. 1590) [incls. flies
of Matanuska Valley, Alaska, also Northwest Territory and Yukon
Territory]   1588

FODOR, EUGENE, ROBERT C. FISHER and BARNETT D. LASCHEVER. Pacific states; Southern California, Northern California, Nevada, Idaho, Oregon, Washington, Alaska. Litchfield, Conn., Fodor's Modern Guides, 1966. 480p. illus.(some col.), maps(some col.) (Fodor Shell Travel Guides U. S. A., vol. 8)   1589

FOFONOFF, N. P. and F. W. DOBSON. Transport computations for the North Pacific Ocean 1950-59; 10-year means and standard deviations by months; wind stress and vertical velocity, annual means 1955-60. Nanaimo, B. C., 1963. 179p. maps, tables, bibliog. (Canada. Fisheries Research Board Ms Report Series, Oceanographic and Limnological, no. 166) [incls. Bering Sea, Aleutian Islands and Gulf of Alaska]   1590

FOFONOFF, N. P. Transport computations for the North Pacific Ocean 1955-58. Ottawa, Queen's Printer, 1960. 4 vols. 9p. in each. tables, maps, bibliog. (Canada. Research Board Ms Report Series Oceanographic and Limnological, no. 77-80)   1591

FOFONOFF, N. P. and C. K. Ross. Transport computations for the North Pacific Ocean 1959-61. Ottawa, Queen's Printer, Feb. 7, Apr. 24, May 23, 1961. 3 vols. 181p.90p.(approx.), 100p.(approx.) maps, tables, bibliog. (Canada. Fisheries Research Board Ms Report Series Oceanographic and Limnological, no. 85, 93, 128)   1592

Foley, L. H., co-auth. SEE no. 4508, Thompson, R.

Fonte, Admiral de. SEE cross-references under: de la Fuente, Bartolome.

FONTICELLI, ANTONIO. Americalogia; ossia osservazioni storiche e fiziologiche sopre gli Americani con un breve ragguaglio delle ultime scoperte fatte dai Russi nel mar Pacifico. Genoa, Eredi di Adamo Scionico, 1790. 123p.   1593

FOOTE, DON CHARLES and SHEILA K. MacBAIN. A selected regional bibliography for human geographical studies of the native populations in Central Alaska. Montreal, McGill University, 1964. 62p. front.(map) [research undertaken for Association on American Indian Affairs]   1594

FOOTE, DON CHARLES. Human geographical studies in northwestern Arctic Alaska, the Point Hope and Upper Kobuk River projects, 1965. Research reports. A. Biological data on selected species of seals and fish, 1 Nov. 1965. B. Meteorological data for Shungnak, Alaska, 6 July to Aug. 27, 1965, 10 Dec. 1965. C. Eskimo stories and songs of the Upper Kobuk River, Alaska, 1 May 1966. Montreal, 1 June 1966. no p. figs. tables, list of tape recordings of stories and songs. [research undertaken for Association on American Indian Affairs]   1595

FOOTE, DON CHARLES. Human geographical studies in northwestern Arctic Alaska. The Upper Kobuk River project, 1965. Final report. Montreal, 1 June 1966. 65p. figs. tables, maps(incl. 1 fold.), bibliog. [research undertaken for Association on American Indian Affairs]   1596

Foote, Don Charles. SEE ALSO no. 4651, van Steensel, M.
   People of light and dark. 1966.

Forbes, Edw., edit. SEE no. 2432, Kellett, Henry.

FORBES, H. A., comp. Gazetteer of northern Canada and parts of Alaska and Greenland. Ottawa, Canadian Geographical Bureau, 1948. 75p. maps. (Department of Mines and Resources)   1597

FORD, COREY. Short cut to Tokyo; the battle for the Aleutians. N. Y., Scribner, 1943. 141p. endmaps.   1598

FORD, COREY. Where the sea breaks its back; the epic story of a pioneer naturalist and the discovery of Alaska. Boston, Little Brown, 1966. 1st ed. 206p. illus. drawings by Lois Darling, endmaps, bibliog. [biog. of Geo. Wilhelm Steller] 1599

Ford, Corey, co-auth. SEE ALSO no.3288,
   Nelson, K. Daughter of gold rush. 1958.

FORD, JAMES ALFRED. Eskimo prehistory in the vicinity of Point Barrow, Alaska. By James A. Ford. With an appendix, *Skeletal remains from the vicinity of Point Barrow, Alaska,* by T. D. Stewart. N. Y., American Museum of Natural History, 1959. 272p. illus. maps, diagrs. tables, bibliog. (Anthropological papers, vol. 47, pt. 1)   1600

FORDE, CYRIL DARYLL. Habit, economy and society, a geographical introduction to ethnology. London, Methuen, 1943. 2d ed. 500p. illus. bibliog. [incls. Haida, Kwakiutl, other Indians and also Eskimos]   1601

Forman, W., co-auth. SEE no. 4144, Siebert, E.

FORREST, ELIZABETH CHABOT. Daylight moon, with 38 reproductions from photographs taken by the author. By Elizabeth C. Forrest. N. Y., F. A. Stokes, 1937. 340p. front. pls. ports. [Eskimos in Alaska]   1602

FORREST, GLADYS and B. FRANK HEINTZLEMAN. Land resources of Alaska; policies and laws controlling their use, prepared by G. Forrest. With a section on forest resources by B. F. Heintzleman. Portland, Oregon, North Pacific Planning Project, June 1944. 80p. 2 maps(fold.), bibliog. (North Pacific Study, no. 14)   1603

Forrest, Linn A., co-auth. SEE no. 572, Blackerby, A. W.

Forrest, Linn A., co-auth. SEE ALSO no. 1685, Garfield, V. E.

Forster, Georg. SEE nos. 1605-8, Forster, Johann Georg Adam.

FÖRSTER, HANS ALBERT. Der weisse Weg; Forscher erobern die Arktis. [TITLE TR. The white way; explorers conquer the Arctic]
Leipzig, Volk und Buch Verlag, 1952. 407p. pls. maps(3 fold.),
chronology, list of narratives, index. [incls. Vitus Bering]1604

FORSTER, JOHANN GEORG ADAM. Cook, der Entdecker. By Georg
Forster. Leipzig, P. G. Kummer, 1789. 232p.   1605

FORSTER, JOHANN GEORG ADAM. Geschichte der Reisen, die seit
Cook an der Nordwest- und Nordost-Küste von Amerika und in dem
nördlichsten Amerika selbst von Mears, Dixon, Portlock, Coxe,
Long u. a. M. unternommen worden sind. Mit vielen Karten und
Kupfern. Aus dem Englischen, mit Zuziehung aller anderweitigen
Hülfsquellen, ausgearbeitet von Georg Forster. Erster[-Dritter]
Band. Berlin, In der Vossischen Buchhandlung, 1791. 3 vols.
x,130,1-302,5,11p.(vol. 1); xxii,314p.(vol. 2); xv,74,1-380p.
(vol. 3) illus. map, tables. [for anr. ed. see no. 1607] 1606

FORSTER, JOHANN GEORG ADAM. Geschichte der Reisen die Seit Cook
an der Nordwest- und Nordost-küste von Amerika; und in dem nördlichsten Amerika selbst von Meares, Dixon, Portlock, Coxe, Long
u. a. m. unternommen worden sind; aus dem Englischen ausgearbeitet von Georg Forster. Berlin, Vossischen Buchhandlung, 1792.
3 vols. front. pls. maps. [see also no. 1606]   1607

FORSTER, JOHANN GEORG ADAM. Kleine Schriften, Ein Beytrag Zur
Volker und Landerkunde. Leipzig and Berlin, 1789-96. 5 vols.
                                                              1608
Forster, Johann Georg Adam. SEE ALSO nos.
     1028, [Cook, Jas.] Des Capitain James Cook's dritte ...1787;
     1028, [Cook, Jas.] Dritte Entdeckungs-Reise ... 1787;
     1030, [Cook, Jas.] Des Capitain Jacob Cook dritte ... 1789;
     1170, Damm, H., edit. Jas. Cook; die suche ... 1922;
     3057, Meares, J. Des Kapitans John Meares ... 1796;
     3651, [Portlock, N.] ... Reisen ... 1796.

Forster, Johann Reinhold. [Alphabetical guide to chronological
     entries]

     Geschichte ... 1609.   History ... 1610, 1611.
     Histoire ... 1612.   Observations ... 1613.

FORSTER, JOHANN REINHOLD. Geschichte der Entdeckungen und Schif-
fahrten im Norden ... Frankfurt, 1784. 2 vols. 446p., 449-596p.
front. maps(fold.) ANR. Berlin, n. d. reprint.   1609

FORSTER, JOHANN REINHOLD.   TRANSLATIONS - Geschichte der
Entdeckungen ... 1784, chronologically.

    History of the voyages and discoveries made in the north.
    London, G. G. J. and J. Robinson, 1786. 489p. plus. (16)p.
    front.(fold. map), maps(fold.), index.   1610

    History of the voyages and discoveries made in the north.
    Translated from the German and elucidated by a new and
    original map of the countries situated about the North
    Pole. Dublin, White and Byrne, 1786. 489p. front.(fold.
    map)   1611

    Histoire des découvertes et des voyages faites dans le nord,
    translated par Broussonnet. Paris, Cuchet, 1788. 2 vols.
    399p. 410p. maps(fold.)   1612

FORSTER, JOHANN REINHOLD. Observations made during a voyage
round the world, on physical geography, natural history, and
ethic philosophy. Especially on: 1. The earth and its strata;
2. Water and the ocean; 3. The atmosphere; 4. The changes
of the globe; 5. Organic bodies; and 6. The human species.
London, G. Robinson, 1778. 649p. [with Capt. Cook]   1613

Forster, Johann Reinhold. SEE ALSO nos.
    1015, [Cook, Jas.] Tagebuch ... 1781;
    1254, deLesseps, J. B. B. Herrn von Lesseps ... 1791;
    1310, Dixon, G. Der kapitaine Portlock's ... 1790;
    2615, [LaPerouse, J. F. G. de] Entdeckungsreise ... 1800.

FORSTINGER, RUDOLF. Durch die Luft zum Nord- und Südpol; Be-
richte und Schilderungen über die seit 1896 in den Polargebieten
ausgeführten Flüge. [TITLE TR. To the North and South Pole by
air; reports and accounts of flights to the polar regions made
since 1896] Breslau, F. Hirt, [1935] 62p. illus. map, diagrs.
append. (Hirts Deutsche Sammlung ... Gruppe 1: Die Erforschung
der Erde. Bd. 6)   1614

Fortier, Ed, edit. SEE no. 70, Alaska hunting ... 1960.

FORTUINE, ROBERT. The health of the Eskimos; a bibliography
1857-1967. Hanover, N. H., Dartmouth College Libraries, 1968.
87p. index, wrps. (The Stefansson Collection)   1615

FOSTER, JOHN W. The Alaskan Boundary Tribunal. Washington,
D. C., Judd and Detweiler, Printers, 1903. 14p.   1616

FOSTER, WALTER BERTRAM. In Alaskan waters. By W. Bert Foster.
Illustrated by Winfield S. Lukens. Philadelphia, Penn Pub. Co.,
1903. 363p. illus. OTHERS 1910 AND 1925.   1617

FOUKE FUR CO. The romance of Alaska sealskin. St. Louis, Mo.,
1954. 7th rev. ed. 47p. illus.   1618

FOUKE FUR CO. The romance of the Alaska fur seal. Greenville, S. C., Fouke Fur Co., 1958. 47p. front endmap, illus. by Robert Hines. 1619

Found, W. A., co-auth. SEE no. 332, Babcock, J. P.

Four thousand miles ... 1896. SEE no. 3451, Pacific Coast Steamship Co.

FOWLER, FRANK S., and CO. Authentic Alaska information. Seattle, F. S. Fowler & Co., [1896 ?] (8)p. 1620

Fox, W. G., co-comp. SEE no. 4655, Van Winkle, L. E.

FRADKIN, NAUM. GRIGOR'EVICH. S. P. Krasheninnikov; pod red. A. I. Solov'eva. [TITLE TR. S. P. Krasheninnikov; edited by A. I. Solov'ev] Moskva, Gos. izd-vo Geogr. lit-ry, 1951. 40p. illus. port. map. 1621

FRAERMAN, RUVIM ISAEVICH and P. D. ZAĬKIN. Plavaniĩa V. M. Golovnina. Pod red. N. N. Zubova. [TITLE TR. Voyages of V. M. Golovnin. N. N. Zubov, editor] Moskva, Gos. izd-vo Geogr. lit-ry, 1948. 118p. illus.(port.), map, bibliog.(of Golovnin's works) 1622

FRAERMAN, RUVIM ISAEVICH and P. D. ZAĬKIN. Zhizn' i neobyknovennye prikliucheniĩa kapitan-leĭtenanta Golovnina, puteshestvennika i morekhodtsa. [TITLE TR. The life and extraordinary adventures of Capt.-Lt. Golovnin, traveler and seafarer] Moskva, Voennoe izd-vo, 1946-48. 2 vols. 280p., 303p. illus. ANR. Moskva, Izd-vo Molodaĩa Gvardiĩa, 1950. 2d ed. 1 vol. 499p. illus. port. pls. [biographical novel] 1623

FRAME, JOHN W. Frame's Alaska pocket pilot; one thousand questions on the most wonderfully misunderstood country in the world asked and answered. Ketchikan, 1929. 49p. 1624

FRANCE, GEORGE W. The struggles for life and home in the northwest by a pioneer home-builder; life, 1865-89. N. Y., Goldman, 1890. 607p. illus. port. facsim. [west and Alaska] 1625

Franchere, Gabriel. A voyage to northwest coast ... 1954. SEE no. 1626.

FRANCHERE, GABRIEL. Narrative of a voyage to the northwest coast of America in the years 1811, 12, 13, and 1814; or, the first American settlement on the Pacific. By Gabriel Franchere. Translated and edited by J. V. Huntington. N. Y., Redfield, 1854. 376p. front. pls. ANR. WITH TITLE A voyage to the northwest coast of America. Edited by Milo Milton Quaife. Chicago, The Lakeside Press, 1954. 321p. front.(port.), illus. maps, append. index. (The Lakeside Classics, Christmas, 1954) [tr. of no. 1627, incls. material on Sitka and Pribilof Islands] 1626

FRANCHERE, GABRIEL. Relation d'un voyage a la cote du Nord-Ouest de Amerique Septentrionale, dans les Annees 1810, 11, 12, 13 et 14. Par G. Franchere, Fils. Montreal, de l'Imprimerie de C. B. Pasteur, 1820. 1st ed. (35),(36),284p. [see no. 1626 for trs., Astor Fur Co.]   1627

FRANCHERE, RUTH. Jack London; the pursuit of a dream. N. Y., Crowell, 1962. 264p.   1628

FRANCIS, FRANCIS. War, waves and wanderings. Cruise in "Lancashire Witch." London, Sampson Low, Marston, 1881. 2 vols.
                                                                   1629

FRANCK, HARRY A. The lure of Alaska. By Harry A. Franck, accompanied by Harry A. Franck, Jr. With 100 reproductions of photographs, most of them taken by the author. N. Y., Frederick A. Stokes, 1939. 1st ed. 306p. illus. front. endmaps. (National Travel Club) ANR. Garden City, N. Y., Blue Ribbon Books, 1943. photos.   1630

FRANKEL, HASKEL. Adventure in Alaska. Illustrated by Anthony Accurso. Garden City, Doubleday, 1963. 1st ed. 142p. illus. (A Signal Book)   1631

FRANKLIN, F. K. The cleft in the rock. N. Y., Thomas Y. Crowell, 1955. 250p. [fict. Aleutian Island setting]   1632

FRANKLIN, JOHN. Narrative of a second expedition to the shores of the Polar Sea, in the years 1825, 1826, and 1827, by John Franklin, Captain R. N. ... Commander of the expedition. Including an account of the progress of a detachment to the eastward by John Richardson, M.D. ... surgeon and naturalist to the expedition. Illustrated by numerous plates and maps. Published by authority of the Right Honourable the Secretary of State for Colonial Affairs. London, John Murray, 1828. 320p. pls. maps (fold.)   1633

Franklin, John. SEE ALSO nos.
     301, Arctic miscellanies ... 1852;
     304, Armstrong, A. Personal narrative ... 1857;
     326, Austin, H. T. Review proceedings ... 1851;
     986, Collinson, R. Journal ... 1889;
    1148, Cyriax, R. J. Cir John Franklin's ... 1939;
    1213, Davydov, I. V. Dzhon Franklin. 1956;
    1819-33, Great Britain (Franklin Search);
    2172, Hooker, Wm. J. Flora boreali-Americana ... 1829-40;
    2177, Hooper, Wm. H. Ten months ... Tuski ... 1853;
    2585, Lamb, G. F. Franklin; happy voyager ... 1956;
    2587, Lambert, R. S. Adventure to Polar Sea. 1950;
    2588, Lambert, R. S. Franklin of Arctic ... 1949;
    3443, Oxley, J. M. D. North overland with Franklin. 1907;
    3766, Recent polar voyages. [187_ ?];
    3804, Richardson, J. Arctic searching expedition. 1851;

Franklin, John. SEE ALSO nos.
    3960, Sargent, Epes. Arctic adventure ... 1857;
    4039, Seemann, B. C. Narrative voyage ... 1853;
    4153-4, Simmonds, P. L. Sir John Franklin ... 1851 and 1852;
    4155, Simmonds, P. L. The Arctic regions ... 1857;
    4156, [Simmonds, P. L.] The Arctic regions ... 1853;
    4173, Skewes, J. H. Sir John Franklin ... 1889;
    4198, Smith Geo. B. Sir John Franklin ... [ca 1896 ?];
    4210, Smucker, S. M. Arctic explorations ... 1857;
    4408, Sutton, A. Endless quest ... 1965.
    4850, Whymper, F. Heroes Arctic ... [ca 1875];
    4974, Wright, Noel. Quest of Franklin. [c1959]

FRANKLIN, LUCIA J. Stories and facts of Alaska; a wonderful book of fascinating and surprising information of Alaska's vast resources; a traveler's guide to the gold mines, the farming valleys, the coal and oil fields, and the different routes to Alaska, and cost of trips. Fairbanks, L. J. Franklin, 1921. 307p. illus. front. pls.   1634

FRASER, C. M. Hydroids of the Pacific coast of Canada and the United States. Toronto, University of Toronto Press, 1937. 207p. pls.   1635

FRASER, CHELSEA CURTIS. Heroes of the air. N. Y., Thomas Y. Crowell, 1926. pls. maps drawn by author.   1636

FRASER, CHELSEA CURTIS. Heroes of the sea. N. Y., Thomas Y. Crowell, 1924.   1637

FRASER, JAMES DUNCAN. The gold fever; or, two years in Alaska. By J. D. Fraser. A true narrative of actual events as experienced by the author. no pl. [Honolulu ?], by author, [c1923] 100p. wrps. [Tanana and Yukon Rivers, city of Circle, 1898]1638

FRAZER, JAMES G. Anthologia anthropologica; the native races of America; a copious selection of passages for the study of social anthropology, from the manuscript notebooks of Sir James Frazer. Arranged and edited from mss. by Robert Angus Downey. London, P. Lund, Humphries & Co., 1939. 351p.   1639

FRAZER, JAMES G. Totemism and exogamy, a treatise on certain early forms of superstition and society. By Sir James Frazer. London, Macmillan, 1910. 4 vols. [vol. 3 contains northwest American material]   1640

FREBOLD, HANS. Grundzüge der geologischen Entwicklung und Struktur des arktischen Sibirien östlich der Lena. [TITLE TR. Fundamentals of the geologic history and structure of arctic Siberia east of the Lena] Berlin, Borntraeger, 1942. 35p. table(fold.) sketch map. (Deutsche Wissenschaftliche Institut zu Kopenhagen. Veröffentlichungen Reihe 1: Arktis, nr. 2) [incls. northern Alaska and Seward Peninsula]   1641

Frechtmann, B., tr. SEE no. 3638, Poncins, G. de M.

FREDE, PIERRE. Aventures lointanes; voyage aux iles Sitka.
Paris, Firmin-Didot, 1887. 128p. illus.   1642

FREDE, PIERRE. Aventures lointaines; voyage aux iles Sitka,
ancienne Amérique Russe. Paris, Firmin-Didot, 1890. illus.
front. pls.   1643

FREDE, PIERRE. Aventures lointaines; voyages, chasses et
peches aux iles Sitka; voyage en caravane a travers la Perse;
un jambon d'hyene; yegor de pisteur d'ours. Paris, Firmin-Didot,
1882, 356p.   1644

Frederick, Chas. SEE nos. 1827 and 1831, Great Britain,
     (Franklin Search)

FREDERICK, ROBERT A., edit. Frontier Alaska, a study in historical interpretation and opportunity. Proceedings of Conference
on Alaskan History, Anchorage, Alaska Methodist University,
June 8-10, 1967. Anchorage, Alaska Methodist University Press,
1968. 172p. illus. bibliogs. (Alaska Review, Fall and Winter
1967-68, vol. 3, no. 1)   1645

FREEMAN, ANDREW A. The case for Doctor Cook. N. Y., Coward-
McCann, 1961. 315p. notes, index. [incls. some material on
Mt. McKinley controversy]   1646

FREEMAN, M. Salmon packers' directory, 1907. Seattle, Pacific
Fisherman, 1908. Others annually to 1923, pub. 1924.   1647.

Freeman, Miller, co-auth. SEE no. 332, Babcock, J. P.

Freeman, N. L., co-auth. SEE no. 4515, Thompson, Wm. F.

Frenaye, Frances, tr. SEE no. 579, Blond, Georges.

French, Cecil, tr. SEE no. 2204, Howay, F. W.

FRENCH, LEIGH HILL. Nome nuggets. Some of the experiences of a
party of gold seekers in northwestern Alaska in 1900. N. Y.,
Montross, Clarke & Emmons, 1901. 102p. front. pls. ports. 1648

FRENCH, LEIGH HILL. Seward's land of gold; five seasons experience with the gold seekers in northwestern Alaska. N. Y., Montross, Clarke & Emmons, [1905 ?] 101p. front. pls. ports. 1649

Freuchen, Dagmar, edit. SEE nos.
     1650, Freuchen, Peter. Adventures in Arctic. 1960;
     1651, Freuchen, Peter. Book of Eskimos. 1961;
     1654, Freuchen, Peter. Men of frozen north. 1962;
     1655, Freuchen, Peter. Peter Freuchen reader. 1965.

FREUCHEN, PETER. Adventures in the Arctic. N. Y., Julian Messner, 1960. 383p. illus. 1650

FREUCHEN, PETER. Book of the Eskimos. Edited and with a preface
by Dagmar Freuchen. Cleveland, World Pub. Co., 1961. 441p. pls.
sketches and photos by Dagmar Freuchen, endmaps. ANR. N. Y.,
Bramhall House, 1961. ANR. Cleveland, World Pub. Co., 1965.
464p. ANR. Greenwich, Conn., Fawcett Pub., 1965. paperback.
(Crest no. M866) 1651

FREUCHEN, PETER. Book of the seven seas. N. Y., Julian Messner,
1957. 512p. front.(port.), illus. maps, endmaps, index. 1652

Freuchen, Peter. Det arktiske år. SEE no. 1657.

FREUCHEN, PETER. It's all adventure. N. Y., Julian Messner,
1938. 508p. photos, endmap. 1653

FREUCHEN, PETER. Men of the frozen north. Edited and with a
preface by Dagmar Freuchen. Cleveland, World Pub. Co., 1962.
315p. drawings by Dagmar Freuchen, endmaps. 1654

FREUCHEN, PETER. Peter Freuchen reader, edited by Dagmar Freuchen. N. Y., Julian Messner, 1965. 1655

FREUCHEN, PETER and FINN SALOMONSEN. The Arctic year. N. Y.,
Putnam, 1958. 438p. illus. maps, endmaps, bibliog. ANR. London,
Jonathan Cape, 1960. 440p. drawings and maps by Erik Petersen,
endmaps, bibliog. index. (Readers' Union) 1656

FREUCHEN, PETER. TRANSLATION - Arctic year. 1958.

  Det arktiske år. København, Gyldendal, 1961. 382p. 1657

FREUCHEN, PETER. The law of Larion. Translated from the Danish
by Evelyn Ramsden. N. Y., McGraw-Hill, 1952. 313p. ANR. London, 1954. 313p. 1658

FREUCHEN, PETER. The legend of Daniel Williams. N. Y., Julian
Messner, 1956. 256p. ANR. London, 1958. 1659

FREUCHEN, PETER. Vagrant viking; my life and adventures.
Translated from the Danish by Johan Hambro. N. Y., Julian Messner, 1953. 312p. illus. endmaps, index. ANR. 9th print. 1963.
422p. photos, endmaps, index. 1660

Freuchen, Peter. SEE ALSO nos.
    1661, Freuchen, Pipaluk. Bogen om ... 1958;
    3746, Rasmussen, K. J. V. Mindeudgave ... 1934-35.

FREUCHEN, PIPALUK, edit. Bogen om Peter Freuchen. [TITLE TR.
The book about Peter Freuchen] København, Forlaget Fremad, 1958.
208p. illus.[edited by Pipaluk Freuchen with others] 1661

FROBESE, F. E. The origin and meaning of the totem poles in southeastern Alaska. Sitka, Alaskan Printing Office, 1897. 14p.   1662

FROMERT-GUIEYSSE, GEORGES. La Pérouse, avec 5 photos et une carte-itineraire de l'expedition La Pérouse. Paris, Éditions de l'Empire français, 1947. 155p. illus. port. map(fold.), bibliog (Collection Les Frande Navigateurs)   1663

Frontier Alaska ... 1967. SEE no. 1645, Frederick, R. A.

FRYE, THEODORE CHRISTIAN and LOIS CLARK. Hepaticae of North America (north of Mexico). Seattle, University of Washington Press, 1937-48. 1022p.   1664

Fryxell, B. L., edit. SEE no. 680, Brooks, A. H.

Fuente, Admiral de la. SEE cross-references under de la Fuente, Bartolome.

FUHRMANN, ERNST. Tlinkit u. Haida, Indianstämme der Westküste von Nordamerika. Kultische Kunst und Mythen des Kulturkreises. [TITLE TR. Tlingit and Haida, Indian tribes of the west coast of North America. Cultic art and myths of the culture area] Hagen i W. und Darmstadt, Folkwangerverlag g.m.b.h., 1922. 41p. 61 pls. on 31 ℓ (Schriftenreihe Kulturen der Erde, material zur Kultur- und Kunstgeschichte Aller Völker [Bilderwerke], Bd. 22)
                                                                1665
Fuller, F. E. SEE no. 1845, Green, J. C.

FULLER, GEORGE W. A history of the Pacific northwest. N. Y., Knopf, 1931. 383p. illus. front. pls. ports. maps(incl. 1 fold.) ANR. 1938. 2d rev. ed. front. pls. ports. maps(incl. 1 fold.)   1666

G

GABRIEL, GILBERT WOLF. I got a country, a novel of Alaska. Garden City, N. Y., Doubleday, 1944. 432p.   1667

GABRIELSON, IRA NOEL and FREDERICK C. LINCOLN. The birds of Alaska. Harrisburg, Penna., Stackpole Co. and Washington, D. C., Wildlife Management Institute, 1959. 922p. illus.(col.), map, diagr. bibliog. gazetteer, index. [illus. by Olaus J. Murie and Edwin R. Kalmbach]   1668

GABRIELSON, IRA NOEL. Wildlife refuges. N. Y., Macmillan, 1943. 257p. illus. bibliog.   1669

GAGE, JOSEPH H. Trail north to danger; mystery in the Yukon. N. Y., Winston, 1952. ANR. Philadelphia and Toronto, 1956. 215p. illus.   1670

Gage, W. L., co-auth. SEE no. 2249, Hyde, A.

GAINES, RUBEN. Chilkoot Charlie. Sitka, Sitka Print. Co., 1951.
26p. drawings by Dale De Armond, wrps. [poetry]   1671

GAINES, RUBEN. Mrs. Maloney. Sitka, Sitka Print. Co., 1955.
11p. illus. wrps. [poetry]   1672

GAINES, RUBEN. The second book of Chilkoot Charlie. Sitka,
Sitka Print. Co., 1955. 27p. drawings by Dale De Armond, wrps.
[poetry]   1673

GAIRDNER, GEORGE W. and A. G. HARRISON. The Gairdner and Harri-
son prospectors guide map and pamphlet to the Omenica, Cassiar,
Liard, Klondyke and Yukon gold fields via the Edmonton Route.
Edmonton, Alberta, Bulletin Print, 1897. 16p. map.   1674

Galaup, Jean F., Comte de la Pérouse. SEE nos. 2609-21,
    La Pérouse, Jean François Galaup de.

[GALIANO, DIONISIO ALCALA] A Spanish voyage to Vancouver and
the north-west coast of America, being the narrative of the
schooners *Sutil* and *Mexicana* to explore the Strait of Fuca.
Translated from the Spanish with an introduction by Cecil Jane.
London, Argonaut Press, 1930. 142p. pls. map. ANR. Fairfield,
Wash., Ye Galleon Press, 1968. facsim ltd. numbered ed. [fac-
sim. of London 1930 ed. with Eng. tr. of Navarette introduction
to 1802 ed. See also no. 1676]   1675

[Galiano, Dionisio Alcala] Atlas ... 1803. SEE no. 1676.

[GALIANO, DIONISIO ALCALA] Relacion del viage hecho por las Goletas *Sutil* y *Mexicana* en el ano le 1792, para reconocer el estrecho de Fuca; con una introduccion en que se de noticia de
las expeditiones executadas anteriormenta por las Espanoles en
busca del paso de noroeste de la America. De Orden del Rey.
[TITLE TR. Narrative of the trip made by the ships *Sutil* and
Mexicana in the year 1792 to survey the Strait of Fuca, with an
introduction giving information on the expeditions made previ-
ously by the Spanish looking for the northwest passage of America. By order of the King] Madrid, En La Imprinta Real, 1802.
186p. table(fold.), vocab. errata. [in 3 pts.: Introduction
by M. F. de Navarette; Text (variously ascribed to Dionisio
Alcala Galiano, Jose Espinosa y Tello, or to Cayetano Valdes);
Appendix by Jose Espinosa y Tello] WITH Atlàs para le viage de
las goletas *Sutil* y *Mexicana* al reconocumento del Estrecho de
Juan de Fuca en 1792. pls.(some fold.), ports. plans, maps
(fold.) ANR. Madrid, 1958. 2 vols. pls. maps. [for tr. see no.
1675]   1676

Galiano, Dionisio Alcala. SEE ALSO nos.
    1495, Espinosa y Tello, J. de. Appendix ... 1806;
    3279, Navarette, M. F. de. ... introd. relacion ... 1802.

Gall, Franz Joseph. SEE no. 925, Choris, L.

Galpin, Wmt SEE no. 1113, Crane, A. R.

Galvin, Pat. SEE no. 1142, Curtin, W. R.

GAMBELL, V. C. The schoolhouse farthest west. St. Lawrence Island, Alaska. N. Y., Woman's Board of Home Missions, 1910. 44p. illus.   1677

Ganzen, A. V., tr. SEE no. 3744, Rasmussen, K. J. V.

GAPP, SAMUEL H. Kolerat Pitsiulret; or, true stories of the early days of the Moravian Mission on the Kuskokwim. Bethlehem, Penna., Christian Education Board of the Moravian Church in America, 1936. 108p. [mission of Rev. J. H. Kilbuck]   1678

GAPP, SAMUEL H. Where polar ice begins; or, the Moravian Mission in Alaska. Bethlehem, Penna., Religious Education Board of the Moravian Church in America, 1928. 126p. pls.   1679

GARBER, CLARK McKINLEY. Stories and legends of the Bering Strait Eskimos. By Clark M. Garber. Boston, Christopher Pub. House, [c1940] 260p. front.(port.), pls. ports. map, plan, glossary. [Wales, Seward Peninsula]   1680

GARDNER, LEE S. The optimist, American Plan; a study in representative government. N. Y., Exposition Press, 1951. 105p.1681

GARFIELD, VIOLA E. Meet the totem. Sitka, Sitka Print. Co., 1951. 54p. pls. drawings by George Federoff. ANR. 1967. 5th print. rev.   1682

GARFIELD, VIOLA E. The Seattle totem pole. Seattle, University of Washington, 1940. 14p. (Extension Series, no. 11, July 1940)   1683

GARFIELD, VIOLA E. and PAUL S. WINGERT. The Tsimshian Indians and their arts. Seattle, University of Washington Press, 1966. 108p. illus. map. ANR. Seattle, University of Washington Press, n. d. 94(4)p. pls. sketches, map, ftntes. wrps. [pts. 1 and 2 of American Ethnological Society Pub. 18, "The Tsimshian; their arts and music," edited by Marian W. Smith. See no. 4202] 1684

GARFIELD, VIOLA E. and LINN A. FORREST. The wolf and the raven; totem poles of southeastern Alaska. Seattle, University of Washington Press, 1948. 151p. illus. ANR. 1961. 2d ed. rev. 156p. front. pls. map, bibliog. addend.   1685

GARFIELD, VIOLA E. Tsimshian clan and society. Seattle, University Press, 1939. 339p. front. pls. maps(fold.) (Pub. in Anthropology, vol. 7, no. 3) [Pt. Simpson, B. C.- Metlakatla, Alaska]   1686

GARLAND, HAMLIN. The long trail; a story of the northwest wilderness. N. Y., Harper, 1907. 262p. front. pls. [to Klondike
via Ashcroft Trail in B. C.]   1687

GARLAND, HAMLIN. The trail of the goldseekers, a record of travel in prose and verse. N. Y., Macmillan, 1899. 264p. ANR.
N. Y., Harper, 1906. [to Klondike via Ashcroft Trail in B. C.]
                                                          1688

GARN, STANLEY MARION, edit. Readings on race. Edited by Stanley M. Garn. Springfield, Ill., Thomas, 1960. 281p. illus.
                                                          1689
Garside, G. W., co-auth. SEE no. 2019, Heid, J. G.

GARST, DORIS SHANNON. Jack London, magnet for adventure. By
Shannon Garst. N. Y., Julian Messner, 1944. 217p. bibliog. 1690

GARST, DORIS SHANNON. John Jewitt's adventure. By Shannon
Garst. Illustrated by Donald McKay. Boston, Houghton Mifflin,
1955. 211p. illus.   1691

GARST, DORIS SHANNON. Scotty Allan, king of the dog-team
drivers. By Shannon Garst. Illustrated by Dan Sweeney. N. Y.,
Julian Messner, 1946. 238p. front.(port.), illus. bibliog.
index.   1692

Gates, Chas. M., co-auth. SEE no. 2364, Johansen, D. O.

Gates, R. W., co-auth. SEE no. 3847, Robinson, E.

Gates, Swiftwater Bill. SEE no. 466, Beebe, Iola.

THE GATEWAY TO THE KLONDIKE and the Atlin gold fields. Skagway,
Fletcher and Hayne, Daily Alaskan Print, 1898.   1693

GAUSSEN, HENRI and P. BARRUEL. Montagnes; la vie aux hautes
altitudes. Paris, Horizones de France, 1955. 207p. illus.
pls.(come col.), map, bibliog. (Collection "La Nature vivante"
no. 5) [incls. Alaskan]   1694

Gay-Tifft, E., tr. SEE no. 4592, Tutein, P.

Gehr, Mary, illus. SEE no. 1069, Copeland, D. A.

Geiger, Ray, edit. SEE no. 188, Almanac Pub. Co.

Geist, Otto. SEE no. 2426, Keim, Chas. J.

GELVIN, E. C. How to build an Alaskan dog sled. [Fairbanks,
Jessen's Print., ca 1968] 6p. diagrs. wrps. [ed. of approx.
500 copies]   1695

Gemeling, Johan G. SEE nos. 1741-42, Gmelin, Johan G.

General hist. Alaska-Yukon-Pac. Exposition ... 1909.
    SEE no. 148, Alaska-Yukon-Pacific Exposition.

Geoghegan, R. H., tr. SEE no. 4675, Veniaminov, I. E. P.

Geographische ... 1772. SEE no. 1472, [Engel, Samuel]

Geography in making. 1952. SEE no. 199, American Geog. Soc.

Geological Soc. of America. SEE no. 3125, Miller, Maynard M.

GEORGE, JEAN CRAIGHEAD. The moon of the gray wolves. N. Y.,
Thomas Y. Crowell, 1969. illus. by Lorence Bjorklund.   1696

GEORGE, MARIAN M., edit. Little journeys to Alaska and Canada;
for intermediate and upper grades, edited by M. M. George. Chicago, A. Flanagan Co., 1901. 80, 93p. front.(col.), pl.(col.),
map. [incls. *A little journey to Alaska* by Edith K. Poyer] ANR.
1923. 80, 93p. illus. (Library of Travel) [incls. *A little
journey to Alaska* by Edith Kingman Kern] ANR. 1928. rev. ed.
167p.   1697

Georgeson, C. C. SEE nos.
    202, American Geog. Soc. Pioneer settlement ... 1932;
    4895, Willoughby, B. Gentlemen unafraid. 1928.

Georgi, J., co-edit. SEE no. 3332, Nordenskiöld, N. A. E.

GERRISH, THEODORE. Life in the world's wonderland; a graphic
description of the northwest, from the Mississippi River to the
land of the midnight sun; beauties of the Oregon and Columbia
Rivers, and the famous inland passage from Tacoma, Washington
Territory, to Sitka, Alaska; descriptions of the old Indian
battle fields; stories of old trappers, freighters, miners and
Indian fighters. no pl., n. d. 421p. front. illus. ANR.
no pl., 1886. ANR. Biddeford, Me., Biddeford Journal, 1886.
ANR. WITH TITLE Life in the world's wonderland ... from St. Paul,
Minnesota to the land of the midnight sun ... Biddeford, Me.,
Biddeford Journal, 1887. 421p. front. illus.   1698

GERSTER, GEORG. Augenschein in Alaska; Ein drücke von einer
Reise durch den 49. Staat der U. S. A. [TITLE TR. Alaska
evaluated. Travel impressions of the 49th state of the U. S. A.]
Bern, A. Scherz, 1961. 112p.   1699

Gerstle, Lewis and Hannah Gerstle. SEE no. 2911, Mack, Gerstle.

GESSAIN, ROBERT. Contribution à l'anthropologie des Eskimo
d'Angmagssalik. København, C. A. Reitzel's forlag, 1960. 167p.
illus. pls. tables, graphs, maps, bibliog. append. (Meddelelser
om Grønland, bd. 161, nr. 4) [incls. Alaskan Eskimos]   1700

GESSAIN, ROBERT. Les Esquimaux du Groenland a l'Alaska. [TITLE TR. The Eskimos from Greenland to Alaska] Paris, Bourrelier, 1947. 121p. illus. photos, drawings, map. ANR. 1953. 3rd ed. 127p. illus. map, bibliog. (La joie de connaitre)   1701

GIANETTI, MICHELANGIOLO. Elogy of Capt. James Cook, composed and publickly recited before the Royal Academy of Florence, translated into English by a member of the Royal Academy of Florence. Florence, Printed for G. Cambiagi, [1785] 87p.   1702

GIBBONS, CHARLES HARRISON. A sourdough samaritan. London and Toronto, Hodder and Stoughton, [1923 ?] 320p. [fict.]   1703

GIBBONS, RUSSELL W. An historical evaluation of the Cook-Peary controversy. Ada, Ohio, Ohio Northern University, 1956. ltd. ed.   1704

GIBBONS, RUSSELL W. Frederick Albert Cook; pioneer American polar explorer. Hamburg, N. Y., Dr. Frederick A. Cook Society, 1965. 23p.   1705

GIBBS, JAMES A., jr. Sentinels of the North Pacific. Portland, Binfords and Mort, 1955. illus. [incls. lighthouses and lightships, Alaska coast]   1706

GIDDINGS, JAMES LOUIS, jr. Ancient men of the Arctic. By J. Louis Giddings. N. Y., Knopf, 1967. [c1967] xxxi,391,i-xvp. photos, drawings, maps, glossary, bibliog. index. [Bering Strait to Greenland]   1707

GIDDINGS, JAMES LOUIS, jr. Dendrochronology in northern Alaska. [Tucson ?], University of Arizona and [College, Alaska ?], University of Alaska, 1941. 107p. illus. map, tables, diagrs. (some fold.), bibliog. (University of Arizona Bulletin, vol. 12, no. 4. Laboratory of Tree-Ring Research, Bulletin no. 1. University of Alaska pub. vol. 4)   1708

GIDDINGS, JAMES LOUIS, jr. The archaeology of Cape Denbigh. Providence, R. I., Brown University Press, 1964. 331p. illus. pls. port. maps, plans, tables, diagrs.(incl. 1 fold.), appends. by James B. Griffin and Roscoe H. Wilmeth, jr. and by Daris R. Swindler. (Brown University Bicentennial Pubs. Studies in the Fields of General Scholarship)   1709

GIDDINGS, JAMES LOUIS, jr. The Arctic woodland culture of the Kobuk River. Philadelphia, University Museum, University of Pennsylvania, 1952. x,144p. illus. pls. figs. maps, plans(incl. 1 fold.), tables, diagrs. bibliog. (University Museum Monographs)   1710

Giddings, James Louis, jr. SEE ALSO nos.
    2631, Larsen, H., edit. Circumpolar ... 1960;

4167, Skarland, Ivar. Flint stations ... 1948;
4264, Spiro, M. E., edit. Context ... anthropol. 1965.

GIFFEN, NAOMI MUSMAKER. The roles of men and women in Eskimo culture. Chicago, University of Chicago, 1930. 113p. table, bibliog. (Pub. in Anthropology, Ethnological Ser.)   1711

GILBERT, GEORGE. The death of Captain James Cook. Honolulu, Paradise of the Pacific Press, 1926. 30p.   1712

Gilbert, Grove Karl. SEE no. 1950, Harriman Alaska Exped.
     1899. vol. 3.

Gilbert, "Kansas" SEE no. 3469, Page, E. M.

GILBERT, KENNETH. Alaskan poker stories. Seattle, Robert D. Seal Pub., 1958. 46p. illus. by Eustace Ziegler, wrps.   1713

GILBERT, KENNETH. Arctic venture. Illustrated by Clifford Geary. N. Y., Holt, 1950. 147p.   1714

Gilbert, Kenneth. SEE ALSO no. 2429,
     Keithahn, E. L. Alaskan igloo tales. 1958.

Gilder, William Henry. [Alphabetical title guide to chronologi-
     cal entries]

     Der Untergang ... 1717.   Ice pack ... 1715.
     Gibel' ekspeditsii ... 1718. In Eis ... 1716.

GILDER, WILLIAM HENRY. Ice-pack and tundra; an account of the search for the *Jeannette* and a sledge journey through Siberia. N. Y., Scribner, 1883. 344p. front. illus. maps(incl. 1 fold.) ANR. London, Sampson & Low, 1883. 344p. front. illus. maps (incl. 1 fold. col.)   1715

   TRANSLATIONS - Ice-pack ... 1883, chronologically.

   In Eis und Schnee Die Aufsuchung der Jeannetteexpedition
      und eine Schlittenfahrtdurch Siberien. pl.?, 1884. 384p.
      illus. pls. maps.   1716

   Der Untergang der Jeannette-Expedition. Leipzig, 1922. abr.
      ed. 158p. illus. pls. maps.   1717

   Gibel' ekspeditsii Zhanetty. [TITLE TR. Loss of the *Jeannette*
      Expedition] Berlin, 1923. abr. ed. 165p. illus. pls.
      maps.   1718

Giles, E. B. SEE no. 4816, White, E. W., Pub. Co.

GILKEY, HELEN M. Weeds of the Pacific northwest. Corvallis, Oregon State University Press, 1957. 472p. pls.(some col.), line drawings, glossary, plant keys, index. [incls. Alaska and B. C.] 1719

Gilkey, Helen M. SEE ALSO no. 4342, Steward, A. N.
    Aquatic plants ... 1963.

GILKEY, J. A. The heroes of the Yukon and other poems. Portland, Oregon, 1932. 67p. 1720

Gillam, Harold. SEE no. 3658, Potter, Jean.

GILLETT, J. M. The gentians of Canada, Alaska, and Greenland. Ottawa, Queen's Printer, 1963. 99p. illus. map, bibliog. (Canada. Department of Agriculture Pub. 1180) 1721

GILLETTE, EDWARD. Facts on Alaska. Report made to the Pacific Construction Co., N. Y., on general condition of Alaska, and on proposed railway; endorsed by the Burlington and Missouri River Railroad Co. Omaha, 1904. 12p. [cf nos. 1510 and 4036] 1722

GILLHAM, CHARLES EDWARD. Beyond the Clapping Mountains; Eskimo stories from Alaska. By Charles E. Gillham. N. Y., Macmillan, 1943. 134p. drawings by Chanimum. 1723

GILLHAM, CHARLES EDWARD. Medicine men of Hooper Bay; or, the Eskimo's Arabian Nights. Eskimo folk-tales from Alaska. By Charles E. Gillham. London, Batchworth Press, 1955. 142p. drawings by Chanimum, map. ANR. N. Y., Macmillan, 1966. 1724

GILLHAM, CHARLES EDWARD. Raw north. By Charles E. Gillham. London, H. Jenkins, 1947. illus. by Bob Hines. ANR. N. Y., A. S. Barnes, 1947. 275p. illus. by Bob Hines. 1725

GILLHAM, CHARLES EDWARD. Sled dog and other poems of the north. By Charles E. Gillham. Hnntington, W. Va., Standard Publications, 1950. 78p. front.(port.), in slipcase. 1726

GILLIS, CHARLES J. Another Summer; the Yellowstone Park and Alaska. N. Y., printed for private distribution, 1893. 76p. 1727

GILLSÄTER, SVEN. Pia i Alaska. Stockholm, Bonnier, 1968. 47p. illus. 1728

GILMAN, ISOBEL AMBLER. Alaska, the American northland. Yonkers-on-Hudson, World Book Co., 1923. 343p. front. pls. maps, index. (Interamerican Geographical Readers) 1729

GILMAN, ISOBEL AMBLER. Alaskaland; a curious contradiction. By Isabel A. Gilman. N. Y., Alice Harriman Co., 1914. 110p. front. pls. [poetry and short stories] 1730

GILMAN, WILLIAM. Our hidden front. N. Y., Reynal & Hitchcock, 1944. 250p. pls. endmaps [Alaska in World War II]   1731

GILPIN, WILLIAM. The cosmopolitan railway compacting and fusing together all the world's continents ... S. F., The History Co., 1849. map(dble.) [proposed railway via Bering Strait]   1732

Gilstrap, W. H., photog. SEE no. 4566, Tozier, D. F.

Ginsburg, C., tr. SEE nos.
     263, Andreyev, A. I. Russ. disc. ... 1952;
     3398, Okun, S. B. Russ.-American Co. 1951.

GJAEREVOLL, O. Botanical investigations in central Alaska, especially in the White Mountains. Part 1, Pteridophytes and Monocotyledons. Trondheim, Detkgl. Norske Videnskabers Selskabs Skrifter, nr. 5, 1958. ALSO 1963. nr. 4 AND 1967. nr. 10.   1733

GJESSING, GUTORM. Circumpolar stone age. København, E. Munksgaard, 1944. 70p. illus. sketchmaps. (Acta Arctica, fasc. 2)
                                                                         1734

"Glacier Pilot" (Robert Reeve) SEE no. 1218, Day, Beth.

"Glacier Priest" SEE nos. 2213-14, Hubbard, Bernard Rosecrans.

GLADFELTER, KATHARINE ELEANOR. Under the North Star; a course on Alaska for junior boys and girls. By Katharine E. Gladfelter. N. Y., Friendship Press, 1928. 135p. pls.(fold.), bibliog.1735

GLANZ, RUDOLPH. The Jews in American Alaska, 1867-1880. N. Y., 1953. 46p. bibliog.   1736

Glazenapp, tr. SEE no. 2678, Lenz, H. F. E.

GLEAVES, ALBERT. The life of an American sailor; Rear Admiral William Hemsley Emory, U. S. N., from his letters and memoirs ... N. Y., George H. Doran, 1923. 359p.   1737

Glimpses of Alaska. A collection of views ... 1897. SEE
     no. 4914, Wilson, Veazie.

Glimpses of Alaska-Yukon-Pac. Exposition ... [c1909] SEE
     no. 149, Alaska-Yukon-Pac. Exposition.

Glimpses of Yukon gold fields ... 1895. SEE no. 4915,
     Wilson, Veazie.

GLODY, ROBERT [pseud.] A shepherd of the far north; the story of William Francis Walsh (1900-1930). S. F., Harr Wagner, 1934. 237p. front. ports. [author is Sister Mary Eustolia]   1738

GLUBOK, SHIRLEY. The art of the Eskimos. N. Y., Harper & Row, 1964. 48p. pls.   1739

GLUBOK, SHIRLEY. The art of the North American Indian. N. Y., Harper & Row, 1964. no p. illus. pls.   1740

GMELIN, JOHANN GEORG. Flora Sibirica, sive Historia plantarum Sibiriae. [TITLE TR. Flora of Siberia, or history of plants of Sibiria] Petropoli, Typogr. Acad. Sci., 1747-69. 4 vols. [incls. Steller's notes on plants collected in Alaska]   1741

GMELIN, JOHANN GEORG. Leben Herrn Georg Wilh. Stellero, gewesnen adiuncti der Kayserl. Frankfurt, 1748. 38p. (Academie der Wiss. zu St. Petersburg)   1742

Gmelin, Johann Georg. SEE ALSO nos.
    3529, Pekarskii, P. P. Istoriia Imp. Akad. Nauk ... 1870-73;
    3623, Plieninger, G. H. T. Joannis Georgii Gmelini ... 1861.

GODDARD, PLINY EARLE. Indians of the northwest coast. N. Y., American Museum of Natural History, 1924. 176p. illus. front. pls. map(fold.), bibliog. (Handbook Series, no. 10) OTHERS 1934 ANR 1945. [from Columbia River to Mt. St. Elias, Alaska; incls. museum collections of J. W. Powell (Haida), Geo. T. Emmons (Tlingit), and Jessup No. Pac. Exped., arranged by Franz Boas]   1743

Goddard, Pliny Earle. SEE ALSO no. 894, Chapman, J. W.
    Ten'a texts ... 1914.

GODSELL, PHILIP HENRY. Arctic trader; the account of twenty years with the Hudsons' Bay Co. N. Y., Putnam, 1934. 329p. front.(port.), pls. endmap, index. ANR. London, n. d. 320p. [no illus. or index in London ed.]   1744

GODSELL, PHILIP HENRY. Red hunters of the snows; an account of thirty years' experience with the primitive Indian and Eskimo tribes of the Canadian north-west and Arctic coast, with a brief history of the early contact between white fur traders and the aborigines. Toronto, Ryerson, 1938. 324p. front. pls. map (fold.)   1745

GODSELL, PHILIP HENRY. The romance of the Alaska Highway. Toronto, Ryerson, 1944. 235p. front. pls. ports. map. ANR. London, Sampson Low, 1946. 210p. append. [London ed. has title: The Alaska Highway]   1746

GODSELL, PHILIP HENRY. The vanishing frontier; a saga of traders, Mounties and men of the last north west. Toronto, Ryerson, 1939. 287p. front. pls. map(fold.)   1747

Godsell, Philip Henry. SEE ALSO no. 2122,
    Hinton, A. C. The Yukon. 1947.

GODWIN, GEORGE STANLEY. Vancouver; a life, 1757-1798. London, Philip Allan, 1930. xi,308p. front.(port.), pls.(incl. 1 fold.), ports. maps(incl. 2 fold.), facsims. append. bibliog. ANR. N. Y., D. Appleton, 1931.   1748

GOEPP, EDOUARD and EMILE L. CORDIER. Les Grands hommes de la France. Navigateurs; par Mm. Edouard Goepp et Emile L. Cordier; ouvrage accompagne de 2 magnifiques cartes imprimees en colour, Bougainville, La Perouse, Dentrecasteaux, Dumont d'Urville. Paris, P. Ducrocq, 1873. 419p. pls. maps(fold.) 1749

GOETZ, DELIA. Arctic tundra. N. Y., Morrow, 1958. 64p. illus. drawings.   1750

GOETZE, O. D. Souvenir of northwestern Alaska. S. F., Wm. Brown Engraving Co., n. d. 48 pls.   1751

GOLD FIELDS OF ALASKA ... Alyekan. The pathway to the gold fields of Alaska. By Louis, a miner returned from the Yukon, 1897. Giving a trip from Juneau down the Yukon to the Alyekan, a region far surpassing the famous Klondike in wealth and extent. The natives furnish the information that leads to the discovery. Kansas City, Mo., Hudson-Kimberly Pub. Co., 1897. 1st ed. 96p.
                                                                    1752

Gold; mining methods ... 1957. SEE
    no. 3615, Pioneers of Alaska, Igloo no. 4.

"Gold Nugget Charlie." SEE no. 2742, Lloyd-Owen, F.

Gold panning ... [ca 1958] SEE no. 104,
    Alaska Prospector's Service.

Goldberg, B. B., edit. SEE no. 3785,
    Research Institute of Alaska.

Goldberg, R. M., edit. SEE no. 3784,
    Research Institute of Alaska.

Golden Heart cook book. n. d. SEE no. 3943,
    Saint Matthew's Episcopal Church.

Golden Klondike guide to the Yukon gold fields ... [1897]
    SEE no. 4749, Washington & Alaska Steamship Co.

GOLDEN PRESS. Eskimos and other peoples of the north. Exciting, authentic punch-out figures ready to assemble, including; totem pole, dog sled, igloo, canoe, kayak. N. Y., Golden Press, 1962. 6 ℓ (col., incl. covers) (Golden Funtime Punch-Out Book) 1753

GOLDEN SANDS MINING CO. OF CAPE NOME, ALASKA. N. Y., [ca 1900] 4p. illus. map.   1754

Golden sands of Cape Nome. 1899. SEE no. 1837,
    Great Northern Railway.

Golden Valley Electric Assoc., Fairbanks. SEE no. 3345,
    North Pacific Consultants.

GOLDER, FRANK ALFRED. Bering's voyages; an account of the efforts of the Russians to determine the relation of Asia and
America. Volume 1; The log books and official reports of the
first and second expeditions, 1725-30 and 1733-42. With a chart
of the second voyage by Ellsworth P. Bertholf. Volume 2: Steller's journal of the sea voyage from Kamchatka to America and
return, on the second expedition 1741-42. Translated and in
part annotated by Leonhard Stejneger. N. Y., American Geographical Society, 1922. 371p.(vol. 1) illus. pls.(incl. 1 fold.),
facsims. maps. (Research Series, no. 1) 291p. (vol. 2) illus.
pls. facsims. maps(2 fold.), index(for both vols.) (Research
Series, no. 2) ANR. N. Y., Octagon House, 1968. 2 vols.
[reprinted for American Geographical Society]   1755

GOLDER, FRANK ALFRED. Father Herman, Alaska's Saint. Pullman,
Washington, by author, [191_ ?] front.(port.)[presented by
Golder as Christmas gift to friends] ANR. WITH TITLE Father
Herman, Alaska's Saint. By F. A. Golder. A preliminary account
of the life and miracles of Blessed Father Herman. S. F., Orthodox Christian Books and Icons, 1968. 66p. front.(port.),
illus. [new edition with added material]   1756

GOLDER, FRANK ALFRED. Guide to materials for American history
in Russian Archives. Edited by J. F. Jameson. Washington, D.C.,
Carnegie Institute, 1917. 177p. (Papers of Department of History, Pub. no. 239) ANR. N. Y., Kraus Reprint Corp., 1966.
2 vols.   1757

GOLDER, FRANK ALFRED. Russian expansion on the Pacific, 1641-
1850. An account of the earliest and later expeditions made by
the Russians along the Pacific Coast of Asia and North America,
including some related expeditions to the Arctic regions. Cleveland, Arthur H. Clark Co., 1914. 368p. illus. front.(map),
facsims. maps, appends. bibliog. index. ANR. Gloucester, Mass.,
Peter Smith, 1960. reprint.   1758

Golder, Frank Alfred. SEE ALSO no. 4335, Stephens, H. M.
    Pacific Ocean in hist. ... 1917.

Goldman, E. A., co-auth. SEE no. 5001, Young, S. P.

GOLDSCHMIDT, WALTER ROCH. Anthropology of Franz Boas; essays
on the centennial of his birth. Menasha, Wisc., American Anthropological Assoc., 1959. 165p. diagrs. tables. (Memoir,
no. 89)   1759

Goldsmith, Rev. J. [pseud.] SEE no. 3576, [Phillips, Richard]

GOLDSON, WILLIAM. Observations on the passage between the Atlantic and Pacific Oceans, in two memoirs on the Straits of Anian,
and the discoveries of De Fonte. Elucidated by a new and original map; to which is prefixed an historical abridgement of
discoveries in the north of America. By William Goldson, M. D.
Portsmouth, W. Mowbray, Printer, 1793. 162p. front.(fold.
map)   1760

GOLDTHWAIT, R. P. and others. Soil development and ecological
succession in a deglaciated area of Muir Inlet, southeast Alaska.
Columbus, Ohio State University, 1966. 167p. (Institute of
Polar Studies, Report no. 20)   1761

GOLENISHCHEV-KUTUZOV, L. I. Puteshestvie v siev. Tikhiĭ Okean
po povelieniĭu Karolia Georgiĭa 3 predpriiatoe ... [TITLE TR.
Voyage of Captains Cook, Clerke and Gore in the *Resolution* and
Discovery, 1776-80, by command of his Majesty George 3rd. St.
Petersburg, 1805-10. 2 vols. 509p.   1762

Golenishchev-Kutuzov, L. I., tr. SEE ALSO nos.
    2617, La Perouse, J. F. G. de. Puteshestvie ... 1800-02;
    3063, Meares, J. Puteshestvie ... 1797.

Golombek, B., tr. SEE no. 4791, Welzl, J.

[GOLOVNIN, VASILIĬ MIKHAILOVICH and K. KHLEIBNIKOV] Materialy
dlĭa istoriĭ russkikh zaseleniĭ po beregam Vostochnogo okeana.
[TITLE TR. Materials on the history of Russian settlements on
the shores of the Eastern Ocean] St. Petersburg, V. tipogra-
phiĭ Morskogo ministerstva, 1861. 4 vols. in 1. 126p.,130p.,
174p. and 240p. tables(fold.), bibliog. (Supplement to Morskoi
Sbornik, no. 1)   1763

GOLOVNIN, VASILIĬ MIKHAILOVICH. Memoirs of a captivity in Japan,
1812-13 ... London, 1824. 3 vols. 302p., 348p. and 302p. [also
in no. 1767, qv. incls. references to Nikolai Khostov and Gav-
ril Ivanovich Davydov]   1764

GOLOVNIN, VASILIĬ MIKHAILOVICH. Puteshestvie vokrug svieta po
povelineiĭu Gosudaria Imperatora sovershennoe na voennom shlĭupie *Kamchatka* v 1817, 1818 i 1819 godakh flota kapitanom Go-
lovninym. [TITLE TR. The round-the-world voyage made by His
Majesty's command on the sloop-of-war *Kamchatka* in 1817-19, by
Captain of the Navy Golovnin] Sanktpeterburg, Morskaĭa tipo-
graphiĭa, 1822. 2 vols. 512(44)p. and 206(217)p. tables(some
fold.), pls.(fold.), map(fold.), supplements.   1765

GOLOVNIN, VASILIĬ MIKHAILOVICH. Recollections of Japan, comprising a particular account of the religion, language, government,
laws and manners of the people, with observations on the geography, climate, population and productions of the country. London,
Henry Colburn, 1819. 302p. [incls. ref. to N. Khostov]   1766

GOLOVNIN, VASILIĬ MIKHAILOVICH. Sochineniĭa i perevody ...
[TITLE TR. Works and translations of Vasiliĭ Mikhailovich Go-
lovnin] St. Petersburg, Naval Printing Occice, 1864. 5 vols.
in 2. 352p., 374p, 284p., 520p. and 204p. front.(port.), pls.
(some fold.), plans, facsims. [vol. 1. biog. by N. Grech and
voyage to Kamchatka: vol. 2. Japan captivity: vol. 3. voyage
to Alaska and California: vol. 4. account of shipwrecks: vol.5.
remarks on Russian-America and R.A. Co.]   1767

GOLOVNIN, VASILIĬ MIKHAILOVICH. Sochineniĭa. Pod red. i s pri-
mechaniĭami I. P. Magidovicha. [TITLE TR. Works. Edited with
notes by I. P. Magidovich] Moskva-Leningrad, Izd-vo Glavsevmorputi, 1949. 507p. illus. maps(incl. 1 fold.), plans, facsims.
                                                               1768

GOLOVNIN, VASILIĬ MIKHAILOVICH. Sok rashcennyia zapiski flota...
o plavannie ego na shlĭupie *Diania* ... St. Petersburg, 1819.
146p. maps.   1769

Golovnin, Vasiliĭ Mikhailovich. SEE ALSO nos.
    516, Berg, L. S. Velikie russkie ... 1950;
    1303, Divin, V. A. V. M. Golovnin. Pod red. M. S.
          Bodnarskogo. 1951;
    1622, Fraerman, K. I. Plavaniĭa V. M. Golovnina. 1948;
    1623, Fraerman, K. I. Zhizn' ... 1946-48;
    1839, Grech, N. Zhizneopisanie ... 1851;
    1948, Harnisch, W. Reise um die Erde ... 1823;
    2623, Lappo, S. D. Plavaniĭa ... 1950;
    2700, Lialina, M. A. Russkie moreplavateli ... 1896;
    3364, Nozikov, N. N. Russkie krugosvetnye ... 1941;
    4620, U. S. S. R. Komitet ob Ustroĭstvĭe Russkikh
          Amerikanskikh Koloniĭ ... append. 1863-64.

Golubtsev, I., tr. SEE no. 1565, Fischer, J. E.

GOODCHILD, G. The Alaskan. London, J. Long, 1926.   1770

GOODCHILD, GEORGE. The land of Eldorado; a tale of the Seal
Islands. London, Jarrolds, 1900. 258p.   1771

GOODENOUGH, WARD H., edit. Explorations in cultural anthropolo-
gy; essays in honor of George Peter Murdock. N. Y., 1964.
[Eskimos of Brooks Range in *Law and societal structure among the
Nunamiut Eskimos*, by L. Pospisil, pp.395-431]   1772

GOODHUE, CORNELIA. Journey into the fog; the story of Vitus
Bering and the Bering Sea. N. Y., Doubleday Doran, 1944. 179p.
endmaps.   1773

GOODMAN, A. E. Klondyke gold fields, Yukon District; map of
routes, mining regulations. no pl., n. d. 32p. front.(fold.
map)   1774

GOODMAN, JOE R. and THOMAS G. THOMPSON. Characteristics of the waters in sections from Dutch Harbor, Alaska, to the Strait of Juan de Fuca and from the Strait of Juan de Fuca to Hawaii. Seattle, University of Washington Press, 1940. append. (Pub. in Physical Oceanography, vol. 3, no. 3. pp.81-103, 1-48)   1775

GOODMAN, JOE R. and others. Physical and chemical investigations Bering Sea, Bering Strait, Chukchi Sea during the summer of 1937 and 1938. Seattle, University of Washington Press, 1942. append. (Pub. in Physical Oceanography, vol. 3, no. 4. pp.105-9, 1-117)   1776

Goodrich, S. G., edit. SEE no. 2356, Jewitt, J. R.

Goodwin, Philip R., illus. SEE no. 2771, London, Jack.

Goodyear guide to State Parks. 1967. SEE no. 4184, Sloane, H. N.

GORBACH, AUGUST B., von. Unter der Mitternachtssonne. Abenteur aus dem leben der Klondyke-goldgraber. Cincinnati, Der Verfasser, 1908. 194p.   1777

GORBATSKIĬ, G. V. Priroda zarubeghnoĭ Arktiki. [TITLE TR. The nature of the non-Russian Arctic] Moskva, Gos. izd-vo geogr. lit-ry, 1951. 204p. illus. append. bibliog.   1778

Gordon, Chas. Wm. SEE no. 1005, Connor, Ralph [pseud.]

GORDON, GEORGE BYRON. In the Alaskan wilderness. By G. B. Gordon. Philadelphia, John C. Winston Co., 1917. 247p. front. (port.), pls. 3 maps(incl. 1 fold. and anr. fold. at back)   1779

GORDON, GRANVILLE ARMYNE. Nootka; a tale of Vancouver Island. By Lord Granville Armyne Gordon. London, Sands, 1899. 245p. front. pls. map.   1780

GORDON, MONA. The mystery of La Pérouse. Christchurch, N. Z., Bascanda, 1961. 187p. ports. maps, bibliog.   1781

GORDON, R. LESLIE. A little journey through Alaska. With pronouncing vocabulary. Chicago, A. Flanagan Co., 1931. 144p. (Library of Travel Series) ANR. 1936. 144p.   1782

GORDON, WILLIAM JOHN. Round about the North Pole. London, J. Murray, 1907. 294p. illus. by Edward Whymper. front. pls. ports. maps, index. ANR. N. Y., Dutton, 1907. [has reference to Bering Strait]   1783

GORE, LOUISE C. Soul of the bearded seal; poems of early Eskimo life. Anchorage, Alaska Methodist University Press, 1967. 112p. glossary, bibliog.   1784

GORHAM MANUFACTURING CO. The soul of Alaska; a comment and a
description, to which is added a Catalogue Raissonne of a series
of bronze statuettes illustrative of Alaskan Indian characteristics and social habitudes, modelled by Louis Potter and cast into bronze by the Gorham Co. N. Y., The Gorham Co., 1905. 96p.
front. pls. wrps.   1785

GORRELL, JOSEPH R. A trip to Alaska. With compliments of the
author, J. R. Gorrell, M.D. Newton, Iowa, Aug. 1905. (40)p.
                                                           1786

Gospel according to St. John, in Haida. 1899. SEE
     no. 665, British & Foreign Bible Soc.

Gospel according to St. Luke, in Haida. 1899. SEE
     no. 666, British & Foreign Bible Soc.

Gospel according to St. Mark. 1916. SEE
     no. 667, British & Foreign Bible Soc.

Gottwaldt, B. L. SEE nos.
     219, Amundsen, R. E. G. Den forste flukt ... 1926;
     220, Amundsen, R. E. G. The first flight ... 1927;
     222, Amundsen, R. E. G. Der erste Flug ... [1927]

GOULD, MAURICE M. and KENNETH BRESSETT. Alaska's coinage
through the years. An illustrated catalog listing all of the recorded issues of tokens used as money by the pioneer settlers of
Alaska including all of the souvenir gold issues and a list of
transportation tokens and medals covering the entire history of
Alaska. Racine, Wisc., Whitman Pub. Co., 1960. 46p. illus.
bibliog. [see also no. 1788]   1787

GOULD, MAURICE M., KENNETH BRESSETT, KAYE and NANCY DETHRIDGE.
Alaska's coinage through the years. An illustrated catalog listing tokens used as money by pioneer Alaskans plus commemorative
medals, souvenir tokens and medals. The odd and curious items
used by the natives as a medium of exchange have been included
as they, too, are a part of the history of Alaska's coinage.
Racine, Wisc. Whitman Pub. Co., 1965. rev. 2d ed. [of no. 1787]
176p. illus. bibliog.   1788

GOULD, RUPERT THOMAS. Captain Cook. London, Duckworth, 1935.
144p. illus. map (Great Lives, no. 49)   1789

GOULET, EMIL OLIVER. Rugged years on the Alaska frontier. By
Emil O. Goulet. Philadelphia, Dorrance, [1949] 304p. ports.
ANR. Philadelphia, 1950. 350p. [autobiog.]   1790

GRABER, ALMA HALL. East to Alaska. Stories of the first Russian voyages to Alaska. Drawings by Dale De Armond, maps by
Lawrence D. Breusch. Sitka, Sitka Printing Co., 1960. 29p.1791

Graded catechism in Innuit. 1951. SEE no. 2792, Lonneux, M. J.

GRAHAM, ANGUS. The golden grandstone, the adventures of George
M. Mitchell. Philadelphia, Lippincott, 1935. 304p. illus.
sketch maps. ANR. Toronto, Oxford University Press, 1935. ANR.
London, Chatto and Windus, 1936.   1792

GRAHAM, J. F. Graham's Alaska "Gold Fields" guide. Third edition. Over 77,700 sold August 14, 1897. Complete information
on mining, prospecting, climate, routes, laws, food, expenses,
maps of gold streams, cuts of quick-mining tools, etc. etc. Official map. Made from U. S. Government Surveys. [Chicago, Lo-
mas Pub. Co., 1897] 30p. illus. maps.   1793

GRAHAME, NIGEL. Bishop Bompas of the frozen north; the adventurous life story of a brave and self-denying missionary amongst
the red Indians and Eskimos of the great northwest. By Nigel
Grahame, B.M. London, Seeley, 1925. 60p. front. illus.
(Seeley's Missionary Lives for Children, vol. 6)   1794

GRAINGER, GEORGE. Little Flip, "The Pribilof Pup," the fur
seal that could not swim. Ann Arbor, Mich., Edwards Bros.
Litho-printers, 1960. 35p. illustrated by J. G. Mosinski. 1795

GRANBERG, WILBUR J. Voyage into darkness. N. Y., Dutton, 1960.
illus. [bering's voyages]   1796

GRANT, DELBERT A. STEWART. Blazing a gospel trail to Alaska;
an Alcan adventure; seven thousand miracle miles by army plane
and jeep through Canada and Alaska. Springfield, Mo., 1944.
55p. illus. ports.   1797

Grant, Gordon, illus. SEE no. 3304, Nicol, John.

GRAVEL, MIKE. Jobs and more jobs. Pasadena, Calif., 1968. 1798

[GRAVES, S. H.] On the "White Pass" pay-roll. By the President
of the White Pass and Yukon Route. Chicago, [Lakeside Press,
R. H. Donnelley and Sons Co.], 1908. 258p. front. pls. ANR.
N. Y., Paladin Press, 1970. 258p. illus.   1799

Gray, P. N., edit. SEE no. 613, Boone and Crockett Club.

Greany, J. M., photog. SEE nos.
    954, Cleveland, B. A. Alaskan cookbook ... 1960;
    955, Cleveland, B. A. Frontier formulas ... 1952.

Great Alaskan earthquake. [1965 ?] SEE no. 162, Alaskan Pub.Co.

Great Alaska earthquake of 1964. 1968. SEE
    no. 3272, National Academy of Sciences.

GREAT BRITAIN. ADMIRALTY. HYDROGRAPHIC DEPARTMENT. Admiralty
tide tables, volume 3, for the year 1960, Pacific Ocean and adjacent seas, including tidal stream tables. London, 1959.
621p. tables. [incls. Gulf of Alaska, Bering Sea and Bering
Strait]   1800

GREAT BRITAIN. ADMIRALTY. HYDROGRAPHIC DEPARTMENT. Alaska and
Bering Sea pilot, including the northeast coast of Siberia.
Originally compiled from various sources by Vice Admiral J. P.
Maclear. Prepared by Staff-Commander J. R. H. MacFarlane. Lon-
don, Printed for the Hydrographic Office, Admiralty, by Eyre &
Spottiswoode, 1908. 620p. 2d ed. [1st ed. in 1898]   1801

GREAT BRITAIN. ADMIRALTY. HYDROGRAPHIC DEPARTMENT. Bering Sea
and Strait pilot, comprising the northwestern and northern
coasts of Alaska from Cape Douglas to Demarcation Point, the
northern coast of Canada from Demarcation Point to Cape Bathurst,
the Aleutian Islands and the northeastern coast of Siberia from
Cape Shipunski to Cape Otto Schmidta. Prepared by Captain G. E.
Sutcliff, R. N. and Lt.-Commander J. Y. G. Torlesse, R. N. London, 1941. 497p. [1st ed. 1920 and supplement no. 12, 1937.
See also no. 1807]   1802

GREAT BRITAIN. ADMIRALTY. HYDROGRAPHIC DEPARTMENT. Sailing
directions for Bering Sea and Alaska. Prepared by J. P. Maclear. London, printed for Hydrographic Office, Admiralty, By
Eyre & Spottiswoode, 1898. 352p.   1803

GREAT BRITAIN. ADMIRALTY. HYDROGRAPHIC DEPARTMENT. Southeast Alaska pilot, comprising the coast and off-lying islands
from Dixon Entrance to Cook Inlet. Prepared by J. N. Tait.
London, 1948. 3rd ed. 577p. [previously in "Alaska and Bering
Sea pilot" - see also nos. 1805 and 1806]   1804

GREAT BRITAIN. ADMIRALTY. HYDROGRAPHIC DEPARTMENT. Southeast Alaska pilot, comprising the coast and off-lying islands
from Dixon Entrance to Cook Inlet. London, 1959. 4th ed.
636p. illus. maps, diagrs. tables, glossary, index.   1805

GREAT BRITAIN. ADMIRALTY. HYDROGRAPHIC DEPARTMENT. Supplement
no. 3, 1953, relating to the Southeast Alaska pilot, third edition 1948, corrected to 11th September 1953. Prepared by H. V.
Silk. London, 1953. 29p.   1806

GREAT BRITAIN. ADMIRALTY. HYDROGRAPHIC DEPARTMENT. Supplement
no. 8, 1953, relating to the Bering Sea and Strait pilot, second
edition 1940, corrected to 11th August, 1953. Prepared by F. M.
Hodgson. London, 1953. 68p.   1807

GREAT BRITAIN. ADMIRALTY. HYDROGRAPHIC DEPARTMENT. The Admiralty list of lights, fog signals and visual time signals,
volume 17, 1953. Corrected to 16th December, 1953. Western
side of South Atlantic Ocean and Eastern Pacific Ocean (Eastern

coast South America, south of Cape Orange; west coasts of South
and North America and Hawaiian Islands.) London, 1953. 528p.
map(text) [also incls. Gulf of Alaska, Bering Sea and Bering
Strait]   1808

GREAT BRITAIN. COLONIAL SECRETARY, EARL OF CARNARVON. Instructions on certain points connected with the Alaska Purchase.
Carnarvon to Seymour, no. 101. London, Downing Street, Dec. 28,
1867. 70p.   1809

Great Britain. Foreign Office. Alaska Boundary Tribunal.
   [Alphabetical title guide to chronological entries]

   Append. to case. 1812.   Case. 1811.
   Append. to counter-case. 1814. Counter-case. 1813.
   Argument. 1810.   Protocols. 1815.

GREAT BRITAIN. FOREIGN OFFICE. ALASKA BOUNDARY TRIBUNAL. Boundary between the Dominion of Canada and the Territory of Alaska.
Argument presented on the part of the government of his Brittanic,
Majesty to the Tribunal constituted under Article I of the Convention signed at Washington, January 24, 1903, between his Brittanic Majesty and the United States of America. London, printed
at the Foreign Office by Harrison & Sons, 1903. 127p.   1810

GREAT BRITAIN. FOREIGN OFFICE. ALASKA BOUNDARY TRIBUNAL. Boundary between the Dominion of Canada and the Territory of Alaska.
Case presented on the part of the government of his Brittanic
Majesty to the Tribunal constituted under Article I of the convention signed at Washington, January 24, 1903, between his
Brittanic Majesty and the United States of America. London,
printed at the Foreign Office by Harrison & Sons, 1903. 105p.
                                                             1811

GREAT BRITAIN. FOREIGN OFFICE. ALASKA BOUNDARY TRIBUNAL. Boun-
dary between the Dominion of Canada and the Territory of Alaska.
Appendix to the case of his Majesty's government before the
Alaska Boundary Tribunal. London, McCorquodale, 1903. maps.
                                                             1812

GREAT BRITAIN. FOREIGN OFFICE. ALASKA BOUNDARY TRIBUNAL. Boundary between the Dominion of Canada and the Territory of Alaska.
Counter-case presented on the part of the government of his
Brittanic Majesty to the Tribunal constituted under Article I of
the convention signed at Washington, January 24, 1903 ... London,
printed at the Foreign Office by Harrison & Sons, 1903. 81p.
                                                             1813

GREAT BRITAIN. FOREIGN OFFICE. ALASKA BOUNDARY TRIBUNAL. Boundary between the Dominion of Canada and the Territory of Alaska.
Appendix to the counter-case of his Majesty's government before
the Alaska Boundary Tribunal. London, McCorquodale, 1903.
2 vols.   1814

GREAT BRITAIN. FOREIGN OFFICE. ALASKA BOUNDARY TRIBUNAL. Boundary between the Dominion of Canada and the Territory of Alaska. Protocols, oral arguments, with index, award of Tribunal, and opinions of its members. September 3 to October 20, 1903. London, printed at Foreign Office by Harrison & Sons, 1903. 978p.
1815

GREAT BRITAIN. PARLIAMENT. (Bering Sea Arbitration) Argument of the United States before the tribunal of arbitration convened at Paris under the provisions of the treaty between the United States of America and Great Britain, concluded February 29, 1892. Presented to both houses of Parliament by command of Her Majesty, March 1893. London, Her Majesty's Stationery Office, printed by Harrison & Sons, 1893. 327p. (U. S. Report no. 8, 1893. Great Britain Parl. Papers no. C-6951)
1816

GREAT BRITAIN. PARLIAMENT. (Bering Sea Arbitration) Dispatch from D'Arcy W. Thompson, forwarding a report of his mission to Bering Sea in 1897. London, Her Majesty's Stationery Office, printed by Harrison & Sons, 1898. 15p. (U. S. Report no. 1, 1898. Great Britain Parl. Papers no. C-8702)
1817

GREAT BRITAIN. PARLIAMENT. (Bering Sea Arbitration) Report on mission to Bering Sea in 1896, dated March 4, 1897, by D'Arcy W. Thompson. London, Eyre & Spottiswoode, 1897. 40p. (U. S. Report no. 3, 1897)
1818

Great Britain. Parliament. House of Commons. (Franklin search) [Alphabetical title guide to chronological entries]

Arctic expedition: further correspondence ... 1826.
Copies of any correspondence ... Belcher's ... 1827.
Copies of any instructions ... 1830.
Copies of any reports ... Collinson ... 1823.
Copies or extracts of any minutes ... 1828.
Copies of instructions ... Franklin ... 1820.
Copies of sailing orders ... Collinson ... 1829.
Copy of any communication ... Consul at Wash. ... 1822.
Copy or extracts correspondence ... Admiralty ... 1824.
Extracts of any proceedings ... Arctic exped. ... 1821.
Further papers relative ... *Erebus* ... Kane ... 1833.
Further papers relative ... *Erebus* ... (Simpson) 1832.
Papers relative to *Erebus* ... 1831.
Report from Select Committee ... Capt. John Ross. 1819.
Report of the committee ... minutes of evidence ... 1825.

GREAT BRITAIN. PARLIAMENT. HOUSE OF COMMONS. (Franklin search, in chronological order) Sessional Papers. Reports from Committees. 1834, vol. 18, no. 250. Report from Select Committee on the expedition to the Arctic Seas, commanded by Captain John Ross. Ordered by the House of Commons to be printed, 28 April 1834. 40p. map(fold. col.) [voyages of Beechey, Richardson, others]
1819

GREAT BRITAIN. PARLIAMENT. HOUSE OF COMMONS. (Franklin search, in chronological order) Sessional Papers. Accounts and Papers. 1847-48, vol. 41, no. 264. Arctic expedition. Return to an address of the Honorable the House of Commons dated 21 March, for: Copies of instructions to Captain Sir John Franklin, in reference to the Arctic expedition of 1845; to any officer or officers appointed by the Admiralty on any expedition in search of Sir John Franklin; and, Copies or extracts of any proceedings and correspondence of the Admiralty in reference to Arctic expeditions from 1845 to the present time, together with copies of charts illustrating the same. Ordered by the House of Commons to be printed, 13 April 1848. 84p. maps(fold.) 1820

GREAT BRITAIN. PARLIAMENT. HOUSE OF COMMONS. (Franklin search, in chronological order) Sessional Papers. Accounts and Papers. 1849, vol. 32, no. 188. Arctic expeditions. Return to an order of the Honorable the House of Commons dated 15 March 1849, for: Extracts of any proceedings or correspondence of the Admiralty in reference to the Arctic expedition, in continuation of Parliamentary papers nos. 264 and 386 of session 1848, up to the present time. Admiralty, 27 March 1849, J. H. Hay, Chief Clerk. Ordered by the House of Commons to be printed, 30 March 1849. 28p. 1821

GREAT BRITAIN. PARLIAMENT. HOUSE OF COMMONS. (Franklin search, in chronological order) Sessional Papers. Accounts and Papers. 1849, vol. 32, no. 387. Arctic expedition. Return to an address of the Honorable the House of Commons dated 11 June 1849, for: Copy of any communication from Her Majesty's Consul at Washington to Her Majesty's principal Secretary of State for Foreign Affairs, in reference to measures adopted by the government of the United States, on the subject of the expedition sent forth by this country under command of Sir John Franklin to the Arctic seas. Correspondence with Her Majesty's charge d'affaires at Washington, respecting the intention of the government of the United States to send two ships of war in search of Sir John Franklin's expedition to the Arctic seas. Ordered by the House of Commons to be printed, 13 June 1849. 2p. 1822

GREAT BRITAIN. PARLIAMENT. HOUSE OF COMMONS. (Franklin search, in chronological order) Sessional Papers. Accounts and Papers. 1850, vol. 35, no. 107. Arctic expedition. Return to an order of the Honorable the House of Commons dated 5 February 1850, for: Copies of any reports or statements from the officers employed in the Arctic expeditions ... resumption of the search for Sir John Franklin's expedition ... Copy or extracts from any correspondence or proceedings of the Board of Admiralty, in relation to the Arctic expeditions ... Copies of the orders ... to the Captains Collinson, Kellett and Moore, and to Lieut. Pullen, and also copies of instructions given to Dr. Rae, through the Hudson's Bay Company; Of any reports made by any officer or officers employed in the late expeditions... And, of the latest chart

of the Polar Sea ... In continuation of Parliamentary papers,
nos. 264 and 386, of session 1848, and of numbers 188 and 387,
of session 1849. Admiralty, 4 March 1850. J. H. Hay, Chief
Clerk, 5 March 1850. 157p. illus. maps(2 fold.)   1823

GREAT BRITAIN. PARLIAMENT. HOUSE OF COMMONS. (Franklin search,
in chronological order) Sessional Papers. Accounts and Papers.
1851, vol. 33, no. 97. Arctic expeditions. Return to an address
of the Honorable the House of Commons dated 7 February 1851, for:
Copy or extracts from any correspondence or proceedings of the
Board of Admiralty in relation to the Arctic expeditions, including those more recently sent forth in resumption of the
search for that under the command of Sir John Franklin; Copies
of any instructions ... to any officers in Her Majesty's service engaged in Arctic expeditions, since the date of ... Parliamentary papers number 107 and number 397 of session 1850;
And, copy or extracts from any correspondence or communications
from the government of the United States, or from Her Majesty's
Minister at Washington ... Admiralty, 7 March 1851. J. H. Hay,
Chief Clerk, 7 March 1851. 106p. maps(2 fold.)   1824

GREAT BRITAIN. PARLIAMENT. HOUSE OF COMMONS. (Franklin search,
in chronological order) Sessional Papers. Accounts and Papers.
1852, vol. 50, no. 1435. Arctic expeditions. Report of the
committee appointed by the Lords Commissioners of the Admiralty
to inquire into and report on the recent Arctic expeditions in
search of Sir John Franklin, together with the minutes of evidence taken before the committee and papers connected with the
subject. London, George Edward Eyre & William Spottiswoode,
1852. 199p.   1825

GREAT BRITAIN. PARLIAMENT. HOUSE OF COMMONS. (Franklin search,
in chronological order) Sessional Papers. Accounts and Papers.
1852, vol. 50, no. 1449. Arctic expedition: further correspondence and proceedings connected with the Arctic expedition. Presented to both Houses of Parliament by command of Her Majesty.
London, Eyre & Spottiswoode, 1852. 216p. illus. maps(4 incl.
1 fold.)   1826

GREAT BRITAIN. PARLIAMENT. HOUSE OF COMMONS. (Franklin search,
in chronological order) Sessional Papers. Accounts and Papers.
18-2-53, vol. 60, no. 82. Arctic expeditions. Return to an
address ... 19 November 1852, for: Copies of any correspondence
... from Sir Edward Belcher's squadron ... and from any other of
the Arctic expeditions since the dates of the last returns from
Mr. Kennedy of the *Prince Albert*, discovery ship; from Commander Inglefield of the screw vessel *Isobel* ... of any plans or
suggestions of search for Rear-Admiral Sir John Franklin ... and
of any further correspondence on the subject of the Arctic regions, since the last laid before this House in ... session
1852. Admiralty, 16 December 1852. J. H. Hay, Chief Clerk,
20 December 1852. 88p. maps(3 fold.)   1827

GREAT BRITAIN. PARLIAMENT. HOUSE OF COMMONS. (Franklin search, in chronological order) Sessional Papers. Accounts and Papers. 1852-53, vol. 60, no. 444. Ship *Rattlesnake*. Return to an order of the Honorable the House of Commons dated 27 April 1853, for: Copies of extracts of any minutes or other documents connected with the selection by the late Board of Admiralty of the ship *Rattlesnake* in preference to a steamer, for the purpose of endeavoring to communicate with the *Plover*; And copies of Instructions given ... to the Captain of the *Rattlesnake*. Admiralty, 3 May 1853. J. H. Hay, Chief Clerk, 4 May 1853. 4p.   1828

GREAT BRITAIN. PARLIAMENT. HOUSE OF COMMONS. (Franklin search, in chronological order) Sessional Papers. Accounts and Papers. 1852-53, vol. 60, no. 1013. Arctic regions. Return to an order of the Honorable the House of Commons dated 1 August 1853, for: Copies of the sailing orders and instructions to Commander Inglefield, of Her Majesty's Ship *Phoenix*, employed in the Arctic regions; Of the instructions to Mr. Kennedy in command of the *Isobel* ... Of any orders and instructions given to Captain Collinson, of the *Enterprise*, of a later date than the 15th day of January 1850; And, of any reports received from Captain Collinson of a later date than the 9th day of July 1851. Admiralty, 19 August 1853. John Jones Dyer, Acting Chief Clerk, 20 August 1853. 4p. [also in Accounts and Papers, 1854, vol. 42, no. 1725]   1829

GREAT BRITAIN. PARLIAMENT. HOUSE OF COMMONS. (Franklin search, in chronological order) Sessional Papers. Accounts and Papers. 1854, vol. 42, no. 171. Arctic expedition. Return to an order of the Honorable the House of Commons dated 4 April 1854, for: Copies of any instructions ... to the commanders of Her Majesty's ships now engaged in the Arctic regions in the search for Sir John Franklin's expedition. Admiralty, 7 April 1854. John Jones Dyer, Chief Clerk, 7 April 1854. 4p.   1830

GREAT BRITAIN. PARLIAMENT. HOUSE OF COMMONS. (Franklin search, in chronological order) Sessional Papers. Accounts and Papers. 1854, vol. 42, no. 1725. Papers relative to the recent Arctic expeditions in search of Sir John Franklin and the crews of H.M.S. *Erebus* and *Terror*. Presented to both Houses of Parliament by command of Her Majesty. London, Eyre & Spottiswoode, 1854. 225p. illus. maps(5 fold.)   1831

GREAT BRITAIN. PARLIAMENT. HOUSE OF COMMONS (Franklin search, in chronological order) Sessional Papers. Accounts and Papers. 1854-55, vol. 35, no. 1898. Further papers relative to the recent Arctic expeditions in search of Sir John Franklin and the crews of H.M.S. *Erebus* and *Terror*. London, Eyre & Spottiswoode, 1855. 958p. illus. 37 maps(some fold.) [contains *Observations on the Western Esquimaux and the country they in habit; from notes taken during two years at Point Barrow, by Mr. John Simpson, R.N., Her Majesty's discovery ship "Plover."* (pp.917-42) reprinted in "Arctic geography and ethnology," Royal Geographic Society, London, 1875. pp.233-75. See no. 3907]   1832

GREAT BRITAIN. PARLIAMENT. HOUSE OF COMMONS. (Franklin search, in chronological order) Sessional Papers. Accounts and Papers. 1856, vol. 41, no. 2124. Further papers relative to the recent Arctic expeditions in search of Sir John Franklin, and the crews of ... *Erebus* and *Terror;* including the reports of Dr. Kane and Messrs. Anderson and Stewart; and correspondence relative to the adjudication of £10,000 as a reward for ascertaining the fate of the crews of *Erebus* and *Terror*. In continuation of papers presented in September 1854-5. Presented to the House of Commons, 1856. London, Harrison & Sons. 95p. 2 maps(1 fold.)
                1833

Great Britain. Parliament. House of Commons. (Franklin search)
    SEE ALSO nos.
    326, Austin, H. T. Review proceedings ... 1851;
    3907, Royal Geographic Soc. Arctic geog. ... 1875;
    4750, Washington, John. Eskimeaux and Eng. vocab. ... 1850.

Great dog races of Nome ... n. d. SEE no. 1182, Darling, E. B.

Great Klondike gold fields ... 1897. SEE no. 132,
    Alaska Transportation, Trading & Mining Co.

Great lesson of great depression. 1934. SEE no. 914,
    Chichagof King Mining Co.

GREAT NORTHERN RAILWAY CO. Alaska and the gold fields of the Yukon. The Klondike, Cook Inlet and other mining regions. Chicago, Poole Bros., 1898. 10p.   1834

GREAT NORTHERN RAILWAY CO. Alaska - Land of gold and glacier. Chicago, Poole Bros., n. d. 61p. illus.   1835

GREAT NORTHERN RAILWAY CO. Alaska tours to the national wonderland. Chicago, Poole Bros., 1898. 59p. illus. maps.   1836

GREAT NORTHERN RAILWAY CO. The golden sands of Cape Nome. The latest and most wonderful of Alaska placer mines. Ten days by steamer from Seattle. All diggings located in American territory. St. Paul, Minn., Dispatch Job Printing, 1899. 24p. ANR. St. Paul, Dispatch Job Printing, 1899. 2d ed. 32p. (Pocket-Books no. 3)   1837

GREAT NORTHERN RAILWAY CO. The northern Pacific tour, from the Lakes and Mississippi River to the Pacific, including Puget Sound and Alaska. St. Paul, W. C. Riley, pub., [c1888] 27p. illus. ANR. St. Paul, 1890.   1838

Great Northern Riilway Co. SEE ALSO no. 2205,
    Howe, R. S., edit. The great northern country ... 1902.

Great Pacific Northwest and Alaska ... [19_ ?]   SEE
    no. 4613, Union Pacific Railroad Co.

Great probability of northwest passage ... 1768. SEE
    no. 2336, [Jefferys, Thomas]

Greater Anchorage, Inc. SEE no. 2705, Life in Anchorage ...1958.

GRECH, N. Zhizneopisanie Vasiliĭa Mikhailovicha Golovnina.
[TITLE TR. Biography of Vasiliĭ Mikhailovich Golovnin]   St.
Petersburg, 1851. 32p.   1839

Grech, N. SEE ALSO no. 1767, Golovnin, V. M.
    Sochinenniĭa ... 1864.

GREELY, ADOLPHUS WASHINGTON. Handbook of Alaska; its resources,
products and attractions. By Major-General A. W. Greely, U.S.A.
With maps and illustrations. N. Y., Scribner's, 1909. 280p.
front. pls. maps(incl. 1 fold. in pocket, 1 dble.), tables, index. ANR. London, Unwin, 1909. 280p. ANR. N. Y., Scribner,
1914. new ed. "... with prefatory chapter on Alaska in 1914
and a map showing proposed railroad routes." 280p. front. pls.
maps(some fold.), tables. ANR. N. Y., Scribner, 1924. 3rd ed.
rev. and enl. "... with new chapters on fisheries, fur-farming,
fur seals, game, goldmining, petroleum and coal, railroads, reindeer, and volcanoes." 330p. front. pls. maps(incl. 1 fold.),
index. ANR. 1925. ANR. Port Washington, N. Y., Kennikat Press,
1970. reprint of 1925 ed.   1840

GREELY, ADOLPHUS WASHINGTON. Handbook of Arctic discoveries.
Boston, Roberts Bros., 1896. 257p. maps(fold.) (Columbian
Knowledge Ser. no. 3) ANR. London, 1896. ANR. Boston, Little
Brown, 1906. 3rd ed. enl. 325p. maps. ANR. 1909. 4th ed. enl.
336p. maps. ANR. WITH TITLE Handbook of polar discoveries.
Boston, Little Brown, 1910. 5th ed. rev. and enl. 336p. front.
(port.), maps(some fold.), bibliogs.   1841

GREELY, ADOLPHUS WASHINGTON. The polar regions in the twentieth
century; their discovery and industrial evolution. By A. W.
Greely, Major-General U. S. Army (Retired) With illustrations
and maps. Boston, Little Brown, 1928. 270p. pls. port. map
(fold.), index. ANR. London, George G. Harrap, 1929. 223p.
front. photos, 2 maps(1 fold.), ftntes.(bibliog.), index. [2
chapters about Alaska plus scattered references]   1842

GREELY, ADOLPHUS WASHINGTON. True tales of Arctic heroism in
the new world. N. Y., Scribner, 1912. 385p. pls. ports. maps.
                                                                  1843
  Greely, Adolphus Washington. SEE ALSO
    no. 3147, Mitchell, Wm. General Greely ... 1936.

Green, Elmer, edit. SEE nos. 3927-8, Rydell, C.

GREEN, FITZHUGH. Bob Bartlett; master mariner. N. Y., Putnam, 1929. 1st ed. 211p. front.(pl.), pls.   1844

Green, John [pseud.] SEE no. 3049, [Mead, Bradock]

GREEN, JOHN C. Nomination of Frederick E. Fuller for Judge in Alaska. Opposition to confirmation by J. C. Green. Washington, 1912. 19p.   1845

GREEN, JONATHAN S. Journal of a tour on the northwest coast of America in the year 1829, containing a description of a part of Oregon, California, and the northwest coast and the numbers, manners and customs of the native tribes. N. Y., C. F. Heartman, 1915. 104p. [reprinted from Missionary Herald, Nov. 1830 with extracts from issues in 1821-30]   1846

GREEN, PAUL and ABBE ABBOTT. I am Eskimo, Aknik my name. By Paul Green, aided by Abbe Abbott. With illustrations by George Aden Ahgupuk. Juneau, Alaska-Northwest Pub. Co., 1959. 86p. illus. endmaps [Kivalina, on Kotzebue Sound]   1847

GREENAWAY, KEITH ROGER and S. E. COLTHORPE. An aerial reconnaissance of Arctic North America. Edited by the Joint Intelligence Bureau, Ottawa. [Montreal, printed by Industrial School for the Deaf], May 1948. 300p. illus. maps(incl. 1 fold.), appends. [4149th A.A.F. Base unit of Air Materiel Command and R.C.A.F. Incls. northeast Alaska]   1848

Greene, Hamilton, illus. SEE no. 481, Bell, Margaret E.

GREENHOW, ROBERT. Geography of Oregon and California and the other territories on the north-west coast of North America, illustrated by a new and beautiful map of those countries. Boston, Freeman, 1845. 120p. map.   1849

GREENHOW, ROBERT. Memoir, historical and political on the northwest coast of North America, and adjacent territories; illustrated by a map and a geographical review of those countries. Washington, D. C., Blair & Reves, 1840. ANR. N. Y., Putnam, 1840. 228p. front.(fold. map)   1850

GREENHOW, ROBERT. The history of Oregon and California; and the other territories on the north-west coast of North America; from their discovery to the present day. Boston, Freeman & Bolles. ANR. "... of North America; accompanied by a geographical view and map of those countries, and a number of documents as proof and illustrations of the history." Boston, C. C. Little & J. Brown, 1844. 482p. front.(fold. map), illus. OTHERS London, Murray, 1844. Boston, Little, 1945. 2d ed. rev. and enl. 492p. map(fold.), wrps. N. Y.,Appleton, 1845. 3rd rev. and enl. Boston, Freeman & Bolles, 1847. 4th rev. and enl. Boston, Little, 1847.   1851

GREENWOOD, AMY.   Rolling north.   N. Y., Crowell, 1955.   218p.
illustrated by Lombard Jones.   [Alcan Highway]   1852

GREGORY, HOMER EWART and KATHLEEN BARNES. North Pacific fisheries,
with special reference to Alaska salmon.   S. F., American Council,
Institute of Pacific Relations, 1939.   322p. tables, diagrs.
figs. ftntes. appends. index.   (Studies of the Pacific, no. 3)
                                                                   1853

Greiner, R., co-auth.   SEE no. 4752, Waterman, T. T.

Grekov, B. D., edit.   SEE no. 3397, Okun, S. B.

GREWINGK, CONSTANTIN CASPAR ANDREAS.   Beitrag zur Kenntniss der
orographischen und geognostischen Beschaffenheit der Nord-West
Küste Amerikas, mit den anliegenden Inseln.   [TITLE TR.   Contribution to the knowledge of the orography and geognosy of the
northwest coast of America and neighboring islands]   St. Petersburg, Gedruckt bey K. Kray, 1850.   351p.   pls. maps(incl. 3
fold.)   (also in Russisch-Kaiserliche Mineralogische Gesellschaft
zu St. Petersburg.   Verhandlungen für die Jahre 1848-49, pub.
1850.   pp.76-424)   1854

GRIER, MARY CATHARINE, comp.   Oceanography of the North Pacific
Ocean, Bering Sea and Bering Strait;   a contribution toward a
bibliography.   Compiled by Mary C. Grier.   Seattle, University of
Washington, 1941.   xxii,290p.   indexes.   (Library Series, vol. 2)
ANR. N. Y., Greenwood Press, n. d.   [1st Greenwood reprint 1969]
                                                                   1855

GRIERSON, JOHN.   Sir Hubert Wilkins;   enigma of exploration.
London, Robert Hale, 1960.   224p.   pls.   maps, bibliog.   1856

Grieve, Jas., tr.   SEE no. 2532, Krasheninnikov, S. P.

GRIFFIN, D. F.   First steps to Tokyo;   the Royal Canadian Air
Force in the Aleutians.   Toronto, Dent, 1944.   50p.   pls. ports.
                                                                   1857

GRIFFIN, HAROLD.   Alaska and the Canadian northwest, our new
frontier.   N. Y., W. W. Norton, 1944.   1st ed.   221p.   illus.
pls. map(dble. by Stephen J. Voorhies), index.   1858

Griffin, Jas. B., co-auth.   SEE no. 1709, Giddings, J. L., jr.

GRIFFITH, WILLIAM.   Report on the Matanuska coal field in the
valley of the Matanuska River, Alaska.   Scranton, Penna., 1905.
20 ℓ illus. with 8 maps and photographic appendix of 22 photos.
                                                                   1859

GRIGGS, ROBERT FISKE and others. Scientific results of the Katmai Expedition of the National Geographic Society, I-X. Columbus, Ohio State University, 1920. 492p. pls. maps(incl. 1
fold.) (Bulletin Contributions in Geographical Exploration,
no. 1, Feb. 1920) [papers from 2d-4th Katmai Expeditions, 1915-
17, by R. F. Griggs, J. S. Hine, J. D. Sayre and P. R. Hagelbarger, J. W. Shipley. Each reprinted from Ohio Journal of
Science, 1918-19]   1860

GRIGGS, ROBERT FISKE. The Valley of Ten Thousand Smokes. By
Robert F. Griggs. Washington, National Geographic Society,
1922. 341p. front.(5-folded pl.), pls. maps(incl. 1 fold. at
back), index.   1861

Grigor'ev, A. A., co-edit. SEE no. 2531, Krasheninnikov, S. P.

Grigor'ev, A. A., edit. SEE ALSO no. 2658, Lebedev, D. M.

Grigor'ev, A. A., tr. SEE ALSO no. 3338, Nordenskiöld, N.O.G.

GRINDALL MINING AND SMELTING CO. Copper and gold mines, Alaska.
Owning the townsite of Grindall, Alaska. Statement. Tacoma,
Wash., 1903. 23p. [on Prince of Wales Island]   1862

Grinnell, Elizabeth, edit. SEE no. 1866, Grinnell, Joseph.

Grinnell, George Bird. SEE nos.
    608, Boone and Crockett Club. Amer. big game ... 1904;
    610, Boone and Crockett Club. Hunting and conserv. ...1925;
    611, Boone and Crockett Club. Hunting at high ... 1913;
    1950, Harriman Alaska Exped. 1899. vol. 1.

GRINNELL, JOSEPH. Birds and mammals of the 1907 Alexander expedition to southeastern Alaska. Berkeley, University of Calif.
Press, 1909. 264p. (Pub. in Zoology, vol. 5, no. 2)   1863

GRINNELL, JOSEPH. Birds of the Kotzebue Sound region, Alaska.
Santa Clara, Calif., Cooper Ornithological Club, 1900. 80p.
map(sketch, fold.), fieldnotes, checklist, bibliog. (Pacific
Coast Avifauna, no. 1)   1864

GRINNELL, JOSEPH. Birds of the 1908 Alexander Alaska Expedition,
with a note on the avifaunal relationships of the Prince William
Sound district. Berkeley, University of California Press, 1910.
428p. (Pub. in Zoology, vol. 5, no. 12)   1865

GRINNELL, JOSEPH. Gold hunting in Alaska as told by Joseph
Grinnell and edited by Elizabeth Grinnell. Elgin, Illinois,
David C. Cook, 1901. 96p. front.(port.), illus. ANR. Seattle,
Shorey Book Store, 1964. facsim. ed.   1866

GRINNELL, MICHAEL. Song of the wild land. N. Y., Pageant Press,
1952. 1st ed. 76p.   1867

Gromov, Michael. SEE no. 2584, Laktionov, A. F.

GRØNLUND, H. Pan Hat Med Jack London. Copenhagen, Carl Allers
Bogforlag, 1944. 204p.   1868

GROVEN, EIVIND. Eskimomelodier fra Alaska; Helge Ingstad's
samling av opptak fra nunamiut; studier over tonesystemer og
rytmer. [TITLE TR. Eskimo melodies from Alaska; Helge Ingstad's collection recorded from Nunamiut; studies of tone
systems and rythmns] Oslo, 1956. 170   map.   1869

GRUBSTAKE PUBLISHING CO. Klondike grubstakes; where to get
them - what to take. Practical information for Yukoners and
others. Issued monthly. Seattle, Grubstake Pub. Co., 1898.
                                                           1870

GRUENING, ERNEST HENRY. An Alaskan reader, 1867-1967; selected
and edited by Ernest Gruening. N. Y., Meredith Press, 1967.
443p. [incls. fict., nonf., poetry]   1871

GRUENING, ERNEST HENRY. Let us end American colonialism. Key-
note address to Alaska Constitutional Convention, November 9,
1955. 24p.   1872

GRUENING, ERNEST HENRY. The battle for Alaska statehood. By
Ernest Gruening. College, University of Alaska Press, 1967.
122p. front.(col. port.), photos. (In cooperation with the
Alaska Purchase Centennial Commission)   1873

GRUENING, ERNEST HENRY. The state of Alaska. By Ernest Gruening. N. Y., Random House, 1954. 607p. 2 textmaps, endmaps,
graphs, bibliog. ANR. 1968. rev. and enl. 661p. illus. maps.
                                                           1874
Gruening, Ernest Henry. SEE ALSO no. 3887,
    Ross, Sherwood. Gruening of Alaska. [c1968]

GUBSER, NICHOLAS J. The Nunamiut Eskimos; hunters of caribou.
New Haven, Yale University Press, 1965. 384p. illus. maps,
bibliog.   1875

GUEMPLE, D. L. Inuit spouse-exchange. Chicago, University of
Chicago, 1961. 133p. tables, bibliog. appends. (Department of
Anthropology)   1876

GUÉRIN, LÉON. Les navigateurs français. Paris, Belin-Lepreur
et Morizot, 1856.   1877

Guernsey, A. H., edit. SEE no. 1981, Hartwig, G. L.

GUERNSEY, ALICE M. Under the northern lights. N. Y., Woman's
Home Missionary Society, 1917. 121p. illus. 5 pls. (Methodist
Episcopal Church)   1878

Guide for Alaskan miners, settlers ... 1902. SEE
   no. 1072, Copper River Mining, Trading & Development Co.

GUIDE, MAP AND HISTORY of the Klondyke Alaska gold fields. Chicago, L. M. Lord & Co., n. d. 46p. map.   1879

GUIDE TO ALASKA. L. A., Calif., [ca 1953] 224p. photos, maps.
                                                             1880
Guide to Alaska and Alcan ... 1963. SEE
   no. 2151, Holiday Pub.

GUIDE TO ALASKA and the Yukon. [S. F.], Alaska-Yukon Transportation Co., [1898] 16p. map(dble.)   1881

GUIDE TO THE KLONDIKE and the Yukon gold fields in Alaska and
the northwest territories. Seattle, Lowman & Hanford, 1897.
115p. illus.   1882

Guil, C., co-auth. SEE no. 885, Chamisso, L. C. A. von.

GUNTHER, ERNA. Art in the life of the Northwest Coast Indian.
With a catalog of the Rasmussen collection of Northwest Indian
art at the Portland Art Museum. Seattle, Superior Pub. Co.,
1966. 275p. front.(col.), photos(some col.), bibliog. [Axel
Rasmussen collection, Portland Art Museum, Portland, Ore.] 1883

GUNTHER, ERNA. Northwest coast Indian art. An exhibit at the
Seattle World's Fair Fine Arts Pavilion, April 21 to October 21,
1962. Seattle, University of Washington Press, 1962. 101p.
photos(some col.), map, list of lending institutions, bibliog.
                                                             1884
Gunther, Erna, tr. SEE ALSO no. 2542, Krause, A.
   The Tlingit Indians. 1956.

GUTENBERG, BENO and C. F. RICHTER. Seismicity of the earth and
associated phenomena. Princeton, N. J., Princeton University
Press, 1949. 273p. illus. tables, maps. [incls. Aleutian Arc,
Alaska and Canadian Shield]   1885

Gutman, K. H., tr. SEE no. 2601, Langsdorff, G. H. von.

GYÖRFFY, ISTVÁN. Addimenta terratologica ad cognitionem florae
peninsulae Alaska et Americae septentrionalis. Kolozsvár, Uni-
versitatis Francisco-Josephina, 1942. (Acta Mathematicarum et
naturalium. 10)   1886

                                H

HAAS, W. H., edit. The American empire. Chicago, 1940. illus.
[pp.151-215 about Alaska]   1887

HACKETT, JOHN A. Rhymes of the north, and other rhymes. Victoria, B. C., Diggon, 1924. 66p.   1888

HADDON, KATHLEEN. Artists in string; string figures; their regional distribution and social significance. N. Y., Dutton, 1930. 174p. diagrs. [incls. Alaskan Eskimo]   1889

HADER, BERTA and ELMER HADER. Reindeer trail; a long journey from Lapland to Alaska. N. Y., Macmillan, 1959. 1st print. (44)p. illus.(some col.)   1890

Hadley, Cora M., illus. SEE no. 4534, Tickasook.

HADMAN, VIRGINIA BALLARD. As the sailor loves the sea. By Ballard Hadman. N. Y., Harper, 1951. 1st ed. 232p. illus. pls. map, endmaps. [autobiog.]   1891

Hadman, Virginia Ballard. SEE ALSO no. 1152,
    Daily Alaska Fishing News. Alaska fisherman's almanac...1946.

Hafling, Jane, illus. SEE nos.
    1751, Fisher, P. Alaskan wild game cook book. 1961;
    2328, James, Sam. Taming Arctic shrew. 1963;
    4222, Snider, G. So was Alaska. 1961.

Hagelbarger, P. R. SEE no. 1860, Griggs, R. F.

HAGGLUND, M. G. Formation, properties and forecast of Arctic sea ice. Toronto, Canada. Meteorological Service, June 1955. 8p. diagr. bibliog. (Circular no. 2673) [resumé U. S. and U.S.S.R. ice observations]   1892

HAIG-BROWN, RODERICK. Captain of the *Discovery*; the story of Captain George Vancouver. Illustrated by Robert Banks. London, Macmillan, 1956. vii,181p. illus.(some col.), maps. (Great Stories of Canada) ANR. N. Y., St. Martin's Press, 1956.   1893

HAIG-BROWN, RODERICK. The whale people. N. Y., William Morrow, 1963. 256p. illus. by Mary Weiler. [Nootka Sound]   1894

HAINES, JOHN. Winter news; poems by John Haines. Middletown, Conn., Wesleyan University Press, [1966] 71p. (The Wesleyan Poetry Program)   1895

HAINES, MADGE and LESLEY MORRILL. John Muir; protector of the wilds. Nashville, Tenn., Abingdon, 1957. illus.   1896

HALCOMBE, JOHN JOSEPH. Stranger than fiction, published under the direction of the Tract Committee. London, Society for Promoting Christian Knowledge, 1872. 256p. front. pls. ports. OTHERS 1873. 3rd ed. and 1874. 4th ed. ALSO 1877, 1878 and 1880. [William Duncan and "Old" Metlakatla]   1897

HALE, CHARLES R. Innocent of Moscow; the apostle of Kamchatka and Alaska. [Davenport], 1888. 23p. bibliog. [Veniaminov and Russian missions 1857-87]   1898

HALE, HORATIO EMMONS. An international idiom; a manual of the Oregon trade language, or "Chinook Jargon." London, Whittaker & Co., 1890. 63(32)p.   1899

HALE, HORATIO EMMONS. Ethnography and philology. U. S. Exploring Expedition, during the years 1838, 1839, 1840, 1841, 1842 under the command of Charles Wilkes, U. S. N. Philadelphia, Printed by C. Sherman, 1846. vol. 6. 666p. ANR. Ridgewood, N. J., Gregg Press, 1966. facsim. reprint. (Edited by Ernest S. Dodge, vol. 4 of "America and the Pacific")   1900

HALE, HORATIO EMMONS. Indians of northwest America and vocabularies of North America; with introduction by Albert Gallatin. pl.?, American Ethnological Society, 1848. 130p. (Transactions vol. 2)   1901

Hale, Ralph T., co-auth. SEE no. 420, Bartlett, R. A.

HALL, ALICE B. Songs of a sourdough. N. Y., 1955. 44p.   1902

Hall, E. Raymond, co-auth. SEE no. 464, Bee, Jas. W.

[HALL, EDWARD H.] Alaska, the Eldorado of the midnight sun; marvels of the Yukon, the Klondike discovery, fortunes made in a day; how to go, what to take and what it costs; routes, rates and distances; attractions and dangers, land laws, practical counsel for prospectors, tourists and stay-at-homes. N. Y., Republic Press, 1897. 62p. front. illus. map(fold.)   1903

HALL, ERNEST FENWICK. Under the northern lights; an intimate disclosure of Alaska, its peoples and traditions of the "Land of the Midnight Sun." Denver, by author, 1932. 70p. illus. port. map(fold.) (Hall's Alaska Travelogs)   1904

HALL, FREDERICK. Laws of Alaska pertaining to civil government, mines and land. L. A., Prack & Blech, 1897. 32p.   1905

HALL, GEORGE LYMAN. Sometime again (E'lot Neg-oo-soo-li). By Major George L. Hall. Seattle, Superior Pub. Co., 1945. 217p. [Army rest camp in Aleutian Islands, WW II]   1906

HALL, JAMES A. Starving on a bed of gold; or, the world's longest fast. Santa Cruz, Calif., Press of the Sentinel, 1909. 149p.   1907

Hall, John C. SEE no. 3578, Pickering, Chas.

HALL, OLOF [pseud.] Youth north. Caldwell, Idaho, Caxton, 1936. 425p. [author is Olof Alfred Hallstrom]   1908

HALL, THOMAS F. Has the North Pole been discovered ? An analytical and synthetic review of the published narratives of ...
Cook and ... Peary ... Boston, 1917. 539p. illus. maps(incl. 1
in pocket), charts, diagrs. tables, index. [incls. Mt. McKinley
controversy]   1909

HALL, WARNER. Even Jericho; a novel. Philadelphia, Macrae-
Smith Co., 1944. 288p.   1910

HALLAGER, MORTEN. Udforlige og troevaerdige efterretninger om
de fra Rusland af langs med kysterne af Iishavet til soes giorte
opdagelser ... [TITLE TR. Complete and trustworthy description
of the Russian discoveries in the Arctic ...] Copenhagen, 1784.
350p. [incls. Bering and Chirikov]   1911

HALLIDAY, WILLIAM MAY. Potlatch and totem; and the recollections of an Indian agent, illustrated from thirty original photographs by the author. London, Dent, 1935. 240p. front. pls.
                                                                1912

HALLOCK, CHARLES. Our new Alaska; or, the Seward Purchase vin-
dicated. N. Y., Forest & Stream Pub. Co., 1886. 209p. front.
sketches by T. J. Richardson, pls.(incl. 1 fold.), map(fold.
col.), appends. ANR. N. Y., Arno Press, 1970. (American Environmental Studies) [reprint of 1886 ed.]   1913

HALLOCK, CHARLES. Peerless Alaska, our cache near the Pole.
N. Y., Broadway Pub. Co., 1908. 224p. front. pls. port.
sketches by George G. Cantwell.   1914

HALLOCK, CONSTANCE M. Forty-eight plus. N. Y., Friendship
Press, 1948. [religious missions in Alaska]   1915

Hallstrom, O. A. SEE no. 1908, Hall, Olof [pseud.]

HALPERN, JOEL MARTIN. Eskimos of the Alaska coast. N. Y.,
American Museum of Natural History, 1955. 6p. (Slide Library)
[villages of Deering and Kotzebue]   1916

HAMBLETON, CHALKLEY J. A gold hunter's experience. Chicago,
1898. 116p.   1917

Hambró, Johan, Lt. SEE no. 1660, Freuchen, P.

HAMILTON, ERNEST W. Forty years on. By Lord Ernest W. Hamilton.
London, Hodder & Stoughton, 1922. 311p. [has one chapt. on
Klondike]   1918

HAMILTON, JOHN TAYLOR. A history of the Church known as the
Moravian Church. Bethlehem, Penna., 1900. [has one chapt. on
Alaska]   1919

HAMILTON, JOHN TAYLOR. A history of the missions of the Moravian Church, during the 18th and 19th centuries. Bethlehem, Penna., 1901. [founding of mission in Alaska on pp.186-93]   1920

HAMILTON, JOHN TAYLOR. Report of the official visit of Bishop J. Taylor Hamilton to the missions in Southern California and Alaska. Bethlehem, Penna., Society for Propagating the Gospel. 1906. 69p.   1921

HAMILTON, JOHN TAYLOR. The beginnings of the Moravian Mission in Alaska. Bethlehem, Penna., The Comenius Press, 1890. 23p.
      1922

Hamilton, John W., *Bishop*. SEE no. 3384, Official record
    Alaska Methodist Episcopal Mission. 1904.

HAMILTON, KATE W. Left on the island. N. Y., Literary Department, Woman's Board of Home Missions, 1905. 16p. [Presbyterian Church]   1923

HAMILTON, WALTER R. The Yukon story; a sourdough's record of gold rush days and Yukon progress from the earliest times to the present day. Vancouver, B. C., Mitchell Press, 1964. 261p. illus. photos, 2 maps(1 fold.), append. bibliog. index. ANR. [pre-1964, date unknown, mimeographed, ltd. print. - Ashcroft Trail, four Robert W. Service poems written for and presented at reunions of Vancouver Sourdough Yukoners included]   1924

HAMLIN, CHARLES SIMEON. Old times on the Yukon; decline of Circle City, romances of the Klondike. L. A., Wetzel Pub. Co., 1928. 172p. front. pls. ports. facsim.   1925

HAMMER, MARIE SIGNE. Alaskan oribatids. København, Ejnar Munksgaard, 1955. 36p. illus. bibliog. (Acta Arctica, fasc. 7)
      1926
Hammond, Edw. P. SEE no. 2012, Headley, P. C.

HAMPTON, KATHLEEN. The Patch. N. Y., Random House, 1960. 1st print. 312p.   1927

HANDBOOK OF BRITISH COLUMBIA, and emigrant's guide to the gold fields, with map and two illustrations from photographs by M. Claudet. London, W. Oliver, [1862 ?] 82p. front.(fold. map), 2 pls.(1 dble.)   1928

Handbook of Church's missions ... 1914. SEE no. 931,
    Church Missions Pub. Co.

HANDBOOK OF VACATION TRIPS in Alaska, Atlin and the Yukon. no pl., n. d. 59p. illus. 3 maps. [cf no. 4834]   1929

HANDLEMAN, HOWARD. Bridge to victory; the story of the recon-
quest of the Aleutians. N. Y., Random House, 1943. 1st print.
275p. front.(port.), pls. endmaps, index. (Random House Wartime Book) [World War II]   1930

HANIGSMAN, ETHEL. Charming Alaska, in verse and picture. By
Ethel Hanigsman. Ketchikan, 1938. [c1938] 25 dble. pages,
sketches, endmaps, wrps.   1931

HANNA, G. DALLAS. Collecting shells in the Arctic. L. A., June
1957. 8p. (Minutes of Conchological Club of Southern California, no. 168)   1932

[HANSBROUGH, HENRY C.] The "looting" of men's character. How
sensationalists and ambitious politicians work their graft.
Washington, D. C., National Pub. Co., 1906. 13p. [has reference
to Rex Beach's "The spoilers."]   1933

HANSEN, A. H. Tundra; romance and adventure on Alaskan trails,
as told by former Deputy United States Marshal Hansen to the
Edingtons. N. Y., Century Co., 1930. 1st print. 334p. ANR.
N. Y., Grosset & Dunlap, 1938. [1930 ed. has on spine "Tundra.
The Edingtons"]   1934

Hansen, Godfred, co-auth. SEE nos.
     225, Amundsen, R. E. G. Nordostpassagen 1921;
     226, Amundsen, R. E. G. Nordvestpassagen ... 1907.

HANSEN, H. P. Cycles and geochronology. S. F., 1961. 24p.
tables, bibliog. (California Academy of Sciences Occasional
Papers, no. 31) [incls. Alaskan area and Bering land bridge
theory]   1935

HANSEN, HENRY P., edit. Arctic biology. Papers presented at
1957 and 1965 Biology Colloquia revised. Corvallis, Oregon
State University, 1967. 2d ed. 294p. illus. bibliog. [for 1st
see Wiggins, Ira L., edit., no. 4865]   1936

HANSEN, MILDRED M. Handbook for the freshman legislator.
Juneau, 1963. ANR. N. Y., Vantage, 1965.   1937

HANSEN, SOPHUS E., comp. Captain Farwell's Hansen handbook for
piloting in the inland waters of the Puget Sound area, British
Columbia, southeastern Alaska, southwestern Alaska, western
Alaska, with some sketches from the original Hansen handbook.
New and revised edition by R. F. Farwell. Seattle, Lowman &
Hanford, 1951. 599p. illus.   1938

HANSEN, SOPHUS E., comp. Hansen handbook for piloting in the
inland waters of Puget Sound, British Columbia, southeastern
Alaska, southwestern Alaska. Revised and enlarged by Raymond F.
Farwell. Seattle, Lowman & Hanford, 1931. 479p. illus.   1939

HANSEN, SOPHUS E., comp. Tacoma to Anchorage and Kodiak via the Inside Passage, compiled by S. E. Hansen ... Seattle, Lowman & Hanford, 1917. 209p. ANR. Seattle, Lowman & Hanford, 1919. 2d ed. rev. and enl. 327p. illus. map. 1940

HANSOME, MARIUS. Appointment with fortune. N. Y., Vantage Press, 1955. 247p. 1941

HANSON, EARL PARKER. Stefansson, prophet of the north. N. Y., Harper, 1941. 241p. pls. ports. map, index. 1942

HANSON, HERBERT CHRISTIAN. Characteristics of some grassland, marsh, and other plant communities in western Alaska. Ecological Monographs, Oct. 1951. append. checklist, bibliog. (vol. 21, no. 4, pp.317-78) 1943

HANSSEN, HELMER JULIUS. Gjennem Isbaksen, atten år med Roald Amundsen. [TITLE TR. Through the ice-pack; 18 years with Roald Amundsen] Oslo, H. Aschehoug & Co.(W. Nygaard), 1941. 218p. front.(dble.map), pls. ports. [tr. of no. 1945] 1944

HANSSEN, HELMER JULIUS. Voyages of a modern viking. London, George Routledge & Sons, 1936. 216p. pls. map(dble.) [see no. 1944 for tr.] 1945

Harben, F. E. SEE no. 4567, Trager, G. L.

Harcourt, Raoul d'. SEE nos. 1232-33, d'Harcourt, Raoul.

HARDCASTLE, ROMAINE. Alaska Day. Sitka. Alaska Day Festival, Inc. Commemorating the purchase transfer of Alaska from Russia to the U. S. A. [Sitka, 1954 ?] 80p. photos, sketches. 1946

Harding, John. SEE no. 4497, Thomas, Lowell.

Harding, Warren G. SEE nos.
    3373, Johnson, W. F. Life Warren G. Harding ... 1923;
    4288, Statement needs of Alaska. Address to president. 1923.

Harkin, W. A.,edit. SEE no. 4588, Tupper, Chas.

HARKNESS, DAVID JAMES. The Great Lakes states and Alaska and Hawaii in literature; a manual for schools and clubs. Knoxville, University of Tennessee, 1959. 59p. (University of Tennessee Newsletter, vol. 38, nos. 5-6) 1947

Harmon, D. W. See no. 3290, Neuman, D. S.

Harms, J. C., co-auth. SEE no. 3773, Reed, J. C.

Harms, Rex E., illus. SEE no. 4824, White, Helen A.

Harney (W. D.) Photogravure Co. SEE no. 312, Artwork ... 1907.

HARNISCH, WILHELM. Reise um die Erde gemacht von Krusenstern u.
Langsdorff; nebst Golownins gefangenschaft in Japan. Fur die
Jugend bearbeitet. Leipzig, 1823. ANR. Wien, 1827. 190p.
2 maps.   1948

HARPER, FRANK. Military ski manual, a handbook for ski and
mountain troops. Harrisburg, Penna., The Military Service Pub.
Co., 1943. 393p.   1949

Harper, Walter. SEE nos.
    4369, Stuck, Hudson. Winter ... 1920;
    4370, Stuck, Hudson. Ten thousand miles ... 1914;
    4372, Stuck, Hudson. Ascent of Denali ... 1914;
    4373, Stuck, Hudson. Voyage on Yukon ... 1917.

HARRIMAN ALASKA EXPEDITION, 1899. Alaska, edited by C. Hart
Merriam. Washington, D. C., Smithsonian Institution, 1910-14.
12 vols. in 13. fronts. in vols. 1-5 and 8-9, illus. pls.(some
col.), maps. (Harriman Alaska Series, vols. 1-5, 8-14) [see
nos. 1951-3 for earlier printings]   1950
    [Content by volume]
    1. Narrative, glaciers, natives. By John Burroughs,
            John Muir, and George Bird Grinnell. 183p. paged
            continuously with vol. 2, which has index for both.
    2. History, geography, resources. By William Healey
            Dall and others. pp.185-383. index(for both vols.)
    3. Glaciers and glaciation. By Grove Karl Gilbert. 231p.
    4. Geology and paleontology. By Benjamin Kendall Emerson
            and others. 173p.
    5. Crytogamic botany. By J. Cardot and others. 424p.
    8. Insects. Pt. 1. By W. H. Ashmead and others. 238p.
    9. Insects. Pt. 2. By W. H. Ashmead and others. 284p.
   10. Crustaceans. By M. J. Rathbun and others. 337p.
   11. Nemerteans ... Bryozoans. By W. R. Coe and A. Robert-
            son. 251p.
   12. Enchytraeids ... Tubicolous annelids. By C. Eisen and
            K. J. Bush. 355p.
   13. Land and fresh water mollusks of Alaska and adjoining
            regions. Hydroids of the expedition. By W. H. Dall
            and C. C. Nutting. 250p.
   14. Monograph of the shallow-water starfishes of the north
            Pacific coast from the Arctic to California. By A. E.
            Verrill. 2 vols. 408p.(vol. 1) and 110 pls.(vol. 2)

HARRIMAN ALASKA EXPEDITION, 1899. Alaska; giving the results
of the Harriman Alaska Expedition carried out with the cooperation of the Washington Academy of Sciences. London, Murray,
1902. 2 vols. illus. pls.(some col.), maps.   1951

HARRIMAN ALASKA EXPEDITION, 1899. Alaska. Harriman Alaska Expedition, with the cooperation of Washington Academy of Sciences. Edited by C. Hart Merriam. N. Y., Doubleday Page,
1902-05. vols. 1-5, 8-13.   1952

HARRIMAN ALASKA EXPEDITION, 1899. Papers from the Harriman
Alaska Expedition. Washington, D. C., The Academy, 1900-02.
30 nos. in 3 vols. pls. (in Washington Academy of Sciences
Proceedings. 1900-02. vols. 2-4) [21 nos. reprinted in vols.
5, 8, 9, 11 and 13 of Smithsonian Harriman Alaska series]   1953

Harriman Alaska Expedition, 1899. SEE ALSO nos.
      745, Burroughs, John. Far and near. 1904;
     2438, Kennan, G. E. H. Harriman, a biog. 1922.

HARRIMAN, ALICE. Wilt thou not sing ? A book of verses. N. Y.,
The Alice Harriman Co., 1912. 94p.   1954

HARRINGTON, J. J., edit. The Esquimeaux. S. F., Turnbull &
Smith, 1867. 12 monthly pts. bd. in 1 vol. 52p. pl.   1955

Harrington, M. R., co-auth. SEE no. 2669, Leechman, J. D.

HARRINGTON, MARK W. The Alaska almanac, with comparison tables
for Puget Sound ... Seattle, M. W. Harrington, 1901.   1956

HARRINGTON, REBIE. Cinderella takes a holiday in the Northland.
Journeys in Alaska and Yukon Territory. By Rebie Harrington with
illustrations. N. Y., Fleming H. Revell Co., [c1937] 269p.
front.(sketch by Eustace Ziegler), pls. map(fold. at back), glossary.   1957

HARRIS, A. C. Alaska and the Klondike gold fields containing a
full account of the discovery of gold; enormous deposits of the
precious metal; routes traversed by miners; how to find gold;
camp life at Klondike; practical instructions for fortune seekers, etc. etc.; including a graphic description of the gold
regions; land of wonders; immense mountains, rivers and plains;
native inhabitants, etc. By A. C. Harris, the well-known author
and traveler; including Mrs. Eli Gage's experiences of a year
among the Yukon mining camps; Mrs. Schwatka's recollections of
her husband as the Alaskan pathfinder; prosaic side of gold
hunting as seen by Joaquin Miller, the poet of the Sierras; embellished with many engravings representing mining and other
scenes in Alaska. Chicago, Philadelphia, Monarch Book Co.(formerly L. P. Miller & Co.), Publishers. [c. J. R. Jones, 1897]
photos, map(fold.) [sold by subscription only] ANR. Philadelphia, National Pub. Co., 1897. 528p. pls. maps(2 fold.) ANR.
Chicago, Smith & Simon, 1897. 528p. ANR. no pl., J. R. Jones,
1897. 528p. front. pls. maps. ANR. Chicago, Monroe Book Co.,
[c. J. R. Jones, 1897] 556p. ANR. Cincinnati, W. H. Ferguson,
1897. 556p. ANR. Chicago, J. S. Ziegler, 1897. 556p. ANR. no
pl., n. d. 556p. front.(pl.), pls. maps(fold.)   1958

Harris, B. K. SEE no. 3837, Robertson, F. C.

HARRIS, CHRISTIE. Once upon a totem. N. Y., Atheneum, 1963.
illus. ANR. 1965. 160p. woodcuts by John Fraser Mills. [Pacific northwest]   1959

HARRIS, CHRISTIE. Raven's cry. N. Y., Atheneum, 1966. 1st ed.
193p. illus. by Bill Reid, map. [Queen Charlotte Island Haidas
and Alaskan Tlingits]   1960

Harris, E., co-auth. SEE no. 4742, Warner, G. C.

HARRIS, JOHN. Navigantium atque Itinerantium Bibliotheca; or,
a complete collection of voyages and travels, consisting of a-
bove six hundred of the most authentic writers ... London, T.
Osborne, H. Whitridge, etc., 1764. 3rd ed. 2 vols. 984p. and
1056(22)p. pls. charts. ANR. EARLIER ED. 1744-48. rev. and
enl. [incls. Bering]   1961

HARRIS, MAE EVANS. You can Alcan. Middleburg, Va., Denlingers,
1959. 96p.   1962

HARRIS, WALTER. Salmon fishing in Alaska. How and where. South
Brunswick, N. J. and N. Y., A. S. Barnes, 1967. 143p. illus.
index. ANR. London, Thos. Yoseloff, 1967.   1963

Harris, Z. S., co-auth. SEE no. 4710, Voegelin, C. F.

Harrison, C. Old Testament stories ... 1893. SEE no. 1966.

HARRISON, CARTER H. A summer outing and the old man's story.
Chicago, Dibble Pub. Co., 1891. 297p. [partially about Alaska]
                                                                       1964

HARRISON, CHARLES. Ancient warriors of the North Pacific; the
Haidas, their laws, customs and legends, with some historical
account of the Queen Charlotte Islands. London, Witherby, 1925.
222p. front. pls. map.   1965

HARRISON, [CHARLES ?] Old Testament stories in the Haida language. By Rev. C. Harrison. London, Society for Promoting
Christian Knowledge, 1893. 92p.   1966

HARRISON, CHARLES. Saint Matthew gie giatlan las St. Matthew,
Haida, translation by Charles Harrison. London, British and
Foreign Bible Society, 1891. 143p.   1967

HARRISON, CHARLES. The Hydah Mission, Queen Charlotte's Island,
an account of the Mission and people. London, C. M. House,
[1884 ?] 23p. illus.   1968

HARRISON, EDWARD SANFORD. Alaska, the sportsman's paradise.
Seattle, Gateway Print. Co., 1909. 12p. illus.   1969

HARRISON, EDWARD SANFORD. Nome and the Seward Peninsula; a
book of information about northwestern Alaska. Seattle, E. S.
Harrison, printed by Metropolitan Press, 1905. 112p. illus.
photos, map(fold. in back) ANR. WITH TITLE Nome and the Seward
Peninsula; history, description, biographies and stories. Seattle, Metropolitan Press, 1905. ltd. ed. [approx. 800 copies
sold by subscription] 392p. illus. pls. ports. (E. S. Harrison Souvenir Edition)   1970

Harrison, Edward Sanford. SEE ALSO no. 28,
    Alaska almanac. 1908-9.

Harrison, Richard Edes, cartog. SEE no. 4300,
    Stefansson, E. Within Circle ... 1945,

Harrison, Richard Edes, co-edit. SEE no. 4783,
    Weigert, H. W. New compass ... 1949.

HARSHBERGER, JOHN WILLIAM. The forests of the Pacific coasts of
British Columbia and southeastern Alaska. Helsinki, 1929. 5p.
(Acta Forestalia Fennica, vol. 34, no. 5)   1971

HART, ALBERT B. and E. CHANNING. Extracts from official papers
relating to the Bering Sea controversy, 1790-1892. Edited by A.
B. Hart and E. Channing. N. Y., A. Lowell & Co., 1893. 26p.
(American History Leaflets, no. 6, Nov. 1892)   1972

HART, ALBERT B. The obvious Orient ... N. Y., D. Appleton,
1911. 369p. [some mention of Alaska]   1973

HART, ROBERT G. McKay's guide to Alaska. N. Y., David McKay
Co., 1959. 330p. maps, endmaps, append. index.   1974

HARTING, JAMES E. The fauna of the Prybilov Islands abridged
from the "Report on the Prybilov group or seal islands of Alaska"
by Henry W. Elliott; with an appendix on the ornithology by Dr.
Elliott Coues, Washington, 1873. London, 1875. 38p. [re-
printed from "The Field" for private circulation]   1975

HARTT, A. C. Movement of salmon in the north Pacific Ocean and
Bering Sea as determined by tagging, 1956-58. Vancouver, B. C.,
1962. 157p. illus. tables, graphs, maps. (International Northern Pacific Fisheries Commission. Bull. no. 6)   1976

Hartwig, Georg Ludwig. [Alphabetical title guide to chronologi-
    cal entries]

    Der Hobe ... 1977.   The polar and tropical ... 1981
    Dwellers ... 1979   The polar world. 1978.
    Heroes ... 1980.

HARTWIG, GEORG LUDWIG. Der Hobe Norden im Natur- und Menschlen-
leben dargestellt. Wiesbaden, 1858.   1977

HARTWIG, GEORG LUDWIG. TRANSLATIONS - Der Hobe Norden ... 1858.

   The polar world; a popular description of man and nature in
     the Arctic and Antarctic regions of the glode, with addi-
     tional chapters. N. Y., Harper, 1869. 486p. illus. front.
     OTHERS London, Longmans, 1869, 1874 and 1886. ANR. London,
     1881. 548p. pls. woodcuts, maps, index. See also no.
     1981]   1978

HARTWIG, GEORG LUDWIG. Dwellers in the Arctic regions; a popular account of the men who live in polar regions. London, Longmans Green, 1887. 158p. illus. pls.   1979

HARTWIG, GEORG LUDWIG. Heroes of the polar world. London,
Longmans Green, 1892. 128p. illus. front.   1980

HARTWIG, GEORG LUDWIG and A. H. GUERNSEY. The polar and tropi-
cal worlds; a description of man and nature in the polar and
equatorial regions of the globe. By Dr. G. Hartwig ... Edited,
with additional chapters, by Dr. A. H. Guernsey. With nearly
two hundred illustrations. Springfield, Mass., Bill, Nichols &
Co., 1871. 761p. front. illus. index. ANR. Springfield, Mass.,
C. A. Nichols & Co., 1874. enl. ed. 811p. maps. ANR. Guelph,
Ontario, 1874. 2 vols. in 1. 811p. illus. maps, index. ANR.
Springfield, Mass., 1877. 2 vols. in 1. [acquisition of Alaska
noted. See also no. 1978]   1981

Hartzell, J. C., edit. SEE no. 2313, Jackson, Sheldon.

Harvey, Fred E., co-edit. SEE no. 643, Brand, D. D.

Harvey, H. P., illus. SEE no. 3770, Reed, Chas. K.

[HASELHURST, MAY A.] Days forever flown. N. Y., privately
printed, by Gillis Bros., 1892. 401p. front.(port.), pls.
[travel in Alaska and northwest]   1982

HASKELL, WILLIAM B. Two years in the Klondike and Alaskan gold-
fields; a thrilling narrative of personal experiences and adventures in the wonderful gold regions of Alaska and the Klondike, with observations of travel and exploration along the Yukon ... including full and authentic information of the countries
described ... Hartford, Conn., Hartford Pub. Co., 1898. 558p.
front. pls. map(fold.)   1903

HASKIN, LESLIE LOREN. Wild flowers of the Pacific coast, in
which is described 332 flowers and shrubs of Washington, Oregon,
Idaho, Central and Northern California and Alaska. With 182
full-page photos by Leslie L. and Lilian G. Haskin. Portland,
Ore., Binfords & Mort, 1934. 409p. pls. glossary, index, errata page. ANR. 1966. 418p. pls. glossary, index.   1984

HASSEL, JOHANN G. H. Vollstandige u. neuste erdbeschreibung des britischen u. russischen Amerikas u. der franzosischen Fischerinseln, mit einer einleitung zur statistik dieser lander. Bearbeitet von dr. G. Hassel. Weimar, Geographische Institut, 1822. 604p.   1985

Hatch, Alden, co-auth. SEE nos.
   3368, Nutchuk. Back to Smoky Sea. 1941;
   3369, Nutchuk. Son of Smoky Sea. 1941.

HATT, DANIEL E. Sitka spruce; songs of Queen Charlotte Islands. Vancouver, B. C., R. P. Latta, 1919. 51p.   1986

HATT, GUDMUND. Arktiste skinddragter; Eurasien og Amerika; en etnografisk studie. [TITLE TR. Arctic fur apparel in Eurasia and America; an ethnographic study] København, J. H. Schultz, 1914. 255p. illus. pls. bibliog. (University of Copenhagen)
                                                                   1987

HATT, GUDMUND. Asiatic influences in American folklore. Copenhagen, E. Munksgaard, 1949. 122p. (Danske Videnskabernes Selskab. Historisk-Filologiske Meddelser. Bd. 31, nr. 6)   1988

HATT, GUDMUND. Mocassins and their relation to Arctic footwear. N. Y., Kraus Reprint Corp., 1966. [reprint from American Anthropological Association Memoirs, 1916. vol. 3, no. 3. pp.149-250. illus.]   1989

HAUSER, WILLIAM E., edit. Thirty hikes in Alaska. Western Chugach. Talkeetna. Kenai. Seattle, The Mountaineers, July 1967. 1st ed. (72)p. illus. photos, maps. (The Mountaineers, Seattle and The Mountaineering Club of Alaska, Anchorage)   1990

Havemeyer, L., co-auth. SEE no. 4649, Van Hise, C. R.

HAVERLY, CHARLES E. Klondyke and fortune by one who has struck it. London, Southwood, Smith & Co., 1897. ANR. WITH TITLE Klondike and fortune; the experiences of a miner who has acquired a fortune in the Yukon Valley. London, Southwood, Smith & Co., 1898. 135p.   1991

HAWKES, CLARENCE. Silversheene, king of sled dogs. Illustrated by Charles Livingston Bull. Springfield, Mass., Milton, 1924. 234p. front. pls.   1992

HAWKES, ERNEST WILLIAM. Eskimo land; a supplementary reader for primary schools. Boston, Ginn & Co., 1914. 90p.   1993

Hawkes, Ernest William. La fete "Des Invites" ... SEE no. 1996.

HAWKES, ERNEST WILLIAM. The dance festivals of the Alaskan Eskimo. By E. W. Hawkes. Philadelphia, University of Pennsylvania, 1914. 41p. pls. plans, diagrs.   1994

HAWKES, ERNEST WILLIAM. The "Inviting-In" feast of the Alaskan Eskimo. Ottawa, Government Print. Bureau, 1913. 20p. illus. plan, diagrs. pls. (Canada. Geol. Survey. Memoir 45, no. 3, Anthropol. Ser.)   1995

   TRANSLATION - "Inviting-In" feast ... 1913.

   La fete "Des Invites" des Esquimaux de l'Alaska. Ottawa, Ca-
      nada National Museum, 1915. (Geol. Survey. Memoir no. 45,
      no. 3)   1996

Hawkesley, Dr. SEE Hawkesworth, John.

HAWKESWORTH, JOHN. The voyages of discovery of Captain James Cook, describing his discoveries and adventures in Tierra del Fuego, Tahiti, New Zealand and Van Diemen's Land, Australia, The Friendly Islands, New Hebrides, New Caledonia, the Sandwich Islands, western North America, etc., partly narrated by the great navigator himself; and partly compiled from his notes and journals by Dr. Hawkesley. Complete unabridged edition. London, Ward, Lock, Bowden & Co., [189_ ?] 2 vols. illus.   1997

Haworth, Paul L., edit. SEE no. 4960, Woollen, Wm. W.

HAWTHORN, AUDREY. Art of the Kwakiutl Indians; and other north-west coast tribes. Seattle, University of Washington Press, 1967. 472p. pls.(some col.)   1998

HAWTHORN, HARRY BERTRAM, C. S. BELSHAW and S. M. JAMIESON. The Indians of British Columbia; a study of contemporary social adjustment. Berkeley, University of California Press, 1958. 499p. maps, tables. [incls. Haida and Tsimshian cultures] 1999

Hawthorne, Mont. SEE nos.
   2918, McKeown, M. F. Alaska silver. 1951;
   2919, McKeown, M. F. Trail led north. 1948.

Haydon, H. E., co-auth. SEE no. 724, Bugbee, J. S.

Hayes, C. E. SEE no. 5004, Yukon Bill [pseud.]

HAYES, FLORENCE SOOY. A land of challenge, Alaska. N. Y., Board of National Missions of the Presbyterian Church in the U. S. A., 1941. 32p. (National Missions Library Series)   2000

HAYES, FLORENCE SOOY. Alaskan hunter, by Florence Hayes. Boston, Houghton, 1959. 248p. illus. by Kurt Wiese.   2001

HAYES, FLORENCE SOOY. Arctic gateway, by Florence Hayes. N. Y., Friendship Press, 1940. 132p. illus. pls. ports. endmaps, bibliog.   2002

HAYES, FLORENCE SOOY. The Eskimo hunter, by Florence Hayes. N. Y., Random House, 1945. 275p. front.(col.), illus. by Kurt Wiese.   2003

HAYES, JAMES GORDON. The conquest of the North Pole; recent Arctic exploration. N. Y., Macmillan, 1934. 317p. front. pls. ports. plan, maps(some fold.), bibliog. index. ANR. London, Butterworth, 1934.   2004

Haygood, W. C., co-auth. SEE no. 737, Burnette, O. L., jr.

HAYNE, M. H. E. and H. WEST TAYLOR. The pioneers of the Klon-dyke; being an account of two years police service on the Yukon narrated by M. H. E. Hayne and recorded by H. West Taylor. Il-lustrated by photos taken on the spot by the narrator. London, Sampson, Low, Marston & Co., 1897. 184p. front.(port.), pls. map. [Royal Northwest Mounted Police]   2005

HAYNES, BESSIE DOAK and EDGAR HAYNES. The grizzly bear; por-traits from life. Norman, University of Oklahoma, 1966. xxi, 386p. illustrated by drawings of Mary Baker.   2006

HAYS, LYDIA A. Kahtlian; a chief of the Raven tribe. N. Y., Woman's Board of Home Missions, 1906. 13p.   2007

HAYS, LYDIA A. Ka-Ta-Da. N. Y., Woman's Board of Home Missions, 1906. 10p.[Presbyterian Church]   2008

HAZARD, JOSEPH TAYLOR. Pacific crest trails from Alaska to Cape Horn. Seattle, Superior Pub. Co., 1946. 317p. front. pls. in-dex. ANR. Seattle, Superior Pub. Co., 1948. enl. and rev.352p. front. pls. index.   2009

HAZELTON, ELIZABETH C. Alaskan forget-me-nots, the northern garden that lured the Portland rose. Seattle, Lowman and Han-ford, 1921. 26p. OTHERS 1923 (28)p. AND 1925.   2010

HEAD, HELEN SMITH. Death below zero. N. Y., Comet Press, 1953. 214p. [fict. setting is Wiseman, Alaska]   2011

HEADLEY, P. C. The reaper and the harvest; or, scenes and in-cidents in connection with the work of the Holy Spirit in the life and labors of Reverend Edward Payson Hammond, M.A. ... with introduction by Reverend A. H. Burlingham, D.D. N. Y., Funk & Wagnalls, 1884. 550p. [pp.498-516 on Alaskan missions]   2012

Hearne, Samuel. SEE no. 4256, Speck, Gordon.

Heath, W. R., co-edit. SEE no. 3198, Morris, F. L.

HEAWOOD, EDWARD. A history of geographical discovery in the seventeenth and eighteenth centuries. Cambridge, Cambridge University Press, 1912. 475p. illus. ports. maps(3 fold.) (Cambridge Geographical Series) ANR. N. Y., Octagon Books, 1965. 475p. illus. maps. 2013

HEER, OSWALD. Flora Fossilis Alaskana. Fossile Flora von Alaska. [TITLE TR. Fossil flora of Alaska] Stockholm, P. A. Norstadt & Söner, 1869. 41p. illus. pls.(col.) (Svenska Vetenskap soka demien. Handlingar. Bd. 8, nr. 4) [also issued as a section of "Flora Fossilis Arctica" Bd. 2, no. 2, 1871. See no. 2015] ANR. Leipzig, Brockhaus, 1871. 41p. 2014

HEER, OSWALD. Flora Fossilis Arctica. Die fossile flora der polarlander, enthaltend die im Nordgroenland, auf der Melville Insel, im Banksland, am Mackenzie, im Island, und im Spitzbergen entdeckten fossilen pflanzen. Zurich, J. Wurster & Co., 1868-83. 7 vols. [see also no. 2014] 2015

HEFLIN, ALMA. Adventure was the compass. Boston, Little Brown, 1942. 285p. illus. by Martha Powell Setchell. [airplane trip to Alaska] 2016

HEGG, ERIC A. Souvenir of Alaska and Yukon Territory. [Skagway, Alaska ?], 1900. 104p. photos. ANR. Seattle, 1902. 126p. 2017

HEGG, ERIC A. Souvenir of Nome, Alaska. Illustrated by E. A. Hegg. Seattle, Wash., 1900. 56 pls., no text. 2018

Hegg, Eric A., photog. SEE ALSO nos.
    463, Becker, E. A. Klondike '98. 1949;
    3183, Morgan, Murray C. One man's gold rush. 1967.

HEID, JOHN G. and G. W. GARSIDE. Local mining laws of Harris mining district, Alaska. Juneau, 1887. 20p. 2019

HEILPRIN, ANGELO. Alaska and the Klondike; a journey to the new Eldorado, with hints to the traveller. N. Y., D. Appleton, 1899. 315p. pl. facsim. maps. ANR. London, G. Arthur Pearson, 1899. 315p. front. pls. diagrs. maps(fold. col.), index. 2020

Heilprin, Angelo. SEE ALSO no. 3631, Pollak, Gustav.
    Michael Heilprin and his sons. 1912.

Heilprin, Michael. SEE no. 3631, Pollak, Gustav.
    Michael Heilprin and his sons. 1912.

Heintzleman, B. Frank, co-auth. SEE no. 1603, Forrest, G.

HEISTAND, HENRY OLCOT SHELDON. The Territory of Alaska. A brief account of its history and purchase; its inhabitants, geographical features and resources, with especial reference to the gold-fields and methods of reaching them. Compiled from official

government records and the latest and most reliable sources.
Kansas City, Mo., Hudson-Kimberly Pub. Co., 1898. 195p. pls.
maps(3 fold.), appends.   2021

HEIZER, ROBERT FLEMING. Archaeology of the Uyak site Kodiak Island, Alaska. Berkeley, University of California Press, 1956.
199p. illus. pls. maps, plans, tables, diagrs. (Anthrological
Record, vol. 17, no. 1)   2022

Helbig, Karl, co-edit. SEE no. 3332, Nordenskiöld, N. A. E.

Held, B., co-auth. SEE no. 949, Clawson, M.

HELLENTHAL, JOHN ALBERTUS. The Alaskan melodrama. By J. A.
Hellenthal. N. Y., Liveright Pub. Corp., 1936. 312p. front.
pls. facsim. map(fold.), index. ANR. London, Allen & Unwin,
1936. 312p. front. pls. map.   2023

HELLER, CHRISTINE A. Wild flowers of Alaska. Portland, Ore.,
Printed by Graphic Arts Center, 1966. 104p. photos(col.), map,
color key, glossary, index.   2024

HELLER, HERBERT L., edit. Sourdough sagas. Cleveland, World
Pub. Co., 1967. 271p. photos. [excerpts from goldrush diaries]
                                                               2025

Helmericks, Bud. SEE nos.
    2027-29, 2031, Helmericks, Constance and Harmon;
    2032-35, Helmericks, Harmon.

HELMERICKS, CONSTANCE. Hunting in North America. By Constance
Helmericks. Harrisburg, Penna., Stackpole, 1956. 298p. illus.
[has scattered references to Alaskan game]   2026

HELMERICKS, CONSTANCE and HARMON HELMERICKS. Our Alaskan winter.
By Constance and Harmon Helmericks. Boston, Little Brown, 1949.
271p. front.(col.), pls. diagrs. endmaps. [Colville River in
Brooks Range, 3rd vol. of trilogy with nos. 2028 and 2031] 2027

HELMERICKS, CONSTANCE and HARMON HELMERICKS. Our summer with
the Eskimos. By Constance and Harmon Helmericks. Boston, Little Brown, 1948. 1st ed. 239p. front.(col.), pls. endmaps.
ANR. London, Museum Press, 1952. 255p. illus. [2d vol. of trilogy with nos. 2027 and 2031]   2028

HELMERICKS, CONSTANCE and HARMON HELMERICKS. The flight of the
Arctic Tern. By Constance and Harmon Helmericks. Boston, Little Brown, 1952. 321p. illus. [bush flying]   2029

HELMERICKS, CONSTANCE. We live in Alaska. By Constance Helme-
ricks. Boston, Little Brown, 1944. 266p. pls. ports. ANR.
Garden City, N. Y., Garden City Pub. Co., 1945. reprint. ANR.
London, Hodder & Stoughton, 1945. 304p. engravings by Gwenda
Morgan.   2030

HELMERICKS, CONSTANCE and HARMON HELMERICKS. We live in the Arctic. By Constance and Harmon Helmericks. Boston, Little Brown, 1947. 1st ed. 329p. pls. port. map, endmaps. ANR. London, 1949. 321p. [1st vol. of trilogy with nos. 2027 and 2028] 2031

HELMERICKS, HARMON. Arctic bush pilot. By Bud Helmericks. Boston, Little Brown, 1956. 180p. illus. photos by author, front. map. 2032

HELMERICKS, HARMON. Arctic hunter. By Bud Helmericks. Boston, Little Brown, 1955. 142p. illus. by Henry Bugbee Kane, endmaps. 2033

HELMERICKS, HARMON. Oolak's brother. By Bud Helmericks. Illustrated by Henry Bugbee Kane. Boston, Little Brown, 1953. 1st ed. 144p. 2034

HELMERICKS, HARMON. The last of the bush pilots. By Harmon Helmericks. N. Y., Knopf, 1969. 1st ed. 361p. front.(dble. map), photos(16p.) 2035

Helmericks, Harmon. SEE ALSO nos.
    2027-29, 2031. Helmericks, Constance and Harmon.

Heltman, Charles C., co-auth. SEE no. 943, Clark, H. F.

HENDERSON, ALICE PALMER. The rainbow's end; Alaska. Chicago, H. S. Stone & Co., 1898. 296p. front. pls. ports. 2036

HENDERSON, DANIEL MacINTYRE. From the Volga to the Yukon; the story of the Russian march to Alaska and California, paralleling our own westward trek to the Pacific. By Daniel Henderson. N. Y., Hastings House, 1944. 256p. endmaps, bibliog. index. 2037

HENDERSON, JOHN B. American diplomatic questions; the fur seals and Bering Sea Award. N. Y., Macmillan, 1901. 529p. 2038

HENDERSON, LESTER D. Alaska; its scenic features, geography, history, and government. Juneau, Daily Alaska Empire, printers, 1928. 112p. pls. ports. diagrs. maps. ANR. 1929. rev. 114p. ANR. 1936. rev and enl. 143p. front. pls. maps. ANR. 1939. rev. 144p. pls. ports. diagrs. maps. 2039

HENDRYX, JAMES BEARDSLEY. Badmen on Halfaday Creek. Garden City, N. Y., Doubleday, 1950. 1st ed. 216p. (Double D Western) [fict. acct. goldrush on the Yukon] 2040

HENDRYX, JAMES BEARDSLEY. Black John of Halfaday Creek. Garden City, N. Y., Doubleday Doran, 1939. 1st ed. 305p. ANR. N. Y., Sundial Press, 1940. 305p. 2041

HENDRYX, JAMES BEARDSLEY. Blood of the North. Garden City,
N. Y., Doubleday Doran, 1938. 278p. ANR. N. Y., Sundial Press,
1939. 278p. [Alaskan setting]   2042

HENDRYX, JAMES BEARDSLEY. Blood on the Yukon Trail; a novel of
Corporal Downey of the Mounted. Garden City, N. Y., Doubleday
Doran, 1930. 305p. ANR. Toronto, 1930. 305p.   2043

HENDRYX, JAMES BEARDSLEY. Connie Morgan hits the trail. Garden
City, N. Y., Doubleday Doran, 1929. 1st ed. 221p. front. illustrated by Ernest Walker. [Alaskan setting]   2044

HENDRYX, JAMES BEARDSLEY. Connie Morgan in Alaska. N. Y., Putnam, 1916. 341p. illus. front.   2045

HENDRYX, JAMES BEARDSLEY. Connie Morgan in the Arctic. N. Y.,
Putnam, 1936. 239p. front.   2046

HENDRYX, JAMES BEARDSLEY. Connie Morgan in the fur country.
N. Y., Putnam, 1921. front.   2047

HENDRYX, JAMES BEARDSLEY. Courage of the north. Garden City,
N. Y., Doubleday, 1946. 251p. [Yukon setting]   2048

HENDRYX, JAMES BEARDSLEY. Gold and guns on Halfaday Creek.
N. Y., Carleton House, 1942. 1st ed. 280p. (Bar H Books) 2049

HENDRYX, JAMES BEARDSLEY. Gold is where you find it. Garden
City, N. Y., Doubleday & Co., 1953. 1st ed. 191p. (Double D
Western)   2050

HENDRYX, JAMES BEARDSLEY. It happened on Halfaday Creek. Garden City, N. Y., Doubleday Doran, 1944. 1st ed. 211p. (Double
D Western)   2051

HENDRYX, JAMES BEARDSLEY. Justice on Halfaday Creek. Garden
City, N. Y., Doubleday, 1949. 220p. (Double D Western) 2052

HENDRYX, JAMES BEARDSLEY. Law and order on Halfaday Creek.
N. Y., Carleton House, 1941. 1st ed. 308p. (Bar H Books) 2053

HENDRYX, JAMES BEARDSLEY. Murder on Halfaday Creek. Garden City,
N. Y., Doubleday, 1951. 1st ed. 191p. (Double D Western)   2054

HENDRYX, JAMES BEARDSLEY. North. N. Y., Putnam, 1923. 334p.
ANR. N. Y., A. L. Burt, n. d. 334p.   2055

HENDRYX, JAMES BEARDSLEY. On the rim of the Arctic. Garden
City, N. Y., Doubleday, 1948. 224p.   2056

HENDRYX, JAMES BEARDSLEY. Outlaws of Halfaday Creek. Garden
City, N. Y., Doubleday Doran, 1935. 1st ed. 299p. ANR. N. Y.,
A. L. Burt, 1935. ANR. N. Y., Triangle Books, 1944.   2057

HENDRYX, JAMES BEARDSLEY. Skullduggery on Halfaday Creek. Garden City, N. Y., Doubleday Doran, 1946. 1st ed. 271p.   2058

HENDRYX, JAMES BEARDSLEY. Snowdrift; a story of the land of the strong cold. N. Y., Putnam, 1922. 381p. [Alaska setting]
2059

HENDRYX, JAMES BEARDSLEY. Strange doings on Halfaday Creek. Garden City, N. Y., Doubleday Doran, 1943. 1st ed. 269p. (Double D Western) ANR. Garden City, N. Y., Sundial Press, 1943.
2060

HENDRYX, JAMES BEARDSLEY. The Czar of Halfaday Creek. Garden City, N. Y., Doubleday Doran, 1940. 1st ed. 271p. (Double D Western) ANR. N. Y., Triangle Books, 1942. 271p.   2061

HENDRYX, JAMES BEARDSLEY. The saga of Halfaday Creek. Garden City, N. Y., Doubleday Doran, 1936. 1st ed. 189p.   2062

HENDRYX, JAMES BEARDSLEY. The Yukon Kid. Garden City, N. Y., Doubleday Doran, 1934. 294p.   2063

Heney, Michael. SEE nos.
   2079, Herron, E. A. Alaska's railroad builder ... 1960;
   4843, Whiting, F. B. Grit, grief and gold ... 1933.

HENLEY, G. F. Guide to the Yukon-Klondike mines; full information of outfit, climate, Dawson City, with notes on alluvial and metalliferous prospecting; routes described in detail; report of William Ogilvie, F.R.G.S. - diary of the late Archbishop Seghers. Victoria, B. C., 1897. 63p. ANR. N. Y., Lipton, 1898. 60p. (People's Handbook Series)   2064

HENNING, CHARLES L. Die Erzlagerstatten der Vereinigten Staaten von Nordamerika, mit Einschluss von Alaska, Cuba, Portorico, und den Philippinen nach Geschichte, Form, Inhalt, und Entstehung. [TITLE TR. Ore deposits of the United States, including Alaska ... history, form, contents and origin] Stuttgart, Ferdinand Enke, 1911. 293p.   2065

HENRIQUES, J. A. Alaska. Facts about the new northwest. Cleveland, Kirtland Society, 1874. 23p. (Natural Science Papers)
2066

HENRY, DAVID and KAY HENRY. Our Indian language. Dinaak'aa. Reading book I. Koyukon dialect of Athapaskan Indian. Fairbanks, Summer Institute of Linguistics, 1966. 24p. illustrated by Marshall Holdstock and Don Drew Canonge. (Wycliffe Bible Translators)   2067

[HENRY, DAVID] Tł'eaka Hok'anaga'. Dictionary of Indian words, Koyukuk, Alaska. no pl., Summer Institute of Linguistics, n. d. 11p.   2068

HENRY, JOSEPH KAYE. Flora of southern British Columbia and Vancouver Island, with many references to Alaska and northern species. Toronto, W. J. Gage, 1915. 363p.   2069

HENRY, MARQUERITE. Alaska, in story and pictures. Chicago, A.
Whitman, 1941. 28p. illustrated by Kurt Wiese (some col.), endmaps.   2070

HENRY, P. F., tr. SEE nos.
     4229, Sobreviela, M. Voyages au LaPérouse ... 1809;
     4640, Vancouver, Geo. Voyage de découvertes ... 1801-02.

HENRY, VICTOR. Esquisse d'une grammaire raisonnée de la langue
aléoute d'après la grammaire et le vocabulaire de Ivan Véniami-
nov. Paris, Maisonneuve & cie, 1879. 73p. (also in: Revue de
Linguistique, vol. 11, pp. 424-57 and vol. 12, pp.1-62. Paris,
1878 and 1879)   2071

HENRY, WILL. The North Star. N. Y., Random House, 1956. 213p.
ANR. N. Y., Bantam Books, 1958. 184p. paperback.   2072

HERBERT, AGNES. The moose. London, Adam & Charles Black, 1913.
248p. front. illustrated by Patten Wilson.   2073

HERBERT, AGNES and A. SHIKARA. Two Dianas in Alaska. London,
J. Lane, 1909. 316p. front.(port.), pls. ANR. London, Nelson,
1909. 2d ed. 256p.   2074

HERBERT, CHARLES F. Alaska mining law manual. Fairbanks,
printed by Jessen's Weekly, n. d. [ca 1966] 77p. illus.
diagrs. maps, index.   2075

Herbert, Henry Howard Molyneux. Fourth Earl of Carnarvon.
     SEE no. 1809, Great Britain. Colonial Secretary.

Herbst, J. F. W., tr. SEE no. 4639, Vancouver, Geo.

Herder, F., von. SEE no. 3775, Regel, E. L.

HERITAGE PRESS. The explorations of Captain James Cook. N. Y.,
Heritage Press, 1948. illustrated by Geoffrey C. Ingleton. 2076

Herman, *Father*. SEE no. 1534, *Father* Herman ... n. d.

Herrington, Wm. C., co-auth. SEE no. 4516, Thompson, Wm. F.

HERRMANN, ERNST. Das Nordpolarmeer das Mittelmeer von morgen.
[TITLE TR. The north polar sea, the Mediterranean of tomorrow]
Berlin, Safari-Verlag, 1949. 343p. bibliog.   2077

HERRON, EDWARD ALBERT. Alaska; land of tomorrow. By Edward A.
Herron. N. Y., McGraw-Hill, 1947. 232p. illus. pls. map.
(Whittlesey House)   2078

HERRON, EDWARD ALBERT. Alaska's railroad builder Mike Heney.
By Edward A. Herron, N. Y., Messner, 1960. 192p. bibliog.
index.   2079

HERRON, EDWARD ALBERT. Dimond of Alaska; adventurer in the far
north. N. Y., Messner, 1957. 190p. bibliog. index. [Anthony
Dimond]   2080

HERRON, EDWARD ALBERT. Dynamite Johnny O'Brien; Alaska's sea
captain. N. Y., Messner, 1962. 189p. bibliog. index.   2081

HERRON, EDWARD ALBERT. First scientist of Alaska; William
Healey Dall. N. Y., Messner, 1958. 192p. bibliog. [Interna-
tional Telegraph Expedition of 1865, and U. S. Geological Sur-
vey]   2082

HERRON, EDWARD ALBERT. The big country (a story of Alaska.)
Illustrated with maps. N. Y., Aladdin Books, 1953. 190p. illus.
maps.   2083

HERRON, EDWARD ALBERT. The conqueror of Mount McKinley. N. Y.,
Messner, 1964. [Hudson Stuck]   2084

HERRON, EDWARD ABLERT. Wings over Alaska; the story of Carl
Ben Eielson. N. Y., Messner, 1959. 192p. bibliog. index. ANR.
N. Y., Washington Square Press, 1967. 217p. bibliog. index.
(Archway Paperback)   2085

HERZOG, WILHELM. Ueber die Verwandtschaft des Yumasprachtstamme.
Mit der Sprache der Aleuten und der Eskimostamme. no pl., n. d.
reprint. (in: Zeitschrift für Ethnologie, vol. 10, Berlin, 1878.
10p.)   2086

Hesse, Josette, tr. SEE no. 3853, Rodahl, Kaare.

HESSE, W. A. Proposed arterial highway system for Alaska.
Juneau, by author, 1940. 11p.   2087

HETZEL, THEODORE B. Indian rights and wrongs in Alaska. Philadelphia, Indian Rights Association, October 1961. 8p. illus.
(Indian Truth, vol. 38, no. 2)   2088

HETZEL, THEODORE B. The meek do not inherit Alaska. Philadelphia, Indian Rights Association, 1962. 8p. illus. (Indian
Truth, vol. 39, nos. 3-4)   2089

HEUSSER, CALVIN JOHN. Juneau Ice Field Research Project; semi-
annual status report. no pl., 1958. 7p. bibliog.   2090

HEUSSER, CALVIN JOHN. Late-Pleistocene environments of North
Pacific North America; elaboration of late-glacial and post-
glacial climatic, physiographic, and biotic changes. N. Y.,

American Geographical Society, 1960. 308p. pls. diagrs. graphs, tables, maps, glossary, append. bibliog. (Special Publication no. 35)   2091

HEWES, AGNES DANFORTH. A hundred bridges to go. N. Y., Dodd Mead, 1950. 275p. [Alaska Highway]   2092

HEWITT, JOHN MICHAEL. The Alaska vagabond, Doctor Skookum; memories of an adventurous life. N. Y., Exposition Press, 1953. 1st ed. 284p.   2093

Heydinger, C., tr. SEE no. 4275, Staehlin, J. v. S.

Heydrich, M. SEE nos. 4332-3, Steller, Geo. W.

HEYE, ARTUR. Im Letzen Westen; mit Trappern, Fischern, Gold-suchern in Alaska. [TITLE TR. In the last west; with trappers, fishermen and golddiggers in Alaska] Zürich, A. Müller, 1939. 334p. pls. ports. endmaps.   2094

HEYE, ARTUR. Nyugat peromen. Alaska. Vass Peter, Ismeretlen Vilagok sor, 1940. 239p. (Athenaeum)   2095

Heye Foundation, N. Y. SEE no. 3259, Museum of American Indians.

[HEYE, GEORGE G. and WILLIAM C. ORCHARD] A rare Salish blanket. N. Y., Museum of the American Indian, 1926. 15p. illus. front. (col.) pl. tipped-in), 3 pls.(tipped-in), sketches. (Heye Foun-dation, Leaflet no. 5)   2096

HEYERDAHL, THOR. American Indians in the Pacific. Boston, Uni-versitets forlaget, 1952. ANR. Chicago, Rand McNally, 1953. 821p. illus. bibliog. index. [relationship of Polynesians to northwest coast Indians]   2097

HEYERDAHL, THOR, SØREN RICHTER and HJALMAR RIISER-LARSEN. Great Norwegian expeditions. Oslo, Dreyers Forlag, [1955 ?] 232p. illus.(some col.), maps(in text) [incls. those of Roald Amund-sen]   2098

HIBBEN, FRANK CUMMINGS. Digging up America. N. Y., Hill & Wang, 1960. photos, index. [from Alaska to Straits of Magellan] 2099

HIBBEN, FRANK CUMMINGS. Hunting American bears. Illustrated by Paul Bransom. Philadelphia, Lippincott, 1945. 247p. illus. [from Admiralty Island, Alaska to Mexico]   2100

HIBBEN, FRANK CUMMINGS. Treasure in the dust; exploring anci-ent North America. Philadelphia, Lippincott, 1951. illus. ANR. WITH TITLE Treasure in the dust; archaeology in the new world. London, Cleaver-Hume Press, 1953. illus. pls. [from Alaskan to Aztec archaeol.]   2101

"Hi Blade Bill." SEE no. 2371, Johnson, Wm. E.

HICK, GEORGE. Pioneer prospector. Edited by Dr. Charles E.
Bunnell. College, University of Alaska, 1954. 32p. front.
(photo), photos, map.   2102

Hieromach Herman. SEE no. 1534, Father Herman ... n. d.

Higgins, H. H. M. SEE no. 3486, Pan Pacific Progress.

HIGGINSON, ELLA RHOADS. Alaska, the great country. N. Y., Macmillan, 1908. 1st ed. 537p. front.(port.), pls. map(dble.),
index. OTHERS 1909, 1910, 1912. ANR. 1917. new ed. with new
material. 583p. front.(port.), pls. map(fold.) OTHERS 1919,
1923, 1926.   2103

HIGGINSON, ELLA RHOADS. The vanishing race and other poems.
Bellingham, Wash., C. M. Sherman, 1911. 28p.   2104

Hildebrand, W., co-auth. SEE no. 434, Baxter, D. V.

Hill, E. E. SEE no. 3290, Neuman, D. S.

HILL, EDGAR P. Reverend Aaron L. Lindsley, Presbyterian statesman of the Pacific northwest. By Reverend E. P. Hill. N. Y.,
1902. 4p. ANR. Seattle, Shorey Book Store, 1964. facsim. ed.
[1964 ed. reprinted as companion piece to reprint of "Aaron
Ladner Lindsley ..." by Mrs. J. Thorburn Ross. See Ross, Emily
Lindsley, no. 3886]   2105

Hill, James J. SEE no. 145, Alaska-Yukon-Pacific Exposition.

HILL-TOUT, C. The far west; the home of the Salish and Dènè.
Toronto, Copp Clark Co., 1907. 263p. front.(photo), pls. map
(fold.), bibliog. index. (The Native Races of the British Empire. British North America 1) [quotes Father Morice exten-
sively on Dènè of western Canada and southeast Alaska]   2106

[HILLER, E. H.] Latest information about the Alaska gold fields;
prospector's guide to Klondike-Yukon. Juneau, [1897] 56p. 2107

HILLS, W. JAMES and B. M. AUSHERMAN, comps. Klondike; mining
laws, rules and regulations of the United States and Canada, ap-
plicable to Alaska and northwest territory. Compiled by W. J.
Hills and B. M. Ausherman. [Seattle, Lowman & Hanford], 1897.
143p. ANR. 1898.   2108

HILLYER, WILLIAM H. The box of daylight. N. Y., Knopf, 1931.
179p. drawings by Erick Berry. [based on *Tsimshian mythology*
by Franz Boas]   2109

HILSCHER, HERBERT HENRY. Alaska now. By Herbert H. Hilscher.
Boston, Little Brown, 1948. 1st ed. 299p. pls. endmaps. ANR.
Boston, 1950. enl. 309p. index.   2110

HILSCHER, HERBERT HENRY and MIRIAM HILSCHER. Alaska, U. S. A.
By Herb and Miriam Hilscher. Boston, Little Brown, 1959. 1st
ed. 243p. pls. map(dble.), index. [revision of no. 2110]2111

HILTON, BUD. Bud Hilton book of nursery rhymes (as heard on
KFRB radio.) no pl., n. d. [Fairbanks, Bud Hilton, Dec. 1967 ?]
(9)p. illus. cartoons, mimeo.   2112

HIMMELHEBER, HANS. Der gefrorene Pfad; Mythen, Märchen und
Legenden der Eskimo. [TITLE TR. Frozen path. Folk tales of
the Eskimo] 3, Auflage. Eisenach, Erich-Röth Verlag, 1951.
130p. front.(port.), illus. (Das Gesicht der Völker ...)
[Nunivak Island]   2113

HIMMELHEBER, HANS. Eskimokünstler; Ergebnisse einer Reise in
Alaska. Zweite Auflage. [TITLE TR. Eskimo artist; results of
a trip to Alaska] Eisenach, Erich-Röth Verlag, 1953. 2d ed.
rev. 136p. front. map, bibliog. (Bücher der Brücke) [rev. of
no. 2115 with added photos]   2114

HIMMELHEBER, HANS. Eskimokünstler; Teilergebnis einer ethno-
graphischen expedition in Alaska von Juni 1936 bis April 1937.
[TITLE TR. Eskimo artist; partial results of the ethnographic
expedition in Alaska, June 1936-April 1937] Stuttgart, Strec-
ker und Schröder, 1938. 111p. pls. map, bibliog.   2115

HINDS, RICHARD BRINSLEY, edit. The botany of the voyage of
H. M. S. *Sulphur*, under the command of Captain Sir Edward Belcher ... during the years 1836-42. Published under the authority of the Lords Commissioners of the Admiralty. Edited and
superintended by Richard Brinsley Hinds, Esq., Surgeon, R. N.
attached to the Expedition. The botanical descriptions by George
Bentham, Esq. London, Smith, Elder & Co., 1846. 195p. pls.
ANR. N. Y., Stechert, 1966. reprint.   2116

HINDS, RICHARD BRINSLEY, edit. The zoology of the voyage of
H. M. S. *Sulphur*, under the command of Captain Sir Edward Belcher ... during the years 1836-42. Published under the authority of the Lords Commissioners of the Admiralty. Edited and superintended by Richard Brinsley Hinds, Esq., Surgeon ... attached
to the expedition. London, Smith, Elder & Co., 1844. 2 vols.
in 1 plus folio atlas [London, 1843-46] 150p.,72p.,v.p. pls.
(some col.)   2117

HINE, CHARLES C. A trip to Alaska; being a report of a lecture
given, with stereopticon illustrations, before the Fire Underwriters' Association of the Northwest, at the 20th annual meeting,
Chicago, Sept. 17, 1889. Copied from the proceedings. Chicago,
King, Fowle & Co., Printers, 1889. 26ℓ . ANR. 1894.64p.   2118

Hine, J. S.   SEE no. 1860, Griggs, R. F.

HINES, JOHN CHESTERFIELD. Minstrel of the Yukon;   an Alaskan adventure. By Jack Hines. N. Y., Greenberg, 1948. 231p.   2119

HINES, JOHN CHESTERFIELD. The blue streak. By Jack Hines.
N. Y., Geo. H. Doran, 1917. 270p. front. pls. [short stories]
                                                                2120

HINES, JOHN CHESTERFIELD. Wolf dogs of the north;   true life
stories of adventure in the 49th state. By Jack Hines. Illustrated by Roger Vernam. Philadelphia, Chilton Co., 1948. 1st
ed. 202p. front. illus. ANR. N. Y., Greenberg, 1948. 241p.
illus. pl. ANR. N. Y., Pocket Book Juniors, 1951. 211p. paperback.   2121

Hines, Robert, illus. SEE nos.
    1364, Dufresne, F. Alaska's animals and fishes. 1946;
    1618, Fouke Fur Co. The romance of Alaska sealskin. 1954;
    1619, Fouke Fur Co. The romance of Alaska fur seal. 1958;
    1725, Gillham, Chas. E. Raw north. 1947;
    3408, Olson, Sigurd. Runes of north. 1963.

HINTON, ARTHUR CHERRY and PHILIP H. GODSELL. The Yukon. Toronto, Ryerson Press, 1947. ANR. Toronto, Ryerson Press, 1954.
184p. pls. photos. ANR. Philadelphia, 1955. illus. [history of
Yukon area from '98 to Alcan]   2122

HINZ, JOHN. Grammar and vocabulary of the Eskimo language as
spoken by the Kuskokwim and southwest coast Eskimos of Alaska.
By Reverend John Hinz. Bethlehem, Penna., The Society for Propagating the Gospel, The Moravian Church, 1944. 194p. ANR.
1955. 2d print. 199p. index of affixes, loose errata page,
tables, ftntes.   2123

HINZ, JOHN. The Passion Week manual. [Eng. tr. of title in Kuskokwim Eskimo language] Herrnhut, 1915.   2124

Hinz, John. SEE ALSO no. 4005, Schmitt, A.
    Untersuchungen zur Geschichte der Schrift ... 1940.

HISCOCK, BARBARA A. *Wawona*; the heritage of sailing in the North
Pacific. Seattle, printed by Craftsman Press for Save Our Ships,
Inc., n. d. [ca 1964] 24p. illus.   2125

Histoire abregee des premier, secund et troisieme voyages ...
    1795. SEE no. 1032, [Cook, Jas.]

Histoire premier, secund et troisieme voyages ... 1796. SEE
    no. 1034, [Cook, Jas.]

HISTOIRE UNIVERSELLE DES VOYAGES, relation succincte et pittoresque des navigations et des decouvertes les plus interssantes
faites dans les temps les plus recuiles par les Egyptiens ... et
de nos jours par Krusenstern, Kotzebue ... Paris, 1856 and 1860.
                                                              2126
HISTOIRE DES VOYAGES curieux et interessans en Chine en Amerique.
Paris, Librairie Universelle, n. d. 3 vols. 3 plans(fold.)
[possibly pirated edition of John Meares' "Voyage de la Chine..."
See no. 3058]   2127

HISTORY AND EXPLANATION of the Russian lands ... along the Pacific coast ... no pl., [ca 1860] 32p.   2128

HISTORY OF THE ADVENTUROUS VOYAGE and terrible shipwreck of the
U. S. steamer "Jeannette" in the Polar Seas, together with a full
and particular account of the death of Lt. DeLong and his brave
shipmates in the Siberian deserts; and the rescue of Danenhower, Melville, and their heroic companions; carefully compiled
from authentic records. N. Y., De Witt, 1882. 95p. illus. 2129

History of location Bering R. coal ... 1912. SEE
     no. 2417, Katalla Pub. League.

History of Matanuska Valley. 1941. SEE
     no. 3482, Palmer Territorial School.

History of wrongs of Alaska ... 1875. SEE
     no. 269, Anti-Monopoly Assoc. of Pac. Coast.

HITCHCOCK, MARY E. Two women in the Klondike; the story of a
journey to the gold-fields of Alaska. N. Y., Putnam, 1899. 485p.
front. illus. pls. map(fold. in pocket), index.   2130

Hiven, F. SEE no. 4833, White Pass and Yukon Ry.

HIXON, ARTHUR T. Canol. Philadelphia, Dorrance, 1946. 284p.
[oil pipeline]   2131

Hobart, C. SEE no. 4651, van Steensel, M.

Hodge, Frederick W., edit. SEE nos.
     1144, Curtis, Edw. S. North Amer. Indian. 1907-15;
     1189, Davidson, D. C. Family hunting terr. ... 1928;
     2295, Irvine, A. How Makah obtained ... Cape Flattery. 1921.

HODGINS, THOMAS. The Alaska Boundary Tribunal and international
law; a review of the decisions. Toronto, Carswell, 1904. 24p.
2 maps.   2132

HODGINS, THOMAS. The Alaska-Canada boundary dispute, under the
Anglo-Russian treaty of 1825; the Russian-American Alaska treaty of 1867; and the Anglo-American conventions of 1892, 94 and
97. An historical and legal review ... Toronto, 1902. 1st ed.

26p. ANR. Toronto, W. Tyrell, 1903. 2d ed. enl. 26p. map. (also in: Contemporary Review, 1902. vol. 82, pp.190-206) 2133

Hodgson, F. M. SEE no. 1807, Great Britain. Admiralty.

HODGSON, ROBERT G. Successful muskrat farming, a practical manual on the raising, breeding of muskrats. Oshawa, Ontario, Fur Trade Journal of Canada, 1925. 109p. pls. map(sketch) [contains regulations for U. S., Canada. Incls. Alaska] 2134

HOFF, SYD. Ogluk the Eskimo. Story and pictures by author. N. Y., Holt, Rinehart & Winston, 1960. 1st ed. (44)p. illus. 2135

HOFF, SYD. Sammy the seal. N. Y., Harper, 1959. illus. by author. 2136

Hoffman, C. W., tr. SEE no. 2528, Kotzebue, Otto von.

HOFFMAN, E., von. Geognostische beobachtungen ausgestellt auf einer reise 1823 bis 1826, unter dem befehl des Hn. Otto v. Kotzebue. Berlin, 1829. 2137

HOFFMAN, WALTER J. Comparison of Eskimo pictographs with those of other American aborigines. Washington, D. C., Judd & Detweiler, 1883. 19p. (reprinted from: Transactions of Anthropological Society of Washington, vol. 2. 1883) 2138

HOFMANN, CHARLES. Frances Densmore; a biography. N. Y., Museum of American Indians, 1967. (Heye Foundation) 2139

HOFSINDE, ROBERT. The Indian medicine man. N. Y., Morrow, 1966. illustrated by author. [incls. northwest coast] 2140

HOGAN, INEZ. Bear twins. N. Y., Dutton, 1935. illus. 2141

HOGAN, INEZ. Twin seals. N. Y., Dutton, 1940. illus. 2142

Hogarth, jr. [pseud.], illus. SEE no. 3489, Paramore, E. E.,jr.

HOIJER, H. and others. Studies in the Athapaskan languages. Berkeley, University of California, 1963. 154p. tables, bibliogs. (Publications in Linguistics, vol. 29) [seminar papers of Summer Institute of Linguistics at University of Oklahoma, Aug. 1958. pp.1-29: *Study of Athapaskan dialects in Alaska and Canadian northwest,* by A. Hoijer] 2143

HOKE, HELEN, edit. Alaska Alaska Alaska; land of yesterday and tomorrow. N. Y., Franklin Watts, 1960. 244p. front. illus. by R. M. Sax, map. 2144

HOKKAIDO, UNIVERSITY. Faculty of Fisheries. Data record of oceanographic observations and exploratory fishing, no. 1. Hako-date, Japan, May 1957. 247p. illus. diagrs. tables. Text in Japanese and English. [studies made partly in Aleutian and Bering Sea waters]   2145

HOKKAIDO, UNIVERSITY. Faculty of Fisheries. Data record of oceanographic observations and exploratory fishing, no. 2. Hako-date, Japan, June 1958. 199p. illus. maps, tables. Text in Japanese and English. [studies made partly in Aleutian waters]
                                                                  2146

[HOLBROOK, SILAS P.] Sketches by a traveller. Boston, 1830. 315p. [Oregon and Alaska]   2147

HOLDEN, RAYMOND PECKHAM. Famous scientific expeditions. N. Y., Random House, 1955. 144p. illustrated by Lee Ames. [Hudson Stuck and Mt. McKinley climb: Stefansson and Canadian Arctic Expedition]   2148

HOLIDAY MAGAZINE. American panorama; west of the Mississippi. Garden City, N. Y., Holiday Magazine Book, 1960. 405p. illus.
                                                                  2149

HOLIDAY PUBLICATIONS, Anchorage. Anchorage; crossroads to adven-ture in Alaska. no pl., 1962. 72p. illus. wrps. ANR. 1963. 88p. illus. wrps.   2150

HOLIDAY PUBLICATIONS, Anchorage. Guide to Alaska and the Alaska Highway. Anchorage, 1963. 414p. illus.   2151

Holiday Publications. SEE ALSO no. 72, Alaska ... 1963.

[HOLLAND,CHARLES WILLIAM] One hundred and fiftieth anniversary of arrival of Captain George Vancouver, R. N. at Burrard Inlet, 1792. no pl., 1942. (8)p. map.   2152

HOLLAND, EDWARD. To the Yukon and the Klondike gold fields. S. F., E. Holland, 1897. 56p. illus. map(fold.), facsims. 2153

HOLLING, HOLLING CLANCY. Pagoo. Boston, Houghton, 1957. illus. [tidal pool inhabitants]   2154

Holm, H. T., co-auth. SEE no. 2945, Macoun, J. M.

HOLM, WILLIAM. Northwest coast Indian art; an analysis of form. By Bill Holm. Seattle, University of Washington Press, 1965. 144p. illus. photos, drawings, bibliog. index. [Bella Coola to Yakutat Bay]   2155

HOLMAN, JOHN PAULISON. Sheep and bear trails; a hunter's wan-derings in Alaska and British Columbia. N. Y., Frank Walters, 1933. 211p. front. pls. ports.   2156

HOLMBERG, HENRIK JOHAN. Ethnographische Skizzen über die völker des russischen Amerika. Helsingfors, Gedruckt bei H. C. Friis, 1855-63. 2 vols. (Finska vetenskaps-societeten. Acta Societatis Scientiarum Fennicae, vol. 4. pp.281-421)   2157

Holmes, Burton, photog. SEE no. 4836, White Pass and Yukon Ry.

HOLMES, JOHN F. and L. V. WORTHINGTON. Project Skijump, conducted during the period Feb. 1951-May 1951. Woods Hole, Mass., Sept. 1951. 66p. illus. maps(text), diagrs. graphs. (Woods Hole Oceanog. Institution, Tech. Report, Ref. no. 51-67)   2158

HOLMES, LEWIS. The Arctic whaleman; or, winter in the Arctic Ocean; being a narrative of the wreck of the whale ship *Citizen*. Together with a brief history of whaling. By the Reverend Lewis Holmes. Boston, Wentworth, 1857. 296p. pls. ANR. Boston, Thayer & Eldridge, 1861.   2159

HOLMES, MAURICE. An introduction to the bibliography of Captain James Cook, R. N. London, Edwards, 1936.   2160

HOLMES, MAURICE. Captain James Cook, R. N. F. R. S., a bibliographical excursion. London, Edwards, 1952.   2161

HOLMES, WILLIAM D. A square in the Arctic Circle; an Alaskan hunt. Hamden, Conn., Shoe String Press, 1960. 168p. illus. 2162

HOLTVED, ERIK. Eskimokunst; with an English summary by the author. København, Foreningen forung dansk kunst, 1947. pls. (Alvedens Kunst, vol. 4, pp.33-64) [incls. Alaskan]   2163

Holtved, Erik, edit. SEE ALSO no. 3749,
     Rasmussen, K. J. V. Alaskan Eskimos ... 1952.

Holy Cross Mission. SEE nos.
     2259, Indian Boys' Press. Catholic prayers ... 1897;
     2260, Indian Boys' Press. Tinneh Indian catechism ... 1897.

Holy Orthodox Church ... Eastern Apostolic Church. 1898. SEE
     no. 1149, Dabovich, S.

HOLZWORTH, JOHN M. The twin grizzlies of Admiralty Island. Philadelphia, Lippincott, 1932. 250p. front. illus.   2164

HOLZWORTH, JOHN M. The wild grizzlies of Alaska; a story of the grizzly and big brown bears of Alaska, their habits, manners and characteristics, together with notes on mountain sheep and caribou, collected by the author for the U. S. Biological Survey. N. Y., Putnam, 1930. 1st ed. 417p. front.(col. pl.), pls. endmaps, map, append. index.   2165

HOLZWORTH, JOHN M. Woof; the half pint bear chaser, the story of a dog who feared cats, but would go after Alaska grizzly bears. Illustrated by Douglas Ryan. N. Y., Gothic Press, 1938. 77p. illus.   2166

HOMESTEADING and natural resources in the Homer district in Alaska. Seldovia, Alaska, 1935. 13p. photos, map.   2167

Homesteading the Kenai-Homer area. [ca 1948] SEE no. 2436,
     Kenai Land Locations.

HONCHARENKO, AHAPIUS. Pervonachaljnoe rukovodstvo dlia izucheniia angliiskago iazyka ... [TITLE TR. The school and family Russo-American primer especially published for use in Alaska by the Alaska Commercial Co.] S. F., E. Bosqui & Co., March 1, 1871. 47p. illus.   2168

HONCHARENKO, AHAPIUS. Russko-Angliiskie razgovorg ... [TITLE TR. Russian and English phrase book, specially adapted for the use of traders, travelers and teachers] S. F., A. Roman & Co., 1868. 100p.   2169

Honcharenko, Ahapius. SEE ALSO no. 2807,
     Luciw, W. Ahapius Honcharenko ... 1963.

Hone, E., edit. SEE no. 197, American Comm. Int'l.
     Wildlife Protection.

HONIGMANN, J. J. The world of man. N. Y., Harper, 1959. 971p. illus. maps, tables, graphs, bibliog. [incls. Alaskan Eskimos and Indians]   2170

HOOKER, WILLIAM JACKSON. A brief memoir of the life of Mr. David Douglas, with extracts from his letters. London, [ca 1837] 104p. [also excerpts from his journal]   2171

HOOKER, WILLIAM JACKSON. Flora Boreali-Americana; or, the botany of the northern parts of British America; compiled principally from the plants collected by Dr. Richardson and Mr. Drummond on the late northern expeditions, under command of Captain Sir John Franklin, R. N. to which are added (by permission of the Horticultural Society of London), those of Mr. Douglas, from north-west America, and of other naturalists. London, H. G. Bohn, 1829-40. 2 vols. 351p. and 328p. front.(fold. map), pls. [originally published in parts]   2172

HOOKER, WILLIAM JACKSON and G. A. WALKER-ARNOTT. The botany of Captain Beechey's voyage; comprising an account of the plants collected by Messrs. Lay and Collie, and other officers of the expedition during the voyage to the Pacific and Behring's Strait, performed in His Majesty's ship *Blossom* under the command of Captain F. W. Beechey in the years 1825, 26, 27 and 28. By Sir

William Jackson Hooker and G. A. W. Arnott. London, H. G. Bohn, 1841. 485p. illus. pls. ANR. N. Y., Stechert-Hafner, 1966. facsim. reprint. 2173

HOOPER, CALVIN LEIGHTON. Arctic ice notes. S. F., A. J. Leary, 1883. 22p. (Geographical Society of the Pacific, Proceedings, 1883. vol. 1, pt. 3) [the *Corwin* and Bering Sea patrol] 2174

HOOPER, CALVIN LEIGHTON. The cruise of the *Corwin* in the Arctic. S. F., Geographical Society of the Pacific, 1882. 32p. table, append. (Proceedings, 1881. vol. 1, pt. 2) 2175

HOOPER, JAMES T. and COTTIE ARTHUR BURLAND. The art of primitive peoples, with 116 photos of specimens from the Hooper collection by R. H. Bomback. London, Fountain Press, [1953] 168p. illus. photos. ANR. N. Y., Philosophical Library, 1954. 2176

HOOPER, WILLIAM HULME. Ten months among the tents of the Tuski, with incidents of an Arctic boat expedition in search of Sir John Franklin, as far as the MacKenzie River, and Cape Bathurst. London, John Murray, 1853. 417p. front.(col.), pls.(some col.), map(fold.) [Capt. T. E. L. Moore, H. M. S. *Plover*, northern Alaskan Eskimos] 2177

Hooper, William Hulme. SEE ALSO no. 1826, Great Britain. Parl.

HOPKINS, DAVID MOODY. The Bering land bridge. Stanford, Stanford University Press, 1967. 495p. illus. photos, figs. tables, maps, endmaps, ftntes. bibliogs. index. [collection of papers presented at 7th Congress, International Assoc. Quaternary Research, Boulder, Colo., Aug. 30-Sept. 5, 1965] 2178

HOPKINS, MARJORIE. The three visitors. N. Y., Parents Magazine Press, 1967. unp. illus.(col.) by Anne Rockwell. 2179

Hoppner, R. B., tr. SEE no. 2561, Krusenstern, A. J. von.

HORETZKY, CHARLES. Canada on the Pacific; being an account of a journey from Edmonton to the Pacific by the Peace River Valley; and of a winter voyage along the western coast of the Dominion; with remarks on the physical features of the Pacific railway route and notices of the Indian tribes of British Columbia. Montreal, Dawson Bros., 1874 244p. plan(fold.), map(fold.) 2180

HORNADAY, WILLIAM T. Camp-fires in the Canadian Rockies. By William T. Hornady, Sc.D. Illustrations by John M. Phillips. With seventy illustrations and two maps. N. Y., Scribner, 1906. 353p. front. pls. maps, index. [scattered references to sheep and mountain goats in Alaska] 2181

HORNADAY, WILLIAM T. Our vanishing wildlife; its extermination and preservation. N. Y., Scribner, 1913. 411p. illus. maps. 2182

HORNADAY, WILLIAM T. Tales from nature's wonderlands. N. Y.,
Scribner, 1924. ANR. N. Y., 1926. 235p. illus. maps.   2183

Horne, Rachel S., illus. SEE nos.
    1365, Dufresne, Frank. My way was north. 1966;
    1366, Dufresne, Frank. No room for bears. 1965.

Horsfall, Bruce, illus. SEE nos.
    1434, Eliot, W. A. Birds of Pac. Coast ... 1923;
    2261, Ingersoll, E., edit. Alaskan bird-life ... 1914.

HORTON, EDITH. The frozen north; an account of Arctic exploration for use in schools. Boston, D. C. Heath, 1904. 157p.
[incls. Schwatka exploration]   2184

Hotovitsky, A., tr. SEE no. 5017, [Zagoskin, L. A.]

HOUBEN, HEINRICH HUBERT. Der Ruf des Nordens; Abenteur und Hel-
dentum der Nordpolfahrer. [TITLE TR. The call of the north; adventure and heroism of Arctic explorers] Berlin, Volksverband
der Bücherfreunde-Wegweiser, 1927. illus. maps. ANR. Leipzig,
Koehler & Amelang, 1928. 298p. [see no. 2186 for abr. and
no. 2187 for tr.]   2185

HOUBEN, HEINRICH HUBERT. Nordpolfahrten. Leipzig, Hase &
Koehler, 1944. 93p. [abr. of no. 2185, with added chapter] 2186

HOUBEN, HEINRICH HUBERT. The call of the north. London, E.
Mathews & Marrot, 1932. 348p. front.(map), pls. ports. drawings.
[tr. of no. 2185]   2187

HOUDENAK, GUNNAR. Roald Amundsens Siste Ferde; med et tillegg
om Krassinferden, av Adolf Hoel. [TITLE TR. Roald Amundsen's
last journey; with an appended section on the voyage of the
Krasin] Oslo, Gyldendal, 1934. 303p. pls. maps(some fold.),
bibliogs.   2188

HOUGH, EMERSON. The Young Alaskans. N. Y., Harper, 1908. 292p.
front. pls. ANR. 1935.   2189

HOUGH, EMERSON. The Young Alaskans in the Rockies. N. Y., Harper, 1913. 326p. front. pls.   2190

HOUGH, EMERSON. The Young Alaskans on the Missouri. N. Y., Harper, 1922. 1st ed. 378p. front. pls.   2191

HOUGH, EMERSON. The Young Alaskans on the trail. N. Y., Harper,
1911. 1st ed. 321p. front. pls.   2192

HOUGH, EMERSON. Young Alaskans in the far north. N. Y., Harper,
1918. 251p. front. pls.   2193

HOUSE, BOYCE. Friendly feudin'; Alaska vs Texas. Illustrated by M. Cox and Tom Jones. San Antonio, Naylor Co., 1959. 64p. illus. 2194

HOUSTON DREDGING AND HYDRAULIC CO. Facts and conditions of the Houston Dredging and Hydraulic Co. no pl., n. d. 15p. 2195

Hover, Joh. SEE no. 219, Amundsen, R. E. G

Hovgaard, A. P., edit. SEE nos.
    3324, Nordenskiöld, N. A. E. ... rejse ... 1881;
    3325, Nordenskiöld, N. A. E. ... voyage ... 1882.

HOVGAARD, WILLIAM. The voyages of the Norsemen to America, with eighty-three illustrations and seven maps. pl.?, pub.?, 1915. [Alaskan and Canadian Indians and Eskimos, Hudson's Bay Co.] 2196

How to build Alaskan dog sled. [ca 1968] SEE
    no. 1695, Gelvin, E. C.

How to raise ... Alaskan malemute. 1963. SEE
    no. 520, Berger, Chas. J.

HOW TO SKIN A SEAL and other Eskimo "How-to" stories. How to do - everyday chores of tundra living - as explained by sixth grade students of the Kolbuk [sic] School, Bethel, Alaska. no pl. [Fairbanks], Jessen's Litho, n. d. [1969] 22p. illus. [should be Kilbuk School] 2197

HOWARD, HARRY WINSMORE and others. Sport fishing for Pacific salmon in Washington-Oregon-Alaska; how, when and where to catch salmon; history of the Pacific salmon. Eugene, Ore., Koke-Chapman Co., 1954. 135p. illus. maps(fold.) 2198

HOWARD, MORT A. Stereopticon lecture on Alaska and the great Klondike stampede of 1897-98. From personal reminiscences. no pl. n. d. 8p. 2199

HOWAY, FREDERICK WILLIAM. Captain George Vancouver. Toronto, Ryerson, 1932. 32p. illus. (Canadian History Readers) 2200

HOWAY, FREDERICK WILLIAM. Presidential address; the early literature of the northwest coast. Ottawa, Royal Society of Canada, 1924. 31p. 2201

HOWAY, FREDERICK WILLIAM. The Dixon-Mears controversy; containing remarks on the voyages of John Meares, by George Dixon; an answer to Mr. George Dixon by John Meares and further remarks on the voyages of John Mears, by George Dixon. Toronto, Ryerson, [c1929] 500 copies printed. 156p. front. illus. facsims. maps, index. ANR. N. Y., 1929. ANR. N. Y. Da Capo Press, 1969. reprint. (Bibliotheca Australiana. Extra Series) [Mears a variant spelling of Meares] 2202

HOWAY, FREDERICK WILLIAM, edit. Voyages of the "Columbia" to the northwest coast 1787 to 1790, and 1790 to 1793. Boston, 1941. 518p. front. ports. facsims. maps, index. (Massachusetts Historical Society Collections, vol. 79) ANR. N. Y. Da Capo Press, 1969. reprint. (Bibliotheca Australiana. Extra Series)   2203

HOWAY, FREDERICK WILLIAM, edit. Zimmermann's Captain Cook. An account of the third voyage of Captain Cook around the world, 1776-1780, by Henry Zimmermann, of Wisslock, in the Palatine, and translated from the Mannheim edition of 1781 by Elsa Michealis, and Cecil French, edited with an introduction and notes by His Honour F. W. Howay. Toronto, Ryerson Press, [c1930] ltd. ed. of 250 copies. xviii,120p. front. illus. facsims. maps(incl. 1 fold.) (The Canadian Historical Studies)   2204

Howay, Frederick William. SEE ALSO nos.
     265, Angus, H. F.   British Columbia ... 1942;
     989, Colnett, Jas.   Journal ... *Argonaut* ... 1940.

Howe, C. P.   SEE no. 3104, Mikkelsen, E.

HOWE, R. S., edit. The great northern country, illustrating and describing the country, opportunities and scenery along the lines of the Great Northern Railway and Northern Steamship Company; Alaska, its resources, scenery and how to get there; the Oriental trade, its beginning, development, and possibilities, expecially for the Pacific Northwest. Edited and illustrated by R. S. Howe. no pl., Great Northern Railway, 1902. 115p. map. ANR. 1903.   2205

Howell, John, edit. SEE no. 3304, Nicol, J.

HOWGATE, HENRY W. Congress and the North Pole. An abstract of Arctic legislation in the Congress of the United States. Kansas City, Mo., Kansas City Review of Science and Industry, 1879. 43p.   2206

Hoy, H. W.   SEE no. 79, [Alaska Life, Seattle]

HRDLIČKA, ALEŠ. Alaska diary, 1926-31; published with the permission of the Secretary of the Smithsonian Institution. Lancaster, Penna., Jaques Cattell Press, 1943. 414p. front. ports. maps, plan, diagr. (Humanizing Science Series)   2207

HRDLIČKA, ALEŠ. An Eskimo brain. N. Y., Knickerbocker Press, 1901. 49p.   2208

HRDLIČKA, ALEŠ. The Aleutian and Commander Islands and their inhabitants. Philadelphia, Wistar Institute of Anatomy and Biology, 1945. 630p. front. illus. maps, bibliog. appends.   2209

HRDLIČKA, ALEŠ. The anthropology of Kodiak Island. Philadelphia, Wistar Institute of Anatomy and Biology, 1944. 486p. front.
illus. ports. maps, plans, facsims. diagr. tables, bibliog. append.   2210

Hrdlička, Aleš. SEE ALSO no. 643,
     Brand, D. D. So live works of men. 1939.

HUBBACK, THEODORE RATHBONE. Ten thousand miles to Alaska for
moose and sheep. Denver, 1921. 14p. illus. ANR. Seattle,
Shorey Book Store, 1967. facsim. of 1921 ed.   2211

HUBBACK, THEODORE RATHBONE. To far western Alaska for big game;
being an account of two journeys to Alaska in search of adventure. London, Rowland Ward, 1929. 232p. illus. front. 3 maps
(incl. 1 fold. in pocket), index.   2212

HUBBARD, BERNARD ROSECRANS. Cradle of the storms. By Bernard R.
Hubbard, S.J. N. Y., Dodd Mead, 1935. 285p. front. pls.(some
dble.), sketches, maps, endmaps, appends. [mountain climbing,
Katmai, Alaska Peninsula]   2213

HUBBARD, BERNARD ROSECRANS. Mush, you malemutes ! By Bernard R.
Hubbard, S.J. N. Y., American Press, 1932. 179p. front. ports.
pls.(some dble.), maps(2 dble.)   2214

Hubbard, Bernard Rosecrans. SEE ALSO nos.
     208, American Press. One hundred pictures ... 1935;
     1338, Douglas, R. D. In land Thunder Mountains... 1932;
     4894, Willoughby, B. Alaskans all. 1933.

HUBBS, CARL LEAVITT and L. P. SCHULTZ. Contribution to the Ich-
thyology of Alaska with descriptions of two new fishes. Ann
Arbor, University of Michigan Press, 1941. 31p. tables(3 fold.)
(Museum of Zoology, Occasional Papers, no. 431)   2215

Huber, Louis R., comp. SEE no. 83, Alaska Magazine Pub. Co.

HUBLEY, RICHARD CARLETON and others. Progress report Juneau Ice
Field Research Project, Alaska, 1954. N. Y., American Geographical Society, Feb. 1955. 53p. graphs, tables, maps, bibliog.
                                                                2216

HUDSON, WILL E. Icy Hell; experiences of a news reel cameraman
in the Aleutian Islands, eastern Siberia and the Arctic fringe of
Alaska; with a map and thirty-two illustrations from photos by
the author. London, Constable & Co., 1937. 307p. front. pls.
ports. map(fold.) ANR. N. Y., Stokes, 1938.   2217

HUGHES, CHARLES CAMPBELL. An Eskimo village in the modern world.
With the collaboration of Jane M. Hughes. Ithaca, Cornell Univ.
Press, 1960. 419p. front. pls. maps, tables, bibliog. (Studies
in Anthropology) [village on St. Lawrence Island]   2218

Hughes, Charles Campbell. SEE ALSO no. 4426,
    Swartz, M. J. Political anthropol. 1966.

Hughes, Everett C., co-edit. SEE no. 4506,
    Thompson, E. T.

Hughes, Jane M., collab. SEE no. 2218, Hughes, C. C.

HUISH, ROBERT, comp. A narrative of the voyages and travels of
Captain Beechey, R. N. ... to the Pacific and Behring's Straits;
performed in the years 1825, 26, 27 and 28. For the purpose of
co-operating with the expeditions under Captain Parry and Franklin. And of Captain Back, R. N. to the Thlew-ee-choh River and
the Arctic Sea in search of the expedition under Captain J. Ross,
R. N., being the conclusion of the series of voyages instituted
for the discovery of the north west passage. Compiled from original and authentic documents by Sir Robert Huish. London, W.
Wright, 1836. 704p. front. pls. map.   2219

HUISH, ROBERT. The north-west passage. A history of the most
remarkable voyages made in search of the north-west passage,
from the earliest periods. By Sir Robert Huish. London, M'Gowan
& Co., 1850. 418p. front. pls. ports.   2220

HULBERT, HOMER B. In search of a Siberian Klondike. N. Y.,
1903. [biog. of Alaskan prospector, Washington B. Vanderlip, in
northeastern Siberia]   2221

HULBERT, WINIFRED. The Bishop of all beyond; Sheldon Jackson.
N. Y., Friendship Press, 1948. 24p.   2222

HULCATT, HUGH. British Columbia, Alaska and the London Artizan
Colony at Moosomin. Seven lectures. no pl., 1889. 40p.   2223

Hulley, Clarence C. Alaska past and present. SEE no. 2224.

HULLEY, CLARENCE C. Alaska 1741-1953. Portland, Ore., Binfords
& Mort, 1953. 406p. pls. photos, endmaps, bibliog. index. ANR.
WITH TITLE Alaska past and present. 1958. rev. and enl. 422p.
ANR. 1970. 3rd ed. rev. and enl. 477p. pls. endmaps, bibliog.
index.   2224

HÜLSEMANN, KUNIGUNDE. Radiolaria in plankton from the Arctic
Drifting Station T-3, including the description of three new
species. Montreal, Arctic Institute of North America, 1963. 51p.
tables, figs. (Technical Paper no. 13)   2225

HULSWITT, IGNATZ von. Tagebuch einer Reisen nach den Vereinigten
Staaten under der Nordwestkuste von Amerika. Munster, Coppen-
rath, 1828. 379p.   2226

HULTÉN, ERIC. Flora of Alaska and neighboring Territories, a manual of the vascular plants. Stanford, Stanford University Press, 1968. 1008p. illus. sketches by Dagney Tande-Lid, photos (col.) by author, endmaps, range maps, glossary, bibliog. indexes. 2227

HULTÉN, ERIC. Flora of Alaska and Yukon. Parts 1-10 and Supplement. Lund, C. W. K. Gleerup, 1941-50. 3 vols. 1902p. (Lunds Universitet, Årsskrift, N. F., Avd. 2, 37:1-46:1) 2228

HULTÉN, ERIC. Flora of the Aleutian Islands and westernmost Alaska Peninsula with notes on the flora of the Commander Islands. Stockholm, Bokförlags aktiebolaget Thule, 1937. 397p. front. pls. diagrs. maps, bibliog. index. ANR. Weinheim, Germany (Hafner), 1960. 2d ed. rev. and enl. 418p. pls. maps, tables, bibliog. index. 2229

HULTÉN, ERIC. Outline of the history of Arctic and Boreal biota during the Quaternary period; their evolution during and after the glacial period as indicated by the equiformal progressive areas of present plant species. Stockholm, Bokförlags Aktiebolaget Thule, 1937. 168p. illus. maps, bibliog. [Kamchatka and Aleutian Islands] 2230

HULTÉN, ERIC. The circumpolar plants, 1: Vascular cryptogams, conifers, monocotyledons. Stockholm, Almqvist & Wiksell, 1962. 275p. maps(col.), references. (Svenska Vetenskapsakademien. Handlingar, Ser. 4, Bd. 8, nr. 5) 2231

HULTKRANTZ, ÅKE. Conceptions of the soul among North American Indians; a study in religious ethnology. Stockholm, 1953. 545p. bibliog. (Stockholm Statens Etnografiska Museum. Monograph Series, pub. nl. 1) [incls. Athabascan and Nadene, as well as Eskimos] 2232

HULTKRANTZ, ÅKE. The North American Indian Orpheus tradition; a contribution to comparative religion. Stockholm, 1957. 340p. map, bibliog. index. (Stockholm Statens Etnografiska Museum. Monograph Series, pub. no. 2) [incls. Tlingit, Haida and Tsimshian] 2233

Humes, Lysons and Sallee. SEE no. 2823, Lysons, Fred. H.

HUNT, CORNELIUS E. The *Shenandoah;* or, the last Confederate cruiser. By Cornelius E. Hunt, (one of her officers) N. Y., G. W. Carleton, and London, S. Low, 1867. 273p. front. ANR. N. Y., W. Abbott, 1910. 135p. 2234

HUNT, HARRIET E. Ketchikan, first city of Alaska. Description, history, resources, schools, etc. Written for use at the Seattle Exposition. Ketchikan, Journal Print., 1909. 64p. illus. 2235

HUNT, LAWRENCE J. The curse of the killer whale. N. Y., Funk & Wagnalls, 1963. 186p.   2236

HUNT, LAWRENCE J. The secret of the haunted crags. N. Y., Funk & Wagnalls, 1965. 154p.   2237

Hunt, Lynn Bogue, illus. SEE no. 2850, McCracken, H.

HUNTER, JOSEPH. Report on boundary line. By Joseph Hunter. Ottawa, 1878. 171p. (Canada. Parliament. Sessional Papers, 5th Sess., 3rd Parl., vol. 2, no. 125)   2238

HUNTING ASSOCIATES LTD. Illustrated case histories; some projects undertaken by the Hunting group of Canada. Toronto, 1959. unp. illus. maps(some fold.) [incls. geophysical surveying in Alaska]   2239

Huntington, J. V., tr. SEE no. 1626, Franchere, G.

HUNTINGTON, JAMES and LAWRENCE ELLIOTT. On the edge of nowhere. By James Huntington as told to Lawrence Elliott. N. Y., Crown Publishers, 1966. 183p. [Koyokuk River area]   2240

Huntington, W. C., tr. SEE no. 3080, Menshutkin, B. N.

Hurd, P. A. SEE no. 4177, Sladen, D. B. W.

Hurst, E. O., illus. SEE no. 2856, McCracken, H.

HUSSEY, KEITH M. and G. S. ANDERSON. Environment and distribution of thermal relief features in the northern foothills section, Alaska. Ames, Iowa, 1963. 76 ℓ illus. maps, cross-sections, tables, bibliog.   2241

HUSSEY, KEITH M. and R. W. FAAS. Foraminiferal paleoecology of the Gubik (Pleistocene) formation of the Barrow area, northern Alaska. Ames, Kowa, 1961. 11ℓ graphs, table, references. 2242

HUSSEY, KEITH M. and R. W. MICHELSON. Tundra relief features near Point Barrow, Alaska. Ames, Iowa, June 1961. 34ℓ illus. maps(incl. 2 fold.), diagr. tables, references.   2243

HUTCHINSON, HORATIO G. Big game shooting. London, Newnes, Office of "Country Life," 1905. 2 vols. [references to Alaska in vol. 1]   2244

HUTCHINSON, JOSEPH H. The wandering Gentile; a story of Alaska. S. F., Press of Commercial News Pub. Co., 1914. 12p.   2245

HUTCHISON, ISOBEL WYLIE. North to the rime-ringed sun; being an Alaskan-Canadian journey made in 1933-34. London, Blackie & Son, 1934. 262p. front.(col.), pls.(some col.), ports. map(fold.), append. ANR. N. Y., Hillman-Curl, 1937. 262p. front.(col.), pls.(some col.), ports. map(fold.), append. [incls. list of plants collected for Royal Herbarium at Kew]   2246

HUTCHISON, ISOBEL WYLIE. Steppingstones from Alaska to Asia. London, Blackie & Son, 1937. 246p. front.(col.), pls.(some col.) map(fold.), endmaps, append. ANR. WITH TITLE The Aleutian Islands; America's back door. London, Blackie & Son, 1942. rev. 182p. front.(col.), pls. ports. endmaps.   2247

Hutchison, Isobel Wylie. The Aleutian Islands ... See no. 2247.

Hutchison, Isobel Wylie. SEE ALSO nos.
    3016, Masik, A. Arctic nights' ... 1935;
    3737, Rasmussen, K. J. V. Eagle's gift ... 1932.

HUTTON, J. E. A history of Moravian Missions. London, Moravian Pub. Office, 1923. 550p. maps, bibliog. index. [incls. Greenland, Labrador and Alaska]   2248

HYDE, ALEXANDER and others. The frozen zone and its explorers; a comprehensive record of voyages, travels, discoveries, adventures and whale-fishing in the Arctic regions for one thousand years. With a ... history of the late expedition ... in the ill-fated "Polaris." Hartford, Conn., Columbian Book Co., 1874. 800p. front. pls. maps(incl. 1 fold.) [other authors A. C.Baldwin, W. L. Gage and C. W. Shields]   2249

HYDE, JOHN. Northern Pacific tour; the Pacific northwest and Alaska, with a description of the country traversed by the Northern Pacific Railroad. St. Paul, Minn., W. C. Riley, 1889. front. illus.   2250

Hyde, John. SEE ALSO no. 4022,
    Schwatka, F. Wonderland ... 1886.

HYLANDER, CLARENCE J. Wildlife community; from the tundra to the tropics in North America. Boston, Houghton, 1965. illus.
                    2251

I

IANKIEVICH, F. de M. Straviteljnyi slovar vsiekh iazykov i nariechii. [TITLE TR. Comparative dictionary of all languages and dialects, alphabetically arranged] St. Petersburg, 1790-91. 4 vols. [incls. Eskimo of Norton Sound, other Alaskan area] 2252

Iditarod Trail Committee, Knik. SEE nos.
    172, All Alaska Sweepstakes ... Souvenir ... 1969;
    1182, Darling, E. B. The great dog races ... 1969.

Iles, Alfred B. SEE no. 56, Alaska Copper Corp.

ILLINGWORTH, FRANK. Highway to the north. London, Ernest Benn,
1955. 297p. map(fold.) ANR. N. Y., Philosophical Library,
1955.   2253

ILLINGWORTH, FRANK. North of the Circle. London, William Hodge
& Co., 1951. 254p. pls. ANR. N. Y., Philosophical Library,
1952. [has one chapter on Alaska; also scattered references]2254

ILLUSTRATED HISTORY OF INDIAN BASKETS and plates made by California Indians and many other tribes now on exhibition at the Pana-
ma-Pacific-International Exposition. All of the baskets shown
in this souvenir are on exhibition in the Lassen County exhibit
at the 1915 Panama-Pacific International Exposition and are the
property of T. A. Roseberry, Susanville, California. no pl.,
Viola M. Roseberry, 1915. unp. 34 pls. with leaves of descriptive text. ANR. Orange Cove, Calif., printed by Leo K. Brown,
1967. facsim. ed., numbered copies. [pls. 12, 28 and 34 contain
Alaskan examples]   2255

ILVESSALO, LAURI and M. JAVALA. Maapallon metsävarat. [TITLE
TR. Forest resources of the world] Helsingfors, 1930. 387p.
tables, diagrs. maps(fold.), bibliog. (Metsätieteelinem tutkim-
uslaitos. Julkaisuja, 16:2) [has Eng. summary and Eng. captions
on diagrs. and tables]   2256

Immaculate Conception Church, Fairbanks. SEE
    no. 2969, Marion Society.

IMRAY, JAMES. North Pacific pilot; Pt. 1. The west coast of
North America, between Panama and Queen Charlotte Islands, including Port Simpson and Sitka Sound. London, James Imray & Son,
1881. 3rd ed. 456p. charts(some fold.)   2257

Incomparable Yukon. [1928 ?] SEE
    no. 4836, White Pass & Yukon Railway.

INDEPENDENT PETROLEUM ASSOCIATION OF AMERICA. The oil producing
industry in your state, 1960-62. Tulsa, Oklahoma, 1961-63.
3 vols. maps, graphs, tables, bibliog.   2258

INDIAN BOYS' PRESS. Catholic prayers and hymns in the Tinneh
language. Kosoreffski, Alaska, Holy Cross Mission, 1897. 39p.
                                                               2259

INDIAN BOYS' PRESS. Tinneh Indian catechism of Christian doc-
trine. Kosoreffski, Alaska, Holy Cross Mission, 1897. 22p.
                                                               2260

Indian rights and wrongs ... 1961. SEE no. 2088, Hetsel, T. B.

Indian Rights Assoc. SEE nos.
  688, Brosius, S. M. Menace to reindeer industry. 1906;
  2088, Hetzel, T. B. Indian rights and wrongs ... 1961;
  2089, Hetzel, T. B. Meek do not inherit Alaska. 1962.

Indian tribes and missions. [c1926] SEE
  no. 931, Church Missions Pub. Co.

Industrial dawn of Alaska. 1904. SEE
  no. 3796, Reynolds-Alaska Development Co.

Industrial progress ... 1909. SEE
  no. 150, Alaska-Yukon-Pacific Exposition.

Influenza epidemic report ... 1919. SEE
  no. 100, Alaska Packers Assoc.

Influenze epidemic ... "Service" ... 1919. SEE
  no. 101, Alaska Packers Assoc.

INGERSOLL, ERNEST, edit. Alaskan bird-life as depicted by many
writers. N. Y., National Association of Audubon Societies, 1914.
ed. of approx. 8000 copies. 72p. front.(col.), 6 pls.(col. with
6 duplicate black and white pls.), map, index. illustrations by
Bruce Horsfall and Allan Brooks.   2261

INGERSOLL, ERNEST. Gold fields of the Klondike and the wonders
of Alaska; a masterly and fascinating description of the newly-
discovered gold mines; how they were found; how worked; what
fortunes have been made; the extent and richness of the gold
fields; how to get there; outfit required; climate; the natives; other vast riches of Alaska; other great gold mines of
the world; the great seal fisheries, etc., with an introduction
by Hon. Henry W. Elliott. no pl., Edgewood Pub. Co., 1897. 512p.
front. pls. OTHERS Philadelphia, World Bible House, 1897. 512p.
N. Y., W. W. Wilson, 1897 and Chicago, 1897.   2262

INGERSOLL, ERNEST. Golden Alaska; a complete account to date of
the Yukon valley; its history, geography, mineral and other resources, opportunities and means of access. Chicago, Rand Mc-
Nally, 1897. 149p. front. pls. maps(incl. 1 fold.)   2263

INGERSOLL, ERNEST and HENRY W. ELLIOTT. In richest Alaska and
the gold fields of the Klondike; how they were found ... together with a history of this wonderful land from its discovery to
the present day ... and practical information for the goldseekers
... prepared under the special supervision of A. J. Munson ...
and written especially by Ernest Ingersoll ... assisted by Henry
W. Elliott. Chicago, Dominion Co., 1897. 487p. front. pls.
map(fold.)   2264

Ingleton, Geoffrey C., illus. SEE no. 2076, Heritage Press.

INGRAHAM, JOSEPH. Friendship Road; the challenge of the Pan American Highway. N. Y., Coward-McCann, 1961. (Challenge Books)   2265

INGSTAD, HELGE. Nunamiut; among Alaska's inland Eskimos. Translated by F. H. Lyon. N. Y., W. W. Norton & Co., 1954. 303p. front. (col.), pls. sketches by Paniaq, map(fold.), Eskimo spelling list, bibliog. index. ANR. London, George Allen & Unwin, 1954. 254p. [Anaktuvak Pass, Brooks Range - tr. of no. 2267]   2266

INGSTAD, HELGE. Nunamiut; blant Alaskas innlands-Eskimoer. Oslo, Gyldendal Norsk Forlag, 1951. 334p. pls. map(fold. col.), sketches by Paniaq. [for tr. see no. 2266]   2267

Ingstad, Helge. SEE ALSO no. 1869,
    Groven, E. Eskimomelodier ... 1956.

Initial performance ... "San Toy" ... n. d. SEE
    no. 1313, Dobbs' Alaska Moving Picture Co.

Inman, H., comp. SEE no. 2378, Jones, C. J.

INNES, M. J. S. Gravity measurements in Canada, January 1, 1954 to December 31, 1956. Ottawa, Queen's Printer, 1957. 14p. maps, bibliog. (Canada. Dominion Observatories Publications, vol. 19, no. 1)   2268

INNIS, HAROLD ADAMS. Settlement and the mining frontier. Toronto, Macmillan, 1936. (vol. 9, pt.2 of "Canadian frontiers of settlement" edited by W. A. MacKintosh and W. L. G. Joerg)   2269

Innis, Harold Adams. The fur trade in Canada ... SEE no. 2270.

INNIS, HAROLD ADAMS. The fur trade of Canada. Toronto, University of Toronto Library, 1927. 172p. table(fold.), appends. ftntes.(bibliog.) (University of Toronto Studies; History and Economics, vol. 1, no. 1) ANR. WITH TITLE The fur trade in Canada; an introduction to Canadian economic history, with a preface by R. M. MacIver. N. Y., Yale University Press, 1930. enl. ed. 444p. pls. maps, appends. ftntes.(bibliog.), index. ANR. Toronto, University of Toronto Press, 1956. 463p. ...edited by S. D. Clark and W. T. Easterbrook. ANR. N. H., Yale University Press, 1962. new ed. of Toronto 1956 ed. 446p. (Yale Western Americana series) [incls. Athabaskan, MacKenzie and Yukon Indians]   2270

Innocent, *Metropolitan of Moscow*. SEE nos. 4670-82,
    Veniaminov, I. E. P.

Innokentiia; metropolita moskovskago ... 1883. SEE
    no. 414, [Barsukov, I. P.]

INSTITUTE OF PACIFIC RELATIONS, Second Conference. Problems of the Pacific; proceedings of the Second Conference of the Institute of Pacific Relations, Honolulu, Hawaii, July 15 to 29, 1927. Edited by J. B. Condliffe. Chicago, University of Chicago Press, 1928. 630p. front.(fold.), diagrs.(some fold.), map(fold.) 2271

INTERESTING ACCOUNT OF THE EARLY VOYAGES, made by the Portugese, Spaniards, etc., to Africa, East and West Indies. The discovery of numerous islands; with particulars of the lives of those eminent navigators. Including the life and voyages of Columbus. To which is prefixed the life of that great circumnavigator Captain Cook ... Extracted from Dr. Kippis. London, Printed for Proprieters and sold at Stalker's, 1790. 276p. front.(port.), pls. maps(fold.) 2272

Interior Alaska, home of opportunity. [1914] SEE no. 1516, Fairbanks Commercial Club.

INTERNATIONAL ASSOCIATION FOR QUATERNARY RESEARCH, 7th Congress. Guidebook for Field Conference F. Central and south central Alaska; Aug.-Sept. 1965. Editors, C. Bertrand Schultz and H. T. U. Smith; Conference Organizer, Troy L. Péwé. Lincoln, Nebraska Academy of Sciences, 1965. 141p. illus. figs.(some fold.), diagrs. maps(some fold.), references. 2273

International Assoc. for Quaternary Research. SEE ALSO no. 2178, Hopkins, D. M. Bering land bridge. 1967.

INTERNATIONAL BOUNDARY COMMISSION. Joint report upon the survey and demarcation of the boundary between Canada and the United States from Tongass Passage to Mount St. Elias. In accordance with the convention of January 24, 1903; the award of the tribunal appointed under the convention, signed at London, October 20, 1903; an exchange of notes between the governments of Great Britain and the United States, relative to the award signed at Washington, March 25, 1905; and the treaty signed at Washington, February 24, 1925. Ottawa, Queen's Printer, 1952. 2 vols. 365p. illus. diagrs. maps(incl. fold. in pocket) WITH atlas: Joint maps of the International Boundary between United States and Canada, from Cape Muzon to Mount St. Elias. 2274

INTERNATIONAL FISHERIES COMMISSION. Regulation and investigation of the Pacific halibut fishery in 1947-49. Seattle, 1948-51. illus. tables, maps. (Reports 13 through 15, separate) 2275

INTERNATIONAL FISHERIES COMMISSION. Report of the International Fisheries Commission, no. 1. Seattle, 1931. 2276

International Fisheries Commission. SEE ALSO nos.
    177, Allen, E. W. Halibut Commission ... 1936;
    332, Babcock, J. P. Investigation ... halibut ... 1930;
    4511, Thompson, Thos. G. Hydrographic ... 1936;
    4513-14, Thompson, Wm. F. Biol. statistics ... 1931, 1934;

International Fisheries Commission. SEE ALSO nos.
    4515, Thompson, Wm. F. Hist. Pac. halibut fishery. 1930;
    4516-17, Thompson, Wm. F. Life hist. Pac. halibut.1930,1936;
    4520, Thompson, Wm. F. Theory ... halibut. 1937.

INTERNATIONAL GEOLOGICAL CONGRESS, 12th, Ottawa, 1913. Guidebook
no. 10. Ottawa, Canada Geological Survey, 1913. [excursions to
Yukon and southeastern Alaska]   2277

INTERNATIONAL HYDROGRAPHIC BUREAU, Monaco. Catalogue of original
charts. Part 3. Pacific Ocean. Corrected to February 1, 1935.
130p. (Special Publication, no. 25. 1935)   2278

INTERNATIONAL NORTH PACIFIC FISHERIES COMMISSION. The exploitation, scientific investigation and management of halibut, *Hippo-
glossus stenolepis* Schmidt, stocks on the Pacific coast of North
America, in relation to the abstention provisions of the North
Pacific Fisheries Convention. Vancouver, 1962. 93p. tables,
graphs, map, bibliog. (Bulletin no. 7)   2279

INTERNATIONAL NORTH PACIFIC FISHERIES COMMISSION. The exploitation, scientific investigation and management of herring, *Clupea
pallasi*, on the Pacific coast of North America in relation to the
abstention provisions of the North Pacific Fisheries Convention.
Vancouver, 1961. 100p. illus. graphs, tables, maps, bibliog.
(Bulletin no. 4)   2280

INTERNATIONAL NORTH PACIFIC FISHERIES COMMISSION. The exploitation, scientific investigation and management of salmon, genus
Oncorhynchus, stocks on the Pacific coast of Canada in relation
to the abstention provisions of the North Pacific Fisheries Convention. Vancouver, 1962. 112p. tables, graphs, map, bibliog.
(Bulletin no. 9)   2281

INTERNATIONAL NORTH PACIFIC FISHERIES COMMISSION. Statistical
yearbook. Vancouver, 1952. in progress. tables, maps.   2282

INTERNATIONAL OIL SCOUTS ASSOCIATION. International oil and gas
development, review 1961. Part 1. Exploration. Austin, Texas,
September 1962. 592p. ports. diagrs. tables, maps, references.
(vol. 32)   2283

INTERNATIONAL PACIFIC HALIBUT COMMISSION. Regulation and investigation of the Pacific halibut fishery in 1957-59.   Seattle,
1958-62. illus. tables, maps. (Reports 26, 27 and 28)   2284

INTERNATIONAL PACIFIC HALIBUT COMMISSION. Regulation and investigation of the Pacific halibut fishery in 1960. Seattle, 1961.
24p. tables, maps. (Report no. 30)   2285

INTERNATIONAL PACIFIC HALIBUT COMMISSION. Utilization of Pacific
halibut stocks; yield per recruitment. Seattle, 1960. 52p.
illus. tables. (Report no. 28)   2286

INTERNATIONAL SOCIETY FOR THE EXPLORATION OF THE ARCTIC REGIONS by means of aircraft. Verhandlungen der II. ordentl. Versammlung in Leningrad, 18-23 Juni 1928. Hrsg. im Auftrage der Gesellschaft von A. Berson und L. Breitfus. [TITLE TR. Proceedings of the second regular meeting in Leningrad, June 18-23, 1928, edited under the direction of the Society by A. Berson and L. Breitfus] Gotha, Justus Perthes, 1929. 76p. illus. pls. (some fold.), diagrs.(fold.), maps. [series of papers in German, English and French]   2287

International Symposium on Arctic Geology. SEE no. 3715,
    Raasch, G. O.

INTERNATIONAL TELEPHONE AND TELEGRAPH CORPORATION. Manning the DEWline. N. Y., [1960 ?] 36p. illus. map.   2288

INTERNATIONAL YUKON POLAR INSTITUTE. Constitution. Headquarters Dawson, Y. T. Founded August 5, 1905. Dawson, Dawson Daily News, 1905. 7p.   2289

INTERNATIONAL YUKON POLAR INSTITUTE. Objects of the Institute. Founded August 5, 1905. Dawson, Y. T. Dawson, Yukon World Press, 1905. 6p.   2290

Introduction to Arctic zool. 2d ed. 1792. SEE
    no. 3531, [Pennant, Thos.]

INVERARITY, ROBERT BRUCE. Art of the northwest coast Indians. Berkeley, University of California, 1950. 243p. pls.(some col.), bibliog. ANR. 1967. 3rd print. [southeastern Alaskan Tlingits, others]   2291

INVERARITY, ROBERT BRUCE. Movable masks and figures of the north Pacific coast Indians. Bloomfield Hills, Mich., Cranbrook Institute of Science, 1941. 4p. pls.(col.)   2292

INVERARITY, ROBERT BRUCE. Northwest coast Indian art; a brief survey. Seattle, University of Washington, 1946. (36)p. illus. (Washington State Museum, ser. no. 1)   2293

INVERARITY, ROBERT BRUCE. Visual files coding index. Bloomington, Indiana University, October 1960. 185p. illus. bibliog. (International Journal American Linguistics, vol. 26, no. 4, pt. 3) [examples incl. Eskimo and Haida]   2294

Iremonger, V., tr. SEE no. 2896, MacGowan, M.

IRVINE, ALBERT. How the Makah obtained possession of Cape Flattery. Translated by Luke Markistun. N. Y., Museum of American Indian, 1921. 10p. (Heye Foundation, Indian Notes and Monographs, Misc. Contrib. no. 6)   2295

IRVINE, TOM A. The ice was all between. N. Y., Longmans Green, 1959. 216p. illus. diagr. ANR. 1954. [northwest passage and Canadian ship *Labrador*]   2296

Irving, W. SEE no. 4651, van Steensel, M., edit.

IRVING, WILLIAM N. Preliminary report on an archaeological re-connaissance in the western part of the Brooks Range of Alaska. no pl., 1954. 20 ℓ plans, maps.   2297

IRWIN, DAVID and JOHN SHERMAN O'BRIEN. Alone across the top of the world; the authorized story of the Arctic journey of David Irwin; As told to Jack O'Brien. Chicago, John C. Winston, 1935. 254p. front.(port.), pls. ports. endmaps. ANR. Chicago, E. M. Hale Co., n. d. (Cadmus Books) [from Nome to Churchill on Hudson's Bay]   2298

IRWIN, DAVID and FRANKLIN M. RECK. One man against the north. With Franklin M. Reck. N. Y., Thos. Y. Crowell, 1940. 244p. front.(pl.), pls. ports. maps, sketches. ANR. London, R. Hale, 1942. 256p. pls. ports. [a later version of no. 2298]   2299

IRWIN, VIOLET MARY. The Shaman's revenge, based on the Arctic diaries of V. Stefansson. Illustrated by Geoffry Grier. N. Y., Macmillan, 1925. 286p. illus.   2300

IRWIN, WILLIAM ROBERT, edit. Challenge;   an anthology of the literature of mountaineering. N. Y., Columbia University Press, 1950. 444p. bibliog.   2301

IS THE TRADE OF ALASKA TERRITORY to be wrested from general com-petition of the merchants of the Pacific Coast by a monopoly ? Extraordinary developments in regard to the Alaska Commercial Company. S. F., November 11, 1871. 8p.   2302

ISLAND PUBLISHING CO. Kodiak earthquake. Kodiak, Island Pub. Co., [ca 1965]   2303

ITJEN, MARTIN. Historic and scenic views in and around Skagway. [Skagway ?], by author, 1933. illus.   2304

ITJEN, MARTIN. The story of the tour on the Skagway, Alaska street car. Owned by Martin Itjen, who built the car and wrote this book - Henry made the chassis. This book contains over one hundred historic and scenic views in and around Skagway, Alaska of the early days of '98. St. Benedict, Ore., 1934. 82p. illus. ANR. no pl. [Skagway ?], by author, 1938. 95p. illus. front. facsims. photos. ANR. no pl. [Skagway ?], by author, 1962 [and George Rapuzzi, successor, 1963] 100p. illus. front. photos, facsims. [much about Soapy Smith]   2305

It's gold ... [1897 ?] SEE no. 5014,
     [Yukon Trading, Mining & Exploration Co.]

ÍŪNGA, EVGENIĬ S. Kolumby rosskie; epizody istoricheskoĭ Khron-
iki xviii veka. [TITLE TR. Russian Columbuses; episodes from
the historical chronicles of the 18th century] Moskva, Gos.
voennomorskoe izd-vo, 1941. 152p. illus. map (Biblioteka Kras-
noflottsa) 2306

IVANHOE, LYTTON FRANCIS. Alaska, geology maps. Bakersfield,
California, 1959. 43 maps incl. index map. 2307

IVANSHINSTOV, H. Obozrienii Russkikh Krugosvietnykh puteshestviĭ
[TITLE TR. Review of Russian voyages around the world] St. Petersburg, 1850. 25 copies printed, not for sale. 306p. tables,
map. (Memoirs of Zapiski Gidrograficheskago Departamenta) ANR.
1872. 2308

Ivie, W., co-auth. SEE no. 882, Chamberlin, Ralph Vary.

J

JACKSON, G. R. and RALPH LOMEN. A suggestion for the reorganiza-
tion of Alaska in anticipation of statehood presented by G. R.
Jackson and Ralph Lomen. Nome, 1953. 6p. 2309

Jackson, G. T. SEE no. 87, Alaska Mining & Engineering Soc.

Jackson, H. H. T., co-auth. SEE no. 5000, Young, S. P.

JACKSON, SHELDON. A statement of facts concerning the difficul-
ties at Sitka, Alaska, in 1885. Washington, D. C., Thomas McGill,
1886. 32p. 2310

JACKSON, SHELDON. Alaska, and missions on the north Pacific
Coast. N. Y., Dodd Mead, 1880. 327p. front.(port.), pls. ports.
map(fold.) ANR. N. Y., Dodd Mead, 1880. 400p. 2311

JACKSON, SHELDON. Facts about Alaska; its people, villages,
missions, schools. N. Y., Woman's Executive Committee of Home
Missions of Presbyterian Church, 1894. 22p. illus. ANR.
[1902 ?] 29p. ANR. 1903. 58p. 2312

JACKSON, SHELDON. The native tribes of Alaska. Ocean Grove,
N. J., National Assembly, 1883. (reprinted from "Sixty addresses
Christian educators in council," edited by J. C. Hartzell.
pp.118-27. 2313

Jackson, Sheldon, SEE ALSO nos.
    640, Brady, Elizabeth P. Sheldon Jackson ... 1911;
    1404, Eaton, John. Sheldon Jackson ... 1898;
    2222, Hulbert, W. Bishop of all beyond ... 1948;
    2366, Johns, Chas. L. Sheldon Jackson School. n. d.;
    2653, Lazell, J. A. Alaskan apostle ... 1960;

3041, Mayberry, G. Sheldon Jackson Junior College ... 1953;
4345, Stewart, R. L. Sheldon Jackson ... [c1908]

Jacobi, U., tr. SEE no. 2355, Jewitt, J.R.

JACOBIN, LOUIS. Lou Jacobin's tourists' and sportsmen's pictorial guide to Alaska; authentic information on where to go, how to
go, what to expect. Juneau, Alaska Tourist Guide Co., 1946. 1st
ed. 208p. illus.(some col.), ports. maps. OTHERS WITH VARIA-
TIONS ON TITLE by Alaska Tourist Guide Co., Juneau; later by
Guide to Alaska Co., Juneau; then by Guide to Alaska, Inc., Anchorage. INCLUDES 1966. (20th Anniversary Edition) and 1967.
(Alaska Centennial Edition)   2314

Jacobin, Louis. SEE ALSO nos.
    74, [Alaska Life, Seattle] Anchorage ... [1945 ?];
    75, [Alaska Life, Seattle] Fairbanks ... [1945 ?];
    76, [Alaska Life, Seattle] Juneau ... [1945 ?];
    77, [Alaska Life, Seattle] Ketchikan ... [1945 ?];
    78, [Alaska Life, Seattle] Nome ... [1945 ?];
    79, [Alaska Life, Seattle] Seward ... [1945 ?]

JACOBSEN, JOHAN ADRIAN. Kapitän Jacobsen's Reise an der Nordwestküste Amerikas, 1881-83, zum Zwecke ethnologischer Sammlungen
und Erdkundigungen, nebst Beschreibung persönlicher Erlebnisse,
für den deutschen Leserkreis bearbeitet, von A. Woldt. [TITLE
TR. Captain Jacobsen's journey to the northwest coast of America,
1881-83, for collecting ethnological materials and information;
with a description of personal experience, edited for German
readers by A. Woldt] Leipzig, M. Spohr, 1884. 431p. illus.
maps(incl. 1 fold.). ANR. Christiana, Norway, 1887. 329p.
[in Norwegian]   2315

JACOBSEN, JOHAN ADRIAN. Unter den Alaska-Eskimos. Berlin, Ullstein, n. d. 155p. maps.   2316

JACOBSEN, JOHAN ADRIAN. Unter Indianern und Eskimos. Berlin,
Hillger, n. d. 32p.   2317

JACOBSEN, N. KINGO and P. P. SVEISTRUP. Erhverv og kultur langs
Polarkredsen. [TITLE TR. Trade and culture along the Arctic
Circle] København, Munksgaard, 1950. 140p. illus. maps.
(Grønlandske selskab)   2318

JÄDERHOLM, AXEL ELOF. Zur Kenntnis der Hydroidenfauna des
Beringsmeeres. [TITLE TR. On the hydroids of Bering Sea]
Stockholm, 1908. 8p. pls. (Arkiv für Zoologi, Bd. 4, no. 8)
[N. A. E. Nordenskiöld"s *Vega* expedition to Bering Strait]   2319

JAGGAR, THOMAS AUGUSTUS. Journal of the Technology Expedition to
the Aleutian Islands, 1907. Boston, Ellis, 1908. 37p. [vol-
canology]   2320

JAGGAR, THOMAS AUGUSTUS. Volcanoes declare war; logistics and strategy of Pacific volcano science. Honolulu, Paradise of Pacific Ltd., 1945. 166p. pls. maps. 2321

JAMES, BUSHROD WASHINGTON. Alaska; its neglected past, its brilliant future. Philadelphia, Sunshine Publishing Co., 1897. 1st ed. 444p. front. pls. maps(some dble.), tables, bibliog. 2322

JAMES, BUSHROD WASHINGTON. Alaskana; or, Alaska in descriptive and legendary poems. By Prof. Bushrod W. James. Philadelphia, Porter & Coates, 1892. 368p. front. pls. append. OTHERS 1893. 402p. AND 1894. 410p. 2323

JAMES, FREDERICK. The Klondike goldfields and how to get there. By Fred. James. With a map. London, George Routledge & Sons, 1897. 68p. front.(map), index. 2324

JAMES, GEORGE WHARTON. Indian basketry; with 300 illustrations. By George Wharton James. Pasadena, Calif., privately printed, 1901. 238p. photos, sketches, bibliog. index. OTHERS 1902 AND 1903. 2325

James, George Wharton. SEE ALSO no. 953,
    Clements, Jas. I. The Klondyke ... 1897.

JAMES, JAMES ALTON. The first scientific exploration of Russian America and the purchase of Alaska. Evanston, Illinois, Northwestern University, 1942. 276p. pls. ports. map(dble.), bibliog. index. (Studies in the Social Sciences, no. 4) [journals of Robert Kennicott and Henry M. Bannister of Smithsonian Institution] 2326

JAMES, JOSEPHINE. Assignment in Alaska. N. Y., Golden Press, 1961. 184p. illustrated by William Plummer. (A Kathy Martin Story) 2327

JAMES, SAM. Taming the Arctic shrew. A northland poem. By Sam James. Illustrated by Jane Hafling. Anchorage, Color Art Printing Co., 1963. (22)p. sketches, wrps. 2328

Jamieson, S. M., co-auth. SEE no. 1999, Hawthorn, H. B.

Jane, Cecil, tr. SEE no. 1675, [Galiano, D. A.]

JANE, FRED T. The Imperial Russian Navy. London, W. Thacker & Co., 1899. 2329

Janvrin, A. J., edit. SEE no. 3817, Ridley, Wm.

JAPAN. MARITIME SAFETY BOARD. Alaska Coast pilot; volume 1, Dixon Entrance to Yakutat Bay. 1961. 2d ed. illus. tables, maps(incl. fold.), references. [text in Japanese, keywords in English] ANR. 1932. 1st ed. 2330

JAQUES, FLORENCE PAGE.   As far as the Yukon.   Illustrated by
Francis Lee Jaques. N. Y., Harper, 1951. 243p. illus. index.
2331

JARVIS, WILLIAM HENRY POPE. The great gold rush; a tale of the
Klondike. Toronto, Macmillan, 1913. 255p.   2332

Javala, M., co-auth. SEE no. 2256, Iivessalo, L.

Jayne, A. G., tr. SEE no. 3107, Mikkelsen, E.

JEANCON, JEAN A. and FREDERIC H. DOUGLAS.   Northwest coast Indians. Denver, Denver Art Museum, 1930. (Leaflet no. 1)   2333

JEBB, RICHARD. Studies in Colonial nationalism. London, Edward
Arnold, 1905. [chapt. 3, pp.25-60, about Alaskan boundary) 2334

JEFFERY, EDMOND C., edit. Alaska; who's here, what's doing,
who's doing it, 1955. Anchorage, 1955. 1st ed. 212p.   2335

[JEFFERYS, THOMAS ?] The great probability of a North West passage;   deduced from observations on the letter of Admiral de
Fonte, who sailed from the Callao of Lima on the discovery of a
communication between the South Sea and the Atlantic Ocean; and
to intercept some navigators from Boston in New England whom he
met with, then in search of a North West passage. Proving the
authenticity of the Admiral's letter, with three explanatory
maps ... 1st. A copy of an authentic Spanish map of America,
published in 1608.   2d. The discoveries made in Hudson's Bay,
by Captain Smith, in 1746 and 1747. 3d. A general map of the
discoveries of Admiral de Fonte. By Thomas Jefferys, Geographer
to the King. With an appendix. Containing the account of a
discovery of part of the coast and inland country of Labrador,
made in 1753. The whole intended for the advancement of trade
and commerce. London, printed for Thomas Jefferys at Charing
Cross, 1768. xxiv,153(1)p. front.(fold. map), maps(fold.)
[text variously ascribed to Theodore Swaine Drage (or Swindrage),
or to Charles Swaine]   2336

Jefferys, Thomas, cartog. SEE ALSO nos.
    2532, Krasheninnikov, S. P. Hist. Kamtschatka ... 1764;
    2533, Krasheninnikov, S. P. Opisanie zemli Kamtschatki.1766;
    3234, Müller, G. F. Voyages from Asia ... 1761.

Jefford, Jack. SEE no. 3658, Potter, Jean.

Jeffries, N. L. SEE no. 53, Alaska Commercial Co.

JENKENS, JAMES TRAVIS. Whales and modern whaling. London, H. F.
& G. Witherby, 1932. pls. [natural history, circumpolar]   2337

JENKINS, THOMAS. The man of Alaska; Peter Trimble Rowe. By the
Rt. Rev. Thomas Jenkins, D.D., Ret. Bishop of Nevada. N. Y.,
Morehouse-Gorham, 1943. 340p. front.(col. port.), pls. ports.
endmaps. [Bishop Rowe was first Episcopalian Bishop of Alaska]
2338

JENNESS, DIAMOND. Comparative vocabulary of the Western Eskimo
dialects. Ottawa, King's Printer, 1928. 134p. (Report Canadian Arctic Expedition, 1913-18, vol. 15, pt. A)   2339

JENNESS, DIAMOND. Dawn in Arctic Alaska. Illustrations by
Giacomo Raimondi. Minneapolis, University of Minnesota Press,
1957. 222p. illus. maps.   2340

JENNESS, DIAMOND. Eskimo administration. Part 1. Alaska. Montreal, 1962. 64p. figs. maps, bibliog. (Arctic Institute of
North America, Technical Paper no. 10)   2341

JENNESS, DIAMOND. Eskimo administration. Part 5. Analysis and
reflections. Montreal, 1968. appends. bibliog. index. 72p.
(Arctic Institute of North America, Technical Paper no. 21)
[index to vols. 1 through 5]   2342

JENNESS, DIAMOND. Eskimo string figures. Ottawa, King's Printer, 1924. 192p. illus. map (Report Canadian Arctic Expedition
1913-18, vol. 13, pt. B)   2343

JENNESS, DIAMOND. Grammatical notes on some Western Eskimo dialects. Southern party, 1913-16. Ottawa, King's Printer, 1944.
34p. ftntes. (Report Canadian Arctic Expedition 1913-18, vol.
15, pt. B)   2344

JENNESS, DIAMOND, edit. The American aborigines; their origin
and antiquity, a collection of papers by ten authors. Toronto,
University of Toronto Press, 1933. 396p. illus. maps (Fifth
Pacific Science Congress)   2345

JENNESS, DIAMOND. The Indians of Canada. Ottawa, 1932. 446p.
(Canada. National Museum, Bulletin no. 65) ANR. 1955. 3rd ed.
452p. illus.(col.), maps(incl. 1 fold.), bibliog. (Canada.
National Museum, Bulletin 65. Anthropological Series no. 15)
OTHERS 1958 AND 1960.   2346

Jenness, Diamond. SEE ALSO nos.
    203, American Geographical Society. Problems ... 1928;
    204, American Geographical Society. Readings ... 1952;
    4427, Swayze, Nansi. Man hunters. 1960.

Jennings, Jesse D., co-edit. SEE no. 4258, Spencer, Robert F.

JENNINGS, ROBERT W. An address; Liberty and home. Delivered by
Robert W. Jennings by request at a mass meeting of citizens of
Ketchikan, June 20, 1917. Ketchikan, published by Citizens of
Ketchikan, 1917. 15p.   2347

JENNINGS, W. T. Report of W. T. Jennings on routes to the Yukon,
printed by order of Parliament. Includes report on highway or
railway route between Stikine River and Teslyn Lake, B. C. Ottawa, Printer S. E. Dawson, 1898. 28p.   2348

JENSEN, CHRISTIAN ALBRECHT THEODOR. Über die grosse atmosphär-
isch-optische Störung von 1912. [TITLE TR. On the great atmospheric optical disturbances of 1912] Berlin, Vereinigung von
Freunden der Astronomie und Kosmischen Physik, Mitteilungen,
1913. 12p. 2 tables. [Katmai eruption]   2349

JENSEN, PAUL. Hunters of the Arctic rim. By Dr. Paul Jensen.
Corvallis, Ore., Chandler Printing, n. d. [ca 195_ ?] (16)p.
illus. photos, map. [St Lawrence Island]   2350

JESUP NORTH PACIFIC EXPEDITION. Ethnographical album of the
north Pacific coasts of America and Asia. Part 1. N. Y., American Museum of Natural History, 1900. 28 pls.   2351

JETTE, JULIUS. Catholic Church, liturgy and ritual in the Tinne
language. Yuyit Rokanaga nulator roka do-daletloye. By Julius
Jette, S.J. Winnipeg, Free Press, no-rodeneletektyar, 1904.
124p.   2352

Jewett, John Rodgers. SEE nos. 2353-56, Jewitt, John Rodgers.

JEWITT, JOHN RODGERS. A journal kept at Nootka Sound, by John R.
Jewitt, one of the surviving crew of the ship *Boston*, of Boston,
John Salter, commander, who was massacred on 22d of March, 1803;
interspersed with some account of the natives, their manners and
customs. Boston, 1807. ANR. WITH TITLE A journal kept at Nootka
Sound by John R. Jewitt, one of the survivors of the crew of the
ship *Boston*, during a captivity among the Indians from March 1803
to July 1805, reprinted from the original edition, Boston, 1807,
with an introduction and a check list of late accounts of Jewitt's
captivity. By Norman L. Dodge. Boston, Goodspeed, 1931. 91p.
front. [100 copies printed]   2353

Jewitt, John Rodgers. John Jewitt Makwinnas ... See no. 2355.

JEWITT, JOHN RODGERS. Narrative of the adventures and sufferings
of John R. Jewitt. Only survivor of the crew of the ship *Boston*,
during a captivity of nearly three years among the savages of
Nootka Sound. With an account of the manners, mode of living,
and religious opinions of the natives. N. Y., 1815. 204p. front.
OTHERS with various publishers and dates edited by Richard Alsop.
ANR. London, Clement Wilson, 1896. 256p. [with introduction and
notes by Robert Brown] front.(port.), pls. ANR. Fairfield,

Washington, Ye Galleon Press, 1967. 161p. front. illus. facsims.
errata note, ftntes. endpapers[facsim. titlepages], appends. bibliog. [facsim. of undated N. Y. ed. 1522 copies printed. Incls.
reprint from B. C. Historical Quarterly, *The later life of John
R. Jewitt*, by Edmond S. Meany, Jr.]   2354

JEWITT, JOHN RODGERS. TRANSLATION - Narrative ... 1815.

   John Jewitt Makwinnas Gefangener Meine ubenteur und Leiden bei
      den Indianern am Nutkafund. Aus dem Englischen uberfecht und
      bearbeitet Prof. Dr. U. Jacobi. Leipzig, F. A. Brockhaus,
      1928.   2355

JEWITT, JOHN RODGERS. The captive of Nootka; or, the adventures
of John R. Jewett [sic] N. Y., Peaslee, 1835. 259p. front.
illus. ANR. 1835. [adapted by Samuel Griswold Goodrich(Peter
Parley's Miscellanies)] ANR. Philadelphia, H. F. Anners, 1841.
(vol. 2 of Peter Parley's Little Library) OTHERS Philadelphia,
Lippincott, 1854 and 1861. ANR. Philadelphia, Clayton, Remson &
Heffelfinger, 1869. OTHERS var. eds.   2356

Jewitt, John Rodgers. SEE ALSO nos.
      324, Aumack, Thos. M. Rivers of rain ... 1948;
      674, Broadus, E. H. John Jewitt, captive ... 1928;
      1691, Garst, Shannon. John Jewitt's adventure. 1955;
      4271, Sproat, G. M. Scenes and studies ... 1868.

Jim Wardner, of Wardner, Idaho. 1900. SEE
      no. 4738, Wardner, Jim.

JOCHELSON, WALDEMAR. Aleut folk lore, grammar and vocabulary.
Edited by Franz Boas. N. Y., Columbia University, n. d.   2357

JOCHELSON, WALDEMAR. Archaeological investigations in the Aleutian Islands. Washington, D. C., Carnegie Institution, 1925.
145p. pls. map(1 fold.), bibliog. (Publication no. 367)   2358

JOCHELSON, WALDEMAR. History, ethnology and anthropology of the
Aleut. Washington, D. C., Carnegie Institution, 1933. 91p. pls.
(Publication no. 432) ANR. The Netherlands, Anthropological Pub-
lications, 1966.   2359

JOERG, WOLFGANG LOUIS GOTTFRIED. Brief history of polar exploration since the introduction of flying. N. Y., American Geographical Society, 1930. 50p. illus. maps(incl. 2 fold. in separate folder) [both in slipcase labelled "Two polar maps with notes
on recent polar exploration"] (Special Publication no. 11) ANR.
1930. 2d rev. ed. 95p. illus. maps(2 fold. as above)   2360

Joerg, Wolfgang Louis Gottfried. SEE ALSO nos.
      202, American Geographical Soc. Pioneer settlement. 1932;
      203, American Geographical Soc. Problems polar ... 1928;
      2270, Innis, H. A. Settlement and mining ... 1936.

JOESTING, HENRY R.   Magnetometer and direct current resistivity studies in Alaska.   Baltimore, American Institute of Mining and Metallurgical Engineers, 1941.   20p.   references.   (Technical Publication no. 1284.   Class L, Geophysics, no. 72)   [author's Ph. D. thesis, Johns Hopkins University, 1941]   2361

Johann, A. E. [pseud.]   Bolyongasok ... 1942.   SEE no. 2363.

JOHANN, A. E. [pseud.]   Pelzjäger, prärien und präsidenten; fahrten und erlebnisse zwischen New York und Alaska.   [TITLE TR. Trappers, prairies and presidents;   travels and experiences between New York and Alaska]   Berlin, Ullstein, 1937.   316p.   pls. ports. maps(incl. 1 fold.)   [author is Alfred Wollschläger]   2362

   TRANSLATION - Pelzjäger ... 1937.

     Bolyongások New Yorktól Alaskáig.   Athenaeum Ismeretlen világok sor, 1942.   260p.   map.   2363

JOHANSEN, DOROTHY O. and CHARLES M. GATES.   Empire of the Columbia;   a history of the Pacific Northwest.   N. Y., 1957.   2364

Johansen, M. A., co-auth.   SEE no. 2703, Lide, Alice A.

JOHN, BETTY.   Seloe, the story of a fur seal.   Drawings by Marie K. Nonnast.   Cleveland, World Pub. Co., 1955.   185p.   illus. 2365

John Muir book ... 1925.   SEE no. 3227, [Muir, John]

John Muir;   pictorial biog. ... 1938.   SEE no. 3222, [Muir, John]

JOHNS, CHARLES L.   Sheldon Jackson School.   N. Y., n. d.   12p. illus.   2366

JOHNSHOY, WALTER.   Apaurak in Alaska;   social pioneering among the Eskimos, compiled from the records of Rev. T. L. Brevig, pioneer missionary to the Eskimos of Alaska from 1894 to 1917. By Dr. Walter Johnshoy.   Philadelphia, Dorrance, 1944.   325p.   front. pls.   2367

Johnson, Edith, illus.   SEE no. 755, Business & Prof. Women's Club.

JOHNSON, ELEANOR M., edit.   North American and island neighbors. Columbus Ohio, Charles E. Merrill Col, 1948.   176p.   illus. photos, maps.   (World Geography Readers by My Weekly Reader Editors) [pp.1-30 about Alaska]   2368

JOHNSON, HUGH A. and HAROLD T. JORGENSON.   The land resources of Alaska;   a Conservation Foundation study.   N. Y., University Publishers, 1963.   551p.   tables, ftntes. maps(in pocket), index. [pub. for University of Alaska, College, Alaska]   2369

Johnson, Jas. R., co-auth. SEE no. 465, Beebe, B. F.

JOHNSON, MADINE. Journey of enchantment; a Texan's tall tale of Alaska. N. Y., Exposition Press, 1956. 1st ed. 67p.   2370

JOHNSON, WILLIAM E. Alaska through the rhymes of a construction stiff; with narrative inserts by J. Patrick O'Neal. Illustrated by Fred Newman. N. Y., Pageant Press, 1956. 72p. illus.   2371

JOHNSON, WILLIS F. A century of expansion. N. Y., Macmillan, 1903. 316p. [some reference to Alaska]   2372

JOHNSON, WILLIS F. The life of Warren G. Harding, from the simple life of the farm to the glamor and power of the White House. Philadelphia, John C. Winston, 1923. 288p. [Chapt. 28 about the fatal trip to Alaska]   2373

JOHNSTON, ALVA. The legendary Mizners. N. Y., Farrar, Straus & Young, 1953. 304p. illus. by Reginald Marsh. [the four Mizner brothers and the Klondike]   2374

JOHNSTON, SAMUEL P., edit. Alaska Commercial Company, 1868-1940; a more or less "documented" history, evidenced by papers from governmental files and books; by old letters from company files; by newspaper articles; by memories of officials and employees of long standing. S. F., Printer, E. E. Wachter, 1940. priv. prtd., numbered ed. 65p. illus.   2375

Joint report ... boundary ... 1952. SEE no. 2274,
    International Boundary Commission.

JONAS, CARL. Beachhead on the wind. Boston, Little Brown, 1945. 212p. [Aleutian Islands, World War II]   2376

[JONES, CHARLES D.] Vagrant verse by charley. Nome, Nome Pub. Co., July 1962. [2d print. Oct. 1962] (13)p.   2377

JONES, CHARLES J. Buffalo Jones' forty years of adventure; a volume of facts gathered from experience by C. J. Jones, whose eventful life has been devoted to the preservation of the American bison and other wild animals ... Compiled by H. Inman. Topeka, Crane & Co., 1899. 469p. illus. pls. ANR. London, 1899. [has a chapt. about the Klondike]   2378

JONES, H. WENDY. Man and the Mountain; life of Sydney Laurence, Alaskan painter. By H. Wendy Jones. Anchorage, Alaskan Pub. Co., and Graphic Arts Press, 1962. 76p. 42 photos of Sydney Laurence paintings, other illus. [Mt. McKinley]   2379

JONES, HERSCHEL V. Adventures in Americana, 1492-1897; the romance of voyage and discovery from Spain to the Indies, the Spanish Main, and North America ... over the Chilkoot Pass to the gold fields of Alaska. N. Y., W. E. Rudge, 1928. 2 vols.   2380

JONES, JOHN WILLIAMS. The salmon. N. Y., Harper, 1959. 192p.
illus. diagrs. tables, bibliog. (The New Naturalist)   2381

JONES, LAURA BUCHAN. Tundra tales. Illustrated by Russell Ahsoak. Fairbanks, Printer, Jessen's Litho, 1959. 19p. illus.
(Soroptimist Club of Fairbanks)   2382

JONES, LIVINGSTON FRENCH. A study of the Thlingets of Alaska.
N. Y., Fleming H. Revell, [1914] 261p. front. pls. map(dble.),
index.   2383

JONES, LIVINGSTON FRENCH. Indian vengeance; a narrative of
Alaskan Indians. Boston, The Stratford Co., 1920. 68p. front.
(port.), 3 pls. [fict. based upon Indian legends of Sitka and
Wrangell]   2384

JONES, M. The story of Captain Cook's three voyages around the
world. Told by M. Jones ... with ... illustrations. London,
Cassell, Petter & Galpin, 1870. 264p. illus.   2385

JONES, N. W. Indian bulletin for 1868. A brief account of Chi-
nese voyages to the northwest coast of America and the interpretation of two hundred Indian names. no pl., C. A. Alvord, 1869.
26p. (Indian bulletin no. 2)   2386

Jonveaux, E., tr. SEE no. 4853, Whymper, F.

JORDAN, DAVID STARR. Matka and Katik; a tale of the Mist Islands. S. F., Whitaker & Ray, 1897. 68p. front. pls. map.
[seals in Bering Sea]   2387

JORDAN, DAVID STARR. The days of man; being memories of a
naturalist, teacher and minor prophet of democracy. Yonkers-on-
Hudson, N. Y., World Book Co., 1922. 2 vols. 710p. and 906p.
illus. index.   2388

JORDAN, DAVID STARR. The story of Matka; a tale of the mist-
islands. S. F., Whitaker & Ray-Wiggin Co., 1910. 80p. front.
pls. map. ANR. Yonkers-on-Hudson, N. Y., World Book Co., 1921.
78p. front. pls. drawings by Chloe Lesley Starks. ANR. Chicago,
World Book Co., 1923. 78p. [with appendix on fur seals by
George A. Clark] ANR. N. Y., World Book Co., 1927. rev. [of
1921 ed.] 78p. (Animal Life Series)   2389

JORDAN, JED. Fool's gold; an unrefined account of Alaska in
1889. As told to M. M. Marberry. N. Y., 1960. 255p. illus. 2390

Jorgenson, H. T., co-auth. SEE no. 2369, Johnson, H. A.

JOSLIN, FALCON. Alaska; proposed legislation for government
construction of railroads and leasing of coal lands. An address
before the 15th session of the American Mining Congress. Spokane,
Washington, November 27, 1912. 20p.   2391

JOSLIN, FALCON.   The needs of Alaska;   an address delivered at the annual meeting of the American Mining Congress, Chicago, October 17-22, 1921. no pl., [1921] 13p.   2392

JOTTI-NERI, ELIGIO [pseud.] Critica alla spedizione Nobile; precede uno studio storico sui tentativi aeronautici di explorazione polare. [TITLE TR. Critical study of the Nobile expedition; including a history of aeronautic exploration]   Milano, Liberia Aeronautica, 1930. 92p. pls. facsims. maps.   2393

Journal Cook's last voyage ... 1781. SEE no. 1014, [Cook, J.]

Journal Cook's last voyage ... 1783. SEE no. 2663, [Ledyard, J.]

JUDGE, CHARLES J. An American missionary; a record of the work of William H. Judge, S.J. Baltimore, J. Murphy, 1904. 293p. front. pls. ports. map(fold.) ANR. Boston, Catholic Foreign Mission Bureau, 1904. 2d ed. rev. 308p.   2394

JUDSON, KATHARINE BERRY. Myths and legends of Alaska; selected and edited by Katharine Berry Judson. Chicago, A. C. McClurg & Co., 1911. 148p. front. pls.   2395

Jülg, B. SEE no. 4657, Vater, Johann Severin.

JUNE DAYS ON ALASKA WATERS; by one of the seven. S. F., W. B. Bancroft, 1887. 28p. [poetry]   2396

Juneau, Alaska. [c1909] SEE no. 4925, Winter & Pond Co.

Juneau - capitol ... [1945 ?] SEE no. 76, [Alaska Life, Seattle]

JUNEAU, CITIZENS OF. Juneau, Alaska; a modern city ... Issued as a souvenir of the visit of the Christian Endeavor Excursion ... July 22, 1907. Juneau, Record-Miner, Printer, 1907. 8p. 2397

JUNEAU COMMERCIAL ASSOCIATION. Juneau, Alaska; capitol of the Territory. no pl., n. d. 8p.   2398

Juneau-Douglas city directory ... 1915. SEE no. 4655,
    Van Winkle, L. E.

JUNEAU EMPIRE PRINT. Development and resources of southeastern Alaska. Juneau, 1923. 37p.   2399

Juneau, gold belt city. 1911. SEE no. 4926, Winter & Pond Co.

JUNEAU RECORD-MINER. Acts of Congress relating to incorporated towns in Alaska, and amendments thereto. Rules and regulations governing common council and ordinances of the city of Juneau, Alaska. Juneau, Juneau Record-Miner, 1904. 98p.   2400

Juneau's...recipes. 1960. SEE no. 870, Catholic Daughters America

K

K stolietnemu jubileiu ... 1894. SEE no. 4631, Valaam Monastery.

KFAR keybook...[c1939] SEE no. 3099, Midnight Sun Broadcasting Co.

Ḳagaḳ, O.   SEE no. 2401, Kaġaḳpak.

KAĠAḲPAK.   Kuliaḳtuat Taimani.   Santa Ana, Calif., Summer Institute of Linguistics, n. d.   15p.   illus. (Wycliffe Bible Translators)   [author is O. Ḳagaḳ]   2401

KAIDANOV, N.   Sistemat. katalog dielam Dep-ta Vnieshnei Torgovliĭ.
[TITLE TR. Systematic catalog of papers of the Department of Ex-
terior Trade]   St. Petersburg, 1887.   2402

KAIDANOV, N.   Sistemat. katalog dielam Gos. Kommerts-kollegiĭ.
[TITLE TR. Systematic catalog of papers of the Imperial College
of Commerce]   St. Petersburg, 1884.   2403

KALLINIKOV, N. F.   Nash kraĭniĭ Severo-Vostok.   [TITLE TR.   Our
far northeast]   St. Petersburg, Tip. Morskogo Ministerstva, 1912.
246p. illus. maps(2 fold.) [incls. ref. economy Alaska]   2404

Kalmbach, Edwin R., illus. SEE nos.
     644, Brandt, H.   Alaska bird trails. 1943;
    1668, Gabrielson, I. N.   Birds of Alaska. 1959.

Kaminin, L. G., co-edit.   SEE no. 2531, Krasheninnikov, S.P.

Kane, Henry Bugbee, illus.   SEE nos.
     849, Carrighar, S.   Icebound summer. 1953;
    2033, Helmericks, Harmon.   Arctic hunter. 1955;
    2034, Helmericks, Harmon.   Oolak's brother. 1953;
    3228, Muir, John.   Wilderness world of ... 1954.

Kane, Paul.   En'kunsters ... 1863.   SEE no. 2407.

KANE, PAUL.   Wanderings of an artist among the Indians of North
America from Canada to Vancouver's Island and Oregon, through the
Hudson's Bay Company's territory and back again.   London, Long-
mans, 1859. 455p. front.(col.), pls. ports.(col.), map(fold.)
ANR. Toronto, Radisson Society of Canada, 1925. ltd. ed. 329p.
front.(port.), ports. (Masterworks of Canadian Authors, no. 7)2405

   TRANSLATIONS - Wanderings ... 1859, chronologically.

   Wanderungen eines Kunstlers unter den Indianern Nordamerika's
      von Canada nach der Vancouver's-Insel und nach Oregon durch
      das Gebiet der Hudsons-Bay-Gesellschaft und zuruck, autoris-
      irte Deutsche ausg. ubersetzt von Luise Hauthal, geb. Vel-
      thusen. Leipzig, H. Mattes, 1862. front. pl. tables.   2406

En'kunstners vandringer blandt Indianerne i Nordamerika fra
Canada til Vancouvers o og Oregon gjennem Hudsons-bai-Kom-
paniets territorium og tilbage igjen, oversat fra engelsk
ved F. F. Kjobenhavn, F. H. Eibes, 1863. 344p.   2407

KANE, THOMAS L. Alaska and the Polar regions. N. Y., 1868.
32p.   2408

KANGUK and WILLIAM ALBEE. Kanguk, a boy of Bering Strait. As
told to William Albee. Boston, Little Brown, 1939. 116p. illus.
(col.) by Kanguk.   2409

"Kansas" Gilbert. SEE no. 3469, Page, E. M.

Kardashinskov, A. L., tr. SEE no. 4319, Stefansson, V.

KARELIN, DMITRIĬ BORISOVICH. Morii͡a nasheĭ rodiny; ocherki po
fizicheskoĭ geografiĭ i istoriĭ issledovanii͡a moreĭ SSSR; 2 izd.
dop. [TITLE TR. Seas of our country; sketches of the physical
geography and history of exploration of the seas of the U.S.S.R.;
second revised edition. Edited by A. V. Zabello] Leningrad,
Gos. izd-vo detskoĭ lit-ry, 1954. 342p. pls.(col.), ports. maps
(some fold.), bibliog.   2410

KARO, H. A. Emergency charting of the Alaska earthquake disaster
area. Manila, 1964. 20p. (United Nations Regional Cartographic
Conference for Asia and the Far East, 4th, Manila, Nov. 21-
Dec. 5, 1964)   2411

Karpf, A., co-auth. SEE no. 903, Chavanne, Josef.

Karr, H. W. S. SEE nos. 4067-69, Seton-Karr, H. W.

Karstens, Harry. SEE nos.
    3509, Pearson, G. H. Seventy-Mile Kid. [c1957];
    4372, Stuck, Hudson. Ascent of Denali ... 1914.

KASAHARA, HIROSHI. Fisheries resources of the North Pacific
Ocean. Vancouver, University of British Columbia, 1961. 135p.
illus. tables, maps, bibliog. (H. R. Macmillan Lectures in
Fisheries, pt. 1, 1960, as delivered Jan.-Feb. 1960)   2412

KASHEVAROFF, ANDREW P. Father Herman (Ascetic and Enlightener of
Alaska.) Translated by A. P. Kashevarov. [Sitka, 1916 ?] 12p.
(from "Ascetics of Valaam Monastery." 1872. cf no. 1534] 2413

KASHEVAROFF, ANDREW P. History of the discovery of Kodiak Island
Juneau, 1938. [tr. from "The chronological history of the discovery of the Aleutian Islands," by Vasilii N. Berkh. 1823. See
nos. 527-8]   2414

KASHEVAROFF, ANDREW P. St. Michael's Cathedral, Sitka, Alaska. By Rev. A. P. Kashevaroff, Juneau, Alaska. Juneau, Empire Printing Co., n. d. 32p. (incl. pls.) pls. photos by Jack Calvin, wrps.   2415

Kashevaroff, Andrew P. SEE ALSO no. 68, Alaska Hist. Assoc. Descriptive booklet Alaska Hist. Museum. 1922.

KASHEVAROV, ALEKSANDR FILIPPOVICH. Otryvki iz dnevnika korpusa flotskikh shturmanov poruchika A. F. Kashevarova, vedennogo im pri obozrĭenīĭ polĭārnogo berega Rossiĭskoĭ Amerika, po porucheniĭū Rossiĭsko-Amerikanskoĭ kompaniĭ v 1838 g. [TITLE TR. Excerpts from the diary of Naval Lietuenant A. F. Kashevarov, written during his survey of the polar coasts of Russian America on behalf of the Russian-American Company in 1838] S.-Peterburg, 1845. 20p. bibliog. [reprinted from Sankt-Peterburgskiĭā vĭedomosti, 1845, nos. 190, 191, 192 and 195)   2416

Kashevarov, Andrew P. SEE nos. 2413-15, Kashevaroff, Andrew P.

KATALLA PUBLICITY LEAGUE. History of the location of the Bering River coal fields. Katalla, Alaska, Jan. 1, 1912. Cordova, printed by Cordova Daily Alaskan Print., 1912. 8p.   2417

KAULFUSS, GEORGE F. Enumeration filicum quas in itinere circa terram legit cl. Adalbertus de Chamisso adiecti sin omnia harum plantarum genera permultasque species non satis cognitae vel novas animadversionibus. Lipsiae, sumtibus C. Cnobloch, 1824. 300p.   2418

KAVANAUGH, ETHEL. Wilderness homesteaders. Caldwell, Idaho, Caxton, 1950. 303p. front. pls. endmaps. [Homer area of Kenai Peninsula]   2419

KEELE, JOSEPH. A reconnaissance across the MacKenzie Mountains on the Pelly, Ross, and Gravel Rivers, Yukon and Northwest Territories. Ottawa, Government Print. Bureau, 1910. 54p. pls. map(fold.)   2420

KEELER, NICHOLAS EDWIN. A trip to Alaska and the Klondike in the summer of 1905. Cincinnati, Ebbert-Richardson Co., 1906. 115p. front. pls. port.   2421

KEEN, J. H., tr. Portions of the Book of Common Prayer in Haida; translated by J. H. Keen. [London ?], Society for Promoting Christian Knowledge, 1899. 39p. [Church of England]   2422

Keenok Club, Nome. SEE no. 4115, Shields, W. C.

Keep, Josiah. West American shells ... 1904. SEE no. 2423.

KEEP, JOSIAH. West coast shells; a familiar description of the marine, fresh water, and land mollusks of the United States found west of the Rocky Mountains, with numerous illustrations by Laura M. Mellen. S. F., Bancroft Bros. & Co., 1887. 230p. front. (col.), illus. OTHERS S. F., Carson, 1888 AND S. F., H. S. Crocker Co., 1893. ANR. WITH TITLE VARIANT West American shells ... including those of British Columbia and Alaska ... S. F., Whitaker & Ray, 1904. 300p. illus. ANR. WITH TITLE West coast shells ... S. F., Whitaker & Ray, 1910. rev. ed. 346p. front.(col.), illus. ANR. WITH TITLE West coast shells; a description in familiar terms of principal marine, fresh-water and land mollusks of the United States, British Columbia, and Alaska, found west of the Sierra. Revised by Joshua L. Bailey, jr. Stanford, Calif., Stanford University Press, 1935. 350p. illus. 2423

KEESING, ELDEE. Gorham's gold. Boston, R. G. Badger, 1915. 357p. [fict.] 2424

Keesing, L. D. SEE no. 2424, Keesing, Eldee.

KEGOZYAH KOZGA SOCIETY. Eleventh annual announcement, Nome, Alaska, 1912-13. Nome, 1912. 24p. 2425

KEIM, CHARLES J. Aghvook, white Eskimo; Otto Geist and Alaskan archaeology. College, University of Alaska Press, 1969. 1st ed. 313p. front.(col.), pls. index. 2426

KEIM, DeBENNEVILLE RANDOLPH. Our Alaskan wonderland and Klondike neighbor; a personal reminiscence and thirty years after. Washington, D. C. Harrisburg Pub. Co., 1898. 352p. front. pls. port. map. 2427

KEITHAHN, EDWARD LINNAEUS. Alaska for the curious. Seattle, Superior Pub. Co., 1966. 1st ed. 160p. illus. facsim. map, bibliog. (Alaska Centennial Edition, 1867-1967) 2428

KEITHAHN, EDWARD LINNAEUS. Alaskan igloo tales; illustrated by George Aden Ahgupuk. Seattle, Robert D. Seal Pub., 1958. 140p. illus. map(sketch), glossary. ANR. EARLIER EDITION WITH TITLE Igloo tales. By Edward L. Kiethahn [sic] Illustrated by George Aden Ahgupuk. Lawrence, Kansas, Haskell Institute, 1944. 122p. illus. map(sketch), glossary. (Indian Life Readers. Alaska series, no. 1. Education Division of U. S. Indian Service) ANR. Lawrence, Kansas, Haskell Institute, 1950. 142p. [Shishmaref, on Sarichef Island] 2429

KEITHAHN, EDWARD LINNAEUS. Eskimo adventure; another journey into the primitive. Seattle, Superior Pub. Co., 1963. 1st ed. 170p. illus. photos by author. [Shishmaref, on Sarichef Island] 2430

Keithahn, Edward Linnaeus. Igloo tales. 1944. SEE no. 2429.

KEITHAHN, EDWARD LINNAEUS. Monuments in cedar. Ketchikan, Roy Anderson, pub., 1945. 160p. illus. ports. pls. map(fold. in back), ethnol. chart, bibliog. ANR. Seattle, Superior Pub. Co., 1963. enl. and rev. 160p. illus.(some col.), bibliog. [totem poles] 2431

Keithahn, Edward Linnaeus. SEE ALSO nos.
    69, Alaska Hist. Assoc. Native Alaskan art ... 1959;
  3178, Morgan, J. Alaska and Hawaii. 1956.

Kejsarens, H. M., tr. SEE no. 2559, Krusenstern, A. J. von.

KELLETT, HENRY. The zoology of the voyage of H. M. S. *Herald*, under the command of Captain Henry Kellett during the years 1845-51. Published under authority Lords Comm. Admiralty. Edited by Prof. Edward Forbes, F.R.S. Vertebrals, including fossil mammals by Sir John Richardson. London, L. Reeve, 1854. 171p. pls. (some fold.) 2432

Kellett, Henry. SEE ALSO nos.
  1820-21; 1823-25; 1831. Great Britain. Parl.
    (Franklin search)
   4039, Seeman, B. C. Narrat. voyage *Herald* ... 1853;
   4041, Seeman, B. C. Botany voyage *Herald* ... 1852-57.

KELLY, NORA. The men of the Mounted. Toronto, J. M. Dent & Sons, 1949. 2433

KELSEY, CLAUDIA. Complete pocket book on how to be a pioneer. By Claudia Kelsey. Hand-screened by the author. "Very limited edition." Auke Bay, Alaska, Kelsey-Shepard Press, 1961. (13)p. sketches, hand-printed, wrps. 2434

KEMP, V. A. M. Without fear, favour or affection. Toronto, Longmans, Green, 1958. 264p. [R.C.M.P., incl. first patrol of northwest passage by the *St. Roch*] 2435

KENAI LAND LOCATIONS. Homesteading the Kenai-Homer area. Anchorage, [ca 1948] 2436

KENDRICK, SYLVESTER J. Chilkoot Pass, and songs of Alaska. L.A., Coast Printing Co., 1926. 61p. port. 2437

KENNAN, GEORGE. E. H. Harriman, a biography. Boston, Houghton, 1922. 2 vols. [has chapt. on Harriman Alaskan Expedition] 2438

KENNECOTT COPPER CORP. Application to have listed ... its stock, Feb. 14, 1916. N. Y., 1916. 8p. (N. Y. Stock Exchange Statement Comm. on Stock List) 2439

KENNECOTT COPPER CORP. First annual report for the period May 27, 1915 to Dec. 31, 1915. 20p. [incls. reports of Alaska Steam Ship Co., 1915 and Copper River and N. W. Railway Co., 1915] OTHERS 1916 AND 1917. ANR. 1918. 4th annual report [incls. Alaska Steam Ship Co., Copper River and N. W. Railway Co., Alaska Development and Mining Co. and Bering River Coal Co., 1918] OTHERS 1919 THROUGH 1924.   2440

KENNEDY, HOWARD ANGUS. The book of the West; the story of western Canada, its birth and early adventures, its youthful combats, its peaceful settlements, its great transformation, and its present ways. Toronto, Ryerson Press, 1925. 205p. front. pls. ports.   2441

KENNEDY, KAY J. The Wien Brothers' story. [Fairbanks ?], 1967. 38p. illus. photos, facsim. map, wrps.   2442

Kennedy, Kay J., co-edit. SEE ALSO no. 4400,
     Sunset. Alaska. 1963.

Kennicott, Robert. SEE no. 2326, James, Jas. Alton.

KENT, ROCKWELL. A northern Christmas; being the story of a peaceful Christmas in the remote and peaceful wilderness of an Alaskan island. N. Y., American Artists' Group, 1941. 26p. illustrated by author. (American Artists' Group Gift Books, no. 1) [Fox Island in Resurrection Bay, Kenai Peninsula - excerpted from no. 2445]   2443

KENT, ROCKWELL. Rockwellkentiana; few words and many pictures by Rockwell Kent and by Carl Zigrosser. A bibliography and list of prints. N. Y., Lakeside Press, 1933. 100p. pls. front.(col.)
                                                                   2444

KENT, ROCKWELL. Wilderness; a journal of quiet adventure in Alaska. With drawings by the author and an introduction by Dorothy Canfield. N. Y., G. P. Putnam, 1920. 217p. illus. front. endmaps. ANR. 1924. 2d ed. ANR. "... with new preface by author." N. Y., Modern Library, 1930. [see also no. 2443] 2445

Kent, Rockwell, illus. SEE ALSO nos.
     3489, Paramore, E. E., jr. Ballad Yukon Jake. 1928;
     4326, Stefansson, V. Unsolved mysteries Arctic. [c1938]

Kern, Edith Kingman [nee Poyer ?] SEE no. 1697, George, M. M.

KERR, MARK B. and R. H. CHAPMAN. Table of elevations within the Pacific Slope; compiled for the Sierra Club. S. F., 1895. 32p. (Sierra Club Pub. no. 8)   2446

KERR, ROBERT. A general history and collection of voyages and travels. Edinburgh, W. Blackwood, 1811-24.   2447

KERSTING, RUDOLF, edit. The white world; life and adventures within the Arctic Circle portrayed by famous living explorers; collected and arranged by R. Kersting. N. Y., Lewis, Scribner & Co., 1902. 386p. front. pls. ports. (Arctic Club)   2448

KESSEL, BRINA, ROBERT B. WEEDEN and GEORGE C. WEST. Bird-finding in Interior and Southcentral Alaska (with addendum including Barrow, Nome, Kotzebue, and Juneau.) no pl., Alaska Ornithological Society, 1967. 42p. maps, cover illus. by R. T. Wallen, bibliog.
2449

Kessel, Brina. SEE ALSO no. 1512, Fairbanks Bird Club.
    Bird-finding interior Alaska's highways. [1965]

KETCHIKAN ALASKA CHRONICLE. Facts about Alaska; a series of questions and answers covering the population, government, history, commerce, resources, industries, and climate of America's last frontier. Ketchikan, Ketchikan Alaska Chronicle, 1932. 82p. illus. photos, map, index. OTHERS 1935. rev. AND 1938. rev.   2450

KETCHIKAN CHAMBER OF COMMERCE. King Salmon Derby. Ketchikan, 1952. illus. map.   2451

KETCHIKAN, CITIZENS OF. The first city, Ketchikan, Saturday, December 23, 1916. A brochure this time and anon at Ketchikan, Alaska. Ketchikan, 1916. ANR. WITH TITLE The first city, Ketchikan, Alaska; Thursday, January 11, 1917; a brochure of facts published in the interests of the citizenry of Alaska's first division. Ketchikan, 1917.   2452

Ketchikan, Citizens of. SEE ALSO no. 2347, Jennings, R. W.
    An address ... 1917.

KETCHIKAN COMMERCIAL CLUB. Ketchikan, Alaska; resources and opportunities. Ketchikan, n. d. [ca 1920 ?] 16p. illus.   2453

Ketchikan "first city in Alaska" [1945 ?] SEE no. 77,
    [Alaska Life, Seattle]

KHLIEBNIKOV, KIRIL TIMOFEEVICH. Pervonaljnoe poselenie Russkikh v Amerikie. [TITLE TR. First settlement of Russians in America] Raduga, Revel, 1833.   2454

KHLIEBNIKOV, KIRIL TIMOFEEVICH. Zhizneopisanie Aleksandra Andreevicha Baranova, glavnago praviteliîa rossiîskikh Koloniî v Amerikie. [TITLE TR. Biography of A. A. Baranov, chief director of the Russian colonies in America] St. Petersburg, Morsk. tip., 1835. 209p.   2455

Khlîebnikov, Kiril Timofeevich. SEE ALSO nos.
    1763, Golovnin, V. M. Materialy dlîa istoriî ... 1861;
    3814, Ricks, M. B. Earliest hist. Alaska ... 1970;
    4706, Vishnevskiî, B. N. Puteshestvennik ... 1957.

KHVAT, LEV BORISOVICH. Tri puteshestviîa k Beringovu prolivu;
zapiski zhurnalista. [TITLE TR. Three voyages to Bering Strait;
notes of a journalist] Leningrad, Izd-vo Glavsevmorputi, 1949.
279p. [Chkalov, Gromov, Levanevskiî]   2456

Khvostov, Nikolai. SEE no. 1211, Davydov, G. I.

KICKBUSH, JOAN AREND. Life in an Eskimo village. Written and
illustrated by Joan Arend Kickbush. A cut-out and color book.
no pl., 1959. 17p. illus. map, wrps.   2457

Kickbush, Joan Arend, illus. SEE ALSO nos.
    3549, Peterson, L. J. This is Alaska. 1958;
    4500, Thomas, Tay. Cry in wilderness. [c1967]

Kidder, Harvey, illus. SEE no. 486, Bell, Margaret E.

Kiethahn, Edward L. SEE nos. 2428-31, Keithahn, Edward Linnaeus.

KILBOURNE, CHARLES E. An Army boy in Alaska. Philadelphia,
Penn Pub. Co., 1915. 346p. illus. by R. L. Boyer.   2458

Kilbuck, J. H. SEE no. 1678, Gapp, S. H.

Kimball, Eastburn and Assoc. SEE nos. 1535-36,
    Fay, Spofford & Thorndike.

Kimball, Yeffe, illus. SEE no. 661, Brindze, Ruth.
    Story of totem pole. 1951.

Kimura, William, illus. SEE no. 107, Alaska Review.

Kinegak, C., co-edit. SEE no. 2746, Lockwood, M. J.

King, James. SEE nos.
    437, [Bayly, Wm.] Orig. astronom. observations ... 1782;
    1013, Cook, Jas. Voyage Pac. Ocean ... 1784;
    4529, Three famous voyages ... n. d.

KING, RICHARD. The Franklin expedition from first to last. London, 1855.   2459

King Salmon Derby. 1952. SEE no. 2451, Ketchikan Chamber of
    Commerce.

KING, W. F. and O. H. TITTMAN. Joint report W. F. King, chief astronomer of the Department and Otto H. Tittman, of the United States Coast and Geodetic Survey, the commissioners appointed under the modus vivendi agreed to between Great Britain and the United States on the 20th October, 1899, to report in regard to the provisional boundary between the Territory of Alaska and the Dominion of Canada, about the head of Lynn Canal; also maps accompanying, and a copy of order in Council of the 20th of February, 1901. Ottawa, 1901. 7p.   2460

KINGSTON, WILLIAM HENRY GILES. Captain Cook; his life, voyages, and discoveries. By William H. G. Kingston. London, Religious Tract Society, n. d. 352p. front. pls. map(dble.)   2461

KINSCELLA, HAZEL GERTRUDE. Flag over Sitka; a story of the Alaska "transfer." Illustrated by Jacob Elshin. Lincoln, Nebraska, University Pub. Co., 1947. 83p. illus. map.   2462

KINZIE, ROBERT A. The Treadwell group of mines, Douglas Island, Alaska. N. Y., 1903. 53p.   2463

KIPPIS, ANDREW. A narrative of the voyages round the world performed by Captain James Cook. With an account of his life during the previous and intervening periods. N. Y., Leavitt & Allen, [1812 ?] 2 vols. in 1. MANY OTHERS, n. d. AND var. dates, var. publishers.   2464

KIPPIS, ANDREW. Captain Cook's voyages, with an account of his life, during the previous and intervening periods, by A. Kippis ... with twelve illustrations reproduced in exact facsimile from drawings made during the voyages. N. Y., Knopf, 1924. 404p. front. pls. ANR. WITH TITLE Captain Cook's voyages with an account of his life during the previous and intervening periods. By Andrew Kippis. N. Y., Knopf, 1925. 410p. front. pls. append. (Blue Jade Library)   2465

KIPPIS, ANDREW. The life of Captain James Cook. London, G. Nichols & G. G. J. & J. Robinson, 1788. 527p. front.(port.) OTHERS Dublin, H. Chamberlaine, 1788. 527p. front.(port.) AND Basil, J. J. Tourneisen, 1788. 2 vols.   2466

TRANSLATIONS - The life of ... 1788, chronologically.

Vie du Capitaine Cook, traduite de l'Anglois du Docteur Kippis, membre de la Société Royale de Londres. Paris, Hotel de Thou, 1789. 546p.   2467

Vie du Capitaine Cook. Traduit de l'Anglois du Docteur Kippis ... par M. Castera. Paris, Berneuse Co., 1789. 2 vols. 2468

KIPPIS, ANDREW. Voyages round the world from the death of Captain Cook to the present time, including remarks on the social condition of the inhabitants in the recently discovered countries, their progress in the arts; and more especially their advancement in religious knowledge. N. Y., Harper, 1844. 401p. (The Family Library, no. 172) OTHERS, var. dates, var. publishers. 2469

KIPPIS, ANDREW. Voyages round the world performed by Captain James Cook, with an account of his life during the previous and intervening periods. London, Cowie, Low & Co., 1826. 2 vols. front.(port.) 2470

Kippis, Andrew. SEE ALSO no. 2272, Interesting account ... extracted from Dr. Kippis. 1790.

KIRCHOF, N. A. J. Auszug aus Cook und Kings reise in den Jahren 1776 bis 80 nebst einem Verzeichnisse ihrer Beobachteten breiten und langen; ingleichen Bemerkungen über die Abweichung der Magnetnadel zum Beweise, dass die Lange der Oerter dadurch mit Gewissheit nicht bestimmet werden konne. Berlin, F. Nikolai, 1794. 62p. 2471

KIRK, ROBERT C. Twelve months in Klondike. By Robert C. Kirk; with one hundred illustrations and a map. London, W. Heinemann, 1899. 273p. front. pls. map. 2472

Kirkland, L., co-auth. SEE no. 4778, Weed, Alberta L.

KIRKWOOD, DEAN. The salmon industry in Alaska. Portland, Ore., C. C. Chapman Co., 1909. 59p. 2473

Kirwan, Archibald Laurence Patrick. A history of polar exploration. 1959. SEE no. 2474.

KIRWAN, ARCHIBALD LAURENCE PATRICK. The white road, a survey of polar exploration. London, Hollis & Carter, 1959. 374p. pls. maps, bibliog. ANR. WITH TITLE A history of polar exploration. N. Y., Norton, 1959. 374p. illus. maps, bibliog. [brief mention of Alaska] 2474

Kirwin, Harry A., co-auth. SEE no. 262, Andrews, R. W.

KITCHENER, LOIS DELANO. Flag over the north. By L. D. Kitchener. Seattle, Superior Pub. Co., 1954. 1st ed. 349p. illus. [the story of the Northern Commercial Co.] 2475

KITSON, ARTHUR. Captain James Cook, R.N.F.R.S., "The circumnavigator." London, John Murray, 1907. 525p. pls. map. ANR. N.Y., Dutton, 1907. [printed at Edinburgh Press] 525p. front.(port.), pls. facsims. map(fold.) 2476

KITSON, ARTHUR. The life of Captain James Cook, the circumnavigator. London, John Murray, 1911. 2d ed. 334p. illus. front. (port.), map(fold.) 2477

KITTLITZ, FRIEDRICH HEINRICH von. Denkwürdigkeiten einer Reise nach dem russischen Amerika nach mikronesien und durch Kamtschatka. Gotha, J. Perthes, 1858. 2 vols. 383p. and 463p. front. pls. 2478

KITTLITZ, FRIEDRICH HEINRICH von. Twenty-four views of the vegetation of the coasts and islands of the Pacific, with explanatory descriptions taken during the exploring voyage of the Russian corvette *Senjawin* under the command of Captain Lutke, 1827-29. London, Longman, Green, Longman & Roberts, 1861. x,68p. pls. [tr. of no. 2480] 2479

KITTLITZ, FRIEDRICH HEINRICH von. Vierundzwanzig Vegetations-Ansichten von Küstenländern und Inseln des Stillen Oceans, aufgenommen in den Jahren 1827, 28 und 29 auf der Entdeckungsreise der Kais. Russ. Corvette *Senjawin* unter Capitain Lütke durch F.H. von Kittlitz. Siegen und Wiesbaden, Friedrich'sche Verlagsbuchhandlung, 1844. 2 vols. [text and atlas] vi,68p. pls. ANR. Siegen, 1845. 1 vol. [text only] ANR. Berlin, Th. Grieben, 1862. 2d ed. [for tr. see no. 2479] 2480

Kittlitz, Friedrich Heinrich von. SEE ALSO no. 2732,
    Litke, F. P. Voyage autour du monde ... 1835.

KITTO, FRANKLIN HUGO. Yukon, land of the Klondike. By F. H. Kitto. Ottawa, 1929. 45p. illus. maps(sketch) (Canada. Northwest Territory and Yukon Branch, Department of the Interior) ANR. 1930. 48p. illus. maps. 2481

KIZER, BENJAMIN HAMILTON. The North Pacific International Planning Project. Based on memoranda by J. C. Rettie et al. N. Y., Institute of Pacific Relations, American Council, 1942. 39ℓ process print. (Paper no. 2) 2482

KIZER, BENJAMIN HAMILTON. The United States-Canadian northwest, a demonstration area for international postwar planning and development. Princeton, N. J., Princeton University Press, 1943. 71p. maps(some fold.), index. 2483

KLABEN, HELEN and BETH DAY. Hey, I'm alive ! N. Y., McGraw-Hill, 1964. illus. [plane crash in the Yukon] 2484

KLAPPHOLZ, LOWELL, edit. Gold ! Gold ! N. Y., McBride, 1959. 207p. illus. bibliog. [incls. chapts. on Klondike and Cape Nome, Alaska] 2485

Kleinenberg, S. E. SEE no. 4180, Sleptsov, M. M.

KLENGENBERG, CHRISTIAN. Klengenberg of the Arctic, an autobiography. Edited by Tom MacInnes. London, J. Cape, 1932. 300p.
front.(port.), pls. [incls. Pt. Hope and Barrow, Alaska]   2486

Klondike; a book for gold seekers. 1897. SEE no. 913,
    Chicago Record.

Klondike and all about it ... 1897. SEE no. 832, [Carey, J. J.]

KLONDIKE AND BOSTON GOLD MINING AND MANUFACTURING CO. Klondike
millions. Prospectus. The Klondike and Boston Gold Mining and
Manufacturing Co. Operating in Klondike District, North West
Territory. Official Brokers, Edw. C. Davis & Co., 244 Washington
St., Boston. 11 Wall Street, New York. Boston, Remington Prin-
ting Co., 1897. 12p. map.   2487

KLONDIKE AND BRITISH COLUMBIA GUIDE. Vancouver, B. C., n. d.
[ca 1896] 45p. illus. (Special Australasian Edition)   2488

"Klondike" Boyle. SEE no. 455, Beattie, Kim.

Klondike gold. 1897. SEE no. 142, Alaska-Yukon-Klondike Synd.

Klondike gold miners. 1897. SEE no. 143,
    Alaska-Yukon-Klondike Synd.

Klondike goldfields on Yukon. 1897. SEE no. 3490,
    [Paramore, H. H. ?]

Klondike grubstakes ... 1898. SEE no. 1870, Grubstake Pub. Co.

"Klondike Kate." SEE nos.
    2866, Lucia, E. Klondike Kate. 1962;
    4893, Willoughby, Barrett. Alaska holiday. 1940.

"Klondike Kid." SEE no. 4861, Wiedemann, Thos.

"Klondike Mike." SEE no. 1265, Denison, Merrill.

Klondike official guide... 1898. SEE no. 3394, Ogilvie, Wm.

Klondike; the Chicago Record's book ... 1897. SEE no. 913,
    Chicago Record.

Klondike; the new gold fields of Alaska ... 1897. SEE no. 4295,
    Steele, Jas. Wm.

"Klondy" Nelson. SEE no. 3288, Nelson, Klondy.

KLONDYKE and the gold fields of Alaska. London, American Jubilee
Co., 1897. 1st ed. 128p. illus. maps, wrps.   2489

Klondyke and Yukon guide ... 1898. SEE no. 3610,
    Pioneer Print. & Pub. Co.

Klondyke gold fields ... n. d. SEE no. 1774, Goodman, A. E.

KLONDYKE MINING LAWS; the Canadian gold fields, how to get there,
where to purchase supplies. Victoria, B. C., Graphic Pub. Co.,
1897. 31p. [incls. White Pass route]   2490

Klondyker ... 1897. SEE no. 4033, Seattle-Alaska Intelligence
    Bureau.

KNABEN, GUNVOR. On the evolution of the *radicatum*-group of the
scapiflora papavers as studied in 70 and 56 chromosome species;
part A, cytotaxonomical aspects. Stockholm, Almqvist & Wicksell,
1959. 74p. illus. pls. tables, bibliog. (Opera botanica,
vol. 2:3) [northern hemisphere, incl. Alaska]   2491

KNAPP, EDWARD J. General convention, 1910. The Church in Alaska
vs the civil law. Shall the Church in Alaska defy the civil law
of marriage and divorce in the case of native marriages ? N. Y.,
C. G. Burgoyne, 1910. 9p.   2492

KNAPP, FRANCES and RHETA LOUISE (CHILDE) DORR. The Thlinkets of
southeastern Alaska. By Frances Knapp and Rheta Louise Childe.
Chicago, Stone & Kimball, 1896. 197p. front. pls. ports.   2493

KNIGHT, CLAYTON and ROBERT C. DURHAM. Hitch your wagon; the
story of Bernt Balchen. Drexel Hill, Penna., Bell Pub. Co.,
1950. 332p. front. pls. ports. sketches by Clayton Knight, endmaps. ANR. 1950. 2d print. with corrections. [reference to
World War II aviation in Alaska]   2494

Knight, Errol Lorne. SEE nos.
    3158, Montgomery, Richard Gill. "Pechuck,"... 1932;
    4314, Stefansson, V. Adventure Wrangel Isl. 1925.

KNIGHT, FRANK. Young Captain Cook. N. Y., Roy Pub. Co., 1966.
                                                             2495

Knight, John Irvine. SEE no. 4314, Stefansson, V.

Knight, Lorne. SEE [cross-references] Knight, Errol Lorne.

KNIGHT'S ISLAND Alaska Copper Co. Seattle, [1905 ?] 16p. illus.
map.   2496

KNIK COMMERCIAL CLUB. Resources of Knik, Alaska. Knik, n. d.
12p.   2497

KNOPOFF, L.   Analytical calculation of the fault-plane problem.
Dominion Observatories, 1961.   (Canada. Pub. vol. 24, no. 10)
pp.309-15.   graphs, tables, bibliog. (also issued as: University
of California Institute of Geophysics Pub. no. 203) [Mt. Fairweather earthquake of July 10, 1958]   2498

KNOPOFF, L.   Statistical accuracy of the fault-plane problem.
Dominion Observatories, 1961.   (Canada. Pub. vol. 24, no. 10)
pp.317-19.   graphs, bibliog. (also issued as: University of
California Institute of Geophysics, Pub. no. 204) [Mt. Fairweather earthquake of July 10, 1958]   2499

Knox, J. A.   SEE no. 171, All about Klondike   ... [1897]

KNOX, OLIVE ELSIE.   By paddle and saddle.   Toronto, Macmillan,
1943.   270p.   [biog. of Sir George Simpson]   2500

Kobuk maiden ... [1903 ?]   SEE no. 3773, Reed, Elmer.

Kodiak earthquake.   [ca 1964]   SEE no. 2303, Island Pub. Co.

KOESTLER, AUGUST E.   Sourdough flights;   Koestler Alaska flight
cover catalogue.   Norfolk, Va., Jesse G. Johnson, 1941.   2d ed.
rev. ltd. 200 autographed copies.   60p.   illus. maps. [1st ed.
in sections in Western Stamp Collector starting with Jan. 11,
1936]   2501

Köhler, J. T., tr.   SEE no. 2533, Krasheninnikov, S. P.

KOHLSTEDT, EDWARD DELOR.   A glimpse of Alaska.   Philadelphia,
Board of Home Missions, n. d.   [ca 1930]   12p.   [Methodist Episcopal Church]   2502

KOHLSTEDT, EDWARD DELOR.   William Duncan, founder and developer
of Alaska's Metlakatla Christian Mission.   Palo Alto, Calif.,
National Press, 1957.   82p.   illus.   2503

KOL, ERZSÉBET.   Tiszaparttól Alaszkáig.   Egy műmelléklettel.
Term. Tud. Tars, 1940.   327p.   pls. maps, bibliog. (No. 12) 2504

Komoda, Kiyoaki, illus.   SEE nos.
   3767, Redding, R. H.   Aluk, Alaskan caribou.   1967;
   3768, Redding, R. H.   Mara, the weasel.   1968.

KONDA, S.   Northern fisheries of Japan.   Sapporo, Japan, School
of Fishery, Hokkaido University, 1933.   pp.1-6 and 1-268. tables,
map(dble.)   (Bulletin, vol. 3) [text in Japanese, summary in
English - incl. crabs in Bering Sea off Alaska]   2505

KOO, TED SWEI-YEN.   Abundance, size and age of red salmon smolts
from the Wood River System, 1959. Seattle, University of Washington, 1960.   9p.   (Fisheries Research Institute Circular no. 118)
[Bristol Bay]   2506

KOO, TED SWEI-YEN. Red salmon smolt enumeration in the Wood River system. Report of field operations and results, 1958. Seattle, University of Washington, 1959. 11p. (Fisheries Research Institute Circular no. 103)   2507

KOO, TED SWEI-YEN. Studies of Alaska red salmon. Seattle, University of Washington, 1962. 449p. photos, figs. tables, maps, glossary, bibliog. (Publications in Fisheries, new ser., vol. 1. Contributions College of Fisheries, no. 105-113)   2508

KOOTENAI GUIDE ... to the mining camps of British Columbia and Klondike. Rossland, Canada, 1898. 78p. map.   2509

KORTRIGHT, FRANCIS H. The ducks, geese and swans of North America, a vade mecum for the naturalist and sportsman. Washington, D. C., American Wildlife Institute, 1942. ltd. ed. of 1000 copies. 476p. pls.(col.), tables(fold.), maps(sketch), bibliog. OTHERS var. dates. ANR. Harrisburg, Penna., Stackpole, 1953. 2510

KOSMOS, GEORGE. Alaska sourdough stories. Illustrated by Eustace Ziegler. Edited by Mary Lou Patton. Seattle, Robert D. Seal Publication, 1956. 30p. illus.   2511

KOSTINENKO, G. I. Stroitel'stvo na vechnoĭ merzlote za rubezhom; Alĭaska, Kanada, Grenlandiĭa. [TITLE TR. Construction on permafront abroad; Alaska, Canada, Greenland] Moskva, Gosstroĭizdat, 1962. 59p. illus. tables, maps, bibliog.   2512

KOSTLIVTŜOV, S. Viedomostj o nastoiashchim polozhenii Ross.-Amer. Kolonii. [TITLE TR. Report of existing conditions in the Russian-American colonies] St. Petersburg, 1860.   2513

Kostlivtsov, S. SEE ALSO no. 4620, U.S.S.R.
     Komitet ob Ustroistvĭe ... 1863-64.

Kostrometinov, S. I., tr. SEE no. 4678, Veniaminov, I. E. P.

KOTZEBUE, AUGUST FRIEDRICH FERDINAND von. Count Benyowsky; or, the conspiracy of Kamtschatka. A tragicomedy in five acts. Translated from the German by the Rev. W. Render, teacher of the German language, in the University of Cambridge. Cambridge, printed for the author and sold by J. Deighton and J. Nicolson, 1798. 210p. (in F. Linge. Collection of plays. vol. 248, no. 4) ANR. Baltimore, printed for Thomas, Andrews and Butler by John W. Butler, 1803. 80p. (no. 2 of: Select plays)
                                                                      2514

KOTZEBUE, AUGUST FRIEDRICH FERDINAND von. La Peyrouse; a comedy in two acts. Translated by Charles Smith. N. Y., 1800.   2515

Kotzebue, Otto von.   [Alphabetical title guide to chronological
     entries]

KOTZEBUE, OTTO von.   Puteshestvie v ĭuzhnyĭ okean i v Beringov
proliv dlĭa ot'iskaniĭa sĭevero-vostochnago morskago prokhoda,
predpriĭatoe v 1815, 1816, 1817 i 1818 godakh izhdiveniem Ego
Sĭatel'stva Grafa Nikolaĭa Petrovicha Rumĭantsova na korablie
Riurikĭe pod nachal'stvom flota leĭtenanta Kotsebu.   [TITLE TR.
Voyage to the Southern Ocean and Bering Straits for the purpose
of finding the Northeast Passage, undertaken in the years 1815-
18, at the expense of the Count N. P. Rumiantsev on the ship
Rurik under the command of Lieutenant of the Navy Kotzebue]
Sanktpeterburg, v tip. Nik. Grecha, 1821-23.   3 vols. 168p. 346p.
and 436p.   pls.(some col., some fold.), tables.   ALSO Atlas k
puteshestviĭu Leĭtenanta Kotzebu no Korablie *Riurikĭe* v ĭuzhnoe
More i v Beringov Proliv.   B. g. i. m.   [TITLE TR.   Atlas to the
voyage of Lt. Kotzebue on the ship *Rurik* into the South Sea and
Bering Strait]
                                                                  2516

     TRANSLATIONS - Puteshestvie v ĭuzhnyĭ okean ... 1821-23,
          chronologically.

     Entdeckungs-Reise in die Süd-See und nach der Beringsstrasse
          zur Erforschung einer nordöstlichen Durchfahrt.   Unternommen
          in den Jahren 1815, 1816, 1817 und 1818, auf Kosten sr. Er-
          laucht des ... Grafen Rumanzoff auf dem Schiffe *Rurick* under
          dem befehle des Lieutenants der russisch-kaiserlichen Marine
          Otto von Kotzebue ... [TITLE TR.   Voyage of discovery in the
          South Sea and to Bering Strait, to explore for a northeast
          passage.   Undertaken in the years 1815-18, at the expense of
          his Highness Count Rumanzoff on the ship *Rurik*, under com-
          mand of Lieutenant of the Imperial Russian Navy Otto von
          Kotzebue]   Weimar, Gebrüder Hoffman, 1821.   3 vols. 168p.
          176p. and 241p.   pls.(col.) some fold.), maps(some fold.),
          tables(some fold.)   ANR. WITH TITLE Entdeckungsreise in die
          Sudsee ... fur die Jugend bearbeitet V. C. Hildebrandt.
          Hanover, 1821.   2 vols.   2517

     A voyage of discovery;   into the South Sea and Beering's
          Straits, for the purpose of exploring a North-East Passage,
          undertaken in the years 1815-18, at the expense of His High-
          ness Count Romanzoff, in the ship *Rurik*, under the command
          of the Lieutenant in the Russian Imperial Navy, Otto von

Kotzebue. London, Longman, Hurst, Rees, Orme, and Brown.
1821. 3 vols. 358p. 433p. and 442p. fronts.(col.), ports.
(col.), pls.(some col.), maps(some fold.) ANR. Amsterdam, N.
Israel and N. Y., Da Capo Press, 1969. facsim. of Longman,
1821 ed. (Bibliotheca Australiana Ser. 2, nos. 17, 18 and
19)   2518

KOTZEBUE, OTTO von. TRANSLATIONS - Puteshestvie v ĭuzhnyĭ
okean ... 1821-23, chronologically.

Voyage of discovery in the South Sea, and to Behring's Straits,
in search of a North-East Passage, undertaken in the years
1815, 16, 17, and 18 in the ship *Rurik*. London, R. Phillips,
1821. abr. 2 pts. in 1. 220p. (Voyage round the world.
Published in "New voyages and travels," edited by Sir Richard
Phillips, vol. 6)   2519

Ontdekkingsreis in der Zuidsee en naar de Beringsstraat in de
jaren 1815-18. Uit het Hgd. Amsterdam, 1822. 3 vols. pls.
maps. [has append. on Krusenstern]   2520

KOTZEBUE, OTTO von. Puteshestvie vokrug svieta, sovershenne po
povelieniĭu Gosudaria Imperatora Aleksandra Pervago, na voennom
shliŭpie *Predpriiatiĭ*, v. 1823, 24, 25 i 26 godakh, pod nachal'-
stvom Flota kapitan-leĭtenanta Koĭsebu. [TITLE TR. A voyage
round the world performed under the order of the Emperor Alexander the First on the war-sloop *Predpriiatie* in 1823-26 under command of Lt.-Commander of the Navy Kotzebue] Sanktpeterburg, V.
morskoi tip., 1828. 200p. maps(fold.)   2521

TRANSLATIONS - Puteshestvie vokrug svieta ... 1828,
chronologically.

Neue reise um die Welt in den Jahren 1823-26. Weimar and St.
Petersburg, Hoffman, 1830. 2 vols. 191p. and 172p. pls.
(col.), maps.   2522

Nieuwe ontdekkingsreise rondom de wereild. Uit het hgd. Haarlem, 1830. 2 vols. 254p. and 271p. pls. maps.   2523

A new voyage round the world, in the years 1823, 24, 25, and
26. London, Henry Colburn & Richard Bentley, 1830. 2 vols.
enl. tr. 341p. and 362p. port. pl. maps. [has append. by
Eschscholtz] ANR. Amsterdam, N. Israel and N. Y., Da Capo
Press, 1967. facsim. ed. 2 vols. (Bibliotheca Australiana,
2d ser. nos. 20 and 21)   2524

Resa omkring jorden, ofversatt af A. W. Stockholm, 1830.
394p. pl.   2525

Nye Reise om Jorden, oversat af Fr. Schaldemose. Copenhagen,
1840.   2526

KOTZEBUE, OTTO von. TRANSLATIONS - Puteshestvie vokrug svieta
... 1828, chronologically.

  Otto v. Kotzebues neue reise um die Welt ... fur die jugend
    bearbeitet. Leipzig, 1847. 2d ed.   2527

  Die neueren entdeckungsreisen fur die Jugend bearbeitet. Leip-
    zig, 1848.   2528

KOTZEBUE, OTTO von. Puteshestviia vokrug sveta. Izdanie vtoroe.
[TITLE TR. Voyages around the world] Second edition. Moskva,
Gos Izd-vo Geogr. lit-ry, 1942. 332p. port. maps(sketch)   2529

Kotzebue, Otto von. SEE ALSO nos.
       884, Chamisso, L. C. A. von. Bemerkungen ... 1821;
       885, Chamisso, L. C. A. von. De animalibus ... [1819];
       886, Chamisso, L. C. A. von. Reise um die Welt ... 1836;
      1493, Eschscholtz, J. F. Zoologischer atlas ... 1829;
      2137, Hoffman, E. von. Geognostiche ... 1829;
      2700, Lialina, M. A., edit. Russkie moreplavateli ... 1896;
      2954, Mahr, August C. Visit of "Rurik" to S. F. 1816. 1932;
      3340, Nordpolarlander ... 1822;
      3689, Price, E. V. Astronomische ... 1830;
      4219, Snelling, Wm. Jos. Polar regions ... 1831.

KRARUP-NIELSEN, AAGE, edit. Jordens erobring; alle tiders store
opdagelsesrejser, redigeret af Aage Krarup Nielsen, skrevet af
dr. phil. Kaj Birket-Smith, dr. phil. Knud Rasmussen, magister
Einar Storgaard, professor, dr. phil. P. Tuxen og redaktøren.
[TITLE TR. The conquest of the earth. The great explorations
of all times. Edited by Aage Krarup Nielsen. Written by Kaj
Birket-Smith, Ph. D, Knud Rasmussen, Ph.D., Einar Storgaard,
M. A., Prof. P. Tuxen, Ph.D. and the editor] København, C.
Erichsen, 1930-32. 6 vols. pls.(some col.), ports. maps(incl.
1 fold.), index. [vol. 6 contains "Polarforskningens saga," by
K. J. V. Rasmussen. See also no. 3747 and no. 3748]   2530

Krasheninnikov, Stefan Petrovich. [Alphabetical title guide to
    chronological entries]

                Aardrykskundige ... 2536.
                Histoire de Kamtschatka ... 2534.
                Histoire et description ... 2535.
                Opisanie zemli Kamchatki ... 2531.
                Opisanie zemli Kamtschatki sotschinennoje ... 2533.
                The history of Kamtschatka ... 2532.

KRASHENINNIKOV, STEFAN PETROVICH. Opisanie zemli Kamchatki sochinennoe. [TITLE TR. A description of Kamchatka] St. Petersburg, Imp. Akademiia nauk, 1755. 2 vols. 438p. and 319p. pls.
(some fold.), maps(some fold.) ANR. St. Petersburg, 1786. 2d
ed. ANR. 1818-19. 3rd ed. 2 vols. 493p. and 486p. ANR. WITH

TITLE Opisanie zemli Kamchatki, v izlozheniĭ po podlinniku i pod
red N. V. Dumetrashko i L. G. Kamanina. Moskva, Gos izd-vo geogr.
lit-ry, 1948. abr. ed. 292p. illus. pl. maps(incl. some fold.)
ANR. Moskva-Leningrad, Izd-glavsevmorputi, Akademiĭa nauk S.S.R.
Institute ètnografiĭ, 1949. 2 vols. in 1. enl. Edited by L. S.
Berg, A. A. Grigor'ev and N. N. Stepanov. 840p. ports. pls.
maps(incl. some fold.), ftntes.   2531

KRASHENINNIKOV, STEFAN PETROVICH. TRANSLATIONS - Opisanie zemli
    Kamchatki ... 1755, chronologically.

  The history of Kamtschatka, and the Kurilski Islands, with the
    countries adjacent; illustrated with maps and cuts. Pub-
    lished at Petersbourg in the Russian language, by order of
    Her Imperial Majesty, and translated into English by James
    Grieve, M.D. Glocester, printed by R. Raikes; London, T.
    Jefferys, 1764. abr. ed. 8,280,8p. front. pls.(some fold.),
    maps(fol..) ANR. Chicago, Quadrangle, 1962. 288p. reprint.
                                                                    2532

  Opisanie zemli Kamtschatki sotschinennoje Stepanom Kraschenin-
    nikowym ... d. i Beschreibung des Landes Kamtschatka ver-
    fasset von Stephan Krascheninnikow ... II Theile 4. Peters-
    burg bey der Academ. der Wissenschaften 1755 in einem Aus-
    zuge in englischer Sprache bekant gemacht von Jacob Grieve...
    und mit Landkarten und Kupferbildern 1764 hrsg. von T. Jef-
    ferys ... nun in das deutsch übersetzet und mit Anmerkungen
    erläutert von Johann Tobias Köhler ... [TITLE TR. Descrip-
    tion of Kamchatka by ... published by the Academy of Sci-
    ences, St. Petersburg, 1755, made known in an extract in Eng-
    lish by James Grieve and published with maps and copper en-
    gravings by J. Jefferys 1764; now translated into German
    with remarks by Johann Tobias Köhler] Lemgo, Meyerische
    Buchhandlung, 1766. 334p. front. pls.(some fold.), map
    (fold.)   2533

  Histoire de Kamtschatka, des iles Kurilski, et des contrees
    voisins, publiee en langue russienne. Tr. par E____ . Ly-
    ons, Benoit Duplain, 1767. 2 vols. 327p. and 359p. maps.
                                                                    2534

  Histoire et description du Kamtchatka ... Trans. du Russe.
    Amsterdam, M. M. Rey, 1770. 2 vols. 439p. and 493p. pls.
    (fold.), tables(fold.), map(fold.)   2535

  Aardrykskundige en natuurlyke beschryving van Kamtschatka, en
    de Kurilsche eilanden, met een gedeelte der kust van Amerika.
    Op Russ-kaiserlyk bevel, te Petersburg, in de Russische taal
    uitg. Vervolgens in het Engelsh en Hoogduitsch, en nu in her
    Nederduitsch vertaald. [TITLE TR. Description of the geogra-
    phy and natural life of Kamchatka and the Kurile Islands, with
    a section on the coast of America ... published in Russian at

Petersburg by the Russian Imperial Command, then translated
into English and German and now into Dutch] Amsterdam, J. W.
Willemsz, 1770. 384p.,14p. pls.(fold.)   2536

Krasheninnikov, Stefan Petrovich. SEE also no. 1621,
    Fradkin, N. G. S. P. Krasheninnikov. 1951.

KRASILOVSKY, PHYLLIS. Benny's flag. Drawings by W. T. Mars.
Cleveland, World Pub. Co., 1960. 34p. illus.   2537

KRASINSKIĬ, G. D. Puti Severa. (Severnye vozdushnye ėkspeditsii
1927 i 1928 gg. Ostrov Vrangeliia lia i pervyĭ Lenskiĭ reis.
[TITLE TR. Routes to the north. (Northern aerial expeditions
1927-28; Wrangel Island and the first Lena trip.) Moskva, Izd-
vo OSOAVIAKHIM, 1929. 159p. illus.   2538

KRATT, IVAN FEDOROVICH. Velikiĭ okean. [TITLE TR. The great
ocean] Leningrad, Izd-vo TSK VLKSM Molodaia guardiia, 1950.
552p. illus. map(fold.) [historical fiction about the Pacific
Ocean]   2539

KRAUSE, ARTHUR and AUREL KRAUSE. Katalog ethnologischer gegen-
stände aus dem Tschuktschenlande und dem südöstlichen Alaska.
Gesammelt von den Gebrüdern Dr. Arthur und Aurel Krause in den
Jahren 1881/82. [TITLE TR. Catalog of ethnographic objects from
Chukchi land and southeast Alaska. Collected by the brothers Dr.
Arthur and Dr. Aurel Krause in 1881-82] Bremen, Deutsche geogra-
phisce Blätter, 1882. 16p. (Bd. 5, Heft. 4, Anlage)   2540

KRAUSE, AUREL. Die Tlingit-Indianer; Ergebnisse einer Reise
nach der Nordwestküste von Amerika und der Beringstrasse ausgeführt im Auftrage der Bremer geographischen Gesellschaft in den
Jhhren 1880-81, durch die Doctoren Arthur und Aurel Krause,
geschildert von Dr. Aurel Krause. [TITLE TR. The Tlingit Indians, results of a trip to the northwest coast of America and
Bering Strait, made by Dr. Arthur and Dr. Aurel Krause, in the
years 1880-81, under the auspices of the Geographical Society of
Bremen, described by Dr. Aurel Krause] Jena, H. Costenoble,
1885. 420p. illus. pls. map(fold.), tables, append. bibliog.
[for tr. see no. 2542]   2541

KRAUSE, AUREL. The Tlingit Indians; results of a trip to the
northwest coast of America and the Bering Straits. Translated by
Erna Gunther. Seattle, University of Washington, 1956. 310p.
pls. sketches, figs. map(fold. separate), notes, glossary, bibliog. index. (American Ethnological Society Monograph) [tr. of
no. 2541]   2542

KRAUSE, EDUARD. Vorgeschichtliche Fischereigeräte und neuere
Vergleichsstücke; eine vergleichende Studie als Beitrag zur Geschichte des Fischereiwesens. [TITLE TR. Prehistoric fishing im-
plements and their new equivalents; a comparative study as a

contribution to the history of the fishing industry] Berlin,
1904. 168p. pls. index. (also in: Zeitschrift für Fischerei
und deren Hilfswissenschaften, 1904. Bd. 11, Heft 304, pp.133-
300) [incls. Aleuts, Eskimos, and west coast Indians]   2543

Krause, J. V., tr. SEE no. 717, [Buache, Philip]

Krenov, D., tr. SEE nos.
    528, Berkh, V. N. Chronolog. hist. ... 1938;
    4537, Tikhmenev, P. A. Hist. ... Russ.-Amer. Co. 1939-40.

KREPS, E. Science of trapping, describing the fur bearing animals, their nature, habits, and distribution, with practical
methods for their capture. St. Louis, Mo., Harding Pub. Co.,
1909. rev. ed. 245p. illus. [incls. Alaskan and B. C.]   2544

Kroeber, A. L. SEE no. 1353, Driver, H. E.

KROTT, PETER. Demon of the north. N. Y., Knopf, 1959. illus.
                                                               2545

KRUBER, A. A., edit. Biblioteka Puteshestvii. Moscow and St.
Petersburg, 1924. (3rd ser., no. 4) [incls. discovery of Kamchatka and Bering's expedition]   2546

KRUG, WERNER G. Sprungbrett Alaska; Land der zukunft. [TITLE
TR. Springboard Alaska; land of the future] Hamburg, Hoffmann
& Campe Verlag, 1953. 367p. illus. map(fold.) [impressions of
personal visit]   2547

KRUGER, CHARLOTTE. Land of tomorrow. Grand Rapids, Mich., Zondervan, 1947. 185p.   2548

Krusenstern, Adam Johann von. [Alphabetical title guide to
    chronological entries]

Atlas ... 2549.	Resa omkring ... 2559.
Beschreibung ... 2558.	Reise omkring ... 2562.
Beyträge ... 2552.	Supplemens ... 2551.
Puteshestvie ... 2553-4.	Uebersicht ... 2557.
Recueil de memoires ... 2550.	Viaggio intorno ... 2563-4.
Reise gutmannschen ... 2566.	Voyage around ... 2561.
Reise om de wereld ... 2560.	Voyage autour ... 2565.
Reise um die Welt ... 2555-6.	Wörter-sammlungen ... 2567.

KRUSENSTERN, ADAM JOHANN von. Atlas de l'Ocean Pacifique dresse
par M. de Krusenstern Contre-Amiral et Directeur de Corps des
Cadets de la Marine ... S. Petersbourg, publie par ordre de sa
Majeste Imperiale, 1827. plans, maps(some dble.) [for accompanying volumes see nos. 2550 and 2551]   2549

KRUSENSTERN, ADAM JOHANN von.   COMPANION VOLUMES TO Atlas...1827.

Recueil de mémoires hydrographiques, pour servir d'analyse et
  d'explication a l'atlas de l'Ocean Pacifique par le Commodore de Krusenstern. [TITLE TR. Collection of hydrographic
  memoirs to serve as analysis and explanation of the Atlas of
  the Pacific Ocean] St. Pétersbourg, de l'Imprimerie de Dé-
  partment de l'Instruction Publique, 1824.   2550

Supplemens au recueil de mémoires hydrographiques ... par le
  Vice-Amiral de Krusenstern. St. Pétersbourg, de l'Imprimerie
  de A. Pluchart, éditeur du dictionnaire encyclopédique,
  1835.   2551

KRUSENSTERN, ADAM JOHANN von.   Beytrage zur Hydrographie der
Grössen Ozeane als Erläuterungen zu einer Charte des ganzen Erd-
kreises nach Mercator's Projection von A. J. von Krusenstern,
Capitain Commodor der Russisch Kaiserlichen Marine. [TITLE TR.
Contribution to the hydrography of the oceans as explanations
for a global map on Mercator's projection] Leipzig, bey Paul
Gotthelf Kummer, 1819. 248p. map.   2552

KRUSENSTERN, ADAM JOHANN von.   Puteshestvie vokrug svieta v 1803,
4, 5 i 1806 godakh. Po poveleniiu Ego Imperatorskago Velichestva Aleksandra Pervago, na korabliakh *Nadezhdie i Nevie*, pod nachal'stvom flota kapitan-leitenanta, nynie kapitana vtorago ranga
Kruzenshterna. [TITLE TR. Voyage round the world, in the years
1803, 1804, 1805, 1806, by order of His Imperial Majesty Alexander the First, on board the ships *Nadezhda* and *Neva*, under the
command of Lieutenant Commander, now Commander Krusenstern]
Sanktpeterburg, Morskoi tipografii, 1809-13. 3 vols. 388p.,
471p. and 449p. + atlas. pls.(some dble.), maps(some dble.),
tables.   2553

KRUSENSTERN, ADAM JOHANN von.   Puteshestvie vokrug sveta v 1803,
1804, 1805 i 1806 godakh na korabliakh "Nadezhde" i "Neve." Pod
red N. N. Zubova. [TITLE TR. Voyage round the world in the
years 1803-06 on board the ships *Nadezhda* and *Neva*. Edited by
N. N. Zubov] Moskva, Gos. izd-vo geogr. lit-ry, 1950. 319p.
illus. port. pls. map, glossary.   2554

TRANSLATIONS - Puteshestvie vokrug svieta ... 1809-13,
  chronologically.

Reise um die Welt in den Jahren 1803, 1804, 1805, und 1806;
  auf Befehl seiner kaiserlichen Majestät Alexander des Ersten
  auf den Schiffen *Nadeshda* und *Newa*, unter dem Commando des
  Capitains von der kaiserlichen Marine, A. J. von Krusenstern.
  St. Petersburg, Gedruckt in der Schnoorschen Buchdruckerey,
  1810-12. 3 vols. 353p., 436p. and 376p. WITH atlas: St.
  Petersburg, 1814. front. pls. maps. ANR. 1810. 1 vol. 2555

KRUSENSTERN, ADAM JOHANN von.   TRANSLATIONS - Puteshestvie vokrug
svieta ... 1809-13, chronologically.

Reise um die Welt, in den Jahren 1803, 1804, 1805 und 1806, auf
Befehl seiner Kaiserl. Majestät Alexanders des Ersten, auf
den Schiffen *Nadeshda* und *Newa*, unter dem Commando des Capi-
täns von der Kaiserl. Marine A. J. von Krusenstern ... Zweite
rechtmässige, mit Bewilligung des Verfassers veranstaltete
und mit dessen Bildniss gezierte, wörtlich nach dem Original
gedruckte Ausaabe.   Berlin, Haude und Spener, 1811.   2 vols.
in 3.   450p.,10p.   8p.,294p. and 8p.269p.   port. fronts. pls.
ANR. Hildburgshausen, 1828.   2556

Uebersicht der Reise um die Welt in den Jahren 1803-06.   Leipzig, 1810-11.   2 vols.   2557

Beschreibung seiner Reise um die Welt.   Fur die Jugend nach
Campe's Lesart bearbeitet.   Magdeburg, n. d.   2558

Resa omkring jorden forrattad aren 1803-6 pa H. M. Kejsarens
of Ryssland befallning.   Ofwersattning.   Orebo, 1811-12.
3 vols.   2559

Reise om de wereld gedaan in de jaren 1803-6, op bevel van
Alexander den Eersten.   Uit het Hgd.   Haarlem, 1811-15. 4
vols. pls. map.   2560

Voyage around the world, in the years 1803, 1804, 1805, and
1806, by order of His Imperial Majesty Alexander the First,
on board the ships *Nadeshda* and *Neva*, under the command of
Capt. A. J. von Krusenstern ... Translated from the original
German by Richard Belgrave Hoppner ... London, J. Murray,
printed by C. Roworth, 1813.   2 vols. 314p. and 404p.   pls.
map.   ANR. Ridgewood, N. J., Gregg Press, 1967.   Edited by
E. S. Dodge.   2 vols.   764p.   (America and the Pacific Series, vol. 7)   ANR. Amsterdam, N. Israel and N. Y., Da Capo
Press, 1967.   2 vols.   facsim. ed.   (Bibliotheca Australiana, 4th ser.)   2561

Reise omkring Jorden, oversat ved A. E. Boye.   Copenhagen,
1818.   2562

Viaggio intorno al mondo fatto negli anni 1803-6 d'ordine di
sua M.I. Alessandro I, su i vacelli la *Nadeshda* e la *Neva* Tr.
dal tedescodal Sig. Angiolini.   Milan, 1818.   3 vols.   2563

Viaggio intorno al mondo fatto negli anni 1803-4-5 e 1806
d'ordine di S. M. imp. Alessandro primo imperatore di Russia
... Raccolta di viaggi ... T. LXXXIX-XCV.   Torino, Dalla
stamperia Alliana, 1830.   2564

KRUSENSTERN, ADAM JOHANN von. TRANSLATIONS - Puteshestvie vokrug
svieta ... 1809-13, chronologically.

Voyage autour du monde, fait dans les années 1803, 1804, 1805,
et 1806, par les ordres de sa majesté impériale Alexandre
ler, empéreur de Russia, sur les vaisseaux la *Nadiejeda* et la
Neva commandés par M. de Krusenstern ... Tr. de l'aveu et
avec des additions de l'auteur, la traduction revue par M.
J.-B.-B. Eyries ... Paris, Gide fils, 1821. 2 vols. and
atlas. 418p. and 531p. pls. maps.   2565

Reise der gutmannschen Zoglinde um unsere Erde. Hannover,
1821. 2 vols. [tr. fr. no. 2565]   2566

KRUSENSTERN, ADAM JOHANN von. Wörter-sammlungen aus den sprachen
einiger völker des östlichen Asiens und der nordwestküste von
Amerika. Bekannt gemacht von A. J. v. Krusenstern. [TITLE TR.
Collection of words from the speech of peoples of eastern Asia
and the northwest coast of America, made known by A. J. von
Krusenstern] St. Petersburg, Gedruckt in der druckerey der
Admiralität, 1813. 69p.   2567

Krusenstern, Adam Johann von. SEE ALSO nos.
    340, Baer, K. E. v. Feier 50-jahrigen Dienstzeit ... 1839;
    537, Bernhardi, C. Memoir ... 1856;
    1767, Golovnin, V. M. Sochinenniía ... 1864;
    1948, Harnisch, W. Reise um die Erde ... 1823;
    2516, Kotzebue, O. v. Puteshestvie ... 1821-23;
    2599, Langsdorff, G. H. v. Bemerkungen ... 1803-07;
    2603, Langsdorff, G. H. v. Plants recueillies ... 1810-18;
    2814, Lupach, V. S. I. F. Kruzenshtern ... 1953;
    2972, Markov, A. Krushenie Korablia *Nevy* ... 1850;
    3291, Nevskiĭ, V. V. Pervoe puteshestvie ... 1951;
    3292, Nevskiĭ, V. V. Vokrug sveta ... 1803-06. 1953;
    3364, Nozikov, N. N. Russkie krugosvetnye ... 1941;
    4136, Shteĭnberg, E. L. I. F. Kruzenshtern ... 1950;

Krusenstern, Ivan Fedorovich [Kruzenshtern, I. F.] SEE
    nos. 2549-67, Krusenstern, Adam Johann von.

KUBLANK, WALTER. Mit flugzeug und luftschiff zum Nordpol.
[TITLE TR. By airplane and airship to the North Pole] Reutlin-
gen, Ensslin & Laiblin, [1930] 31p. illus. [Andree, Amundsen
and Nobile]   2568

KUGELMASS, J. ALVIN. Roald Amundsen; a saga of the polar seas.
N. Y., Julian Messner, 1955. 191p. illus.   2569

Kul'tura indeĭtsev ... 1963. SEE no. 4616,
    U.S.S.R. Akademiía nauk.

KUMMER, FREDERIC ARNOLD. The perilous island; a story of mystery in the Aleutians. Philadelphia, Winston, 1942. 212p.   2570

KUNST, JAAP. Ethnomusicology; a study of its nature, its problems, methods and representative personalities, to which is added a bibliography. The Hague, Martinus Nijhoff, 1959. 3rd ed. enl. of "Musicologica" 303p. ports. illus. tables, indexes. 2571

KUPFFER, A. T. Observations météorologiques, faites à Sitka, sur l côte N. O. de l'Amérique (latitude 57°3' longitude 222°15' à l'est de Paris.) Moskva, Akademiia nauk S.S.S.R., 1950. 144p. tables, append. (Sciences mathematique et physique, t.4; Mémoires, Ser., 1850) 2572

Kupriīanov, A. B., co-auth. SEE nos.
    19, Agranat, G. A. Naselenie ... 1963;
    21, Agranat, G. A. Promyshlennost' ... 1962.

KURSH, HARRY. This is Alaska. Englewood Cliffs, N. J., Prentice-Hall, 1961. 286p. pls. map, endmap, bibliog. index. 2573

KURTEN, BJÖRN and R.L. RAUSCH. Biometric comparisons between North American and European mammals. København, Munksgaard, 1959. 44p. illus. tables, diagrs. bibliog. (Acta Arctica, fasc. 11) [Alaskan and Fennescandian wolverines and lynxes] 2574

Kushnarev, E. G., co-auth. SEE no. 4239, Sokalov, A. V.

KUZNETSOV, I. V., edit. Lîudi russkoĭ nauki. [TITLE TR. Men of Russian science] Moskva, Ogiz, 1948- ? 2 vols. 641p. and pp.642-1197. illus. ports. maps. 2575

KUZNETSOV, I. V., edit. Lîudi russkoĭ nauki; ocherki v vydaīu shchikhsia deīateliākh estestvoznaniīa i tekhniki: geologiīa, geografiīa. [TITLE TR. Men of Russian science; accounts of outstanding individuals active in the natural sciences and technology; geology, geography] Moskva, Gos. izd-vo fiziko-matematicheskoĭ lit-ry, 1962. 580p. illus. maps(some fold.), bibliog. 2576

L

L., B. V. Die Glaubwürdigkeit von Maldonados nordwestlicher Schiffahrt. Gotha, 1712. 52p. 2577

L., B. V. SEE ALSO no. 1548,
    Ferrer Maldonado, L. Viaggio dal Mare ... 1588.

L., C. SEE no. 3653, [Portlock, N.]

L., L., tr. SEE no. 1374, Dumont d'Urville, J. S. C.

Labillardiere, J. J. H. de. SEE nos. 1234-36, de Labillardiere, J. J. H.

Labor, Earle, edit. SEE no. 2759, London, Jack.

Labarce, B., co-auth. SEE no. 434, Baxter, D. V.

LaCasse, W. J., co-auth. SEE no. 848, Carpenter, Stanley J.

LaCHAPPELLE, EDWARD R. Snow studies on the Juneau Ice Field.
N. Y., American Geographical Society, March 1954. 31p. illus.
diagrs.(incl. 1 fold.), graphs, cross-sections, profiles(fold.),
map(sketch), bibliog. (Juneau Ice Field Research Project Report
no. 9)   2578

Lacour, Louis, edit. SEE no. 3986, Savvage, Jehan.

LaCroix, Robert de. SEE no. 1238, de LaCroix, Robert.

LADA-MOCARSKI, VALERIAN. Bibliography of books on Alaska published before 1868. New Haven, Yale University Press, 1969. 567p.
front. illus. facsims. indexes. [has separate titlepage and index in Cyrillic]   2579

LADUE, JOSEPH. Klondyke facts; being a complete guide book to
the gold regions of the great Canadian Northwest Territories and
Alaska. By Joseph Ladue, author of "Klondyke Nuggets," and founder of Dawson City, N. W. T. N. Y., American Technical Book Co.,
1897. 205p. front.(port.), pls. maps(incl. 1 fold.), append.
ANR. WITH TITLE Klondyke facts; being a complete guide book to
the great gold regions of the Yukon and Klondyke and the Northwest Territories and Alaska. Montreal, J. Lovell, 1897. 205p.
pls. maps.   2580

LADUE, JOSEPH. Klondyke nuggets; being a brief description of
the famous gold regions of the great Canadian northwest and
Alaska. N. Y., American Technical Book Co., 1897. 92p. (American Technical Series, no. 5) ANR. Montreal, John Lovell & Son,
1897.   2581

LAFORTUNE, BELLARMINE. A collection of prayers, hymns and instructions for the use of the Catholic Eskimos on Seward Peninsula, Alaska. By B. Lafortune, S.J. Nome, 1916. 49p.   2582

LaGrassierie, Raoul de. SEE no. 1239, de La Grasserie, Raoul.

Laguna, Frederica De. SEE nos. 1240-48, De Laguna, Frederica.

Laharpe, J. F. de. SEE no. 3781, Relation abregce ...
     La Pérouse ... l'hist. generale des voyages ... 1799.

Laing, Alexander, edit. SEE no. 3304, Nicol, J.

LAING, HAMILTON MACK. Birds collected and observed during the
cruise of the *Thiepval* in the North Pacific, 1924. Ottawa, F. A.
Acland, 1925. 43p. front.(pl.), pls. fig. bibliog. wrps. (Victoria Memorial Museum Bull. no. 40, Biol. Ser. no. 9, Nov. 1925)
[Nikolski and Unalaska, Aleutians; support Brit. world flight]2583

311

Lake Advertising Agency, Salt Lake City. SEE no. 133,
    Alaska travel guide. 1965.

Laktionov, Aleksandr Fedorovich. Nordpolen. SEE no. 2584.

LAKTIONOV, ALEKSANDR FEDOROVICH. Severny ĭ polĭūs; ocherk istoriĭ puteshestviĭ k t͡sentru Arktiki. [TITLE TR. North Pole;
historical sketch of voyages to the center of the Arctic] Arkh-
angelsk, Ark'hangel'skoe oblastnoe Izd-vo, 1939. 236p. illus.
maps. ANR. Moskva, Izd-vo glavsevmorputi, 1949. 394p. illus.
maps, bibliog. ANR. Moskva, Izd-vo "Morskoi transport," 1955.
rev. and enl. 472p. ports. illus. maps(incl. 1 fold.), bibliog.
indexes. ANR.Moskva, Izd-vo "Morskoi transport," 1960. 525p.
rev. and enl. illus. diagrs. tables, graphs, maps(incl. 1 fold.),
bibliog. ALSO IN SWEDISH WITH TITLE Nordpolen.   2584

LAMB, G. F. Franklin, happy voyager. Being the life and death
of Sir John Franklin. London, 1956. 293p. index.   2585

LAMBERT, CLARA. The story of Alaska. N. Y., Harper, 1940.
(40)p. illus.(some col.) by C. H. DeWitt.   2586

LAMBERT, RICHARD S. Adventure to the Polar Sea; the story of
Sir John Franklin. Indianapolis, Ind., Bobbs-Merrill, 1950. 2587

LAMBERT, RICHARD S. Franklin of the Arctic; a life of adventure;
maps by Julius Griffith. Toronto, McClelland & Stewart, 1949.
354p. photos, maps, endmaps, errata slip. (Cadmus Edition) 2588

Lambert, T. R., illus. SEE nos.
    3099, Midnight Sun Broadcasting Co. KFAR keybook...[c1939];
    3615, Pioneers of Alaska. Gold; mining ... 1957.

Lamont Geological Observatory. SEE no. 3128, Miller, Maynard M.

L'AMOUR, LOUIS. Sitka, a novel of Alaska. N. Y., Appleton-Century-Crofts, 1957. 282p. ANR. N. Y., Bantam Editions, 1958.
245p. paperback.   2589

LANCASTER, G. B. [pseud.] The world is yours. N. Y., Appleton,
1934. 322p. [author is Edith J. Lyttleton - fict. acct. Yukon
in the 1920s]   2590

Land of promise ... 1962. SEE no. 4043, Seattle, Century 21.

Land of the midnight sun missions ... 1925. SEE no. 3585,
    [Piet, J. M.]

LANDRU, HORTENSE. Sled dog of Alaska. By Jack Landru. N. Y.,
Dodd Mead, 1953. 184p.   2591

Lane, Adolf. SEE no. 4791, Welzl, J.

LANE, ANNE W. and LOUISE H. WALL. The letters of Franklin K. Lane, personal and political ... Boston, Houghton, 1922. 473p. [pp.259-61 about Alaska Railroad and Alaska purchase]   2592

LANE, FREDERICK A. The greatest adventure; a story of Jack London. Illustrated by Sidney Quinn. N. Y., Aladdin Books, 1954. 192p. (American Heritage Series)   2593

Lane, Louis. SEE no. 4894, Willoughby, Barrett.

LANE, ROSE WILDER. He was a man. N. Y., Harper, 1925. 380p. ANR. WITH TITLE Gordon Blake. London, Harper, 1925. 380p. [fict. based upon life of Jack London]   2594

LANG, JOHN. The story of Captain Cook. London, T. C. & E. C. Jack, and N. Y., E. P. Dutton, 1906. 119p. pls.(col.)   2595

LANGE, ANN. The Eskimo store. Illustrated by Gladys Rourke Blackwood. Chicago, Albert Whitman, 1948. (23)p. front. illus. (some col.)   2596

L'ANGE-GARDIEN, MARIE de. En Alaska. L'Oeuvre des Soeurs de Sainte-Anne Parmi las Sauvages et les Blancs. Recit de voyage par Sr. Marie de L'Ange-Gardien. Montreal, Arbour & Laperle, imprimeurs-editeurs, 1900. 24p.   2597

LANGLE, PAUL-ANTOINE FLEURIOT de. La tragique expedition de Lapérouse et Langle. Paris, Hachette, 1954. 249p. illus. bibliog.   2598

Langsdorff, Georg Heinrich von. [Alphabetical title guide to chronological entries]

>   Bemerkungen ... 2599.
>   Plantes recueillies ... 2603.
>   Reis rondom de wereld ... 2602.
>   Reise um die Welt ... 2601.
>   Voyages and travels ... 2600.

LANGSDORFF, GEORG HEINRICH von. Bemerkungen auf einer reise um die Welt in den Jahren 1803 bis 1807. [TITLE TR. Observations on a voyage around the world in the years 1803 to 1807] Frankfurt am Mayn, F. Wilmans, 1812. 2 vols. 304p. and 336p. front. ports. pls. diagrs. ANR. 1813. [Krusenstern voyage]   2599

TRANSLATIONS - Bemerkungen ... 1812, CHRONOLOGICALLY.

Voyages and travels in various parts of the world, during the years 1803, 1804, 1805, 1806, and 1807. By G. H. von Langsdorff ... Illustrated by engravings from original drawings. London, H. Colburn, 1813-14. 2 vols. 362p. and 386p. pls. (incl. fronts. ports. music), map(fold.) ANR. Carlisle, Penna., printed by George Philips, 1817. 617p. front.(fold.)

[sold under various imprints of publishers in several cities in U. S.] ANR. Ridgewood, N. J., Gregg Press, 1967. 2 vols. Edited by E. S. Dodge. (America and the Pacific. First ser. vol. 5) ANR. Amsterdam, N. Israel and N. Y., Da Capo Press, 1967. 2 vols. (Bibliotheca Australiana, 4th ser.) 2600

LANGSDORFF, GEORG HEINRICH von. TRANSLATIONS - Bemerkingen ... 1818, CHRONOLOGICALLY.

Reise um die Welt, fur die Jugend bearbeitet von K. H. Cutman. Vienna, 1816. 2601

Reis rondom de wereld in de jaren 1803 tot 1807. Uit het Hgd. door M. Stuart. Haarlem and Amsterdam, 1813. [vols. 1 and 2] and Amsterdam, 1819. [vols. 3 and 4] [a new ed. of vols. 1 and 2 in 1818] 2602

LANGSDORFF, GEORG HEINRICH von and F. FISCHER. Plantes recueillies pendant le voyage des russes autor du monde. Expedition dirigee par M. Krusenstern. Tubingen, J. C. Cotta, 1810-18. 26p. pls. 2603

Langsdorff, Georg Heinrich von. SEE ALSO nos.
1948, Harnisch, W. Reise um die Erde ... 1823;
3920, Russell, Thos. C. Langsdorff's narrat. Rezanov...1927.

LANKS, HERBERT C. Highway to Alaska. Photographs by the author. N. Y., Appleton-Century Co., 1944. 200p. front. photos, endmaps by Gladys C. Lanks, index. [World War 11 contruction of Alcan Highway] 2604

LANTIS, DAVID W. Alaska. Garden City, N. Y., Doubleday, 1957. 64p. illus.(some col.) (American Geographical Society, Know Your America Series) 2605

LANTIS, MARGARET. Alaskan Eskimo ceremonialism. N. Y., J. J. Augustin, 1947. 127p. front. illus. map, bibliog. (American Ethnological Society Monographs, no. 11) ANR. Seattle, University of Washington Press, 1966. reissue. 143p. maps, bibliog. 2606

LANTIS, MARGARET. Eskimo childhood and interpersonal relationships; Nunivak biographies and genealogies. Seattle, University of Washington Press, 1960. 215p. illus. map, tables, append. bibliog. (American Ethnological Society Monographs, no. 33) ANR. 1966. reissue. 236p. photos, sketches, map, appends. bibliog.2607

Lantis, Margaret. SEE ALSO no. 4262,
Spicer, Edw. H., edit. Human problems ... 1952.

LANTZEFF, GEORGE V. Siberia in the Seventeenth Century. A study of the colonial administration. Berkeley, University of California Press, 1943. 2608

La Pérouse, Jean François Galaup de. [Alphabetical title guide
    to chronological entries]

A voyage ... 2611, 2612, 2614.   The first French ... 2621.
Découvertes ... 2609.   The voyage of ... 2613.
Entdeckungsreise ... 2615.   Viaggi di ... 2618.
Le voyage ... 2620.   Voyage ... Autor ... 2610.
Ontdekkingen ... 2616.   Voyage de ... 2619.
Puteshestvie ... 2617.

[La PÉROUSE, JEAN FRANÇOIS GALAUP de] Découvertes dans le mer du
Sud. Nouvelles de la Peyrouse, jusqu'en 1794. Traces de son
passage trouvees en diverses isles et terres de l'Ocean pacifique;
grande isle peuplee d'emigres français. Paris, Chez Everat,
1798. 397p.   2609

[La PÉROUSE, JEAN FRANÇOIS GALAUP de] Voyage de La Pérouse Autor
du Monde, Publié Conformément au Décret de 22 Avril 1791, et
Rédigé par M. L. A. Milet-Mureau ... Paris, Imprimerie de la Ré-
publique, An V [1797] 4 vols. bd. in 2 and atlas. 346p., 398p.,
422p. and 309p. pls. maps. ANR. Paris, Plassan, L'An VI de la
Republique [1798] 4 vols. and atlas. pls. maps.   2610

TRANSLATIONS - Voyage ... Autor du Monde ... [1797],
CHRONOLOGICALLY.

A voyage round the world, performed in the years 1785, 86, 87,
and 88, by the *Boussole* and *Astrolabe*, under the command of
J. F. G. de La Pérouse; pub. by order of the National Assembly under the superintendence of L. A. Milet-Mureau. Tr. fr.
the French. London, G. G. & J. Robinson, 1798. 2 vols. and
atlas. 539p. and 531p. front. port. pls. maps.   2611

A voyage round the world, in the years 1785, 86, 87 and 1788,
by J. F. G. de La Pérouse; pub. conformably to the decree of
the National Assembly and ed. by M. L. A. Milet-Mureau. Tr.
from the French. London, Johnson, 1798. 3 vols. pls. maps.
OTHERS London, Johnson, 1799. 2 vols. and atlas AND 1807.
3 vols. and atlas. ANR. London, Lackington, Allen & Co.,
1807. 3 vols. and atlas.   2612

The voyage of La Pérouse round the world, in the years 1785, 86,
87, and 88, with the nautical tables. Arranged by M. L. A.
Milet Mureau ... To which is prefixed narrative of an interesting voyage from Manila to St. Blaise. And annexed, travels over the continent, with the dispatches of La Pérouse
in 1787 and 1788, by M. de Lesseps. Tr. fr. the French.
London, J. Stockdale, 1798. 2 vols. pls. maps.   2613

A voyage round the world; in the years 1785, 86, 87, and 88,
by M. de La Pérouse; abr. fr. the orig. French journal...
lately published by M. Milet-Mureau ... To which are added;
A voyage from Manilla to California, by Don Antonio Maurelle;

315

and an abstract of the voyage and discoveries of the late
Captain G. Vancouver. Edinburgh, printed by J. Moir for T.
Brown, 1798. 336p.,31p.,61p. pls. maps(fold.) ANR. Boston,
J. Bumstead, 1801. 336p.   2614

[La PEROUSE, JEAN FRANÇOIS GALAUP de] TRANSLATIONS - Voyage ...
Autor du Monde ... [1797], CHRONOLOGICALLY.

Entdeckungsreise in den jahren 1785, 86, 87, 88. Herausgegeben
von Mar. C. Ant. Milet-Mureau. Aus dem Franz. ubersetzt und
mit Anmerkungen begleitet von J. R. Forster und C. L. Sprengel. Berlin, 1798. ANR. Berlin, 1799. ANR. Berlin, 1800.
2 vols. 358p. and 344p. map. ANR. Leipzig, Reinicke unde
Hinrichs, 1799. 2 vols.   2615

Ontdekkingen in de Zuidzee, en berichten aanaaende de La Pérouse enlzijne tochtgenoten, opgemaakt uit sporen van zijne
reis, op onderscheidene eilanden en landen der Stille zee
gevonden; alsmede aangaande een groot eiland thans door
Fransche vluchtelingen bevolkt. Uit det Fransche vertaald.
Haarlem, F. Bohn, 1799. 480p. pl.   2616

Puteshestvie Laperuza v iuzhnom i sievernom Tikhom okeanie v
prodolzhenie 1785-88 godov. Izvlechenno is opisaniia iz-
dannago v Parizhie v 1798 godu. [TITLE TR. La Pérouse's
voyage in the south and north Pacific Ocean during the years
1785-88. Extracted from the work published at Paris, 1798]
By L. I. Golenishchev-Kutuzov. St. Petersbourg, 1800-02.
2 pts.   2617

Viaggi di La Pérouse intorno al mondo...Milano, Tipografia,
Sonzozno e comp., 1815. 4 vols. OTHERS Livorno, Tip. Vig-
nozzi, 1827. 3 vols. AND Torino, Dalla Stamperia Alleana,
1829. 7 vols.   2618

Voyage de Lapérouse, rédigé d'apres ses manuscrits origineaux,
suivi d'un appendice renfermant tout ce que l'on a decouvert
depuis le naufrage jusqua nos jours, et enrichi de notes par
M. de Lesseps ... seul debris vivant de l'expedition dont il
etait interprete; accompagne d'une carte generale du voyage,
orne du portrait et d'un fac-simile de Lapérouse. Paris,
A. Bertrand, 1831. 436p. pls. facsims. map(fold.)   2619

Le voyage de Lapérouse sur les côtes de l'Alaska et de la California (1786) avec une introduction et des notes par Gilbert
Chinard. Baltimore, Johns Hopkins Press, 1937. 144p. front.
(port.), pls. maps, plans, facsims. (Historical Documents,
Institut Français de Washington. Cahier 10)   2620

The first French expedition to California; Lapérouse in 1786.
Translated with introduction and notes by Charles N. Rudkin.
L. A., G. Dawson, 1959. 145p. illus. port. maps, facsims.
bibliog. notes. (Early Calif. Travel Ser. no. 46)ltd.ed.2621

La Pérouse, Jean François Galaup de. SEE ALSO nos.
  177, Allen, Edw. W. ... Lapérouse, a checklist. 1941;
  180, Allen, Edw. W. "Vanishing Frenchman" ... 1959;
  436, Bayly, Geo. Sea-life ... relics ... la Pérouse. 1886;
  492, Bellesort, A. La Pérouse, avec un portrait ... 1926;
  739, Burney, Jas. Memoir D'Entrecasteaux ... 1820;
  876, Centinaire de la mort de Lapérouse. 1888;
  1234, de Labillardiere, J. J. H. Relation voyage recherche
        ... 1799;
  1251, de Lesseps, J. B. B. Journal voyage ... 1790;
  1273, D"Entrecasteaux, A. R. J. B. Voyage ... recherche...
        1808;
  1296, Dillon, Peter. Narrative ... fate La Pérouse ... 1829;
  1371, Dumont d'Urville, J. S. C. Voyage ... recherche...1832;
  1456, Emmanuel, M. La France ... 1959;
  1507, Exploration et ... naufrage ... 1945;
  1663, Froment-Guieysse, G. La Pérouse ... 1947;
  1781, Gordon, Mona. Mystery of La Pérouse. 1961;
  2515, Kotzebue, A. F. F. von. La Peyrouse ... two acts. 1800;
  2598, Langle, Paul-Antoine Fleuriot de. La tragique exped.
        ... 1954;
  2964, Marcel, Gabriel. Une exped. oubliee recherche ...1888;
  3554, Petit-Thouars, A. A. Du. Fragments du dernier...1797;
  3781, Relation abregee du voyage ... 1799;
  4229, Sobreviela, M. Voyages au ... 1809;
  4356, Story La Peyrouse. 1841;
  4636, Valentin, F. Voyages ... 1841;
  4644, Vanderbourg. Le Pérouse ... 1810;
  4646, Van der Linden, M. J. Reize naar de zuider zee...1805;
  4716, Voyage de découverte ... 1832-3.

La Pérouse; ou, le voyage ... 1810. SEE no. 4644,
  Vanderbourg.

LAPPO, S. D. Okeanograficheskiĭ spravochnik arkticheskikh moreĭ
SSSR (obshchaĩe lotsiĩa). [TITLE TR. Oceanographic handbook of
the Arctic Seas of the USSR (general sailing directions)] Leningrad, Izd-vo glavsevmorputi, 1940. 182p. illus. sketch maps,
table, errata slip.   2622

LAPPO, S. D. Plavaniĩa Vasiliĩa Mikhailovicha Golovnina. [TITLE
TR. The voyages of Vasiliĭ Mikhailovich Golovnin] Moskva, Izd-
vo "Pravda," 1950. 23p. port. (Vsesoũĩznoe obshchestvo po
rasprostraneniĩu politicheskikh i nauchnykh znaniĭ)   2623

LARDNER, D. The history of maritime and inland discoveries. By
Rev. D. Lardner. London, Longmans, 1830. 3 vols. (The Cabinet
Cyclopedia. Geography)   2624

LARGE, R. C. Prince Rupert; a gateway to Alaska. Vancouver,
B. C., Mitchell Press, 1951. 210p. photos.   2625

LaROCHE, FRANK. En route to the Klondike, Chilkoot Pass and Skaguay Trail. Chicago, H. O. Shepherd Co., 1897. 57p. illus.
2626

LaROCHE, FRANK. En route to the Klondike; a series of photographic views of the picturesque land of gold and glaciers, picturing the actual places traveled over by the gold seekers en route to the land of treasure, presenting to the eye its beauties, its grandeurs and its dangers; also showing many camps and parties of Argonauts going to the gold fields. Chicago, W. B. Conkey, 1898. 6 pts. in 1 vol. illus. map(fold.)
2627

LaROCQUE, JOSEPH ALFRED AURELE. Catalogue of the recent Mollusca of Canada. Ottawa, Queen's Printer, 1953. 406p. bibliog. index. (Canada. National Museum Bull. no. 129, Biol. Series no. 44) [adjacent Alaskan and Sea of Okhotsk]
2628

LARSEN, HELGE. Eskimokulturen. [TITLE TR. The Eskimo culture] København, Munksgaards Forlag, 1960. 83p. [also in: Grønland, Apr.-Sept. 1960. nos. 4, 5, 6, 7 and 8, var. paging]
2629

LARSEN, HELGE and FROELICH RAINEY. Ipiutak and the arctic whale hunting culture. N. Y., 1948. 276p. illus. pls. map(fold.), plans, tables, diagrs. (Anthropological Papers, American Museum of Natural History, vol. 42)
2630

LARSEN, HELGE, edit. The Circumpolar Conference in Copenhagen 1958. København, Ejnar Munksgaard, 1960. 92p. maps. [pp.27-33, *A view of archaeology about Bering Strait*, by James Louis Giddings]
2631

Larsen, Helge. SEE ALSO no. 4465,
    Tax, Sol, edit. Indian tribes ... 1952. vol. 3.

Larssen, A. K., co-auth. SEE no. 260, Andrews, Ralph W.

Laschever, B. D., co-edit. SEE no. 1589, Fodor, E, edit.

LASKY, SAMUEL GROSSMAN. Transverse faults at Kennecott and their relation to the main fault systems. N. Y., American Institute of Mining and Metallurgical Engineers, 1928. 17p. (Technical Pub. no. 152)
2632

Latest information about Alaska gold fields ... [1897] SEE
    no. 2107, [Hiller, E. H.]

LATHAM, EDWARD, edit. Statehood for Hawaii and Alaska. N. Y., Wilson, 1953. 197p. maps, bibliog. (The Reference Shelf, vol. 25, no. 5)
2633

LATHAM, ROBERT GORDON. The native races of the Russian Empire. London, Hippolite Bailliere, 1854. 340p. [chapt. 19, history of Russian America]
2634

LATHROP, GRACE G. Tashekah. Chicago, Womans' American Baptist
Home Mission, n. d. 4p. 2635

LATHROP HIGH SCHOOL, Fairbanks. Arctic oil, magic in the north.
no pl. [Fairbanks], March 15, 1969. 27p.(9p. append.) illus.
maps. (Distributive Education Class) 2636

LATHROP, WEST. Dogsled danger. Illustrated by Richard M. Powers.
N. Y., Random House, 1956. 247p. illus. 2637

LATHROP, WEST. Jet, sled dog of the north. London, 1958. 254p.
front. 2638

LATHROP, WEST. Juneau, the sleigh dog. N. Y., Random House,
1942. 1st print. 279p. illustrated by Kurt Wiese. ANR. London, Museum Press, 1946. 224p. illus. 2639

LATHROP, WEST. Northern trail adventure. N. Y., Random House,
1944. 217p. 2640

Laufe, A., edit. SEE no. 1575, Fitzgerald, E. M.

LAUNAY de VALERY, CORDIER de. Tableau topographique et politique
de la Sibérie, de la Chine, de la zone moyenne d'Asie et du nord
de l'Amérique. Berlin, 1806. 130p. ltd. ed. of 400 copies.2641

Laurence, Sydney. SEE no. 2379, Jones, H. Wendy.

LAURIDSEN, PETER. Vitus Bering; the discoverer of Bering Strait.
Translated from Danish by Julius E. Olsen. Chicago, S. C. Griggs
& Co., 1889. xvi,223p. maps(fold.) [tr. of no. 2643] 2642

LAURIDSEN, PETER. Vitus J. Bering og de russiske opdagelsesrejser fra 1725-43. København, F. Hegel & Sons, 1885. 210p.
pls. maps(fold.), table. [for tr. see no. 2642] 2643

LAUT, AGNES CHRISTIAN. Pioneers of the Pacific Coast; a chronicle of sea robbers and fur hunters. Toronto, Brook & Co.,
1915. 139p. illus. front.(col.), pls. ports. map(fold.) (Chronicles of Canada Series) 2644

LAUT, AGNES CHRISTIAN. The fur trade of America. N. Y., Macmillan, 1921. 341p. illus. front. pls. 2645

LAUT, AGNES CHRISTIAN. Vikings of the Pacific. By A. C. Laut.
The adventures of the explorers who came from the west, eastward;
Bering, the Dane; the outlaw hunters of Russia; Benyowsky, the
Polish pirate; Cook and Vancouver, the English navigators;
Gray of Boston, the discoverer of the Columbia; Drake, Ledyard,
and other soldiers of fortune on the west coast of America. N.Y.,
Macmillan, 1905. [c1905] xviii,349p. front.(pl.), pls. ports.
maps. index. ANR. 1914. 2646

LaVERNE'S KLONDIKE SONGSTER. no pl., [1898 ?] 16p. 2647

Lavrov, A. M., cartog. SEE no. 3717, Rabot, Chas.

LAWING, NELLIE (TROSPER) NEAL. Alaska Nellie. By Nellie Neal
Lawing. Seattle, Published at Chieftain Press, Seattle Printing
and Publishing Co., [c1940] 1st print. 201p. front.(port.),
pls. ports. endmaps. [autobiog., Lake Kenai area] 2648

LAWRENCE, EDWARD A. Clover Passage. Caldwell, Idaho, Caxton,
1954. 260p. pls. [fishing in southeastern Alaska] 2649

LAWRENCE, GUY. Forty years on the Yukon Telegraph. Vancouver,
B. C., Mitchell Press, 1965. 121p. photos, map, append. index.
2650

Lawton, Joseph. SEE no. 107, Alaska Review.

LAZAREV, ALEKSEĬ PETROVICH. Plavanie vokrug svi͡eta na shli͡upie
Ladogie v 1822-24 godakh, shli͡upom nachaljstvoval Cap.-Leit.
A. P. Lazarev. [TITLE TR. Voyage round the world in the sloop
Ladoga, 1822-24, commanded by Capt.-Lieut. A. P. Lazarev] St.
Petersburg, 1832. 275p. map. 2651

LAZAREV, ALEKSEĬ PETROVICH. Zapiski o plavanii͡ voennogo shli͡upa
Blagonamerennogo v Beringov proliv i vokrug sveta dli͡a otkrytii͡
v 1819, 1820, 1821 i 1822 godalh vedennye gvardeĭskogo ekipazha
leĭtenantom A. P. Lazarevym. [TITLE TR. Notes on the voyage of
the naval sloop *Blagonamerennyi* into the Bering Strait and around
the world for discoveries in 1819, 1820, 1821 and 1822, kept by
the Guard's Lt. A. P. Lazarev] Moskva, Gosudarstvennoe izd-vo
geograficheskoi literatury, 1950. 475p. illus. maps(2 fold.)
2652

LAZELL, J. ARTHUR. Alaskan apostle, the life story of Sheldon
Jackson. N. Y., HARPER, 1960. 218p. front. illus. map(dblep.)
index. [Presbyterian Church] 2653

LEACOCK, STEPHEN BUTLER. Adventurers of the far North, a chronicle of the frozen seas. Toronto, Brook & Co., 1914. 152p.
front.(col.), pls. ports. map(fold.) (Chronicles of Canada Ser.
vol. 20) [from Elizabethan times to Franklin search with brief
chapt. on subsequent expeditions] 2654

Leacock, Stephen Butler. SEE ALSO no. 4326,
    Stefansson, V. Unsolved mysteries ... [c1938]

LEAGUE OF WOMEN VOTERS OF THE NORTH STAR BOROUGH. Fairbanks,
golden heart city. Fairbanks, 1968. 28p. illus. 2655

LEAHEY, A. H. Preliminary report on exploratory soil survey
along the Alaska Military Highway and the Yukon River system.
Ottawa, Canada. Experimental Farms Service, 1943. 16p. 2656

LEAHEY, A. H.   Report on trip to Experimental Substation, Whitehorse, Y. T., 1946. Ottawa, Canada. Experimental Farms Service,
[1946 ?] 6p. [incls. visit to Palmer and Matanuska Valley in
Alaska]   2657

Lebas, tr. SEE no. 1309, Dixon, George.

LEBEDEV, D. M.   Plavanie A. I. Chirikova na paketbote "Sv. Pavel"
k poberezh'iam Ameriki; s prilozheniem sudovogo zhurnala 1741
g. Otv. red. akademik A. A. Grigor'ev. [TITLE TR. Voyage of
A. I. Chirikov on the vessel *St. Paul* to the coast of America;
with the log book of 1741 in supplement. Editor, Academician
A. A. Grigor'ev] Moskva, Izd-vo Akademii nauk SSSR, 1951. 429p.
illus. tables, maps(some fold.), facsims. bibliog.   2658

Le BOURDAIS, DONAT MARC.   Northward on the new frontier. Ottawa,
Graphic Pub., 1931. 311p. pls. ports. endmaps. ANR. Toronto,
T. Nelson & Sons, 1931.   2659

Le BOURDAIS, DONAT MARC.   Stefansson, ambassador of the North.
Montreal, Harvest House, 1963. 204p. map(fold.) [incls. Canadian Arctic Expedition of 1913-18]   2660

Le Bourdais, Donat Marc. SEE ALSO no. 4314,
     Stefansson, V. Adventure Wrangel Island. 1925.

Le CLERC, C.   Bibliotheca Americana; histoire, geographie, voyages, archeologie et linguistique des deux Amériques et des
Philippines. Paris, Maisonneuve & Co., 1878. 737p.   2661

LEBEDOUR, KARL FRIEDRICH von.   Flora Rossica; sive, Enumeratio
plantarum in totius Imperii Rossici provinciis europaeis, asiati-
cus et americanis hucusque observatarum. [TITLE TR. Flora of
Russia; or, enumeration of all plants of European, Asiatic and
American provinces of the Russian Empire] Stuttgartiae, Sumtibus Librariae E. Schweizerbart, 1841-53] 4 vols. map(fold.)2662

LEDYARD, JOHN.   A journal of Captain Cook's last voyage to the
Pacific Ocean, and in quest of a North-West Passage between Asia
and America; performed in the years 1776, 1777, 1778 and 1779,
illustrated with a chart shewing the tracts of the ships employed
in this expedition, faithfully narrated from the original ms of
John Ledyard. Hartford, N. Patten, 1783. 208p. front.(fold.
map)   2663

[LEDYARD, JOHN] The adventures of a Yankee; or, the singular
life of John Ledyard; with an account of his voyage round the
world with the celebrated Captain Cook. Designed for youth. By
a Yankee. Boston, Carter, Hendee & Babcock, 1831. 90p. illus.
                                                                 2664

Ledyard, John.   SEE ALSO nos.
    323, Augur, Helen.   Passage to glory.   1946;
    3237, Mumford, Jas. K.   John Ledyard, Amer. Marco Polo. 1939;
    3238, Mumford, Jas. K., edit.   John Ledyard's journal. [c1963];
    4253, Sparks, Jared.   Life of John Ledyard ... 1828.

LEE, CHARLES A., comp.   Aleutian Indian and English dictionary;
common words in the dialects of the Aleutian Indian language as
spoken by the Oogashik, Egashik, Egekik, Anangashuk and Misremie
tribes around Sulima River and neighboring parts of the Alaska
Peninsula.   By Rev. Charles A. Lee.   Seattle, Lowman & Hanford
Stationery and Printing Co., 1896.   23p.   wrps.   ANR. Seattle,
Shorey Photocopy, 1965.   facsim. ed.   2665

LEE, CLIFTON.   Alaska in sketches.   Anchorage, Young Printing,
1962.   (47)p.   [artist's sketches of southcentral Alaska]   2666

LEE, FRANK C.   Alaska Highway poems.   Mason City, Iowa, Klipto
Pub. Co., [c1944]   (34)p.   photos.   2667

Lee, William H.   SEE no. 149, Alaska-Yukon-Pacific Exposition.

Leech, Wm. H., edit.   SEE no. 3089, Methodist Alaska Yukon
    Pcific Commission.

LEECHMAN, DOUGLAS.   Vanta Kutchin.   Ottawa, Department of Northern
Affairs and Natural Resources, National Parks Branch, National
Museum of Canada, 1954.   35p.   illus. front. sketches, photos,
endmaps, bibliog.   (Bulletin no. 130, Anthropology Ser. no. 33)
[Indians of Old Crow, Canada, their cultural tie-in with Indians
of Alaska]   2668

LEECHMAN, JOHN DOUGLAS   and M. R. HARRINGTON.   String-records of
the Northwest.   N. Y., Heye Foundation, Museum of the American
Indians, 1921.   64p.   front. illus. pls.   (Indian Notes and Monographs, Misc. no. 16)   2669

LEEHEY, MAURICE DANIEL.   Mining code for the use of miners and
prospectors in Washington and Alaska, with notes and annotations
and forms for general use.   [Seattle, c1900].   103p.   2670

LEEHEY, MAURICE DANIEL.   The public land policy of the United
States in Alaska;   an address before the Northwest Mining Conven-
tion.   Spokane, Franklin Press, 1912.   16p.   ANR. Seattle, Shorey
Book Store, 1965.   facsim. ed.   2671

[Le FEBRE, H. B.]   The "Soapy" Smith tragedy.   Skagway, printed
by Daily Alaskan, 1907.   24p.   pls. ports.   ANR. [or same ?]
compiled by Shea and Patten.   2672

LEGAL DIRECTORIES PUBLISHING CO. The Pacific Coast legal direc-
tory. States of Alaska, Arizona, California, Hawaii, Nevada,
Oregon and Washington. 1961-62. Revised to July 10, 1961. L.A.,
Legal Directories Pub. Co., 1961. 636p. annual.   2673

Leffingwell, E. deK. SEE nos.
  3104, Mikkelsen, E. Conquering Arctic ice. 1909;
  3108, Mikkelsen, E. Ukendt Mandt til Ukendt Land. 1954;
  3109, Mikkelsen, E. Mirage in Arctic. 1955.

LEIBERMAN, ELIAS. The American short story; a study of the influence of locality in its development. Ridgewood, N. J. The
Editor, 1912. [contains chapt. on Jack London]   2674

[LEISHER, J. J.] The decline and fall of Samuel Sawbones, M.D.,
on the Klondike; by his next best friend. Chicago, The Neely
Co., 1900. 197p. front. pls.   2675

LELAND, CHARLES E. Fusang; or, the discovery of America by Chi-
nese Buddhist priests in the fifth century. London, Trubner &
Co., 1875. 212p.   2676

Le Monnier, Franz. SEE no. 903, Chavanne, Josef.

LENSEN, GEORGE ALEXANDER, edit. Russia's eastward expansion.
Englewood Cliffs, N. J., Prentice-Hall, 1964. (A Spectrum Book,
no. S-94)   2677

LENZ, H. F. E. Nabliudeniia nad nakloneniam i stepenjiu sily
magnitoi strielki. [TITLE TR. Observation on the magnetic dip
and intensity.] St. Petersburg, 1836. 30p. [made by Dr. Lenz
during voyage round the world with Naval Captain Litke on the
sloop *Seniavin*, translated from the German by Lieut. Glazenapp]
                                                                 2678

LEONARD, JOHN WILLIAM. The gold fields of the Klondike; fortune
seeker's guide to the Yukon region of Alaska and British America;
the story as told by Ladue, Berry, Phiscator and other gold fin-
ders. With maps, diagrams and illustrations. Chicago, A. N.
Marquis & Co., 1897. 216p. front. pls. ports. maps(incl.1 fold.)
ANR. London, Fisher Unwin, 1897.   2679

LEONHARDY, ALMA and others. Directed study guides for London's
The call of the wild and other stories. N. Y., Macmillan, 1929.
72p.   2680

LEONOV, ALEKSANDR KUZ'MICH. Regional'naia okeanografiia, chast'
1; Beringovo, Okhotskoe, Iaponskoe, Kaspiiskoe i Chernoe Moria.
[TITLE TR. Regional oceanography, part 1; Bering, Okhotsk,
Japan, Caspian and Black Seas] Leningrad, Gidrometeorologiches-
koe izd-vo, 1960. 765p. tables, diagrs. maps(some fold.),
bibliog.   2681

LEOPOLD, ALDO STARKER and FRANK FRASER DARLING. Wildlife in
Alaska; an ecological reconnaissance. By A. Starker Leopold and
F. Fraser Darling. N. Y., Ronald Press, 1953. 129p. pls.
tables, maps, bibliog. index.   2682

LEPOTIER, ADOLPHE AUGUSTE MARIE. Les Russes en Amerique. Paris,
A. Fayard, 1958. 252p. illus.   2683

Le Rebeller, A., tr. SEE no. 3901, Rouquette, L.-F.

LEROI-GOURHAN, A. Archéologie de Pacifique-nord. Materiaux pour
l'étude des relations entre les peuples riverains d'Asie et
d'Amérique. Paris, Université de Paris, 1946. 542p. (Travaux
et Mémoires de l'Institut d'Ethnologie, no. 47) [incls. Aleut]
                                                                     2684

LESCHEN, A, AND SONS ROPE CO. Leschen's Hercules; how vessels
are unloaded at Nome, Alaska. St. Louis, A. Leschen & Sons Rope
Co., April 1914. 4p.   2685

LESLIE, ALEXANDER, comp. Die Nordpolarreisen Adolf Erik Nordenskiöld's 1858 bis 1879. Aus dem Englischen. Autorisirte
deutsche Ausg. Leipzig, F. A. Brockhaus, 1880. 443p. illus.
maps(incl. 1 fold., 2 dble.) [tr. of no. 2687]   2686

LESLIE, ALEXANDER, comp. The Arctic voyages of Adolf Erik Nordenskiöld, 1858-1879. London, Macmillan, 1879. 447(40)p. front.
illus. maps(fold.), append. [see no. 2686 for tr.]   2687

Leslie, Alexander. SEE ALSO no. 3330,
     Nordenskiöld, N. A. E. Voyage of *Vega*. 1881.

Leslie, John. Discovery and adventure ... 1860. SEE no. 2688.

LESLIE, JOHN and others. Narrative of discovery and adventure in
the polar seas and regions with illustrations of their climate,
geology and natural history, and an account of the whale fishery.
Edinburgh, Oliver & Boyd, 1830. 424p. pls. map(fold.) ANR.
1835. ANR. N. Y., Harper, 1839. 373p. illus. map(fold.)
(Stereotype Edition) OTHERS 1844, 1853, 1859. ANR. WITH TITLE
Discovery and adventure in the polar seas and regions; with a
narrative of the recent expeditions in search of Sir John Franklin, including the voyage of the "Fox" and the discovery of the
fate of the Franklin expedition. By John Leslie and others.
London, T. Nelson, 1860. 652p. front.   2688

Lesseps, J. B. B. de. SEE nos. 1251-56, deLesseps, J. B. B.

Lesser, E. and M., tr. SEE no. 3365, Nozikov, N. N.

LESSNER, ERWIN. Cradle of conquerors; Siberia. N. Y., Doubleday, 1955. 774p. endmaps. [incls. refs. to Alaska]   2689

LES TINA, DOROTHY. Alaska; a book to begin on. Illustrated by
Aliki. N. Y., Holt, Rinehart and Winston, 1962. 1st ed. unp.
illus.   2690

LES TINA, DOROTHY. Icicles on the roof. N. Y., Abelard-Schuman,
1961. 181p.   2691

LESURE, THOMAS B. How to see and enjoy Arizona, California,
Hawaii - plus Alaska and the Pacific Northwest. N. Y., Harian
Publications, 1966. 2 vols.   2692

Let's go sailing sheltered seas. [c1948] SEE no. 119,
    Alaska Steamship Co.

Letter from Russian sea-officer ... 1754. SEE nos.
    1311, [Dobbs, Arthur], tr.
    2693, Lettre d'un officier ... 1753.

Letters lately published ... subject present dispute Spain ...
    1790. SEE no. 4762, [Webb, Francis ?]

LETTRE D'UN OFFICIER de la marine russienne a un seigneur de la
cour concernant la carte des novelles découvertes au nord de la
mer du Sud. Trad. l'orig. Russe. Publie par M. de l'Isle a
Paris en 1752. Berlin, 1753. 60p. ANR. Berlin, [1753 ?] 54p.
[has been variously attributed to G. F. Müller, Sven Waxell, or
to Philip Buache]   2693

Levanevskiĭ, Sigismund. SEE nos.
    2584, Laktionev, A. F. Severny i polīus ... 1955;
    4326, Stefansson, V. Unsolved mysteries ... [c1938];
    4496, Thomas, Lowell. Sir Hubert Wilkins. [c1961];
    4717, Voyage Chelyuskin. By members Exped. 1935;
    4872, Wilkins, G. H. Thoughts through space. 1942.

LEVCHENKO, G. I., edit. Morskoi atlas, tom. 3; voenno-istori-
cheskiĭ, chast' 1; opisaniīā k kartam. Pod obshcheĭ redaktsīēi
admirala G. I. Levchenko. [TITLE TR. Marine atlas, vol. 3;
military history, pt. 1; descriptions to the maps. Admiral
G. I. Levchenko, General Editor] Moskva-Leningrad, Izd. Glavnogo
shtaba voenno-morskogo flota, 1959. 920p. illus. tables, pls.
maps(some fold.), bibliog.   2694

Leveque, James, illus. SEE no. 4243, Sourdough Jack.

Levine, Joseph, co-auth. SEE no. 3601, Pine, T. S.

LEWIS AND DRYDEN'S MARINE HISTORY of the Pacific northwest; an
illustrated review of the growth and development of the maritime
industry, from the advent of the earliest navigators to the present time, with sketches and portraits of a number of well-known
marine men. Edited by Edgar Wilson Wright. Portland, Ore.,
Lewis and Dryden Printing Co., 1895. 494p. front. pls. ports.

ANR. N. Y., Antiquarian Press, 1959. 2 vols. facsim. reprint,
ltd. ed. of 750 copies.   2695

Lewis and Dryden's Marine history ... 1895. SEE ALSO
     no. 2859, McCurdy, H. W. ... Marine hist. ... 1966.

LEWIS, GEORGE EDWARD. Yukon lyrics. Portland, Ore., 1925. 69p.
illus. [poetry]   2696

Lewis, George Edward. SEE ALSO nos.
     573, Blacklock, Alaska. Nick of woods. 1916;
     770, Caldwell, E. N. Alaska trail dogs. 1945;
     2697, Lewis, Jas. C. Black Beaver ... 1911.

LEWIS, JAMES CONRAD. Black Beaver, the trapper; the only book
ever written by a trapper. Twenty-two years with Black Beaver.
Lewis and Clark a hundred years later, from the Amazon to the
MacKenzie River. Written by George E. Lewis at the dictation of
James C. Lewis. Chicago, printed by Robert O. Law Co., 1911.
58p.   2697

Lewis, James Conrad. SEE ALSO no. 770,
     Caldwell, E. N. Alaska trail dogs. 1945.

LEWIS, MICHAEL. England's sea officers. London, Allen & Unwin,
1939. [incls. George Vancouver]   2698

Lewis, Richard, illus. SEE no. 4505, Thompson, D.S.

Lewis, Wm. S., co-edit. SEE no. 2871, MacDonald, Ranald.

L'HOMMEDIEU, DOROTHY K. Togo, the little Husky. Philadelphia,
Lippincott, 1951. 61p. illus.(some col.) by Marquerite Kirmise

LĪALINA, MARĪĪA ALEKSANDROVNA, edit. Russkie moreplavateli; V.
Golovnin (V plīenu u īaponīsev); O. F. Kotsebu (Plavanie na
"Rīurikīe"); G. Nevel'skoī (Prisoedinenie Amurskago kraīa).
Obratotany po podlinnym sochinenīam puteshestvennikov M. A.
Līalinoī. [TITLE TR. Russian sea-farers; V. Golovnin (in
Japanese captivity); O. F. Kotsebue (voyages on the *Rurik*); G.
Nevel'skoī (annexation of the Amur area); edited from the com-
plete reports of the travelers by M. A. Līalina] St. Petersburg,
A. F. Devrien, 1896. 380p. illus. ports. (Russkie puteshest-
venniki-issledovateli)   2700

LIBBY, WILLARD FRANK. Radiocarbon dating. Chicago, University
of Chicago Press, 1955. 2d ed. rev. and enl. 175p. illus.
textmap, diagrs. graphs, tables, bibliog. [incls. some ref. to
Alaska]   2701

LIBERATE ALASKA FROM THE FISH TRAP, by Ketchikan and Cordova fishermen in support of legislation introduced by Delegate E. L. Bartlett of Alaska to prohibit the use of traps, weirs, and pound nets for fishing in the waters of the Territory of Alaska, and legislation to transfer control of Alaskan fisheries to the Territory of Alaska. Ketchikan, 1949. 96p. illus. charts(incl. 3 fold.), tables. 2702

LIDE, ALICE A. and MARGARET A. JOHANSEN. Ood-le-uk the Wanderer. Boston, Little Brown, 1930. 265p. [juvenile fict.] 2703

Life and work Innocent ... 1897. SEE no. 415, [Barsukov, I.P.]

LIFE IN ALASKA. Juneau, 1914. 4p. 2704

LIFE IN ANCHORAGE, ALASKA. 1958 Fur Rendezvous-Dog Mushers' Annual. Anchorage, Greater Anchorage, Inc. and Alaskan Sled Dog and Racing Association, 1958. 64p. illus. photos. ANR. Special 49th Star Edition. 1959 Fur Rendezvous-Dog Mushers' Annual. Anchorage, Greater Anchorage, Inc. and Alaskan Sled Dog and Racing Association, 1959. (72)p. illus. photos. 2705

LIFE OF CAPTAIN COOK. no pl., n. d. 32p. 2706

LIFE OF CAPTAIN JAMES COOK. Dublin, J. Jones, 1924. 179p. front. illus. 2707

LIFE OF CAPTAIN JAMES COOK, a new edition. London, C. F. Cook, 1831. 170p. front. pls. 2708

Life of John Ledyard ... 1828. SEE no. 4252, [Sparks, Jared]

LIFE OF THE REVEREND MOTHER AMADEUS OF THE HEART OF JESUS; foundress of the Ursuline Missions of Montana and Alaska; sketch compiled from convent annals by an Ursuline of Alaska. N. Y., Paulist Press, 1923. 233p. front.(port.) 2709

LIFE, VOYAGES AND DISCOVERIES OF CAPTAIN JAMES COOK. London, J. W. Parker, 1859. 6th ed. 220p. front. pls. ports. 2710

Lincoln, F. C., co-auth. SEE no. 1668, Gabrielson, I. N.

LIND, JENS VILHELM AUGUST. Fungi (micromycetes) collected in Arctic North America (King William Land, King Point and Herschel Island) by the Gjøa Expedition under Captain Roald Amundsen, 1904-1906. Christiana, Jacob Dybwad, 1910. 25p. (Norske videnskapsakademi. Skrifter 1. Matematisk-naturvidenskapelig klasse, 1909, no. 9) 2711

LIND PRINTING CO. Alaska salmon recipe book. Ketchikan, Lind Print. Co., 1961. 2712

LINDBERGH, ANNE MORROW.   North to the Orient.   With maps by
Charles A. Lindbergh. N. Y., Harcourt Brace, 1935. 255p. front.
maps, endmaps, appends. ANR. London, Penquin Books, 1937. 215p.
maps, append. paperback. (Golden Library)   2713

LINDQUIST, WILLIS. Alaska, The forty-ninth state. Drawings by
P. A. Hutchinson. N. Y., McGraw-Hill, 1959. 111p. illus. maps,
chronology. (Whittlesey House)   2714

LINDQUIST, WILLIS. Call of the white fox. Illustrated by P. A.
Hutchinson. N. Y., McGraw-Hill, 1957. 192p. front. (Whittlesey
House)   2715

Lindsay, Matthew, J., comp. SEE no. 5002,
    Yukon and Klondyke ... Alaska. [c1897]

LINDSEY, DOUGLAS. Alaska.   A complete book of reference and
guide to Alaska with three maps, the latest mining laws and all
necessary information in regard to outfits, distances, rates of
fare, etc. By Douglas Lindsey. Stockton, Calif., T. W. Hummel
Pub. House, 1897. 24p. front.(fold. map), illus. maps.   2716

LINDSLEY, AARON LADNER.   Sketches of an excursion to southern
Alaska. By the Reverend Aaron L. Lindsley. [Portland, Ore.,
1879 ?] 73p. ANR. Portland, Ore., 1881. ANR. Seattle, Shorey
Book Store, 1966. facsim. of 1881 ed. [Presbyterian Church] 2717

Lindsley, Aaron Ladner. SEE ALSO nos.
    2105, Hill, E. P. ... Presbyt. statesman ... 1902;
    3886, Ross, Emily L. ... founder Alaska missions ...
            [ca 1910 ?]

LINNAEUS, CAROLUS. Plantae Rariores Camtschatcenses. By Carl
von Linne. Upsaliae, 1750. var. p. [also in his "Amoenitates
Academicae" vol. 2 (1st ed. Holmiae, 1751: 2d ed. Lugduni Bata-
vorum, 1764; 3rd ed. Erlangae, 1787) His dissertation, Upsala,
J. P. Halenius, Respondent. Incls. plants observed by G. W.
Steller in Russian America]   2718

Linnaeus, Carolus. SEE ALSO no. 3623, Plieninger, G. H. T.
    J. G. Gmelini ... epistolici ... 1861.

Linne, Carl von. SEE no. 2718, Linnaeus, Carolus.

LINEBERRY, WILLIAM P., edit. The new states; Alaska and Hawaii.
N. Y.,   H. W. Wilson Co., 1963. 208p. maps, bibliog.   2719

LIPKE, ALICE C. Under the aurora. L. A. and N. Y., Suttonhouse,
1938. 286p. illus. photos.   2720

LIPKIND, WILLIAM. Boy with a harpoon. Illustrated by Nicolas
Mordinoff. N. Y., Harcourt Brace, 1952. 1st ed. 58p. illus.
                                                              2721

LIPS, EVA. Das Indianerbuch. [TITLE TR. The book on Indians] Leipzig, F. A. Brockhaus Verlag, 1956. 443p. illus. maps(incl. fold.) [has reference to Bering land bridge] 2722

LISĪĀNSKIĬ ĪŪRIĬ FEDEROVICH. Puteshestvie vokrug svĭeta v 1803, 4, 5, i 1806 godakh, po povelĭenĭĭu Ego Imperatorskago Velichestva Aleksandra Pervago, na korablĭe *Nevĭe*, pod nachal'stvom. Sanktpeterburg, V. tipogr. F. Drekhslera, 1812. 2 vols. 346p. and 335p. illus. port. WITH ATLAS Sobranie kart i risunkov ... [TITLE TR. Collection of maps and plates belonging to the voyage of ...] St. Petersburg, Naval Printing Office, 1812. pls. maps. ANR. Moskva, Gos. izd-vo geogr. lit-ry, 1947. abr. reprint of 1812 ed. illus. map. [for tr. see no. 2724] 2723

LISĪĀNSKIĬ ĪŪRIĬ FEDEROVICH. Voyage round the world in the years 1803-15, and 1806, performed by order of His Imperial Majesty Alexander the First, emperor of Russia, in the ship *Neva*. London, printed for J. Booth, 1814. 388p. illus.(some col. pls.), port. maps(some col.), charts(some fold.), appends. ANR. Ridgewood, N. J., Gregg Press, 1967. Edited by Ernest S. Dodge. (First Series, America and the Pacific. vol. 6) reprint of London 1814 ed. ANR. Amsterdam, N. Israel and N. Y., Da Capo Press, 1967. (Bibliotheca Australiana, Fourth Series) facsim. reprint of London 1814 ed. [tr. of no. 2723] 2724

Lisĭānskiĭ, Ĭuriĭ Federovich. SEE ALSO nos.
    928, Chukovskiĭ, N. K. Vodeteli fregatov. 1947;
    2814, Lupach, V. S. Kruzenshtern i Lisĭānskiĭ ... 1953;
    3291, Nevskiĭ, V. V. Pervoe puteshestvie ... 1951;
    3364, Nozikov, N. N. Russkie krugosvetnye ... 1941;
    4136, Shteĭnberg, E. L. Kruzenshtern, Lisĭānskiĭ. 1950;
    4137, Shteĭnberg, E. L. Zhizneopisanie russkogo ... 1948.

Lisiansky, Urey. SEE nos. 2723-24, Lisĭānskiĭ, Ĭuriĭ Federovich.

LISITZSKY, GENE. Four ways of being human. N. Y., Viking, 1956. 304p. illus. (Compass no. C128) ANR. N. Y., Viking, 1960. 2725

l'Isle, J. N. De. SEE no. 1257, Delisle, Joseph Nicolas.

LITSHFIELD, SARAH. Hello Alaska. Chicago, A. Whitman & Co., 1945. 31p. illus.(some col.), endmaps. 2726

Litke, Fedor Petrovich. [Alphabetical title guide to chronological entries]

Atlas du voyage ... 2734. Viermalige reise ... 2728.
Chetyrekratnoe ... 2727. Voyage ... 2732, 2735.
Observations ... 2729. Voyage ... [atlas] 2731.
Puteshestvie ... 2730, 2733.

LITKE, FEDOR PETROVICH. Chetyrekratnoe puteshestvie v Sĭevernyĭ Ledovityĭ okean, sovershennoe po povelĭeniĭu Imperatora Aleksandra I. na voennom brigĭe "Novaĭa Zemlĭa," v 1821, 1822, 1823 i 1824 godakh. S prisovokupleniem puteshestviĭ leĭtenanta Dimidova v Bĭeloe more i Shturmana Ivanova na rĭeku Pechoru. [TITLE TR. Four voyages into the Arctic Ocean, undertaken at the command of Emperor Alexander I, in the naval brig *Novaya Zemlya* in 1821-24, with the addition of the voyages of Lt. Demidov into the White Sea and Mate Ivanov to Pechora River] Sanktpeterburg, V. Morskoĭ Tip., 1828. 2 vols. 321p. and 251p. pls.(incl. 1 fold.), maps (some fold.) ANR. 2 vols. in 1. 581p. pls. maps(some fold.) ANR. Moskva, Gos. izd-vo geogr. lit-ry, 1948. 333p. pls. maps (some fold.) enl. from 1828 ed. [for tr. see no. 2728] 2727

LITKE, FEDOR PETROVICH. Viermalige reise durch das nordliche Eismeer, auf der brigg *Nowaja Semlja*, in den jahren 1821 bis 1824. Aus dem Russ. ubersetzt von A. Erman. Berlin, 1825. [tr. of no. 2727] 2728

LITKE, FEDOR PETROVICH. Observations du pendule invariable exécutées dans un voyage autor du monde, pendant les années 1826, 1827, 1828 et 1829. [TITLE TR. Pendulum observations made during the voyage around the world, 1826-1829] Leningrad, Akademiia nauk SSSR, 1937. (Mémoires par divers savants, T.3 242p. pls. (incl. 1 fold.) [incls. those made at Sitka] 2729

LITKE, FEDOR PETROVICH. Puteshestvie vokrug svĭeta, sovershennoe po povelĭeniĭu Imperatora Nikolaĭa I, na voennom shlĭupie *Seniavinĭe* v 1826-9 godakh, flota Kap. Federom Litke. Otdĭelenie istoricheskoe. [TITLE TR. Voyage around the world, carried out by order of Emperor Nicholas I in the Navy sloop *Seniavin*, by Captain Fedor Litke, 1826-29. Historical section] St. Petersburg, Printing Office of H. I. M.'s Chancellery, 1834(1835, 1836) 3 vols. with atlas. 294p., 282p. and 270p. pls. [see no. 2731 for atlas] 2730

ATLAS TO Puteshestvie ... Otdĭelenie istoricheskoe. 1834 (1835, 1836)

Voyage autour de monde ... sur la corvette Le *Séniavine* ... Partie historique ... Lithographié de Engelmann et Compagne. Paris, Cité Bergère, No. 1, n. d. 38p. pls. maps(some fold.) [text and captions in French - same atlas accompanies also no. 2732] 2731

TRANSLATION - Puteshestvie ... Otdĭelenie istoricheskoe. 1834 (1835, 1836)

Voyage autour du monde, exécuté par ordre de sa Majesté l'Empereur Nicolas I, sur la corvette Le *Séniavine*, dans les années 1826, 1827, 1828 et 1829, par Frédérick Lutké, Captaine de vaisseau, Aide-de-Camp de S. M. l'Empereur, Commandant de l'Expédition, partie historique, avec un atlas, lithographié d'après les dessins originaux d'Alexandre Postels et du Baron Kittlitz. Traduit du Russe sur le manuscrit original, sous les yeux de l'auteur, par le Conseiller d'État J. Boyé. Tome premier [Tomes second et troisième] Paris, Typographie de Firmin Didot Freres, 1835-36. 3 vols. 410p., 387p. and 352p. pls. maps. [see no. 2731 for atlas] 2732

LITKE, FEDOR PETROVICH. Puteshestvie vokrug svieta, sovershennoe po povelieniiu Imperatora Nikolaia I, na voennom shliupie "Seniavenie," v 1826, 1827, 1828 i 1829 godakh ... Otdielenie morekhodnoe s atlasom. [TITLE TR. Voyage around the world carried out by order of Emperor Nicholas I on the Navy sloop *Seniavin* in the years 1826-29, by Navy Captain Fedor Litke. Nautical section with an atlas] Sanktpeterburg, Kh. Gintze, 1835. 356p. pls. (some fold.), maps(some fold.) [has captions in Russian and French - for atlas see no. 2734] 2733

ATLAS TO Puteshestvie ... Otdielenie morekhodnoe s atlasom. 1835.

Atlas du voyage autour du monde de la corvette *Séniavine* fait en 1826, 1827, 1828 et 1829 sous les ordres de Frédéric Lutké Capitaine de premier rang de la Marine Imperiale de Russie, Membre du Comite Scientifique de l'État Major de la Marine, de l'Academie Imperiale des Sciences, de las Société Geographique de Londres ... [St. Petersburg, Hydrographic Depot, Naval General Staff of H. I. M., 1832] plans, maps. [title, text and captions in French and Russian - same atlas accompanies no. 2735] 2734

TRANSLATION - Puteshestvie ... Otdielenie morekhodnoe s atlasom. 1835.

Voyage autour du monde, éxécuté par ordre de Sa Majesté l'Empereur Nicolas I, sur la corvette Le *Séniavine*, dans les années 1826, 1827, 1828 et 1829, sous le commandement de Frédéric Lutké, Capitaine de la Marine Imperiale de Russie, Commandant de l'Expédition; traduit du Russe, sous les yeux de l'auteur, par le Conseiller d'État J. Boyé. Partie nautique avec un atlas. St. Petersburg, Kh. Gintze, 1836. 343p. pls. (some fold.), tables, index. [captions in French and Russian - accompanied by same atlas as described, see no. 2734] 2735

Litke, Fedor Petrovich. SEE ALSO nos.
    557, Biogaphie du dr. Mertens ... n. d.;
    1314, Dobrovol'skii, A. D. Plavaniia F. P. Litke ... 1948;
    2479, Kittlitz, F. H. von. Vierundzwanzig ... 1844;
    2678, Lenz, H. F. E. Nabliudeniia ... 1836;
    2967, Marich, M. [pseud.] Zhizn' i plavaniia ... 1949;
    3418, Orlov, B. P. Fedor Petrovich Litke ... 1948;
    3654, Postels, A. Illustrationes algarum ... 1840.

LITTEN, FREDERIC N. Air trails north. N. Y., Dodd Mead, 1939.
236p.   2736

LITTEN, FREDERIC N. Pilot of the north country; a Johnny
Caruthers flying story. N. Y., Dodd Mead, 1938. 244p.   2737

LITTLE KLONDYKE NUGGET. Story of the discovery. Official reports - who ought to go - medical advice - how to avoid many
hardships - best outfit - shortest routes - precious items about
mining useful to all - Canadian customs deputies - maps and illustrations - calendar - department for expense account, receipts,
memoranda - etc. etc. U. S. and Canada mining laws in full. From
official documents. Chicago, Laird & Lee, Pub., 1897. 150p.
front. pls. 21 ruled ℓ , calendar, maps(incl. 1 fold.)   2738

LITURGY AND HYMNS IN THE ESKIMO LANGUAGE of the Kuskokwim district, Alaska, as used by the Moravian Mission. Green Bay, 1945.
                                                             2739
Liturgy and ritual in Tinne ... 1904. SEE
     no. 2352, Jette, Julius.

LLORENTE, SEGUNDO. A Orillas del "Kusko." [TITLE TR. The banks
of the "Kusko." Bilbao, Spain, 1951.   2740

LLOYD, CHARLES CHRISTOPHER, edit. The voyages of Captain James
Cook round the world. Selected from his journals ... London,
Cresset Press, 1949. 384p. maps, endmaps. (The Cresset Library)
ANR. [in French] Paris, R. Juilliard, 1951. 403p. map.   2741

Lloyd, Charles Christopher. SEE ALSO no. 3533, [Penrose, C. V.]
     Memoir James Trevenen ... 1959.

LLOYD-OWEN, FRANCES. Gold Nugget Charlie; a narrative compiled
from the notes of Charles E. Masson. Saga of the west and the
great white northland. London, Geo. Harrap & Co., 1939. 259p.
front. pls. ports. endmaps.   2742

LLWYD, JOHN PLUMMER DERWENT. The message of an Indian relic.
Seattle, Lowman & Hanford, 1909. 21p. pls.   2743

LOBANOV-ROSTOVSKIĬ, ALEKSANDR ĨAKOVLEVICH. Kratkaĩa relĩatsiĩa o
Sibirskoĭ ėkspediťsiĭ flota Kap. Beringa. [TITLE TR. Short ac-
count of the Siberian expedition of Naval Captain Bering] St.
Petersburg, 1824. 28p.   2744

Lobel, Loïcq de. SEE no. 4436, Syndicat Français du Trans-
     Alaska-Sibérien.

Locella, G., tr. SEE no. 1228, deFilippo, Filippo.

LOCKLEY, FRED. Alaska's first free mail delivery in 1900. Portland, Ore., n. d. 9p. ANR. Seattle, Shorey Book Store, 1967.
facsim. reprint.   2745

LOCKWOOD, MARY JANE and CYRUS KINEGAK, edits. Writings from Alaska, University of Alaska Upward Bound, Summer 69. no pl., n. d. [Fairbanks, 1969 ?] 36p. sketches, collages. [short stories, poetry, essays]   2746

LODOCHNIKOV, ANDRE. Molitvy i Piesnopiennia Pravoslavnoĭ Tserkvi na Aleutskom Nariechiĭ, perevodie na Aleutskiĭ jazyk bivshiv Psalomshchik Unalashkinskoĭ Tserkvi Andrei Lodochnikov. [TITLE TR. Prayers and canticles of the Orthodox Church in the Aleutian dialect by the Psalmodist of the Unalaskan Church, Andre Lodoch-nikov] N. Y., Amerikanskiĭ Pravda Viēstnik, 1898. 77p.   2747

LOFTUS, AUDREY. According to Grandfather (the Medicine Man). Fairbanks, by author, 1965. 1st print. 33p. illus. sketches. [Athabaskan Indians of the Interior - Tanana region]   2748

Loftus, Audrey. SEE ALSO nos.
    249, Anderson, Laura David. According to Mama. 1956;
    3506, Paul, David. According to Papa. 1957.

LOKKE, CARL L. Klondike saga. Minneapolis, University of Minne-sota, 1965. illus.   2749

Lomen Brothers, photog. SEE nos.
    222, Amundsen, R. E. G. First crossing polar sea. 1928;
    1182, Darling, E. B. The great dog races of Nome. n. d.;
    3123, Miller, Max. Great trek ... reindeer ... 1935.

LOMEN, CARL JOYS. Fifty years in Alaska. By Carl J. Lomen. N. Y., David McKay, 1954. 302p. endmaps. [autobiog.]   2750

LOMEN, HELEN and MARJORIE FLACK. Taktuk; an Arctic boy. Garden City, N. Y., Doubleday Doran, 1928. 1st ed. 139p. front.(col.), pls.(some col.), endmaps.   2751

Lomen, Ralph, co-auth. SEE no. 2309, Jackson, G. R.

LOMONOSOV, MIKHAIL VASIL'EVICH. Kratkoe opisanie raznykh puteshestviĭ po Sĭevernym morĭam, i pokazanie vozmozhnago prokho-da Sibirskim okeanom v. Vostochnuĭu Indiĭu. [TITLE TR. Brief account of sundry voyages in the northern waters and demonstra-tion of the possibility of a passage by Siberian waters to the East Indies] St. Petersburg, 1847. 150p. [with two supplements] ANR. 1854. (vol. 7 of "Sochinenĭu." 1091 1934)   2752

LOMONOSOV, MIKHAIL VASIL'EVICH. Razsuzhdenie o boljshoi Tochnos-ti morskago puti, chitannoe v publichnom sobraniĭ Akademiĭ Nauk, Maiĭa 8 dnia 1759 goda. [TITLE TR. Dissertation on the maximum of precision in sea travel, read at a public meeting of the Im-perial Academy of Sciences, 8 May, 1759] St. Petersburg, 1759. 52p. [Chichagof's voyage based on this]   2753

Lomonosov, Mikhail Vasil'evich. Sochineniia. SEE no. 2752.

Lomonosov, Mikhail Vasil'evich. SEE ALSO nos.
   3080, Menshutkin, B. N. Russia's Lomonosov. 1952;
   3081, Menshutkin, B. N. Zhizneopisanie ... 1937;
   3535, Perevalov, V. A. Lomonosov i Arktika ... 1949;
   4236, Sokolov, A. P. Proekt Lomonosova...Chichagova. 1854.

LONDON, JACK. A daughter of the snows. With illustrations in
color by Frederick C. Yohn. Philadelphia, Lippincott, 1902.
334p. OTHERS var. reprints and translations.   2754

London, Jack. An odyssey of the North. SEE no. 2783.

LONDON, JACK. Best short stories of Jack London. Garden City,
N. Y., Sun Dial Press, 1945. 311p. OTHERS var. dates and editions.   2755

LONDON, JACK. Brown wolf and other Jack London stories as chosen
by Franklin K. Mathews, Editor. Chief Scout Librarian, B. S. A.
N. Y., Macmillan, 1920. 312p. front. pl. OTHERS var. dates. 2756

LONDON, JACK. Burning Daylight. N. Y., Macmillan, 1910. 361p.
front. pls. OTHERS var. editions, reprints and translations.2757

LONDON, JACK. Children of the frost. N. Y., Macmillan, 1902.
261p. illustrated by Raphael M. Reay. OTHERS var. reprints and
translations.   2758

LONDON, JACK. Great short works of Jack London. Edited and with
an introduction by Earle Labor. N. Y., Harper & Row, 1965. 379p.
bibliog.   2759

LONDON, JACK. Jack London's stories for boys. N. Y., Cupples
and Leon, 1936. 121p. illustrated by C. Richard Schaare.   2760

LONDON, JACK. Jack London's tales of adventure. Edited by Irving Shepard. Garden City, N. Y., Hanover House, 1956. 531p.
                                                                 2761

LONDON, JACK. Lost face. N. Y., Macmillan, 1910. 240p. front.
illus. OTHERS var. reprints. [short stories]   2762

LONDON, JACK. Love of life, and other stories. N. Y., Macmillan,
1907. 265p. OTHERS var. reprints and translations. SEE ALSO
no. 2781.   2763

LONDON, JACK. Moon-face, and other stories. N. Y., Macmillan,
1906. 273p. OTHERS var. reprints and translations.   2764

LONDON, JACK. Revolution, and other essays. N. Y., Macmillan,
1910. 309p. OTHERS var. reprints and translations.   2765

LONDON, JACK. Smoke Bellew. Illustrated by P. J. Monahan. N. Y., Century Co., 1912. 385p. front. illus. OTHERS var. reprints and translations. 2766

LONDON, JACK. Stories of the North. Selected by Betty M. Owen. N. Y., Scholastic Book Services, 1966. [c1965] 1st print. 248p. paperback. (Scholastic Library Edition, no. T660) 2767

LONDON, JACK. Tales of the far North. Girard, Kansas, Haldeman-Julius Co., n. d. [ca 1920] (Little Blue Book, no. 288) 2768

LONDON, JACK. Tales of the white silence. Girard, Kansas, Haldeman-Julius Co., n. d. [ca 1920] (Little Blue Book, no. 1024) 2769

LONDON, JACK. The Bodley Head Jack London. Edited by Arthur Calder-Marshall. London, John Lane, 1963. 377p. (The Bodley Head) [short stories] 2770

LONDON, JACK. The call of the wild. Illustrated by Philip R. Goodwin and Charles Livingston Bull. N. Y., Macmillan, 1903. 231p. front.(col.), pls.(col.) OTHERS in many printings, editions and translations. SEE ALSO no. 2780. 2771

LONDON, JACK. The call of the wild and other stories, with biographical illustrations and pictures of contemporary scenes together with introduction and captions by Louis B. Salomon. N. Y., Dodd Mead, 1960. 142p. (Great Illustrated Classics) 2772

LONDON, JACK. The call of the wild and other stories, with introduction by Frank Luther Mott. N. Y., Macmillan, 1926. 268p. front. (Modern Readers' Series) ANR. 1935. 2773

LONDON, JACK. The call of the wild and selected stories. N. Y., New American Library, 1960. 176p. paperback. (Signet Classic, no. CD20) 2774

LONDON, JACK. The call of the wild and White Fang. N. Y., Washington Square Press, 1962. ANR. N. Y., 1966. 11th print. 337p. front.(map), paperback. (A Washington Square Press Book, no. W-275) 2775

LONDON, JACK. The call of the wild. The cruise of the *Dazzler*. And other stories of adventure. With the author's special report; Gold hunters of the North. N. Y., Platt & Munk, 1960. 528p. (Platt & Munk Great Writers Collection) 2776

LONDON, JACK. The call of the wild, White Fang and The scarlet plague. Introduction by Bernard Fergusson. London, Collins, 1953. 384p. 3 vols. in 1. (Collins New Classic Series) 2777

LONDON, JACK. The faith of men, and other stories. N. Y., Macmillan, 1904. 286p. OTHERS var. reprints and translations. 2778

LONDON, JACK. The god of his fathers, and other stories. N. Y.,
McClure Phillips, 1901. 299p. ANR. WITH TITLE The God of his
fathers, tales of the Klondyke. London, Isbester, 1902. 308p.
ANR. London, Pitman, 1907. OTHERS var. reprints and translations.
2779

LONDON, JACK. The scarlet plague and The call of the wild.
N. Y., Collier, 1931. (Seven Seas Edition) SEE ALSO no. 2777.
2780

LONDON, JACK. The scarlet plague. Love of life. The unexpected.
Three stories. London, Staples Press, 1946. 100p.   2781

LONDON, JACK. The sea-wolf. Illustrated by W. J. Aylward.
N. Y., Macmillan, 1904. 466p. illus. OTHERS var. reprints and
translations.   2782

LONDON, JACK. The son of the wolf. Tales of the far North.
Boston, Houghton, 1900. 251p. front. OTHERS var. reprints and
translations. ANR. WITH TITLE An odyssey of the North. London,
Mills & Boon, 1915. 284p. (Mills & Boon Shilling Cloth Library)
2783

LONDON, JACK. The sun-dog trail, and other stories. Cleveland,
World Pub. Co., [c1951] 1st ed. 251p.   2784

LONDON, JACK. White Fang. N. Y., Macmillan, 1906. 327p. front.
pls.(col.) OTHERS var. reprints and translations. SEE ALSO nos.
2775 and 2777.   2785

London, Jack. SEE ALSO nos.
 769, Calder-Marshall, A. Lone wolf; story of ... 1961;
 1628, Franchere, R. Jack London ... 1962;
 1690, Garst, Shannon. Jack London ... 1944;
 1868, Grønlund, H. Pan hat med Jack London. 1944;
 2593, Lane, F. A. Greatest adventure ... 1954;
 2594, Lane, R. W. Gordon Blake. 1925;
 2594, Lane, R. W. He was a man. 1925;
 2674, Leiberman, E. American short story ... 1912;
 2680, Leonhardy, A. Directed study ... Call of wild ... 1929;
 2786, London, Joan. Jack London ... 1939;
 3012, Martino, S. Jak London. Spunti ... 1934;
 3378, O'Connor, R. Jack London ... 1964;
 3415, Ordaz, Luis. Jack London; el rey ... 1946;
 3503, Pattee, F. L. Sidelights Amer. lit. 1922;
 3860, Roden, D. London's Call of wild ... 1965;
 3874, Romano, V. Jack London. [in Ital.] 1952;
 4062, Service, R. W. Spell ... plus Terrible Solomons...1943;
 4228, Sobotka, H. A. Kraj Bohaterów Jacka Londona. 1929;
 4235, Sokolicz, A. Jack London. 1925;
 4353, Stone, I. Sailor on horseback. 1938;
 4499, Thomas, L., jr. Trail of '98. [c1962];

4668, Vedde, S. Jack London ! Introd. til ... 1943;
4728, Walcutt, C. C. Jack London. 1966;
4955, Woodbridge, H. C. Jack London; a bibliog. 1966.

LONDON, JOAN. Jack London and his times; an unconventional
biography. N. Y., Doubleday, 1939. 387p. index. ANR. N. Y.,
Book League of America, 1939. 387p. ANR. Seattle, University of
Washington Press, 1968. (Americana Library)   2786

London, John, co-edit. SEE no. 4955, Woodbridge, H. C.

London, John Griffith. SEE nos. 2754-85, London, Jack.

Long, John, tr. SEE no. 3649, [Portlock, N.]

LONGSTRETH, THOMAS MORRIS. The Force carries on; the sequel to
The scarlet Force. Illustrated by Clare Bice. Toronto, Macmillan, 1954. 182p. illus.(some col.) (Great Stories of Canada)
[incls. acct. of Canadian icebreaker, *St. Roch*]   2787

LONGSTRETH, THOMAS MORRIS. The scarlet Force; the making of
the Mounted Police. Illustrated by Ruth M. Collins. N. Y., Macmillan, 1953. 182p. illus. endmaps(col.) (Great Stories of
Canada) [incls. Yukon gold rush]   2788

LONGSTRETH, THOMAS MORRIS. The silent Force; scenes from the
life of the Mounted Police of Canada. N. Y., The Century Co.,
1927. 383p. front. pls. maps, index. ANR. London, Philip Alan
& Col, 1928. [much about Yukon gold rush]   2789

Longyear Co., E. J. SEE no. 3125, Miller, Maynard.

LONNEUX, MARTIN J. Catholic manual of prayers in Innuit. no pl.,
n. d. [Chaneliak, Alaska, ca 1950 ?]   2790

LONNEUX, MARTIN J. Mass book and hymnal in Innuit. Missarchutit
Kalikat. Chaneliak (Hamilton P. O.), Alaska, Aug. 15, 1950. 129p.
index.   2791

LONNEUX, MARTIN J. The graded catechism in Innuit. Chaneliak,
Alaska, 1951. 292p.   2792

"Looting of men's character ... " 1906. SEE no. 1933,
    [Hansbrough, H. C.]

LOPP, WILLIAM THOMAS. Alaska; a year alone in Alaska. N. Y.,
American Missionary Association, n. d. 11p.   2793

LOPP, WILLIAM THOMAS. White Sox; the story of the reindeer in
Alaska. Drawings by H. Boylston Dummer. Yonkers-on-Hudson,
N. Y., World Book Co., 1924. 76p. front. (Animal Life Series)
ANR. 1927.   2794

Lopp, William Thomas. SEE ALSO no. 4528,
    Thornton, H. R. Report Alaska Mission, 1892-93. n. d.

LORD, CLIFFORD SYMINGTON. Geological reconnaissance along the
Alaska Highway between Watson Lake and Teslin River, Yukon and
British Columbia. Ottawa, 1944. 20p. map(fold.) (Canada.
Geological Survey Paper no. 42-25)   2795

Lord, L. M., & Co., pub. SEE no. 1879, Guide, map and
    hist. Klondyke ... n. d.

LORENZ, LUDWIG von. Das Becken der Stellerschen Seekuh. [TITLE
TR. The pelvis of Steller's sea cow] Wien, R. Lechner(W. Müller),
1904. 11p. (Geologische Bundesanstalt, Abhandlungen. Bd. 19,
Heft 3)   2796

LORING, CHARLES G. Memoir of the Hon. William Sturgis. Prepared
agreeably to a resolution of the Massachusetts Historical Society.
By Charles G. Loring. Boston, Press of John Wilson & Son, 1864.
64p. appends. [Sturgis was master of ship trading for furs on
northwest coast]   2797

Lothian, W. F. SEE no. 816, Canada. Yukon Terr. 1947.

Lotsiia Chukotskogo moriia. 1938. SEE no. 4618,U. S. S. R.
    Gidrograficheskoe upravlenie.

LOTZ, JAMES ROBERT. Some notes on a journey from Whitehorse to
Juneau, Alaska, via Skagway and Haines, July 25-26th, 1962. Ottawa, August 1962. 9p. illus.   2798

Louderback, Walt, illus. SEE no. 1146, Curwood, Jas. O.

LOUDON, W. J. A Canadian geologist. Toronto, Macmillan, 1930.
                                                               2799
Louis [pseud.] SEE no. 1752, Gold fields ... 1897.

LOUVAIN, ROBERT and others. White wilderness. N. Y., Simon &
Schuster, 1958. 54p. illus.(col.), index. (Walt Disney Productions) ANR. N. Y., Golden Press, 1958.   2800

LOVE, W. T. Placer mining laws of Alaska for the prospector.
Nome, 1901. 28p.   2801

LOW, CHARLES RATHBONE. Captain Cook's three voyages round the
world; with a sketch of his life. By Commander Charles Rathbone
Low. London, Geo. Routledge, n. d. 512p. illus. pls.(col.)
ANR. 1875. 1st ed. OTHERS var. dates.   2802

Low-down truth ... 1923. SEE no. 1520,
    Fairbanks Daily News-Miner.

LOWE, CHARLES WILLIAM. Freshwater algae and freshwater diatoms. Ottawa, King's Printer, 1923. 53p. pls. map. (Canadian Arctic Expedition Report, vol. 4, Botany, Pt. A) [incls. Teller, Alaska] 2803

LOYAL LEAGUE, THE. Popular national songs to be sung at the meetings of the League at Ruby, Long, Poorman and Tanana. Ruby, Record Citizen Print., 1918. 20p. 2804

LUCAS, F. A. Animals of the past; an account of some of the creatures of the ancient world. N. Y., American Museum of Natural History, 1922. (Handbook Series no. 4, 6th ed.) [incls. refs. to bones of mammoths and mastodons found in Alaska] 2805

LUCIA, ELLIS. Klondike Kate; the life and legend of Kitty Rockwell, the queen of the Yukon. N. Y., Hastings House, 1962. 305p. illus. bibliog. index. 2806

LUCIW, WASYL and THEODORE LUCIW. Ahapius Honcharenko and The Alaska Herald; the editor's life and an analysis of his newspaper. Toronto, Slavia Library, 1963. 120p. front.(port.), pls. ports. facsims. bibliog. index, wrps. [has cover title: Ahapius Honcharenko "Alaska Man"] 2807

LUGRIN, CHARLES HENRY, Pub. Yukon gold fields; map showing routes from Victoria, B. C., to the various mining camps on the Yukon River and its branches; mining regulations of the Dominion Government and forms of application together with table of distances, extracts from Mr. Ogilvie's reports, and other information. Published by Chas. H. Lugren. Victoria, B. C., Colonist Print. & Pub. Co., 1897. 32p. map(fold.) 2808

LUKENS, MATILDA BARNS. The Inland Passage; a journal of a trip to Alaska. no pl., 1889. 84p. 2809

LULL, RICHARD S. The evolution of the elephant. N. H., Yale University, 1908. 44p. (Peabody Museum of Natural History, Guide no. 2) 2810

LULL, RODERICK. Call to battle; a novel. Garden City, N. Y., Doubleday, 1943. 304p. [World War II, Japanese attack on Pacific Coast] 2811

LUND, MORTEN. The Inside Passage to Alaska. Philadelphia, Lippincott, 1965. illus. maps (Sports Illustrated Cruise Book) 2812

LUND, ROBERT. The Alaskan. N. Y., John Day Co., 1953. ANR. N. Y., Bantam Books, 1955. 1st paperback ed. 366p. [fict.] 2813

Lung, Edw. B. SEE no. 3013, Martinsen, E. L.

LUPACH, V. S. I. F. Kruzenshtern i Ĩŭ. F. Lisĩanskiĩ; pod red.
M. S. Bodnarskogo. [TITLE TR. I. F. Krusenstern and Ĩŭ. F.
Lisĩanskiĩ; edited by M. S. Bodnarskiĩ]. Moskva, Gos. izd-vo
geogr. lit-ry, 1953. 46p. illus. map. [voyages of *Neva* and
Nadezhda round the world, 1803-06]   2814

LUPACH, V. S., edit. Russkie moreplavateli. [TITLE TR. Russian
navigators] Moskva, Voennoe izd-vo Ministerstva oborony, 1953.
671p. illus. ports. map, maps(text), supplements, indexes. 2815

LÜTGEN, KURT. Two against the Arctic. The story of a restless
life between Greenland and Alaska. Translated from German by
Isabel and Florence McHugh. N. Y., Pantheon, 1957. 239p. illustrated by K. J. Blisch, drawings, maps(incl. front.) [ori-
ginally published in German as "Kein Winter für Wölfe,"by Georg
Westermann Verlag, Braunschweig]   2816

Lutke, Fedor (Fyodor) Petrovich. SEE nos. 2727-35,
    Litke, Fedor Petrovich.

LUTZ, HAROLD JOHN. Aboriginal man and white man as historical
causes of fires in the boreal forest, with particular reference
to Alaska. N. H., Yale University, 1959. 49p. bibliog. (School
of Forestry Bulletin, no. 65)   2817

L'VOV, V. E. Zavoevanie polĩarnykh pustyn'. [TITLE TR. Conquest of the polar wastes] Leningrad, Viestnik znaniĩa, 1928.
62p. illus. maps. (Priroda i lĩudi, no. 10) [Roald Amundsen
and other explorers]   2818

LYNCH, JEREMIAH. Three years in the Klondike. London, Edward
Arnold, 1904. 280p. front. pls. map(fold.) ANR. Chicago, Lakeside Press, 1967. 375p. front.(port.), illus. map(dble.), notes,
index. [for tr. see no. 2820]   2819

LYNCH, JEREMIAH. Trois ans au Klondike, traduit de l'anglais par
Paul Lefevre. Paris, Librarie Ch. Delagrave, [1905] 302p. front.
pls. map(fold.) [tr. of no. 2819]   2820

LYNGE, BERNT. Lichens from the *Gjøa* Expedition. Kristiana,
Jacob Dybwad, 1921. 7p. (Norske videnskaps-akademi, Oslo, Skrif-
ter. I. Matematisk-naturhistoriske klasse, 1921, no. 15) [incls.
King Point on Arctic Yukon coast]   2821

Lynner, J., tr. SEE no. 3071, Meldgaard, J.

Lyon, F. H., tr. SEE nos.
    2266, Ingstad, H. Nunamiut. 1954;
    2892, MacFie, H. Wasa Wasa. 1951.

Lyons, Esther, comp. SEE no. 4914, Wilson, Veazie.

LYONS, HENRY. The Royal Society, 1660-1940. By Sir Henry Lyons.
Cambridge, Cambridge University Press, 1944.   2822

LYSONS, FRED H. Map-guide; Seattle to Dawson. Over the Chilkoot, through the lakes and down the Yukon. Seattle, Humes,
Lysons & Sallee, 1897. 80p. map.   2823

Lyttleton, E. SEE no. 2590, Lancaster, G. B. [pseud.]

M

MABEE, JACK. Sourdough Jack's cookery; authentic sourdough
cookery from his country kitchen. S. F., Argonaut House, dist.,
1965. 6th print. 48p. illus. index. [first printed in 1959]
                                                               2824

McAFEE, ADAH B. Haines Hospital, Alaska. N. Y., Woman's Board
Home Missions of the Presbyterian Church in U. S. A., 1911. 8p.
(leaflet no. 2)   2825

McALLISTER, D. E. List of the marine fishes of Canada. Ottawa,
Department of Northern Affairs and Natural Resources, 1960. 76p.
bibliog. index. (National Museum of Canada. Bull. no. 168,
Biol. Ser. no. 62)   2826

McALLISTER, D. E. and R. J. Krejsa. Placement of the prowfishes,
Zaproridae, in the superfamily *Stichaeoidae*. Ottawa, Department
of Northern Affairs and Natural Resources, 1961. 4p. bibliog.
(National Museum of Canada. Natural History Papers no. 11,
July 24, 1961)   2827

McArthur, C. A., illus. SEE no. 4382, Sullivan, May K.

McArthur, James, co-auth. SEE no. 447, Beach, Rex.

McBain, Sheila K., co-edit. SEE no. 1594, Foote, D. C.

MacBETH, RODERICK GEORGE. Policing the plains; being the real-
life record of the famous Royal Northwest Mounted Police. London,
Hodder & Stoughton, 1920. 320p. front. pls. ports. OTHERS var.
editions. ANR. Toronto, Musson, 1931. rev. & enl. 252p. front.
pls. ports. [has some Yukon gold rush refs.]   2828

McBRIDGE, JAMES LLOYD. Golden glacier. Garden City, N. Y.,
Doubleday Doran, 1932. 244p.   2829

McBRIDE, JAMES LLOYD. The Smoky Valley claim. Illustrated by
E. Joseph Dreany. Caldwell, Idaho, Caxton, 1948. 260p. illus.
[fict. with Kenai Peninsula locale]   2830

McBRIDE, WILLIAM D.   The saga of the riverboats.   Compiled by
W. D. McBride.   Saga of famed packets and other steamboats of
mighty Yukon River.   no pl., n. d.   var. pagings. [extract from
Cariboo and Northwest Digest, Winter 1948-Spring 1949 issues]2831

McCAIN, CHARLES W.   History of the S. S. *Beaver*; being a graphic
and vivid sketch of this noted pioneer steamer and her romantic
cruise for over half a century on the placid island-dotted waters
of the North Pacific, also containing a description of the Hudson's Bay Company from its formation in 1670, down to the present
time.   Vancouver, B. C., Evans & Hasting, 1894.   99p.   illus. pls.
ports. facsim.   2832

McCALLEN, BARBARA (GEAN)   The ivory carver.   As told and illustrated by Barbara (Gean) McCallen.   Anchorage, Anchorage Printing
Co., 1964.   19p.   illus. wrps.[five and one-half by four and one-
quarter inches in size]   2833

McCLELLAN, ROLANDER GUY.   The golden state;   a history of the
region west of the Rocky Mountains;   embracing California, Oregon, Nevada, Utah, Arizona, Idaho, Washington Territory, British
Columbia, and Alaska, from the earliest period to the present
time ... with a history of Mormonism and the Mormons.   By R. Guy
McClellan.   Philadelphia, W. Flint & Co., 1872.   685p.   front.
pls. ports. maps. ANR. 1872.   711p.   OTHERS 1874 AND 1875.   ANR.
1876.   820p.   2834

McClintock, Eva, edit.   SEE no. 4875, Willard, Carrie M. White.

M'CLURE, ROBERT JOHN Le MESURIER.   The discovery of the northwest passage by H. M. S. "Investigator,"   Captain R. M'Clure,
1850, 1851, 1852, 1853, 1854.   Edited by Commander Sherard Osborn,
from the logs and journals of Captain Robert Le M. M'Clure.   Illustrated by Commander S. Gurney Cresswell.   London, Longman,
Brown, Green, Longmans & Roberts, 1856.   (20)405(1)p.   front. pls.
map(fold.)   OTHERS London, Longman, 1857.   2d ed.   463p.   front.
(port.), pls. map.   ALSO 1859.   3d ed. AND Edinburgh, Blackwood,
1865.   4th ed.   358p.   map(fold.)   ANR. Rutland, Vt. and Tokyo,
Japan, Charles E. Tuttle, 1969.   405p.   facsim. of 1856 ed. [has
append. by R. Maguire at Pt. Barrow]   2835

M'CLURE, ROBERT JOHN Le MESURIER and others.   The melancholy fate
of Sir John Franklin and his party, as disclosed in Dr. Rae's
report;   with the despatches and letters of Captain M'Clure, and
other officers employed in the Arctic expedition.   London,
J. Betts, 1854.   56p.   [contains summary of exploration for northwest passage]   2836

M'Clure, Robert John Le Mesurier.   SEE ALSO nos.
       23, Aick, Gerhard.   Scheres Eis voraus ! 1953;
      304, Armstrong, Alexander.   Personal narrat. ... 1857;
      498, Benham, D.   Sketches ... Miert ... 1854;
     1823-4, Great Britain.   Parl. (Franklin Search);

3093, Meyer, K.-H. Fünf Jahre ... [1950];
3102, Miertsching, J. A. Reise-Tagebuch ... 1855.

McCONNELL, RICHARD GEORGE. Preliminary report on the Klondike gold fields, Yukon District, Canada. Ottawa, Government Printing Bureau, 1900. 44p. pls. diagrs. map(fold.) (Canada. Geological Survey)　　　　　　　　　　　　　　　　　　　　　2837

McCONNELL, RICHARD GEORGE. Report on an exploration in the Yukon and Mackenzie Basins, Northwest Territory. [with atlas] Montreal, 1890. 163p. maps(some fold.) (Canada. Geological Survey, Annual Report, vol. 4, pt. D, Geology and Natural History Survey of Canada, 1888-89)　　　　　　　　　　　　　　2838

McCONNELL, RICHARD GEORGE. Report on gold values in the Klondike high level gravels. Ottawa, Government Printing Bureau, 1907. 34p. pls.(some fold.), map(col. fold.) (Canada. Geological Survey, Bulletin no. 979)　　　　　　　　　　　　　　　2839

McCONNELL, RICHARD GEORGE. Report on the Klondike gold fields. Ottawa, S. E. Dawson, 1905. 71p. pls. diagrs. maps(col.fold.) (Canada. Geological Survey, Annual Report, vol. 14, pt. B, n.s., 1901)　　　　　　　　　　　　　　　　　　　　　2840

McConnell, Richard George. SEE ALSO no. 1216,
　　　Dawson, Geo. M. Report Yukon district ... 1898.

McCORKLE, RUTH. The Alaskan ten-footed bear and other legends. Illustrated by Wilbur Walluk. Seattle, Robert D. Seal,pub., 1958. 39p. illus.　　　　　　　　　　　　　　　　　2841

McCRACKEN, HAROLD. Alaska bear trails. Illustrated with photos by the author. Garden City, N. Y., Doubleday Doran, 1931. 1st ed. 260p. front.(pl.), pls. ports. [Stoll-McCracken exped. for American Museum of Natural History to Alaska Peninsula] 2842

McCRACKEN, HAROLD. Beyond the frozen frontier. N. Y., Robert Speller Pub. Corp., 1936. 1st ed. 233p. [fict.]　　　　2843

McCRACKEN, HAROLD. God's frozen children. Animals, men and mummies of the far north. Garden City, N. Y., Doubleday Doran, 1930. 1st ed. 291p. front. pls. endmaps, append. [Stoll-McCracken exped. for American Museum of Natural History,and Aleutian Islanders]　　　　　　　　　　　　　　　2844

McCRACKEN, HAROLD. Hunters of the stormy sea. Garden City, N. Y., Doubleday, 1957. 1st ed. 312p. illus. maps, bibliog. notes, index. [history of Aleutians, sea otters and fur trade]
　　　　　　　　　　　　　　　　　　　　　　　2845

McCRACKEN, HAROLD. Iglaome. N. Y., Century Co., 1930. [short stories of Bering Sea coastal Eskimos]　　　　　　　2846

McCRACKEN, HAROLD. Pirate of the north. Drawings by Ernest Tonk. Philadelphia, Lippincott, 1953. 1st ed. 213p. illus. [fict. account of wolverine]   2847

McCRACKEN, HAROLD. Roughnecks and gentlemen. Garden City, N. Y., Doubleday & Co., 1968. 1st ed. 441p. illus. photos, index. [autobiog.]   2848

McCRACKEN, HAROLD. Sentinel of the snow peaks; a story of the Alaskan wild mountain sheep. Philadelphia, Lippincott, 1945. 151p. illustrated by Enos B. Comstock. pls. map. [fict. - setting is St. Elias Range]   2849

McCRACKEN, HAROLD. Son of the walrus king. Philadelphia, Lippincott, 1944. 129p. drawings by Lynn Bogue Hunt. front.(col.), pls. [natural history - Little Diomede Island]   2850

McCRACKEN, HAROLD. The beast that walks like man; the story of the grizzly bear. Garden City, N. Y., Hanover House, 1955. 319p. pls. append. bibliog. notes, index. [Alaska Peninsula]   2851

McCRACKEN, HAROLD. The biggest bear on earth. Philadelphia, Lippincott, 1943. 114p. drawings by Paul Bransom. front.(col.), pls. [fict. account of Alaska Peninsula brown bear]   2852

McCRACKEN, HAROLD. The caribou traveler. Philadelphia, Lippincott, 1949. 204p. illus. map [migrations of Barren Ground caribou]   2853

McCRACKEN, HAROLD. The flaming bear. Philadelphia, Lippincott, 1951. 1st ed. 222p. illus. [fict. based on Aleut legend]   2854

McCRACKEN, HAROLD. The last of the sea otters. Philadelphia, Frederick A. Stokes, 1942. 99p. illustrated by Paul Bransom. front.(col.)   2855

McCRACKEN, HAROLD. The story of Alaska. Garden City, N. Y., Garden City Books, 1956. 1st ed. 57p. drawings by Earl Oliver Hurst. endmaps. [juv. hist.]   2856

McCRACKEN, HAROLD. Toughy; bulldog of the Arctic. Philadelphia, Lippincott, 1948. 202p. illustrated by Carl Burger. [mascot of Stoll-McCracken Expedition]   2857

McCRACKEN, HAROLD and HARRY VAN CLEVE. Trapping; the craft and science of catching fur-bearing animals, by Harold McCracken and Harry Van Cleve. N. Y., A. S. Barnes, 1947. 196p. illustrated by Howard L. Hastings.   2858

McCullough, J. G., edit. SEE no. 3567, Phelps, Edw. J.

McCURDY, HORACE WINSLOW. The H. W. McCurdy marine history of the Pacific Northwest; an illustrated review of the growth and development of the maritime industry from 1895, the date of publication of the last such comprehensive history (Lewis and Dryden's marine history of the Pacific Northwest) to the present time, with sketches and portraits of a number of well known marine men. Edited by Gordon Newell. Seattle, Superior Pub. Co., 1966. 706p. illus. ports. endmaps, index. 2859

McCurdy, Horace Winslow. SEE ALSO no. 2695,
    Lewis and Dryden's marine history ... 1895.

McCURDY, JAMES G. By Juan de Fuca's Strait; pioneering along the northwestern edge of the continent. Portland, Ore., Metropolitan Press, 1937. 312p. front.(map), ports. facsims. ANR. Portland, Ore., Binfords & Mort, 1949. 2860

McDANIEL, ESTHER K. Rainbow to the storms. N. Y., Exposition Press, 1964. [poetry] 2861

MacDONALD, ALEXANDER. In search of Eldorado; a wanderer's experiences, with an introduction by Admiral Moresby. London, T. Fisher Unwin, 1905. 291p. front.(port.), pls. ports. OTHERS 1906. 2d impr. AND 1910. 3rd impr. 2862

MacDONALD, ALEXANDER. The white trail; a story of the early days of Klondike. N. Y., H. M. Caldwell, 1908. front. illustrated by William Rainey. ANR. London, Blackie, 1908. 392p. front. pls. map. ANR. Toronto, Musson, 1908. 2863

McDONALD, JOSEPH LANE. Hidden treasures; or, fisheries around the northwest coast. Gloucester, Mass., Proctor Bros., Printers, 1871. 110(10)p. [incls. extract from report of General Jefferson C. Davis when military governor of Alaska] 2864

McDONALD, LUCILE SAUNDERS. Bering's potlatch. Illustrated by Nils Hogner. London, Oxford University Press, 1944. 232p. front.(map), illus. [fict.] 2865

McDONALD, LUCILE SAUNDERS. Search for the northwest passage. Portland, Ore., Binfords & Mort, 1958. 142p. illus. endmap, index. [Cook, Vancouver, others] 2866

MacDONALD, MALCOLM. Down North. London, Oxford University Press, 1943. 274p. front.(map), bibliog. index. ANR. WITH TITLE Down North; a view of northwest Canada. N. Y., Farrar, 1943. 274p. front.(map), pls. [incls. ref. to Fort Yukon, Alaska] 2867

MacDONALD, MALCOLM. The favorites of fate; a novel. N. Y., Exposition Press, 1954. 1st ed. 134p. 2868

McDONALD, NORMAN C. Fish the strong waters. By N. C. McDonald.
N. Y., Ballantine Books, 1956. 184p. ANR. 1956. (Ballantine
Books Original Novel, no. 175) paperback. [southeastern locale]
2869

McDONALD, NORMAN C. Witch doctor. N. Y., Ballantine Books,
1959. 1st ed. ANR. 1959. 1st Canadian ed. ANR. N. Y., Ballantine Books, 1968. 1st Bal-Hi ed. 143p. paperback. [free
tr. of Tlingit story]   2870

MacDONALD, RANALD. Ranald MacDonald, the narrative of his early
life on the Columbia under the Hudson's Bay Company's regime; of
his experiences in the Pacific whale fisheries; and of his great
adventure to Japan; with a sketch of his later life on the western frontier, 1824-1894;   edited and annotated by William S.
Lewis and Naojiro Murakami. Spokane, printed by Inland-American
Printing Co., 1923. 333p. pls. ports. plan, facsim. maps.
(published for Eastern Washington State Historical Society) 2871

McDONALD, ROBERT, tr. Book of common prayer according to the use
of the church of England and Ireland. Translated into Takudh by
Archdeacon McDonald, D. D. London, Society for Promoting Christian Knowledge, 1873. 123p. ANR. WITH TITLE in English and
Takudh. Book of common prayer and administration of the sacraments...Translated into the Takudh tongue by Ven. Archdeacon
McDonald, D. D. Ettunetle tutthug enjit gichinchik akǫ sakrament
rsikotitinyoo akǫ chizi thlelchil nutinde akǫ kindi kwunttlutri-
tili ingland thlelchil tungittiyin kwikit. Takudh tsha zit
thleteteitazya Ven. Archdeacon McDonald, D. D., Kirkhe. London,
1899. [printed by Richard Clay & Sons, London and Bungay] 426p.
ANR. WITH TITLE in English and Takudh. London, 1912. 460p. ANR
London, n. d. 221p. pls.   2872

McDONALD, ROBERT. Chilig Takudh tshah zit. [TITLE TR. Hymns in
Takudh language] London, Society for Promoting Christian Know-
ledge, 1890. 89p. [composed and translated by Ven. Robert Mc-
Donald, Archdeacon of Mackenzie River] ANR. London, 1893. ANR.
Anchorage, printed by Anchorage Times, n. d. 69p. [printed for
St. Stephen's Mission, Fort Yukon, Alaska, ca 1940]   2873

McDONALD, ROBERT and JULES L. PREVOST, trs. Cilicu whut ana
kunacu yit tatluonu khuvo whykainiwhylit lowhulud bu khutitash
towhutotuwon cithlotalton yulh. [TITLE TR. Hymns, the Creed,
the Lord's Prayer and the Ten Commandments] Tanana, Alaska,
1901. 36p. [translated by Ven. Archdeacon McDonald and Jules
L. Prevost. See also Prevost's "Culic whutana ... " [1915],
no. 3686]   2874

McDONALD, ROBERT, tr. David vi Psalmnut, Takudh tsha zit thleteteitazya Ven. Archdeacon McDonald, D. D. Kirkhe. Winnipeg, Manitoba, Society for Promoting Christian Knowledge, 1886. 195p.
[printed by Robert D. Richardson]   2875

McDONALD, ROBERT, tr. Ettunetle rsotitinyoo, thlukwinadhun sheg akǫ ketchid kwitugwatsui Takudh ttshah zit thleteteitazya. Archdeacon McDonald, D. D. Kirkhe. London, British and Foreign Bible Society, 1898. 1,876p. [the Bible translated into Takudh] 2876

McDONALD, ROBERT, tr. Fourth and fifth Books of Moses, called Numbers, and Deuteronomy. Moses vit ettunetle ttyig akǫ ttankthut nikendo Trigwitittittshi akǫ Deuteronomi kutrahnyoo. Tukudh ttsha zit thleteteitazya. By Archdeacon McDonald, D. D. London, printed for the British and Foreign Bible Society, 1891. 191p. wrps. [title in English and Takudh] 2877

McDONALD, ROBERT. Grammar of the Tukudh language. London, Society for Promoting Christian Knowledge, 1911. 201p. 2878

McDONALD, ROBERT, tr. Joshua to 1. Samuel. Joshua enjit ettenettle. Tukudh ttsha zit thleteteitazya. Archdeacon McDonald, D. D. Kirkhe. London, printed for the British and Foreign Bible Society, 1892. 203p. [printed by Richard Clay & Sons, London and Bungay] 2879

McDONALD, ROBERT, tr. Kwunduk nirzi Mathyoo akǫ Mark rsotitinyoo Kirkhe Kwitinyithutluth. Takudh ttsha zit Thleteteitazya Ven. Archdeacon McDonald, D. D., Kirkhe. London, British and Foreign Bible Society, 1885. 122p. 2880

McDONALD, ROBERT, tr. Moses vit ettunetle ttyig Genesis, Exodus, Levitikus. Genesis ettunetle. Archdeacon McDonald, D. D. Kirkhe Thleteteitazya. London, British and Foreign Bible Society, 1890. 282p. 2881

[McDONALD, ROBERT, tr. ?] Nuwheh kukwadhud Jesus Christ vih kwunduk nirzi, Matthew, Mark, Luke, John, ha rsiotitinyokhai kirre, kwitinyithutluth kwikit. John rsiotitinyoo vih etunetle tig ha, Tukudh tsha zit. Thleteteitazy. London, [no pub.], 1874. 267p. [HAS COVER TITLE Tukudh four gospels] 2882

McDONALD, ROBERT, tr. Ochikthud ettunetle trootshid akǫ ettunetle choh trorsi ochikthud ettunetle akǫ thlukwinadhun ketchid trorzi kah, Dr. Isaac Watts, Kirkhe. Thleteteitazya Archdeacon McDonald, D. D., Kirkhe. London, Religious Tract Society, 1885. 2883

[McDonald, Robert, tr. ?] Tukudh four gospels. SEE no. 2882.

McDONALD, ROBERT, tr. Tunutrunatli koogwiinyathun. Ingland thlitrelchil kyo. Takudh tsha zit thleteteitazya Archdeacon McDonald, Kirkhe. Winnipeg, Robert D. Richardson, printer, 1886. 21p. 2884

McDONALD, ROBERT, tr. Zzehkke enjit gichinchik nekwazzi ttrin ihthlog kenjit akǫ gichinchik ttrin kittekookwichiltshei kenjit kah. Bp. Oxenden vut sun kwut sut thleteteitazya chizi gichinchik kah tikyinchiknut akǫ trinyunnut enjit. Chutrua kenjit

347

gichinchik tthui, akǫ chunkyo rsotitinyoo enjit gichinchik Arch-
deacon McDonald. [TITLE TR. Prayers extracted from Oxenden and
Ramsden's family prayers and translated by R. McDonald into
Takudh dialect of the natives of the Mackenzie River district,
Canada] London, Society for Promoting Christian Knowledge,
1885. 50p.   2885

McDONALD, T. P. Why one rule for the States and reverse rule for
Alaska ? A petition to the Congress of the United States. Seattle, 1914. 8p. [refers to coal mining]   2886

McDowell, Kay, co-auth. SEE no. 1545, Fernald, K.

MacDowell, Lloyd W. SEE nos.
    114, Alaska Steamship Co. Alaska glaciers ... 1906;
    115, Alaska Steamship Co. Alaska Indian basketry. 1904;
    126, Alaska Steamship Co. Totem poles ... 1905.

McELRAY, ROBERT McNUTT. The winning of the far west; a history
of the regaining of Texas, of the Mexican War, and the Oregon
question, and of the successive additions to the territory of the
United States 1829-1867. N. Y., Putnam, 1914. 384p. front.
(col.), pls. maps(fold.) [incls. Alaska purchase]   2887

McELWAINE, EUGENE. The truth about Alaska, the golden land of
the midnight sun. Chicago, privately printed, 1901. 445p.
front.(port.), pls. ports. maps. [primarily about Nome]   2888

McEWEN, G. F., THOMAS G. THOMPSON and R. VAN CLEVE. Hydrographic
sections and calculated currents in the Gulf of Alaska, 1927 and
1928. Seattle, International Fisheries Commission, 1930. 36p.
tables, diagrs.(incl. 1 fold.), charts(sketch) (Report no. 4,
Vancouver, B. C.)   2889

McEwen, G. F., co-auth. SEE ALSO no. 4511,
    Thompson, Thos. G. Hydrographic sects. ... 1936.

McFarland, Mrs. A. E. SEE no. 641, Brady, Mrs. John G.

McFARLAND, JEANNETTE. One mad scramble. Cambridge, Ohio, Southeastern Printing Co., 1940. 116p. [travel, partly in southeast
Alaska]   2890

MacFarlane, J. R. H. SEE no. 1801, Great Britain. Admiralty.

McFEAT, TOM, edit. Indians of the north Pacific coast. Seattle,
University of Washington Press, 1967. 270p. tables, bibliog.
append. ANR. Seattle, University of Washington Press, 1967.
(WP-21) paperback. [northwest coast, Yakutat Bay to Straits of
Juan de Fuca]   2891

MacFIE, HARRY and HANS G. WESTERLUND. Wasa-Wasa; a tale of trails and treasures in the far North. Translated from Swedish by F. H. Lyon. N. Y., W. W. Norton & Co., 1951. 1st ed. 288p. ANR. London, Allen and Unwin, 1951. 244p. map. ANR. London, Reader's Union, 1953. 248p. [a Swedish edition was printed in 1945]   2892

McGARVEY, LOIS. Along Alaska trails. N. Y., Vantage, 1960. 1st ed. 200p. illus. photos. [autobiog.]   2893

McGERR, PAT. Pick your victim. Garden City, N. Y., Doubleday, 1947. [c1947] 1st ed. 22p. (Published for The Crime Club)
                                                                   2894

MacGOWAN, KENNETH. Early man in the new world. N. Y., Macmillan, 1950. 260p. illus. maps, bibliog. ANR. WITH Joseph F. Hester, Jr. N. Y., Doubleday, 1962. rev. 333p. illus. drawings. ANR. Gloucester, Mass., Peter Smith, 1962.   2895

MacGOWAN, M. The hard road to Klondike. Translated from Irish by Valentin Iremonger. London, Routledge & Kegan Paul, 1962. 150p. illus. maps.   2896

MacGREGOR, ELLEN. Miss Pickerell goes to the Arctic. Illustrated by Paul Galdone. N. Y., McGraw-Hill, 1954. 126p. front. illus. (Whittlesey House)   2897

MacGREGOR, JOHN. The progress of America, from the discovery by Columbus to ... 1846. London, 1847. 2 vols. 1,520p. and 1,334p. [incls. voyages to northwest coast and fur trade]   2898

McGUIRE, JOHN A. In the Alaska-Yukon gamelands. By J. A. McGuire. Cincinnati, Stewart Kidd Co., 1921. 251p. photos by author, pls. ports. map. [trip sponsored by Colorado Museum of Natural History]   2899

MACHETANZ, FREDERICK. On Arctic ice. With illustrations by the author. N. Y., Scribner's, [c1940] 105p. illus.(some dble., col.)   2900

MACHETANZ, FREDERICK. Panuck, Eskimo sled dog. Illustrated by the author. N. Y., Scribner's, [c1939] 95p. illus.(some col.)
                                                                   2901

Machetanz, Frederick, illus. SEE ALSO nos.
        107, Alaska Review. Three artists of Alaska. 1965;
       2902, Machetanz, Sara. A puppy named Gih. 1957;
       2903, Machetanz, Sara. Barney hits the trail. 1950;
       2904, Machetanz, Sara. Rick of High Ridge. 1952;
       2905, Machetanz, Sara. Robbie and sled dog race. 1964;
       2906, Machetanz, Sara. Seegoo, dog of Alaska. 1961;
       2907, Machetanz, Sara. The howl of malemute. 1961;
       2908, Machetanz, Sara. Where else but Alaska ? [c1954];

4299, Stefansson, E. Here is Alaska. 1943;
4428, Swenson, M. C. Kayoo, Eskimo boy. 1939.

MACHETANZ, SARA. A puppy named Gih. Illustrated by Frederick
Machetanz. N. Y., Scribner's, 1957. 28p. illus.(col.)   2902

MACHETANZ, SARA. Barney hits the trail. Illustrated by Frederick Machetanz. N. Y., Scribner's, 1950. 195p. front. illus.
2903

MACHETANZ, SARA. Rick of High Ridge. Illustrated by Frederick
Machetanz. N. Y., Scribner's, 1952. 177p. illus. front.   2904

MACHETANZ, SARA. Robbie and the sled dog race. Illustrated by
Frederick Machetanz. N. Y., Scribner's, 1964.   2905

MACHETANZ, SARA. Seegoo, dog of Alaska. London, 1961. 204p.
illus.   2906

MACHETANZ, SARA. The howl of the malemute; the story of an
Alaskan winter. Illustrated with photographs by Frederick
Machetanz. N. Y., Wm. Sloane, 1961. 204p. photos.   2907

MACHETANZ, SARA. Where else but Alaska ? Illustrated with
lithographs and photographs by Frederick Machetanz. N. Y.,
Scribner's, [c1954] 214p. illus.   2908

Machetanz, Sara. SEE ALSO no. 107,
    Alaska Review. Three artists of Alaska. 1965.

MACHOWSKI, JACEK. Alaska. Wyd. 1. Warszawa, Wildza Powszechna,
1965. 421p. illus. ports. maps(some fold.)   2909

McHugh, Isabel and Florence, trs. SEE no. 2816, Lütgen, K.

McILRAITH, JOHN. Life of Sir John Richardson. London, Longmans
Green, 1868. 280p. front.(port.)   2910

MacInnes, T., edit. SEE no. 2486, Klengenberg, C.

MACK, GERSTLE. Lewis and Hannah Gerstle. N. Y., 1953. [early
history of Hutchinson, Kohl & Co., later to become Alaska Com-
merical Co.]   2911

MACKAY, ANGUS (OSCAR DHU). By trench and trail in song and story
by Angus Mackey (Oscar Dhu). Illustrated by Lt. William R. Mac-
ķay. Seattle, Mackay Printing & Pub. Co., 1918. 144p. front.
pls.   2912

McKay, David. SEE no. 1974, Hart, Robert G.

MacKay, DOUGLAS. The Honourable Company; a history of the Hudson's Bay Co. Indianapolis, Bobbs-Merrill, 1936. 1st ed. 396p. front.(port.), pls. facsims. plans, maps by R. H. H. Macaulay, append. bibliog. index. ANR. Toronto, McClelland & Stewart, 1937. 2d ed. corrected and revised. 396p. ANR. London, Cassell & Co., 1937. ANR. N. Y., Tudor Pub. Co., 1938.   2913

MACKAYE, BENTON. An act proposed as a solution of the conservation problem in Alaska, with explanation of the same. [pl. ?], Allied Printing Trades Council, n. d.   2914

McKEE, LANIER. The land of Nome; a narrative sketch of the rush to our Bering Sea gold-fields, the country, its mines and its people, and the history of a great conspiracy 1900-1901. N. Y., Grafton Press, 1902. 260p.   2915

McKENNAN, ROBERT A. The Chandalar Kutchin. Montreal, Arctic Institute of North America, 1965. 156p. pls. figs. (Technical Paper no. 17)   2916

McKENNAN, ROBERT A. The Upper Tanana Indians. N. H., Yale University Press, 1959. 226p. pls. maps, bibliog. (Publication in Anthropology no. 55)   2917

McKEOWN, MARTHA FERGUSON. Alaska silver; another Mont Hawthorne story. N. Y., Macmillan, 1951. 1st print. 274p. endmaps. [salmon canneries, southeastern Alaska]   2918

McKEOWN, MARTHA FERGUSON. The trail led north; Mont Hawthorne's story. N. Y., Macmillan, 1948. 1st ed. 222p. front.(map), map.   2919

McKINLEY, CHARLES and others. Case for limited modification of cabotage to facilitate economical integration of Canadian and United States railroad and steamship transportation in the North Pacific. Portland, Ore., North Pacific Planning Project, 1944. 28p. tables. (North Pacific Study no. 10)   2920

McKINLEY, CHARLES and others. United States - Canadian postwar civil aviation relationships in the North Pacific. Portland, Ore., North Pacific Planning Project, 1944. 15p. tables. (North Pacific Study no. 6)   2921

McKinley, Charles, co-auth. SEE ALSO no. 4393,
     Sundborg, Geo. Proposal ... fisheries ... 1944.

MacKintosh, W. A., edit. SEE no. 2269, Innis, H. A.

M'KONOCHIE, ALEXANDER. A summary view of the statistics and existing commerce of the principal shores of the Pacific Ocean. ... establishment of a central free port within its limits; and also of one in the southern Atlantic ... By Capt. M'Konochie. London, J. M. Richardson, 1818. 366p. map.   2922

McLAIN, CARRIE M. Gold-rush Nome. An illustrated historical
chronicle of gold-rush Nome. Portland, Ore., printed by Graphic
Arts Center, [c1969] 46(23)p. illus. wrps. [photos from collections of Nome Historical Museum and author]   2923

McLAIN, CARRIE M. Pioneer teacher. Portland, Ore., printed by
Graphic Arts Center, [c1970] 70p. illus. wrps. [Teller, Hay-
cock and Nome at turn of century]   2924

McLAIN, JOHN SCUDDER. Alaska and the Klondike. Illustrated
from photographs. N. Y., McClure, Phillips & Co., 1905. 330p.
front. illus. map(fold.), index.   2925

MacLAREN, J. MALCOLM. Gold; its geological occurence and geographical distribution. London, The Mining Journal, 1908. 687p.
[has short section on Alaska and Yukon]   2926

MacLEAN, ALISTAIR. Ice Station Zebra. N. Y., Doubleday & Co.,
1963. 276p. [fict.]   2927

MacLEAN, JOHN KENNEDY and CHELSEA FRASER. Heroes of the farthest
North and farthest South. N. Y., Thomas Y. Crowell, 1938.
484p.+18p. front. pls. ports. maps. [rev. of no. 2929 - later
explorations of Stefansson, Amundsen, others]   2928

MacLEAN, JOHN KENNEDY and OTHERS. Heroes of the Polar Seas. London, W. & R. Chambers, 1910. ANR. N. Y., Thomas Y. Crowell,
1923. [SEE ALSO no. 2928]   2929

MacLEAN, T. A. Lode mining in Yukon; an investigation of quartz
deposits in the Klondike division. Ottawa, Government Printing
Bureau, 1914. 205p. front. pls. maps(some fold.), diagrs.
index. (Canada. Department of Mines)   2930

Maclear, J. P. SEE nos.
   1801, Great Britain Admiralty. Alaska Bering Sea pilot. 1898;
   1803, Great Britain Admiralty. Sailing Bering Sea ... 1898.

MacLENNAN, EWEN and CHARLES WILBERT SNOW. Songs of the Neukluk.
Council, Alaska, privately printed, May 15, 1912. 30p. front.
(pl.) [poetry]   2931

MacLEOD, ELLEN JANE. Alaska star. Fort Washington, Penna.,
1957. (Christian Literature Crusade) ANR. London, Bickering
& Inglis, 1957. 96p. front.(col.) ANR. 1960.   2932

MacLEOD, J. A., co-auth. SEE nos.
   3847, Robinson, E. Field observ. ... ice fog ... 1954;
   3849, Robinson, E. Wiresonde observ. ... 1954.

McMANUS, ROBERT. The tourist's pictorial guide and hand book to
British Columbia and the northern Pacific waters. Victoria, B. C.,
Tourist's Pictorial Guide Pub. Co., 1890. 48p. illus.   2933

MacMASTER, DONALD. The seal arbitration, 1893. By Sir Donald
MacMaster. Montreal, Brown, 1894. 65p. map.   2934

McMICKEN, E. G. Seattle to the Nome gold coast. Seattle, W. D.
Richardson, pub., Press of Denny-Coryell, Feb. 1900. 44p. illus.
(pub. for Pacific Clipper Line, Cape Nome Steamers)   2935

McMILLAN, A. J. The mineral resources of British Columbia and
the Yukon; a lecture delivered at the Imperial Institute, London, on December 6, 1897. London, Cassell, n. d. 20p.   2936

McMILLION, OVID MILLER. New Alaska. Ann Arbor, Mich., Edwards
Bros., 1939. 216p. pls. maps(some fold.), bibliog.   2937

McMINN, HOWARD EARNEST and EVELYN MAINO. An illustrated manual
of Pacific Coast trees; with lists of trees recommended for
various uses on the Pacific Coast, by H. W. Shepherd. Berkeley,
University of California Press, 1935. 409p. front.(col.),
illus. glossary, bibliog. ANR. 1937. 2d ed.   2938

MacMULLEN, JERRY. *Star of India*; the log of an iron ship.
Berkeley, Howell-North, 1961. 133p. front. illus. photos, fac-
sims. endmaps, append. index. [in salmon trade, Alaska Packer's
Star fleet]   2939

McMURRAY, DeVON. All aboard for Alaska ! Boston, Heath, 1941.
159p. photos.   2940

McNEER, MAY. The Alaska gold rush. Drawings by Lynd Ward. N.Y.,
Random House, 1960. 186p. illus. index. (Landmark 92)   2941

McNEILLY, MILDRED MASTERSON. Heaven is too high. N. Y, Morrow,
1944. 432p. [hist. fict. Baranov in Alaska]   2942

NcNEILLY, MILDRED MASTERSON. Praise at morning. N. Y., Morrow,
1947. [hist. fict. Russian fleet in American waters, Civil War
period]   2943

MacNEISH, RICHARD S. Investigations in southwest Yukon; ar-
chaeological excavation. Comparisons and speculations. Andover,
Mass., Robert S. Peabody Foundation for Archaeology, 1964.
(Papers, vol. 6, no. 2)   2944

MACOUN, JAMES MELVILLE and H. T. HOLM. Vascular plants. Ottawa,
King's Printer, 1921. 50p. pls. map. (Canadian Arctic Expedition, Report, vol. 5: Botany, Pt. A) [incls. Pt. Barrow]   2945

Macoun, James Melville, co-auth. SEE ALSO no. 2946,
   Macoun, John. Catalogue Canadian birds. 1909.

MACOUN, JOHN. Catalogue of Canadian birds. Ottawa, King's Printer, 1900-04. in 3 pts. [1900, 1903 and 1904] 733p. (Geology Survey of Canada) ANR. 1909. 1 vol. 2d ed. rewritten and enl. by John Macoun and James Melville Macoun.   2946

MACOUN, JOHN. Climate and soil of the Yukon. Evidence of Mr. John Macoun, Assistant Director and Naturalist, Geological Survey, before the select standing committee on agriculture and colonization, 1903. Printed by order of Parliament as advance sheets of the Committee's final report. Ottawa, S. E. Dawson, 1903. 18p. (Canada. Committee on Agriculture and Colonization)
2947

McPherson, Duncan, illus. SEE no. 545, Berton, Pierre.

McPHERSON, MURDOCK. Condensed statement from Mr. Bell's report to Prince Rupert's Land governor of Hudson's Bay Company. By Murdock McPherson, MacKenzie District, Hudson's Bay Company, November 18, 1845. [ref. to Yukon River exploration]   2948

MAC'S PHOTO SERVICE, Anchorage. Alaska earthquake pictorial. Anchorage, 1964. 40p. photos.   2949

McWHINNIE, MRS. JAMES. A trip to Alaska. Chicago, Woman's American Baptist Home Mission Society, n. d. [1909 ?] 22p.   2950

McWHINNIE, MRS. JAMES. History of Kodiak Orphanage, Wood Island, Alaska. Chicago, Woman's American Baptist Home Mission Society, 1912. rev. 23p.   2951

MADSEN, CHARLES and JOHN SCOTT DOUGLAS. Arctic trader. N. Y., Dodd Mead, 1956. 273p. pls. [Nome]   2952

MAGIDOVICH, I. P. Istoriīa otkrytiīa i issledovaniīa Severnoĭ Ameriki. [TITLE TR. History of the discovery and exploration of North America] Moskva, Gos. izd-vo geograf. lit-ry, 1962. 467p. illus. maps, bibliog. indexes.   2953

Magidovich, I. P., edit. SEE ALSO no. 1768,
    Golovnin, V. M. Sochineniīa. 1949.

Maguire, Rochfort. SEE nos.
    1827-8, Great Britain. Parl. (Franklin Search);
    1831-2, Great Britain. Parl. (Franklin Search);
    2835, M'Clure, R. J. LeM. Discovery n.w. passage ... 1856.

Maher, R., co-auth. SEE no. 4780, Weeks, Tim.

Mahoney, Michael Ambrose. SEE no. 1265, Denison, Merrill.

MAHR, AUGUST C.   The visit of the "Rurik" to San Francisco in 1816.   Stanford, Calif., Stanford University Press, 1932.   (Pub. University Series History, Economics and Political Science, vol. 2, no. 2)   2954

MAILER, NORMAN.   Why are we in Vietnam ?   A novel.   N. Y., Putnam, [c1967]   208p.   2955

Maino, E., co-auth.   SEE no. 2938, McMinn, H. E.

Makarov, S. O.   SEE no. 4967, Wrangell, F. F.

Maksutov, D. P.   SEE no. 3582, Pierce, R. A.

MALASPINA, ALEJANDRO.   Viaje politico-cientifico alrededor del mundo por las corbetas *Descubierta* y *Atrevida* al mundo de los capitanes de navio Di Alejandro Malaspina y Don Jose de Busta-mante y Guerra des de 1789 a 1794, publicado con una introduccion por Don Pedro de Novo y Colson.   Madrid, Imp. de la viuda ehijos de Abienze, 1885.   681p.   port.   pls.   map.   2956

Malaspina, Alejandro.   SEE ALSO nos.
    1496, Espinosa y Tello, José de.   Memorias ... 1809;
    1546, Fernandez, J.   Tomás de Suria ... 1939;
    4696, Viana, F. J. de.   Diario del viage explorador ... 1849;
    4724, Wagner, H. R.   Journal Tomás de Suria ... 1936.

Maldonado, Lorenzo Ferrer.   SEE nos. 1547-49,
    Ferrer Maldonado, Lorenz.

MALLETTE, GERTRUDE ETHEL.   Chee-chá-ko.   Illustrated by Herbert Morton Stoops.   N. Y., Doubleday Doran, 1938.   299p.   front.(col.) [juv. fict.]   2957

MALLINSON, FLORENCE LEE.   My travels and adventures in Alaska, by Mrs. Florence Lee Mallinson, for nine years a resident in the northland.   Seattle, Seattle-Alaska Co., 1914.   200p.   front. (port.), pls.   2958

Malmgren, Finn.   SEE no. 219, Amundsen, R. E. G.

Malmquist, L., illus.   SEE no. 4730, Walford, L. A.

MALUQUER, JUAN J.   Exploracion aeropolar.   [TITLE TR.   Aerial exploration of the Arctic]   Barcelona, I. G. Seix y Barral Huos, 1945.   67p.   ports.   illus.   maps.   (Coleccion estudio de conoci-mientos generales, 44)   [Roald Amundsen and *Norge*, Sir Hubert Wilkins, others]   2959

Manifest of Pacific Northwest.   SEE no. 3698, Production Surveys.

MANNING, CLARENCE AUGUSTUS.   Russian influence on early America. N. Y., Library Publishers, 1953.   216p.   2960

ALASKAN BIBLIOGRAPHY

MANSFIELD, NORMA BICKNELL. Keeper of the wolves. By Norma B. Mansfield. N. Y., Farrar & Rinehart, 1938. 308p. front. glossary.
2961

MANSFIELD, NORMA BICKNELL. The girl from Frozen Bend. By Norma B. Mansfield. N. Y., Farrar & Rinehart, 1938. 279p.
2962

MANWARING, G. E. My friend the Admiral; the life, letters, and journals of Rear-Admiral James Burney, F.R.S., the companion of Captain Cook and friend of Charles Lamb. London, Geo. Routledge & Sons, 1931. xvi,314p. front. port. pls.
2963

Map-guide; Seattle to Dawson ... 1897. SEE no. 2823, Lysons,F.H.

Map of surveyed route ... 1903. SEE no. 43,
    Alaska Central Railroad Co.

Marberry, M. M., co-auth. SEE no. 2390, Jordan, Jed.

MARCEL, GABRIEL. Une expedition oublieé a la recherché de Lapérouse. Paris, L. Baudoin, 1888. 23p.
2964

Marchand, Etienne. SEE no. 1579, Fleurieu, Chas. C. P.

MARCUS, MELVIN GERALD. Climate-glacier studies in the Juneau ice field region, Alaska. Chicago, University of Chicago, 1964. 128p. (Department of Geography, Research Paper no. 88)
2965

MARGESON, CHARLES ANSON. Experiences of gold hunters in Alaska. Hornellsville, N. Y, by author, 1899. 297p. front.(port.), pls.
2966

MARICH, M. [pseud.] Zhizn' i plavaniía flota kapitan-leĭtenanta Fedora Litke. [TITLE TR. The life and voyages of Capt. Lt. of the Navy Litke] Moskva, Izd-vo Glavsemorputi, 1949. 278p. port. [author is Mariía Davydovna Cherneysheva]
2967

MARINE RESEARCH SOCIETY, Salem, Mass. The sea, the ship and the sailor; tales of adventure from log books and original narratives. Salem, Mass., Marine Research Society, 1925. illus. [incls. an abridgment of John Nicol narrative]
2968

MARION SOCIETY, IMMACULATE CONCEPTION CHURCH, Fairbanks. Cooking favorites of Fairbanks. no pl., n. d. [ca 1965 ?] 68p. append. (8)p.
2969

MARIS, OMER. Sketches from Alaska. Chicago, 1897. 63p. 2970

MARKHAM, CLEMENTS ROBERTS and F. H. H. GUILLEMARD. The lands of silence; a history of Arctic and Antarctic exploration. Cambridge, University Press, 1921. 539p. front. pls. ports. facsims. maps(some fold.), bibliog. [incls. Russian Arctic exploration and northwest passage]
2971

356

Markistun, Luke, tr. SEE no. 2295, Irvine, A.

MARKOV, ALEKSANDR. Krushenie korablia *Nevy* u Novo-Arkhangeljska-
go porta. Razskaz ochevidsta. [TITLE TR. Account of an eyewit-
ness of the shipwreck of the ship *Neva* at New Archangel] St.
Petersburg, 1850. 36p. [Krusenstern voyage round the world,
1803-06]   2972

MARKOV, ALEKSANDR. Russkie na Vostochnom Okeanie. Vostochnaía
Sibiri-Rossiískiía vladieniía v Amerikie-Byt dikarei-Kaliforniía-
Proekt Krugosvietnoí torgovoí ékspedifsií. [TITLE TR. The Russians on the Pacific Ocean-Eastern Siberia-Russian possession in
America-condition of the natives-California-plan for a trading
expedition round the world] Moscow, University Press, 1849.
148p. ANR. St. Petersburg, A. Dmitriev, 1856. 2d ed. enl. 263p.
                                                              2973

MARKOV, SERGEĬ. Letopis' Alíaski. Izd. 2. [TITLE TR. Annals
of Alaska] Moscow-Leningrad, Izd-vo glavsevmorputi, 1948. 220p.
illus. ports. maps(some fold.), append. index.   2974

MARKS, ALFRED, pub. On to Klondike ! and the great Alaska gold
discoveries. A concise treatise answering the two questions.
How to get there and what to take with you. Also containing much
essential information including maps and illustrations by a
Practical Miner. N. Y., Published by Alfred Marks, 1897. 62p.
illus. maps.   2975

Marsden, Edward. SEE no. 456, Beattie, Wm. Gilbert.

MARSH, GORDON H. and WILLIAM S. LAUGHLIN. Human anatomical knowledge among the Aleutian Islanders. Albuquerque, University of
New Mexico, 1956. 78p. glossary, ftntes. bibliog. (reprinted
from Southwestern Journal of Anthropology, vol. 12, no. 1,
Spring 1956)   2976

MARSH, ROY SIMPSON. Kang. Philadelphia, Macrae Smith Co., 1962.
illus.   2977

MARSH, ROY SIMPSON. Moog. Philadelphia, Macrae Smith Co., 1958.
2d print. 188p. front. endmaps.   2978

MARSHALL, EDISON. Child of the wild. Illustrated by Herbert M.
Stoops. N. Y., Cosmopolitan Book Corp., 1926. 297p. front.
pls.   2979

MARSHALL, EDISON. Ocean gold; a novel for young people. N. Y.,
Harper, 1925. 383p. front. pls.   2980

MARSHALL, EDISON. Princess Sophia; a novel of Alaska. Garden
City, N. Y., Doubleday, 1958. 1st ed. 381p. notes, endmaps.
                                                              2981

MARSHALL, EDISON. Seward's folly. N. Y., Little Brown, 1924.
312p.   2982

MARSHALL, EDISON. The deadfall; a romance and adventure in
America's last frontier, Alaska. Illustrated by George W. Gage.
N. Y., Cosmopolitan Book Corp., 1927. 290p. illus.   2983

MARSHALL, EDISON. The deputy at Snow Mountain. N. Y., H. C. Kin-
sey, 1932. 284p.   2984

MARSHALL, EDISON. The doctor of Lonesome River. N. Y., Cosmopolitan Book Corp., 1931. 294p. ANR. N. Y., A. L. Burt, n. d.
                                                             2985

MARSHALL, EDISON. The far call. Illustrated by Walt Louderback.
N. Y., Cosmopolitan Book Corp., 1928. 284p. front. pls.   2986

MARSHALL, EDISON. The fish hawk. N. Y., A. L. Burt, n. d. 290p.
                                                             2987

MARSHALL, EDISON. The land of forgotten men. Illustrated by W.
Herbert Dunton. Boston, Little Urown, 1923. 306p. front.   2988

MARSHALL, EDISON. The missionary. Illustrated by Jules Gotlieb.
N. Y., Cosmopolitan Book Corp., 1930. 288p. front. pls.   2989

MARSHALL, EDISON. The sleeper of the moonlit ranges; a new
novel. Illustrated by Jes W. Schlaikjer. N. Y., Cosmopolitan
Book Corp., 1925. 311p. front. pls.(incl. 1 col. dble.)   2990

MARSHALL, EDISON. The snowshoe trail. Boston, Little Brown,
1921. 324p. front.   2991

MARSHALL, J. B. Captain Cook's voyages of discovery. Abridged
with notes. pl.?, Leeds & Co., n. d. 96p. front. (Bright's
Story Readers, no. 146, Grade IV)   2992

MARSHALL, JAMES STIRRAT and CARRIE MARSHALL. Adventures in two
hemispheres, including Captain Vancouver's voyage. Vancouver,
B. C., Talex Print. Service, 1955. 208p. facsims. charts, maps.
[2d ed. has different title, see no. 2995]   2993

MARSHALL, JAMES STIRRAT and CARRIE MARSHALL. Pacific voyages.
Selections from Scots Magazine, 1771-1808. Portland, Ore., Binfords & Mort, 1960. 100p. pls. charts.   2994

MARSHALL, JAMES STIRRAT and CARRIE MARSHALL. Vancouver's voyage;
by James Stirrat Marshall and Carrie Marshall. Vancouver, B. C.,
Mitchell Press, 1967. 2d ed. 228p. illus. maps, bibliog.
[first pub. in 1955 with different title, see no. 2993]   2995

MARSHALL, JAMES VANCE. A river ran out of Eden. London, Hodder
& Stoughton, 1962. ANR. N.Y., Wm. Morrow & Co., 1963. 128p.
illustrated by Maurice Wilson.   2996

Marshall, Robert. Alaska wilderness. 1970. SEE no. 2998.

MARSHALL, ROBERT. Arctic village. N. Y., Harrison Smith & Robert
Haas, 1933. 399p. front. pls. ports. tables, endmaps, append.
indexes. ANR. N. Y., Literary Guild, 1933. 399p. ANR. London,
1934. 319p. illus. [village of Wiseman on Koyukuk River drain-
age]   2997

MARSHALL, ROBERT. Arctic wilderness. Berkeley, Calif., University of California Press, 1956. 171p. front.(pl.), pls. maps
(incl. 1 fold. at back) ANR. REISSUED WITH TITLE Alaska wilderness; exploring the Central Brooks Range. 1970. 2d ed. 173p.
                                                                  2998

MARSHALL, ROBERT. Doonerak or bust. A letter to friends about
an Arctic vacation. By Bob Marshall. no pl., privately printed,
n. d. [1938 ?] 36p. front.(port.), map, wrps. [author's letters; Doonerak, a mountain in the Brooks Range]   2999

MARSHALL, ROBERT. North Doonerak, Amawk and Apoon. Another letter to friends about an Arctic exploration between June 23 and
July 16, 1939 from Bob Marshall. no pl., n. d. 31p. front.
(photo tipped-in), map(dble.), wrps.   3000

Marshall, Robert. SEE ALSO no. 4506, Thompson, E. T.
     Race; individual and collective behavior. 1958.

MARSTON, MARVIN R. Men of the tundra; Eskimos at war. By Muk-
tuk Marston (Marvin R. Marston, Lt. Col. USAF ret.) N. Y.,
October House, 1969. 227p. illus. photos, appends. [First and
Second Battalions, Alaska Territorial Guard - World War II] 3001

MARTIN, ANNA. Around and about Alaska. N. Y., Vantage Press,
1959. 95p. map. [author's travels in Alaska]   3002

MARTIN, FRANCES G. Nine tales of Raven. By Frances Martin. Pictures by Dorothy McEntee. N. Y., Harper & Row, 1951. 60p.
illus.   3003

MARTIN, FREDERICKA I. Sea bears; the story of the fur seal.
Philadelphia, Chilton Co., Book Division, 1960. 1st ed. 201p.
photos, index. ANR. Toronto, Ambassador Books, 1960. [portions
of "Sea bears" originally published as "The hunting of the silver
fleece." See no. 3005   3004

MARTIN, FREDERICKA I. The hunting of the silver fleece; epic of
the fur seal. N. Y., Greenberg, 1946. 328p. pls. ports. append.
bibliog. index. [cf no. 3004]   3005

Martin, Fredericka I. SEE ALSO no. 4676,
    Veniaminov, I. E. P. Opyt ... 1846.

MARTIN, LAWRENCE. Some features of glaciers and glaciation in
College Fiord, Prince William Sound, Alaska. Berlin, Gebruder
Borntraeger, 1913. illus. maps. (reprinted from Zeitschrift für
Gletscherskunde, Band VII, heft 5, Oct. 1913. pp.289-333)
[author's Ph. D. thesis, Cornell University, 1913]   3006

Martin, Lawrence, co-auth. SEE ALSO no. 4459, Tarr, Ralph S.
    Alaskan glacier studies. 1914.

MARTIN, LOUISE ANITA. North to Nome. Illustrated with photographs. Chicago, A. Whitman & Co., 1939. 316p. front.(pl.)-
pls. (Junior Press Books) [fict.]   3007

MARTIN, MARTHA [pseud.] Home on the bear's domain. N. Y., Macmillan, 1954. 246p. ANR. London, Gollanz, 1954. 253p. [auto-
biog. - author is Helen Bolyan - locale is Chichagof Island,
southeastern Alaska]   3008

MARTIN, MARTHA [pseud.] O rugged land of gold. N. Y., Macmillan,
1953. 223p. endmaps. [autobiog. - author is Helen Bolyan -
locale is Chicagof Island, southeastern Alaska]   3009

MARTIN, PAUL SIDNEY, GEORGE I. QUIMBY and DONALD COLLIER. Indians
before Columbus; twenty thousand years of North American history
as revealed by archaeology. Chicago, University of Chicago
Press, 1947. xxiii,582p. front. illus. tables, charts, glossary,
bibliog. (Contribution of Chicago Natural History Museum)
[incls. Haida, Tlingit Indian, Okvik, Old Bering Sea, Late Aleut
cultures, others]   3010

MARTINDALE, THOMAS. Hunting in the upper Yukon. Philadelphia,
G. W. Jacobs, 1913. 320p. front. pls. ports. map(fold.) [Skag-
way and International Boundary areas]   3011

MARTINO, SALVATORE. Jak London. Catanio, Italy, 1934. 51p.
(Spunti per uno studio critico, Studio ed. moderno)   3012

MARTINSEN, ELLA LUNG and EDWARD BURCHALL LUNG. Black sand and
gold. As told by Edward Burchall Lung to Ella Lung Martinsen.
N. Y., Vantage Press, 1956. 1st ed. 419p. photos. ANR.
Portland, Ore., Metropolitan Press, 1967. Centennial Edition.
419p. photos. [for sequel see no. 3014]   3013

MARTINSEN, ELLA LUNG and EDWARD BURCHALL LUNG. Trail to north
star gold. Portland, Ore., Metropolitan Press, 1969. 359p.
[sequel to no. 3013]   3014

Martz, Henry. SEE no. 146, Alaska-Yukon-Pacific Exposition,
    1909.

MARVIN, FREDERIC ROWLAND. The Yukon overland; the gold-digger's hand-book. By Frederic R. Marvin. Cincinnati, The Editor Pub. Co., 1898. 170p. front. pls. map(fold.) [overland route from Spokane, Wash. - book has section on Chinook vocabulary]   3015

Mary Eustolia, *Sister*, auth. SEE no. 1738, Glody, Robert [pseud.]

Mary Mildred, *Sister*, tr. SEE no. 1224, deBaets, Maurice.

MASIK, AUGUST and ISOBEL WYLIE HUTCHISON. Arctic nights' entertainments; being the narrative of an Alaskan-Estonian digger August Masik as told to Isobel Wylie Hutchison during the Arctic night of 1933-34 near Martin Point, Alaska. London, Blackie & Son, 1935. 234p. front.(col.), pls. ports. (reprinted in Travel Library, Sept. 1936, 1938) [Masik's biog. - with Stefansson on Canadian Arctic Expedition, 1913-18]   3016

MASON, ALPHEUS THOMAS. Bureaucracy convicts itself. The Ballinger-Pinchot controversy of 1910. N. Y., Viking, 1941. 224p. pls. [legal status of coal mining claims, Prince William Sound region]   3017

MASON, GEORGE F. The bear family. Drawings by author. N. Y., Morrow, 1960. 96p. illus. maps.   3018

Mason, Herbert L., co-auth. SEE no. 889, Chaney, Ralph Works.

MASON, MICHAEL HENRY. The Arctic forests. London, Hodder & Stoughton, 1924. 1st ed. 320p. front. pls.(incl. 1 col.), ports. maps(incl. 2 fold.), index. ANR. London, 1934. 299p. illus. maps.   3019

MASON, OTIS T. Indian basketry; studies in a textile art without machinery. N. Y., Doubleday Page, 1904. 2 vols. (from author's *Aboriginal American basketry* in U. S. National Museum Report for 1902, pp.171-548)   3020

MASON, WALTER E. Dogs of all nations; a complete work, profusely illus'd., bearing on the world's different varieties of the dog, grouped under their several nationalities, with descriptive matter explaining the characteristics and utility of each. S. F., Hicks Judd, 1915. 144p. illus.   3021

MASON, WINFIELD SCOTT. The frozen northland; life with the Esquimo in his own country. Cincinnati, Jennings & Graham and N. Y., Eaton & Mains, 1910. 160p. front.(map), pls. maps. [partially about Alaska]   3022

Mass book and hymnal in Innuit. 1950. SEE no. 2791, Lonneux, M. J.

Masson, Chas. E. SEE no. 2742, Lloyd-Owen, F.

MASTERSON, JAMES R. and HELEN BROWER. Bering's successors, 1745-1780; contributions of Peter Simon Pallas to the history of Russian exploration toward Alaska. Seattle, University of Washington Press, 1948. 96p. maps(some fold.) (reprinted from Pacific Northwest Quarterly, Jan. and Apr., 1947, vol. 38, pp.35-83 and pp.109-155)   3023

MATANUSKA ELECTRIC ASSOCIATION, INC., Palmer. A report on agriculture - past and future - in the State of Alaska. Palmer, 1967. 40p.   3024

THE MATANUSKA VALLEY. Palmer, n. d. 15p. illus. map.   3025

Materialy dlīā istoriĭ russkikh ... 1861. SEE no. 1763, Golovnin, V. M.

Mathews, F. K., edit. SEE no. 2756, London, J.

MATHEWS, RICHARD. The Yukon. N. Y., Holt, Rinehart & Winston, 1968. 313p. illus. maps, bibliog. (Rivers of America Series)   3026

MATHIASSEN, THERKEL. Archaeological collections from the western Eskimos. Translated by W. E. Calvert. Copenhagen, Gyldendalske boghandel, 1930. 100p. illus. pls. map. (Report of the Fifth Thule Expedition 1921-24, vol. 10, no. 1)   3027

MATHIASSEN, THERKEL. Eskimoerne i nutid og fortid. [TITLE TR. The Eskimos in modern times and in the past] København, P. Haase & soner forlag, 1929. 196p. illus. map, bibliog.   3028

MATHIASSEN, THERKEL. Report on the expedition. Copenhagen, Gyldendal, 1945. 121p. illus. ports. maps, tables, append. (Report of the Fifth Thule Expedition 1921-24, vol. 1, no. 1)3029

Mathiassen, Therkel. SEE ALSO no. 3746, Rasmussen, K. Mindeudgave; udgivet af Peter Freuchen. 1934-35.

MATLOCK, ALMA HARWELL. Teaching above the Arctic Circle. no pl., n. d. [ca 1967] 24p. illus. photos, sketches [teacher at Eskimo village of Selawik, on Kotzebue Sound, 1928-37]   3030

MATTESON, H. H. The trap. N. Y., W. J. Watt, 1921. 293p. illustrated by George W. Gage.   3031

MATTHES, FRANÇOIS ÉMILE. Variations of glaciers in the continental United States and Alaska 1933-1938. Paris, Gauthier-Villars, 1939. 22p. bibliog. (International Geodetic & Geophysical Union, Assoc. of Scientific Hydrology, Reunion de Washington, 1939. Comptes rendus des séances et rapports. T.2, Commission des glaciers. Question 1, rapport 7)   3032

MATTHEWS, COURTLAND W. Aleutian interval. Seattle, Frank Mc-
Caffrey, Pub., 1949. 61p. [poetry]   3033

MATTHIESSEN, PETER. Oomingmak; the expedition to the musk ox
island in the Bering Sea. N. Y., Hastings House, 1967. 85p.
illus. photos, index. [Nunivak Island]   3034

MAULE, FRANCIS I. El Dorado "29" along with other weird Alaskan
tales, done into verse by Francis I. Maule. Philadelphia, John
C. Winston Co., 1910. 124p. front. illus.   3035

MAURELLE, FRANCISCO ANTIONIO. Journal of a voyage in 1775, to
explore the coast of America, northward of California, by Don
Francisco Antonio Maurelle. London, J. Nicols, 1781. (in
"Miscellanies of Daines Barrington" pp.469-534. map, index. Also
separate. Translated from Spanish manuscript) ANR. London,
1798. Translated from French.ANR. S. F., 1920. ltd. ed. of
230 copies. 121p. port. maps. (also in Pallas, Peter Simon.
"Neue nordische beiträge ... " 1782, as *Tagebuch einer im Jahre
1775 zur Untersuchung der nördlich von Californien fortgesetzten
Küsten geschehenen Reise (u.s.w.)* See no. 3475)   3036

Maurelle, Francisco Antonio. Tagebuch ... SEE no. 3036.

Maurelle, Francisco Antonio. SEE ALSO nos.
   407, Barrington, D. Miscellanies. 1781;
   2614, La Pérouse, J. F. G. de. Voyage ... 1798;
   3475, Pallas, Peter Simon. Neue nordische ... 1781-96.

MAURY, JEAN WEST. Old Raven's world. Boston, Little Brown, 1931L
284p. illus. [Tlingit legends]   3037

Maxwell, M. W., co-auth. SEE no. 800, Camsell, Chas.

MAY, CHARLES P. Animals of the far North. N. Y., Abelard-Schuman, 1963.   3038

MAYBERRY, FLORENCE. Dachshunds of Mama Island. N. Y., Doubleday,
1963. [juv. - Sitka area]   3039

MAYBERRY, GENEVIEVE. Eskimo of Little Diomede. Chicago, Follett
Pub. Co., 1961.   3040

MAYBERRY, GENEVIEVE. Sheldon Jackson Junior College; an intimate history. N. Y., Board of National Missions of Presbyterian
Church in the United States of America, 1953. 40p. illus.   3041

Mayhew, E. R., co-auth. SEE no. 4798, West, E. L.

Mayhew, Isobel. SEE no. 4193, Smith, Chas. W.

MAYNE, FANNY, edit. Voyages and discoveries in the Arctic regions. London, Longman, Brown, Green & Longmans, 1855. 140p. append. (The Traveller's Library, vol. 73)   3042

MAYOKOK, ROBERT. Eskimo customs. [Nome], Nome Nugget Press, 1951. 36p. illus. sketches by author. ANR. 1965. wrps.   3043

MAYOKOK, ROBERT. Eskimo life. Told by an Eskimo artist. Nome, Nome Nugget Press, 1951. 36p. illus. ANR. 1965. 21p. ANR. no pl., n. d. 21p. illustrated by author, wrps.   3044

MAYOKOK, ROBERT. Eskimo stories. [Nome], Nome Nugget Press, 1960. 42p. illus. ANR. no pl., n. d. [printed by Instant Printing, Anchorage] 42p. illustrated by author, wrps.   3045

MAYOKOK, ROBERT. The Alaskan Eskimo. no pl., n. d. 11p. illustrated by author, wrps.   3046

MAYOKOK, ROBERT. True Eskimo stories. no pl. [Anchorage ?], Northern Pub. Co., n. d. 36p. illus. by author, wrps. ANR. Sitka, Sitka Printing Co., n. d. [ca 1958 ?] 40p. illus. by author, wrps.   3047

Mayokok, Robert. SEE ALSO nos.
    3987, Say it in Eskimo. 1965;
    4150, Silook, R. In the beginning. [c1970]

MAZURMOVICH, BORIS NIKOLAEVICH. Vydaĩushchĩesĩa otechestvennye zoologi. [TITLE TR. Outstanding zoologists of our country; a textbook for the middle schools] Moskva, Gos. uchebno-pedagog. izd-vo, 1960. 427p. ports. bibliog. [incls. M. V. Lomonosov, S. P. Krasheninnikov, others]   3048

[MEAD, BRADOCK] Remarks in support of the new chart of North and South America; in six sheets. By J. Green, Esq. London, printed for Thomas Jeffreys, 1753. 48p. maps.   3049

MEANY, EDMOND STEPHEN, edit. A new Vancouver journal on the discovery of Puget Sound by a member of the *Chatham's* crew, edited by Edmond S. Meany. Seattle, 1915. 43p.   3050

MEANY, EDMOND STEPHEN. Vancouver's discovery of Puget Sound; portraits and biographies of the men honored in the naming of geographic features of northwestern America. N. Y., Macmillan, 1907. 344(43)p. front.(port.), pls. ports. maps(incl. 1 dble.), charts. OTHERS Portland, Ore., Binfords & Mort, 1935, 1949 AND 1957.   3051

Meany, Edmond Stephen, jr. SEE no. 2354,
    Jewitt, J. R. Narrative adventure ... *Boston* ... 1967.

Meares, John.   [Alphabetical title guide to chronological entries]

MEARES, JOHN. An answer to Mr. George Dixon, late commander of
the *Queen Charlotte* in the services of Messrs. Etches and Co.,
in which the remarks of Mr. Dixon on the voyages to the northwest
coast of America, etc., lately pub'd. are fully considered and
refuted. London, Logographic Press, 1791. 32p.   3052

MEARES, JOHN. Authentic copy of the memorial to the Right Honourable William Wyndham Grenville, one of his Majesty's principal secretaries of state, by Lieutenant John Mears [sic], of the
Royal Navy; dated 30th April, 1790, and presented to the House
of Commons, May 13, 1790. Containing every particular respecting
the capture of the vessels in Nootka Sound. London, printed for
J. Debrett, 1750 [sic] 65p. ANR. London, 1810.   3053

[MEARES, JOHN] Mr. Mear's [sic] memorial dated 30th Apr. 1790
(14 enclosures) to the Rt. Hon. Wm. Wyndham Grenville, one of
his Majesty's principal secretaries of state. [London ?,
1790 ?] 31p. table(fold.)   3054

[MEARES, JOHN] The memorial of John Mears [sic] to the House of
Commons, respecting the capture of vessels in Nootka Sound, with
an introduction and notes by Nellie B. Pipes. Portland, Ore.,
Metropolitan Press, 1933. 92p. ltd. ed. of 300 copies.   3055

MEARES, JOHN. Voyages made in the years 1788 and 1789, from
China to the northwest coast of America, to which are prefixed,
an introductory narrative of a voyage performed in 1786, from
Bengal, in the ship *Nootka;* observations on the probable existence of a northwest passage; and some account of the trade between the north west coast of America and China; and the latter
country and Great Britain. Comp. by W. Combe from papers of J.
Meares. London, Logographic Press, 1790. 372(108)p. front.
pls. maps, append. ANR. 1791. 2d ed. 2 vols. 363p., 332(108)p.
front. pls. maps, append. ANR. Amsterdam, N. Israel and N. Y.,
Da Capo Press, 1967. facsim. of 1790 ed. (Bibliotheca Australiana, no. 22)   3056

TRANSLATIONS - Voyages ... 1790, chronologically.

Des Kapitans John Meares und des Kapitans Wm. Douglas Reisen
   nach der Nordwestkuste von Amerika, in den Jahren 1786 bis
   1789, aus dem Englischen ubersetzt und mit Anmerkungen er-
   lautert von George Forster; nebst einer Abhandlung von eben
   demselben, uber die Nordwestkuste von Amerika, und den

dortigen Pelzhandel ... Berlin, Voss, 1796. 302p. pls.
ports. maps(2 fold.) [an earlier German translation made in
Berlin in 1791]   3057

Voyage de la Chine a la côte nord-ouest d'Amérique, faits dans
les années 1788 et 1789; precédés de la relation d'un autre
voyage exécuté en 1786 sur le vaisseau le *Nootka*, parti du
Bangale; d'un recueil d'observations sur la probabilité
d'un passage nord-ouest; et d'un traite abrégé du commerce
entré la côte nord-ouest et la Chine, etc. etc., tr. de
l'anglois par J. B. L. J. Billecocq avec une collection de
cartes geographiques, vues, marines, plans et portraits.
Paris, F. Buisson, [1793] 3 vols. and atlas. pls. ports.
maps. ANR. Paris, [1794] 3 vols. and atlas. (24)391p.,
(4)386p. and (2)372p. pls. port. maps.   3058

Viaggi dalla China alla costa nord-ovest d'America, fatti negli
anni 1788 e 1789 dal capitano G. Meares; prima traduzione
Italiana, arricchita di note istoriche-scientifiche di vedute,
marine, ritratti carta geografica etc. Firenze, G. Pagani,
1796. 4 vols. front.(port.), pls. charts, map(fold.)   3059

Viaggi dalla China alla costa nord-ovest d'America, fatti negli
anni 1788 e 1789 dal capitano G. Meares; Italiana corretta
et accresciuta, coll' aggiunta di uno estratto de' Viaggi di
Milord Mackartney. Napoli, Giuseppe Policarpo Merande, 1796.
4 vols. in 2. front. pls. maps.   3060

Viaggi dalla China alla costa nord-ovest d'America, fatti negli
anni 1788 e 1789 dal capitano G. Meares; prima versione
Italiana. Torino, Soffietti, 1797-98. 4 vols. front.(port.)
pls. ports. maps.   3061

Tvanne resor fran Ostindien till Americas nordvastra kust, aren
1786, 1788 och 1789; af Johan Meares; sammandrag utur en-
gelska originalet Samuel Odmann. Stockholm, I. Utter, 1797.
404p.   3062

Puteshestvie Kap. Mirsa k Siev.-Zap. beregam Ameriki v pro-
dolzhenii 1788-89. [TITLE TR. Capt. Meare's voyage to the
northwest shores of America during the years 1788-89] St.
Petersburg, 1797. in 2 pts. 96p.,41p.   3063

Meares, John. SEE ALSO nos.
    1306, Dixon, Geo. Further remarks ... 1791;
    1307, Dixon, Geo. Remarks ... 1790;
    1497, [Etches, J. C.] Continuation authentic ... 1790;
    1498, [Etches, J. C.] Authentic statement ... 1790;
    1607, Forster, J. G. A. Geschichte ... 1792;
    2127, Histoire des voyages ... n. d.;
    2202, Howay, F. Wm., edit. Dixon-Mears [sic.] ... [c1929];
    3780, Reisen nach nordwestlichen Kuste ... 1795.

MEARS, ELIOT GRINNELL. Maritime trade of western United States. Stanford, Calif., Stanford University Press, 1935. 538p. front. diagrs. maps. (Business Series)
3064

MEARS, ELIOT GRINNELL. Pacific Ocean handbook. Stanford, Calif., James Ladd Delkin, 1944.
3065

MECKING, LUDWIG. Die Polarländer. [TITLE TR. The Polar lands] Leipzig, Bibliographisces Institut, 1925. 158p. pls.(1 col., 1 dble.), table(1 fold.), diagr. maps(2 dble.), bibliog. (Allgemeine Länderkunde)
3066

Mecking, Ludwig. SEE ALSO no. 3339, Nordenskiöld, N. O. G. Geography Polar regions ... 1928.

MEDILL, ROBERT BELL. Klondike diary; true account of the Klondike rush of 1897-98. Portland, Ore., Beattie & Co., 1949. 188p. illus. ports.
3067

Meek do not inherit Alaska. 1962. SEE no. 2089, Hetzel, T. B.

MEEKER, EZRA. The busy life of eighty-five years of Ezra Meeker. Ventures and adventures. Sixty-three years of pioneer life in the old Oregon country; an account of the author's trip across the plains with an ox team, 1852; return trip, 1906-7; his cruise on Puget Sound, 1853; trip through the Natchess Pass, 1854; over the Chilcoot Pass; flat-boating on the Yukon, 1898. The Oregon Trail. Seattle, published by the author, Press of Wm. B. Burford, Indianapolis, [c1916] 399p. front.(port.), pls.
3068

MEIJI DAIGAKU. Arasuka chiiki Gakujutsu Chōsadan. Tokyo, 1961. 267p. illus.(some col.), tables, diagrs. map(fold. col. in pocket) [travel in Alaska]
3069

MEISNER, HANS OTTO. Bezanbernde Wildnis; Wandern, Jagen, Fliegen in Alaska. Stuttgart, Cotta, 1963. 400p. illus.(some col.), ports.(some col.), maps.
3070

Melady, Eva, illus. SEE no. 3663, Potter, Louise.

MELDGAARD, JØRGEN. Eskimo sculpture; translated by Jotte Lynner and Peter Wait. London, Methuen, 1960. 48p. pls. bibliog. ANR. N. Y., Clarkson N. Potter, 1962. [tr. of no. 3072]
3071

MELDGAARD, JØRGEN. Eskimo skulptur. København, Schultz, 1959. 48p. illus. pls. bibliog. [has examples from Alaska. See no. 3071 for tr.]
3072

MELIN, MARGARET. Modern pioneering in Alaska. N. Y., Pageant Press, 1954. 78p. illus. [autobiog.]
3073

MELVILLE, EVOLYN. Fort Yukon, Alaska, established 1847 north of the Arctic Circle. By Evolyn Melville. Fort Yukon, May, 1949. [printed by Jessen's Weekly, Fairbanks] (8)p. ANR. April, 1953. 2d print. [printed by Jessens' Weekly, Fairbanks. 16p.   3074

MELVILLE, GEORGE WALLACE. In the Lena Delta; a narrative of the search for Lieutenant Commander DeLong and his companions, followed by an account of the Greely relief expedition and a proposed method of reaching the North Pole. By George W. Melville, Chief Engineer, U. S. N. Edited by Melville Philips. London, Longmans Green, 1885. 497p. pls. maps. ANR. Boston, Houghton Mifflin, 1885. 497p. pls. maps.   3075

Melville, George Wallace. SEE ALSO nos.
    1445, Ellsberg, Edw. Hell on ice. 1938;
    2129, History ... rescue Danenhower, Melville ... 1882.

Melvin, G., co-auth. SEE no. 393, Barbeau, Chas. M.

MELZACK, RONALD. The day Tuk became a hunter and other Eskimo stories, retold by Ronald Melzack. Illustrated by Carol Jones. N. Y., Dodd Mead, 1967. 92p. illus.(col.)   3076

Memoir of James Trevenen ... 1959. SEE no. 3533, [Penrose, C.V.]

Mémoires et observations ... 1765. SEE no. 1471, [Engel, Samuel]

MEMORANDUM ON THE BOUNDARY between Canada and Alaska showing the position of the Canadian Government in respect thereto. [Quebec ?], 1899. 129p. map(fold.)   3077

Memorial to Sec. of Interior. 1912. SEE no. 4633,
    Valdez, Citizens of.

MÉNAGER, FRANCIS M. The kingdom of the seal. Illustrated by the author. Chicago, Loyola University Press, 1962. 203p. front. illus. map. [Catholic missionary at Hooper Bay]   3078

MENDÖL, TIBOR. Az Északi-sark felfedézése és meghóditása. A föld fefedezöi és meghóditói v. köt. Révai, 1939.   3079

MENSHUTKIN, BORIS NIKOLAEVICH. Russia's Lomonosov. Translated by W. C. Huntington. Princeton, N. J., Princeton University Press, 1952.   3080

MENSHUTKIN, BORIS NIKOLAEVICH. Zhizneopisanie Mikhaila Vasil'-evicha Lomonosova. Tret'e izdanie s dopolneniiami. [TITLE TR. Biography of Mikhail Vasil'evich Lomonosov. Third edition, with additions] Moskva, Izd-vo Akademii Nauk SSSR, 1947. 294p. pls. facsims. bibliog. AN EARLIER EDIT. 1937. 237p.   3081

MENZEL, B. Dans la toundra de l'Alaska. Neychatel, 1938. [Moravian Church in Alaska]   3082

MENZIES, DONALD, edit. The Alaska Highway, a saga of the North.
Edited by Don Menzies. Edmonton, Stuart Douglas, 1943. rev.
ed.   (46)p. photos, sketches, maps.   3083

MENZIES, ROBERT JAMES. A review of the systematics and ecology
of the genus "Exosphaeroma," with the description of a new genus,
a new species, and a new subspecies. Crustacea, Isopoda, Sphaero-
midae. N. Y., American Museum of Natural History, 1954. 24p.
illus. bibliog. (American Museum Novitates, Aug. 11, 1954.
no. 1683) [incls. species in Alaskan habitat]   3084

MERK, FREDERICK, edit. Fur trade and empire; George Simpson's
journal; remarks connected with the fur trade in the course of
a voyage from York Factory 1824-25; together with accompanying
documents. Edited with an introduction by Frederick Merk. Cambridge, Harvard University Press, 1931. 370p. map(fold.)
(Harvard Historical Studies, vol. 31) ANR. 1968. rev. ed. 370p.
tables, map.   3085

MERRETT, JOHN. Captain James Cook. N. Y., Criterion, 1957.
illus.   3086

Merriam, C. H., edit. SEE nos.
    1950, Harriman Alaska Exped. 1899;
    4098, Sheldon, Chas. Wilderness of Denali. 1930.

MERRILL, ELMER DREW. The botany of Cook's voyages and its unexpected significance in relation to anthropology, biogeography
and history. Waltham, Mass., Chronica Botanica, 1954. iv,224p.
illus. ports. facsims. (vol. 14, no. 5/6)   3087

MERRILL, G. K. Lichens. Ottawa, King's Printer, 1924. 12p.
bibliog. (Canadian Arctic Expedition, 1833-18, Report. vol. 4,
Botany. pt. D)   3088

Mertens, H. SEE nos.
    557, Biographie du docteur Mertens ... *Seniavine.* n. d.;
    645, Brandt, J. F. Prodromus descript. ... 1835.

Messchaert, N., tr. SEE no. 3969, Sarychev, G. A.

METHODIST ALASKA YUKON PACIFIC COMMISSION. 1834-1909; Diamond
Jubilee of Methodism of the Pacific, authorized by annual conferences of the northwest, approved by the General Assembly of
the Methodist Episcopal Church, edited by William H. Leech.
Seattle, [1909] 80p. illus.   3089

Methodist Episcopal Mission. SEE nos. 3384-5, Official record
    ... 1904 and 1905.

Metlahkatla; ten years' ... 1869. SEE no. 1382, [Duncan, Wm.]

Metlakahtla. 1907. SEE no. 4365, Stromstadt, D. M.

METLAKAHTLA and the North Pacific Mission of the Church Mission- ary Society. London, Church Missionary House, 1800. 130p. front. (col. map) ANR. 1881. 2d ed. [written by Eugene Stock. Prior to 1887, Metlakatla was in British Columbia] 3090

METLAKATLA, ALASKA: church manual. no pl., n.d. [a "new" Metla- katla was established on Annette Island, Alaska in 1887] 3091

MEYER, ALMA E. Wassara and his tale of the far North. Indiana- polis, E. C. Seale & Co., 1962. (30)p. 3092

MEYER, KARL-HEINZ. Fünf Jahre im Eis; die Geschichte einer Nord- polexpedition 1850-1854. [TITLE TR. Five years in the ice; the history of a North Pole expedition, 1850-1854] Wuppertal-Barmen, Emil Müller, [1950] 75p. map. [Sir Robert M'Clure and ship *Investigator*, based on journal of J. A. Miertsching, SEE no. 3102] 3093

Meyer, Richard E., illus. SEE no. 954, Cleveland, Bess A.

MEYERS, WALTER E. Eskimo village. N. Y., Vantage Press, 1957. 125p. illus. glossary. [teacher in village of Koyuk on Seward Peninsula] 3094

MEZHOV, VLADIMIR IZMAĬLOVICH. Sibirskaĭa bibliografiĭa; ukazatel' knig i stateĭ o Sibiri na russkom ĭazykĭe i odnĭekh tol'ko knig na inostrannykh ĭazykakh za ves' period knigopechataniĭa.[TITLE TR. The Siberian bibliography; an index of books and articles on Siberia in the Russian language and books (only) in foreign lan- guages, for the period since the beginning of printing] S.-Peter- burg, Tip. I. N. Skorokhodova, 1891-92. 3 vols. plus index vol. 485p., 470p., 303p. and 188p. (index vol.) [for second printing, SEE no. 3096] 3095

MEZHOV, VLADIMIR IZMAILOVICH. Sibirskaĭa bibliografiĭa; ukazatel' knig i stateĭ o Sibiri na russkom ĭazykĭe i odnĭekh tol'ko knig na inostrannykh ĭazykakh za ves' period knigopechataniĭa. S.-Peterburg, A. S. Semenov, 1903. 3 vols. in 2. [2d print. of no. 3095] 3096

MICHAEL, CHARLES D. 'Mid snow and ice; stories of peril in Polar Seas. Toronto, n. d. 318p. illus. 3097

Michael, H. N., edit. SEE no. 5018, Zagoskin, L.A.

Michael, M. A., tr. SEE no. 4758, Waxell, Sven L.

Michael, Maurice, tr. SEE no. 3109, Mikkelsen, E.

Michaelis, Elsa, tr. SEE no. 2204, Howay, F. W.

Michelson, R. W., co-auth. SEE no. 2243, Hussey, K. M.

MIDDENDORFF, W.   Ueber die Tlinkit in Russischen Amerika.   St.
Petersburg, 1861.   3098

MIDNIGHT SUN BROADCASTING CO., Fairbanks.   KFAR Keybook of Interior Alaska "From the top of the world to you."   KFAR Key for
Alaska's riches.   Fairbanks, Midnight Sun Broadcasting Co.,
[c1939]   Printed by Frank McCaffrey, Seattle.   Book designed by
T. R. Lambert.   Drawings by Eustace P. Ziegler and T. R. Lambert.
64p.   illus. sketches, photos, maps.   [Fairbanks as it was in
1938]   3099

Midshipman's diary ... 1862.   SEE no. 1500,
    Euryalus; tales of sea ... 1860.

MIERS, HENRY ALEXANDER.   Yukon;   a visit to the Yukon gold-fields.
Letter from Henry A. Miers, addressed to Hon. Clifford Sifton,
Minister of the Interior.   [Ottawa], 1901.   32p.   3100

Miert, Jan August.   SEE nos. 3101-02, Miertsching, Johann August.

MIERTSCHING, JOHANN AUGUST.   Journal de M. Miertsching, inter-
prète du Capitaine MacClure dan son voyage au Pole Nord.   Genèvre, Paris, Joel Cher buliez, 1857.   Seconde édition.   143p.   map
(fold.)   (Tiré de la Bibliothèque universelle de Genèvre, janvier
et fevrier 1857)   ANR. Genèvre, Imprimerie Ramboz et Schuchard,
1857.   172p.   map(fold.)   [tr. of no. 3102]   3101

MIERTSCHING, JOHANN AUGUST.   Reise-tagebuch des Missionars Johann
August Miertsching, welcher als Dolmetscher die Nordpol Expedition zur Aufsuchung Sir John Franklins auf dem Schiffe *Investiga-*
tor begleitete.   In den Jahren 1850 bis 1854.   [TITLE TR.   Travel
diary of missionary Johann August Miertsching, who accompanied,
as interpreter, the Arctic expedition on the *Investigator* in
search of Sir John Franklin in the years 1850 to 1854]   Leipzig,
Gnadau, Im Verlag der Unitats Buchhandlung bei E. Kummer, 1855.
196p.   map(fold.), append.   ANR. 1856.   2d ed.   206p.   [see
no. 3101 for tr.]   3102

Miertsching, Johann August.   SEE ALSO nos.
    23, Aick, Gerhard.   Schweres Eis voraus ! 1953;
    489, Benham, Daniel.   Sketches life Miert ... 1854;
    1823, Great Britain.   Parl. (Franklin search);
    3093, Meyer, K.-H.   Fünf Jahre im Eis.   [1950]

MIGHELS, ELLA S.   Wawona;   an Indian story of the Northwest.
S. F., Harr Wagner Pub. Co., 1921.   117p.   illus. map.   3103

Mikkelsen, Ejnar.   [Alphabetical title guide to chronological
    entries]

    Conquering ... 3104.   Mirage ... 3109.
    Frozen justice ... 3107.   Norden for lov. 3106.
    John Dale ... 3105.   Ukendt Mand ... 3108.

MIKKELSEN, EJNAR. Conquering the Arctic ice. London, W. Heinemann, 1909. 470p. front. ports. diagrs. maps(incl. 1 fold.),
appends. ANR. Philadelphia, Geo. W. Jacobs, 1909. 470p. [polar
expedition of 1906-07, by Mikkelsen and E. deK. Leffingwell -
third appendix has medical notes on northern Alaska by G. P. Howe]
3104

MIKKELSEN, EJNAR. John Dale; en roman fra Polhavets kyster.
København, Gyldendal, 1921. 242p.   3105

MIKKELSEN, EJNAR. Norden for lov og ret, en Alaska - historie.
[TITLE TR. Northern law and justice; an Alaskan story] København, og Kristiana, Gyldendal, 1920. 217p. map.   3106

   TRANSLATIONS - Norden for lov ... 1920.

   Frozen justice; a story of Alaska. Copenhagen, Gyldendal,
      1922. 309p. map(fold. in back) ANR. London, 1922. 309p.
      map(fold.) ANR. N. Y., Knopf, 1922. 230p. Translated from
      the Danish by A. G. Jayne. illustrated with scenes from
      motion picture, endmaps.   3107

MIKKELSEN, EJNAR. Ukendt Mand til Ukendt Land. København,
Gyldendal, 1954. 191p. illus.   3108

   TRANSLATION - Ukendt Mand ... 1954.

   Mirage in the Arctic. London, Rupert Hart-Davis, 1955. 216p.
      front.(port.), photos, map. Translated from the Danish by
      Maurice Michael.   3109

MIKLUKHO-MAKLAĬ, NIKOLAĬ NIKOLAEVICH. Über einige Schwämme des
nordlichen Stillen Oceans und des Eismeeres, welche im zoologischen Museum der K. Akademie der Wissenschaften in St. Petersburg
aufgestellt sind. Ein Beitrag zur Morphologie und Verbreitung
der Spongien. [TITLE TR. On some sponges of the North Pacific
and Arctic Oceans, in the St. Petersburg Academy of Science]. A
contribution to the morphology and distribution of sponges]
St.-Pétersbourg, 1870. 24p. pls. (Akademiĩa nauk SSSR. Mémoires. Ser. 7, t. 15, no. 3)   3110

MILANOWSKI, PAUL G. and TRUDE A. MILANOWSKI. Dindee Shuu Aandeeg.
[TITLE TR. Dictionary of Upper Tanana Athabaskan] Tetlin,
Alaska, Wycliffe Bible Translators, 1961. 7p. (Summer Institute
of Linguistics)   3111

MILANOWSKI, PAUL G. Uusii dinahtt'aa'. I. [TITLE TR. Begin-
ner's reader. I.] Tetlin, Alaska, Wycliffe Bible Translators,
July 1965. 24p. illustrated by R. Gilman. (Summer Institute of
Linguistics) [Upper Tanana Athabaskan]   3112

MILANOWSKI, PAUL G. Uusii dinahtt'aa'. II. [TITLE TR. Beginner's reader. II.] Tetlin, Alaska, Wycliffe Bible Translators, July 1965. 28p. illustrated by R. Gilman. (Summer Institute of Linguistics) [Upper Tanana Athabaskan]   3113

THE MILEPOST. Anchorage, Alaska Research Co., 1949. 1st ed. annual. Edited by William A. Wallace. illus. map(fold.) LATER EDITIONS published by: Alaska Highway Research Co., Anchorage; published by: Alaska Travel Research Co., Anchorage; and published by: Alaska Northwest Pub. Co., Juneau. var. p. illus. maps.   3114

MILES, CHARLES. Indian and Eskimo artifacts of North America. Chicago, Henry Regnery, 1963. 244p. illus. pls.(some col.), bibliog. index. ANR. N. Y., Bonanza Books, n. d.   3115

Milet-Mureau, M. L. A., edit. SEE no. 2610, La Pérouse, J.F.G.de

MILLER, BASIL WILLIAM. Ken in Alaska. By Basil Miller. Grand Rapids, Mich., Zondervan Pub. House, 1944. 71p.   3116

MILLER, BASIL WILLIAM. Koko and the Eskimo doctor. By Basil Miller. Grand Rapids, Mich., Zondervan Pub. House, 1949. 88p.
                                                                  3117

MILLER, BASIL WILLIAM. Koko - king of the Arctic trail. By Basil Miller. Grand Rapids, Mich., Zondervan Pub. House, 1947.
                                                                  3118

MILLER, BASIL WILLIAM. Koko on the Yukon. By Basil Miller. Grand Rapids, Mich., Zondervan Pub. House, 1954. 88p.   3119

MILLER, INEZ. This is Alaska ! [Homer, Alaska ?], 1967.
[poetry]   3120

MILLER, JAMES MARTIN, edit. Discovery of the North Pole. Dr. Frederick A. Cook's own story of how he reached the North Pole April 21st, 1908; and the story of Commander Robert E. Peary's discovery April 6, 1909 ... special introduction by General A.W. Greely ... edited by Honorable J. Martin Miller ... also containing a true and authentic account of other great Polar expeditions, including Franklin, Greely, Abruzzi, Nares, Nordenskjold, Nansen, Sverdrup, Shackelton, etc. Illustrated with half-tone reproductions of photographs of many expeditions. Philadelphia, George A. Parker, [c1909] 428p. front.(dble. ports.), illus. many facsims. of newspaper cartoons. ANR. no pl., n. d. [c1909] 428p.   3121

Miller, Joaquin. SEE nos.
    3550, Peterson, M. S. Joaquin Miller ... [c1937];
    4406, Sutherland, H. V. Out of North. 1913.

Miller, Leon Gordon. SEE no. 3133, Miller, Polly.

MILLER, MAX. Fog and men on Bering Sea. Illustrated with pictures mostly taken by Bill (Ensign A. E. Harned) and by Ole (Ensign George Olsson). N. Y., E. P. Dutton, 1936. [c1936] 1st
ed. 272p. front.(map), pls. [U. S. Coast Guard ship *Northland*]
3122

MILLER, MAX. The great trek; the story of the five-year drive
of a reindeer herd through the icy wastes of Alaska and northwestern Canada. Garden City, N. Y., Doubleday Doran, 1935. 1st
ed. 224p. illus. sketch, photos by Lomen Bros. ftntes. endmap.
3123

MILLER, MAYNARD MALCOLM. Juneau Ice Field Research Project,
Alaska, 1950 summer field season. N. Y., American Geographical
Society, Sept. 1954. 102, 96ℓ cross-sections, graphs, diagrs.
tables, text maps, bibliog. append. (Juneau Ice Field Research
Project Report no. 7)   3124

MILLER, MAYNARD MALCOLM. Mechanical core drilling in firn and
ice; with a report on related investigations in the Taku Glacier,
S. E. Alaska, 1950-53. Prepared for The E. J. Longyear Co., The
Eastman Oil Well Survey Co., and the Geological Society of America. 40, 21ℓ illus. diagrs.(3 fold.), maps, tables, bibliog.
no pl., June 1954.   3125

MILLER, MAYNARD MALCOLM. Preliminary report of field operations,
the Juneau Ice Field Research Project, 1949 season. N. Y., American Geographical Society, Jan. 20, 1950. 36(13)p. diagrs. map,
appends. (Juneau Ice Field Research Project Report no. 2)   3126

MILLER, MAYNARD MALCOLM. Progress report of the Juneau Ice Field
Research Project, 1948, written and compiled from the field notes
and reports of members of the party. N. Y., American Geographical
Society, May 1949. 108p. pls. maps, appends. (Dept. of Explor-
ation and Field Research, American Geographical Soc. and Juneau
Ice Field Research Project Report no. 1)   3127

MILLER, MAYNARD MALCOLM. Prospectus of new research facilities
and scientific investigations on the Taku-Llewellyn Glacier
system, Alaska-B. C., in relation to the forthcoming International
Geophysical Year, Part 1 (plans for 1955-57) prepared for the
Lamont Geological Observatory, Columbia University. N. Y., Oct.
1954. rev. May 1955. 19p. maps(fold.), bibliog. (Foundation
for Glacier Research, Internal Memorandum no. 11)   3128

MILLER, MAYNARD MALCOLM. Scientific observations of the Juneau
Ice Field Research Project, Alaska 1949 field season. N. Y.,
American Geographical Society, July 1952. 163p. illus. sketch
maps, diagrs. (Juneau Ice Field Research Project Report no. 6)
3129

MILLER, MAYNARD MALCOLM. Status reports of the Juneau Ice Field Research Project, Alaska, from 1948 to 1952. N. Y., American Geographical Society, July 1953. 29p. text map. (Internal Memorandum no. 4)   3130

MILLER, MIKE. Off the beaten path in Alaska. Illustrated by Rudy J. Ripley. Juneau, Alaskabooks, 1970. printed and bound by Evergreen Press, Vancouver, Canada. 116p. sketches, sketch maps, paperback. (An Alaskabook, no. 101)   3131

MILLER, MIKE. Soapy. With illustrations by Rudy J. Ripley. Juneau, Alaskabooks, 1970. printed by Evergreen Press, Vancouver, Canada. 122p. illus. paperback. (An Alaskabook no. 102)   3132

Miller, Mike, co-edit. SEE ALSO no. 3406,
     Olson, B. G. Blood on Arctic snow. 1956.

MILLER, POLLY and LEON GORDON MILLER. Lost heritage of Alaska; the adventures and art of the Alaskan coastal Indians. Cleveland, World Pub. Co., 1967. 1st print. 320p. illus.endmaps.
                                                                 3133

Miller, S. W. SEE no. 3666, Poulter, Thos. C.

Milligrock, A., illus. SEE no. 4535, Tickasook.

MILLROY'S PATHFINDER to Alaska and the Klondyke gold fields. no pl., [1897 ?]   3134

MILLS, DAVID. The Canadian view of the Alaskan boundary dispute as stated by Hon. David Mills, Minister of Justice, in an interview with the correspondent of the Chicago Tribune on the 14th Aug., 1899. Ottawa, Gov't Print. Bur., 1899. 23p.   3135

MILLS, ENOS ABIJAH. The grizzly; our greatest wild animal. Boston, Houghton Mifflin, 1919. 289p. pls.   3136

MILLS, JAMES. Airborne to the mountains. N. Y., A. S. Barnes, 1961. 261p. photos, maps, glossary, appends. [Muldrow Glacier, Mt. McKinley]   3137

Mills, John Fraser, illus. SEE no. 1959, Harris, Christie.

MILLS, STEPHEN E. and JAMES W. PHILLIPS. Sourdough sky; a pictorial history of flights and flyers in the bush country. Seattle, Superior Pub. Co., [c1969] 1st ed. 176p. pls. map, facsims. list of Alaskan airmen, index.   3138

MILTON, JOHN P. Nameless valleys, shining mountains; the record of an expedition into the vanishing wilderness of Alaska's Brooks Range. N. Y., Walker & Co., 1970. photos, drawings.   3139

MINER'S GUIDE to Alaskan and Yukon River gold fields. Published by Alaskan and Yukon River Gold Fields Bureau of Information, 330 Pine, San Francisco, California. [S. F., 1898] unp.(16p.+ 12 ruled blank p.), diagrs. maps(incl. 1 fold.), calendar. 3140

Miners' manual. 1898. SEE no. 943, Clark, Horace F.

Miners' News Pub. Co. SEE no. 171,All about Klondike mines.[1897]

MINERS' SUPPLEMENT to the Royal Baker and Pastry Cook. N. Y., 1898. 29p. 3141

Mirabeau, de, M. SEE no. 3383, Official papers ...
    Nootka Sound. 1790.

MIRICK, SUSANNAH and others. Feasibility of automobile ferry service connecting southeastern Alaska with the Canadian highway system at Prince Rupert and with the Alaska Highway via Haines. (A preliminary study) Portland, Ore., 1944. 36p. tables, map. (North Pacific Planning Project, North Pacific Study no. 5) 3142

Mirick, Susannah, co-auth. SEE ALSO no. 3787,
    Rettie, Jas. C. Comparisons ... costs ... commodities. 1944.

MIRSKY, JEANNETTE. To the Arctic ! The story of northern exploration from earliest times to the present. N. Y., Knopf, 1948. 1st Borzoi ed. 334p. pls. maps(some fold.) ANR. N. Y. and London, Allan Wingate, 1949. 334p. illus. maps. [rev. and expanded ed. of no. 3144] 3143

MIRSKY, JEANNETTE. To the North ! The story of Arctic exploration from earliest times to the present. N. Y., Viking, 1934. 386p. pls. ports. facsims. maps(incl. 1 fold.), appends. bibliog. ANR. WITH TITLE Northern conquest. London, H. Hamilton, 1-34. 386p. pls. ports. facsims. maps(incl. 1 fold.) [see also no. 3143] 3144

Mission of Russian Church to Aleoutine Isl. 1849. SEE
    no. 991, Colonial Church Chronicle.

MISSIONARY LAUNCH "Princeton." no pl., [ca 1925] [Presbyterian Church leaflet, Indians of southeastern Alaska] 3145

Mr. Mear's [sic] memorial ... [1790 ?] SEE no. 3054,
    [Meares, John]

Mitchell, Geo. M. SEE no. 1792, Graham, A.

MITCHELL, MAIRIN. The maritime history of Russia, 1848-1948. London, Sedgwick & Jackson, 1949. 544p. illus. maps, bibliog. index. 3146

MITCHELL, WILLIAM. General Greely; the story of a great American. N. Y., Putnam, 1936. 242p. pls. ports. map.   3147

MITCHELL, WILLIAM. Skyways. Philadelphia, Lippincott, 1930.3148

MIZNER, ADDISON. The many Mizners. N. Y., Vere Pub. Co., 1932.
305p.   3149

Mizner, Addison. SEE ALSO nos.
    2374, Johnston, A. Legendary Mizners. 1953;
    4380, Sullivan, Edw. D. Fabulous Wilson Mizner. 1935.

Mizner, Edgar, William, and Wilson. SEE nos.
    2374, Johnston, A. Legendary Mizners. 1953;
    3149, Mizner, Addison. Many Mizners. 1932;
    4380, Sullivan, Edw. D. Fabulous Wilson Mizner. 1935.

MJELDE, MICHAEL JAY. *Glory of the Seas*.Middletown, Conn., Wesleyan University Press, 1969. 303p. illus. photos, maps, appends. bibliog. index. (published for Marine Historical Association) [whaling and salmon fleets]   3150

Modern El Dorado. 1897. SEE no. 1428, El Dorado Pub. Co.

MOFFETT, THOMAS C. The American Indian on the new trail; the
red man of the United States and the Christian gospel. N. Y.,
Missionary Education Movement of U. S. and Canada, 1914. 302p.
                                                             3151

MOIR, GEORGE T. Sinners and saints. Victoria, B. C., privately
printed, 1947.   3152

Moiseev, P. A., edit. Soviet fisheries ... no. 1. 1968.
    SEE no. 4249, Sovetskie Rybokhoziaistvennye ... 1963.

MOLCHUL'SKIĬ, VIKTOR IVANOVICH. Die Kaefer Russlands. I. In-
secta Carabica. [TITLE TR. Beetles of Russia. I. Carabida] Mos-
cau, Buchdruch. v. W. Gautier, 1850. 91p. tables(fold.)   3153

MOLCHUL'SKIĬ, VIKTOR IVANOVICH. Genres et espèces d'insects publiés dans differents ouvrages par Victor Motschoulsky. [TITLE
TR. Genera and species of insects published in various papers of
Victor Mochul'skij St. Petersburg, Impr. V. Besobrasoff & Co.,
1868. 118p. bibliog. index. (Russkoe entomologicheskoe obshchestvo, St. Petersburg. Trudy(Horae). t.6. Suppl.) [incls.
those of southeastern Alaska]   3154

Moll, Herman, cartog. SEE nos. 932-3, Churchill, A.
    Collection voyages ... 1732-47 and 1745.

Moller, Fred. SEE no. 3658, Potter, Jean.

MÖLLER, JOACHIM VAN. Auf nach Alaska. Ein Fuhrer für Wagemutige von Joachim van Möller (Mit 50 Illustrationem und einer Doppel-karte). Charlottenburg, Germany, Verlag von Friedrich Thiel, 1897. 198p. illus. maps(2 fold. in back pocket)   3155

Monahan, P. J., illus. SEE no. 2766, London, Jack.

Mondria, Ramon, tr. SEE no. 934, Cipolla, A.

Monk Herman. SEE no. 1534, Father Herman ... n. d.

MONTAGUE, PHILIP S. Ready reference and hand book of the Klon-dyke and Alaskan gold fields. Containing maps of both routes, mining laws, boundary lines, how and when to go, necessary outfit and supplies to take, etc. Carefully compiled from official reports, correspondence, and the private diaries of several miners just returned from the phenomenal gold fields of the Klon-dyke. Compiled by Phil. S. Montague. S. F., The Hicks-Judd Co. Print., 1897. 58p. pls. map(fold.)   3156

Montgomery, Richard Gill. Adventures in the Arctic. SEE
    no. 3158.

MONTGOMERY, RICHARD GILL. Husky; co-pilot of the *Pilgrim*. N. Y., Holt, 1942. illus. ANR. N. Y., 1949. 213p. wrps.   3157

MONTGOMERY, RICHARD GILL. "Pechuck;" Lorne Knight's adventures in the Arctic. N. Y., Dodd Mead, 1932. 291p. front. pls. ports. endmaps. ANR. Caldwell, Idaho, Caxton, 1932. 291p. front. pls. ports. endmaps. ANR. WITH TITLE Adventures in the Arctic; ori-ginally published under the title "Pechuck." N. Y., Dodd Mead, 1932. 281p. front.(port.), pls. ports. endmaps. ANR. N. Y., Grosset & Dunlap, n. d. reissue rev. 281p. front.(port.), pls. ports. endmaps. [Knight on whaling cruises with Capt. Louis Lane and with Stefansson in the Arctic, also on Wrangel Island]   3158

MONTGOMERY, RUTHERFORD GEORGE. Amikuk. Drawings by Marie Non-nast. N. Y., World, 1955. 205p. illus.   3159

MONTGOMERY, RUTHERFORD GEORGE. Iceblink. By Rutherford Mont-gomery. Illustrated by Rudolf Freund. N. Y., Henry Holt, 1941. 288p. front.(dble. map), pls.(1 dble.) OTHERS 2d print. 1944; 3rd print. 1945.   3160

MONTGOMERY, RUTHERFORD GEORGE. Seecatch; a story of a fur seal. Boston, Ginn & Co., 1955. illus.   3161

Moore, Captain Billie. SEE nos.
    900, Chase, Will H. Reminiscences Capt. Billie Moore.[c1947];
    3162, Moore, J. Bernard. Skagway ... 1968.

Moore, *Bishop* D. H. SEE no. 3385, Official record Alaska
    Mission Methodist Episcopal Church. 1905.

MOORE, J. BERNARD. Skagway in days primeval. N. Y., Vantage
Press, 1968. 202p. [based on diary of Capt. Billie Moore] 3162

MOORE, OTIS M., edit. The new northwest. Edited by O. M. Moore.
Seattle, Puget Sound Bureau of Information, 1900. vol. 1, no. 1,
August 1900. [only issue printed] 3163

MOORE, OTIS M., comp. Washington illustrated; including views
of the Puget Sound country, and Seattle, gateway of the Orient,
with glimpses of Alaska. Seattle, Puget Sound Bureau of Information, [1901 ?] (116)p. illus. ports. 3164

MOORE, TERRIS. Alaska. N. Y., American Geographical Society,
1962. 6p. maps, bibliog. pamphlet(fold.) (Focus, vol. 13,
no. 3, November 1962) 3165

MOORE, TERRIS. Mt. McKinley; the pioneer climbs. College,
University of Alaska Press, 1967. 202p. front.(col.), pls.
maps, ftntes. glossary, bibliog. index. 3166

Moore, William. SEE nos.
    900, Chase, Will H.Reminiscences Capt. Billie Moore.[c1947];
    3162, Moore, J. Bernard. Skagway in days primeval. 1968.

MOOREES, COENRAAD F. The Aleut dentition; a correlative study
of dental characteristics in an Eskimoid people. Cambridge, Harvard University Press, 1957. 196p. illus. ports. maps, diagrs.
tables, bibliog. 3167

THE MORAVIAN CHURCH IN ALASKA. The Board of Christian Education
and Evangelism. Bethlehem, Penna., n. d. 3168

MORAVIAN MISSION among the Esquimeaux in Alaska. A brief report
issued by the Society for Propagating the Gospel among the Heathen. Bethlehem, Penna., January 1, 1887. 4p. 3169

THE MORAVIAN MISSION in Alaska; published to commemorate the completion of its first decade. A. L. O'Erter, editor. Bethlehem,
Penna., June 19, 1895. pls. folio. 3170

Morellet, A., tr. SEE no. 4640,
    Vancouver, Geo. Voyage de découvertes ... 1790-95. 1800.

MORENUS, RICHARD. Alaska sourdough; the story of Slim Williams.
N. Y., Rand McNally, 1956. 278p. illus. [Chitina, 1900-33,
hunting, trapping, breeding sled dogs] 3171

MORENUS, RICHARD. Dew line; Distant Early Warning, the miracle
of America's first line of defense. N. Y., Rand McNally, 1957.
184p. illus. 3172

MOREY, WALTER. Gentle Ben. By Walt Morey. N. Y., E. P. Dutton,
1965. 191p. front. illus. [Alaskan brown bear] 3173

MOREY, WALTER. Gloomy Gus. By Walt Morey. N. Y., E. P. Dutton, 1970. 256p. illus. [Kodiak brown bear]   3174

MOREY, WALTER. Home is the North. By Walt Morey. N. Y., E. P. Dutton, 1967. 1st ed. 223p. front. illus.   3175

MOREY, WALTER. Kävik the wolf dog. By Walt Morey. N. Y., E. P. Dutton, 1968. 192p. illus. [sled dog]   3176

Morey, Walter. SEE ALSO no. 728, Burford, Virgil.
     North to danger. 1954.

MORGAN, BERNICE BANGS. The very thought of thee; adventures of an Arctic missionary. Grand Rapids, Zondervan Pub. House, 1952. 136p. illus.   3177

Morgan, Edw. E. P., co-auth. SEE no. 4958, Woods, H. F.

MORGAN, JULIET and EDWARD L. KEITHAHN. Alaska and Hawaii. N.Y., Macmillan, 1956. 312p. illus. text maps. (Around the world; a series of geography readers)   3178

MORGAN, LAEL. The woman's guide to boating and cooking. Free-port, Me., B. Wheelwright Co., 1968. 246p. illus.(some col.), bibliog.   3179

MORGAN, LEN. Klondike adventure. N. Y., Thomas Nelson & Sons, 1940. 199p. front. illus. map.   3180

MORGAN, MURRAY CROMWELL. Bridge to Russia; those amazing Aleutians. By Murray Morgan. N. Y., E. P. Dutton, 1947. 1st ed. 222p. endmaps, append. bibliog.   3181

MORGAN, MURRAY CROMWELL. Dixie raider; the saga of the C. S. S. *Shenandoah*. By Murray Morgan. N. Y., E. P. Dutton, 1948. 1st ed. 336p. pls. endmaps, bibliog.   3182

MORGAN, MURRAY CROMWELL. One man's goldrush; a Klondike album. Seattle, University of Washington Press, 1967. 215p. illus. [photos by E. A. Hegg]   3183

MORGAN, MURRAY CROMWELL. Skid road; an informal portrait of Seattle. N. Y., Viking Press, 1951. [c1951] 280p. ftntes. endmaps, index.   3184

MORGAN, WILLIAM G. The trail of a cheechako in Alaska. Washington, D. C., H. L. & J. B. McQueen, 1928. 46p.   3185

MORICE, ADRIAN GABRIEL. Essai sur l'origine des Dènès de l'Amér-ique du Nord. [TITLE TR. Essay on the origin of the Dènès of North America] Quebec, Impr. de "L'Evénement," 1915. 245p. pls. port.   3186

MORICE, ADRIAN GABRIEL. Fifty years in western Canada; being the
abridged memoirs of Reverend A. G. Morice. Toronto, 1930. 267p.
3187

MORICE, ADRIAN GABRIEL. Notes on the western Dènès. Toronto,
1894. 222p. (reprinted from Transactions Canadian Institute,
1894. vol. 4, pt. 1)
3188

MORICE, ADRIAN GABRIEL. Thawing out the Eskimo. By Rev. Adrian
G. Morice, O.M.I., translated by Mary T. Loughlin. Boston, The
Society of the Propagation of the Faith, 1943. 2d ed. 188p.
front.(map), pls. [brief mention of Alaskan missionaries in translator's prologue]
3189

MORICE, ADRIAN GABRIEL. The history of the northern interior of
British Columbia (formerly New Caledonia) 1660-1880. Toronto,
1904. pls. map(fold.) ANR. Toronto, 1905. 3rd ed. 368p. illus.
map. ANR. London, 1906. ANR. Fairfield, Washington, Ye Galleon
Press, 1969. facsim. of London 1906 ed.
3190

MORICE, ADRIAN GABRIEL. The new methodical, easy and complete
Dènè syllabary. Stuart's Lake Mission, British Columbia, 1890.
3p.
3192

Morice, Adrian Gabriel. SEE ALSO nos.
    2106, Hill-Tout, C. Far west. 1907;
    3591, Pinart, A. L. A few words on Alaska Dènè ... n. d.

MORISON, SAMUEL ELIOT. Aleutians, Gilberts and Marshalls; June
1942-April 1944. Boston, Little Brown, 1951. [vol. 7 of author's
"History of U. S. Naval operations in Worl War II"]
3192

MORISON, SAMUEL ELIOT. The maritime history of Massachusetts,
1783-1860. Boston, 1921. ltd. ed. of 385 copies. ANR. Boston,
Houghton, 1961. reprint of 1921 ed. (Sentry 6)
3193

Mornas, Buy de. Cosmographie Methodique et Elementaire. Paris,
1770. 568p. pls. maps. [incls. Pacific coastal waters and
de la Fuente's northwest]
3194

Morning and evening prayer ... Eskimo ... 1923. SEE
    no. 1480, Episcopal Church.

MOROZEWICZ, JÓZEF MARIAN. Komandory; studjum geograficzno-
przyrodnicze. [TITLE TR. The Commander Islands; a study, geography and natural history] Warszawa, Wydawn. Kasy im. Mianow-
skiego, 1925. 230p. illus. pls. figs. tables, maps(2 fold. col.)
[incls. references to Aleutian and Pribilof Islands]
3195

MORRELL, BENJAMIN. A narrative of four voyages; to the South
Sea, North and South Pacific ... 1822-31. N. Y., 1832. 492(4)p.
port. OTHERS 1841 and 1853. [incls. northwest coast]
3196

MORRELL, WILLIAM PARKER. The gold rushes. London, Adam & Charles Black, 1940. 426p. maps(4 fold.), bibliog. (The Pioneer Histories, edited by V. T. Harlow and J. A. Williamson) ANR. Chester Springs, Penna., Dufour Editions, 1940.   3197

Morrill, Lesley, co-auth. SEE no. 1896, Haines, Madge.

Morris, Chas., edit. SEE no. 1009, Cook, F. A.

MORRIS, FRANK LEMERISE, W. R. HEATH and AMOS BURG. Marine atlas, volume II. Port Hardy, [B. C.] to Skagway, Alaska. Seattle, P. B. I. Co., 1959. tables, charts(some col., some fold.) [incls. Inland Passage]   3198

MORRIS, IDA DORMAN. A Pacific Coast vacation, by Mrs. James Edwin Morris; illustrated from photographs taken enroute by James Edwin Morris. N. Y., The Abbey Press, 1901. 255p. front.(port.) pls. ports. ANR. London, 1901.   3199

Morris, Mrs. James Edwin. SEE no. 3199, Morris, Ida Dorman.

MORRISON, HUGH A. Alaskan newspapers and periodicals; preliminary checklist prepared for the use of James Wickersham, delegate from Alaska. Washington, D. C., 1915. 28p.   3200

MORROW, HONORÉ. Argonaut. N. Y., Wm. Morrow, 1933. 316p. endmaps.   3201

MORROW, WILLIAM W. "The spoilers" Berkeley, Calif., Lederer, Street and Zeus Co., Printers, 1916. 113p. (reprinted from California Law Review, vol. 4, no. 2, Jan. 1916) [Cape Nome gold mining case which formed theme of Rex Beach novel]   3202

Morskoi Sbornik. SEE no. 1763, [Golovnin, V. M.]

MORTIMER, GEORGE. Observations and remarks made during a voyage to the islands of Teneriffe, Amsterdam, Maria's Islands near Van Diemen's Land; Otaheite, Sandwich Islands; Owhyhee, the Fox Islands on the north west coast of America, Tinian, and from thence to Canton, in the brig *Mercury* commanded by John Henry Cox, Esq. ... by Lieut. George Mortimer ... London, printed for the author; and sold by T. Cadell ... 1791. 72p. pl. maps(2) ANR. Dublin, 1791. 119p. [for tr. see no. 3204]   3203

MORTIMER, GEORGE. Waarnem, en aanmerk. geduw. eene reize naar Teneriffe, Van Diemensland, Sandwich-Eiland, de Noord-West-Kust van Amerika, enz. on der bevel van J. H. Cox. Uit h. Eng. Vert. Leyden, 1793. [tr. of no. 3203]   3204

Mortimer, George. SEE ALSO no. 3651, Portlock, N.
    Nathaniel Portlock's und Georg Mortimer's Reisen ... 1796.

MORTON, ARTHUR SILVER. A history of the Canadian West to 1870-71; being a history of Rupert's Land (The Hudson's Bay Company's territory) and of the North-West Territory (including the Pacific Slope) London, T. Nelson & Sons, 1939. 987p. maps(some fold.), bibliog. index.   3205

MORTON, ARTHUR SILVER. Sir George Simpson, overseas governor of the Hudson's Bay Company; a pen picture of a man of action. Portland, Binfords & Mort, 1944. front. pls. ports.   3206

MORTON, ARTHUR SILVER. The Northwest Company. Toronto, Ryerson, 1930. 32p. (Canadian History Readers)   3207

MOTHER LODE COPPER MINES COMPANY OF ALASKA. Report of W. G. Clark and C. M. Eaton. N. Y., n. d. 27p.   3208

Mott, F. L., edit. SEE no. 2773, London, J.

MOTT, SARAH M. Fishing and hunting (in Alaska with Ola) Chicago, American Book Co., 1905.   3209

MOUNT McKINLEY NATURAL HISTORY ASSOC., Mt. McKinley Park. Mt. McKinley National Park. Alaska storybook to color. Amsterdam, N. Y., The Noteworthy Co., Printer, 1968. (34)p. illus. maps, wrps.   3210

MOUNT WRANGELL CO. Short story of Alaska and the Yukon up to date, as told by the Mt. Wrangell Company's explorer, 1897-98. Boston, 1898.   3211

Mountain wonderland ... Revilla Island ... [ca 1945] SEE no. 84, Alaska Magazine Pub. Co.

MOUNTEVANS, EDWARD RATCLIFFE GARTH RUSSELL EVANS. Arctic solitudes. London, Lutterworth Press, 1953. 143p. pls. bibliog. endmap. ANR. N. Y., Philosophical Library, 1953. 143p. pls. endmap.   3212

MOUNTEVANS, EDWARD RATCLIFFE GARTH RUSSELL EVANS. British Polar explorers. London, W. Collins, 1943. 48p. pls.(some col.), ports.(some col.) (Britain in Pictures) [incls. James Cook]3213

MOUNTEVANS, EDWARD RATCLIFFE GARTH RUSSELL EVANS. From husky to Sno-Cat; a short survey of Polar exploration yesterday and today. London, 1957. 173p. photos, endmaps, bibliog. index. 3214

Mourelle, Francisco A. SEE no. 3036, Maurelle, F. A.

MOWRY, WILLIAM. Heart of the North. N. Y., 1930. 331p.   3215

MOWRY, WILLIAM A. The territorial growth of the United States. N. Y., 1902.   3216

MOZEE, BEN. The reindeer problems in Alaska. Nome, June 1933.
3217

MUDGE, ZACHARIAH ATWELL. Arctic heroes; facts and incidents of
Arctic explorations, from the earliest voyages to the discovery
of the fate of Sir John Franklin, embracing sketches of commercial
and religious results. By Rev. Z. A. Mudge. Four illustrations.
N. Y., Nelson & Phillips and Cincinnati, Hitchcock & Waldon,
[c1875] 304p. front. pls. [children's general survey of Arctic
with scattered Alaskan-Bering Sea references] 3218

MUDGE, ZACHARIAH ATWELL. Fur-clad adventurers; or, travels in
skin-canoes, on dog-sledges, on reindeer, and on snow-shoes,
through Alaska, Kamchatka, and eastern Siberia. N. Y., Phillips
& Hunt and Cincinnati, Walden & Stowe, 1880. 342p. front. pls.
[Western Union Telegraph Expedition, 1865-68] 3219

Mudge, Zachariah Atwell. SEE ALSO no. 1582,
Flint, S. R. Mudge memoirs ... 1883.

MUELLER, R. J. A short illustrated topical dictionary of western
Kutchin. Fairbanks, Summer Institute of Linguistics, 1964. 52p.
(Wycliffe Bible Translators) illus. 3220

MUIR, JOHN. Alaska. no pl., Northern Pacific Railroad Co., n.d.
[ca 1893-95 ?] folder. [cf no. 3353] 3221

[MUIR, JOHN] John Muir; a pictorial biography, compiled by the
pupils of the John Muir School, Seattle, Washington, in commemoration of the one hundredth anniversary of the birth of John
Muir, 1838-1938. Seattle, Lowman & Hanford, 1938. (105)p. front.
ports. facsims. 3222

MUIR, JOHN. Our national parks. Boston, Houghton Mifflin, 1901.
382p. front. illus. index. [has brief, scattered references to
Alaskan national parks] 3223

MUIR, JOHN, edit. Picturesque California and the region West of
the Rocky Mountains, from Alaska to Mexico. N. Y., J. Dewing,
[c1887-1888] folio, in 30 pts. pls. wrps. ANR. 1894. folio,
in 32 pts. pls. wrps. 3224

MUIR, JOHN. Stickeen. Boston, Houghton Mifflin, [c1909] 73p.
ANR. 1912. 2d ed. ANR. Boston, Houghton Mifflin, n. d. 81p.
(The Riverside Literature Series) 3225

MUIR, JOHN. The cruise of the *Corwin*; journal of the Arctic expedition of 1881 in search of DeLong and the *Jeannette*. Edited
by William Frederic Badè. Boston, Houghton Mifflin, 1917. 279p.
front. photos, sketches, map, appends. index. ANR. Boston, 1917.
ltd. numbered edit. on large paper. 3226

[MUIR, JOHN]   The John Muir book; by the pupils of the John Muir
School, Seattle, Washington.   Seattle, Cooperative Printing Co.,
1925. 71p.   3227

MUIR, JOHN.   The wilderness world of John Muir.   With an introduction and interpretive comments by Edwin Way Teale.   Illustrated
by Henry B. Kane.   Boston, Houghton Mifflin, 1954. 332p. illus.
index.   [excerpts from Muir's writings, incl. "Travels in Alaska,"
"Stickeen," and "Cruise of the *Corwin*"]   3228

MUIR, JOHN.   The writings of John Muir, edited by William Fred-
eric Badè.   Boston, Houghton Mifflin, 1915-24. 10 vols. illus.
(Sierra Edition)   ANR. 1916-24. 10 vols. illus.   (Manuscript
Edition)   [both editions include editor's "Life and letters of
John Muir," vols. 9 and 10. See no. 334]   3229

MUIR, JOHN.   Travels in Alaska.   Boston, Houghton Mifflin, 1915.
327p. front.(pl.), pls. glossary of Chinook Jargon, index. ANR.
1915. ltd. ed. of 450 copies on large paper. 236p. front.(col.),
index.   3230

Muir, John.   SEE ALSO nos.
    334, Badè, Wm. F.   Life and letters John Muir. 1924;
    1896, Haines, M.   John Muir, protector wilds. 1957;
    1950, Harriman Alaska Exped. 1899. vol. 1;
    4941, Wolfe, L. M., edit.   John of Mtns.; unpub. journals ...
        1938;
    4942, Wolfe, L. M.   Son of wilderness ... 1945;
    4997, Young, S. Hall.   Alaska days ... [c1915]

MUIR, JOHN REID.   The life and achievements of Captain James
Cook ... explorer, navigator, surveyor and physician.   London,
Blackie, 1939. 310p. illus. port. map, bibliog.   3231

"Muktuk" Marston.   SEE no. 3001, Marston, Marvin R.

MÜLLER, GERHARD FRIEDRICH.   Herrn v. Tschitschagow russischkayser-
lichen admirals reise nach dem Eissmeer.   St. Petersburg, J. Z.
Logan, 1793. 104p.   3232

MÜLLER, GERHARD FRIEDRICH.   Nachrichten von Seereisen, und zur
See gemachten Entdeckungen, die von Russland aus längst den Küsten
des Eissmeeres und auf dem Ostlichen Weltmeere gegen Japon und
Amerika geschehen sind; die Erlauterung einer bey der Akademie
der Wissenschaften verfertigten Landkarte. [TITLE TR. Description of voyages and discoveries by sea from Russia along the
coasts of the Frozen Sea and on the Eastern Ocean toward Japan
and America; explanation of the map compiled at the Academy of
Sciences].   St. Petersburg, 1758. 304p. bibliog. [vol. 3(of 4)
of author's "Sammlung Russischer Geschichte"]   3233

Müller, Gerhard Friedrich.   Voyages et découvertes ... 1766.
    See no. 3235.

Müller, Gerhard Friedrich. Voyages from Asia ... 1761. SEE
no. 3234.

MÜLLER, GERHARD FRIEDRICH. TRANSLATIONS AND ENL. - Nachrichten
... 1758, chronologically.

Voyages from Asia to America, for completing the discoveries
of the North West coast of America; to which is prefixed a
summary of the voyages made by the Russians on the Frozen
Sea, in search of a North East passage; serving as an explanation of a map of the Russian discoveries, published by
the Academy of Sciences at Petersburgh. Translated from the
High Dutch of S. [sic] Muller with the addition of three new
maps by Thomas Jefferys. London, T. Jefferys, 1761. 76p.
maps, bibliog. [enl. of no. 3233] ANR. London, 1764. 120p.
ANR. Amsterdam, N. Israel and N. Y., Da Capo Press, 1967.
facsim. of 1761 Eng. ed. (Bibliotheca Australiana, 3rd ser.,
no. 26)   3234

Voyages et découvertes faites par les Russes le long des côtes
de la mer Glaciale et sur l'Ocean Oriental, tant vers le
Japon que vers l'Amérique. On y a joint l'Histoire du fleuve
Amur et des pays adjacens, depuis la conquete des Russes. Tr.
de L'Allemand par C. F. G. Dumas. Amsterdam, Chez Marc-
Michel Rey, 1766. 2 vols. (12)388p. and (4)207(22)p. map
(fold.) ANR. Amsterdam, Rozet, 1768. [in French] 2 vols.
same paging.   3235

Müller, Gerhard Friedrich. SEE ALSO no. 493,
Bellin, J. N. Carte ... l'Ocean Septentrional ... 1766.

[Müller, Gerhard Friedrich] SEE ALSO no. 2693,
Lettre d'un officier ... 1753.

Müller, Gerhard Friedrich. SEE ALSO no. 3529,
Pekarskiĭ, P. O. Istoriĭa Akad. nauk ... 1870-73.

MÜLLER, MARTIN. Koloniale wirstchaft und besiedlung des sub-
arktischen westens von Nordamerika. [TITLE TR. Colonial economy
and settlement of subarctic western North America] Leipzig,
Skriptofot-Druck Dr. jur. Stein & Co., 1935. 79p. pls. diagr.
sketch maps, bibliog. [author's doctoral thesis, Leipzig Uni-
versity]   3236

Müller, S. SEE nos. 3232-35, Müller, Gerhard Friedrich.

MUNFORD, JAMES KENNETH. John Ledyard; an American Marco Polo.
By Kenneth Munford. Portland, Binfords & Mort, 1939. 308p.
front.(map)   3237

MUNFORD, JAMES KENNETH, edit. John Ledyard's journal of Captain Cook's last voyage. Edited by James Kenneth Munford. With an introduction by Sinclair H. Hitchings. And with notes on plants by Helen M. Gilkey and notes on animals by Robert M Storm. Corvallis, Oregon State University Press, [c1963] (41)264p. illus. facsims. maps, endmaps, ftntes. append. bibliog. index. (Oregon State Studies in History, no. 3)   3238

Munford, Kenneth. SEE nos. 3237-38, Munford, James Kenneth.

MUNGER, JAMES F. Two years in the Pacific and Arctic Oceans and China, being a journal of every day life on board ship. Interesting information in regard to the inhabitants of different countries and the exciting events peculiar to a whaling voyage. Vernon, N. Y., J. R. Howlett, Printer, 1852. 80p. ANR. Fairfield, Wash., Ye Galleon Press, 1967. facsim. ed. ltd. to 401 copies.   3239

MUNN, HENRY TOKE. Prairie trails and Arctic by-ways. London, Hurst & Blackett, 1932. 288p. illus. [gold rush, Dawson in Yukon Terr. and St. Michael, Alaska]   3240

MUÑOZ, JUAN. Juneau; a study of the Gastineau Channel area. Juneau, Totem Press, 1956. 120p. photos, graphs, wrps.   3241

MUÑOZ, RIE. Nursing in the North 1867-1967. Written and illustrated by Rie Muñoz. Published under the auspices of The Alaska Nurses' Association. Anchorage, Ken Wray's Print Shop, [c1967] 50p. illus. bibliog.   3242

MUNRO, WILFRED HAROLD. Tales of an old seaport; a general sketch of the history of Bristol, Rhode Island, including, incidentally, an account of the voyages of the Norsemen, so far as they may have been connected with Narragansett Bay and personal narratives of some notable voyages accomplished by sailors from the Mt. Hope lands. Princeton, N. J., Princeton University Press, 1917. 292p. pls. [incls. D'Wolfe's "Voyage to North Pacific... 1861. See no. 1287]   3243

MUNROE, KIRK. Snow-shoes and sledges; a sequel to "The fur-seal's tooth." N. Y. Harper, 1895. 271p. front. illus. ANR. N. Y , 1923.   3244

MUNROE, KIRK. The fur-seal's tooth; a story of Alaskan adventure. N. Y., Harper, 1894. 1st ed. 267p. front. pls. map.3245

Munson, A. J., edit. SEE no. 2264, Ingersoll, E.

Murakami, N., co-edit. SEE no. 2871, MacDonald, Ranald.

MURDOCK, GEORGE PETER. Ethnographic bibliography of North America. New Haven, Yale University Press, 1941. 168p. map(fold.) (Yale Anthropological Studies, vol. 1) ANR. New Haven, Human Relations Area Files Press, 1960. 3rd reprint. 393p. map, append. index. (Behavior Science Bibliographies)　　　　　　　3246

MURDOCK, GEORGE PETER. Our primitive contemporaries. N. Y., Macmillan, 1934. 614p. front. illus. endmaps, index. [incls. Eskimos and Haida Indians]　　　　　　　　　　　　　3247

MURDOCK, GEORGE PETER. Rank and potlatch among the Haidas. New Haven, Yale University Press, 1936. 20p. (Publications in Anthropology, no. 13)　　　　　　　　　　　　　　　　3248

Murdock, George Peter. SEE ALSO no. 1772,
　　Goodenough, W. H., edit. Explorations anthropol. ... 1964.

MURIE, ADOLPH. A naturalist in Alaska. Illustrated by Olaus J. Murie. Photos by author and Charles J. Ott. N. Y., Devin-Adair Co., 1961. 302p. illus. index. (American Naturalists Series)
　　　　　　　　　　　　　　　　　　　　　　3249

MURIE, ADOLPH. Birds of Mount McKinley, Alaska. By Adolph Murie. Illustrated by Olaus Murie with photographs by Charles Ott. no pl., published by The Mt. McKinley Natural History Assoc., [c1963] [printed by Pisani Printing Co., S. F.] 86p. illus. checklist, wrps.　　　　　　　　　　　　3250

MURIE, ADOLPH. Mammals of Mount McKinley National Park Alaska. By Adolph Murie. Sketches by Olaus Murie. Photographs by Charles J. Ott. no pl., published by The Mt. McKinley Natural History Assoc., [cAug. 1962] [printed by Pisani Printing Co., S. F.] 56p. illus. checklist, wrps.　　　　　　　　3251

MURIE, MARGARET E. Two in the far north. Illustrated by Olaus J. Murie. N. Y., Knopf, 1962. 1st ed. 438p. front.(map), sketches. [author is Mrs. Olaus J. Murie]　　　　　　　3252

Murie, Olaus J. SEE nos.
　　644, Brandt, H. Alaska bird trails.1943;
　1203, Davis, Mary Lee. Alaska ... 1930;
　1206, Davis, Mary Lee. We are Alaskans. 1931;
　1668, Gabrielson, I. N. Birds of Alaska. 1959;
　3249, Murie, Adolph. A naturalist ... 1961;
　3250, Murie, Adolph. Birds of Mt. McKinley ... [c1963];
　3251, Murie, Adolph. Mammals of Mt. McKinley ... [c1962];
　3252, Murie, Margaret E. Two in far north. 1962.

MURPHY, EMILY FERGUSON. Bishop Bompas. Toronto, Ryerson, n. d. 30p. illus. (Canadian History Readers)　　　　　　3253

MURPHY, ROBERT. The haunted voyage. N. Y., Doubleday, 1961. [that of Vitus Bering]　　　　　　　　　　　　　3254

MURPHY, ROBERT. The warmhearted polar bear, by Robert Murphy, pictures by Louis Slobodkin. Boston, Little Brown, 1957. 48p. illus.   3255

MURRAY, ALEXANDER HUNTER. Journal of the Yukon, 1847-1848, by A. H. Murry [sic] no pl., 1848. 93(11)p. illus. plan. ANR. ... by Alexander Hunter Murray; edited with notes by L. J. Burpee ... Ottawa, Govt. Print. Bureau, 1910. 125ℓ   pls. plan, tables, map(fold.), ftntes. bibliog. (Publications of the Canadian Archives, no. 4) ANR. [in French] 1910. 138p.   3256

MURRAY, GLADYS HALL. Mystery of the talking totem pole. N. Y., Dodd Mead, 1965. 208p.   3257

MURRAY, HUGH. Historical account of discoveries and travels in North America; including the United States, Canada, the shores of the Polar Sea, and the voyages in search of a Northwest Passage; with observations on emigration. London, Longman, Rees, Orme, Brown & Green, 1829. 2 vols. map(fold.)   3258

MUSEUM FÜR VOLKERKUNDE. SEE nos. 534 and 536,
    Berlin, Königlichen Museen.

MUSEUM OF AMERICAN INDIANS, Heye Foundation, N. Y. Guide to the Museum. Second floor. N. Y., 1922. 251p. front.(fold. plan) (Indian Notes and Monographs, Misc. Pub. no. 31)   3259

"Mushing Parson." SEE no. 4998, Young, S. Hall.

Mustard, J. H. SEE no. 3290, Neuman, D. S.

My Alaska cruise. [19_ ?] SEE no. 120, Alaska Steamship Co.

MYERS, C. V. Oil to Alaska. [Edmonton, Alberta, Canada, Provincial News Co., 1944 ?] 40p. illus. map.   3260

MYERS, C. V. Through Hell to Alaska; a novel. N. Y., Exposition Press, 1955. 1st ed. 264p.   3261

MYERS, HARRY M. and WILLIAM A. MYERS. Adventures in McKinley Park. no pl. [Lapeer, Mich. ?], privately printed, 1933.   3262

MYERS, HARRY M. and WILLIAM A. MYERS. Back trails. [Lapeer, Michigan, privately printed, 1933] ltd. ed. of 500 copies. 269p. [McKinley Park]   3263

MYERS, HORTENSE and RUTH BURNETT. Carl Ben Eielson, young Alaskan pilot. By Hortense Myers and Ruth Burnett. Illustrated by Gray Morrow. Indianapolis, Bobbs-Merrill, [c1960] 192p. illus. (col.) (Childhood of Famous Americans) [Alaskan content, pp.110-192]   3264

MYERS, HORTENSE and RUTH BURNETT. Vilhjalmur Stefansson, young
Arctic explorer. Indianapolis, Bobbs-Merrill, 1966. (Childhood
of Famous Americans)   3265

MYERS, JOHN L. The Great Land. N. Y., Board of Home Missions,
n. d. 6p.   3266

MYERS, WILLIAM. Through wonderland to Alaska. Reading, Penna.,
1895. 271p.   3267

Myerson Printing Co. SEE nos.
    3490, [Paramore, H. H. ?] Klondike gold fields ... 1897;
    3491, Paramore, H. H. Pract. guide ... 1897.

MYRON, ROBERT. Mounds, towns and totems; Indians of North America. Cleveland, World Pub., 1966. 127p. illus.   3268

                              N

N. N., tr. SEE no. 410, Barrow, John.

N. N. SEE no. 1311, [Dobbs, Arthur]

Nach, Jas., edit. SEE no. 4339, Sterling Pub. Co.

NADAILLAC, *Marquis de*. Prehistoric America. Edited by William
Healey Dall and translated by N. D'Anvers. N. Y., G. P. Putnam,
1884. 566p. illus. ANR. 1890.   3269

NADEZHDIN, IVAN. Sbornik tserkovnykh pīesnopīenĭi i molitvos-
lovii na koloshinskom nariechii. [TITLE TR. Collection of church
canticles and liturgies in the Kolosh dialect] S. F., published
by Rev. Bishop Nikolai, 1896. 51p.   3270

NAISH, CONSTANCE and GILLIAN STORY, comps. English-Tlingit dictionary. Nouns. Fairbanks, Summer Institute of Linguistics,
March 1963. 81p. wrps. (Wycliffe Bible Translators)   3271

Narrative of negotiations ... England and Spain ... 1791. SEE
    no. 730, [Burges, Jas. B.]

NASHOALOOK, A., co-tr. SEE no. 4445, Tagarook, P.

Nathaniel Portlock's und Georg Mortimer's Reisen ... 1796. SEE
    no. 3651, [Portlock, N.]

Nation needs coal. 1917. SEE no. 39, Alaska Bureau, Seattle.

NATIONAL ACADEMY OF SCIENCES, Washington, D. C. The great Alaska
earthquake of 1964; hydrology. Washington, D. C. National Academy of Sciences, 1968. (18)446p. maps(in sep. slipcase) (Pub.
no. 1603)   3272

NATIONAL BOARD OF FIRE UNDERWRITERS and PACIFIC FIRE RATING BU-
REAU. The Alaska earthquake, March 27, 1964. S. F., distributed
by American Insurance Assoc., 1964. 35p.   3273

National Conference Stratospheric Meteorology. SEE no. 430,
    Batten, E.

NATIONAL GEOGRAPHIC SOCIETY, Washington, D. C. America's wonderlands. Washington, D. C., National Geographic Society, 1966.
Enlarged Edition. 552p. photos(col.), maps. [national parks]
                                                            3274

NATIONAL GEOGRAPHIC SOCIETY, Washington, D. C. Contributed tech-
nical papers. Volume 1. Katmai Series, volume 1. Numbers 1-4.
Washington, D. C., 1923-29. illus. diagrs. maps. [papers by
E. T. Allen, C. N. Fenner, and E. G. Zies. Results of the Fifth
Katmai Expedition of the National Geographic Society, 1919.
Papers from The Geophysical Laboratory, Carnegie Institution of
Washington]   3275

NATIONAL GEOGRAPHIC SOCIETY, Washington, D. C. Great adventures
with National Geographic. Edited by M. Severy. Washington, D. C.,
1963. 504p. illus. maps. [incls. Katmai, Mt. St. Elias and
Mt. McKinley]   3276

National Geographic Society. SEE ALSO nos.
    1860, Griggs, R. F. Sci. results Katmai ... 1920;
    3286, Nelson, E. W. Wild animals N. A. ... 1918;
    4648, Van Dyke, E. C. Coleoptera collected Katmai ... 1924.

NATIONAL PUBLISHING CO. Seattle of today, illustrated; the
metropolis of the Pacific Coast, the gateway to Alaska and the
Orient, the most progressive city of the 20th Century. [Seattle,
1907 ?] 231p. front. ports.   3277

Native Alaskan art ... 1959. SEE no. 69, Alaska Hist. Assoc.

Na-tor-uck. SEE no. 4586, Tucker, Minnie.

NATSIONALMUSEET, ETNOGRAFISKE SAMLING, København, Polar folk og
indianerne. [TITLE TR. Arctic peoples and Indians] København,
1960. 121p. illus.   3278

NAVARETTE, MARTIN FERNANDEZ de. Noticia historica de las expedi-
ciones hechas por las Españoles en busca del paso del noroeste de
la America, para serir de introduccion a la relacion del viage
executado en 1792 por las goletas *Sutil* y *Mexicana* con el objete
de reconocer el estrecho de Fuca. Madrid, Imprenta Real, 1802.
168p.   3279

Navarette, Martin Fernandez de. SEE ALSO no. 1676,
    [Galiano, D. A.] Relacion viage ... 1802.

Navigantium atque Itinerantium Bibliotheca ... 1764. SEE
    no. 1961, Harris, John.

Navigazioni de Cook ... 1826 and 1830. SEE nos. 1043 and
    no. 1045, [Cook, Jas.]

NEATBY, LESLIE H. Conquest of the last frontier, by L. H. Neatby.
Athens, Ohio University Press, 1966. 425p. pls. maps, bibliog.
                                                                3280

NEATBY, LESLIE H. In quest of the North West Passage. Toronto,
Longmans Green, 1958. 194p. illus. maps(some fold.), bibliog.
ANR. N. Y., Thos. Y. Crowell Co., 1962. 194p. illus. maps,
bibliog. paperback. (Apollo Edition A-49)   3281

NEELANDS, BARBARA S. The coming of the reindeer. N. Y., Lantern
Press, 1966. (26)p. illus. front.   3282

NELSON, EDWARD WILLIAM. A sledge journey in the delta of the
Yukon, northern Alaska. London, 1883. maps.   3283

NELSON, EDWARD WILLIAM. The Alaska Longspur. N. Y., National
Association of Audubon Societies, 1913. (Educational Leaflet
no. 67. Also in Bird-Lore, May-June 1913, vol. 15, pp.202-5.
pl.)   3284

NELSON, EDWARD WILLIAM. The Emperor Goose. N. Y., National Association of Audubon Societies, 1913. (Educational Leaflet no.
64. Also in Bird-Lore, Mar.-Apr. 1913, vol. 15, pp.129-32. pl.)
                                                                3285

NELSON, EDWARD WILLIAM. Wild animals of North America; intimate
studies of big and little creatures of the mammal kingdom.
Washington, D. C., National Geographic Society, 1918.   3286

Nelson, Edward William. SEE ALSO no. 4098, Sheldon, Charles.
    Wilderness of Denali. 1930.

Nelson, Erick. SEE no. 4497, Thomas, Lowell.
    First world flight ... 1925.

NELSON, GRACE MIX. The blue of Alaska and other poems. By Grace
Mix Nelson. N. Y., Bookcraft Pub. Co., [c1936] (14)15-102p.
photos, sketches. [several of the poems and photos about Alaska]
                                                                3287

NELSON, KLONDY and COREY FORD. Daughter of the gold rush. N. Y.,
Random House, 1958. 173p. illus. ANR. London, 1958. 176p.
illus.   3288

Nelson, Klondy. SEE ALSO no. 1365, Dufresne, Frank.
    My way was North. 1966.

NELSON, RICHARD K. Hunters of the northern ice. Chicago, University of Chicago Press, 1969. 429p. illus.   3289

Neĉsvietov, I. SEE nos.
    554, Bielkov, Z. Molitvy ... 1896;
    4670, Veniaminov, I. E. P. Gospoda ... [1840];
    4671, Veniaminov, I. E. P. Kratkaĭa ... 1840;
    4673, Veniaminov, I. E. P. Nachatki ... 1840.

Neue nachrichten ... Insuln ... 1776. SEE no. 3933,
    S., J. L.

NEUMAN, DANIEL SAHEYAUSE. Practical medical manual for Alaska
missionaries and teachers: Appendix; pharmacy and drugs, by
E. E. Hill; asepsis and antisepsis, by J. H. Mustard; obstetrics
by J. M. Sloan; outlines of first aid, by D. W. Harmon. Nome,
Press of Nombe Daily Nugget, 1911. 100p.   3290

Neuman, Daniel Saheyause. SEE ALSO no. 3823,
    Riggs, R. C. Animal stories ... 1923.

Neuste Reise um die Welt ... n. d. SEE no. 1581,
    Fleurieu, C. P. C.

Neuste Reisbeschreibungen ... dritte ... 1786. SEE
    no. 1027, [Cook, Jas.]

NEVSKIĬ, VLADIMIR VASIL'EVICH. Pervoe puteshestvie Rossian vokrug
sveta. Moskva, Gos. izd-vo geograficheskoĭ literatury, 1951.
272p. illus. tables, maps(incl. 1 fold.), bibliog. [A. J. von
Krusenstern and Ĭu. F. Lisĭanskiĭ]   3291

NEVSKIĬ, VLADIMIR VASIL'EVICH. Vokrug sveta pod russkim flagom;
pervoe krugosvetnoe puteshestvie russkikh na korablĭakh Nadezhda
i Neva ... v. 1803-1806 godakh. [TITLE TR. Round-the-world under
the Russian flag; the first Russian round-the-world voyage on
ships Nadezhda and Neva ... in 1803-06] Moskva-Leningrad, Gos.
izd-vo detskoi lit-ry, 1953. 215p. illus. ports. pl.(fold.),
maps(incl. 1 fold.) [revision of no. 3291]   3202

New Alaska Highway packet ... 1948. SEE no. 3357,
    Northwest Mapping Service.

New America in songs. n. d. SEE no. 3680, Presbyterian Church.

New northwest. 1900. SEE no. 3163, Moore, Otis M.

NEW OFFICIAL MAP of Alaska and the Klondike gold fields. Chicago,
1897. 28p. map(fold.) ANR. Philadelphia, 1897. 28p. map
(fold.)   3293

NEW SOUTH WALES PUBLIC LIBRARY, Sydney. Bibliography of Captain
James Cook, R.N., F.R.S., Circumnavigator. Sydney, Alfred James
Kent, Govt. Print., 1928. 172p. ANR. [Edited by M. K. Beddie]
Sydney, Mitchell Library, 1970. 2d ed. 894p. (Council of the
Library of New South Wales, Sydney) [catalogue of bi-centenary
of birth of Cook]   3294

New state of Alaska. [1959 ?] SEE no. 89, Alaska National Bank.

New What ! No igloos ? 1963. SEE no. 3534, PEO Sisterhood.

New York Legislature, Albany. SEE nos.
     155 and 157, Alaska-Yukon-Pacific Exposition, 1909.

NEWCOMB, RAYMOND LEE. Our lost explorers; the narrative of the
Jeannette Arctic expedition, as related by the survivors and in
the records and last journals of Lieutenant De Long. Revised by
Raymond Lee Newcomb, naturalist of the expedition ... Also an account of the *Jeannette* search expeditions, their discoveries ...
the burning of the *Rodgers* ... Hartford, American Pub. Co., 1882.
xv,479p. illus. maps, plans.   3295

NEWELL, EDYTHE W. The rescue of the sun, and other tales from
the far North. By Edythe W. Newell. Illustrated by Franz Alt-
schuler. Chicago, A. Whitman, 1970. 142p. illus. glossary.
[Eskimo legends]   3296

NEWELL, GORDON R. and JOE WILLIAMSON. Pacific steamboats; from
sidewheeler to motor ferry. Seattle, Superior Pub. Co., 1958.
196(4)p. photos, photo index. ANR. N. Y., Bonanza Books, n.d.
reprint.   3297

NEWELL, GORDON R. SOS North Pacific; tales of shipwrecks off
the Washington, British Columbia, and Alaska coasts. Portland,
Binfords & Mort, 1955. 216p. illus. photos, index.   3298

Newell, Gordon R., edit. SEE ALSO no. 2859,
     McCurdy, H. W. Marine hist. Pac. northwest. 1966.

NEWELL, IRWIN MAYER. *Copidognathus curtus* Hall, 1912, and other
species of *Copidognathus* from western North America. (Acari,
Halacaridae) N. Y., American Museum of Natural History, 1951.
27p. pls. bibliog. (American Museum Novitates, no. 1499) [in-
cludes Aleut and Northern Alaskan]   3299

NEWELL, IRWIN MAYER. Further studies on Alaskan Halacaridae
(Acari) N. Y., American Museum of Natural History, 1951. 56p.
pls. bibliog. (American Museum Novitates, no. 1536)   3300

NEWELL, IRWIN MAYER. New species of *Agaue* and *Thalassarachna*
from the Aleutians (Acari, Halacaridae) N. Y., American Museum
of Natural History, 1951. 19p. pls. (American Museum Novitates,
no. 1489)   3301

NEWELL, IRWIN MAYER. New species of *Copidognathus* (Acari, Halacaridae) from the Aleutians. N. Y., American Museum of Natural
History, 1950. 19p. pls. (American Museum Novitates, no. 1476)
3302

Niblett, Mollie G., edit. SEE no. 4296, Steele, Samuel B.

Nicholas, *Bishop of the Aleutians and Alaska.* SEE nos. 3308-10,
    Nikolai, *Bishop of the Aleutians and Alaska.*

NICHOLS, JEANNETTE PADDOCK. Alaska, a history of its administration, exploitation, and industrial development during its first
half century under the rule of the United States. Cleveland,
Arthur H. Clark Co., 1924. 456p. front.(map), ports. map(fold.),
bibliog. periodical bibliog. index. ANR. N. Y., Russell and
Russell, 1963. reprint.
3303

Nicholson, Wm., tr. SEE no. 499, Beniowski, M. A.

NICOL, JOHN. The life and adventures of John Nicol, mariner,
edited by John Howell. Edinburgh, Blackwood, and London, T.
Cadell, 1822. 216(12)p. ANR. WITH TITLE The life and adventures
of John Nicol, mariner. His service in King's ships in war and
peace, his travels and explorations by sea ... N. Y., Farrar &
Rinehart, 1936. 214p. front. port. illus. by Gordon Grant. ANR.
London, Cassell, 1937. 246p. front.(port.), illus.
3304

Nicol, John. SEE ALSO no. 2968, Marine Research Soc.
    Sea, ship and sailor ... 1925.

Niedieck, Paul. Cruises ... 1909. SEE no. 3307.

NIEDIECK, PAUL. Kreuzfahrten im Beringmeer; neue jagden und
reisen von Paul Niedieck ... mit 32 tafeln, einer karte und 100
text abbildungen nach originalaufnahmen. Berlin, P. Parey, 1907.
253p. pls. ports. map(fold.), appends.
3305

   TRANSLATIONS - Kreuzfahrten ... 1907, CHRONOLOGICALLY.

   Mes Croisieres dans le mer de Behring; nouvelles chasses et
      noveaux voyages ... tr. de l'allemand par L. Roustan ... avec
      123 gravures d'apres les photographies de l'auteur et une
      carte. Paris, Plon-Nourrit, 1908. 296p. front.(port.), pls.
      map(fold.)
      3306

   Cruises in the Bering Sea; being records of further sport and
      travel. By Paul Niedieck. Translated from the original Ger-
      man by R. A. Ploetz. London, Rowland Ward, and N. Y., Charles
      Scribner's Sons, 1909. 252p. front.(port.), pls. map(fold.
      in pocket)
      3307

NIKOLAI, *Bishop of the Aleutians and Alaska*. Archpastoral epistle, on occasion of centenary of foundation of Orthodox Mission in North America, 1794-1894. S. F., Sept. 25, 1894. 4p.   3308

NIKOLAI, *Bishop of the Aleutians and Alaska*. Molitvy na koloshinskim narîechiî. Izdanie Prêôsvîashshennago Nikolaîa, episkopa Aleutskago i Alîaskinskaqo, v pamîat' stolîetnîago îubileîa Pravoslavnoî Missiî po Alîaskie.   [TITLE TR. Prayers in the Koloshi dialect. Published by His Grace Nikolai, Bishop of the Aleutians and Alaska in commemoration of the centennial of the Orthodox Mission in Alaska. Translated by Vladimir Donskoi, a priest in Sitka, and printed in New York by G. Vainshtein] Sitkha, 1895. 23p.   3309

NIKOLAI, *Bishop of the Aleutians and Alaska*. Propovîedi prêôsvîashshennago Nikolaîa episkopa Aleutskago i Alîaskiskago. [TITLE TR. Sermons of his eminence Nikolai, Bishop of the Aleutians and Alaska] N. Y., Tip. Amerikanskii Pravda Viestnik, 1897. 355p.
                                                                3310

Nikolai, *Bishop of the Aleutians and Alaska*. SEE ALSO
    no. 3270, Nadezhdin, I. Sbornik ... 1896.

NILSSON, GUSTAF ADOLF. Sjöfarare; Kåserier om sjöskildrare genom tiderna. [TITLE TR. Seafarers; talks about men who have described the sea over the years] Malmö, Allhem, 1957. 222p. ports. maps. [incls. Sven Waxell, Roald Amundsen, others]   3311

NISHIMOTO, SETSUO. Report on whale marking in the North Pacific, 1950. No. 2. The North Pacific area. Tokyo, Fisheries Agency of the Japanese Government, June 1951. 245p. charts. (Committee for Improvement of Equipment of Whaling Vessels)   3312

NOBILE, UMBERTO. Gli Italiani al Polo Nord. [TITLE TR. The Italians at the North Pole] Roma, Associazone culturale aeronautica, 1945. 32p. wrps. [*Norge* and *Italia*]   3313

NOBILE, UMBERTO. In volo alla conquista del segreto polare (da Roma a Teller attraverso il Polo Nord) [TITLE TR. Flying in conquest of the unknown Pole; from Rome to Teller across the North Pole] Milano, A. Mondodori, 1928. 405p. pls. ports. diagrs. maps(incl.1 fold.), appends.   3314

NOBILE, UMBERTO. My polar flights. An account of the voyages of the airships *Italia* and *Norge*. N. Y., 1961. 1st American ed. 288p. pls. map.   3315

Nobile, Umberto. SEE ALSO nos.
    203, American Geog. Soc. Problems of polar research. 1928;
    219, Amundsen, R. E. G. Den forste flukt ... 1926;
    1446, Ellsworth, Lincoln. Beyond horizons. 1938;
    2393, Jotti-Neri, E. Critica alla spedizione Nobile ...1930;
    3342, "Norge" al Polo Nord ... 1926.

NOICE, HAROLD H. With Stefansson in the Arctic. N. Y., Dodd Mead, 1924. 269p. pls. ports. map(fold.) ANR. London, 1925.
3316

Nomad in North America ... 1927. SEE no. 313, [Assher, Ben]

NOME, a wonderland of wealth - Seward Peninsula and its resources. Seattle, Trade Register Print, 1905. 26p. 3317

Nome, Alaska. Information ... 1932. SEE no. 3358, Alaska Chamber of Commerce, Nome.

Nome and northwestern Alaska. [1945 ?] SEE no. 78, [Alaska life, Seattle]

NOME BOARD OF EDUCATION. The Nome Schools; course of study and rules and regulations adopted by Board of Education. Nome, Nome News, 1903. 19p. 3318

Nome cook book. [1968 ?] SEE no. 4950, Women's Society of Christian Service, Nome.

Nome Kennel Club. SEE nos.
172, All Alaska Sweepstakes. 1909;
1182, Darling, E. B. The great dog races. n. d.

Nome Nugget, pub. SEE no. 3358, Northwestern Alaska Chamber of Commerce, Nome ... 1932.

NOME-SEWARD PENINSULA CHAMBER OF COMMERCE. Petition to locate home for aged prospectors at Kruzgamepa Hot Springs, Second Division. no pl., Nome-Seward Peninsula Chamber of Commerce, 1916. 4p. 3319

NOONAN, DOMINIC A. Alaska, the land of now. Seattle, Sherman Printing Co., 1921. 134p. front. ANR.. Seattle, 1923. 146p. [poetry] 3320

NOONAN, DOMINIC A. Alaska, the land of plenty. N. Y., Pageant Press, 1960. 163p. append. [poetry] 3321

Norbeg, Ingv. L. SEE no. 4242, Soot-Ryen, T.

NORD, SVERRE. A logger's odyssey. Caldwell, Idaho, Caxton, 1943. 255p. front.(port.) [gold mining in Alaska; logging on Columbia River] 3323

Nordenskiöld, Adolf Erik. SEE nos. 3323-35, Nordenskiöld, Nils Adolf Erik.

Nordendskiöld, Nils Adolf Erik.   [Alphabetical title guide to
    chronological entries]

Die Unsegelung ... 3334.   Studier och ... 3326.
Im Eis ... 3332.   The voyage *Vega* ... 3330.
Lettres ... 3323.   Vega-exped. ... 3328.
... rejse ... 3324.   *Vegas* färd ... 3329.
... Vegafahrt ... 3335.   *Vegas* reise ... 3333.
... voyage ... 3325.   Voyage de la *Vega* ... 3331.
Studien ... 3327.

NORDENSKIÖLD, NILS ADOLF ERIK.   Lettres de A. E. Nordenskiöld
racontant la découverte du passage Nord-Est du pôle nord 1878-
1879, avec une préface pa M. Daubrée.   [TITLE TR. Letters from
A. E. Nordenskiöld, describing the discovery of the north polar
North East Passage, 1878-1879, with a preface by Mr. Daubrée]
Paris, M. Dreyfous, 1880. 276p. front.(port.), map(fold.), facsim.(fold.)   3323

NORDENSKIÖLD, NILS ADOLF ERIK.   Nordenskiöld's rejse omkring
Asien og Europa.   Edited by A. Hovgaard.   Populairt fremstillet
efter mine dagboeger.   København, 1881. 356p. illus. maps. 3324

NORDENSKIÖLD, NILS ADOLF ERIK.   Nordenskiöld's voyage round Asia
and Europe.   A popular account of the North-East Passage of the
Vega, 1878-80.   By A. Hovgaard, Lieutenant in the Royal Danish
Navy, and member of the *Vega* expedition.   Translated from the
Danish by H. L. Brackstad.   London, Sampson Low, 1882. 293p.
pls. maps. [tr. of no. 3324]   3325

NORDENSKIÖLD, NILS ADOLF ERIK.   Studier och forskningar föranledda
af mina resor i höga Norden.   Ett populärt vetenskapligt bihang
till "*Vegas* färd kring Asien och Europa."   [TITLE TR. Studies
and investigations occasioned by my voyages in the far North;
a popular, scientific supplement to "*Vegas* färd kring Asien och
Europa."]   Stockholm, F. & G. Beijer, [1883-84] 546p. pls.
maps.   3326

    TRANSLATION - Studier ... [1883-84]

    Studien und Forschungen veranlasst durch emine Reisen im hohen
      Norden.   Ein populär-wissenschaftlichen Supplement zu "Die
      Umsegelung Asiens und Europas auf der *Vega*."   Autorisierte
      deutsche Ausgabe.   Mit über 200 Abbildungen, 8 Tafeln und
      Karten.   [TITLE TR. Studies and investigations occasioned by
      my travels in the far North; a popular-scientific supplement
      to "Die Umsegelung Asiens und Europas auf der *Vega*."   Author-
      ized German edition with over 200 illustrations, eight plates
      and maps]   Leipzig, F. A. Brockhaus, 1885. 521p. front. pls.
      (some col., some fold.), maps(some fold.), facsims.   3327

NORDENSKIÖLD, NILS ADOLF ERIK. Vega-expeditionens vetenskaplige iakttagelser bearbetade af deltagare i resan och andra forskare. [TITLE TR. Scientific observations of the *Vega* Expedition prepared by members of the expedition and other scientists] Stockholm, F. & G. Beijer, 1882-87. 5 vols. 812p., 516p., 529p., 582p. and 535p. pls.(fold. dble. col.), tables(fold.), diagrs. (fold. dble. col.), maps(fold.)   3328

NORDENSKIÖLD, NILS ADOLF ERIK. *Vegas* färd kring Asien och Europa; jemte en historisk återblick på föregående resor längs Gamla Verldens nordkust, af A. E. Nordenskiöld. [TITLE TR. The voyage of the *Vega* round Asia and Europe; with a historical review of previous journeys along the north coast of the Old World] Stockholm, F. & G. Beijer, [1880-812 2 vols. 510p. and 486p. illus. pls. ports. maps(fold.)   3329

   TRANSLATIONS, ABRIDGMENTS - *Vegas* färd ... [1880-81], CHRONO-
   LOGICALLY.

   The voyage of the *Vega* round Asia and Europe; with a historical review of previous journeys along the north coast of the Old World. Translated by Alexander Leslie. London, Macmillan, 1881. 2 vols. 524p. and 482p. ports. maps. ANR. N. Y., Macmillan, 1886. abr. ed. 413p. port. maps(some fold.)   3330

   Voyage de la *Vega* autour de l'Asie et de l'Europe. Paris, 1885. 2 vols.   3331

   Im Eis des Nordens; die erste Umsegelung Asiens durch A. E. von Nordenskiöld auf der "Vega" 1878-1880; frei nacherzählt von Johannes George mit Unterstützung von Karl Helbig. [TITLE TR. In northern ice; the first circumnavigation of Asia by A. E. Nordenskiöld on the *Vega* 1878-1880; freely retold by Johannes Georgi assisted by Karl Helbig] Stuttgart, Franckh, 1953. 164p. port. maps(text), append.   3332

NORDENSKIÖLD, NILS ADOLF ERIK. *Vegas* reise omkring Asia og Europa. Kristiana, 1881. 2 vols.   3333

   TRANSLATIONS, ABRIDGMENTS - *Vegas* reise ... 1881, CHRONOLOGI-
   CALLY.

   Die Umsegelung Asiens und Europas auf der *Vega*. [TITLE TR. The voyage of the *Vega* around Asia and Europe] Leipzig, F. A. Brockhaus, 1882. 2 vols. ANR. Leipzig, F. A. Brockhaus, 1921. 158p. front. pls. maps. [1921 ed. a summary of 1882 ed.]   3334

   Nordenskiölds Vegafahrt um Asien und Europa. Nach Nordenskiölds Berichten für weitere Kreise bearbeitet von E. Erman. [TITLE TR. Nordenskiöld's voyage in the *Vega* around Asia and Europe. Rewritten by E. Erman for the ... public from Nordenskiöld's

reports] Leipzig, F. A. Brockhaus, 1886. 397p. front.(port.)
pls. ports. plans, maps(fold.) [based upon no. 3334]   3335

Nordenskiöld, Nils Adolf Erik. SEE ALSO nos.
    308, Arnell, H. W. Die mosse der Vega-exped. 1917;
    2686, Leslie, Alexander. Die Nordpolarreisen ... 1880;
    2687, Leslie, Alexander. Arctic voyages ... 1879.

Nordenskiöld, Nils Otto Gustaf. [Alphabetical title guide to
    chronological entries]

                    Die Polar welt ... 3337.
                    Polarvärlden ... 3336.
                    Poliarnyĭ ... 3338.
                    The geography of Polar ... 3339.

NORDENSKIOLD, NILS OTTO GUSTAF. Polarvärlden och dess granlän-
der. [TITLE TR. The polar world and its neighboring lands]
Stockholm, A. Bonnier, 1907. 214p. illus. (Populärt veten-
skapliga föreläsningar vid Göteborgs högskola, ny följd-V]   3336

    TRANSLATIONS - Polarvärlden ... 1907, CHRONOLOGICALLY.

    Die Polarwelt und ihre Nachbarländer, mit 77 abbildungen, im
      text und einem Fargigen Titlebund. Leipzig and Berlin, B. G.
      Tuebner Verlag, 1909. 220p. front.(col.), illus.   3337

    Poliarnyĭ mir i sosĭedniĭa emu strany. Perevod s nĭemefsk.
      A. A. Grigor'eva, pod redakĭsiĭ prof. D. N. Anuchina. Pril-
      ozhenie k "Zemleviĭedeniĭu za 1912 g Moskva, 1912. [TITLE TR.
      Polar world and its neighboring countries. Translation from
      the German by A. A. Grigof'ev, under the editorship of Prof.
      D. N. Anuchin. Supplement to "Zemlevedenie" for 1912]
      Moskva, 1912. 64p. [append. to Zemlevedenie, t.19, 1912,
      in pts. 1-3. (pt. 4 not comp.)]   3338

NORDENSKIÖLD, NILS OTTO GUSTAF and LUDWIG MECKING. The geography
of the Polar regions; consisting of a general characterization
of polar nature by Otto Nordenskiöld, and a regional geography of
of the Arctic and the Antarctic by Ludwig Mecking. N. Y., American Geographic Society, 1928. 359p. diagrs. maps. (Special
Pub. no. 8) ANR. N. Y., American Geographic Society, 1950. 359p.
illus. maps, bibliogs. (Special Pub. no. 8) [incls. tr. of
Mecking's "Die Polarländer" see no. 3066]   3339

Nordenskiöld, Otto Gustaf. SEE nos. 3336-9,
    Nordenskiöld, Nils Otto Gustaf.

NORDPOLARLANDER nach altern u. neuesten reisebeschreibungen,
namentlich Mackenzie ... Kotzebue. Budapest, 1822. 3 vols. 3340

NORFORD, B. SEELEY. Illustrations of Canadian fossils; Cambrian, Ordovician and Silurian of the western Cordillera. Ottawa, Queen's Printer, 1962. 25p. pls. bibliog. (Canada. Geological Survey, Paper no. 62-14) [incls. southeastern Alaska]   3341

"NORGE" al polo nord; da Roma allo stretto di Behring in dirigible, 13,000 km in 172 ore di volo; note del commandante Y. H. [TITLE TR. The "Norge" over the North Pole; from Rome to Bering Strait in a dirigible, 13,000 km in 172 hours of flight] Bologna, L. Capelli, 1926. 218p. pls. plans, sketch maps, map(fold.)3342

Norris, [Luther] "Doc" SEE nos.
    1059, Cooke, C. Fascinating Alaska. 1947;
    4862, Wiedemann, Thos., sr. Saga of Alaska. [c1946]

NORTH-AMERICAN TRANSPORTATION AND TRADING COMPANY. Alaska and the gold fields of the Yukon, Koyukuk, Tanana, Klondike and their tributaries. By the North-American Transportation and Trading Co. [Chicago ? 1899 ?] 119p. photos, 3 maps, wrps. ANR. WITH TITLE Alaska and the gold fields of Nome, Golovin Bay, Forty Mile. the Klondike and other districts. Chicago and Seattle, [1900 ?] 136p. ANR. WITH TITLE Alaska and the gold fields of Nome, Port Clarence, Golovin Bay, Kougarok, the Klondike and other districts. [Chicago, 1900 ?] 168p. illus. wrps.   3343

North Pacific almanac. 1890. SEE no. 3348,
    North Pacific Pub. Co.

NORTH PACIFIC COAST COUNTRY. Chicago, Chicago, Milwaukee and St. Paul Railway, 1907. 59p. ANR. Chicago, Chicago, Milwaukee, St. Paul and Pacific Railroad Co., 1909. 63p. front. illus. maps.
                                                                3344

NORTH PACIFIC CONSULTANTS. Economic analysis of Fairbanks and contiguous area, Alaska. Prepared by North Pacific Consultants for Golden Valley Electric Assiciation, Inc. Anchorage, North Pacific Consultants, 1959.   3345

North Pacific International Planning Project. SEE no. 2482,
    Kizer, B. H.

NORTH PACIFIC PLANNING PROJECT. Preliminary memorandum on peacetime use and maintenance of the Alaska military highway. Preliminary draft. Portland, Ore., 1943. 23ℓ tables, map(fold.), diagr.(fold.) (North Pacific Study, no. 2)   3346

NORTH PACIFIC PLANNING PROJECT. The North Pacific study; general summary of research memoranda prepared by the staff of the U. S. section. Portland, Ore., 1944. 18 numbered ℓ (North Pacific Study, no. 1)   3347

North Pacific Planning Project. SEE ALSO no. 800,
    Camsell, Chas. Canada's new northwest ... 1947.

North Pacific Planning Project, North Pacific Studies, nos. 3
    through 15. SEE under individual author:

    No. 3. Rettie, Jas. C. Supplement Prelim. Alaska Highway.
                1944. no. 3791;
    No. 4. Rettie, Jas. C. Comparisons transport. costs
                commodities ... 1944. no. 3787;
    No. 5. Mirick, S. Feasibility automobile ferry ... 1944;
    No. 6. McKinley, C. U.S.-Canadian postwar civil aviation
                ... North Pacific. 1944. no. 2921;
    No. 7. Rettie, Jas. C. Problems postwar Skagway-Whitehorse-
                Fairbanks petroleum pipeline ... 1944. no. 3789;
    No. 8. Rettie, Jas. C. Shipping services ... 1944. no.3790;
    No. 9. Sundborg, Geo. Shipping ... Pt. 2. 1944. no. 4397;
    No.10. McKinley, C. Case limited cabotage ... 1944.no.2920;
    No.11. Sundborg, Geo. Int'l. fisheries ... 1943. no. 4395;
    No.12. Sundborg, Geo. Proposal protect. minor fisheries
                ... U. S. and Canada. 1944. no. 4393;
    No.13. Sundborg, Geo. Agric. development ... 1944.no. 4394;
    No.14. Forrest, G. Land resources ... 1944. no. 1603;
    No.15. Rettie, Jas. C. Population trends ... 1944. no.3788.

North Pacific ports ... 1914. SEE no. 4478, Terminal Pub. Co.

NORTH PACIFIC PUBLISHING CO., Portland, Oregon. North Pacific
almanac; information relating to Oregon, Washington, Idaho,
Alaska and British Columbia. Portland, Ore., 1890. ANR. WITH
TITLE North Pacific almanac and statistical handbook for 1890,
containing valuable information about Oregon, Washington, Idaho,
Alaska, and British Columbia. Portland, Ore., Steel, 1890. 2d
ed.   3348

North Star Borough, Fairbanks. SEE no. 2655, League of
    Women Voters.

NORTH TO ALASKA AND THE YUKON; a guide to the travellers in the
"land of the future." Victoria, B. C., 20th Century Advertising
Ltd., 1968. 86p. illus.(incl. 8 col. postcards), maps.   3349

Northern Commercial Co. SEE nos.
    49-54, Alaska Commercial Co.;
    2475, Kitchener, L. D. Flag over North. 1954.

NORTHERN EXPLORATION AND DEVELOPMENT CO. The right way to conserve the enormous resources of Alaska for the people. Seattle,
n. d. 15p.   3350

NORTHERN NAVIGATION CO. The Alaska gold fields. S. F., n. d.
28p.   3351

"Northern Nuggets" Recipes ... 1961. SEE no. 3941,
    Saint Joseph's Hospital, Fairbanks.

NORTHERN PACIFIC RAILROAD CO. Across the continent via the Northern Pacific from the Lakes and Mississippi River to the Pacific, Columbia River, Puget Sound and Alaska. St. Paul, W. C. Riley, [1890 ?] (30)p.   3352

NORTHERN PACIFIC RAILROAD CO. Alaska. [St Paul, 19_ ?] 31p. illus. [cf no. 3221]   3353

NORTHERN PACIFIC RAILROAD CO. Puget Sound and Alaska. [St. Paul, 19_ ?] 32p. illus. maps. ANR. [1916]   3354

Northern Pacific Railroad Co. SEE ALSO nos.
    147, Alaska-Yukon-Pac. Exposition. 1909;
    2250, Hyde, J. Northern Pac. tour ... 1889;
    3513, Peattie, Ella W. Journey through wonderland. 1890;
    4022, Schwatka, F. Wonderland ... 1886.

Northern Pacific Railway. SEE no. 4808, Wheeler, Olin D.
    Wonderland '98 ... 1898.

Northern Pacific tour ... [1888] SEE no. 1838,
    Great Northern Railway.

NORTHLAND TRANSPORTATION CO., Seattle. Sea voyage vacations, Alaska, wonder, waterway cruise. Season 1941. Seattle, 1941. 32p. illus.(col.)   3355

NORTHRUP, TRUMAN. The phantom code. Boston, W. A. Wilde Co., 1937. 294p.   3356

NORTHWEST MAPPING SERVICE, Seattle. New Alaska Highway packet; full color maps, travel guide, latest tourist information. Seattle, 1948. 8p. illus. map(fold.col.)   3357

NORTHWESTERN ALASKA CHAMBER OF COMMERCE, Nome. Nome, Alaska; information concerning Nome and northwestern Alaska published by Northwestern Alaska Chamber of Commerce. Nome, From the press of The Nome Nugget, 1932. 40p. illus. maps, wrps.   3358

NORTHWOOD, T. D. and F. W. SIMPSON. Depth measurements in the Seward ice field by sonic echo-ranging. Ottawa, National Research Council of Canada, Dec. 1948. 13ℓ photos, diagrs. maps. National Research Council Division of Physics Report PS-300 and Arctic Institute of N. A. Project Snow Cornice)   3359

NOURSE, JOSEPH EVERETT. American explorations in the ice zones. The expeditions of De Haven, Kane, Rodgers, Hayes, Hall, Schwatka and DeLong ... relief voyages ... naval exploration in Alaska ... Lts. Ray and Stoney ... By Prof. J. E. Nourse, U.S.N. Boston, D. Lothrop, 1884. 608p. front. pls. map, bibliog. index. ANR. Boston, n. d. 3rd ed. 624p. front. pls. ports. maps(1 in pocket), bibliog. index.   3360

NOVO y COLSON, PEDRO de. Historia de las exploraciones articas hechas en busca del paso del nordeste con un prologo del Ilmo, Sr. D. Cesareo Fernandez Dura. Madrid, Fortanet, 1880. 260p. port. map(fold.) ANR. 1882. 2d ed.   3361

NOVO y COLSON, PEDRO de. Sobre los viajes apocrifos de Juan de Fuca y de Lorenzo Ferrer Maldonado recapilacion y estudio, contiene tambien este libro la disertacion del mismo autor titulada ultima terria sobre la Atlantida. Madrid, Fortanet, 1881. 223p.   3362

Novo y Colson, Pedro de. SEE ALSO no. 2956, Malaspina, A. Viaje politico-cientifico ... 1885.

Nowell, Frank, photographer. SEE no. 312, Artwork of Seattle and Alaska. 1907.

Nowell, Thomas, co-auth. SEE no. 312, Artwork of Seattle and Alaska. 1907.

NOYES, SHERMAN A. Faith Creek. N. Y., Vantage Press, 1956. 1st ed. 150p.   3363

Nozikov, Nikolaĭ Nikolevich. Russian voyages ... n. d. SEE no. 3365.

NOZIKOV, NIKOLAĬ NIKOLEVICH. Russkie krugosvetnye moreplavateli. Pod redaktŝieĭ is vstupitel'noĭ stat'eĭ M. A. Sergeeva. Izd-ie vtorae. [TITLE TR. Russian round-the-world navigators] Moskva, Voennoe izd-vo ministerstva vooruzhennykh sil soĭuza SSSR, 1947. 294p. illus. maps(fold.) ANR. 1941. 1st ed.   3364

   TRANSLATION - Russkie ... 1941.

   Russian voyages round the world. Edited with an introduction
      by M. A. Sergeyev. Translated from the Russian by Ernst and
      Mira Lesser. London, Hutchinson, n. d. [ca 1941] 165p.
      endmaps. [Krusenstern, Lisĭanskiĭ,Golovnin, Litke]   3365

NULSEN, ROBERT HOVEY, edit. Trailering to Alaska; a complete guide for trailering up the Alaska Highway. Beverly Hills, Calif., Trail-R-Club of America, 1960. 112p. illus. maps, bibliog. wrps.   3366

NUNN, GEORGE EMRA. Origin of the Strait of Anian concept. Philadelphia, 1929. 1td. ed. of 200 copies printed by author. 36p. front.(map), illus. sketch maps.   3367

NUTCHUK and ALDEN HATCH. Back to the Smoky Sea. By Nutchuk with Alden Hatch. Illustrated by Nutchuk. N. Y., Messner, 1946.225p. pls. ports. sketches. [autobiog. of Simeon Oliver of Unalaska in Aleutian Islands - continuation of no. 3369]   3368

NUTCHUK and ALDEN HATCH. Son of the Smoky Sea. By Nutchuk with Alden Hatch. Illustrated by Nutchuk. N. Y., Messner, 1941. 245p. front.(port.), pls. sketches, endmaps. [autobiog. of Simeon Oliver (Nutchuk), continued in no. 3368]   3369

Nutting, C. C. SEE no. 1950, Harriman Alaska Exped. 1899.

Nuwheh kukwadhud Jesus Christ ... 1874. SEE no. 2882,
    [McDonald, Robert, tr. ?]

O

OAKES, PATRICIA. A state is born. N. Y., Harcourt Brace, 1958. maps. (Harbrace Teachers' Notebook in Social Studies)   3370

OAKES, PATRICIA. The Alaska voters' guidebook. Central, Alaska, 1962. ltd. ed. of 300 numbered copies. 88p.   3371

Obeler, A., co-auth. SEE no. 3808, Rickard, M. E. C. (H.)

OBERG, KALERVO. The social economy of the Tlingit Indians. Chicago, University of Chicago, 1940. (abstract from Ph.D. dissertation, University of Chicago, 1937. pp.133-61)   3372

O'BRIEN, ESSE FORESTER. Reindeer roundup. Austin, Texas, Steck Co., 1959. 108p. photos(col.) by Grady Carothers.   3373

O'Brien, John. SEE nos.
    1153, Dalby, M. A. Sea saga Dynamite Johnny O'Brien. 1933;
    2081, Herron, E. A. ... Alaska's sea captain. 1962;
    4958, Woods, H. T. God's loaded dice ... 1948.

O'Brien, John Sherman, co-auth. SEE no. 2298, Irwin, D.

O'BRIEN, P. J. Will Rogers, ambassador of good will, prince of wit and wisdom. By P. J. O'Brien. Illustrated. Philadelphia, John C. Winston Co., [c1935] 288p. front.(port.), pls. ports. facsim. [biog. - chapts. 1 and 13 concern plane crash near Barrow, Alaska in 1935 which killed Will Rogers and pilot, Wiley Post]   3374

Oceanic observations ... 1963. SEE no. 4029, Scripps Inst.
    Oceanography.

Ocherki obshcheĭ ètnografiĭ ... 1957. SEE no. 4617,
    U. S. S. R. Akademiĭa nauk.

O'CONNOR, DONALD J. Alaska's Interior gateway. Vienna, Va., 1953. 46p. tables. [rail transporation]   3375

O'Connor, Mrs. Larry, auth. SEE nos. 4893-4905,
    Willoughby, Barrett.

O'CONNOR, PAUL. Eskimo parish. By Paul O'Connor, S.J. Milwaukee, Bruce Pub. Co., [c1947] 134p. pls. [Yukon Delta, Kotzebue Sound areas]   3376

O'CONNOR, RICHARD. High jinks on the Klondike. Indianapolis, Bobbs-Merrill, [c1954] 1st ed. 284p. endmaps, bibliog. index.
                                                                  3377

O'CONNOR, RICHARD. Jack London; a biography. Boston, Little Brown, 1964. 430p.   3378

O'COTTER, PAT [pseud.] Rhymes of a roughneck. Seward, Pat O'Cotter, 1918. 92p. [author is Frank J. Cotter]   3379

O'Dell, Scott. Island of the blue dolphins. Boston, Houghton Mifflin, 1960. 184p. [juv. fict.]   3380

Odlum, J., co-auth. SEE no. 1574, Fitz, F. E.

Odmann, S., tr. SEE no. 3062, Meares, J.

O'Enter, A. L., edit. SEE no. 3170, Moravian mission in
    Alaska ... 1895.

OETTEKING, BRUNO. Craniology of the North Pacific coast. Leiden, E. J. Brill and N. Y., G. E. Stechert, 1930. 391(93)p. pls. (incl. 1 fold.), diagrs. tables. (Jesup North Pacific Expedition Pubs. vol. 11, pt. 1; published as Memoir of American Museum of Natural History, vol. 15, pt. 1) [incls. Athabaskan Indians, also Eskimo of St. Lawrence Island]   3381

Oetteking, Bruno. SEE ALSO no. 1247, De Laguna, F.
    Archaeol. Cook Inlet ... 1934.

Officers, committees ... 1910. SEE no. 299, Arctic Club.

OFFICERS OF U. S. REVENUE CUTTER SERVICE, and some of their friends. Below zero; songs and verses from Bering Sea and the Arctic. Astoria, Ore., J. S. Dellinger & Co., 1903. 28p. illus.
                                                                  3382

Official Alaska cook book. 1969. SEE no. 3568, Phelps, Sue.

Official catalogue ... 1909. SEE no. 151, Alaska-Yukon-Pac.Expo.

Official daily program. 1909. SEE no. 152, Alaska-Yukon-Pac.
    Expo.

Official guide ... 1909. SEE no. 153, Alaska-Yukon-Pac. Expo.

Official guide to Klondyke ... 1897. SEE no. 1001,
    Conkey, W. B., Co.

OFFICIAL PAPERS relative to the dispute between the courts of Great Britain and Spain, on the subject of the ships captured in Nootka Sound, with the proceedings in both houses of Parliament on the King's message; to which are added the report of M. de Mirabeau and the subsequent decrees of the National Assembly of France on the Family Compact. London, Debrett, 1790. 100p. 3383

Official prospectus. 1902. SEE no. 44, Alaska Central R.R. Co.

OFFICIAL RECORD OF THE ALASKA METHODIST EPISCOPAL MISSION. John W. Hamilton, D.D., L.L.D., Presiding Bishop. First Session 1904 held at Juneau, Alaska. Juneau, Juneau Record Miner Print., 1904. 22p. 3384

OFFICIAL RECORD OF THE ALASKA MISSION of the Methodist Episcopal Church. David H. Moore, Presiding Bishop. Second Annual Session. no pl., 1905. 22p. 3385

OGDEN, ADELE. The California sea otter trade, 1784-1848. Berkeley, University of California Press, 1941. 251p. index. (Publications in History, vol. 26) 3386

Ogden, Henry. SEE no. 4497, Thomas, Lowell.

OGILVIE, DAVID SHEPHERD. A kandid view of Kiska. N. Y., William-Frederick Press, 1945. 31p. (William-Frederick Poets) [Aleutian Island setting] 3387

OGILVIE, WILLIAM. Copy of further report of William Ogilvie, Esq., and evidence accompanying the same. Ottawa, S. E. Dawson, print., 1899. 36p. (Canada. Sessional Papers, no. 87b-c, 1899) 3388

OGILVIE, WILLIAM. Early days on the Yukon and the story of its gold finds. London, John Lane and Toronto, Bell & Cockburn, 1913. 306p. front.(port.), pls. ports. ANR. Ottawa, Thorburn & Abbott, 1913. 306p. illus. 3389

OGILVIE, WILLIAM. Evidence taken before the Commission appointed to investigate charges of alleged malfeasance of the officials of the Yukon territory. Ottawa, S. E. Dawson, print., 1899. 264p. (Canada. Sessional Papers, no. 87a. Ogilvie Committee of Inquiry, 1899) 3390

Ogilvie, William. Guide officiel du Klondike ... 1898.
     SEE no. 3394.

OGILVIE, WILLIAM. Information respecting the Yukon district, from the reports of William Ogilvie, Dominion Land Surveyor, and from other sources. Ottawa, Government Print. Bureau, 1897. 64p. pls. maps(2 dble.) 3391

OGILVIE, WILLIAM. Lecture on the Klondike mining district by Wm. Ogilvie, F.R.G.S., Surveyor to the Dominion of Canada, delivered at Victoria, B. C., Nov. 5th, 1897. Victoria, B. C., printed by Richard Wolfenden, 1897. 14p.   3392

OGILVIE, WILLIAM. Lecture on the Yukon gold fields (Canada) delivered at Victoria, B. C., by Mr. Wm. Ogilvie ... explorer and surveyor of the Government of Canada in the Canadian Yukon. Revised, amplified and authorized by the lecturer. Victoria, B. C., The Colonist Press, 1897. 32p. illus.   3393

OGILVIE, WILLIAM. The Klondike official guide; Canada's great gold field, the Yukon district, with ... regulations governing placer mining. Toronto, Hunter Rose Co., 1898. 153p. front. illus. maps(2 fold.) (Published by authority of Canada. Dept. of the Interior) ANR. WITH TITLE Guide officiel du Klondike ..., Toronto, 1898.   3394

OGILVIE, WILLIAM. Truths about the Klondike. Information respecting the Yukon district from the reports of Wm. Ogilvie. Ottawa, Government Print. Bureau, 1897. 59p. (Canada. Dept. of the Interior) ANR. Ottawa, 1897. 66p. ANR. N. Y., British-American Pub. Co., 1897.   3395

Ogilvie, William. SEE ALSO nos.
    1113, Crane, A. R. Smiles and tears ... 1901;
    1168, Dall, Wm. H. Yukon Territory ... 1898;
    2064, Henley, G. F. Guide to Yukon-Klondike mines ... 1898;
    4494, Thomas, L., jr. Trail of '98. [c1962];
    5003, Yukon Basin Gold Dredging Co. Prospectus. [ca 1908]

Ohlson, O. F. SEE no. 3486, Pan Pacific Progress.

OKAKOK, GUY. Okakok's Alaska; selections from Pt. Barrow news submitted to Fairbanks Daily News-Miner 1955-59. Sitka, Sitka Print. Co., 1959. 31p. sketches, wrps. (Sponsored by PEO Sisterhood, Chapt. B., Fairbanks) ANR. 1960. 2d ed.   3396

O'Kane, W. C., illus. SEE no. 4729, Walden, A. T.

OKUN', SEMEN BENTCIONOVICH. Rossiĭsko-Amerikanskaĭa Kompaniĭa (pod redakt͡sei i s predisloviem Akademika B. D. Grekova). [TITLE TR. The Russian-American Company. Edited with a preface by B. D. Grekov] Moskva-Leningrad, Gos sotsial'no-ekonomicheskoe izd-vo, 1939. 260p. (Istoricheskiĭ fokul'tet. Universitet. Leningrad) [See no. 3398 for tr.]   3397

OKUN', SEMEN BENTCIONOVICH. The Russian-American Company. S. B. Okun. Edited, with introduction by B. D. Grekov ... Translated from the Russian by Carl Ginsburg ... Cambridge, Harvard University Press, 1951. 311p. notes, index, wrps. (Russian Translation Project Series of American Council of Learned Societies) [tr. of no. 3397]   3398

OLDROYD, IDA SHEPHERD. The marine shells of the west coast of North America. Stanford, Stanford University Press, 1924-27. 2 vols. in 4. pls. (Pub. University Series, Geological Sciences) 3399

OLDS, LEE. Too much sun; a novel. N. Y., Vanguard Press, 1960. 245p. 3400

OLIVER, EDMUND H., edit. The Canadian Northwest; its early development and legislative records; minutes of the Councils of the Red River Colony and the Northern Department of Rupert's Land. Edited by Prof. E. H. Oliver. Ottawa, Public Archives of Canada, 1914. 2 vols. 1,348p. [incls. documents between Hudson's Bay Co. and Russian-American Co.] 3401

OLIVER, ETHEL ROSS. Aleutian boy. Portland, Ore., Binfords and Mort, 1959. 1st ed. 193p. illus. endmaps, glossary. 3402

OLIVER, NOLA NANCE. Alaskan Indian legends. Illustrated by Frances Brandon. N. Y., House of Field-Doubleday, [c1947] 69p. front. illus. 3403

Oliver, Pasfield, edit. SEE no. 499, Beniowski, M. A.

Oliver, Simeon. SEE nos. 3368-69, Nutchuk.

Olsen, J. E., tr. SEE no. 2642, Lauridsen, P.

OLSEN, MICHAEL L., comp. A preliminary list of references for the history of agriculture in the Pacific northwest and Alaska. Compiled and edited by Michael L. Olsen, University of Washington, Seattle. A cooperative project by the Agricultural History Branch, Economic Research Service, U. S. Department of Agriculture and the Agriculture History Center. Davis, Calif., University of California, 1968. 58p. index. (Agriculture History Center, March 1968) 3404

OLSEN, STANLEY J. Postcranial skeletal characters of *Bison* and *Bos*. Cambridge, Harvard University Press, 1960. 15p. pls. diagrs. map, bibliog. (Peabody Mus-um Archeological and Ethnological Papers, vol. 35, no. 4) [incls. Yukon River to Norton Sound area] 3405

OLSON, B. G. and MIKE MILLER, edits. Blood on the Arctic snow and other true tales of far North adventure from the Alaska Sportsman. Seattle, Superior Pub. Co., 1956. 279p. illus. 3406

OLSON, RONALD LeROY. Adze, canoe and house types of the northwest coast. Seattle, University of Washington Press, 1927. 38p. illus. maps. (Pub. in Anthropology, vol. 2, no. 1) ANR. [reissue bound with author's "The Quinalt Indians"] Seattle, University of Washington Press, 1967. 234p. illus. maps. (Pub. in Anthropology, vol. 4, no. 1 and vol. 2, no. 1)[incls. Athabaskans] 3407

OLSON, SIGURD F. Runes of the North. By Sigurd F. Olson. N. Y., Knopf, 1963. 1st ed. 254p. illustrated by Robert Hines, map (dble.)   3408

O'Malley, Henry, co-auth. SEE no. 332, Babcock, J. P.

OMAN, LEILA. Eskimo legends; authentic Eskimo tales of suspense and excitement translated from the native tongue. Nome, Alaska, Nome, Nome Pub. Co., print., 1965. 3rd print. sketches, wrps.
                                                                3409

O'MEARA, WALTER ANDREW. The savage country; a history of the men of the Northwest Company, and the lands they conquered. By Walter O'Meara. Boston, Houghton Mifflin, 1960.   3410

On the Klondike ... 1897. SEE no. 4208, Smith's Cash Store.

On the "White Pass" payroll ... 1908. SEE no. 1799,
    [Graves, S. H.]

On to Klondike ! 1897. SEE no. 2975, Marks, Alfred, pub.

One hundred and fifty latest views ... 1909. SEE no. 154,
    Alaska-Yukon-Pacific Exposition.

One hundred events ... 1944. SEE no. 83, Alaska Mag. Pub. Co.

One hundred fiftieth anniv. arrival Capt. Geo. Vancouver ...
    1942. SEE no. 2152, [Holland, Chas. Wm.]

One hundred pictures little known Alaska. 1935. SEE no. 208,
    American Press.

One thousand miles ... fiords of B. C. ... 1936. SEE no. 822,
    Canadian Pacific Railway Co.

O'Neal, J. Patrick. SEE no. 2371, Johnson, Wm. E.

O'NEILL, HAROLD E. The auroral drama. Aurora, Missouri, Burney Bros. Pub. Co., 1937. 327p. [incls. references to Pt. Barrow]
                                                                3411

O'NEILL, HESTER. The picture story of Alaska. N. Y., David McKay Co., 1951. (49)p. illus.(col.) by Ursula Koering, maps.
                                                                3412

ORCHARD, WILLIAM G. Beads and beadwork of the North American Indians. N. Y., Museum of the American Indian, Heye Foundation, 1929. 140p. pls. (Contribution from the Museum, vol. XI) 3413

ORCHARD, WILLIAM C. The technique of porcupine quill decoration among the North American Indians. N. Y., Museum of the American Indian, Heye Foundation, 1916. 53p. pls. (Contribution from the Museum, vol. IV, no. 1)   3414

Orchard, William C. SEE ALSO no. 2096,
    [Heye, Geo. G.] Rare Salish blanket. 1926.

ORDAZ, LUIS. Jack London; el rey de los vagabundos. Buenos Aires, 1946. 143p. (Coleccion: La marcha de los heroes, Editorial Abril)   3415

ORDIN, A. Velikiĭ lĕtchik nashego vremeni Valeriĭ Pavlovich Chkalov. Stenogramma publichnoĭ lekt͡siĭ prochitanoĭ v. [TITLE TR. The great flier of our time, Valeriĭ Pavlovich Chkalov. Stenogram of a public lecture delivered in Moscow] Moskva, Pravda, 1949. 24p. (Vsesoi͡uznoe obshchestvo po rasprostrane-nii͡u politicheskikh i nauchnykh znaniĭ)   3614

OREGON. STATE. Committee for A-Y-P Exposition. SEE no. 158,
    Alaska-Yukon-Pacific Exposition. Report ... 1909.

OREGON. STATE. Department of Education. A resource unit on Alaska, our 49th State. Prepared by G. Arnold. Edited by M. Burcham. Salem, 1961. 50p. illus. maps(some fold.), bibliog.
                                                            3417

Oregon, Washington and Alaska gaz. and bus. dir. 1901.
    SEE no. 3630, Polk, R. L., & Co.

Oregon-Washington Railroad and Navigation Co., pub. SEE no. 37,
    Alaska Bureau, Seattle Chamber of Commerce.

Origin, activities and supporters of Bureau. 1915. SEE no. 40,
    Alaska Bureau, Seattle.

Original astronom. observations ... 1782. SEE no. 437,
    [Bayly, Wm.]

ORLOV, B. P. Fedor Petrovich Litke, zamechatel'nyĭ russkiĭ put-eshestvennik i uchenyĭ, (k 150-letii͡u so dni͡a rozhdennii͡a); stenogramma publichnoĭ lekt͡siĭ, prochitannoĭ 8 apreli͡a 1948 goda v t͡sentral'nom lektoriĭ obshchestva v Moskve. [TITLE TR. Fedor Petrovich Litke, remarkable Russian navigator and scientist, (on the occasion of the 150th anniversary of his birth); stenogram of the public lecture delivered on the 8th of April, 1948, in the central lecture hall of the Society in Moscow] Moskva, Izd-vo "Pravda," 1948. 22p. port. map. (Vsesoi͡uznoe obshchestvo po rasprostranenii͡u politicheskikh i nauchnyk znaniĭ)   3418

Orlova, N. S., comp. SEE no. 1420, Efimov, A. V.

ORMOND, CLYDE. Bear ! Black, grizzly, brown, polar. Harrisburg, Penna., Stackpole, 1961. 291p. illus. [hunting]   3419

ORTELIUS, ABRAHAM. Theatrum orbis terrarum. Antverpiae, 20, Apud AEgid. Coppenium Diesth, Maii 1570. (De Mona Druidum inshia ... epistola Humfredi Lhuyd p.1-6(3rd group). ANR. N. Y., American Elsevier Pub. and Lausanne, Sequoia, 1964. (16)53(56)p. 70 maps(col., some fold.) facsim. ed. [Straits of Anian concept]   3420

Orthodox schools in Alaska in 1904. 1905. SEE no. 4676, [Veniaminov, I. E. P. ?]

ORVIG, SVENN, edit. McCall Glacier, Alaska; meteorological observations 1957-58. Montreal, Arctic Institute of North America, 1961. 30p. illus. tables, refs. (Arctic Institute Research Paper, no. 8, May 1961. IGY Brooks Range Project 4, 17, station AD48: McCall Glacier)   3421

OSBORN, HENRY FAIRFIELD. The age of mammals in Europe, Asia and North America. N. Y., 1919.   3422

Osborn, Sherard, edit. SEE no. 2835, M'Clure, R. J. Le M.

Osborne, Thomas. SEE nos. 932-3, Churchill, A.

OSCHINSKY, LAWRENCE. The most ancient Eskimos. Ottawa, University of Ottawa, 1964. 112p. illus. tables, map, bibliog. (Canadian Research Centre for Anthropology)   3423

OSGOOD, CORNELIUS B. Contributions to the ethnography of the Kutchin. New Haven, Yale University Press, 1936. 188p. pls. port. map, bibliog. (Yale University Publications in Anthropology, no. 14)   3424

OSGOOD, CORNELIUS B. Ingalik material culture. New Haven, Yale University Press, 1940. 500p. front.(col.), pls. plans, tables, diagrs. maps, bibliog. (Yale University Publications in Anthropology, no. 22) ANR. N. Y., Taplinger Human Relations Area Files Press, 1964. reissue.   3425

OSGOOD, CORNELIUS B. Ingalik mental culture. New Haven, Yale University Press, 1959. 195p. illus. maps, glossaries, phonetic key, appends. bibliog. (Yale University Publications in Anthropology, no. 56)   3426

OSGOOD, CORNELIUS B. Ingalik social culture. New Haven, Yale University Press, 1958. 289p. illus. maps, figures, append. bibliog. (Yale University Publications in Anthropology, no. 53)   3427

OSGOOD, CORNELIUS B. The distribution of the northern Athapaskan Indian. New Haven, Yale University Press, 1936. 23p. illus. map, bibliog. (Yale University Publications in Anthropology, no. 7) 3428

OSGOOD, CORNELIUS B. The ethnography of the Tanaina. New Haven, Yale University Press, 1937. 229p. pls. tables, plans, diagrs. maps, bibliog. (Yale University Publications in Anthropology, no. 16) ANR. N. Y., Taplinger Human Relations Area Files Press, 1966. reissue. 3429

OSGOOD, CORNELIUS B. Winter; the strange and haunting story of a lone man's experiences in the far North. London, 1955. 255p. illus. drawings. 3430

OSGOOD, HARRIET KEENEY. Yukon River children. By Harriet Osgood. N. Y., Oxford University Press, 1944. 80p. illus. front. map. 3431

OSGOOD, WILFRED HUDSON. A peculiar bear from Alaska. Chicago, 1909. 3p. (Field Museum of Natural History Pub., no. 138. Zool Ser., vol. X, no. 1) [glacier bear, Mt. St. Elias] 3432

Osgood, Wilfred Hudson. SEE ALSO no. 1012, Cook, F. A.
    To top of continent ... 1908.

OSIPOV, K. Pervye russkie poliarnye morekhody. [TITLE TR. The first Russian arctic seamen] Moskva, 1949. 101p. illus. bibliog. (Gosudarstvennoe uchebno-pedagogicheskoe izd-vo Ministerstva Prosveshcheniia RSFSR) 3433

Ostenso, N. A., co-auth. SEE no. 569, Black, D. J.

Ostermann, H., edit. SEE nos.
    3734, Rasmussen, K. J. V. Alaskan Eskimo words ... 1941;
    3749, Rasmussen, K. J. V. The Alaskan Eskimos ... 1952.

OSTERVALD, JEAN FREDERIC. Ettunetle rsyotitinyoo kwunduk nyukwun treltsei. Ostervald kirkhe. [TITLE TR. Ostervald's summary of Bible history translated into Takudh] London, Society for Promoting Christian Knowledge, 1899. 23(29)p. bound with Oxenden, Ashton. Zzehkko enjit gichinchik nukwazzi ttrin ihthlog kenjit ako ttrin kittekookwichilttsei kenjit kah. [TITLE TR. Oxenden's family prayers for one week, also prayers for special days ...] ANR. 1922. 78p. 3434

OSTROVSKII, BORIS GERMANOVICH. Velikaia severnaia ékspeditsiia 1733-1743. Izdanie vtoroe dopolnennoe. [TITLE TR. The Great Northern Expedition 1733-1743. Second enlarged edition] Arkhangel'sk, Severnoe izd-vo, 1937. 206p. illus. bibliog. ANR. 1935. 1st ed. 137p. [Vitus Bering, A. I. Chirikov, others] 3435

OSWALT, WENDELL H.   Alaskan Eskimos.   S. F., Chandler Pub. Co.,
1967.   [distributed by Science Research Associates, Chicago]
297p.   illus.(some col.), maps(incl. 2 fold.), tables, bibliog.
index.   (Chandler Publications in Anthropology and Sociology)
ANR. paperback.   3436

OSWALT, WENDELL H.   Mission of change in Alaska.   Eskimos and
Moravians on the Kuskokwim.   San Marino, Calif., The Huntington
Library, 1963.   [c1963]   170p.   front.(map), endmaps, ftntes.
index.   3437

OSWALT, WENDELL H.   Napaskiak; an Alaskan Eskimo community.
Tucson, University of Arizona Press, 1963.   178p.   illus. maps,
bibliog. [revision of "Napaskiak; an Eskimo village in western
Alaska."   Fort Wainwright, Alaskan Air Command, 1961.   130p.
illus. maps, bibliog.   (Arctic Aeromedical Laboratory, Fort
Wainwright.   Technical Report, 57-23)]   3438

OSWALT, WENDELL H.   This land was theirs; a study of the North
American Indian.   N. Y., Wiley, 1966.   560p.   maps, bibliog.
[incls. Kuskokwim Eskimos and Tlingit Indians]   3439

Ott, Charles J., photog.   SEE nos.
     728, Burford, V.   North to danger.   [c1969];
     3249, Murie, Adolph.   A naturalist ... 1961;
     3250, Murie, Adolph.   Birds of Mt. McKinley, Alaska.   1963;
     3251, Murie, Adolph.   Mammals of Mt. McKinley National
               Park ... 1962.
Our coastal trips.   n. d.   SEE no. 4620, Union Steamship
     Co. of B. C.

OUR COUNTRY: West.   Boston, Perry Mason & Co., 1900.   [c1897]
256p.   illus.   ANR. 1902.   (Companion Series)   3440

Our northern domain ... 1910.   SEE no. 1329, [Dole, N. H.]

Out of Alaska's kitchens.   1948.   SEE no. 58,
     Alaska Crippled Children's Assoc.

OUT OF DOOR LIBRARY.   Mountain climbing.   N. Y., Scribner, 1897.
358p.   illus.   [Alaskan mountains included]   3441

Over the Chilkoot ... 1897.   SEE no. 2823, Lysons, Fred H.

Overland to Klondike through Cariboo ... 1898.   SEE no. 670,
     British Columbia Mining Journal.

Overland to Klondike via Spokane route.   1897.   SEE no. 4266,
     Spokane Chamber of commerce.

Owen, Betty M., edit.   SEE no. 2767, London, Jack.

OWENS, FERN ROYER. The sky pilot of Alaska. Mountain View, California, 1949. 175p. illus. maps. [biog. of Harold Wood, Seventh Day Adventist]   3442

Oxenden, Ashton. SEE no. 3434, Ostervald, J. F.

OXLEY, JAMES McDONALD. North overland with Franklin. N.Y., T.Y. Crowell, 1907. 286p.   3443

P

PEO Sisterhood. SEE nos.
      3396, Okakok, G. Okakok's Alaska. 1959;
      3534, PEO Sisterhood, Chapt. B. What ? No Igloos ? [c1954]

P. T. A. cook book. 1941. SEE no. 3546, Peterburg P. T. A.

Pacific Clipper Line. SEE no. 2935, McMicken, E. G.

Pacific coast legal directory. 1961. SEE no. 2673,
      Legal Directories Pub. Co.

PACIFIC COAST STEAMSHIP CO., S. F. Alaska cruises, via "Totem Pole" Route, Season 1912. SS *Spokane* tourists' souvenir diary. [S. F., 1912 ?] illus.   3444

PACIFIC COAST STEAMSHIP CO., S. F. Alaska excursion. Season of 1915. Totem Pole Route. Chicago, Poole Bros., 1915. 18p.   3445

PACIFIC COAST STEAMSHIP CO., S. F. Alaska excursions. Season 1901. S. F., 1901. 12p. illus. plans, map.   3446

PACIFIC COAST STEAMSHIP CO., S. F. Alaska; the marvelous land of gold and glacier. By Patrick Donan. S. F., 1899. 37p. illus.   3447

PACIFIC COAST STEAMSHIP CO., S. F. Alaska, via Totem Pole Route. Summer excursions. S. F., 1906. 16p. ANR. 1911. 16p.   3448

PACIFIC COAST STEAMSHIP CO., S. F. All about Alaska. S. F., 1887. 32p. ANR. S. F., printed by Payot, Upham & Co., 1892. 72p. illus. diagrs. wrps. OTHERS 1888, 1890, 1891, 1894, 1898. var. p.   3449

PACIFIC COAST STEAMSHIP CO., S. F. California, British Columbia, Washington, Alaska, Mexico. S. F., Feb. 1904. 20p. ANR. Apr. 1907. 20p.   3450

PACIFIC COAST STEAMSHIP CO., S. F. Four thousand miles north and south from San Francisco, covering coast travel from Mexico to Alaska. S. F., 1896. 75p. illus. plans, map.   3451

PACIFIC COAST STEAMSHIP CO., S. F.   The Alaska Indian mythology;
their legends and traditions, history of the totem pole, description of a potlatch. By C. D. Dunnan. [Chicago ?], 1915. 12p.
3452

PACIFIC COAST STEAMSHIP CO., S. F. Yukon Territory, Alaska and
Puget Sound; a general review of the mineral, lumber, shipping
and industrial resources. By A. S. Allen. [S. F., 1902 ?] 72p.
illus.   3453

Pacific Coast Steamship Co., S. F.   SEE ALSO nos.
    3464-5, Pacific Steamship Co.;
    4912, Wilson, Jas. A. Bits of Alaska [c1908]

Pacific Construction Co., N. Y.   SEE no. 1722, Gillette, Edw.

Pacific Fire Rating Bureau.   SEE no. 3273, National Board
    Fire Underwriters.

PACIFIC NORTHWEST AND ALASKA; an empire of matchless pleasure-
lands. [Chicago, Poole Bros., 1915 ?] 48p. illus. maps.
OTHERS 1925, 1930 and n. d. [railroad brochures of Chicago and
Northwestern Railway Co. and Chicago, Milwaukee, St. Paul and
Pacific Railroad Co.]   3455

Pacific Northwest and Alaska. Issued ... 1927. SEE
    no. 4614, Union Pacific System.

PACIFIC NORTHWEST INDUSTRIES. Alaska; frontier fur industry.
[pl. ?], 1954. 12p. illus. charts, map, append. bibliog.
(Special Supplement)   3456

Pacific Science Association. SEE nos. 3457-62,
    Pacific Science Congress.

PACIFIC SCIENCE CONGRESS, 5th, Victoria and Vancouver, B. C.,
1933. Proceedings. Toronto, 1934. [incls. some papers of Alaskan interest]   3457

PACIFIC SCIENCE CONGRESS, 5th, Victoria and Vancouver, B. C.,
1933. Trade of Canada with Asia, Oceania, Alaska, Mexico ... Bureau of Statistics, Canada. Specially compiled for the Fifth
Pacific Science Congress at Vancouver, B. C., June 1, 1933. Ottawa, Acting King's Printer, J. O. Patenaude, 1933. 45p.   3458

PACIFIC SCIENCE CONGRESS, 9th, Bangkok, Thailand, 1957. Ninth
Pacific Science Congress of the Pacific Science Association;
abstracts of papers. Bangkok, 1957. 265p. [incls. some papers
of Alaskan interest]   3459

PACIFIC SCIENCE CONGRESS, 9th, Bangkok, Thailand, 1957. Proceedings of the Ninth Pacific Science Congress of the Pacific Science Association. Bangkok, Nov. 18-Dec. 9, 1957; vol. 16. Oceanography. Bangkok, 1958. 240p. charts, graphs, tables, bibliog. [some papers of Alaskan interest]   3460

PACIFIC SCIENCE CONGRESS, 10th, Honolulu, Hawaii, 1961. Abstracts of symposium papers. Honolulu, Pacific Science Assoc., 1961. 487p. [has some papers of Alaskan interest]   3461

PACIFIC SCIENCE CONGRESS, 10th, Honolulu, Hawaii, 1961. Proceedings. L. D. Tuthill, editor. Honolulu, Bishop Museum Press, 1963. 464p. [some papers with Alaskan interest]   3462

PACIFIC STATES NEWSPAPER DIRECTORY containing a carefully prepared list of all the newspapers and periodicals published in California, Oregon, Washington, Idaho, Utah, Nevada, Arizona, New Mexico, Montana, Alaska, Wyoming, British Columbia, Texas, Colorado, Sandwich Islands, Mexico; arranged alphabetically by towns and also by counties, with a brief description of each state, territory and county. S. F., Palmer and Rey, 1888. 3rd ed. 348p. ANR. 1890. 320p.   3463

PACIFIC STEAMSHIP CO. Alaska; top o' the world tours. Seattle, 1924. 31p. illus. maps. ANR. 1927.   3464

PACIFIC STEAMSHIP CO. Cruising the world's smoothest waterway thru the Inside Passage and 10,000 islands of Alaska. [Seattle?], 1929. 27p. front.(col.), photos, tables, map(col. fold.) ANR. [Seattle ?], n. d. 12p. photos, tables, map.   3465

Pacific Steamship Co. SEE ALSO nos. 3444-53, Pacific Coast Steamship Co.

PACIFIC TIN MINES CO. A few facts about tin mining. S. F., Press of John Partridge, n. d. 7p.   3466

PACIFIC UNIVERSITY, Forest Grove, Oregon. A souvenir bulletin of articles exhibited by Pacific University at the Alaska-Yukon-Pacific Exposition, 1909. [Forest Grove, Ore., 1909] 24p.   3467

PACKARD, WINTHROP. The young ice whalers. Boston, Houghton Mifflin, 1903, 397p.   3468

PAGE, ELIZABETH MERWIN. Wild horses and gold; from Wyoming to the Yukon. By Elizabeth Page. N. Y., Farrar & Rinehart, [c1932] 362p. front. illus. historical notes, list of Klondike parties, map(fold.) (Pioneer Edition) [Old Edmonton Trail and biog. of "Kansas" Gilbert]   3469

PAGE, ROGER. This is Kodiak; compiled, edited and published by Roger Page. Kodiak, 1969. 64p. photos.   3470

PAILLARD, LOUIS. Un Lyonnaise au Klondike. Correspondence de
M. L. Paillard Administrateur delegue du Syndicat Lyonnais du
Klondike. Bourg, Imprimérie "Francisque Allombert," 1900. 214p.
front.(port.), pls. map(fold.)   3471

Palacios, R., cartog. SEE no. 1401, Dyson, Jas. L.

Pallas, Peter Simon. [Alphabetical title guide to chronological
    entries]

            Flora rossica ... 3472.
            Neue nordische Beyträge ... 3475
            Neueste nordische Beyträge. 3475.
            Opisanie rastĭeniĭ ... 3473, 3474.
            Zoographia ... 3476.

PALLAS, PETER SIMON. Flora rossica; seu Stirpium imperii rossici per Europam et Asiam indigenarum descriptiones et icones.
Jussu et auspiciis Catharinae II Augustae. [TITLE TR. Russian
flora; or description of plants of the European and Asiatic
parts of the Russian Empire and their illustrations. Edited by
the order and at the expense of Empress Catherine II] Petropoli,
Typogr. J. J. Weibrecht, 1784-88. 2 vols. [pt. 1 published in
1784. vii,80p. pls.: pt. 2 published in 1788. 114p. pls.]
folio. ANR. Francafurti et Lipsiae, 1789-1790. 2 vols. without
pls. [pt. 1 published in 1789. xxii,191p.: pt. 2 published in
1790. 229p.]   3472

    TRANSLATIONS - Flora rossica ... 1784-88, CHRONOLOGICALLY.

    Opisanie rastĭeniĭ Rossiĭskago gosudarstva s ikh izobrazheniĭa-
        mi. Po Vyevysochaĭshemu povelĭeniĭu i na izhdeveniĭ Eĭa Im-
        peratorskago Velichestva, izdannoe P. S. Pallasom. S. ruko-
        pisnago sochineniĭa perevel Vasileĭ Zuev. Chast' I. [TITLE
        TR. Description of plants of the Russian Empire with their
        illustrations, edited at the order and expense of Her Majes-
        ty. Translated from the manuscript by Vasiliĭ Zuev. Part I]
        S. Peterburg, 1786. 204p. pls.   3473

    Opisanie rastĭeniĭ Rossiĭskago gosudarstva. Izdannoe P. S.
        Pallasom. Tobolsk, Typogr. V. Kornil'eva, 1792. 233p. 3474

[PALLAS, PETER SIMON, edit.] Neue nordische Beyträge zur physikalischen und geographischen Erd-und Völkerbeschreibung, Naturgeschichte und Oekonomie. [TITLE TR. New northern contributions
to physical geography, anthropology, natural history and economy]
St. Petersburg & Leipzig, 1781-96. 7 vols. var. p. pls.(some
col.), maps. [vols. 5-7 HAVE ADDED EXTRA TITLEPAGE Neueste nordische Beyträge. St. Petersburg & Leipzig, Cnobloch, 1793-96.
In these volumes will be found Maurelle, F. A. "Tagebuch einer
im Jahre 1775 ..." See no. 3036 and G. W. Steller's "Reise von
Kamtschatka ... " See no. 4333]   3475

PALLAS, PETER SIMON. Zoographia Rosso-Asiatica, sistens Omnium Animalium in extenso imperio Rossico et adjacentibus maribus observatorum Recensionem, Domicilia, Mores et Descriptiones, anatomen atque Icones plurimorum. Auctore Petro Pallas, Eq. Aur. Academico-Petropolitano. Volumen tertium. Petropoli in Officina Caes. Academiae Scientiarum Impress. M.DCC.CXI. Edit. MDCCCXXXI. St. Petersburg, 1811(1831). (vii)428p. pls. [printed in 1811, published in 1831, a few advance copies distributed prior to 1831]   3476

Pallas, Peter Simon. SEE ALSO nos.
    3023, Masterson, Jas. R. Bering's successors ... 1948;
    4102-3, Shelekhov, G. I. Rossiiskago kuptsa ... 1791 and
           1793-92.

PALMEDO, ROLAND. Ski new horizons. By Roland Palmedo. A guide to skiing round the world with illustrations. With supplemental information supplied by Pan American Airways' network of offices on all six continents. Garden City, N. Y,, Doubleday, 1961. [c1956] 1st rev. ed., 1st print. 319p. front. illus. endmaps, index. [pt. 8, chapt. 2 about Alaska]   3477

PALMER, ARTIS. There's no place like Nome. N. Y., William Morrow, 1963. 215p. front. [autobiog.]   3478

PALMER, FREDERICK. In the Klondyke; including an account of a winter's journey to Dawson. N. Y., Scribner, 1899. 218p. front. pls.   3479

PALMER, FREDERICK. With my own eyes; a personal story of battle years. Indianapolis, 1933. 395p. photos, index. [World War I and Klondike]   3480

PALMER, J. FREDERICK. Kodiak bear hunt; stalking the giant bears of Alaska. N. Y., Exposition Press, 1958. 79p.   3481

PALMER TERRITORIAL SCHOOL. History of the Matanuska Valley. Palmer, 1941. [written by the school children]   3482

Pamiatnik trudov ... 1857. SEE no. 4378, [Sturdza, A.]

PAN AMERICAN AIRWAYS, INC. Alaska Division. Pan American Airways System; the Panair way, handbook of information for personnel [Seattle ? 1943] 63p. illus. port. map.   3483

Pan American Airways, Inc. SEE ALSO no. 3477,
    Palmedo, R. Ski new horizons. 1961.

PAN AMERICAN HIGHWAY SYSTEM. Washington, D. C., Pan American Union, 1959.   3484

PAN AMERICANA PUB. CO. Alaska opportunities; register. Hollywood, Calif., 1947.   3485

PAN PACIFIC PROGRESS. Alaska. Los Angeles, March 1930. 45p.
illus. port. map. (Volume 12) [contains articles by G. A. Parks,
S. C. Bone, O. F. Ohlson, E. W. Sawyer, J. L. Steele, H. H. M.
Higgins and Malcolm Elliott]   3486

Panama-Pacific Historical Congress. SEE no. 4335,
    Stephens, H. M.

Panama-Pacific Int'l. Exposition, 1915. SEE no. 2255,
    Illustrated hist. Indian baskets ... 1915.

PANETH, PHILIP. Alaskan backdoor to Japan. London, Alliance
Press, 1943. 108p. pls. maps.   3487

PAPE, RICHARD. Poles apart; a fast-moving account of his adventures from Alaska to Antarctica. London, Odhams Press, 1960.
256p. pls. [Alaska Highway, Vancouver to Fairbanks and return]
                                                               3488

PARAMORE, EDWARD E., jr. The ballad of Yukon Jake. N. Y.,
Coward-McCann, 1928. 42p. front. illustrated by Hogarth, jr.
[Hogarth, jr. a pseudonym for Rockwell Kent]   3489

[PARAMORE, H. H. ?] Klondike gold fields on the Yukon. St.
Louis, Mo., Myerson Printing Co., 1897. wrps.   3490

PARAMORE, H. H. The practical guide to Klondike gold fields;
being a compendium of reliable information bearing upon the gold
regions of Alaska. St. Louis and S. F., Myerson Printing Co.,
1897. 64p. pls. map(fold.)   3491

PARISH, PEGGY. Ootah's lucky day. Pictures by Mamoru Funai.
N. Y., Harper & Row, 1970. 63p. illus.(col.) (An I can read
book)   3492

Parker, Herschel. SEE no. 699, Browne, Belmore.

PARKER, MARY M. This was Alaska. Seattle, Tewkesbury Pub. Co.,
1950. 237p. front. [fict.]   3493

Parkes, Mrs. G. R. SEE nos. 3843-45, Robins, Elizabeth.

PARKINSON, EDWARD S. Wonderland; or, twelve weeks in and out of
the U. S. Brief account of a trip across the continent, short
run into Mexico, steamer voyage to Alaska. Trenton, N. J., Mac-
Crellish & Quigley, Printers, 1894. 259p. illus.   3494

Parks, G. A. SEE no. 3486, Pan Pacific Progress.

PARRAN, THOMAS and others. Alaska's health; a survey report to
the United States Department of the Interior by the Alaska Health
Survey Team. Pittsburgh, University of Pittsburgh Graduate School
of Public Health, 1954. var. p. figs. tables, bibliog.   3495

PARRISH, MAUD. Nines pounds of luggage. London, 1940. [autobiog., incls. Nome and Dawson gold rushes] 3496

PARTRIDGE, BELLAMY. Amundsen; the splendid Norseman. N. Y., F. A. Stokes, 1929. 276p. photos, endmaps. ANR. London, Hale, 1953. 206p. 3497

PARTRIDGE, WELLS MORTIMER. Some facts about Alaska and its missions. [Peabody, Mass., C. H. Shepard, 1900] 46p. illus. 3498

PASETSKIĬ, VASILIĬ MIKHAILOVICH. Vitus Bering. Moskva, Gos. izd-vo geogr. lit-ry, 1958. 46p. illus. port. map, bibliog. 3499

PASTEUR, JAN DAVID. Reizen rondom de waereld door J. Cook; vertaald door J. D. Pasteur. Bladwijzer. Leyden, Honkoop, Allart en Van Cleef, 1795-1809. 14 vols. and atlas. pls. ports. charts, tables, maps, index. ANR. Leyden, Amsterdam en S. Haage, 1797-1809. 14 vols. 3500

PATCHIN, F. The Pony Rider Boys in Alaska; or, the gold diggers of Taku Pass. N. Y., 1924. 212p. illus. 3501

PATERSON, THOMAS THOMSON. Eskimo string figures and their origin. København, E. Munksgaard, 1949. 98p. illus. sketch map. (Acta Arctica, fasc. 3) 3502

PATTEE, FRED LEWIS. Sidelights on American literature. N. Y., Century, 1922. 342p. [has chapt. on Jack London, *The prophet of the last frontier*] 3503

PATTERSON, SAMUEL. Narrative of the adventures and sufferings of Samuel Patterson, experienced in the Pacific Ocean, and many other parts of the world with an account of the Feegee and Sandwich Islands. From the Press in Palmer, May 1, 1817. 144p. [Compiled by Ezekiel Terry, vicinity of Wilbraham, May 1, 1817] ANR. WITH SLIGHTLY CHANGED TITLE. Providence, Printed at the Journal Office, 1825. 2d ed. enl. 164p. ANR. Fairfield, Wash., Ye Galleon Press, 1967. (18)144p. facsims. bibliog. notes. facsim. of 1817 ed., ltd. to 481 numbered copies. [1817 ed. published in Massachusetts ?] 3504

Patton, Mary Lou, edit. SEE no. 2511, Kosmos, Geo.

PATTY, ERNEST N. North country challenge. N.Y., David McKay, 1969. 272p. illus. endmaps. [autobiog., President Emeritus of University of Alaska] 3505

PAUL, DAVID and AUDREY LOFTUS. According to Papa; as told to Audrey Loftus. Fairbanks, St. Matthews's Episcopal Guild, Oct. 1957. 1st print. 33p. illus. wrps. [Athabaskan lore] 3506

Pavlovskiĭ, E. N., edit. SEE no. 338, Baer, Karl Ernst von.

Payzant, Chas., co-auth. SEE no. 4089, Shannon, Terry.

Pḗ nēl´lŭ ʳ ghā ... 1910. SEE no. 791, Campbell, Edgar O.

PEABODY MUSEUM OF ARCHAEOLOGY AND ETHNOLOGY, Cambridge. Author and subject catalogues of the Library of the Peabody Museum of Archaeology and Ethnology, Harvard University. Boston, G. K. Hall & Co., 1963. 54 vols. index to subject headings. 1st Supplement, 1970. 12 vols. 2d Supplement, in progress. 6 vols.
3507

PEARSON, GRANT HAROLD. My life of high adventure. By Grant H. Pearson with Philip Newill. Englewood Cliffs, N. J., Prentice-Hall, [c1962] 234p. illus. photos, endmaps. [autobiog., former Superintendent of Mount McKinley National Park]   3508

PEARSON, GRANT HAROLD. The Seventy Mile Kid; wilderness superintendent of Mount McKinley National Park. By Grant H. Pearson. Los Altos, Calif., by author, printed by Signal Press, [c1957] 13p. illus. photos, wrps. [about Harry Karstens, Supt. 1921-28]   3509

PEARSON, GRANT HAROLD. The taming of Denali; now Mt. McKinley. Los Altos, Calif., 1957. 21p. wrps.   3510

PEARSON, T. GILBERT. Birds of America. Edited by T. G. Pearson. Garden City, N. Y., Garden City Pub. Co., 1936. in 3 pts. var.p. pls.(some col.), index.   3511

PEARY, ROBERT EDWIN and others. Vilhjalmur Stefansson. N. Y., Nomad Pub. Co., 1925. 53p. pls. ports. map, bibliog.   3512

PEATTIE, ELLA W. A journey through wonderland; or, the Pacific northwest and Alaska, with a description of the country traversed by the Northern Pacific Railroad. Issued by Northern Pacific Railroad. Chicago, Rand McNally, 1890. 94p. front.   3513

"Pechuck" SEE no. 3158, Montgomery, Richard G.

PEDERSEN, ELSA. Alaska. N. Y., Coward-McCann, 1969. [c1968] (7)8-125(3)p. front.(dble. map), illus. maps, index. (States of the Nations, 49)   3514

PEDERSEN, ELSA. Alaska harvest. N. Y., Abingdon Press, 1961. 192p. illus. ANR. Eau Claire, Wisc., Hale, 1961.   3515

PEDERSEN, ELSA. Cook Inlet decision. N. Y., Atheneum Press, 1963. illus.   3516

PEDERSEN, ELSA. Dangerous flight. N. Y., Abingdon Press, 1960. 224p. illus.   3517

PEDERSEN, ELSA. Fisherman's choice. N. Y., Atheneum Press, 1964. illus. 3518

PEDERSEN, ELSA. House upon a rock. N. Y., Atheneum Press, 1968. 1st ed. 218p. illus. 3519

PEDERSEN, ELSA. Mystery on Malina Straits. N. Y., Ives Washburn, 1963. 116p. illus. 3520

PEDERSEN, ELSA. Petticoat fisherman. N. Y., Atheneum Press, 1969. 1st ed. 231p. illus. 3521

PEDERSEN, ELSA. The mountain of gold mystery. N. Y., Ives Washburn, 1964. 122p. illus. 3522

PEDERSEN, ELSA. The mountain of the sun. N. Y., Abingdon Press, 1962. 224p. illus. 3523

PEDERSEN, ELSA. The mystery of the *Alaska Queen*. N. Y., Ives Washburn, 1969. 145p. illus. 3524

PEDERSEN, ELSA. Victory at Bear Cove; a story of Alaska. N. Y., Abingdon Press, 1959. 207p. illus. 3525

PEDERSEN, HANS HARTVIG SEEDORFF. Vitus Berings minde. København, Rasmus Naver, printed by Langkjaers Bogtrykkeri, 1943. ltd. ed. of 200 copies. 30p. illus. wrps. (Julehilsner, 1943) [poetry] 3526

PEISSON, ÉDOUARD. Pôles; l'etonnante aventure de Roald Amundsen. [TITLE TR. Poles; the amazing adventure of Roald Amundsen] Paris, B. Grasset, 1952. 275p. illus. maps, bibliog. 3527

PEKARSKIĬ, PETR PETROVICH. Arkhivnyĭa razyskaniĭa ob izobrazheniĭ nesushchestvuĭushchago nynĭe zhivotnago *Rhytina borealis*. [TITLE TR. Archival research concerning the representation of the now extinct animal *Rhytina borealis*] Sanktpeterburg, 1869. 33p. pl. (Akademiĭa nauk SSSR. Zapiski. t.15, suppl. no. 1) [Steller's seacow and Vitus Bering voyage to Alaska] 3528

PEKARSKIĬ, PETR PETROVICH. Istoriĭa Imperatorskoĭ Akademiĭa nauk v Peterburgie. [TITLE TR. History of the Imperial Academy of Sciences in Petersburg] Sanktpeterburg, Tip. Akademiĭa nauk, 1870-73. 2 vols. 775p. and 1,042p. front.(facsim.) [has biogs. of G. F. Müller, J. G. Gmelin, G. W. Steller, others] 3529

PENDER, JANE. Kotzebue; two worlds. Text and photos by Jane Pender. Published by Kotzebue Enupiak. Fairbanks, printed by The Lettershop, [c1970] 20p. illus. photos, wrps. 3530

[PENNANT, THOMAS] Arctic zoology. London, printed by H. Hughs, 1784-87. 2 vols. and supplement. pp.1-186, pp.187-586 and 163p. supplement. pls. maps(fold.) [supplement also issued separately] ANR. WITH TITLE Introduction to the Arctic Zoology. Second edition. London, R. Faulder, 1792. 2 vols. in 3. illus. maps (fold.) [see no. 3532 for tr.]   3531

[PENNANT, THOMAS] Introduction to Arctic zoology. 1792. SEE no. 3531.

[PENNANT, THOMAS] Thiergeschichte der nordlichen polarlander. Aus dem englischen des Herrn Thom. Pennant, mit Anmerkungen und zusatzen durch E. A. W. Zimmermann. Leipzig, S. L. Crusius, 1787. 2 vols. [tr. of no. 3531]   3532

[PENROSE, CHARLES VINICOMBE] A memoir of James Trevenen, edited by Christopher Lloyd and R. C. Anderson. London, Navy Records Society, 1959. [voyages of Capt. James Cook]   3533

PEO SISTERHOOD, Chapter B., Fairbanks. What ! No igloos ? Diary of a Fairbanks housewife. Fairbanks, PEO Sisterhood, Chapt. B, [c1954] 43p. ANR. WITH TITLE The new What ! No igloos ? Sitka, Sitka Print. Co., July 1963. [cJuly 1954. reprinted Sept. 1954 and June 1955] 47p. illus.   3534

PEO Sisterhood, Chapter B., Fairbanks. SEE ALSO no. 3396, Okakok, Guy. Okakok's Alaska ... 1959.

PEREVALOV, V. A. Lomonosov i Arktika, Iz istoriĭ geograficheskoĭ nauki i geograficheskikh otkrytiĭ. [TITLE TR. Lomonosov and the Arctic. From the history of geographical science and geographical discoveries] Moskva-Leningrad, Izd-vo Glavsemorputi, 1949. 504p. illus. ports. facsims. maps(some fold.), suppl. append. bibliog.   3535

PERKINS, ANGIE VILLETTE WARREN. San Diego to Sitka; with notes by the way. Illustrated by the author. Knoxville, Tenn., S. B. Newman & Co., 1902. 88p. illus.   3536

PÉRON, [FRANÇOIS ?] Mémoires du Capitaine Péron, sur ses Voyages aux Côtes d'Afrique, en Arabie, a l'Ile d'Amsterdam, d'Anjouan et de Mavotte, aux Côtes Nord-Ouest de l'Amérique, aux Iles Sandwich, a la Chine, etc. Paris, Brissot-Thivars, Libraire, Bossange Fréres, Printed Imprimerie la Lachevardière Fils, Successeur de Cellot, 1824. 2 vols. in 1. 328p. and 359p. pls.(fold.), maps (fold.) [voyage of *Otter*, northwest coast, 1796]   3537

PERREY, ALEXIS. Documents sur les tremblements de terre et les phénomènes volcaniques dans l'Archipel des Kouriles et au Kamtschatka. [TITLE TR. Documents on the earthquakes and volcanic phenomena of the Kurile Archipelago and Kamchatka] Lyon, 1863.
3538

PERREY, ALEXIS. Documents sur les tremblements de terre et les phénomènes volcaniques des Îles aleutiennes, de la péninsule d'Alaska et de la côte No. d'Amérique. [TITLE TR. Documents on the earthquakes and volcanic phenomena of the Aleutian Islands, of the Alaska Peninsula, and of the Northwest coast of America] Dijon, J. E. Rabutut, 1866. 131p. (Academie de Sciences Mémoire, 2d ser., vol. 13, sec. sc.) 3539

Perry Mason & Co. SEE no. 3440, Our country: West. 1900.

PERRY, RICHARD. The *Jeannette*; and a complete and authentic narrative encyclopedia of all voyages ... North Polar ... scientific and geographical ... By Capt. Richard Perry. Elegantly illustrated with two hundred engravings. Chicago, Coburn and Cook Pub. Co., 1882. 840p. illus. maps, index. ANR. Kansas City, Kansas City Pub. Co., 1883. 3540

PERRY, RICHARD. The world of the polar bear. Seattle, University of Washington Press, 1966. 195p. photos, map, bibliog. index. 3541

PERRY, RICHARD. The world of the walrus. N. Y., Taplinger, 1968. [c1967] [first pub. in U.S. in 1968] 162p. photos, map (dble.), bibliog. index. 3542

Perry, William. SEE no. 326, Austin, H. T.

Perseverance Mine meeting ... 1918. SEE no. 87,
    Alaska Mining & Engr. Soc.

PERTEK, JERZY. Polacy na szlakach morskich świata. [TITLE TR. The Poles on the world's sea routes] Gdańsk, Zakład narodowy im. Ossolińskich we Wrocławiu 1957. 662p. illus. ports. maps, bibliog. (Gdańskie towarzystwo naukowe) [incls. account of Count M. A. Beniowski] 3543

PERUGIA, PAUL del. Le grand nord. [TITLE TR. The Arctic] Paris, Presses Universitaires de France, 1951. 128p. maps, bibliog. ("Que sais-je ?" Le point des connaissances actuelles, no. 512) [Russian and North American economies] 3544

PETERSBURG HIGH SCHOOL. Flood tide. Published by Petersburg High. Petersburg, 1925. 18p. illus. wrps. (vol. 1, no. 1)3545

PETERSBURG PARENT AND TEACHERS ASSOC. P. T. A. cookbook. Petersburg, 1941. 168p. illus. 3546

PETERSBURG VETERANS OF FOREIGN WARS AUXILIARY. V. F. W. Auxiliary cookbook. Petersburg, 1964. 3547

Petersen, Erik, illus. SEE no. 1656, Freuchen, P.

PETERSON, HAROLD C. American Indian tomahawks. N. Y., Museum of the American Indian, 1965. 142p. pls. (Contribution from the Museum, Heye Foundation)   3548

PETERSON, LEAH JANE. This is Alaska. Drawings by Joan Arend Kickbush. Seattle, Pacific Books, 1958. 107p. illus. endmaps.
                                                                    3549

PETERSON, MARTIN SEVERIN. Joaquin Miller, literary frontiersman. Stanford, Stanford University Press, [c1937] 198p. front.(port.)
                                                                    3550

PETERSON, RAYMOND ALFRED. Report seismograph air shooting tests, Naval Petroleum Reserve no. 4, August 1948. no pl., United Geophysical Co., 1949. 13ℓ diagrs. [Barrow, Alaska]   3551

PETERSON, ROGER TORY. A field guide to western birds. Boston, Houghton Mifflin, 1941. 240p. front.(col.), pls.(some col.), map, index. ANR. 1961. 2d ed. rev. and enl. [2d ed. expanded to incl. Alaska, western Canada and Hawaii. 1st briefly refers to species found in Alaska]   3552

PETERSON, ROGER TORY and JAMES FISHER. Wild America; the record of a 30,000-mile journey around the continent by a distinguished naturalist and his British colleague. By Roger Tory Peterson and James Fisher. Illustrated by Roger Tory Peterson. Boston, Houghton Mifflin, 1955. [c1955] 1st print. Sept. 1955 434p. illus. endmaps, append. index. [incls. Chevak, in western Alaska and Pribilof Islands]   3553

PETIT-THOUARS, ABEL AUBERT Du. Fragments du dernier voyage de La Pérouse. Paris, Quimper, 1797.   3554

PETIT-THOUARS, ABEL AUBERT Du. Voyage autour du monde sur le frégate *La Vénus*, pendant les années 1836-1839, publiée par ordre du Roi, sous les auspices de Ministre de la Marine ... Paris, Gide, 1840-49. 10 vols. and atlas. var. p. pls.(some col.), maps. ANR. Paris, Gide, 1840-55. 10 vols. and atlas of 3 vols. bd. in 2. var. p. pls.(some col.), maps. [incls. views of Alaska]3555

PETITE, IRVING. Meander to Alaska. Garden City, N. Y., Doubleday, 1970. 223p. maps. [via Inside Passage]   3556

PETITOT, ÉMILE FORTUNÉ STANISLAS JOSEPH. Dictionnaire de la langue Dènè-dindjié, dialectes Montagnais ou Chippewayan, Peaux de lièvre et Loucheux, renferment en outre un grand nombre de termes propres à sept autres dialectes de la même langue; précédé d'une monographie des Dènè-dindjié, d'une grammaire et de tableaux synoptiques des conjugaisons. [TITLE TR. Dictionary of the Dènè-dindjié language, Mountain or Chippewyan, Hare and Loucheux dialects including also a large number of expressions peculiar to seven other dialects of the same language; preceded

by a mongraphy of the Dènè-dindjié, a grammar, and a synoptic table of conjugations] Paris, E. Leroux and S. F., A. L. Bancroft & Co., 1876. ltd. to 15, 50 and 150 copies in var. papers. 367p. map(fold.) [published as vol. 2 of "Bibliotheque de linguistique ... " 1876, edited by A. L. Pinart. See no. 3592]
3557

PETITOT, ÉMILE FORTUNÉ STANISLAS JOSEPH. Origine asiatique des Esquimaux; nouvelle étude ethnographique. Par le R. P. Émile Petitot. [TITLE TR. Asiatic origin of the Eskimos; new ethnographic study] Rouen, E. Gagniard, 1890. 33p. (extracted from Le Bulletin de la Société normande de Geographie, and also in Les Missions Catholiques, Paris, Oct. to Dec. 1879. ouzième année, nos. 543-550. var. p.)
3558

PETITOT, ÉMILE FORTUNÉ STANISLAS JOSEPH. Vocabulaire français-esquimau; dialecte des Tchiglit des bouches du Mackenzie et de l'Anderson; précédé d'une monographie de cette tribe et des notes grammaticales. Par le R. P. É. Petitot. [TITLE TR. French-Eskimo vocabulary; dialect of the Tshiglit at the mouth of the Mackenzie and Anderson Rivers; with a monographic introduction on this tribe and some grammatical notes] Paris, E. Leroux and S. F., A. L. Bancroft & Co., 1876. 75p. illus. [published as vol. 3 of "Bibliotheque de linguistique ... " 1876, edited by A. L. Pinart. See no. 3592]
3559

Petrus, J. SEE no. 4261, Sperry, Armstrong.

Petterson, Carl, illus. SEE no. 618, Booth, E. S.

PETTIBONE, MARIAN HOPE. Polychaetous annelids of the Polynoidae from the northeastern Pacific, with a description of a new species. N. Y., American Museum of Natural History, 1949. 5p. pl. (American Museum Novitates, no. 1414)
3560

PETTINGILL, OLIN SEWALL, jr., edit. The bird watcher's America. Illustrated by John Henry Dick. N. Y., McGraw-Hill, 1966. 441p. illus.
3561

PETTITT, GEORGE ALBERT. Primitive education in North America. Berkeley, University of California Press, 1946. 182p. bibliog. (Publication in American Archaeology and Ethnography, vol. 43)
3562

PÉWÉ, TROY LEWIS. Permafrost and its effect on life in the North. By Troy L. Péwé. Corvallis, Oregon State University Press, [c1966] 40p. illus. figs. table, map, bibliog. wrps. [originally published in Arctic Biology, Proc. 18th Annual Colloquium, 1957 and rev. in Arctic Biology, 1967. 2d ed. See nos. 1936 and 4865]
3563

PÉWÉ, TROY LEWIS, edit. The periglacial environment, past and present. Montreal, McGill-Queen's University Press, 1969. 487p. illus. maps. [based on Symposium on cold climate environments and processes, VIIth Congress of International Assoc. for Quaternary Research, Fairbanks, Aug. 18-25, 1965. SEE no. 2273] 3564

PFIZMAIER, AUGUST. Aufklärungen über die Sprache der Koloschen. Wien, 1883. (reprinted from Kaiserliche Akademie der Wissenschaften, Philosophisch-Historische Classe, Sitzungsberichte, 1883. Bd. 105, Heft 1. pp.169-234) [a tr. of no. 4681] 3565

PFIZMAIER, AUGUST. Die Sprache der Aleuten und Fuchsinseln. By Dr. A. Pfizmaier. Wien, 1884. 82p. (reprinted from Kaiserliche Akademia der Wissenschaften, Philosophisch-Historische Classe, Sitzungsberichte, 1883. vol. 105, pp.801-80 and vol. 106, 1884. pp.237-316) [a tr. of no. 4675] 3566

PHELPS, EDWARD J. Orations and essays of Edward J. Phelps, diplomat and statesman; edited by J. G. McCullough, with a memoir by John W. Stewart. N. Y., Harper, 1901. 475p. [Bering Sea controversy, pp.427-51] 3567

PHELPS, SUE. The official Alaska cook book; a collector's edition. [Juneau], Southeast Alaska Empire, 1969. unp. illus. 3568

PHILIPS, CARROLL. Alaska ... homesteaders, by Carroll Philips, and family. As published in the Fairbanks Daily News-Miner of January 18, 19, and 29, 1940. [Fairbanks, 1940 ?] 12p. illus.3569

Philips, Melville, edit. SEE no. 3075, Melville, G. W.

PHILLIPS, ALAN. The living legend; the story of the Royal Canadian Mounted Police. By Alan Phillips. Boston, Little Brown, [c1957] 328p. [incls. Alaska-Yukon border, Dawson gold rush] 3570

PHILLIPS, ELLIS L., jr. Alaska summer, 1938. Glen Head, L. I., N. Y., by author, 1938. ltd. to 500 numbered copies. 32p. front. sketches, bds. 3571

Phillips, Jas. W., co-auth. SEE no. 3138, Mills, Stephen E.

Phillips, John, edit. SEE no. 609, Boone and Crockett club.

Phillips, L. K., edit. SEE no. 4255, Speck, Gordon.

Phillips, Merton O. SEE no. 4199, Smith, Jos. R.

PHILLIPS, PHILIP LEE. Alaska and the northwest part of North America, 1588-1898; maps in the Library of Congress. By P. L. Phillips. N. Y., Burt Franklin, Pub., 1970. 119p. maps. [reprint of 1898 edition, U. S. Gov't. Print. Office, Washington, D. C.] 3572

PHILLIPS, R. A. J. Canada's North. Toronto, Macmillan of Canada, 1967. 306p. illus. photos, pls.(some col.), maps, index. (Published for the Centennial of Canadian Confederation) [many scattered references to Alaska and Alaska Highway]   3573

PHILLIPS, RICHARD. A collection of modern and contemporary voyages and travels. By Sir Richard Phillips. London, 1805-10. [vol. 5, no. 1 and vol. 6, no. 2 published in 1806 and 1807 contain Sarychev's "Account of voyage ... " tr. from "Puteshestvie ... " 1802. See no. 3965]   3574

PHILLIPS, RICHARD. A general collection of voyages and travels, from the discovery of America to the commencement of the nineteenth century. By Sir Richard Phillips. London, printed for Phillips, 1809-1810. 2d ed. 28 vols. front. illus. maps. ANR. 1813. [vols. 4-10 in 2d ed. contain voyages of James Cook] 3575

[PHILLIPS, RICHARD] A view of the character, manners, and customs of the North-Americans, comprehending an account of the Northern Indians; of the inhabitants of Oonalashka and Nootka Sound; of the five Indian Nations of Canada; of the inhabitants of the United States, &c. In which are displayed all the remarkable curiosities which are to be found in those countries. Ornamented with plates. By the Rev. J. Goldsmith, Vicar of Dunnington, and formerly of Trinity College, Cambridge. Philadelphia, J. Bouview for Johnson and Warner, 1810. 22ℓ front. illus. wrps.   3576

Phillips, Walter Shelley. Indian fairy tales. SEE no. 3577.

PHILLIPS, WALTER SHELLEY. Totem tales; Indian stories Indian told, gathered in the Pacific Northwest; with a glossary of words, customs and history of the Indian. Chicago, Star Pub. Co., 1896. 326p. front. pls. glossary. ANR. WITH TITLE Indian fairy tales; folklore-legends-myths; totem tales as told by the Indians, gathered in the Pacific Northwest, with a glossary of words, customs and history of the Indians, fully illustrated by the author. Chicago, Star Pub. Co., [c1902] reissue of author's "Totem tales ..." 1896. 326p. front. pls. glossary. 3577

PICKERING, CHARLES. The races of man; and their geographical distribution, new edition to which is prefixed an analytical synopsis of the natural history of man, by John C. Hall. London, H. G. Bohn, 1863. 445p.   3578

Picturesque Alaska. 1888. SEE no. 4939, [Witteman, A.]

PIERCE, EDWARD L. Memoirs and letters of Charles Sumner. Boston, Roberts Bros., 1877-93. 4 vols. illus. [pp.318-28 about Alaska]   3579

PIERCE, FRANK RICHARDSON. Rugged Alaska stories. Seattle, 1950. 432p. illus.(some col.)   3580

PIERCE, RICHARD A. Alaska in 1867 as viewed from Victoria.
[Kingston, Canada, 1967] (8)p. (reprinted from Queen's Quarterly, Winter 1967. vol. 74, no. 4)   3581

PIERCE, RICHARD A. Prince D. P. Maksutov; last governor of
Russian America. [L. A., 1967] illus. (reprinted from Journal
of the West, July, 1967. vol. 6, no. 3. pp.395-416)   3582

PIERCE, W. H. Thirteen years of travel and exploration in
Alaska, by W. H. Pierce; edited by Prof. and Mrs. J. H. Carruth.
Lawrence, Kansas, Journal Pub. Co., 1890. 224p. illus. [1886,
mining in Yukon, also Treadwell Mine in southeastern Alaska] 3583

PIERREPONT, EDWARD WILLOUGHBY. Fifth Avenue to Alaska, with maps
by Leonard Forbes Beckwith. N. Y., Putnam, 1884. 329p. maps
(4 fold.) ANR. 1885. 3rd ed.   3584

[PIET, JOSEPHUS M.] The land of the midnight sun; the missions
of Alaska. no pl., Schinner, 1925. 20p. illus. ports.   3585

Pijardiere, Louis de La Coeur de la. SEE no. 3986,
     Savvage, Jehan.

PIKE, GORDON CHESLEY. Guide to the whales, porpoises and dol-
phins of the northeast Pacific and Arctic waters of Canada and
Alaska. Nanaimo, B. C., May 1954. 6p. (Fisheries Research
Board of Canada, Pacific Biology Station Circ. no. 32)   3586

PIKE, WARBURTON MAYER. Through the subarctic forest; a record
of a canoe journey from Ft. Wrangel to the Pelly Lakes and down the
Yukon River to the Behring Sea. London, Edward Arnold, 1896.
295p. front. pls. maps(2 fold.), appends. ANR. N. Y., Arno
Press for Abercrombie Fitch, 1967. facsim reprint. 310p. illus.
                                                                 3587

PILDER, HANS. Die Russisch-Amerikansiche handelskompanie bis
1825; von dr. phil. H. Pilder. [TITLE TR. The Russian-American
Company up to 1825] Berlin and Leipzig, G. J. Göschen, 1914.
174p. appends. bibliog. ftntes.   3588

PILGRIM, MARIETTE SHAW. Alaska; its history, resources, geography, and government. Caldwell, Idaho, Caxton Printers, 1939.
296p. front.(fold. map), illus. ANR. 1943. rev. ed., 2d print.
334p. front.(fold. map), illus. append. index. OTHERS 1945,
1952 and 1954.   3589

PILGRIM, MARIETTE SHAW. Oogaruk, the Aleut. Illustrated by
Helen Hughes Wilson. Caldwell, Idaho, Caxton Printers, 1947.
223p. front.(col.), pls.   3590

Pilot; guide to s. e. Alaska ... 1966. SEE no. 4555,
     Tongass Pub. Co.

Pim, Bedford Chapperton Trevelyan. SEE nos. 1831 and 1833,
    Great Britain. Parl. (Franklin search)

PINART, ALPHONSE LOUIS. A few words on the Alaska Dene in answer
to Father Morice, accompanied by a short vocabulary of the A'tana
or Copper River Indian language. no pl., n. d. (extr. fr.
Anthropos, Ephemeris, 1906. Bd. 1. pp.907-13)   3591

PINART, ALPHONSE LOUIS. Bibliotheque de Linguistique et d'Ethnographie Americaines. Paris, E. Leroux, 1876. [vol. 2 is Petitot's "Dictionnaire de la langue Dènè-dindjié ... " 1876. See
no. 3557]   3592

PINART, ALPHONSE LOUIS. Catalogue des collections rapportées de
l'Amérique russe (aujourd'hui territoire d'Aliaska) ... exposées
dans l'une des galeries du Museum d'histoire naturelle de Paris
(section d'anthropologie) [TITLE TR. Catalog of collections
brought back from Russian America, now the Territory of Alaska
... exhibited at the Museum of Natural History] Paris, Imprimerie de J. Claye, 1872. 30p.   3593

PINART, ALPHONSE LOUIS. Eskimaux et Koloches; idées religeieuses
et traditions des Kaniagmioutes. Par M. Alphonse Pinart. Paris,
Typographie A. Hennuyer, 1873. (extr. fr. Revue d'Anthropologie,
Paris, 1873. t.2. pp.673-80)   3594

PINART, ALPHONSE LOUIS. La caverne d'Aknañh, île d'ounga (Archipel Shumagin, Alaska) [TITLE TR. The cave of Aknañh, Unga Island (Shumagin Archipelago, Alaska)] Paris, Ernest Lewoux, 1875.
11p. pls.(col.), tables, map.   3595

PINART, ALPHONSE LOUIS. La Chasse aux Animaux Marins et les
Pêcheries chez les Indigénes de la côte, nord-ouest d'Amérique.
[TITLE TR. The hunting of marine animals and the fisheries of
the natives of the northwest coast of America] Boulogne-sur-Mer,
Imp. de C. aigre, 1875. 15p. [incls. Aleuts, as well as the
Indians of southeastern Alaska]   3596

PINART, ALPHONSE LOUIS. Notes sur les Koloches. Paris, A. Hennuyer, 1873. 23p. (extr. fr. Bulletin de la Société d'Anthropologie, Paris, 1872. ser. 2, vol. 7)   3597

PINART, ALPHONSE LOUIS. Sur les Atnahs. Paris, E. Leroux, 1875.
8p. (extr. fr. Revue de Philogie et d'Ethnographie, no. 2)   3598

PINART, ALPHONSE LOUIS. Voyages a la côte Nord-ouest de l'Amérique éxécutes durant les années 1870-72 par Alphonse L. Pinart.
Paris, E. Leroux and S. F., A. L. Bancroft, 1875. 51p. (Histoire
naturelle, vol. 1, pt. 1)   3599

Pinart, Alphonse Louis, edit. SEE ALSO nos.
    3557, Petitot, E. F. S. J. Dictionnaire ... 1876;
    3559, Petitot, E. F. S. J. Vocabulaire ... 1876.

Pinchot, Amos, co-auth. SEE no. 4211, Smyth, Nathan A.

PINCHOT, GIFFORD. Who shall own Alaska ? Some facts about its
farm lands, forests, mines and harbors. no pl., 1911. 14p.
(reprinted from Saturday Evening Post, Dec. 16, 1911) [Ballinger-
Pinchot investigation]   3600

Pinchot, Gifford. See also no. 4211, Smuth, Nathan A.

PINE, TILLIE S. and JOSEPH L. LEVINE. The Eskimos know. Illustrated by Exra Jack Keats. N. Y., McGraw-Hill, 1957. 32p.
illus.   3601

Pinegin, N. V. See no. 3909, Rubakin, N. A.

PINGRY, Mrs. J. F. The message of an Alaskan life. N. Y.,Woman's
Board of Home Missions, 1905. 8p.   3602

PINKERTON, JOHN. A general collection of the best and most interesting voyages and travels in all parts of the world, i.e.,
America, Asia, Asiatic Islands, Europe, many of which are now
first translated into English. London, Longman, Hurst, Rees and
Orme, 1808-14. 17 vols. pls. maps, bibliog. [vol. 2. pub. 1812.
pp.498-738, voyages of Capt. Jas. Cook. vol. 17. published in
1814. 225p. (bibliog. of voyages)]   3603

PINKERTON, KATHRENE SUTHERLAND (GEDNEY) Hidden Harbor. By
Kathrene Pinkerton. N. Y., Harcourt Brace, 1951. 278p. front.
(map)   3604

PINKERTON, KATHRENE SUTHERLAND (GEDNEY) Second meeting. By
Kathrene Pinkerton. N. Y., Harcourt Brace, 1956. 204p.   3605

PINKERTON, KATHRENE SUTHERLAND (GEDNEY) Steer North ! By Kathrene Pinkerton. N. Y., Harcourt Brace, 1962. 219p.   3606

PINKERTON, KATHRENE SUTHERLAND (GEDNEY) Three's a crew. By
Kathrene Pinkerton. Illustrated by author and Stewart Edward
White. N. Y., Carrick & Evans, [c1940] 316p. front.(pl.), pls.
endmaps. ANR. London, H. Jenkins Ltd., 1941. 286p. front. pls.
ports. endmaps. (A Herbert Jenkins Book) [cruising waters off
southeastern Alaska]   3607

PINKERTON, KATHRENE SUTHERLAND (GEDNEY) Tomorrow Island. By
Kathrene Pinkerton. N. Y., Harcourt Brace, 1960. 217p.   3608

PINKERTON, KATHRENE SUTHERLAND (GEDNEY) Year of enchantment. By
Kathrene Pinkerton. N. Y., Harcourt Brace, 1957. 224p.   3609

PIONEER PRINTING AND PUBLISHING CO., Seattle. Klondyke and Yukon
guide; Alaska and Northwest Territory gold fields. Where they
are. How to get there. What to take along. When to go and what

to do to secure a claim. Compiled and published by Alaska illus-
trators. Seattle, Press of Pioneer Printing and Pub. Co., 1898.
31p. illus. maps.   3610

PIONEER WOMEN OF ALASKA, Igloo no. 3, Fairbanks. Constitution
and by-laws, Fairbanks Igloo no. 3, organized February 19, 1916.
[Fairbanks], The Alaska Citizen Printing Co., 1916. 24p.   3611

PIONEERS OF ALASKA, Grand Igloo, Nome. Constitution and by-laws.
Nome, Nugget Job Printing, 1907. 40p.   3612

PIONEERS OF ALASKA, Grand Igloo, Nome. Constitution of the Grand
Igloo. Constitution and by-laws of subordinate Igloos, as adopted
by the Grand Igloo, 1908, with amendments by the Grand Igloo,
1909, 1910, 1911. Nome, Alaska Printing Co., 1911. 38p. ANR.
... as adopted 1908 ... amended ... 1912. Nome, Alaska Printing
Co., n. d. 43p. ANR. ... as adopted 1908 ... amended ... including 1921. [no pl., 1921 ?] 44p.   3613

Pioneers of Alaska, Grand Igloo, Nome. SEE ALSO no. 899,
     Chase, Will H. Pioneers of Alaska ... 1951.

PIONEERS OF ALASKA, Igloo no 4, Fairbanks. By-laws and list of
members of Igloo no. 4, Fairbanks, Alaska. July 1, 1913. [Fair-
banks, 1913 ?]   3614

PIONEERS OF ALASKA, Igloo no. 4, Fairbanks. Gold; mining methods
used in the goldfields of the Klondike and Fairbanks. Fairbanks,
printed by Commercial Printing Co., 1957. (9)p. front. by T. R.
Lambert, illus. diagr. wrps.   3615

Pipes, Nellie B., edit. SEE no. 3055, [Meares, John]

Pis'ma Innokentiĭa, metropolita moskovskago ... 1897-1901. SEE
     no. 416, [Barsukov, Ivan]

PITELKA, FRANK ALOIS. Geographic variation and the species problem in shore-bird genus *Limnodromus*. Berkeley, University of
California Press, 1950. 107p. pls. tables, maps, append. bibliog. [incls. Alaskan and northern Canadian]   3616

Pittsburgh, University of. Graduate School of Public Health.
     SEE no. 3495, Parran, Thos.

PIVER, JACK. Alaska insurance quiz. S. F., Jack Piver, 1969.
77p.   3617

PLACE, MARIAN TEMPLETON. The Yukon. N. Y., Ives Washburn, 1967.
211p. map, bibliog.   3618

Placer mining. A hand-book ... 1897.   SEE no. 978, Colliery
     Engr. Co.

Placer mining laws of Alaska ... 1901. SEE no. 2801, Love, W. T.

PLANCHAT, HENRI. Le Klondike; sa civilisation - son or, sa situation economique - son avenir. Paris, E. Bernard et cie, Imprimeurs, 1901. 30p.   3619

"PLATINUM BILL" [pseud.] Under the northern lights, by "Platinum Bill." Illustrated with fotografs by J. Doody. Portland, Ore., W. R. Smith, 1916. [printed by The Columbian Printing Co.] 95p. front. pls. [poetry - author assumed to be Wilfred Robert Smith]
                                                                    3620

PLATZMANN, JULIUS. Amerikanisch-Asiatiche Etymologieen via Behrings-strasse "from the east to the west." Leipzig, B. G. Taubner, 1871. 112p. [50 copies printed for private circulation]
                                                                    3621

Plea for Mount McKinley Nat. Park ... 1916. SEE no. 797,
    Camp Fire Club of America.

Plea for protection Amer. labor ... proposed railway. 1910. SEE
    no. 4329, Stein, Robert.

Plea for sale ... "Panhandle" ... 1911. SEE no. 4328,
    Stein, Robert.

PLEMPEL, CHARLES A. The Klondyke gold fields; their discovery, development and future possibilities. Baltimore, Maryland Pub. Co., 1897. 63p.   3622

PLIENINGER, GUIL. HENR. THEODOR. Joannis Georgii Gmelini ... Reliquias quae supersunt commercii epistolici cum Carolo Linnaeo, Alberto Hallero, Guilielmo Stellero et al. Floran Gmelini sibiricam ejusque Iter sibiricum potissimum concernentis, ex mandato et sumtibus Academiae scientiarum Caesareae petropolitanae publicandas curavit Dr. Guil. Henr. Theodor Plieninger ... Addita autographa lapide impressa. [TITLE TR. Letters left by J. G. Gmelin from correspondence with Carl Linnaeus, Albrecht Haller, Wilhelm Steller and others, chiefly concerning Gmelin's "Flora Sibirica" and his "Reise durch Sibirien." Edited by G. H. T. Plieninger by order and with funds of the Royal Academy of Sciences in Petersburg. Lithographic reproductions of autographs added] Stuttgartiae, typis C. F. Heringianis, 1861. 196p. facsim.(fold.)   3623

Ploetz, R. A., tr. SEE no. 3307, Niedieck, Paul.

Pocket dictionary Chinook Jargon ... 1898. SEE no. 1342,
    Downing & Clarke, pub.

POETRY SOCIETY OF ALASKA. One hundred years of Alaska poetry, 1867-1967. Denver, Alan Swan, pub., 1966. [printed by Big Mountain Press, Denver] illus. laminated birch covers.   3624

Pohl, Frederick J., edit. SEE no. 1011, Cook, F. A.

Pohl, Ruchard W. SEE no. 247, Anderson, Jacob Peter.

POKROVSKIĬ, ALEKSEI ALEKSEEVICH, edit. Ėkspedit͡sii͡a Beringa; sbornik dokumentov; podgotovil k pechati A. Pokrovskiĭ. [TITLE TR. Bering's expedition; collection of documents edited by A. Pokrovskiĭ] Moskva, Glavnoe arkhivnoe upravlenie NKVD SSSR, 1941. 417p. illus. maps(fold.) 3625

POLAR BEAR CITIZEN BAND CLUB, Fort Wainwright. Alaska citizen band radio directory. Fort Wainwright (Fairbanks), June 1968. 32p. 3626

Polar folk og indianerne. 1960. SEE no. 3278,
    Nationalmuseet, Etnografiske samling, København.

POLITOVSKIĬ, V. G. Kratkoĭ istoricheskoĭ obrozani obrazovani i dei͡stviĭ R. A. Ka. [TITLE TR. Short historical review of the origin and transactions of the R. A. Co.] St. Petersburg, 1861. 3627

R. L. POLK AND COMPANY, Seattle. Alaska-Yukon gazetteer and business directory for 1901-02. Seattle and St. Paul, R. L. Polk & Co., 1901. OTHERS var. years, var. p. 3628

R. L. POLK AND COMPANY, Kansas City. Polk's Fairbanks city directory, 1959. volume one, including College and North Pole. Kansas City, R. L. Polk & Co., 1960. 455p. OTHERS var. dates, var. p. 3629

R. L. POLK AND COMPANY, Portland, Ore. Oregon, Washington and Alaska gazetteer and business directory, 1901-02. Issued biennially. Portland, Ore., R. L. Polk & Co., 1901. 3630

POLLAK, GUSTAV. Michael Heilprin and his sons. N. Y., 1912. illus. photos. [excerpts from Angelo Heilprin's writings. See no. 2020] 3631

POLLOCK, ELLEN. Helene of the Yukon. no pl., by author, 1940. 257p. illus. wrps. [Klondike gold rush] 3632

POLLOCK, HOWARD W. The State of the 70's; an action plan for Alaska. N. Y., Boyer Organization, Inc., 1970. 162p. wrps.3633

POLLOG, CARL HANNS and ERICH TILGENKAMP. In Eis und Sturm. Die verwegenen und abenteuerlichen Expeditionen in die Arktis und zum Nordpol, mit Schiffen, Ski, Schlitten und Luftfahrzeugen. Erste Sammlung. [TITLE TR. In ice and storm. Bold and adventurous expeditions in the Arctic and to the North Pole, by ship, ski, sledge, and aircraft. First selection] Zurich, Aero-Verlag, [c1946] 3634

POLUNIN, NICHOLAS VLADIMIR. Circumpolar Arctic flora. Oxford, Clarendon Press, 1959. 514p. illus. map, glossary, index. 3635

Pomerans, A. J., tr. SEE no. 4183, Slijper, E. J.

POMEROY, EARL SPENCER. The Pacific Slope; a history of California, Oregon, Washington, Idaho, Utah and Nevada. By Earl S. Pomeroy. N. Y., Knopf, 1965. 1st ed. 403p. illus. map(fold.) 3636

POMEROY, EARL SPENCER. The Territories and the United States, 1861-1890; studies in colonial administration. By Earl S. Pomeroy. Philadelphia, University of Pennsylvania Press and London, G. Cumberlege, Oxford University Press, 1947. 163p. bibliog. (The American Historical Association) ANR. Seattle, University of Washington Press, 1969. (Americana Library, no. 15) 3637

PONCINS, GONTRAN de MONTAIGNE, *Vicomte* de. Par le détroit de Bering; avec 16 photos de l'autour. [TITLE TR. Through Bering Strait] Paris, Stock, 1953. 204p. front.(map), photos. ANR. Garden City, N. Y., Doubleday, 1954. HAS TITLE The ghost voyage; out of Eskimo land. Translated by Bernard Frechtmann. 222p. endmaps. ANR. [in Eng.] London, Victor Gollancz Ltd., 1955. [trip in small boat from Coppermine in Arctic to Vancouver] 3638

Poncins, Gontran de Montaigne, *Vicomte* de. The ghost voyage. See no. 3638.

PONIATOWSKI, MICHEL. Histoire de la Russie d'Amérique et de l'Alaska. Paris, Horizons de France, 1958. 362p. illus. maps. 3639

Pont, Chas. E., illus. SEE no. 4761, Wead, F. W.

Poole, Gray, co-auth. SEE no. 3640, Poole, Lynn.

POOLE, LYNN and GRAY POOLE. Danger ! Iceberg ahead ! By Lynn and Gray Poole. N. Y., Random House, [C1961] 81p. illus.(some col.) (Easy to Read Book) 3640

POOR, HENRY VARNUM. An artist sees Alaska. By Henry Varnum Poor. Illustrated by the author. N. Y., Viking Press, 1945. 279p. pls. ports. map. 3641

Poor, Val A. SEE no. 76, [Alaska Life, Seattle]

POPE, G. D., jr. Eskimo exhibit. [Bloomfield Hills], Cranbrook Institute of Science, 1941. (7)p. wrps. 3642

Poppoff, I. G., co-auth. SEE no. 4531, Thuman, Wm. C.

Popular national songs ... 1918. SEE no. 2804, Loyal League.

PORSILD, ALF ERLING. Reindeer grazing in Northwest Canada; report of an investigation of pastoral possibilities in the area from the Alaska-Yukon boundary to Coppermine River. Ottawa, F. A. Acland, printers, 1929. 46p. illus. maps. [has reference to reindeer in Alaska]   3643

PORT ORCHARD NAVIGATION CO., Tacoma. Stikine River route to the Klondike. Shortest, safest, quickest and best. Tacoma, Van Duzen, printer, 1898. 12p.   3644

PORTER, KENNETH WIGGINS. John Jacob Astor; businessman. Cambridge, Harvard University Press, 1931. 2 vols. fronts. pls. ports. facsim. (Harvard Studies in Business History, no. 1) ANR. N. Y., Russell and Russell, 1965. reprint. [Astor's agreement with Russia to purchase R.-A. sea otter furs, aborted by War of 1812]   3645

Porter, O. R., co-auth. SEE no. 724, Bugbee, J. A.

PORTER, STEPHEN C. Pleistocene geology of Anaktuvuk Pass, Central Brooks Range, Alaska. Montreal, Arctic Institute of North America, 1966. 100p. pls. graphs, maps(incl. 1 fold.), bibliog. (Arctic Institute Technical Paper no. 18)   3646

PORTER, ZOE. The Alaska primer. S. F., Harr Wagner Pub. Co., 1926. 174p. illus.   3647

Porteus, S., edit. SEE no. 788, Campbell, Archibald.

PORTLOCK, NATHANIEL. A voyage round the world; but more particularly to the north-west coast of America; performed in 1785, 1786, 1787, and 1788, in the *King George* and *Queen Charlotte,* Captains Portlock and Dixon. Embellished with twenty copperplates. Dedicated, by permission, to his majesty. By Captain Nathaniel Portlock. London, printed for John Stockdale and George Goulding, [1789] xii,384(xl)p. front.(port.), pls.(some fold.), port. maps(some fold.), append. ANR. Amsterdam, N. Israel and N. Y., Da Capo Press, 1968. facsim. ed. (Bibliotheca Australiana, no. 43)   3648

[PORTLOCK, NATHANIEL and GEORGE DIXON] A voyage round the world in the years 1785, 1786, 1787, and 1788, performed in the *King George,* commanded by Captain Portlock, and the *Queen Charlotte,* commanded by Captain Dixon, under the direction of the incorporated Society for the Advancement of the Fur Trade. London, printed for R. Randal, 1789. vi,146p. [pages misnumbered 151] front. [has preface signed by C. L.] ANR. Dublin, printed for J. Whitworth, 1789. 144p. front.   3649

[PORTLOCK, NATHANIEL and GEORGE DIXON] An abridgement of Portlock and Dixon's voyage round the world, performed in 1785, 6, 7, and 8. London, Stockdale, 1789. 272p. pl. map.   3650

[PORTLOCK, NATHANIEL and GEORGE MORTIMER] Nathaniel Portlock's und Georg Mortimer's Reisen an die Nortvestkuste von Amerika; nebst den Reisen eines Amerikanischen Dolmetschers und Pelzandlers, welch eine Beschreibung der Sitten und Gebrauche des Nord amerikanischen Wilden anthalten; hrsg. von John Long;   aus dem Englischen ubersetzt und mit einer vorlaufigen Schilderung des Nordens von Amerika, begleitet von Georg Forster. Berlin, Bossischen Buchhandlung, 1796. viii,384p. front. pls. maps.   3651

[PORTLOCK, NATHANIEL and GEORGE DIXON] Reis naar de nord-west kust van Amerika. Gedaan in de jaren 1785, 1786, 1787 en 1788. Door de Kapteins Nathaniel Portlock en George Dixon. Uit derzelver oorspronklijke reisverhalen zamengesteld en vertaald. Met platen. Amsterdam, bij Matthijs Schalekamp, 1795. xvi,265p. pls.(fold.), ports. map(fold.)   3652

[PORTLOCK, NATHANIEL and GEORGE DIXON] Voyage of Captains Portlock and Dixon to King George's Sound and round the world. Philadelphia, Cruikshank, 1803. 120p.   3653

Portlock, Nathaniel. SEE ALSO nos.
    1308, Dixon, Geo. Voyage ... ded. Sir Jos. Banks ... 1789;
    1809, Dixon, Geo. Voyage autour du monde ... 1789;
    1310, Dixon, Geo. Der Kapitaine Portlock's ... 1790;
    1606, Forster, J. G. A. Geschichte der Reisen ... 1791;
    3304, Nicol, John. Life and adventures ... 1822;
    3780, Reisen nach nordwestlichen Kuste ... 1795.

Position of San Francisco canned salmon trade. 1904. SEE
    no. 303, Armsby, J. K., Co.

Pospisil, L. SEE no. 1772, Goodenough, W. H., edit.

Post, Wiley, SEE no. 3374, O'Brien, P. J.

POSTELS, ALEXANDR FILIPPOVICH and FRANTZ JOSEPH RUPRECHT. Illustrationes algarum in itinere circa orbem iussu Imp. Nicolaie I atque auspiciis navarchi F. Lutke annis 1826-29 celoce *Seniavin* executo collectarum ... [with titlepage and text also in Russian, Izobrazheniĩa i opisaniĩa...] [TITLE TR. Illustrations and descriptions of marine plants collected in the North Pacific Ocean, near the shores of the Russian possession in Asia and America, during the voyage around the world made by order of Emperor Nicolas I; on the naval sloop *Seniavine* in 1826 to 1829, under the command of Fleet Captain Fedor Litke. Published by Alexandr Postels and Frank Ruprecht] St. Petersburg, Press of Edward Pratz, 1840. 28(2)22(2)p. pls. indexes.   3654

Postels, Alexandr Filippovich and Frantz Joseph Ruprecht. Izobrazheniĩa i opisaniĩa ... 1840. SEE no. 3654.

Postels, Alexandr Filippovich and Frantz Joseph Ruprecht. SEE ALSO no. 2732. Litke, F. P. Voyage ... 1835.

POTT, AUGUST FRIEDRICH. Die quinare and vigesimale Zählmethode bei Völkern aller Welttheile. Nebst ausführlicheren Bemerkungen über die Zahlwörter indogermanischen Stammes und einen Anhange über Fingernamen. Von Dr. August Friedrich Pott. Halle, C. A. Schwetschke und Sohn, 1847. viii,304p. [pp.59-61, numerals of Aleut, Kadjak, Eskimo as well as Tschuktschi, Tschugazi and Kolkasck] 3655

POTTER, CLINT. Sitka sketches. By Clint Potter. Text by Roberley Reh Potter. Anchorage, Alaska Northwest Publishing Co., 1970. 52p. watercolor, and pen and ink sketches. 3656

POTTER, JEAN CLARK. Alaska under arms. N. Y., Macmillan, 1942. 1st print. 200p. endmaps, index. [World War II] 3657

POTTER, JEAN CLARK. Flying frontiersmen. By Jean Potter. N. Y., Macmillan, 1956. [c1956] 1st print. x,212p. pls. ports. endmaps by Richard Edes Harrison. [children's adaptation of no. 3659] 3658

POTTER, JEAN CLARK. The flying north. N. Y., Macmillan, 1947. 261p. pls. ports. endmaps. ANR. 1965. [pioneer bush aviation] 3659

POTTER, LOUISE. A study of a frontier town in Alaska; Wasilla to 1959. Hanover, N. H., printed by R. E. Burt Lithographer, 1963. 104p. illus. photos, tables, map, bibliog. 3660

POTTER, LOUISE. Alaska Highway flowers; a list of wild flowers which may be found near the road between Mile Zero at Dawson Creek, British Columbia and Mile 1520 at Fairbanks, Alaska. Compiled by Louise Potter, Thetford Center, Vermont and Wasilla, Alaska. no pl., Louise Potter, [c1966] 40p. illus. bibliog. wrps. 3661

POTTER, LOUISE. Old times on Upper Cook's Inlet. Anchorage, published by Book Cache, 1967. [printed by Commercial Printing Co., Fairbanks] 43p. illus. facsims. map(fold.), bibliog. wrps. 3662

POTTER, LOUISE. Roadside flowers of Alaska. Illustrated by Eva Melady. Thetford Center, Vt., 1962. 610p. illus. bibliog. ANR. Hanover, N. H., printed for author by Roger Burt, 1963. 2d print. 590p. illus. field list, color key, geog. index, common and botanical names index, bibliog. 3663

POTTER, LOUISE. Wild flowers along Mt. McKinley Park Road. Hanover, N. H., printed by Roger Burt, 1969. 145p. illus. color key, bibliog. index. 3664

POUGH, RICHARD H. Audubon bird guide. Garden City, Doubleday & Co., 1946. 312p. illus. 3665

POULTER, THOMAS C., C. F. ALLEN and STEPHEN W. MILLER. Seismic measurements on the Taku Glacier. Stanford, Stanford Research Institute, 1949. 16ℓ pls. tables, bibliog. (Juneau Ice Field Research Project, American Geographical Society)   3666

POWELL, ADDISON MONROE. Echoes from the frontier; poems on Oregon, Alaska and the West. N. Y., 1909.   3667

POWELL, ADDISON MONROE. Trailing and camping in Alaska. N. Y., A. Wessels, 1909. 379p. front. pls. port. ANR. N. Y., Wessels and Bissel, 1910. 379p. pls. port.   3668

POWELL, EDWARD ALEXANDER. Marches of the North; from Cape Breton to the Klondyke, illustrated with photographs. By E. Alexander Powell. N. Y., Century Co., [c1931] 1st print. 311p. front. pls. map(fold.), endmaps.   3669

POWELL, J. L. Journey to Alaska; a description of a tour from Framingham, Mass. to Alaska. Rutland, Vt., The Tuttle Co., 1891. 36p.   3670

POWERS, ALFRED. Alaska, America's last frontier. Cleveland, Travel League, [1921 ?] 14p. port.   3671

POWERS, ALFRED. Animals of the Arctic in action and adventure. N. Y., David McKay, 1965. 272p. illus. index.   3672

Poyer, Edith K. SEE no. 1697, George, M. M., edit.

PRATHER, J. B. The land of the Midnight Sun; a beautiful collection of Alaska and Northwest Territory views, including totems, glaciers; also a trip to the gold fields of the Klondike. Douglas, Alaska, [c1899] [printed by Albertype Co., Brooklyn, N. Y.]   front.(port.), pls.   3673

Pratt, John F. SEE no. 1062, Coolidge, L. A.

PRATT, WILLIAM A. The gold fields of Cape Nome, Alaska. By W. A. Pratt, from personal observation during his two years search for "pay dirt" in the Nome country. Providence, R. I., Card, The Printer, 1900. 80p. map(fold.), errata slip.   3674

PREDPRIĬĀTIE IMPERATRITSY EKATERINY 2 dlĩā puteshestviĩā vokrug svieta v 1786 godu. [TITLE TR. The enterprise of the Empress Catharine II toward a circumnavigation of the globe, 1786] St. Petersburg, 1840. 16p.   3675

Preliminary report Bering Strait ... 1960. SEE no. 1377, Dunbar, M. J.

PRENTICE, HARRY. The Boy Explorers; or, The adventures of two boys in Alaska. N. Y., A. L. Burt, 1895. 314p.   3676

PRENTISS, HENRY MELLEN. The great Polar current; polar papers
old and new. Cambridge, Riverside Press, 1897. 153p. ANR. WITH
TITLE The great Polar current; polar papers DeLong-Nansen-Peary.
N. Y., F. A. Stokes, 1897.   3677

PRESBYTERIAN CHURCH. Board of Home Missions. Alaska, "The
Great Land." Four programs for Junior meetings. N. Y., n. d.
7p. (Young People's Department)   3678

PRESBYTERIAN CHURCH. Board of Home Missions. Alaska, "The treasure house of the nation." Alaska to the immigrant. Poem by
Rev. S. Hall Young. no pl., n. d. 6p. (Publication no. 455)
                                                              3679

PRESBYTERIAN CHURCH. Board of Home Missions. New America in
songs. no pl., n. d. 7ℓ (Publication no. 454) [incls.poem by
Rev. S. Hall Young, *Alaska to the immigrant*]   3680

PRESBYTERIAN CHURCH. Board of Home Missions. The experience of
Chilcat George. N. Y., 1911. 3p.   3681

PRESBYTERIAN CHURCH. Board of National Missions. The Presbyterian Church in Alaska; an official sketch of its rise and progress,
1877-1884, with the minutes of the first meeting of the Presbytery
of Alaska, Sheldon Jackson, D.D., stated clerk. Washington, D.C.,
Press of Thomas McGill & Co., 1886. 13p.   3682

PRESBYTERIAN CHURCH. Presbytery of Portland, Oregon. The relation of this Presbytery to the beginning of missionary work in
Alaska. Portland, Ore., Ellis Printing Co., 1900. 12p.   3683

Presbyterian Church. SEE ALSO no. 1403, Eastman, Fred.
    Unfinished business ... 1921.

PRESCOTT, ADA M. Alaskan Indian totems. [N. Y., Industrial
Arts Cooperative Service, 1941] 11ℓ pls. map.   3684

Present status musk-ox ... 1934. SEE no. 197, American Comm.
    Int'l. Wildlife Protection.

[PREVOST, JULES L.] Culic whutana kunacu yit. Tadluonu khuvu
whykainiwhulit. Kowhulud by khudidash. Dowhudoduwon cithlotalton yulh. [By Rev. Jules L. Prevost] Tanana, Alaska, 1907.
[1st ed.] 32p. [hymnal]   3685

[PREVOST, JULES L.] Culic whutana kunacu yit whukowneltunh
yilh. [Nenana, May 26, 1915. 2d ed.] 32p. [hymns and cate-
chism]   3686

PREVOST, JULES L. and T. H. CANHAM, trs. Tennatla bu chilichu
Christtsun. Translated by Jules L. Prevost and *Archdeacon* Canham.
[TITLE TR. Book of songs to Christ] Ft. Adams, Alaska, St.
James Mission, 1894. 16p.   3687

Prevost, Jules L., tr. SEE ALSO nos.
    1481, [Episcopal Church] Service book ... 1908;
    2874, McDonald, Robert. Cilicu whut ana kunacu ... 1901.

PRICE, ARCHIBALD GRENFELL. The explorations of Captain Cook in
the Pacific as told by selections of his own journals, 1768-79.
Edited by A. Grenfell Price. N. Y., Limited Editions Club,
1957. illus. boxed.   3688

Price, Arthur, illus. SEE nos.
    389, Barbeau, Chas. M. Alaska beckons. 1947;
    392, Barbeau, Chas. M. Pathfinders ... 1958.

Price, E. B., co-auth. SEE no. 570, Black, M. L. P.

Price, E. V. Astronomicheskiĭ nabliŭdeniĭa ... 1832. SEE
    no. 3690.

PRICE, E. V. Astronomishce beobachtungen auf des Hn. Otto v.
Kotzebue zweiten reise um die welt in den landurg splatzen an-
gestellt. [TITLE TR. Astronomical observations made by E. V.
Price on Kotzebue's second voyage] Dorpat, Hsgb. v. W. Struve,
1930.   3689

    TRANSLATION - Astronomische ... 1830.

    Astronomicheskiĭ nabliŭdeniĭa proĭzvedenniĭa E. V. Preisom vo
    vtorom puteshestviĭ Kap. Kotsebu. St. Petersburg, 1832. 47p.
    tables. [translated by Lt. A. Borisov from Struve's German
    work. Supplement by P. Tarkhanov]   3690

PRICE, JULIUS MENDES. From Euston to the Klondike; the narrative of a journey through British Columbia and the North-West
Territory in the summer of 1898. With map and illustrations
from sketches by the author and photographs ... London, Sampson,
Low, Marston & Co., 1898. 301p. front. pls. map(fold.)   3691

PRICE, OLIVE. Reindeer Island. Philadelphia, The Westminster
Press, 1960. 158p. illus.   3692

PRIKLONSKIĬ, VASILIĬ L'VOVICH. Lĭetopis' ĭakutskago kraĭa,
sostavlennaĭa po offiĭsial'nym i istoricheskim dannym. Izdanie
G. I. Ĭudina. [TITLE TR. Chronicle of the Yakutsk region, compiled from official and historical data. Published by G. V.
Yudin] Krasnoyarsk, Eniseĭskaĭa gub. tipografiĭa, 1896. (2)205,
xvip. index. [incls. Aleutian Islands]   3693

PRINCE, BERNADINE LeMAY. The Alaska Railroad in pictures, 1914-
1964. Anchorage, Ken Wray Print Shop, printer, 1964. 2 vols.
1st ed. ltd. to 1000 numbered copies. 466p. and 467-1,092p.
photos, facsims. addend.   3694

Prince Rupert; gateway ... 1951. SEE no. 2625, Large, R. C.

PRINGLE, GEORGE CHARLES FRASER. Adventures in service. Toronto, McClelland and Stewart, 1929. [Presbyterian missionaries in Canada, some mention of Klondike]   3695

PRINGLE, GEORGE CHARLES FRASER. Tillicums of the trail; being Klondike yarns told to Canadian soldiers overseas by a sourdough padre. Toronto, McClelland and Stewart, [c1922] 253p.   3696

PRITCHARD, A. L. Pacific salmon migration; the tagging of the pink salmon and the chum salmon in British Columbia in 1928. no pl., Biological Board of Canada, 1930. 17p. (Canada. Biol. Bd. Bulletin no. 14)   3697

Proceedings ... 1909. SEE no. 155, Alaska-Yukon-Pac. Exposition.

Proceedings Grand Camp ... 1901-17. SEE nos. 281-96,
     Arctic Brotherhood.

PRODUCTION SURVEYS. This is Alaska today; unveiling a rich empire, the vast potentials, its golden future. [Portland, Ore.?], 1954. pp.133-204. illus.(col.), maps. [compiled from Alaska Section of "A manifest of the Pacific Northwest"]   3698

A PROPOSED SYSTEM of highways for interior and western Alaska.
no pl., 1945. 8p. map.   3699

Prospectus. 1871. SEE no. 46, Alaska Coal Co.

Prospectus. n. d. SEE no. 94, Alaska-Northwestern Railroad.

Prospectus. n. d. SEE no. 102, Alaska Petroleum & Coal Co.

Prospectus. n. d. SEE no. 110, Alaska Smelting & Develop. Co.

Prospectus of Wrangel ... 1901. SEE no. 4966.
     [Wrangell] Bd. of Trade.

PROSSER, WILLIAM THORNTON. History of Alaska and the Klondike. Prospectus for three volumes. N. Y. and Seattle, The Northern Historical Assoc., 1912. 12ℓ pls. map, wrps. [most likely was never published]   3700

PRUITT, WILLIAM O., jr. Animals of the North. N. Y., Harper and Row, 1967. 173p. drawings by William D. Berry, glossary. [Interior of Alaska, Tanana River area]   3701

Puget Sound and Alaska. [19_ ?] SEE no. 3354, Northern Pac. R.R.

Puget Sound Bur. of Information. SEE nos.
     3163, Moore, Otis M. New Northwest ... 1900;
     3164, Moore, Otis M. Washington illus. ... [1901 ?]

PUHR, CONRAD. Modern Alaska. no pl., n. d. [ca 1955] 108p.
photos by Conrad Puhr, no text, ringbound. 3702

Pullen, "Mother" Harriet. SEE no. 4894, Willoughby, B.

Pullen, W. J. L. SEE nos.
   1823-26, Great Britain. Parl. (Franklin search)

PURDY, ANNE. Dark boundary. N. Y., Vantage Press, 1954. 79p.
3703

PUSTINSKIĬ, INNOKENTIĬ. Otchet o sostvianiĭ Alĭaskanskago
vikariatstva za 1906 godu. By the Most Rev. Innokentiĭ Pustinskiĭ. [TITLE TR. Report on the condition of the Alaska diocese
in the year 1906] N. Y., Tip. Amerikanskiĭ Pravda Viestnik,
1906. 34p. 3704

PUTNAM, GEORGE PALMER. Mariner of the North; the life of Captain Bob Bartlett. N. Y., Duell, Sloan and Pearce, [c1947]
246p. appends. bibliog. index. 3705

PUTNAM, GEORGE ROCKWELL. Lighthouses and lightships of the
United States. Boston, Houghton Mifflin, 1917. 308p. 3706

Puzanova, V. F., co-auth. SEE nos.
   18, Agranat, G. A. Energetika ... 1962;
   19, Agranat, G. A. Naselenie ... 1963;
   21, Agranat, G. A. Promyshlennost' ... 1962.

PYLE, ERNEST TAYLOR. Home country. By Ernie Pyle. N. Y., Wm.
Sloane Assoc., [c1947] 1st print. vii,472p. index. [incls.
references to Interior Alaska, Salmon River, Berglund sisters:
see no. 4130] 3707

Q

Quaife, M. M., edit. SEE no. 1626, Franchere, G.

QUEENY, EDGAR MONSANTO. Cheechako; the story of an Alaskan bear
hunt. Photos by author. N. Y., Scribner's, 1941. 133p.
front.(col.), pls.(some col.), ports. endmaps, bibliog. 3708

QUIETT, GLENN CHESNEY. Pay dirt; a panorama of American gold
rushes. N. Y., Appleton-Century Co., 1936. 506p. front. pls.
ports. 3709

QUIMBY, GEROGE IRVING. Aleutian Islanders; Eskimos of the North
Pacific. By George I. Quimby. Drawings by Helen Z. Quimby.
Chicago, Field Museum of Natural History, 1944. 48p. pls. draw-
ings, bibliog. index. (Dept. Anthropology Leaflet, no. 35) 3710

QUIMBY, GEORGE IRVING. Periods of prehistoric art in the Aleutian
Islands. By George I. Quimby. no pl., 1945. (reprint from
American Antiquity, Oct. 1945)   3711

QUIMBY, GEORGE IRVING. Prehistoric art of the Aleutian Islands.
By George I. Quimby. Chicago, Field Museum of Natural History,
1948. 16p. (reprint from Fieldiana. Anthropology, vol. 36,
no. 3, Dec. 1948)   3712

QUIMBY, GEORGE IRVING. The sadiron lamp of Kamchatka as a clue
to the chronology of the Aleut. By George I. Quimby. no pl.,
1946. (reprint from American Antiquity, Jan. 1946)   3713

Quimby, George Irving. SEE ALSO no. 3010,
    Martin, Paul S. Indians before Columbus. 1947.

QUINN, VERNON. Picture map geography of Canada and Alaska. With
maps and drawings by Da Osimo. Toronto, 1944. illus. maps. ANR.
Philadelphia, Lippincott, 1954. 6th impr. rev. ed. 122p. illus.
maps. ANR. Philadelphia, Lippincott, 1960. rev. ed. illus.
maps. (Picture Map Geography Series)   3714

R

RAASCH, GILBERT OSCAR, edit. Geology of the Arctic; proceedings
of the first International Symposium on Arctic Geology, held in
Calgary, Alberta, January 11-13, 1960 under the auspices of the
Alberta Society of Petroleum Geologists. Toronto, University of
Toronto Press, 1961. 3 vols. 1,196p. illus. diagrs. graphs,
tables, maps(fold.), bibliog.   3715

RABLING, HAROLD. The story of the Pacific. N. Y., W. W. Norton
& Co., 1965. illus.   3716

RABOT, CHARLES and P. VITTENBURG. Poliarnye strany, 1914-1924 gg.
S kartoi plavanii ėkspeditsii v Severnom Ledovitom okeane s 1914
po 1924 gg. sost. A. M. Lavrovym. [TITLE TR. The polar regions,
1914-1924. With a sailing-chart of the expeditions in the north
polar ocean during the period 1914-1924 by A. M. Lavrov] Leningrad, Redaktsionno-izdatel'skii otdel Morskogo vedomstva, 1924.
182p. pls. table, maps(some fold.). [incls. northern Alaska]
                                                               3717

RADAU, HANNS. Little Fox, Alaskan trapper. London, Abelard-
Schuman, 1963. 158p. illus.   3718

RADAU, HANNS. The last chief; Alaskan trapper. London, Abelard-
Schuman, 1962. 157p. illus.   3719

RADCLIFFE, JESSIE W. Our northernmost possessions. N. Y.,
Woman's Executive Committee of Home Missions, 1894. 14p.   3720

RADCLYFFE, CHARLES ROBERT EUSTACE. Big game shooting in Alaska.
By Captain C. R. E. Radclyffe. London, Rowland Ward Ltd., 1904.
292p. front. pls. ports. map(fold. in pocket)   3721

Radde, G. SEE no. 3775, Regel, E. L.

RADICAL CONTRUCTION on the basis of one sovereign republic with
dependent states and territories, uniformly constituted throughout the public domain, and with the corruptions of party politics
abolished, being an address delivered at an interior town in Nevada, and printed by request as an appeal to all Americans for
new nationality with the South and Russian America, looking also
to union with Mexico and Canada. Sacramento, Russell and Winterburn, printers, 1867. 17p.   3722

RADLOV, LEOPOL'D FEODOROVICH. Leopold Radloff's Wörterbuch der
Kinai-Sprache, herausgegeben von A. Schiefner. [TITLE TR. Leopold Radlov's dictionary of the Kinai language, prepared for publication by A. Schiefner. St. Petersbourg, 1874. x,33p.
(Akademiîa nauk SSSR. Mémoires, serie 7, t. 21, no. 8) [in German and Kinai (Tanaina Indian)]   3723

Rae, John. SEE nos.
    1820, Great Britain. Parl. (Franklin search);
    1823, Great Britain. Parl. (Franklin search);
    2836, M'Clure, R. J. LeM. Melancholy fate ... 1854.

Raĭkov, B. E., tr. SEE no. 338, Baer, Karl Ernst von.

Railroad building in Seward Peninsula ... [1904 ?] SEE
    no. 4799, Western Alaska Construction Co.

Raimond, C. E. SEE nos. 3843-45, Robins, Elizabeth [pseud.]

Raimondi, G., illus. SEE no. 2340, Jenness, D.

RAINE, EDGAR C. Here, there and everywhere; a factual story of
unusual events encountered during forty-seven years of lecturing
at universities, colleges, and clubs. By Edgar C. Raine. N.Y.,
Greenwich Publishers, [c1959] 1st ed. 49p. [incls. lecture-
vignettes of Alaska and other subjects]   3724

RAINE, WILLIAM MacLEOD. The Yukon Trail; a tale of the North.
With illustrations by George Ellis Wolfe. Boston, Houghton Mifflin, [c1917] 324p. front. illus. ANR. N. Y., Grosset and Dunlap, n. d. [c1917] reprint.   3725

RAINEY, FROELICH G. Archaeology in central Alaska. N. Y., American Museum of Natural History, 1939. illus. map, wrps. (Anthropological Papers, vol. 36, pt. 4, pp.351-405)   3726

RAINEY, FROELICH G. Eskimo prehistory; the Okvik site on the
Punuk Islands. N. Y., American Museum of Natural History, 1941.
illus. map, bibliog. wrps. (Anthropological Papers, vol. 37,
pt. 4, pp.453-569)   3727

RAINEY, FROELICH G. The whale hunters of Tigara. N. Y., American Museum of Natural History, 1947. ftntes. wrps. (Anthropological Papers, vol. 41, pt. 2, pp.227-84)   3728

Rainey, Froelich G. SEE ALSO no. 2630,
     Larsen, H. Ipiutak ... 1948.

RAMPART HYDRAULIC MINING CO., operating on Hunter Creek near
Rampart, Alaska. L. A., 1904. 23p.   3729

Ramsden, Evelyn, tr. SEE no. 1658, Freuchen, Peter.

RAND, AUSTIN LOOMER. Mammals of the Yukon. Ottawa, King's
Printer, 1945. 93p. illus. map. (Canada. National Museum.
Bulletin 100, Biol. Ser. no. 29)   3730

RAND McNALLY & CO. Rand McNally guide to Alaska and Yukon for
tourists, investors, homeseekers and sportsmen. With maps and
illustrations. N. Y. and Chicago, Rand McNally & Co., [c1922]
175p. pls. maps(incl. 1 fold. at back)   3731

RAND McNALLY & CO. The Rand-McNally guide to the great Northwest; containing information regarding the states of Montana,
Idaho, Washington, Oregon, Minnesota, North Dakota, Alaska, also
western Canada and British Columbia, with a description of the
route along the Chicago and Northwestern, Union Pacific, Oregon
Short Line, and Oregon River and Navigation Co. railways. Sidney Howard Soule, editor. Chicago, Rand McNally, [c1903] 365p.
front. illus. map.   3732

RAPAPORT, STELLA F. Reindeer rescue. N. Y., Putnam, 1955.
120p. illus. endmaps. [juv. hist. Eskimos, 1898]   3733

Rare Salish blanket. 1926. SEE no. 2096, Heye, Geo. G.

Rasmussen, Knud Johan Victor. [Alphabetical title guide to
     chronological entries]

Across Arctic...3740.   Fra Grønland...3739.
Alaskan Eskimo...3734.   Heldenbuch...3748.
Dansk udlaengsel...3735.   Mindeudgave...3746.
Den store...3742.   Polarforskningens...3747.
Die Gabe...3738.   ...Thulefahrt...3743.
Die Grosse...3745.   The Alaskan Eskimos...3749.
Du Groenland...3741.   The eagle's gift...3737.
Festens gave...3736.   Velikiĭ sannyĭ put' ...3744.

RASMUSSEN, KNUD JOHAN VICTOR. Alaskan Eskimo words; compiled by Knud Rasmussen, edited by H. Ostermann. Copenhagen, Gyldendalske Boghandel, Nordisk Forlag, 1941. 83p. map(fold.) (Report of Fifth Thule Expedition, 1921-24, vol. 3, no. 4)   3734

RASMUSSEN, KNUD JOHAN VICTOR. Dansk udlaengsel; Tale ved Raebild-Festen 4 Juli 1930. [TITLE TR. Danish longing for afar. Speech made at celebration of July 4, 1930, in Raebild] København, Levin and Munksgaard, 1931. 23p. [Vitus Bering]   3735

RASMUSSEN, KNUD JOHAN VICTOR. Festens gave; eskimoiske Alaska-aeventyr, med teyninger of Ernst Hansen. København, Nordisk Forlag, 1929. 207p. front. pls.(col.), map.   3736

   TRANSLATIONS - Festens ... 1929, CHRONOLOGICALLY.

   The eagle's gift, Alaska Eskimo tales. Translated by Isobel
      Hutchison. Illustrated by Ernst Hansen. Garden City, N. Y.,
      Doubleday Doran, 1932. 235p. front. pls.(some col.)   3737

   Die Gabe des Adlers. Eskimoische Maerchen aus Alaska. Frank-
      furt am Main, [1937 ?]   3738

RASMUSSEN, KNUD JOHAN VICTOR. Fra Grønland til Stillehavet, rejser og mennesker; fra 5. Thule-ekspedition 1921-24. [TITLE TR. From Greenland to the Pacific; journeys and people from the Fifth Thule Expedition] København, Gyldendal, 1925. 2 vols. 464p. and 415p. ports. pls. maps. [also in author's "Mindeudgave ... " no. 3746]   3739

   TRANSLATIONS - Fra Grønland ... 1925, CHRONOLOGICALLY.

   Across Arctic America; narrative of the Fifth Thule Expedition.
      N. Y., Putnam, 1927. 388p. front. pls. ports. maps, endmaps.
                                                                3740

   Du Groenland au Pacifique. Paris, 1929.   3741

   Den store slaederejse. [TITLE TR. The great sledge trip]
      København, Gyldendalske Boghandel, Nordisk Forlag, 1932.
      148p. front.(port.), pls. map(fold.) ANR. 1937. [see also
      author's "Velikii sanny put' ..." no. 3744, and his "Die
      Grosse Schlittenreise ..." no. 3745]   3742

   Rasmussen's Thulefahrt; zwei Jahre im Schlitten durch uner-
      forschtes Eskimoland. [TITLE TR. Rasmussen's Thule expedi-
      tion; two years by sledge throughout unexplored Eskimoland.
      Edited by Friedrich Sieburg] Frankfurt am Main, Societats-
      verlag, 1934. 346p. illus. maps.   3743

Velikiĭ sannyĭ put'; 18,000 kilometrov po neissledovannym
oblastĭām arkticheskoĭ Ameriki. Perevod s datskogo A. V. Ganzen pod red. i s predisloviam M. A. D'ĭākonova. [TITLE TR.
The great sledge trip; 18,000 km. in unexplored areas of the
Arctic America. Translated from Danish by A. V. Ganzen; preface by the editor M. A. D'ĭākonov] Leningrad, Izd-vo Glavsevmorputi, 1935. 250p. illus. map. ANR. WITH TITLE Velikiĭ
sannyĭ put'. Perevod s datskogo A. V. Ganzen. Predislovie i
primechanĭā L. A. Fainberga. [TITLE TR. The great sledge
trip. Translated from Danish by A. V. Ganzen. Preface and
notes by L. A. Fainberg] Moskva, Gos. izd-vo geograf. lit-ry,
1958. 182p. illus. map. (Puteshestvĭā, priklĭūchenĭā,
fantazĭā) [cf no. 3742]   3744

Die Grosse Schlittenreise; mit einer Einführung; Knud Rasmussen, ein Heldenleben der Arktis, von Aenne Schmücker. [TITLE
TR. The great sledge trip; with an introduction, Knud Rasmussen, the life of an Arctic hero, by Aenne Schmücker]
Essen, H. V. Chamier, 1946. 245p. pls. port. map(fold.)
[cf no. 3742]   3745

RASMUSSEN, KNUD JOHAN VICTOR. Mindeudgave; udgivet af Peter
Freuchen, Therkel Mathiassen, Kaj Birket-Smith. [TITLE TR.
Memorial edition; edited by Peter Freuchen, Therkel Mathiassen,
Kaj Birket-Smith] København, Gyldendal, 1934-35. 3 vols. 348p.,
416p. and 393p. pls. diagrs. maps(some fold.) [vol. 2 contains
author's "Fra Grønland til Stillehavet ... " no. 3739]   3746

RASMUSSEN, KNUD JOHAN VICTOR. Polarforskningens saga. [TITLE TR.
The saga of polar exploration] By Knud Rasmussen. København,
C. Erichsen, 1930-32. 398p. maps, index. [vol. 6 of "Jordens
erobring ... " 1930-32, edited by Aage Krarup-Nielsen, see
no. 2530]   3747

TRANSLATION - Polarforskningens ... 1930-32.

Heldenbuch der Arktis; Entdeckungsreisen zum Nord un Südpol.
[TITLE TR. Book of heroes of the Arctic] Leipzig. F. A.
Brockhaus, 1933. 318p. illus. maps.   3748

RASMUSSEN, KNUD JOHAN VICTOR. The Alaskan Eskimos, as described
in the posthumous notes of Dr. Knud Rasmussen, by H. Ostermann.
Edited after the latter's death with the assistance of E. Holtved.
Translated from the Danish by W. E. Calvert. Copenhagen, Gylden-
dalske Boghandel, Nordisk Forlag, 1952. 291p. illus. ports.
(Report of Fith Thule Expedition, 1921-24, vol. 10, no. 3) 3749

Rasmussen, Knud Johan Victor. SEE ALSO nos.
    233, American Geog. Soc. Problems polar research. 1928;
    431, Bauer, H. Ein Leben für die Eskimo ... 1960;
    2530, Krarup-Nielsen, A., edit. Jordens erobring ... 1930-32.

Rathbun, M. J. SEE no. 1950, Harriman Alaska Exped. 1899.

RAUSCH, ROBERT LLOYD. Notes on the Nunamiut Eskimo and mammals of the Anaktuvuk Pass region, Brooks Range, Alaska. Montreal, 1951. 50p. (reprint from Arctic, vol. 4, no. 3, 1951)   3750

RAUSCH, ROBERT LLOYD. Observations on a cyclic decline of lemmings (*Lemmus*) on the Arctic coast of Alaska during the Spring of 1949. Montreal, 1950. 12p. (reprint from Arctic, vol. 3, no. 3, 1950)   3751

RAUSCH, ROBERT LLOYD. On the status of some Arctic mammals. Montreal, 1953. 58p. (reprint from Arctic, vol. 6, no. 2, 1952)
          3752

Rausch, Robert Lloyd, co-auth. SEE ALSO nos.
    2574, Kurten, B. Biometric compar. ... 1959;
    4001, Schiller, E. L. Mammals Katmai ... 1956.

RAVENHILL, ALICE. A corner stone of Canadian culture; an outline of the arts and crafts of the Indian tribes of British Columbia. Victoria, B. C., King's Printer, Photo Offset by Don McDiarmid, 1944. 103p. pls. bibliog. (Canada. British Columbia Provincial Museum Occas. Papers, no. 5) [incls. Haida and Tlingit]   3753

RAY, DOROTHY JEAN. Artists of the tundra and the sea. Seattle, University of Washington Press, 1961. 170p. photos, sketches, map, append. bibliog. [Eskimo ivory carving]   3754

RAY, DOROTHY JEAN. Eskimo masks; art and ceremony. Seattle, University of Washington Press, 1967. pls.(some col.), map, bibliog. index.   3755

RAYMOND AND WHITCOMB CO. A series of summer and autumn tours to Alaska, the Pacific Northwest, the Yellowstone Park, Utah, Colorado, and California. Season of 1902. Boston, Raymond and Whitcomb Co., 1902. 104p. ANR. ... Season of 1907. Boston, 1907. 112p.   3756

RAYMOND AND WHITCOMB CO. Alaska, California, the Yellowstone. Tours. 1924. Boston, Raymond and Whitcomb Co., 1925. 59p. illus.   3757

RAYMOND AND WHITCOMB CO. Raymond and Whitcomb land cruises; Canadian Rockies, Alaska National Parks ... Summer 1930. Boston and N. Y., Raymond and Whitcomb Co., 1930. 112p. illus.   3758

RAYMOND AND WHITCOMB CO. Spring tour ... 1906. Boston, Raymond and Whitcomb Co., 1906. 16p. ANR. Spring tour ... 1907. Boston, 1907. 16p.   3759

RAZIN, A. Otkrytie Ameriki. [TITLE TR. Discovery of America]
St. Petersburg, M. O. Wolf, 1860. 272p. pls. maps. [a child's
history, incls. Aleutian Islands] 3760

REA, ELLA M. Castaways of the Yukon. Boston, Meador Publishing
Co., 1936. 298p. front.(port.) [fict. - has introductory poem
by William Yanert of Purgatory] 3761

READ, FRANCIS W. G. I. Parson. N. Y., Morehouse-Gorham Co.,
1945. 117p. [Aleutian Islands in World War II] 3762

READ, J. E. Nansen in the frozen world ... followed by a brief
history of the principal earlier Arctic explorations from the
Ninth century to the Peary expedition, including Cabot, Frobisher,
Bering, Sir John Franklin, Kane, Hayes, Hall, Nordenskjold, Nares,
Schwatka, DeLong, Greely and others. Philadelphia, A. J. Holman
Co., 1897. 560p. front.(port.), illus. 3763

Ready reference ... Klondyke ... 1897. SEE no. 3156,
Montague, Philip S.

THE REASONS WHY NOME, ALASKA is entitled to a harbor and breakwa-
ter. [Nome ?], 1915. 16p. 3764

REAT, LORRAINE. Alaskan days. By Loraine Reat. Seattle, Far-
west, print., [c1944] (45)p. illus. wrps. [photos with captions, no text, has cover title "Alaskan pages"] 3765

Reay, Raphael M., illus. SEE no. 2758, London, Jack.

RECENT POLAR VOYAGES: a record of discovery and adventure, from
the search after Franklin to the British Polar Expedition, 1875-
76. London, T. Nelson & Sons, [187_ ?] pls. map(fold.) 3766

Reck, Franklin M., co-auth. SEE no. 2299, Irwin, David.

REDDING, ROBERT H. Aluk, an Alaskan caribou. Garden City, N. Y.,
Doubleday & Co., 1967. 1st ed. 107p. illus. by Kiyoaki Komoda.
3767

REDDING, ROBERT H. Mara, the weasel. Garden City, N. Y., Doubleday & Co., 1968. 1st ed. 138p. illus. by Kiyoaki Komoda. 3768

REDDING, ROBERT H. North to the wilderness; the story of an
Alaskan boy. Garden City, N. Y., Doubleday & Co., 1970. 1st ed.
187p. endmaps. 3769

REED, CHARLES K. Western bird guide; birds of the Rockies and
west to the Pacific, illustrated by Chester A. Reed, Harry F.
Harvey, R. I. Brasher. Worcester, Mass., 1913. 255p. front.
(col.), illus.(some col.) ANR. Garden City, N. Y., Doubleday,
1917. 252p. illus. (Pocket Nature Series) 3770

REED, CHESTER ALBERT. North American birds eggs. N. Y., Doubleday Page, 1904. 356p. pls. [Alaskan eggs noted]   3771

Reed, Chester Albert, illus. SEE ALSO no. 3770,
    Reed, Chas. K. Western bird guide ... 1913.

REED, ELMER. The Kobuk maiden and other Alaska sourdough verses.
A collection of Alaska verses compiled from newspapers published
in the Territory from 1866 to 1933. Dedicated to the pioneers of
Alaska, empire builders of the Northland. Juneau, Elmer Reed,
[1933 ?]   3772

REED, JOHN CALVIN and J. C. HARMS. Rates of tree growth and
forest succession in the Anchorage-Matanuska Valley area. Montreal, 1956. illus. diagrs. graphs, textmap, ref. (reprint
from Arctic, vol. 9, no. 4, 1956. pp.239-48)   3773

REED, JOHN and H. S. BOSTOCK. Research in geology and geomor-
phology in the North American Arctic and Subarctic. Montreal,
1955. ref. (reprint from Arctic, vol. 7, no.3-4, 1954. pub. in
1955. pp.129-40) [Alaska, Yukon and N. W. T. in Canada)   3774

Reeve, Robert. SEE nos.
    1218, Day, Beth. Glacier pilot ... 1957;
    3658, Potter, J. Flying frontiersmen. 1956.

REGEL, E. L. and FERDINAND von HERDER. Plantae Raddeanae (G.
Radde: Reisen in den Süden von Ost-Sibirien im Auftrage der
Kaiserlichen russischen geographischen Gesellschaft ausgeführt in
den Jahren 1855-59; durch Botanische Abteilung, Nachträge zur
Flora der Gebiete des Russischen Reichs östlich vom Altai bis
Kamtschatka und Sitka) [1862-87] vols. 1-4.   3775

Reichelderfer, F. W. Meteorological services in Alaska. Montreal, 1948. 8p. (reprint from Arctic, vol. 1, no. 1, 1948)   3776

Reid, Bill, illus. SEE no. 1960, Harris, Christie.

REID, CHARLES F. Education in the Territories and outlying
possessions of the United States. N. Y., Columbia University
Press, 1940. 593p. bibliog. (Columbia University. Teacher's
College, Contribution to Education, no. 825) [author's Ph.D.
thesis]   3777

Reid, Robert Allan, photog. SEE no. 154, Alaska-Yukon-Pacific
    Exposition. One hundred and fifty views... 1909.

REID, VIRGINIA HANCOCK. The purchase of Alaska; contemporary
opinion. By Virginia Reid Hancock. [Long Beach, printed by
Press-Telegram, 1939] 134p. bibliog. ANR. 1940.   3778

452

REID, W. A. Chips from the ship's log of the "Helen Gould," the
Y.M.C.A. launch of the Yukon. no pl., [1906 ?] 47p. illus.3779

Reis naar de noord-west kust ... 1795. SEE no. 3652,
    [Portlock, N. and Geo. Dixon]

Reise nach dem Stillen Ocean ... 1785. SEE no. 1024,
    [Cook, James and James King]

REISEN NACH DER NORDWESTLICHEN KUSTE von Amerika von dem kapi-
tainen Meares, Dixon, Portlak, u. a. Ein Auszug aus der Gros-
seren sammlung dieser reisen für liebhaber und lesekabinete.
Nurnberg, E. O. Grattenauer, 1795. 440p.   3780

Relacion del viage hecho por las goletas *Sutil* y *Mexicana* ...
    1802. SEE no. 1676, [Galiano, A. D.]

RELATION ABREGEE DU VOYAGE DE LA PEROUSE, pendant les annees
1785, 86, 87, et 1788; pour faire suite a l'abrege ... de l'histoire generale des voyages, par Laharpe; avec portrait figures
et carte. Leipsick, 1799. 562p. pls. map(fold.)   3781

Remarks and conjectures ... 1780. SEE no. 679, [Brooks, R. ?]

Remarks in support ... 1753. SEE no. 3049, [Mead, Bradock]

[Remington, Chas. Henry] SEE no. 1071, "Copper River Joe"

RENDAHL, HJALMAR. Fische aus dem östlichen Sibirischen Eismeer
und dem Nordpazifik. [TITLE TR. Fishes of the East Siberian Sea
and North Pacific] [Stockholm, 1931] 81p. tables, diagrs.
(Arkhiv för zoologi. Bd. 22A, no. 10) [incls. those of Bering
Strait and Bering Sea collected by *Vega* expedition, 1878-79] 3782

Render, Wilhelm, tr. SEE no. 2514, Kotzebue, A. F. F. von.

REPLOGLE, CHARLES. Among the Indians of Alaska. London, Headley
Bros., 1904. 182p. pls. ports.   3783

Reply of Alaska Commercial Co. ... [1887 ?] SEE no. 52,
    Alaska Commercial Co.

Report of Al red B. Iles. 1913. SEE no. 56, Alaska Copper Co.

Report of Alaska-Yukon-Pacific Exposition. State of Washington.
    1910. SEE no. 156, Alaska-Yukon-Pacific Exposition.

Report of Board of Directors ... [1913] SEE no. 526,Bering Sea
    Co.

Report of Legislative Comm. N. Y. 1909. SEE no. 157,
    Alaska-Yukon-Pacific Exposition.

Report on agriculture ... 1967.   SEE no. 3024,
    Matanuska Elec. Assoc.

Report on Jualin Mine ... 1929.   SEE no. 4245,
    Southeastern Alaska Mining Corp.

Report on properties ... 1907.   SEE no. 137,
    Alaska United Copper Exploration Co.

Report on proposed highway ... 1941.   SEE no. 672,
    British Columbia-Yukon-Alaska Highway Commission.

Report to the 25th Legislative Assembly ... [Oregon] 1909.   SEE
    no. 158, Alaska-Yukon-Pacific Exposition.

Report with respect to Yukon ... 1907.   SEE no. 3904,
    [Rowatt, H. H.]

RESEARCH INSTITUTE OF ALASKA, Anchorage.   Alaska survey and re-
port: 1970-71.   Volume 1.   Editors in chief, Stephen M. Brent
and Robert M. Goldberg.   [Anchorage], printed by Pyramid Print.
Co., [c1970]   441p.   graphs, maps, directories, index, wrps.
(The Research Institute of Alaska, Inc. in conjunction with The
Anchorage Daily News)   3784

RESEARCH INSTITUTE OF ALASKA, Anchorage.   Alaska survey and report: 1970-71.   Volume 2.   Edited by Barbara B. Goldberg.
[Anchorage], printed by Pyramid Print. Co., [c1970]   261p. charts,
graphs, map, append. wrps. (The Research Institute of Alaska, Inc.
in conjunction with The Anchorage Daily News)   3785

RESOLUTION REQUESTING GOVERNMENT AID in railroad construction on
Seward Peninsula, passed at a mass meeting of Nome businessmen,
miners and operators on March 14, 1914, at Nome, Alaska. [Nome ?],
1914.   4p.   3786

Resolutions ... 1874.   SEE no. 270, Anti-Monopoly Assoc. Pac.
    Coast.

Resources of Knik ... n. d.   SEE no. 2497, Knik Commercial Club.

RETTIE, JAMES CARDNO and S. MIRICK.   Comparisons of transportation costs for 88 specified commodities between midwestern and
eastern points and Seattle, Washington, or Prince Rupert, British Columbia, between Seattle and various points in Alaska;
between Anchorage, Alaska and Fairbanks, Alaska.   Portland, Ore.,
North Pacific Planning Project, 1944.   10p.   tables, diagrs.
(fold.)   (North Pacific Study [no. 4])   3787

RETTIE, JAMES CARDNO and others.   Population trends, living conditions and employment opportunities in Alaska.   Preliminary
draft.   Portland, Ore., North Pacific Planning Project, 1944.111p.
pls. diagrs. map(fold.) (North Pacific Study [no. 15])   3788

454

RETTIE, JAMES CARDNO and others. Problems in postwar commercial utilization of the Skagway-Whitehorse-Fairbanks petroleum products pipeline system in Alaska. Portland, Ore., North Pacific Planning Project, 1944. 33p. tables, diagr.(fold.), map(fold.) (North Pacific Study [no. 7])   3789

RETTIE, JAMES CARDNO and others. Shipping services in the American North Pacific, United States and Canadian. Part 1. Economic analysis. Preliminary draft. Portland, Ore., North Pacific Planning Project, 1944. 40p. front.(diagr.), tables, map(fold.) (North Pacific Study [no. 8])   3790

RETTIE, JAMES CARDNO and others. Supplement to preliminary memorandum on peacetime use and maintenance of the Alaska Highway. Portland, Ore., North Pacific Planning Project, 1944. 17p. tables. (North Pacific Study [no. 3])   3791

Review of the salmon industry ... 1935. SEE no. 1358, Drumheller, Ehrlichman Co.

REX, ROBERT W. Hydrodynamic analysis of circulation and orientation of lakes in northern Alaska. La Habra, California Research Corporation, 1960. 39p. tables, graphs, diagrs. bibliog.   3792

REX, ROBERT W. Microrelief produced by sea ice grounding in the Chukchi Sea near Barrow, Alaska. Montreal, 1955. 10p. (reprint from Arctic, vol. 8, no. 3, 1955)   3793

REYNOLDS-ALASKA DEVELOPMENT CO. A concrete statement of facts by the President of the company, with Governor Brady's advisement. N. Y., June 30, 1904. 4ℓ .   3794

REYNOLDS-ALASKA DEVELOPMENT CO. Annual report of June 8, 1907 and special report of November 18, 1907. Boston, The Barta Press, 1907.   3795

REYNOLDS-ALASKA DEVELOPMENT CO. The industrial dawn of Alaska. N. Y., 1904.   3796

REYNOLDS, CHARLES. The animal suite of Alaska. Eagle River, Alaska, published by Charles Reynolds, [c1968] (18)p. photos, [words and music of songs for children]   3797

REYNOLDS, JOSEPH W. Reynold's handbook of the mining laws of the United States and Canada; arranged with reference to Alaska and the Northwest Territories ... forms and glossary, parts 1 and 2. Chicago, W. B. Conkey Co., 1898. 359p.   3798

Rezanov, Nikolai Petrovich. SEE nos.
    314, Atherton, G. Rezanov. 1906;
    910, Chevigny, H. Lost empire ... 1937;
    3920, Russell, Thos. C. Langsdorff's narrat. ... 1927.

[RHODES, CHARLES C.] Professor Sonntag's thrilling narrative of the Grinnell Exploring Expedition to the Arctic Ocean in the years 1853, 1854, 1855, in search of Sir John Franklin, under the command of Dr. E. K. Kane, U.S.N., containing the history of all previous explorations of the Arctic Ocean, from the year 1618 down to the present time; showing how far they advanced north-ward, what discoveries they made, and their scientific observa-tions ... With nearly one hundred splendid engravings. Philadel-phia, Cincinnati, J. T. Lloyd, 1857. 176p. front. pls. OTHERS var. editions and issues. [authorship denied by Prof. August Sonntag; book ascribed to Charles C. Rhodes]   3799

RĪABOV, NIKOLAĬ IVANOVICH and M. G. SHTEĬN. Ocherki istoriĭ russkogo Dal'nego Vostoka, xvii-nachalo xx veka. [TITLE TR. Sketches of the history of the Russian Far East, 17th to early 20th centuries] Khabarovsk, Khabarovskoe knizhnoe izd-vo, 1958. 174p. illus. map, bibliog. [much on the Russian-American Co.]
                                                                 3800

RICH, EDWIN ERNEST, edit. Hudson's Bay Company, 1670-1870. Toronto, Macmillan, 1960. 3 vols. 687p,974p. illus. maps(some col.), index.   3801

RICHARDS, EVA LOUISE ALVEY. Arctic mood; a narrative of Arctic adventures. By Eva Alvey Richards. Caldwell, Idaho, Caxton, 1949. [c1949] 282p. photos, drawings, endmaps, addend. [school teacher at village of Wainwright]   3802

RICHARDS, H. G. and R. W. FAIRBRIDGE. Annotated bibliography of Quaternary shorelines 1945-1964. Philadelphia, 1965. 280p. (Academy of Natural Sciences of Philadelphia, Special Pub. no. 6)
                                                                 3803
Richardson, Harold W. SEE no. 632, Bowman, Waldo G.

RICHARDSON, JOHN. Arctic searching expedition; a journal of a boat-voyage through Rupert's Land and the Arctic Sea, in search of the discovery ships under command of Sir John Franklin, with an appendix on the physical geography of North America. By Sir John Richardson. London, Longman, Brown, Green and Longmans, 1851. 2 vols. viii,413p. and vii,426p. pls. map. ANR. N.Y., Harper, 1852. 516p. no pls. or map.   3804

RICHARDSON, JOHN. The Polar regions. By Sir John Richardson. Edinburgh, A. & C. Black, 1861. ix,400p. map(fold.)   3805

Richardson, John. SEE ALSO nos.
    469, Beechey, F. W. Zoology ... voyage ... 1839;
    1633, Franklin, John. Narrat. second exped. ... 1828;
    1820-1, Great Britain. Parl. (Franklin search);
    2432, Kellett, Henry. Zoology voyage ... 1854;
    2910, McIlraith, John. Life of ... 1868.

Richardson, T. J., illus. SEE no. 1913, Hallock, Chas.

RICHET, ETIENNE. Les Esquimaux de l'Alaska. I. (Moeurs et coutumes) Paris, Librairie Littéraire et Scientifique, 1921. 244p. (extracted from Bulletin de la Société Royale de Geographie d'Anvers) 3806

RICHMAN, IRVING BERDINE. California under Spain and Mexico, 1535-1847. A contribution toward the history of the Pacific coast of the United States, basee on original sources ... in the Spanish and Mexican archives and other repositories. With maps, charts, and plans. Boston, Houghton, 1911. 541p. 3807

Richter, C. F., co-auth. SEE no. 1885, Gutenberg, B.

Richter, S., co-auth. SEE no. 2098, Heyerdahl, Thor.

RICKARD, MAXINE ELLIOTT (HODGES). Everything happened to him; by Mrs. "Tex" Rickard with Arch Obeler. N. Y., Stokes, 1936. 368p. front.(port.) 3808

Rickard, "Tex" (George Lewis Rickard) SEE nos.
3808, Rickard, M. E. (H.) Everything happened ... 1936;
3952, Samuels, Chas. Magnificent Rube ... [c1957]

RICKARD, THOMAS ARTHUR. The romance of mining. By T. A. Rickard. Toronto, Macmillan of Canada, 1945.[c1944) reprint. 450p. front. pls. ports. maps. [has chapts. on Alaska and the Klondike] 3809

RICKARD, THOMAS ARTHUR. Through the Yukon and Alaska. By T. A. Rickard. S. F., Mining and Scientific Press, 1909. [c1909] 392p. front. pls. figs. maps, bibliog. index. 3810

Rickard, Thomas Arthur. SEE ALSO no. 4499,
Thomas, Lowell, jr. Trail of '98. [c1962]

RICKER, ELIZABETH M. Seppala, Alaskan dog driver. Boston, Little Brown, 1930. 295p. front. pls. ports. ANR. N. Y., Grosset and Dunlap, n. d. [reprinted Jan. 1931] [biog. Leonhard Seppala of Nome and the Seward Peninsula] 3811

RICKETTS, EDWARD FLANDERS and JOHN CALVIN. Between Pacific tides; an account of the habits and habitats of some five hundred of the common, conspicuous seashore invertebrates of the Pacific Coast between Sitka, Alaska, and northern Mexico. By Edward F. Ricketts and Jack Calvin. Stanford, Stanford University Press, 1939. 320p. pls. diagrs. bibliog. index. ANR. 1948. 2d ed. rev. 365p. pls. diagrs. append. bibliog. index. ANR. 1962. 3rd ed. rev. by Joel W. Hedgpeth. ANR. 1968. 4th ed. rev. by Joel W. Hedgpeth. 614p. 3812

[Rickman, J.]   SEE nos.
     437, [Bayly, Wm.] Orig. astronom. ... 1782;
    1014, [Cook, Jas.] Journal ... 1781;
    1016, [Cook, Jas.] Troisieme voyage ... 1782;
    1017, [Cook, Jas.] Authentic narrat. ... 1783.

RICKS, MELVIN B. Directory of Alaska postmasters and postoffices,
1867-1963. Ketchikan, Tongass Publishing Co., 1965. 72p. front.
illus. wrps.   3813

RICKS, MELVIN B. The earliest history of Alaska. By Melvin B.
Ricks. Contained herein are first English editions of three
Russian works: Shelekhov's voyage to Alaska, 1793 - Berkh's
history of the Aleutian Islands, 1823 - Khlebnikov's life of
Baranov, 1835. Anchorage, Cook Inlet Historical Society, 1970.
[c1963 by Melvin B. Ricks. Pub. 1970 by special permission of
Louise Ricks Wright] ltd. to 300 copies. 64   front. facsim.
endmaps.   3814

RIDGER, ARTHUR LOTON. A wanderer's trail; being a faithful record
of travel in many lands, by A. Loton Ridger ... Illustrated with
sixty reproductions from photographs. N. Y., Holt, 1914. 403p.
front.(port.), pls.   3815

RIDLEY, WILLIAM. Senator MacDonald's misleading account of his
visit to Metlakatla exposed by the Bishop of Caledonia. no pl.,
1882. 12p. [refers to Metlakatla in British Columbia, Canada
prior to move to Annette Island, Alaska in 1887]   3816

RIDLEY, WILLIAM. Snapshots from the North Pacific; letters written by Bishop Ridley of Caledonia, edited by Alice J. Janvrin.
London, Church Missionary Society, 1903. 192p. front.(port.),
illus. map. ANR. 1904. 2d ed.   3817

RIEDER, KEITH KOCH. Cheechako first class. Portland, Maine,
House of Falmouth, 1953. 200p. [autobiog.]   3818

RIEGEL, ROBERT EDGAR and ROBERT G. ATHEARN. America moves west.
By Robert E. Riegel and Robert G. Athearn. N. Y., Holt Rinehart
and Winston, 1964. 4th ed. xiv,651p. illus. maps, bibliog.
[4th ed. incls. refs. to Alaska and Yukon]   3819

RIEHL, HERBERT and C. R. ELFORD. Ocean analysis from coastal
reports. Chicago, University of Chicago, 1943. 18p. figs.
tables, bibliog. (Institute of Meteorology Misc. Report, no. 9)
[Pacific Coast, Alaska and Hawaii]   3820

RIENITS, REX and THEA RIENITS. The voyages of Captain Cook.
London, Paul Hamlyn, 1968. 157p. illus.(some col.), facsims.
maps, index.   3821

RIESENFELD, STEFAN A. Protection of coastal fisheries under international law. Washington, D. C., 1942. 296p. (Carnegie Endowment for International Peace, Division of International Law, Monograph Series, no. 5)   3822

RIGGS, RENÉE COUDERT. Animal stories from Eskimo land; adapted from the original Eskimo stories collected by Dr. Daniel S. Neuman. Illustrated and decorated by George W. Hood. N. Y., F. A. Stokes, 1923. 113p. front.(col.), illus.(col.)   3823

RIGGS, RENÉE COUDERT. Igloo tales from Eskimo land. N. Y., F. A. Stokes, 1928. 132p.   3824

Right way to conserve ... n. d. SEE no. 3350,
    Northern Exploration & Development Co.

Riiser-Larsen, Hj. SEE nos.
    219, Amundsen, R. E. G. Den forste flukt ... 1926;
    2098, Heyerdahl, T. Great Norwegian expeditions. [1955 ?]

RILEY, JANE. The little seal with meal appeal. Minneapolis, T. S. Denison & Co., 1963. illus.   3825

RINFRET, RAOUL. Le Yukon et son or. Montreal, Imprimerie du "Cultivateur," 1898. 89p.   3826

RINK, HINRICH JOHANNES. The Eskimo tribes; their distribution and characteristics, especially as regards language. With a comparative vocabulary and a sketch-map. By Dr. Henry Rink. Copenhagen, C. A. Reitzel, 1887-1891. 2 vols. 163p. and 124p. map. ANR. London, Williams and Norgate, 1887-91. 2 vols. in 1. ANR. London, Longmans, Green, 1891.   3827

Ripley, Rudy J., illus. SEE nos.
    3131, Miller, Mike. Off beaten path ... 1970;
    3132, Miller, Mike. Soapy. 1970.

RISWOLD, MILDRED. Albert, an Eskimo boy. Photos by George Riswold. Anchorage, Alaskan Publishing Co., 1960. 36p. illus. wrps.   3828

Ritualistic ceremony ... 1900. SEE no. 297, Arctic Brotherhood.

Roads of adventure ... 1932. SEE no. 823, Canadian Pac. Ry. Co.

ROBARTS, VICTORIA P. Lets go to Alaska; a factual picture story for young people and travelers. L. A., Wetzel Publishing Co., [c1951] 108p. illus.   3829

RABAU, *Father*. Catholic prayers and hymns in Innuit. Holy Cross, Alaska, October 1899. 21p.   3830

ROBBIN, IRVING. Polar regions how and why book. N. Y., Grosset and Dunlap, 1965. illus. wrps. (Wonder Books)   3831

ROBBINS, LEONARD H. Mountains and men. By Leonard H. Robbins. Illustrated. N. Y., Dodd Mead & Co., 1931. [1931] 324p. front. (pl.), pls. maps, endmaps, index. [Mt. McKinley, pp.72-115 and Mt. Logan, pp.246-60]   3832

Robert de Vaugondy, Didier. SEE nos. 4660-2,
    Vaugondy, Didier Robert de.

ROBERTS, DAVID. Deborah; a wilderness narrative. N. Y., Van-guart Press, 1970. 188p. illus. [climbing east side of Mt. Deborah, 1964, Cantwell-Healy area]   3833

ROBERTS, DAVID. The mountain of my fear. N. Y., Vanguard Press, 1968. photos, maps, glossary, appends. [climbing Mt. Huntington just south of Mt. McKinley]   3834

ROBERTS, LLOYD. Samuel Hearne. Toronto, Ryerson, 1930. 27p. illus. port. (Canadian History Reader)   3835

Roberts, Marjorie, edit. SEE nos.
        42, Alaska Centennial ... [1967];
        61, Alaska earthquake. 1964;
        72, Alaska, land of promise ... 1963;
      1494, Eskimo life in Alaska. 1964;
      4488, This is Alaska ... 1964.

Robertson, A. SEE no. 1950, Harriman Alaska Exped. 1899.

ROBERTSON, DOUGLAS S. To the Arctic with the Mounties. Toronto, Macmillan, 1934. 309p. front. illus. map, index. [pp.237-42, reindeer trek from Alaska to Canada - some other slight mention of Alaska]   3836

ROBERTSON, FRANK C. and BETH KAY HARRIS. Soapy Smith, king of the frontier con men. N. Y., Hastings House, 1961. 244p. illus. photos, bibliog. append. index.   3837

ROBERTSON, JAMES ROOD. A Kentuckian at the Court of the Tsars; the Ministry of Cassius Marcellus Clay to Russia, 1861-1862 and 1863-1869. Berea, Ky., Berea College, 1935.   3838

ROBERTSON, WILLIAM NORRIE. Yukon memories; sourdough tells of chaos and changes in the Klondyke vale. Toronto, Hunter-Rose, 1930. 359p. front.(map), pls. ports. append.   3839

ROBERTSON, WYNDHAM. Oregon, our rights and title; containing an account of the condition of the Oregon Teritory ... statement of the claims of Russia, Spain, Great Britain, and the United States; accompanied with a map prepared by the author. Washington, D. C., Gideon, 1846. 203p. front.(fold. map), tables.   3840

ROBINETTE, ALLAN M., comp. Facts about Cape Nome and its golden sands; a resume of the statements of people who were present at the great placer diggings, from the date of their discovery until the winter of 1899, together with the mining laws in force, processes of mining, names of districts, rivers and creeks embraced therein; routes of travel, rates of fare, equipment needed, and other information of value to every one interested in the Alaskan country. Seattle, Cape Nome Information and Supply Bureau, 1900. 64p. illus. 3841

ROBINETTE, GRADY. Rebel of the Yukon and other writings. [Anchorage ?], by June Robinette, [c1967] 49p. wrps. [poetry and personal experiences] 3842

ROBINS, ELIZABETH [pseud.] Come and find me. Illustrated by E. L. Blumenschein. N. Y., Century Co., 1908. 531p. front. pls. [author is C. E. Raimond (Mrs. G. R. Parkes)] 3843

ROBINS, ELIZABETH [pseud.] Raymond and I. N. Y., Macmillan, 1956. [c1956] 1st print. ANR. London, Hogarth Press, 1956. [autobiog. - author is C. E. Raimond (Mrs. G. R. Parkes)] 3844

ROBINS, ELIZABETH [pseud.] The magnetic North. N. Y., F. A. Stokes, 1904. 417p. front.(fold. map) ANR. London, 1904. 387p. map(fold.) [gold rush - author is C. E. Raimond (Mrs. G. R. Parkes)] 3845

ROBINSON, ELMER. An investigation of the ice fog phenomena in the Alaskan area. Stanford, Calif., Stanford University, Oct. 1952. 24p. tables, refs. (Stanford Research Institute Report, no. 4) ANR. 1953. 28(3)p. illus. text map, diagrs. graphs, tables. (Report no. 5) ANR. May 1953. 11p. illus. refs. (Report no. 7) ANR. Aug. 1953. 17p. diagrs. graphs, tables, refs. (Report no. 8) ANR. May 1954. 65p. illus. text map, diagrs. graphs, tables, refs. (Report no. 15) [Tanana Valley] 3846

ROBINSON, ELMER and others. Field observations and methods relating to ice fog at Eielson Air Force Base, Alaska, December 1952- February 1953. By Elmer Robinson, E. J. Wiggins, W. C. Thuman, J. A. MacLeod and R. W. Gates. Stanford, Calif., Stanford University, February 1954. 99p. illus. diagrs. tables, refs. (Stanford Research Institute Report, no. 13. Sci. Report, no. 4) 3847

ROBINSON, ELMER. Some instances of unstable surface temperature conditions during an Arctic winter. Montreal, 1955. illus. graphs, tables, refs. (reprint from Arctic, vol. 8, no. 3, pp.148-57) [Eielson AFB near Fairbanks, Tanana Valley] 3848

ROBINSON, ELMER and J. A. MacLEOD. Wiresonde observations during 1952-1953 winter at Eielson Air Force Base, Alaska. Stanford, Calif., Stanford University, Jan. 1954. 10p. illus. graphs, table, refs. (Stanford Research Institute Report, no. 12. Sci. Report, no. 3) 3849

Robinson, Elmer, co-auth. SEE no. 4530, Thuman, Wm. C.
   Technique ... determination water in air ... 1953.

ROBINSON, MARGARET KING. Sea temperature in the Gulf of Alaska
and in the Northeast Pacific Ocean, 1941-1952. Berkeley, University of California Press, 1957. vii,98p. illus. chart(fold.),
tables, refs. (Scripps Institution of Oceanography Bulletin,
vol. 7, no. 1. Also published as Contribution from Scripps Institution of Oceanograpy, no. 917)   3850

ROBOLSKY, M. The life, voyages and discoveries of Captain J. C.
Englisches Lesebuch für deutsche Schulen. Quedlinburg, 1864.
[Captain James Cook ?]   3851

Rockwell, Kitty. ("Klondike Kate") SEE nos.
   2806, Lucia, E. Klondike Kate ... 1962;
   4893, Willoughby, B. Alaska holiday. 1940.

RODAHL, KAARE. Eskimo metabolism; a study of racial factors in
basal metabolism. By Kaare Rodahl, M.D. Oslo, Brøgger, 1954.
83p. illus. tables, maps, refs. (Norway. Norsk Polarinstitutt.
Skrifter no. 99) [studies made at Arctic Aeromedical Laboratory,
near Fairbanks - refers to villages of Barter Island, Anaktuvuk
Pass, Kotzebue and Gambell, the latter on St. Lawrence Island]
                                                            3852

RODAHL, KAARE. North, the nature and drama of the polar world.
By Kaare Rodahl, M.D. N. Y., Harper, [c1953] 1st ed. 237p.
pls. endmaps, bibliog. index. ANR. Melbourne, 1954. 224p. photos, bibliog. index. ANR. London, Heinemann, 1954. 224p. photos,
bibliog. index. ANR. [in French] L'archipel flottant(North); preface du Colonel J.-O. Fletcher; traduction de Josette Hesse.
Paris, Arthaud, [c1954] 226p. illus. maps.[Fletcher Ice Island,
cf no. 3857]   3853

RODAHL, KAARE. Nutritional requirements under Arctic conditions.
By Kaare Rodahl, M.D. Oslo, 1960. 58p. tables, refs. (Norway.
Norsk Polarinstitutt. Skrifter no. 118) [studies made at Arctic
Aeromedical Laboratory near Fairbanks]   3854

RODAHL, KAARE. Smilet Folk. By Kaare Rodahl, M.D. [TITLE TR.
The smiling people] Oslo, Gyldendal, 1957. 188p. illus. ports.
map [Eskimos of Kotzebue, others]   3855

RODAHL, KAARE. Studies on the blood and blood pressure in the
Eskimo and the significance of ketosis under Arctic conditions.
By Kaare Rodahl, M.D. Oslo, 1954. 79p. illus. tables, refs.
(Norway. Norsk Polarinstitutt. Skrifter no. 102) [studies
made at Arctic Aeromedical Laboratory near Fairbanks]   3856

RODAHL, KAARE. T-3, beretningen om tre menns eventyrlige opphold på en flytende is-øy ved Nordpolen og om livet i den arktiske verden. By Kaare Rodahl, M.D. [TITLE TR. T-3, account of three men's incredible sojourn on a floating ice island near the North Pole and of life in Arctic regions] Oslo, Gyldendal, Norsk Forlag, 1954. 180p. illus. [cf no. 3853] 3857

RODAHL, KAARE. The last of the few. By Kaare Rodahl, M.D. N.Y., Harper and Row, [c1963] 1st ed. 208p. pls. photos, line drawings by Dorothy Robinson, map(fold. col.), endmaps, index. [Eskimos of Barter Island, Anaktuvuk Pass, Kotzebue, Gambell and the Pribilof Island Aleuts] 3858

RODAHL, KAARE. United States Air Force survival ration studies in Alaska. By Kaare Rodahl, M.D. Montreal, 1950. illus. (reprint from Arctic, Aug. 1950. vol. 3. pp.124-5) [studies made at Arctic Aeromedical Laboratory near Fairbanks] 3859

RODEN, DONALD. London's The call of the wild; also, White fang. N. Y., Monarch Press, 1965. 74p. 3860

RODEN, HENRY. Alaska mining law, Federal and Territorial, covering lode, placer, oil and coal locations, water rights, mill sites and tunnels, with forms and explanations. Juneau, by author, 1950. rev. wrps. ANR. Fairbanks, Jessen's Pub. Co., 1955. 3861

RODEN, HENRY. Compiled laws of Alaska 1933; containing the General Laws of the Territory of Alaska, annotated with decisions of the courts of the Territory of Alaska and the United States. Juneau, [1934 ?] 1,224p. index. 3862

RODEN, HENRY. The Alaska mining law, with explanatory notes, effective July 30, 1913. no pl., 1913. 20p. 3863

RODLI, AGNES SYLVIA. North of Heaven; a teaching ministry among the Alaskan Indians. Chicago, Moody Press, 1963. 180p. [village of Nikolai] 3864

ROGERS, GEORGE WILLIAM. Alaska in transition; the southeast region. Baltimore, Johns Hopkins University Press, 1960. 384p. illus. tables, figs. ftntes. maps(fold.), endmaps, appends. index. (Sponsored by Arctic Institute of North America, and Resources for the Future) 3865

ROGERS, GEORGE WILLIAM. The future of Alaska, economic consequences of statehood. Baltimore, Johns Hopkins Press, 1962. 311p. illus. tables, graphs, bibliog. (Sponsored by Arctic Institute of North America, and Resources for the Future) 3866

ROGERS, LISPENARD [pseud.] On and off the saddle; characteris-
tic sights and scenes from the great Northwest to the Antilles.
By Lispenard Rogers. N. Y., Putnam, 1894. 201p. [author is
Henry E. Smith]   3867

Rogers, Will. SEE no. 3374, O'Brien, P. J.

ROHAN-CSERMAK, G. de. Sturgeon hooks of Eurasia. N. Y., Wenner-
Gren Foundation, 1963. 155p. illus. maps, bibliog. (Viking
Fund. Publications in Anthropology, no. 35) [incls. Alaskan]
                                                                   3868

ROLFE, MARY A. Our national parks. Chicago, Benjamin H. Sanborn,
1928. illus. [reference to Mt. McKinley National Park, pp.157-
197]   3869

ROLFSRUD, ERLING NICOLAI. Brother to the eagle; the story of
Carl Ben Eielson. With a preface by Sir Hubert Wilkins. Alexan-
dria, Minn., Lantern Books, 1952. 181p. illus. endmaps.   3870

ROLLINS, ALICE M. WELLINGTON. From palm to glacier with an interlude; Brazil, Bermuda, and Alaska. N. Y., Putnam, 1892.
145p.   3871

Rollins, Alice M. Wellington. SEE ALSO no. 1113,
    Crane, Alice Rollins [same ?]

ROLT-WHEELER, FRANCIS W. The boy with the U. S. Life-Savers.
With forty-eight illustrations, nearly all from photographs
loaned by bureaus of the U. S. government. Boston, Lothrop, Lee
and Shepard, 1915. 346p. illus. (U. S. Service Series)   3872

ROLT-WHEELER, FRANCIS W. The boy with the U. S. Survey. By
Francis Rolt-Wheeler. With thirty-seven illustrations from pho-
tographs taken by the U. S. Geological Survey. Boston, Lothrop,
Lee and Shepard, [c1909] xii,381(4)p. front.(pl.), pls. (U. S.
Service Series)   3873

Romance of Alaska sealskin. 1954. SEE no. 1618, Fouke Fur Co.

Romance of the Alaska fur seal. 1958. SEE no. 1619, Fouke Fur
    Co.

ROMANO, VINCENZO. Jack London, Firenze, Marzocco-Bemporad, 1952.
31p.   3874

ROMIG, EMILY CRAIG. The life and travels of a pioneer woman in
Alaska. Colorado Springs, privately printed, 1945. 136p. front.
pls. ports. ANR. WITH TITLE A pioneer woman in Alaska. Caldwell,
Idaho, Caxton, 1948. rev. enl. ed. 140p. front. pls. ports. 3875

ROMIG, JOSEPH HERMAN. A medical handbook for missionaries in cold climates. By Dr. Joseph H. Romig. Philadelphia, Boericke and Tafel, 1904. 259p.   3876

ROMIG, JOSEPH HERMAN. Annual report of the Moravian Mission at Bethel, Alaska. By Dr. Joseph H. Romig. Bethlehem, Penna., 1899. (extracted from Proceedings, Society of United Brethren for Propagating the Gospel Among the Heathen, 1899)   3877

ROMIG, JOSEPH HERMAN. The raven of the Eskimos. Colorado Springs, privately printed, 1943. 34p.   3878

Romig, Joseph Herman. SEE ALSO no. 243,
     Anderson, Eva G. Dog-team doctor ... 1940.

ROOSEVELT, THEODORE and others. The deer family. By Theodore Roosevelt, T. S. Van Dyke, D. G. Elliot and A. J. Stone. N. Y., Macmillan, 1902. 334p. illus. by Carl Rungius and others, index.   3879

ROPER, EDWARD. A claim on Klondyke; a romance of the Arctic El Dorado. Edinburgh, W. Blackwood and Sons, 1899. 312(32)p.front. pls. [fict.]   3880

RØRDAM, VALDEMAR. Dansk Liv. [TITLE TR. Danish life] Kjøbenhavn, A. Busck, Nyt Nordisk Forlag, 1938. 159p. [incls. expeditions of Vitus Bering]   3881

ROSCOE, W. F. Ice bound. N. Y., Vantage Press, 1954. 132p. pls. [fict. account of commercial salmon fishing in Alaska] 3882

Roseberry, Vida M. SEE no. 2255, Illustrated hist. Indian baskets ... 1915.

ROSENBERG, FRANTZ. Big game shooting in British Columbia and Norway. London, M. Hopkinson & Co., 1928. 261p. front.(port.), pls. index. [also incls. Alaska]   3883

ROSENBERG, FRANTZ. Storvildtjagt; Norge og Alaska. Oslo, Gyldendal, Norsk Forlag, 1926. 192p. pls.   3884

Rosin, A., tr. SEE no. 1233, d'Harcourt, Raoul.

ROSS, EDWARD A. Proposed cession of Alaska panhandle to Canada by sale or exchange. no pl., 1914. 10p.   3885

ROSS, EMILY LINDSLEY. Aaron Ladner Lindsley, founder of Alaska missions and leader of other great enterprises in the Northwest. By Mrs. J. Thorburn Ross. Published with the approval of the Board of National Missions in the U. S. A. no pl., [ca 1910 ?] ANR. Seattle, Shorey Book Store, 1964. facsim. reprint. (9)p. port. [reprint has leaflet(fold. in pocket, by Rev. Edgar P. Hill) 3886

Ross, Emily Lindsley. SEE ALSO nos.
  2105, Hill, Edgar P. Rev. Aaron L. Lindsley ... 1964;
  2717, Lindsley, A. L. Sketches ... so. Alaska. [1879 ?]

Ross, James Clark. SEE no. 703, Browne, Wm. H. J.

ROSS, SHERWOOD. Gruening of Alaska; the dynamic career of a remarkable U. S. Senator. N. Y., Best Books, [c1968] 224p. photos,
index, paperback. (Best Books, no. 95-8062)   3887

ROSSIĬSKO-AMERIKANSKAĬA KOLONIĬA. Otchet Komiteta ob ustroĭstve
Russkikh Amerikanskikh Koloniĭ. [TITLE TR. Report of Committee
on the establishment of the Russian-American colonies] St.
Petersburg, 1863. [cf no. 4619]   3888

ROSSIĬSKO-AMERIKANSKAĬA KOLONIĬA. Prilozheniĭa k otchet Komiteta
ob ustroĭstve Russkikh Amerikanskikh Koloniĭ. [TITLE TR. Supplement to the report of the Committee on the establishment of
the Russian-American colonies] St. Petersburg, 1863.   3889

ROSSIĬSKO-AMERIKANSKAĬA KOMPANIĬA. K istoriĭ Rossiĭsko-Amerikanskoĭ Kompaniĭ. [TITLE TR. Contribution to the history of the
Russian-American Company] Krasnoyarsk, 1957. 180p.(Krasnoĭar-
skiĭ kraevoĭ gosudarstvennyĭ arkhiv)   3890

ROSSIĬSKO-AMERIKANSKAĬA KOMPANIĬA. Otchet Rossiĭsko-Amerikanskaĭa
Kompaniĭa za 1852 god. [TITLE TR. Report of the Russian-American
Company by the governors. For the year 1852] St. Petersburg,
Pechatano v Tipografiĭ Shtava Inspektora po Intsenornoĭ chasti,
1853. OTHERS var. years, var.p.   3891

Rossiĭsko-Amerikanskaĭa Kompaniĭa. SEE ALSO no. 5023,
    Zavalishin, D. I.

ROSSITER, HARRIET. Alaska calling; a laugh on every page. By
Harriet Rossiter. N. Y., Vantage Press, [c1954] 200p. front.
(pl.), sketches, pls. ports. endmaps, index.   3892

ROSSITER, HARRIET. Indian legends from the land of Al-ay-ek-sa.
Ketchikan, Ketchikan Alaska Chronicle, E. C. Howard, pub., 1925.
(27)p. front. illus. map, wrps.   3893

ROSSITER, HARRIET. The twins birthday surprise. N. Y., Vantage
Press, 1954. 40p.   3894

ROSSMAN, EARL. Black sunlight; a log of the Arctic. N. Y. and
London, Oxford University Press, 1926. 231p. front. pls. ports.
map(fold.) [southeast Alaska as well as Barrow and Wainwright in
the Arctic]   3895

ROST, ERNEST CHRISTIAN. Mount McKinley, its bearing on the polar controversy; a brief review of attempts - successful and otherwise - to reach the top of the continent and a few logical deductions therefrom. Washington, D. C., printed by J. D. Milane & Sons, 1914. 33p. illus. wrps. [defends Frederick Cook] 3896

ROSTEN, NORMAN. The big road; a narrative poem. N. Y., Rinehart & Co., 1946. 8,xv-xvii,232p. illus. maps. 3897

ROSTLUND, ERHARD. Freshwater fish and fishing in native North America. Berkeley, University of California Press, 1952. 313p. fig. tables, maps, bibliog. index. (University of California Publications in Geography, vol. 9) [incls. Arctic] 3898

Roswig, B. B., co-auth. SEE no. 250, Anderson, R. M.

ROUCH, JULES ALFRED PIERRE. Les mers polaires. [TITLE TR. The Polar seas] Paris, Flammarion, 1954. 251p. (Bibliothèque de philosphie scientifique) [has separate chapters on Bering Sea and Arctic Ocean] 3899

ROULET, MARY F. N. Our little Alaskan cousin. Boston, L. C. Page, 1907. 138p. 3900

ROUQUETTE, LOUIS-FREDERIC. Le grand silence blanc. Roman vecu d'Alaska. Paris, Ferenczi, [1921] ANR. [Paris], Editions Mornay, 1928. ANR. Paris, Aux Editions Arcen-Ciel, [1944] ANR. Paris, Les Editons de la Nouvelle France, [1945] ANR. Paris, Editions G. P. 1951. ANR. [in Eng.] The great white silence; translated from the French by O. W. Allen and A. Le Rebeller; decorations by Ludmila Tchirikova. N. Y., Macmillan, 1930. 236p. illus. 3901

Rouquette, Louis-Frederic. The great white silence ... SEE no. 3901.

ROUSE, J. J. Pioneer work in Canada, practically presented by J. J. Rouse. Kilmarnock, Scotland, Ritchie, [1935 ?] 182p. front.(port.) 3902

Roustan, L., tr. SEE no. 3306, Niedieck, Paul.

ROVIER, VICTOR. Pioneer Pete's Christmas at Ophir Creek. By Victor Rovier. no pl., by Victor Rovier, 1963. 14p. sketches. [Council, near Nome] 3903

[ROWATT, H. H.] Report with respect to the Yukon Territory, 1907. 20p. (Canada. Department of the Interior) 3904

Rowe, Peter Trimble. SEE nos.
1104, Cox, Mary. Peter Trimble Rowe. 1959;
2338, Jenkins, Thos. Man of Alaska ... 1943;
4781, Weems, C. Bishop of Arctic. 1912.

ROWLEY, DIANA, edit. Arctic research; the current status of research and some immediate problems in the North American Arctic and Subarctic. Edited by Diana Rowley. Montreal, Arctic Institute of North America, 1955. 261p. illus. port. maps(incl. 1 fold.) (Special Publication, no. 2, Dec. 1955. Also published as: Arctic. 1954. vol. 7, nos. 3-4, 1955)   3905

ROY, ELIZABETH LILLIAN. Polly in Alaska. Illustrated by H. S. Barbour. N. Y., Grosset and Dunlap, n. d. [c1926] 274p. pls. (The Polly Brewster Series)   3906

ROYAL GEOGRAPHIC SOCIETY, London. Arctic geography and ethnology. A selection of papers on Arctic geography and ethnology. Reprinted and presented to the Arctic Expedition of 1875, by the president, council, and fellows of the Royal Geographic Society. London, J. Murray, 1875. 292p. illus. maps(fold.) [incls. reports by Collinson on Bering Strait and by J. Simpson on western Eskimos]   3907

Royal Society of Canada, Ottawa. SEE no. 2201, Howay, F. Wm.

ROYAL, CHARLES ELLIOTT. The trail of a sourdough; rhymes and ballads. Toronto, McClelland and Stewart, 1919. 168p.   3908

RUBAKIN, NIKOLAĬ ALEXSANDROVICH. Na plavaĭushchikh l'dinakh po Ledovitomu okeanu; so stat'eĭ N. V. Pinegina "Puteshestviĭa k severnomu poliŭsu." [TITLE TR. On floating ice in the Arctic Ocean; with an article by N. V. Pinegin "Travels to the North Pole."] Moskva-Leningrad, Gosud. izd-vo, 1927. 80p. illus. [Pinegin's "Travels ... " incls. DeLong, Amundsen, others]   3909

RUDENKO, SERGEI IVANOVICH. Drevniĭaĭa Kul'tura Beringova moriĭa i eskimosskaĭa problema. Pod obshcheĭ red, L. S. Berga i v. I. Ravdonikasa. [TITLE TR. The ancient culture of the Bering Sea and the Eskimo problem] Moskva-Leningrad, Izdatel'stvo Glavsevmorputi, 1947. 131p. illus. tables, bibliog. [for Eng. tr. see no. 3911]   3910

RUDENKO, SERGEI IVANOVICH. The ancient culture of the Bering Sea and the Eskimo problem. Translated by Paul Tolstoy. Toronto, University of Toronto Press, 1961. 186p. illus. pls. plans, map. (Published for Arctic Institute of North America. Anthropology of the North, Translations from Russian Sources, no. 1) [tr. of no. 3910]   3911

Rüdiger, H., edit. SEE no. 4322, Stefansson, V.

Rudkin, Chas. N., tr. SEE no. 2621, La Perouse, J. F. G. de.

RUE, LEONARD LEE, III. The world of the red fox. N. Y., Lippincott, [c1969] 1st ed. 204p. front. illus. append. bibliog. index. (Living World Books, John K. Terres, Editor) [many scattered refs. Mt. McKinley Pk. - text and photos by author]   3912

RUGGIERI, VINCENZO. Du Transvaal a l'Alaska. Traduit de l'Italien et suivi d'un vocabulaire esquimeau. Paris, Plon-Nourrit et Cie, 1901. 291p. 3913

Rungius, Carl, illus. SEE nos.
 452, Beach, Wm. N. In shadow Mt. McKinley. 1931;
 3879, Roosevelt, T. Deer family. 1902;
 4099, Sheldon, Chas. Wilderness No. Pac. islands. 1912.

Ruprecht, F. J., co-auth. SEE no. 3654, Postels, A.

Russell and Winterburn, printers. SEE no. 3722,
 Radical construction ... Russ. Amer. ... 1867.

RUSSELL, ANDREW. Grizzly country. By Andy Russell. N. Y., Knopf, 1967. 302p. photos. [Alaska and western Canada] 3914

RUSSELL, FREDERICK STRATTEN and CHARLES MAURICE YONGE. The seas; our knowledge of life in the sea and how it is gained. By F. S. Russell and C. M. Yonge. London and N. Y., Warne, [1963] xiii, 376p. illus.(some col.), diagrs. maps(some col.), bibliog. AN EARLIER ED. N. Y., Frederick Warne & Co., 1928. 3915

RUSSELL, ISRAEL COOK. Glaciers of North America; a reading lesson for students of geography and geology. Boston, Ginn & Co., 1897. 210p. illus. diagrs. text maps. ANR. London, 1897. 111p. illus. photos, maps. [Alaskan glaciers on pp.74-130] 3916

RUSSELL, ISRAEL COOK. Volcanoes of North America; a reading lesson for students of geography and geology. N. Y., Macmillan, 1897. 346p. illus. [some refs. to Alaska] 3917

RUSSELL, JOSEPH ALBERT, edit. Industrial operations under extremes of weather. Boston, American Meteorological Society, 1957. 121p. diagr. graphs, tables, maps, refs. (Meteorological Monographs, vol. 2, no. 9. May 1957) [discussion of Alaska Railroad operations and oil field problems at Pt. Barrow] 3918

RUSSELL, TERRY and RENNY RUSSELL. On the loose. S. F., Sierra Club, [c1967] 122p. photos(some col.) 3919

RUSSELL, THOMAS C., edit. Langsdorff's narrative of the Rezanov voyage to Nueva California in 1806, being that division of Dr. Georg H. von Langsdorff's *Bemerkungen auf einer Reise um die Welt*, when, as personal physician, he accompanied Rezanov to Nueva California from Sitka, Alaska, and back; an English translation revised, with the Teutonisms of the original Hispaniolized, Russianized, or Anglicized, by Thomas C. Russell; illustrated with portraits and map. S. F., Thomas C. Russell, 1927. ltd. ed. of 260 copies. 158p. front. pls.(incl. 1 dble.), ports. facsims. maps(incl. 1 fold.) (Russell California Reprints) 3920

RUSSELL, THOMAS C., edit. The Rezanov voyage to Nueva California in 1806; the report of Count Nikolai Petrovich Rezanov of his voyage to that provincia of Nueva Espana from New Archangel; an English translation revised and corrected, with notes, etc. by Thomas C. Russell. Annotated, the Count Rezanov; the Russian American Company; the Krusenstern expedition; the settlements in Alaska; the Dona Concepcion Arguello; her family, her romantic and pathetic history ... S. F., Thos. C. Russell, 1926. ltd. ed. of 260 copies. 104p. front.(port.), pls. (Russell California Reprints)   3921

Russell, Thomas C. SEE ALSO no. 4162,
    Simpson, Geo. Narrative voyage ... 1930.

RUSSELL, THOMAS H. The illustrious life and work of Warren G. Harding, twenty-ninth president of the United States. Chicago, 1923. [Chapt. 19, Harding's trip to Alaska]   3922

Russian American Colony. SEE nos. 3888-89,
    Rossiĭsko-Amerikanskaĭa Koloniĭa.

Russian American Company. SEE nos. 3890-91,
    Rossiĭsko-Amerikanskaĭa Kompaniĭa.

RUSTGARD, JOHN. Home rule for Alaska; a discussion of legislation and legislators; speech delivered at Anchorage, Alaska, September 30, 1927. Juneau, 1927. 39p.   3923

RUTZEBECK, HJALMAR. Alaska man's luck; a romance of fact. N. Y., Boni and Liveright, 1920. 260p. endmaps. ANR. 1925.   3924

RUTZEBECK, HJALMAR. My Alaskan idyll. N. Y., Boni and Liveright, 1920. 296p. ANR. 1922. [autobiog.]   3925

RYAN, JOHN JOSEPH. The *Maggie Murphy*. N. Y., W. W. Norton & Co., [c1951] 1st ed. 224p. [commercial fishing, based in Ketchikan]   3926

Ryan, John Joseph. SEE ALSO no. 4243, Sourdough Jack.

RYDELL, CARL. Adventures of Carl Rydell; the autobiography of a seafaring man. Edited by Elmer Green. London, E. Arnold & Co., 1924. 308(16)p. front.(port.), pls. map. [expanded version of no. 3928]   3927

RYDELL, CARL. On Pacific frontiers; a story of life at sea and in outlying possessions of the United States. By Captain Carl Rydell. Edited by Elmer Green. Illustrated with drawings by H. Boylston Dummer. Yonkers-on-Hudson, World Book Co., 1924. 267p. front. sketches, map. (Pioneer Life Series) [also issued with title "Adventures of Carl Rydell ... " See no. 3927]   3928

RYDER, CHARLES J. Alaska - history - condition - needs. N. Y.,
American Missionary Association, n. d. 4p. 3929

RYDER, THEODORE. Compilation and study of ice thicknesses in the
Northern Hemisphere, 1952-1953. N. Y., American Geographical
Society, 1953. 2 vols. 20p. and 59(26)p. graphs, map, bibliog.
supplements. [data for Arctic stations in Alaska incl.] 3930

RYLEEF, K. F. Polnoe sobranie sochineniĭ. [TITLE TR. Complete
collected works] Leningrad, Akademiiā nauk SSSR, 1934. [Russian
American Co.] 3931

RYLEEF, K. F. Sochineniiā i perepiska. [TITLE TR. Works and
correspondence. Second edition] K. F. Ryleeva, edited by P.
Efremov. St. Petersburg, 1874. [Russian-American Co.] 3932

S

S, J. B., edit. SEE no. 4332, Steller, Geo. W.

S., J. L. Neue Nachrichten von denen neuentdekten Insuln in der
See Zwischen Asien und Amerika ... verfasset von J. L. S. Hamburg und Leipzig, Bey Friedrich Ludwig Gieditsch, 1776. 173p.
[variously ascribed to Johann Ludwig Schultz, Jean-Benoît Schérer,
August Ludwig Schlözer, or J. L. Schulz(e)] 3933

S. S. S. R. SEE nos. 4615-19, U. S. S. R.

S, Z. Ozhizni i podvigakh Innokentiiā; sostavleno po knigie
I. P. Barsukova. [TITLE TR. On the life and work of Innocent;
compiled from I. P. Barsukov's book] St. Petersburg, A. Kastan-
skiĭ & Co., 1893. 36p. pls. [refers to *Father* Veniaminov,
Metropolitan of Moscow] 3934

SABIN, EDWIN LEGRAND. Klondike pardners; wherein are told the
haps and mishaps of two fortune-seekers who in the Klondike stampede hit the trail of rain and mud, snow and ice, mountains,
lakes, and rivers, for six hundred miles to that rainbow's end in
a frozen land of "gold is where you find it" if you don't quit
first. By Edwin L. Sabin with some illustrations by Lyle Justis.
Philadelphia, Lippincott Co., 1929. [c1929] 286p. front.(col.),
illus.(some col.), endmaps. (The American Trail Blazers Series)
3935

SABINE, BERTHA W. A summer trip among Alaskan missions. By
Bertha W. Sabine, Deaconess. Hartford, Church Missions Pub. Co.,
[ca 1910 ?] (Church in Story and Pageant) [Episcopalian missionary at Anvik in early 1900s] 3936

SACHOT, OCTAVE L. M. La Sibérie orientale et l'Amérique Russe,
le pole nord et ses habitants, recits et voyages. Paris, P. Ducrocq, 1875. 370p. map. ANR. Paris, 1883. 266p. map. 3937

Sage, W. N.   SEE no. 265, Angus, H. F., edit.

SAILER, REECE IVAN.   Invertebrate research in Alaska.   Montreal,
1954.   9p.   (reprint from Arctic, vol. 7, nos. 3-4, 1954)   3938

Sailing sheltered seas ... 1933.   SEE no. 121, Alaska Steamship
    Co.

SAINT ANN'S ACADEMY.   Saint Ann's in British Columbia and Alaska,
1853-1924.   Victoria, British Columbia, n. d.   106p.   ports. 3939

SAINT GEORGE and CATHCART.   Alaska mining laws passed by the
Alaska Territorial Legislature, 1915.   Signed by the Governor,
April 23, 1915.   Effective July 22, 1915.   Fairbanks, News Miner
Press, 1915.   15p.   3940

Saint Herman.   SEE no. 1534, *Father* Herman, Russ.
    missionary to Alaska.   n. d.

Saint John, G. A., co-auth.   SEE no. 4531, Thuman, Wm.

SAINT JOSEPH'S HOSPITAL, Women's Auxiliary, Fairbanks.   "Northern
nuggets"   Recipes from members and friends of the Women's Auxiliary of St. Joseph's Hospital, Fairbanks, Alaska.   Kansas City,
Mo., Bev-Ron Pub. Co., Dec. 1961.   1st ed. of 250 copies.   ANR.
Feb. 1962.   2d ed. of 500 copies.   ANR. May 1962.   3rd ed. of
1000 copies.   96(8)p.   illus. index, wrps. ringbound.   3941

Saint Mark's kloosh yiem ... 1912.   SEE no. 668, British
    & Foreign Bible Soc.

SAINT MATTHEW'S EPISCOPAL CHURCH, The Ladies' Guild, Fairbanks.
Favorite recipes.   [Fairbanks ?], 1944.   162p.   index, ringbound.
                                                                3942

SAINT MATTHEW'S EPISCOPAL CHURCH, The Ladies' Guild, Fairbanks.
The Golden Heart cook book.   Compiled and edited by The Ladies'
Guild of Saint Matthew's Episcopal Church, Fairbanks.   [Fair-
banks ?], ca 1950 ?]   149p.   wrps.   3943

SALIN, EDGAR.   Die wirtschaftliche Entwicklung von Alaska (und
Yukon Territory);   ein Beitrag zur Geschichte und Theorie der
Konzentrationsbewegung, von Edgar Salin, mit einer karte von
Alaska.   [TITLE TR.   The economic development of Alaska (and
Yukon Territory); a contribution to the history and theory of
syndicalism] Tübingen, J. C. B. Mohr, 1914.   226p.   map(fold.),
bibliog.   (Archiv für Sozialwissenschaft und Sozialpolitik;
Ergänzungsheft 12)   3944

SALISBURY, HAROLD.   Alaskan songs and ballads.   By Harold Salisbury.   Illustrated by the author.   Portland, Ore., Metropolitan
Press, 1967.   111p.   illus.   3945

SALISBURY, HAROLD. Poems of Alaska. Nome, 1954. 64p. illus.
3946

SALISBURY, HAROLD. The Great Land, poems of Alaska. Illustrated by the author. Anchorage, Ken Wray Press, 1969. 79p. illus.
3947

SALISBURY, OLIVER MAXSON. "Quoth the Raven," a little journey into the primitive. By O. M. Salisbury. Seattle, Superior Pub. Co., 1962. [c1962] 1st ed. 275p. pls. photos by author. [school teacher and wife during 1920s in Klawock, southeastern Tlingit village]
3948

Salomon, Louis B., edit. SEE no. 2772, London, Jack.

Salomonsen, Finn, co-auth. SEE no. 1656, Freuchen, Peter.

SAMOĬLOV, VĬACHESLAV ALEKSANDROVICH. Semen Dezhnev i ego vremiĭa. [TITLE TR. Semen Dezhnev and his time] Moskva, Izd-vo Glavsevmorputi, 1945. 148p. pls. maps(some fold.), append. bibliog. [biog. account voyage of 1648 through Bering Strait]
3949

SAMOĬLOVICH, RUDOL'F LAZAREVICH. Put'k poliŭsu. 2. izd. [TITLE TR. The route to the Pole. 2d edition] Leningrad, Izd-vo Vsesoiŭznogo arktichesnogo instituta, 1933. 63p. illus. ports. map(fold.) (Poliãrnaiã biblioteka) [DeLong, Amundsen, others]
3950

SAMSON, SAM and MIGNON MAYNARD CHISAM. The Eskimo Princess; a story of a million dollar gold discovery in the Cyrus Noble in Nome, Alaska, at told to Mignon Maynard Chisam. Stevenson, Wash., Columbia Gorge Pub. Co., 1941. 48p. ports. (Souvenir Edition, July 1941) ANR. Boston, Christopher Pub. House, 1951. 50p. 3951

SAMUELS, CHARLES. The magnificent rube, the life and gaudy times of Tex Rickard. N. Y., McGraw-Hill, [c1957] 301p. illus. photos, bibliog. [chapts. 4 through 6 about Yukon gold rush]
3952

SAMWELL, DAVID. A narrative of the death of Captain James Cook. Edited and indexed by B. Cartwright, jr. Honolulu, 1916. 1td. ed. of 500 copies. 26p. (Hawaiian Historical Society Reprint no. 2) [See no. 3954]
3953

SAMWELL, DAVID. A narrative of the death of Captain James Cook. To which are added some particulars, concerning his life and character, and observations respecting the introduction of the venereal disease into the Sandwich Islands. By David Samwell, Surgeon of the *Discovery*. London, Printed for G. G. J. and J. Robinson, 1786. 34p.
3954

[SAMWELL, DAVID] Details nouveaux et circonstanciés sur la mort du Capitaine Cook; traduits de l'Anglois. Paris, chez Née de la Rochelle, 1786. 56p. [See no. 3954]
3955

SAN FRANCISCO-ALASKA CLUB. Constitution and by-laws, adopted
October 6, 1911. S. F., 1911. 15p.   3957

SANDERSON, IVAN T. The continent we live on. N. Y., Random House,
1961. 299p. illus. maps. ANR. 1962. adapted by Anne Terry
White. (Special Young Readers Edition) [incls. Alaska and Alaska
Highway]   3956

Santa Fe Route. SEE no. 4295, Steele, Jas. Wm.

SANTOS, ANGEL. Jesuitos en el Polo Norte. Madrid, 1943. 546p.
[Aleutian Islands and Kuskokwim River delta]   3958

SARGENT, CHARLES SPRAGUE. Manual of the trees of North America
(exclusive of Mexico) Edition 2 with corrections. Boston,
Houghton Mifflin, 1926. 910p. illus. glossary. AN EARLIER ED.
1905. ANR. 1933. ANR. Gloucester, Mass., Peter Smith, 1962. reprint. 2 vols. ANR. N. Y., Dover, 1966. 2 vols. wrps. reprint.
                                                                3959

SARGENT, EPES, edit. Arctic adventure by sea and land, from the
earliest date to the last expeditions in search of Sir John
Franklin. Boston, Phillips, Sampson & Co., and London, S. Low,
Son & Co., 1857. 480p. front.(port.), pls. maps(incl. 1 fold.)
ANR. 1858. reissue.   3960

Sargent, Epes and William H. Cunnington. The Arctic world and
     its explorers. See no. 3961.

SARGENT, EPES and WILLIAM H. CUNNINGTON. The wonders of the Arc-
tic world; a history of all the researches and discoveries in the
frozen regions of the North from the earliest times ... By Epes
Sargent. Together with a complete and reliable history of the
Polaris expedition, by William H. Cunnington. N. H., Wm. Gay &
Co., 1873. [has title on spine "The Arctic world and its ex-
plorers"] 651p. front. ports. pls. map. ANR. Philadelphia,
J. E. Potter, 1873. 651p.   3961

SARNOFF, PAUL. Ice pilot; Bob Bartlett. N. Y., Julian Messner,
1966. 191p. bibliog.   3962

SARS, GEORG OSSIAN. Fresh-water Ostracoda from Canada and Alaska.
Ottawa, King's Printer, 1926. 22p. pls. (Canadian Arctic Expedition, 1913-18. Report, vol. 7; Crustacea, pt. 1)   3963

Sarychev, Gavriil Andreevich. [Alphabetical title guide to
     chronological entries]

     Account ... 3967.   Puteshestvie ... 3965, 3970,3971.
     Achtjährige ... 3966.   Reis in het ... 3969.
     Atlas ... 3964.   Voyage dans ... 3968.

SARYCHEV, GAVRIIL ANDREEVICH. Atlas Svernoy chasti Vostochnago Okeana, sostavlen v chertezhnoy Gosudarstvennago Admiraltezhkago Departamenta, a Novg yshikh opisey i kart, 1826, Pod Rukovodstvom Viche-Admirala i Gidrografa Sarycheva. [TITLE TR. Atlas of the northern part of the Pacific Ocean, compiled in sheets by the Imperial Navy Department from latest reports and maps, 1826, under the direction of Vice-Admiral and Hydrographer Sarychev] St. Petersburg, 1826. maps. 3964

SARYCHEV, GAVRIIL ANDREEVICH. Puteshestvie flota Kapitana Sarycheva po sîeverovostochnoĭ chasti Sibiri, Ledovitomu morĭu i Vostochnomu okeanu, v prodolzhenie os'mi iĭet, pri Geografisheskoĭ i Astronomicheskoĭ morskoĭ Ėkspeditŝii, byvsheĭ pod nachal'stvom flota Kapitana Billingsa, s 1785 po 1793 god. [TITLE TR. The voyage of Captain Sarychev to the northeastern part of Siberia, the Arctic Sea and Eastern Ocean in the course of eight years, with the Geographical and Astronomical Expedition under command of Captain Billings in 1785-1793] Sanktpeterburg, Tip. Shnora, 1802. 2 pts. in 1. 187p., 192p. table(fold.), errata list. atlas(folio) pls. maps. 3965

TRANSLATIONS - Puteshestvie ... 1802, CHRONOLOGICALLY.

Achtjährige Reise im nordöstlichen Siberien auf dem Eismeere und dem nordöstlichen ozean. Aus dem Russ. übersetzt von J. H. Busse. Leipzig, 1805-15. 3 vols. pls. map. ANR. Leipzig, W. Reim & Co., 1805-06. 2 vols. 190p. and 196p. pls. map. 3966

Account of a voyage of discovery to the North-East of Siberia, the Frozen Ocean, and the North-East Sea. By Gawrila Sarytschew, Russian Imperial Major-General to the Expedition. Translated from the Russian and embellished with engravings. London, Printed for Richard Phillips, by J. G. Barnard, 1806-1807. abridged with some added material. 2 vols. in 1. 71p.,80p. pls.(fold. some col.), index. (also in "A collection of modern and contemporary voyages and travels," by Sir Richard Phillips. 1805-1810. See no. 3574) ANR. Amsterdam, N. Israel and N. Y., Da Capo Press, 1969. 2 vols. in 1. facsim. of 1806 Phillips edition. (Bibliotheca Australiana, no. 64) 3967

Voyage dans la Sibérie orientale la mer glaciale, l'ocean pacifique septentrional et a la côte nord de l'Amérique, translated par L. G. Coutousove. Paris, 1807. pls. maps. 3968

Reis in het noordoostlijke Siberie, en op de Ijszee en den noordoostelijken oceaan; uit de hoogduitsche vertaling van Johann Heinrich Busse, overgezet door N. Messchaert. [TITLE TR. Voyage to northeastern Siberia, the Arctic Sea and Northeastern Ocean; from Johann Heinrich Busse's German translation, translated by N. Messchaert] Amsterdam, Johannes Allart, 1808. abr. enl. 2 vols. xxxii,190p. x,334p. pls. map. 3969

SARYCHEV, GAVRIIL ANDREEVICH. Puteshestvie Kapitana Billingsa cherez chukotskuíu zemlíu ot Beringova proliva do Nizhnekolymsko-go ostroga, i plavanie Kapitana Galla na sudníe *Chernom Orĺīe* po Síeverovostochnomu Okeanu v 1791 godu. [TITLE TR. The journey of Captain Billings from Bering Strait to Fort Nizhe-Kolymst, and the voyage of Captain Hall on the *Chernyĭ Orel* in the Northeastern Ocean in 1791] Sanktpeterburg, Morskaía tipografiía, 1811. 191p. pls.(fold.), maps(fold.), vocabularies.   3970

[SARYCHEV, GAVRIIL ANDREEVICH] Puteshestvie po severo-vostochnoĭ chasti Sibiri, Ledovitomu moríu i Vostochnomu okeanu. [Pod red N. N. Zubova] [TITLE TR. Expedition to the northeastern part of Siberia, the Arctic Sea and the Eastern Ocean. [N. N. Zubov, edi-tor]] Moskva, Gos. izd-vo geogr. lit-ry, 1952. 325p. illus. map(fold. in pocket) [combines elements of both nos. 3965 and 3970 with added append. glossary and index]   3971

Sarychev, Gavriil Andreevich. SEE ALSO no. 3574,
    Phillips, R. Collection modern and contemporary ... 1805-10.

SATTERFIELD, ARCHIE and LLOYD JARMAN. Alaska bush pilot in the float country. Seattle, Superior Pub. Co., 1969. 160p. photos. [southeastern Alaska]   3972

Sauer, Martin. [Alphabetical title guide to chronological entries]

    An account ... 3973.   Viaggio ... 3978.
    Geographische ... 3975.   Voyage fait ... 3974.
    Reise nach ... 3976, 3977.

SAUER, MARTIN. An account of a geographical and astronomical ex-pedition to the northern parts of Russia, for ascertaining the degrees of latitude and longitude of the mouth of the River Kovi-ma; of the whole coast of the Tshutski, to East cape; and of the islands in the Eastern Ocean, stretching to the American coast. Performed, by command of Her Imperial Majesty Catherine the Se-cond ... by Commodore Joseph Billings, in the years 1785, &c. to 1794. The whole narrated from the original papers, by Martin Sauer, Secretary to the Expedition. London, Printed by A. Stra-han, for T. Cadell, Jun. and W. Davies, 1802. 332p., 58p. pls. map(fold.), append. vocabularies, glossary. [Russian Northeastern Expedition of 1785-93]   3973

    TRANSLATIONS - An account ... 1802, CHRONOLOGICALLY.

    Voyage fait par ordre de l'impératrice de Russie Catherine II, dans le nord de la Russie Asiatique, dans la mer Glaciale, dans la mer d'Anadyr, et sur les côtes de l'Amérique, depuis 1785 jusqu'en 1794, par le commodore Billings; rédigé par M. Sauer, Secrétaire-Interprète de l'Expedition, et traduit de l'anglais avec des notes par J. Castéra. Avec une Collec-tion de quinze Planches ... Paris, chez F. Buisson, Imprimeur-

Libraire, [1802] 2 vols. 385p. and 417p. atlas. pls. maps.
[vol. 2 contains Aleut and Kodiak vocabularies on pp.296-303
and pp.304-311]   3974

Geographische-astronomische Reise nach den nördlichen gegenden
Russlands und zur untersuchung der Mündung des Kowima-Flusses
... Berlin, 1802. 334p. pls. map. [cf no. 3977]   3975

Reise nach den nördlichen gegenden vom Russischen Asien und
Amerika unter dem Commodor Joseph Billings in den Jahren
1785-1794; Aus original-paperien verfasset vom Martin Sauer.
Aus dem Englischen übersetzt von M. C. Sprengel. Weimar, Verlag des Landes-Industrie-Comptoirs, 1803. 296p. map.(Bibliothek der Neuesten und Wichtigsten Reisebeschreibungen. Bd. 8)
                                                            3976

Reise nach Siberien, Kamtschatka, und zur Untersuchung der Mündung des Kowima-Flusses, der ganzen Küste der Tschutschen und
der zwischen dem festen Lande von Asien und Amerika befind-
lichen Inslen aug Besehl der Kaiserin von Russland, Catharina
der Zweiten, in den Jahren 1785 bis 1794, unternommen von Kapitan Joseph Billings und nach den original Papieren heraus
gegeben, von Martin Sauer, Sekretär der Expedition. Aus dem
Englischen übersetzt. Mit Kupfern and Karte. Berlin und
Hamburg, 1803. 334p. pls.(fold.), map(fold.) [cf no. 3975-
Aleut and Kodiak vocabularies on pp.325-30]   3977

Viaggio fatto nel nord della Russia Asiatica dal 1785 fino al
1794, scritto dal Sign. Sauer, tradotto dal Conte L. Bossi.
Milano, 1816. 2 vols. 288p. and 324p. pls.(some col.) 3978

SAVAGE, ALMA HELEN. Dogsled apostles. By Alma Savage. N. Y.,
Sheed and Ward, 1942. 231p. front. pls. ports. facsims. index.
ANR. Freeport, N. Y., Books for Libraries Press, 1968. [c1942]
(Essay Index Reprint Series) [much about *Monseigneur* Joseph
Crimont, S.J.]   3979

SAVAGE, ALMA HELEN. Eben the crane. By Alma Savage. Illustrated
by Charles Keller. N. Y., Sheed and Ward, 1944. 74p. illus.
(col.), endmaps.   3980

SAVAGE, ALMA HELEN. Forty-ninth star. By Alma Savage. N. Y.,
Benziger Bros., 1959. illus.   3981

SAVAGE, ALMA HELEN. Holiday in Alaska. By Alma Savage. Boston,
D. C. Heath & Co., 1944. [c1944] 80p. front. illus.(some col.)
by Jon Nielsen, endmaps, glossary. (New World Neighbors Series)
                                                            3982

SAVAGE, ALMA HELEN. Kulik's first seal hunt. By Alma Savage.
Paterson, N. J., St. Anthony Guild Press, [c1948] 114p. illus.
by Anthony A. McGrath.   3983

SAVAGE, ALMA HELEN. Smoozie, the story of an Alaskan reindeer fawn. By Alma Savage. Illustrated by Charles Keller with maps by LeRoy Appleton. N. Y., Sheed and Ward, 1941. 68p. illus. maps. 3984

SAVAGE, RICHARD HENRY. The Princess of Alaska; a tale of two countries. A novel. Chicago, F. T. Neely, 1894. [c1894] 420p. (Neely's Library of Choice Literature, no. 33) ANR. London, Routledge, 1895. 3985

SAVVAGE, JEHAN. Mémoire du voyage en Russie fait en 1586 par Jehan Savvage, suivi de l'expedition de Fr. Drake en Amérique a la méme epogue. Publies pour la prémiere fois d'apres les manuscripts de la Bibliotheque Imperiale, par Louis Lacour. Paris, A. Aubry, 1855. 30p. 3986

Sawyer, E. W. SEE no. 3486, Pan Pacific Progress.

SAY IT IN ESKIMO; an informal phonetic guide to Northern Alaska Eskimo speech. Nome, printed at The Nome Nugget, E. P. "Speedy" Strom, [c1965] (73)p. illus. by Robert Mayokok, wrps. [two and three -quarters inch by four and one-half inch in size] 3987

SAYLER, HARRY L. The Airship Boys due North; or, by balloon to the Pole. By H. L. Sayler. Illustrated by S. H. Riesenberg. Chicago, Reilly & Britton Co., [c1910] 335p. front.(pl.), pls. (The Airship Boys Series) [fict. - coastal Alaska through Bering Strait] 3988

Sayler, Harry L. SEE ALSO nos. 4844-46, Whitney, Elliott [pseud.]

Sayre, J. D. SEE no. 1860, Griggs, R. F.

SBORNIK TSERKOVNYKH PĨESNOPĨENIĨ i molitvosloviĩ na aglomiutsko-kuskovimskom narĩechiĩ. [TITLE TR. Collection of church canticles and liturgies in Anglomut-Kuskokwim dialect. N. Y., 1896. 3989

SCAMMON, CHARLES MELVILLE. The marine mammals of the north-western coast of North America, described and illustrated together with an account of the American whale-fishery. S. F., John H. Carmany and N. Y., Putnam, 1874. 319p. front. pls.(some dble.), glossary, append. ANR. N. Y., Dover, 1968. reprint with added biog. of Scammon and introd. by Victor B. Scheffer. [catalog of North Pacific whales] 3990

SCARFF, R. F. Distribution and origin of life in America, with twenty-one maps. no pl., 1911. [contains fauna of Alaska] 3991

SCARTH, W. H. Report on trip to the Yukon. By Inspector W. H. Scarth, Royal Canadian Mounted Police. Ottawa, Government Printing Bureau, 1897. 13p. 3992

SCEARCE, STANLEY.   Northern lights to fields of gold. Illustrated by R. H. Hall. Caldwell, Idaho, Caxton Printers, 1939. [c1939] 390p. front.(col.), pls. map.   3993

Scenery ahead in Alaska ... n. d. SEE no. 122,
     Alaska Steamship Co.

SCENES FROM THE LAND OF THE MIDNIGHT SUN ... Yukon and Alaska. Dawson, n. d. 44p. photos. [poetry]   3994

SCHAFER, JOSEPH.   The Pacific Slope and Alaska. Philadelphia, G. Barrie's Sons, 1904. 436p. front.(col.), pl.(col.), ports. (History of North America, vol. 10) ANR. Philadelphia, 1904. 442p. front.(col.), pls. ports. plans, facsims. maps. ANR. Philadelphia, 1905. [has title "The Pacific Slope and Alaska; a history 1500-1900 ..."] 442p.   3995

Schaldemose, Fr., tr. SEE no. 2526, Kotzebue, Otto von.

SCHANZ, MORITZ.   Ein zug nach Osten.   [TITLE TR. March to the East] Hamburg, W. Mauke Sohne, 1897. 2 vols. [Alaska in vol. 2]   3996

SCHEFFER, VICTOR B.   Seals, sea lions, and walruses; a review of the Pinnipedia. Stanford, Stanford University Press and London, Oxford University Press, 1958. 179p. pls. tables, figs. synoptic key, bibliog. index.   3997

SCHEFFER, VICTOR B.   The year of the seal. N. Y., Charles Scribnerls Sons, [c1970] 205p. illus. maps. [fur seal of Pribilof Islands]   3998

SCHEFFER, VICTOR B.   The year of the whale. N. Y., Charles Scribner's Sons, [c1969] 213p. front. illus. bibliog. index. ANR. N. Y., Scribner, [c1969] 244p. front. illus. bibliog. index, paperback. (Special Members Edition, American Museum of Natural History) [fict. natural history of sperm whale with scattered refs. to Aleutian Islands, Alaskan waters in general]   3999

Scheffer, Victor B. SEE ALSO no. 3990, Scammon, C. M.
     Marine mammals ... 1968.

Schiefner, A., edit. SEE no. 3723, Radlov, L. F.

Schenkofsky, Milt, illus. SEE no. 4932, Wirt, Sherwood.

SCHÉRER, JEAN-BENOÎT.   Rècherches Historiques et Géographiques sur le Nouveau-Monde. Par Jean-Benoît Schérer ... Paris, Brunet, [1777] 352p. pls. map. [incls. northwest coast of America and Russian Kamchatka - comparison of Arctic languages]   4000

[Schérer, Jean-Benoît?] SEE ALSO no. 3933, S., J. L.
Neue Nachrichten ... Insuln ... 1776.

[Schérer, Jean-Benoît, edit. ?] SEE ALSO no. 4332,
Steller, Geo. W. ... Beschreibung ... Kamchatka ... 1774.

Scherer, Johann Benedict. SEE no. 4000, Schérer, Jean-Benoît.

SCHILLER, EVERETT L. and ROBERT LLOYD RAUSCH. Mammals of the
Katmai National Monument, Alaska. Montreal, 1956. maps, refs.
(reprint from Arctic, vol. 9, no. 3, pp.191-201)   4001

SCHLEIN, MIRIAM. Oomi, the new hunter, illustrated by George F.
Mason. N. Y., Abelard-Schuman, 1955. 109p. illus. [juv. fict.
with general Arctic setting]   4002

SCHLÖZER, AUGUST LUDWIG. Neue Erdbeschreibung von ganz Amerika.
Gottingen und Leipzig, 1777. 2 vols. pls.(fold.), maps(fold.)
[Russian America in vol. 2]   4003

[Schlözer, August Ludwig ?] SEE ALSO no. 3933,
S., J. L. Neue Nachrichten ... Insuln ... 1776.

SCHMITT, ALFRED. Die Alaska-Schrift und ihre schriftgestliche
bedeutung. Abbildungsheft. Marburg, Simons Verlag, 1951. 200p.
append. (Munstersche Forschungen. Herausgegeben von Jost Trier
und Herbert Grundmann, Heft 4)   4004

SCHMITT, ALFRED and JOHN HINZ. Untersuchungen zur Geschichte der
Schrift (Eine Schriftentwicklung um 1900 in Alaska) von Dr. Alfred
Schmitt, Professor der vergleichenden Sprachwissenshaft an der
Universität Erlangen unter Mitarbeit von Rev. John Hinz, Spring-
field, Minnesota, U.S.A. [TITLE TR. Research in the history of
writing. Evolution of writing around 1900 in Alaska] Leipzig,
Otto Harrassovitz, 1940. 2 vols. 534p. illus. facsims.(some
fold.), map.   4005

SCHMITZ, C. A. and R. WILDHABER, edits. Festschrift Alfred
Bühler. Basel, Pharos-Verlag, 1965. 466p. illus. refs. (Basler
Beiträge zur Geographie und Ethnologie. Ethnologische Reihe,
vol. 2) [contains *Speculations on origin of Eskimo culture*, by
H. G. Bandi, on pp.39-53. Refers to Bering land bridge]   4006

Schmücker, A., edit. SEE no. 3745, Rasmussen, K. J. V.

SCHNEIDER, A. In beautiful Alaska, respectfully dedicated to the
Pioneers of Alaska and the Yukon. no pl, by author, 1909. 4007

SCHNEIDER, A. The Alaskan Trail. Valdez, published by author,
1903.   4008

Schneider, Paul, tr. SEE no. 1052, [Cook, Jas.]

Schoolhouse farthest west. SEE no. 1677, Gambell, V. C.

SCHOOLING, WILLIAM. The Hudson's Bay Company; the Governor and Company of Adventurers trading into Hudson's Bay during 250 years, 1670-1920. By Sir William Schooling. London, Hudson's Bay Co., 1920. xvi,129p. illus. maps(incl. 1 fold.), wrps. [commemorating 250th anniversary]   4009

SCHUCHERT, CHARLES. Atlas of paleogeographic maps of North America. With an introduction by Carl O. Dunbar. N. Y., John Wiley and London, Chapman & Hall, 1955. xi,177p. maps, refs. index.
4010

SCHULENBURG, ALBRECHT CONAN. Die Sprache der Zimshian-Indianer in Nordwest-Amerika. Braunschweig, Richard Sattler, 1894. 372p.
4011

Schultz, C. Bertrand, co-edit. SEE no. 2273, International Assoc. Quatenary Research.

Schultz, Carl Joh., tr. SEE no. 1212, Davydov, G. I.

SCHULTZ, GWEN. Glaciers and the Ice Age; earth and its inhabitants during the Pleistocene. N. Y., Holt, Rinehart & Winston, 1963. 128p. photos, charts, maps, glossary, bibliog. index. (Holt Library of Science, Ser. 1, no. 4)   4012

[Schultz, Johann Ludwig ?] SEE no. 3933, S., J. L.

Schultz, L. P., co-auth. SEE no. 2215, Hubbs, C. L.

SCHULTZE, AUGUSTUS. A brief grammar and vocabulary of the Eskimo language of north-western Alaska. Bethlehem, Penna., The Comenius Press, 1899. 21p. (Society for Propagating the Gospel Among the Heathen) [for enl. ed. in 1894, see no. 4014]   4013

SCHULTZE, AUGUSTUS. Grammar and vocabulary of the Eskimo language of north-western Alaska, Kuskoquim District, by Augustus Schultze, D.D., President Moravian College, Bethlehem, Pa. Bethlehem, Penna., Moravian Publication Office, 1894. 67p. [enl. of no. 4013]   4014

SCHULTZE, AUGUSTUS. Liturgy, hymns and scripture lessons in the Eskimo language of the Kuskoquim District, north-western Alaska. Compiled from translations of missionaries. Bethelehem, Penna., 1902. 17p. ANR. 1908. 2d print. 19p.   4015

[Schultze, Johann L. ?] SEE no. 3933, S., J. L.

Schuster, Carl. SEE no. 4465, Tax, Sol.

SCHWALBE, ANNA BUXBAUM. Dayspring on the Kuskokwim; the story of Moravian missions in Alaska. Bethlehem, Penna., Moravian Press, 1951. 264p.   4016

Schwartz, J. A. SEE no. 4309, Stefansson, V.

SCHWARTZKOPF, KARL-AAGE. The Alaska pilot. N. Y., Franklin Watts, [c1956] ANR. N. Y., Wats, 1962. 118p. AN EARLIER ED. [in Swedish] Stockholm, Albert Bonniers, 1956.   4017

SCHWATKA, FREDERICK. A summer in Alaska. A popular account of the travels of an Alaska exploring expedition along the great Yukon River, from its source to its mouth, in the British North-West Territory, and in the Territory of Alaska. By Frederick Schwatka. Philadelphia, J. Y. Huber, 1891. 418p. front.(port.), pls. sketches, map, append. index. OTHERS St. Louis, Mo., J. W. Henry, 1893 AND 1894. ANR. St. Louis, J. W. Henry, n. d. [enl. of no. 4019, with added chapters, no fold. map]   4018

SCHWATKA, FREDERICK. Along Alaska's great river. A popular account of the travels of the Alaska Exploring Expedition of 1883, along the Great Yukon River, from its source to its mouth, in the British North-West Territory, and in the Territory of Alaska. By Frederick Schwatka ... Commander of the Expedition. N. Y., Cassell & Co., [c1885] 360p. front. pls. sketches, maps(incl. 1 fold. in front pocket), appends. index. ANR. Chicago, Henry,1898. enl. ANR. N. Y., Cassell, 1900. ANR. Chicago, Hill, 1900. [cf no. 4018]   4019

SCHWATKA, FREDERICK. Exploring the great Yukon; an adventurous expedition down the great Yukon River from its source in the British North-West to its mouth in the Territory of Alaska. no pl., Art and Science Pub. Co., n. d. 418p. illus. diagrs. [See also nos. 4018 and 4019]   4020

SCHWATKA, FREDERICK. Nimrod in the North; or, hunting and fishing adventures in the Arctic regions. By Frederick Schwatka. N. Y., Cassell, 1885. [c1885] 198p. front.(port.), pls. sketches. ANR. Boston, Educational Pub. Co., n. d. [c1885]   4021

SCHWATKA, FREDERICK and JOHN HYDE. Wonderland;or, Alaska and the Inland Passage, by Lieut. Frederick Schwatka. With a description of the country traversed by the Northern Pacific Railroad, by John Hyde. Chicago, Rand McNally, 1886. 96p. front.(col.), illus. ANR. WITH TITLE Wonderland; or, the Pacific Northwest and Alaska; with a description of the country traversed by the Northern Pacific Railroad. Chicago, Rand McNally, 1888. 94p. front. illus. map. [cf no. 2250]   4022

Schwatka, Frederick. SEE ALSO no. 4068, Seton-Karr, H. W.
    Shores and alps of Alaska. 1887.

SCHWIEBERT, ERNEST. Salmon of the world. N. Y., Winchester
Press, 1970. 63p. illus. 4023

SCIDMORE, ELIZA RUHAMAH. Alaska, its southern coast and the Sitkan Archipelago. Boston, D. Lothrop, 1885. 333p. front.(dble.
map), pls. [variant title Journeyings ... 1889 ? See no. 4027]
4024

SCIDMORE, ELIZA RUHAMAH. Appleton's guide-book to Alaska and the
Northwest coast; including the shores of Washington, British
Columbia, southeastern Alaska, the Aleutian and the Seal Islands,
the Bering and the Arctic coasts, with maps and many illustrations.
N. Y., D. Appleton, 1893. 156p. pls. maps(some fold.), bibliog.
ANR. N. Y., 1898. enl. ed. with chapt. on Klondike. 167p. pls.
maps(some fold., incl. 2 fold. in pocket), bibliog. ANR. N. Y.,
1899. 167p. [cf no. 4026] 4025

SCIDMORE, ELIZA RUHAMAH. Guide-book to Alaska and the Northwest
coast, including the shores of Washington, British Columbia,
southern Alaska, the Aleutian and Seal Islands, the Bering and
the Arctic coasts. London, Heinemann, 1893. 156p. pls. maps
(some fold.) [London ed. of no. 4025] 4026

SCIDMORE, ELIZA RUHAMAH. Journeyings in Alaska. Boston, D.
Lothrop, 1889. [possibly same as no. 4024 ?] 4027

SCOTT, ERASTUS HOWARD. Alaska days. With an account of the trip
from Chicago to Seattle and return. By Erastus Howard Scott.
Chicago, Scott, Foresman & Co., [c1923] 106p. illus. maps. [In-
side Passage, then Alaska Railroad to Fairbanks] 4028

Scott, James Foster. SEE no. 1204, Davis, M. L.

SCRIPPS INSTITUTION OF OCEANOGRAPHY. Oceanic observations of the
Pacific: 1956. Berkeley and Los Angeles, University of California Press, 1963. 458p. maps, tables, bibliog. 4029

SCULL, EDWARD MARSHALL. Hunting in the Arctic and Alaska. Philadelphia, John C. Winston, 1914. 304p. front. pls. maps. ANR.
London, Duckworth & Co., 1914. 304p. front. pls. maps. 4030

Sea, ship ... 1925. SEE no. 2968, Marine Research Soc.

Sea voyage ... 1941. SEE no. 3355. Northland Transportation Co.

Seafood ... [c1970] SEE no. 4244, Southeast Alaska
    Trollers Assoc.

Seal and seal islands. 1870. SEE no. 53, Alaska Commercial Co.

SEALOCK, RICHARD BURL and PAULINE A. SEELY. Bibliography of place
name literature, United States, Canada, Alaska and Newfoundland.
Chicago, American Library Assoc., 1948. 331p. 4031

SEAMAN, J. V. New general atlas, chiefly intended for the use of schools and private libraries. N. Y., Seaman, 1821. maps(some dble.) [contains explorations of Capt. Jas. Cook in Pacific Ocean]   4032

SEATTLE-ALASKA INTELLIGENCE BUREAU. The Klondyker; a compendium of useful and authentic information conerning the gold fields of Alaska. Seattle, 1897.   4033

SEATTLE CENTURY 21 EXPOSITION 1962; land of promise, souvenir travel guide to the Northwest: Washington, Alaska, Alaska Highway, British Columbia, Yukon, Alberta, Montana. Anchorage, Armed Forces Publications, 1962. var. pagings, illus. [cf no. 72]4034

SEATTLE CHAMBER OF COMMERCE. Business friendhsip tour. Seattle, 1933. illus. itinerary.   4035

Seattle Chamber of Commerce. SEE ALSO nos. 35-40, Alaska
    Bureau, Seattle Chamber of Commerce.

Seattle Electric Co. SEE no. 160, Alaska-Yukon-Pacific Exposi-
    tion. Souvenir guide ... [1909]

Seattle of today...[1907 ?] SEE no. 3277, National Pub. Co.

SEATTLE POST-INTELLIGENCER. Facts on Alaska. [Seattle, 1904 ?] 16p. [cf nos. 1510 and 1722]   4036

Seattle, the gateway ... 1909. SEE no. 159, Alaska-Yukon-
    Pacific Exposition.

Seattle to Nome gold coast. 1900. SEE no. 2935, McMicken, E.G.

Seattle World's Fair Fine Arts Pavilion. SEE no. 1884,
    Gunther, Erna.

Second report Bering Strait dam. 1962. SEE no. 1378,
    Dunbar, M. J.

SECRETAN, JAMES HENRY EDWARD. The Klondyke and back; a journey down the Yukon from its source to its mouth, with hints to intending prospectors. London, Hurst & Blackett, 1898. 260p. front.(port.), pls. diagrs.   4037

SEED, H. G. and S. D. WILSON. The Turnagain Heights landslide in Anchorage, Alaska. Berkeley, University of California, 1966. 37p. illus. graphs, tables, refs. (Dept. of Civil Engineering, Soil Mechanics and Bituminous Materials Research Laboratory. Also in Proceedings of American Society of Civil Engineers, 1967. vol. 93, no. SM4, pp.325-53)   4038

SEEMANN,BERTHOLD CARL. Narrative of the voyage of H. M. S. *Herald* during the years 1845-51, under the command of Captain Henry Kellett ... being a circumnavigation of the globe, and three cruizes [sic] to the Arctic regions in search of Sir John Franklin. By Berthold Seemann. London, Reeve & Co., 1853. 2 vols. in 1. xvi, 322p. and vii,302p. fronts.(col.), map(fold.), index. [for tr. see no. 4040]   4039

SEEMANN, BERTHOLD CARL. Reise um die Welt; und drei Fahrten der Königlich Britischen Fregatte *Herald* nach dem nördlichen Polarmeere zur Aufsuchung Sir John Franklin's in den Jahren 1845-1851. Von Berthold Seemann. Hannover, Carl Rümpler, 1853. 2 vols. in 1. xi,335p. and vi,294p. pls. [a tr. of no. 4039]   4040

SEEMANN, BERTHOLD CARL. The botany of the voyage of H. M. S. *Herald* under the command of Captain Henry Kellett ... during the years 1845-51. By Berthold Seemann, naturalist of the Expedition, with one hundred plates. London, Lovell Reeve, 1852-57. 483p. pls. [incls. Norton Sound]   4041

Seemann, Berthold Carl. SEE ALSO no. 2479,
    Kittlitz, F. H. von. Twenty-four views ... 1861.

SEGAL, LOUIS. The conquest of the Arctic. London, G. G. Harrap & Co., 1939. 284p. pls. ports. maps(1 fold.), append. [append. contains chronology of Arctic voyages, 1870-1918]   4042

Seghers, Charles John, *Archbishop*. SEE nos.
    623, Bosco, Antoinette. Chas. John Seghers ... 1960;
    1223, deBaets, Maurice. *Monseigneur* Seghers. 1896;
    2064, Henley, G. F. Guide to Yukon-Klondike ... diary
        late *Archbishop* Seghers. 1897.

Selections. Tsimshian. n. d. SEE no. 929, Church of England.

Sella, Vittorio, illus. SEE no. 1226, deFilippi, Filippo.

SELLE, RALPH ABRAHAM. A daughter of the midnight sun. By Ralph A. Selle. Houston, Texas, Carroll Printing Co., [c1933] 32p. wrps. (Outdoor Nature Series) [short stories]   4043

SELLE, RALPH ABRAHAM. Luck and Alaska. By Ralph A. Selle. Houston, Texas, Carroll Printing Co., 1932. [c1932] 186p. (outdoor Nature Series) [sketches taken from articles appearing in Houston Chronicle]   4044

SELLE, RALPH ABRAHAM. The lure of gold; luck and Alaska. By Ralph A. Selle. Houston, Texas, Carroll Printing Co., 1932. 32p. (outdoor Nature Series)   4045

SELSAM, MILLICENT ELLIS. The quest of Captain Cook, by M. E. Selsam; illustrated by L. J. Ames. N. Y., Doubleday, 1962. 128p. port. map.   4046

Selver, P., tr.   SEE no. 4792, Welzl, J.

SENTER, GANO E.   Kawoo of Alaska.   Denver, Sage Books, [c1964]
113p. front. illus. photos, endmaps. [experiences of marooned
seaman with Tlingit Indians of southeatern Alaska]   4047

Seppala, Leonhard. SEE nos.
    3811, Ricker, E. M. Seppala ... 1930;
    4508, Thompson, R. Siberian Husky. 1962.

Seppala Siberian Husky Club. SEE no. 4508, Thompson, R.

Sergeant, Judson T., illus. SEE no. 4525, Thorne, Jas. F.

Sergeyev, M. A., edit. SEE no. 3364, Nozikov, N. N.

Series of summer and autumn tours ... 1902. SEE no. 3756,
    Raymond and Whitcomb Co.

Service book ... Qliyukuwhutana Indians ... Tanana ... 1908. SEE
    no. 1481, [Episcopal Church]

SERVICE, ROBERT W. and LARRY BECK. Alaska-Yukon favorites. Three
by Service.   Three by Beck.   Seattle, Golden Nugget, [1967 ?] 29p.
illustrated by David Murphey, wrps. [a retitled edition of no.
4057]   4048

SERVICE, ROBERT W. Ballads of a cheechako. Toronto, [c1909] 1st
ed. 146p. illus. ANR. Toronto, Briggs, 1909. 137p. front.
(port.) ANR. Philadelphia, E. Stern & Co., 1909. 137p. ANR.
N. Y., Barse & Hopkins, n. d. [c1921] 220p. front.(port.)
OTHERS var. pubs. and dates. [See also var. collections of author's poems]   4049

SERVICE, ROBERT W. Bar-room ballads; a book of verse. N. Y.,
Dodd Mead, 1940. 169p.   4050

SERVICE, ROBERT W. Collected poems of Robert Service. N. Y.,
Dodd Mead, 1944. 738p. OTHERS var. dates. [contains author's
Ballads of a cheechako, Spell of the Yukon, others]   4051

SERVICE, ROBERT W. Collected verse of Robert Service. London,
E. Benn, [c1930] 811p. [contains author's Ballads of a cheechako, Songs of a sourdough and Rhymes of a rolling stone, others]
                                                             4052

SERVICE, ROBERT W. Complete poetical works of Robert W. Service.
N. Y. and N. J., Barse & Co., [c1921] var. p.   4053

SERVICE, ROBERT W. My adventures in the North. Excerpts from
"Ploughman of the moon" an autobiography of Robert Service. Foreword by Larry Beck. no pl., [1967 ?] 62p. illus. sketches,
wrps.   4054

SERVICE, ROBERT W. Ploughman of the moon; an adventure into memory. N. Y., Dodd Mead, 1945. 472p. front.(port.) [autobiog. See also no. 4054]   4055

SERVICE, ROBERT W. Rhymes of a rolling stone. Toronto, Briggs, 1912. 195p. OTHERS N. Y., Dodd Mead, 1912. 172p. illus. and 1918. ANR. N. Y., Barse & Hopkins, n. d. [c1912]   4056

SERVICE, ROBERT W. and LARRY BECK. Robert W. Service favorites. Seattle, Published by Golden Nugget, [1967 ?] 32p. illustrated by David Murphey, wrps. [See also no. 4048]   4057

SERVICE, ROBERT W. Songs of a sourdough. Toronto, Ryerson, [c1907] ANR. Toronto, Briggs, 1908. 13th ed. 106p. ANR. London, R. F. Unwin, 1910. 22d impr. OTHERS var. pubs. and dates. Also reprinted with title Spell of Yukon. See no. 4063]   4058

SERVICE, ROBERT W. The best of Robert Service. N. Y., Apollo Editions, 1963. 223p. paperback.   4059

SERVICE, ROBERT W. The complete poems of Robert Service. N. Y., Dodd Mead, 1933. var. p. ANR. N. Y., Dodd Mead, 1942. var.p. (1,032p.) [contains author's Ballads of a cheechako, Rhymes of a rolling stone, Spell of Yukon, others]   4060

SERVICE, ROBERT W. The shooting of Dan McGrew. The cremation of Sam McGee. Illustrated by Rosemary Wells. Designed by Susan Jeffers. N. Y., William R. Scott, 1969. (52)p. illus.(col.) (Young Scott Books)   4061

SERVICE, ROBERT W. The spell of the Yukon and Ballads of a chee- chako. Plus The terrible Solomons by Jack London. Sandusky, Ohio, The American Reader's Library, 1943. 158p.   4062

SERVICE, ROBERT W. The spell of the Yukon and other verses. Philadelphia, Edward Stern, [c1907] 99p. ANR. N. Y., Barse & Hopkins, n. d. [c1907] 126p. 4"X6" in size. ANR. N. Y., Dodd Mead, 1935. OTHERS var. pubs. and printings. [Author's Songs of a sourdough, reprinted with new title. See also no. 4058]   4063

SERVICE, ROBERT W. The trail of ninety-eight, a northland ro- mance. With illustrations by Maynard Dixon. N. Y., Dodd Mead, 1911 [c1910] 514p. front. pls. ANR. Toronto, Ryerson, 1928. 514p. front. pls. ANR. London, E. Benn, 1936. 320p. OTHERS var. pubs. and printings.   4064

SERVICE, ROBERT W. Yukon poems of Robert W. Service. Palmer Lake, Colorado, Filter Press, 1967. 30p. illus. wrps. (Sour- dough Edition)   4065

Service, Robert W. SEE ALSO nos.
    1172, Dana, Marvin. Shooting Dan McGrew; novel ... [c1915];
    4499, Thomas, Lowell, jr. Trail of '98. [c1962]

SESSIONS, FRANCIS CHARLES. From Yellowstone Park to Alaska. By Francis C. Sessions. Illustrated by C. H. Warren. N. Y., Welch, Fracker Co., 1890. 186p. front. pls.   4066

SETON-KARR, HEYWOOD WALTER. Bear-hunting in the White Mountains; or, Alaska and British Columbia revisited. By H. W. Seton-Karr. London, Chapman & Hall, 1891. 156p. front. sketches by author, map(fold.)   4067

SETON-KARR, HEYWOOD WALTER. Shores and alps of Alaska. By H. W. Seton-Karr. London, S. Low, Marston, Searle & Rivington, 1887. 248p. pls. ports. maps(incl. 1 fold.), append. index. [short references to journal of John Bremner and also to Frederick Schwatka]   4068

SETON-KARR, HEYWOOD WALTER. Ten years' travel and sport in foreign lands; or, travels in the eighties. London, Chapman & Hall, 1890. 2d ed. with additions. [an earlier edition with title Ten years' wild sports in foreign lands. London, 1889 ?]   4069

"Seventy-Mile Kid." SEE nos.
     3509, Pearson, Grant H. The Seventy-Mile Kid. [c1957];
     4372, Stuck, Hudson. Ascent of Denali ... 1914.

Severy, M., edit. SEE no. 3276, National Geographic Soc.

Seward - gateway to Kenai empire. SEE no. 79,
     [Alaska Life, Seattle]

SEWARD, FREDERICK W. Reminiscences of a wartime statesman and diplomat, 1830-1915. By Frederick W. Seward, the Assistant Secretary of State during the administrations of Lincoln, Johnson and Hayes ... N. Y., Putnam, 1916. x,489p. [biog. of Wm. Henry Seward - has references to Alaska purchase]   4070

SEWARD, FREDERICK W. The autobiography of William Henry Seward from 1801 to 1834, with a memoir of his life and selections from his letters from 1851 to 1876. N. Y., 1877. 822p. ANR. WITH TITLE William H. Seward; an autobiography from 1801 to 1834. With a memoir of his life and selections from his letters. By Frederick W. Seward. N. Y., Derby & Miller, 1891. 3 vols. fronts. pls. ports. map(fold.) [vols. 2 and 3 have separate title: Seward at Washington as Senator and Secretary of State. Purchase of Alaska refered to in vol. 3]   4071

Seward, Frederick W. Seward at Washington ... 1891. SEE no.4071.

Seward, Frederick W. Wm. H. Seward; an autobiog. ... 1891. SEE no. 4071.

SEWARD, OLIVE R., edit. William Henry Seward's travels around the world. N. Y., 1873. 788p. illus.   4072

SEWARD, WILLIAM HENRY. Address on Alaska at Sitka, August 12,
1869. Published by the Directors of The Old South Works, Old
South Meeting House, Boston, Mass. Boston, n. d. 16p. (Old
South Leaflets, no. 133)   4073

SEWARD, WILLIAM HENRY. Alaska. Speech of William H. Seward, at
Sitka, August 12, 1869. Washington, D. C., Philp & Solomons,
1869. 31p. [offprint from no. 4078] ANR. Seattle, Shorey Book
Store, 1966. facsim. of 1869 print. [HAS COVER TITLE Our North
Pacific States ... 1869. SEE no. 4078]   4074

SEWARD, WILLIAM HENRY. Alaska; speech of William H. Seward at
Sitka, August 12, 1869. Washington, D. C., James J. Chapman,
1879. 14p.   4075

Seward, William Henry. Commerce in Pacific Ocean. 1852. SEE
     no. 4077.

Seward, William Henry. Diplomatic history ... 1853-84. SEE
     no. 4079.

Seward, William Henry. Our North Pacific States. 1869. SEE
     no. 4078.

SEWARD, WILLIAM HENRY. Speech of Mr. Seward, at Sitka. August 12,
1869. In the daily British Colonist and Victoria Chronicle.
Volume 22, no. 66. Victoria, V. I., B. C. Saturday morning,
August 28, 1869.   4076

SEWARD, WILLIAM HENRY. Speech of William H. Seward in the Senate
of the United States July 29, 1852. Commerce in the Pacific
Ocean. Washington, D. C., [Buell & Blanchard], 1852. 14p. 4077

SEWARD, WILLIAM HENRY. Speeches of William H. Seward in Alaska,
Vancouver's and Oregon, August, 1869. Washington, D. C., Philp
& Solomons, 1869. 31p. wrps. [speeches at Sitka, Victoria,
B. C., and at Salem, Ore. - HAS COVER TITLE Our North Pacific
States]   4078

Seward, William Henry. The diplomatic history of the war for
     the union. See no. 4079.

SEWARD, WILLIAM HENRY. The works of William H. Seward. Edited
by George E. Baker. N. Y., Redfield, 1853-84. 5 vols. fronts.
(ports.), facsim. [vol. 5 HAS IMPRINT Boston, Houghton Mifflin
AND SPECIAL TITLEPAGE The diplomatic history of the war for the
union] ANR. Boston, Houghton Mifflin, 1888. 5 vols. [vol. 5
contains references to purchase of Alaska]   4079

Seward, William Henry. SEE ALSO nos.
     155, Alaska-Yukon-Pac. Expo. Proceedings ... 1909;
     157, Alaska-Yukon-Pac. Expo. Report ... N. Y. ... 1910;
     377, Bancroft, Frederic. Life Wm. H. Seward ... 1900;

```
1006, Conrad, Earl.  Governor and his lady.  1960;
4070, Seward, F. W.  Reminiscences war statesman ... 1916;
4071, Seward, F. W.  Autobiog. Wm. H. Seward ... 1877;
4071, Seward, F. W.  Seward at Washington.  1891;
4072, Seward, Olive.  Wm. H. Seward's travels ... 1873;
4647, Van Deusen, Glyndon G.  Wm. Henry Seward.  1967;
4885, Williams, Sherman.  New York's part in history. 1915.
```

SEYMORE, WILLIAM C. The Klondike Katakism. One hundred and fifty practical questions answered. Tacoma,Steinbach & Pritchard, 1897. 52p.   4080

SGROI, PETER P. Why the United States purchased Alaska. College, University of Alaska Press, [c1970] 64p. front. ftntes. bibliog. wrps.   4081

SHABELSKI, ACHILLE. Voyage aux colonies russes de l'Amérique fait à bord du sloop de guerre l'*Apollon*, pendant les années 1821, 1822 et 1823. St. Petersburg, N. Gretsch, 1826. 106p.   4082

SHAĪASHNIKOV, I.   Kratkoe pravilo dlĩa blagochestivoĭ zhizni. [TITLE TR. Short rule for a pious life] N. Y., Tipografiĩa Amerikanskiĭ Pravoslavnyĭ Viestnik, 1902. 15p. [in Aleut dialect]   4083

SHALAMOV, TIKHON. Po Missii; iz pokhodnago zhurnala Aliaskinskago provoslavnago missionera. By *Father* Tikhon Shalamov. [TITLE TR. On mission;   from the field journal of an Alaskan Orthodox missionary] N. Y. Tipografiĩa Amerikanskiĭ Pravoslavnyĭ Viestnik, 1904. 68p.   4084

SHALAMOV, TIKHON. Ocherk iz pokhodnago zhurnala Aliaskinskago pravoslavnago missionera. By *Father* Tikhon Shalamov.   [TITLE TR. Sketch from a journal of travel of an Alaskan Orthodox missionary] N. Y., Tipografiĩa Amerikanskiĭ Pravoslavnyĭ Viestnik, 1904. 68p.   4085

SHAND, MARGARET CLARK and ORA M. SHAND.   The summit and beyond. By Margaret Clark Shand and Ora M. Shand.   Illustrated with photographs. Caldwell, Idaho, Caxton Printers, 1959. [c1959] 326p. front.(pl., pls. [Dyea and Chilkoot Pass briefly described] 4086

Shand, Ora M., co-auth. SEE no. 4086, Shand, Margaret Clark.

SHANNON, TERRY. A dog team for Ongluk. Chicago, Children's Press, 1962. 32p. illus.   4087

SHANNON, TERRY. Kidlik's kayak. Chicago, Albert Whitman & Co., 1959. illus.   4088

SHANNON, TERRY and CHARLES PAYZANT. Ride the ice down ! United States and Canadian icebreakers in Arctic seas.   San Carlos, Calif., Golden Gate Junior Books, [c1970] 78p. illus. maps. 4089

SHANNON, TERRY. Tyee's totem pole. Chicago, Albert Whitman & Co., 1955. 48p. illus. 4090

SHAPIRO, H. L. The Alaskan Eskimo, a study of the relationship between the Eskimo and the Chipewyan Indians of Central Canada. N. Y., American Museum of Natural History, 1931. illus. tables, maps, refs. wrps. (Anthropological Papers, vol. 31, pt. 6, pp.347-84) 4091

SHARP, ROBERT P. Glaciers. Eugene, University of Oregon Press, 1960. 78p. illus. table, diagrs. maps, glossary, bibliog. (Condon Lectures) [glaciers in Alaska, Canada and Greenland] 4092

SHARPLES, ADA WHITE. Alaska wild flowers. Stanford, Calif., Stanford University Press, 1938. 156p. front. illus. index. ANR. Stanford, Stanford University Press, 1958. 2d print. 156p. front. illus. index. 4093

SHARPLES, ADA WHITE. Two against the North. N. Y., Dial Press, 1961. 252p. map. [autobiog.] 4094

SHASKOV, S. S. Istoricheskie stiudy S. S. Shashkova; Izdanie N. A. Shigin. [TITLE TR. S. S. Shashkov's historical studies; edited by N. A. Shigin] St. Petersburg, A. Morigerov, 1872. 2 vols. 4095

SHAW, CHARLES GARDNER and R. SPRAGUE. Additions to Alaskan fungi. Pullman, Washington State College, 1954. bibliog. (Agriculture Experimental Stations Scientific Paper no. 1334.Also in: Research studies, vol. 22, no. 3, Sept. 1954. pp.170-78) 4096

SHAW, EARL B. Anglo-America, a regional geography. N. Y., Wiley, 1959. 480p. illus. maps, bibliog. [a textbook with section on Alaska] 4097

Shaw, Flora. SEE no. 480, Bell, E. Moberly.

Shea and Patten, comp. SEE no. 2672, [Le Febre, H. B.]

Sheffield, W. M., comp. SEE no. 28, Alaska almanac. 1905-07.

SHELDON, CHARLES. The wilderness of Denali, explorations of a hunter-naturalist in northern Alaska. Edited by C. Hart Merriam and E. W. Nelson. N. Y., Charles Scribner's Sons, 1930. [c1930] 412p. front.(port), pls. map(fold. in back), appends. index. ANR. N. Y. Scribner, 1960. 412p. [has appends. and index, no pls. or map] [Toklat River area of Mt. McKinley National Park] 4098

SHELDON, CHARLES. The wilderness of the North Pacific Coast islands, a hunter's experiences while searching for wapiti,bears, and caribou on the larger coast islands of British Columbia and Alaska. N. Y., Charles Scribner's Sons, 1912. [c1912] front.

pls. by Carl Rungius, photos, maps(incl. 1 fold.), ftntes. appends. index. [Montague and Admiralty Islands, southeastern Alaska]   4099

SHELDON, CHARLES. The wilderness of the Upper Yukon, a hunter's explorations for wild sheep in sub-Arctic mountains. N. Y., Charles Scribner's Sons, 1911. [c1911] 354p. front.(col. pl.), pls.(some col.), maps, appendixes, index. ANR. London, Unwin, 1911. 354p. front.(col. pl.), pls.(some col.), maps(some fold.) ANR. Toronto, Copp Clark, 1911. ANR. N. Y., Charles Scribner's Sons, 1919. 2d ed. rev. 364p. front.(col. pl.), pls.(some col.), maps(incl. 1 fold.), appends. index.   4100

Sheldon, Charles. SEE ALSO nos.
    610, Boone and Crockett Club. Hunting ... 1925;
    1012, Cook, F. A. To top continent ... 1908;
    4809, Whelen, T., edit. Hunting big game ... vol. 2. 1946.

Shelekhov, Grigorii Ivanovich. Grigori Schelechof Russischen Kaufmanns Erste ... 1793. SEE no. 4104.

Shelekhov, Grigorii Ivanovich. Istoricheskoe i geograficheskoe ... 1793. SEE no. 4103.

SHELEKHOV, GRIGORII IVANOVICH. Puteshestvie G. Shelekhova s 1783 po 1790 iz Okhotska po Vostochnomu okeanu k Amerikanskim beregam ... s kartinkoiu. Sanktpeterburg, Tip. Gubernskago pravleniia, 1812. 2 pts. in 1. 172p. illus. map [See earlier editions with different titles in 1791 and 1793,1792 (nos. 4102-3) and also translations (nos. 4104-5)]   4101

Shelekhov, Grigorii Ivanovich. Rossiiskago kuptsa Grigor'ia Shelekhova prodolzhenie ... 1792. SEE no. 4103.

SHELEKHOV, GRIGORII IVANOVICH. Rossiiskago kuptsa Grigor'ia Shelekhova stranstvovanie v 1783 ... godu ... V Sanktpeterburgie, 1791 goda. [TITLE TR. Journey of the Russian merchant Grigorii Shelekhov in 1783 from Okhotsk across the Eastern Ocean to the American coast ...] St. Petersburg, 1791. iv,74p. front. map (fold.) [cf no. 4103 and no. 4101. See also trs. nos. 4104-5]
                                                                      4102

SHELEKHOV, GRIGORII IVANOVICH. Rossiiskago kuptsa imenitago ryl'skago grazhdanina Grigor'ia Shelekhova pervoe stranstvovanie s 1783 po 1787 god iz Okhotska po Vostochnomu okeanu k Amerikanskim beregam, i vozvrashchenie ego v Rossiiu s obstoiatel'nym uviedomleniem ob otkrytii novoobrietennykh im ostrovov Kyktaka i Afagnaka ... S geograficheskim chertezhem, so izobrazheniem samago morehkhodtsa i naidennykh im dikikh liudei. [TITLE TR. First voyage of the Russian merchant Grigorii Shelekhov of Ryl'sk in 1783-87 from Okhotsk over the Eastern Ocean to the coasts of American and return to Russia, with a circumstantial account of his discovery of the newly acquired islands of Kuktat

and Afognak ... With geographic map and illustrations fo the seafarer and the savages he found]   St. Petersburg, 1793, 1792.   2
vols. in 1 (vol. 1 in 2 pts.) 86,87-172p. and 95p. illus. port.
map.[Separate titles for pt. 2 of vol. 1 and for vol. 2 follow]
VOLUME 1, PART 2, pub. in 1793, pp.87-172 (this pt. not in 1791
printing) HAS TITLE Istoricheskoe i geograficheskoe opisanie Kuril'skikh, Aleutskikh, Andreĭanovskikh i Lis'evskikh ostrovov,
prostiraĭushchikysĭa ot Kamchatki do Ameriki na vostochnom okeane.
[TITLE TR. Historical and geographic description of the Kuril,
Aleutian, Andreanof and Fox Islands, extending from Kamchatka to
America in the Eastern Ocean]
VOLUME 2 pub. in 1792, 95p. HAS TITLE Rossiĭskago kupĉsa Grigor'
ia Shelekhova prodolzhenie stranstvovaniĭa po vostochnomu okeanu
k Amerikanskim beregam v 1788 godu ... [TITLE TR. Continuation of
the Russian merchant Grigoriĭ Shelekhov's voyage over the Eastern
Ocean to the American coast in 1788 ...]   4103

TRANSLATION of vol. 1, pt. 1 and vol. 2 - Rossiĭskago kupĉsa
    imenitago ... 1793, 1792.

Grigori Schelechof Russischen Kaufmanns Erste und Zweyte Reise
    von Ochotsk in Sibirien durch den östlichen Ocean nach den
    Küsten von Amerika in den Jahre- 1783 bis 1789. Nebst um-
    ständlicher Beschreibung der von ihm neuentdeckten Inseln
    Rüktak, Ufagnak und mehrerer andrer, zu welchen selbst der
    berühmte Cap. Cook nicht gekommen und die sich der Russischen
    Herrschaft unterworfen haben. Aus dem Russischen übersetz
    von J. Z. Logan. St. Petersburg, bey Johann Kacharias Logan,
    1793. 84p.   4104

TRANSLATION of vol. 1(pt. 1 only) - Rossiĭskago kuptsa imeni-
    tago ... 1793, 1792.

Voyage of Gregory Shelekhof, a Russian merchant, from Okhotzk,
    on the Eastern Ocean, to the coast of America, in the years
    1783, 1784, 1785, 1786, 1787 and his return to Russia. From
    his own journal. no pl., n. d. 42p. [also in no. 4656] 4105

Shelekhov, Grigoriĭ Ivanovich. SEE ALSO nos.
    4, Adamov, A. G. G. I. Shelikhov; pod red ... 1952;
    5, Adamov, A. G. G. I. Shelikhov ... 1951;
    3475, Pallas, P. S. Neue nordische Beyträge ... 1781-96;
    3814, Ricks, M. B. Earliest hist. Alaska ... 1970;
    4656, Varieties of literature ... 1795.

SHELFORD, VICTOR E. The ecology of North America. Urbana, University of Illinois Press, 1963. xxii,610p. illus. graphs,
tables, maps, bibliog. index. [pp.211-37 refer to parts of
Alaska, Canada and Greenland]   4106

SHEMELIN, FEDOR. Istoricheskoe izviestĭe o pervom puteshestviĭa
Rossiian vokrug svieta. [TITLE TR. Information about the first
Russian voyages round the world] [St. Petersburg?], 1823.33p.4107

SHEMELIN, FEDOR. Zhurnal pervago puteshestviia Rossiian vokrug zemnago shara, sochinennyi pod vysochaishim Ego Imperatorskago Velichestva pokrovitel'stvom Rossiisko-Amerikanskoi kompanii glavnym kommissionerom moskovskim kuptsom Fedorom Shemelinym. [TITLE TR. Journal of the first voyage of the Russians around the globe, written by Moscow merchant, Fedor Shemelin, chief commissioner of the Russian American Company which is under the sovereign patronage of His Imperial Majesty] Sanktpeterburg, Meditsinskaia tipografiia, 1816[1818] in 2 pts. 168p. and 428p. tables.   4108

SHENITZ, HELEN A. Alaska's good Father, the story of an Alaskan priest who became head of the Russian Orthodox Church. Wilkes Barre, Penna., 1962. 10p. wrps. [*Father* Veniaminov]   4109

SHEPARD, F. P. and R. F. DILL. Submarine canyons and other sea valleys. Chicago, Rand McNally, 1966. 381p. illus. maps. [scattered references to Bering Sea, Aleutian waters, and those of southeastern Alaska]   4110

Shepard, Irving, edit. SEE no. 2761, London, Jack.

SHEPARD, ISABEL SHARPE. The cruise of the U. S. Steamer "Rush" in Behring Sea, summer of 1889. S. F., Bancroft Co., 1889. 257p. 2 fronts.(pl. and fold. map), pls.   4111

SHEPARD, THOMAS ROCHESTER. Placer mining law in Alaska; a lecture delivered to the graduate class of the Yale Law School, March 4, 1909, by Thomas R. Shepard ... New Haven, Press of S. Z. Field, 1909. 16p. (reprint from Yale Law Journal, March-May, 1909)   4112

Shepherd, H. W., co-auth. SEE no. 2938, McMinn, H. E.

SHERMAN, DEAN F., edit. Alaska cavalcade. Compiled and edited by Dean F. Sherman. Seattle, Alaska Life Pub. Co., Edwin A. Kraft, Pub., [c1943] [printed by Pioneer, Inc., Tacoma, Wash.] 300p. front. ports. pls. facsim. endmaps.   4113

Sherman, H. M., co-auth. SEE no. 3872, Wilkins, G. H.

SHERWOOD, MORGAN B. Exploration of Alaska 1865-1900. New Haven, Yale University Press, 1965. 207(18)p. pls.(in unp. sect.), maps, ftntes. chronol. index. (Yale Western Americana Series 7)   4114

Shields, G. W., co-auth. SEE no. 2249, Hyde, A.

SHIELDS, WALTER C. The ancient ground. Poetry. Seattle, Press of Loman and Hanford, 1918. 47p. (Privately Printed by The Keenok Club, of Nome, Alaska) 47p.   4115

ALASKAN BIBLIOGRAPHY

SHIELS, ARCHIBALD WILLIAMSON. Early voyages to the Pacific, a few notes on the days of iron men and wooden ships. Compiled by Archie W. Shiels. [Bellingham, Wash., Union Printing Co., c1931] 1st ed. 61p. ANR. Seattle, Shorey Book Store, 1964. facsim. of [c1931] ed. 61p. wrps. [pp.36-61 about Alaska] 4116

SHIELS, ARCHIBALD WILLIAMSON. Little journeys into the history of Russian America and the purchase of Alaska. Compiled by Archie W. Shiels. [Bellingham, Wash., Union Printing Co., c1949] 116p. ltd. ed. of 125 autographed copies. ANR. Seattle, Shorey Book Store, 1965. facsim. of [c1949] ed. 4117

SHIELS, ARCHIBALD WILLIAMSON. Seward's icebox, a few notes on the development of Alaska 1867-1932. By Archie W. Shiels. [Bellingham, Wash., Union Printing Co., c1933] ltd. ed. of 500 copies. 419p. 4118

SHIELS, ARCHIBALD WILLIAMSON. "Tell me a 'stowry'" no pl., n.d. [Bellingham, Wash., ca 1942 ?] var. p. [15 short stories for children about Alaskan Indians] 4119

SHIELS, ARCHIBALD WILLIAMSON. The purchase of Alaska. By Archie W. Shiels. College, University of Alaska Press, 1967. 207p. bibliog. (Alaska Purchase Centennial Commission) [incls. speech by Charles Sumner] 4120

SHIELS, ARCHIBALD WILLIAMSON. The story of two dreams, early plans for a transcontinental railroad to Alaska ... By Archie W. Shiels. [Bellingham, Wash., Union Printing Co., c1957] 31p. ANR. Seattle, Shorey Book Store, 1965. facsim. of [c1957] ed. 4124

SHIELS, ARCHIBALD WILLIAMSON. The work of Veniaminov in Alaska. Victoria, B. C., 1947. (reprinted from author's *Father Herman*, in British Columbia Historical Quarterly, Oct. 1947) 4122

Shigin, N. A., edit. SEE no. 4095, Shashkov, S. S.

Shikari, A., co-auth. SEE no. 2074, Herbert, Agnes.

SHILLINGLAW, JOHN JOSEPH. A narrative of Arctic discovery from the earliest period to the present time; with the details of the measures adopted by Her Majesty's government for the relief of the expedition under Sir John Franklin. London, W. Shoberl, 1850. 348p. front.(port.), maps(fold.) 4123

SHIMKIN, DEMITRI BORIS. The economy of a trapping center, the case of Fort Yukon, Alaska. N. Y., Johnson Reprint Corp., 1966. (reprinted from Economic Development and Cultural Chance, vol.3, 1954/55. Chicago, 1955. pp.219-40. map, tables.) 4124

SHINEN, DAVID and MARILENE SHINEN. Yapigum Atiḫtoosi. A beginning reading book in Yupik Eskimo, the language spoken by the Eskimos who live on St. Lawrence Island. Gambell, Alaska, Summer Institute of Linguistics, 1966. ltd. ed. of 100 copies. 28p. illus. wrps. (Wycliffe Bible Translators) 4125

SHINEN, MARILENE. Marriage customs of the St. Lawrence Island Eskimos. (reprint from Anthropologica, vol. 5, no. 2, 1963. pp.199-208. wrps. 4126

Shinen, Marilene. SEE ALSO no. 4125, Shinen, David.

Shipley, J. W. SEE no. 1860, Griggs, R. F.

Shishmaref Day School. SEE no. 57, Alaska Crippled Children's Assoc.

SHLIÂMIN, BORIS ALEKSANDROVICH. Beringovo more. [TITLE TR. Bering Sea] Moskva, Gos. izd-vo geograficheskoĭ lit-ry, 1958. 96p. illus. maps, bibliog. 4127

SHMIDT, PETR ĨUL'EVICH. Ryby Tikhogo okeana. Ocherk sovremennykh teoriĭ i voyzreniĭ na rasprostranenie i razvitie fauny ryb Tikhogo okeana. [TITLE TR. Fishes of the Pacific Ocean] Moskva, Pishchepromizdat, 1948. 123p. tables, maps, bibliog. 4128

SHNEĬDEROV, VLADIMIR ADOL'FOVICH. Phokhod "Sibiriâkova." [TITLE TR. The voyage of the *Sibiriâkov*] Moskva, "Molodaiâ gvardiiâ," 1933. 207p. illus. ports. (Bibliotheka ėkspeditŝiĭ i puteshestviĭ) [mention of Alaskan coastal waters] 4129

Shoot 'em ... ! [19__] SEE no. 106, Alaska Range Guides Assoc.

SHORE, EVELYN BERGLUND. Born on snowshoes. Illustrated with photographs and with decorations by Courtney Allen. Boston, Houghton Mifflin, 1954. [c1954] 209p. front.(sketch), photos, sketches, endmaps. [autobiog. - trapping in Salmon River area, near Fort Yukon] 4130

Shore, Evelyn Berglund. SEE ALSO no. 3707, Pyle, E. T.

Short story of Alaska ... 1898. SEE no. 3211, Mount Wrangell Co.

SHORT, WAYNE. The cheechakoes. Drawings by Peter Parnall. N. Y., Random House, [c1964] 1st print. 244p. sketches, map [autobiog. - southeastern Alaska - for sequel SEE no. 4132] 4131

SHORT, WAYNE. This raw land. N. Y., Random House, 1968. [autobiog. - southeastern Alaska - sequel to no. 4131] 4132

SHORTALL, LEONARD. Eric in Alaska. N. Y., Morrow, 1967. 48p. [juv. fict.] 4133

SHORTT, T. M.   The summer birds of Yakutat Bay, Alaska.   Toronto, Royal Ontario Museum of Zoology, 1939.   30p.   bibliog.   (Contribution no. 17)   4134

SHRIEVER, LUCILLE W.   Alaskan verses from native folklore.   Montreal, Marlin Publishing Co., 1969.   57p.   [four and one-half inch by six and one-quarter inch in size]   4135

Shteĭn, M. G., co-auth.   SEE no. 3800, Rĭabov, N. I.

SHTEĬNBERG, EVGENIĬ L'VOVICH.   I. F. Kruzenshtern, Ĭu. F. Lisĭanskiĭ;   pod red, A. I. Solov'eva.   [TITLE TR.   I. F. Krusenstern, I. F. Lisianskiĭ;   edited by A. I. Solov'ev]   Moskva, Gos. izd-vo geogr. lit-ry, 1950.   40p.   ports.   illus.   maps.   4136

SHTEĬNBERG, EVGENIĬ L'VOVICH.   Zhizneopisanie russkogo moreplavatelĭa Ĭuriĭa Lisĭanskogo, soderzhashchee istoriĭu ego sluzhby na voennom flote rossiĭskom, ego plavaniĭ v Zapadnuĭu i Vostochnuĭu Indiĭu, Severnuĭu Ameriku i Ĭuzhnuĭu Ameriky, a takzhe o znamenitom pervom voĭazhe russkikh morĭakov vokrug sveta s 1803 po 1806 god.   [TITLE TR.   Biography of the Russian navigator Ĭuriĭ Lisĭanskiĭ, including a history of his service in the Russian Navy, his trips to the West and East Indies, North and South America, and also the first around-the-world voyage of Russian navigators from 1803 to 1806]   Moskva, Voen. izd-vo, 1948.   212(4)p.   port.   map(fold.)   4137

SHUMAKER, CECIL LEE.   Do you know ?   Nature essays of Prince William Sound.   Illustrated by the author.   N. Y., Exposition Press, 1967.   illus.   4138

SHURTLEFF, BERTRAND LESLIE.   Colt of the Alcan Road.   By Bertrand Shurtleff.   Indianapolis, Bobbs-Merrill, 1951.   4139

SHURTLEFF, BERTRAND LESLIE.   Escape from the icecap.   A tale of Huskie and Spareribs.   By Bertrand Shurtleff.   Indianapolis, Bobbs-Merrill, 1952.   282p.   illus. by Diana Thorne.   4140

SHURTLEFF, BERTRAND LESLIE.   Long lash.   By Bertrand Shurtleff.   Indianapolis, Bobbs-Merrill, 1947.   273p.   illus. by Diana Thorne.   4141

SHURTLEFF, BERTRAND LESLIE.   Two against the North, a story of Huskie and Spareribs.   By Bertrand Shurtleff.   Illustrated by Diana Thorne.   Indianapolis, Bobbs-Merrill, 1949.   1st ed.   274p.   front.(dble.), illus.   4142

Siberian Husky News.   SEE no. 4508, Thompson, Raymond.

SICKELS, DOROTHY J.   Eskimos, hunters of the Arctic.   Garden City, N. Y., Garden City Pub. Co., 1941.   20p.   [juv.]   4143

SIEBERT, ERNA and WERNER FORMAN.   North American Indian art.
N. Y., Tudor Pub. Co., 1967. pls.(col.) [Tlingit included] 4144

Sieburt, F., edit.   SEE no. 3743, Rasmussen, K. J. V.

SIEM, CONRAD. Memorial on the introduction of domesticated rein-
deer into Canada. By Conrad Siem. Written at the request of Rt.
Hon. R. L. Borden, Premier of the Dominion of Canada.   N. Y.,
McConnell Printing Co., 1911. 31p.   4145

SIEM, CONRAD. The C. S. L. T., containing views on Abraham Lincoln as expressed by Bismarck in 1878 from the recollections of
the author. [pl. ?, pub. ?], 1915. 61p. [discusses proposed
plan for Alaska on the Community System of Land Tenure]   4146

SIEM, CONRAD. The menace, a semi-scientific story of particular
interest to the people of Nome.   Dedicated to the miners of
Seward Peninsula. Nome, 1903. 22p.   4147

SIERRA CLUB, San Francisco. Wilderness in a changing world.
S. F., Sierra Club, 1966. 255p. photos, maps. (Wilderness Conference, 9th, S. F., 1965) [incls. references to proposed dams
in Alaska]   4148

Sierra Club. SEE ALSO no. 595, Bohn, David. Glacier Bay. 1967.

Sifton, Clifford. SEE nos.
    1151, Dafoe, John W. Clifford Sifton ... 1931;
    3100, Miers, H. A. Yukon. Visit ... 1901.

Sights and scenes ... 1890. SEE no. 4612, Union Pacific R.R. Co.

Silk, H. V. SEE no. 1806, Great Britain. Admiralty.

SILLARS, ROBERTSON. The North Pacific and Alaska. N. Y., Columbia University, Teacher's College, 1942. 19p. reading list,
maps. (Institute of Adult Education, Theaters of War, Series 1,
no. 3)   4149

SILOOK, ROGER. ... in the beginning. By Roger Silook. Illustrated by Robert Mayokok. Anchorage, The Anchorage Printing Co.,
[c1970] (31)p. illus. wrps. [Eskimo legend as told by a St.
Lawrence Islander]   4150

SILVERBERG, ROBERT. Scientists and scoundrels. N. Y., Thomas Y.
Crowell, 1965. [incls. references to Frederick Cook]   4151

SILVERS, CONNIE.   Alaska Highway sketches souvenir and travel
guide. Anchorage, by author, n. d. [1963 ?] 200p. illus. maps,
wrps. [from Dawson Creek, B.C., Canada, to Fairbanks, Alaska.
Incls. other Alaskan roads]   4152

SIMMONDS,PETER LUND. Sir John Franklin and the Arctic regions; showing the progress of British enterprise for the discovery of the Northwest Passage during the 19th century. With more detailed notices of the recent expeditions in search of the missing vessels under Captain Sir John Franklin. London, G. Routledge & Co., 1851. 375p. front. maps(fold.), bibliog. [for separate American edition, SEE no. 4154]   4153

SIMMONDS, PETER LUND. Sir John Franklin and the Arctic regions, with detailed notices of the expeditions in search of the missing vessels under Sir John Franklin. To which is added an account of the American expedition under the patronage of Henry Grinnell with an introduction to the American edition. Buffalo, G. H. Derby & Co., 1852. 396p. front. pls. map(fold.) [does not have bibliog. of no. 4153. Later reprinted, SEE no. 4156]   4154

SIMMONDS, PETER LUND. The Arctic regions; a narrative of British enterprise to discover the North-West Passage. London, Routledge, 1857. 8th ed. xi,284p. front. ANR. WITH TITLE The Arctic regions and polar discoveries during the nineteenth century, with an account of the new British exploring expedition fitted out in 1875, its objects and prospects. London, Routledge, 1875. 10th ed. [with textual changes]. 387p. front. map(fold.)
4155

[SIMMONDS, PETER LUND] The Arctic regions; being an account of the American expedition in search of Sir John Franklin, under the patronage of Henry Grinnell, Esq. of New York. Auburn and Buffalo, N. Y., Derby, Orton and Mulligan, 1853. 396p. front. illus. [reprint of no. 4154]   4156

Simmonds, S., tr. SEE no. 4746, Wartes, Wm. C., edit.

SIMMONS, GEORGE. Target: Arctic; men in the skies at the top of the world. Philadelphia, Chilton Books, 1965. 1st ed. [pub. simultaneously by Ambassador Books, Toronto] xii,420p. illus. maps, bibliog. appends. index.   4157

SIMOENS de SILVA, ANTONIO CARLOS. Viagens aos Estados Unidos da America, Colombia britannica, territorio do Alaska e archipelago do Hawaii. De 1914 a 1915 - 1915 a 1916 - 1928 a 1929 em missões scientificas, de caracter official, do governo do Brasil perante os Congressos internacionaes de americanistas e pan-americanos. Rio de Janeiro, Imprensa nacional, 1932. 236p.   4158

SIMONSEN, SIGURD J. Among the sourdoughs. N. Y., Fortuny's, Pub., 1940. 1st ed. 153p. [fict.]   4159

SIMPSON, ALEXANDER. The life and travels of Thomas Simpson, the Arctic discoverer, by his brother, Alexander Simpson. London, Richard Bentley, 1845. 424p. front.(port.), map(fold.). [Dease and Simpson, Pt. Barrow to Back River for Hudson's Bay Co.]   4160

Simpson, F. W.   SEE no. 3359, Northwood, T. D.

Simpson, George.   An overland journey ... 1847.   SEE no. 4161.

SIMPSON, GEORGE.   Narrative of a journey round the world, during
the years 1841 and 1842.   By Sir George Simpson, Governor-in-Chief
of the Hudson's Bay Company's territories in North America.   In
two volumes.   London, Henry Colburn, Publisher, 1847.   [printed
by F. Shoberl, Jun.]   xi(1)438p. and vii,469p. front.(port.),
map(fold.) ANR. WITH TITLE An overland journey around the world,
during the years 1841 and 1842. Philadelphia, Lea & Blanchard,
1847.   2 pts. in 1.   273p. and 230p.   4161

SIMPSON, GEORGE.   Narrative of a voyage to California ports in
1841-42, together with voyages to Sitka, the Sandwich Islands and
Okhotsk.   From the narrative of a journey round the world by Sir
George Simpson.   S. F., From the Press of T. C. Russell, 1930.
ltd. ed. of 250 copies.   232p. (The Russell California series)4162

Simpson, George.   SEE ALSO nos.
     880, Chalmers, J. W.   Fur trade governor ... 1960;
     2500, Knox, O. E.   By paddle and saddle.   1943;
     3085, Merk, F.   Fur trade and empire ... 1931;
     3206, Morton, A. S.   Sir George Simpson ... 1944;
     4326, Stefansson, V.   Unsolved mysteries ... [c1938]

Simpson, John.   SEE nos.
     1826, and 1832.   Great Britain.   Parl. (Franklin search);
     3907, Royal Geographic Soc.   Arctic geog. ... 1875.

SIMPSON, THOMAS.   Narrative of the discoveries on the North Coast
of America; effected by the officers of the Hudson's Bay Company
during the years 1836-39.   By Thomas Simpson, Esq.   London,
Richard Bentley, Publisher, 1843.   [printed by S. J. Bentley,
Wilson and Flay] xix,419p. maps(fold. in pocket), append. [incls.
Pt. Barrow and Alaskan Arctic coast]   4163

Simpson, Thomas.   SEE ALSO nos.
     4160, Simpson, Alexander.   Life and travels ... 1845;
     4326, Stefansson, V.   Unsolved mysteries ... [c1938]

Sinkiel, M., tr.   SEE no. 1332, Donskoi, V.

Sitka spruce ... 1927.   SEE no. 4797, West Coast Lumber Trade
     Extension Bureau.

Six month's prospecting ... 1898.   SEE no. 48,
     Alaska Coast Exploration Co.

SKAGUAY COMMERCIAL CLUB.   Skaguay, the gateway to the Klondike, a
brief history of its rapid growth from a city of tents to a city
of substantial buildings.   Skaguay, Daily Alaskan Print, 1898.
unp. illus. [Published by Fletcher & Hayne]   4164

SKAGWAY CHAMBER OF COMMERCE. Constitution and by-laws. Skagway,
Daily Alaskan Print, 1900. 8p.   4165

SKAGWAY COMMERCIAL CLUB. Skagway, Alaska. Skagway, The Daily
Alaskan, n. d. 46p.   4166

Skalberg, Johann, tr. SEE no. 4759, Waxell, S. L.

SKARLAND, IVAR and JAMES LOUIS GIDDINGS, jr. Flint stations in
Central Alaska. By Ivar Skarland and J. L. Giddings, jr. Menasha, Wisc., 1948. illus. pl. map (reprinted from American Antiquity, vol. 14, pp.116-20)   4167

Skarland, Ivar. SEE ALSO no. 4535, Tickasook. Inipiut homes.

Skellings, E., edit. SEE no. 141, Alaska Writers Workshop.

SKELTON, RALEIGH ASHLIN. Captain James Cook after two hundred
years. A commemorative address delivered before th Hakluyt Society. By R. A. Skelton. Published by the Trustees of the British
Museum. London, British Museum, 1969. 32p.+ 24p.(pls.) front.
(port.), pls. facsims. maps.   4168

SKELTON, RAILEIGH ASHLIN. Captain James Cook as a hydrographer;
annual lecture to the Society for Nautical Research, 1953. London, 1954. (reprinted from The Mariner's Mirror, vol. 40, no. 2,
May 1954. pp.92-119)   4169

SKELTON, RALEIGH ASHLIN. Charts and views drawn by Cook and his
officers and reproduced from the original manuscripts. Cambridge,
University Press, 1955. (Hakluyt Society)   4170

SKELTON, RALEIGH ASHLIN. Explorer's maps, chapters in the cartographic record of geographical discovery. London, Routledge &
Kegan Paul, 1958. 337p. illus. maps, bibliog. ANR. 1960.
reprint. [those of Capt. James Cook, others]   4171

SKELTON, RALEIGH ASHLIN and R. V. Tooley. The marine surveys of
James Cook in North America, 1758-68. London, The Map Collectors
Circle, 1967. 34p. illus. (Map Collectors Circle, 4th series,
no. 37)   4172

Sketches by a Traveller. 1830   SEE no. 2147, [Holbrook, S.P.]

SKEWES, JOSEPH HENRY. Sir John Franklin, the true secret of the
discovery of his fate. A "revelation." London, Bemrose & Sons,
1889. 243p. illus. maps. [TITLE ON COVER Sir John Franklin, the
discovery of his fate, after forty years' silence, now made pub-
lic] ANR. London, 1890. with supplement.   4173

SKINNER, CONSTANCE LINDSAY. The search relentless. London,1925.
252p. ANR. N. Y., Coward-McCann, 1928. vii,311p. ANR.Toronto,
McClelland, 1928. [fict. acct. Yukon goldrush]   4174

SKINNER, J. W. and G. L. WILDE. Permian fusulinids from Pacific Northwest and Alaska. Lawrence, Kansas, 1966. 64p. illus. refs. (Kansas. University. Paleontological contributions, paper no.4) [Alaska-Yukon border between Fairbanks and Dawson, Y. T.]   4175

SKINNER, MORRIS F. and OVE C. KAISEN. The fossil bison of Alaska and preliminary revision of the genus. N. Y., American Museum of Natural History, 1947. 133p. pls. figs. tables, maps, wrps. (Frick Laboratory Bull. vol. 89, art. 3)   4176

SLADEN, DOUGLAS BROOKE WHEELTON. On the cars and off, being a journal of a pilgrimage along the Queen's Highway to the east from Halifax in Nova Scotia to Victoria in Vancouver's Island, with additional matter on the Klondike by P. A. Hurd. London, 1898. 512p. front. pls. maps, index. ANR. London, n. d. 512p. [also has added Yukon material] OTHERS London, 1874 and 1875, prior to gold rush.   4177

Slavin, S. V., edit. SEE no. 21, Agranat, G. A.

SLAYDEN, THELMA THOMPSON. Miracle in Alaska. N. Y., Frederick Fell, 1963. 1st print. 260p. [fict.]   4178

SLEATOR, WILLIAM. The angry moon. Retold by William Sleator, with pictures by Blair Lent. Boston, Little Brown, [c1970] 1st ed. 45(3)p. front. illus.(col.) (An Atlantic Monthly Press Book) [juv. based upon a Tlingit legend recorded by Dr. John R. Swanton. SEE no. 4420]   4179

Slepnov, M. SEE no. 4717, Voyage *Chelyuskin.*

SLEPTSOV, M. M. Biologiĭa i promysl kitov dal'nevostochnykh moreĭ. Pod red. S. E. Kleĭnenberga. [TITLE TR. Biology of the whales and whaling of the Far Eastern Seas] Moskva, Pishche-promizdat, 1955. 63p. illus. tables, maps. [studies of Academy of Science and Ministry of Fisheries in 1948 and 1951-54, Okhotsk, Bering and Chukchi Seas]   4180

SLEVIN, JOSEPH RICHARD. The amphibians of western North America; an account of the species known to inhabit California, Alaska, British Columbia, Washington, Oregon, Idaho, Utah, Nevada, Arizona, Sonora, and Lower California. S. F., California Academy of Sciences, 1928. 152p. pls. (Occasional Papers, no. 16)   4181

SLIJPER, EVERHARD JOHANNES. Walvisson. Amsterdam, D. B. Centen, 1958. [SEE no. 4183 for tr.]   4182

SLIJPER, EVERHARD JOHANNES. Whales. Translated by A. J. Pomerans. London, Hutchinson & Co., 1962. 475p. illus. tables, maps, appends. bibliog. ANR. N. Y., Basic Books, 1962. [tr. of no. 4182]   4183

Sloan, J. M. SEE no. 3290, Neuman, D. C.

SLOANE, HOWARD N. and LUCILLE L. SLOANE. The Goodyear guide to State Parks. Region 2, California, Washington, Oregon, Alaska, Hawaii, including campsites, beaches, national parks, historic sites, forests, and other vacation and recreational areas. N. Y., Crown Publishers, 1967. illus. photos. [Alaska, pp.1-27]   4184

Sloane, Lucille L. SEE no. 4184, Sloane, H. N.

Small, Adrian, illus. SEE no. 4703, Villiers, A. J.

SMALL, AUSTIN J. The frozen trail. Boston, Houghton, 1924. 305p. [fict.]   4185

SMALL, MARIE. Four fares to Juneau. Illustrated by Erna Karolyi. N. Y., McGraw-Hill and London, Whittlesey House, [c1947] 237p. sketches, endmaps. [autobiog.]   4186

SMETANA, A. Staphylinini und Quediini von Kanada und Alaska, Col. Staphylinidae. Lund, C. W. K. Gleerup, 1965. 18p. illus. refs. (Lund. Univ. Acta, sectio 2, no. 13) [rove beetles] 4187

SMILEY, CHARLES HUGH. Atmospheric refraction at low altitudes. Toronto, 1950. 9p. table, bibliog. (Royal Meteorological Society, Canadian Branch. Papers, vol. 1, no. 7, Oct. 1950) [incls. Alaska and North Pole "Ptarmigan" flights]   4188

SMIRNOV, NESTOR ALEKSANDROVICH. Zveri Arktiki. [TITLE TR. Wild animals of the Arctic] Leningrad, Izd-vo Glavsevmorputi, 1935. 579p. illus. bibliogs. [by var. authors, on Arctic fauna, incl. marine mammals]   4189

SMITH, ARTHUR M. On to Alaska with Buchanan. Complete story of the trips to Alaska made annually by G. E. Buchanan of Detroit, and the eighty or more boys and girls who earn the right to make the trip with him. Los Angeles, Ward Ritchie Press, 1937. 124p. front. pls. ports.   4190

Smith, Charles, tr. SEE no. 2515, Kotzebue, A. F. F. von.

SMITH, CHARLES W., comp. A union list of manuscripts in libraries of the Pacific Northwest. Seattle, University of Washington Press, 1932. 57p. (Pacific Northwest Library Assoc., Committee on Bibliography)   4191

SMITH, CHARLES W., comp. Check-list of books and pamphlets relating to the history of the Pacific Northwest to be found in representative libraries of that region. Olympia, Washington State Library Assoc., 1909. 1st ed. 191p. [for later ed. SEE no. 4193]   4192

SMITH, CHARLES W., comp. Pacific Northwest Americana; a check list of books and pamphlets relating to the history of the Pacific Northwest. Compiled by Charles W. Smith. N. Y., H. W. Wilson, 1921. rev. and enl. 329p. (University of Washington Library) ANR. rev. and extended by Isabel Mayhew. Portland, Ore., Binfords and Mort, 1950. 381p. [also issued interleaved] (Oregon Historical Society) [both later editions of no. 4192]   4193

Smith, Cynthia Roe, co-auth. SEE no. 1207, Davis, Phyllis Eileen.

SMITH, DARRELL HEVENOR. The Bureau of Education; its history, activities, and organization. Baltimore, Johns Hopkins Press, 1923. 157p. [U. S. Bureau of Education]   4194

SMITH, DAVID MURRAY. Arctic expeditions from British and foreign shores; from the earliest times to the expedition of 1875-76. By D. Murray Smith. Glasgow, R. Liddell, 1877. xv,824p. front. pls.(some col.), ports. charts(fold.), map. OTHERS in 1877, Edinburgh, pub. by Thomas C. Jack, Grange Pub. Works: London, J. G. Murdock. ANR. London, Fullerton and Jack, 1880. [incls. Franklin search by way of Bering Strait]   4195

SMITH, FRANCES C. Men at work in Alaska. N. Y., Putnam, 1967. 127p. illus. map. [juv.]   4196

SMITH, FRANCES C. The world of the Arctic. Philadelphia, Lippincott, 1960. 126p. illus. [juv. incls. Alaska]   4197

SMITH, GEORGE BARNETT. Sir John Franklin and the romance of the Northwest Passage. N. Y., F. H. Revell, n. d. [ca 1896 ?]   4198

Smith, H. T. U., co-edit. SEE no. 2273, International Assoc. Quaternary Research.

Smith, Henry E. SEE no. 3867, Rogers, Lispenard.

Smith, Jefferson Davis "Soapy" SEE nos.
    977, Collier, Wm. K. Reign of ... 1935;
    2305, Itjen, Martin. Story tour Skagway street car. 1934;
    2672, [Le Febre, H. B.] "Soapy" Smith tragedy. 1907;
    3132, Miller, Mike. Soapy. 1970;
    3837, Robertson, F. C. Soapy Smith ... 1961.

Smith, Jessica, tr. SEE no. 345, Baidukov, G. F.

SMITH, JOSEPH RUSSELL and MERTON OGDEN PHILLIPS. North America, its people and the resources, development, and prospects of the continent as the home of man. N. Y., Harcourt Brace, 1942. rev. ed. 1,106p. [has chapters on southwestern Alaska and the Yukon Valley]   4199

SMITH, LAURA ROUNTREE. Little Eskimo. Chicago, A. Flanagan Co.,
1931. 159p. front. illus. (Little People of Other Lands series)
[juv. with locale general Arctic]   4200

Smith, Lowell. SEE no. 4497, Thomas, Lowell.

SMITH, MARIAN WESLEY, comp. Asia and North America, transpacific
contacts. Salt Lake City, 1953. 97p. illus. maps. (supplement
to American Antiquities, vol. 15, no. 3, pt. 2, Jan. 1953. Society for American Archaeology. Memoir, no. 9. AAAS Section on
Anthropology) [contains *Preliminary statement pottery Cape Denbigh* ... by James B. Griffin, pp. 40-42 and *Significance* ...
archaeol. ... *inland Alaska,* by F. G. Rainey, pp. 43-46]   4201

SMITH, MARIAN WESLEY, edit. The Tsimshian; their arts and music.
Edited by M. W. Smith. N. Y., J. J. Augustin, 1951. xii,290p.
pls. figs. music notes, maps, bibliog. index. (American Ethnographical Society. Pub. vol. 18) [contains *The Tsimshian and
their neighbors,* by V. E. Garfield, pp.3-70: *Tsimshian sculpture,*
by P. S. Wingert, pp.73-94: and *Tsimshian songs,* by C. M. Barbeau, pp.97-280. SEE ALSO no. 1684]   4202

SMITH, MAUDE PARSON, comp. Alaska. Hartford, Church Missions
Pub. Co., [1909]-1910. 89p. (Missionary Leaflet, series 6,
1-6)   4203

SMITH, RICHARD AUSTIN, edit. The frontier states; Alaska and
Hawaii, by Richard Austin Smith and the editors of Time-Life
Books. N. Y., Time-Life, 1968. 192p. illus.(some col.), ports.
maps(col.) (Time-Life Library of America Series) ANR. Boston,
Little Brown, 1970.   4204

Smith, "Soapy" SEE nos.
     977, Collier, Wm. K. Reign of ... 1935;
     2305, Itjen, Martin. Story tour Skagway street car. 1934;
     2672, [Le Febre, H. B.] "Soapy" Smith tragedy. 1907;
     3132, Miller, Mike. Soapy. 1970;
     3837, Robertson, F. C. Soapy Smith ... 1961.

SMITH, W. W. Alaska, the Eldorado of the North. Hartford, 1910.
3 vols. [vols. 2 and 3 have different titles. vol. 2: In the
heart of the Alaska gold fields. vol. 3: From the gold fields
to the land of the midnight sun]   4205

SMITH, WALTER S. Heredity and environment, a novel of Alaska and
the North. Boston, Meador, 1930. 125p.   4206

Smith, Wilfred Robert [assumed author] SEE no. 3620,
     "Platinum Bill"

SMITH, WILLIAM D. Northwest Passage, historic voyage of the S.S.
Manhattan. N. Y., American Heritage Press, 1970. 204p. illus.
endmaps. [oil tanker to Prudhoe Bay]   4207

SMITH'S CASH STORE. On the Klondike; how to go, when to go, where to go. [pl.?], Valleau and Peterson, 1897. 12p. 4208

SMITTER, WESSEL. Another morning. N. Y., Harper, 1941. 355p. [Matanuska Valley homesteaders] 4209

SMUCKER, SAMUEL MOSHEIM, edit. Arctic explorations and discoveries during the nineteenth century. Being detailed accounts of several expeditions to the north seas, both English and American, conducted by Ross, Parry, Back, Franklin, M'Clure and others. Including the First Grinnell Expedition under Lietuenant DeHaven, and the final effort of Dr. E. Kane in search of Sir John Franklin. N. Y., Miller & orton, 1857. 517p. illus. ANR. WITH VAR. TITLE. N. Y., W. L. Allison, 1886. enl. 640p. 4210

SMYTH, NATHAN A. and AMOS PINCHOT. Brief on the Cunningham coal entries in Alaska, submitted to the President in behalf of G. Pinchot. no pl., 1912. 127p. [Ballinger-Pinchot investigation] 4211

SNELL, ROY JUDSON. An Eskimo Robinson Crusoe. Boston, Little Brown, 1917. 4212

SNELL, ROY JUDSON. Arctic stowaways. By Roy J. Snell. Chicago, 1935. 180p. 4213

SNELL, ROY JUDSON. Captain Kituk, with illustrations by George F. Kerr. Boston, Little Brown, 1918. 225p. illus. ANR. Chicago and N. Y., Reilly and Lee Co., 1931. 225p. illus. 4214

SNELL, ROY JUDSON. Eskimo legends. Illustrated by Florence J. Hoopes. Boston, Little Brown, 1925. 203p. front.(col.), pls. 4215

SNELL, ROY JUDSON. Little White Fox and his Arctic friends. Illustrated by George F. Kerr. Boston, Little Brown, 1916. 130p. 4216

SNELL, ROY JUDSON. On the Yukon Trail. Chicago, 1922. 322p. 4217

SNELL, ROY JUDSON. Told beneath the Northern Lights, a book of Eskimo legends. Boston, 1925. 238p. illus. 4218

SNELLING, WILLIAM JOSEPH. The Polar regions of the western continent explored; embracing a geographical account of Iceland, Greenland, the islands of the frozen sea, and the northern parts of the American continent ... Together with ... navigators in those regions. Boston, W. W. Reed, 1831. 501p. front.(map), pls. [incls. account of Otto von Kotzebue] 4219

SNIDER, GERRIT "HEINIE" Centennial; one hundred stories of Alaska. By Gerrit Heinie Snider. Anchorage, Color Art Print. Co., [c1966] 192p. illus. ports. wrps. [several stories appeared in The Frontiersman, Palmer, Alaska weekly newspaper] 4220

SNIDER, GERRIT "HEINIE" Mink raising in Alaska. By Gerrit Snider. [Anchorage, The Times Pub. Co., 1929] 51p. illus. ports. plans. 4221

SNIDER, GERRIT "HEINIE" So was Alaska. Sketches by Jane Hafling. Anchorage, printed by Color Art Print., 1961. 95p. illus. photos, wrps. [1909 to 1961] 4222

SNIFFEN, MATTHEW K. and THOMAS SPEES CARRINGTON. The Indians of the Yukon and Tanana Valleys, Alaska. By M. K. Sniffen and T. S. Carrington. Philadelphia, 1914. 35p. front. pls. (Indian Rights Assoc. Pub., Second Series, no. 98) 4223

SNODGRASS, JEANNE O. American Indian painters, a biographical directory. N. Y., Museum of the American Indian, 1967. (Contribution from the Museum, vol. 21) 4224

Snow, Chas. W., co-auth. SEE no. 2931, MacLennan, Ewen.

SNYDER, LESTER LYNNE. A study of the sharp-tailed grouse. Toronto, 1935. 66p. front. illus. bibliog. (University of Toronto Studies in Biological Science, no. 40) [incls. those of central Alaska] 4225

SNYDER, LESTER LYNNE. The birds of Wrangell Island, with special reference to the Crawford collection of 1922. Toronto, 1926. 20p. bibliog. (University of Toronto Studies in Biological Science, no. 28) 4226

SNYDER, LESTER LYNNE. The Northwest coast sharp-shinned hawk. Toronto, 1938. 6p. (Royal Ontario Museum Occas. Papers, no. 4) 4227

So you think you will have a flower garden ... [1953] SEE no. 238, Anchorage Garden Club.

"Soapy" Smith tragedy. 1907. SEE no. 2672, [Le Febre, H. B.]

SOBOTKA, HENRYK ANDRZEJ. Kraj Bohaterów Jacka Londona. Stany zjiednoczone Pólnocnej ameryki w prawdziwym świetle. Lów, Poland, Ksiaznica Atlas, 1929. 494p. 4228

SOBREVIELA, MANUEL and NARCISSO y BARCELO. Voyages au Pérous, faits dans les années 1791 à 1794 - d'apres l'original espagnol, traduits par P. F. Henry. Paris, 1809. 3 vols. pls.(col.), map(fold. col.) 4229

SOCIETY FOR PROMOTING CHRISTIAN KNOWLEDGE. A Kwagutl version of portions of the Book of Common Prayer. London, n. d. 62p.   4230

SOCIETY FOR PROMOTING CHRISTIAN KNOWLEDGE. Am da malshk ga na Damsh, St. John; ligi; the Gospel according to St. John, translated into Zimshian. London, 1889. 47p.   4231

SOCIETY FOR PROMOTING CHRISTIAN KNOWLEDGE. Am da malshk ga na Damsh, St. Luke; ligi; the Gospel according to St. Luke, translated into Zimshian. London, [1889?] 63p.   4232

SOCIETY FOR PROMOTING CHRISTIAN KNOWLEDGE. Am da malshk ga na Damsh, St. Mark; ligi; the Gospel according to St. Mark, translated into Zimshian. London, [1889 ?] 40p.   4233

SOCIETY FOR PROMOTING CHRISTIAN KNOWLEDGE. Am da malshk ga na Damsh, St. Matthew; ligi; the Gospel according to St. Matthew, translated into Zimshian. London, [1889 ?] 59p.   4234

SOKOLICZ, ANTONINA. Jack London. Wasšaw, Ksiazka, 1925. 32p. [in Polish]   4235

SOKOLOV, A. P. Proekt Lomonosova i ekspeditsiia Chichagova 1765-1766. [TITLE TR. Lomonosov's project and Chicagov's expedition] St. Petersburg, 1854. 156p.   4236

SOKOLOV, A. P. Russkaia Morskaia Biblioteka 1701-1851, ischislenie i opisanie knig, rukopisei i statei po morskomu dielu za 150 liet. [TITLE TR. Russian Naval Library 1701-1851, an enumeration and description of books, manuscripts, and articles on marine affairs for 150 years. Edited by V. K. Shultz] St. Petersburg, 1883. 2d ed. 404p.   4237

SOKOLOV, A. P. Sievernaia ekspeditsiia 1733-43. [TITLE TR. Northern expedition 1733-43] St. Petersburg, 1851. 271p. maps. [voyages of Vitus Bering and A. I. Chirikov to Alaska]   4238

SOKOLOV, A. P. and E. G. KUSHNAREV. Tri krugosvetnykh plavaniia M. P. Lazareva. [TITLE TR. M. P. Lazarev's three voyages around the world] Moskva, Gos. izd-vo geograficheskoi literatury, 1951. 207p. illus. maps, ftntes.   4239

SOLA, A. E. IRONMONGER. Klondyke, truth and facts of the new Eldorado. London, Mining and Geographical Institute, [c1897] 92(12)p. front.(port.), pls. maps(incl. 1 fold.)   4240

SOLDIER's SOUVENIR HANDY BOOK; especially prepared for servicemen in Alaska. [pl., pub., 1944 ?] 250p. map. [sold by Alaska Specialties Co., Ketchikan. Contains data on Alaska, poem "Alaska's flag," space for personnel record and notes]   4241

Solov'ev, A. I., edit. SEE nos.
   1621, Fradkin, N. G. S. P. Krasheninnikov ... 1951.
   4136, Shteĭnberg, E. L. I. F. Kruzenshtern, Ĩu. F. Lisĩanskiĭ
      ... 1950.

Sommer, L., co-auth. SEE no. 4713, Voigtlander, O.

Sonntag, August. SEE no. 3799, [Rhodes, Chas. C.]

SOOT-RYEN, TRON. Notes on fishes from Alaska collected by Ingv.
L. Norberg. Tromsø, Norway, K. Karlsen, 1940. (Museum. Aarshef-
ter, Naturhistorisk avd. nr. 14, Bd. 57, nr. 3, 1934) 10p. pl.
                                                              4242

Soroka, Leonid, co-auth. SEE no. 835, Carlson, S. W.

Sougez, E., photog. SEE no. 1232, d'Harcourt, R.

Soul of Alaska ... 1905. SEE no. 1785, Gorham Mfg. Co.

Soule, Sidney Howard, edit. SEE no. 3732, Rand McNally and Co.

SOURDOUGH JACK [pseud.] Sourdough Jack sez ... Fairbanks, Fairbanks Pub. Co., [c1954] 1st print. Nov. 1954. 28p. cartoons by
Jim Leveque, wrps. [four and five-eighths inches by six inches
in size - author is John J. Ryan]   4243

Sourdough Jack's cookery. 1959. SEE no. 2824, Mabee, Jack.

Sourdough Stampede Assoc. SEE no. 319, Atwood, F.

SOUTHEAST ALASKA TROLLERS ASSOC., Ladies Auxiliary, Sitka. Seafood secrets. Sitka, printed by Sitka Printing Co., [c1970] 104p.
illus. sketches, photos.   4244

SOUTHEASTERN ALASKA MINING CORPORATION. Report on Jualin Mine,
Berners Bay region; Alaska, January 15, 1929. [no pl., 1929]
[mine near Juneau, report in Eng. and French]   4245

Southeastern Alaska route. 1907. SEE no. 47, Alaska Coast Co.

SOUTHWEST OPERATING CO. The Chief Wholecheeze Alaskan coloring
book. Juneau, printed by Juneau Publishers, [c1966] (24)p,
illus.   4246

Southworth, R. G. SEE no. 897, Charles, S. D.

Souvenir, Feb. 13, 1909. SEE no. 1522, Fairbanks Harmonie Soc.

Souvenir guide of ... 1909. SEE no. 160, Alaska-Yukon-Pac. Expo.

Souvenir of Alaska and Yukon ... 1900. SEE no. 2017, Hegg, E. A.

Souvenir of Nome ... 1900. SEE no. 2018, Hegg, E. A.

Souvenir of northwestern Alaska. n. d. SEE no. 1751, Goetze,O.D.

Souvenir of 2d annual All Alaska Sweepstakes. 1909. SEE
    no. 172, All Alaska Sweepstakes.

SOVETSKIE RYBOKHOZĪAĪSTVENNYE ISSLEDOVANIĪA v severo-vostochnoĭ
chasti Tikhogo okeana, vyp. 1, 1963. [TITLE TR. Soviet fisheries
investigations in the northeastern part of the Pacific Ocean,
no.1] Moskva and Vladivostok, 1963. 317p. illus. tables, graphs,
maps, bibliog. (Vsesoĭuznoe nauchno-issledovatel'-skiĭ institut
morskogo rybnogo khozĪaĪstva i okeanografiĭ. Isvestiĭa. Trudy
v. 48, Moskva. Tikhookeanskiĭ nauchno-issledovatel'-skiĭ institut morskogo rybnogo khozĪaĪstva i okeanografiĭ. Izvestiĭa no.
50, Vladivostok) [papers on oceanog. and fishery research in
Bering Sea and Gulf of Alaska, 1958-62. for tr. SEE no. 4249]
                                                              4247

SOVETSKIE RYBOKHOZĪAĪSTVENNYE ISSLEDOVANIĪA v severo-vostochnoĭ
chasti Tikhogo okeana, vyp. 4. [TITLE TR. Soviet fisheries investigations in the northeastern part of the Pacific Ocean, no.4]
Moskva, Izd-vo Pishevaĭa promyshlennost', 1965. 347p. illus.
tables, graphs, maps, bibliog. (Vsesoĭuznoe nauchno-issledovatel'
-skiĭ institut morskogo rybnogo khozĪaĪstva i okeanografiĭ. Trudy v. 58, Moskva. Tikhookeanskiĭ nauchno-issledovatel'-skiĭ
institut morskogo rybnogo khozĪaĪstva i okeanografiĭ. Izvestiĭa,
v. 53, Vladivostok) [oceanog., hydrochemistry, ichthyological
research in eastern Bering Sea and Gulf of Alaska, 1958]   4248

SOVIET FISHERIES INVESTIGATIONS in the Northeast Pacific, no. 1.
P. A. Moiseev, editor. Jerusalem, Israel Program for Scientific
Translations, 1968. 333p. illus. graphs, tables, map, bibliog.
[tr. of no. 4247]   4249

Sowerby, G. B., illus. SEE no. 469, Beechey, F. Wm.

Spackman, W., jr., co-auth. SEE no. 1395, Dutcher, R. R.

SPARKS, JARED. Leben des beruhmten Amerikanischen reisenden John
Ledyard, des Begleiters von Cook; nach seinen Tagebuchern und
seinem Briefwechsel dargestellt von Jared Sparks; aus den Englischen von D. E. F. Michaelis. Leipzig, J. C. Hinrichssche
Buchhandlung, 1829. x,350p. front. [tr. of no. 4252]   4250

Sparks, Jared. Life and travels John Ledyard. SEE no. 4253.

SPARKS, JARED. Memoirs of the life and travels of John Ledyard,
from his journals and correspondence. London, H. Colburn, 1828.
xii,428p.   4251

SPARKS, JARED. The life of John Ledyard, the American traveller; comprising selections from his journals and correspondence. Cambridge, Mass., Hilliard and Brown, 1828. xii,325p. ANR. Cambridge, Mass., Hilliard and brown, 1829. 2d ed. xii,310p. ANR. Boston, C. C. Little and J. Brown, 1847. 419p. (Library of American Biography, 2d ser., vol. 14) ANR. Boston, Little, Brown & Co., 1864. [SEE ALSO no. 4250 for tr.]   4252

[SPARKS, JARED] Travels and adventures of John Ledyard, comprising his voyage with Capt. Cook's third and last expedition, his journey on foot 1300 miles round the Gulf of Bothnia to St. Petersburgh, his adventures and residence in Siberia, and his exploratory mission to Africa. London, published for H. Colburn by R. Bentley, 1834. xii,428p. WITH HALF-TITLE Life and travels of John Ledyard. ANR. London, published for H. Colburn by R. Bentley, 1834. 2d ed. xii,428p. WITH HALF-TITLE Life and travels of John Ledyard.   4253

Sparrman, A., tr. SEE no. 4641, Vancouver, Geo.

SPAULDING, ALBERT C. Archaeological investigations on Agattu, Aleutian Islands. Ann Arbor, 1962. 79p. pls. figs. tables, drawings by Anta Montet White, bibliog. wrps. (University of Michigan Anthropological Papers, Museum of Anthropology, no. 18)

SPECK, GORDON. Northwest exploration. Edited by L. K. Phillips. Portland, Ore., Binfords and Mort, 1954. 394p. illus. ports. maps, bibliog.   4255

SPECK, GORDON. Samuel Hearne and the Northwest Passage. Caldwell, Idaho, Caxton Printers, 1963. 337p. illus. maps, bibliog.   4256

"Speedy" Strom. SEE no. 3987, Say it in Eskimo ... [c1965]

SPENCE, SYDNEY ALFRED. Captain James Cook, R. N., 1728-1779; a bibliography of his voyages, to which is added other works relating to his life, conduct and nautical achievement ... Compiled by S. A. Spence. Mitcham, Sy., England, by the author, 1960. iv,50p. ports.   4257

SPENCER, ROBERT F and JESSE D. JENNINGS, edits. The native Americans. N. Y., Harper and Row, 1965. 593p. illus. [incls. Eskimos and Indians from Arctic to mid-America]   4258

SPERRY, ARMSTRONG. All about Captain Cook. Rev. ed. London, W. H. Allen, 1960. 147p. illus. endmaps. (All About Books Series)   4259

SPERRY, ARMSTRONG. All about the Arctic and Antarctic. N. Y., Random House, 1957. illus.   4260

SPERRY, ARMSTRONG. Le Capitaine Cook explore le Pacifique, by A. Sperry; adapte par J. Petrus. Paris, F. Nathan, 1965. 157p. illus. ports. maps. (Histoire et Documents ser.)　　　　4261

Sperry, Armstrong, illus. SEE ALSO no. 1093, Coryell, H. V. Klondike gold. 1938.

SPICER, EDWARD HOLLAND, edit. Human problems in technological change ... a casebook. N. Y., Russell Sage Foundation, 1952. 301p. illus. [pp.127-48, *Eskimo herdsmen; introduction of reindeer herding to the natives of Alaska*, by Margaret Lantis]　4262

SPICER, GEORGE WASHINGTON. The constitutional status and government of Alaska. Baltimore, Johns Hopkins Press, 1927. 121p. bibliog. wrps. (John Hopkins University Studies in Historical and Political Science, series 45, no. 4) [author's Ph.D. thesis at Johns Hopkins University, 1926]　　　　　　　4263

SPIRO, MELFORD E., edit. Context and meaning in cultural anthropology. In honor of A. Irving Hallowell. N. Y. and London, Free Press, 1965. 442p. illus. diagr. [pp.189-205 contains *A long record of Eskimos and Indians at the forest edge* by James Louis Giddings]　　　　　　　　　　　　　　　　　4264

SPOKANE, Washington, CHAMBER OF COMMERCE. Are you going to Klondike. Take the Spokane Overland route and save $700.00. Spokane, Winship Quick Print, 1897. 31p. map(fold.tipped-in at front), wrps.　　　　　　　　　　　　　　　　　　　　　4265

SPOKANE, Washington, CHAMBER OF COMMERCE. Overland to Klondike via the Spokane route. The easiest, cheapest, safest route. Travelers on Second-Class or Tourist Tickets may stop over for ten days in Spokane. Spokane, Pigott-French-Greenberg Co., Printers, 1897. 32p. map(fold. tipped-in at front.), wrps. [describes the Ashcroft Trail, British Columbia]　　　　　　　　　4266

Sportsman's guide to Alaska [ca 1952] SEE no. 123, Alaska Steamship Co.

SPRAGUE, RODERICK. Some fungi on Alaskan species of *Carex*. Pullman, Washington, 1954. (Agricultural Experiment Stations Scientific Paper, no. 1316. Also in Washington State College Research Studies, Sept. 1954, vol. 22, no. 3, pp.161-9. illus. bibliog. [species from southeastern Alaska]　　　　　4267

Sprague, Roderick. SEE ALSO no. 4096, Shaw, G. G. Additions Alaskan fungi. 1954.

Sprengel, C. L., tr. SEE no. 2615, La Pérouse, J. F. G. de.

Sprengel, M. C., tr. SEE nos.
    3976, Sauer, M. Reise nach nördlichen ... 1803;
    4638, Vancouver, Geo. Entdeckungsreise ... 1799.

Spring, Ira, photog. SEE nos.
   1566, Fish, Byron. Alaska. 1965;
   4268, Spring, Norma. Alaska, pioneer state. 1967;
   4269, Spring, Norma. Alaska, complete travel ... [c1970]

SPRING, NORMA. Alaska, pioneer state. Camden, N. J., Thos. Nelson & Sons, 1967. photos by Bob and Ira Spring. 234p. illus.
                                                                    4268

SPRING, NORMA. Alaska, the complete travel book. Photographs by Bob and Ira Spring. N. Y., Macmillan, [c1970] 2d print. 248p. front. photos, endmaps, index.   4269

Spring, Robert, photog. SEE nos.
   1566, Fish, Byron. Alaska. 1965;
   4268, Spring, Norma. Alaska, pioneer state. 1967;
   4269, Spring, Norma. Alaska, complete travel ... [c1970]

Spring tour ... 1906. SEE no. 3759, Raymond & Whitcomb Co.

SPRINGER, JOHN A. Innocent in Alaska; the story of Margaret Knudsen Burke. N. Y., Coward-McCann, 1963. 319p. illus.   4270

SPROAT, GILBERT MALCOLM. Scenes and studies of savage life. By Gilbert Malcolm Sproat. London, Smith, Elder & Co., 1868. xii, 317p. front. [John R. Jewitt and ship *Boston* in Nootka Sound, 1803]   4271

SPRUNGMAN, ORMAL I. Photography afield. Harrisburg, Penna., Stackpole, 1951. 449p. illus.(some col.) [has one chapt. about Alaska]   4272

Spuhn, Carl. SEE no. 95, Alaska Oil and Guano Co.

SPURR, JOSIAH EDWARD. Through the Yukon gold diggings, a narrative of personal travel. Boston, Eastern Pub. Co., 1900. 276p. front. illus. [by a geologist]   4273

Square deal for fur seal. 1910. SEE no. 798, Camp Fire Club of America.

STABLES, GORDON. Off to Klondike; or, a cowboy's rush to the gold fields. N. Y., 1898. 327p. ANR. London, n. d. 327p. 4274

STAEHLIN, JAKOB von STORCKSBURG. An account of the new northern archipelago, lately discovered by the Russians in the Seas of Kamtschatka and Anadir. By Mr. J. von Staehlin, Secretary to the Imperial Academy of Sciences at St. Petersburg, and Member of the Royal Society of London. Translated from the German original. London, printed for C. Heydinger, 1774. xx,118p. ANR. London, C. Heydinger, 1774. xx,118p. front.(fold. map) ... translated from German original, revised by Matthew Maty. [tr. of no. 4276, vol. also contains a separate narrative re East-Spitzbergen] 4275

STAEHLIN, JAKOB von STORCKSBURG. Das von den Russen in den Jahren 1765, 66, 67 entdekte nordliche Insel-Meer, zwischen Kamtschatka und Nordamerika beschrieben von Herrn. von Staehlin ... nebst einer landcharte ... Stuttgart, bey Christoph Friedrich Cotta, 1774. 40p. map(fold.) [Dezhnev, Bering, Chirikov, others - for tr. see nos. 4275 and 4277]   4276

STAEHLIN, JAKOB von STORCKSBURG. Relation du nouvel archipel septentrional découvert depuis peu par les Russes dans les mers de Kamtschatka & d'Anadir, tr. en anglois de l'original allemand, & de l'anglois en françois. [London,, Du Museum Britannique, 1774] 96p. ANR. Paris, 1782. 2 pts. in l. 60p. and 96p. [tr. of no. 4276]   4277

STAENDER, GILBERT and VIVIAN STAENDER. Adventures with Arctic wildlife. Caldwell, Idaho, Caxton, 1970. 260p. illus.(some col.)   4278

STALINSKIĬ MARSHRUT PRODOLZHEN: Moskva - Severnyĭ polĩus - Severnaĩa Amerika. [TITLE TR. The Stalin route has been extended; Moscow - North Pole - North America] Moskva, Partizdat TSK VKP9(b), 1937. 105p. [fliers V. P. Chkalov, A. V. Belĩakov and G. F. Baĭdukov]   4279

STANĨUKOVICH, T. V. Kunstkamera Peterburgskoĭ Akademiĭ Nauk. [TITLE TR. The Museum of the Academy of Sciences of St. Petersburg] Moskva-Leningrad, Izd-vo Akademiĭ nauk SSSR, 1953. 239p.,72p. illus. ports. index. (Akademiĭ nauk SSSR, Institut Etnografiĭ) [incls. collections from Alaska]   4280

Stankevich, K. B., co-auth. SEE no. 4281, Stankevich, V. B.

STANKEVICH, VLADIMIR BENEDIKTOVICH and K. B. STANKEVICH. Na velikom Severe; iz istoriĭ russkikh polĩarnykh puteshestviĭ. [TITLE TR. The great North; from the history of Russian polar voyages] Berlin, Amerikanskoe izd-vo, 1923. 168p. map(fold.)   4281

STANLEY, WILLIAM M. A mile of gold; strange adventures on the Yukon, illustrated with views taken on the spot. Chicago, Laird and Lee, 1898. 219p. illus. map. (Pastime Series, no. 60) 4282

STANSBURY, CHARLES FREDERICK. Klondike, the land of gold, illustrated; containing all available practical information of every description concerning the new gold fields, what they are and how to reach them, a short history of Alaska, a synopsis of the personal testimony of miners who have been on the ground, a digest of the mining laws of the United States and Canada, the latest authentic maps, with a review of the famous gold rushes of the world. N. Y., F. T. Neely, 1897. 190p. pls. maps. (Neely's Popular Library, no. 96)   4283

Stanton, Stephen Berrien. The Bering Sea controversy. SEE no. 4284.

STANTON, STEPHEN BERRIEN. The Behring Sea dispute. N. Y., A. B. King, 1890. [printed for private distribution] 58p. ANR. WITH TITLE The Bering Sea controversy. N. Y., A. B. King, 1892. 102p. bibliog. [author's Ph.D. thesis, Columbia University, N. Y., 1889, relates to commercial sealing, U. S. and Great Britain] 4284

STARBUCK, ALEXANDER. History of the American whale fishery from its earliest inception to the year 1876. Waltham, Mass., 1878. 767p. pls. tables. ANR. N. Y., Argosy-Antiquarian, 1964. 2 vols. special ltd. ed. of 50 numbered copies, reprint of 1878 ed. vii, 770p. [earliest printing: Part 4 of "Report of U. S. Commissioner of Fish and Fishing," in 1875] 4285

STARK, CHARLES R., jr. The Bering Sea eagle. Caldwell, Idaho, Caxton, 1957. 170p. photos, endmaps. [biog. of Harry L. Blunt, aviator] 4286

STARR, WALTER AUGUSTUS. My adventures in the Klondike and Alaska, 1898-1900, written for my grandchildren in 1960. S. F., 1960. [designed and printed by Lawton Kennedy] 68p. front.(fold. map) 4287

State of Alaska; air trade ... 1962. SEE nos. 1568-69, Fisher Assoc.

Statement by Alaska Steamship Co. ... 1923. SEE no. 124, Alaska Steamship Co.

Statement in relation to Alaska fisheries ... 1910. SEE no. 95, Alaska Oil & Guano Co.

STATEMENT OF THE NEEDS OF ALASKA. An address to the President. By the people of Ketchikan. Ketchikan, 1923. 20p. [to then President Harding] 4288

STATON, FRANCES M. and MARIE TREMAINE. A bibliography of Canadiana. By Frances M. Staton amd Marie Tremaine. Toronto, Public Library, [c1935] 828p. facsims. ANR. 1965. reprint. WITH First Supplement, edited by Gertrude M. Boyle. 1959. [c1959] 333p. facsims. 4289

Steamer "Eliza Anderson" [1940] SEE no. 4694, Veteran Steamboatmen's Assoc. of West.

STEAMSHIP COMPANIES OF PUGET SOUND AND ALASKA. An appeal to Congress. An argument for wiredrag survey of Alaska waters; suitable steamships for U. S. Coast and Geodetic Survey, charting Alaskan water-courses ... Seattle, 1914. 7ℓ. 4290

Stearns, F., co-auth. SEE no. 881, Chamberlin, J. L.

STEEL, WILL A. Home rule measure for Alaska; an act to provide for Comptroller and Board of control. Juneau, Feb. 16, 1927. 11p.   4291

STEELE, G. P. *Seadragon*, northwest under the ice. N. Y., Dutton, 1962. 255p. illus. maps. [Northwest Passage by nuclear submarine, Aug. 1-Sept. 5, 1960]   4292

STEELE, HARWOOD ELMES ROBERT. Policing the Arctic, the story of the conquest of the Arctic by the Royal Canadian (formerly North-West) Mounted Police. Toronto, Ryerson, 1935. 390p. front. pls. ports. map(fold.), bibliog. index. ANR. London, Jarrolds, 1936. 390p. [incls. Yukon gold rush]   4293

Steele, J. L. SEE no. 3486, Pan Pacific Progress.

STEELE, JAMES WILLIAM. A golden era. The new gold fields of the United States. The facts and figures, with a brief description of mines, miners, and the art of gold-finding. [Chicago], published by the Passenger Dept. of the Chicago, Milwaukee and St. Paul Railway, 1897. 60p. illus. map(fold.)   4294

STEELE, JAMES WILLIAM. The Klondike; the new gold fields of Alaska and the far North-West. Chicago, The Steel Pub. Assoc., 1897. 80p. illus. maps, wrps. (The Klondike and Alaska, Special Edition) ANR. Chicago, The Steele Pub. Assoc. 1897. (The Klondike Santa Fe Route Special Editon) ANR. Chicago, Britton Co., 1897. 80p.   4295

STEELE, SAMUEL B. Forty years in Canada, reminiscences of the great North-West. By Col. S. B. Steele. Edited by Mollie Green Niblett, with an introduction by J. G. Colmer. London, H. Jenkins, 1915. 428p. pls. ANR. Toronto, McClelland, Goodchild and Stewart, 1918. [autobiog. frontier Klondike, N. W. M. P.]
                                                                          4296

STEENSBY, HANS PEDER. Om Eskimokulturens Oprindelse; En etnografisk og Antropogeografisk studie. [TITLE TR. On the origin of Eskimo culture; an ethnographical and anthropogeographical study] Copenhagen, 1905. 219p. (also in Meddelselser om Grønland, Bd. 53, 1917. pp.39-228. rev. and tr. into English] 4297

Steensel, M. Van. SEE no. 4651, Van Steensel, M.

STEERE, WILLIAM CAMPBELL. Bryophyta of Arctic America. 1. Species from Little Diomede Island, Bering Strait, Alaska. Ann Arbor, 1938. (Papers from the Department of Botany and the Herbarium of the University of Michigan, no. 646)   4298

STEFANSSON, EVELYN (SCHWARTZ) BAIRD. Here is Alaska. By Evelyn Stefansson. N. Y., Scribner, 1943. 154p. illus. photos by Frederick Machetanz, others, endmaps, index. ANR. 1959. 178p. illus. maps. (Revised Statehood Edition)   4299

STEFANSSON, EVELYN (SCHWARTZ) BAIRD. Within the Circle; portrait of the Arctic. By Evelyn Stefansson. N. Y., Scribner, 1945. 1st ed. 160p. front. port. photos, maps by Richard Edes Harrison, index. ANR. N. Y., Scribner, 1954. 160p. front. port. photos, maps by Richard Edes Harrison, index. [pp.101-128 about Alaska]   4300

STEFANSSON, VILHJALMUR. Arctic manual. Prepared under direction of the Chief of the Air Corps United States Army. With a special introduction and index. N. Y., Macmillan, 1944. [c1944] Trade Edition. 556(16)p. pls. photos, diagrs. errata, index. EARLIER EDITIONS Washington, D. C., Government Printing Office, 1940. 2 vols. in 1. 536p. (U. S. Army, Chief of the Air corps) ANR. Washington, D. C., G. P. O., 1942. condensed ed. 74p. (U. S. Army Technical Manual, no. TM 1-240. April 1, 1942) ANR. Washington, D. C., G. P. O., 1944. 131p. illus. map(fold.) (U. S. Army Technical Manual, no. TM 1-240, Jan. 17, 1944. Superseding TM 1-240, April 1, 1942)   4301

STEFANSSON, VILHJALMUR and others. Blueprint for hemispheric defense. Chicago, 1941. 19p. map. [Roundtable radio discussion, July 13, 1941]   4302

Stefansson, Vilhjalmur. Das Geheimnis ... 1925. SEE no. 4308.

STEFANSSON, VILHJALMUR. Discovery, the autobiography of Vilhjalmur Stefansson. [Reymond Peckham Holden, editor] N. Y., McGraw-Hill, [c1964] 1st ed. 411p. front.(port.), illus. endmaps, index.   4303

Stefansson, Vilhjalmur. Goste primnaîa arktika. 1935. SEE no. 4319.

STEFANSSON, VILHJALMUR and OLIVE RATHBUN WILCOX. Great adventures and explorations from the earliest times to the present as told by the explorers themselves; edited by ... Vilhjalmur Stefansson with the collaboration of Olive Rathbun Wilcox. N. Y., Dial Press, 1947. 788p. maps by Richard Edes Harrison, bibliog. ANR. London, Robert Hale, 1947.   4304

STEFANSSON, VILHJALMUR. Hunters of the great North. By Vilhjalmur Stefansson. With illustrations. N. Y., Harcourt, Brace & Co., [c1922] vii,301p. front. pls. maps(fold.) ANR. London, G. G. Harrap, 1923. 287p. front. pls. maps(fold.)   4305

    TRANSLATION - Hunters of great North. [c1922]

    Jäger des hohen Nordens. Leipzig, F. A. Brockhaus, 1924. abr.
    ed. 159p. front.(port.), pls. map. (Reisen und Abenteur)
                                                           4306

Stefansson, Vilhjalmur. Länder der Zukunft ... 1923. SEE no. 4318.

STEFANSSON, VILHJALMUR. My life with the Eskimo. By Vilhjálmur Stefánsson. Illustrated. N. Y., Macmillan Co., 1913. [pub. Nov. 1913] 538p. front. pls. ports. maps(fold.), append. by Rudolph Martin Anderson. [var. editions through 1926 retain plural spelling "Eskimo" and appendix by R. M. Anderson] ANR. ENTITLED My life with the Eskimos (Abridged Editon) by Vilhjalmur Stefansson with forewords by Henry Fairfield Osborn ... and Reginald Walter Brock ... N. Y., Macmillan Co., 1927. [abr. ed. pub. Mar. 1927] 382p. front.(dble.), pls. ports. endmaps. [1927 ed. used plural spelling "Eskimos" - Anderson appendix omitted, one about Blonde Eskimos added] ANR. WITH TITLE My life with the Eskimo. By Vilhjálmur Stefánsson. N. Y., Collier Books, 1962. [1st Collier edition 1962] 447p. index, paperback. [no illus. maps, or appendixes, plural spelling of "Eskimo"] (Collier Books no. 09670) [Stefansson-Anderson Arctic Expedition of American Museum of Natural History, in 1908-1912] 4307

TRANSLATION - My life with the Eskimo. 1913.

Das Geheimnis der Eskimos, vier Jahre im nördlichsten Kanada; mit 85 Abbildungen und 2 Karten. [TITLE TR. The secret of the Eskimo, four years in northernmost Canada; with 85 illustrations and 2 maps] Leipzig, F. A. Brockhaus, 1925. abr. ed. 273p. pls. maps. 4308

Stefansson, Vilhjalmur. Neuland ... 1928. SEE no. 4322.

STEFANSSON, VILHJALMUR and JULIA AUGUSTA SCHWARTZ. Northward Ho! An account of the far North and its people. Selected from the writings of Vilhjalmur Stefansson and adapted for boys and girls by Julia Augusta Schwartz. N. Y., Macmillan Co., 1925. [c1925] 181p. front.(map), illus. [scattered refs. to Alaska] 4309

STEFANSSON, Northwest to fortune; the search of western man for a commercially practical route to the Far East. By Vilhjalmur Stefansson. Maps designed by James MacDonald. N.Y., Duell, Sloan and Pearce, [c1958] 1st ed. 356p. maps, endmaps, index. ANR. London, 1958. maps. 4310

STEFANSSON, VILHJALMUR. Not by bread alone. N. Y., Macmillan Co., 1946. 339p. bibliog. index. ANR. WITH TITLE The fat of the land. N. Y., Macmillan Co., 1956. enl. ed. 339p. bibliog. index. [some references to nutrition of Alaskan Eskimos] 4311

STEFANSSON, VILHJALMUR. Prehistoric and present commerce among the Arctic Coast Eskimo. Ottawa, 1914. 29p. map(fold.) (Canada. National Museum. Bull. 6, Anthropological Series, no. 3) 4312

STEFANSSON, VILHJALMUR. Routes to Alaska. N. Y., Council on Foreign Relations, 1941. 11p. map. (reprinted from Foreign Affairs, July 1941) 4313

STEFANSSON, VILHJALMUR.   The adventure of Wrangel Island; based
mainly on the diary of Errol Lorne Knight.   N. Y., Macmillan,
1925. 1st ed. 424p. front. pls. ports. maps(incl. 1 fold.),
facsims. appends. ANR. London, Jonathan Cape, 1926. rev. 416p.
front. pls. ports. maps(incl. 1 fold.), facsims. appends.   4314

STEFANSSON, VILHJALMUR. The American far North. N. Y., 1939.
(reprinted from Foreign Affairs, vol. 17, April 1939. pp.508-23.
map)   4315

STEFANSSON, VILHJALMUR. The Arctic in fact and fable.   N. Y.,
Foreign Policy Assoc., 1945.   96p.   diagrs. maps.   (Headline
Series, no. 51. March-April 1945)   4316

Stefansson, Vilhjalmur. The fat of the land. 1956. SEE no. 4311.

STEFANSSON, VILHJALMUR. The friendly Arctic; the story of five
years in polar regions.   N. Y., Macmillan, 1921.   xxxi,784p.
front. pls. maps(incl. 2 fold. in pocket) ANR. N. Y., Macmillan,
1943. enl. ed. 812p. front. pls. maps(incl. 2 fold. in pocket),
appends. index. ANR. Westport, Conn.,   Greenwood Press, 1970.
reprint of 1943 ed.   4317

   TRANSLATIONS - Friendly Arctic ... 1921, CHRONOLOGICALLY.

   Länder der Zukunft, fünf Jahre Reisen im höchstein Norden, mit
      119 Abbildungen und 8 Karten. [TITLE TR. Lands of the fu-
      ture; five years in the far north, with 119 illustrations
      and 8 maps] Leipzig, F. A. Brockhaus, 1923. 2 vols. 385p.
      and 418p. pls. maps.   4318

   Goste priimnaīa Arktika.   Perevod A. L. Kardashinskogo i R. A.
      Braude. Leningrad, Izd-vo Glavsevmorputi, 1935. abr. ed.
      512p. pls. maps. ANR. Moskva, Gos. izd-vo geogr. lit-ry,
      1948. 2d abr. Russ. ed. 328p. illus. maps(incl. 1 fold.)4319

STEFANSSON, VILHJALMUR. The friendly North. N. Y., The Grolier
Society, 1930. 16p. illus. maps.   4320

STEFANSSON, VILHJALMUR. The northward course of empire. By
Vilhjalmur Stefansson. With an introduction by Dr. Edward William
Nelson ... With illustrations and a map. N. Y., Harcourt, Brace
& Co., [c1922] 274p. front. pls. map(fold.), append bibliog,
                                                             4321

   TRANSLATION - Northward course ... 1922.

   Neuland im Norden; die Bedeutung der Arktis für Siedlung,
      Verkehr und Wirtschaft der Zukinft. [TITLE TR. New North-
      land; the future role of the Arctic in settlement, commerce
      and industry] [edited by H. Rüdiger] Leipzig, F. A. Brock-
      haus, 1928. enl. ed. xii,288p. pls. diagr. map.   4322

STEFANSSON, VILHJALMUR. The Stefánsson-Anderson Arctic Expedi-
dition of the American Museum. N. Y., 1919. 2 pts. in 1. vii,
475p. illus. maps(fold.), corrections, index. (Anthropological
Papers of the American Museum of Natural History, vol. 14, pts.1
and 2) [contains author's preliminary report, SEE no. 4324, also
Harpoons and darts in Stefánsson collection by Clark Wissler
dated 1916, SEE no. 4936]   4323

STEFANSSON, VILHJALMUR. The Stefánsson-Anderson Arctic Expedition of the American Museum; preliminary ethnological report.
By Vilhjálmur Stefánsson. N. Y., 1914. pp.1-395. figs. maps.
(Anthropological Papers of the American Museum of Natural History,
vol. 14, pt. 1)   4324

STEFANSSON, VILHJALMUR. Ultima Thule; further mysteries of the
Arctic. N. Y., Macmillan Co., 1940. 383p. pls. maps, bibliog.
[much about Alaska]   4325

STEFANSSON, VILHJALMUR. Unsolved mysteries of the Arctic. By
Vilhjalmur Stefansson. Introduction by Stephen Leacock telling
how this book came to be written. N. Y., Macmillan, [c1938]
381p. illus. maps(incl. 1 dble.), bibliog. in slipcase. [Special
Edition printed for Explorer's Club ltd. to 200 numbered copies,
with frontispiece by Rockwell Kent, autographed by Stefansson and
Kent] ANR. N. Y., Macmillan, 1939. [c1938] trade edition. 381p.
maps(incl. 1 dble.), bibliog. ANR. London, G. G. Harrap, 1939.
351p. maps(incl. 1 dble.), bibliog. ANR. N. Y., Collier Books,
1962.1st Collier edition [cover has spelling Vilhjálmur Stefán-
sson] 320p. maps(incl. 1 dble.), bibliog. paperback. (Collier
Books, no. 03768) [of five mysteries, two have Alaskan interest:
Thomas Simpson and Northwest Passage; Sir Hubert Wilkins and
search for missing Russian fliers on North Polar flight]   4326

Stefansson, Vilhjalmur. SEE ALSO nos.
    420, Bartlett, R. A. Last voyage *Karluk* ... 1916;
    539, Berry, Erick. Mr. Arctic ... 1966;
   1187, Dartmouth College Library. Dictionary catalog ... 1967;
   1578, Fletcher, Inglis. Vilhjalmur Stefansson. 1925;
   1942, Hanson, E. P. Stefansson ... 1941;
   2148, Holden, R. P. Famous scientific expeditions. 1955;
   2300, Irwin, V. M. Shaman's revenge. 1925;
   2660, Le Bourdaus, D. M. Stefansson ... 1963;
   3016, Masik, A. Arctic nights entertainment ... 1935;
   3158, Montgomery, Richard Gill. "Pechuck" ... 1932;
   3265, Myers, H. Vilhjalmur Stefansson ... 1966;
   3316, Noice, H. H. With Stefansson in Arctic. 1924;
   3512, Peary, R. E. Vilhjalmur Stefansson. 1925;
   4496, Thomas, Lowell. Sir Hubert Wilkins ... [c1961];
   4782, Weigert, H. W. Compass of world ... 1944;
   4783, Weigert, H. W. New compass of world ... 1949;
   4809, Whelen, T. Hunting big game ... vol. 2. 1946;
   4936, Wissler, C. Harpoons and darts ... 1916.

Steger, Friedrich. SEE no. 4849, Whymper, F.

STEGNER, WALLACE EARLE. The Big Rock Candy Mountain. N. Y.,
Duell, Sloan and Pearce, 1943. 515p. [fict. Alaska, western U.S.
and Canada]   4327

STEIN, ROBERT. Can a nation be a gentleman ? Address delivered
before the third National Peace Congress at Baltimore, May 4,
1911 (Revised). A plea for the sale or exchange to Canada of
the "Panhandle" or part of Alaska southeast of Mount St. Elias.
Washington, D. C., Judd & Detweiler, 1911. 11p.   4328

STEIN, ROBERT. The defense of Alaska. A plea for the protection
of American labor. With a map of proposed railway. Washington,
D. C., Judd and Detweiler, 1910. 2d ed. 23p. map(fold.)   4329

STEJNEGER, LEONHARD HESS. Georg Wilhelm Steller, the pioneer of
Alaskan natural history. Cambridge, Harvard University Press,
1936. 623p. front. pls.(incl. 1 col.), ports, facsims. maps
(incl. 1 fold.), appends. bibliog. index.   4330

Stejneger, Leonhard Hess. SEE ALSO nos.
     203, American Geog. Soc. Problems polar research ... 1928;
     1755, Golder, F. A. Bering's voyages ... vol. 2. 1922.

STELLER, GEORG WILHELM. Georg Wilhelm Steller's ausfuhrliche
Beschreibung von sonderbaren Meer-thieren mit Erlauterungen und
nothigen Kupfern versehn. [TITLE TR. George Wilhelm Steller's
detailed description of singular sea-animals ...] Halle, 1753.
                                                               4331

STELLER, GEORG WILHELM. Georg Wilhelm Steller's ... Beschreibung
von dem lande Kamtschatka, dessen Einwohnern, deren Sitten, Nah-
men, Lebensart und verschiedenen Gewohnheiten, berausgegeben von
J. B. S. mit vielen kupfern. Frankfurt und Leipzig, bey Johann
Georg Fleischer, 1774. var. p. pls. maps. [J. B. S. assumed to
be Jean-Benoît Schérer] ANR. WITH TITLE Von Kamtschatka nach
Amerika. Leipzig, F. A. Brockhaus, 1926. 158p. pls. maps.
[abr. by M. Heydrich of nos. 4332 and 4333]   4332

STELLER, GEORG WILHELM. G. W. Steller's ... Reise von Kamtschatka nach Amerika mit dem Commandeur-Capitän Bering; ein Pendant
zu dessen Beschreibung von Kamtschatka. [TITLE TR. G. W. Steller's voyage from Kamchatka to America with Commander Captain
Bering; an appendix to his description of Kamchatka] St. Petersburg, bey Johann Zacharias Logan, 1793. 134p. [also in no.
3475, Pallas, P. S. Bd. 5-6 of "Neue nordische Beyträge ..."
1793-96, with same imprint, date and paging. For abr. version
SEE no. 4332. Also cf no. 4334]   4333

STELLER, GEORG WILHELM. Tagebuch seiner Seereise ... St. Petersburg, Johann Zacharias Logan, 1793. 2 pts. in 1. var. p.[cf
no. 4333]   4334

Steller, Georg Wilhelm.   SEE ALSO nos.
   488, Bell, Margaret E.   Touched with fire ... 1960;
   1599, Ford, Corey.   Where sea breaks its back.   1966;
   1741, Gmelin, J. G.   Flora sibirica ... 1747-69;
   1742, Gmelin, J. G.   Leben Herrn Georg Wilh. Steller ... 1748;
   1755, Golder, F. A.   Bering's voyages ... vol. 2. 1922;
   2718, Linnaeus, Carolus.   Plantae Rariores ... 1750;
   3475, Pallas, P. S.   Neue nordische Beyträge ... Bd.5-6.1793-
         1796;
   3528, Pekarskiĭ, P. P.   Arkhionyĭa ... *Rhytina borealis*.1869;
   3529, Pekarskiĭ, P. P.   Istoriĭa Imp. Akad. nauk v Peter-
         burgie, 1870-73;
   3623, Plieninger, G. H. T.   J. G. Gmelin ... epistolici ...
         1861.
   4330, Stejneger, L. H.   Georg Wilhelm Steller ... 1936;
   4407, Sutton, A.   Steller of North.   1961;
   4794, Wendt, H.   Entdeckungsfahrt durchs Robbenmeer ... 1952;
   4965, Wotte, H.   In blauer Ferne lag Amerika ... 1966.

Stepanov, N. N., co-edit.   SEE no. 2533, Krasheninnikov, S. P.

STEPHENS, H. MORSE and HERBERT E. BOLTON, edits.   The Pacific
Ocean in history;   papers and addresses presented at the Panama-
Pacific Historical congress, held at San Francisco, Berkeley and
Palo Alto, July 19-23, 1915.   N. Y., Macmillan, 1917.   535p.
[contains paper by F. A. Golder on Alaska]   4335

STEPHENS, LORENZO DOW.   Life sketches of a Jayhawker of '49.
[San Jose], 1916.   ltd. ed. of 300 copies.   68p.   illus. wrps.
[has some Alaskan content]   4336

STEPHENSON, WILFRED S.   A collection of pen sketches and tinted
wash drawings of sailing ships, passenger liners and war ships
familiar in Pacific Coast and Alaskan ports.   Vancouver, Wash.,
Ben Kreis Agency, 1947.   25p.   pls. port.   4337

STEPHENSON, WILLIAM B., jr.   The land of tomorrow.   By William B.
Stephenson, Jr.   formerly United States Commissioner in Alaska.
Illustrated.   N. Y., George H. Doran Col, [c1919]   240p.   front.
(pl.), pls.   [St. Michael in 1909, other areas of Alaska]   4338

STERLING PUBLISHING CO., N. Y.   Alaska - the 49th state - in pictures.   Introduction by Alaska's Delegate to Congress E. L. (Bob)
Bartlett.   N. Y., Sterling Pub. Co., [c1958]   64p.   illus. maps,
wrps.   ANR. [edited by James Nach]   N. Y., Sterling Pub. Co. and
London, Oak Tree Press, 1966.   rev. ed. [first London ed. c1965]
64p.   illus. maps, wrps. (Visual Geography Series)   4339

STEVENS, GLENHOPE RUSSELL.   Gold hungry.   Sherman, Calif., Tribune Pub. Co., 1927.   256p.   [fict. with Alaskan setting]   4340

STEVENSON, ADLAI EWING.   From New York to Alaska and back again.
N. Y., priv. printed, 1893.   [by Vice-Pres. of U.S. 1893-97] 4341

STEWARD, ALBERT N., LaREA J. DENNIS and HELEN M. GILKEY. Aquatic plants of the Pacific Northwest. With vegetative keys. Corvallis, Oregon State University, 1963. 2d ed. 272p. pls. figs. glossary, bibliog. index. [incls. Alaska and B. C.]   4342

STEWART, ELIHU. Down the Mackenzie and up the Yukon in 1906. London and N. Y., John Lane, 1913. 270p. front. pls. map(fold.) [also gold rush by way of Chilkoot Pass]   4343

STEWART, GEORGE R. N. A. 1 looking North. From the Canadian border to Circle, Alaska. Boston, Houghton Mifflin, 1957. 1st print. 176p. photos, maps, endmaps by Ervin Raisz. [vol. 1 of 2 vols. with title "N. A. 1; The North-South continental highway"]
4344

Stewart, John W. SEE no. 3567, Phelps, Edw. J.

STEWART, ROBERT LAIRD. Sheldon Jackson, pathfinder and prospector of the missionary vanguard in the Rocky Mountains and Alaska. Illustrated. N. Y., Fleming H. Revell, [c1908] 488p. front. (ports.), pls. ports. facsims. maps(incl. 1 fold.), append. index.   4345

Stewart, T. D., co-auth. SEE no. 1600, Ford, Jas. A.

Stikine River route to Klondike. 1898. SEE no. 3644, Port Orchard Navigation Co.

STIMPLE, BERT. Fun on the farm in Alaska. N. Y., Carlton Press, 1962. [c1962] (A Geneva Book) [homesteading in Tanana Valley in modern times]   4346

STIMPSON, WILLIAM. Prodromus descriptionis animalium evertebratorum, quae in expeditione ad oceanum Pacificum Septentrionalem, a Republica Federata missa, Cadwaladero Ringold et Johanne Rogers ducibus, observavit et descripsit W. Stimpson. Philadelphia, 1857 and 1860. 116p. (extracted from Proceedings of Philadelphia Academy of Natural Science, Feb. 1857 and Jan. 1860) [specimens of vertebrates from North Pacific Exploring Expedition of Capts. John Rodgers and C. Ringgold, U.S.N., in 1854-55]   4347

STIMPSON, WILLIAM. The crustacea and echinodermata of the Pacific shore of North America. Cambridge, printed by H. O. Houghton, 1857. 92p. (extracted from Journal of Boston Society of Natural History, vol. 6)   4348

STIRLING, MATTHEW W. and others. Indians of the Americas. Washington, D. C., National Geographic Society, 1965. 7th print. rev. ed. 423p. illus. [incls. Eskimos of Arctic]   4349

[Stock, Eugene] SEE no. 3090, Metlakahtla... 1800.

STODDARD, CHARLES WARREN. Over the Rocky Mountains to Alaska. St. Louis, Mo., B. Herder, 1899. 168p. ANR. St. Louis, Mo., B. Herder, 1904. [c1899] 3rd ed. 168p.   4350

STODDARD, GORDON. Go North, young man; modern homesteading in Alaska. Portland, Ore., Binfords and Mort, 1957. 260p. photos, endmaps. [Kenai Peninsula]   4351

Stolietnemu jubileiu ... 1894. SEE no. 4631, Valaam Monastery.

STONE, ANDREW J. Saw-tooth power; its value, its importance, its possibilities. S. F., 1914. 83p.   4352

Stone, Andrew J. SEE ALSO nos.
     206, American Mus. Natural Hist. ... explorat. Arctic. 1905;
     3879, Roosevelt, T. Deer family. 1902.

STONE, IRVING. Sailor on horseback, the biography of Jack London. Boston, Houghton Mifflin, 1938. 338p. illus. ANR. Garden City, N. Y., Doubleday, 1947. 338p. illus.   4353

STONEY, GEORGE M. Explorations in Alaska; extracts. Seattle, Shorey Book Store, 1965. facsim. of U.S.N. 1899 print. 102p. illus. map, ringbound. (reprinted from Proceedings U. S. Naval Institute, vol. 25, 1899. Sept. issue pp.533-84 and Dec. issue pp.799-849)   4354

STOREY, MOORFIELD. Charles Sumner. Boston, Houghton Mifflin, 1900. 466p. front.(port.), illus. pls. index. (American Statesmen, Standard Library Edition, edited by John T. Morse, Jr. in thirty-two volumes. Vol. XXX. The Civil War. Charles Sumner) [pp.338-340 of Alaskan interest]   4355

Storia de'viaggi intrapresi ... SEE no. 1022, [Cook, Jas.]

Story, Gillian, co-comp. SEE no. 3271, Naish, C.

Story of a fox. n. d. SEE no. 109, Alaska Silver Fox & Fur
     Farms Co.

Story of Klondike. 1898. SEE no. 144, Alaska-Yukon-Klondike
     Gold Syndicate.

THE STORY OF La PEYROUSE: with engravings. Philadelphia, 1841. 282p. illus. ANR. Philadelphia, 1854. illus. (Peter Parley's Little Library, no. 5) ANR. London, n. d. 282p. illus.   4356

Story of salmon. 1934. SEE no. 4994, Young, Isobel Nelson.

Story of the silver fox. 1909. SEE no. 63, Alaska Fur and
     Silver Fox Co.

STRAHORN, CARRIE ADELL. Fifteen thousand miles by stage ... thirty years of path finding and pioneering from the Missouri to the Pacific and from Alaska to Mexico. N. Y., Putnam, 1911. 673p. pls.(some col.)
4357

STRANG, HERBERT, edit. Pioneers in Canada; explorers and settlers in the far North and West. London, H. Frowde, and Hodder & Stoughton, [19_] 320p. front.(col.), pls.(col.), maps. (in editor's The Romance of the World Series) [John Franklin, others]
4358

STRANGE, HENRY GEORGE LATIMER and MRS. KATHLEEN (REDMAN) STRANGE. Never a dull moment. Toronto, 1941. [autobiog. Harry Strange, in Klondike and Alberta, B. C.]
4359

STRANGE, JAMES. James Strange's journal and narrative of the commercial expedition from Bombay to the Northwest coast of America, together with a chart showing the tract of the expedition. With an introduction by A. V. Venkaturama Ayyar ... Curator, Madras Record Office. Madras, printed by the Superintendent, Government Press, 1928. 63p. map(fold.) (printed from manuscript in Madras Record Office "Records of Ft. St. George." Public Sundries, vol. 37) ANR. 1929. reprint. ANR. Seattle, Shorey Book Store, 1966. facsim of 1928 ed. [has vocabularies of Prince William Sound and Nootka Sound Indians]
4360

STRATEMEYER, EDWARD. To Alaska for gold; or, the fortune hunters of the Yukon. Illustrated by A. B. Shute. Boston, Lee and Shepard, [c1899] 248p. illus. ANR. Boston, Lee and Shepard, 1905. [c1899] 248p. front. pls. (Bound to Succeed Series) 4361

Stratemeyer, Edward. SEE ALSO no. 4920, Winfield, Arthur M. Rover Boys in Alaska. n. d.

STREET, P. Vanishing animals, preserving natures's rarities. N. Y., Dutton, 1963. 232p. illus. [sea otters and fur seals of Aleutian Island waters, polar and Kodiak bears, among others]4362

STRETCH, RICHARD HENRY. Placer mines and their origin. Seattle, Lowman and Hanford, 1897. 24p.
4363

STRINGER, ARTHUR J. A. The lamp in the valley, a novel of Alaska. Indianapolis, Bobbs-Merrill, 1938. 314p.
4364

[Strom, R. P. "Speedy"] SEE no. 3987, Say it in Eskimo. [c1965]

STROMSTADT, DAZIE M. Metlakahtla. Seattle, Hill Pub. Co., 1907. 20p.
4365

STROMSTADT, DAZIE M. Sitka the beautiful. Seattle, Homer Hill, 1906. 12p.
4366

STRONG, CHARLES S.   King ram, a novel.   N. Y.,   John Day Co.,
[c1961] 192p.   illus. (The Your-Fair-Land Series) [setting is
Mt. McKinley National Park]   4367

Struve, W. SEE nos.
  3689, Price, E. V. Astronomische beobachtungen ... 1830;
  3690, Price, E. V. Astronomische nabliŭdeniĭa ... 1832.

Stuart, M., tr. SEE no. 2602, Langsdorff, G. H. von.

STUART-STUBBS, B. Maps relating to Alexander Mackenzie; a keep-
sake distributed at a meeting of the Bibliographical Soceity of
Canada; Société Bibliographique du Canada. Vancouver, University of British Columbia, 1968. unp. maps. [contains 21 annotated facsim. maps of northwestern Canada and Alaska]   4368

Stubbs, B. Stuart. SEE no. 4368, Stuart-Stubbs, B.

STUCK, HUDSON. A winter circuit of our Arctic coast; a narrative of a journey with dog-sleds around the entire Arctic coast
of Alaska. By Hudson Stuck. With maps and illustrations. N. Y.,
Scribner, 1920. [c1920] 360p. front.(pl.), pls. maps(2 fold.),
errata slip, index. ANR. London, T. Werner Laurie, 1920. 360p.
illus. maps(2), index.   4369

STUCK, HUDSON. Ten thousand miles with a dog sled; a narrative
of winter travel in Interior Alaska. By Hudson Stuck, Archdeacon
of the Yukon. Illustrated. N. Y., Scribner, 1914. [c1914] 420p.
front.(port.), pls.(some col.), map(fold. col.), index. ANR. London, T. Werner Laurie, 1914. ANR. N. Y., Scribner, 1927. 2d ed.
OTHERS var. dates. [travels in Arctic Alaska as well as the
Interior]   4370

STUCK, HUDSON. The Alaskan missions of the Episcopal Church; a
brief sketch, historical and descriptive, with a preface by the
Right Reverend Peter Trimble Rowe. N. Y., Domestic and Foreign
Missionary Society, 1920. 179p. pls. ports. map(fold.)   4371

STUCK, HUDSON. The ascent of Denali (Mount McKinley); a narrative of the first complete ascent of the highest peak in North
America. By Hudson Stuck, D.D., Archdeacon of the Yukon. Illustrated. N. Y., Scribner, 1914. [c19142 188p. front.(pl.), pls.
map(fold.) ANR. London, Bickers & Son, 1914. ANR. N. Y., Scribner, 1918. [c1914] 188p. front.(pl.), pls. map(fold.) [Stuck-
Karstens Expedition to climb Mt. McKinley, 1913]   4372

STUCK, HUDSON. Voyages on the Yukon and its tributaries; a nar-
rative of summer travel in the Interior of Alaska. By Hudson
Stuck, with maps and illustrations. N. Y., Scribner, 1917.
[c1917] 397p. front.(pl.), pls. maps(2 fold. col.), index. ANR.
N. Y., Scribner, 1925. [c1917] 397p. [one of the maps by William
Yanert]   4373

Stuck, Hudson.   SEE ALSO nos.
   918, Chitty, A. B. Hudson Stuck of Alaska. 1962;
   2148, Holden, R. P. Famous scientific expeditions.   1955;
   3509, Pearson, G. H. Seventy-Mile Kid. [c1957];
   3510, Pearson, G. H. Taming of Denali ... 1957.

STUDLEY, J. T. The journal of a sporting nomad; with thirty-nine
illustrations. London and N. Y., John Lane, 1912. xvi,803p.
front.(port.), pls.   4374

STULL, EDITH. The first book of Alaska. N. Y., Franklin Watts,
1965. 88p. photos, map, index.   4375

STURDZA, ALEXANDRU. Missions de Camtchatka. Quelques faits au-
thentiques sur les progres de l'église de Russie dans les îles
et parages de l'Amérique-russe. no pl., n. d.   4376

STURDZA, ALEXANDRU. Oeuvres posthumes. Notions sur la Russie.
Missions de Kamtchatka. Paris, 1858.   4377

[STURDZA, ALEXANDRU] Pamiatnik trudov pravoslavnykh blagoviest-
nikov russkikh s 1793 do 1853 goda. [TITLE TR. Memoirs of the
labors of the Orthodox missionaries, 1793-1853] Moskva, Tipografiia V. Got'ai, 1857. 377p.   4378

Sturgis, William. SEE no. 2797, Loring, Charles G.

STURSBERG, PETER. Journey into victory; up the Alaska Highway
and to Sicily and Italy. London, Geo. G. Harrap & Co., 1944.
160p. front. port. maps.   4379

SULLIVAN, EDWARD DEAN. The fabulous Wilson Mizner. N. Y., The
Henkle Co., 1935. [one of four Mizner brothers in Alaska and the
Klondike]   4380

SULLIVAN, MAY KELLOGG. A woman who went to Alaska. By May Kellogg Sullivan. Boston, J. H. Earle & Co., [c1902] 392p. front.
(port.), pls. map(dble.) ANR. Boston, J. H. Earle & Co., [c1903]
4th ed. 392p. front.(port.), pls. OTHERS 1910 and 1912.
[autobiographical, primarily Nome and the Swedish Luthern Mission
at Chinik (now Golovin) on Golovin Bay]   4381

SULLIVAN, MAY KELLOGG. The trail of a sourdough, life in Alaska.
By May Kellogg Sullivan. Boston, Richard G. Badger, The Gorham
Press, [c1910] 258p. front.(pl.), pls. sketches. [short word
sketches of Alaskan life]   4382

SULLIVAN, R. J. The Ten'a food quest. Washington, D. C., Catholic University of America, 1942. 142p. pls. bibliog. (Catholic
University Anthropological Ser., no. XI) [author's Ph.D. dissertation, about Athabaskan Indians of lower Yukon River, western
Alaska]   4383

SULLIVAN, WALTER. The Polar regions; the geography, climate, and life of the Arctic and Antarctic, and the explorers and scientists who discovered them. N. Y., Golden Press, 1962. 54p. illus.(col.), maps. 4384

Summary observations ... 1776. SEE no. 4570, [Travers, de Val ?]

SUMMER INSTITUTE OF LINGUISTICS, Fairbanks. The order for morning prayer. Excerpts in Eskimo Point Hope dialect. Fairbanks, n. d. (6)p. wrps. 4385

SUMMER INSTITUTE OF LINGUISTICS, Fairbanks. Tlingit reading book. One. Juneau, 1962. 47p. illus. map, wrps. 4386

SUMMER INSTITUTE OF LINGUISTICS, Fairbanks. Tlingit reading book. Two. Fairbanks, n. d. 53p. wrps. 4387

[SUMMER INSTITUTE OF LINGUISTICS, Fairbanks] Ukpiktuat Nigiugik-kaŋat. Fairbanks, n. d. 19p. illus. wrps. [sampling of New Testament translated into Eskimo dialect] 4388

SUMMER INSTITUTE OF LINGUISTICS, Fairbanks. Unipkaat coloring book in Iñupiat. Illustrated by Thelma Webster. Fairbanks, Feb. 1960. 29p. illus. wrps. 4389

Summer Institute of Linguistics, Fairbanks. SEE ALSO nos.
    22, Ahmaogak, Roy. Iñupiam ukaluŋi ... [1963 ?];
   984, Collins, Raymond. Dinak'i. 1966;
   985, Collins, Raymond. Dinak'i Ch'its'utozre. 1966;
  2067, Henry, David. Our Indian language. 1966;
  2068, [Henry, David] Tł'eaka Hok'anaga'. n. d.;
  2143, Hoijer, A. Studies in Athapaskan languages. 1963;
  2401, Kaǵakpak. Kuliaktuat Taimani. n. d.;
  3111, Milanowski, Paul G. Dindee Shuu Aandeeg. 1961;
  3112, Milanowski, Paul G. Uusii dinahtt'aa'. I. 1965;
  3113, Milanowski, Paul G. Uusii dinahtt'aa'. II. 1965;
  3271, Naish, Constance. English-Tlingit dict. Nouns. 1963;
  4125, Shinen, David. Yapigum Atihtoosi. 1966;
  4445, Tagarook, P. Jesus Kamanaktuat. n. d.;
  4767, [Webster, D. H.] Brief introd. Eskimo. n. d.;
  4768, Webster, D. H. [Can you read English ? ...] 1968;
  4769, Webster, D. H. Iḷisaaǵviŋich. Iñupiam. n.d.;
  4770, Webster, D. H. Iḷisaaǵviŋich Iñupiat. n.d.;
  4771, Webster, D. H. Iñupiat Eskimo dictionary. 1970;
  4772, Webster, D. H. Iñupiat Suuvat ? 1968;
  4773, Webster, D. H. Iñupiat Taiguangich. 1. n. d.;
  4774, Webster, D. H. Iñupiat Taiguangich. 2. n. d.;
  4775, Webster, D. H. Let's learn Eskimo. 1967;
  4978, Wycliffe Bible Translators. Jesus nts'aa' hondai
           ndiign. I. 1965;
  4979, Wycliffe Bible Translators. Brass serpent ... n. d.;
  4980, Wycliffe Bible Translators. Utk'-Uheenee X'usheex'ee.
           1963;

528

4981, Wycliffe Bible Translators. Ut K'Uheenih X'Usheeyee
      Yuh. [ca 1963];
5026, Zibell, W. Atuutit mumiksat. 1967;
5027, Zibell, W. Iñupiam ukałhi. 1966;
5028, Zibell, W. Iñupiam ukałhi. [1968];
5029, Zibell, W. Unipchaat. 1. 1969;
5030, Zibell, W. Unipchaat. 2. 1969;
5031, Zibell, W. Unipchaat. 3. 1970.

Summer journeys to Alaska and Yukon ... 1931. SEE no. 1125,
    Criswell Travel Service.

Summer tours ... 1927. SEE no. 198, American Express.

SUMNER, B. H. A short history of Russia. N. Y., Harcourt, 1944.
                                                                4390

SUMNER, CHARLES. Speech of Honorable Charles Sumner, of Massachusetts, on the cession of Russian America to the United States.
Washington, D. C., Congressional Globe Office, 1867. 48p. front.
(fold. map.) [map not in all copies]   4391

SUMNER, CHARLES. Works. Boston, Lee & Shepard. 1870-1883. 15
vols. [vol. XI contains references to Alaska purchase on pp.
183-4 and p.241]   4392

Sumner, Charles. SEE ALSO nos.
    3579, Pierce, Edw. L. Memoirs and letters ... 1877-93;
    4120, Shiels, Archie W. Purchase of Alaska ... 1967;
    4355, Storey, Moorfield. Charles Sumner. 1900.

SUNDBORG, GEORGE and C. McKINLEY. A proposal for protection of
the minor fisheries of the North Pacific through cooperative
action of the United States and Canada. Portland, Ore., 1944.
28p. (North Pacific Planning Project. North Pacific Study,
no. 12)   4393

SUNDBORG, GEORGE. Agricultural development in Alaska; further
possibilities and problems. Portland, Ore., 1944. 46p. diagr.
(fold.), maps(fold.) (North Pacific Planning Project. North
Pacific Study, no. 13)   4394

SUNDBORG, GEORGE. International fisheries cooperation between
Canada and the United States in the North Pacific. A memorandum
for the Joint Economic Committees of Canada and the United States.
Preliminary draft. Portland, Ore., 1943. 68p. append. (North
Pacific Planning Project. North Pacific Study, no. 11) 4395

SUNDBORG, GEORGE. Opportunity in Alaska. N. Y., Macmillan, 1945.
[c1945] 1st print. ix,302p. pls. map(fold.), index. [post
World War II economic outlook]   4396

SUNDBORG, GEORGE. Shipping services in the American North Pacific, United States and Canada. Part 2. Historical background. Portland, Ore., 1944. 92p. tables, diagrs.(some fold.), map (fold.), bibliog. (North Pacific Planning Project. North Pacific Study, no. 9)   4397

SUNDBORG, GEORGE. Statehood for Alaska; the issues involved and the facts about the issues. Anchorage, Alaska Statehood Association, 1946. 35p. wrps.   4398

SUNDERMAN, JAMES F., edit. World War II in the air. The Pacific. Edited by Major James F. Sunderman, U.S.A.F. N. Y., Franklin Watts, [c1962] ANR. N. Y., Bramhall House, n. d. xi,306p. front. (dble. map), photos, ports. facsim. glossaries (aircraft), index. [pp.145-51 of Bramhall ed. about Aleutian Islands]   4399

SUNSET EDITORS. Alaska, by the editors of Sunset Books and Sunset Magazine, assisted by Kay Kennedy. Menlo Park, Calif., Lane Book Co., 1963. 79p. illus. wrps. (A Sunset Discovery Book) ANR. Menlo Park, Calif., Lane Book Co., 1966. rev. ed. 96p. photos, maps, bibliog. wrps. (A Sunset Travel Book)   4400

SUPF, PETER. Flieger erobern die Pole. [TITLE TR. Flyers conquer the Poles] München, Nymphenburger Verlagshandlung, 1957. 200p. illus. bibliog. [contains account of Sir Hubert Wilkins, others]   4401

SUR, FOREST JOHN. Placer gold mining and prospecting. How to find & mine gold bearing gravels. A practical handbook for prospectors & miners. By Forest John Sur, Mining Engineer and Geologist. Hollywood, Calif., Stanley Rose, 1934. 1st ed. 116p. illus. photos(fold.), figs. facsims. index. [many references to Alaska]   4402

Suria, Tomás de. SEE nos.
    1546, Fernandez, J. Tomás de Suria ... 1939;
    4724, Wagner, H. R. Journal ... 1936.

SURVEY ASSOCIATES. American-Russian frontiers. no pl., 1944. 96p. illus. maps, wrps. (Calling America Series)   4403

SUSHKOV, BORIS ALEKSANDROVICH. Dal'nevostochnye moria i ikh poberezh'ia; istoriko-geograficheskiĭ obzor. [TITLE TR. Far Eastern seas and their coasts; historical and geographical outline] Vladivostok, Primorskoe knizhnoe izd-vo, 1958. 118p. maps, bibliog. [incls. Aleutian Islands and Alaskan mainland coast]
                                                                 4404

Sutcliff, G. E. SEE no. 1802, Great Britain. Admiralty.

SUTHERLAND, HOWARD V. Biggs' Bar, and other Klondyke ballads. Philadelphia, D. Biddle, 1901. 78p.   4405

530

SUTHERLAND, HOWARD V. Out of the North; with a foreword by
Joaquin Miller. N. Y., Desmond Fitzgerald, Inc., 1913. 20p.
[poetry]   4406

Sutherland, Howard V. SEE ALSO no. 4924,
    Winslow, Kathryn. Big pan-out ... [c1951]

Sutherland, L., co-auth. SEE no. 4739, Ware, Kay.

SUTTON, ANN and MYRON SUTTON. Steller of the North. Chicago,
Rand McNally, 1961. 231p. illus. by L. E. Fisher, maps, bibliog.
[Georg Wilhelm Steller, naturalist on Bering's last voyage] 4407

SUTTON, ANN and MYRON SUTTON. The endless quest; the life of
John Franklin, explorer. London, Constable Young, 1965. 244p.
illus. maps, bibliog.   4408

Sutton, Myron, co-auth. SEE nos. 4407-8, Sutton, Ann.

Sveistrup, P. P., co-auth. SEE no. 2318, Jacobsen, N. K.

SVENSKA MISSIONSFÖRBUNDET I AMERIKA. Alaska förr och nu, en
naturskildring, kulturbild och missionsberättelse, enligt muntliga
och skriftliga meddelanden af missionärer, utgifven af Svenska
Missionsförbundet i Amerika till förmån för dess missioner. Chicago, P. G. Almberg & Co., 1897. 152(6)p. front.(map), photos,
ports. sketches. [Unalakleet, Yakutat, Golovin Bay missions,
others]   4409

SVERDRUP, HARALD ULRIK. Dynamics of tides on the North Siberian
shelf; results from the *Maud* Expedition. Oslo, Cammermeyer,
1926. 75p. charts, tables, diagrs. (Geofysiske publikasjoner,
vol. 4, no. 5) [from Pt. Barrow, Alaska to Cape Chelyuskin,
Russia]   4410

SVERDRUP, HARALD ULRIK. General report of the expedition. Bergen, John Grieg, 1933. 22p. pls. (Scientific results, vol. 1,
no. 1) [*Maud* Expedition, 1918-25]   4411

SVERDRUP, HARALD ULRIK. Meteorology, part 2. Bergen, John Grieg,
1933. 22p. pls. (Scientific results, vol. 3) [*Maud* Expedition
1918-25, incl. data for Alaskan coast at Nome]   4412

SVERDRUP, HARALD ULRIK. Tre aar i isen med "Maud" med et tillaeg
om en slaedereise rundt Tsjuktsjerhal vøen. [TITLE TR. Three
years in the ice with the "Maud" with a supplement on a sledge
trip around the Chukotsk Peninsula] Oslo, Gyldendal, Norsk forlag, 1926. 285p. front. pls. ports. maps. [*Maud* Expedition
of 1918-25]   4413

Sverdrup, Harald Ulrik. SEE ALSO no. 225,
    Amundsen, R. E. G. Nordostpassagen ... 1921.

SVET, Ĭa. M. Moreplavatel' tumannago Al'biona; Dzhems Kuk.
[TITLE TR. The seafarer from the misty Albion; James Cook]
Moskva, Gos. izd-vo Geograficheskoi Literatury, 1963. 80p. illus.
maps. (Zamelchatel'nye geografy i puteshestvenniki)   4414

Sviatoe evangelie ot Ioanna Aleutsko-lisjevskom nariechiĭ. 1902.
    SEE no. 4538, Tikhon, *Bishop*.

Sviatoe evangelie ot Luki, Aleutsko-lisjevskom nariechiĭ. 1903.
    SEE no. 4539, Tikhon, *Bishop*.

[Swaine, Charles]   SEE nos.
    1344, [Drage, Theodore Swaine] Account voyage ... 1748;
    2336, [Jefferys, Thos. ?]   Great probability North West
                passage ... 1768.

SWANTON, JOHN REED.   Contributions to the ethnology of the Haida.
N. Y., Stechert, 1905.   300p.   pls.   table(fold.), maps(fold.)
(Memoir American Museum of Natural History, vol. 8, no. 1.   Pub.
Jesup North Pacific Expedition, vol. 5, pt. 1)   4415

SWANTON, JOHN REED and FRANZ BOAS.   Haida songs.   Tsimshian texts
(new series) by Franz Boas.   Leyden, Late E. J. Brill, 1912.
284p.   (Pub. American Ethnological Society, vol. 3)   4416

SWANTON, JOHN REED.   Indian tribes of Alaska and Canada.   Seattle,
Shorey Book Store, 1965.   facsim. reprint.   map(fold.), wrps.
[pp.529-608 extracted from no. 4419]   4417

SWANTON, JOHN REED.   Social conditions, beliefs and linguistic
relationship of the Tlingit Indians.   N. Y., Johnson Reprint
Corp., 1970.   pls. [pp.391-485 extracted from Annual Report,
1904-05 of U. S. Bureau of American Ethnology, published in
1908]   4418

SWANTON, JOHN REED.   The Indian tribes of North America.   St.
Clair Shores, Mich., Scholarly Press, 1968.   [reprint of U. S.
Bureau of American Ethnology Bulletin no. 145, published in
1952]   4419

SWANTON, JOHN REED.   Tlingit myths and texts.   N. Y., Johnson Re-
print Corp., 1970.   451p.   [facsim. reprint of U. S. Bureau of
American Ethnology Bulletin no. 39 published in 1909.   Indians of
Sitka and Wrangell areas]   4420

SWARTH, HARRY SCHELWALD.   Birds and mammals of the 1909 Alexander
Alaska Expedition.   By Harry S. Swarth.   Berkeley, University of
California Press, 1911.   pls. maps(incl. 1 fold.), bibliog. (Uni-
versity of California Pub. in Zoology, vol. 7, no. 2.   pp.9-172)
                                                          4421

SWARTH, HARRY SCHELWALD. Birds and mammals of the Stikine River region of northern British Columbia and southeast Alaska. By Harry S. Swarth. Berkeley, University of California Press, 1922. pls. map, bibliog. (University of California Pub. in Zoology, vol. 24, 1922. pp.125-314) 4422

SWARTH, HARRY SCHELWALD. Birds of Nunivak Island, Alaska. By Harry S. Swarth. Los Angeles, Calif., Cooper Ornithological Club, 1934. 64p. front.(port.), illus. map, bibliog. index. (Pacific Coast Avifauna, no. 22. Published by the Club, March 31, 1934) 4423

SWARTH, HARRY SCHELWALD. Report on a collection of birds and mammals from the Atlin region, northern British Columbia. By Harry S. Swarth. Berkeley, University of California Press, 1926. pls. bibliog. (University of California Pub. in Zoology, vol.30, no. 4. Sept. 24, 1926. pp.51-162) [British Columbia - Yukon - Alaskan borders] 4424

SWARTH, HARRY SCHELWALD. Report on a collection of birds and mammals from Vancouver Island. By Harry S. Swarth. Berkeley, University of California Press, 1912. pls. bibliog. (University of California Pub. in Zoology, Feb. 13, 1912. vol. 10, no. 1. pp.1-124) [Vancouver Island and Alaskan specimens] 4425

SWARTZ, MARC J., VICTOR W. TURNER and ARTHUR TUDEN, co-edits. Political anthropology. 1964 annual general meeting of The American Anthropology Association. Chicago, Aldine Pub. Co., 1966. 309p. diagrs. bibliogs. [pp.255-63, *From contest to council; social control among the St. Lawrence Eskimos*, by Charles Campbell Hughes] 4426

SWAYZE, NANSI. The man hunters; Jenness, Barbeau, Wintemberg. Toronto, Clarke, Irwin, 1960. 180p. (Canadian Portraits series) 4427

Swedish Missionary Foundation of America. SEE no. 4409, Svenska Missionsförbundet i Amerika.

SWANSON, MARGARET C. Kayoo, the Eskimo boy. N. Y., Scribner, 1939. 112p. illustrated by Frederick Machetanz. 4428

SWENSON, OLAF. Northwest of the world; forty years trading and hunting in northern Siberia. N. Y., Dodd Mead, 1944. 270p. front. pls. port. [proprietor of trading post at Nome] 4429

Swenson, Olaf. SEE ALSO no. 4508, Thompson, R. The Siberian Husky. 1962.

SWERDLOFF, HERMAN G. Yarns of the Yukon; recollections of a sourdough under the Midnight Sun, by Herman G. Swerdloff. Perth Amboy, N. J., Yukon Press, [1966] 232p. [poetry] 4430

SWIFT, HILDEGARDE (HOYT). Edge of April; a biography of John Burroughs. N. Y., Morrow, 1957. illus. 4431

SWIFT, HILDEGARDE (HOYT). From the eagle's wing; a biography of John Muir. Illustrated by Lynd Ward. N. Y., Morrow, 1962. 287p. 4432

Swiftwater Bill. SEE no. 466, Beebe, Iola.

Swindler, Daris R. SEE no. 1709, Giddings, J. L., jr.

[Swindrage, Theodore S.] SEE nos.
 1344, [Drage, Theodore Swaine] Account voyage ... 1748;
 2336, [Jefferys, Thos. ?] Great probability North West
 passage ... 1768.

SWINEFORD, ALFRED P. Alaska. Its history, climate and natural resources. By Hon. A. P. Swineford, Ex-Governor of Alaska. With map and illustrations. Chicago, Rand McNally & Co., [c1898] 256p. illus. front.(pl.), map(fold. at back), append. 4433

Swineford, Alfred P. SEE ALSO no. 52,
 Alaska Commercial Co. Reply ... to ... Swineford ... 1887.

SWITHINBANK, CHARLES WINTHROP MOLESWORTH. Ice atlas of Arctic Canada. Ottawa, 1960. 67p. graphs(col.), table, maps(col.), bibliog. folio. (Canada. Defense Research Board) [from Icy Cape, Alaska to Canada's Smith Sound] 4434

SYME, RONALD. Captain Cook; Pacific explorer. By R. Syme. Illustrated by W. Stobbs. N. Y., W. Morrow, 1960. 96p. illus. (Morrow Junior Books) 4435

SYNDICAT FRANÇAIS du TRANS-ALASKA SIBÉRIEN. Le chemin de fer trans-Alaska-Sibérien (projet Loïcq de Lobel) Rapport présenté au gouvernment imperial de Sa Majeste l'empereur de Russie. [Paris ? 1902 ?] 32p. map(fold.) 4436

SYNGE, MARGARET BERTHA. A book of discovery. Edinburgh, Nelson, 1962. illus. map. [pp.229-35, account of Capt. James Cook's third voyage and death] 4437

SYNGE, MARGARET BERTHA. Captain Cook's voyages round the world; with an introduction ... by M. B. Synge. London, T. Nelson & Sons, 1897. xiv,ix,11-152p. illus. ports. maps. ANR. London, T. Nelson, 1903. xiv,ix,11-152p. illus. ports. maps. 4438

SYNGE, MARGARET BERTHA. Cook's voyages; the text reduced, with introduction and notes, by M. B. Synge. London, Rivington, Perceval, 1894. [An earlier ed. published in 1892] 4439

SZÉCHÉNYI, ZSIGMOND. Alaszkában vadásztam. Eine abenteuerliche Jagdreise durchs weite Land. München-Bonn, Wien, Übers v. Paul Palffy Pal., 1959. 275p. [cf no. 4441]   4440

SZÉCHÉNYI, ZSIGMOND. Alaszkában vadásztam. 1935 aug.-okt. Buda-pest, Bibliotheca Kaidó, 1957. 256p. pls. ports. endmaps. ANR. N. Y. Bibliotheca Kossuth, 1957. 256p. (Vilá-gjárók 8) [cf no. 4440]   4441

T

TABER, RALPH G. Stray gold; a rambler's clean-up. St. Paul, Minn., St. Paul Book and Stationery Co., 1915. 191p. [poetry]
4442

TACOMA CHAMBER OF COMMERCE, Tacoma, Washington. Tacoma, the gateway to the Klondike. Tacoma, Advertising Committee of Tacoma Chamber of Commerce, 1897. 122p. map.   4443

TACOMA DAILY NEWS, Tacoma, Washington. Tacoma, the gate way to the Klondike. Tacoma, 1897. 16p. illus. ports. maps. [special issue of December 14, 1897]   4444

TAGAROOK, P. and A. NASHOALOOK. Jesus kamanaktuat savaani. Translated by P. Tagarook and A. Nashoalook. Edited by R. Ahmao-gak. Illustrated by T. Webster. Fairbanks, Wycliffe Bible Translators, n. d. 27p. front. illus. wrps. [western Arctic Eskimo]   4445

Tagebuch ... J. R. Forster. 1781. SEE no. 1015, [Cook, Jas.]

Tait, J. N. SEE no. 1804, Great Britain. Admiralty.

TANANA CLUB. The constitution and by-laws of the Tanana Club, organized January 1, 1906. [Fairbanks], Press of Daily News-Miner, 1914. 15p.   4446

TANANA DIRECTORY CO. Directory of the Tanana Valley, 1907. Fairbanks, 1907. 222p.   4447

TANANA DREDGING CO. Memorandum and subscription agreement. no pl., n. d. 7p.   4448

TANANA, TOWN OF. Ordinance no. VII. Revised ordinances of the town of Tanana. Enacted February 13, 1914. [Tanana ?], 1914. 58p.   4449

TANANA VALLEY RAILROAD CO. Annual report of the Tanana Valley Railroad Company. Chicago and N. Y., 1909. OTHERS for years 1910 through 1916.   4450

TANFIL'EV, GAVRIIL IVANOVICH. Morīā; Kaspiĭskoe, Chernoe, Bal-
tiĭskoe, Ledovitoe, Sibirskoe i Vostochnyĭ okean. Istoriīā issle-
dovaniīā, morfometriīā, gidrologiīā, biologiīā. [TITLE TR. The
Caspian, Black, Baltic, Glacial, Siberian Seas, and the Pacific
Ocean. History of exploration, morphometry, hydrology, biology]
Moskva, Leningrad, Glavnauka, NKP RSFSR, 1931. 246p. illus.
maps, bibliogs. [incls. Bering Sea]   4451

TANSILL, CHARLES CALLAN. Canadian-American relations, 1875-1911.
New Haven, Yale University Press, 1943. ANR. Gloucester, Mass.,
Peter Smith, 1964. [Bering Sea sealing controversy]   4452

TANSILL, CHARLES CALLAN. The foreign policy of Thomas F. Bayard,
1885-1897. N. Y., Fordham University Press, 1940. [Bering Sea
sealing controversy - Bayard was U. S. Secretary of State, 1885-
89; became U. S. Ambassador to Great Britain, 1893-97]   4453

TAPP, GENE and LOIS TAPP. Alaskan designs for crafts, hobbies.
North Pole, designed and printed by Jon-Hunt Advertising, n. d.
[ca 1967] (18)p. illus. wrps. (No. 1, The Mukluk Shop, Fairbanks)   4454

TAPP, GENE and LOIS TAPP. Alaskan designs for crafts, hobbies.
North Pole, designed and printed by Jon-Hunt Advertising, n. d.
[cal967] (22)p. illus. wrps. (No. 2, The Mukluk Shop, Fairbanks)   4455

TAPP, GENE and LOIS TAPP. Alaskan mukluks for the family. Complete instructions for making all sizes of mukluks on your own
sewing machine. North Pole, designed and printed by Jon-Hunt
Advertising, n. d. [ca 1967] 8p. illus. wrps.   4456

TARANETS, ANATOLIĬ ĪA. Kratkiĭ opredelitel'ryb sovetskogo
Dal'nego Vostoka i prilezhashchikh vod. [TITLE TR. Handbook for
identification of fishes of Soviet Far East and adjacent waters]
Vladivostok, 1937. 200p. illus. map(fold.), checklist, keys,
indexes in Russian and Latin, with English summary. (Vladivostok.
Tikhookeanskiĭ nauchno-issledovatel'skiĭ institut rybnogo kho-
ziāĭstva i okeanografiĭ. Izvestiīā, t. 11)   4457

TARENETSKIĬ, ALEKSANDR IVANOVICH. Beiträge zur Skelet- und
Schädelkunde der Aleuten, Konaegen, Kenai und Koljuschen; mit
vergleichend anthropologischen Bemerkungen. Von Professor A.
Tarenetzky. [TITLE TR. Contributions to the knowledge of skele-
tons and skulls of the Aleuts, Konags, Kenai, and Kolosh, with
comparative anthropological observations] St. Petersburg, 1900.
73p. pls.(some col.), tables. (Zapiski Imperatorskoĭ Akademiīā
nauk ... VIIIe serie. Po Fiziko-matematishekomu ‚otdīēleniīū.
tom. IX, no. 4)   4458

Tarkhanov, P. SEE no. 3690, Price, E. V.

TARR, RALPH STOCKMAN and LAWRENCE MARTIN. Alaskan glacier studies. Results of the National Geographic Society Alaskan expeditions 1909-1910, and subsequent investigations by the authors,
1913 in the Yakutat Bay, Prince William Sound and lower Copper
River regions. Washington, D. C., National Geographic Society,
1914. 498p. illus. pls. maps(incl. some fold.)   4459

TATE, CHARLES MONTGOMERY. Chinook as spoken by the Indians of
Washington Territory, British Columbia, and Alaska; for the use
of traders, tourists and others who have business intercourse
with the Indians. Chinook-English, English-Chinook. Victoria,
B. C., M. W. Waitt, 1889. 47p.   4460

TATE, CHARLES MONTGOMERY. Chinook jargon as spoken by the Indians
of the Pacific Coast; for the use of missionaries, traders,
tourists and others who have business intercourse with the Indians. Chinook-English, English-Chinook. Victoria, B. C., T. R.
Cusack, 1914. 48p. wrps.   4461

TAVERNER, PERCY ALGERNON. A study of *Buteo borealis*, the red-
tailed hawk, and its varieties in Canada. Ottawa, King's Printer,
1927. 20p. pls. textmap, bibliog. (Canada. National Museum of
Canada Bull. no. 48. Biol. Ser. no. 13) [also Alaskan varieties]
          4462

TAVERNER, PERCY ALGERNON. Birds of Canada. Ottawa, 1934. 445p.
pls.(incl. some col.), glossary, indexes. (Canada. Department
of Mines. National Museum of Canada Bull. no. 72, Biol. Ser.
no. 19) ANR. Toronto, Musson Book Co., 1938. 455p. pls.(incl.
some col.) [Alaskan species included]   4463

TAVERNER, PERCY ALGERNON. Birds of western Canada. Ottawa,
King's Printer, 1926. 380p. pls.(col.), bibliog. index. (Cana-
da. Geological Survey. National Museum of Canada Bull. no. 41.
Biol. Ser. no. 10)   4464

TAX, SOL, edit. Indian tribes of aboriginal America, selected
papers of the 29th International Congress of Americanists ...
Chicago, 1952. ANR. N. Y., Cooper Square Publishers, 1967. reprint ed. illus. (29th International Congress of Americanists)
[contains *The Ipiutak culture; its origin and relationships*, by
Helge Larsen, pp. 22-34, and *A survival of the Eurasiatic animal
style in modern Alaskan Eskimo art*, by Carl Schuster, pp.33-45.
illus.]   4465

TAXAY, DON. Money of the American Indians and other primitive
currencies of the Americas. N. Y., Nummus Press, [c1970] 158p.
front. pls. ftntes. bibliog. index. [has scattered references to
Alaskan]   4466

TAYLOR, BARBARA A. Alaska, last frontier. N. Y., Carlton Press,
1963. 174p. photos and drawings by author, map(dble.) (A Re-
flection Book)   4467

TAYLOR, CHARLES MAUS, jr. Touring Alaska and the Yellowstone. By Charles M. Taylor, Jr. Profusely illustrated from photographs by the author. Philadelphia, George W. Jacobs & Co., [c1901] 388p. front. pls. [travel in southeastern Alaska]   4468

TAYLOR, FRANK J. High horizons; daredevil flying postmen to modern magic carpet - the United Air Lines story. N. Y., McGraw-Hill, [c1951] 198p. illus. photos. [pp.125-40, World War II, transport flying in Aleutian Islands and other parts of Alaska]
                                                                4469

Taylor, Frank J. SEE ALSO no. 165, Albright, H. M.
    "Oh Ranger !" 1928.

Taylor, H. P., jr. SEE no. 4982, Wyllie, P. J.

Taylor, H. West, co-auth. SEE no. 2005, Hayne, M. H. E.

TAYLOR, L. D. Ice structures, Burroughs Glacier, southeast Alaska. Columbus, Ohio, 1962. 106p. illus. graphs, tables, maps, bibliog. (University of Ohio Institute of Polar Studies, Report no. 3)   4470

TAYLOR, LYTTON. Alaska and the Yukon Valley. How to get there; journey fully described; land of gold; its mineral fields - seals - fisheries - furbearing animals - reindeer and people. Nashville, Tenn., Brandon Printing Co., 1897. 124p.   4471

TAYLOR, RICHARD C. Statistics of coal. The geographical and geological distribution of mineral combustibles or fossil fuel. Philadelphia, 1848. 1st ed. 148p.754p. index. [first quarter of book about western North America, incl. Russian America and British America]   4472

TAYLOR, SARAH DRURY. Lure of the Northland; poems of the Yukon and Alaska. Vancouver, 1955. 43p.   4473

Taylor, W. E., jr. SEE no. 4651, Van Steensel, M.

Teacher's guide to "Alaska's Silver Millions." 1936. SEE
    no. 625, Boutwell, W. D.

Teale, E. W., edit. SEE no. 3228, Muir, John.

TEBEN'KOV, MIKHAIL DMITRÍEVICH. Atlas Sĭeverozapadnykh beregov Ameriki ot Beringova proliva do mysa Korriéntes i ostrovov Aleut-skikh s privosokupleniem nĭekotorykh mĭest Sĭeverovostochnago berega Azii. Sostavil kapitan-I-go ranga Tebĭen'kov. [TITLE TR. Atlas of the Northwest coast of America from Bering Stait to Cape Corrientes and of the Aleutian Islands, supplemented by some places of the Northeast coast of Asia. Compiled by Capt. Teben'-kov] Sanktpeterburg, 1852. maps(incl. 1 dble.), folio. [with 2d vol., SEE no. 4475]   4474

TEBEN'KOV, MIKHAIL DMITRÍEVICH. Gidrograficheskiîa zamiechaniîa k atlasu Sîeverozapadnykh beregov Ameriki ostrovov Aleutskikh i nîekotorykh drugikh mîest Sîevernago Tikhago okeana. Kapitan I ranga Tebîen'kov. [TITLE TR. Hydrographic notes to the atlas of the Northwest coast of America, the Aleutian Islands and some other places of the North Pacific Ocean. Compiled by Capt. Teben'kov] Sanktpeterburg, v Tipografiî Morskago Kadetskago Korpusa, 1852. 148p.,17p. errata slip. [companion vol. to no. 4474]   4475

TEDROW, J. C. F. Morphological evidence of frost action in Arctic soils. New Brunswick, N. J., Rutgers University, 1962. (N. J. Agriculture Experimental Station, Journal Series paper: also in Biuletyn peryglacjalny, no. 11. Łódz, 1962. pp.343-53. illus. bibliog.) [Northern Alaska and Canada]   4476

TEICHMANN, EMIL. A journey to Alaska in the year 1868; being a diary of the late Emil Teichmann. Edited with an introduction by his son Oskar. Kensington, privately printed by The Cayme Press, 1925. 272p. illus. ports. maps. ltd. ed. of 100 copies. ANR. N. Y., Argosy, 1963. facsim reprint, ltd. ed. of 750 and deluxe ltd. ed. of 87 copies. [commerce with Russian American Fur Co. by agent for M. Oppenheim & Co. of London and N. Y., 1866]   4477

Teichmann, Oskar, edit. SEE no. 4477, Teichmann, Emil.

Ten thousand Alaska and west coast fishing jobs. 1946. SEE
    no. 3454, Pacific Industrial Research Burea.

Terminal facilities No. Pac. ports. 1914. SEE no. 4479,
    Terminal Pub. Co.

TERMINAL PUBLISHING CO., comp. North Pacific ports; a compilation of useful marine, exporting and importing information for Alaska and the western coasts of Canada and the United States. Seattle, 1914.   4478

TERMINAL PUBLISHING CO., comp. Terminal facilities of North Pacific ports; a compilation of all useful information concerning Alaska, British Columbia, Washington, Oregon, and California shipping. Seattle, 1914.   4479

Territorial Sportsmen's Assoc. SEE no. 93,
    Alaska Northwest Pub. Co.

TEWKESBURY, WILLIAM, comp. Alaska business directory, travel guide and almanac with homestead laws, hunting, living costs,etc. Seattle and Anchorage, Tewkesbury Pub., [c1948] 518p. illus. maps, index, wrps.   4480

TEWKESBURY, WILLIAM, edit. Alaska highway and travel guide, business directory and almanac. Compiled and edited by William Tewkesbury. Anchorage and Seattle, published by Tewkesbury Publishers, David Tewkesbury and William Tewkesbury, [c1950] [lithgraphed by Lowman and Hanford, Seattle] 712p. illus. maps(incl. 1 fold.), indexes. 4481

TEWKESBURY, WILLIAM, [comp.] Tewkesbury's who's who in Alaska and Alaska business index. Volume 1, 1947. Containing a biographical index of personal sketches of prominent living Alaskans, an alphabetical directory of business concerns and their owners, a complete directory of the fur trade and of the fishing, mining, and lumber industries, a list of Federal and Territorial government agencies and welfare institutions, and much information of a miscellaneous character. Juneau and Seattle, Tewkesbury Publishers, [c1947] 320p. map(fold. in back), indexes. 4482

Tewsley, U., tr. SEE no. 5037, Zimmermann, H.

Thane meeting ... 1918. SEE no. 88, Alaska Mining & Engr. Soc.

THIBERT, ARTHUR. English-Eskimo, Eskimo-English dictionary. Ottawa, Ottawa University, 1958. rev. ed. 173p. (Research Centre for Amerindian Anthropology) 4483

Thiergeschichte ... 1787. SEE no. 3532, [Pennant, Thos.]

Thiery, Maurice. Captain Cook ... 1930. SEE no. 4486.

THIÉRY, MAURICE. La vie et les voyages du Capitaine Cook; illus. par A. Zaccagnino. Paris, P. Roger, 1929. 238p. port. map. (La Vie des Grands Navigateurs) 4484

   TRANSLATIONS - La Vie ... 1929, CHRONOLOGICALLY.

   The life and voyages of Captain Cook, by M. Thiéry. London,
      Geoffrey Blas, 1929. ix,238p. front.(port.), pls. ports.
      map, endmaps. 4485

   Captain Cook navigator and discoverer. By M. Thiéry. N. Y.,
      R. M. McBride, 1930. x,265p. illus. port. facsim. endmaps.
                                                              4486

THIRRING, GUSZTAV. A magyarországi Kivándorlás és a Külföldi magyarság. Kilián, 1905. 366p. 4487

Thirty-six years seafaring ... 1864. SEE no. 460,
      [Bechervaise, John ?]

THIS IS ALASKA, America's last frontier; a pictorial. Edited by Marjorie Roberts. Anchorage, Alaska Publications, 1964. 79p. illus. ports. facsims. wrps. 4488

This is Alaska; sailing ... [c1948] SEE no. 125,
   Alaska Steamship Co.

This is Alaska today... 1954. SEE no. 3698, Production Surveys.

This is Kodiak. 1969. SEE no. 3470, Page, Roger.

Thomas, B. D. SEE no. 4510, Thompson, Thos. Gordon.

THOMAS, BENJAMIN PLATT. Russo-American relations 1815-1867. By
Benjamin P. Thomas. Baltimore, Johns Hopkins Press, 1930. [c1930]
viii,9-185p. ftntes. index. (Johns Hopkins University Studies
in Historical and Political Science, Ser. 48, no. 2) ANR. N. Y.,
Da Capo Press, 1970. reprint. [author's Ph.D. thesis, 1929:
has chapt. on Alaska purchase]   4489

THOMAS, CHARLES W. Ice is where you find it. By Captain Charles
W. Thomas, U.S.C.G. Indianapolis, Bobbs-Merrill, [c1951] 1st ed.
378p. front.(pl.), maps, index. [pp.317-66, Bering Sea patrol]
                                                                 4490

Thomas Cook Co. SEE no. 1058, Cook Co., Thomas.

THOMAS, EDITH LUCRETIA RICHMOND. A night in Sitka; Alaskan tales
told in verse. By Edith Lucretia Richmond Thomas. N. Y., Har-
binger House, 1948. [c1948] 84p. [of gold rush days]   4491

THOMAS, EDWARD HARPER. Chinook, a history and dictionary of the
Northwest Coast trade jargon; the centuries-old trade language of
the Indians of the Pacific; a history of its origin and its
adoption and use by the traders, trappers, pioneers and early
settlers of the Northwest coast. Portland, Ore., Metropolitan
Press, 1935. 179p. ANR. Portland, Ore., Binfords and Mort, 1954.
ANR. Portland, Ore., Binfords and Mort, [c1970] 2d ed. xi,171p.
front.(port.), append. bibliog.   4492

Thomas, J. H., co-auth. SEE no. 4864, Wiggins, Ira L.

THOMAS, LOWELL and LOWELL THOMAS, jr. Famous first flights that
changed history. Garden City, N. Y., Doubleday, 1968. [c1968]
1st ed. 340p. front.(port.), photos, ports. bibliog. index.
[many references to Alaska, to Sir Hubert Wilkins, Carl Ben
Elelson, others]   4493

THOMAS, LOWELL. Kabluk of the Eskimo. By Lowell Thomas. Boston,
Little Brown, 1932. [c1932] 276p. front.(port.), pls. ports.
[biog. of Louis Romanet of Hudson's Bay Co. in eastern Canadian
Arctic. One brief mention of Alaska only]   4494

THOMAS, LOWELL. Lowell Thomas' book of the high mountains. N.Y.,
Julian Messner, [c1964] 512p. front.(port.), photos, drawings,
maps, index. [many scattered references to Alaska]   4495

THOMAS, LOWELL. Sir Hubert Wilkins, his world of adventure; a biography by Lowell Thomas. N. Y., McGraw-Hill, [c1961] 296p. illus. photos. ANR. London, 1962. 278p.   4496

THOMAS, LOWELL. The first world flight, being the personal narratives of Lowell Smith, Erick Nelson, Leigh Wade, Leslie Arnold, Henry Ogden, John Harding. Boston, Houghton, 1925. [U. S. around the world flight of 1924, planes *Seattle, Boston, New Orleans* and *Chicago*]   4497

THOMAS, LOWELL. Woodfill of the Regulars; a true story of adventure from the Arctic to the Argonne. By Lowell Thomas. Garden City, N. Y., Doubleday Doran & Co., 1929. [c1929] 1st ed. 325p. front.(port.), photos, facsims. [several chapts. tell of Army service of Samuel Woodfill on Ft. Egbert at Eagle and Ft. Gibbon near Tanana, early 1900's]   4498

THOMAS, LOWELL, jr. The trail of '98; an anthology of the Klondike. N. Y., Duell, Sloan and Pearce, [c1962] 1st ed. 191p.   4499

Thomas, Mary. SEE nos. 4500-02, Thomas, Tay.

THOMAS, TAY. Cry in the wilderness. "Hear ye the voice of the Lord." By Tay Thomas. Anchorage, Color Art Printing Co., [c1967] 125p. front.(map), photos, cover illus. by Joan Kickbush, ftntes. bibliog. wrps. (Issued under the auspices of the Alaska Council of Churches)   4500

THOMAS, TAY. Follow the North Star. By Tay Thomas. Garden City, N. Y., Doubleday, 1960. 1st ed. 165p. illus. [flying in Alaska]   4501

THOMAS, TAY. Only in Alaska. By Tay Thomas. Garden City, N. Y., Doubleday, 1969. 252p. illus. ports. endmaps(col.) [biog.]   4502

THOMAS, WILLIAM S. Trails and tramps in Alaska and Newfoundland, with 147 illustrations from original photographs. N. Y., Putnam, 1913. xv,330(6)p. front. illus. index. [mountain climbing, hunting in southeast Alaska, on Kenai Peninsula and Kodiak Island]   4503

THOMPSON, ARTHUR RIPLEY. Gold-seeking on the Dalton Trail; being the adventures of two New England boys in Alaska and the Northwest Territory. Boston, Little, 1900. 352p. front. pls. maps. ANR. Boston, Little, 1925. 327p. illus. in color by George Avison. front. pls. (Beacon Hill Bookshelf)   4504

Thompson, D'Arcy W. SEE nos. 1817-8,
    Great Britain. Parl. Papers.

THOMPSON, DONNIS STARK. The Loon Lake mystery; an Alaskan tale. By Donnis Thompson. Illustrated by Richard Lewis. N. Y., Criterion Books, [c1966] 144p. illus. [juv. with Kenai Peninsula setting]   4505

THOMPSON, EDGAR T. and EVERETT C. HUGHES, edits. Race, individual and collective behavior. Glencoe, Illinois, 1958. 619p. bibliog. [pp.98-101, *Northern Alaska*, excerpted from Robert Marshall's "Arctic Village," 1933. (pp.230-6)]   4506

THOMPSON, J. WALTER, CO., N. Y. The Alaskan market, 1958; this concise description of Alaska as a market is an introductory survey. N. Y., J. Walter Thompson Co., 1958. 39p. illus. maps, tables, bibliog.   4507

Thompson, N., co-auth. SEE no. 1410, Edgar J. H.

THOMPSON, RAYMOND and LOUISE H. FOLEY. The Siberian Husky. Adderwood Manor, Washington, Raymond Thompson Co., 1962. 69p. illus. maps, wrps. (Volume 1. Historical Edition. Edited by the staff of The Siberian Husky News, official organ of The Seppala Siberian Husky Club) [references to Leonhard Seppala and Olaf Swanson as breeders of Alaskan Huskies]   4508

THOMPSON, STITH, edit. Tales of the North American Indians. Cambridge, Harvard University Press, 1929. 386p. map(fold.), bibliog. [anthology incls. Alaskan Eskimo as well as Alaskan Indian tales]   4509

THOMPSON, THOMAS GORDON, B. D. THOMAS and C. A. Barnes. Distribution of dissolved oxygen in the North Pacific Ocean. Pullman, Washington, Washington State University, 1934. tables, diagrs. (Publications in Oceanography, Ser. 21. Also in James Johnstone Memorial Volume, University of Liverpool, 1934. pp.203-34) [includes Gulf of Alaska and Bering Sea north of Aleutian Islands]   4510

THOMPSON, THOMAS GORDON, G. F. McEWEN and R. VAN CLEVE. Hydrographic sections and calculated currents in the Gulf of Alaska, 1929. Seattle, printed by Wrigley Printing Co., 1936. 32p. tables, diagrs. charts. (International Fisheries Commission Report no. 10. Vancouver, B. C.)   4511

Thompson, Thomas Gordon. SEE ALSO nos.
    1775, Goodman, J. Characteristics ... Dutch Harbor ... 1940;
    2889, McEwen, G. F. Hydrographic ... Gulf Alaska ... 1930.

Thompson, W. F. ("Wrong Font") SEE no. 1516,
    Fairbanks Commercial Club.

THOMPSON, WILLIAM FRANCIS. An outline for salmon research in
Alaska, prepared for the meeting of the International Council for
Exploration of the Sea at Amsterdam, Oct. 1-9, 1951. Seattle,
1951. 49p. (University of Washington. Fisheries Research Institute, Circular no. 18)   4512

THOMPSON, WILLIAM FRANCIS, HARRY A. DUNLAP and F. HOWARD BELL.
Biological statistics of the Pacific halibut fishery, no. 1.
Changes in yield of a standardized unit of year. Vancouver, B.C.,
1931. 108p. pls. tables(incl. 1 fold.), charts(incl. 1 fold.)
(International Fisheries Commission, Report no. 6)   4513

THOMPSON, WILLIAM FRANCIS and F. HOWARD BELL. Biological statistics of the Pacific halibut fisheries, no. 2. Effect of changes
in intensity upon total yield and yield per unit of year. Seattle, 1934. 49p. diagrs. charts. (International Fisheries Commission, Report no. 8)   4514

THOMPSON, WILLIAM FRANCIS and NORMAN L. FREEMAN. History of the
Pacific halibut fishery. Vancouver, B. C., 1930. 61p. pls.
diagrs. charts(incl. 1 fold.) (International Fisheries Commission, Report no. 5)   4515

THOMPSON, WILLIAM FRANCIS and WILLIAM C. HERRINGTON. Life history of the Pacific halibut. No. 1. Marking experiments. Victoria, B. C., 1930. 137p. pls. tables, diagrs.(incl. some fold.)
charts(incl. 1 fold.) (International Fisheries Commission,
Report no. 2)   4516

THOMPSON, WILLIAM FRANCIS and RICHARD VAN CLEVE. Life history of
the Pacific halibut. No. 2. Distribution and early life history.
Seattle, 1936. 184p. pls. tables, diagrs. charts, appends.
bibliog. (International Fisheries Commission, Report no. 9) 4517

THOMPSON, WILLIAM FRANCIS. Some salmon research problems in
Alaska, prepared for the meeting held by the National Research
Council on scientific research in Alaska, Washington, D. C.,
November 9, 1950. Seattle, 1950. 19p. (University of Washing-
ton. Fisheries Research Institute. Circular no. 11)   4518

THOMPSON, WILLIAM FRANCIS. The effect of fishing on stocks of
halibut in the Pacific. Seattle, University of Washington Press,
1950. 60p. illus. tables, diagrs. (University of Washington
Publications Fisheries Research Institute)   4519

THOMPSON, WILLIAM FRANCIS. Theory of the effect of fishing on
the stock of halibut. Seattle, 1937. 22p. diagrs. bibliog.
(International Fisheries Commission, Report no. 12)   4520

Thompson, "Wrong Font" SEE no. 1516, Fairbanks Commercial Club.

THOMSON, JAY EARLE. Our Pacific possessions. N. Y., Scribner,
1931. 264p. index.   5421

THOMSON STATISTICAL SERVICE, Seattle. Thomson's manual of Pacific
Northwest finance; a digest of securities in, or pertaining to
the Territory of Alaska, the Province of British Columbia, the
State of Iowa, the State of Montana, the State of Oregon, the
State of Washington. Seattle, 1930. vol. 1. 487p.   4522

Thorburn, Don. SEE no. 4523, Thorburn, Lois.

THORBURN, LOIS and DON THORBURN. No tumult, no shouting; the
story of the PBY. N. Y., Holt, 1945. 148p. illus. ports. [U.S.
Navy Air Force in Aleutian Islands, World War II]   4523

THOREN, RAGNAR. Picture atlas of the Arctic. N. Y., American
Elsevier Publishing Co., 1969. 475p. photos, figs. maps, bibliog.   4524

THORNE, J. FREDERIC. In the time that was, dedicated to Ah-Koo.
Done into English by J. Frederic Thorne (Kitchakahaech). Illustrated by Judson T. Sergeant (To-u-sucka). Being the first volume of a series of legends of the tribe of Alaskan Indians known
as the Chilkats - of the Klingats. As told by Zachook the "Bear"
to Kitchakahaech the "Raven." Seattled, Published by the Raven,
[c1909] (28)p. front.(col.), illus.(col.), wrps.   4525

THORNTON, HARRISON ROBERTSON. Among the Eskimos of Wales, Alaska,
1890-93. By Harrison Robertson Thornton. Edited and annotated
by Neda S. Thornton and William M. Thornton, Jr. Baltimore, Johns
Hopkins Press and London, Humphrey Milford, 1931. [c1931] xxxviii,
234p. front.(port.), pls. ports. map, sketches, ftntes. [Seward
Peninsula]   4526

THORNTON, HARRISON ROBERTSON. Our Alaska Mission. N. Y., American Missionary Association, n. d. 4p.   4527

THORNTON, HARRISON ROBERTSON and WILLIAM T. LOPP. Report of
Alaska Mission, 1892-1893. N. Y., American Missionary Association, n. d. 8p.   4528

Thornton, Neda S., co-edit. SEE no. 4526, Thornton, H. R.

Thornton, Wm. M., jr., co-edit. SEE no. 4526, Thornton, H. R.

Three artists of Alaska ... 1965. SEE no. 107, Alaska Review.

THREE FAMOUS VOYAGES of Captain James Cook round the world, nar-
rating his discoveries and adventures in Tierra del Fuego ... together with an account of his murder at Hawaii and the subsequent
voyage of Captain King to Kamtschatka, Japan and China. London,
Ward, Lock, Bowden & Co., [189_ ?] xx,1,176p. illus. ports.
maps. (Hawkesworth Edition) ANR. London, Ward, Lock & Co.,
[189_ ?] xx,1,152p. illus. ports. maps, append.(abr.) (Hawkesworth Edition)   4529

Three voyages Cook ... n. d. SEE no. 1053, [Cook, Jas.]

Three voyages Jas. Cook...1821. SEE no. 1042, [Cook, Jas.]

Three voyages to Pacific ... 1897. SEE no. 1050, [Cook, Jas.]

Through Alaska gateway ... 1906. SEE no. 45, Alaska Central R.R.

Through hell and high water. 1941. SEE no. 1508, Explorers Club.

THUMAN, WILLIAM C. and ELMER ROBINSON. A technique for the determination of water in air at temperatures below freezing. Stanford, Calif., 1953. 14p. diagrs. tables, bibliog. (Stanford Research Institute, Report no. 9, Scientific Report no. 1. Sept.
1953) [at Eielson AFB near Fairbanks]   4530

THUMAN, WILLIAM C., G. A. St. JOHN and I. G. Poppoff. Studies of
the intensity of light scattered by water fogs and ice aerosols.
Stanford, Calif., 1955. 45p. illus. diagrs. graphs, bibliog.
(Stanford Research Institute, Report no. 18. Scientific Report
no. 5. Mar. 1955) [at Eielson AFB near Fairbanks]   4531

Thuman, William C., co-auth. SEE ALSO no. 3847,
     Robinson, E. Field observ. ... ice fog ... 1954.

Ticasuk. SEE nos. 4534-5, Tickasook.

TICHY, HERBERT. Alaska; ein Paradies des Nordens. [TITLE TR.
Alaska; a paradise of the North] München, Wilhelm Goldmann Ver-
lag, 1951. 3rd ed. 277p. pls. endmaps. ANR. 1939. 1st ed.
[SEE ALSO no. 4533]   4532

TICHY, HERBERT. Alaszka. Észak paradicsoma. Tizenhat táblával.
Ford. Konroly Kálmán. Singer és Wolfner, 1941. 240p. [tr. of
no. 4532]   4533

[TICKASOOK] Eskimo legend of Kotzebue. [Fairbanks ?], [c1959]
(14)p. cover illus. by Isaac Eben, interior sketches by Cora W.
Hadley, wrps. [author is Emily Ivanoff Brown]   4534

TICKASOOK. Inipiut homes. Foreword by Ivan Skarland. Sketches
by Alfred Milligrock. Unalakleet, Tickasook, 1956. 14p. [author
is Emily Ivanoff Brown]   4535

TIKHMENEV, PETR ALEKSANDROVICH. Istoricheskoe obozrienīe obra-
zovaniīa Rossiīsko-Amerikanskoī Kompanii i dīeistviīa eīe do
nastoīashchago vremeni; chast' 1 i 2. [TITLE TR. Historical
survey of the establishment of the Russian-American Company and
of its activities to the present time; parts 1 and 2] Sanktpeterburg, Tipografiīa Edmunda Veīmara, 1861 and 1863. 2 vols.
386p.+66p. 11p.,388p.,79p.+292p. illus. ports. tables, maps
(fold.), bibliog. index. [pt. 2 contains appends. SEE no.
4537 for tr.]   4536

TIKHMENEV, PETR ALEKSANDROVICH. The historical review of formation of the Russian-American Company. St. Petersburg, 1861, pt.1. 1863, pt. 2. Translated by Dimitri Krenov. Seattle, U. S. Works Pregress Administration, 1939-40. [tr. of no. 4536]   4537

Tikhmenev, Petr Aleksandrovich. SEE ALSO no. 4693,
    Veselev, F. F. Razbor vtoroi chasti ... 1864.

TIKHON, *Bishop*. Sviatoe evangelie ot Ioanna, na Aleutsko-lisjevskom nariechiĭ. [TITLE TR. Holy Gospel from John in the Aleutian-Fox dialect] N. Y., Amerikanskiĭ Pravoslavnyi Viestnik, 1902. 95p. [Vasili Ivanovich Belyavin, later to become *Patriarch of Moscow*]   4538

TIKHON, *Bishop*. Sviatoe evangelie ot Luki,na Aleutsko-lisjevskom nariechiĭ. [TITLE TR. Holy Gospel from Luke, in the Aleutian-Fox dialect] N. Y., Amerikanskiĭ Pravoslavnyi Viestnik,1903. 124p. [Vasili Ivanovich Belyavin, later to become *Patriarch of Moscow*]   4539

Tilgenkamp, E., co-auth. SEE no. 3634, Pollog, C. H.

TILLEY, H. A. Japan, the Amoor, the Pacific; with notices of other places comprised in a voyage of circumnavigation in the Imperial corvette *Rynda* in 1858-1860. London, 1861.   4540

TILTON, GEORGE FRED. "Cap'n George Fred himself." Garden City, N. Y., 1929. 295p. illus. map. [autobiog. - whaling in Alaskan Arctic waters]   4541

Time-Life Books. SEE no. 4204, Smith, Richard Austin, edit.

Tin in U. S. ... Alaska. 1904. SEE no. 418, Bartels Tin
    Mining Co.

Tinneh Indian catechism ... 1897. SEE no. 2260, Indian Boys'
    Press.

Tishnoff, Elias. SEE nos. 4600-03, Tyzhnov, Il'ia.

Tł'eaka Hok'anaga' dictionary ... n. d. SEE no. 2068,
    [Henry, David]

Tlingit reading book. 1962 and n. d. SEE nos. 4386-7,
    Summer Institute of Linguistics.

To the Klondike and Alaska ... [1897] SEE no. 54,
    Alaska Commercial Co.

To the Klondike gold fields ... [1898] SEE no. 54,
    Alaska Commercial Co.

To the Yukon ... 1897. SEE no. 2153, Holland, Edw.

Today's facts about Anchorage ... 1944. SEE no. 233,
    Anchorage Chamber of Commerce.

TOKAREV, SERGEĬ ALEKSANDROVICH and I. A. ZOLOTOREVSKAIĬA, edits.
Indeitsy Ameriki; étnograficheskiĭ sbornik. [TITLE TR. The
Indians of America; an ethnographic collection] Moskva, Akademiĭa nauk SSSR, 1955. 264p. illus. table, maps. (Institut étnografiĭ. Trudy, nov. seriĭa, t.25) [incl. those of Russian colonies in America, others]   4542

Tokarev, Sergeĭ Aleksandrovich, co-edit. SEE ALSO no. 1419,
    Efimov, A. V. Narody Ameriki. 1959.

TOKYO AGRICULTURE TECHNICAL RESEARCH SOCIETY.   Information on
oceanographic conditions in northern waters, 1887-1953. Tokyo,
1954. 13p.+556p. maps, tables. (Weather Damage Series: Thun-
derstorms, Hail, Cold, no. 1. Mar. 1954) [title of tables in
both Japanese and/or English - incls. Bering Sea and Aleutian
waters]   4543

TOLAND, J. Ships in the sky; the story of the great dirigibles.
N. Y., Holt, 1957. 352p. illus. [incls. Amundsen-Nobile polar
flight of the *Norge* in 1926]   4544

TOLLEMACHE, STRATFORD H. R. L. Reminiscences of the Yukon. London, Longmans, 1911. 316p. front. pls. ANR. London, E. Arnold,
1912. 216p. ANR. Toronto, Wm. W. Briggs, 1912.   4545

TOLMACHEV, ALEKSANDR INNOKENT'EVICH. O kolichestvennoĭ kharak-
teristike flor i floristicheskikh oblastei. [TITLE TR. On quan-
titative characteristics of floras and floristic regions] Moskva-
Leningrad, 1941. 36p. bibliog. (Akademiĭa nauk SSSR. Sever-
naĭa baza. Trudy, vyp. 8) [incl. those of Alaska]   4546

TOLMIE, W. FRASER and GEORGE M. DAWSON. Comparative vocabularies
of the Indian tribes of British Columbia, with a map illustrating
distribution. Montreal, Dawson Bros., 1884. 131p. table(fold.),
map(col. fold.), wrps. (Canada. Geological and Natural History
Survey)   4547

Tolstoy, Paul, tr. SEE no. 3911, Rudenko, S. I.

TOMASEVIC, JOZO. International agreements on conservation of
marine resources, with special reference to the North Pacific.
Stanford, Calif., 1943. 297p. illus. tables, diagrs. maps.
(Stanford University Food Research Institute. Commodity Policy
Studies no. 1)   4548

TOMASHEVSKIĬ, VSEVOLOD VSEVOLODOVICH. Materialy k bibligrafiĭ Sibiri i Dal'nego Vostoka; xv-pervaĭa polovina xix veka. [TITLE TR.
Contributions to the bibliography of Siberia and the Far East;
15th to the first half of the 19th century] Vladivostok, 1957.
213p. (Akad. nauk SSSR. Dal'nevostochnyĭ filial im V. L.Komarova)
                                                               4549

Tombstone Nugget Pub. Co. SEE no. 913, Chicago Record.

TOMIN, MIKHAIL PETROVICH. Opredelitel' kustistykh i listovatykh lishaĭnikov SSSR. [TITLE TR. A manual for identification of bushy and leafy lichens of the USSR] Moskva, 1937. 311p. bibliog. index. [incl. those of Arctic North America]   4550

TOMLINSON, EVERETT T. Three boys in Alaska. N. Y. and London, D. Appleton & Co., 1928. 224p.   4551

Tomlinson, Robert, co-auth. SEE no. 1383, Duncan, Wm.

TOMPKINS, STUART RAMSAY. Alaska, Promyshlennik and sourdough. By Stuart Ramsay Tompkins. Norman, University of Oklahoma Press, 1945. [c1945] 1st ed. 350p. illus. photos, maps, bibliog. index.   4552

TOMPKINS, STUART RAMSAY. Let's read about Alaska. Illustrated by Richard Gringhuis. Grand Rapids, Fideler Co., 1949. 112p. illus. photos. (Life in Other Lands Library)   4553

TOMPKINS, STUART RAMSAY. Life in America; Alaska. Grand Rapids, Fideler Co., 1958. 128p. illus. maps, glossary, index. OTHERS 1960, 1961 and 1963. [geography textbook]   4554

TONGASS PUBLISHING CO. Pilot; guide to scenic southeast Alaska and Northern British Columbia. [Juneau ?], Tongass Pub. Co., 1966.   4555

Tonk, Ernest, illus. SEE no. 2847, McCracken, H.

Tooke, Wm., tr. SEE no. 4656, Varieties of literature... 1795.

Tooley, R. V., co-auth. SEE no. 4172, Skelton, R. A.

Torlesse, J. Y. G. SEE no. 1802, Great Britain. Admiralty.

TORONTO PUBLIC LIBRARY. The Canadian catalogue of books published in Canada, about Canada, as well as those written by Canadians, with imprint 1921-1949. Toronto, 1959. 2 vols. [originally published in series of 28 annual lists]   4556

TORONTO PUBLIC LIBRARY. The Canadian North West; a bibliography of the sources of information in the Public Reference Library of the City of Toronto, Canada in regard to the Hudson's Bay Company, the fur trade and the early history of the Canadian North West. Toronto, 1931. 52p.   4557

Toronto Public Library. SEE ALSO no. 4289,
     Staton, F. M. Bibliog. Canadiana ... 1934.

TORRUBIA, JOSE GIUSEPPE.   I Moscoviti nella California ossia
Dimostrazione della Verita del Passo all' America Settentrionale
nuovamente scoperto dai Russi, e di quelle anticament praticato
dalli Popolatori, che vi transmigrarono dall'Asia ... By Giuseppe
Torrubia. Rome, 1759. ANR. Venice, 1760. [incls. northwest
coast and Russian voyages prior to Vitus Bering]   4558

TOSI, PASQUALE. La Missione dell' Alaska. Memoria de R. P.
Pasquale Tosi, D.C.D.G. Superione della Missione Roma. [pl.?],
1893. 72p.   4559

THE TOTEM POLE; legends and traditions of Alaska Indians. no
pl., n. d. (4)p.   4560

Totem poles of Alaska ... 1905. SEE no. 126, Alaska Steamship
    Co.

The totems of Alaska. [c1905]   SEE no. 4927, Winter and Pond Co.

Tour through land nightless days ... [190_ ?] SEE no. 4829,
    White Pass and Yukon Railway.

TOWNLEY, SIDNEY DEAN and M. W. ALLEN. Descriptive catalogue of
earthquakes of the Pacific Coast of the United States, 1769 to
1928. Berkeley, University of California Press, 1939. 297p.
(Seismological Society of America Bull., no. 1, vol. 29. Jan.
1939)   4561

TOWNSEND, CHARLES HASKIN. The Crested Auklet. N. Y., National
Association of Audubon Societies, 1913. (Education Leaflet no.65.
Also in Bird-Lore, Mar.-Apr. 1913. vol. 15, pp.133-6. pl.)
[Bering Strait, Aleutian Islands]   4562

TOWNSEND, EARL C., jr. Birdstones of the North American Indian.
Indianapolis, 1959. 719p. pls.(incl. some col.)   4563

TOWNSEND, LAWRENCE D. Variations in the meristic characters of
flounders from the Northeastern Pacific. Seattle, 1936. 24p.
tables. (International Fisheries Commission Report no. 11)
[from Puget Sound to Bering Sea]   4564

TOWNSEND, MILLICENT D. Alaska calling. Juneau, Empire Printing
Co., [c1938] 17ℓ illus. [poetry]   4565

TOZIER, D. F. Arts and crafts of the Totem Indians, collected by
Captain D. F. Tozier, classified and photographed by W. H. Gil-
strap. Tacoma, Washington, Central News, n. d. 32p. illus.
OTHERS (39)p. and (41)p.   4566

TRAGER, GEORGE LEONARD and F. E. HARBEN. North American Indian
languages; classification and maps. Buffalo, N. Y., 1958. 35p.
tables, maps, bibliog. (University of Buffalo, Dept. Anthropology and Linguistics. Studies in Linguistics Occasional Papers no.

5)   [sectional maps incl. Alaska-Western Canada, language areas
incl. Eskimo]   4567

Trail blazers of bygone days. 1951. SEE no. 899,
     Chase, Wm. H.

TRANSCONTINENTAL RESEARCH BUREAU. Jobs in Alaska. Hollywood,
Calif., 1946.   4568

TRANTER, GLADDIS JOY. Plowing the Arctic. London, Hodder and
Stoughton, 1944. 256p. front. pls. ports. ANR. Toronto, Longmans, 1945. 311p. ANR. N. Y., 1945. 311p. [R.C.M.P. *St. Roch*
and northwest passage, west to east]   4569

Trask, Willard R., tr. SEE no. 1433, Eliade, Mircea.

Travels ... John Ledyard ... 1834. SEE no. 4253, [Sparks, Jared]

[TRAVERS, de VAL ?] Summary observations and facts collected
from late and authentic accounts of Russian and other navigators,
to show the practicability and good prospect of success in enterprises to discover a northern passage for vessels by sea, between
the Atlantic and Pacific Oceans, or nearly to approach the North
Pole; for which the offers of reward are renewed by a late Act
of Parliament. London, Sold by John Nourse, 1776. 29p. [pos-
sibly by Daines Barrington ?]   4570

TREADGOLD, ARTHUR NEWTON CHRISTIAN. Report on the gold fields of
the Klondike. Toronto, George V. Morang & Co., 1899. vii,94p.
front. illus. maps(dble.)   4571

TREADWELL, AARON LOUIS. *Neosabellides alaskensis*, a new species
of polychaetous annelid from Alaska. N. Y., 1943. 2p. illus.
(American Museum of Natural History Novitates, no. 1235)   4572

TREADWELL, AARON LOUIS. Polychaetous annelids collected by Captain R. A. Bartlett in Alaska, in 1924, with descriptions of new
species. N. Y., 1926. 8p. illus. (American Museum of Natural
History Novitates, no. 223)   4573

TREFETHEN, JAMES B. Crusade for wildlife. Harrisburg, Penna.,
Stackpole Co., 1961.   4574

TREFZGER, HARDY. My fifty years of hunting, fishing, prospecting,
guiding, trading and trapping in Alaska. N. Y., Exposition Press,
[c1963] 118p. illus. maps. [southeast Alaska]   4575

TRELAWNY-ANSELL, EDWARD CLARENCE. I followed gold. London,
Peter Davies, 1938. ANR. N. Y., Lee Furman, 1939. 321p.   4576

Tremaine, M., co-edit. SEE no. 4289, Staton, F. M.

Trevenen, Jas. SEE no. 3533, [Penrose, C. V.]

TREZONA, C. E.   Cape Nome and the northern placer mines;   written from personal observations.   Seattle, Denny-Coryell, 1900.   45p. pls.   4577

Triggs, O. L., edit.   SEE no. 1220, Deans, Jas.

Trip to wonderful Alaska.   1905.   SEE no. 127, Alaska Steamship Co.

Troisieme voyage de Cook; ou, Journal ... 1782.   SEE no. 1016, [Cook, Jas.]

Troisieme voyage de Cook; ou, voyage ... 1785.   SEE no. 1025, [Cook, Jas.]

Troisieme voyage de Jas. Cook ... 1804.   SEE no. 1037, [Cook, Jas.]

Trolloppe, H.   SEE nos. 1828, 1830-32, Great Britain. Parl. (Franklin search)

Trotter, C. L., co-auth.   SEE no. 1395, Dutcher, R. R.

TROUT, PETER L.   My experiences at Cape Nome, Alaska.   Seattle, Lowman and Hanford, 1899.   42p.   4578

TROUT, PETER L.   New theory concerning the origin and deposition of placer gold.   Seattle, Pigott, 1901.   82p.   4579

TROUTMAN, ARTHUR, edit.   The Alaska oil and gas handbook.   Austin, Texas, Oil Frontiers Pub. Co., 1958.   vi,76p.   illus.   4580

TRUE, BARBARA and MARGUERITE HENRY.   Their first igloo.   Illustrated by Gladys Blackwood.   Chicago, Albert Whitman & Co., 1943. illus.(col.)   4581

TRUMAN, BENJAMIN C.   Occidental sketches.   S. F., San Francisco News Co., 1881.   212p.   [by Special Agent of U. S. Post Office in Aleutian Islands]   4582

TRUSLER, JOHN.   A descriptive account of the islands lately discovered in the South Seas, with some account of the country of Camchatka.   London, 1778.   4583

TUCCI, JOANNA LUCY.   Stone-age people and American Indians.   Juvenile sketches of life and customs of ancient man.   By J. L. Tucci.   Illustrated by Stina Nagel.   N. Y., Exposition Press, [c1959]   1st ed.   23p.   illus.   4584

TUCKER, EPHRAIM W. History of Oregon, containing a condensed account of the most important voyages and discoveries of the Spanish, American and English navigators on the Northwest coast of America, and of the different treaties relative to the same; the claim of the United States to that territory. Buffalo, N.Y., A. W. Wilgus, 1844. 84p.   4585

TUCKER, MINNIE, tr. Jesus will give you rest. Fairbanks, printed for Gold Pan Trading Post, [ca 1967] 1p.(fold.) port. biog. sketch, in envelope. [words of hymn in English, translated into Eskimo picture writing by Minnie (Na-tor-uck) Tucker of Rock Point, Yukon-Kuskokwim Delta]   4586

Tuden, Arthur, co-edit. SEE no. 4426, Swartz, M. J.

Tukudh four gospels ... [cover title] SEE no. 2882,
    [McDonald, Robert, tr. ?] Nuwheh Kukwadhud Jesus Christ.1874.

Tukudh primer ... Tinne Indians. n.d. SEE no. 1482,
    [Episcopal Church]

TULLY, JOHN PATRICK. Assessment of temperature structure in the eastern subArctic Pacific Ocean. Nanaimo, British Columbia, 1961. 22p. illus. graphs, maps, bibliog. (Canada. Fisheries Research Board, Ms. Report Series, Oceanographic and Limnological, no. 103)   4587

TUPPER, CHARLES. Political reminiscences. By Sir Charles Tupper. Edited by W. A. Harkin. London, 1914. [Canadian statesman; Bering Sea fur seal controversy]   4588

TUPPER, CHARLES. Recollections of sixty years. By Sir Charles Tupper. N. Y., Cassell & Co., 1914. ANR. London. 1914. [Canadian statesman; Bering Sea fur seal controversy]   4589

Turner, George. SEE no. 4910, Wilson, George.

TURNER, MICHAEL. The king bear. Racine, Wisc., Golden Press, 1968.   4590

TURNER-TURNER, J. Three years' hunting and trapping in America and the great North-West. London, Maclure & Co., 1888. 182p. front.(port.), illus. by Constance Hoare, maps. ANR. N. Y., Arno Press, 1967. facsim. ed. (Abercrombie and Fitch Library)   4591

Turner, Victor W., co-edit. SEE no. 4426, Swartz, M. J.

TUTEIN, PETER. The sealers. Translated from Danish by Eugene Gay-Tifft. N. Y., Putnam, 1938. 247p. [an earlier Danish edition entitled "Faengstmaend."]   4592

Tuthill, L. D., edit. SEE no. 3462, Pacific Science Congress, 10th. Proceedings. 1963.

TUTTLE, CHARLES RICHARD. Alaska; its meaning to the world, its resources, its opportunities. By Charles R. Tuttle. Illustrated. Seattle, Franklin Shuey & Co., 1914. [c1914] 318p. front.(map), pls. ports. map, directory of Territorial officials.   4593

TUTTLE, CHARLES RICHARD. The golden north; a vast country of inexhaustible gold fields and a land of illimitable cereal and stock raising capabilities. Illustrated with maps and engravings. Chicago, Rand McNally, 1897. 307p. front.(fold. map), maps, appends.   4594

Tvoreniĩa Innokentiĩa, metropolita moskovskago. 1887. SEE no. 417, [Barsukov, I. P.]

Tweney, Geo. H., co-edit. SEE no. 4955, Woodbridge, H. C.

Twenty-three opinions on Alaska tin ... 1908. SEE no. 749, Burton, John E.

Twice through Northwest Passage. 1945. SEE no. 4611, Union Diesel Engine Co.

Two hundred questions ... 1914. SEE no. 105, Alaska Publicity & Trade Agency.

TYLER, ALICE (FELT). The foreign policy of James G. Blaine. Minneapolis, University of Minnesota Press, 1927. ANR. Hamden, Conn., Shoestring Press, 1965. (Archon Books) [Bering Sea fur seal controversy]   4595

TYLER, CHARLES MARION. The island world of the Pacific Ocean. S. F., 1887. 387p. [has section on Alaska and Aleutian Islands]   4596

Types of Alaska natives. [c1905] SEE no. 4928, Winter & Pond Co.

Tyrrell, Edith. SEE no. 4598, Tyrrell, Mary Edith (Carey).

TYRRELL, JOSEPH BURR, edit. Documents relating to the early history of Hudson Bay. Edited with introduction and notes by J. B. Tyrrell. Toronto, 1931. ltd. ed. of 550 copies. 419p. front. pls. facsims. maps(incl. 2 fold.), index. (Champlain Society Pub. no. 18)   4597

TYRRELL, MARY EDITH (CAREY). I was there; a book of reminiscences. By Edith Tyrrell. Toronto, Ryerson Press, [c1938] ix,131p. front.(port.), pls. ports. ANR. Toronto, Ryerson, 1939. with introduction by J. E. Middleton. [autobiog. by wife of Canadian geologist in Klondike]   4598

TYTLER, PATRICK FRASER. Historical view of the progress of discovery on the more northern coasts of America; from the earliest period to the present time. By Patrick Fraser Tytler. With descriptive sketches of the natural history of the North American regions. By James Wilson...to which is added an appendix containing remarks on a late memoir of Sebastian Cabot with a vindication of Richard Hakluyt. Illustrated by a map, and nine engravings by Jackson. Edinburgh, Oliver and Boyd, 1832. 2(7)-444p. front.(fold. map), pls. port. (Edinburgh Cabinet Library, vol.9) ANR. Edinburgh and London, 1833. 2(7)-444p. front.(fold. map), pls. port. ANR. N. Y., Harper, 1833. 360p. front.(fold. map) pls. append. OTHERS N. Y., Harper, 1839, 1844, 1846, and 1886.
4599

[TYZHNOV, IL'IA ?] Aleutskiĭ bukvar'. [TITLE TR. Aleutian primer (or, Aleutian abecedarium)] [St. Petersburg, ca 1839 or 1840] ANR. Moscow, Synod Press, 1846. 30p. ANR. St. Petersburg, 1893. 32p. [sometimes bound with nos. 4671 and 4673] 4600

TYZHNOV, IL'IA, comp. ... Aleutsko-Kad'iakskiĭ bukvar' ...[TITLE TR. Aleutian-Kodiak primer compiled by Il'ia Tyzhnov] St. Petersburg, at the Synod Press, 1848. (34)p. ANR. St. Petersburg, Synod Press, 1848. (52)p. errata. [by *Father* Tyzhnov. Printing of (52)p. has some textual differences from that of (34)p.] 4601

TYZHNOV, IL'IA, comp. and tr. Khrishtianat ... Illiam Tyzhnavym pil'ia. [TITLE TR. Christian guide book together with the history of St. Michael and the Michael Catechism. Compiled by Il'ia Tzyhnov] St. Petersburg, at the Synod Press, 1847. 96p. [based on a section (*Short sacred history*) of no. 4673, Nachatki khristrianskago ... 1840, by I. E. P. Veniaminov and Ĭa. Netsvĭetov] 4602

TYZHNOV, IL'IA, comp. ... Ot Matfeĭa ... [TITLE TR. The Gospel according to Saint Matthew. Translated by I. Tyzhnov into the Aleutian-Kodiak language] St. Petersburg, at the Synod Press, 1848. ii,(272)p. [in double columns] 4603

U

UDALL, STEWART L. The quiet crisis. N. Y., Holt, Rinehart & Winston, 1963. 209p. illus.(some col.), ports.(some col.) [incls. Mt. McKinley National Park as well as other Alaskan areas] 4604

UHLENBECK, CHRISTIANUS CORNELIUS. Ontwerp van eene vergelijkende vormleer der eskimo-talen. [TITLE TR. Project of a comparative etymology of Eskimo languages] Amsterdam, Johannes Müller, 1907. 76p. tables. (Akademie van Wetenschappen. Afdeeling letterkunde. Verhandlingen, 1908. n. reeks, deel 8, no. 3) 4605

UHLENBECK, CHRISTIANUS CORNELIUS. Oude aziatische contacten van het eskimo. [TITLE TR. Old Asiatic contacts of the Eskimos] Amsterdam, N. V. Noord-hollandsche uitgevers maatschappij, 1941. 27p. bibliog. (Akademie van Wetenschappen. Afdeeling letter-kunde. Mededeelingen, n. reeks, deel 4, no. 7)   4606

Ukpiktuat Nigiugikkaṇat. n. d. SEE no. 4388,
     [Summer Institute of Linguistics]

ULRICH, E. O. and G. A. COOPER. Ozarkian and Canadian brachio-poda. N. Y., 1938. 323p. pls. figs. (Geological Society of America, Spec. Paper no. 13) (Yukon-Alaskan boundary area]   4607

Under Cook's flag ... [19_ ?]   SEE no. 4814, Whitcombe & Tombs.

Underwood, Clarence F., illus. SEE no. 447, Beach, Rex.

UNDERWOOD, JOHN JASPER. Alaska; an empire in the making. By John J. Underwood. N. Y., Dodd Mead, 1913. [c1913] 440p. front. pls. ports. map(fold.) OTHERS 1915, 1918, 1920. ANR. N. Y., Dodd Mead, 1925. rev. ed. ANR. London, John Lane, 1925. ANR. N. Y., Dodd Mead, 1928. [c1925]   4608

Unfinished business of Presbyterian Church ... 1921. SEE
     no. 1403, Eastman, Fred.

UNGERMANN, KENNETH A. The race to Nome. N. Y., Harper, 1963. illus. [juv. fict.]   4609

UNION BOOK AND PUBLISHING CO., Chicago. Alaska and the Yukon Territory. [Chicago, 19__] (16)p. illus. (America, Her Gran-deur and Her Beauty Series, part 13)   4610

UNION DIESEL ENGINE CO. Twice through the Northwest Passage. Oakland, Calif., privately printed by the Company, 1945. (21)p. illus. sketch maps. (Bulletin no. 75) [R.C.M.P. *St. Roch*, 1940-42 and 1944]   4611

UNION PACIFIC RAILROAD CO. Sights and scenes in Oregon, Washing-ton and Alaska for tourists. Chicago, Rand McNally, 1890. 2d ed. 58p. ANR. Chicago, Knight, Leonard & Co., 1891. 3rd ed. 66p. ANR. [Chicago ?], Knight, Leonard & Co., 1892. 4th ed. 80p.   4612

UNION PACIFIC RAILROAD CO. The great Pacific Northwest and Alas-ka; a panorama of grandeur, a revelation of accomplishment, a vision of opportunity. [Chicago, Newman, 19__ ?] 47p. illus. map.   4613

UNION PACIFIC RAILROAD CO. The Pacific Northwest and Alaska. Issued by the Union Pacific System. Omaha, Neb., printed by the Acorn Press, 1927. [c1927] 48p. illus. maps, wrps. ANR. [with slight changes] Chicago, Poole Bros., [1935 ?] 48p. illus. maps, wrps. OTHERS var. dates. [cf no. 3455]   4614

U. S. S. R. AKADEMIĪA NAUK. Institut étnografiĭ. Atlas geograficheskikh otkrytiĭ v Sibiri i v Severo-Zapadnoi Amerike. [TITLE TR. Atlas of geographical discoveries in Siberia and Northwestern America] Moskva, Hayka, 1964. 134p. maps(incl. some fold.) [17th and 18th centuries]   4615

U. S. S. R. AKADEMIĪA NAUK. Institut étnografiĭ. Kul'tura indeĭtsev; voklad korennogo naseleniĭa Ameriki v mirovuĭu kul'tura. [TITLE TR. Culture of the Indians; contributions of the aboriginal American population to world culturá] Moskva, Izd-vo Akademii nauk SSSR, 1963. 328p. illus. bibliog. [incls. Alaskan place names]   4616

U. S. S. R. AKADEMIĪA NAUK. Institut étnografiĭ. Ocherki obshcheĭ etnografiĭ; vyp. 1, obshchie svedeniĭa, Avstraliĭa i Oceaniĭa, Amerika, Afrika. [TITLE TR. Sketches on general ethnography; no. 1, general information, Australia and Oceania, America, Africa] Moskva, Izd-vo Akademii nauk SSSR, 1957. 342p. illus. maps(fold.), bibliog. [chapt. on America has references to Eskimos, Aleuts and Indians of Alaska and Canada, pp.134-53 and pp.163-4]   4617

U. S. S. R. Akademiĭa nauk. Institut étnografiĭ. SEE ALSO
    no. 1419, Efimov, A. V. Narody Ameriki. 1959.

U. S. S. R. GIDROGRAFICHESKOE UPRAVLENIE. Lotsiĭa Chukotskogo morĭa. [TITLE TR. Chukchi sea pilot] Leningrad, 1938. 159p. tables, sketch charts, charts(fold.) [incls. American coast, Cape York to Pt. Barrow]   4618

U. S. S. R. KOMITET OB USTROĬSTVIĒ RUSSKIKH AMERIKANSKIKH KOLONIĬ Doklad komiteta ob ustroĭstvīē russkikh amerikanskikh koloniĭ. [TITLE TR. Report of the committee for settlement of the RussianAmerican colonies] St. Petersburg, v Tip. Departamenta vnieshnĭaĭa torgovlĭa, 1863-64. 2 vols. 403(2)p. and 613(110)p. tables(incl. some fold.), append. [incls. reports of S. Kostlivtsov and V. M. Golovnin. cf no. 3888]   4619

U. S. S. R. Morskoi Sbornik. SEE no. 1763, [Golovnin, V. M.]

UNION STEAMSHIP COMPANY of British Columbia. Our coastal trips. [Vancouver,B. C., Sun Publishing Co., n. d.] 32p. illus.   4620

United Geophysical Co. SEE no. 3551, Peterson, Raymond A.

UNITED STATES ALASKA TIN MINING CO., Milwaukee. Annual statement 1905. Milwaukee, 1905. OTHERS yearly for 1906 through 1911. [at Tin City, near Cape Prince of Wales]   4621

UNITED STATES ALASKA TIN MINING CO., Milwaukee. Facts and history of the tin discoveries in Alaska. Milwaukee, 1904. 23p.
                                                            4622

United States Alaska Tin Mining Co., Milwaukee. SEE ALSO
    no. 749, Burton, John E. Twenty-three opinions ... 1908.

U. S. Alaskan Air Command. SEE nos.
    3438, Oswalt, W. H. Napaskiak ... 1961;
    4653, VanStone, Jas. W. Point Hope ... 1961.

U. S. Army Air Force. SEE no. 1848,
    Greenaway, K. R.

U. S. Army Corps of Engineers. SEE no. 1562, Finnie, R.

UNITED STATES-BRITISH COLUMBIA CORPORATION. Alaska; its resources. A timely brochure. Seattle, n. d. 12p.   4623

U. S. Coast and Geodetic Survey. SEE no. 4765, Weber, G. A.

U. S. International Boundary Commission. SEE no. 2274,
    International Boundary Commission.

U. S. Joint Economic Committee of Canada and United States. SEE
    no. 800, Camsell, Charles.

United States mail route, freight ... 1907. SEE no. 1097,
    Council City & Solomon River Railroad.

United States mining laws ... 1906. SEE no. 897, Charles, S. D.

U. S. Revenue Cutter Service. SEE no. 3382, Officers of
    U. S. Revenue Cutter Service. Below zero ... 1903.

University of California, Agric. Hist. Center, Davis. SEE
    no. 3404, Olsen, Michael L.

UYEDA, CLIFFORD. The Deer Mountain; the adventures of a New
England youth during a violent summer in Alaska. N. Y., Exposition Press, 1959.   4624

                                V

VACHON, ANDREW WILLIAM. Fish without chips. By Andrew William
Vachon, S. J. Juneau, Men of the Cathedral, 1960. unp.
sketches by author, wrps.   4625

VACHON, ANDREW WILLIAM. Ketchikan sketchings. By Andrew William
Vachon, S. J. Seattle, R. D. Seal, 1959. unp. sketches by
author, portfolio.   ,   4626

VAETH, J. GORDON. To the ends of the earth; the explorations of
Roald Amundsen. By J. Gordon Vaeth. Illustrated with photographs
and maps. N. Y., Harper & Row, [c1962] 219p. front. pls. maps,
bibliog. index.   4627

                               558

Vagrant verse ... 1962. SEE no. 2377, [Jones, Chas. D.]

VAHL, JENS. Alaska; folket og missionen. [TITLE TR. Alaska; the
people and the missions] København, G. E. C. Gad Boghandel, 1872.
108p.   4628

VAIL, ISAAC NEWTON. Alaska, land of the nugget. Why ? A critical examination of geological and other testimony, showing how and
why gold was deposited in polar lands. Pasadena, Calif., Press
of G. A. Swerdfiger, 1897. 68p.   4629

VAKHTIN, V. Russkie truzheniki morïa. Pervaïa morskaïa ekspe-
ditsiïa Beringa. [TITLE TR. Russian toilers of the deep.
Bering's first expedition] St. Petersburg, 1890.   4630

VALAAM MONASTERY. K stolietnemu jubileïu pravoslaviïa v Amerikie
(1794-1894). Ocherki iz istorii Amerikanskoï pravoslavnoï duk-
hovnoï missii (Kad'ïakskoi missii 1794-1847 gg.). [TITLE TR.
Centenary of the Russian Church in America, 1794-1894. Sketch of
the history of the American Russian Orthodox religious mission
(Kodiak mission 1794-1837)] St. Petersburg, M. Merkushev, 1894.
292p. pls. port.   4631

[VALAAM MONASTERY] Zhiznj Valaamskago monakha Germana, Amerikan-
skago missionera. [TITLE TR. Life of the monk Herman of Valaam,
American missionary] St. Petersburg, Synod Press, 1894. 24p.
                                                                4632

[Valdes, Cayetano] SEE no. 1676, [Galiano, D. A.]

VALDEZ, CITIZENS OF. Memorial to the Secretary of the Interior.
Valdez, 1912. 3p.   4633

VALDEZ MINER. Alaska, the Richardson Road, Valdez to Fairbanks,
an illustrated booklet descriptive of the road, the towns at
either end and the surrounding country with beauties and possibilities of Alaska. Valdez, Valdex Miner, 1922. 40p. illus.
map(fold.)   4634

Valenta, Edw., tr. SEE no. 4791, Welzl, J.

VALENTIN, FRANÇOIS. Voyages and adventures of La Pérouse. From
the fourteenth edition of the F. Valentin abridgment, Tours,
1875. Translated from the French. Honolulu, University of Hawaii
Press, 1969. 161p. illus. map (Published for Friends of the
Library of Hawaii) [an earlier French edition, no. 4636]   4635

VALENTIN, FRANÇOIS. Voyages et adventures de Lapérouse par F.
Valentin. Tours, A. Mame et cie, 1841. 2d ed. 288p. pls. [SEE
no. 4635 for tr.]   4636

Van Cleve, H., co-auth. SEE no. 2858, McCracken, H.

Van Cleve, Richard, co-auth. SEE nos.
    2889, McEwen, G. F. Hydrog. sect. ... Gulf of Alaska. 1930;
    4511, Thompson, Thos. G. Hydrog. sects. ... 1936;
    4517, Thompson, Wm. F. Life hist. Pac. halibut ... 1936.

Vancouver, George. [Alphabetical title guide to chronological
    entries]

        A voyage of discovery ... 1748. 4637.
        Entdeckungsreise ... 1799. 4638.
        Narrative or journal ... 1802. 4643.
        Puteshestvie ... 1827-1838. 4642.
        Reisen nach ... 1799-1800. 4639.
        En upptacksta-resa ... 1800. 4641.
        Voyage de decouvertes ... 1800. 4640.

VANCOUVER, GEORGE. A voyage of discovery to the North Pacific
Ocean, and round the world; in which the coast of Northwest
America has been carefully examined and accurately surveyed. Undertaken by His Majesty's command, principally with a view to
ascertain the existence of any navigable communication between
the North Pacific and North Atlantic Oceans; and performed in
the years 1790, 1791, 1792, 1793, 1794, and 1795, in the *Discovery*
Sloop of War, and Armed Tender *Chatham*, under the command of Captain George Vancouver. In three volumes. London, printed for
G. G. & J. Robinson, and J. Edwards, 1798. atlas(folio) and 3
vols. paged as follows: vol. 1, xxix,432p.   vol. 2, 504p. and
vol. 3, 505(3)p. pls. maps. ANR. London, J. Stockdale, 1801.
6 vols. paged as follows: vol. 1, 410p. vol. 2, 418p. vol. 3,
435p. vol. 4, 419p. vol. 5, 454p. and vol. 6, 412(2)p. pls.
(fold.), maps(fold.) ANR. Amsterdam, N. Israel and N. Y., Da
Capo Press, 1968. facsim. of London 1798 edition. 3 vols. and
atlas. (Bibliotheca Australiana, nos. 30-33)   4637

TRANSLATIONS - A voyage of discovery ... 1798, CHRONOLOGICALLY.

Entdeckungsreise in den nordlichen Gewassern der Sudsee und
    langst den westlichen Kusten von Amerika, von 1790 bis 1795;
    aus dem Englischen von M. C. Sprengel. Halle, Rengerschen
    Buchhandlung, 1799. 308p.   4638

Reisen nach dem nordlichen theile der Sudsee wahrend der jahre
    1790 bis 1795, aus dem englischen ubersicht und mit anmer-
    kungen begleitet von Joh. Friedr. Wilh. Herbst. Berlin,
    1799-1800. 2 vols. pls.   4639

Voyage de découvertes a l'ocean Pacifique de Nord, et autour du
    monde; dans lequel la côte nord-ouest de l'Amérique a ete
    soigneusement reconnue et exactement relevée; ordonne par le
    roi d'Angleterre, principalement dans la vue de constater
    s'il existe, a travers le continent de l'Amérique, un passage
    pour les vaisseaux, de l'ocean Pacifique du Nord a l'ocean
    Atlantique septentrianal; et execute en 1790, 1, 2, 3, 4, et

1795, par le capitaine Geo. Vancouver. Tr. de langlais. J.N. Demeunier & A. Morellet. Ouvrage enrichi de figures, avec grande atlas. Paris, Impr. de la Republique, 1800. atlas (folio) and 3 vols. paged as follows: vol. 1, 491p. vol. 2, 516p. and vol. 3, 562p. ANR. Paris, De l'imprimerie de Didot Jeune, 1801-1802. 6 vols.(incl. atlas) pls. maps. ANR. Paris, Lecointe, 1883. 6 vols.   4640

En upptacksts-resa till Norra stilla hafvet och kring jordklo-tet, att pa kongl engelsk befallning och segellart sammanbang imellan Norra stilla och Norra Atlantiska hafven, forrattad ahren 1790, 1791, 1792, 1793, 1794, 1795, under commando af captiain George Vancouver; ifran engelskan i sammandrag ut-gifven af Anders Sparrman. Stockholm, A. Zetterberg, 1800. 2 vols. in 1. pls. map(fold.)   4641

Puteshestvie v sieverniîu chasti Tikhago Okeana i vokrug svie-ta, sovershennoe v 1791-5 godakh Kap. G. Vankuverom pervom s angliskago. Izdano ot Gosudarstvennogo admiralteiskago de-partamenta. St. Petersburg, V. Morskoi Tipografii, 1827-1838. 6 vols.   4642

[VANCOUVER, GEORGE] Narrative or journal of a voyage of disco-very to the North Pacific Ocean, and around the world, performed in the years 1791, 2, 3, 4, and 1795, by Captain George Vancouver and Lieutenant Broughton. London, Lee, 1802. 80p. pl. [chap-book]   4643

Vancouver, George.   SEE ALSO nos.
    242, Anderson, B. Surveyor of sea ... 1960;
    357, Baker, J. N. L. Hist. geog. discovery ... 1931;
    617, Boone, L. R. Capt. Geo. Vancouver ... 1934;
   1013, Cook, Jas. Voyage to Pacific ... 1784;
   1272, Denton, V. L. Far west coast. 1924;
   1748, Godwin, Geo. S. Vancouver, a life ... 1930;
   1893, Haig-Brown, R. Capt. of *Discovery* ... 1956;
   2152, [Holland, Chas. Wm.] 150th anniv. arrival Burrard
         Inlet. 1942;
   2200, Howay, F. Wm. Captain Geo. Vancouver. 1932;
   2614, La Perouse, J. F. G. de. Voyage ... added Vancouver...
         1798;
   2992, Marshall, Jas. S. Adventures in two hemispheres.1955;
   2994, Marshall, Jas. S. Pacific voyages. 1960;
   2995, Marshall, Jas. S. Vancouver's voyage ... 1967;
   3051, Meany, E. S. New Vancouver journal ... 1915;
   3051, Meany, E. S. Vancouver's discovery Puget Sd. 1907;
   4878, Williams, G. British search for N. W. Passage. 1962.

VANDERBOURG. La Pérouse; ou, le voyage atour du monde, tableau historique, avec un prologue en vaudeville, intitule; le Marin provençal. Paris, 1810.   4644

VANDERCOOK, JOHN WOMACK. Great sailor; a life of the discoverer Captain James Cook. N. Y., Dial Press, 1951. viii,339p. front. (port.), endmaps. 4645

VAN DER LINDEN, M. J. Reize naar de zuider zee in 1785-88 naar het fransch de M. J. van der Linden. Groningen, 1805. 3 vols. [voyage of La Perouse] 4646

Vanderlip, W. B. SEE no. 2221, Hulbert, H. B.

VAN DEUSEN, GLYNDON G. William Henry Seward. N. Y., Oxford University Press, 1967. 4647

VAN DYKE, EDWIN COOPER. The Coleoptera collected by the Katmai expeditions. Washington, D. C., National Geographic Society, 1924. 26p. (Contributed Technical Papers, Katmai Series, vol.2, no. 1) 4648

Van Dyke, T. S., co-auth. SEE no. 3879, Roosevelt, T.

VAN HISE, C. R. and L. HAVEMEYER. Conservation of our natural resources. N. Y., 1930. ANR. N. Y., Kraus, 1970. reprint. 4649

VAN LOON, DIRK. Papeek. By Dirk Van Loon. Illustrated by Louis S. Glanzman. Philadelphia, Lippincott, 1970. 93p. illus. [juv. general Arctic setting] 4650

VAN STEENSEL, M., edit. People of light and dark, edited by M. Van Steensel. Foreword by H. R. H. Prince Philip. Ottawa, Queen's Printer, 1966. xx,156p. illus. maps, bibliog. (Canada. Department of Indian Affairs and Northern Development) [series of radio broadcast essays called "The changing North," Canadian Broadcasting System. Those pertinent to Alaska: ... *and then came man*, by W. E. Taylor; ... *of whales and whalers*, by D. C. Foote; *Alaska*, by W. Irving; and *Local schools versus hostels*, by C. Hobart] 4651

VANSTONE, JAMES W. Eskimos of the Nushagak River; an ethnographic history. Seattle, University of Washington Press, 1967. 192p. maps, bibliog. 4652

VANSTONE, JAMES W. Point Hope; an Eskimo village in transition. Seattle, University of Washington Press, 1962. x,177p. illus. plans, maps, bibliog. (The American Ethnological Society) ANR. [earlier edition with title] Point Hope; an Eskimo community in Northwest Alaska. Fort Wainwright, 1961. 166p. diagr. map, bibliog. (U.S.A.F. Alaskan Air Command, Arctic Aeromedical Laboratory Technical Report no. 52-22) [Ft. Wainwright near Fairbanks] 4653

VAN VALIN, WILLIAM B. Eskimoland speaks; midnight sunlight and nocturnal noon. Caldwell, Idaho, Caxton Printers, 1941. 242p. front. pls. ports. index. ANR. London, Museum Press, 1945. 202p. pls. ports. endmaps. [western Arctic coast]   4654

Van Valkenburg, R. R. SEE no. 86, Alaska Mining & Engr. Soc.

VAN WINKLE, L. E. and WALTER GARFIELD FOX, comps. Juneau-Douglas city directory for the years 1914-15. Juneau, published by L. E. Van Winkle and Walter Garfield Fox, 1915.   4655

VARIETIES OF LITERATURE from foreign literary journals and original Mss. now first published. London, printed for J. Debrett, 1795. 2 vols. in 1. 552p. and 754p. [in 2d vol. a translation by Rev. Wm. Tooke of Shelekhov's "Reise von Ochotsk ..." SEE no. 4105]   4656

Varner, Reed W. SEE no. 433, Baxter, D. V.

VATER, JOHANN SEVERIN. Grammatiken, Lexika und Wörtersammlungen aller Sprachen der Erde von Johann Severin Vater. Zweite, völlig umgearbeitete Ausgabe von B. Jülg. Berlin, In der Nicolaischen Buchhandlung, 1847. i-xii,592p. indexes.   4657

VATER, JOHANN SEVERIN. Lingarum totius orbis Index alphabeticus, quarum Grammaticae, Lexica, collectiones vocabulorum recesnentur, patria significatur, historia adumbratur a Joanne Severino Vatero ... Berolini In officina libraria Fr. Nicolai, MDCCCXV [1815] iv,259p. [in 2 columns of German and Latin - incls. Aleut, Kodiak, Norton and Prince William Sound dialects - later printed in German. SEE no. 4657]   4658

Vater, Johann Severin. SEE ALSO no. 12,
    Adelung, J. C. Mithridates ... 1806[-1817]

Vattemore, H. SEE no. 4852, Whymper, F.

VAUDRIN, BILL. Tanaina tales from Alaska. By Bill Vaudrin. With an introduction by Joan B. Townsend. Norman, University of Oklahoma, 1969. 1st ed. 133p. illus. map, glossary. (The Civilization of the American Indian Series, no. 96)   4659

VAUGONDY, DIDIER ROBERT de. Lettre de M. Robert de Vaugondy Au sujet d'une Carte Systèmatique de pays septentronaux de l'Asie et de l'Amérique. [Paris, printed by Imprimerie d'Antoine Boudet, Imprimeur du Roi, 1768] 8p. map.   4660

VAUGONDY, DIDIER ROBERT de. Mémoire sur les Pays de l'Asie et de l'Amérique, situes au nord de la mer du Sud; Accompagné d'une carte, intitulée; Nouveau Systéme Géographique, par lequel on concile les anciennes connoissances sur les pays nord-ouest de l'Amérique, avec les nouvelles découvertes des Russes au nord de

la mer du Sud. Par M. de Vaugondy. Paris, Chez l'Auteur, printed by Antoine Boudet, 1774. viii,32(3)p. map(fold.), wrps.4661

VAUGONDY, DIDIER ROBERT de. Observations Critiques sur Les
Nouvelles Découvertes de l'Amiral de la Fuente. Présentées à
l'Académie Royale des Sciences, le 26 Mai 1753. Par M. Robert de
Vaugondy, fils, Géographe ordinaire du Roi. Paris, Chez Antoine
Boudet, 1753. 23p. wrps.   4662

VAURIE, CHARLES. Systematic notes on palearctic birds; no. 9
Sylviianae; the genus *Phylloscopus*. N. Y., 1954. 23p. table,
map. (American Museum of Natural History Novitates no. 1685.
Aug. 1954)   4663

VAURIE, CHARLES. Systematic notes on palearctic birds; no. 14
Turdinae; the genera *Erithacus, Luscinia, Tarsiger, Phoenicurus,
Monticola, Erythropygia,* and *Oenante.* N. Y., 1955. 30p. tables.
(American Museum of Natural History Novitates no. 1731. June
1955)   4664

VAURIE, CHARLES. Systematic notes on paleartic birds; no. 20
Fringillidae; the genera *Leucosticte, Rhodopechys, Carpodacus,
Pinicola, Loxia, Uragus, Urocynchramus* and *Propyrrhula.* N. Y.,
1956. 37p. illus. (American Museum of Natural History Novi-
tates no. 1786. Sept. 1956) [incls. Aleutian and Pribilof
Islands]   4665

VAURIE, CHARLES. Systematic notes on palearctic birds; no. 22
Fringillidae *Emberiza schoeniclus;* no. 25 *Motacillidae;* the
genus *Motacilla.* N. Y., 1956-57. 13+16p. illus. tables.
(American Museum of Natural History Novitates, no. 1795 and no.
1832) [incls. St. Michael, western Alaska]   4666

VDOVIN, INNOKENTIĬ STEPANOVICH. Istoriia izucheniia paleoazi-
atskikh iazykov. [TITLE TR. History of Paleoasiatic language
studies] Moskva-Leningrad, Izd-vo Akademii nauk SSSR, 1954.
165p. bibliog. (Akademiia nauk SSSR. Institut iazykozanniia)
[incls. studies by I. E. P. Veniaminov]   4667

VEDDE, SIGURD. Jack London ! Introduktion til et Forfatterskab.
København, Ejnar Munksgaard, 1943. 140p.   4668

VENEGAS, MIGUEL. Noticia de la California, y desu conquista tem-
poral y espiritual hasta el tiempo presente. Sacada de la historia manuscrita, formada en Mexico año de 1739, por el *Padre* Miguel Venegas, de la Compañia de Jesus; y de otras Noticias, y
Relaciones antiquas, y modernas. Añadida de algunos mapas par-
ticulares, y uno general de la America Septentrional, Asia Oriental, y Mar del Sùr intermedio, sormados sobre las Memorias mas
recientes, y exactas, que se publican juntamente. Dedicada al
Rey N.^{tro} Senor por la Provincia de Nueve-España, de la Compañia
de Jesus. Con Licencia, En Madrid, En la Imprenta de la Viuta de

Manuel Fernandez, y del Supremo Consejo de la Inquisicion, Año de
M.D.CCLVII [1757] 3 vols. xxiv,240p. viii,564p. viii,436p. maps
(fold.) [vol. 3 has notes by *Father* Burriel on Russians in the
North Pacific, de la Fuente, Buache, Delisle, others]   4669

VENIAMINOV, IVAN EVSĪEEVICH POPOV. Gospoda nashego iīusa Khrista
evangelie napissanoe apostolom Matfeem. S. Russkago īazyka na
Aleutsko-Lis'evskiĭ perevel *Svīashchennik* Ioann Veniaminov 1828
goda, i v 1836 godu ispravil; a *Svīashchennik* Īakov Netsvīetov,
razsmatrivaīa ego okonchatel'no, svoimi poīasneniīami sdīelal ikh
poniatnymi i dlīa Ashkhintsev imīeīushchikhsvoe narīechīe. [TITLE
TR. The Gospel of our Lord Jesus Christ as written by the apostle
Matthew. Translated from Russian into the Aleut-Fox language in
the year 1828 by the *Reverend* Ivan Veniaminov and revised in 1836;
final revision with added notes, made by the *Reverend* Īakov
Netsvīetov, for the Atkans who have a dialect of their own] [Mos-
kva, V Sinodal'noi tipografii, 1840] xiv,258p. ANR. [Moskva,
V Sinodal'noi tip., ca 1848] xiv,247p.[in error for 237p.],21p.
ANR. Santpeterburg, Synodal'naīa tipografiīa, 1896. 261p.   4670

VENIAMINOV, IVAN EVSĪEEVICH POPOV. Kratkaīa Khristianskaīa
katikhizis, s Russkago īazyka na Aleutsko-Lis'evskiĭ perevel
Svīashchennik Ioann Veniaminov 1827 goda, i v 1837 godu ispravil;
a *Svīashchennik* Īakov Netsvīetov razsmatrivaīa onyia, svoimi
poīasneniīami sdīelal ikh poniatnymi i dlīa Ashkhintsev, imīeīushchikhsvoe narīechīe. [TITLE TR. The Christian catechism translated into the Aleut-Fox language from Russian in the year 1827
by the *Reverend* Ivan Veniaminov and revised in 1837; final revision with added notes, made by the *Reverend* Īakov Netsvīetov for
the Atkans who have a dialect of their own] Sanktpeterburg, 1840.
ANR. 1893. [sometimes bound with no. 4673, or with no. 4600] 4671

VENIAMINOV, IVAN EVSĪEEVICH POPOV. Langues de l'Amérique Russe.
Par Ivan Veniaminoff. Paris, n. d. (extracted from Nouvelles
Annales des voyages, vol. 1, 1850. pp.359-64)   4672

VENIAMINOV, IVAN EVSĪEEVICH POPOV. Nachatki Khristianskago u-
cheniīa ili kratkaīa svīashchennaīa istoriīa i kratkiĭ Khristian-
skiĭ katikhizis; s Russkago īazyka na Aleutsko-Lis'evskiĭ perevel *Svīashchennik* Ioann Veniaminov 1827 goda, i v 1837 godu ispravil; a *Svīashchennik* Īakov Netsvīetov, razsmatrivaīa onyia,
svoimi poīasneniīami sdīelal ikh poniatnymi i dlīa Ashkhintsev,
imīeīushchikhsvoe narīechīe. [TITLE TR. The rudiments of Christian teaching, or a brief sacred history and a short Christian
catechism; translated from Russian into the Aleut-Fox language
by the *Reverend* Ivan Veniaminov in the year 1827 and revised in
1837; final revision with added notes, made by the *Reverend*
Īakov Netsvīetov, for the Atkans who have a dialect of their own]
Sanktpeterburg, Synodal'naīa tipografiīa, 1840. xxiii,24p.+104p.
+51p. ANR. Sanktpeterburg, Synodal'naīa tip., 1893. [sometimes
bound with no. 4671, or with no. 4600]   4673

VENIAMINOV, IVAN EVSĪEEVICH POPOV. Natavlenie *Vysokopreosvīash-chennago* Innokentiīa, byvshago *Arkhiepiskopa* Kamchatskago, Kuril'-skago, i Aleutskago. [TITLE TR. Teachings of the *Most Reverend Innocent*, late *Archbishop* of Kamchatka and the Kuril and Aleutian Islands] N. Y., Amerikanskiĭ Pravoslavnyi Viestnik, 1899. 40p.

4674

VENIAMINOV, IVAN EVSĪEEVICH POPOV. Opyt grammatiki Aleutsko-Lis'evskago īazyka. *Svīashchennika* I. Veniaminova v Unalashkie. [TITLE TR. Essay on the grammar of the Aleutian-Fox language. By *Reverend* I. Veniaminov, at Unalaska] Sanktpeterburg, V Tipogra-fiīa Imp. Akademiīa nauk, 1846. 2 pts. in 1. XV,iii,87p.+vi,120p. tables(fold.) [tr. made by Henry, SEE no. 2071 and by Pfizmaier, SEE no. 3566. Also may be found in U. S. Dept. of Interior "The Aleut language" tr. by Richard H. Geoghegan and edited by Fredericka I. Martin, Washington, D. C., G. P. O., 1944. 169p.]

4675

[VENIAMINOV, IVAN EVSĪEEVICH POPOV ?] The Orthodox schools in Alaska in 1904. By Innocent, *Bishop of Alaska*. N. Y., 1905. 68p.

4676

VENIAMINOV, IVAN EVSĪEEVICH POPOV. Sostoianīa pravoslavnoĭ tserkvi na rossiĭsko-amerikanskikh. *Svīashchennika* I. Veniami-nova. [TITLE TR. The state of the Orthodox Church in Russian America. Written by the *Reverend* I. Veniaminov] Sanktpeterburg, V Tipografiīa Imp. Akademiīa nauk, 1840. 44p. (also in Journal of Ministry of Public Instruction, vol. 26, no. 6. 1840. pp.16-58)

4677

VENIAMINOV, IVAN EVSĪEEVICH POPOV. Ukazanie puti v tsartstvīe nebesnoe. Besieda *Preosvīashchennago* Innokentiīa (Veniaminova), perevedennaīa na Indianskiĭ īazyk S. I. Kostrometinoyvm. Ka-vak-shii Ev-u-tu-tsi-no-i dte tiki An-ku-u Kha-te ... [TITLE TR. Guide road into Heavenly Kingdom. A discourse of *Most Reverend Innocent Veniaminov*, translated into Indian language by S. I. Kostrometinov] N. Y., Tip. Amerikanskiĭ Pravoslavnyi Viestnik, 1901. 16p. [title in Russian and Tlingit]

4678

VENIAMINOV, IVAN EVSĪEEVICH POPOV. Ukazanie puti tsarstvie ne-besnoe pouchenie, na Aleutsko-Lis'evskom iazykie sochinennoe *Svīashchennikom* Ioannom Veniaminovym 1833 goda. [TITLE TR. Guide to the Heavenly Kingdom, lesson in the Aleutian-Fox language, composed by the *Reverend* Ivan Veniaminov in 1833] Moskva, Syno-dal'noĭ tipografiĭ, 1840. iv,4p.+134p.

4679

TRANSLATION - Ukazanie puti ... 1840.

Wegweiser zum Himmelreich, oder Vortrage sur Belehrung des neugetauften Christen im Russ-Amerika. Aus dem Russ. uber-setzt von Julie v. Z. Odessa, 1848.

4680

VENIAMINOV, IVAN EVSĪEEVICH POPOV. Zamiechaniīa o koloshenskom i kad'īakskom īazykakh i otchasti o prochikh rossiīsko-amerikan- skikh, s prisovokupleniem rossiīsko-koloshenskago slovarīa soder- zhashchago bolīee 1000 slov, iz koikh na nīekotoryīa sdīelany poīasneniīa. [TITLE TR. Remarks on the Koloshi and Kodiak lan- guages, also on other languages of Russian-America, with added Russian-Koloshi vocabulary of more than 1000 words, some with ex- planations] Sanktpeterburg, Tip. Imp. Akademiīa nauk, 1846. 81p. tables(some fold.), wrps. [refer to Pfizmaier, no. 3565]   4681

Veniaminov, Ivan Evsīeevich Popov. Zapiski ob Atkhinskikh ... 1840. SEE no. 4682.

VENIAMINOV, IVAN EVSĪEEVICH POPOV. Zapiski ob ostrovakh Unalash- kinskago otdīela, sostavlennyīa I. Veniaminovym.[TITLE TR. Notes on the Unalaska Islands District. Compiled by I. Veniaminov, published under auspices of the Russian American Company] Sankt- peterburg, Izdano izhdiveniem Rossiīsko-Amerikanskoĭ Kompaniĭ, 1840. 3 vols. in 2.   ix,364p., (viii) 409p., (iv)154p. tables (some fold.) [third part has different title: Zapiski ob Atkhinskikh Aleutskh i Koloshakh ...]   4682

Veniaminov, Ivan Evsīeevich Popov. SEE ALSO nos.
    414, [Barsukov, I. P.] Innokentiīa ... 1883;
    415, [Barsukov, I. P.] Life and work ... 1897;
    416, [Barsukov, I. P.] Pis'ma Innokentiīa ... 1897-1901;
    417, [Barsukov, I. P.] Tvoreniīa Innokentiīa ... 1887;
    1898, Hale, Chas. R. Innocent of Moscow ... 1888;
    2071, Henry, V. Esquisse d'une grammaire ... aleoute ...1879;
    3565, Pfizmaier, A. Aufklärungen ... 1883;
    3566, Pfizmaier, A. Die Sprache der Aleuten ... 1884;
    3934, S., Z. O zhizni i podvigakh Innokentiīa. 1893;
    4109, Shenitz, H. Alaska's good *Father* ... 1962;
    4122, Shiels, A. W. Work of Veniaminov ... 1947;
    4667, Vdovin, I. S. Istoriīa izucheniīa ... 1954.

Ver Mehr, John. SEE no. 4924, Winslow, Kathryn.

VERCEL, ROGER. Northern lights. Translated from the French by Katherine Woods. N. Y., Random House, [c1948] 251p. [fict. polar Arctic setting with some slight mention of Alaska]   4683

VERHOEVEN, L. A. A report to the salmon fishing industry of Alaska on the results of the 1947 tagging experiments. Seattle, University of Washington, 1952. 21p.+50p. illus. graphs, tables, maps. (Fisheries Research Institute Circular no. 28) [southeast Alaska waters]   4684

Vernam, Roger, illus. SEE no. 2121, Hines, J. C.

VERNE, JULES. Bekannte und unbekannte Welten. Wien, A. Hartle- ben, 1881. [vols. 33-34 contain author's *Die Vorläufer des Kapi- tän Cook*. illus. port.]   4685

Verne, Jules. Die Vorläufer ... 1881. SEE no. 4685.

VERNE, JULES. Flood and flame. Part two of The golden volcano. By Jules Verne. Translated from the French by I. O. Evans. Westport, Conn., Associated Booksellers, n. d. [c1962 in England by Arco Publications] 190p. (The Fitzroy Edition of Jules Verne Edited by I. O. Evans) [Part one, The claim on Forty Mile Creek. SEE no. 4689]   4686

Verne, Jules. Le volcan d'or. SEE nos. 4686 and 4689.

VERNE, JULES. Les Grands navigateurs du XVIII siècle. Paris, Bibliothèque d'éducation et de récréation, [1880 ?] illus. maps. (Histoire générale des Grands voyages et de Grands voyageurs) [contains Cook's voyages, pp.108-226. SEE ALSO no. 4688]   4687

VERNE, JULES. Premier voyage du Capitaine Cook. Edited by H. Wiltshire. Sydney, H. Wiltshire, 1926. 74p. [reprint of Les Grands navigateurs ... SEE no. 4687]   4688

VERNE, JULES. The claim on Forty Mile Creek. Part one of The golden volcano. By Jules Verne. Translated from the French by I. O. Evans. Westport, Conn., Associated Booksellers, n. d. [c1962 in England by Arco Publications] 191p. (The Fitzroy Edition of Jules Verne Edited by I. O. Evans) [cf no. 4686. First printed as Le volcan d'or in 1906]   4689

VERNE, JULES. The fur country or seventy degrees North latitude. Translated from the French of Jules Verne by N. D'Anvers. With one hundred illustrations. Boston, James R. Osgood & Co., 1874. 334p. front. pls. [fict. adventure polar passage via drifting iceberg/island through Bering Strait]   4690

Verne, Jules. The golden volcano. SEE nos. 4686 and 4689.

Verrill, A. E. SEE nos. 1950-53, Harriman Alaska Exped.

VER WIEBE, W. A. Oil fields in North America. Wichita, Kansas, Edwards Bros., 1949. iv,251p. illus.   4691

VESANEN, EIJO. On Alaska earthquakes. Helsinki, 1947. 21p. diagrs. (Suomalainen tiedeakatemia. Toimituksia. Ser. A, III, Geologica-Geographica, 14)   4692

VESELEV, F. F. Razbor vtoroi chasti ... St. Petersburg, Imperial Academy of Sciences, 1864. 47p. [a review of Tikhmenev's Istoricheskoe ... Pt. 2. SEE no. 4536]   4693

VETERAN STEAMBOATMEN'S ASSOCIATION OF THE WEST. Steamer "Eliza Anderson." [Champoeg, Oregon, 1940] (6)p. illus.   4694

Veterans of Foreign Wars Auxil. cookbook. 1964. SEE no. 3547, Petersburg V. F. W. Auxiliary.

VEVERS, GWYNNE. Animals of the Arctic. N. Y., McGraw-Hill,
illus.   4695

VIANA, FRANCISCO JAVIER de. Diario del viage explorador de las
corbetas españolas "Descubierta" y "Atrevida," en los años de
1789 à 1794, llevado por el teniente de navio D. Francisco Javier
de Viana, y ofrecido para su publicacion, en su original inedito,
por el Sr. D. Francisco Javier de Viana, y demas hijos del autor.
Cerrito de la Victoria, Imprenta del Ejercito, 1849. 360p. wrps.
[diary account of Malaspina voyage from California to Alaska in
1791. pp.185-219]   4696

VICTOR, RALPH. The Boy Scouts of the Yukon. Illustrated by
Rudolf Mencl. N. Y., A. L. Chatterton, [c1912] 194p. front.
pls.   4697

VIDAL, GORE. Williwaw, a novel. N. Y., Dutton, 1946. 222p.
[locale, Aleutian Islands]   4698

VIERECK, PHILLIP. Eskimo Island; a story of the Bering Sea
hunters. N. Y., John Day, [c196]] 160p. illus.(some col.)
[King Island]   4699

View of character ... Oonalashka ... 1810. SEE no. 3576,
   [Phillips, Richard]

VIKSTEN, ALBERT. I Guldjägares Spår; resan till Yukon och
Alaska; 2 uppl. Stockholm, Ltis förlag, 1951. 336p. illus.
                                                               4700

VIKSTEN, ALBERT. Pälsjägarnas Paradis. Stockholm, Ltis förlag,
1955. 184p.   4701

Village people. 1966. SEE no. 236, Anchorage Daily News.

VILLARD, HENRY. A journey to Alaska. N. Y., 1899. 48p.   4702

Villari, Linda. SEE no. 1227, de Filippi, Filippo.

Villaume, Herrn Prof. SEE no. 1253, de Lesseps, J. B. B.

VILLIERS, ALAN JOHN. Captain Cook, the seaman's seaman. A study
of the great discoverer. Illustrations by Adrian Small, master
mariner in sail. London, Hodder & Stoughton, 1967. ix,10-256p.
pls. ports. maps, bibliog. ANR. [SEE no. 4704]   4703

VILLIERS, ALAN JOHN. Captain James Cook. N. Y., Scribner,
[c1967] 307p. illus. front.(port.), ports. maps, endmaps, appends. bibliog. index. [ANR. SEE no. 4703]   4704

VILLIERS, ALAN JOHN. Pioneers of the seven seas. London, Routledge & Kegan Paul, 1956. illus. [pp.78-85, Capt. Jas. Cook]
                                                               4705

Vincent, La Belle Brooks. SEE no. 687, Brooks-Vincent, La Belle.

VISHNEVSKIĬ, BORIS NIKOLAEVICH. Puteshestvennik Kirill Khlebnikov. [TITLE TR. The traveler Kiril Khlebnikov] Permi, Permskoe
knizhnoe izd-vo, 1957. 60p. illus. maps(incl. 1 fold.), bibliog.
(Zamechatel'nye liūdi prikam'ĩa) [of the Russian-American Co.]
4706

Vittenburg, P., co-auth. SEE no. 3717, Rabot, Chas.

VITVITSKIĬ, G. N. Klimaty Severnoĭ Ameriki. [TITLE TR. Climates
of North America] Moskva, Gos. izd-dat. geogr. lit., 1953. 287p.
illus. tables, bibliog. [incl. Alaska and Canada] 4707

VIZE, VLADIMIR ĨUL'EVICH. Morĩa Sovetskoĭ Arktiki; ocherki po
istoriĭ issledovaniĩa. [TITLE TR. Seas of the Soviet Arctic;
historical outline of their investigation] Moskva, Izd-vo glavsemorputi, 1948. 3rd ed. rev. and enl. 413p. illus. ports.
maps(incl. 2 fold.), bibliogs. indexes. [earlier editions in
1936 and 1939] 4708

VIZE, VLADIMIR ĨUL'EVICH. Russkie poliārnye morekhody iz promysh-
lennyk, torgovykh isluzhilykh liūdei XVII-XIX vv; biografiches-
kiĭ slovar'. [TITLE TR. Russian polar seafarers from among the
hunters, traders and government officials of the 17th-19th century; a biographical dictionary] Moskva-Leningrad, Izd-vo
glavsemorputi, 1948. 72p. illus. map, bibliog. 4709

VOEGELIN, C. F. and Z. S. HARRIS. Index to the Franz Boas collection of material for American linguistics. Baltimore, Waverly Press, 1945. 43p. bibliog. (Language monograph no. 22.
Language, vol. 21, no. 3, suppl.) [incls. ms. papers on Northwest Indian and Eskimo-Aleut languages by various authors] 4710

VOEGELIN, C. F. and F. M. VOEGELIN. Languages of the world,
native America fascicle one. Bloomington, Indiana, 1964. 149p.
bibliog. (Anthropological linguistics, vol. 6, no. 6) [much on
Alaskan Indian and Eskimo-Aleut languages) 4711

Voegelin, F. M. SEE no. 4711, Voegelin, C. F.

THE VOICE OF THE YUKON; as heard by some who "mushed" the great
stampede to the river of the Thron Diuck for the gathering of
gold in the year 1898, written down by one of them, with pen
drawings by R. P. Wilson. Vancouver, B. C., Wrigley, 1930. 45p.
illus. [poetry anthology] 4712

VOIGTLÄNDER, O. Drei jahre in Alaska. Nach eigenen erlebnissen
von O. Voigtländer, erzhalt von L. Sommer. [TITLE TR. Three
years in Alaska. Experiences of O. Voigtländer, related by L.
Sommer] Berlin, C. Hause, [190_ ?] 30p. illus. map. (Hauses
Volks- und Jugend Bibliothek, Hft. 1) [gold prospecting, 1902
through 1905] 4713

Voix de'Alaska ... 1930. SEE no. 767, [Calasanctius, *Sister*
    Mary Joseph]

Volckmann, Erwin. SEE no. 365, Balch, Thos. W.

VOLMAR, F. A. Das Bärenbuch. [TITLE TR. The bear book] Bern,
Vorlag Paul Haupt, 1940. 404p. illus. bibliog. (incls. bear
cults of Alaskan Eskimos and Indians]   4714

VON BERNEWITZ, M. W. Handbook for prospectors. By M. W. von
Bernewitz. First Edition. N. Y. and London, McGraw-Hill, 1926.
[c1926] ix,319p. front. figs. charts, glossary, °index. ANR.
WITH TITLE Handbook for prospectors and operators of small mines.
Fourth Edition. Revised by Harry C. Chellson. N. Y., McGraw-
Hill, 1943. [scattered textual references to Alaskan mining]4715

VOYAGE DE DÉCOUVERTES AUTOUR DU MONDE et a la recherche de la
Pérouse ... sur la corvette *L'Astrolabe*, pendant les années 1826-
1829. Paris, de Roret, 1832-1833. 5 vols.   4716

Voyage of Captains Portlock and Dixon ... 1803. SEE
    no. 3653, [Portlock, N.]

THE VOYAGE OF THE *CHELYUSKIN*. By members of the expedition.
Translated by Alex Brown. With numerous plates and maps. N. Y.,
Macmillan, 1935. [c1935] xii,325p. front.(port.), pls. ports.
maps(incl. 1 dble.) [incls. flight (by way of Alaska) by Soviet
airmen, M. Slepnov, S. Levanevski and G. A. Ushagov, to aid
marooned crew of *Chelyuskin*]   4717

The voyage of the *Chelyuskin*. SEE ALSO no. 877,
    Centkiewicz, C. J. *Czeluskin* ... 1953.

Voyage round world ... Fur Trade. 1789. SEE no. 3649,
    [Portlock, N.]

Voyage to Pacific Ocean ... SEE nos. 1035, 1041 and 1046,
    [Cook, Jas.]

Voyages of Captain James Cook ... SEE nos. 1044, 1047, 1048,
    and 1049, [Cook, Jas.]

Voyages round the world ... n. d. SEE no. 1054, [Cook, Jas.]

Vrangel', Ferdinand Petrovich. SEE no. 4968,
    Wrangell, Ferdinand Petrovich.

VYVYAN, CLARA COLTMAN (ROGERS). Arctic adventure. London, P.
Owen, 1961. 172p. pls. map. ANR. Hollywood-by-the-Sea, Fla.,
Transatlantic Arts, 1962. illus. [author's journeys by steamer
and canoe, Inside Passage, Yukon, other rivers, 1926]   4718

W

W., A., tr. SEE no. 2525, Kotzebue, O. v.

WACHEL, PAT. Oscar Winchell; Alaska's flying cowboy. Minneapolis, T. S. Denison & Co., [c1967] 210p. (Men of Achievement Series)   4719

WADE, FREDERICK COATE. Treaties affecting the North Pacific coast. Read before the 6th Annual Conference, Association of Canadian Clubs, Vancouver, August 4, 1914. [Vancouver, Saturday Sunset Presses, n. d.] 19p. [Alaskan boundary]   4720

Wade, Leigh. SEE no. 4497, Thomas, Lowell.

Wadsworth, F. H., co-auth. SEE no. 432, Baxter, D. V.

Waggoner, J. H. SEE no. 4816, White, E. W., Pub. Co.

WAGNER, ELBY. Partners three. N. Y., Thomas Y. Crowell, 1928. 295p. [fict.]   4721

WAGNER, HENRY RAUP. Apocryphal voyages to the Northwest coast of America. Worcester, Mass., American Antiquarian Society, 1931.
                                                                    4722

WAGNER, HENRY RAUP. Cartography of the Northwest coast of America to the year 1800. By H. R. Wagner. Berkeley, University of California Press, 1937. 2 vols. 279p. and pp.271-543. illus. maps(some fold.), bibliog. index. ANR. Amsterdam, Israel, 1968. 2 vols. in 1. reprint of 1937 ed. xi,543p.   4723

WAGNER, HENRY RAUP. Journal of Tomas de Suria of his voyage with Malaspina to the Northwest coast of America in 1791. Glendale, Calif., 1936. ed. ltd. to 100 copies. pls. (also in Pacific Historical Review, vol. 5, pp.234-76. Sept. 1936)   4724

WAGNER, HENRY RAUP. Some imaginary California geography. Worcester, Mass., American Antiquarian Society, 1926. 49p. maps. [early North Pacific voyages noted also]   4725

WAGNER, HENRY RAUP. Spanish voyages to the Northwest coast of America in the 16th century. S. F., 1929. 571p. pls. port. maps(incl. some fold.), append. index. (California Historical Society Special Publication no. 14) ANR. Amsterdam, N. Israel, 1966. reprint of 1929 ed.   4726

WAID, EVA CLARK. Alaska; the land of the totem. Compiled by Eva Clark Waid. N. Y., [1910] 127p. (Woman's Board of Home Missions of the Presbyterian Church in the U. S. A.) ANR. N. Y., [191_ ?] 135p. wrps.   4727

Wait, Peter, tr. SEE no. 3072, Meldgaard, J.

WALCUTT, C. C. Jack London. Minneapolis, University of Minnesota Press, 1966. 48p. (University of Minnesota Pamphlets on American Writers no. 57)   4728

WALDEN, ARTHUR TREADWELL. A dog-puncher on the Yukon. By Arthur Treadwell Walden. With an introduction by Walter Collins O'Kane. And with illustrations. Boston, Houghton Mifflin, 1928. [c1928] 289p. front.(pl.), pls. endmaps. ANR. Montreal, Louis Carrier & Co., 1928. 289p. illus. [several of the photographic plates by Asahel Curtis]   4729

WALFORD, LIONEL ALBERT. Marine game fishes of the Pacific coast from Alaska to the equator. Berkeley, University of California Press, 1937. 205p. front.(col.), pls.(incl. some col.), diagr. map. [paintings by Link Malmquist and photos by Ralph Emerson]
                                                                   4730

Walker-Arnott, G. A., co-auth. SEE no. 2173, Hooker, Wm. J.

WALKER, FRANKLIN. Jack London and the Klondike. San Marino, California, 1966.   4731

WALKER, ROBERT J. Letter of the Hon. R. J. Walker on the purchase of Alaska, St. Thomas and St. John. Washington, D. C., Washington Chronicle Printing, 1868. 11p. (reprinted from Washington Daily Morning Chronicle of Jan. 28, 1868)   4732

WALKER, THEODORE J. Whale primer. With special attention to the California gray whale. [Cabrillo Historical Society, 1962] 58p. illus. map. [has background and appended scientific names North American cetaceans]   4733

Wall, Louise H., co-auth. SEE no. 2592, Lane, A. W.

WALLACE, F. T. A dream of Alaska. [Cleveland, Ohio ?], n. d.
                                                                   4734

Wallace, Wm. A., edit. SEE no. 3114, Milepost. 1949.

Wallis, J. P. R., edit. SEE no. 353, Baines, Thos.

Walluk, Wilbur, illus. SEE no. 2841, McCorkle, R.

Walsh, Wm. F. SEE no. 1738, Glody, R.

WALTON, JOHN. Six explorers. London, Oxford University Press, 1942. map. (Living Names Series)   4735

WALTON, W. B. Eskimo or Innuit dictionary; as spoken by all those strange people on the Alaska Peninsula, the coast of Bering Sea and the Arctic Ocean, including settlements on all streams emptying into those waters. Seattle, Metropolitan Print. and Binding Co., 1901. 32p.   4736

Ward, Gerard, co-edit. SEE no. 1316, Dodge, E. S.

WARDMAN, GEORGE. A trip to Alaska; a narrative of what was seen and heard during a summer cruise in Alaskan waters. By George Wardman, United States Treasury Agent at the seal islands. Boston, Lee & Shepard Pub. and N. Y., Charles T. Dillingham, 1884. [c1884] 237p. ANR. S. F., S. Carson & Co. and Boston, Lee & Shepard, [1884] 237p. [on revenue cutter, *Rush*]   4737

[WARDNER, JAMES F.] Jim Wardner of Wardner, Idaho. By Himself. N. Y., The Anglo-American Pub. Co., 1900. [c1900] 154(2)p. illus. port. facsims. [three chapts. on Nome and Klondike, with many facims. of gold rush advertisements]   4738

Wardwell, Allen. SEE no. 311, Art Institute of Chicago.

WARE, KAY and L. SUTHERLAND. Let's read about Alaska. Illustrated by E. Joseph Dreany. St. Louis, Mo., Webster Pub. Co., 1960. 32p. illus.   4739

WARFEL, KENNETH. Fow ! and other fingerprints. Philadelphia, Dorrance & Co., 1966. [poetry]   4740

WARNER, DONALD F. The idea of continental union; agitation for the annexation of Canada to the United States 1849-1893. By Donald F. Warner. [Lexington], University of Kentucky Press, [c1960] ix,276p. maps, bibliog(notes & ftntes.), index. (Published for the Mississippi Valley Historical Association) [has references to Seward, Sumner, and Alaska purchase]   4741

WARNER, GERTRUDE CHANDLER. Windows into Alaska; a course for primary children, stories and notes for teachers; worship services by Elizabeth Harris. Teachers Edition. N. Y., Friendship Press, 1928. 104p. pl.(fold.), bibliog.   4742

WARNER, OLIVER MARTIN WILSON. English maritime writing. London, Longmans, Green, 1958. (Published for The British Council and National Book League. British Book News Bibliography. Series of supplements, no. 105) [pp.29-31 about Cook voyages]   4743

WARNER, OLIVER MARTIN WILSON. Great seamen. London, G. Bell, 1961. 226p. pls. ports. ANR. Chester Springs, Penna., Dufour Editions, 1961. [pp.82-115 about James Cook]   4744

WARREN, HENRY MATHER. To and fro. Philadelphia, William F. Fell Co., [c1908] [section about Chilkoot Pass]   4745

WARTES, WILLIAM C., ROY AHMAOGAK and SAMUEL SIMMONDS. The Utḳiaġvik Iñupiat hymn book. Alaska North Slope Iñupiat (Eskimo) dialect. Cuernavaca, Morelos, Mexico, Tipografica Indigena, 1959. unp. append. wrps.   4746

Washburn, Bradford. SEE nos. 4747-48, Washburn, Henry Bradford.

WASHBURN, HENRY BRADFORD. Bradford on Mount Fairweather. N. Y.,
Putnam, 1930. 127p. front.(ports.), pls. maps. [photos and
sketchmaps by author]   4747

WASHBURN, HENRY BRADFORD. Mount McKinley and the Alaska Range in
literature. By Bradford Washburn. A descriptive bibliography.
Special advance edition prepared for the Alaska Science Conference
to be held at Mount McKinley National Park, Alaska, September,
1951. Boston, Museum of Science, 1951. 88p. wrps.   4748

Washburn, Henry Bradford. SEE ALSO no. 699,
     Browne, Belmore. Conquest Mt. McKinley. 1913.

WASHINGTON AND ALASKA STEAMSHIP CO. Golden Klondike. Guide to
the Yukon gold fields giving latest and reliable maps and data.
Washington and Alaska Steamship Company, operating the finest and
fastest steamships between Tacoma, Seattle, Victoria and Vancouver, and Juneau, Dyea, Skaguay, Haines Mission and Wrangel. Tacoma, Allen & Lamborn Printing Co., [1897] 24p. map(fold.) 4749

Washington illustrated. [1901 ?] SEE no. 3164,
     Moore, Otis M.

WASHINGTON, JOHN. Eskimaux and English vocabulary, for the use
of the Arctic expedition. Published by order of the Lords Commissioners of the Admiralty. London, John Murray, 1850. xvi,
160p.   4750

Washington, State of. SEE no. 156, Alaska-Yukon-Pacific Exped.
     Report of ... Committee ... 1910.

WASOWICZ, JÓSEF. Granica śniegu w Selkirkach oraz Kordyljerach
Alaski i Kanady. [TITLE TR. Studies on the snow line in Canada
and Alaska] Krakow, Polska Adademja umiejętności, 1934. tables,
sketchmaps. (Prace Komisji Geograficznaj. n^r 4. Nakl. Pol-
skiej Akademji umiejętności)   4751

WATERMAN, THOMAS TALBOT and RUTH GREINER. Indian houses of Puget
Sound. N. Y., Museum of the American Indian, Heye Foundation,
1921. vi,59p. illus. (Indian Notes and Monographs, Misc. ser.
no. 9) [comparison with housing of Indians in southeastern
Alaska)   4752

WATERMAN, THOMAS TALBOT and others. Native houses of western
North America. N. Y., Museum of the American Indian, Heye Foun-
dation, 1921. 97p. front.(fold. map), pl. bibliog. (Indian
Notes and Monographs, Misc. ser. no. 11)   4753

WATERMAN, THOMAS TALBOT and GERALDINE COFFIN. Types of canoes on
Puget Sound. N. Y., Museum of the American Indian, Heye Foundation, 1920. 43p. illus. (Indian Notes and Monographs, Misc.
ser. no. 5)   4754

WATSON, ARTHUR CHACE. The long harpoon; a collection of whaling anecdotes. New Bedford, Mass., G. H. Ryenolds, 1929. 165p. illus. [incls. Bering Strait and Arctic Alaskan waters] 4755

WATSON, JANE WERNER. Walt Disney's Seal Island. Adapted by Jane Werner Watson. N. Y., Golden Press, 1958. 32p. photos(col.) 4756

WATSON, W. W. Our Alaskan trip, in letter. Salina, Kansas, 1910. 78p. front.(port.), pls. sketch. [ltd. printing - by steamer *Spokane* to southeastern Alaska] 4757

WAXELL, SVEN LARSSON. The American expedition. By Sven Waxell, with an introduction and note by M. A. Michael. London, William Hodge & Co., [1952] 236p. front.(port.), pl.(fold.), maps, endmaps, append. bibliog. index. [translated from Johan Skalberg's Danish verson. SEE no. 4759] 4758

WAXELL, SVEN LARSSON. Vitus Berings eventyrlige opdagerfærd 1733-1743, skildret af hans rejsefacile og første officer. Forord af Hakon Mielche; med uddrag af A. J. Andrejef's indledning til den russiske udg. [TITLE TR. Vitus Bering's adventurous voyage of discovery 1733-1743, portrayed by his fellow voyager and first officer. Preface by Hakon Mielche; with an extract from A. J. Andreev's introduction to the Russian edition] København, Rosenkilde og Bagger, 1948. 139p. pls. maps(fold.) [cf nos. 4758 and 4760] 4759

WAXELL, SVEN LARSSON. Vtoraĩa Kamchatskaĩa ėkspeditsiĩa Vitusa Beringa; perevod s rukopisi na nemetskom ĩazyke ĩu. I. Bronshteĩna, pod red. i s predisl. A. I. Andreeva. [TITLE TR. The Second Kamchatka Expedition of Vitus Bering; translation from the manuscript in German by ĩu. I. Bronshtein, edited with an introduction by A. I. Andreev] Leningrad, Izd-vo Glavsevmorputi, 1940. 127p. illus. maps(some fold.), facsims. [cf nos. 4758 and 4759] 4760

Waxell, Sven Larsson. SEE ALSO nos.
   721, Büchner, Eug. Die Abbildungen ... Seekuh ... 1891;
   1311, Dobbs, A. Letter ... 1754.
   2693, Lettre d'un officier ... 1752;
   3311, Nilsson, G. A. Sjöfarare ... 1957.

WEAD, FRANK. Gales, ice and men; a biography of the steam barkentine *Bear*. By Frank Wead. Decorations by Charles E. Pont. N. Y., Dodd Mead, 1937. [c1937] 272p. front.(col. pl.), pls. (incl. 1 dble.), endmaps, appends. [pp.61-238, in Alaskan waters] 4761

Weatherall, M., tr. SEE no. 4791, Welzl, J.

Weatherall, R., tr. SEE no. 4791, Welzl, J.

[WEBB, FRANCIS ?] Letters lately published ... on the subject of the present dispute with Spain ... London, 1790. 101p. [Nootka Sound controversy - also ascribed to James B. Burges] 4762

WEBB, NANCY M. Aguk of Alaska. Englewood Cliffs, Prentice-Hall, 1963. 64p. illus. [juv.] 4763

Webb, Samuel B., co-edit. SEE nos. 614-15, Boone and Crockett Club.

WEBB, WILLIAM SEWARD. California and Alaska; and over the Canadian Pacific Railway. N. Y., Putnam, 1890. 190p. front. pls. ANR. 1891. 268p. front. pls. 4764

WEBER, GUSTAVUS A. The Coast and Geodetic Survey; its history, activities and organization. Baltimore, Johns Hopkins Press, 1923. 107p. bibliog. (Brookings Institution. Institute for Government Research Monograph no. 16) 4765

WEBER, HEINRICH. Die Entwickelung der physikalischen Geographie der Nord-Polarländer bis auf Cooks Zeiten. [TITLE TR. The evolution of physical geography of the North Polar lands up to the time of Cook] München, T. Ackermann, 1898. 250p. (Münchener geographische Studien ... 4. Stück) 4766

[WEBSTER, DONALD HUMPHRY] A brief introduction to Eskimo (Arctic slope dialect) with useful phrases. Wainwright, Alaska, D. H. Webster, n. d. 14p. bibliog. wrps. (Summer Institute of Linguistics and Wycliffe Bible Translators) 4767

WEBSTER, DONALD HUMPHRY. [Can you read English ? Then you can] also read Eskimo. It's very easy, even easier than reading English, because ... . Illustrated by T. A. Webster. Fairbanks, Summer Institute of Linguistics, 1968. 60p. illus. wrps. (Wycliffe Bible Translators) 4768

WEBSTER, DONALD HUMPHRY. Iḷisaaġviŋich Iñupiam. Santa Ana, Calif., Summer Institute of Linguistics, n. d. 24p. illus. wrps. (Wycliffe Bible Translators) 4769

WEBSTER, DONALD HUMPHRY. Iḷisaaġviŋich Iñupiat. D. H. Webster. [on cover] [Fairbanks, Summer Institute of Linguistics, n. d.] 24p. illus. wrps. (Wycliffe Bible Translators) [on title page, Iñupiam aglaŋi] 4770

WEBSTER, DONALD HUMPHRY and WILFRIED ZIBELL. Iñupiat Eskimo dictionary. Donald H. Webster and Wilfried Zibell. Illustrated by Thelma A. Webster. [Fairbanks, Summer Institute of Linguistics, c1970] 211p. illus. map, index, wrps. (Wycliffe Bible Translators) [Kobuk River and North Slope dialects] 4771

WEBSTER, DONALD HUMPHRY and ROY AHMAOGAK. Iñupiat suuvat ? What about the Eskimo ? Compiled and edited by Donald H. Webster and Roy Ahmaogak. Illustrated by Thelma Webster. Fairbanks, Summer Institute of Linguistics, [c1968] 29p. illus. maps. [Eskimo and English in parallel columns]   4772

WEBSTER, DONALD HUMPHRY. Iñupiat taiguangich. I. no pl., Summer Institute of Linguistics, n. d. 10p. wrps. (Wycliffe Bible Translators) [Eskimo primer no. 1]   4773

WEBSTER, DONALD HUMPHRY. Iñupiat taiguangich. II. no pl., Summer Institute of Linguistics, n. d. (16)p. wrps. (Wycliffe Bible Translators) [Eskimo primer no. 2]   4774

WEBSTER, DONALD HUMPHRY. Let's learn Eskimo. By D. H. Webster. Illustrated by T. Webster. Fairbanks, Summer Institute of Linguistics, [c1967] 53p. illus. diagrs. chart, wrps. ANR.[c1968] 2d ed. 66p. (Wycliffe Bible Translators) [North Slope dialect]
                                                                       4775

Webster, Donald Humphry. SEE ALSO no. 22,
    Ahmaogak, R. Iñupiam Uḵaluŋi. [1963 ?]

WEBSTER, FRANK V. Two boy gold miners; or, lost in the mountains. N. Y., Cupples & Leon, 1909. 205p. front. illus. [Alaskan and Montana settings]   4776

WEBSTER, FRANK V. The young treasure hunter; or, Fred Stanley's trip to Alaska. By Frank V. Webster. N. Y., Cupples & Leon, [c1909] 204p. front. pls.   4777

Webster, Thelma, illus. SEE nos.
    4445, Tagarook, A. Jesus kamanaḵtuat ... n. d.;
    4768, Webster, D. H. Can you read ... 1968;
    4771, Webster, D. H. Iñupiat Eskimo dictionary. [c1970];
    4772, Webster, D. H. Iñupiat suuvat ? [c1968];
    4775, Webster, D. H. Let's learn ... [c1967]

WEED, ALBERTA L. Grandma goes to the Arctic. Philadelphia, Dorrance, 1957. 279p. illus. ANR. 1961. (as told by Alberta L. Weed to Lola Kirkland]   4778

WEED, WALTER H. The copper mines of the world. N. Y., Hill Pub. Co., 1907. 375p.   4779

Weeden, R. B. SEE nos.
    1512, Fairbanks Bird Club. Bird-finding ... highways. [1965]
    2449, Kessel, B. Bird-finding Interior ... 1967.

WEEKS, TIM and RAMONA MAHER. Ice Island; polar science and the Arctic Research Laboratory. N. Y., John Day, 1965. 220p.   4780

WEEMS, CARRINGTON. The Bishop of the Arctic. N. Y., 1912. 11p. illus. [biog. of Peter Trimble Rowe]   4781

WEIGERT, HANS WERNER and VILHJALMUR STEFANSSON, co-edits. Compass of the world; a symposium on political geography edited by Hans W. Weigert and Vilhjalmur Stefansson. Maps by Richard E. Harrison. N. Y., Macmillan, 1944. 1st print. xvi,466p. illus. diagrs. maps, index. ANR. London, n. d. maps.   4782

WEIGERT, HANS WERNER, VILHJALMUR STEFANSSON and RICHARD EDES HARRISON, co-edits. New compass of the world, a symposium on political geography. Editors Hans W. Weigert, Vilhjalmur Stefansson, Richard Edes Harrison. N. Y., Macmillan, 1949. xix,375p. illus. maps.   4783

Weil, C. K., illus. SEE nos.
    80, Alaska Magazine Pub. Co. Book of animals. 1940;
    81, Alaska Magazine Pub. Co. Book of ... frontier. 1941;
    82, Alaska Magazine Pub. Co. Book of totems ... 1942.

WEIMER, M. D. K. Klondyke. M. D. K. Weimer's true story of the Alaska gold fields. no pl., [ca1903] 312p. front.(port.), pls.   4784

WELLCOME, HENRY SOLOMON. The story of Metlakahtla. London, Saxon, 1887. xx,483p. front. pls. ports. ANR. London, Saxon, 1887. 2d ed. xx,483p. front. pls. ports. ANR. London, Saxon, 1887. 3rd ed. xx,483p.,ii,45p. front.(port.), pls. [has added 45p.] ANR. London, Saxon, 1887. 4th ed. xx,483p. front.(port.), pls. append.   4785

WELLING, JAMES CLARKE. The Bering Sea arbitration; or, "pelagic sealing," juridically considered according to a particular analogy of municipal law. Washington, D. C., The University Press, 1893. 18p. (Columbian University Studies)   4786

WELLINGTON, JOHN L. The gold fields of Alaska; how to reach and operate them. A thrilling account of Mr. Wellington's successful trip into that country during the past season. In which he gives all the maps, statistics and such other general advice and information of interest to prospecting parties. Cripple Creek, Colo., Buckner Printing Co., 1896. 72p.   4787

WELLS, HARRY LAURENZ. Alaska and the Klondike; the new gold fields and how to reach them. Portland, Ore., Harry L. Wells, 1897. [printed by Multnomah Printing Co.] 72p. front. pls. maps.   4788

WELLS, HARRY LAURENZ. Alaska, the new Eldorado; its history,its gold fields, its scenery, its routes of travel. Portland, Ore., J. K. Gill Co., 1897. 88p. front. pls. maps(cold.) ANR. 1898.   4789

WELLS, RAYMOND M. Great Circle enroute temperatures for military application at heights of 10,000, 20,000, 30,000, 40,000 and 53,000 feet with supplementary surface temperatures. Renton, Washington, Boeing Co., Transport Division, 1962. 17ℓ [Reviews in Geophysics no. 8)   4790

Welzl, Jan. Auf den Spuren ... [c1937] SEE no. 4791.

Welzl, Jan. Ein leben ... SEE no. 4792.

Welzl, Jan. La vie ... SEE no. 4792.

Welzl, Jan. Po stopach ... 1930. SEE no. 4791.

WELZL, JAN. The quest for polar treasures. Translated by M. and R. Weatherall. N. Y., Macmillan, 1933. 352p. ANR. in Czech, Po stopach polarnich pokladu, published in 1930. ANR. in German, Auf den Spuren der Polarschätze aus dem Bescheschriften übertragen von Adolf Lane, Berlin, Scherl, [c1937]. 299(3)p. maps (incl. 1 fold.) [sequel to no. 4792]   4791

WELZL, JAN. Thirty years in the golden North. Translated by Paul Selver. N. Y., Macmillan, 1932. 336p. map(fold.) ANR. in Czech, Tricet let na zlatem Severu. OTHERS Ein Leben in der Arktis, ANR La vie des Esquimaux. [for sequel, SEE no. 4791]4792

Welzl, Jan. Tricet let na zlatem Severu. SEE no. 4792.

WENDT, FLORENCE. Life along the Yukon in 1935 as seen by a tourist. Madison, Wisconsin, The author, 1936. 118p. wrps.4793

WENDT, HERBERT. Entdeckungsfahrt durchs Robbenmeer; Georg Wilhelm Stellers Reise ans "Ende der Welt." [TITLE TR. Voyage of discovery across the seal sea; Georg Wilhelm Steller's journey to the "end of the world."] Stuttgart, Franckh'sche Verlagshandlung, 1952. 173p. pls. maps, bibliog. append. [biog. of Steller, and his part in Bering's Great Northern Expedition, 1741-42, also other Russian north Pacific voyages]   4794

WENTWORTH, ELAINE. Mission to Metlakatla. Boston, Houghton Mifflin, 1968. 192p. [*Father* Duncan and Tsimshian Indians] 4795

WERENSKIOLD, WERNER. Mean monthly air transport over the North Pacific Ocean. Kristiania, Grøndahl & Sons, 1922. 55p. charts, diagrs. (Geofysiske publikationer, vol. 2, no. 9) [incls. coasts of southern Alaska and Aleutian Islands]   4796

WEST COAST LUMBER TRADE EXTENSION BUREAU. Sitka spruce, a quality wood of high service. Seattle, 1927. 17p. illus.   4797

WEST, ELLSWORTH LUCE and ELEANOR RANSOM MAYHEW. Captain's papers; a log of whaling and other sea experiences. By Captain Ellsworth Luce West as told to Eleanor Ransom Mayhew. Barre, Mass., Barre Publishers, 1965. [c1965] front.(map), pls. [whaling and coastal freighting by owner and captain of *Corwin* after ship was retired from U. S. Revenue Cutter service] 4798

West, Geo. C., co-auth. SEE no. 2449, Kessel, B.

Westerlund, H. G., co-auth. SEE no. 2892, MacFie, H.

WESTERN ALASKA CONSTRUCTION CO. Railroad building in the Seward Peninsula; by Western Alaska Construction Company. [N. Y., 1904 ?] 2d ed. 24p. pls. map(fold.) [Council City and Solomon River Railroad] 4799

WESTERN UNION TELEGRAPH COMPANY. To the stockholders of the Western Union (and Russian Extension) Telegraph Company. Statement of the origin, organization and progress of the Russian-American Telegraph Western Union Extension, Collins' Overland Line, via Behring Strait and Asiatic Russia to Europe. Collated and prepared from official documents on file in the "Russian Bureau" of the Western Union Telegraph Company, by order of the Board of Directors. O. H. Palmer, Secretary. Rochester, N. Y., "Evening Express" Book and Job Printing Office, 1866. 165(3)p. 4800

Westersheim, *Ritter* von. SEE no. 4802, Wettstein, Richard.

Westrate, E. V., co-auth. SEE no. 977, Collier, Wm. R.

WETHERELL, J. E. Strange corners of the world. By J. E. Wetherell. Illustrated. N. Y., Thomas Nelson & Sons, 1927. [c1927] 244p. illus. ports. maps. [pp.6-12 Polar flights with brief mention of Amundsen's *Norge* and map of its flight. pp.149-54 Valley of 10,000 Smokes] 4801

WETTSTEIN, RICHARD, *Ritter* von Westersheim. Monographie der Gattung *Euphrasia*. [TITLE TR. Monograph of the genus *Euphrasia*] Leipzig, W. Engelmann, 1896. 316p. pls. maps. (Botanisches Institut. Arbeiten. No. 9. Deutsche Universität, Prague) [incls. Aleutian Island, other Alaskan species] 4802

Wetzel, J. L., tr. SEE no. 1029, [Cook, Jas.]

WEYER, EDWARD MOFFAT, jr. An Aleutian burial. N. Y., American Museum of Natural History, 1929. illus. ftntes. wrps. (Anthropological Papers, vol. 31, pt. 3, 1929. pp.219-38) [Stoll-McCracken Expedition, 1928] 4803

ALASKAN BIBLIOGRAPHY

WEYER, EDWARD MOFFAT, jr. Archaeological material from the vil-
lage site at Hot Springs, Port Möller, Alaska. N. Y., American
Museum of Natural History, 1930. illus. map, bibliog. wrps.
(Anthropological Papers, vol. 31, pt. 4, 1930. pp.239-79)[Stoll-
McCracken Expedition, 1928]   4804

WEYER, EDWARD MOFFAT, jr. The Eskimos; their environment and
folkways. New Haven, Yale University Press and London, Oxford
University Press, 1932. 491p. illus. tables(incl. 1 fold.),
diagr. maps(incl. some fold.), bibliog. index. (Lewis Stern
Memorial Fund Publication) ANR. Hamden, Conn., Archon Books,
1962. reprint. [Stoll-McCracken Expedition, 1928]   4805

What Fairbanks, Alaska's golden heart ... 1911. SEE
    no. 1517, Fairbanks Commercial Club.

What ! No igloos ? 1954. SEE no. 3534, PEO Sisterhood.

What's doing in Anchorage. 1955. SEE no. 239,
    Anchorage Guide Pub. Co.

WHEATON, HELEN. Prekaska's wife; a year in the Aleutians. By
Helen Wheaton. Illustrated. N. Y., Dodd Mead, 1945. [c1945]
251p. pls. ports. endmaps.   4806

Wheeler, Francis Rolt. SEE nos. 3872-3, Rolt-Wheeler, Francis.

WHEELER, JAMES COOPER. Captain Pete in Alaska. N. Y., Dutton,
1910. 302p. front. pls.   4807

WHEELER, OLIN D. Wonderland '98 ... Read it, then profit by your
reading, and go see it. Reached by the Northern Pacific Railway.
Chicago, Rand McNally, 1898. 103p. [printed yearly to 1906 with
minor title variations]   4808

WHELEN, TOWNSEND, edit. Hunting big game; an anthology of true
and thrilling adventures. Volume II. The Americas. Harrisburg,
Penna., Military Service Pub. Co., 1946. 282p. [incls. extracts
from writings of Charles Sheldon and Vilhjalmur Stefansson] 4809

WHERRY, JOSEPH H. Indian masks and myths of the West. N. Y.,
Funk & Wagnalls, [c1969] xiii,273p. fronts.(maps), photos,
ports. bibliog. indexes. ANR. N. Y., Bonanza books, n. d. reprint. [much about Alaskan Eskimos and Indians]   4810

WHERRY, JOSEPH H. The totem pole Indians. N. Y., Funk & Wagnalls, 1965. 152p. illus. map, append. index.   4811

JAY WHIPPLE MINING CO. Prospectus. Seattle, Ogden & Co., printers, n. d. 8p.   4812

WHITCOMBE AND TOMBS, LTD. Captain James Cook, for ages 12 to 14 years. Auckland, Whitcombe & Tombs, n. d. 59p. illus. front. (port.), maps. (Whitcombe's Story Books, no. 653)   4813

WHITCOMBE AND TOMBS, LTD. Under Cook's flag, with chronology of Cook's life. Auckland, Whitcombe & Tombs, [19_ ?] 148p. illus. port. maps. (Whitcombe's Historical Story Books)   4814

White, Anne Terry, edit. SEE no. 3956, Sanderson, Ivan T.

WHITE, ELMER J. "Stroller" White, tales of a Klondike newsman. Compiled and edited by R. N. De Armond. Vancouver, Canada, Mitchell Press, [c1969] 182p. [excerpts from 1900-1930 Klondike newspapers edited by White and others]   4815

White, Elmer J. SEE ALSO no. 4894, Willoughby, B.
     Alaskans all. 1933.

WHITE, E. W., PUBLISHING CO. Chips and sticks; with pictures. Battle Creek, Mich., E. W. White Pub. Co., 1886. 208p. front. pls. [articles by Rev. J. H. Waggoner, Eva Belle Giles, Will Carleton, others]   4816

WHITE, HELEN A. Alaska big game animals. [Anchorage, Anchorage Printing Co., ca 1961 ?] 20p. illus. by author, wrps.[four and one-half by six inches in size]   4817

WHITE, HELEN A. Alaska wildberry trails (with recipes). Anchorage, [Anchorage Printing Co., c1959] 68p. illus. by author, wrps. [four and one-half by five and seven-eighths inches in size]   4818

WHITE, HELEN A. Alaska wildflower trails. Anchorage, [Anchorage Printing Co., n. d. 1958 ?] 48p. illus. by author, index, wrps. [four and one-half by six inches in size]   4819

WHITE, HELEN A. Bird sampler; a pocket guide to fifty Alaskan birds. Anchorage, [Anchorage Printing Co., c1963] 51p. illus. by author, wrps. [four and one-half by six inches in size] 4820

WHITE, HELEN A. It's true about Alaska. A collection of little known facts about the 49th State. By Helen A. White, Wasilla, Alaska. [Anchorage, Anchorage Printing Co., ca 1962 ?] 12p. illus. by author, wrps. [five and one-half by eight and one-half inches in size]   4821

WHITE, HELEN A. Landscaping for Alaskans. Anchorage, [Anchorage Printing Co., c1962] 31p. sketches, glossary, append. bibliog. wrps. [five and one-half by eight and one-half inches in size]
          4822

583

WHITE, HELEN A. More about Alaska wildflower trails. Anchorage, [Anchorage Printing Co., c1962] 48p. front.(photo), photos, sketches by author, index, wrps. [four and one-half by six inches in size]   4823

WHITE, HELEN A. More about what's cooking in Alaska. Cover design and illustrations by Rex E. Harms. Anchorage, [Anchorage Printing Co., c1962] 44p. illus. bibliog. [five and one-half by eight and one-half inches in size]   4824

WHITE, HELEN A. What's cookin' in Alaska; recipes for Alaskan fish and game. Anchorage, [Anchorage Printing Co., c1961] 51p. illus. glossary, wrps. [five and one-half by eight and one-quarter inches in size]   4825

WHITE, JAMES. Boundary disputes and treaties, by James White. Toronto, Brook & Co., 1914. 958p. maps. [also in "Canada and its provinces" by Adam Shortt and Arthur G. Doughty, published in 1914]   4826

WHITE, JAMES. Treaty of 1825 - correspondence respecting the boundary between Russian America (Alaska) and British North America. By James White. Ottawa, printed for The Royal Society of Canada, 1915. wrps. (from Transactions of The Royal Society of Canada, vol. 9, ser. 3, 1915. pp.67-77) [letters of Sir Charles Bagot (British ambassador to Russia) to George Canning (British Secretary of State for Foreign Affairs) in 1823-24]   4827

WHITE PASS AND YUKON RAILWAY. A handbook of vacation trips in Alaska, Atlin and the Yukon on the White Pass and Yukon Route. [Seattle, 1928 ?] 59p. pls. tables, maps. [cf no. 1929]   4828

WHITE PASS AND YUKON RAILWAY. A tour through the land of nightless days; Alaska and the Canadian Yukon. [Chicago, 190_ ?] 24p. illus. photos.   4829

WHITE PASS AND YUKON RAILWAY. Alaska, along the shore and beyond. Chicago, Franklin Printers, [191_ ?] 24p. pls.(col.), wrps.4830

WHITE PASS AND YUKON RAILWAY. Alaska and the scenic Yukon and Atlin Lake country. [Seattle ? 19__ ?] (30)p. illus.   4831

WHITE PASS AND YUKON RAILWAY. Alaska and the Yukon Territory. Seattle, 1916. 22p. illus. map.   4832

WHITE PASS AND YUKON RAILWAY. Alaska, Atlin and the Yukon; the land where the world stays young. [Chicago, Poole Bros., 1928 ?] 46p. illus. photos, tables, map(col.) OTHERS[title varies] [Seattle, 1928 and 1930 ?] (46)p. ANR. no pl., n. d. 32p. photos, map(dble. col.) [32p. printing has text with title *Go North*, by Frederick Hiven]   4833

WHITE PASS AND YUKON RAILWAY. Alaska, Yukon and the scenic lake country. [Seattle ? 1939] (7)p. illus.   4834

WHITE PASS AND YUKON RAILWAY. Comments; Alaska, Atlin and the Yukon, by travelers over the White Pass and Yukon Route. [Seattle, 19__ ?] 24p. pls.   4835

White Pass and Yukon Railway. Go North. n. d. SEE no. 4833.

WHITE PASS AND YUKON RAILWAY. The incomparable Yukon. Chicago, Poole Bros., [1928 ?] 46p. illus. map. [photos courtesy Burton Holmes lectures, poem by Robert W. Service]   4836

WHITE PASS AND YUKON RAILWAY. The White Pass and Yukon Route; the scenic railway of the world. Descriptive and scenic souvenir. The Atlin gold fields, White Horse copper belt, Klondike, Yukon, and Cape Nome gold fields. To which is added a compendium of the principal points of interest along this picturesque route. Compiled and edited by Trevor Corry. [Seattle, Century Printing Co., 1901 ?] 144p. illus. map(col. fold.), adverts.   4837

WHITE PASS AND YUKON RAILWAY. White Pass and Yukon Route. no pl., 1925. 12p. illus.   4838

WHITE PASS AND YUKON RAILWAY. White Pass and Yukon Route to the land where beauty does abide. Chicago, [Poole Bros., c1923] 31p. illus.   4839

White, Richard. SEE no. 278, Arctic Brotherhood.

White, Ruth Taylor, illus. SEE no. 165, Albright, H. M.

WHITE, STEWART EDWARD and HARRY De VIGHNE. Pole star. By Stewart Edward White and Harry Devighne. N. Y., Doubleday Doran, 1935. [c1935] 1st ed. 452p. [fict. biog. of Alexander Baranov in Sitka]   4840

WHITE, STEWART EDWARD. Wild geese calling. Garden City, N. Y., Doubleday Doran, 1940. [c1940] viii,477p. ANR. 1942. viii,577p. endmaps. [logging in southeastern Alaska and state of Washington - fict.]   4841

White, Stewart Edward. SEE ALSO no. 3607,
    Pinkerton, Kathrene S. Three's a crew. [c1940]

White, "Stroller" SEE no. 4815, White, Elmer J.

White, W. R. H. SEE no. 4863, Wigan, S. O.

WHITEHEAD, ROBERT. The first book of bears. By Robert Whitehead. Illustrations by James Teason. N. Y., Franklin Watts, [c1966] 54p. front. illus. map, index. [chapt. on Alaskan brown and Kodiak bears]   4842

WHITING, FENTON BLAKEMORE. Grit, grief and gold; a true narrative of an Alaskan pathfinder. By Dr. Fenton B. Whiting. Seattle, Peacock Pub. Co., 1933. 247p. front. pls. ports. [biog. M. J. Heney, builder of White Pass and Yukon Railway]   4843

WHITNEY, ELLIOTT [pseud.] The black fox of the Yukon. Illustrated by Harry W. Armstrong. Chicago, Reilly & Britton, 1917. 272p. illus. [fict. - author is Harry L. Sayler]   4844

WHITNEY, ELLIOTT [pseud.] The bully of the frozen north. By Elliott Whitney. Chicago, Reilly & Lee, Pub., [c1936]   268p. [fict. Kodiak bear hunt - author is Harry L. Sayler]   4845

WHITNEY, ELLIOTT [pseud.] The king bear of Kodiak Island. Illustrated by Don Sayre Groesbeck. Chicago, Reilly & Britton, 1912. 268p. illus. [fict. - author is Harry L. Sayler]   4846

WHITTLE, WILLIAM C. Cruises of the Confederate States steamers "Shenandoah" and "Nashville." Norfolk, Va., 1910.   32p. [CSS *Shenandoah* and whaling vessels off Alaskan Arctic coast]   4847

WHYMPER, FREDERICK. A journey from Norton Sound, Bering Sea, to Fort Youkon (junction of Porcupine and Youkon Rivers).   London, W. Clowes & Son, 1868. 19p. map(fold.) (extracted from J. Royal Geographical Society, vol. 38, 1868. pp.219-37)   4848

WHYMPER, FREDERICK. Alaska; Reisen und Erlebnisse im hoben Norden, autorisirte Deutsche ausgabe von Dr. Friedrich Steger. Braunschweig, Druck und Verlag von G. Westermann, 1869.   351p. front. pls. map. [a tr. of no. 4851]   4849

WHYMPER, FREDERICK. The heroes of the Arctic and their adventures. London, Society for Promoting Christian Knowledge, and N. Y., Pott, Young & Co., n. d. [ca 1875] 302p. pls. map(fold.) [John Franklin, others]   4850

WHYMPER, FREDERICK. Travel and adventure in the Territory of Alaska, formerly Russian America - now ceded to the United States - and in various other parts of the North Pacific. By Frederick Whymper. With map and illustrations. London, John Murray, 1868. xx,331p. front. pls. map(fold.) ANR. London, 1869. ANR. N. Y., Harper, 1869. xix,21-353p. front. pls. map(fold.) ANR. N. Y., Harper, 1871. ANR. Ann Arbor, Mich., University Microfilms, 1966. facsim. reprint of 1868 ed. xx,331p. front. pls. map. (March of America Facsimile Series no. 93) [Russo-American Telegraph Expedition, Western Union Telegraph System. For translations SEE nos. 4848, 4852 and 4853]   4851

WHYMPER, FREDERICK. Voyages et aventures dans la Colombia anglaise, l'ile Vancouver, le territoire d'Alaska et la California, abrégé par H. Vattemore. Paris, Hachette et Cie, 1880. abr. ed. 192p. illus. maps. [a tr. of no. 4851]   4852

WHYMPER, FREDERICK. Voyages et aventures dans l'Alaska (anciennes Amerique russe) ouvrage tr. de l'anglais avec l'autorisation de l'auteur par Emile Jonveaux, illustre de 37 gravures sur bois. Paris, Hachette et Cie, 187. 412p. pls. map(fold.) [a tr. of no. 4851. For a later French ed. SEE no. 4852]   4853

Whymper, Frederick. SEE ALSO no. 1783,
    Gordon, W. J. Round about North Pole. 1907.

WICK, CARL IRVING. Ocean harvest; the story of commercial fishing in Pacific Coast waters. Seattle, Superior Pub. Co., 1946. 185p. pls. charts, diagrs. plans. [hist. Alaskan salmon canning industry]   4854

WICKERSHAM, JAMES. Address at the driving of the golden spike and the completion of the Tanana Mines Railway, at Fairbanks, Alaska, July 17, 1905. Fairbanks, 1905. 9p.   4855

WICKERSHAM, JAMES. An address delivered at the laying of the cornerstone of the Alaska Agricultural College and School of Mines on July 4th, 1915, by Hon. James Wickersham, Delegate to Congress from Alaska. [Fairbanks ? 1915] (7)p.   4856

WICKERSHAM, JAMES. Alaska, its resources, present condition and needed legislation, being a synopsis of an address delivered by Hon. James Wickersham, U. S. District Judge of Alaska, before the respective Chambers of Commerce of Seattle on November 5, 1902 and Tacoma, November 11, 1902. Tacoma, Allen & Lamborn Print. Co., 1902. 15(1)p.   4857

WICKERSHAM, JAMES. Old Yukon. Tales - Trails - and Trials. By Hon. James Wickersham of Juneau, Alaska. Washington, D. C., Washington Law Book Co., 1938. [c1938] 514p. front.(map), illus. ports. facsims. map, index.   4858

WICKERSHAM, JAMES. Speech of Hon. James Wickersham, Delegate to Congress, delivered before joint session first Alaska territorial legislature, Juneau, Alaska, March 10, 1913. [Juneau ? 1913] (8)p.   4859

WICKERSHAM, JAMES. The organization of territorial government in Alaska. Do you favor a government by the people of Alaska, or a government by the Federal bureaus ? Which kind is your legislature organizing ? An appeal to Alaskans by James Wickersham. [Juneau ? 1927] 32p.   4860

WIEDEMANN, THOMAS. Cheechako into sourdough, by Thomas Wiedemann, (the Klondike Kid). Portland, Ore., Binfords & Mort, [c1942] 266p. front. pls. endmaps, index. [steamers *Eliza Anderson* and *W. K. Mervin*, Klondike 1897]   4861

WIEDEMANN, THOMAS and LUTHER NORRIS. The saga of Alaska. By Thomas Wiedemann, Sr. and Luther ("Doc") Norris. Prairie City, Ill., The Press of James A. Decker, [c1946] 85p. front.(2 sep. ports.), pls. sketches. [poetry] 4862

Wien, Fritz, Harold, Noel, Ralph and Sigurd. SEE nos.
    2442, Kennedy, Kay J. Wien brothers' story. 1967;
    3658, Potter, J. Flying frontiersmen. 1956.

Wiese, Kurt, illus. SEE nos.
    2002, Hayes, F. S. Alaskan hunter. 1959;
    2004, Hayes, F. S. Eskimo hunter. 1945;
    2070, Henry, M. Alaska, in story ... 1941;
    2639, Lathrop, W. Juneau, sleigh dog. 1942.

WIGAN, S. O. and W. R. H. WHITE. Tsunami of March 27-29, 1964, west coast of Canada. Ottawa, 1964. 12p. (Canada. Dept. of Mines and Technical Surveys) 4863

Wiggins, E. J., co-auth. SEE no. 3847, Robinson, E.

WIGGINS, IRA LOREN and JOHN H. THOMAS. A flora of the Alaskan Arctic slope. Toronto, University of Toronto Press, 1962. 452p. illus. tables, gazetteer, glossary, maps, bibliog. index. (Arctic Institute of North America Special Pub. no. 4) 4864

WIGGINS, IRA LOREN, edit. Arctic biology. Corvallis, Oregon State University Press, 1957. illus. pls. bibliogs. (18th Biology Colloquium, 1957) [for 2d Colloquia, SEE no. 1936] 4865

WIGGINS, IRA LOREN, edit. Current biological research in the Alaskan Arctic. Stanford, Calif., Stanford University Press, 1953. vii,55p. diagrs. tables, maps. (Stanford University Pubs. University ser. Biol. sciences, vol. XI, no. 1) 4866

WIKSTROM, ROBERT. Alaska oddities, a collection of true and fascinating facts about Alaska, the 49th star in our flag. Compiled and drawn in cartoon style by Robert Wikstrom. Seattle, R. D. Seal, 1958. (80)p. illus. 4867

Wilbur, M. E., tr. SEE no. 1362, Duflot de Mofras, E.

Wilby, G. V., co-auth. SEE no. 952, Clemens, W. A.

Wilcox, O. R., co-edit. SEE no. 4304, Stefansson, V.

Wilde, G. L., co-auth. SEE no. 4175, Skinner, J. W.

Wilderness Conference, 9th, S. F., 1965. SEE no. 4148, Sierra Club.

Wilderness in a changing world. 1966. SEE no. 4148, Sierra Club.

Wildhaber, R., co-edit. SEE no. 4006, Schmitz, C. A.

WILEY, S. C. Colonization and settlement in the Americas; a selected bibliography. Ottawa, 1960. 68p. (Canada. Dept. of Mines and Technical Surveys. Geographical Branch. Bibliographical Series, no. 25) [text in Eng. and French by region]   4868

Wiley, Sarah King, co-auth. SEE no. 4869, Wiley, Wm. H.

WILEY, WILLIAM HALSTEAD and SARAH KING WILEY. The Yosemite, Alaska, and the Yellowstone. London, Offices of "Engineering," and N. Y., J. Wiley & Sons, 1893. 230p. front.(port.), illus. map(fold.) [reprint from Engineering]   4869

WILKERSON, ALBERT SAMUEL. Some frozen deposits in the gold fields of Interior Alaska; a study of the Pleistocene deposits of Alaska. N. Y., American Museum of Natural History, 1932. 22p. illus. figs. diagrs. maps. (Novitates, no. 525. May 1932)   4870

WILKINS, GEORGE HUBERT. Flying the Arctic. By Captain George H. Wilkins. With 31 illustrations. N. Y., Putnam, 1928. [c1928] 1st print. xv,336p. front.(port.), pls. ports. append. [Detroit Arctic Expedition and Carl Ben Eielson]   4871

WILKINS, GEORGE HUBERT and H. M. SHERMAN. Thoughts through space; a remarkable adventure in the realm of the mind. N. Y., Creative Press, 1942. [c1942] 421p. front.(port.), pls. ports. facsims. ANR. Westport, Conn., Associated Booksellers, 1957. ANR. N. Y., C. & R. Anthony, Publishers, 1961. [attempts to locate missing Russian flier, S. Levanevskiĭ in Arctic in 1937]   4872

Wilkins, George Hubert. SEE ALSO nos.
    203, American Geog. Soc. Problems polar research ... 1928;
    1856, Grierson, J. Sir Hubert Wilkins ... 1960;
    4326, Stefansson, V. Unsolved mysteries ... 1938;
    4401, Supf, P. Flieger erobern die Pole. 1957;
    4493, Thomas, L. Famous first flights. 1968;
    4496, Thomas, L. Sir Hubert Wilkins ... 1961.

Wilkins, Sir Hubert. SEE nos. 4871-2, Wilkins, George Hubert.

Will you hear knock of opportunity ? 1914. SEE no. 139,
    Alaska Utilities Development Co.

Willard, Caroline (McCoy). SEE nos. 4873-5,
    Willard, Carrie M. White.

WILLARD, CARRIE M. WHITE. Children of the far North. By Mrs. Eugene S. Willard. N. Y., Woman's Board of Home Missions, n. d. 12p. [Presbyterian]   4873

WILLARD, CARRIE M. WHITE. Kin-da-shon's wife; an Alaskan story. By Mrs. Eugene S. Willard. N. Y., Fleming H. Revell, [c1892] v,6-281p. front. pls. ANR. N. Y., Fleming H. Revell, n. d. [c1892] 4th ed. xi,6-281p. front.(pl.), pls. [Chilkat Indians]
4874

WILLARD, CARRIE M. WHITE. Life in Alaska. Letters of Mrs. Eugene S. Willard, edited by her sister, Mrs. Eva McClintock. Philadelphia, Presbyterian Board of Publications, 1884. 384p. front. pls. maps. [mission to Tlingit Indians in southeastern Alaska]
4875

Willard, Mrs. Eugene S. SEE nos. 4873-5,
    Willard, Carrie M. White.

WILLIAMS, ARCHIBALD. Conquering the air; the romance of the development and use of aircraft. N. Y., Thomas Nelson & Sons, 1926. [Chapt. 19 on polar flights. Chapt. 20 about first around the world flight in 1924]
4876

Williams, Beryl. SEE no. 1483, Epstein, S.

Williams, Daniel. SEE no. 1659, Freuchen, Peter.

Williams, Eliza Azelia. SEE no. 4879, Williams, Harold, edit.

WILLIAMS, FRANCES. I asked for it. By Mrs. Frances Williams. Philadelphia, Dorrance, 1954. 140p. illus. [driving the Alaska Highway]
4877

WILLIAMS, GLYNDWR. The British search for the Northwest Passage in the eighteenth century. London, Longmans, 1962. 306p. illus. maps, bibliog. (Royal Commonwealth Society Imperial Studies, no. 24) [incls. James Cook and George Vancouver]
4878

WILLIAMS, HAROLD, edit. One whaling family. Edited by Harold Williams. Illustrated with photographs. Boston, Houghton Mifflin, 1964. [c1964] xii,401p. pls. ports. endmaps, appends. [diary of Eliza Williams, whaler *Florida*, 1858-61 and the William Williams manuscript, whaler *Florence*, 1873-74]
4879

WILLIAMS, HENRY LLEWELYN. History of the adventurous voyage and terrible shipwreck of the U. S. Steamer "Jeannette," in the Polar Seas. N. Y., A. T. B. DeWitt, 1882. 95p. illus.
4880

WILLIAMS, HOWEL, edit. Landscapes of Alaska, their geologic evolution. Prepared by members of the United States Geological Survey. Published in coöperation with the National Park Service, United States Department of the Interior. Edited by Howel Williams. Berkeley, University of California Press, 1958. [c1958] xii,148p. front.(tipped-in col. pl.), pls. figs. maps, glossary, append. index.
4881

WILLIAMS, JAY P. Alaskan adventure. Harrisburg, Penna., Stackpole, 1952. 299p. pls. diagrs. appends. [wildlife in southeastern Alaska]   4882

WILLIAMS, JOHN G. A Forty-Niner's experience in the Klondike.
How to get there. When to start. General information. Boston,
Pinkham Press, 1897. 29p. port.   4883

Williams, Marilyn B. SEE no. 600, Bolanz, Marie [pseud.]

WILLIAMS, MAXCINE MORGAN. Alaska wildflower glimpses. Juneau,
printed at the Totem Press, 1952. 47p. illus. photos. ANR.
Juneau, Totem Press, 1953. 2d ed. 52p. front.(photo), photos
by author, sketches by Claudia Kelsey, list of botanical names,
wrps.   4884

WILLIAMS, SHERMAN. New York's part in history. N. Y., Appleton,
1915. 390p. [references to Wm. H. Seward and Alaska purchase]
                                                                4885

Williams, "Slim." SEE no. 3171, Morenus, R.

Williams, Wm. F. SEE no. 4879, Williams, Harold.

WILLIAMSON, JAMES ALEXANDER. Builders of the empire. Oxford,
Clarendon Press, 1942. reprint. illus. port. maps.[has section
on James Cook]   4886

WILLIAMSON, JAMES ALEXANDER. Cook and the opening of the Pacific.
N. Y., Macmillan, 1948. 251p. front.(port.), pls. maps. (Teach
Yourself History Library, edited by A. L. Rowse)   4887

Williamson, Joe, co-auth. SEE no. 3297, Newell, G.

WILLIAMSON, THAMES ROSS. Far north country. N. Y., Duell, Sloan
& Pearce, [c1944] xi,235p. endmaps, index. (American Folkways
ser., edited by Erskine Caldwell)   4888

WILLIAMSON, THAMES ROSS. North after seals. Boston, Houghton
Mifflin, 1934. 266p.   4889

WILLIAMSON, THAMES ROSS. On the reindeer trail. Illustrated by
Lee Townsend. Boston, Houghton Mifflin, 1932. 242p. front.
pls.   4890

WILLIAMSON, THAMES ROSS. The earth told me. N. Y., Simon &
Schuster, 1930. 350p. ANR. London, 1931. 287p. [fict.]   4891

WILLIS, A. R. North of the Yukon. N. Y., Avalon Books, n. d.
reprint. 254p. [c1940 by Stovel Press and c1955 by Bouregy &
Curl]   4892

WILLOUGHBY, BARRETT. Alaska holiday. By Barrett Willoughby. Boston, Little Brown, 1940. [c1940] 295p. front.(pl.), pls. ports.   4893

WILLOUGHBY, BARRETT. Alaskans all. By Barrett Willoughby. Boston, Houghton Mifflin, 1933. 234p. front. pls. ports. facsim.
4894

WILLOUGHBY, BARRETT. Gentlemen unafraid. N. Y., Putnam, 1928. 285p. front. pls. ports.   4895

WILLOUGHBY, BARRETT. River House. Boston, Little Brown, 1936. 389p. ANR. N. Y., Triangle Books, 1936. [fict. - southeastern Alaska setting]   4896

WILLOUGHBY, BARRETT. Rocking moon; a romance of Alaska. N. Y., Putnam, 1925. [c1925] 360p. front.(pl.) ANR. N. Y., A. L. Burt, 1925. [fict. - Aleutian Islands setting - SEE ALSO no. 4902]   4897

WILLOUGHBY, BARRETT. Sitka, portal to romance. With illustrations. Boston, Houghton Mifflin, 1930. [c1930] x,233p. front. (pl.), pls. ports. facsim.   4898

WILLOUGHBY, BARRETT. Sitka, to know Alaska one must first know Sitka. London, Hodder & Stoughton, n. d. [c1930] 248p. illus. ports.   4899

WILLOUGHBY, BARRETT. Sondra O'Moore. Boston, Little Brown, 1939. 320p. ANR. N. Y., Grosset & Dunlap, n. d. reprint. [fict.]   4900

WILLOUGHBY, BARRETT. Spawn of the North. Boston, Houghton Mifflin, 1932. [c1932] 349p. ANR. N. Y., Triangle Books, n. d. reprint. [fict. - Ketchikan setting]   4901

WILLOUGHBY, BARRETT. The fur trail omnibus; containing two complete novels. Where the sun swings North. Rocking moon. N. Y., Grosset & Dunlap, n. d. [c1925] 360p. [refer to nos. 4897 and 4905]   4902

WILLOUGHBY, BARRETT. The golden totem; a novel of modern Alaska. Boston, Little brown, 1945. 315p.   4903

WILLOUGHBY, BARRETT. The trail eater. A romance of the All-Alaska Sweepstakes. N. Y., Putnam, 1929. [c1929] 1st ed. vii, 400p. glossary. [fict. based on Nome sled dog races]   4904

WILLOUGHBY, BARRETT. Where the sun swings North. N. Y., Putnam, 1922. viii,355p. ANR. N. Y., A. L. Burt, n. d. reprint. [also in omnibus vol., SEE no. 4902]   4905

Willoughby, Barrett. SEE ALSO no. 888,
    Chandler, Edna W. Pioneer ... skies ... Ben Eielson. 1959.

Willoughby, Florance (Barrett). SEE nos. 4893-4905,
    Willoughby, Barrett.

WILLOUGHBY, WILLIAM FRANKLIN. Territories and dependencies of
the United States. Their government and administration. By
William Franklin Willoughby, Treasurer of Porto Rico. N. Y.,
Century Co., 1905. [c1905] xi,334p. append. index. [contains
brief textual references to Alaska]   4906

WILLSON, BECKLES. The great company; being a history of the
honourable company of merchants-adventurers trading into Hudson's
Bay. By Beckles Willson with an introduction by Lord Strathcona
and Mount Royal, present Governor of the Hudson's Bay Company with
original drawings by Arthur Heming and maps, plans and illustrations. Toronto, Copp, Clark Co., 1899. [c1899] xxii,17-541p.
front.(port.), pls. ports. sketches, facsims. maps(incl. 1 fold.),
appends. index. ANR. London, Smith, Elder & Co., 1900. 2 vols.
rev. and enl. xxxii,339p.+xii,369p. fronts. pls. ports. facsims.
(incl. 1 fold.), maps, appends. index. [incls. Alaska boundary
documents with map, and references to Alaska purchase]   4907

Wilmeth, R. H., jr., co-auth. SEE no. 1709, Giddings, L. J., jr.

WILMOVSKY, N. J. The utilization of fishery resources by the
Arctic Alaskan Eskimos. Stanford, Calif., Stanford University,
1956. 8p. (Stanford University Natural History Museum Occas.
Papers, no. 2)   4908

WILSON, CAROL GREEN. Alice Eastwood's wonderland; the adventures
of a botanist. S. F., [c1955] ed. ltd. to 2000 copies. 222p.
front.(port.) [has one chapt. on Alaska and Yukon]   4909

WILSON, GEORGE. George Turner's betrayal of his country.[Lexing-
ton, Mo. ?], 1904. 4p. map. [railroad prospects and coal deposits in Alaska]   4910

WILSON, H. P. A comparison of theoretical-actual surface wind
data. Toronto, 1961. 16p. tables. (Canada. Meteorological
Branch, Circ. Cir-3518, TEC 364. Aug. 1, 1961) [incls. date for
Pt. Barrow]   4911

Wilson, Jas., co-auth. SEE no.4599, Tytler, P. F.

WILSON, JAMES A. Bits of Alaska. Illustrated with photos by
courtesy of Pacific Coast Steamship Co. [S. F., c1908] 59p.4912

WILSON, KATHERINE. Copper-Tints. A book of Cordova sketches. By
Katherine Wilson. Drawings by Eustace P. Ziegler. Cordova, Cordova Daily Times Press, 1923. 44p. front.(port.), sketches,

wrps. ANR. Seattle, Shorey Book Store, 1966. facsim. reprint ltd. to 500 copies. [Shorey print. a facsimile reproduction published by The Cordova Centennial Committee, 1967]   4913

Wilson, Patten, illus. SEE no. 2073, Herbert, A.

Wilson, R. P., illus. SEE no. 4712, The voice of Yukon ... 1930.

Wilson, Riley, co-auth. SEE no. 1427, Eisenlohr, L. H.

Wilson, S. D., co-auth. SEE no. 4038, Seed, H. G.

WILSON, VEAZIE. Glimpses of Alaska. A collection of views of the interior of Alaska and the Klondike District. From photographs by Veazie Wilson. Compiled by Miss Esther Lyons. Chicago, Rand McNally, 1897. 96ℓ photos with captions. [cf no. 4915]
4914

WILSON, VEAZIE. Glimpses of the Yukon gold fields and Dawson Route. Vancouver, Thomson Stationery Co., 1895. 96ℓ photos. [SEE ALSO no. 4914]   4915

WILSON, VEAZIE. Guide to the Yukon gold fields, where they are and how to reach them. With maps and many illustrations. Seattle, Calvert Co., 1895. front. pls. maps(fold.) 72p.,13p.,22p. ANR. Seattle, 1897. rev. ed.   4916

WILT, RICHARD. E-Tooka-Shoo, the cold little Eskimo boy. N. Y., Julian Messner, 1941. 47p. illus.(col.)   4917

WINCHELL, MARY E. Home by the Bering Sea. Caldwell, Idaho, Caxton, 1951. [c1951] 226p. photos, endmaps. [by matron of Jessie Lee Home, Methodist mission school for Aleut children at Unalaska in 1900]   4918

Winchell, Oscar. SEE no. 4719, Wachel, Pat.

WINCHESTER, J. D. Capt. J. D. Winchester's experience on a voyage from Lynn, Massachusetts to San Francisco, Cal. and to the Alaskan gold fields. Salem, Mass., Newcomb & Gauss, Printers, 1900. [c1900] 251p. front. sketches by author.   4919

WINFIELD, ARTHUR M. [pseud.] The Rover Boys in Alaska; or, lost in the fields of ice. By Arthur M. Winfield. Illustrated. N. Y., Grosset & Dunlap, n. d. [c1914] 285p. front.(pl.), pls. (The Rover Boys' Series for Young Americans) [author is Edward Stratemeyer]   4920

Wingert, P. S., co-auth. SEE nos.
     1684, Garfield, V. E. Tsimshian Indians and arts. 1966;
     4202, Smith, Marian W. Tsimshian arts and music. 1951.

WINKLER, HEINRICH. Uralaltaische Völker und Sprachen von Dr. Heinrich Winkler. Berlin, Ferd. Dümmlers Verlagsbuchhandlung Harrwitz und Gossman, 1884. 480p. [compares North American and Asiatic Eskimo languages]   4921

WINSLOW, ISAAC O. Our American neighbors. Boston, D. C. Heath, 1921. rev. 200p. [Alaska on pp.34-49]   4922

WINSLOW, KATHRYN. Alaska bound. N. Y., Dodd Mead, 1960. 281p. pls. maps.   4923

WINSLOW, KATHRYN. Big pan-out; the story of the Klondike gold rush. N. Y., W. W. Norton & Co., [c1951] 1st ed. x,247p. pls. endmaps. [based partially on diaries of Howard V. Sutherland and John Ver Mehr]   4924

WINTER AND POND CO., Juneau. Juneau, Alaska. [Juneau, Winter & Pond Co., c1909] (22)ℓ photos(mounted, incl. 2 fold.), cover photo, wrps. [oblong photograph album]   4925

WINTER AND POND CO., Juneau. Juneau, gold belt city. Juneau, 1911. 24p. ANR. Seattle, Shorey Book Store, 1964. facsim. ed. [photograph album]   4926

WINTER AND POND CO., Juneau. The totems of Alaska. [Juneau, Winter & Pond Co., c1905] 12p. pls. OTHERS 1909 and 1915. var. pagings. [photograph album]   4927

WINTER AND POND CO., Juneau. Types of Alaska natives. [Juneau, Winter & Pond Co., c1905] (12)ℓ photos(mounted), cover photo, wrps. [photograph album]   4928

WINTER, JAMES M. New York to Alaska. Voyage of steamer "Dolphin" May to July, 1900. A day to day personal narrative by James M. Winter, Chief Engineer. Middletown, N. Y., privately printed, 1943.   4929

WINTHER, OSCAR OSBURN. The great northwest; a history. N. Y., Knopf, 1947. 383p. illus. port. maps. ANR. N. Y., Knopf, 1950. 2d ed. rev. and enl. xviii,491p.,xxxp. bibliog. (Western Ameri-cana series)   4930

WIRT, LOYAL LINCOLN. Alaskan adventure; a tale of our last frontier and of "Whiskers" the gallant leader of the first dog team to cross Alaska. N. Y., Fleming H. Revell, 1937. 124p. front.(port.), pls. ANR. London, n. d. [c1937] 124p.   4931

WIRT, SHERWOOD ELIOT. Cracked ice; a symposium of Alaskan de-mentia, designed more to harrow than to beguile. Illustrated by Milt Schenkofsky. Juneau, [c1937] 32p. illus.[poetry]   4932

WISHART, ANDREW. The Bering Sea question; the arbitration treaty and the award, with a map. By Andrew Wishart. Edinburgh, W. Green & Sons, 1893. 54p. front.(fold. map)   4933

WISHAW, LORNA. As far as you'll take me. N. Y., Dodd Mead, 1958. 216p. [Alaska Highway]   4934

Wisner, Wm. L., co-auth. SEE nos.
    1056, Cook, Jos. J. Killer whale ! 1963;
    1057, Cook, Jos. J. Warrior whale. 1966.

WISSLER, CLARK. Archaeology of the Polar Eskimo. By Clark Wiss-ler. N. Y., American Museum of Natural History, 1918. illus. figs.(in text), map(fold.), wrps. (Anthropological Papers, vol. 22, pt. 3, 1918. pp.105-66) [incls. comparison artifacts found in Crocker Land, Greenland in 1813-18 with those in Alaskan and other Arctic locations]   4935

WISSLER, CLARK. Harpoons and darts in the Stefánsson collection. By Clark Wissler. N. Y., American Museum of Natural History, 1916. illus. figs.(in text), wrps. (Anthropological Papers, vol. 14, pt. 2, 1916. pp.397-443) [compares Alaskan and Green-landic - paper also in no. 4324, qv]   4936

WISTING, OSCAR. 16 år med Roald Amundsen; fra pol til pol. [TITLE TR. 16 years with Roald Amundsen, from Pole to Pole] Oslo, Gyldendal, 1930. 206p. pls. ports.   4937

WITEMAN, GEORGE (TWEEDDALE) North of '62. A story of adventure, Buffalo, N. Y., Foster & Stewart Pub. Co., 1946. [c1946] 235p. endmaps. [Chisana, Wrangell Mtns.]   4938

[WITTEMANN, A.] Picturesque Alaska. N. Y., The Albertype Co., 1888. 4p.,12ℓ photos. ANR. WITH TITLE Picturesque Alaska in photo-gravure. From recent negatives. N. Y., Albertype Co., 1892. 1p.,18ℓ photos. [photograph album]   4939

Woldt, A., edit. SEE no. 2315, Jacobsen, J. A.

WOLFE, ALFRED. In Alaskan waters. Caldwell, Idaho, Caxton, 1942. [c1942] 1st print. 196p. front. pls. port. diagr. [commercial salmon and halibut fishing, southeastern and Kodiak waters]   4940

WOLFE, LINNIE MARSH, edit. John of the mountains; the unpub-lished journals of John Muir. Boston, Houghton Mifflin, 1938. 459p.   4941

WOLFE, LINNIE MARSH. Son of the wilderness; the life of John Muir. N. Y., Knopf, 1945. 364p. front. pls. ports. facsim. (fold.)   4942

WOLFE, LOUIS. Let's go to the Klondike gold rush. N. Y., Putnam, 1964. illus. 4943

WOLFF, ERNEST. Handbook for the Alaskan prospector. By Ernest Wolff. With contributions by Donald J. Cook and Mrs. Claude Matthews. Containing Part I, Geology, and Part II, Prospecting techniques. Edited by Richard H. Byrns. Fort Collins, Colorado, published by The Burnt River Exploration and Development Co., [c1964] xvii,428p. front. figs. tables, maps, endmaps, glossary, append. bibliog. index. 4944

WOLFF, FERDINAND LUDWIG, von. Der Vulkanismus. Bd. 2: Specieller Teil, Tl., Häfte 1-2. [TITLE TR. Volcanology. vol. 2, Special Part, pt. 1, sect. 1-2] Stuttgart, F. Enke, 1923-29. 828p. illus. tables, maps(sketch), maps(fold.) [incls. Aleutian Arc, Wrangell volcano group and Kamchatka-Kurile Arc] 4945

WOLFF, ODIN. Levnetsefterretninger om den berømte søemand og udødelige Landopdager commandeur Vitus Jonassen Beering ... af Professor og Dr. Odin Wolff. København, P. D. Køpping, 1822. 60p. [biog. of Vitus Bering] 4946

Wollschläger, Alfred. SEE nos.
    2362, Johann, A. E. [pseud.] Pelzjäger ... 1937;
    2363, Johann, A. E. [pseud.] Bolyongások New Yorktól...1942.

WOMAN'S AMERICAN BAPTIST HOME MISSION SOCIETY. Alaska; pocket edition studies in home missions. Chicago, 1916. 31p. 4947

WOMAN'S AMERICAN BAPTIST HOME MISSION SOCIETY. Alaska; totem poles, polygamy, slavery, ingenuity, thrift and pride of office. Chicago, 1911. 7p. 4948

WOMAN'S SOCIETY OF CHRISTIAN SERVICE, Juneau. Come into my kitchen. A sharing of recipes by the Woman's Society of Christian Service from members and friends of the Juneau Methodist Church. Juneau, Alaska. Cover and illustrations by Claudia Kelsey. [no pl., Oct. 1967] 90p. illus. wrps. ringbound. 4949

WOMAN'S SOCIETY OF CHRISTIAN SERVICE OF METHODIST CHURCH, Nome. Nome cook book. [Nome ?, 1968 ?] 48p. illus. wrps. 4950

Wonderland '98 ... Read it ... 1898. SEE no. 4808, Wheeler, O.D.

Wonderland; or, Alaska ... 1886. SEE no. 4022, Schwatka, F.

Wonderland; or, the Pacific ... 1888. SEE no. 4022, Schwatka, F.

Wonderland; or, twelve weeks ... 1894. SEE no. 3494, Parkinson, Edw. S.

WOOD, FRANCES ELIZABETH. Mount Rainier, Mount McKinley, Olympic;
with Crater Lake, Lassen Volcanic,Lava Beds, Craters of the Moon,
Katmai, by Frances Wood. Chicago, Follet Pub. Co., 1964. 32p.
illus.(col.) (Our National Parks Series)   4951

Wood, Harold. SEE no. 3442, Owens, F. R.

WOOD, JAMES PLAYSTED. Alaska, the great land. N. Y., Meredith
Press, 1967. 1st ed. 181p. endmaps, bibliog. index.   4952

WOOD, PETER. Peter Wood's 1945 Alaska business directory. [Fair-
banks ?, 1945]   4953

WOOD, PETER. Unbelievable years; the truth about Alaska. Playa
del Rey, Calif., Littlepage Press, [c1969] 236p. illus. photos,
facsims. [by editor of Alaska Newsletter]   4954

WOODBRIDGE, HENSLEY C., JOHN LONDON and GEORGE H. TWENEY. Jack
London, a bibliography. Georgetown, Calif., Talsiman Press,
1966. [c1966] 422p. front.(port.), photos, facsims.(title
pages), indexes.   4955

WOODCOCK, GEORGE. Ravens and prophets;an account of journeyings
in British Columbia, Alberta, and southern Alaska. London, A.
Wingate, [c1952] 244p. illus.   4956

WOODMAN, ABBY JOHNSON. Picturesque Alaska; a journal of a tour
among the mountains, seas and islands of the northwest, from San
Francisco to Sitka. Boston, Houghton Mifflin, 1889. [c1889]
212p. front.(dble. map), pls. OTHERS 1889, 1890 and 1898. 4957

WOODS, HENRY FITZWILLIAM and EDWARD E. P. MORGAN. God's loaded
dice, Alaska 1897-1930. By Edward E. P. Morgan in collaboration
with Henry F. Woods. Limited edition. Caldwell, Idaho, Caxton
Printers, 1948. [c1948] ltd. numbered signed ed. of 1000 copies.
298p. pls. ports.   4958

WOODWORTH, JAMES. Kodiak bear, Alaskan adventure. Harrisburg,
Penna., Stackpole, 1959. illus. map. [by a professional guide]
                                                              4959

WOOLLEN, WILLIAM WATSON. The inside passage to Alaska, 1792-1920,
with an account of the North Pacific coast from Cape Mendocino
to Cook Inlet, from the accounts left by Vancouver and other
early explorers, and from the author's journals of exploration
and travel in that region, edited from his original manuscripts
by Paul L. Haworth. Cleveland, A. H. Clark Co., 1924. 2 vols.
fronts. pls. ports. maps.   4960

THE WORKING MAN'S GUIDE TO ALASKA. Fairbanks, 1953.   4961

World's most beautiful Exposition ... 1909. SEE no. 161,
    Alaska-Yukon-Pacific Exposition.

WORTHINGTON, LAWRENCE VALENTINE. Oceanographic observations made from the ice island T-3. Woods Hole, Mass., 1953. 7p. graph, table, map, bibliog. (Woods Hole Oceanographic Institution, Technical Report Ref. no. 53-92, Dec. 1953)   4962

Worthington, Lawrence Valentine, co-auth. SEE ALSO no. 2158, Holmes, J. F. Project Skijump ... 1951.

WORTHYLAKE, MARY. Moolack; young salmon fisherman, illustrated by Roy Schroeder. Chicago, Melmont Publishers, 1963. 48p. illus. [Tsimshian Indians of southeastern Alaska]   4963

WORTHYLAKE, MARY. Nika Illahee (my homeland). Illustrated by Henry Luhrs. Chicago, Melmont Publishers, 1962. 32p. illus. [Tsimshian Indians of southeastern Alaska]   4964

WOTTE, HERBERT. In blauer Ferne lag Amerika. Reisen und Abenteur des deutschen naturforschers Georg Wilhelm Steller. (Mit 32 Schwarzweisstafeln, 1 textkarte und 1 Ausschlagkarte) Leipzig, Brockhaus, 1966. 321p. bibliog.   4965

[WRANGELL] BOARD OF TRADE. A prospectus of Wrangel,[sic] Alaska, giving statistics and general information relative to the resources and industries of the Wrangel district. [Wrangell], Board of Trade, 1901. 54p. front. pls.   4966

WRANGELL, FERDINAND FERDINANDOVICH. Vitze-Admiral Stepan Osipovich Makarov; biograficheskii ocherk. Chast' 1 i 2. [TITLE TR. Vice-Admiral Stepan Osipovich Makarov; a biographical sketch, parts 1 and 2] Sanktpeterburg, Izd. Glavnogo Morskogo Shtaba, 1911. 2 vols. 317p. and 550p. illus. ports. tables, bibliog. [round the world voyage of *Vitiaz*, 1886-1889, Okhotsk and Bering Seas]   4967

WRANGELL, FERDINAND PETROVICH. Ocherki puti iz Sitkhi v Sanktpeterburg. [TITLE TR. Sketch of the journey from Sitka to St. Petersburg] St. Petersburg, Press of N. Grech, 1836. 117p. [brief sect. on Alaska]   4968

Wrangell, Ferdinand Petrovich. SEE ALSO no. 342, Baer, K. E., von. Statische ... 1839.

Wright, Edgar W., edit. SEE no. 2695, Lewis & Dryden's marine history. 1895.

WRIGHT, GEORGE FREDERICK. The ice age in North America and its bearing upon the antiquity of man. N. Y., 1889. 662p. OTHERS 1890, 1891 and 1896. ANR. Oberlin, Ohio, Bibliotheca Sacra Co., 1911. 5th ed. 763p. front. pls. diagrs. maps(some fold.)   4969

WRIGHT, GEORGE FREDERICK. The Muir Glacier, Alaska. Philadelphia, printed for the Society by the American Printing House, [1889 ?] 22p. illus. maps. (Society of Alaskan Natural History and Ethnology Bulletin no. 2)   4970

WRIGHT, HAMILTON and OTHERS. America across the seas; our colonial empire described by Hamilton Wright, C. H. Forbes-Lindsay and others. N. Y., C. S. Hammond Co., 1909. 106p. [*Alaska*, by W. W. Atwood]   4971

WRIGHT, HELEN SAUNDERS. The great white North; the story of polar exploration from the earliest times to the discovery of the Pole. By Helen S. Wright. N. Y., Macmillan, 1910. [c1901] xx,489p. front.(port.), pls. maps, glossary, index.   4972

Wright, John K. SEE no. 199, American Geog. Soc.

WRIGHT, JULIA NcNAIR. Among the Alaskans. Philadelphia, Presbyterian Board of Publications, [c1883] 351p. front.(map), pls. maps(incl. 1 col.)   4973

Wright, "Luke." SEE no. 4976, Wright, Wm. Preston.

WRIGHT, NOEL. Quest for Franklin. London, Heinemann, [c1959] xii,258p. front.(port.), pls. drawings, maps, bibliog. index.
                                                              4974

WRIGHT, THEON. The big nail; the story of the Cook-Peary feud. N. Y., John Day Co., [c1970] 368p. photos, maps, bibliog.(notes), append. [much also about Cook's Mt. McKinley climb]   4975

WRIGHT, WILLIAM PRESTON. The Alaska Highway; how we may put it to peacetime work, an investigation sponsored by the Great Falls Tribune, Great Falls, Montana. Prepared by staff correspondent W. P. (Luke) Wright. [Great Falls, Montana], 1945. 35p. illus. map. [12 articles first published in The Great Falls Tribune]
                                                              4976

"Wrong Font" Thompson. SEE no. 1516, Fairbanks Commercial Club.

WURMBRAND, DEGENHARD. Herrn der wildnis; jagdfahrten im westen Nordamerikas und Kanadas. [TITLE TR. Masters of the wild; hunting trips in western North America nad Canada] Berlin, P. Parey, [1936] 287p. pls. maps(fold.)   4977

WYCLIFFE BIBLE TRANSLATORS. Jesus nts'aa' hondai ndiign. I. [TITLE TR. Life of Jesus. Book I] Tetlin, 1965. [printed by Standard Pub. Co., Cincinnati, Ohio] 48p. illus.(col.), wrps. [in Upper Tanana dialect of Athapaskan Indians]   4978

WYCLIFFE BIBLE TRANSLATORS. The brass serpent and other stories. Fairbanks, n. d. 17p. illus. wrps. [in Tlingit]   4979

WYCLIFFE BIBLE TRANSLATORS.   Utk'-Uheenee X'usheex'ee.   Fairbanks,
1963.   44p.   wrps.   [hymns in Tlingit]   4980

WYCLIFFE BIBLE TRANSLATORS.   Ut K'Uheenih X'Usheeyee Yuh.   [Fair-
banks, ca 1963 ?]   37p.   wrps.   [hymns in Tlingit]   4981

Wycliffe Bible Translators.   SEE ALSO nos.
    22, Ahmaogak, Roy.   Iñupiam uḳaluṇi ... [1963 ?];
   984, Collins, Raymond.   Dinak'i.   1966;
   985, Collins, Raymond.   Dinak'i Ch'its'utozre.   1966;
  2067, Henry, David.   Our Indian language.   1966;
  2068, [Henry, David]   Tł'eaka Hok'anaga'.   n. d.;
  2143, Hoijer, A.   Studies in Athapaskan languages.   1963;
  2401, Kaḍaḳpak.   Ḳuliaḳtuat Taimani.   n. d.;
  3111, Milanowski, Paul G.   Dindee Shuu Aandeeg.   1961;
  3112, Milanowski, Paul G.   Uusii dinahtt'aa'. I.   1965;
  3113, Milanowski, Paul G.   Uusii dinahtt'aa'. II.   1965;
  3271, Naish, Constance.   English-Tlingit dict. Nouns.   1963;
  4125, Shinen, David.   Yapigum Atiḥtoosi.   1966;
  4385, Summer Institute of Linguistics.   Order for morning
          prayer ... Pt. Hope ... n. d.;
  4386, Summer Inst. Ling.   Tlingit reading book. 1.   1962;
  4387, Summer Inst. Ling.   Tlingit reading book 2.   n. d.;
  4388, Summer Inst. Ling.   Ukpiḳtuat Nigiugikkaṇat.   n. d.;
  4389, Summer Inst. Ling.   Unipkaat coloring book Eskimo.   1960;
  4445, Tagarook, P.   Jesus Kamanaḳtuat.   n. d.;
  4767, [Webster, D. H.]   Brief introd. Eskimo.   n. d.;
  4768, Webster, D. H.   [Can you read English ? ...]   1968;
  4769, Webster, D. H.   Iḷisaaġviṇich. Iñupiam.   n. d.;
  4770, Webster, D. H.   Iḷisaaġviṇich. Iñupiat.   n. d.;
  4771, Webster, D. H.   Iñupiat Eskimo dictionary.   1970;
  4772, Webster, D. H.   Iñupiat Suuvat ?   1968;
  4773, Webster, D. H.   Iñupiat Taiguangich. 1.   n. d.;
  4774, Webster, D. H.   Iñupiat Taiguangich. 2.   n. d.;
  4775, Webster, D. H.   Let's learn Eskimo.   1967;
  5026, Zibell, W.   Atuutit mumiksat.   1967;
  5027, Zibell, W.   Iñupiam ukałhi.   1966;
  5028, Zibell, W.   Iñupiam ukałhi.   [1968];
  5029, Zibell, W.   Unipchaat. 1.   1969;
  5030, Zibell, W.   Unipchaat. 2.   1969;
  5031, Zibell, W.   Unipchaat. 3.   1970.

Wyeth, N. C., illus.   SEE no. 906, Cheney, Warren.

WYLLIE, P. J., edit.   Ultramafic and related rocks.   N. Y.   and
London, John Wiley & Sons, 1967.   464p.   illus. tables.   [has
article by H. P. Taylor, jr., *The zoned ultramafic complexes of
southeastern Alaska.* pp.97-121]   4982

WYMAN, GILBERT.   Public land and mining laws of Alaska, the Northwest Territory, and the province of British Columbia ... The United States mining laws and regulations are also inserted in full.
Fruitvale, Calif., G. Wyman, 1898.   776p.   4983

WYTFLIET, CORNELIUS. Descriptionis Ptolemaicae augmentum, siue Occidentis notitia breui commentario illustrata studio et operata Cornely Wytfliet Louaniensis. Louvain, Johannes Bogardus, 1597. 2 pts. in 1. 191p.+atlas(folio) maps. ANR. Louvain, Gerard Riuij, 1598. 2 pts. in 1. 191p.+atlas(quarto) maps. OTHERS Douai, 1603, 1605, 1607, 1611 and Arnhem, 1615. varying no. of maps. ANR. Amsterdam, 1965. facsim. reprint. 116p. maps(dble.) folio. [map 14 depicts Straits of Anian in same position as Bering Strait]   4984

X - Y

Yakutat South. 1964. SEE no. 311, Art Institute of Chicago.

YANERT, WILLIAM. A dab o' sourdough. no pl., n. d. [ca 1935 ?] sketches by author, wrps. [poetry]   4985

YANERT, WILLIAM. Yukon breezes. Purgatory (P. O. Beaver) and Seattle, Peacock Printing, 1935(1937) ltd. print. 193p. sketches(col.) by author interleaved with text, index. [poetry]
4986

Yanert, William. SEE ALSO nos.
    3761, Rea, Ella M. Castaways of Yukon. 1936;
    4373, Stuck, Hudson. Voyages on Yukon ... 1917.

YARD, ROBERT STERLING. The book of national parks. N. Y., Scrib-ner, 1919. 420p. illus. maps.   4987

Yard, Robert Sterling. SEE ALSO no. 797,
    Camp Fire Club of America. Plea for Mt. McKinley ... 1916.

YARMOLINSKY, AVRAHAM, edit. Aleutian manuscript collections. N. Y., 1944. 12p. bibliog. (reprinted from New York Public Library Bulletin, Aug. 1944)   4988

YARMOLINSKY, AVRAHAM, edit. Kamchadal and Asiatic Eskimo manu-script collections. A recent accession. N. Y., 1947. 13p. front. ftntes. bibliog. (reprinted from New York Public Library Bulletin, Nov. 1947)   4989

Ybarra y Berge, Javier de. SEE no. 1288, de Ybarra y Berge, Javier.

Yohn, F. C. SEE no. 2754, London, Jack.

Yonge, C. M., co-auth. SEE no. 3915, Russell, Frederick S.

C. Y. YOUNG CO. Alaska information. Compliments of the company. Mining and fishing supplies. Juneau, Press of E. D. Beattie, 1916. 104p.   4990

YOUNG, DAVID L.   Millions want to.   Tucson, Arizona, Three Flags
Pub. Co., 1963.   [c1963] 192p. illus. front.(dble. maps) [tra-
vel by trailer, incl. trip by Alcan Highway in 1947]   4991

YOUNG, GEORGE ORVILLE. Alaskan trophies won and lost, by G. O.
Young. Boston, Christopher Pub. House, [c1928] 248p. front.
pls. plan, map(fold.)   4992

YOUNG, GEORGE ORVILLE. Alaskan-Yukon trophies won and lost, by
G. O. Young. Huntington, W. Va., Standard Pub. Co., 1947.
273p.+iv p. front. pls. map, endmaps. [in Wrangell Mtns.] 4993

YOUNG, ISOBEL NELSON. The story of salmon. N. Y., American Can
Co., 1934. 48p. illus.(some col.), map, diagrs.   4994

Young Men's Christian Assoc. SEE no. 3779, Reid, W. A.

YOUNG, R. B. British Columbia pilot (Canadian edition). Volume
II. Northern portion of the coast of British Columbia, including
the coast of British Columbia from Cape Caution to Portland Inlet,
and the southern coast of Alaska together with the Queen Charlotte Islands. 1953. Third edition. Prepared by R. B. Young.
Ottawa, Queen's Printer, 1954. 305p. tables, maps(fold.) (Canada. Hydrographic Service [second edition in 1945]   4995

YOUNG, SAMUEL HALL. Adventures in Alaska. By S. Hall Young.
Illustrated. N. Y., Fleming H. Revell, [c1919] 181p. front.
pls.   4996

YOUNG, SAMUEL HALL. Alaska days with John Muir. By S. Hall
Young. Illustrated. N. Y., Fleming H. Revell, [c1915] 226p.
front.(port.), pls. port. map.   4997

YOUNG, SAMUEL HALL. Hall Young of Alaska, "The Mushing Parson,"
the autobiography of S. Hall Young. N. Y., Fleming H. Revell,
[c1927] 448p. front. pls. ports. map, index.   4998

YOUNG, SAMUEL HALL. The Klondike clan. A tale of the great stampede. By S. Hall Young. Illustrated. N. Y., Fleming H. Revell,
[c1916] 393p. front.(pl.), pls. map. [historical fict.]   4999

Young, Samuel Hall. SEE ALSO nos.
     3679, Presbyterian Church. Alaska ... "treasure" ... n. d.;
     3680, Presbyterian Church. New America ... n. d.

YOUNG, STANLEY PAUL and H. H. T. JACKSON. The clever coyote.
Part 1. Its history, life habits, economic status, and control,
by S. P. Young. Part 2. Classification of the races of the
coyote, by H. H. T. Jackson. Washington, D. C., Stackpole Co.
and Wildlife Management Institute, 1951. 411p. front. pls. maps.
bibliog.   5000

YOUNG, STANLEY PAUL and EDWARD A. GOLDMAN. The wolves of North America. Part 1. Their history, life habits, economic status and control, by Stanley P. Young. Part 2. Classification of wolves, by Edward A. Goldman. Washington, D. C., American Wildlife Institute, 1944. 2 pts. in 1. 636p. pls.(col.), figs. tables, maps, bibliog. index. ANR. N. Y., Dover, 1964. 2 vols. reprint. pp.1-388 and pp.389-636. ANR. Gloucester, Mass., Peter Smith, 1966. 2 vols. reprint. 5001

Yukon-Alaska Int'l. Boundary ... 1914. SEE no. 766,
    Cairnes, DeL. D.

YUKON AND KLONDYKE GOLD FIELDS OF ALASKA. Compiled by Matthew J. Lindsay. S. F., [c1897] 48p. illus. maps, wrps. 5002

YUKON BASIN GOLD DREDGING CO. Prospectus. Kansas City, Mo., [ca 1908] 40p. illus. map, wrps. [William Ogilvie, President] 5003

YUKON BILL [pseud.] Derby days in the Yukon and other poems of the "Northland." By Yukon Bill. N. Y., George H. Doran, [1910] 128p. front. pls.(col.) ANR. Toronto, [1910] 128p. [author is C. E. Hayes] 5004

YUKON GOLD COMPANY. An abridged history with illustrations of the operations of the Yukon Gold Company, June 1911. [Philadelphia, Press of Ferris & Leach, 1911] 11p. pls. 5005

YUKON GOLD COMPANY. Annual statement and report. [N. Y. ?, 19__] [for year ending Dec. 31] 5006

YUKON GOLD COMPANY. Letter from the president to the stockholders of the Yukon Gold Co. [N. Y. ?, 1909] (4)p. 5007

Yukon gold fields; map showing routes ... 1897. SEE no. 2808,
    Lugrin, Chas. H.

Yukon, land of Klondike. 1929. SEE no. 2481, Kitto, F. H.

YUKON PUBLISHING CO. Facts for Klondikers, experiences of some of the most noted miners ... authentic accounts of different trails ... Seattle as an outfitting point. Seattle and S. F., Yukon Publishing Co., 1898. 40p. 5008

A YUKON SOUVENIR. Published by the Bennett News Company. Whitehorse, Y. T., n. d. [photograph album] 5009

Yukon Territory, Alaska and Puget Sound ... [1902 ?] SEE
    no. 3453, Pacific Coast Steamship Co.

Yukon Territory, brief descript. ... 1938. SEE no. 816, Canada.

YUKON TERRITORY, Commissioner of. Interim report of the Commissioner of Yukon Territory. Ottawa, printed by S. E. Dawson, 1906. 11p. (Canada. Dept. of Interior. Sessional Papers, no. 25aA)
5010

Yukon Territory; history ... 1907. SEE no. 817, Canada.

YUKON TRADING, MINING AND EXPLORATION COMPANY. Alaska, its gold and its best company. [Rochester, N. Y., Press of A. J. Wegman, 1897 ?] (14)p. illus. pl.
5011

[YUKON TRADING, MINING AND EXPLORATION COMPANY] Dredging for gold on the Yukon and its tributaries. [Boston ?, Yukon Trading, Mining and Exploration Co., 1897 ?] 4p.
5012

YUKON TRADING, MINING AND EXPLORATION COMPANY. Facts ... finds and figures. Boston, 1897. 23p.
5013

[YUKON TRADING, MINING AND EXPLORATION COMPANY] It's gold, gold, gold all over. [Boston ?, 1897 ?] 22p.
5014

Z

Z., Julie v., tr. SEE no. 4680, Veniaminov, I. E. P.

Z., Q. Alaska, a spectacular extravaganza in Rhino-Russian rhymes and two acts. Published by the author. N. Y., E. J. Hale & Sons, 1868. 35p.
5015

Zabello, A. V., edit. SEE no. 2410, Karelin, D. B.

Zaccagnino, A., illus. SEE no. 4484, Thiéry, M.

ZACCARELLI, JOHN. Zaccarelli's pictorial souvenir book of the golden northland with 192 original photographic reproductions. Dawson, Y. T., John Zaccarelli, n. d. photos, map.
5016

[ZAGOSKIN, LAVRENTIĬ ALEKSIEEVICH] Account of pedestrian journeys in the Russian possessions in America by Lieutenant L. A. Zagoskin in 1842, 1843 and 1844. no pl., n. d. 422 maps(fold. incl. 1 in pocket), mimeographed. ANR. 1961. 2d mimeo. reproduction. [translation by Antoinette Hotovitzky in 1935, of Zagoskin's "Peshekhodnaĩa ... " SEE no. 5019]
5017

[ZAGOSKIN, LAVRENTIĬ ALEKSIEEVICH] Lieutenant Zagoskin's travels in Russian America, 1842-1844; the first ethnographic and geographic investigations in the Yukon and Kuskokwim valleys of Alaska. Edited by Henry N. Michael. Toronto, University of Toronto Press, [c1967] xiv,358p. illus. port. maps(incl. 1 fold. at back), glossaries, bibliog. (Anthropology of the North; Translations from Russian Sources, no. 7) SEE no. 5019]
5018

605

ZAGOSKIN, LAVRENTIĬ ALEKSIEEVICH. Peshekhodnaia opis' chasti russkikh vladīeniĭ v Amerikie. Proizvedennaia leĭtenantom L. Zagoskinym v 1842, 1843 i 1844 godakh. [TITLE TR. Description based on explorations on foot of parts of the Russian territories in America by Lt. L. Zagoskin in 1842, 1843 and 1844] St. Petersburg, Pechatano v Tipografiĭ Karla Kraiīa, 1847-1848. 2 vols. 182p. and 120p.+43p. tables(fold.), map(fold.) [for translations SEE nos. 5017 and 5018. For enl. SEE no. 5020] 5019

[ZAGOSKIN, LAVRENTIĬ ALEKSIEEVICH] Puteshestviia i issledovaniia leĭtenanta Lavrentiia Zagoskina v Russkoĭ Amerike v 1842-1844 godakh. [TITLE TR. Travels and explorations of Lt. Zagoskin in Russian America in 1842-44] Moskva, Gosudarstvennoe Izdatel'stvo Geograficheskoĭ Literatury, 1956. 453p. front.(port.), pls. maps. [an enl. of no. 5019, edited by M. B. Chernenko, G. A. Agranat, and E. E. Blomkvist] 5020

Zagoskin, Lavrentiĭ Aleksieevich. SEE ALSO no. 1270,
    Denkschriften der russischen ... 1849.

ZAHM, JOHN AUGUSTINE. Alaska; the country and its inhabitants, a lecture by the Rev. J. A. Zahm ... delivered before the students of Notre Dame University, December 9, 1885. Notre Dame, Indiana, University Press, 1886. 27p. illus. 5021

Zaĭkin, P. D., co-auth. SEE nos.
    1622, Fraerman, R. I. Plavaniia V. M. Golovnina. 1948;
    1623, Fraerman, R. I. Zhizn' ... Golovnina ... 1946-48.

ZAĬKOV, S. Kratkoĭ obrazanie put. na ostrovakh vostochnago okeana. [TITLE TR. Short sketch of Zaikov's cruises to the islands in the Eastern Ocean] St. Petersburg, 1820. 5022

[ZAVALISHIN, DMITRIĬ IRINARKHOVICH] Rossiĭsko-Amerikanskaia Kompaniia. Moscow, University Press, 1865. 46p. 5023

ZEIDLER, PAUL GERHARD. Polarfahrten; die wichtigsten Entdeckungsreisen in den Eismeeren, mit Berichten der Forscher und ihrer Gefährten. Schluszwort und zwei Polarkarten von Dr. Leonid Breitfus. [TITLE TR. Polar voyages; important voyages of discovery in the polar seas, with accounts of the explorers and their companions. Epilogue and 2 polar maps by Leonid Breitfus] Berlin, Deutsche Buch-Gemeinschaft,1927. 510p. illus. maps, bibliog. 5024

ZEVALLOS, CIRIACO de. Memorias sobre los viajes apocrifos de Maldonado. Madrid, 1798. 5025

Zevallos, Ciriaco de. SEE ALSO no. 712,
    Buache, J. N. Disertaciones sobre ... 1798.

Zhiznj Valaamskago monakha Germana ... 1894. SEE no. 4632,
    [Valaam Monastery]

Zibell, Aḵuǵluk Wilfried. SEE nos. 5026-31, Zibell, Wilfried.

ZIBELL, WILFRIED, edit. Atuutit Mumiksat. Edited by Aḵuǵluk
Wilfried Zibell. Fairbanks, Wycliffe Bible Translators, n. d.
[Ambler, Alaska, Feb. 1967] 48(4)p. index in English and Eski-
mo, wrps. [Eskimo hymnal]   5026

ZIBELL, WILFRIED. Iñupiam Ukaⱡhi; Eskimo reader for the Kobuk
River-Kotzebue Sound area. Illustrated by Don Drew Canonge.
Fairbanks, Summer Institute of Linguistics, 1966. 40p. illus.
(col.), wrps. (Wycliffe Bible Translators) [SEE ALSO no. 5028]
                                                                  5027

ZIBELL, WILFRIED. Iñupiam Ukaⱡhi; Eskimo reader for the Kobuk
River-Kotzebue Sound area. Illustrated by C. E. P. Platts. Fair-
banks, Summer Institute of Linguistics, [1968] 41p. illus.
(Wycliffe Bible Translators) [for ANR. SEE no. 5027]   5028

ZIBELL, WILFRIED. Unipchaat 1. Animal stories of the Kobuk
River Eskimos. Edited by Aḵuǵluk Wilfried Zibell. Fairbanks,
Summer Institute of Linguistics, [c1969] illus. wrps. (Wycliffe
Bible Translators)   5029

ZIBELL, WILFRIED. Unipchaat 2. Animal stories of the Kobuk
River Eskimos. Edited by Aḵuǵluk Wilfried Zibell. Illustrated
by C. E. Platts. Fairbanks, Summer Institute of Linguistics,
[c1969] 500 copies printed. 26p. illus. wrps. (Wycliffe Bible
Translators)   5030

ZIBELL, WILFRIED. Unipchaat 3. Animal stories of the Kobuk
River Eskimos. Edited by Aḵuǵluk Wilfried Zibell. Illustrated
by LeRoy Frye. Fairbanks, Summer Institute of Linguistics,
[c1970] illus. wrps. (Wycliffe Bible Translators)   5031

Zibell, Wilfried. SEE ALSO no. 4771, Webster, D. H.
    Iñupiat Eskimo dictionary. [c1970]

Ziegler, Eustace, illus. SEE nos.
    1713, Gilbert, K. Alaskan poker stories. 1958;
    2511, Kosmos, George. Alaska sourdough stories. 1956;
    3099, Midnight Sun Broadcasting Co. KFAR ... 1939;
    4913, Wilson, K. Copper-tints ... 1923.

Zies, E. G. SEE no. 3275, National Geog. Soc.

Zigrosser, Carl. SEE no. 2444, Kent, Rockwell.

ZIMMERMANN, E. A. W. von. Taschenbuch der Reisen oder unterhal-
tende Darstellung der Entdeckungen des 18ten Jahrhunderts, in
Rücksicht der Länder, Menschen und Productenkunde. Für jede
Klasse von Lesern. Achter Jahrgang ... für das Jahr 1809. Leipzig, [1809] 2 vols. 356p. and 288p. pls.(some fold.), maps(fold.)
[has some Alaskan and Siberian Arctic content]   5032

Zimmermann, E. A. W. von. SEE ALSO no. 3532, [Pennant, Thos.]
    Thiergeschichte der nordlichen polarlander. 1787.

Zimmermann, Heinrich. [Alphabetical title guide to chronological
    entries]

    Dernier voyage ... 1782.   Reize rondom ... 5035.
    Heinrich Zimmermanns...5033. Zimmermann's acct. ... 5037.
    Posliednee ... 5036.

ZIMMERMANN, HEINRICH. Heinrich Zimmermanns von Wiszloch in der
Pfalz, Reise um die Welt, mit Capitain Cook. Manheim, bei E. F.
Schwann, kuhrfürstl. Hofbuchhändler, 1781. (9),10-110p.   5033

    TRANSLATIONS - Heinrich Zimmermanns ... 1781, CHRONOLOGICALLY.

    Dernier voyage du Capitaine Cook autour du monde, où se trou-
        vent les circonstances de sa mort; publié en Allemand par
        Henri Zimmerman. Berne, Nouvelle Société Typographique,
        1782. xvi,200p. ANR. Berne, Nouvelle Société Typographique,
        1783. xvi,200p. reprint.   5034

    Reize rondom de waereld. Met Kapitein Cook. Uit het Hoog-
        duitsch Vertaald. Te Leyden, by A. en J. Honkoop, 1784.
        (2),6p.+116p. ANR. Leyden, L. van der Spyk, 1791.6p.+116p.5035

    Posliednee puteshestvie okolo svieta Kap. Kuka, slavnago ny-
        nieshniago vieka morekhodtsa, s obstoiatel'stvani o ego smerti
        i priobshcheniem kratkago opisaniīa ego zhizni. Izdano Gen-
        rikom Tsimmermanom, ego soputnikom i ochevidnymsvidietelem
        vsiekh proizshestviĭ, sluchivshikhsiīa s nim do vremiīa sego
        posliedniago ego puteshestviīa. [TITLE TR. Last voyage a-
        round the world of Capt. Cook, famous naviagor of the present
        century, with circumstances of his death and a short account
        of his life. Edited by Henry Zimmermann, a fellow voyager
        and eye-witness to all the events that happened to him up to
        the time of his last journey. St. Petersburg, Petr Bogdano-
        vich, 1786. 265p. ANR. St. Petersburg, 1788. 2d ed. 411p.
                                                                    5036

    Zimmermann's account of the third voyage of Captain Cook, 1776-
        1780. Translated by Miss U. Tewsley ... under direction of
        Johannes C. Andersen ... with a few explanatory notes. Wel-
        lington, N. Z., W. A. G. Skinner, government printer, 1926.
        49p. pls. facsim. map(fold.) (Alexander Turnbull Library
        Bulletin, no. 2)   5037

Zimmermann, Heinrich. SEE ALSO no. 2204, Howay, F. W., edit.
    Zimmermann's Capt. Cook. 1930.

ZOLOTAREV, ALEKSANDR MIKHAILOVICH. Perezhitki totemizma u narodov Sibiri. [TITLE TR. Survivals of totemism among the peoples
of Siberia] Leningrad, Izd-vo Instituta Narodov Severa, 1934.
52p. bibliog. [discusses Alaskan Eskimos as well as Asiatic]5038

Zolotorevskaiîà, I. A., co-edit. SEE no. 4542, Tokarev, S. A.

ZUBKOVA, Z. N. Aleutskie ostrova, fiziko-geograficheskiĭ ocherk.
[TITLE TR. The Aleutian Islands, a physical geographical outline]
Moskva, OGIZ Gosudarstvennoe izd-vo geograficheskoĭ literatury,
1948. 287p. illus. bibliog. (Vsesoiūznoe geograficheskoe
obshchestvo Zapiski, novaîà seriîà, T.4)   5039

ZUBOV, NIKOLAI NIKOLAEVICH. Otechestvennye moreplavateli-
issledovateli moreĭ i okeana. [TITLE TR. Our native explorer-
navigators of the oceans and seas] Moskva, Gosudarstvennoe izd-
vo geograficheskoĭ literatury, 1954. 473p. illus. maps(in text),
glossary, chronology, table of voyages, index.   5040

Zubov, Nikolai Nikolaevich. SEE ALSO nos.
     1314, Dobrovol'skiĭ, A. D. Plavaniîà F. P. Litke ... 1948;
     1622, Fraerman, R. I. Plavaniîà V. M. Golovnina. 1948;
     2554, Krusenstern, A. J. von. Puteshestvie ... 1950;
     3971, Sarychev, G. A. Puteshestvie ... 1952.

Zuev, Vasiliĭ, tr. SEE no. 1786, Pallas, P. S.

Zuverlassige Nachricht ... Capts. Cook and Clerke ... 1783.
     SEE no. 1018, [Cook, Jas.]

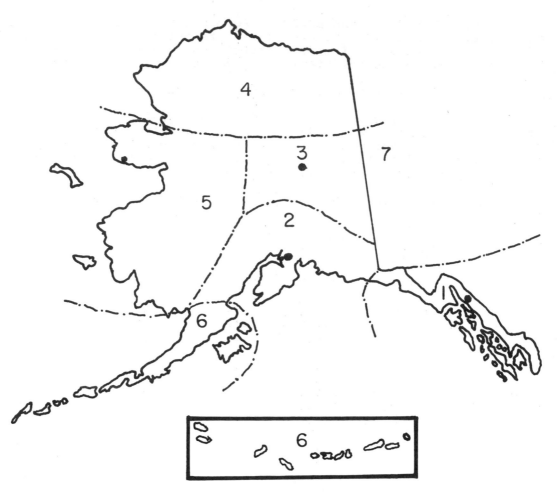

An outline map of Alaska and Yukon Territory with index-coded geographic areas.

EXPLANATORY NOTE FOR MAP AND INDEX

The index consists of alphabetized subjects. Under each subject heading, alphabetical entries are composed of author, abbreviated title, date, and bibliography number followed by geographic code number in parentheses. The geographic classifications employed are terms in common usage. A list and brief description of the geographic regions denoted is provided.

ALASKAN BIBLIOGRAPHY

A list of geographic code numbers with descriptions of regions follows:

0. So designated when the area covered pertains to two or more of the regions below.

1. *Southeast*. The area south and east of a line extending into the Gulf of Alaska from the Alaska-Yukon border.

2. *South-central*. The area west of the Yukon border, along the Gulf of Alaska on the south, and bounded by the Alaska Range on the north and west to include Mt. McKinley.

3. *Interior*. South of the Arctic Circle on the north, to the Alaska Range on the south, with the Yukon border to the east, to a line formed approximately at the headwaters of the Kuskokwim River, to the junction of Yukon-Tanana Rivers on the west.

4. *Arctic*. Bounded on the south by the Arctic Circle, and extending poleward into the Arctic Ocean on the north.

5. *Western*. Bounded by the western boundaries of the Interior and South-central regions and extending westward into the Bering Sea to include all Bering Sea islands.

6. *Southwestern*. Takes in the Alaska Peninsula, Aleutian Islands, and Kodiak Island.

7. *Yukon Territory*, Canada.

8. So designated when the area covered is undetermined, either through lack of specific regional setting or inability to ascertain setting.

INDEX

AGRICULTURE-Homesteading(cont.)

Philips, C. ... homesteaders
... [1940?]   3569(3)
Sharples, A. W. Two against
North. 1961.   4094(2)
Smitter, W. Another morning.
1941.   4209(2)
Snider, G. So was Alaska.
1961.   4222(2)
Stimple, B. Fun on farm ...
1962.   4346(3)
Stoddard, G. ... modern home-
steading. 1957.   4351(2)

ALASKA HIGHWAY (ALCAN)

Alaska Bur., Great Falls.
Hy. log ... [ca 1959] 34(0)
Alaska Highway.
[ca 1944]   66(0)
Alaska Highway guide ... maps
... Alcan. [ca 1947] 67(0)
Amer. Auto. Assoc. ...
Alaska Highway. 1949. 192(0)
Atwood, G. H. Along the
Alcan. 1960.   320(0)
Baskine, G. Hitch-hiking
... 1944.   425(0)
B.C.-Yukon-Alaska Hy. Comm.
Report ... 1941.   672(0)
Camsell, C. Canada's new
northwest... 1947.   800(0)
Canada. Alaska Highway.
1955.   802(0)
Coe, D. Alaska Highway ...
[ca 1943]   968(0)
Coe, D. La route de l'Alaska.
1946.   969(0)
Coe, D. Vägen till Alaska.
1946.   970(0)
Crowe, G. R. ... flight guide
Alaska Hy. 1968.   1135(0)
Davies, R. A. ... Canada's
4 year plan. 1944.   1196(0)
Dawson, C. A. New Northwest.
1947.   1215(0)
Dick, J. W. Down north.
1944.   1290(0)
Dozois, L. O. R. ... leveling
B.C. and Y.T. 1951. 1343(0)
Evans, A. R. Northward Ho!
1947.   1502(0)

Godsell, P. H. Alaska Highway.
1946.   1746(0)
Godsell, P. H. Romance Alaska
Highway. 1944.   1746(0)
Grant, D. A. S. ... gospel
trail...jeep...1944. 1797(0)
Greenwood, A. Rolling North.
1955.   1852(0)
Harris, M. E. You can
Alcan. 1959.   1962(0)
Hinton, A. C. The Yukon.
1947.   2122(0)
Holiday Pub. Guide ...
1963.   2151(0)
Illingworth, F. Highway to
north. 1955.   2253(0)
Lanks, H. C. Highway to
Alaska. 1944.   2604(0)
Leahey, A. H. ... surveys ...
Military Hy....1943. 2656(0)
Lee, F. C. Alaska Hy.
poems. [c1944]   2667(0)
Lord, C. A. Geol. reconnais.
... 1944.   2795(0)
Menzies, D. Alaska Highway
... 1943.   3083(0)
North Pac. Plan. Proj....peace
Military Hy. 1943.   3346(0)
Northwest Mapping Service.
Hy. packet. 1948.   3357(0)
Nulsen, R. H. Trailering to
Alaska. 1960.   3366(0)
Pape, R. Poles ... Alaska to
Antarctic. 1960.   3488(0)
Phillips, R. A. J. Canada's
north. 1967.   3573(0)
Potter, L. Alaska Hy. flowers.
[c1966]   3661(0)
Puhr, C. Modern Alaska.
n. d.   3702(0)
Rettie, J. C. ... peacetime
maint. ... 1944.   3791(0)
Rosten, N. Big road.
1946.   3897(0)
Sanderson, I. T. Continent we
live on. 1961.   3956(0)
Stewart, G. R. NA 1 looking
north ... 1957.   4344(0)
Stursberg, P. ...victory
Sicily & Italy.1944. 4379(0)
Williams, F. I asked for it.
1954.   4877(0)

ALASKA HIGHWAY (cont.)

Wishaw, L. As far as you'll
  take me. 1958.   4934(0)
Wright, W. P. ... peacetime
  work ... 1945.   4976(0)
Young, D. L. Millions want
  to. 1963.   4991(0)

ANTHOLOGIES.

Alaska League West. Writers.
  ... poetry ... 1956.   73(0)
Explorers Club. Hell and high
  water. 1941.   1508(0)
Gruening, E. ... reader ...
  1967.   1871(0)
Heller, H. L. Sourdough sagas.
  1967.   2025(0)
Hoke, H. Alaska Alaska Alaska.
  1960.   2144(0)
Irwin, W. R. ... mountaineering. 1950.   2301(0)
MacGowan, K. Early man ...
  new world. 1950.   2895(0)
Olson, B. G. Blood on Arctic
  snow. 1956.   3406(0)
Poetry Soc. of Alaska. One
  hundred yrs. ... 1966.3624(0)
Reed, E. Kobuk maiden ...
  verses ... [1933?]   3772(0)
Thomas, L., jr. Trail of
  [c1962]   4499(0)
Thompson, S. Tales ... Indians.
  1929.   4509(0)
Voice of the Yukon ...
  1930.   4712(7)
Whelen, T. Hunting big game
  ... 1946.   4809(0)

ARTISTS.

Alaska Review. ... Machetanz
  ... Kimura ... 1965.   107(0)
Jones, H. W. ... Sydney
  Laurence. 1962.   2379(2)
Kent., R. Rockwellkentiana
  ... 1933.   2444(2)
Lee, C. Alaska in sketches
  1962.   2666(2)
Potter, C. Sitka sketches.
  1970.   3656(1)

Snodgrass, J. O. Amer. Indian
  painters ... 1967.   4224(0)
Vachon, A. W. Fish without
  chips. 1960.   4625(1)
Vachon, A. W. Ketchikan
  sketchings. 1959.   4626(1)

ATLASES.

Amer. Geog. Soc. ... glacier
  maps ... 1960.   200(0)
Amer. Geog. Soc. Physical map
  Arctic. 1930.   201(4)
Dodimead, A. J. ... oceanog.
  data ... 1960.   1320(2)
Dodimead, A. J. ... Pac. sub-
  arctic ... 1961.   1321(5)
Eschscholtz, J. F. Zool. ...
  Kotzebue ... 1829.   1493(0)
G.B., F.O. Boundary...append.
  to case ... 1903.   1812(0)
Int'l. Boundary Comm. ... re-
  port ... 1952.   2274(1)
Ivanhoe, L. F. ... geol. maps.
  1959.   2307(0)
Krusenstern, A. J. v. ... de
  l'ocean Pac....1827. 2549(0)
Levchenko, G. I. Morskoi
  1959.   2694(0)
Morris, F. L. Marine atlas
  ... Skagway ... 1959.3198(1)
Sarychev, G. A. Atlas Svernoy
  ... 1826.   3964(0)
Schuchert, C. ... paleogeogra-
  phic maps N.A.1955. 4010(0)
Seaman, J. V. ...general atlas
  ... schools. 1821.   4032(0)
Swithinbank, C.W.M. Ice atlas
  ... 1960.   4434(4)
Teben'kov, M. D. ... Sievero-
  padnykh ... 1852.   4474(0)
Teben'kov, M. D. Gidrogra-
  ficheskiia ... 1852. 4475(0)
Thoren, R. ... Arctic ...
  1969.   4524(4)
U.S.S.R. ... geograficheskikh
  ... 1964.   4616(0)

AVIATION.

Amer. Geog. Soc. Problems polar research...1928.   203(4)

AVIATION. (cont.)

Amundsen, R.E.G. Air pioneer-
ing ... 1929.   213(4)
Amundsen, R.E.G. ... pol-
flyoning ... 1925.   214(4)
Amundsen, R.E.G. ... polar
flight ... 1925.   215(4)
Amundsen, R.E.G. En avion
... pole ... 1925.   216(4)
Amundsen, R.E.G. My polar
flight. 1925.   217(4)
Amundsen, R.E.G Our
polar flight. 1925.   218(4)
Amundsen,R.E.G. ... forste
... Polhavet ... 1926. 219(4)
Amundsen, R.E.G. ... Flug
... Polarmeer ... 1927.220(4)
Amundsen, R.E.G. First
flight ... 1927.   221(4)
Amundsen, R.E.G. First
crossing ... 1928.   222(4)
Baidukov, G.F. Nash polet
... Amerika. 1937.   344(4)
Baidukov, G.F. Over the North
Pole. 1938.   345(4)
Baidukov, G.F. O Chkalove.
1939.   346(4)
Balchen, B. Come North with
me. 1958.   368(4)
Beliakov, A.V. Iz Moskvy ...
Amerika ... 1938.   478(4)
Bobrov, N. N. Chkalov.
1940.   590(4)
Carlson, W.S. Lifelines ...
Arctic. 1962.   837(4)
Chandler, E.W. ... Ben Eielson
... 1959.   888(0)
Chkalov, V.P. Dva pereleta
1938.   919(4)
Chkalov, V.P. Nash transpo-
liarnyi ... 1938.   920(4)
Chkalov, V.P. Unser transpo-
larflug. 1939.   921(4)
Chkalov, V.P. Shturmanskiĭ...
NO-25. [1939?]   922(4)
Chkalov, V.P. ... log book ...
NO-25 ... 1939.   923(4)
Clark, H.T. ...Amundsen-Ells-
worth ... 1928.   940(4)
Crowe, G.R. Plan-a-flight ...
1968.   1135(0)

Day, B. ... story Bob Reeve
... 1957.   1218(0)
Ellis, F. H. Canada's flying
... 1954.   1441(0)
Forstinger, R. Nord-und
Südpol ... [1935]   1614(4)
Fraser, C.C. Heroes of air.
1926.   1636(0)
Heflin, A. Adventure was
compass. 1942.   2016(0)
Helmericks, C. Flight *Arctic
Tern*. 1952.   2029(0)
Helmericks, H. Arctic bush
pilot. 1956.   2032(0)
Helmericks, H. Last of bush
pilots. 1969.   2035(0)
Houdenak, G. Roald Amundsen's
Siste ... 1934.   2188(4)
Int'l. Soc. Explorat. Arctic
... Versamml. 1929. 2287(4)
Joerg, W. L. G. ...history ...
polar ... 1930.   2360(4)
Jotti-Neri, E. ... Nobile ...
aeronautici ... 1930.2393(4)
Kennedy, K.J. Wien brothers'
story. 1967.   2442(0)
Khvat, L.B. Tri puteshest-
viia...Bering. 1949. 2456(0)
Knight, C. Hitch wagon ...
Balchen. 1950.   2494(0)
Krasinskiĭ, G.D. Puti
Severa. 1929.   2538(0)
Kublank, W. ... Nordpol.
[1930]   2568(4)
Laktionov, A. F. Severny i
poliùs ... 1939.   2584(4)
Lindbergh, A.M. North to
Orient. 1935.   2713(0)
Lvov, V.E. Zavoevanie po-
liàrnykh ... 1928.   2818(4)
Maluquer, J. J. Exploracion
aeropolar. 1945.   2959(4)
Mills, J. Airborne to mtns.
1961.   3137(2)
Mills, S.E. Sourdough sky
... [c1969]   3138(0)
Mitchell, W. Skyways.
1930.   3148(0)
Nobile, U. Gli Italiani al
Polo Nord. 1945.   3313(4)
Nobile, U. ...segreto polare
... 1928.   3314(4)

AVIATION. (cont.)

Nobile, U. My polar flights.
  1961.   3315(4)
"Norge" al Polo Nord ...
  1926.   3342(4)
O'Brien, P.J. Will Rogers
  ... [c1935]   3374(4)
Ordin, A. ... Valeriĭ Pavlo-
  vich Chkalov. 1949. 3416(4)
Owens, F.R. Sky pilot of
  Alaska. 1949.   3442(0)
Pollog, C.H. In Eis und Sturm.
  [c1946]   3634(4)
Potter, J. C. Flying fron-
  tiersmen. 1956.   3658(0)
Potter, J.C. Flying North.
  1947.   3659(0)
Satterfield, A. Alaska bush
  pilot ... 1969.   3972(1)
Simmons, G. Target: Arctic
  ... 1965.   4157(4)
Smiley, C.H. Atmospheric re-
  fract. ... 1950.   4188(0)
Stalinskiĭ Marshrut Prodolzhen
  ... 1937.   4279(0)
Stark, C.R.,jr. Bering Sea
  eagle. 1957.   4286(0)
Sunderman, J.F. World War II
  in air ... [c1962]   4399(6)
Supf, P. Flieger ... Pole.
  1957.   4401(4)
Taylor, F. J. High horizons
  ...[c1951]   4469(0)
Thomas, L. Famous first
  flights ... 1968.   4493(0)
Thomas, L. Sir Hubert Wilkins
  ... [c1961]   4496(0)
Thomas, L. First world flight
  ... 1925.   4497(0)
Thomas, T. Follow North
  Star. 1960.   4501(0)
Thorburn, L. No tumult ...
  PBY. 1945.   4523(6)
Toland, J. Ships...dirigibles.
  1957.   4544(4)
Voyage *Chelyuskin*.By members
  Expedition. 1935.   4717(0)
Wachel, P. Oscar Winchell
  ... [c1967]   4719(0)
Wells, R. M. Great Circle ...
  surface temp. 1962. 4790(0)

Wilkins, G.H. Flying the
  Arctic. 1928.   4871(4)
Wilkins, G.H. Thoughts ...
  space. 1942.   4872(4)
Williams, A. Conquering air
  ... 1926.   4876(0)
Wisting, O. år Roald Amund-
  sen ... 1930.   4937(4)
Zeidler, P.G. Polarfahrten
  ... 1927.   5024(4)

BIBLIOGRAPHY.

Adams, J. Canad. plant
  geog. 1928-47.   11(0)
Allen, E.W. ... de Laperouse.
  check list. 1941.   177(0)
Arctic Inst. N.A. Catalogue
  ... 1968.   300(0)
Berton, P. Klondike bibliog.
  1958.   543(7)
Boone & Crockett Club. Ameri-
  can game ... 1930.   609(0)
Breitfus, L.L. Polargebiete
  ... 1950.   653(4)
Brinsmade, E. M. ... young
  people ... 1961.   662(0)
Brinsmade, E. M. Children's
  books. 1956.   663(0)
Chavanne, J. ... Polar-Region-
  en ... 1878.   903(0)
Dartmouth College Lib. Stefans-
  son Collect. ...1967.1187(0)
Dutilly, A.A. ... bibliogs.
  Arctic. 1945.   1396(0)
Farquhar, F.P. List...mtns.
  ... 1934.   1528(0)
Foote, D.C. ... human geog....
  central ... 1964.   1594(0)
Fortuine, R. Health Eskimos
  classified ... 1968. 1615(0)
Golder, F.A. ... materials
  Russ. archives.1917. 1757(0)
Giles, M. C. Oceanog....con
  tribution ...1941.   1855(0)
Harkness, D.J. Great Lakes &
  ...literature.1959. 1947(0)
Harris, J. Navigantium atque
  ... 1764.   1961(6)
Holmes, M. Introd. ... Jas.
  Cook. 1936.   2160(2)
Holmes, M. Cook, bibliog.
  excursion. 1952.   2161(2)

BIBLIOGRAPHY. (cont.)

Kaidanov, N. ...Dep-ta Vniesh-
nei Torgovliĭ. 1887. 2402(6)
Kaidanov, N. ... Kommerts-
kollegiĭ. 1884. 2403(6)
Kent, R. Rockwellkentiana ...
1933. 2444(2)
Kruber, A. A. Biblioteka
Puteshestviĭ. 1924. 2546(6)
Lada-Mocarski, V. ... books
before 1868. 1969. 2579(0)
LeClerc, C. Bibliotheca Ameri-
cana ... 1878. 2661(0)
Mezhov, V. I. Sibirskaĭa bib-
liografiĭa. 1891-92. 3095(5)
Murdock, G. P. Ethnographic...
N. A. 1941. 3246(0)
New South Wales Pub. Lib. ...
Jas. Cook ... 1928. 3294(0)
Olsen, M. L. ... list...agric.
... 1968. 3404(0)
Peabody Mus. Archaeol.&Ethnol.
Auth. subj. ...1963. 3507(0)
Richards, H. G. Annot. Quater-
nary ... 1965. 3803(0)
Sealock, R. B. ... place name
... 1948. 4031(0)
Smith, C. W. Union list ms. ...
Pac. N. W. 1932. 4191(0)
Smith, C. W. Check-list ...bks.
pamphlets ...1909. 4192(0)
Smith, C. W. Pacific Northwest
Americana. 1921. 4193(0)
Sokolov, A. P. ... Morskaĭa
Biblioteka ... 1883. 4237(0)
Spence, S. A. Capt. Jas. Cook
... 1960. 4257(0)
Staton, F. M. Bibliog.Cana-
diana... [c1935] 4289(0)
Tomashevskiĭ, V. V. ... Sibiri
i Dal'nego ... 1957.
Toronto Pub. Lib. Canadian
catalogue ... 1959. 4556(0)
Toronto Pub. Lib. Canadian
northwest ... 1931. 4557(0)
Warner, O. M. W. English mari-
time writing. 1958. 4743(0)
Washburn, H. B. Mt. McKinley
...descript. ...1951. 4748(2)
Wiley, S.C. Colonization
Americas...1960. 4868(0)

Woodbridge, H. C. Jack London
... 1966. 4955(0)
Yarmolinsky, A. Aleutian ms.
collect. ... 1944. 4988(6)
Yarmolinsky, A. Kamchadal and
Asiatic ms. ...1947. 4989(6)

BIOGRAPHY - Collective.

Berkh, V. N. ... Ross.
Admiralov...1831-36. 533(0)
Dabovich, S. Lives of Saints
... 1898. 1150(0)
Kuznetŝov, I. V.Lĭudi russkoĭ
nauki. 1948-[?] 2575(0)
Kuznetŝov, I. V. Lĭudi russkoĭ
nauki ... 1962. 2576(0)
Snodgrass, J. O. Amer. Indian
painters ... 1967. 4224(0)
Tewkesbury, W. ... who's
who ... [c1947] 4482(0)
Vize, V. I. Russkie Polĭarnye
... slovar. 1948. 4709(0)

BIOGRAPHY - General.

Amundsen, R.E.G. Mitt ...
polarforsker. 1927. 223(4)
Amundsen, R.E.G. ... life ...
explorer. 1928. 224(4)
Anderson, B. ... Vancouver ...
... 1960. 242(1)
Anderson, E. G. Dog-team dr.
...Romig. 1940. 243(5)
Arctander, J. W. Apostle...
Duncan ... [c1909] 276(1)
Arneson, O. R. Amundsen ...
1929. 309(4)
[Assher, B.] Nomad in North
America. 1927. 313(0)
Badè, W. F. Life and letters
J. Muir. 1924. 334(1)
Baer, K. E. Avtobiografiĭa
... 1950. 338(0)
Baer, K. E. Selbstbiographie
... 1912. 339(0)
Baer, K.E. Nachrichten ...
Leben ... 1865. 341(0)
Bancroft, F. Life Wm. H.
Seward ... 1900. 377(0)
[Barsukov, I.P.] Innokentiĭa
... 1883. 414(6)

BIOGRAPHY. (cont.)

[Barsukov, I. P.] Life work
Innocent ... 1897.   415(6)
Bartlett, R.A. ... Log "Bob"
Bartlett. 1928.   421(4)
Bauer, H. Ein Leben Rasmussen
... 1960.   431(4)
Beach, R. Personal exposures
... [c1940]   441(0)
Beattie, K. Brother...Klondike
Boyle. 1940.   455(7)
Beattie, W. Gilbert Marsden
... 1955.   456(0)
Bellesort, A. Lapérouse ...
1926.   492(1)
Belov, M. Semen
Dezhnev. 1955. . . .   495(6)
Benham, D. Sketches Jan August
Miert ... 1853.   498(4)
Bernhardi, C. ... Krusenstern
... 1856.   537(0)
Besant, W. Capt. Cook.
1890.   549(2)
Biographie dr. Mertens ...
n. d.   557(0)
Black, M.L.P. My seventy
years. 1938.   570(7)
Brewer, Chas. Reminiscences.
1884.   654(0)
Brower, Chas. D. Fifty years
... 1942.   691(4)
Brower, Chas. D. King of
Arctic. 1958.   692(4)
Burkholder, M. Capt. Cook.
1928.   735(2)
Camsell, Chas. Son of North.
1954.   801(7)
Carpenter, H. M. Three years
in Alaska. 1901.   845(7)
Carrington, H. Life Capt.
Cook. 1939.   852(2)
Carruthers, Jose, Capt. Jas.
Cook ... 1930.   855(2)
Caughey, J. W. Hubert Howe
Bancroft ... 1946.   873(0)
Chase, Wm. H. ...Capt. Billie
Moore. [c1947]   900(0)
Chukovskiĭ, N. K. Bering. [in
Russ.] 1961.   927(6)
Cody, H.A. Apostle of North.
1908. [Bompas]   966(7)

Cole, Cornelius. Memoirs
... 1908.   976(0)
Connelly, J. B. Master ...
Amasa Delano. 1943. 1004(0)
Conrad, E. Gov. and lady...
Wm. H. Seward. 1960. 1006(0)
Dafoe, J. W. Clifford Sifton
... 1931.   1151(0)
Dalby, M. A. Dynamite Johnny
O'Brien. 1933.   1153(0)
Davis, M.L. Sourdough...[Dr.
J. F. Scott] 1933.   1204(7)
Davydov, I. V. Dzhon Franklin.
1956.   1213(4)
Day, B. Glacier pilot...Bob
Reeve. 1957.   1218(0)
deBaets, M. Monseigneur
Seghers ... 1896.   1223(0)
deBaets, M. Apostle...Seghers.
1943.   1224(0)
DeLong, E. Explorer's wife.
1938.   1259(0)
Denison, M. Klondike Mike.
1943.   1265(7)
Desjardin, J.-A. En Alaska;
deux mois ... 1930. 1278(0)
De Vigne, H. L. Time of life
... doctor. 1942. 1381(0)
De Windt, H. My restless life.
1909.   1285(0)
Divin, V. A. A. I. Chirikov
vydaiush. ... 1953. 1300(6)
Divin, V. A. A.I. Chirikov
zamechatel'nyi. 1950.1301(6)
Divin, V. A. Velikiĭ russkiĭ
... Chirikov. 1953. 1302(6)
Divin, V. A. V. M. Golovnin.
... 1951.   1303(0)
Drebert, F. Alaska missionary.
1959.   1349(5)
Dufresne, F. My way was
North. 1966.   1365(0)
Dunn, R. World alive ...
1956.   1391(0)
Eaton, J. Sheldon Jackson.
1898.   1404(0)
Ellsworth, L. Beyond horizons.
1938.   1446(4)
Englund, J. F. På äventyr;
vilda västern...1924.1475(0)
Engstrom, E. John Engstrom.
[c1956]   1476(3)

BIOGRAPHY. (cont.)

Evans, E. D. Sailor's log.
 1902.   1503(6)
Fitz, F. E. Lady sourdough.
 1941.   1574(5)
Fitzgerald, E. Army doctor's
 wife. Letters. 1962. 1575(1)
Fletcher, I. Vilhjalmur
 Stefansson. 1925.   1578(0)
Flint, S. R. Mudge memoirs...
 1883.   1582(1)
Ford, C. Where sea...[Geo.
 Steller] 1966.   1599(6)
Fradkin, N. G. Krasheninnikov
 ... 1951.   1621(0)
Fraerman, R. I. Zhizn'...V.M.
 Golovnin. 1945-48.   1623(0)
France, Geo. W. Struggles for
 life ... 1890.   1625(0)
Freuchen, P. Vagrant viking
 ... 1953.   1660(4)
Freuchen, Pipaluk. Bogen om
 Peter Freuchen. 1958. 1661(4)
Gillham, C. E. Raw North.
 1947.   1725(0)
Gleaves, A. ... Wm. Hemsley
 Emory ... 1923.   1737(0)
Glody, R. ... Wm. Francis
 Walsh ... 1934.   1738(4)
Gmelin, J. G. Leben Georg
 Wilh. Stellero...1748.1742(0)
Godsell, P. H. Arctic trader.
 1934.   1744(4)
Godsell, P. H. Red hunters of
 snows ... 1938.   1745(4)
Godwin, G. S. Vancouver; a
 life. 1930.   1748(1)
Golder, F. A. *Father* Herman...
 [191__?]   1756(2)
Goodhue, C. Journey ...
 V. Bering... 1944.   1773(6)
Gould, R. T. Capt. Cook.
 1935.   1789(2)
Goulet, E. O. Rugged years
 ... [1949]   1790(0)
Graham, A. ... Geo. M. Mitchell
 ... 1935.   1792(7)
Grech, N. Zhizneopisanie V. M.
 Golovnina. 1851.   1839(0)
Green, F. Bob Bartlett.
 mariner. 1929.   1844(0)

Green, P. I am Eskimo, Aknik
 ... 1959.   1847(4)
Grierson, J. Sir Hubert
 Wilkins. 1960.   1856(0)
Hadman, B. As sailor loves
 sea. 1951.   1891(1)
Hale, C. R. Innocent of
 Moscow. 1888.   1898(6)
Hamilton, W. Yukon story.
 1964.   1924(7)
Hanson, E. P. Stefansson...
 1941.   1942(4)
Hanssen, H. J. Gjennem ...
 Amundsen. 1941.   1944(4)
Hayne, M. H. E. Pioneers...
 police...1897.   2006(7)
Hays, L. Kahtlian...Raven
 tribe. 1906.   2007(1)
Headley, P. C. ... Rev. Edw.
 Payson Hammond. 1884.2012(0)
Helmericks, C. Our Alaskan
 winter. 1949.   2027(4)
Helmericks, C. Our summer with
 Eskimos. 1948.   2028(4)
Helmericks, C. We live in
 Alaska. 1944.   2030(4)
Helmericks, C. We live in
 Arctic. 1947.   2031(4)
Herbert, A. Two Dianas in
 Alaska. 1909.   2074(6)
Hewitt, J. M. Alaska vagabond
 ... 1953.   2093(0)
Hick, Geo. Pioneer prospector.
 1954.   2102(0)
Hill, E. P. Rev. Aaron L.
 Lindsley. 1902.   2105(0)
Hitchcock, M. E. Two women in
 Klondike ... 1899.   2130(7)
Hofmann, Chas. Frances Dens-
 1967.   2139(0)
Hooker, Wm. J. ... David
 Douglas ... [ca 1837]2171(0)
Howay, F. Wm. Capt. Geo.
 Vancouver. 1932.   2200(1)
Hrdlička, A. Alaska diary.
 1943.   2207(0)
Hulbert, W. Bishop ... Shel-
 don Jackson. 1948.   2222(0)
Huntington, Jas. On edge of
 nowhere. 1966.   2240(5)
Jenkins, Thos. ... Peter Trim-
 ble Rowe. 1943.   2338(0)

BIOGRAPHY. (cont.)

Johnshoy, W. Apaurak...[T. L. Brevig] 1944.   2367(5)
Johnson, W. F. Life Warren G. Harding. 1923.   2373(0)
Johnston, A. Legendary Mizners. 1953.   2374(0)
Jones, Chas. J. Buffalo Jones' 40 yrs. ... 1899.   2378(7)
Jones, H. W. Man and mtn. Sydney Laurence. 1962.   2379(2)
Judge, Chas. J. American missionary ... 1904.   2394(0)
Kane, P. Wanderings of artist ... 1859.   2405(7)
Kane, P. Wanderungen ... 1862. . . . . . .   2406(7)
Kane, P. En'Kunsters vandringger ... 1863.   2407(7)
Kanguk. ... boy of Bering Strait. 1939.   2409(5)
Kashevaroff, A. P. *Father* Herman. [1916?]   2413(6)
Kavanaugh, E. Wilderness homesteaders. 1950.   2419(2)
Keim, Chas. J. Aghvook...Otto Geist ... 1969.   2426(0)
Kennan, Geo. E. H. Harriman 1922.   2438(0)
Kennedy, K. J. Wien brothers story. 1967.   2442(0)
Kent, R. Northern Christmas. 1941.   2443(2)
Kent, R. Wilderness ... 1920.   2445(2)
Khlĩebnikov, K. T. Zhizn. A. A. Baranova.1835.   2455(1)
Kingston, W. H. G. Capt. Cook. n. d.   2461(2)
Kippis, A. Life Capt. Jas. Cook. 1788.   2466(2)
Kippis, A. Vie du Capt. Cook ... 1789.   2467(2)
Kippis, A. Vie du Capt. Cook ... 1789.   2468(2)
Kirk, R. C. 12 mos. in Klondike. 1899.   2472(7)
Kitson, A. Life Capt. Jas. Cook ... 1911.   2477(2)
Klengenberg, C. Klengenberg of Arctic. 1932.   2486(4)

Knight, C. Hitch wagon... Balchen. 1950.   2494(0)
Kohlstedt, E. D. William Duncan...1957.   2503(1)
Lane, A. W. Letters Franklin K. Lane ... 1922.   2592(0)
Lane, R. W. He was man.[Jack London] 1925.   2594(0)
Lane, R. W. Gordon Blake.[Jack London] 1925.   2594(0)
Lang, J. Story Capt. Cook. 1906.   2595(2)
L'Ange-Gardien, M. de. En Alaska...Soeurs...1900.   2597(0)
Lauridsen, P. Vitus Bering... .889.   2642(6)
Lauridsen, P. Vitus J. Bering og de ... 1885.   2643(6)
Lawing, N. N. Alaska Nellie. [c1940]   2648(2)
Lawrence, G. 40 yrs. Yukon Telegraph. 1965.   2650(7)
Lazell, J. A. Alaskan apostle S. Jackson. 1960.   2653(0)
LeBourdais, D. M. Stefansson ... 1963.   2660(0)
Lewis, J. C. Black Beaver, trapper. 1911.   2697(0)
Life of Capt. Cook. n. d. . . . . . .   2706(2)
Life of Capt. Jas. Cook. 1824.   2707(2)
Life of Capt. Jas. Cook, a new ... 1831.   2708(2)
Life of Rev. Mother Amadeus ... 1923.   2709(0)
Life, voyages ... Capt. Jas. Cook. 1859.   2710(2)
Lloyd-Owen, F. Gold Nugget Charlie...Masson.1939.2742(0)
Lomen, C. J. 50 yrs. Alaska. 1954.   2750(5)
London, Joan. Jack London and his times. 1939.   2786(0)
Loring, Chas. G. Memoir Wm. Sturgis. 1864.   2797(1)
Low, Chas. R. Capt. Cook's three ... n. d.   2802(2)
Lucia, E. Klondike Kate... 1962.   2806(7)
Luciw, W. Ahapius Honcharenko ... 1963.   2807(0)

BIOGRAPHY. (cont.)

Lütgen, K. Two against Arctic.
  1957.   2816(4)
Lynch, J. 3 yrs. in Klondike.
  1904.   2819(7)
Lynch, J. Trois ans Klondike.
  [1905]   2820(7)
McCracken, H. Roughnecks and
  gentlemen. 1968.   2848(0)
McIlraith, J. Life Sir John
  Richardson. 1868.   2910(0)
Mack, G. Lewis and Hannah
  Gerstle. 1953.   2911(0)
McKeown, M. F. Alaska silver
  Mont Hawthorne. 1951. 2918(1)
McKeown, M. F. Trail led North.
  Mont Hawthorne. 1948. 2919(0)
McLain, C. M. Pioneer teacher.
  [c1970]   2924(5)
Mallinson, F. My travels ...
  in Alaska. 1914.   2958(0)
Manwaring, G. E. ... Admiral ...
  Jas. Burney ... 1931. 2963(2)
Marich, M. Zhizn' ... Fedora
  Litke. 1949.   2967(0)
Martin, M. Home on bear's
  domain. 1954.   3008(1)
Martin, M. O rugged land of
  gold. 1953.   3009(1)
Martinsen, E. L. Black sand...
  E. B. Lung. 1956.   3013(7)
Martinsen, E. L. Trail to north
  ...E. B. Lung. 1969. 3014(7)
Masik, A. Arctic...entertain-
  ments ... 1935.   3016(4)
Matlock, A. H. Teaching ...
  Arctic...[ca 1967]   3030(4)
Mayokok, R. Eskimo life.
  1951.   3044(5)
Meany, E. S. Vancouver's dis-
  covery...1907.   3051(1)
Medill, R. B. Klondike diary
  ... 1949.   3067(7)
Meeker, E. Busy life 85 yrs.
  [c1916]   3068(0)
Melin, M. Modern pioneering
  ... 1954.   3073(2)
Menager, F. M. Kingdom of seal.
  1962.   3078(5)
Menshutkin, B. N. Russia's
  Lomonosov. 1952.   3080(0)

Menshutkin, B. N. Zhizn. M. V.
  Lomonosova. 1947.   3081(0)
Miller, M. Soapy.
  1970. . . . .   3132(0)
Mitchell, Wm. General Greely
  ... 1936.   3147(4)
Montgomery, R. G. Adventures
  ...Lorne Knight.1932.3158(4)
Montgomery, R.G. "Pechuck"
  Lorne Knight.1932.   3158(4)
Moore, J. B. Skagway in days
  primeval. 1968.   3162(1)
Morenus, R. Alaska sourdough
  Slim Williams. 1956. 3171(2)
Morgan, Wm. G. Trail of
  cheechako. 1928.   3185(0)
Morice, A. G. 50 yrs. in w.
  Canada. 1930.   3187(7)
[Muir, J.] ...pictorial biog.
  ... 1938.   3222(0)
Muir, J. Wilderness world...
  1954.   3228(0)
Muir, J. Writings of ...
  1915-24.   3229(0)
Muir, J. R. Life of Capt.
  Jas. Cook. 1939.   3231(2)
Munger, Jas. F. Two yrs. in
  Pacific ... 1852.   3239(4)
Munn, H. T. Prairie trails...
  Arctic ... 1932.   3240(0)
Murie, A. Naturalist in
  Alaska. 1961.   3249(0)
Murie, M. Two in far North.
  1962.   3252(0)
Murphy, E. F. Bishop Bompas.
  n. d.   3253(7)
Nelson, K. Daughter of gold
  rush. 1958.   3288(5)
Nicol, J. Life and adventures
  ... 1822.   3304(0)
Noice, H. With Stefansson in
  Arctic. 1924.   3316(4)
Nord, S. Logger's odyssey.
  1943.   3322(0)
Nutchuk. Back to Smoky Sea.
  1946.   3368(6)
Nutchuk. Son of Smoky Sea.
  1941.   ,   3369(6)
O'Connor, P. Eskimo parish.
  [c1947]   3376(5)
O'Connor, R. Jack London...
  1964.   3378(0)

BIOGRAPHY. (cont.)

Ordaz, L. Jack London; el rey
  ... 1946.   3415(0)
Ordin, A. Velikiĭ lĕtchik...
  V. P. Chkalov. 1949. 3416(0)
Orlov, B. P. F. P. Litke...
  1948.   3418(0)
Osgood, C. Winter.
  1955. . . . . 3430(3)
Owens, F. R. Sky pilot...
  [Harold Wood] 1949. 3442(0)
Page, E.M. Wild horses...[Kan-
  sas Gilbert]]c1932] 3469(7)
Palmer, A. There's no place
  like Nome. 1963.   3478(5)
Palmer, F. In Klondyke ...
  1899.   3479(7)
Palmer, F. With my own eyes.
  1933.   3480(7)
Parrish, M. 9 pounds of lug-
  gage. 1940.   3496(0)
Partridge, B. Amundsen ...
  1929.   3497(0)
Pasetskiĭ, V. M. Vitus Bering.
  1958.   3499(6)
Patterson, S. Narrative of
  sufferings...1817.   3504(0)
Patty, E. N. North country
  challenge.   3505(3)
Pearson, G. H. My life of high
  adventure. [c1962]   3508(2)
Pearson, G. H. Seventy Mile Kid
  ...[c1957]   3509(2)
Peary, R. E. V. Stefansson.
  1925.   3512(4)
Peisson, É. Pôles ... Roald
  Amundsen. 1952.   3527(4)
[Penrose, C. V.] Memoir Jas.
  Trevenen...1959.   3533(2)
Perevalov, V. A. Lomonosov i
  Arktika...1949.   3535(0)
Peterson, M. S. Joaquin Miller
  ... [c1937]   3550(7)
Philips, C. Alaska...home-
  steading ...[1940?]   3569(3)
Pierce, E. L. Memoirs, letters
  Chas. Sumner.1877-93. 3579(0)
Pierce, R. A. Prince D. P. Mak-
  sutov...[1967]   3582(1)
Pierce, W. H. 13 years ...
  1890.   3583(0)

Pinkerton, K. Three's a crew.
  [c1940]   3607(1)
Pollak, G. Michael Heilprin.
  1912.   3631(0)
Porter, K. W. John Jacob Astor.
  1931.   3645(6)
Putnam, G. P. Mariner...Bob
  Bartlett. [c1947]   3705(0)
Richards, E.L.A. Arctic mood.
  1949.   3802(4)
Rickard, M.E. Everything...
  Tex Rickard. 1936.   3808(0)
Rickard, T.A. Through Yukon
  and Alaska. 1909.   3810(0)
Ridley, Wm. Snapshots from
  No.Pac.letters.1903.   3817(1)
Rieder, K. Cheechako first
  class. 1953.   3818(0)
Roberts, L. Samuel Hearne.
  1930.   3835(1)
Robertson, F. C. Soapy Smith
  1961.   3837(0)
Robertson, J. R. [C. M. Clay]
  ...Tsars. 1935.   3838(0)
Robertson, W. N. Yukon memo-
  ries ... 1930.   3839(7)
Robins, E. Raymond and I.
  1956.   3844(7)
Robins, E. Magnetic north.
  1904.   3845(7)
Robolsky, M. Life, voyages
  ... Capt. J. C. 1864.3851(2)
Rodli, A. S. North of Heaven
  1963.   3864(5)
Romano, V. Jack London.
  1952.   3874(0)
Romig, E. C. Life and travels
  pioneer woman. 1945. 3875(1)
Romig, E. C. Pioneer woman in
  Alaska. 1948.   3875(0)
Rørdam. V. Dansk Liv. [Vitus
  Bering] 1938.   3881(6)
Ross, E. L. Aaron Ladner Linds-
  ley. [ca 1910?]   3886(0)
Ross, S. Gruening of Alaska.
  [c1968]   3887(0)
Rossman, E. Black sunlight...
  1926.
Russell, Thos. H. ... life ...
  W. G. Harding. 1923. 3922(0)
Rydell, C. Adventures...auto-
  biog. ... 1924.   3927(0)

BIOGRAPHY. (cont.)

Rydell, C. On Pacific fron-
tiers...1924.   3928(0)
S., Z. O zhizni ... Innoken-
tiĭa ... 1893.   3934(6)
Sabine, B. W. Summer trip...
missions. [ca 1910]   3936(5)
Samoĭlov, V. A. Semen Dezhnev
... 1945.   3949(0)
Samuels, C. Magnificent Rube
Tex Rickard. [c1957] 3952(0)
Service, R. W. My adventures
... [1967?]   4054(7)
Service, R. W. Ploughman of
moon. 1945.   4055(7)
Seward, F. W. Remininscences...
1916.   4070(0)
Seward, F. W. Autobiog. Wm. H.
Seward. 1877.   4071(0)
Seward, F. W. Seward at Wash-
ington...1891.   4071(0)
Seward, F. W. Wm. H. Seward...
autobiog. 1891.   4071(0)
Seward, Wm. H. Diplomatic
hist. 1853-84.   4079(0)
Seward, Wm. H. Works ...
1853-84.   4079(0)
Shand, M. C. Summit and beyond
... 1959.   4086(1)
Sharples, A. W. Two against
North. 1961.   4094(2)
Shenitz, H. Alaska's ...
[Veniaminov] 1962.   4109(6)
Shore, E. B. Born on snowshoes.
1954.   4130(3)
Short, W. Cheechakoes.
[c1964]   4131(1)
Short, W. This raw land.
1968.   4132(1)
Shteĭnberg, E. L. Kruzenshtern,
Lisĭanskiĭ. 1950.   4136(0)
Shteĭnberg, E. L. Zhizn. Iuriĭa
Lisĭanskogo ... 1948. 4137(0)
Simpson, A. Life...Thos. Simp-
son. 1845.   4160(4)
Small, M. Four fares to
Juneau. [c1947]   4186(1)
Sobotka, H. A. Kraj...Jacka
Londona. 1929.   4228(0)
Sokolicz, A. Jack London.[in
Polish] 1925.   4235(0)

Sparks, J. Leben...John Led-
yard...1829.   4250(2)
Sparks, J. Memoirs life...
J. Ledyard. 1828.   4251(2)
Sparks, J. Life John Ledyard.
1828.   4252(2)
Sparks, J. Life and travels
J. Ledyard. 1843.   4253(2)
Sparks, J. Travels ... John
Ledyard. 1834.   4253(2)
Speck, G. Samuel Hearne.
1963.   4256(0)
Springer, J. A. Innocent...
M. K. Burke. 1963.   4270(3)
Spurr, J. E. Through Yukon gol
gold diggings. 1900. 4273(7)
Stark, C. R. Bering Sea...
[H. L. Blunt] 1957. 4286(0)
Starr, W. A. Adventures in
Klondike. 1960.   4287(0)
Steele, S. B. 40 yrs. in
Canada. 1915.   4296(7)
Stefansson, V. Discovery...
[c1964]   4303(4)
Stefansson, V. My life with
Eskimo. 1913.   4307(4)
Stefansson, V. Das Geheimnis
der Eskimos. 1925.   4308(4)
Stejneger, L. H. Georg Wilhelm
Steller. 1936.   4330(6)
Stephens, L. D. Life sketches
Jayhawker. 1916.   4336(0)
Stewart, R. L. Sheldon Jackson
... [c1908]   4345(0)
Stoddard, G. Go North ...
1957.   4351(2)
Stone, I. Sailor on horseback
Jack London. 1938.   4353(0)
Storey, M. Charles Sumner.
1900.   4355(0)
Strahorn, C. A. 1500 miles...
30 yrs. ... 1911.   4357(0)
Strange, H.G.L. Never a dull
moment. 1941.   4359(7)
Strange, Jas. ...journal and
narrat. ... 1928.   4360(2)
Sullivan,E.D. Fabulous Wilson
Mizner. 1935.   4380(0)
Sullivan, M. K. Woman who
went ... [c1902]   4381(5)
Svet, Ĭa. M. Moreplavatel'
Dzhems Kuk. 1963.   4414(2)

BIOGRAPHY. (cont.)

Swayze, N. Manhunters ...
 1960.   4427(0)
Swenson, O.   Northwest of
 world ... 1944.   4429(5)
Teichmann, E.   Journey to
 ... diary. 1925.   4477(1)
Thiéry, M. La vie...Capt. Cook
 ... 1929.   4484(2)
Thiéry, M. Life...Capt. Cook.
 1929.   4485(2)
Thiéry, M. Capt. Cook ...
 1930.   4486(2)
Thirring, G. A magyarországi
 ... 1905.   4487(0)
Thomas, L. Sir Hubert Wilkins
 ... [c1961]   4496(0)
Thomas, L. Woodfill of Regu-
 lars...1929.   4498(3)
Thomas, T. Follow North Star.
 1960.   4501(0)
Thomas, T. Only in Alaska.
 1969.   4502(0)
Thornton, H. R. Among Eskimos
 of Wales...1931.   4526(5)
Tilton, G. F. "Cap'n George
 Fred himself." 1929. 4541(0)
Tollemache, S.H.R.L. Reminis-
 cences. 1911.   4545(7)
Trefzger, H. 50 yrs. hunting,
 ... [c1963]   4575(1)
Tupper, C. Political reminis-
 cences. 1914.   4588(0)
Tupper, C. Recollections 60
 yrs. 1914.   4589(0)
Tyrrell, M. E. I was there...
 [c1938]   4598(7)
Vaeth, J. G. To ends earth...
 R. Amundsen. [c1962] 4627(0)
[Valaam Monastery] Zhiznj ...
 Germana ... 1894.   4632(6)
Van Deusen, G. G. Wm. Henry
 Seward. 1967.   4647(0)
Villiers, A. J. Capt. Cook...
 1967.   4703(2)
Villiers, A. J. Capt. Jas.
 Cook. [c1967]   4704(2)
Wachel, P. Oscar Winchell...
 [c1967]   4719(0)
Walcutt, C. C. Jack London.
 1966.   4728(0)

Walden, A. T. Dog-puncher on
 Yukon. 1928.   4729(7)
Walker, F. Jack London and
 Klondike. 1966.   4731(7)
[Wardner, J.] Jim Wardner of
 Wardner, Idaho. 1900.4738(7)
Weed, A. L. Grandma goes to
 Arctic. 1957.   4778(4)
Weems, C. Bishop of Arctic.
 1912. [P. T. Rowe] 4781(0)
Welzl, J. Quest for polar
 treasures. 1933.   4791(4)
Welzl. J. Po stopach polarnich
 ... 1930.   4791(4)
Welzl. J. Auf den Spuren ...
 [c1937]   4791(4)
Welzl, J. 30 yrs. golden north.
 1932.   4792(4)
Wentworth, E. ... to Metlakat-
 la. 1968.[W. Duncan] 4795(1)
Wheaton, H. Prekaska's wife.
 ...Aleutians. 1945. 4806(6)
White, S. E. Pole star.
 1935. [A.A.Baranov] 4840(1)
Whiting, F. B. Grit... M. J.
 Heney. 1933.   4843(1)
Wiedemann, Thos. Cheechako into
 sourdough. [c1942] 4861(7)
Wilkins, G. H. Flying Arctic.
 1928.   4871(4)
Wisting, O. 16 år med Roald
 Amundsen. 1930.   4937(0)
Wolfe, A. In Alaskan waters.
 1942.   4940(0)
Wolfe, L. M. Son of wilderness
 J. Muir. 1945.   4942(0)
Woods, H. F. God's loaded dice
 ... 1948.   4958(0)
Wrangell, F. F. Vitze-Admiral
 S. O. Makarov. 1911. 4967(0)
Young, S. H. Adventures in
 Alaska. [c1919]   4996(1)
Young, S. H. Alaska days with
 J. Muir. [c1915]   4997(1)
Young, S. H. Hall Young of
 Alaska. [c1927]   4998(1)

BIOLOGICAL SCIENCES - General.

Bade, Wm. F. Life and letters
 J. Muir. 1924.   334(0)

BIOLOGICAL SCIENCES - General.
(cont.)

B. C. Natural Resources Conf.
Transactions. 1959.   671(7)
Carrighar, S. Icebound summer.
1953.   849(5)
Carrighar, S. Moonlight at mid-
day. 1958.   850(5)
Darling, F. F. Pelican in wil-
derness. 1956.   1184(0)
Dufresne, F. Alaska's animals
and fishes. 1946.   1364(0)
Dufresne, F. No room for bears.
1965.   1366(1)
Dugdale, V. Album N. A. ani-
mals. 1966.   1367(0)
Forster, J. R. Observ. phys.
geog. nat. hist. 1778.1613(0)
Freuchen, P. Arctic year.
1958.   1656(4)
Freuchen, P. Det arktiske år.
1961.   1657(4)
Hansen, H. P. Arctic biology.
1967.   1936(0)
Hylander, C. J. Wildlife com-
munity ... 1965.   2251(0)
Morozewicz, J. M. Komandory...
1925.   3195(6)
Muir, J. Cruise of *Corwin*.
1917.   3226(0)
[Muir, J.] John Muir book ...
1925.   3227(0)
Murie, A. Naturalist in Alaska.
1961.   3249(2)
Murie, M. E. Two in far north.
1962.   3252(2)
Olson, S. Runes of North.
1963.   3408(0)
Perevalov, V. A. Lomonosov i
Arktika ... 1949.   3535(6)
Peterson, R. T. Wild America.
1955.   3553(6)
Sanderson, I. T. Continent we
live on. 1961.   3956(0)
Scarff, R. F. Distrib. origin
life ... 1911.   3991(0)
Sheldon, C. Wilderness of
Denali. 1930.   4098(2)
Sheldon, C. Wilderness North
Pac. islands. 1912.   4099(6)
Sheldon, C. Wilderness Upper
Yukon. 1911.   4100(0)

Shelford, V. E. Ecol. N. A.
1963.   4106(0)
Shumaker, C. L. Do you know?
Pr. Wm. Sd. 1967.   4138(2)
Staender, G. Adventures Arctic
wildlife. 1970.   4278(4)
Stejneger, L. H. Georg Wilhelm
Steller...1936.   4330(6)
Tytler, P. F. Hist. view ...
nat. history. 1832.   4599(0)
Wiggins, I. L. Arctic biology
... 1957.   4865(0)
Wiggins, I. L. Current biolo-
gical research.1953. 4866(0)
Wilson, Jas. A. Bits of Alaska
... [c1908]   4912(1)
Wotte, H. In blauer Ferne lag
...Steller. 1966.   4965(6)

BIOLOGICAL SCIENCES - Botany.

Adams, J. Bibliog. Canadian
plantgeog. 1928-47.   11(0)
Anderson, J. P. Alaska-grown
plants. 1918.   246(1)
Anderson, J. P. Flora of
Alaska. 1959.   247(0)
Arnell, H. W. Die mosse Vega-
exped. 1917.   308(0)
Baxter, D. V. Forest and fun-
gus lower Yukon. 1939.432(0)
Baxter, D. V. Importance fungi
...spruce. 1942.   433(0)
Black, M. L. P. Yukon wild
flowers. [1940?]   571(7)
Britton, M. E. Vegetation
Arctic tundra. 1966. 673(4)
Cheney, R. W. Pleistocene flo-
ra Fairbanks. 1936.   889(3)
Cooper, W. S. Contrib. Glacier
Bay ... 1956.   1067(1)
Cooper, W. S. Vegetation Pr.
Wm. Sd. 1942.   1068(2)
Drury, W. H. Bog flats ... Up-
per Kuskokwim. 1956. 1359(5)
Eliot, W. A. Forest trees Pac.
Coast. 1938.   1435(0)
Fink, B. Lichen flora U. A.
1935.   1559(0)
Floderus, B. G. O. Strange spe-
cies *Salix*...1935. 1583(2)

BIOLOGICAL SCIENCES - Botany.
(cont.)
Floderus, B.G.O. 2 Linnean
Salix ... 1940.   1584(0)
Frye, T. C. Hepaticae of N. A.
1937-48.   1664(0)
Giddings, J. L. Dendrochrono-
logy no. Alaska.1941. 1708(4)
Gilky, H. M. Weeds of Pacific
n. w. 1957.   1719(0)
Gillett, J.M. Gentians Canada,
Alaska...1963.   1721(0)
Gjaerevoll, O. Bot. investig.
Pteridophytes...1958. 1733(3)
Gmelin, J. G. Flora Sibirica
1747-69.   1741(6)
Györffy, I. ... florae penin-
sula Alaska. 1942.   1886(6)
Hanson, H. C. ... grassland...
1951.   1943(5)
Harriman Alaska Exped. Crytoga-
mic. Vol. 5. 1910.   1950(0)
Harshberger, J. W. Forests Pac.
... 1929.   1971(1)
Haskin, L. L. Wild flowers Pac.
coast...1934.   1984(0)
Heer, O. Flora Fossilis Alas-
kana. 1869.   2014(0)
Heer, O. Flora Fossilis Arcti-
ca. 1868-83.   2015(4)
Heller, C. A. Wild flowers of
Alaska. 1966.   2024(0)
Henry, J. K. Flora B. C....
1915.   2069(1)
Hinds, R. B. Bot. *Sulphur* ...
Belcher. 1846.   2116(0)
Hooker, W. J. Brief memoir Da-
vid Douglas.[ca1837] 2171(0)
Hooker, W. J. Flora Boreali-
Americana. 1829-40. 2172(0)
Hooker, W. J. Bot. Beechey's
Blossom ... 1841.   2173(0)
Hultén, E. Flora of Alaska.
1968.   2227(0)
Hultén, E. Flora Alaska and
Yukon. 1941-50.   2228(0)
Hultén, E. Flora Aleutian Isls.
... 1937.   2229(6)
Hultén, E. Outline...Arctic and
boreal biota...1937. 2230(6)
Hultén, E. Circumpol. plants...
Vasc. 1962.   2231(0)

Hutchison, I. W. North to
rime-ringed sun.1934.2246(4)
Hutchison, I. W. Stepping
stones ... 1937.   2247(6)
Hutchison, I. W. Aleutian
Islands...1942.   2247(6)
Ilvessalo, L. Maapallon met-
sävarat. 1930.   2256(0)
Kaulfuss, G. F. Enumeration
filicum ... 1824.   2418(0)
Knaben, G. Evolution...papavers
... 1959.   2491(0)
Langsdorff, G. H. Plants re-
cueillies...1810-18. 2603(0)
Lebedour, K. F. Flora Rossica
... 1841-53.   2662(6)
Lind, J. V. A. Fungi(micromy-
cetes)...*Gjøa*. 1910. 2711(4)
Linnaeus, C. Plantae Rariores
Camtschatcences.1750.2718(6)
Lynge, B. Lichens *Gjøa* exped.
1921.   2821(4)
McMinn, H.E. Illus. manual Pac.
coast trees...1935. 2938(0)
Macoun, J. M. Vascular plants.
1921.   2945(4)
Mason, M. H. Arctic forests.
1924.   3019(0)
Merrill, E. D. Botany Cook's
voyages. 1954.   3087(2)
Merrill, G. K. Lichens.
1924.   3088(4)
Pallas, P. S. Flora Rossica...
1784-88.   3472(6)
Pallas, P. S. Opisanie ...
1786.   3473(6)
Pallas, P. S. Opisanie ...
1792.   3474(6)
Plieninger, G. H. T....Gmelin
epistolici...1861.   3623(6)
Polunin, N. V. Circumpolar
Arctic ... 1959.   3635(4)
Postels, A. F. Illus. algarum
...Lutke ... 1840.   3654(6)
Potter, L. Alaska Highway
flowers. [c1966]   3661(0)
Potter, L. Roadside flowers
... 1962.   3663(0)
Potter, L. Wildflowers along
Mt. McKinley Rd.1969.3664(2)
Reed, J. C. Rates tree growth
...1956.   3773(2)

BIOLOGICAL SCIENCES - Botany.
(cont.)
Sargent, Chas. S. Manual trees
N. A. 1926. 3959(0)
Seemann, B. C. Bot. *Herald*...
Kellett...1852-57. 4041(0)
Sharples, A. W. Alaska wild
flowers. 1938. 4093(0)
Shaw, C. G. Additions to Alas-
kan fungi. 1954. 4096(1)
Sprague, R. Some fungi Alas-
kan *Carex*. 1954. 4267(1)
Steere, Wm. C. Bryophyta Arctic
Bering Strait. 1938. 4298(6)
Steward, A. N. Aquatic plants
Pac. n. w. 1963. 4342(0)
Tolmachev, A.I....flor i flori-
sticheskikh...1941. 4546(0)
Tomin, M. P. ...lishaĭnikov...
1937. 4550(4)
Wettstein, R. Monographie der
...*Euphrasia*. 1896. 4802(6)
White, H. A. Alaska wildberry
trails...[c1959] 4818(0)
White, H. A. Alaska wildflower
trails. n.d. 4819(0)
White, H. A. More...wildflower
trails. [c1962] 4823(0)
Wiggins, I. L. Flora Alaskan
Arctic Slope. 1962. 4864(4)
Williams, M. M. Alaska wild-
flower ... 1952. 4884(0)
Wilson, C.G. Alice Eastwood's
wonderland. 1955. 4909(0)

BIOLOGICAL SCIENCES -
Entomology.

Alexander, C. P. Crane flies...
Erioptera Meigen. 1955.169(0)
Carpenter, S. J. Mosquitos
N. A. 1955. 848(0)
Chamberlin, R. V. Spiders of
Alaska. 1947. 882(0)
Darsie, R. F....mosquito pupae
Aedes riparius...1954.1186(0)
Fluke, C.L. *Metasyrphus* species
(Diptera...) 1952. 1588(2)
Hammer, M. S. Alaskan oribatids
1955. 1926(0)
Harriman Alaska Exped. Insects.
Pt.1. 1910. Vol. 8. 1950(0)

Harriman Alaska Exped. Insects.
Pt.2. 1910. Vol. 9. 1950(0)
Mochul'skiĭ, V. I. ...Insecta
Carabica. 1850. 3153(6)
Mochul'skiĭ, V. I. Genres et
especes insects.1868.3154(6)
Newell, I. M. *Copidognathus
curtus* Hall...1951. 3299(0)
Newell, I. M. ...Halacaridae
(Acari). 1951. 3300(6)
Newell, I. M. *Agaue* and *Thalas-
sarachna* ... 1951. 3301(6)
Newell, I. M. *Copidognathus*
... 1950. 3302(6)
Smetana, A. Staphylinini und
Quediini ... 1965. 4187(0)
Van Dyke, E. C. Coleoptera...
Katmai...1924. 4648(6)

BIOLOGICAL SCIENCES -
Ichthyology.

Clemens, W. A. Fishes Pac. ...
Canada. 1946. 952(1)
Crandell, J. V. Story Pacific
salmon. 1946. 1112(0)
Hubbs, C. L. Contrib....2 new
fishes. 1941. 2215(0)
Jones, J. W. The salmon.
1959. 2381(0)
McAllister, D. E. List marine
fishes Canada. 1960. 2826(0)
McAllister, D. E. Prowfishes,
Zaproridae ...1961. 2827(0)
Pritchard, A. L. Pac. salmon
... 1930. 3697(1)
Rendahl, H. Fische...Nord-
pazifik. [1931] 3782(0)
Rostlund, E. Freshwater fish
... 1952. 3898(4)
Schwiebert, E. Salmon of world.
1970. 4023(0)
Shmidt, P. I. Ryby Tikhogo
okeana. 1948. 4128(0)
Soot-Ryen, T. Notes...fishes...
I.L.Norberg. 1940. 4242(2)
Taraneĉs, A. I. Kratkiĭ opre-
delitel'ryb...1937. 4457(0)
Thompson, W.F. Biol. Pacific
halibut.no.1. 1931. 4513(0)
Thompson, W. F. Biol. Pacific
halibut.no.2. 1934. 4514(0)

BIOLOGICAL SCIENCES -
                Ichthyology. (cont.)

Thompson, W. F. Life hist. Pac.
    halibut, no. 1. 1930. 4516(0)
Thompson, W. F. Life hist. Pac.
    halibut, no. 2. 1936. 4517(0)
Walford, L. A. Marime game
    fishes ... 1937.   4730(0)

BIOLOGICAL SCIENCES -
                Limnology.

Harriman Alaska Exped....mol-
    lusks. 1910. Vol. 13. 1950(0)
Lowe, Chas. Wm. Freshwater
    algae...diatoms.1923. 2803(5)
Sars, G. O. Fresh-water Ostra-
    coda ... 1926.   3963(0)

BIOLOGICAL SCIENCES - Marine.

Barrow, H. D. Paradise North.
    1956. [tide pools]   408(0)
Beklemishev, K. V. Distrib.
    zooplankton...1959.   473(0)
Bidenkap, O. Fortegnelse...
    bryozoer. 1906.   553(0)
Broch, H. Oktokorallen...
    1936.   675(0)
Broch, H....Stylasteriden (Hy-
    drokorallen)...1936.   676(0)
Broch, H....Stylasteriden (Hy-
    drokorallen)...1942.   677(0)
Chamberlin, J. L. ...*Spisula
    polynyma* 1963.   881(0)
Clark, A. H. Arctic...mollusks
    ... 1960.   936(4)
Clemens, W. A. Check list...
    fauna and flora...1933.951(1)
Dall, W. H. Catalogue shells
    Bering Strait.1874.   1156(4)
Dall, W. H. Descript....Mol-
    lusca ... 1873.   1157(0)
Dall, W. H. Descript....Mol-
    lusca...1872.   1158(0)
Dall, W. H. Descript...Crus-
    tacea ... 1872.   1159(0)
Dall, W. H. New parasitic
    crustacea...1874.   1162(0)
Dall, W. H. Parasites of ceta-
    ceans ... 1872.   1163(0)

Dall, W. H. Prelim. ... mol-
    lusks ... 1872.   1164(0)
Dall, W. H. Prelim. ... mol-
    lusks ... 1877.   1165(0)
Darling, L. Seals and wal-
    ruses. 1955.   1185(0)
Flora, Chas. Sound and sea.
    1968.   1586(0)
Flower, R. H. Cephalopods
    Seward Penin....1941.1587(5)
Fraser, C. M. Hydroids Pac.
    ... 1937.   1635(1)
Hanna, G. D. Collecting shells
    in Arctic. 1957.   1932(4)
Harriman Alaska Exped. Crusta-
    ceans. 1910. Vol. 10.1950(0)
Harriman Alaska Exped. Nemer-
    teans. 1910.Vol. 11. 1950(0)
Harriman Alaska Exped. Enchy-
    traeids.1910. Vol.12.1950(0)
Harriman Alaska Exped....star-
    fishes. 1910. Vol.14.1950(0)
Hülsemann, K. Radiolaria in
    plankton...1963.   2225(4)
Jäderholm, A. E....Hydroiden-
    fauna...1908.   2319(0)
Keep, J. West coast shells...
    1887.   .   2423(0)
LaRocque, J. A. A. Catalogue
    ...mollusca...1953. 2628(0)
Menzies, R. J...."Exosphaeroma"
    Isopoda... 1954.   3084(0)
Miklukho-Maklaĭ, N. N. ...
    Schwämme ... 1870.   3110(0)
Oldroyd, I. S. Marine shells
    ... 1924-27.   3399(0)
Perry, R. World of walrus.
    1968.   3542(0)
Pettibone, M. H. Polychaetous
    annelids...1949.   3560(0)
Pike, G. C. ...whales, por-
    poises...1954.   3586(0)
Ricketts, E. F. Between Pacific
    tides. 1939.   3812(1)
Scammon, C. M. Marine mammals
    ... 1874.   3990(0)
Scheffer, V. B. Seals, sea
    lions...1958.   3997(0)
Scheffer, V. B. Year of seal.
    [c1970]   3998(6)
Scheffer, V. B. Year of whale.
    [c1969]   3999(0)

BIOLOGICAL SCIENCES - Marine.
(cont.)
Sleptsov, M. M. Biologiíã i
promysel. kitov.1955. 4180(0)
Slevin, J. R. Amphibians ...
1928.   4181(0)
Slijper, E. J. Walvisson.
1958.   4182(0)
Slijper, E. J. Whales.
1962. . . . . 4183(0)
Smirnov, N. A. Zveri Arktiki.
1935.   4189(4)
Steller, G. W. ...sonderbaren
Meer-thieren...1753. 4331(6)
Stimpson, W. ... animalium ever-
tebratorum...1857.   4347(0)
Stimpson, W. Crustacea and
echinodermata. 1857. 4348(0)
Tanfil'ev, G. I. Moríã; Kaspiĭ-
skoe, Chernoe...1931. 4451(0)
Treadwell, A. L. *Neosabellides
alaskensis* ... 1943. 4572(2)
Treadwell, A. L. Polychaetous
annelids...1926.   4573(0)
Walker, T. J. Whale primer.
[1962]   4733(0)

BIOLOGICAL SCIENCES -
Ornithology.

Alaska Mag. Pub. Book animals
and birds. 1940.   80(0)
Amer. Ornithol. Union. Check-
list N.A. ... 1886.   207(0)
Bailey, A. M. Birds Arctic
Alaska. 1948.   347(4)
Bailey, A. M. Birds Cape Prince
of Wales ... 1943.   348(5)
Booth, E. S. Birds of west.
1948.   618(0)
Booth, E. S. Birds of western
... Alaska. 1960.   619(0)
Brandt, H. Alaska bird trails.
1943.   644(5)
Brooks, A. Distrib. list birds
B. C. 1925.   684(1)
Cassin, J. Illus. birds Calif.
... R. A. 1856.   863(0)
Cassin, J. Mammalogy and or-
nithol. 1859.   864(0)
Dall, W. H. ...avifauna Aleut.
Isl. ... 1874.   1160(6)

Dall, W. H. ...avifauna Aleut.
Isl. ...1873.   1161(6)
Delacour, J. T. Prelim. Canada
geese...1951.   1237(0)
Einarsen, A. S. Black brant
... 1965.   1426(0)
Eliot, W. A. Birds Pac. coast.
1923.   1434(0)
Fairbanks Bird Club. ... In-
terior ... [1965]   1512(3)
Fisher, J. The fulmar.
1952. . . . . 1570(6)
Gabrielson, I. N. Birds of
Alaska. 1959.   1668(0)
Grinnell, J. Birds and mammals
southeast. 1909.   1863(1)
Grinnell, J. Birds Kotzebue
Sound. 1900.   1864(5)
Grinnell, J. Birds...avifaunal
Pr. Wm. Sd. 1910.   1865(2)
Ingersoll, E. Alaskan bird-
life. 1914.   2261(0)
Kessel, B. ... Interior,So.Cen-
tral, Barrow.1967.   2449(0)
Kortright, F. H. Ducks, geese,
swans N. A. 1942.   2510(0)
Laing, H. M. Birds...*Thiepval*
...1925.   2583(6)
Macoun, J. Catalogue Canadian
birds. 1900-04.   2946(0)
Murie, A. Birds Mt. McKinley.
[c1963]   3250(2)
Nelson, E. W. Alaska longspur.
1913.   3284(6)
Nelson, E. W. Emporer goose.
1913.   3285(5)
Pearson, T. G. Birds of
America. 1936.   3511(0)
Peterson, R. T. Field guide to
western ... 1941.   3552(0)
Pettingill, O.S. Bird watcher's
America. 1966.   3561(0)
Pitelka, F. A. Geog. ...*Limno-
dromus*. 1950.   3616(0)
Pough, R. H. Audubon bird
guide. 1946.   3665(0)
Reed, Chas. K. Western bird
guide. 1913.   3770(0)
Reed, Chester A. N. A. bird's
eggs. 1904.   3771(0)
Shortt, T. M. Summer birds
Yakutat Bay. 1939.   4134(1)

BIOLOGICAL SCIENCES -
        Ornithology. (cont.)

Snyder, L. L. Study sharp-
tailed grouse. 1935. 4225(0)
Snyder, L. L. Birds Wrangell
Isl. ... 1926.   4226(4)
Snyder, L. L. ... sharpshinned
hawk. 1938.   4227(0)
Swarth, H. S. Birds and mam-
mals ... 1911.   4421(1)
Swarth, H. S. Birds and mam-
mals Stikine...1922. 4422(1)
Swarth, H. S. Birds Nunivak
Island. 1934.   4423(5)
Swarth, H. S. ...collect.birds
Atlin...1926.   4424(1)
Swarth, H. S....collect. birds
Vancouver Isl. 1912. 4425(1)
Taverner, P. A. Study *Buteo
borealis* ...hawk.1927.4462(0)
Taverner, P. A. Birds Canada.
1934.   4463(0)
Taverner, P. A. Birds western
Canada. 1926.   4464(0)
Townsend, C. H. Crested auklet.
1913.   4562(0)
Vaurie, C. ...palearctic...
Sylviinae ... 1954. 4663(0)
Vaurie, C. ...palearctic ...
Turdinae... 1955. 4664(0)
Vaurie, C. ...palearctic...
Fringillidae...1956. 4665(6)
Vaurie, C. ...palearctic...
Fringillidae...1956-7.4666(5)
White, H. A. Bird sampler.
[c1963]   4820(0)

BIOLOGICAL SCIENCES -
        Physiology.

Garn, S. M. Readings on race.
1960.   1689(0)
Rodahl, K. Eskimo metabolism.
1954.   3852(0)
Rodahl, K. Nutritional ...
Arctic ... 1960.   3854(0)
Rodahl, K. ...blood...Eskimo
...ketosis...1954. 3856(0)
Rodahl, K. U. S. survival
ration studies...1950.3859(0)

Stefansson, V. Not by bread
alone. 1946.   4311(0)
Stefansson, V. The fat of the
land. 1956.   4311(0)

BIOLOGICAL SCIENCES - Zoology.

Alaska Mag. Pub. Book of ani-
mals and birds. 1940. 80(0)
Alfthan, A. E. Hafsutterns och
pelssälens...1903. 170(0)
Allen, J. A. ... caribou ...
Kenai ... [1901] 181(2)
Allen, J. A. On eared seals...
no. fur seals...1870. 182(0)
Aron, Wm. Distrib. animals
east. no. Pac. 1960. 310(0)
Banfield, A.W.F. Revision
reindeer...1961.   384(0)
Bee, J. W. Mammals no. Alaska
Arctic Slope. 1956. 464(4)
Beechey, F. W. Zoology...
voyage...1839.   469(0)
Brandt, J. F. Prodromus desc.
animalium. 1835. 645(0)
Büchner, E. ...Seekuh (*Rhytina
gigas* Zimm.)...1891. 721(1)
Callison, J. P. Wolf predation
... 1948.   781(0)
Caras, R. A....Deadman Bay...
Kodiak bear. 1969. 831(6)
Cassin, J. Mammalogy and
ornithol. 1859.   864(0)
Chamisso, L.C.A. Animalibus...
Kotzebue...[1819] 885(0)
Chase, W. H. Alaska's mammoth
brown bears. 1947. 898(0)
Crisler, L. Arctic wild.
1958.   1124(4)
Dice, L. R. Land vertebrate
assoc. ... 1920. 1389(3)
Digby, G. B. Mammoth...n. e.
Siberia. 1926.   1294(0)
Dove, W. E. Progr. parasites
reindeer. [1929?] 1338(5)
Elton, C. Voles, mice and
lemmings. 1942. 1449(0)
Eschscholtz, J. F. Zool. atlas
Kotzebue...1829. 1493(0)
Grinnell, J.Birds and mammals
... 1909.   1863(1)

BIOLOGICAL SCIENCES - Zoology.
(cont.)
Harting, J. E. Fauna Prybilov
... Coues. 1875.   1975(6)
Haynes, B. D. Grizzly bear.
1966.   2006(0)
Hinds, R. B. Zool. ... *Sulphur*
Belcher. 1844.   2117(0)
Holzworth, J. M. Wild grizzlies
... 1930.   2165(0)
Hornaday, W. T. Camp-fires in
Canadian ... 1906.   2181(0)
Hornaday, W. T. Our vanishing
wildlife...1913.   2182(0)
Hornaday, W. T. Tales...
nature...1924.   2183(0)
Kellett, H. Zoology *Herald* ...
Vertebrals...1854.   2432(0)
Kurten, B. Biometric compari-
sons ... 1959.   2574(0)
Leopold, A. S. Wildlife in
Alaska ... 1953.   2682(0)
Lorenz, L. Becken Stellerschen
Seekuh. 1904.   2796(6)
Lucas, F. A. Animals of past.
1922.   2805(0)
Lull, R. S. Evolution elephant.
1908.   2810(0)
McCracken, H. Alaska bear
trails. 1931.   2842(6)
McCracken, H. Hunters stormy
sea. 1957.   2845(6)
McCracken, H. Beast that walks
...grizzly...1955.   2851(6)
McCracken, H. Biggest bear on
earth. 1943.   2852(6)
McCracken, H. Caribou traveler.
1949.   2853(0)
McCracken, H. Last of sea
otters. 1942.   2855(6)
McGuire, J.A. In Alaska-Yukon
game land. 1921.   2899(2)
Mazurmovich, B. N. Vydaĭush.
...zoologi. 1960.   3048(0)
Mills, E. A. Grizzly ...
1919.   3136(0)
Murie, A. Mammals of Mt.
McKinley. [c1962]   3251(2)
Nelson, E. W. Wild animals
N. A. ... 1918.   3286(0)
Olsen, S. J. Postcranial ...
Bison and *Bos*. 1960. 3405(5)

Osborn, H. F. Age of mammals.
1919.   3422(0)
Osgood, W. H. Peculiar bear
from Alaska. 1909.   3432(2)
Pallas, P. S. Zoographia-Rosso
Asiatica...1811(1831).3476(0)
Pekarskiĭ, P. P. ... *Rhytina*
borealis. 1869.   3528(6)
[Pennant, T.] Arctic zoology.
1784-87.   3531(0)
[Pennant, T.] Introduction to
Arctic zool. 1792.   3531(0)
Pennant, T. Thiergeschichte
nordl. ... 1787.   3532(0)
Perry, R. World of polar
bear. 1966.   3541(4)
Powers, A. Animals of Arctic.
1965.   3672(4)
Pruitt, W. O. Animals of
North. 1967.   3701(3)
Rand, A. L. Mammals of Yukon.
1945.   3730(7)
Rausch, R. Notes...mammals
Anaktuvuk Pass.1951. 3750(4)
Rausch, R. Observations ...
Lemmings ... 1950.   3751(4)
Rausch, R. On status...Arctic
mammals. 1953.   3752(4)
Roosevelt, T. Deer family.
1902.   3879(0)
Rue, L. L. World of red fox.
[c1969]   3912(2)
Russell, A. Grizzly country.
1967.   3914(0)
Sailer, R. I. Inverteb. ...
Alaska. 1954.   3938(0)
Schiller, E. L. Mammals
Katmai ... 1956.   4001(6)
Skinner, J. W. Permian fusuli-
nids ... 1966.   4175(0)
Skinner, M. F. Fossil bison
revision...1947.   4176(0)
Smirnov, N. A. Zveri Arktiki.
1935.   4189(4)
Swarth, H. S. Birds and mam-
mals ... 1911.   4421(1)
Swarth, H. S. Birds and mam-
mals Stikine...1922. 4422(1)
Swarth, H. S....collect. birds
& mammals Atlin.1926.4424(1)
Swarth, H. S. ...collect. ...
Vancouver Isl.1912. 4425(0)

BIOLOGICAL SCIENCES - Zoology.
(cont.)
White, H. A. Alaska big game
animals. [ca 1961 ?] 4817(0)
Williams, J. P. Alaskan adventure. 1952. 4882(1)
Young, S. P. Clever coyote.
1951. 5000(0)
Young, S. P. Wolves of N. A.
1944. 5001(0)

CARTOGRAPHY.

Bellin, J. N. Carte ...Ocean
Sept. ... 1766. 493(0)
Bellin, J. N. Hydrographie
Françoise. 1802. 493(0)
Bellin, J. N. Remarques ...
Russes...1766. 494(0)
Breitfus, L. L. Arktis ...
1939. 651(4)
Brown, L. A. Story of maps.
1949. 697(0)
Buache, J. N. Mémoire ...
Engel ... 1775. 713(0)
Buache, P. Carte...de l'Isle.
1752. 714(0)
Buache, P. Considerations
Grande Mer...1753[-55] 715(0)
[Buache, P.] Explication...
Mer du Sud. 1752. 716(0)
[Buache, P.] Erklarung ...
Norden...1753. 717(0)
Buache, P. Expose découvertes
au nord...[1753] 718(0)
Buache, P. Liste des Cartes...
[1755] 719(0)
Colquhoun, A. R. Greater
America maps...1904. 994(0)
Davidson, G. Glaciers...Russ.
charts...1904. 1192(0)
Davidson, G. Tracks and land-
falls Bering...[1901] 1193(6)
Delisle, J. N. Nouvelles cartes
... Fonte ... 1753. 1257(0)
[Dobbs, A.] Letter from Russ.
sea-officer...1754. 1311(0)
Greenaway, K. R. Aerial reconn.
Arctic...1948. 1848(4)
[Mead, Bradock] Remarks new
chart...1753. 3049(0)

Nunn, G. E. Origin Strait of
Anian concept. 1929. 3367(0)
Ortelius, A. Theatrum orbis
terrarum. 1570. 3420(0)
Phillips, P. L. Alaska...Lib.
of Congress. 1970. 3572(0)
Skelton, R. A. Capt. Jas.Cook
hydrog....1953. 4169(2)
Skelton, R. A. Charts ...
Cook ... 1955. 4170(2)
Skelton, R. A. Explorer's
maps ... 1958. 4171(0)
Skelton, R. A. Marine surveys
Jas. Cook ... 1967. 4172(2)
Stuart-Stubbs, B. Maps...
A. Mackenzie...1968. 4368(0)
Wagner, H. R. Cartography
N. W. Coast...1937. 4723(0)
Wytfliet, C. Descriptionis
Ptolemaicae ... 1597.4984(0)

CIVIC CLUBS, GROUPS,
ORGANIZATIONS.

Alaska Crippled Children's As-
soc. Eskimo...n.d. 57(5)
Alaska Crippled Children's As-
soc....kitchen...1958. 58(0)
Alaska Hist. Assoc....booklet
Museum...1922. 68(1)
Alaska Hist. Assoc. Native...
art...Museum. 1959. 69(0)
Alaska League Western Writers.
poetry. 1956. 73(0)
Alaska Native Brotherhood.
Constitution...1922. 90(0)
Alaska Northwest Pub. Co. ...
camp cook...1962.[Terr.
Sportsmen's Assoc.] 93(0)
Alaska Press Club. Alaska blue
book. 1963. 103(0)
Alaska Range Guides Assoc.
Shoot ... [19__] 106(0)
Alaska State Fair. Premium
list ... 1960. 111(2)
Alaska Writer's Workshop.
Alaska poetry. n.d. 141(0)
All-Alaska Sweepstakes.[Nome
Kennel Club] 172(5)
Anchorage Chamber of Commerce.
Anchorage...1918. 232(2)

CIVIC CLUBS, GROUPS,
            ORGANIZATIONS. (cont.)

Anchorage Chamber of Commerce.
    Today's ... 1944.   233(2)
Anchorage Garden Club. So ...
    flower ... n. d.   238(0)
Anchorage Women's Club. Alas-
    ka's cooking. 1959.   240(0)
Arctic Brotherhood. ... history
    of order. 1909.   278(0)
Arctic Brotherhood. Constitu-
    tion Grand Camp. n.d.   279(0)
Arctic Brotherhood. Convention
    ... n. d.   280(0)
Arctic Brotherhood. Proc.Grand
    Camp.1901-17.   281-296(0)
Arctic Brotherhood. Ritualistic
    ... 1900.   297(0)
Arctic Club. ...50th anniv.
    [1958 ?]   298(0)
Arctic Club. Officers ...
    by-laws...1910.   299(0)
Atwood, F. [Sourdough Stampede
    Assoc.]roster.1930.   319(0)
Business & Prof. Women's Club.
    ...cookbook...1962.   755(1)
Chase, W. H. Pioneers of
    Alaska...1951.   899(0)
Cone, E. ...Igloo 15, Pioneers
    of Alaska...1923.   1000(5)
Cordova Common Council...facts
    about Cordova. 1914.   1080(2)
Cordova Common Council. Rules,
    by-laws...1914.   1081(2)
Crewe, F. ... Arctic Brother-
    hood...1910.   1120(3)
Douglas, R. D. Boy Scout...
    grizzly ... 1929.   1336(2)
Douglas, R.D. [Boy Scouts]...
    Fr. Hubbard. 1932.   1337(6)
Eastern Star. By-laws...Fair-
    banks. 1914.   1402(3)
Fairbanks Chamber of Commerce.
    Tanana Valley. 1908.   1513(3)
Fairbanks Commercial Club.
    Fairbanks...1916.   1515(3)
Fairbanks Commercial Club.
    Interior...[1914]   1516(3)
Fairbanks Commercial Club.
    What ... 1911.   1517(3)

Fairbanks Community Hospital
    Assoc. Survey.1961. 1518(3)
Fairbanks Harmonie Soc. Sou-
    venir. 1909.   1522(3)
Farmer's Loop Homemakers Club.
    Family ...[ca1955]   1526(3)
Fletcher, A. L. Boy Scouts in
    Alaska. 1913.   1577(1)
Hamilton, W. R. Yukon story.
    1964. [Vancouver Sourdough
    Yukoners]   1924(7)
Int'l. Yukon Polar Institute.
    Constitution. 1905. 2289(7)
Int'l. Yukon Polar Institute.
    Objects...1905.   2290(7)
Jones, L. B. Tundra tales.[So-
    roptimist Club]1959. 2382(5)
Juneau, Citizens. Juneau...
    1907.   2397(1)
Juneau Commercial Assoc. Ju-
    neau ... n. d.   2398(1)
Katalla Publicity League.Hist.
    Bering R.coal. 1912. 2417(2)
Kegoayah Kozga Soc.11th an-
    nual...1912.   2425(5)
Ketchikan Chamber of Commerce.
    King salmon...1952. 2451(2)
Ketchikan, Citizens. First
    city...1916.   2452(2)
Ketchikan Commercial Club.
    ...resources...n.d. 2453(2)
Knik Commercial Club.Resources
    Knik. n.d.   2497(2)
League of Women Voters. Fair-
    banks ... 1968.   2655(3)
Life...[Alaska Sled Dog and
    Racing Assoc.]1958. 2705(2)
Loyal League. Popular...songs
    ...meetings. 1918.   2804(5)
Muñoz, R. Nursing...[Alaska
    Nurses'Assoc.][1967] 3242(0)
Nome-Seward Peninsula Chamber
    of Commerce. 1916.   3319(5)
Northwestern Alaska Chamber of
    Commerce.Nome.1932. 3358(5)
PEO Sisterhood...Fairbanks...
    [c1964]   3534(3)
Petersburg PTA. Cook book.
    1941.   3546(1)
Petersburg Vet. of For.Wars
    Aux. cook book.1964. 3547(1)

CIVIC CLUBS, GROUPS,
        ORGANIZATIONS. (cont.)

Pioneer Women of Alaska...by-
  laws ... 1916.   3611(3)
Pioneers of Alaska, Grand Ig-
  loo. By-laws. 1907. 3612(5)
Pioneers of Alaska, Grand Ig-
  loo. By-laws. 1911. 3613(5)
Pioneers of Alaska, Igloo 4.
  By-laws. [1913?]   3614(3)
Pioneers of Alaska, Igloo 4.
  Gold ... 1957.   3615(3)
Polar Bear Citizen Band Club.
  ...directory. 1968. 3626(0)
Reid, W. A. "Helen Gould"
  Y.M.C.A. [1906?]   3779(0)
St. Joseph's Hosp. Women's Aux.
  ...recipes...1961.   3941(3)
S.F.-Alaska Club...by-laws.
  1911.   3957(0)
Shields, W. C. Ancient ...
  [Keenok Club] 1918. 4115(5)
Skaguay Commercial Club. Skag-
  uay ... 1898.   4164(1)
Skagway Chamber of Commerce.
  Constitution...1900. 4165(1)
Skagway Commercial Club.
  Skagway...n.d.   4166(1)
Tanana Club. Constitution...
  1914.   4446(3)
Victor, R. Boy Scouts of
  Yukon. [c1912]   4697(7)

COMMERCE - General.

Alaska Pub. and Trade Agency.
  200 questions. 1914. 105(0)
Anti-Monopoly Assoc. Hist.
  wrongs ... 1875.   269(0)
Anti-Monopoly Assoc. Resolutions ... 1874.   270(0)
Bering Sea Commercial Co.
  ...whaling...n.d.   525(4)
Bering Sea Co. Report ...
  [1913]   526(0)
Burford, V. North to danger.
  1954.   728(0)
Cooney, E. Alaskamo.
  1966. . . . . 1065(1)
Eberhart, B. Crew of two.
  1961.   1405(0)

Ellsworth, L. Halibut
  schooner. 1953.   1448(2)
Erskine, W. F. White water.
  1960.   1491(0)
Horetzky, C. Canada on Paci-
  fic. 1874.   2180(1)
Leschen, A., & Sons Rope Co.
  ...vessels Nome.1914.2685(5)
Mears, E. G. Maritime trade of
  west. U. S. 1935.   3064(0)
Newell, G. Pacific steamboats.
  1958.   3297(0)
Northern Exploration & Develop.
  Co. Resources. n.d. 3350(0)
Pacific Sci. Congress, 5th.
  Trade ... 1933.   3458(0)
Ryan, J. J. The *Maggie Murphy*.
  [c1951]   3926(2)
Tanana Dredging Co. Memoran-
  dum. n. d.   4448(3)
West Coast Lumber Trade Ext.
  Bur. ...spruce. 1927.4797(1)

COMMERCE - Fisheries.

Alaska Oil & Guano Co. Statement ... 1910.   95(6)
Alaska Packers Assoc. Argo red
  salmon cook book.1911. 99(6)
Alaska Packers Assoc. Influenza...Bristol Bay.1919.100(6)
Alaska Packers Assoc. Influenza...epidemic. 1919. 101(6)
Allen, E. W. Halibut commission
  ... 1936.   179(0)
Andrews, R. W. Fish and ships.
  1959.   260(0)
Armsby, J. C., Co. ... canned
  salmon. 1904.   303(0)
Babcock, J. P. Investig. halibut ... 1930.   332(0)
Beklemishev, K. V. Distrib.
  zooplankton ... 1959. 473(0)
Bingham, J. W. Report,,,law
  coastal fish. 1938. 556(0)
Boutwell, W. D. Alaska's silver
  millions. 1936.   625(0)
Canada. Physical & chemical
  record. 1955-1958. 806-9(0)
Canada. Proc. ... sealing
  fisheries. 1934.   810(0)

COMMERCE - Fisheries.   (cont.)

Carrothers, W. A. B. C. fisheries. 1941.   854(1)
Clark, E. D. Salmon canning industry. [1927?]   938(0)
Cobb, J. N. Canning fishery products...1919.   963(0)
Cooley, R. A. Politics and... salmon. 1963.   1061(0)
Crandell, J. V. Story Pacific salmon. 1946.   1112(0)
Daily Alaska Fishing News. ... almanac. 1946.   1152(0)
DeLoach, D. B. Salmon canning industry. 1939.   1258(0)
Drumheller, Ehrlichman Co. ... salmon industry. 1935.1358(0)
Freeman, M. Salmon packer's directory. 1908.   1647(0)
Gregory, H. E. No. Pac. fisheries...1939.   1853(0)
Hartt, A. C. Movement salmon ...1962.   1976(0)
Hassel, J. G. H. Vollstandige ... 1822.   1985(0)
Hiscock, B. O. The *Wawona*. n. d.   2125(0)
Hokkaido Univ. ... exploration fishing.No. 1. 1957.   2145(0)
Hokkaido Univ. ...exploration fishing.No. 2. 1958.   2146(0)
Int'l. Fisheries Commission. ...halibut...1948.   2275(0)
Int'l. Fisheries Commission. Report. No. 1. 1931. 2276(0)
Int'l. No. Pac. Fish. Comm. ...halibut...1962.   2279(0)
Int'l. No. Pac. Fish. Comm. ...herring...1961.   2280(0)
Int'l. No. Pac. Fish. Comm. ...salmon...1962.   2281(0)
Int'l. No. Pac. Fish. Comm. ...yearbook. 1952.   2282(0)
Int'l. Pac. Halibut Comm. ... investig.1958-62.   228405(0)
Int'l. Pac. Halibut Comm. Utilization...1960.   2286(0)
Kasahara, H. Fisheries resources ... 1961.   2412(0)
Kirkwood, D. Salmon industry in Alaska. 1909.   2473(0)

Konda, S. No. fisheries of Japan. 1933.   2505(0)
Koo, T.S.-Y. Abundance...salmon smolts...1959.   2506(6)
Koo, T.S.-Y. Red salmon smolt Wood River. 1959.   2507(6)
Koo, T.S.-Y. Studies Alaska red salmon. 1962.   2508(6)
Krause, E. Vorgeschichtliche ... 1904.   2543(0)
Liberate ...from fish trap... 1949.   2702(0)
McDonald, J. L. Hidden treasures ... 1871.   2864(0)
McKeown, M. F. Alaska silver. 1951.   2918(1)
MacMullen, J. *Star of India* iron ship. 1961.   2939(0)
Mjelde, M. J. *Glory of the Seas*. 1969.   3150(0)
Pacific Industrial Research Bur. ...jobs. 1946. 3454(0)
Reisenfeld, S. A. Protection ...law. 1942.   3822(0)
Russell, F. S. Seas. [1963] . . . . . . 3915(0)
Sovetskie Rybokhoziaĭstvennye ...vyp. 1. 1963.   4147(0)
Sovetskie Rybokhoziaĭstvennye ...vyp. 4. 1965.   4148(0)
Soviet fisheries investigations ... no. 1. 1968.   4249(0)
Sundborg, G. Proposal ... fisheries...1944.   4393(0)
Sundborg, G. Int'l. fisheries ... 1943.   4395(0)
Thompson, T. G. Hydrographic ...1936.   4511(0)
Thompson, W. F. Outline salmon research...1951.   4512(0)
Thompson, W. F. Biol. statistics. halibut...1931.4513(0)
Thompson, W. F. Biol. statistics. halibut. 1934. 4514(0)
Thompson, W. F. Hist. Pac. halibut fishery. 1930. 4515(0)
Thompson, W. F. Life...halibut no. 1. 1930.   4516(0)
Thompson, W. F. Life...halibut no. 2. 1936.   4517(0)
Thompson, W. F. Some salmon research...1950.   4518(0)

COMMERCE - Fisheries.   (cont.)

Thompson, W. F. Effect fishing
...halibut. 1950.   4519(0)
Thompson, W. F. Theory...fish-
ing ...halibut. 1937. 4520(0)
Tomasevic, J. Int'l. agreements
... 1943.   4548(0)
Townsend, L. D. Variations ...
...flounders...1936. 4564(0)
Verhoeven, L. A. Report salmon
fishing...1952.   4684(1)
Wick, C. I. Ocean harvest...
1946.   4854(0)
Wilmovsky, N. J. Util. fishery
... 1956.   4908(4)
Young, C. W., Co. Alaska information ... 1916.   4990(0)
Young, I. N. Story of salmon.
1934.   4994(0)

COMMERCE - Fur Industry.

Alaska Commercial Co. By-laws.
1870.   51(0)
Alaska Commercial Co. Reply
... [1887 ?]   52(0)
Amer.-Russ. Commercial Co.
Alaska fur-seal...1869.209(0)
Amer.-Russ. Commercial Co. By-
laws...1855.   210(0)
Anti-Monopoly Assoc. History of
wrongs...1875.   269(0)
Anti-Monopoly Assoc. Resolu-
tions...1874.   270(0)
Belden, A. L. Fur trade ...
1917.   477(0)
Canada. Report rights Hudsons
Bay Co. 1857.   812(0)
Chalmers, J. W. Fur trade gov-
ernor, Simpson. 1960. 880(1)
Davidson, G. C. Northwest Co.
1918.   1194(0)
Dobbs, A. Acct. countries...
1744.   1312(0)
Dunn, J. Hist. Ore. Terr. ...
1844.   1386(0)
Dunn, J. Ore. Terr. and Brit.
No. Amer. 1845.   1387(0)
Fisher, R. H. Russian fur trade
1943.   1572(0)

Innis, H. A. Fur-trade ...
1927.   2270(0)
Is trade of Alaska Terr. ...
1871.   2303(0)
Johnston, S.P. Alaska Commer-
cial Co. ... 1940.   2375(0)
Kitchener, L. D. Flag over
North. 1954.   2475(0)
Laut, A. C. Fur trade of
America. 1921.   2645(0)
Loring, C. G. Memoir Wm.
Sturgis. 1864.   2797(0)
McCain, C. W. Hist. *Beaver*.
1894.   2832(0)
MacGregor, J. Progress of
America. 1847.   2898(0)
Mack, G. Lewis and Hannah
Gerstle. 1953.   2911(0)
MacKay, D. Honourable Co.
... 1936.   2913(0)
McPherson, M. Condensed state-
ment...Bell. 1845.   2948(7)
Merk, F. Fur trade and empire.
Simpson journ.1931.   3085(0)
Morton, A. S. History Canadian
west ... 1939.   3205(0)
Morton, A. S. Sir Geo. Simpson
... 1944.   3206(0)
Morton, A. S. Northwest Co.
1930.   3207(0)
Murray, A. H. Journal of Yukon.
1848.   3256(7)
Oliver, E. H. Canadian n. w.
...1914.   3401(0)
Pacific Northwest Industries.
Alaska...fur...1954. 3456(0)
Porter, K. W. John Jacob Astor.
1931.   3645(0)
Rich, E. E. Hist. Hudson's
Bay Co. 1960.   3801(0)
Rossiĭsko-Amerikanskaĭa Kompa-
niĭa.K istoriĭ.1957. 3890(0)
Rossiĭsko-Amerikanskaĭa Kompa-
niĭa. Otchet. 1853. 3891(0)
Ryleev, K. F. Polnoe sobranie
sochineniĭ. 1934.   3931(0)
Ryleev, K. F. Sochineniĭa...
1874.   3932(0)
Schooling, W. Hudson's Bay
1920.   4009(0)
Simpson, A. Life...Thomas
Simpson. 1845.   4160(4)

COMMERCE - Fur Industry.(cont.)

Simpson, G. Narrative ...
    1847.   4161(0)
Simpson, G. Overland ...
    1847.   4161(0)
Simpson, G. ... voyage...
    1930.   4162(1)
Teichmann, E. Journey ...
    1925.   4477(1)
Tikhmenev, P. A. Hist. review
    R.-A. Co. 1939-40.   4537(0)
Toronto Pub. Lib. Canadian
    n. w. bibliog. 1931. 4557(0)
Tyrrell, J. B. Documents...
    Hudson Bay. 1931.   4597(0)
Willson, B. Great company ...
    1899.   4907(0)
[Zavalishin, D. I.] Rossiĭsko-
    Amer. Komp. 1865.   5023(0)

COMMERCE - Fur seal and
                    Sea otter.

Alaska Commercial Co. Alaska
    fur seals. [1870]   49(6)
Alaska Commercial Co. Alaska
    seal fisheries. [1870] 50(6)
Alaska Commercial Co. Seal and
    seal isls. 1870.   53(6)
Allan, A. Hunting sea otter.
    1910.   173(0)
Amer.-Russ. Commercial Co.
    ...fur-seal bill.1869. 209(6)
Barrett-Hamilton, G.E.H. Report
    ... 1898.   406(6)
Boitsov, L. V. Kotikovoe
    Khoziaĭstvo. 1934.   598(6)
Camp Fire Club. Square deal for
    fur seal. 1910.   798(0)
Canada. Proc. Spec. Comm. seal-
    ing ... 1934.   810(0)
Carter, J. C. Fur-seal arbitra-
    tion ... 1893.   857(0)
Evans, R. D. Sailor's log ...
    1902.   1503(6)
Fouke Fur Co. Romance Alaska
    sealskin. 1954.   1618(6)
Fouke Fur Co. Romance Alaska
    fur seal. 1958.   1619(6)

Henderson, J. B. Amer. diploma-
    tic questions. 1901. 2038(6)
Martin, F. I. Sea bears ...
    1960.   3004(6)
Martin, F. I. Hunting silver
    fleece. 1946.   3005(6)
Ogden, A. Calif. sea otter
    trade. 1941.   3386(0)
Williamson, T. R. North after
    seals. 1934.   4889(6)

COMMERCE - Fur trapping,
                    Trading, Ranches.

Alaska Fur and Silver Fox Co.
    Story silver fox.1909. 63(0)
Alaska Silver Fox & Fur Farms
    Co. Story of fox.n.d. 109(3)
Beaver, C. M. Fort Yukon tra-
    der. [c1955]   459(3)
Carroll, J. A. First ten yrs.
    Ft. Yukon...1957.   853(3)
Godsell, P. H. Arctic trader
    ...Hudson's...1934.   1744(0)
Godsell, P. H. Red hunters...
    1938.   1745(0)
Hodgson, R. G. ... muskrat
    farming...1925.   2134(0)
Klengenberg, C. Klengenberg of
    Arctic. 1932.   2486(4)
Kreps, E. ... trapping...
    1909.   2544(0)
Laut, A. C. Pioneers of Pac.
    coast. 1915.   2644(0)
Lewis, J. Black Beaver, trap-
    per. 1911.   2697(3)
McCracken, H. Trapping; craft
    ... 1947.   2858(0)
Morenus, R. Alaska sourdough
    ...1956.   3171(2)
O'Meara, W. A.Savage country
    ... 1960.   3410(0)
Shimkin, D. B. Econ. ... Ft.
    Yukon ... 1955.   4124(3)
Snider, G. H. Mink raising...
    [1929]   4221(2)
Swenson, O. Northwest of world
    ... 1944.   4429(5)
Trefzger, H. My 50 years...
    [c1963]   4575(1)
Turner-Turner, J. 3 yrs. hun-
    ting & trapping.1888.4591(0)

COMMERCE - Fur trapping,
Trading, Ranches.

Wheaton, H. Prekaska's wife...
Aleut. [Isl.] 1945.   4806(6)

COMMERCE - Insurance.

National Bd. Fire Underwriters.
...earthquake...1964. 3273(0)
Piver, J. Alaska insurance.
quiz. n. d.   3617(0)

COMMUNICATIONS.

B. C. Distr. Tel. & Delivery
Co. 50 yrs....1941.   669(1)
Harrington, J. J. Esquimeaux.
1867.   1955(0)
Hewitt, J. M. Alaska vagabond
... 1953.   2093(0)
Int'l. Tel. & Tel. Corp. Man-
ning DEWline. [1960?] 2288(0)
James, J. A. First scientific
exploration.1942.   2326(0)
Lawrence, G. 40 yrs. Yukon
telegraph. 1965.   2650(7)
Midnight Sun Broadcasting Co.
KFAR Keybook...[c1939]3099(3)
Mitchell, Wm. General Greely
... 1936.   3147(0)
Morenus, R. DEWline ...
1957.   3172(0)
Mudge, Z. A. Fur-clad adven-
turers ... 1880.   3219(0)
Polar Bear CB Club. Alaska
directory. 1968.   3626(0)
Ricks, M. B. Directory...post-
offices. 1964.   3813(0)
Western Union Tel. Co. To the
stockholders. 1866.   4800(0)
Whymper, F. Journey Norton Sd.
1868.   4848(0)
Whymper, F. Alaska; Reisen...
1869.   4849(0)
Whymper, F. Travel and adven-
ture...1868.   4851(0)
Whymper, F. Voyages et aventures...1880.   4852(0)
Whymper, F. Voyages et aventures...1871.   4853(0)

CONSERVATION.

Allen, D. L. Our wildlife
legacy. 1954.   176(0)
Amer. Comm. Int'l. Willife
Prot. ...musk-ox.1934.197(4)
Boone & Crockett Club. Hunting
& conserv. 1925.   610(2)
Butcher, D. Exploring national
parks. 1949.   756(0)
Butcher, D. Exploring national
refuges. 1963.   757(0)
Butcher, D. Seeing wildlife...
nat. refuges. 1955.   758(0)
Camp Fire Club. Plea for Mt.
McKinley...1916.   797(2)
Camp Fire Club. Square deal for
fur seal. 1910.   798(0)
Cooley, R. A. Alaska..conser-
vation. 1966.   1060(0)
Cooley, R. A. Politics & con-
servation. 1963.   1061(0)
Gabrielson, I. N. Wildlife
refuges. 1943.   1669(0)
Haines, M. J. Muir; protector
... 1957.   1896(0)
Hornaday, W. T. Our vanishing
wildlife ... 1913.   2182(0)
Johnson, H. A. Land resources
... 1963.   2369(0)
Leopold, A. S. Wildlife...ecol.
reconn. 1953.   2682(0)
Lutz, H. J. Aboriginal...fires
boreal forest. 1959. 2817(0)
Mackaye, B. Act proposed...
conservation. n.d.   2914(0)
Milton, J. P. Nameless valleys
...1970.   3139(4)
Muir, J. Our national parks.
1901.   3223(0)
Northern Explor. & Develop.Co.
...resources...n.d. 3350(0)
Robertson, D.S. To Arctic with
Mounties. 1934.   3036(0)
Russell, T. On the loose.
[c1967]   3919(0)
Sierra Club. Wilderness in
changing world. 1966.4148(0)
Street, P. Vanishing animals
... 1963.   4362(0)
Swift, H. H. Edge April...John
Burroughs. 1957.   4431(0)

ALASKAN BIBLIOGRAPHY

CONSERVATION. (cont.)

Swift, H. H. From eagle's wing;
J. Muir. 1962.   4432(0)
Tomasevic, J. Int'l. agreements
marine...1943.   4548(0)
Trefethen, J. B. Crusade for
wildlife. 1961.   4574(0)
Udall, S. L. The quiet crisis.
1963.   4604(0)
Van Hise, C. R. Conservation
nat. resources. 1931. 4649(0)
Wolfe, L. M. John of mtns.;
journ. J. Muir. 1938. 4941(0)
Wolfe, L. M. Son of wilderness;
J. Muir. 1945.   4942(0)

COOK BOOKS.

Alaska Crippled Children's As-
soc. Eskimo...n.d.   57(5)
Alaska Crippled Children's As-
soc....kitchens...1958. 58(0)
Alaska Northwest Pub. Co.Alas-
kan camp cook. 1962.   93(0)
Alaska Packers Assoc. Argo red
salmon...1911.   99(0)
Anchorage Women's Club. Alas-
ka's cooking. 1959.   240(2)
Business & Prof. Women's Club.
Capitol...1962.   755(1)
Catholic Daughters of America.
Juneau...1960.   870(1)
Cleveland, B. A. Alaskan cook
book. 1960.   954(0)
Cleveland, B. A. Frontier for-
mulas. 1952.   955(0)
Fairbanks cook book...Ladies
Presbyt. Ch. 1913.   1519(3)
Farmers Loop Homemakers Club.
Family...[ca1955]   1526(3)
Fisher, P. Alaskan wild game
... 1961.   1571(0)
Lind Print. Co. Alaska salmon
recipe book. 1961.   2712(0)
Mabee, Sourdough Jack. ...
cookery. 1959.   2824(0)
Marion Soc. Cooking...Fair-
banks. [ca1965?]   2969(3)
Miners' supplement Royal baker
... 1898.   3141(0)

Morgan, L. Woman's guide to
boating...1968.   3179(0)
Petersburg P.T.A. Cookbook.
1941.   3546(1)
Petersburg V.F.W. Aux. cook-
book. 1964.   3547(1)
Phelps, S. Official...cook
book. 1969.   3568(1)
St. Joseph's Hospital Aux.
...nuggets...1961.   3941(3)
St. Matthews Episcopal Church.
Favorite ... 1944.   3942(3)
St. Matthews Episcopal Church.
Golden... [ca1950?]   3943(3)
Southeast Alaska Trollers As-
soc. Cook...[c1970]   4244(1)
White, H. A. Alaska wildberry
trails. [c1959]   4818(0)
White, H. A. More...what's
cookin'...[c1962]   4824(0)
White, H. A. What's cookin'
...[c1961]   4825(0)
Woman's Soc. Christian Serv.
...kitchen.[1967]   4949(1)
Women's Soc. Christian Serv.
Nome cook...[1968]   4950(5)

DOGS and DOG MUSHING.

All Alaska Sweepstakes Dog
Souvenir...1909.   172(5)
Allan, A. A. Gold, men and
dogs. 1931.   175(5)
Berger, C. J. How to raise ...
malemute...1963.   520(5)
Caldwell, E. N. Alaska trail
dogs. 1945.   770(0)
Carrighar, S. Wild voice of
North. 1959.   851(5)
Darling, E. B. For honor and
glory France. n.d.   1177(0)
Darling, E. B. Dog races of
Nome. n.d.   1182(5)
Garst, S. Scotty Allan...
1946.   1692(5)
Gelvin, E. C. How to build...
dog sled. [ca 1968] 1695(0)
Hines, J. Wolf dogs of north.
1948.   2121(0)
Life in Anchorage.
1958. . . . . .2705(2)

DOGS and DOG MUSHING. (cont.)

McCracken, H. Toughy; bulldog
of Arctic. 1948.   2857(4)
Mason, W. E. Dogs of all
nations. 1915.   3021(0)
Morenus, R. Alaska sourdough.
1956.   3171(2)
Muir, J. Stickeen.
[c1909]   3225(1)
Muir, J. Wilderness world ...
1954.   3228(1)
Ricker, E. M. Seppala, Alaskan
dog driver. 1930.   3811(5)
Thompson, R. Siberian husky.
1962.   4508(0)
Walden, A. T. Dog puncher on
Yukon. 1928.   4729(7)
Wirt, L. L. Alaskan adventure.
1937.   4931(0)

ECONOMIC CONDITIONS.

Agranat, G. A. Energetika ...
1962.   18(0)
Agranat, G. A. Naselenie...
1963.   19(0)
Agranat, G. A. Novaîa teknika
... 1960.   20(0)
Agranat, G. A. Promyshlennoist'
... 1962.   21(0)
Alaska Bureau. Alaska.
1915. . . . . 35(0)
Alaska Bureau. ... frontier
... 1913.   36(0)
Alaska Bureau. Alaska tour.
1913.   37(0)
Alaska Bureau. Develop Alaska
dinner. 1911.   38(0)
Alaska Bureau. Nation needs
coal. 1917.   39(0)
Alaska Bureau. Origin ...
1915.   40(0)
Alaska Utilities Develop. Co.
...opportunity. 1914.   139(0)
Alcan Pub. Co. ...register...
[ca 1946]   166(0)
Baker, J. Southeastern opportunity...[ca1953]   358(1)
Bartz, F. Fischgründe ...
1942.   424(0)

Benton & Bowles.   49th State
...marketing. 1959.   510(0)
Bloch, I. ...resources...
mineral...1956.   577(0)
Boyce, W. D. Alaska, present
and future. 1913.   634(0)
Brandt, K. Whale oil economic
... 1940.   646(0)
Brandt, K. Whaling and whale
oil...1948.   647(0)
Camsell, C. Canada's new
northwest...1947.   800(0)
Canada. Yukon Terr. brief
descript. 1938.   816(7)
Canada. Yukon Terr. history...
1909.   817(7)
Carlson, W. Opportunities...
s.e. ...[ca1939]   836(1)
Chichagof King Mining Co.Great
lesson...1934.   814(1)
Davies, R. A. Arctic eldorado
Canada. 1944.   1196(0)
Dawson, C. A. New northwest.
1947.   1215(0)
Dunbar, M. J. Prelim. Bering
Strait scheme. 1960. 1377(4)
Dunbar, M. Second rpt. Bering
Strait dam. 1962.   1378(4)
Erdmann, H. Alaska; ein Beitrag
... 1909.   1484(0)
Fairbanks, Chamber of Commerce.
Fairbanks ... 1908. 1513(3)
Fairbanks Commercial Club.
Descriptive...1916. 1515(3)
Fairbanks Commercial Club.
Interior ... [1914] 1516(3)
Fairbanks Commercial Club. What
Fairbanks...1911.   1517(3)
Finnie, R. Canada moves North.
1942.   1561(0)
Forrest, G. Land resources...
1944.   1603(0)
Gillette, E. Facts...railway
...1904.   1722(0)
Gravel, M. Jobs and more jobs.
1968.   1798(0)
Greely, A. W. Polar regions...
1928.   1842(0)
Hellenthal, J. A. Alaskan
melodrama. 1936.   2023(0)
Hermann, E. Das Nordpolarmeer
... 1949.   2077(4)

ECONOMIC CONDITIONS. (cont.)

Homesteading ... Homer.
1935. . . . . 2167(2)
Illingworth, F. North of
Circle. 1951. 2254(0)
Institute Pac. Relations. Prob-
lems Pac. ... 1928. 2271(0)
James, B. W. Alaska ...
1897. 2322(0)
Jeffery, E. C. Alaska who's
here ... 1955. 2335(0)
Juneau Commercial Assoc.
Juneau. n.d. 2398(1)
Juneau Empire Print. Develop-
ment ... 1923. 2399(1)
Kallinikov, N. F. Nash Kraĭniĭ
...1912. 2404(4)
Ketchikan Alaska Chronicle.
Facts ... 1932. 2450(2)
Ketchikan Commercial Club.
Ketchikan. n.d. 2453(2)
Kizer, B. H. No. Pac. Int'l.
Plan. Project. 1942. 2482(0)
Kizer, B. H. U.S.-Canadian n.w.
... 1943. 2483(0)
Knik Commercial Club. Resources
... n.d. 2497(2)
McKinley, C. Case...cabotage...
1944. 2920(0)
McKinley, C. U.S.-Canadian...
aviation ... 1944. 2921(0)
M'Konochie, A. Summary...free
port...1818. 2922(0)
Morgan, M. Skid Road...Seattle.
1951. 3184(0)
Müller, M. Koloniale wirtschaft
... 1935. 3236(0)
Muñoz, J. Juneau, study...
1956. 3241(1)
No. Pac. Consultants. Econ.
...Fairbanks...1959. 3345(3)
No. Pac. Planning Project. No.
Pac. study...1944. 3347(0)
Pac. Coast SS Co. Yukon Terr.,
Alaska...[1902?] 3453(0)
Pan American Pub. Co. Alaska
opportunities.1947. 3485(0)
Pan Pacific Progress. Alaska.
1930. 3486(0)
Paneth, P. Alaskan backdoor
to Japan. 1943. 3487(0)

Perugia, P. Le grande nord.
1951. 3544(0)
Phillips, R.A.J. Canada's
North. 1967. 3573(0)
Production Surveys. This is
Alaska...1954. 3698(0)
Reasons why Nome entitled to
harbor ... 1915. 3764(5)
Rettie, J. C. Comparisons
...commodities. 1944.3787(0)
Rettie, J. C. Population
trends ... 1944. 3788(0)
Rettie, J. C. Problems ...
pipeline ... 1944. 3789(0)
Rettie, J. C. Shipping ser-
vices... 1944. 3790(0)
Rettie, J. C. Suppl. ...use...
Alaska Hy. 1944. 3791(0)
Rogers, G. W. Alaska in tran-
sition ... 1960. 3865(1)
Rogers, G. W. Future Alaska...
statehood...1962. 3866(0)
Russell, J. A. Industrial
...weather. 1957. 3918(0)
Salin, E. Wirtschaftliche...
1914. 3944(0)
Smith, F. C. Men at work in
Alaska. 1967. 4196(0)
Stefansson, V. Fat of land.
1956. 4311(0)
Stefansson, V. Not by bread
alone. 1946. 4311(0)
Stefansson, V. Routes to
Alaska. 1941. 4313(0)
Stefansson, V. Northward
course... [c1922] 4321(0)
Stefansson, V. Neuland im
Norden...1928. 4322(0)
Stein, R. Defense of Alaska...
railway. 1910. 4329(0)
Stone, A. J. Saw-tooth power
...1914. 4352(0)
Sundborg, G. Opportunity in
Alaska. 1945. 4396(0)
Thompson, J. W., Co. Alaskan
market...1958. 4507(0)
Thomson Statistical Service.
...finance...1930. 4522(0)
Transcontinental Research Bur.
Jobs in Alaska. 1946.4568(0)
Tuttle, C. R. Alaska...re-
sources...1914. 4593(0)

ECONOMIC CONDITIONS. (cont.)

Tuttle, C. R. Golden north...
   1897.   4594(0)
U.S.-B.C. Corp. Alaska;
   resources...n.d.   4623(0)
Weigert, H. W. Compass of
   world ... 1944.   4782(0)
Weigert, H. W. New compass of
   world ... 1949.   4783(0)
Wickersham, J. Alaska; its
   resources...1902.   4857(0)
Wiley, S. C. Colonization ...
   bibliog. 1960.   4868(0)
Wood, J. P. Alaska, great
   land. 1967.   4952(0)
Wood, P. Unbelievable years...
   [c1969]   4954(0)
Workingman's guide to Alaska.
   1953.   4961(0)
[Wrangell] Board of Trade.
   Prospectus ... 1901. 4966(1)
Zimmermann, E.A.W. Taschenbuch
   ... [1809]   5032(4)

EDUCATION - Schools, Teachers.

Albee, W. Alaska challenge.
   1940.   164(5)
Anderson, H. D. Alaska natives;
   survey...1935.   244(0)
Berto, H. D. North to Alaska's
   shining river. 1959.   541(5)
Brooks, A. M. Clenched fist.
   1948.   683(2)
Buchan, L. Hearth in snow.
   1952.   720(6)
Carlson, G. F. Two on the
   rocks ... 1967.   833(5)
Eide, A. H. Drums of Diomede.
   1952.   1425(5)
Forrest, E. C. Daylight moon...
   1937.   1602(0)
Gambell, V. C. Schoolhouse...
   St. Lawrence I. 1910. 1677(5)
Johns, C. L. Sheldon Jackson
   School. n.d.   2366(1)
McLain, C. M. Pioneer teacher.
   [c1970]   2924(5)
Matlock, A. H. Teaching above
   Arctic Circle. n.d.   3030(5)

Mayberry, G. Sheldon Jackson
   Jr. College...1953. 3041(1)
Pacific Univ. Souvenir...
   [1909]   3467(0)
Patty, E. N. North country
   challenge. 1969.   3505(3)
Petersburg High School. Flood
   tide. 1925.   3545(1)
Pettitt, G. A. Primitive education in N.A. 1946. 3562(0)
Reid, C. F. Educ. Territories
   ... 1940.   3777(0)
Richards, E. L. A. Arctic mood.
   1949.   3802(4)
Rodli, A. S. North of Heaven.
   1963.   3864(5)
Smith, D. H. Bureau of Education ... 1923.   4194(0)
van Steensel, M. People of
   light and dark. 1966.4651(0)
[Veniaminov, I.E.P.] Orthodox
   schools ... 1905.   4676(6)
Wickersham, J. Address...Alas-
   ka Agric. Col.[1915] 4856(3)
Winchell, M.E. Home by
   Bering Sea. 1951.   4918(2)

EDUCATION - Texts.

Adamov, A. G. Pervye Russkie...
   1950.   6(0)
Ahmaogak, R. Iñupiam uḳaluŋi.
   [1963?]   22(4)
Bompas, W. C. Western Esqui-
   maux primer. n.d.   605(4)
Boutwell, W. D. Teacher's
   guide ... 1936.   625(0)
Burkholder, M. Capt. Cook.
   1928.   735(2)
Buynitzky, S. N. Eng.-Aleut.
   vocabulary. 1871.   760(6)
Campbell, E. O. Pĕ nēl' ...
   ... 1910.   791(4)
Canada. Fifth book of reading
   lessons. 1883.   805(7)
Carpenter, F. G. North
   America... 1910.   844(0)
Collins, R. Dinak'i ...
   1966.   985(4)
Efimova, A.A. Otechestvennye
   ...geog....1954.   1422(0)

643

EDUCATION - Texts. (cont.)

Eggleston, E. Stories Amer.
  life ... 1895.   1423(0)
George, M. M. Little journeys
  ... 1901.   1697(0)
Gilman, I. A. Alaska ...
  1923.   1729(0)
Gladfelter, K. E. Under North
  Star; course...1928. 1735(0)
Harkness, D. J. Great Lakes
  ... in lit. 1959.   1947(0)
Hawkes, E. W. Eskimo land...
  suppl. reader...1914. 1993(0)
Henry, D. Our Indian language.
  1966.   2067(5)
[Henry, D.] Tł'eaka Hok'anaga'.
  n.d.   2068(5)
Honcharenko, A. Pervonachaljnoe
  ... 1871.   2168(6)
Honcharenko, A. Russko-Angliis-
  kie razgovorg...1868. 2169(6)
Horton, E. Frozen North...
  1904.   2184(4)
Howay, F. W. Capt. Geo. Van-
  couver. 1932.   2200(1)
Inverarity, R.B. Visual files
  coding index. 1960.   2294(0)
Johnson, E.M. N.A. & island
  neighbors. 1948.   2368(0)
Kaġaḳpak. Ḳuliaḳtuat Taimani.
  n. d.   2401(5)
Keithahn, E. L. Alaskan igloo
  tales. 1958.   2429(5)
Keithahn, E. L. Igloo tales.
  1944.   2429(5)
Lantis, D. W. Alaska.
  1957.   2605(0)
Leonhardy, A. Directed study
  guides ... 1929.   2680(0)
Marshall, J. B. Capt. Cook's
  voyages...n.d.   2992(2)
Mazurmovich, B. N. Vydaiush.
  ...zool. 1960.   3048(0)
Milanowski, P. G. Dindee Shuu
  Aandeeg. 1961.   3111(3)
Milanowski, P. G. Uusii di-
  nahtt'aa'. I. 1965.   3112(3)
Milanowski, P. G. Uusii di-
  nahtt'aa'. II. 1965. 3113(3)
Morgan, J. Alaska and Hawaii.
  1956.   3178(0)

Morice, A. G. New methodical...
  Déné syllabary. 1890.3191(1)
Murphy, E. F. Bishop Bompas.
  n. d.   3253(7)
Nome Bd. Educ. Nome schools.
  1903.   3318(5)
Oakes, P. A State is born.
  1958.   3370(0)
Oregon. Dept. Educ. Resource
  unit...1961.   3417(0)
Osipov, K. Pervye russkie
  ... 1949.   3433(4)
Pattee, F. L. Sidelights Amer.
  lit. 1922.   3503(0)
Pedersen, E. Alaska.
  1969. . . . .   3514(0)
Porter, Zoe. Alaska primer.
  1926.   3647(0)
Quinn, V. Picture map geog.
  Canada & Alaska.1944.3714(0)
Robolsky, M. Life...Capt.J.C.
  Eng.Lesebuch...1864. 3851(2)
Russell, I. C. Glaciers N. A.
  reading ...1897.   3916(0)
Russell, I. C. Volcanoes N.A.
  reading ...1897.   3917(0)
Seaman, J.V. New general atlas
  ...1821.   4032(0)
Shaw, E.B. Anglo-America, reg.
  geog. 1959.   4097(0)
Shinen, D. Yapigum Atiḥtoosi
  1966.   4125(5)
Sillars, R. No. Pac. & Alaska.
  1942.   4149(0)
Sterling Pub. Co.Alaska-49th
  State...[c1958]   4339(0)
Summer Inst. Linguistics.Tlin-
  git reading...1.1962.4386(1)
Summer Inst. Linguistics.Tlin-
  git reading...2.n.d. 4387(1)
Tompkins, S. R. Let's read
  about Alaska. 1949.   4553(0)
Tompkins, S. R. Life in Ameri-
  ca; Alaska. 1958.   4554(0)
[Tyzhnov, I.?] Aleutskiĭ buk-
  var'. [ca1839]   4600(6)
Tyzhnov, I.Aleutsko-Kad'iak-
  skiĭ bukvar'.1848.   4601(6)
Warner, G. C. Windows into
  Alaska...1928.   4742(0)
[Webster, D. H.] Brief introd.
  Eskimo...n.d.   4767(4)

EDUCATION - Texts. (cont.)

Webster, D. H. Can you read
English? 1968.   4768(4)
Webster, D. H. Iḷisaaġviṇich
Iñupiam. n.d.   4769(4)
Webster, D. H. Iḷisaaġviṇich
Iñupiat ... n.d.   4770(4)
Webster, D. H. Iñupiat Suuvat?
[c1968]   4772(4)
Webster, D. H. Iñupiat taiguan-
gich. 1. n.d.   4773(4)
Webster, D. H. Iñupiat taiguan-
gich. 2. n.d.   4774(4)
Webster, D. H. Let's learn
Eskimo. [c1967]   4775(4)
Zibell, W. Iñupiam Ukaḷhi.
1966.   5027(4)
Zibell, W. Iñupiam Ukaḷhi.
[1968]   5028(4)
Zimmermann, E.A.W. Taschenbuch
... [1809]   5032(4)

ENGINEERING.

Alaska Mining & Engr. Soc. Con-
stitution...n.d.   86(0)
Alaska Mining & Engr. Soc. Per-
severance mine...1918. 87(0)
Alaska Mining & Engr. Soc.
Thane meeting. 1918.   88(0)
Atwood, G. H. Along the Alcan.
1960.   320(0)
Bowman, W. G. Bulldozers come
first...1944.   632(0)
Camsell, C. Canada's new north-
west...1947.   800(0)
Davidson, D.T. Geol. & engr.
...soils. 1959.   1190(0)
Davies, R.A. Arctic eldorado...
Canada...1944.   1196(0)
Finnie, R. Canol. Sub-Arctic
pipeline...1945.   1562(4)
Flood, M. Arctic journal...
1950.   1585(4)
Hixon, A. T. Canol.
1946. . . . . 2131(4)
Kostinenko, G.I. Stroitel'stvo
... 1962.   2512(0)
Myers, C. V. Oil to Alaska.
[1944?]   3260(0)

ETHNOLOGY - Arts, Crafts.

Adam, L. Nordwestamerikanische
Indianerkunst. [1923]   3(0)
Adler, B.W.K.A. Nordasiatische
Pfeil...1901.   13(0)
Alaska Crippled Children's As-
soc. ...cook...1952.   57(5)
Alaska Mag. Pub. Co. Book of
totems...1942.   82(0)
Alaska Steamship Co. Alaska
Indian basketry. 1904.115(0)
Alaska Steamship Co. Totem
poles...1905.   126(1)
Appleton, L. H. Indian art...
1950.   274(0)
Art Institute of Chicago. Yaku-
tat south...1964.   311(1)
Balcom, M. G. Ketchikan...
totem...[c1961]   371(1)
Barbeau, C.M. Haida myths...
argillite. 1953.   390(1)
Barbeau, C.M. Totem poles.
1950.   394(1)
Boas, F. Primitive art.
1927.   587(0)
Cadzow, D. A. Native copper
objects...1920.   765(0)
Cavana, V.V. Alaska basketry.
1917.   874(0)
Collins, H. B. Okvik artifact
...1959.   981(5)
Collins, H. B. Prehist. harpoon heads...[1941?] 983(5)
Cooper, J. M. Snares, deadfalls
... 1938.   1066(0)
Covarrubias, M. Eagle, jaguar
... 1954.   1099(0)
Davis, R.T. Introd. native
arts...1949.   1209(0)
d'Harcourt, R. Arts de l'Amérique. 1948.   1232(0)
d'Harcourt, R. Primitive art
of Americas. 1950.   1233(0)
Dockstader, F. J. Indian art
in America. 1960.   1315(0)
Douglas, F. H. Indian art of
U. S. 1941.   1334(0)
Durham, B. Canoes and kayaks
west. America. 1960. 1393(0)
Emmons, G.T. Jade in B. C. and
Alaska. 1923.   1457(0)

ETHNOLOGY - Arts, Crafts.
(cont.)
Emmons, G. T. Slate mirrors Tsimshian. 1921. 1458(1)
Emmons, G. T. Basketry of Tlingit. 1903. 1459(1)
Emmons, G. T. Chilkat blanket ... 1907. 1460(1)
Emmons, G. T. Tahltan Indians ... 1911. 1462(1)
Emmons, G. T. Whale house of Chilkat. 1916. 1463(1)
Fast, E. G. Catalogue antiquities... [1869?] 1533(0)
Frazer, J. G. Totemism and ... 1910. 1640(0)
Frobese, F. E. Origin ... totem...1897. 1662(1)
Fuhrmann, E. Tlinkit u. Haida ... 1922. 1665(1)
Garfield, V. E. Meet the totem. 1951. 1682(1)
Garfied, V. E. Seattle totem pole. 1940. 1683(1)
Garfield, V. E. Tsimshian Indians...1966. 1684(1)
Garfield, V. E. Wolf and raven ...1948. 1685(1)
Gorham Mfg. Co. Soul of Alaska ...Louis Potter.1905. 1785(0)
Groven, E. Eskimomelodier... 1956. 1869(5)
Haddon, K. Artists in string ... 1930. 1889(0)
Halliday, W. M. Potlatch and totem. 1935. 1912(1)
Hatt, G. Arktiste skinddragter ... 1914. 1987(0)
Hatt, G. Mocassins and relation to Arctic...1966. 1989(0)
Hawthorn, A. Art of Kwakiutl ...1967. 1998(1)
[Heye, G. G.] Rare Salish blanket. 1926. 2096(1)
Himmelheber, H. Eskimokünstler ... 1953. 2114(5)
Himmelheber, H. Eskimokünstler ...1938. 2115(5)
Holm, W. Northwest coast Indian art. 1965.

Holtved, E. Eskimokunst ... 1947. 2163(5)
Hooper, J. T. Art of primitive peoples. [1953] 2176(0)
How to skin a seal ... n. d. 2197(5)
Illus. hist. Indian baskets... 1915. 2255(0)
Inverarity, R. B. Art of n.w. coast ... 1950. 2291(1)
Inverarity, R. B. Movable masks and figures...1941. 2292(1)
Inverarity, R. B. Northwest ...Indian art. 1946. 2293(1)
James, G. W. Indian basketry ...1901. 2325(0)
Jenness, D. Eskimo string figures. 1924. 2343(0)
Keithahn, E. L. Monuments in cedar...1945. 2431(1)
Krause, A. Katalog ethnologischer...1882. 2540(1)
Krause, E. Vorgeschichtliche ...1904. 2543(0)
Leechman, J. D. String-records...1921. 2669(0)
McCallen, B. G. Ivory carver. 1964. 2833(5)
Mason, O. T. Indian basketry. 1904. 3020(0)
Meldgaard, J. Eskimo sculpture. 1960. 3071(0)
Meldgaard, J. Eskimo skulptur. 1959. 3072(0)
Miles, C. Indian and Eskimo artifacts...1963. 3115(0)
Olson, R. L. Adze, canoe and house type...1927. 3407(0)
Orchard, W. C. Beads and beadwork...1929. 3413(0)
Orchard, W. C. Technique porcupine-quill. 1916. 3414(0)
Pac. Coast Steamship Co. ... totem ... 1915. 3452(1)
Paterson, T. T. Eskimo string figures...1949. 3502(0)
Peterson, H. C. American Indian tomahawks. 1965.3548(0)
Pope, G. D. Eskimo exhibit. 1941. 3642(0)

ETHNOLOGY - Arts, Crafts.
(cont.)
Prescott, A.M. Alaskan Indian
totems. [1941]   3684(1)
Quimby, G.I. Periods prehist.
art Aleut. ...1945.   3711(6)
Quimby, G.I. Prehist. art
Aleut. ... 1948.   3712(6)
Ravenhill, A. ...tribes of
B.C. 1944.   3753(1)
Ray, D.J. Artists of tundra
and sea. 1961.   3754(0)
Ray, D. J. Eskimo masks...
1967.   3755(0)
Rohan-Csermak, G. Sturgeon
hooks Eurasia. 1963. 3868(0)
Siebert, E. North Amer. Indian
art. 1967.   4144(1)
Smith, M.W. Tsimshian; arts
and music. 1951.   4202(1)
Snodgrass, J.O. Amer. Indian
painters; biog. 1967. 4224(0)
Tickasook. Inipiut homes.
1956.   4535(5)
Totem pole; legends and tra-
ditions. n.d.   4560(1)
Townsend, E.C. Birdstones N.A.
Indian. 1959.   4563(0)
Tozier, D.F. Arts and crafts
Totem Indians. n.d. 4566(1)
Waterman, T.T. Indian houses
Puget Sd. 1921.   4752(1)
Waterman, T.T. Native houses
west. N.A. 1921.   4753(1)
Waterman, T.T. Types of canoes
Puget Sd. 1920.   4754(1)
Wherry, J.H. Indian masks
and myths. [c1969]   4810(0)
Wherry, J.H. Totem Pole In-
dians. 1965.   4811(1)
Winter & Pond Co. Totems of
Alaska. [c1905]   4927(1)
Wissler, C. Harpoons and darts
...1916.   4936(0)

ETHNOLOGY - Culture.

Anchorage Daily News. Village
people. 1966.   236(0)
Anderson, H.D. Alaska natives;
survey. 1935.   244(0)
Andrews, C.L. Eskimo and reindeer ... 1939.   254(5)

Averkieva, I.P. Razlozhenie
... 1961.   331(0)
Beattie, W.G. Marsden of
Alaska...1955.   456(0)
Birket-Smith, K. Moeurs et
coutumes...1955.   563(0)
Bojesen, H.H. Alaskai
Indianusok...1921.   599(0)
Buchan, L. Hearth in snow.
1952.   720(6)
Butler, E. Alaska land and
people. 1957.   759(0)
Chapman, N.N. Animistic be-
liefs Ten'a...1939.   895(5)
Clairmont, D.H.J. Deviance...
1963.   935(0)
Cross, J.F. Eskimo adoption.
n.d.   1130(0)
Cross, J.F. Eskimo children.
n.d.   1131(0)
Cross, J.F. The Eskimos. Eski-
mo women. n.d.   1132(0)
Davidson, D.S. Family hunting
terr. ... 1928.   1189(0)
Davy, G. La foi jurée ...
1922.   1210(1)
De Laguna, F. ...dynamic forces Tlingit. 1952.   1246(1)
Drucker, P. Cultures No. Pac.
... 1965.   1356(0)
Durlach, T.M. ...Tlingit, Hai-
da, Tsimshian. 1928. 1394(1)
Edmonson, M.S. Status...soci-
al...Indians. 1958. 1413(0)
Eliade, M. Le chamanisme ...
1951.   1432(0)
Eliade, M. Shamanism ...
ecstasy. 1964.   1433(0)
Ernst, A.H. Wolf ritual...
1952.   1488(0)
Eskimo life in Alaska ...
1964.   1494(0)
Fejes, C. People of Noatak.
1966.   1537(4)
Findeisen, H. Das Tier als
Gott...1956.   1555(0)
Foote, D.C. Human geog. ...Pt.
Hope...1966.   1595(4)
Foote, D.C. Human geog. ...
Upper Kobuk. 1966.   1596(4)
Forde, C.D. Habit, econ. and
soc. geog. ...1943. 1601(0)

ETHNOLOGY - Culture. (cont.)

Forrest, E. C. Daylight moon.
 1937.   1602(0)
Freuchen, P. Book of Eskimos.
 1961.   1651(0)
Garfield, V. E. Tsimshian clan
 ...1939.   1686(1)
Giddings, J. L. Arctic woodland
 Kobuk R. 1952.   1710(4)
Giffen, N. M. Roles men and wo-
 men Eskimo...1930.   1711(0)
Gordon, G. B. In Alaskan wil-
 derness. 1917.   1779(0)
Gore, L. C. Soul of bearded
 seal. 1967.   1784(0)
Green, P. I am Eskimo ...
 1959.   1847(4)
Guemple, D. L. Inuit spouse-
 exchange. 1961.   1876(0)
Haig-Brown, R. Whale people.
 1963.   1894(1)
Halpern, J. M. Eskimos Alaska
 Coast. 1955.   1916(4)
Hawkes, E. W. Dance festivals
 ...Eskimo. 1914.   1994(0)
Hawkes, E. W. "Inviting-in"
 feast...1913.   1995(0)
Hawkes, E. W. La fete "Des In-
 vites"...1915.   1996(0)
Hawthorn, H. B.   Indians of
 B. C. ...1958.   1999(1)
Hays, L. A. Kahtlian, chief
 Raven tribe. 1906.   2007(1)
Hays, L. A. Ka-Ta-Da.
 1906. . . . .   2008(1)
Hetzel, T. B.   Indian rights
 ...1961.   2088(0)
Hetzel, T. B.   Meek do not in-
 herit Alaska. 1962.   2089(0)
Hughes, C. C. Eskimo village
 ...1960.   2218(5)
Hultkrantz, A. Concept. soul
 ...1953.   2232(0)
Hultkrantz, A. ...Orpheus tra-
 dition. 1957.   2233(0)
Huntington, J. On edge of
 nowhere. 1966.   2240(5)
Ingstad, H. Nunamiut...inland
 Eskimos. 1954.   2266(4)
Ingstad, H. Nunamiut ... inn-
 lands Eskimoer. 1951. 2267(4)

Jacobsen, N. K. Erhverv og kul-
 tur ... 1950.   2318(4)
Jenness, D. Dawn in Arctic
 Alaska. 1957.   2340(4)
Jenness, D. Eskimo admin. I.
 Alaska. 1962.   2341(0)
Jenness, D. Eskimo admin. V.
 Analysis...1968.   2342(0)
Jenness, D. American aborigines
 ...1933.   2345(0)
Jenness, D. Indians of Canada.
 1932.   2346(0)
Jensen, P. Hunters Arctic rim.
 n.d.   2350(5)
Jones, L. F. Study Thlingets
 ...1914.   2383(1)
Kangkuk.   ... boy of Bering
 Strait. 1939.   2409(5)
Keithahn, E. L. Eskimo adven-
 ture...1963.   2430(5)
Kunst, J. Ethnomusicology.
 1959.   2571(0)
Lantis, M. Alaskan Eskimo
 ceremonialism. 1947. 2606(5)
Lantis, M. Eskimo childhood
 ...Nunivak...1960.   2607(5)
Larsen, H. Eskimokulturen.
 1960.   2629(0)
Larsen, H. Circumpolar conf.
 ...1960.   2631(5)
Leechman, D. Vanta Kutchin.
 1954.   2668(0)
Lips, E. Das Indianerbuch.
 1956.   2722(0)
McCracken, H. Hunters stormy
 sea. 1957.   2845(6)
McKennan, R. A. Chandalar
 Kutchin. 1965.   2916(4)
McKennan, R. A. Upper Tanana
 Indians. 1959.   2917(0)
Marsh, G. H. Human anatomical
 knowl. Aleut. 1956. 2976(6)
Marshall, R. Arctic Village.
 1933.   2997(4)
Marston, M. R. Men of tundra.
 1969.   3001(0)
Mathiassen, T. Eskimoerne i
 nutid...1929.   3028(0)
Mayokok, R. Eskimo customs.
 1951.   3043(5)
Mayokok, R. Eskimo life.
 1951.   3044(5)

ETHNOLOGY - Culture. (cont.)

Mayokok, R. Alaskan Eskimo.
n. d.   3046(5)
Meyers, W. E. Eskimo village.
1957.   3094(5)
Moorrees, C. F. Aleut dentition.
Eskimoid...1957.   3167(6)
Morice, A. G. Thawing out
Eskimo. 1943.   3189(0)
Murdock, G. P. Our primitive
contemporaries. 1934. 3247(0)
Murdock, G.P. Rank and potlatch
...Haidas. 1936.   3248(1)
Nelson, R. K. Hunters of nor-
thern ice. 1969.   3289(4)
Nutchuk. Back to Smoky Sea.
1946.   3368(6)
Nutchuk. Son of Smoky Sea.
1941.   3369(6)
Oberg, K. Social econ.Tlingit
Indians. 1940.   3372(1)
Oetteking, B. Craniology no.
Pac. coast. 1930.   3381(0)
Okakok, G. Okakok's Alaska...
Pt. Barrow...1959.   3396(4)
Olson, S. Runes of North.
1963.   3408(0)
Osgood, C. B. Contrib. ethno-
graphy Kutchin. 1936. 3424(0)
Osgood, C. B. Ingalik material
culture. 1940.   3425(0)
Osgood, C. B. Ingalik mental
culture. 1959.   3426(0)
Osgood, C. B. Ingalik social
culture. 1958.   3427(0)
Osgood, C. B. Distrib. no.
Athapaskan ... 1936. 3428(0)
Osgood, C. B. Ethnography
Tanaina. 1937.   3429(0)
Oswalt, W. H. Alaskan Eskimos.
1967.   3436(0)
Oswalt, W. H. Mission of
change...1963.   3437(5)
Oswalt, W. H. Napaskiak...
1961.   3438(5)
Pender, J. Kotzebue, two
worlds. [c1970]   3530(4)
Pettitt, G. A. Primitive educa-
tion. 1946.   3562(0)
Pinart, A. L. Eskimaux et
Koloches...1873.   3594(0)

Pinart, A. L. La Chasse aux
Animaux Marins. 1875.3596(0)
Pinart, A. L. Notes sur les
Koloches. 1873.   3597(6)
Pinart, A. L. Sur les Atnahs.
1875.   3598(6)
Rainey, F. G. Whale hunters
Tigara. 1947.   3728(4)
Rasmussen, K.J.V. Alaskan
Eskimos...1952.   3749(0)
Rausch, R. L. Notes Nunamiut
Anaktuvuk...1951.   3750(4)
Richet, E. Esquimaux...1.
1921.   3806(0)
Rodahl, K. Smilets folk.
1957.   3855(0)
Rodahl, K. Last of few.
[c1963]   3858(0)
Rostlund, E. Freshwater fish
...1952.   3898(4)
Senter, G. E. Kawoo of Alaska.
[c1964]   4047(1)
Shapiro, H. L. Alaskan Eskimos
...1931.   4091(0)
Shinen, D. Marriage customs
St. Lawrence ...1963.4126(5)
Sniffen, M. K. Indians Yukon
& Tanana...1914.   4223(0)
Spicer, E. H. Human problems...
1952.   4262(5)
Spiro, M. E. Context and
meaning...1965.   4264(0)
Stefansson, V. Hunters of ...
North. [c1922]   4305(0)
Stefansson, V. Jäger des hohen
Nordens. 1924.   4306(0)
Stefansson, V. Prehistoric
commerce...1914.   4312(4)
Sullivan, R. J. Ten'a food
quest. 1941.   4383(5)
Swanton, J. R. Contrib. ...
Haida. 1905.   4415(1)
Swanton, J. R. Social condi-
tions...Tlingit.1970.4418(1)
Swartz, M. J. Political an-
thropology. 1966.   4426(5)
Tax, S. Indian tribes...
1952.   4465(0)
Taxay, D. Money Amer. Indian
... [c1970]   4466(0)
Thibert, A. English-Eskimo...
dict. 1958.   4483(0)

ETHNOLOGY - Culture. (cont.)

Thompson, E. T. Race; indivi-
dual ...1958.   4506(4)
Thornton, H. R. Among Eskimos
Wales...1931.   4526(5)
U.S.S.R. Akad. Nauk. Kul'tura
...1963.   4616(0)
U.S.S.R. Akad. Nauk. Ocherki
...1957.   4617(0)
Van Steensel, M. People of
light & dark. 1966.   4651(0)
VanStone, J. W. Eskimos of
Nushagak R. 1967.   4652(6)
VanStone, J. W. Point Hope...
1962.   4653(4)
Van Valin, W. B. Eskimoland
speaks...1941.   4654(4)
Wilmovsky, N. J. Util. fishery
resources...1956.   4908(4)
Woman's Amer. Baptist Home
Mission ... totem poles ...
1911.   4948(1)
Zolotarev, A. M. Perezhitki
totemizma...1934.   5038(0)

ETHNOLOGY - Legends, Tales,
                        Myths.

Anderson, L. D. According to
Mama. 1956.   249(3)
Bagley, C. B. Indian myths
n. w. coast. 1930.   343(1)
Barbeau, C. M. Indian speaks.
1943.   393(0)
Barbeau, C. M. Tsimsyan myths.
1961.   395(1)
Bayliss, C. K. Treasury Eskimo
tales. 1922.   435(0)
Beck, G. J. Soncth-Shan (The
Old Hat) 1909.   461(1)
Boas, F. Indianische Sagen...
nordpac. ... 1895.   586(1)
Chapman, J. W. Ten'a texts and
tales...Anvik. 1914.   894(5)
Clark, E. E. Indian legends
Pac. n.w. 1953.   937(1)
Corser, H. P. Legendary lore...
totem. 1910.   1086(1)
Corser, H. P. Totem lore and
land of totem. n.d.   1089(1)

Corser, H. P. Totem lore Alas-
kan Indians. n.d.   1090(1)
Costello, J. A. Siwash...
Pac. n.w. 1895.   1094(1)
Crane, W. E. Totem tales.
1932.   1115(1)
Cunningham, C. Talking stone.
Indians & Esk. 1939.   1139(0)
Deans, J. Tales from totems
hidery...1899.   1220(1)
Driggs, J. B. Short sketches
...1905.   1350(4)
Garber, C. M. Stories...Bering
Strait. [c1940]   1680(5)
Gillham, C. E. Beyond Clapping
Mtns. 1943.   1723(5)
Gillham, C. E. Medicine men of
Hooper Bay. 1955.   1724(5)
Hatt, G. Asiatic influences...
folklore. 1949.   1988(0)
Hillyer, W. H. Box of daylight
Tsimshian...1931.   2109(1)
Himmelheber, H. Der gefrorene
Pfad...1951.   2113(5)
Irvine, A. How Makah...Cape
Flattery. 1921.   2295(1)
Jones, L. B. Tundra tales.
1959.   2382(4)
Jones, L. F. Indian vengeance.
1920.   2384(1)
Judson, K. B. Myths and le-
gends...1911.   2395(0)
Keithahn, E. L. Alaskan igloo
tales. 1958.   2429(5)
Keithahn, E. L. Igloo tales.
1944.   2429(5)
Loftus, A. According to Grand-
father. 1965.   2748(3)
McCorkle, R. Alaskan ten-
footed bear. 1958.   2841(0)
Maury, J. W. Old raven's
world. 1931.   3037(1)
Mayokok, R. Eskimo stories.
1960.   3045(5)
Mayokok, R. True Eskimo
stories. n.d.   3047(5)
Newell, E. W. Rescue of sun...
1970.   3296(0)
Oman, L. Eskimo legends.
1965.   3409(5)
Paul, D. According to Papa.
1957.   3506(3)

ETHNOLOGY - Legends, Tales,
    Myths, (cont.)

Phillips, W. S. Indian fairy
    tales...[c1902]   3577(1)
Phillips, W. S. Totem tales...
    1896.   3577(1)
Rasmussen, K.J.V. Festens
    gave...1929.   3736(4)
Rasmussen, K.J.V. Eagle's
    gift. 1932.   3737(4)
Rasmussen, J.J.V. Die Gabe
    des Adlers. [1937?]   3738(4)
Riggs, R. C. Animal stories...
    1923.   3823(5)
Riggs, R. C. Igloo tales ...
    1928.   3824(5)
Romig, J. H. Raven of Eskimos.
    1943.   3878(5)
Rossiter, H. Indian legends
    ...1925.   3893(0)
Salisbury, O. M. "Quoth the
    Raven." 1962.   3948(1)
Shiels, A. W. "Tell me a
    'stowry' " n.d.   4119(0)
Shriever, L. W. Alaskan verses
    from native lore.1969.4135(0)
Silook, R. ...in the begin-
    ning. [c1970]   4150(5)
Sleator, Wm. The angry moon.
    [c1970]   4179(1)
Thompson, S. Tales N. A. In-
    dians. 1929.   4509(0)
Thorne, J. F. In time that was.
    Chilkats. [c1909]   4525(1)
[Tickasook] Eskimo legends
    Kotzebue. [c1959]   4534(4)
Vaudrin, B. Tainaina tales...
    1969.   4659(3)
Volmar, F. A. Das Bärenbuch.
    1940.   4714(0)
Zibell, W. Unipchaat 1. Kobuk
    ...[c1969]   5029(4)
Zibell, W. Unipchaat 2. ...
    Kobuk...[c1969]   5030(4)
Zibell, W. Unipchaat 3. ...
    Kobuk...[c1970]   5031(4)

ETHNOLOGY - Origins.

Ackerman, R. E. Archaeol. surv.
    Glacier Bay. 1964.   1(1)

Ackerman, R. E. Prehistory Kus-
    kokwim-Bristol Bay.1964.2(5)
Anatolii, A. Indiane Aliaski
    ...[1907?]   230(1)
Anatolii, A. Indianskoe ...
    Tlingit. 1899.   231(1)
Averkieva, I. P. Rabstvo...
    Indietsev...1941.   330(0)
Baer, K. E. Statische ...
    v. Wrangell...1839.   342(0)
Baity, E. C. Americans before
    Columbus. 1951.   356(0)
Balbi, A. Atlas ethnog. ...
    peuples...1826.   360(0)
Bancroft, H. H. Native races
    ...1874-75.   381(0)
Bandi, H. G. Alaska, Urgesch-
    ichte...1967.   382(0)
Bandi, H. G. Eskimo prehistory.
    [c1969]   383(0)
Bandi, H. G. Urgeschichte der
    Eskimo. 1965.   383(0)
Bank, T. P. Birthplace of
    winds. 1956.   385(6)
Barbeau, C. M. Alaska beckons.
    1947.   389(0)
Barbeau, C. M. Medicine men on
    No. Pac. coast. 1958. 391(1)
Barbeau, C. M. Pathfinders in
    No. Pac. 1958.   392(0)
Beach, W. W. Indian miscellany.
    1877.   451(1)
Birket-Smith, K. Eskimoerne.
    1927.   559(0)
Birket-Smith, K. Eskimos.
    1936.   560(0)
Birket-Smith, K. Eskimos.
    1959.   561(0)
Birket-Smith, K. Menneskets...
    1958.   562(0)
Birket-Smith, K. Naturmen-
    nesker. 1934.   564(0)
Birket-Smith, K. Chugach
    Eskimo. 1953.   565(2)
Birket-Smith, K. Eyak Indians
    Copper delta.1938.   566(3)
Block, B. Rimelig formod-
    ning...1804.   578(0)
Boas anniversary volume ...
    1906.   582(0)
Boas, F. Contrib. ethnology
    Kwakiutl. 1925.   583(1)

ETHNOLOGY - Origins. (cont.)

Boas, F. Facial paintings
Indians...1898.   584(1)
Boas, F. Race, language and
culture. 1940.   588(0)
Boas, F. Use masks and head-
ornaments ... 1890.   589(1)
Brand, D. D. So live works of
men. 1939.   643(0)
Brooks, C. W. Japanese wrecks
... n.w. ...1876.   685(0)
Burge, M. S. Indians of Upper
Tanana...1938.   729(2)
Byhan, A. Die Polarvölker ...
1909.   761(0)
Campbell, J. M. Prehistoric
cultural... 1962.   792(0)
Casagrande, J. B. In company
of man. 1960.   860(0)
Chance, N. A. Eskimo of North
Alaska. 1967.   887(4)
Collins, H. B. Arctic area,
indigenous...1954.   982(0)
Cressman, L. S. Research...
Naknek ... 1962.   1118(6)
Dall, W. H. Native tribes...
1885.   1167(0)
de Laguna, F. Anthropol. ...
no. Tlingit. [1949] 1240(1)
de Laguna, F. Anthropol. Tlingit Chatham Str.[1950]1241(1)
de Laguna, F. Archaeol. ...no.
Tlingit...[1949?]   1242(1)
de Laguna, F. Chugach prehist.
Pr. Wm. Sd. 1956.   1243(2)
de Laguna, F. Selected papers
...1960.   1245(0)
de Laguna, F. Archaeol. Cook
Inlet...1934.   1247(2)
de Laguna, F. Prehistory no.
Yukon. 1947.   1248(0)
Driver, H. E. Indians N. A.
1961.   1352(0)
Drucker, P. Indians n.w. coast.
1955.   1357(1)
Edmonds, H.M.W. Eskimo of St.
Michael ... 1966.   1412(5)
Efimov, A.V. Narody Ameriki.
1959.   1419(0)
Eleonskaîa, E. N. Aleuty.
1929.   1431(6)

Ford, J. A. Eskimo prehistory
...P. Barrow. 1959. 1600(4)
Forster, J.G.A. Kleine Schrif-
ten...1789-96.   1608(0)
Forster, J. R. Observations
...1778.   1613(2)
Frazer, J. G. Anthologia an-
thropologica...1939. 1639(0)
Garn, S. M. Readings on race.
1960.   1689(0)
Gessain, R. Contrib....Eski-
mo ... 1960.   1700(0)
Gessain, R. Esquimeaux Groen-
land a l'Alaska.1947.1701(0)
Giddings, J. L. Ancient men of
Arctic. 1967.   1707(0)
Giddings, J. L. Archaeol. Cape
Denbigh. 1964.   1709(5)
Gjessing, G. Circumpolar stone
age. 1944.   1734(0)
Goddard, P. E. Indians North-
west coast. 1924.   1743(1)
Goldschmidt, W. Anthropology
Franz Boas. 1959.   1759(0)
Goodenough, W. H. Explorations
cultural...1964.   1772(4)
Green, J. S. Journal tour...
n.w. 1915.   1846(1)
Gubser, N. J. Nunamiut Eskimos.
1965.   1875(4)
Hale, H. E. Ethnog. ...Wilkes
...1846.   1900(0)
Hale, H. E. Indians n. w.Amer.
vocabs....1848.   1901(0)
Harriman Alaska Exped.vol. 1.
1902.   1950(0)
Harrison, C. Ancient warriors
...1925.   1965(1)
Hartwig, G. L. Dwellers
Arctic ... 1887.   1979(0)
Heizer, R. F. Archaeol. Uyak
...Kodiak Isl. 1956. 2022(6)
Heyerdahl, T. American Indians
in Pac. 1952.   2097(1)
Hibben, F. C. Digging up
America. 1960.   2099(0)
Hibben, F. C. Treasure in the
dust. 1951.   2101(0)
Hill-Tout, C. Far west...Salish
& Dene. 1907.   2106(1)
Hoffman, W. J. ...Eskimo
pictographs...1883. 2138(0)

ETHNOLOGY - Origins. (cont.)

Hofmann, C. Frances Densmore, biog. 1967.   2139(0)
Holmberg, H. J. Ethnog. Skizzen russ. Amer. 1855063. 2157(0)
Honigmann, J.J. World of man. 1959.   2170(0)
Hopkins, D. M. Bering land bridge. 1967.   2178(4)
Hrdlička, A. Alaska diary ... 1943.   2207(0)
Hrdlička, A. Eskimo brain. 1901.   2208(0)
Hrdlička, A. Aleutian & Commander Isl. ...1945.   2209(6)
Hrdlička, A. Anthropol. Kodiak Isl. 1944.   2210(6)
Irving, W. N. ...archaeol.... Brooks Range. 1954. 2297(4)
Jackson, S. Native tribes of Alaska. 1883.   2313(0)
Jacobsen, J. A. Kapitän Jacobsen's Reise. 1884.   2315(0)
Jacobsen, J. A. Unter den Alaska-Eskimos. n.d.   2316(0)
Jacobsen, J. A. ...Indianern und Eskimos. n.d.   2317(0)
Jeancon, J. A. Northwest coast Indians. 1930.   2333(1)
Jesup No. Pac. Exped. Ethnog. album...Pt.1. 1900. 2351(0)
Jochelson, W. Archaeol. Aleut. Isl. 1925.   2358(6)
Jochelson, W. Hist. ethnol. anthrop. Aleut. 1933. 2359(6)
Keim, C. J. Aghvook, white Eskimo. 1969.   2426(5)
Knapp, F. Thlinkets S.E. Alaska. 1896.   2493(1)
Krause, A. Die Tlingit-Indianer...1885.   2541(1)
Krause, A. Tlingit Indians... 1956.   2542(1)
Larsen, H. Ipiutak and Arctic whale hunting...1948. 2630(4)
Latham, R. G. Native races, Russ. empire. 1854. 2634(0)
Leroi-Gourhan, A. Archéol. du Pac.-nord. 1946.   2684(6)
Llwyd, J.P.D. Message Indian relic. 1909.   2743(1)

McCracken, H. God's frozen children. 1930.   2844(6)
McFeat, T. Tindians No. Pac. coast. 1967.   2891(1)
MacNeish, R. S. Investig. s.w. Yukon...1964.   2944(7)
Martin, P. S. Indians before Columbus...1947.   3010(0)
Mason, W. S. Frozen northland ...Esquimo...1910. 3022(0)
Mathiassen, T. Archaeol. ... Eskimos. 1930.   3027(0)
Middendorff, W. Ueber Tlinkit R. A. 1861.   3098(1)
Miller, L. G. Lost heritage of Alaska. 1967.   3133(1)
Morice, A. G. Essai sur ... Dènè ... 1915.   3186(0)
Morice, A. G. Notes western Dènès. 1894.   3188(0)
Nadaillac, M. Prehistoric American. 1884.   3269(0)
Oschinsky, L. Most ancient Eskimos. 1964.   3423(0)
Oswalt, W. H. This land was theirs. 1966.   3439(0)
Petitot, É.F.S.J. Origine ... Esquimaux...1890.   3558(0)
[Phillips, R.] View...Oonalashka ... 1810.   3576(6)
Pickering, C. Races of man... 1863.   3578(0)
Pinart, A. L. ...d'Aknanh Île d'Ounga. 1875.   3595(6)
Quimby, G. I. Aleut. Islanders ... 1944.   3710(6)
Quimby, G. I. Sadiron lamp of Kamchatka...1946.   3713(6)
Rainey, F. G. Archaeology Central Alaska. 1939.   3726(3)
Rainey, F. G. ...Okvik...Punuk ... 1941.   3727(5)
Replogle, C. Among Indians of Alaska. 1904.   3783(0)
Royal Geog. Soc. Arctic geog. & ethnol. ... 1875. 3907(4)
Rudenko, S. I. Drevnīaīa Kul'-tura Beringova. 1947.3910(0)
Rudenko, S. I. Ancient culture Bering Sea. 1961. 3911(0)
Schmitz, C. A. Festschrift Alfred Bühler. 1965.   4006(0)

ETHNOLOGY - Origins. (cont.)

Skarland, I. Flint stations
central Alaska. 1948. 4167(3)
Smith, M. W. Asia and N. A.
...1953.   4201(0)
Spaulding, A. C. Archaeol. ...
Agattu ... 1962.   4254(6)
Spencer, R. F. Native Americans
...1965.   4258(0)
Steensby, H. P. Om Eskimokul-
turens ... 1905.   4297(0)
Stefansson, V. ...Arctic exped.
1919.   4323(4)
Stefansson, V. ...Arctic exped.
prelim. ...1914.   4324(4)
Stirling, M.W. Indians of
Americas. 1965.   4349(0)
Swanton, J. R. Indian tribes
Alaska & Canada. 1965.4417(0)
Swanton, J. R. Indian tribes
of N. A. 1968.   4419(0)
Swayze, N. Man hunters ...
1960.   4427(0)
Taranetskiĭ, A. I. Beiträge...
Aleuten ... 1900.   4458(0)
Tokarev, S. A. Indeitsy Ameriki
... 1955.   4542(0)
Veniaminov, I.E.P. Zapiski...
Unalashkinskago. 1840.4682(6)
Weyer, E. M. Aleutian
burial. 1929.   4803(6)
Weyer, E. M. Archaeol. ...
Port Moller...1930.   4804(6)
Weyer, E. M. The Eskimos.
1932.   4805(0)
Wissler, C. Archaeol. Polar
Eskimo. 1918.   4935(0)

EXPLORATION - Collective.

Adamov, A. G. Pervye russkie...
1950.   6(0)
Adamov, A. G. Po neizvedannym
putiam. 1950.   7(0)
Amer. Geog. Soc. Problems of
polar research. 1928. 203(4)
Andreyev, A. I. Russ. disc.
Pac. 1952.   263(0)
Andreyev, A.I. Russkie otkry-
tiĭa...1948.   264(0)
Baker, J.N.L. Hist. geog.
... 1931.   357(0)

Barrington, D. Miscellanies...
1781.   407(1)
Barrow, J. Chronological ...
voyages...1818.   409(0)
Barrow, J. Storia cronologica
...viaggi ... 1820.   410(0)
Beaglehole, J. C. Exploration
of Pacific. 1934.   453(0)
Berg, L. S. Ocherki po istorii
russkikh...1946.   512(0)
Bergman, S. Beröm upptöckts-
färder...1939.   521(0)
Berkh, V. N.Khronologicheskaĭa
...Aleutskikh...1823. 527(6)
Berkh, V. N. Chronological
Aleutian Isls. 1938.   528(6)
Berkh, V. N.Khronologicheskaĭa
siev. ...1821-23.   529(0)
Berkh, V. N. Zhizn. Ross. ad-
miralov. 1831-36.   533(0)
Breitfus, L. L. Arktis...
1939.   651(4)
Breitfus, L. L. Das Nordpolar-
gebiet ... 1943.   652(4)
Breitfus, L. L. Die Erforschung
Polar...1950.   653(4)
[Brooks, R. ?] Remarks ...
Cook. 1780.   679(2)
Bryce, G. Seige and conquest
North Pole. 1910.   711(4)
Burney, J. Chronolog. hist.
...voyages...1819.   738(0)
Canada. Fifth book reading...
1883.[Yukon R. disc.] 805(7)
Caswell, J. E. Arctic fron-
tiers. 1956.   866(0)
Caswell, J. E. Utilization
sci. reports. 1951.   867(0)
Chukovskiĭ, N. K. Voditeli
fregatov. 1947.   928(0)
Churchill, A. Collect. voyages
...1732-47.   932(0)
Churchill, A. Collect. voyages
...1745.   933(0)
Clowes, W. L. Royal Navy...
1899-1903.   960(0)
Coxe, W. Acct. Russian dis-
coveries. 1780.   1106(0)
Coxe, W. Nouvelles découvertes
Russes...1781.   1107(0)
Coxe, W. Die neuen Entdeck....
Russen. 1783.   1108(0)

EXPLORATION - Collective.
(cont.)
Croft, A. Polar exploration.
1939.   1126(4)
Crouse, N.M. Search for n.w.
passage. 1934.   1134(4)
Davis, H. Record Japanese
vessels...1872.   1202(0)
de La Croix, R. Mysteries No.
Pole. 1954.   1238(4)
Delisle, J. N. Nouvelles cartes
...de Fonte...1753.   1257(0)
[de Marbault, M.?] Essai ...
Russie...1777.   1261(0)
Denkschriften der russ. geog.
... 1849.   1270(0)
Denton, V. L. Far west coast.
1924.   1272(0)
Dieck, H. Marvelous wonders
Polar... 1885.   1292(0)
Dodge, E. S. American activi-
ties Cent. Pac. 1966. 1316(0)
Dodge, E. S. Northwest by sea.
1961.   1317(0)
Dolan, E. F. White battle-
ground. 1961.   1326(4)
Douglas, M. Frozen North.
n. d.   1335(4)
Edwards, D. M. Toll of Arctic
Seas. 1910.   1414(0)
Efimov, A. V. Iz istoriĭ russ.
èksped. ... 1948.   1416(0)
Efimov, A. V. Iz istoriĭ russ.
èksped. ... 1949.   1417(0)
Efimov, A. V. Iz istoriĭ russ.
èksped. ... 1950.   1418(0)
Efimov, A. V. Otkrytiĭa russ.
... 1951.   1420(0)
Efimov, A. V. Velikie russkie
geog. ... 1949.   1421(0)
Efimova, A. A. Otechestvennye
putesh. ... 1954.   1422(0)
Emmanuel, M. La France et ...
polaire ... 1959.   1456(0)
Explorers Club. Through Hell
and high water. 1941. 1508(0)
Farquhar, F. P. Brief chronology ... 1943.   1527(0)
Fischer, J. E. Sibirskaĭa
istoriĭa ... 1774.   1565(0)
Förster, H. A. Der weisse Weg
1952.   1604(4)

Forster, J.G.A. Geschichte
Reisen Cook...1792. 1607(0)
Forster, J. R. Geschichte der
Entdeck...1784.   1609(0)
Forster, J.R. Hist. voyages
& disc. 1786.   1610(0)
Forster, J.R. Hist. voyages
& disc. 1786.   1611(0)
Forster, J.R. Histoire des
découvertes. 1788.   1612(0)
Fraser, C.C.Heroes of sea.
1924.   1637(0)
Freuchen, P. Book of seven
seas. 1957.   1652(0)
Freuchen, P. Men of frozen
north. 1962.   1654(0)
Goepp, E. Grande hommes de la
France...1873.   1749(0)
Golder, F.A. Russ. expansion
Pacific. 1914.   1758(0)
Great Britain. Parl. (Franklin
search)   1820-33(4)
Greely, A. W. Handbook Arctic
discoveries. 1896.   1841(0)
Greely, A. W. Polar regions
20th cent. 1928.   1842(0)
Greely, A. W. True tales
Arctic ... 1912.   1843(0)
Guérin, L. Les navigateurs
français. 1856.   1877(0)
Hallager, M. Udforlige og
troevaerdige...1784. 1911(0)
Harris, J. Navigantium ...
bibliotheca ... 1764.1961(0)
Hartwig, G. L. Der Hobe Norden
...1858.   1977(0)
Hartwig, G. L. Polar world ...
1869.   1978(0)
Hartwig, G. L. Heroes Polar
world. 1892.   1980(0)
Hartwig, G.L. Polar and tropi-
cal worlds. 1871.   1981(0)
Hayes, J. G. Conquest North
Pole. 1934.   2004(4)
Heawood, E. Geog. disc. 17th
& 18th cent. 1912.   2013(0)
Heyerdahl, T. Great Norwegian
expeditions. [1955?] 2098(0)
Histoire universelle ...
1856.   2126(0)
Histoire des voyages...en Chine
... n. d.   2127(0)

EXPLORATION - Collective.
(cont.)
Hist. & exploration Russ. ...
Pacific. [ca 1860]   2128(0)
Holden, R. P. Famous scienti-
fic exped. 1955.   2148(0)
Horton, E. Frozen North.
1904.   2184(4)
Houben, H. H. Der Ruf des
Nordens. 1927.   2185(0)
Houben, H. H. Nordpolfahrten.
1944.   2186(0)
Houben, H. H. Call of North.
1932.   2187(0)
Hovgaard, W. Voyages Norsemen
... 1915.   2196(0)
Hyde, A. Frozen zone ...
1874.   2249(4)
Interesting accts. ...voyages
...Cook...1790.   2272(2)
Int'l. Yukon Polar Institute.
Constitution. 1905.   2289(4)
Int'l. Yukon Polar Institute.
Objects ... 1905.   2290(4)
Ivanshinstov, N. Obozrieniĭ
Russ. ... 1850.   2308(0)
Jane, F. T. Imperial Russian
Navy. 1899.   2329(0)
Kerr, R. General hist. ...
voyages ... 1811-24.   2447(0)
Kersting, R. White world ...
1902.   2448(4)
Kippis, A. Voyages from death
Cook ... 1844.   2469(0)
Kirwan, A.L.P. White road ...
1959.   2474(4)
Krarup-Nielsen, A. Jordens
erobring...1930-32.   2530(0)
Kruber, A. A. Biblioteka ...
1924.   2546(0)
Kuznetsov, I.V. Lĭudi russkoĭ
nauki. 1948-[?]   2575(0)
Lardner, D. Hist. maritime &
inland disc. 1830.   2624(0)
Laut, A. C. Vikings of Pacific.
1905.   2646(0)
Leacock, S. B. Adventures far
north. 1914.   2654(4)
Leslie, J. Discovery polar
seas. 1860.   2688(0)
Leslie, J. Narrat. polar seas
... 1830.   2688(0)

Lewis, M. England's sea offi-
cers. 1939.   2698(0)
Lupach, V. S. Russkie morepla-
vateli. 1953.   2815(0)
Lyons, H. Royal Soc. 1660-1940.
1944.   2822(0)
McDonald, L. Search northwest
passage. 1958.   2866(0)
MacGregor, J. Progress of
America. 1847.   2898(0)
MacLean, J. K. Heroes Polar
Seas. 1910.   2929(4)
Magidovich, I. P. Istoriĩa...
Severnoĭ Amer. 1962. 2953(0)
Markham, C. R. Lands of si-
lence. 1921.   2971(4)
Marshall, J. S. Pacific
voyages. 1960.   2994(0)
Masterman, J. R. Bering's
successors. 1948.   3023(0)
Mayne, F. Voyages and disc.
Arctic ... 1855.   3042(4)
Michael, C. D. 'Mid snow and
ice...polar...n.d.   3097(4)
Mirsky, J. To Arctic !
1948.   3143(4)
Mirsky, J. To the North !
1934.   3144(4)
Mirsky, J. Northern conquest.
1934.   3144(4)
Mitchell, M. Maritime hist.
Russ. 1949.   3146(0)
Mountevans, E.R.G.R.E. Arctic
solitudes. 1953.   3212(4)
Mountevans, E.R.G.E.R. British
polar ... 1943.   3213(4)
Mountevans, E.R.G.R.E. ...hus-
ky to sno-cat.1957.   3214(4)
Müller, G. F. Herrn v.
Tschitschagow...1793.3232(0)
Müller, G. F. Nachrichten...
1758.   3233(0)
Müller, G. F. Voyages Asia to
America. 1761.   3234(0)
Müller, G. F. Voyages et
découvertes...1766.   3235(0)
Murray, H. Hist. acct. ...
Polar ... 1829.'   3258(0)
Nat. Geog. Soc. Great adven-
tures...1963.   3276(0)
Neatby, L. H. Conquest last
frontier. 1966.   3280(0)

EXPLORATION - Collective.
(cont.)
Neatby, L. H. In quest north-
west passage. 1958.   3281(0)
New South Wales Pub. Library.
Bibliog....Cook.1928. 3294(2)
Nilsson, G. A. Sjöfarare ...
1957.   3311(0)
Nordpolarlander...Mackenzie
...Kotzebue. 1822.   3340(0)
Nourse, J. E. Amer. exploration
ice zones. 1884.   3360(0)
Nozikov, N. N. Russkie krugo-
svetnye...1947.   3364(0)
Nozikov, N. N. Russian voyages
... n.d.   3365(0)
Osipov, K. Pervye russkie
... 1949.   3433(0)
Perry, R. *Jeannette*...voyages
North Pole. 1882.   3540(0)
Pertek, J. Polacy na szlakach
... 1957.   3543(0)
Phillips, R. Collect. ... voy-
ages ... 1805-10.   3574(0)
Phillips, R. General collect.
voyages.1809-10.   3575(2)
Pinkerton, J. General collect.
voyages. 1808-14.   3603(2)
Prentiss, H. M. Great polar
current...1897.   3677(4)
Rabot, C. Poliarnye strany...
1924.   3717(4)
Read, J. E. Nansen in frozen
world ... 1897.   3763(0)
Recent polar voyages ...
[187_?]   3766(0)
Reisen nach...Meares, Dixon,
Portlak...1795.   3780(0)
[Rhodes, C.C.] Prof. Sonntag's
...explorations.1857. 3799(0)
Riabov, N. I. Ocherki istorii
russ. ... 1958.   3800(0)
Ricks, M. B. Earliest hist.
...1970.   3814(0)
Rowley, D. Arctic research...
1955.   3905(0)
Sargent, E. Arctic adventure...
1857.   3960(4)
Sargent, E. Wonders of Arctic.
world.   3961(4)
Segal, L. Conquest of Arctic.
1939.   4042(4)

Sherwood, M. B. Exploration
Alaska. 1965.   4114(0)
Shillinglaw, J. J. Narrative
Arctic disc. 1850.   4123(4)
Silverburg, R. Scientists and
scoundrels. 1965.   4151(2)
Simmonds, P.L. Sir John Frank-
lin ... 1851.   4153(4)
Simmonds, P.L. Sir John Frank-
lin ... 1852.   4154(4)
Simmonds, P.L. Arctic regions
...n.w. passage.1857.4155(4)
[Simmonds, P.L.] Arctic
regions ... 1853.   4156(4)
Smith, D. M. Arctic expedi-
tions ... 1877.   4195(4)
Smith, G. B. Sir John Frank-
lin ... [ca 1896?]   4198(0)
Smucker, S. M. Arctic explora-
tions...1857.   4210(4)
Snelling, W.J. Polar regions
... 1831.   4219(4)
Speck, G. Northwest explora-
tion. 1954.   4255(0)
Stankevich, V. B. Na velikom
Severe ... 1923.   4281(0)
Stefansson, V. Great adven-
tures...1947.   4304(0)
Stefansson, V. Northwest to
fortune. [c1958]   4310(4)
Stefansson, V. Routes to
Alaska. 1941.   4313(0)
Stefansson, V. Ultima Thule;
mysteries...1940.   4325(4)
Stefansson, V. Unsolved
mysteries...[c1938] 4326(0)
Strang, H. Pioneers Canada.
[19__]   4358(0)
Sumner, B.H. Short hist. of
Russia. 1944.   4390(0)
Synge, M. B. Book of discovery.
1962.   4437(2)
Tanfil'ev, G. I. Moria; Kas-
piiskoe...1931.   4451(0)
[Travers, de Val?] Summary...
no. passage. 1776.   4570(0)
Tucker, E. W. Hist. Oregon
... 1844.   4585(0)
Tytler, P. F. Hist. view...
disc. 1832.   4599(0)
Varieties lit. ... now first
published. 1795.   4656(6)

EXPLORATION - Collective.
(cont.)

Villiers, A. J. Pioneers of
seven seas. 1956.   4705(0)

Vize, V. I. Morîa Sovetskoĭ
arktiki...1948.   4708(0)

Vize, V. I. Russkie polîarnye
morekhody...1948.   4709(0)

Wagner, H. A. Apocryphal
voyages...1931.   4722(0)

Wagner, H.R. Some imaginery
Calif. geog. 1926.   4725(0)

Wagner, H. R. Spanish voyages
n.w. coast...1929.   4726(1)

Walton, J. Six explorers.
1942.   4735(0)

Whymper, F. Heroes of Arctic
... [ca 1875]   4850(0)

Williams, G. British search
n.w. passage. 1962.   4878(2)

Williamson, J. A. Builders of
empire. 1925.   4886(2)

Wright, H. S. Great white
North. 1910.   4972(0)

Wright, N. Quest for Franklin.
[c1959]   4974(0)

Zeidler, P. G. Polarfahrten...
1927.   5024(4)

Zubov, N. N. Otechestvennye
... 1954.   5040(0)

EXPLORATION - Before 1867.

Adamov, A. G. G. I. Shelekhov
... 1952.   4(0)

Adamov, A. G. G. I. Shelekhov
... 1951.   5(0)

Allen, E. W. "Vanishing Frenchman" La Pérouse.1959. 180(0)

Anderson, B. Life...Vancouver.
1966.   242(1)

Anderson, B. Surveyor of sea...
Vancouver. 1960.   242(1)

Arctic miscellany ...
1852.   301(0)

Armstrong, A. Personal narrat.
"Investigator" 1857.   304(4)

Augur, H. Passage...J. Ledyard
...1946.   323(1)

Aumack, T.M. Rivers ...J.R.
Jewitt. 1948.   324(1)

Austin, H. T. Review...Austin
and Perry. 1851.   326(4)

Baer, K.E. Avtobiografiîa
... 1950.   338(0)

Baer, K.E. Eine Selbst-
biographie...1912.   339(0)

Baer, K.E. ...50-jahrigen...
Krusenstern. 1839.   340(0)

Baer, K.E. Nachrichten
Leben ... 1865.   341(0)

Baer, K.E. Statische und
ethnog. 1839.   342(0)

Barrell, G. Notes of voyages
...1890.   405(0)

Barrow, J. Cook's voyages...
1904.   411(2)

Barrow, J. Cook's voyages...
1860.   412(2)

Barrow, J. Voyages discovery
... 1846.   413(0)

Bayly, G. Sea-life 60 yrs.
...la Pérouse. 1886.   436(1)

[Bayly, Wm.] Orig. astronom.
obs. ...Cooke...1782.   437(2)

Beaglehole, J. C. Journals
...Cook. Vol.3. 1956.   454(2)

Beauties Capt. Cook's voyages
... 1785.   458(2)

[Bechervaise, J.?] 36 years
...[Beechey] 1864.   460(1)

Beechey, F. W. Narrat. voyage
...*Blossom*...1831.   467(0)

Beechey, F. W. Reise nach dem
Stillen ...1832.   468(0)

Beechey, F. W. Zool....voyage
...1839.   469(0)

Belcher, E. Narrat. voyage
Sulphur...1843.   475(0)

Bellesort, A. La Pérouse, avec
port. 1926.   492(1)

Belov, M. Semën Dezhnev.
1955.   495(0)

Benham, D. ...Jan August Miert
"Investigator" 1853.   498(4)

Beniowski, M. A. Memoirs...
1898.   499(6)

Berg, L. S. Otkrytie Kamchatki
...Beringa...1935.   513(6)

Berg, L.S. Otkrytie ...
Beringa. 1946.   514(6)

Berg, L.S. Otkrytie...Kam-
chatki...Beringa.1924.515(0)

Berkh, V. N. Opisanie...R.-A.
Nevy ... 1817.   530(1)

EXPLORATION - Before 1867.
(cont.)

[Cook, J.] Dritte und letzte
Reise...1787.   1029(])

[Cook, J.] Des Capitain Jacob
Cook dritte...1789.   1030(2)

[Cook, J.] Capt. Cook's three
voyages...1792.   1031(2)

[Cook, J.] Histoire abregee...
1795.   1032(2)

[Cook, J.] Capt. Cook's third
... 1795.   1033(2)

[Cook, J.] Histoire ...trois
voyages...1796.   1034(2)

[Cook, J.] Voyage to Pac. O.
...elegant...1796.   1035(2)

[Cook, J.] Capt. Cook's three
...life...1797.   1036(2)

[Cook, J.] Troisième voyage
...J.B.J.Breton.1804. 1037(2)

[Cook, J.] Capt. Cook's third
...life...1809.   1038(2)

[Cook, J.] Capt. Cook's...No.
& So. Poles.1811.   1039(2)

[Cook, J.] Capt. Cook's three
...abr. 1814.   1040(2)

[Cook, J.] Voyage to Pac. O.
...unpub. 1818.   1041(2)

[Cook, J.] Three voyages...
1821.   1042(2)

[Cook, J.] Navigazioni de
Cook...1826.   1043(2)

[Cook, J.] Voyages...round
world...1826.   1044(2)

[Cook, J.] Navigazioni de Cook
...1830.   1045(2)

[Cook, J.] Voyage to Pac. O.
review...1831.   1046(2)

[Cook, J.] Voyages...with
maps...1842.   1047(2)

[Cook, J.] Voyages Capt. Jas.
Cook...1853-54.   1048(2)

[Cook, J.] Voyages Capt. Jas.
Cook ... 1853-54.   1049(2)

[Cook, J.] Three voyages...
1897.   1050(2)

[Cook, J.] Capt. Cook's voyages
...Synge. 1897.   1051(2)

[Cook, J.] Auf unbekannten...
n.d.   1052(2)

[Cook, J.] Three voyages ...
n.d.   1053(2)

[Cook, J.] Voyages...third and
last ... n. d.   1054(2)

Corney, P. Puteshestvie G. P.
Kornea...1822,23.   1983(0)

Corney, P. Voyages No. Pac. ...
1896.   1084(0)

Cyriax, R. J. Sir John Franklin ... 1939.   1148(4)

Dall, W. H. Yukon Territory.
1898.   1168(7)

Damm, H. Jas. Cook...bearbeitet
... 1922.   1170(2)

Davydov, G.I. Dvukratnoe...
1810-12.   1211(0)

Davydov, G.I. Reise der russ.-
kaiserlichen...1816. 1212(0)

Davydov, I.V. Dzhon Franklin.
1956.   1213(0)

deLabillardiere, J.J.H. Relat.
...La Pérouse...1799.1234(0)

deLabillardiere, J.J.H. Acct.
voyage...1800.   1235(0)

deLabillardiere, J.J.H. Voyage
search Pérouse.1800. 1236(0)

deLesseps, J.B.B. Journ. hist.
...La Pérouse...1790.1251(1)

deLesseps, J.B.B. Travels Kamtschatka...1790.   1252(1)

deLesseps, J.B.B. Des Herrn
von Lesseps...1791.   1253(1)

deLesseps, J.B.B. Herrn von
Lesseps...1791.   1254(1)

deLesseps, J.B.B. Hist. dagverhaal ... 1792.   1255(1)

deLesseps, J.B.B. Voyage de...
n.d.   1256(1)

D'Entrecasteaux, A.R.J.B....re-
cherche Pérouse.1808.1273(0)

deRoquefeuil, C. Journ. voyage
autour...1823.   1274(0)

deRoquefeuil, C. Reise um die
Welt...1823.   1275(0)

deRoquefeuil, C. Voyage ...
1823.   1276(0)

D'Wolf, J. Voyage North Pac.
...1861.   1287(0)

Dillon, P. Narrat. ... voyage
La Pérouse...1829.   1296(0)

Dillon, P. Voyage aux iles...
1830.   1297(0)

Divin, V. A. A.I. Chirikov...
1953.   1300(0)

EXPLORATION -Before 1867.
                    (cont.)
Divin, V. A. A.I. Chirikov...
  1950.   1301(0)
Divin, V. A. Velikii russkiĭ
  ...Chirikov. 1953.   1302(0)
Divin, V.A. V.M. Golovnin...
  1951.   1303(0)
Dixon, G. Further remarks...
  1791.   1306(0)
Dixon, G. Remarks ...
  1790. . . . . 1307(0)
Dixon, G. Voyage...*King George*
  ... 1789.   1308(0)
Dixon, G. Voyage autour ...
  1789.   1309(0)
Dixon, G. Der Kapitaine ...
  1790.   1310(0)
Dobrovol'skiĭ, A.D. Plavaniîa
  F. P. Litke...1948. 1314(0)
[Drage, T. S.] Acct. voyage...
  California ... 1748. 1344(0)
Duflot de Mofras' travels...
  1937.   1362(0)
Duflot de Mofras, E. Explora-
  tion ... 1844.   1363(0)
DuHalde, J.-B. Descript. géog.
  ... 1735.   1369(5)
DuHalde, J.-B. General hist.
  China. 1736.   1370(5)
Dumont d'Urville, J.S.C.Voyage
  de La Pérouse. 1832. 1371(0)
Dumont d'Urville, J. Voyage
  pittoresq. ...1834035.1372(0)
Dumont d'Urville, J. Maler-
  ische Reise...1835-37.1373(0)
Dumont d'Urville, J. Viaggio...
  1841.   1374(0)
Dumont d'Urville, J. Puteshest-
  vie...1843.   1375(0)
Ellis, Wm. Authentic narrat.
  Cook & Clerke...1782. 1443(2)
Engel, S. Anmerkungen ...
  Cook...1780.   1469(0)
Engel, S. Remarques...Cook...
  1781.   1470(0)
[Engel, S.] Mémoires et ob-
  servations. 1765. 1471(0)
[Engel, S.] Geographische...
  1772.   1472(0)
[Engel, S.] Extraits raissones
  ... 1779.   1473(0)

Erman, G.A. Reise um die
  Erde...1833-48.   1486(0)
Eschscholtz, J.F. Zool. atlas
  Kotzebue ... 1829.   1493(0)
Espinosa y Tello, J. Appen-
  dix Relacion...1806. 1495(0)
Espinosa y Tello, J. Memorias
  sobre...1809.   1496(0)
[Etches, J.C.] Continuation...
  Argonaut. 1790.   1497(0)
[Etches, J.C.] Authent. state-
  ment ... 1790.   1498(0)
Exploration et le...naufrage
  Lapérouse. 1945.   1507(0)
Fernandez, J. Tomas de Suria...
  Malaspina. 1939.   1546(1)
Ferrer Maldonado, L. Appendix
  Viaggio ... 1813.   1547(0)
Ferrer Maldonado, L. Viaggio
  ...1810.   1548(0)
Ferrer Maldonado, L. Voyage
  de la mer ... 1812. 1549(0)
Fischer, J. E. Sibirische...
  1768.   1564(0)
Fischer, J. E. Sibirskaîa...
  1774.   1565(0)
Fleurieu, C.P.C. Voyage autour
  ...[1798-1800]   1579(0)
Fleurieu, C.P.C. Voyage ...
  1801.   1580(0)
Fleurieu, C.P.C. Die neuste
  Reise...n.d.   1581(0)
Flint, S.R. Mudge memoirs...
  1883.   1582(1)
Fonticelli, A. Americalogie...
  Russi...1790.   1593(0)
Ford, C. Where sea breaks...
  1966. [Bering]   1599(6)
Forster, J.G.A. Cook, der Ent-
  decker. 1789.   1605(2)
Forster, J.G.A. Geschichte...
  Cook. 1791.   1606(0)
Forster, J.G.A. Geschichte...
  Cook. 1792.   1607(0)
Forster, J.R. Observations...
  1778.   1613(2)
Fradkin, N.G. S.P.Krashen-
  innikov...1951.   1621(6)
Fraerman, R.I. Plavaniîa
  V.M. Golovnina.1948. 1622(0)
Fraerman, R.I. Zhizn' ...
  Golovnina.1946-48.   1623(0)

EXPLORATION - Before 1867.

Franchere, G. Narrative ...
  1854.   1626(0)
Franchere, G. Voyage to n.w.
  coast...1954.   1626(0)
Franchere, G. Relation voyage
  nord-ouest...1820.   1627(0)
Franklin, J. Narrat. 2d exped.
  polar sea...1828.   1633(0)
Froment-Guieysse, G. La Perouse
  ... 1947.   1663(0)
[Galiano, D.A.] Spanish voyage
  ... Sutil ... 1930.   1675(1)
[Galiano, D.A.] Relacion del
  ... Sutil ... 1802.   1676(1)
Gianetti, M. Elogy Capt. Jas.
  Cook...[1785]   1702(2)
Gilbert, G. Death of Capt.
  Jas. Cook. 1926.   1712(2)
Gmelin, J.G. Leben Herrn
  ...Steller...1748.   1742(6)
Godwin, G.S. Vancouver, a
  life. 1930.   1748(2)
Golder, F. A. Bering's voyages
  ... 1922.   1755(0)
Goldson, Wm. Observ. passage
  De Fonte...1793.   1760(0)
Golenishchev-Kutuzov, L. I.
  Puteshestvie...1805. 1762(2)
Golovnin, V.M. Memoirs ...
  1824.   1764(0)
Golovnin, V.M. Puteshestvie
  ...Kamchatka...1822. 1765(0)
Golovnin, V.M. Recollections
  ... 1819.   1766(0)
Golovnin, V.M. Sochineniĩa
  ...1864.   1767(0)
Golovnin, V.M. Sochineniĩa
  ... 1949.   1768(0)
Golovnin, V.M. Sok rashcennyia
  ... Diania...1819.   1769(0)
Goodhue, C. Journey ...Vitus
  Bering...1944.   1773(6)
Gordon, M. Mystery of La Perouse
  ... 1961.   1781(0)
Gould, R. T. Capt. Cook.
  1935.   1789(2)
Granberg, W.J. Voyage ...
  Bering. 1960.   1796(6)
Great Britain. Parl. (Franklin
  search)   1819-33(0)

Grech, N. Zhizneopisanie V. M.
  Golovnina. 1851.   1839(0)
Haig-Brown, R. Capt. Discovery
  ...Vancouver. 1956. 1893(2)
Hale, H. E. Ethnog....U.S. Ex-
  ploring Exped. 1846. 1900(0)
Harnisch, W. Reise...Krusen-
  stern...1823.   1948(0)
Hawkesworth, J. Voyages...Cook
  ... [189_?]   1997(2)
Heritage Press. Explorations
  ... Cook. 1948.   2076(2)
Hinds, R. B. Botany Sulphur
  Belcher. 1846.   2116(0)
Hinds, R.B. Zool. voyage Sul-
  phur...Belcher. 1844.2117(0)
Hoffman, E. Geognostiche ...
  Kotzebue. 1829.   2137(0)
[Holland, C.W.] 150th anniv.
  Vancouver...1942.   2152(2)
Holmes, M. Introd. bibliog.
  Cook. 1936.   2160(2)
Holmes, M. Capt. Jas. Cook...
  bibliog. 1952.   2161(2)
Hooker, W. J. Flora Boreali-
  American...1829-40. 2172(0)
Hooker, W. J. Botany Beechey...
  Blossom...1841.   2173(0)
Hooper, C. L. Arctic ice notes.
  1883. [Corwin]   2174(4)
Hooper, C. L. Cruise of Corwin
  in Arctic. 1882.   2175(4)
Hooper, W.H. Ten months...
  Tuski...1853.   2177(4)
Howay, F.W. Capt. Geo. Van-
  couver. 1932.   2200(0)
Howay, F.W. Dixon-Mears
  controversy. [c1929] 2202(0)
Howay, F.W. Voyages Columbia
  ... 1941.   2203(0)
Howay, F.W. Zimmermann's
  Capt. Cook. [c1930] 2204(2)
Huish, R. Narrat. voyages...
  Beechey...1836.   2219(0)
Huish, R. North-west passage.
  1850.   2220(0)
Hulswitt, I. Tagebuch...
  1828.   ˙   2226(0)
Ĩunga, E.S. Kolumby rosskie...
  1941.   2306(0)
[Jefferys, T.?] Great probabi-
  lity n.w.pass. 1768. 2336(0)

EXPLORATION - Before 1867.
(cont.)
Krusenstern, A. J. Reise om-
kring Jorden...1818. 2562(0)
Krusenstern, A.J. Viaggio in-
torno ... 1818.   2563(0)
Krusenstern, A.J. Viaggio in-
torno ... 1830.   2564(0)
Krusenstern, A.J. Voyage autour
... 1821.   2565(0)
Krusenstern, A. J. Reise der
gutmannschen...1821. 2566(0)
L.,B.V. Die Glaubwürdigkeit
Maldonados...1712.   2577(0)
Lang, J. Story of Capt. Cook.
1906.   2595(2)
Langle, F. de. La tragique ex-
ped. Lapérouse. 1954. 2598(0)
Langsdorff, G.H. Bemerkingen
reise...1812.   2599(0)
Langsdorff, G.H. Voyages ...
1813-14.   2600(0)
Langsdorff, G.H. Reise um die
Welt...1816.   2601(0)
Langsdorff, G.H. Reis rondom
... 1813.   2602(0)
Langsdorff, G.H. Plants re-
cueillies...1810-18. 2603(0)
[La Pérouse, J.F.G.] Décou-
vertes ... 1798.   2609(0)
[La Pérouse, J.F.G.] Voyage...
autor ... [1797]   2610(0)
[La Pérouse, J.F.G.] Voyage
round world. 1798.   2611(0)
[La Pérouse, J.F.G.] Voyage
round world. 1798.   2612(0)
[La Pérouse, J.F.G.] Voyage of
... 1798.   2613(0)
[La Pérouse, J.F.G.] Voyage
round world...1798.   2614(0)
[La Pérouse, J.F.G.] Entdeck-
ungsreise ...1798.   2615(0)
[La Pérouse, J.F.G.] Ontdekkin-
gen Zuidzee...1799.   2616(0)
[La Pérouse, J.F.G.] Puteshest.
Laperuza...1800-02.   2617(0)
[La Pérouse, J.F.G.] Viaggi di
... 1815.   2618(0)
[La Pérouse, J.F.G.] Voyage de
...1831.   2619(0)
[La Pérouse, J.F.G.] Le voyage
...1937.   2620(0)

[La Pérouse, J.F.G.] First
French...1959.   2621(0)
Lappo, S. D. Plavaniĭa...Gol-
ovnina. 1950.   2623(0)
Lauridsen, P. Vitus Bering...
1889.   2642(0)
Lauridsen, P. Vitus J. Bering
og de ... 1885.   2643(0)
Lazarev, A.P. Plavanie vokrug
...Ladoga. 1832.   2651(0)
Lazarev, A.P. Zapiski...Blago-
namerennogo...1950.   2652(0)
Lebedev, D.M. Plavanie...Chi-
rikova...1951.   2658(0)
Ledyard, J. Journal...Cook's
last ... 1783.   2663(2)
[Ledyard, J.] Adventures...
Life...1831.   2664(2)
Leland, C.E. Fusang...disc.
...1875.   2676(0)
Lettre d'un officier ...
1752.   2693(0)
Lialina, M.A. Russkie...Go-
lovnin; Kotsebu.1896.2700(0)
Life of Capt. Cook.
n. d. . . . . .2706(2)
Life of Capt. Jas. Cook.
1824.   2707(2)
Life of Capt. Jas. Cook, new
edition. 1831.   2708(2)
Life, voyages...Capt. Cook.
1859.   2710(2)
Lisīanskiĭ, I. F. Puteshestvie
...Nevie. 1812.   2723(0)
Lisīanskiĭ, I. F. Voyage...
Neva 1814.   2724(0)
Litke, F.P. Chetyrekratnoe...
"Novaĭa Zemlĭa" 1828.2727(0)
Litke, F.P. Viermalige reise...
Nowaja Semlja. 1825. 2728(0)
Litke, F.P. Observations ...
1937.   2729(2)
Litke, F.P. Puteshestvie...
Seniavine.1834.   2730(0)
Litke, F.P. ... Otdĭelene
atlasom. n.d.   2731(0)
Litke, F.P. Voyage autour ...
Séniavine...1835-36. 2732(0)
Litke, F.P. Puteshestvie...
1835.   2733(0)
Litke, F.P. Atlas...Séniavine
... [1832]   2734(0)

ALASKAN BIBLIOGRAPHY

EXPLORATION - Before 1867.
(cont.)
Litke, F.P. Voyage autour du
monde. 1836.   2735(0)
Lloyd, C. Voyages Capt. Cook...
1949.   2741(2)
Lobanov-Rostovskiĭ, A. I.
Kratkaīà ... 1824.   2744(0)
Lomonosov, M.V. Kratkoe opi-
sanie...1847.   2752(0)
Lomonosov, M.V. Razsuzhdenie
... 1759.   2753(0)
Low, C. R. Capt. Cook's three
voyages ... n.d.   2802(2)
Lupach, V.S. Kruzenshtern i
Lisīānskiĭ ... 1953. 2814(0)
M'Clure, R.J.Le M. Discovery
Investigator. 1856.   2835(4)
M'Clure, R.J.Le M. Melancholy
...Franklin...1854.   2836(4)
McIlraith, J. Life Sir John
Richardson. 1868.   2910(4)
Mahr, A. C. Visit "Rurik"
1932.   2954(0)
Malaspina, A. Viaje pol.-cient.
Descubierta...1885.   2956(0)
Manwaring, G. E. ...Admiral...
Jas. Burney. 1931.   2963(2)
Marcel, G. Une exped. ... La-
pérouse. 1888.   2964(0)
Marine Research Soc. Sea, ship
...1925.   2968(0)
Marshall, J.B. Capt. Cook's
voyages. n. d.   2992(2)
Marshall, J.B. Vancouver's
voyage...1967.   2995(2)
Maurelle, F. A. Journal voyage
... 1781.   3036(1)
Meany, E.S. ...Vancouver jour-
nal *Chatham*. 1915.   3050(1)
Meany, E. S. Vancouver's disc.
...1907.   3051(0)
Meares, J. Answer...remarks...
1791.   3052(0)
Meares, J. Authentic...memori-
al ... 1790.   3053(0)
[Meares, J.] Mr. Mear's memorial...[1790?]   3054(0)
[Meares, J.] Memorial of ...
1933.   3055(0)
Meares, J. Voyages...*Nootka*
... 1790.   3056(0)

Meares, J. Des Kapitans...
1796.   3057(0)
Meares, J. Voyages de Chine...
Nootka ... [1793]   3058(0)
Meares, J. Viaggi dalla China.
...1796.   3059(0)
Meares, J. Viaggi dalla China.
...1796.   3060(0)
Meares, J. Viaggi dalla China
...1797-98.   3061(0)
Meares, J. Tvanne resor fran
Ostindien...1797.   3062(0)
Meares, J. Puteshestvie Kap.
Mirsa ... 1897.   3063(0)
Menshutkin, B. N. Russia's
Lomonosov. 1952.   3080(0)
Menshutkin, B. N. Zhizn.
Lomonosova. 1937.   3081(0)
Merrett, J. Capt. Jas. Cook.
1957.   3086(2)
Meyer, K.-H. Fünf Jahre...
[1950]   3093(4)
Miertsching, J. A. Journal
interprete...1857.   3101(4)
Miertsching, J.A. Reise-tage-
buch ... 1855.   3102(0)
Mornas, B. Cosmographie...
1770.   3194(0)
Morrell, B. Narrat. four...
1832.   3196(0)
Mortimer, G. Observations...
Mercury. 1791.   3203(6)
Mortimer, G. Waarnem ...
1793.   3204(6)
Muir, J. R. Life...Jas. Cook.
1939.   3231(2)
Munford, J.K. J. Ledyard...
1939.   3237(2)
Munford, J.K. J. Ledyard's
journal Cook.[c1963] 3238(2)
Munro, W. H. Tales ... sea
port. 1917.   3243(0)
Navarette, M.F. Noticia...
Sutil 1802.   3279(1)
Nevskii, V.V. Pervoe ...
1951.   3291(0)
Nevskii, V.V. Vokrug...*Nadezh-
da i Neva*.1953.   3292(0)
Nicol, J. Life ...
1822. . . . . .3304(0)
Novo y Colson, P. Hist. ...
nordeste...1880.   3361(0)

EXPLORATION - Before 1867.
(cont.)
Novo y Colson, P. Sobre...
apocrifos...1881. 3362(0)
Official papers...Nootka Sd.
1790. 3383(0)
Orlov, B. P. F. P. Litke ...
russki ... 1948. 3418(0)
Ostrovskiĭ, B. G. Velikai͡a
...1937. 3435(0)
Oxley, J. McD. North overland
Franklin. 1907. 3443(4)
[Pallas, P.S.] Neue nordische
... 1781-96. 3475(0)
Pasetskiĭ, V.M. V. Bering.
1958. [in Russ.] 3499(0)
Pasteur, J.D. Reizen rondom
Cook...1797-1809. 3500(2)
Patterson, S. Narrative...
1817. 3504(0)
Pekarskiĭ, P.P. Arkhivnyi͡a
razyskanii͡a. 1869. 3528(0)
[Penrose, C.V.] Memoir Jas.
Trevenen...1959. 3533(2)
Péron, [F?] Memoires ...
1824. 3537(1)
Petit-Thouars, A.A. Fragments
...La Pérouse. 1797. 3554(0)
Petit-Thouars, A.A. Voyage au-
tour...*Venus*. 1840. 3555(0)
Pokrovskiĭ, A.A. Ékspedit͡sii͡a
Beringa...1941. 3625(0)
Portlock, N. Voy. *King George*
...[1789] 3648(1)
[Portlock, N.] Voyage *King
George* ...1789. 3649(1)
[Portlock, N.] Abr. voyage
...1789. 3650(1)
[Portlock, N.] ...Reisen die
...1796. 3651(1)
[Portlock, N.] Reis naar...
1795. 3652(1)
[Portlock, N.] Voyage...King
George's Sd. 1803. 3653(1)
Postels, A. Illus. algarum...
Lutke...1840. 3654(0)
Predprii͡atie Imperatritsy Ekat-
eriny...1840. 3675(0)
Price, A. G. Explorations...
Cook. 1957. 3688(2)
Price, E. V. Astronomische...
Kotzebue...1830. 3689(0)

Rasmussen, K.J.V. Dansk
udlaengsel...1930. 3735(0)
Reisen nach ... Meares, Dixon,
Portlak...1795. 3780(0)
Relation abregee... de La
Pérouse...1799. 3781(0)
Richardson, J. Arctic searching
exped. 1851. 3804(0)
Richardson, J. Polar regions.
1861. 3805(0)
Rienits, R. Voyages Capt.
Cook. 1968. 3821(2)
Robolsky, M. Life Capt. J. C.
Lesebuch...1864. 3851(2)
Rørdam, V. Dansk Liv.[Bering]
1938. 3881(0)
Russell, T.C. Langsdorff's...
1927. 3920(1)
Samoilov, V. A. Semen Dezhnev
1945. 3949(0)
Samwell, D. Narrat. death...
Cook. 1916. 3953(2)
Samwell, D. Narrat. ... Cook
...*Discovery*. 1786. 3954(2)
[Samwell, D.] Details...mort
...Cook. 1786. 3955(2)
Sarychev, G.A. Puteshestvie
...1802. 3965(0)
Sarychev, G.A. Achtjährige
Reise...1805-15. 3966(0)
Sarychev, G.A. Acct. voyage
...1806-07. 3967(0)
Sarychev, G.A. Voyage dans
Siberie...1807. 3968(0)
Sarychev, G.A. Reis in het
...Siberie...1808. 3969(0)
Sarychev, G.A. Puteshestvie
Billingsa...1811. 3970(0)
Sarychev, G.A. Puteshestvie
Sibiri...1952. 3971(0)
Sauer, M. Acct. geog. ...
Billings. 1802. 3973(6)
Sauer, M. Voyage fait ...
[1802] 3974(6)
Sauer, M. Geographische-astron-
omische...1802. 3975(6)
Sauer, M. Reise nach nordli-
chen ... 1803. 3976(6)
Sauer, M. Reise nach Siberien
...1803. 3977(0)
Sauer, M. Viaggio fatto nel
...1816. 3978(6)

EXPLORATION - Before 1867.
                 (cont.)

Savvage, J. Mémoire du voyage.
  1855.   3986(0)
Seemann, B.C. Narrat. *Herald*
  Kellett. 1853.   4039(0)
Seemann, B.C. Reise um die
  Welt...1853.   4040(0)
Seemann, B.C. Botany voyage
  Herald. 1852-7.   4041(5)
Selsam, M.E. Quest of Capt.
  Cook. 1962.   4046(2)
Shabelski, A. Voyage aux ...
  Apollon ... 1826.   4082(0)
Shelekhov,G.I. Puteshestvie...
  Okhotska...1812.   4101(6)
Shelekhov, G.I. Rossiĭskago
  kuptsa...1791.   4102(6)
Shelekhov, G.I. Rossiĭskago
  kuptsa...1793,1792. 4103(6)
Shelekhov, G.I. ...Russ.
  Kaufmanns...1793.   4104(6)
Shelekhov, G.I. Voyage of...
  n.d.   4105(6)
Shemelin, F. Istoricheskoe...
  1823.   4107(0)
Shemelin, F. Zhurnal pervago...
  1816-[1818]   4108(0)
Shteinberg, E.L. Kruzenshtern,
  Lisĭanskiĭ...1950.   4136(0)
Shteĭnberg, E.L. Zhizn. ...
  Lisĭanskago...1948. 4137(0)
Simpson, T. Narrative...
  1843.   4163(4)
Skelton, R. A. Capt. Jas. Cook
  commem. ... 1969.   4168(2)
Skelton, R.A. Capt. Jas. Cook
  hydrog. 1954.   4169(2)
Skewes, J.H. Sir J. Franklin
  ...revelation. 1889. 4173(0)
Smith, G.B. Sir John Franklin
  ...[ca 1896?]   4198(0)
Sobreviela, M. Voyages au
  Pérous ... 1809.   4229(0)
Sokolov, A.P. Proekt Lomono-
  sova...1854.   4236(0)
Sokolov, A.P. Sĭevernaĭa
  éksped. 1851.   4238(0)
Sokolov, A.P. Tri krugosvet-
  nykh...Lazareva. 1951.4239(0)
Sparks, J. Leben John Ledyard
  ...1829.   4250(2)

Sparks, J. Memoirs life J.
  Ledyard. 1828.   4251(2)
Sparks, J. Life J. Ledyard.
  1828.   4252(2)
[Sparks, J.] Travels ... John
  Ledyard. 1834.   4253(2)
Speck, G. Samuel Hearne ...
  1963.   4256(4)
Spence, S.A. Capt. Jas. Cook
  bibliog. ...1960.   4257(2)
Sproat, G.M. Scenes ...
  savage life. 1868. 4271(0)
Staehlin, J.v.S. Acct. new no.
  archipelago. 1774. 4275(0)
Staehlin, J.v.S. Das von den
  Russen ... 1774.   4276(0)
Staehlin, J.v.S. Relation du
  ...[1774]   4277(0)
Stejneger, L.H. G. W. Steller
  ...1936.   4330(0)
Steller, G.W. ...Beschreibung
  ...1774.   4332(0)
Steller, G.W. ...Reise...
  1793.   4333(0)
Steller, G.W. Tagebuch...
  1793.   4334(0)
Story of La Peyrouse.
  1841.   4356(0)
Strange, J. ...journal...
  1928.   4360(0)
Stuart-Stubbs, B. Maps ...
  A. Mackenzie...1968. 4368(4)
Sumner, B. H. Short history of
  Russia. 1944.   4390(0)
Sutton, A. Steller of North.
  1961.   4407(0)
Sutton, A. Endless quest...
  1965.   4408(0)
Svet, I.M. Moreplavatel'
  Dzhems Kuk. 1963.   4414(2)
Synge, M.B. Capt. Cook's
  voyages...1897.   4438(2)
Synge, M.B. Cook's voyages...
  1894.   4439(2)
Teben'kov, M.D. Gidrografich-
  eskiĭa...1852.   4475(0)
Thiéry, M. La Vie et voyages
  Capt. Cook. 1929.   4484(2)
Thiéry, M. Life and voyages
  Capt. Cook. 1929.   4485(2)
Thiéry, M. Captain Cook ...
  1930.   4486(2)

EXPLORATION - Before 1867.
(cont.)
Three famous voyages Capt.
Cook ... [189_?]   4529(2)
Tilley, H.A. Japan, Amoor...
Rynda ... 1861.   4540(0)
Torrubia, J.G. I Moscoviti
... 1759.   4558(0)
Trusler, J. Descript. account
... 1778.   4583(0)
Vakhtin, V. Russkie truzheniki
morîa. 1890. [Bering] 4630(0)
Valentin, F. Voyages ... La
Pérouse. 1969.   4635(0)
Valentin, F. Voyages et ...
Lapérouse...1841.   4636(0)
Vancouver, G. Voyage ... *Dis-
covery*... 1798.   4637(2)
Vancouver, G. Entdeckungsreise
...1799.   4638(2)
Vancouver, G. Reisen nach den
...1799-1800.   4639(2)
Vancouver, G. Voyage de decou-
vertes...1800.   4640(2)
Vancouver, G. En upptackst-
resa...1800.   4641(2)
Vancouver, G. Puteshestvie v
sîeverniîu...1827-38. 4642(2)
[Vancouver, G.] Narrat. or
journal. 1802.   4643(2)
Vanderbourg. La Pérouse ...
tableau...1810.   4644(0)
Vandercook, J.W. Great sailor
Cook. 1951.   4645(2)
van der Linden, M.J. Reize...
Zuider Zee...1805.   4646(0)
Vaugondy, D. R. Lettre ...
Carte...[1768]   4660(0)
Vaugondy, D. R. Mémoire...
1774.   4661(0)
Vaugondy, D. R. Observations
...Fuente. 1753.   4662(0)
Verne, J. Bekannte und ...
Welten. 1881.   4685(0)
Verne, J. Les Grands naviga-
teurs...[1880?]   4687(2)
Verne, J. Premier voyage du
...Cook. 1926.   4688(0)
Viana, F.J. Diario del viage
"Descubierta"...1849. 4696(1)
Villiers, A. J. Capt. Jas.
Cook. 1967.   4703(2)

Villiers, A. J. Capt. James
Cook. [c1967]   4704(2)
Voyage de découvertes...la
la Perouse...1832-3. 4716(0)
Wagner, H.R. Journ. Tomás de
Suria...1936.   4724(1)
Waxell, S. L. American expedi-
tion. [1952]   4758(0)
Waxell, S.L. Vitus Berings
eventyrlige...1948. 4759(0)
Waxell, S.L. ...Kamchatskaîa
...Beringa...1940.   4760(0)
Wendt, H. Entdeckungsfahrt...
Stellers...1952.   4794(0)
Whymper, F. Journey Norton Sd.
...Ft. Youkon.1868.   4848(0)
Whymper, F. Travel ... Alaska.
1868.   4851(0)
Whymper, F. Voyages et...
1880.   4852(0)
Williamson, J. A. Cook and
...Pacific. 1948.   4887(2)
Wolff, O. Levnetsefterretnin-
ger...Beering...1822.4946(0)
Wrangell, F.F. ...Makarov...
1911.   4967(0)
Wrangell, F.F. Ocherki ...
Sitkhi...1836.   4968(1)
[Zagoskin, L.A.] Acct. jour-
neys...n.d.   5017(0)
[Zagoskin, L.A.] ...travels
...[c1967]   5018(0)
Zagoskin, L.A. Peshekhodnaîa
...1847-48.   5019(0)
[Zagoskin, L.A.] Puteshestviîa
...1956.   5020(0)
Zaikov, S. Kratkoî obrazanie
put. 1820.   5022(6)
Zevallos, C. de. Memorias
...Maldonado. 1798. 5025(0)
Zimmermann, H. ... Reise um
die welt...Cook.1781.5033(2)
Zimmermann, H. Dernier voyage
du Cook...1782.   5034(2)
Zimmermann, H. Reize rondom de
waereld. 1784.   5035(2)
Zimmermann, H. Posliednee
...1786.   5036(2)
Zimmermann, H. ...acct. third
voyage Cook. 1926.   5037(2)

EXPLORATION - After 1967.

Aick, G. Schweres Eis voraus!
1953.   23(4)
American Mus. Nat. Hist. A. J.
Stone ... 1905.   206(0)
Amundsen, R.E.G. Mitt liv ...
1927.   223(0)
Amundsen, R.E.G. My life ...
1928.   224(0)
Amundsen, R.E.G. Nordostpassa-
gen Maud ...1921.   225(4)
Amundsen, R.E.G. Nordvestpass.
...Gjøa...1907.   226(4)
Amundsen, R.E.G. "The Northwest
Passage" Gjøa.1908.   227(4)
Amundsen, R.E.G. Norwestpassa-
gen. 1922.   228(4)
Amundsen, R.E.G. Scientific
...Gjøa. [1930-33]   229(4)
Anderson, Wm. R. First under
North Pole. 1959.   251(4)
Anderson, Wm. R. Nautilus 90°
North. 1959.   252(4)
Arnell, H.W. Die mosse
Vega...1917.   308(4)
Arneson, O. Roald Amundsen
som har var. 1929.   309(0)
Back, H. S. Something...Yukon
Plateau. 1927.   333(0)
Balch, E.S. No. Pole & Brad-
ley Land. 1913.   363(4)
Balch, E.S. Der Nordpol ...
1914.   364(4)
Bartlett, R.A. Sails over ice.
1934.   419(0)
Bartlett, R.A. Last voyage
Karluk ... 1916.   420(4)
Bartlett, R.A. Log of "Bob"
Bartlett. 1928.   421(0)
Bauer, H. Ein Leben für Eskimo
...Rasmussen. 1960.   431(0)
Bixby, W. Track of Bear.
1965.   568(0)
Boni, A. Roald Amundsen.
1946. [in Dutch]   607(0)
Borden, C.L. Cruise of Northern
Light. 1928.   621(0)
Burroughs, J. Far and near.
1904.   745(0)
Campbell, R. Discovery and ex-
plorat. Youcon.1885.   794(0)

Campbell, R. Two journals.
1958.   795(0)
Canada. Fifth book [disc.
Yukon] 1883.   805(0)
Centkiewicz, C.J. Czeluskin...
1953.   877(0)
Cook, F.A. Finding North
Pole. [c1909]   1009(4)
Cook, F.A. My attainment Pole.
1911.   1010(4)
Cook, F.A. Return from Pole
...1951.   1011(0)
Cook, F.A. To top continent
...McKinley. 1908.   1012(2)
Cummings, H. Synopsis ...
"Tuscarora" 1874.   1138(0)
Dalby, M.A. Sea...Dynamite
Johnny O'Brien.1933. 1153(0)
Dall, W.H. Spencer Fullerton
Baird...1915.   1166(0)
Danenhower, J. W. ... narrat.
"Jeannette" 1882.   1173(0)
Dawson, G.M. Report...Yukon
...1898.   1216(7)
DeLong, E. Explorer's wife.
1938.   1259(0)
DeLong, G. W. Voyage Jeannette
...1883.   1260(0)
Ellsberg, E. Cruise Jeannette
... 1949.   1444(0)
Ellsberg, E. Hell on ice...
Jeannette. 1938.   1445(0)
Farrar, F.S. Arctic assign-
ment.1955.[St. Roch] 1529(4)
Fletcher, I. V.Stefansson.
1925.   1578(4)
Freuchen, P. Adventures in
Arctic. 1960.   1650(4)
Freuchen, P. It's all adven-
ture. 1938.   1653(0)
Freuchen, P. ... reader.
1965.   1655(0)
Freuchen, P. Vagrant viking...
1953.   1660(0)
Freuchen, Pipaluk. Bogen om
Peter Freuchen.1958. 1661(0)
Gibbon, R.W. Hist. evaluation
Cook-Peary...1956.   1704(4)
Gibbons, R. W. F. A. Cook.
...explorer. 1965.   1705(0)
Gilder, W. H. Ice-pack ...
Jeannette...1883.   1715(0)

EXPLORATION - After 1867.
                          (cont.)
Gilder, W. H. In Eis und
   Schnee. 1884.   1716(0)
Gilder, W.H. Der Untergang...
   1922.   1717(0)
Gilder, W.H. Gibel' ėkspedi-
   t͡sĭĭ Zhanetty. 1923. 1718(0)
Gordon, W. J. Round North
   Pole. 1907.   1783(0)
Green, F. Bob Bartlett ...
   mariner. 1929.   1844(0)
Grierson, J. Sir Hubert
   Wilkins. 1960.   1856(0)
Griggs, R. F. Sci. results
   Katmai ... 1920.   1860(6)
Griggs, R.F. Valley 10,000
   Smokes. 1922.   1861(6)
Grinnell, J. Birds and mammals
   Alexander Exped. 1909.1863(1)
Grinnell, J. Birds Alexander
   Exped. ... 1901.   1865(0)
Hall, T. F. Has North Pole
   been discovered? 1917.1909(0)
Hanson, E.P.   Stefansson,
   prophet ... 1941.   1942(4)
Hanssen, H.J. Gjennem Isbaksen
   ...R. Amundsen.1941. 1944(4)
Hanssen, H.J. Voyages modern
   viking. 1936.   1945(4)
Harriman Alaska Exped. 1899.
   1910-14.   1950(0)
Harriman Alaska Exped. Alaska
   ...results...1902.   1951(0)
Harriman Alaska Exped. Alaska
   ...1902-05.   1952(0)
Harriman Alaska Exped. Papers
   ...1900-02.   1953(0)
History ... "Jeannette" ...
   1882.   2129(0)
Hooper, C.L. Arctic ice notes.
   1883.   2174(4)
Hooper, C.L. Cruise of *Corwin*
   ... 1882.   2175(4)
Irvine, T.A. Ice all between.
   1959. [*Labrador*]   2296(4)
Jacobsen, J.A. Capt. Jacob-
   sen's Reise...1884.   2315(0)
James, J.A. First scientific
   explor. R.A. 1942.   2326(0)
Keele, J. Reconn. Mackenzie
   Mtns. ... 1910.   2420(7)

Kemp, V.A.M. Without fear ...
   1958. [*St. Roch*]   2435(4)
Kennan, G. E.H.Harriman,
   biog. 1922.   2438(0)
LeBourdais, D. M. Stefansson
   ... 1963.   2660(0)
Leslie, A. Nordpolarreisen...
   Nordenskiöld. 1880. 2686(4)
Leslie, A. Arctic...Norden-
   skiöld...1879.   2687(4)
Longstreth, T.M. Force carries
   on ... 1954.   2787(4)
Lütgen, K. Two against Arctic.
   1957.   2816(0)
McConnell, R.G. Report explor.
   Yukon ... 1890.   2838(7)
McCracken, H. Toughy ...
   1948.   2857(0)
Marshall, J.S. Adventures in
   two hemispheres.1955.2993(0)
Marshall, R. Arctic wilderness.
   1956.   2998(4)
Marshall, R. Doonerak or
   bust. n.d.   2999(4)
Marshall, R. North Doonerak,
   Amawk ... n.d.   3000(4)
Masik, A. Arctic night's enter-
   tainment...1935.   3016(4)
Mathiassen, T. Report on ex-
   ped. 1945.[5th Thule]3029(4)
Melville, G.W. In Lena Delta.
   1885.   3075(0)
Mikkelsen, E. Conquering
   Arctic ice. 1909.   3104(4)
Mikkelsen, E. Ukendt mand til
   ukendt Land. 1954.   3108(4)
Mikkelsen, E. Mirage in Arctic.
   1955.   3109(4)
Miller, J. M. Discovery North
   Pole...Cook. [c1909] 3121(0)
Mitchell, Wm. General Greely...
   1936.   3147(4)
Montgomery, R.G. "Pechuck"
   ... 1932.   3158(5)
Montgomery, R.G. Adventures
   Lorne Knight. 1932.   3158(5)
Muir, J.   Stickeen.
   [c1909] . . . . .3225(1)
Muir, J. Cruise of *Corwin* ...
   1917.   3226(0)
Muir, J. Wilderness world...
   1954.   3228(0)

EXPLORATION - After 1867.
(cont.)
Nelson, E.W. Sledge journey...
delta Yukon...1883.   3283(5)
Newcombe, R.L. Our lost ...
Jeannette ... 1882.   3295(4)
Niedieck, P. Kreuzfahrten im
Beringmeer...1907.   3305(0)
Niedieck, P. Mes Croisieres...
Behring...1908.   3306(0)
Niedieck, P. Cruises in Bering
Sea...1909.   3307(0)
Noice, H.H. With Stefansson in
Arctic. 1924.   3316(4)
Nordenskiöld, N.A.E. Lettres...
du pole nord. 1880.   3323(4)
Nordenskiöld, N.A.E. ...rejse.
...Asien...1881.   3324(4)
Nordenskiöld, N.A.E. ...voyage
Asia...*Vega*. 1882.   3325(4)
Nordenskiöld, N.A.E. Studier
... [1883-84]   3326(4)
Nordenskiöld, N.A.E. Studien
...1885.   3327(4)
Nordenskiöld, N.A.E. *Vega*-
expeditionens...1882. 3328(4)
Nordenskiöld, N.A.E. *Vegas*
färd... [1880-81]   3329(4)
Nordenskiöld, N.A.E. Voyage of
Vega ... 1881.   3330(4)
Nordenskiöld, N.A.E. Voyage de
la *Vega* ... 1885.   3331(4)
Nordenskiöld, N.A.E. Im Eis des
Nordens...*Vega*. 1953. 3332(4)
Nordenskiöld, N.A.E. *Vegas*
reise ... 1881.   3333(4)
Nordenskiöld, N.A.E. Die Umse-
gelung...*Vega*. 1882. 3334(4)
Nordenskiöld, N.A.E. *Vega*-
fahrt... 1886.   3335(4)
Partridge, B. Amundsen ...
1929.   3497(0)
Peary, R. E. Vilhjalmur
Stefansson 1925.   3512(4)
Peisson, E. Pôles ...
1952. . . . . 3527(0)
Pike, W.M. Through subarctic
...canoe. 1896.   3587(0)
Pinart, A. L. Voyages a la cote
... 1875.   3599(0)
Pollog, C.H. In Eis und Sturm.
[c1946]   3634(4)

Poncins, G. de M. Par le de-
troit Bering. 1953.   3638(4)
Poncins, G. de M. Ghost voyage.
1954.   3638(4)
Putnam, G.P. Mariner of North.
...Bartlett.[c1947]   3705(0)
Rasmussen, K.J.V. Fra Grønlund
...Thule...1925.   3739(4)
Rasmussen, K.J.V. Across Arctic
America. 1927.   3740(4)
Rasmussen, K.J.V. Du Groenland
... 1929.   3741(4)
Rasmussen, K.J.V. Den store
slaederejse. 1932.   3742(4)
Rasmussen, K.J.V. ...Thule-
fahrt...1934.   3743(4)
Rasmussen, K.J.V. Velikiĭ...
put' ... 1935.   3744(4)
Rasmussen, K.J.V. Die Grosse
Schlittenreise.1946. 3745(4)
Rasmussen, K.J.V. Mindeudgave
...1934-5.   3746(4)
Rasmussen, K.J.V. Polarforsk-
ningens saga. 1930-2.3747(4)
Rasmussen, K.J.V. Heldenbuch
Arktis ... 1933.   3748(4)
Rubakin, N.A. Na plavaĭush-
chikh ... 1927.   3909(4)
Samoilovich, R.L. Put'k pol-
ĭusu. 1933.   3950(4)
Schwatka, F. Summer in Alaska.
1891.   4018(0)
Schwatka, F. Along Alaska's
great river.[c1885]   4019(0)
Schwatka, F. Exploring great
Yukon...n.d.   4020(0)
Shneĭderov, V.A. Phokhod
"Sibirĭakova." 1933. 4129(0)
Smith, W.D. Northwest Passage
Manhattan. 1970.   4207(4)
Steele, G.P. *Seadragon* n. w.
under ice. 1962.   4292(4)
Stefansson, V. Discovery ...
[c1964]   4303(0)
Stefansson, V. My life with
Eskimo. 1913.   4307(4)
Stefansson, V. Das Geheimnis...
1925.   4308(4)
Stefansson, V. Adventure Wran-
gel Isl. 1925.   4314(5)
Stefansson, V. Friendly
Arctic. 1921.   4317(4)

EXPLORATION - After 1867.
(cont.)
Stefansson, V. Länder der
Zukunft...1923.   4318(4)
Stefansson, V. Goste priimnaîa
Arktika. 1935.   4319(4)
Stefansson, V. Stefánsson-An-
derson Exped. 1919.   4323(4)
Stoney, G.M. Explorations in
Alaska...1965.   4354(0)
Sverdrup, H.U. General report
..."Maud" ... 1933.   4411(4)
Sverdrup, H.U. Tre aar i isen
"Maud" ... 1926.   4413(0)
Thomas, L. Famous first
flights. 1968.   4493(0)
Thomas, L. Sir Hubert Wilkins
... [cl961]   4496(0)
Tranter, G.J. Plowing Atlantic.
1944. [*St. Roch*]   4569(4)
Union Diesel Engine Co. Twice
...N.W. Passage. 1945.4611(4)
Vaeth, J.G. To ends earth ...
[cl962]   4627(0)
Williams, A. Conquering air...
1926.   4876(0)
Williams, H.L. Hist....voyage
..."Jeannette" 1882. 4880(0)
Wright, T. Big nail.
[cl970] . . . . . . 4975(2)
Young, S. H. Alaska days with
J. Muir. [cl915]   4997(0)

EXPOSITIONS.

Alaska-Yukon-Pac. Exposition.
Address...1909.   145(0)
Alaska-Yukon-Pac. Exposition.
International...1908. 146(0)
Alaska-Yukon-Pac. Exposition.
A-Y-P ... 1909.   147(0)
Alaska-Yukon-Pac. Exposition.
General hist. ...1909. 148(0)
Alaska-Yukon-Pac. Exposition.
Glimpses...[cl909]   149(0)
Alaska-Yukon-Pac. Exposition.
Industrial ... 1909.   150(0)
Alaska-Yukon-Pac. Exposition.
Official...1909.   151(0)
Alaska-Yukon-Pac. Exposition.
Official daily...1909. 152(0)
Alaska-Yukon-Pac. Exposition.
Official guide...1909. 153(0)

Alaska-Yukon-Pac. Exposition.
150 latest ... 1909.   154(0)
Alaska-Yukon-Pac. Exposition.
Proceedings...1909.   155(0)
Alaska-Yukon-Pac. Exposition.
Report A-Y-P...1910.   156(0)
Alaska-Yukon-Pac. Exposition.
Report...N.Y. 1910.   157(0)
Alaska-Yukon-Pac. Exposition.
Report...Oregon. 1909.158(0)
Alaska-Yukon-Pac. Exposition.
Seattle ... 1909.   159(0)
Alaska-Yukon-Pac. Exposition.
Souvenir...[1909]   160(0)
Alaska-Yukon-Pac. Exposition.
World's ... 1909.   161(0)
Edgren, A. Jubel kantat...
A-Y-P. 1909.   1411(0)
Gunther, E. Northwest Coast
Indian art. 1962.   1884(0)
Illus. Indian baskets Panama-
Pac. Int'l. 1915.   2255(0)
Pacific Univ. Souvenir ...
A-Y-P...[1909]   3467(0)
Seattle Century 21 Exposition
1962...1962.   4034(0)

FICTION.

Ames, R. A. Cheechako.
1958.   212(0)
Andrews, C. L. Wrangell and
gold Cassiar. [cl937] 258(2)
Arctander, J.W. Lady in blue.
1911.   277(1)
Atherton, G. Rezanov.
1906. . . . . 314(1)
Aumack, T.M. Rivers of rain...
1948.   324(1)
Auzias de Turenne, R. Le dernier mamouth. 1904.   327(8)
Auzias de Turenne, R. Le roi
du Klondike. [18__?]   328(7)
Balcom, M.G. Creek Street.
1963.   369(1)
Ball, J. Arctic showdown.
1966.   374(8)
Beach, R. Alaskan adventures
...3 in 1. n.d.   438(0)
Beach, R. Barrier.
[cl908] . . . . . . 442(0)
Beach, R. Iron trail.
1913. . . . . 445(1)

ALASKAN BIBLIOGRAPHY

FICTION. (cont.)

Beach, R. Silver horde.
[c1909] . . . . . . 446(0)
Beach, R. Spoilers.
1906. . . . . 447(5)
Beach, R. Spoilers; a play...
n. d. 447(5)
Beach, R. Winds of chance.
[c1918] 448(7)
Beach, R. Valley of thunder.
1939. 449(8)
Beach, R. World in his arms.
1945. 450(1)
Bell, B. E. Alaska snowtrapped.
1960. 479(8)
Bigelow, M. J. Urdag the
Aleut. 1955. 555(6)
Bishop, E. F. Timber wolf of
Yukon. 1923. 567(7)
Blacklock, Alaska. Nick of
the woods. 1916. 573(0)
Blond, George. Plunderers.
1951. 579(6)
Bolanz, Maria. So Hago.
1963. 600(1)
Bone, Scott C. Chechachco and
sourdough. 1926. 606(0)
Boyd, Aubrey. Smoky Pass.
1932. 636(8)
Boyd, E. M. Doom in midnight
sun. [c1944] 637(3)
Boyd, E. M. Murderer wears
mukluks. 1945. 638(5)
Browne, Belmore. Frozen bar-
rier...1921. 700(5)
Browne, Belmore. Quest of gol-
den valley...1916. 701(0)
Browne, Belmore. White blanket
... 1917. 702(8)
Bryant, C.K. Top o' the
world. 1951. 710(3)
Buhro, Harry. Rough-stuff and
moonlight. 1948. 725(8)
Burnett, W. R. Goldseekers.
1962. 736(0)
Calvin, Jack. Fisherman 28.
1930. 782(1)
Calvin, Jack. Square-rigged.
1929. 784(0)
Carter, Nicholas. Klondike
claim...1897. 858(7)

Case, R. O. Yukon drive.
1929. 861(7)
Case, R. O. West of Barter
River. 1941. 862(8)
Cheesman, E. Sealskins for
silk. 1956. 904(0)
Cheney, Warren. His wife.
1907. 905(8)
Cheney, Warren. The challenge.
1906. 906(8)
Cheney, Warren. Way of North
... Baranof. 1905. 907(1)
Chevigny, H. Lord of Alaska;
Baranov. 1942. 909(1)
Chevigny, H. Lost empire...
Rezanov. 1937. 910(1)
Clark, Susie C. Lorita, Alaskan
maid. 1892. 944(1)
Collins, A. F. Jack Heaton ...
1921. 979(7)
Connor, Ralph. Corp. Cameron
N.W.M.P. 1906. 1005(7)
Conrad, Earl. Governor and
his lady. 1960. 1006(0)
Corey, A. L. White angel of
trails. 1968. 1082(7)
Cullum, Ridgwell. Bull moose.
1931. 1137(1)
Curtis, Jack. Kloochman.
1966. 1145(0)
Curwood, J. O. Alaskan.
1922. 1146(5)
Dana, Marvin. Shooting Dan
McGrew...[c1915] 1172(7)
Dee, Harry. James Griffin's
adventures...1903. 1225(8)
Dodge, H.L. Attraction of com-
pass.1916. 1318(8)
Dorrance, J. F. Golden Alaskan.
1931. 1333(8)
Downes, A. M. Natalia, novel
of old Alaska. 1960. 1340(1)
Droonberg, E. Das Siwash mad-
chen ... 1925. 1354(0)
Droonberg, E. Die goldwascher
...1925. 1355(0)
Dunn, Robert. Youngest world
...1914. 1390(8)
Ellis, E.S. Klondike nuggets.
1898. 1439(7)
Ellis, E. S. Young goldseekers
of Klondike. 1912. 1440(7)

673

FICTION. (cont.)

Ellis, T. M. Tales of Klondike. 1898.   1442(7)

Erspamer, A. M. Klondike widow.   1492(7)

Felps, J. I. Such a folly. 1956.   1540(8)

Fenwick, G. Athabascan princess. 1910.   1542(3)

Ferber, Edna. Great son. 1944.   1543(0)

Ferber, Edna. Ice palace. 1958.   1544(0)

Franklin, F.K. Cleft in rock. 1955.   1632(6)

Gabriel, G.W. I got a country. 1944.   1667(0)

Gage, J. H. Trail north to danger. 1952.   1670(7)

Garland, Hamlin. Long trail... 1907.   1687(7)

Garland, Hamlin. Trail of gold seekers...1899.   1688(7)

Gibbons, C.H. Sourdough samaritan. [1923?]   1703(7)

Gillsäter, S. Pia i Alaska. 1968.   1728(8)

Goodchild, G. The Alaskan. 1926.   1770(8)

Goodchild, G. Land of Eldorado; Seal Islands. 1900.   1771(6)

Gordon, G.A. Nootka; tale of Vancouver Isl. 1899. 1780(1)

Grinnell, M. Song of wild land. 1952.   1867(8)

Hall, Olof. Youth North. 1936.   1908(0)

Hall, Warner. Even Jericho. 1944.   1910(8)

Hampton, K. The patch. 1960.   1927(8)

Hansome, M. Appointment with fortune. 1955.   1941(8)

Head, H.S. Death below zero. 1953.   2011(4)

Hendryx, J. B. Badmen on Halfaday creek. 1950.   2040(7)

Hendryx, J. B. Black John of Halfaday Creek. 1939. 2041(7)

Hendryx, J. B. Blood of North. 1938.   2042(0)

Hendryx, J. B. Blood on Yukon Trail...1930.   2043(7)

Hendryx, J. B. Courage of North. 1946.   2048(7)

Hendryx, J. B. Gold and guns Halfaday Creek.1942. 2049(7)

Hendryx, J. B. Gold is where you find it. 1953.   2050(7)

Hendryx, J. B. It happened on Halfaday Creek. 1944.2051(7)

Hendryx, J. B. Justice on Halfaday Creek. 1949.   2052(7)

Hendryx, J. B. Law ... Halfaday Creek. 1941.   2053(7)

Hendryx, J. B. Murder on Halfaday Creek. 1951.   2054(7)

Hendryx, J. B. North. 1923.   2055(5)

Hendryx, J. B. On rim of Arctic. 1948.   2056(4)

Hendryx, J. B. Outlaws of Halfaday Creek. 1935.   2057(7)

Hendryx, J. B. Skullduggery on Halfaday Creek. 1946.2058(7)

Hendryx, J. B. Snowdrift ... 1922.   2059(5)

Hendryx, J. B. Strange...Halfaday Creek. 1943.   2060(7)

Hendryx, J. B. Czar Halfaday Creek. 1940.   2061(7)

Hendryx, J. B. Saga of Halfaday Creek. 1936.   2062(7)

Hendryx, J. B. Yukon Kid. 1934.   2063(7)

Henry, Will. North Star. 1956.   2072(8)

Herbert, Agnes. The moose. 1913.   2073(8)

Hines, J. C. Minstrel of Yukon ... 1948.   2119(7)

Hutchinson, J. H. Wandering gentile ... 1914.   2245(0)

Jarvis, W.H.P. Great gold rush ... 1913.   2332(7)

Jonas, C. Beachhead on the wind. 1945.   2376(6)

Keesing, L.D. Gorham's gold. 1915.   2424(8)

Kratt, I.F. Velikiĭ okean. 1950.   2539(0)

Kummer, F. A. Perilous Island. 1942.   2570(6)

FICTION. (cont.)

L'Amour, Louis. Sitka.
1957. . . . . 2589(1)
Lancaster, G. B. World is
yours. 1934. 2590(7)
Lane, R. W. Gordon Blake.
1925. 2594(0)
Lane, R. W. He was a man.
1925. 2594(0)
London, Jack. Daughter of
snows. 1902. 2754(0)
London, Jack. Burning Daylight.
1910. 2757(7)
London, Jack. Smoke Bellew.
1912. 2766(7)
London, Jack. Call of wild.
1903. 2771(0)
London, Jack. Sea-wolf.
1904. 2782
London, Jack. White fang.
1906. 2785(0)
Lull, Roderick. Call to battle.
1943. 2811(6)
Lund, Robert. Alaskan.
1953. 2813(2)
McCracken, Harold. Beyond
frozen frontier.1936. 2843(0)
MacDonald, A. White trail...
1908. 2863(7)
MacDonald, Malcolm. Favorites
of fate. 1954. 2868(8)
McDonald, N.C. Fish strong
waters. 1956. 2869(1)
McDonald, N.C. Witch doctor.
1959. 2870(1)
McGerr, Pat. Pick your victim.
1946. 2894(6)
MacLean, Alistair. Ice Station
Zebra. 1963. 2927(4)
McNeilly, M. M. Heaven is too
high. 1944. 2942(1)
McNeilly, M.M. Praise at
morning. 1947. 2943(0)
Mailer, Norman. Why are we in
Vietnam? [c1967] 2955(0)
Mansfield, N. B. Keeper of
wolves. 1934. 2961(8)
Mansfield, N. B. Girl from
Frozen Bend. 1938. 2962(8)
Marshall, Edison. Child of
wild. 1926. 2979(8)

Marshall, Edison. Princess
Sophia. 1958. 2981(1)
Marshall, Edison. Seward's
folly. 1924. 2982(0)
Marshall, Edison. Deadfall.
1927. 2983(8)
Marshall, Edison. Deputy at
Snow Mtn. 1932. 2984(8)
Marshall, Edison. Doctor Lone-
some River. 1931. 2985(8)
Marshall, Edison. Far call.
1928. 2986(6)
Marshall, Edison. Fish hawk.
n. d. 2987(6)
Marshall, Edison. Land of for-
gotten men. 1923. 2988(8)
Marshall, Edison. Missionary.
1930. 2989(8)
Marshall, Edison. Sleeper of
moonlit range. 1925. 2990(8)
Marshall, Edison. Snowshoe
trail. 1921. 2991(8)
Marshall, J. V. River ran out
of Eden. 1962. 2996(6)
Matteson, H. H. The trap.
1921. 3031(8)
Mighels, E. S. Wawona; Indian
story...1921. 3103(1)
Mikkelsen, E. John Dale...pol-
havets...1921. 3105(8)
Mikkelsen, E. Norden for lov
og ret ... 1920. 3106(4)
Mikkelsen, E. Frozen justice.
1922. 3107(4)
Morrow, Honore. Argonaut.
1933. 3201(7)
Mowry, Wm. Heart of North.
1930. 3215(8)
Myers, C. V. Through Hell to
Alaska. 1955. 3261(8)
Noyes, Sherman A. Faith
1956. 3363(3)
Olds, Lee. Too much sun.
1960. 3400(8)
Parker, M.M. This was Alaska.
1950. 3493(3)
Pilgrim, M.S. Oogaruk the
Aleut. 1947. 3590(6)
Pollock, Ellen. Helene of the
Yukon. 1940. 3632(7)
Purdy, Anne. Dark boundary.
1954. 3703(3)

FICTION. (cont.)

Raine, W. M. Yukon trail.
[c1917]   3725(7)
Rea, Ella M. Castaways of
Yukon. 1936.   3761(7)
Robins, E. Come and find me.
1908.   3843(7)
Robins, E. Magnetic North.
1904.   3845(7)
Roper, Edw. Claim on Klondyke
...1899.   3880(7)
Roscoe, W. F. Ice bound.
1954.   3882(4)
Rouquette, L.-F. Le grand
silence blanc. [1921.]3901(4)
Savage, R. H. Princess of
Alaska. [c1894]   3985(1)
Service, R. W. Trail of '98.
1911.   4064(7)
Simonsen, S.J. Among sour-
doughs. 1940.   4159(7)
Skinner, C. L. Search relent-
less. 1925.   4174(7)
Slayden, T. T. Miracle in
Alaska. 1963.   4178(8)
Small, A. J. Frozen trail.
1924.   4185(7)
Smith, W. S. Heredity and en-
vironment...1930.   4206(8)
Smitter, Wessel. Another
morning. 1941.   4209(2)
Stegner, W. E. Big Rock Candy
Mtn. 1943.   4327(8)
Stevens, G. R. Gold hungry.
1927.   4340(8)
Stringer, A.J. Lamp in
valley. 1938.   4364(8)
Tutein, P. The sealers.
1938.   4592(6)
Vercel, R. Northern lights.
[c1948]   4683(4)
Verne, Jules. Flood and flame.
n.d.   4686(0)
Verne, Jules. Claim on 40 Mile
Creek. n.d.   4689(7)
Verne, Jules. The fur country.
1874.   4690(4)
Verne, Jules. The golden vol-
cano. pt. 1. n.d.   4686(0)

Verne, Jules. The golden volcano. pt. 2. n.d.   4689(7)
Vidal, G. Williwaw.
1946.   4698(6)
Wagner, E. Partners three.
1928.   4721(7)
White, S. E. Pole star.
1935.   4840(1)
White, S. E. Wild geese
calling. 1940.   4841(1)
Williamson, T. R. Earth told
me. 1930.   4891(8)
Willis, A. R. North of Yukon.
n.d.   4892(7)
Willoughby, B. River House.
1936.   4896(1)
Willoughby, B. Sondra O'Moore.
1939.   4900(1)
Willoughby, B. Spawn of North.
1932.   4901(1)
Willoughby, B. The golden
totem. 1945.   4903(1)
Willoughby, B. Trail eater.
1929.   4904(5)
Willoughby, B. Where sun
swings North. 1922. 4905(0)
Witeman, Geo. North of '62.
1946.   4938(2)
Young, S. Hall. Klondike clan.
[c1916]   4999(7)

FICTION - Criticism.

Leiberman, E. Amer. short
story...1912.   2674(0)
Martino, S. Jak London. Spunti
...1934.   3012(0)
Roden, D. London's Call wild,
White Fang.1965.   3860(7)
Vedde, S. Jack London!...For-
fatterskab. 1943.   4668(0)

FICTION - Short Stories.

Beach, R. Pardners.
1905. . . . . 440(7)
Beach, R. Crimson gardenia.
[1916]   443(7)
Beach, R. Goose woman.
1925.   444(7)

FICTION - Short Stories.(cont.)

Crane, A. R. Smiles and tears
...1901.   1113(7)
Gilbert, K. Alaskan poker
stories. 1958.   1713(0)
Hines, J. C. The blue streak.
1917.   2120(0)
Lockwood, M. J. Writing from
Alaska. n.d.   2746(0)
London, Jack. Best short
stories. 1945.   2755(0)
London, Jack. Brown Wolf and
other... 1920.   2756(0)
London, Jack. Children of
frost. 1902.   2758(0)
London, Jack. Great short
works ... 1965.   2759(0)
London, Jack. ...stories...
1936.   2760(0)
London, Jack. ...tales of ad-
venture. 1956.   2761(0)
London, Jack. Lost face.
1910.   2762(0)
London, Jack. Love of life...
1907.   2763(0)
London, Jack. Moon-face and
other ... 1906.   2764(0)
London, Jack. Stories of North.
1966.   2767(7)
London, Jack. Tales of far
north. n.d.   2768(7)
London, Jack. Tales of white
silence. n.d.   2769(7)
London, Jack. Bodley Head Jack
London. 1963.   2770(0)
London, Jack. Call of wild and
other...1960.   2772(0)
London, Jack. Call of wild and
other...1926.   2773(0)
London, Jack. Call of wild and
selected...1960.   2774(0)
London, Jack. Call of wild.
Cruise...1960.   2776(0)
London, Jack. Faith of men ...
1904.   2778(0)
London, Jack. God of his
father ... 1901.   2779(7)
London, Jack. Son of wolf.
1900.   2783(7)
London, Jack. Sun-dog trail
... [1951]   2784(7)

McCracken, Harold. Iglaome.
1930.   2846(5)
Pierce, F. R. Rugged Alaska
stories. 1950.   3580(0)
Selle, R. A. Daughter midnight
sun. [c1933]   4043(0)

FISHING, Sport. See HUNTING.

GEOGRAPHY. See HISTORY
                and Geography.

GOLD RUSHES - Books published
              [1862?] to 1910.

Adney, T. Klondike stampede.
1900.   14(7)
Akif'ev, I. N. Na delekiĭ
Siever ... 1902.   26(0)
Alaska Commercial Co.To Klon-
dike...fields.[1898]   54(7)
Alaska Trade Comm. Are you
going ... 1898.   131(0)
Alaska Transportation, Trading
& Mining Co. ... gold fields
... 1897.   132(7)
Alaska-Yukon-Klondike Gold
Synd. Klondike. 1897. 142(7)
Alaska-Yukon-Klondike Gold
Synd. ...gold...1897. 143(7)
Alaska-Yukon-Klondike Gold
Synd. Klondike. 1898. 144(7)
All about Klondike ...
[1897]   171(7)
Appeal Yukon miners ...
[1898]   272(7)
Auzias de Turenne, R. Voyage
au pays...1898.   329(7)
Barber, J. W. Alaskan gold
fields...1897.   396(2)
Barfus, E. Die Goldsucher...
[ca 1880]   398(7)
Barnum, F. To Yukon River...
[1896?]   404(7)
Beebe, Iola. True life story
Swiftwater... 1908.   466(7)
Belcher, H. A. All about Klon-
dike...1897.   476(7)
Bellard, W. Klondyke mines...
1897.   491(7)
Boillot, Leon. Aux mines d'or
... 1899.   597(7)

GOLD RUSHES - Books Published
          [1862?] to 1910.
                    (cont.)
Bordman, P. Capt. ... Klondike
...guide. 1897.   622(7)
Bramble, C.A. Klondike; manual
... 1897.   642(7)
B.C. Mining Journal. Overland
...Cariboo...1898.   670(7)
Brooks-Vincent, La Belle. Scar-
let life Dawson.[1900] 687(0)
Brostrom, I. New gold fields
Cape Nome. 1899.   689(5)
Brown, Gus, Co. Gold fields
Alaska. 1897.   695(0)
Caldwell, J. B. Calgary route
to Klondike. n.d.   773(7)
Campbell, Colin. White Pass and
Yukon route...1901.   790(7)
Campbell, L. E. Age of gold...
1909.   793(0)
Campion Mining and Trading Co.
Facts...Nome. 1903.   799(5)
Cantwell, G. Kondike, sou-
venir. 1901.   826(7)
[Carey, T. J.] Klondike and all
about it. 1897.   832(7)
Carpenter, H. M. Three years
in Alaska. 1901.   845(0)
Chicago Record. Klondike ...
1897.   813(7)
Clark, F. M. Roadhouse tales...
Nome. 1902.   939(5)
Clark, H. F. Miner's manual ...
1898.   943(0)
Clements, Jas. I. Klondyke...
1897.   953(7)
Clum, J. P. Trip to Klondike...
stereoscope. 1899.   961(7)
Colliery Engr. Co. Placer
mining...1897.   978(7)
Conkey, W. B., Co. Official
guide...1897.   1001(0)
Coolidge, L. A. Klondike and
Yukon...1897.   1062(0)
Copper River Mining, Trading &
...Co. Guide. 1902.   1072(2)
Corbett, J. Lake country.
1898.   1074(2)
Crewe, E. O. Gold fields of
Yukon ... 1897.   1119(7)
Crewe, F. Camp Hades #23 ...
1910.   1120(3)

Crewe, F. Log sloop "North"
Cook's Inlet. 1896.   1121(2)
Cross, V. Girl of Klondike.
1898.   1133(7)
Day, L. Tragedy of Klondike.
1906.   1219(7)
deFonvielle, W. Aventures...
Klondike. 1900.   1229(7)
deFonvielle, W. Aventures d'un
Français...1901.   1230(7)
Devine, Edw. J. A travers...
Bering. [1905?]   1282(5)
Devine, Edw. J. Across widest
...Bering. 1905.   1283(5)
DeWindt, H. Through gold-
fields...1898.   1286(5)
Donnelly, E. C. Klondike pic-
nic...1898.   1331(7)
Downie, Wm. Hunting for gold
1893.   1341(0)
Dyer, E. J. Gold fields...
1898.   1397(7)
Dyer, E. J. Routes and mineral
...1898.   1398(7)
Edwards, Wm. S. In to the
Yukon. 1904.   1415(7)
El Dorado Pub. Co. Modern El
Dorado...1897.   1428(0)
Fair, Agnes T. Sourdough's
bible. 1910.   1511(0)
Fenn, G. M. To win or to die.
[ca 1900]   1541(7)
French, L. H. Nome nuggets...
1901.   1648(5)
French, L. H. Seward's land
gold...[1905?]   1649(5)
Gairdner, G.W. ...guide map
... 1897.   1674(7)
Gateway to Klondike and Atlin.
1898.   1693(7)
Gold fields of Alaska...
By Louis...1897.   1752(0)
Golden Sands Mining Co....Cape
Nome...[ca1900]   1754(5)
Goodman, A. E. Klondyke gold
fields...n.d.   1774(7)
Gorbach, A. B. Unter der Mit-
ternachtssone...1908.1777(7)
Graham, J. F. ... gold fields
guide. [1897]   1793(0)
Great Northern Railway Co.
Alaska ... 1898.   1834(0)

GOLD RUSHES - Books Published
          [1862?] to 1910.
                    (cont.)
Great Northern Railway Co....
    Cape Nome. 1899.   1837(5)
Grinnell, J. Gold hunting in
    Alaska. 1901.   1866(0)
Grubstake Pub. Co. Klondike
    grubstakes...1898.   1870(7)
Guide, map and history ...
    n. d.   1879(0)
Guide to Alaska and Yukon.
    [1898]   1881(0)
Guide to Klondike and Yukon
    gold fields. 1897.   1882(0)
[Hall, Edw. H.] Alaska, Eldora-
    do ... 1897.   1903(0)
Hall, J. A. Starving on bed of
    gold. 1909.   1907(0)
Hambleton, C. J. Gold hunter's
    experience. 1898.   1917(0)
Handbook of B. C. emigrant's
    guide ... [1862?]   1928(7)
Harris, A. C. Alaska and Klon-
    dike gold ... 1897. 1958(0)
Haskell, W. B. Two years Klon-
    dike...1898.   1983(0)
Haverly, C. E. Klondyke and
    fortune... 1897.   1991(7)
Hayne, M.H.E. Pioneers of
    Klondyke...1897.   2005(7)
Hegg, Eric A. Souvenir Alaska
    & Yukon...1900.   2017(0)
Hegg, Eric A. Souvenir of
    Nome... 1900.   2018(5)
Heilprin, A. Alaska and Klon-
    dike. 1899.   2020(0)
Heistand, H.O.S. Territory of
    Alaska ... 1898.   2021(0)
Henderson, A. P. Rainbow's end
    ... 1898.   2036(0)
Henley, G. F. Guide to Yukon...
    1898.   2064(7)
[Hiller, E.H.] Latest infor-
    mation ... [1897]   2107(0)
Hitchcock, M. E. Two women in
    Klondike. 1899.   2130(7)
Holland, Edw. To Yukon and Klon-
    dike ... 1897.   2153(7)
Howard, M. A. Stereopticon...
    Alaska ... n.d.   2199(0)
Hulbert, H.B. In search of Si-
    berian Klondike. 1903.2221(5)

Ingersoll, E. Gold fields ...
    1897.   2262(0)
Ingersoll, E. Golden Alaska...
    1897.   2263(0)
Ingersoll, E. In richest
    Alaska ... 1897.   2264(0)
James, F. Klondike goldfields
    1897.   2324(7)
Jennings, W. T. Report...
    1898.   2348(7)
Jones, C. J. Buffalo Jones'
    40 yrs. 1899.   2378(7)
Keim, DeB. R. Our Alaskan won-
    derland...1898.   2427(0)
Klondike and B. C. guide ...
    n. d.   2488(7)
Klondyke and gold fields of
    Alaska. 1897.   2489(0)
Klondyke mining laws ...
    1897.   2490(7)
Kootenai guide to mining camps
    ...1898.   2509(7)
Ladue, Jos. Klondyke facts...
    1897.   2580(7)
Ladue, Jos. Klondyke nuggets...
    1897.   2581(7)
LaRoche, Frank. En route to
    Klondike...1897.   2626(7)
LaRoche, Frank. En route to
    Klondike views. 1898.2627(7)
[Le Febre, H.B.] "Soapy" Smith
    tragedy. 1907.   2672(1)
[Leisher, J.J.] Decline and
    fall ... 1900.   2675(7)
Leonard, J. W. Gold fields
    Klondike...1897.   2679(7)
Lindsey, D. Alaska...reference
    ... 1897.   2716(0)
Little Klondike Nugget ...
    laws... 1897.   2738(7)
Lugrin, C. H. Yukon gold
    fields ... 1897.   2808(7)
Lynch, J. Three years Klon-
    dike...1904.   2819(7)
Lynch, J. Trois ans au
    Klondike. [1905]   2820(7)
Lysons, F.H. Map-guide...
    1897.   2823(7)
MacDonald, A. In search of
    Eldorado. 1905.   2862(0)
McElwaine, E. Truth about
    Alaska...1901.   2888(5)

GOLD RUSHES - Books Published
[1862?] to 1910.
(cont.)
McKee, Lanier. Land of Nome.
1902.   2915(5)
McLain, J. S. Alaska and Klon-
dike. 1905.   2925(0)
Margeson, C.A. Experiences
gold hunters...1899. 2966(0)
Maris, Omer. Sketches from
Alaska. 1897.   2970(0)
Marks, Alfred. On to Klondike!
1897.   2975(7)
Marvin, F. R. Yukon overland
... 1898.   3015(7)
Miers, H.A. Yukon. Visit ...
1901.   3100(7)
Millroy's pathfinder ...
[1897?]   3134(0)
Miners' guide ...
[1898] . . . . . .   3140(7)
Miner's supplement to Royal
Baker ... 1898.   3141(0)
Möller, J.V. Auf nach Alaska.
1897.   3155(0)
Montague, P.S. Ready reference
... 1897.   3156(7)
Mt. Wrangell Co. Short story
Alaska ... 1898.   3211(0)
New official map ...
1897.   3293(7)
North-Amer. Transp. & Trading
Co. Alaska ...[1899?] 3343(0)
Northern Navigation Co. ...
gold fields. n.d.   3351(0)
Paillard, L. Un Lyonnaise au
Klondike... 1900.   3471(7)
Palmer, F. In Klondyke...
1899.   3479(7)
[Paramore, H.H. ?] Klondike
gold fields. 1897.   3490(7)
Paramore, H.H. Practical guide
... 1897.   3491(7)
Pierce, W.H. Thirteen yrs.
... 1890.   3583(0)
Pioneer Print. & Pub. Co. Klon-
dike ... guide.1898. 3610(7)
Planchat, H. Le Klondike ...
1901.   3619(7)
Plempel, C. A. Klondyke gold
fields ... 1897.   3622(7)
Port Orchard Navig. Co.Stikine
River ... 1898.   3644(7)

Powell, A. M. Trailing & camp--
ping ... 1909.   3668(0)
Prather, J. B. Land of mid-
night sun ... [c1899]3673(0)
Pratt, W. A. Gold fields ...
Cape Nome. 1900.   3674(5)
Price, J. M. From Euston to
Klondike...1898.   3691(7)
Prosser, W. T. Prospectus:
Hist. ... 1912.   3700(0)
Rickard, T. A. Through Yukon
... 1909.   3810(0)
Rinfret, R. Le Yukon et son...
or. 1898.   3826(7)
Robinette, A.M. Facts about
Cape Nome ... 1900.   3841(5)
[Rowatt, H.H.] Report...Yukon
... 1907.   3904(7)
Seattle-Alaska Intelligence
Bur. Klondyker. 1897.4033(7)
Secretan, J.H.E. To Klondyke
and back. 1898.   4037(0)
Seymore, W.C. Klondike Kata-
kism...1897.   4080(7)
Siem, C. The menace ...
1903.   4147(5)
Sladen, D.B.W. On the cars and
off ... 1898.   4177(7)
Smith, W. W. Alaska ...
1910.   4205(0)
Smith's Cash Store. On Klon-
dike...1897.   4208(7)
Sola, A.E.I. Klondyke, truth
...[c1897]   4240(7)
Spokane Chamber of Commerce.
Are you going...1897.4265(7)
Spokane Chamber of Commerce.
Overland...1897.   4266(7)
Spurr, J.E. Through Yukon
... 1900.   4273(7)
Stanley, W.M. A mile of gold.
1898.   4282(7)
Stansbury, C.F. Klondike...
1897.   4283(0)
Steele, J. W. Golden era ...
1897.   4294(0)
Steele, J. W. Klondike ...
1897.   4295(0)
Stoddard, C. W. Over Rocky
Mtns. ... 1899.   4350(0)
Sullivan, M.K. Woman who went
to Alaska. [c1902]   4381(5)

GOLD RUSHES - Books Published
    [1862?] to 1910.
             (cont.)
Sullivan, M. K. Trail of sour-
  dough. [c1910]   4382(5)
Tacoma Chamber of Commerce.
  Tacoma ... 1897.   4443(7)
Tacoma Daily News. Tacoma,
  gateway ... 1897.   4444(7)
Taylor, L. Alaska and Yukon
  ... 1897.   4471(0)
Treadgold, A.N.C. Report gold
  fields...1899.   4571(7)
Trezona, C. E. Cape Nome and
  ...placer mines.1900. 4577(5)
Trout, P. L. My experience at
  Cape Nome...1899.   4578(5)
[Wardner, J.] Jim Wardner of
  Wardner, Idaho. 1900. 4738(0)
Warren, H. M. To and fro.
  [c1908]   4745(1)
Washington & Alaska S.S. Co.
  Golden ... [1897]   4749(1)
Weimer, M.D.K. True story
  ...[ca 1903]   4784(7)
Wellington, J. L. Gold fields
  ...1896.   4787(0)
Wells, H. L. Alaska and Klon-
  dike. 1897.   4788(0)
Wells, H. L. Alaska, new
  Eldorado ... 1897.   4789(0)
Wheeler, O. D. Wonderland '98
  ... 1898.   4808(0)
White, E. J. "Stroller" White
  ...[c1969]   4815(7)
White Pass & Yukon Ry. White
  Pass... [1901?]   4837(7)
Williams, J.G. Forty-niner's
  experience...1897. 4883(7)
Wilson, V. Glimpses of Alaska.
  1897.   4914(0)
Wilson, V. Glimpses of Yukon
  ... 1895.   4915(7)
Wilson, V. Guide to Yukon
  ... 1895.   4916(7)
Winchester, J. D. ... voyage
  from Lynn...1900.   4919(0)
Yukon and Klondyke ...
  Alaska. [c1897]   5002(7)
Yukon Pub. Co. Facts for
  Klondikers. 1898.   5008(7)
Yukon souvenir ...
  n. d.   5009(7)

Zaccarelli, J. ...pictorial
  souvenir. n.d.   5016(7)

GOLD RUSHES - Books Published
    1911 to 1970.

Allan, A. A. Gold, men and
  dogs. 1931.   174(5)
Ames, R. A. Cheechako.
  1958.   212(7)
Anzer, R. C. Klondike gold
  rush...1959.   271(7)
Armstrong, N.A.D. Yukon
  yesterdays. 1936.   306(7)
Atwood, F. Alaska-Yukon
  gold book. 1930.   319(0)
Austin, Basil. Diary ninety-
  eighter. 1968.   325(2)
Baines, T. Northern goldfield
  diaries. 1965.   353(0)
Baird, A. 60 years on Klondike
  ... 1965.   354(7)
Bankson, R. A. Klondike
  Nugget. 1935.   386(7)
Banow, E.M. Diary of ...
  1948.   387(7)
Beattie, Kim. Brother...Klon-
  dike Boyle. 1940.   455(7)
Becker, E. A. Treasury of
  Alaskana. 1969.   462(7)
Becker, E. A. Klondike '98.
  1949.   463(7)
Bell, E. M. Flora Shaw.
  1947.   480(7)
Berton, L. B. I married
  Klondike. [c1954]   542(7)
Berton, P. A. Klondike bibliog.
  1958.   543(7)
Berton, P. Steampede for gold.
  1955.   544(7)
Berton, P. Golden trail.
  1957.   545(7)
Berton, P. Klondike.
  1958.   546(7)
Berton, P. The Klondike fever.
  1958.   547(7)
Berton, P. The mysterious
  North. 1956.   548(7)
Cadwallader, C. L. Reminis-
  cences Iditarod. n.d. 764(0)
Cameron, C. Cheechako in
  Alaska & Yukon. 1920. 785(7)

GOLD RUSHES - Books Published
1911 to 1970.
(cont.)
Canton, F. M. Frontier trails
... 1930.   825(0)
Carmack, G. W. My experiences
in Yukon. 1933.   838(7)
Chase, W. H. Pioneers of
Alaska. 1951.   899(0)
Chase, W. H. Reminiscences of
Billie Moore. [c1947] 900(0)
Chase, W. H. Sourdough pot.
1923.   901(0)
Clifton, V. Book of Talbot.
1933.   959(0)
Collier, W. R. Reign of Soapy
Smith. 1935.   977(0)
Colp, H.D. Strangest story
ever told. 1953.   993(1)
Copper River Joe. Golden cross
Valdez... 1939.   1071(2)
Cotten, B. Adventure in Alaska
... 1922.   1095(0)
Crewe, F. Poems Klondyke's
...days...1921.   1122(7)
Cunynghame, F. Lost trail.
1953.   1140(7)
Curtin, W. R. Yukon voyage...
Yukoner. 1938.   1142(0)
Denison, M. Klondike Mike.
1943.   1265(7)
Dietz, A. A. Mad rush for gold
...1914.   1293(0)
Dill, W.S. Long day ...
1926.   1295(7)
Dunn, Robert. World alive.
1956.   1391(7)
Fraser, J. D. Gold fever...
[c1923]   1638(3)
Goulet, E. O. Rugged years
... [1949]   1790(0)
Graham, A. Golden grindstone...
G.M.Mitchell. 1935.   1792(0)
Hamilton, E. W. 40 years on.
1922.   1918(7)
Hamilton, W. R. Yukon story.
1964.   1924(7)
Hamlin, C.S. Old timers on
Yukon. 1928.   1925(3)
Heller, H. L. Sourdough sagas.
1967.   2025(7)
Hewitt, J. M. Alaska vagabond
1953.   2093(0)

Hick, G. Pioneer prospector.
1954.   2102(0)
Johnston, A. Legendary Mizners.
1953.   2374(7)
Jones, H. V. Adventures in
Americana...1928.   2380(7)
Jordan, J. Fool's gold...
1960.   2390(0)
Kitto, F. H. Yukon ...
1929.   2481(7)
Klappholz, L. Gold! Gold!
1959.   2485(0)
Lloyd-Owen, F. Gold Nugget
Charlie. 1939.   2742(0)
Lokke, C. L. Klondike saga.
1965.   2749(7)
London, Jack. Revolution and
other essarys.1910. 2765(7)
Longstreth, T. M. Scarlet...
Mounted Police. 1953.2788(7)
Longstreth, T. M. Silent ...
Mounted Police. 1927.2789(7)
Lucia, E. Klondike Kate...
1962.   2806(7)
MacBeth, R. G. Policing plains
...R.N.M.P. 1920.   2828(7)
McBride, W.D. Saga of river-
boats. n.d.   2831(7)
MacFie, H. Wasa Wasa ...
1951.   2892(0)
MacGowan, M. Hard road to
Klondike. 1962.   2896(7)
McKeown, M.F. Trail led North.
1948.   2919(0)
McLain, C. M. Gold-rush Nome.
[c1969]   2923(5)
Martinsen, E.L. Black sand
and gold. 1956.   3013(0)
Martinsen, E.L. Trail to North
Star gold. 1969.   3014(0)
Masik, A. Arctic night's en-
tertainment. 1935. 3016(7)
Mathews, R. Yukon.
1968.   3026(0)
Medill, R.B. Klondike diary.
1949.   3067(7)
Meeker, E. Busy life of 85 yrs.
[c1916]   3068(0)
Miller, Mike. Soapy.
1970.   3132(0)
Mizner, Addison. Many Mizners.
1932.   3149(7)

GOLD RUSHES - Books Published
1911 to 1970.
(cont.)

Moir, G. T. Sinners and saints.
1947.   3152(0)

Moore, J. B. Skagway in days
primeval. 1968.   3162(1)

Morgan, M.C. One man's gold
rush. 1967.   3183(7)

Morgan, M. C.   Skid road...
Seattle. 1951.

Morrell, W.P. Gold rushes.
1940.   3197(0)

Munn, H. T. Prairie trials and
arctic ... 1932.   3240(0)

Nelson, K. Daughter of gold
rush. 1958.   3288(5)

Nord, Sverre. Logger's odyssey.
1943.   3322(0)

O'Connor, R. High jinks on
Klondike. [c1954]   3377(7)

Ogilvie, W. Early days on Yukon
... 1913.   3389(7)

Page, E. M. Wild horses and
gold. [c1932]   3469(7)

Palmer, F. With my own eyes.
1933.   3480(7)

Parrish, M. Nine pounds of
luggage. 1940.   3496(0)

Peterson, M.S. Joaquin Miller,
... [c1937]   3550(7)

Phillips, A. Living legend...
R.C.M.P. [c1957]   3570(7)

Pollak, G. Michael Heilprin...
1912.   3631(7)

Potter, L. Old times Upper
Cook's Inlet. 1967.   3662(2)

Powell, E. A. Marches of North.
... [c1931]   3669(7)

Pringle, G.C.F. Adventures in
service. 1929.   3695(7)

Quiett, G. C. Pay dirt...
1936.   3709(0)

Rickard, M.E.(H.) Everything
...Tex Rickard. 1936. 3808(7)

Robertson, F. C. Soapy Smith...
1961.   3837(0)

Robertson, W. N. Yukon memories.
1930.   3839(7)

Robinette, G. Rebel of Yukon.
[c1967]   3842(7)

Robins, E. Raymond and I.
1956.   3844(7)

Romig, E. C. Life and travels
... 1945.   3875(0)

Rutzebeck, H. Alaska man's
luck...1920.   3924(1)

Rutzebeck, H. My Alaskan
idyll. 1920.   3925(1)

Samuels, C. Magnificent Rube...
Tex Rickard. [c1957] 3952(7)

Scearce, S. Northern lights to
fields of gold.1939. 3993(0)

Shand, M. C. Summit and beyond. 1959.   4086(1)

Springer, J. Innocent...M. K.
Burke. 1963.   4270(3)

Starr, W. A. My adventures in
Klondike...1960.   4287(0)

Steele, H.E.R. Policing the
Arctic. 1935.   4293(7)

Steele, S.B. Forty years in
Canada...1915.   4296(7)

Stephens, L.D. Life sketches
Jayhawker...1916.   4336(0)

Stewart, E. Down Mackenzie and
up Yukon...1913.   4343(7)

Strange, H.G.L. Never a dull
moment. 1941.   4359(7)

Sullivan, E.D. Fabulous Wilson
Mizner. 1935.   4380(7)

Thomas, E.L.R. Night in
Sitka...1948.   4491(1)

Thomas, L.J. Woodfill of the
Regulars...1929.   4498(3)

Thomas, L. J., jr. Trail of
'98. [c1962]   4499(7)

Tollemache, S.H.R.L. Reminiscences Yukon. 1911. 4545(7)

Trelawney-Ansell, E. C. I followed gold. 1938.   4576(7)

Tyrell, M.E.(C.) I was there
...[c1938]   4598(7)

Verne, Jules. Claim on 40 Mile
Creek. n.d.   4689(7)

Veteran Steamboatmen's Assoc.
of West. "Eliza Anderson"
[1940]   4694(0)

Viksten, A. I Guldjägares
Spår...1951.   4700(7)

Walden, A. T. Dog puncher on
Yukon. 1928.   4729(7)

Walker, F. Jack London and
Klondike. 1966.   4731(7)

Welzl, J. Quest for polar
treasures. 1933.   4791(0)

GOLD RUSHES - Books Published
1911-1970.
(cont.)
Welzl, J. 30 yrs. in golden
north. 1932.   4792(0)
White, E. J. "Stroller" White
...[c1969]   4815(7)
Wiedemann, T. Cheechako into
sourdough. [c1942]   4861(7)
Winslow, K. Big pan-out.
[c1951]   4924(7)
Woods, H. F. God's loaded dice.
... 1948.   4958(7)
Young, S. H. Adventures in
Alaska...[c1919]   4996(0)

GOVERNMENT - City and State.

Adrian, C. R. Governing our
50 states. 1963.   15(0)
Anderson, R. M. Planning ...
50 states. 1966.   250(0)
Commerce Clearing House.Alaska
tax reporter. 1963.   998(0)
Cooley, R. A. Alaska, challenge
...1966.   1060(0)
Cooley, R. A. Politics...
1963.   1061(0)
Cordova, Town of. Rules, by-
laws ... 1914.   1081(2)
Fairbanks. Ordinances.
1907.   1523(3)
Fairbanks. Revised ordinances.
1912.   1524(3)
Fernald, K. Rubles to state
hood. 1965.   1545(0)
Gardner, L.S. Optimist ...
1951.   1681(0)
Gruening, E. Let us end Amer.
colonialism. 1955.   1872(0)
Gruening, E. Battle for Alaska
statehood. 1967.   1873(0)
Gruening, E. State of Alaska.
1954.   1874(0)
Hansen, M. M. Handbook freshmen
legislator. 1963.   1937(0)
Jackson, G. R. Suggestion reor-
ganization...1953.   2309(0)
Juneau Record-Miner. ...incorp.
city Juneau. 1904.   2400(1)
Latham, E. Statehood for Hawaii
and Alaska. 1953.   2633(0)

League of Women Voters No.Star
Bor. Fairbanks.1968. 2655(2)
Legal Directories Pub. Co. Pac.
Coast legal...1961. 2673(0)
Oakes, P. A state is born.
1958.   3370(0)
Oakes, P. Alaska voter's
guidebook. 1962.   3371(0)
Pollock, H. State of 70's...
1970.   3633(0)
Ross, S. Gruening of Alaska.
[c1968]   3887(0)
Sundborg, G. Statehood for
Alaska. 1946.   4398(0)
Tanana, Town of. Ordinance...
1914.   4449(3)
Wood, P. Unbelievable years.
[c1969]   4954(0)

GOVERNMENT - Federal.

Carstenson, V. Public lands...
1968.   856(0)
Clawson, M. Federal lands...
1957.   949(0)
Leehey, M.D. Public land policy in Alaska. 1912. 2671(0)

GOVERNMENT - Territorial.

Alaska Bar Assoc. ...sketch of
judiciary...1901.   31(0)
Alaska Bar Assoc. Proceedings.
... 1899.   32(0)
Allen, E. W. Halibut Comm.
... 1936.   179(0)
Altsheler, W.B. Maladministration Ballinger...1910.190(2)
American-Russian Co. Alaska
fur-seal bill. 1969.   209(0)
Anchorage Daily Times. Alaska's
struggle ... 1950.   237(0)
Campbell, W. Arctic patrols...
1936.   796(7)
Canada. Reports N.W.M.P.
1896-1901.   814(7)
Castle, N. H. Treatise searches
...prohibition.1922.   865(0)
Catto, W. Yukon administration.
1902.   871(7)
Chambers, E. J. R.N.M.P. ...
history. 1906.   883(7)

GOVERNMENT - Territorial.
                    (cont.)
Coffin, C. C. Seat of empire.
  1870.   972(0)
Corson, J. W. Home rule ...
  1908.   1091(0)
Corson, J. W. Is ordinance of
  1787 to apply. 1907. 1092(0)
Cowles, B.K. Alaska...Organic
  Act...1885.   1101(0)
Duncan, W. Appeal...Metlakahtla
  Indians..1886.   1380(1)
Dunning, W. A. Paying for
  Alaska. 1912.   1392(0)
Evans, R.D. Sailor's log ...
  1902.   1503(6)
Farrar, J. Purchase of Alaska.
  1934.   1532(0)
Fink, A. "As to Wickersham..."
  1910.   1557(0)
Fink, A. Alaska situation.
  n. d.   1558(0)
Green, J. C. Nomination F.E.
  Fuller Judge...1912. 1845(0)
Hall, F. Laws of Alaska ...
  1827.   1905(0)
[Hansbrough, H.C.] "Looting"
  character...1906.   1933(5)
Hansen, A. H. Tundra...Deputy
  Marshall...1930.   1934(0)
Hardcastle, R. Alaska Day,
  Sitka. [1954?]   1946(1)
Hayne, M.H.E. Pioneers of
  Klondyke. 1897.   2005(7)
Herron, E. A. Dimond of
  Alaska ... 1957.   2080(0)
Howgate, H. W. Congress and
  North Pole. 1879.   2206(4)
Jackson, S. Statement...Sitka
  ... 1886.   2310(1)
Jennings, R. W. Address ...
  Ketchikan... 1917. 2347(0)
Johnson, W. F. Century of ex-
  pansion. 1903.   2372(0)
Johnson, W. F. Life Warren G.
  Harding. 1923.   2373(0)
Joslin, F. Alaska...legislation
  ... 1912.   2391(0)
Kelly, N. Men of Mounted.
  1949.   2433(7)
Kirk, R. C. Twelve months in
  Klondike. 1899.   2472(7)

Knapp, E. J. General convention
  ... 1910.   2492(0)
Liberate Alaska from fish trap
  ... 1949.   2702(0)
Longstreth, T. M. Scarlet Force
  Mounted Police. 1953.2788(7)
Longstreth, T. M. Silent Force
  Mounted Police. 1927.2789(7)
MacBeth, R.G. Policing plains
  ... R.N.W.M.P. 1920. 2828(7)
McDonald, T. P. Why one rule
  ...petition...1914. 2886(0)
McElray, R. McN. Winning of
  far west. 1914.   2887(0)
Mackaye, B. Act proposed ...
  conservation...n.d. 2914(0)
McKee, L. Land of Nome...
  1902.   2915(5)
Mowry, W. A. Territorial
  growth...1902.   3216(0)
Ogilvie, Wm. Copy further re-
  port...1899.   3388(7)
Ogilvie, Wm. Evidence...mal-
  feasance...1899.   3390(7)
Phillips, A. Living legend...
  R.C.M.P. [c1957]   3570(7)
Pinchot, G. Who shall own
  Alaska? 1911.   3600(2)
Robertson, D. S. To Arctic with
  Mounties. 1934.   3836(0)
Russell, T. H. Illus. Warren
  G. Harding. 1923.   3922(0)
Rustgard, J. Home rule ...
  1927.   3923(0)
Scarth, W. H. Report trip to
  Yukon. 1897.   3992(7)
Shepard, I. S. Cruise "Rush"
  Behring...1889.   4111(0)
Shepard, T. R. Placer mining
  laws ... 1909.   4112(0)
Siem, C. C.S.L.T. ...
  1915.   4146(0)
Smyth, N. A. Brief Cunningham
  coal 1912.   4211(0)
Spicer, G. W. Constitutional
  status...1927.   4263(0)
Statement needs of Alaska.
  1923.   4288(0)
Steel, W. A. Home rule measure
  ... 1927.   4291(0)
Steele, H.E.R. Policing the
  Arctic. 1935.   4293(7)

GOVERNMENT - Territorial.
(cont.)
Steele, S. B. 40 years...
1915.   4296(7)
Thomas, C. W. Ice is where...
[c1951]   4490(0)
Truman, B. C. Occidental
sketches. 1881.   4582(6)
Wardman, G. Trip to Alaska...
1884.   4737(6)
Wead, F. W. Gales, ice ...
Bear. 1937.   4761(0)
West, E. L. Captain's papers...
1965.   4798(0)
Wickersham, J. Old Yukon.
1938.   4858(0)
Wickersham, J. Speech...Terr.
legislature.[1913]   4859(0)
Wickersham, J. Organization...
terr. gov. [1927]   4860(0)
Willoughby, W. F. Territories
... 1905.   4906(0)
Wilson, G. Geo. Turner's be-
trayal ... 1904.   4910(0)
Wyman, G. Public land...laws
... 1898.   4983(0)
Yukon Terr. Interim report...
1906.   5010(7)

GOVERNMENT - Treaties and
Foreign Relations.

Bailey, T.A. Diplomatic hist.
... 1958.   350(0)
Balch, E. S. Letters and papers
...frontier. 1904.   361(0)
Balch, T. W. Die Alaska-Grenze
... 1922.   365(0)
Balch, T. W. Alaska frontier.
1903.   366(0)
Balch, T. W. Alasko-Canadian
frontier. 1902.   367(0)
Bancroft, F. Life Wm. H.
Seward ... 1900.   377(0)
Batchelor, G. Unification N.A.
1967.   426(0)
Begg, A. Report relative to
Alaska boundary...1896.470(0)
Begg, A. Review Alaskan boun-
dary...1900.   471(0)
Bethune, W. C. Canada's western
northland. 1937.   551(0)

Bingham, J. W. Report int'l
law...fisheries.1938. 556(0)
[Blowitz, H.G.S.A.O.] Bering
Sea arbitration ...
1893.   581(0)
[Burges, J.B.] Narrat....dis-
pute Eng.Spain.1791. 730(1)
Cairnes, D.D. Yukon-Alaska
Boundary...1914.   766(0)
Callahan, J. M. Amer. foreign
policy...1967.   777(0)
Callahan, J. M. Amer. relations
Pacific. 1901.   778(0)
Callahan, J. M. Russo-Amer.
relations. 1908.   779(0)
Callahan, J. M. Alaska Purchase
... 1908.   780(0)
Canada's Alaskan dismemberment.
1904.   818(0)
Carter, J. C. Fur-seal arbitra-
tion ... 1893.   857(0)
Clay, C. M. Oration Alaska
annex. ... 1896.   950(0)
Cole, Cornelius. Memoirs...
1908.   976(0)
Comments...Spain...Nootka Sd.
1790.   997(1)
Conant, M. Long polar watch...
defense...1962.   999(0)
Convention U.S. Japan...Russ.
posses. 1868.   1007(0)
Correspondence...seizure Brit.
Amer. vessels...1887.1085(0)
Dafoe, J.W. Clifford Sifton...
1931.   1151(0)
Dallas, A. G. San Juan, Alaska
... 1873.   1169(0)
Davidson, G. Alaska boundary.
1903.   1191(0)
Dickinson, J. McG. Alaska's
boundary...1904.   1291(0)
Dodge, W. S. Oration...Sitka...
1868.   1319(0)
Duane, R. Case of "Sayward"
... 1891.   1360(0)
Edelstein, J.C. Alaska comes
of age. 1942.   1408(0)
[Etches, J.C.] Continuation
...Nootka Sd. 1790. 1497(1)
[Etches, J.C.] Authentic ...
Nootka Sd. 1790.   1498(1)
Ewart, J. S. Kingdom of Canada.
1908.   1505(0)

GOVERNMENT - Treaties and
          Foreign Relations.
          (cont.)
Foster, J. W. Alaskan boundary.
  1903.   1616(0)
G.B. Colonial Sec. Instructions
  ...Purchase. 1867.   1809(0)
G.B. For. Off. Boundary ...
  Argument. 1903.   1810(0)
G.B. For. Off. Boundary ...
  Case ... 1903.   1811(0)
G.B. For. Off. Boundary...Ap-
  pendix...1903.   1812(0)
G.B. For. Off. Boundary...Coun-
  tercase...1903.   1813(0)
G.N. For. Off. Boundary...Ap-
  pend. counterc. 1903. 1814(0)
G.B. For. Off. Protocols...
  Boundary. 1903.   1815(0)
G.B. Parl. Papers. Bering Sea
  Argument... 1893.   1816(0)
G.B. Parl. Paper. Dispatch...
  Thompson...1898.   1817(0)
G.B. Parl. Papers. Report...
  Thompson. 1897.   1818(0)
Hart, A. B. Extracts offic.
  papers...1893.   1972(0)
Henderson, J.B. Amer. diplomat.
  fur seals...1901.   2038(0)
Hodgins, T. Alaska boundary.
  1904.   2132(0)
Hodgins, T. Alaska-Canada boun-
  dary...1902.   2133(0)
Hunter, J. Report on boundary
  line. 1878.   2238(0)
Int'l. Boundary Comm.Jt. report
  ... 1952.   2274(0)
James, J.A. First sci.
  explora. R.A. 1942. 2326(0)
Jebb, R. Studies colonial
  nationalism. 1905.   2334(0)
Jordan, D.S. Days of man ...
  1922.   2388(0)
King, W. F. Jt. report boun
  dary. 1901.   2460(0)
Lane, A. W. Letters Franklin
  K. Lane...1922.   2592(0)
McElray, R. McN. Winning far
  west...1914.   2887(0)
MacMaster, D. Seal arbitration
  ... 1894.   2934(0)
Mason, A. T. Bureaucracy con-
  victs itself. 1941. 3017(2)

Meares, J. Answer to Mr. Geo.
  Dixon ... 1791.   3052(1)
Meares, J. Authentic...Nootka
  Sd. 1750.[sic]   3053(1)
[Meares, J.] Mr. Mear's memo-
  rial..[1790?]   3054(1)
[Meares, J.] Memorial of ...
  1933.   3055(1)
Memorandum boundary ...
  1899.   3077(0)
Mills, D. Canadian view ...
  boundary ... 1899. 3135(0)
Niedieck, P. Kreuzfahrten
  Beringmeer...1907. 3305(0)
Niedieck, P. Croisieres ...
  Behring...1908.   3306(0)
Niedieck, P. Cruises in Bering
  Sea...1909.   3307(0)
Oliver, E. H. Canadian north-
  west ... 1914.   3401(0)
Phelps, E. J. Orations and es-
  says...1901.   3567(0)
Pierce, E.L. Memoirs...Chas.
  Sumner...1877-93.   3579(0)
Pomeroy, E. S. Terr....colonial
  administration.1947. 3637(0)
Radical construction...R.A.
  ... 1867.   3722(0)
Reid, V.H. Purchase of Alaska.
  [1939]   3778(0)
Riesenfeld, S. A. Protection
  ...fisheries.1942. 3822(0)
Robertson, J.R. Kentuckian...
  Tsars...Clay.1935. 3838(0)
Robertson, W. Oregon ...
  1846.   3840(1)
Ross, E. A. Proposed cession
  ...panhandle.1914. 3885(1)
Seward, F.W. Reminiscences...
  1916.   4070(0)
Seward, F.W. Autobiog. ...
  1877.   4071(0)
Seward, Olive R. Wm. H. Seward
  ... 1873   4072(0)
Seward, Wm. H. Address on
  Alaska ... n.d.   4073(0)
Seward, Wm. H. Alaska Speech
  Sitka...1869.   4074(0)
Seward, Wm. H. Alaska; speech
  at Sitka...1879.   4075(0)
Seward, Wm. H. Speech of Mr.
  Seward...1869.   4076(0)

GOVERNMENT - Treaties and
          Foreign Relations.
          (cont.)
Seward, Wm. H. Speech in Senate
  ...1852.   4077(0)
Seward, Wm. H. Speeches in
  Alaska...1869.   4078(0)
Seward, Wm. H. Works ...
  1853-84.   4079(0)
Sgroi, P. P. Why U.S. pur-
  chased...[c1970]   4081(0)
Shiels, A. W. Little journeys
  ... [c1949]   4117(0)
Shiels, A. W. Seward's icebox.
  [c1933]   4118(0)
Shiels, A. W. Purchase of
  Alaska. 1967.   4120(0)
Stanton, S. B. Behring Sea...
  dispute. 1890.   4284(0)
Stein, R. Can a nation be a
  gentleman ? 1911.   4328(1)
Storey, M. Charles Sumner.
  1900.   4355(0)
Sumner, C. Speech Chas. Sumner
  ... 1867.   4391(0)
Sumner, C. Works.
  1870-83. . . . . . . .4392(0)
Sundborg, G. Proposal protect.
  fisheries...1944.   4393(0)
Sundborg, G. Int'l. fisheries
  ... 1943.   4395(0)
Sundborg, G. Shipping services
  ... 1944.   4397(0)
Survey Assoc. Amer.-Russ. fron-
  tiers. 1944.   4403(0)
Tansill, C. C. Canadian-Amer.
  relations. 1943.   4452(0)
Tansill, C.C. Foreign policy
  T. F. Bayard. 1940. 4453(0)
Thomas, B.P. Russo-American
  relations. 1930.   4489(0)
Tomasevic, J. Int'l. agreements
  ... 1943.   4548(0)
Tucker, E. W. History Oregon
  1844.   4585(1)
Tupper, C. Political remin-
  iscences. 1914.   4588(0)
Tupper, C. Recollections 60
  yrs. 1914.   4589(0)
Tyler, A.(F.) Foreign policy
  Jas. G. Blaine.1927. 4595(0)
Van Deusen, G.G. Wm. Henry
  Seward. 1967.   4647(0)

Wade, F. C. Treaties affecting
  ... 1914.   4720(0)
Walker, R. J. Letter of ...
  purchase. 1968.   4732(0)
Warner, D. F. Idea of continen-
  tal union.[c1960] 4741(0)
[Webb, F.?] Letters lately
  pub. Spain. 1790. 4762(1)
Weigert, H. W. Compass of
  world...1944.   4782(0)
Weigert, H.W. New compass of
  world...1949.   4783(0)
Welling, J.C. Bering Sea ar-
  bitration...1893. 4786(0)
White, J. Boundary disputes
  ... 1914.   4826(0)
White, J. Treaty of 1825...R.A.
  & Brit. N.A. 1915. 4827(0)
Williams, S.N. N.Y.'s part in
  history. 1915.   4885(0)
Willson, B. Great Company.
  1899.   4907(0)
Wishart, A. Bering Sea ques-
  tion ... 1893.   4933(0)

GUIDEBOOKS.

Alaska.
  n. d. . . . . 27(0)
Alaska Bureau. Alaska, direct
  route...[ca1949]   34(0)
Alaska Bureau. Alaska tour.
  1913.   37(0)
Alaska Centennial...Anchorage
  ... [1967]   42(0)
Alaska Highway guide with
  maps. [ca1947]   67(0)
Alaska, land of promise ...
  1963.   72(0)
[Alaska Life] Anchorage ...
  [1945?]   74(2)
[Alaska Life] Fairbanks ...
  [1945?]   75(3)
[Alaska Life] Juneau...Douglas
  ...[1945?]   76(1)
[Alaska Life] Ketchikan ...
  [1945?]   77(1)
[Alaska Life] Nome ...
  [1945?]   78(5)
[Alaska Life] Seward ...
  [1945?]   79(2)
Alaska Mag. Pub. Co. ...Revilla
  Isl. [ca1945]   84(1)

GUIDEBOOKS. (cont.)

Alaska Northwest Pub. Co.
Alaska traveler. 1963.   92(0)
Alaska Opportunist. Alaska –
last frontier. 1947.   96(0)
Alaska Opportunities.
1953. . . . . 97(0)
Alaska travel guide.
1965.   133(0)
Allen, L. H. Alaska's Kenai
... [ca 1947]   183(2)
Amer. Express Travel Dept. Sum-
mer tours...1927.   198(0)
Anchorage, crossroads ...
[ca 1945]   234(0)
Anchorage Guide Pub. Co. What's
doing...1955.   239(2)
Atwood, E. Anchorage, all
Alaska city. 1957.   317(2)
Baedecker, K. Dominion of Cana-
da...1894.   336(0)
Baedecker, K. United States,
excursions. 1909.   337(0)
Cook, Thos., Co. Alaska,
Pacific. 1924.   1058(0)
Cordova Daily Times. Cordova
... 1914.   1079(2)
Criswell Travel service. Sum-
mer journeys. 1931.   1125(0)
Dynes, W. M. ...directory and
guide...1920.   1399(0)
Dynes, W. M. ... tours Alaska
... 1921.   1400(1)
Fodor, E. Pacific States ...
Alaska. 1966.   1589(0)
Frame, J. W. ... Alaska pocket
pilot...1929.   1624(0)
Guide to Alaska.
[ca 1953] . . . . . 1880(0)
Handbook of vacation trips.
n.d.   1929(0)
Hart, R. G. McKay's guide...
1959.   1974(0)
Holiday Pub. Guide to Alaska...
Highway. 1963.   2151(0)
Int'l. Geol. Cong. Guide book
... 1913.   2277(0)
Jacobin, L. ...tourist's ...
guide ... 1946.   2314(0)
Lesure, T. B. How to see and
enjoy ... 1966.   2692(0)

McManus, R. Tourist's pictorial
guide. 1890.   2933(0)
Milepost.
1949. . . . . .3114(0)
Moore, O. M. New northwest.
1900.   3163(0)
North to Alaska and Yukon.
1968.   3349(0)
Northwest Mapping Service. New
Alaska Hy. ...1948.   3357(0)
Nulsen, R. H. Trailering to
Alaska. 1960.   3366(0)
Rand McNally & Co. ...Alaska
and Yukon. [c1922]   3731(0)
Rand McNally & Co. ...guide to
great n.w. [c1903]   3732(0)
Scidmore, E. R. Appleton's
guidebook...1893.   4025(0)
Scidmore, E. R. Guide-book to
Alaska...1893.   4026(0)
Seattle Century 21 Expo. 1962.
Land promise.1962.   4034(0)
Silvers, C. Alaska Highway
sketches. n.d.   4152(0)
Tewkesbury, W. Alaska Hy. tra-
vel guide.[c1950]   4481(0)
This is Alaska ... 1964.
1964. . . . . . . .4488(0)
Tongass Pub. Co. Pilot; guide
to s.e. 1966.   4555(1)

HEALTH.

Alaska Packers Assoc. Influ-
enza epidemic. 1919. 100(2)
Alaska Packers Assoc. Influ-
enza epidemic. 1919. 101(2)
Anderson, E. G. Dog-team doc-
tor...1940.   243(5)
Burke, C. H. Doctor Hap.
1961.   734(0)
DeVighne, H. C. Time of my
life. 1942.   1281(0)
Fairbanks Community Hosp.Assoc.
Survey ... 1961.   1518(3)
Fortuine, R. Health of Eskimos
...bibliog. 1968.   1615(0)
Hewitt, J. M. Alaska vagabond
Dr. Skookum. 1953.   2093(0)
McAfee, A. B. Haines Hospital.
1911.   2825(2)
Mikkelsen, E. Conquering Arctic
ice. 1909.   3104(4)

HEALTH. (cont.)

Muñoz, Rie. Nursing in
North. [c1967]   3242(0)
Neuman, D. S. Practical medi-
cal manual...1911.   3290(0)
Parran, T. Alaska's health...
1954.   3495(0)
Rodahl, K. Eskimo metabolism
... 1954.   3852(0)
Rodahl, K. Nutrition require-
ments...1960.   3854(0)
Rodahl, K. Studies blood...
Eskimo...1954.   3856(0)
Rodahl, K. U.S.A.F. survival
ration ...1950.   3859(0)
Romig, J. H. Medical handbook
...cold...1904.   3876(5)

HISTORY and Geography.

Adams, Ben. Last frontier...
[c1961]   10(0)
Alaska & Yukon general ...
1937.   30(0)
Alaska facts ...
1945. . . . . 62(0)
Alaska Mag. Pub. Co. Book of
...Frontier. 1941.   81(0)
Alaska Mag. Pub. Co. 100 events
built Alaska. 1944.   83(0)
Alaska National Bank. New
state ... [1959?]   89(0)
Alaska Northwest Pub. Co.
Alaska traveler...1963. 92(0)
Alaska story.
1951. . . . . .128(0)
Allen, E. W. North Pacific
1936.   178(0)
American Geog. Soc. Geog. in
making. 1952.   199(0)
American Geog. Soc. Pioneer
settlement. 1932.   202(0)
American Geog. Soc. Readings
geog. N.A. 1952.   204(0)
Andrews, C.L. Story of
Alaska. 1931.   256(0)
Andrews, C.L. Story of Sitka.
1922.   257(1)
Angus, H.F. B.C. and U.S.
... 1942.   265(0)
Armstrong, T.E. Russian
settlement...1965.   307(0)

Atkins, B. Modern antiquities
... 1898.   315(0)
Aubert, F. L'Ouest Canadien
... 1907.   321(0)
Balcom, M. G. Ghost towns of
Alaska. 1965.   370(0)
Bancroft, H.H. Chronicles of
builders...1891-92.   378(0)
Bancroft, H.H. Hist. Alaska
... 1886.   379(0)
Bancroft, H.H. Hist. n.w.
coast. 1884.   380(0)
Bandi, H.G. Alaska, urgesch-
ichte...1967.   382(0)
Baranskiĭ, N.N. Amerikanskiĭ
Sever...1950.   388(0)
Bartz, F. Alaska.
1950. [in German]   423(0)
Bennett, J. E. Alaska ...
1899.   501(0)
Berton, P. Mysterious North.
1956.   548(0)
Bicknell, E. Territorial
acquisition...1899.   552(0)
Brown, D. M. Metlakahtla.
1907.   694(1)
Brown, J. W. Abridged hist.
Alaska. 1909.   696(0)
Brown, R.N.R. Polar regions
... 1927.   698(4)
Bruce, H.A. Romance of Amer.
expansion. 1909.   704(0)
Bruce, M.W. Alaska; history
... 1895.   705(0)
Bruet, E. L'Alaska; geog. ...
1945.   706(0)
Bruhl, G. Zwischen Alaska
und Feuerland.1896.   707(0)
Burnette, O. L. Soviet view
Amer. past. 1964.   737(0)
Burpee, L.J. On old Athabaska
Trail. 1926.   741(7)
Burpee, L.J. Search for wes-
tern sea. 1908.   742(0)
Cadwallader, C.L. Reminisc.
Iditarod Trail...n.d. 764(0)
Caldwell, H. W. Alaska and
Hawaii. 1900.   772(0)
Caldwell, J. B. Introducing
Alaska. 1947.   774(0)
Caldwell, J.B. What to expect
... 1945.   775(0)

HISTORY and Geography. (cont.)

Calvin, Jack. Sitka.
1936.   783(1)
Canada. Yukon Territory.
1938.
Canada. Yukon Territory,
history. 1909.   817(7)
Carpenter, F.G. Alaska;
northern...1923.   843(0)
Carpenter, F.G. North America
...reader. 1910.   844(0)
Caughey, J.W. Hist. Pacific
Coast. 1933.   872(0)
Caughey, J.W. Hubert Howe
Bancroft. 1946.   873(0)
Chaffin, Y.M. Koniag to king
crab. 1967.   879(6)
Clark, H.W. Alaska, last
frontier. n.d.   941(0)
Clowes, W.L. Royal Navy ...
1899-1903.   960(0)
Colquhoun, A.R. Greater Amer.
maps...1904.   994(0)
Cooke, C. Fascinating Alaska.
1947.   1059(0)
Cordova Daily Times. All-
Alaska...1928.   1076(2)
Cordova Daily Times. All-
Alaska ... 1930.   1077(2)
Corser, H.P. Seventy-six
page hist. 1927.   1088(0)
Cox, J. Our own country...
1913.   1102(0)
Cushman, Dan. Great North
Trail. 1966.   1147(0)
Dall, W. H. Alaska and its
resources. 1870.   1155(0)
Davis, M. L. Alaska, great
bear's cub. 1930.   1203(0)
Davis, M.L. Uncle Sam's attic.
... [c1930]   1205(0)
DeArmond, R.N. Founding of
Juneau. 1967.   1001(1)
DeArmond, R.N. Some names
around Juneau.1957.   1222(1)
Denison, B.W. Alaska today.
1949.   1264(0)
Dow, Peter. Alaska ...
1927.   1339(0)
Drake, M. Alaskana ...
1938.   1345(0)

Eggleston, E. Stories Amer.
life. 1895.   1423(0)
Elliott, H. W. Alaska og
Salorne ... 1888.   1436(0)
Elliott, H.W. Our Arctic
province. 1886.   1437(0)
Engstrom, E. John Engstrom.
[c1956]   1476(3)
Erskine, W. F. Katmai.
1962.   1489(6)
Facts on Alaska.
[1902?] . . . . . .1510(0)
Fairbanks Daily News-Miner.
Low-down truth.1923. 1520(0)
Farrar, V.J. Elementary sylla-
bus...hist.1924.   1530(0)
Fernald, K. Rubles to state-
hood. 1965.   1545(0)
Field, H.M. Our western archi-
pelago. 1895.   1552(0)
Fish, Byron. Alaska.
1965.   1566(0)
Fowler, F.S. Authentic Alaska
information.[1896?] 1620(0)
Frederick, R.A. Frontier
Alaska ... 1968.   1645(0)
Freuchen, Peter. Law of
Larion. 1925.   1658(0)
Freuchen, Peter. Legend Daniel
Williams. 1956.   1659(0)
Glanz, R. Jews in Amer.
Alaska...1953.   1736(0)
Godsell, P. H. Vanishing
frontier...1939.   1747(0)
Gorbatskiĭ, G.V. Priroda
zarubeghnoĭ...1951. 1778(0)
Greely, A.W. Handbook of
Alaska. 1909.   1840(0)
Greenhow, R. Geog. Oregon...
1845.   1849(0)
Greenhow, R. Memoir, history
...1840.   1850(0)
Greenhow, R. History Oregon
1840   1851(0)
Grewingk, C. Beitrag zur Kennt-
niss...1850.   1854(0)
Griffin, H. Alaska and Cana-
dian northwest.1944. 1858(0)
Grønlund, H. Pan hat med Jack
London. 1944.   1868(0)
Haas, W.H. American empire.
1940.   1887(0)

ALASKAN BIBLIOGRAPHY

HISTORY and Geography.(cont.)

Hallock, Chas. Our new Alaska.
1886. 1913(0)
Hallock, Chas. Peerless
Alaska. 1908. 1914(0)
Harriman Alaska Exped. vol. 2.
1910-14. 1950(0)
Harrison, E.S. Nome and Seward
Peninsula. 1905. 1970(5)
Hart, A. B. Obvious Orient ...
1911. 1973(0)
Heawood, E. A. Hist. geog.
discovery. 1912. 2013(0)
Heistand, H.O.S. Territory of
Alaska. 1898. 2021(0)
Henderson, L. D. Alaska ...
1928. 2039(0)
Henriques, J.A. Alaska, facts
... 1874. 2066(0)
Heye, A. Im Letzen Westen ...
1939. 2094(0)
Heye, A. Nyugat peremen ...
1940. 2095(0)
Higginson, E. R. Alaska, great
country...1908. 2103(0)
Hilscher, H. Alaska now.
1948. 2110(0)
Hilscher, H. Alaska U.S.A.
1959. 2111(0)
Hinton, A. C. The Yukon.
1947. 2122(7)
Howay, F.W. Presidential ad-
dress ... 1924. 2201(0)
Hulcatt, H. B.C., Alaska ...
1889. 2223(0)
Hulley, C.C. Alaska 1741-1953.
1953. 2224(0)
Hunt, H.E. Ketchikan, first
city...1909. 2235(1)
Jackson, S. Alaska and mis-
sions No. Pac. 1880. 2311(0)
Jackson, S. Facts about Alaska.
1894. 2312(0)
Johansen, D.O. Empire of
Columbia...1957. 2364(1)
Kane, T. L. Alaska and polar
regions. 1868. 2408(0)
Keithahn, E. L. Alaska for the
curious. 1966. 2428(0)
Kennedy, H.A. Book of the west.
1925. 2441(0)

Ketchikan, Citizens of. First
city...1916. 2452(1)
Kursh, H. This is Alaska.
1961. 2573(0)
Lantis, D. W. Alaska.
1957. 2605(0)
Laut, A. C. Pioneers Pacific
Coast. 1915. 2644(0)
Laut, A. C. Fur trade of Amer.
1921. 2645(0)
LeBourdais, D. M. Northward
new frontier. 1931. 2659(0)
Lewis & Dryden marine history.
1895. 2695(0)
Life in Alaska.
1914. . . . . 2704(0)
Lineberry, W. P. New states
... 1963. 2719(0)
London, Joan. Jack London and
times...1939. 2786(0)
McClellan, R.G. Golden states
... history. 1872. 2834(0)
McCracken, H. Roughnecks and
gentlemen. 1968. 2848(0)
McCurdy, H.W. ...marine hist.
Pac. 1966. 2859(0)
McCurdy, J.G. By Juan de
Fuca's Strait...1937. 2860(0)
Machowski, J. Alaska.
1965. [in Polish] 2909(0)
MacKay, D. Honourable Company.
1936. 2913(0)
McMillion. O.M. New Alaska
1939. 2937(0)
Mecking, L. Die Polarländer.
1925. 3066(4)
Melville, E. Fort Yukon ...
1949. 3074(3)
Moore, Terris. Alaska.
1962. 3165(0)
Morgan, J. Alaska and Hawaii.
1956. 3178(0)
Morice, A.G. Hist. no. in-
terior B.C. 1904. 3190(1)
Morton, A.S. Hist. Canadian
west ... 1939. 3205(0)
Nicols, J.P. Alaska ...
1924. 3303(0)
Nordenskiöld, N.O.G. Polar-
världen...1907. 3336(4)
Nordenskiöld, N.O.G. Die Polar-
welt...1909. 3337(4)

692

HISTORY and Geography. (cont.)

Nordenskiöld, N.O.G. Poliarnyĭ
  ... 1912.   3338(4)
Nordenskiöld, N.O.G. Geography
  Polar...1928.   3339(4)
Our country: West.
  1900.   3457(0)
Pacific Science Congress, 5th.
  Proceedings. 1934.   3457(0)
Pacific Science Congress, 9th.
  Abstracts...1957.   3459(0)
Pacific Science Congress, 9th.
  Proceedings...1958.   3460(0)
Pacific Science Congress, 10th.
  Abstracts...1961.   3461(0)
Pacific Science Congress, 10th.
  Proceedings. 1963.   3462(0)
Palmer Terr. School. History
  Matanuska Valley.1941.3482(2)
Pedersen, E. Alaska.
  1969.   3514(0)
Phillips, P.L. Alaska and
  n.w. ... 1970.   3572(0)
Phillips, R.A.J. Canada's
  north. 1967.   3573(0)
Pilgrim, M.A. Alaska, history
  resources...1939.   3589(0)
Place, M. T. The Yukon.
  1967.   3618(0)
Pomeroy, E.S. Pacific slope ...
  1965.   3636(0)
Potter, L. Study frontier town
  ...Wasilla. 1963.   3660(2)
Potter, L. Old times on Upper
  Cook's Inlet. 1967. 2662(2)
Prince, B. LeM. Alaska Railroad
  in pictures. 1964.   3694(0)
Prosser, W.T. Prospectus;
  Hist. Alaska...1912. 3700(0)
Puhr, C. Modern Alaska and
  Alcan. n.d.   3702(0)
Richman, I.B. Calif. under
  Spain...1911.   3807(0)
Riegel, R.E. America moves
  west. 1964.   3819(0)
Schafer, J. Pacific slope and
  Alaska. 1904.   3995(0)
Schanz, M. Ein zug nach Osten.
  1897.   3996(0)
Seattle Post-Intelligencer.
  Facts ... [1904?]   4036(0)

Shaw, E.B. Anglo-America,
  regional...1959.   4097(0)
Shiels, A.W. Seward's ice box.
  [c1933]   4118(0)
Skaguay Commercial Club.
  Skaguay ... 1898.   4164(1)
Skagway Commercial Club. Skag-
  way, Alaska. n.d.   4166(1)
Smith, J.R. North America...
  1942.   4199(0)
Smith, R.A. Frontier states...
  1968.   4204(0)
Snider, G. Centennial; 100
  stories...[c1966]   4220(0)
Spring, N. Alaska, pioneer
  state. 1967.   4268(0)
Stefansson, E. Here is Alaska.
  1943.   4299(0)
Stefansson, E. Within the
  circle...1945.   4300(0)
Stefansson, V. American far
  North. 1939.   4315(0)
Stefansson, V. Arctic in fact
  and fable. 1945.   4316(4)
Stefansson, V. Friendly North.
  1930.   4320(0)
Stephens, H.M. Pacific Ocean
  ... 1917.   4335(0)
Stephenson, W.B. Land of to-
  morrow. [c1919]   4338(0)
Stone, I. Sailor on horseback
  Jack London. 1938. 4353(0)
Stromstadt, D.M. Metlakahtla.
  1907.   4365(1)
Stromstadt, D.M. Sitka the
  beautiful. 1906.   4366(1)
Sushkov, B.A. Dal'nevostoch-
  nye moria...1958.   4404(0)
Swineford, A.P. Alaska, hist.
  ... [c1898]   4433(0)
Taylor, B.A. Alaska. last
  frontier. 1963.   4467(0)
Thomas, L. Book of high mtns.
  [c1964]   4495(0)
Thomas, Tay. Only in Alaska.
  1969.   4502(0)
Thomson, J.E. Our Pacific
  possessions. 1931. 4521(0)
Tompkins, S.R. Alaska, Promy-
  shlennik ... 1945.   4552(0)
Tyler, C.M. Island world of
  Pacific Ocean.1887. 4596(0)

HISTORY and Geography. (cont.)

Underwood, J.J. Alaska, em-
pire...1913.   4608(0)
Union Book & Pub. Co. Alaska &
Yukon Terr. [19__]   4610(0)
Weber, G.A. Coast and Geodetic
Survey...1923.   4765(0)
White, H.A. It's true about
Alaska. [ca1962?]   4821(0)
Wikstrom, R. Alaska oddities...
1958.   4867(0)
Williamson, T.R. Far North
country. [c1944]   4888(0)
Willoughby, B. Alaskans all.
1933.   4894(0)
Willoughby, B. Gentlemen una-
fraid. 1928.   4895(0)
Willoughby, B. Sitka ...
1930.   4898(1)
Willoughby, B. Sitka ...
n.d.   4899(1)
Wilson, K. Copper-tints. Cor-
dova sketches. 1923. 4913(2)
Winslow, I.O. Our American
neighbors. 1921.   4922(0)
Winther, O.O. Great northwest
... 1947.   4930(0)
Wood, J.P. Alaska. the great
land. 1967.   4952(0)
Woollen, W.W. Inside Passage
... 1924.   4960(0)
Wright, H. America across the
seas...1909.   4971(0)
Zahm, J.A. Alaska, country &
inhabitants. 1886.   5021(0)
Zimmermann,E.A.W. Taschenbuch
... [1809]   5032(0)

HISTORY - Russian America.

Alekseev, A. I. Okhotsk
... 1958.   168(0)
Andrews, C. L. Story of Sitka.
1922.   257(1)
Atherton, G. Rezanov.
1906.   314(1)
Baer, K.E. Statistische...
Wrangell...1839.   342(0)
Barrett-Hamilton, G.E.H.
Report...seal...1898. 406(6)
Beach, R. World in his arms.
1945.   450(0)

Blaschke, E.L. Topographia...
1842.   574(1)
Bodnarskiĭ, M.S. Ocherki po
istoriĭ...1947.   592(0)
Bolotov, I. Kratkoe opisanie...
1805.   601(6)
Cassin, J. Illus. birds ...
1856.   863(0)
Chevigny, H. Lord of Alaska.
1942.   909(0)
Chevigny, H. Lost empire...
1937.   910(0)
Chevigny, H. Russian America.
1965.   911(0)
Colyer, V. Bombardment Wrangel
... 1870.   995(1)
Convention between U.S. and
Japan...1868.   1007(0)
Coxe, W. Comparative view ...
Russ. disc. ... 1787.1105(0)
Coxe, W. Acct. Russ. disc.
... 1780.   1106(0)
Denis, F.J. Les Californies...
1849.   1263(0)
de Ybarra y Berge, J. De Cali-
fornia...1945.   1288(0)
Farrar, V.J. Annexation Russ.
Amer. ... 1937.   1531(0)
Farrar, V.J. Purchase of
Alaska. 1934.   1532(0)
Fonticelli, A. Americalogie
... 1790.   1593(0)
Freuchen, P. Law of Larion.
1952.   1658(0)
Golder, F.A. Guide ... Russ.
archives.1917.   1757(0)
[Golovnin, V.M.] Materialy
dlĭa ... 1861.   1763(0)
Grewingk, C. Beitrag zur
Kenntniss...1850.   1854(0)
Hassel, J.G.H. Vollstandigeu.
neueste...1822.   1985(0)
Henderson, D. From Volga to
Yukon. 1944.   2037(0)
Holmberg, H.J. Ethnog. Skiz-
zen ... 1855-63.   2157(0)
Jane, F.T. Imperial Russian
Navy. 1899.   2329(0)
Kaidanov, N. Sistemat.kat. ...
Vniesh. Tor. 1887.   2402(0)
Kaidanov, N. Sistemat.kat.Gos.
Kommerts-koll. 1884. 2403(0)

HISTORY - Russian America.
(cont.)
Karelin, D.B. Morîà nasheî...
1954.   2419(0)
Kashevaroff, A.P. Hist. disc.
Kodiak Isl. 1938.   2414(6)
Khlîëbnikov, K.T. Pervonalj-
noe...1833.   2454(0)
Khlîëbnikov, K.T. Zhizn.
Baranova. 1835.   2455(0)
Kittlitz, F.H. Denkwürdig-
keiten...1858.   2478(0)
Kostlivt͡sov, S. Viedomostj...
1860.   2513(0)
Krasheninnikov, S.P. Opisanie
...Kamchatki...1755. 2531(0)
Krasheninnikov, S.P. History
Kamtschatka...1764.   2532(0)
Krasheninnikov, S.P. Opisanie
...sotschin....1766. 2533(0)
Krasheninnikov, S.P. Histoire
...Kamtschatka.1770. 2535(0)
Krasheninnikov, S.P. Aardryks-
kundige...1770.   2536(0)
Lantzeff, G.V. Siberia ...
1943.   2608(0)
Latham, R.G. Native races...
1854.   2634(0)
Launay de Valery, C. Tableau...
1806.   2641(0)
Ledebour, K.F. Flora Rossica
...1841-53.   2662(0)
Lensen, G.A. Russia's east-
ward expansion. 1964. 2677(0)
Lepotier, A.A.M. Les Russes
Amérique. 1958.   2683(0)
Lessner, E. Cradle of conquer-
ors; Siberia. 1955. 2689(0)
Levchenko, G.I. Morskoi atlas.
Tom. 3. 1959.   2694(0)
Lisîanskiî, I.F. Puteshestvie
vokrug...1812.   2723(0)
Magidovich, I.P. Istoriîà ...
1962.   2953(0)
Manning, C.A. Russian influ-
ence ... 1953.   2960(0)
Markov, A. Krushenie korablie
Nevy ... 1850.   2972(1)
Markov, A. Russkie na Vostoch-
nom Okeanie. 1849.   2973(0)
Markov, S. Letopis' Alîaski.
1948.   2974(0)

Mezhov, V.I. Sibirskaîà
bibliog. ...1891-92. 3096(0)
Middendorff, W. Ueber Tlinkit
Russ. Amer. 1861.   3098(1)
Okun', S.B. Ross.-Amer. Komp.
1939.   3397(0)
Okun', S.B. Russ.-Amer. Co.
1951.   3398(0)
Pekarskiî, P.P. Istoriîà Im-
peratorskoî...1870. 3529(0)
Pierce, R.A. Alaska in 1867.
[1967]   3581(0)
Pierce, R.A. Prince D.P. Mak-
sutov...[1967]   3582(0)
Pilder, H. Die Russ.-Amer.
komp. ... 1914.   3588(0)
Pinart, A.L. Catalogue col-
lections...1872.   3593(0)
Politovskiî, V.G. Kratkoî...
1861.   3627(0)
Poniatowski, M. Hist. de la
Russie...1958.   3639(0)
Priklonskiî, V.L. Lîëtopis'
Îakutskago...1896.   3693(0)
Pustinskiî, I. Otchet...Alîas-
kanskago...1906.   3704(0)
Razin, A. Otkrytie Ameriki.
1860.   3760(6)
Rîàbov, N.I. Ocherki istoriĭ
... 1958.   3800(0)
Ross.-Amer. Koloniĭ. Otchet
...1863.   3888(0)
Ross.-Amer. Koloniĭ. Priloz-
heniîà...1863.   3889(0)
Ross.-Amer. Komp. K istoriĭ
...1957.   3890(0)
Ross.-Amer. Komp. Otchet
... 1853.   3891(0)
S., J.L. Neue nachrichten...
1776.   3993(0)
Sachot, O.L.M. La Siberie
...1875.   3937(0)
Schérer, J.-B. Recherches Hist.
et Geog. [177]   4000(0)
Schlözer, A.L. Neue Erdbeschreibung...1777.   4003(0)
Shashkov, S.S. Istoricheskie
... 1872.   4095(0)
Shelekhov, G.I. Ross. kupt͡sa
... 1791.   4102(6)
Shiels, A.W. Early voyages...
1931.   4116(0)

HISTORY - Russian America.
                    (cont.)
Shiels, A.W. Little journeys
    ...[c1949]   4117(0)
Syndicat Français du Trans-
    Alaska-Sibirien. Le Chemin
    ...[1902?]   4436(0)
Taylor, R.C. Statistic of coal
    geog. ... 1848.   4472(0)
Tikhmenev, P.A. Istoricheskoe
    ... 1861.   4536(0)
Tikhmenev, P.A. Hist. review
    ... 1839-40.   4537(0)
Tomashevskiĭ, V.V. Materialy
    ...bibliog. 1957.   4549(0)
U.S.S.R. Komitet...R.A.Koloniĭ.
    Doklad. 1863-64.   4619(0)
Venegas, M. Noticia de la
    Calif. ... [1757]   4669(0)
Veselev, F.F. Razbor vtoroi
    ...1864.   4693(0)
Vishnevskiĭ, B.N. Putesh.
    K. Khlebnikov. 1957. 4706(0)
Yarmolinsky, A. Aleut. ms. col-
    lections. 1944.   4988(6)
Yarmolinsky, A. Kamchadal ...
    ms. collections.1947. 4989(0)
[Zavalishin, D.I.] Ross.-Amer.
    Komp. 1865.   5023(0)

HOLIDAYS.

Alaska-Yukon-Pac. Exposition.
    Proceedings...1909.   155(0)
Best, Eva. Alaska Christmas
    candles. n.d.   550(8)
Burgess, Thornton W. Christmas
    reindeer. 1926.   731(0)
Corser, H.P. Mere man ...
    Kemper's Christmas.
    1915.   1087(0)
Crawford, J.W. Souvenir ...
    New Year. 1898.   1116(0)
Dunn, Robert. Santa Claus on
    beach. 1914.   1388(0)
Fairbanks Fourth of July Cele-
    bration...1909.   1521(3)
Kent, Rockwell. Northern
    Christmas. 1941.   2443(2)
Rovier, V. Pioneer Pete's
    Christmas. 1963.   3903(5)

HOMECRAFTS.

Brown, A.M. How to know and
    select furs. 1966.   693(0)
Gelvin, E.C. How to build...
    dog sled. [ca1968]   1695(0)
Tapp, G. Alaskan designs
    crafts. no. 1. n.d.   4454(0)
Tapp, G. Alaskan designs
    crafts. no. 2. n.d.   4455(0)
Tapp, G. Alaskan mukluks ...
    n. d.   4456(0)

HUMOR.

Bowen, R.O. Alaskan
    dictionary. 1965.   629(0)
Couzens, F.S. Sayings Dr.
    Bushwacker...1867.   1098(0)
Emmons, L.A. Prophetic...Tro-
    jan Soc. ... 1870.   1464(0)
Fisher, P. Alaska wild game
    cook book. 1961.   1571(0)
Gaines, R. Chilkoot Charlie.
    1951.   1671(0)
Gaines, R. Mrs. Maloney.
    1955.   1672(0)
Gaines, R. Second book Chil-
    koot Charlie. 1955.   1673(0)
Hilton, Bud. ...book of nursery
    rhymes. n.d.   2112(0)
House, B. Friendly feudin' ...
    Texas. 1959.   2194(0)
James, S. Taming Arctic shrew.
    1963.   2328(4)
Kelsey, C. Complete...how to
    be pioneer. 1961.   2434(1)
Kosmos, G. Alaska sourdough
    stories. 1956.   2511(0)
PEO Sisterhood. What! No ig-
    loos? [c1954]   3534(3)
Rossiter, H. Alaska calling.
    [c1954]   3892(0)
Sourdough Jack. Sourdough Jack
    sez. [c1954]   4243(3)
Stimple, Bert. Fun on farm
    in Alaska. 1962.   4346(3)
Wikstrom, R. Alaska oddities.
    1958.   4867(0)
Wirt, Sherwood. Cracked ice.
    [c1937]   4932(0)

HUNTING and Sport Fishing.

Alaska hunting and fishing
  guide. 1960.   70(0)
Alaska Range Guides Assoc.
  Shoot 'em...[19__]   106(0)
Alaska Steamship Co. Sportsman
  guide...[ca1952]   123(0)
Annabel, Russell. Alaskan
  tales. 1953.   266(0)
Annabel, Russell. Hunting and
  fishing...1948.   267(0)
Annabel, Russell. Tales big
  game guide. 1938.   268(0)
Armstrong, N.A.D. After big
  game upper Yukon.1937. 305(0)
Auer, H.A. Campfires in
  Yukon. 1916.   322(7)
Baillie-Grohman, W.A. 15 yrs.
  sport...1900.   352(0)
Beach, R. Oh shoot!...sports-
  man. 1921.   439(2)
Berg, Ben. Guide...hunting
  grounds. [ca1962]   511(0)
Bergen, H. Jagdfahrten ...
  1928.   517(0)
Berger, Andre. Dans les Neiges
  ... 1930.   519(0)
Boone & Crockett Club. Amer.
  big game...1904.   608(0)
Boone & Crockett Club. Amer.
  mammals & birds.1930. 609(0)
Boone & Crockett Club. Hunting
  conservation. 1925. 610(0)
Boone & Crockett Club. Hunting
  high altitudes.1913. 611(0)
Boone & Crockett Club. N. A.
  big game. 1939.   612(0)
Boone & Crockett Club. Records
  N.A. big game. 1932. 613(0)
Boone & Crockett Club. Records
  N.A. big game. 1952. 614(0)
Boone & Crockett Club. Records
  N.A. big game. 1958. 615(0)
Boone & Crockett Club. Records
  N.A. big game. 1964. 616(0)
Bovet, L.A. Moose hunting in
  Alaska. 1933.   626(0)
Bradner, E. Northwest angling.
  1950.   639(0)
Cane, C.R.J. Summer and fall
  ...Cook's Inlet.1903. 824(2)

Carpenter, R.R.M. Game trails
  ... 1938.   846(1)
Carpenter, R.R.M. Game trails
  ... 1940.   847(3)
Coffey, L. Wild of Alaska big-
  game...1963.   971(0)
Cordier, A.H. Some big game
  hunts...1911.   1075(0)
Eddy, J.W. Hunting on Kenai
  Peninsula. 1924.   1406(2)
Eddy, J.W. Hunting Alaska
  brown bear...1930. 1407(2)
Endicott, W. Adventures...
  trail...1928.   1466(0)
Finton, W.L. Alaskan bear ad-
  ventures. 1937.   1563(6)
Fleischman, M.C. After big
  game ... 1909.   1576(0)
Frede, P. Aventures lointaines
  ...Sitka. 1882.   1644(1)
Harris, Walter. Salmon fishing
  ... Alaska. 1967.   1963(0)
Harrison, E.S. ...sports-
  man's paradise. 1909.1969(0)
Helmericks, C. Hunting in
  N. A. 1956.   2026(0)
Hibben, F.C. Hunting American
  bears. 1945.   2100(1)
Holman, J.P. Sheep and bear
  trails...1933.   2156(0)
Holmes, W.D. Square in Arctic
  Circle. 1960.   2162(4)
Howard, H.W. Sport fishing
  ...salmon...1954.   2198(0)
Hubback, T.R. 10,000 miles
  moose & sheep.1921. 2211(0)
Hubback, T. R. To far western
  Alaska big game.1929.2212(0)
Hutchinson, H.G. Big game
  shooting. 1905.   2244(0)
Ketchikan Chamb. Comm. King
  salmon derby. 1952. 2451(1)
Lawrence, E.A. Clover Passage.
  1954.   2649(1)
Martindale, T. Hunting in Up-
  per Yukon. 1913.   3011(1)
Meisner, H.O. Bezanbernde
  ... 1963.   3070(0)
Mott, S.M. Fishing and hunting
  ... 1905.   3209(1)
Olson, B.G. Blood on Arctic
  snow. 1956.   3406(0)

HUNTING and Sport Fishing.
                              (cont.)
Ormond, Clyde. Bear!
   1961.   3419(0)
Palmer, J.F. Kodiak bear hunt.
   1958.   3481(6)
Queeny, E.M. Cheechako...bear
   hunt. 1941.   3708(0)
Radcliffe, C.R.E. Big game
   shooting...1904.   3721(0)
Rosenberg, F. Big game shooting
   ... 1928.   3883(0)
Rosenberg, F. Storvildtjagt...
   1926.   3884(8)
Schwatka, F. Nimrod in North
   ... 1885.   4021(0)
Scull, E.M. Hunting in Arctic.
   1914.   4030(0)
Seton-Karr, H.W. Bear-hunting
   White Mtns. 1891.   4067(3)
Studley, J.T. Journal sporting
   nomad. 1912.   4374(0)
Széchényi, Z. Alaszkában ...
   1959.   4440(0)
Széchényi, Z. Alaszkában ...
   1957.   4441(0)
Thomas, W.S. Trails and
   tramps...1913.   4503(0)
Trefzger, H. My 50 yrs. hunting
   fishing...[c1963]   4575(1)
Turner-Turner, J. 3 yrs. hunt-
   ing & trapping.1888.   4591(0)
Whelen, T. Hunting big game...
   vol. 2. 1946.   4809(0)
Woodworth, J. Kodiak bear ...
   1959.   4959(6)
Wurmbrand, D. Herrn der Wildnis
   ... [1936]   4977(0)
Young, G.O. Alaskan trophies
   won and lost. [c1928] 4992(2)
Young, G.O. Alaska-Yukon trophies...1947.   4993(2)

JOURNALS, Diaries, Letters.

Akif'ev, I.N. Na dalekiĭ
   ... 1902.   26(5)
Atwood, G.H. Along the
   Alcan. 1960.   320(0)
Austin, Basil. Diary ninety-
   eighter. 1968.   325(2)
Baines, T. Northern goldfield
   diaries. 1965.   353(0)

Banow, E.M. Diary of ...
   1948.   387(7)
Berkh, V.N. Pervoe morskoe
   ... 1823.   531(6)
Briggs, H. Letters from
   Alaska...1889.   658(0)
Broke, H.G. With sack and
   stock ... 1891.   678(1)
Bush, R.J. Reindeer, dogs...
   1871.   754(5)
Campbell, R. Two journals
   ... 1958.   795(0)
Chkalov, V.P. Shturmanskiĭ
   ... [1939?]   922(0)
Chkalov, V.P. Navigator's log
   book ... 1939.   923(0)
Clifton, V. Book of Talbot.
   1933.   959(0)
Collinson, R. Journal Enter-
   prise ... 1889.   986(4)
Colnett, J. Journal ...
   Argonaut ... 1940.   989(0)
[Cook, J.] Journal ...
   1781.   1014(2)
[Cook, J.] Tagebuch ...
   1781.   1015(2)
Crewe, F. Log sloop "North"
   ... 1896.   1121(2)
Curtin, W.R. Yukon voyage...
   1938.   1142(0)
Davis, M.L. Sourdough gold...
   1933.   1204(7)
Dunn, R. Shameless diary...
   explorer. 1907.   1389(2)
Emmons, G.T. Emmons journal.
   n. d.   1461(0)
Euryalus...diary midshipman.
   1860.   1499(0)
Evans, R.D. Sailor's log.
   1902.   1503(6)
Flood, Milford. Arctic journal
   ... 1950.   1585(4)
Golder, F.A. Bering's voyages.
   1922.   1755(6)
Green, J.S. Journal tour...
   1915.   1846(1)
Grinnell, J. Gold hunting in
   Alaska. 1901.   1866(0)
Henley, G.F. Guide ... diary
   Seghers. 1898.   2064(7)
Hooker, W.J. ...memoir David
   Douglas.[ca1837]   2171(1)

JOURNALS, Diaries, Letters.
                              (cont.)
Hrdlička, A. Alaska diary.
    1943.   2207(0)
Hulswitt, I. Tagebuch einer
    Reisen...1828.   2226(0)
Jaggar, T.A. Journal of Tech-
    nology Exped. 1908.   2320(6)
Jewitt, J.R. Journal ... at
    Nootka Sd. 1807.   2353(1)
Johnshoy, W. Apaurak in
    Alaska. 1944.   2367(5)
Kashevarov, A.F. Otryvki ...
    R.A. Komp. 1845.   2416(0)
Kent, Rockwell. Wilderness...
    1920.   2445(2)
Lloyd, C.C. Voyages Capt.
    J. Cook. 1949.   2741(2)
Manwaring, G.E. My friend...
    Jas. Burney...1931.   2963(2)
Marine Research Soc. Sea, ship
    ... 1925.   2968(0)
Marshall, R. Arctic wilderness.
    1956.   2998(4)
Marshall, R. Doonerak or bust
    letter...[1938?]   2999(4)
Marshall, R. North Doonerak...
    letter...n.d.   3000(4)
Maurelle, F.A. Journal of
    voyage...1781.   3036(1)
Maurelle, F.A. Tagebuch...
    1782.   3475(1)
Meany, E.S. New Vancouver
    journal...1915.   3050(2)
Medill, R.B. Klondike diary...
    1949.   3067(7)
Merk, F. Fur trade...Simpson
    journal. 1931.   3085(1)
Midshipman's diary...
    1862.   1500(0)
Miertsching, J.A. Journal
    de ... 1857.   3101(0)
Miertsching, J.A. Reise-tage-
    buch...1855.   3102(0)
Moore, J.B. Skagway in days
    primeval. 1968.   3162(1)
Munford, J.K. John Ledyard's
    journal. [c1963]   3238(2)
Munger, J.F. 2 yrs. Pac. and
    Arctic O. ...1852.   3239(0)
Murray, A.H. Journal of
    Yukon. 1848.   3256(7)

Newcomb, R.L. Our lost ex-
    plorers. 1882.   3295(0)
Nordenskiöld, N.A.E. Lettres
    ... 1880.   3323(4)
Page, E.M. Wild horses and
    gold...[c1932]   3469(7)
Paillard, L. Un Lyonnaise
    ... 1900.   3471(7)
Pierce, E.L. ...letters C.
    Sumner. 1877-93.   3579(0)
Price, A.G. Explor. Cook...
    journals. 1957.   3688(2)
Richards, E.A.L. Arctic mood.
    1949.   3802(4)
Ridley, W. Snapshots No. Pac.
    ...letters.1903.   3817(1)
Seton-Karr, H. W. Shores &
    alps ... 1887.   4068(2)
Shalamov, T. Po Missii...
    1904.   4084(6)
Shalamov, T. Ocherk...zhurnala
    ...1904.   4085(6)
Shelekhov, G.I. Voyage of...
    from journal. n.d.   4105(6)
Shemelin, F. Zhurnal ...
    1816[1818]   4108(0)
Stefansson, V. Adventure Wran-
    gel Isl. 1925.   4314(5)
Steller, G.W. Tagebuch seiner
    Seereise. 1793.   4334(6)
Studley, J.T. Journal sporting
    nomad...1912.   4374(0)
[Vancouver, G.] Narrat. or
    journal...1802.   4643(2)
Vaugondy, D.R. Lettre de
    ... [1768]   4660(0)
Viana, F.J. Diario del viage
    ...1849.   4696(1)
Wagner, H.R. Journal Tomás de
    Suria...1936.   4724(1)
Walker, R.J. Letter R.J.
    Walker ... 1868.   4732(0)
Watson, W.W. Our Alaskan trip
    ...letter. 1910.   4757(1)
[Webb, F.?]Letters lately pub
    lished ... 1790.   4762(1)
West, E.L. Captain's papers.
    1965.   4798(0)
Willard, C.M.W. Life in Alaska
    letters...1884.   4875(1)
Williams, H. One whaling
    family. 1964.   4879(4)

JOURNALS, Diaries, Letters.
                              (cont.)
Winslow, K. Big pan-out ...
    [c1951]   4924(7)
Wolfe, L.M. John of Mountains.
    1938.   4941(0)
Woodman, A.J. Picturesque
    Alaska. 1889.   4957(1)
Woollen, W.W. Inside Passage.
    1924.   4960(0)

JUVENILE - Fiction.

Adams, Andy. Alaska ghost
    mystery. [c1961]   8(8)
Agnew, E.J. Leo of Alaska.
    1958.   16(8)
Akers, F. Boy fortune hunters
    in Alaska. [1908]   25(8)
Allen, T.D. Prisoners polar
    ice. 1959.   184(4)
Allen, W.B. Gold hunters of
    Alaska. 1889.   185(7)
Allen, W.B. Gulf and glacier
    ... 1892.   186(1)
Allen, W.B. Red mtn. of
    Alaska. 1889.   187(7)
Appel, B. We were there in
    Klondike...1956.   273(7)
Barlow, R. Secret mission to
    Alaska. 1959.   400(0)
Beaty, J.Y. Sharp ears;
    baby whale. 1938.   457(0)
Beim, L. Little igloo.
    1941.   472(4)
Bell, M.E. Danger on Old
    Baldy. 1944.   481(1)
Bell, M.E. Daughter of Wolf
    House. 1957.   482(1)
Bell, M.E. Enemies in Icy
    Strait. 1945.   483(1)
Bell, M.E. Love is forever.
    1954.   484(1)
Bell, M.E. Ride out the storm.
    1951.   485(1)
Bell, M.E. Pirates Icy Strait.
    1943.   486(1)
Bell, M.E. Totem casts
    shadow. 1949.   487(1)
Bell, M.E. Watch for tall
    white sail. 1948.   489(1)
Benton, Bell. ABC for Alaska.
    1967.   509(0)

Blackerby, A.W. Tale of Alaska
    whale. 1955.   572(1)
Bowen, R.S. Red Randall in
    Aleutians. 1945.   630(6)
Bowen, V. Lazy beaver.
    1948.   631(0)
Breckenridge, G. Radio Boys
    rescue...[1922?]   649(0)
Bryant, C.K. Terry Twins in
    Alaska. 1957.   708(0)
Bryant, C.K. Terry Twins ...
    find treasure.1961.   709(0)
Bunn, I.F. Growing up in
    Alaska. 1965.   727(5)
Burgess, T.W. Christmas
    reindeer. 1926.   731(4)
Burglon, N. Lost Island.
    1939.   732(0)
Burrows, E. Irene of Tundra
    Towers. 1928.   747(1)
Burrows, E. Judy of Whale
    Gate. 1930.   748(0)
Byrd, E.N. Black wolf of
    Black River. 1959.   762(7)
Byrd, E.N. Ice King.
    1965.   763(4)
Caldwell, F. Wolf the storm
    leader. 1929.   771(0)
Carpenter, F. Our little
    friends Eskimo...1931.842(4)
Catherall, A. Arctic sealer.
    1960.   868(4)
Catherall, A. Lone seal pup.
    1965.   869(4)
Cawston, V. Matuk, Eskimo
    boy. 1965.   875(0)
Chaffee, Allen. Sitka, snow
    baby. 1923.   878(0)
Chipperfield, J.E. Boru, dog
    of O'Malley. 1966.   916(0)
Clarke, T.E. Alaska challenge.
    1959.   945(0)
Clarke, T.E. Back to Anchorage.
    1961.   946(2)
Clarke, T.E. No furs for
    Czar. 1962.   947(0)
Clarke, T.E. Puddle jumper...
    flyer...1960.   948(2)
Comfort, M.H. Peter and Nancy
    U.S. & Alaska. 1940.   996(0)
Cook, J.J. Killer whale!
    1963.   1056(5)

JUVENILE - Fiction.   (cont.)

Cook, J.J.   Warrior whale.
  1966.   1057(5)
Coryell, H.V.   Klondike gold.
  1938.   1093(7)
Craig, Jas.   On Yukon Trail.
  [c1922]   1109(7)
Creekmore, R.   Lokoshi learns
  to hunt seals. 1946.   1117(4)
Darling, E.B.   Baldy of Nome.
  1912.   1175(5)
Darling, E.B. Boris, grandson
  of Baldy. 1936.   1176(5)
Darling, E.B.   Luck of the
  trail. 1933.   1178(5)
Darling, E.B. Navarre of
  North. 1930.   1179(5)
Darling, E.B. No boundary
  line. 1942.   1180(5)
Darling, E.B.   The break-up.
  1928.   1181(5)
Davis, P.E.   Anchorage fun
  book. 1967.   1207(2)
Denison, M.   Susannah, little
  girl...Mounties.1961. 1266(7)
Denison, M. Susannah of Moun-
  ties. 1959.   1267(7)
Denison, M. Susannah of Yukon.
  1937.   1268(7)
Denison, M. Susannah rides
  again. 1941.   1269(7)
Desmond, A.C.   Sea cats.
  1944.   1279(6)
Desmond, A.C.   Talking tree.
  1949.   1280(1)
Diven, R.J.   Rowdy.
  1927. . . . . 1299(0)
Dixon, F.W. Mystery at Devil's
  Paw. 1959.   1304(8)
Dixon, F.W. Through air to
  Alaska. 1930.   1305(0)
Dolch, E.W. Stories from
  Alaska. 1961.   1327(0)
Douglas, R.D. Boy scout in
  grizzly country.1929. 1336(2)
Emerson, A.B. Ruth Fielding
  in Alaska. 1926.   1450(0)
Emery, R.G. Adventure North.
  1947.   1455(0)
Erskine, W.F. Trap pirate in
  Alaska. 1964.   1490(6)

Finney, G.B. To survive we
  must be clever.1966. 1560(6)
Foster, W.B. In Alaskan waters.
  1903.   1617(0)
Frankel, H. Adventure in
  Alaska. 1963.   1631(0)
George, J.C. Moon of grey
  wolves. 1969.   1696(0)
Gilbert, K. Arctic venture.
  1950.   1714(4)
Golden Press. Eskimos...punch-
  out figures...1962.   1753(0)
Grainger, G. Little Flip ...
  fur seal. 1960.   1795(6)
Harris, C. Raven's cry.
  1966.   1960(1)
Hawkes, C. Silversheene, king
  sled dogs. 1924.   1992(4)
Hayes, F.S. Alaskan hunter.
  1959.   2001(0)
Hayes, F.S. Eskimo hunter.
  1945.   2003(4)
Helmericks, H. Arctic bush
  pilot. 1956.   2032(0)
Helmericks, H. Arctic hunter.
  1955.   2033(4)
Helmericks, H. Oolak's
  brother. 1953.   2034(4)
Hendryx, J.B. Connie Morgan
  hits trail. 1929.   2044(0)
Hendryx, J.B. Connie Morgan in
  Alaska. 1916.   2045(0)
Hendryx, J.B. Connie Morgan in
  Arctic. 1936.   2046(4)
Hendryx, J.B. Connie Morgan in
  fur country. 1921.   2047(0)
Herron, E.A. Big country.
  1953.   2083(0)
Hoff, Syd. Ogluk the Eskimo.
  1960.   2135(4)
Hoff, Syd. Sammy the seal.
  1959.   2136(6)
Hogan, Inez. Bear twins.
  1935.   2141(0)
Hogan, Inez. Twin seals.
  1940.   2142(0)
Hoke, H. Alaska Alaska Alaska.
  1960.   2144(0)
Holling, H.C. Pagoo.
  1957.   2154(1)
Holzworth, J.M. Woof ... bear
  chaser. 1938.   2166(1)

JUVENILE - Fiction.   (cont.)

Hopkins, M. The three visitors.
    1967.   2179(0)
Hough, E.   Young Alaskans.
    1908.   2189(0)
Hough, E. Young Alaskans in
    Rockies. 1913.   2190(0)
Hough, E. Young Alaskans on
    Missouri. 1922.   2191(0)
Hough, E. Young Alaskans on
    trail. 1911.   2192(0)
Hough, E. Young Alaskans in
    far North. 1918.   2193(0)
Hunt, L.J. Curse of killer
    whale. 1963.   2236(0)
Hunt, L.J. Secret of
    haunted crags. 1965.   2237(0)
Irwin, V.M.   Shaman's
    revenge. 1925.   2300(4)
James, J. Assignment in
    Alaska. 1961.   2327(1)
John, Betty. Seloe, story of
    fur seal. 1955.   2365(6)
Kickbush, J. ...Eskimo village
    coloring bk. 1959.   2457(5)
Kilbourne, C.E. Army boy in
    Alaska. 1915.   2458(0)
Krott, P.   Demon of North.
    1959.   2545(0)
Landru, Jack. Sled dog of
    Alaska. 1953.   2591(3)
Lange, Ann.   Eskimo store.
    1948.   2596(0)
Lathrop, W.   Dogsled danger.
    1956.   2637(0)
Lathrop, W. Jet, sled dog of
    North. 1938.   2638(0)
Lathrop, W. Juneau, sleigh
    dog. 1942.   2639(1)
Lathrop, W. Northern Trail ad-
    venture. 1944.   2640(0)
Les Tina, D. Alaska; book to
    begin on. 1962.   2690(0)
Les Tina, D. Icicles on roof.
    1961.   2691(0)
L'Hommedieu, D.K. Togo, little
    husky. 1951.   2699(5)
Lide, A.A. Ood-le-uk wanderer.
    1930.   2703(0)
Lindquist, W. Call of white
    fox. 1957.   2715(0)

Lipkind, Wm. Boy with harpoon.
    1952.   2721(5)
Litten, F.N. Air trails
    north. 1939.   2736(0)
Litten, F.N. Pilot of north
    country...1938.   2737(0)
Lomen, H. Taktuk, Arctic
    boy. 1928.   2751(4)
McBride, J.L. Golden glacier.
    1932.   2829(0)
McBride, J.L. Smoky Valley
    claim. 1948.   2830(2)
McCracken, H. Pirate of North.
    1953.   2847(3)
McCracken, H. Sentinel of snow
    peaks. 1945.   2849(1)
McCracken, H. Son of walrus
    king. 1944.   2850(5)
McCracken, H. The flaming
    bear. 1951.   2854(6)
McCracken, H. Last of sea
    otters. 1942.   2855(6)
McDonald, L. Bering's potlatch.
    1944.   2865(1)
MacGregor, E. Miss Pickerell
    goes to Arctic.1954. 2897(4)
Machetanz, F. On Arctic ice.
    [c1940]   2900(5)
Machetanz, F. Panuck, Eskimo
    sled dog. [c1939]   2901(5)
Machetanz, F. A puppy named
    Gih. 1957.   2902(5)
Machetanz, F. Barney hits
    trail. 1950.   2903(5)
Machetanz, S. Rick of High
    Ridge. 1952.   2904(2)
Machetanz, S. Robbie and sled
    dog race. 1964.   2905(5)
Machetanz, S. Seegoo, dog of
    Alaska. 1961.   2906(5)
Machetanz, S. Howl of male-
    mute. 1961.   2907(5)
MacLeod, E.J. Alaska star.
    1957.   2932(0)
Mallette, G.E. Chee-chá-ko.
    1938.   2957(0)
Marsh, R. S. Kang.
    1962. . . . . .2977(0)
Marsh, R. A. Moog.
    1958. . . . . .2978(0)
Marshall, E. Ocean gold.
    1925.   2980(0)

JUVENILE - Fiction.   (cont.)

Martin, F. Nine tales of
    Raven. 1951.   3003(1)
Melzack, R. Day Tuk became
    hunter. 1967.   3076(4)
Meyer, A.E. Wassara and his
    tale ... 1962.   3092(0)
Miller, B.W. Ken in Alaska.
    1944.   3116(0)
Miller, B.W. Koko and Eskimo
    doctor. 1949.   3117(0)
Miller, B.W. Koko - king of
    Arctic Trail.1947.   3118(4)
Miller, B.W. Koko on Yukon.
    1954.   3119(7)
Montgomery, Richard Gill.
    Husky. 1942.   3157(0)
Montgomery, Rutherford G.
    Amikuk. 1955.   3159(6)
Montgomery, Rutherford G. Ice-
    blink. 1941.   3160(4)
Montgomery, Rutherford G. See-
    catch...furseal.1955. 3161(6)
Morey, Walt.   Gentle Ben.
    1965.   3173(1)
Morey, Walt.   Gloomy Gus.
    1970.   3174(6)
Morey, Walt. Home is North.
    1967.   3175(1)
Morey, Walt. Kăvik wolf dog.
    1968.   3176(0)
Morgan, Len. Klondike adven-
    ture. 1940.   3180(7)
Mount McKinley Nat. Hist.Assoc.
    ...book to color...
    1968.   3210(2)
Munroe, K. Snow-shoes and
    sledges...1895.   3244(0)
Munroe, K. Fur-seal's tooth
    ... 1894.   3245(0)
Murphy, R. Warmhearted polar
    bear. 1957.   3255(4)
Murray, G.H. Mystery talking
    totem pole. 1965.   3257(1)
Neelands, B.S. Coming of
    reindeer. 1966.   3282(0)
Northrup, T. Phantom code.
    1937.   3356(0)
O'Dell, Scott. Island Blue
    Dolphins. 1960.   3380(0)
Oliver, E.R. Aleutian boy.
    1959.   3402(7)

Parish, P. Ootah's lucky day.
    1970.   3492(4)
Patchin, F. Pony Rider Boys
    in Alaska. 1924.   3501(1)
Pedersen, E. Alaska harvest.
    1961.   3515(1)
Pedersen, E. Cook Inlet deci-
    sion. 1963.   3516(2)
Pedersen, E. Dangerous flight.
    1960.   3517(2)
Pedersen, E. Fisherman's
    choice. 1964.   3518(1)
Pedersen, E. House upon a
    rock. 1968.   3519(1)
Pedersen, E. Mystery of Malina
    Straits. 1963.   3520(1)
Pedersen, E. Petticoat fisher-
    man. 1969.   3521(1)
Pedersen, E. Mountain of gold
    mystery. 1964.   3522(1)
Pedersen, E. Mountain of the
    sun. 1962.   3523(1)
Pedersen, E. Mystery of *Alaska
    Queen*. 1969.   3524(2)
Pedersen, E. Victory at Bear
    Cove. 1959.   3525(2)
Pinkerton, K.S.(G.) Hidden
    Harbor. 1951.   3604(1)
Pinkerton, K.S.(G.) Second
    meeting. 1956.   3603(1)
Pinkerton, K.S.(G.) Steer
    North. 1962.   3606(0)
Pinkerton, K.S.(G.) Tomorrow
    Island. 1960.   3608(1)
Pinkerton, K.S.(G.) Year of
    enchantment.1957.   3609(1)
Poole, L. Danger! Iceberg
    ahead! [c1961]   3640(4)
Prentice, H. Boy Explorers...
    in Alaska. 1895.   3676(0)
Radau, H. Little Fox ...
    trapper. 1963.   3718(0)
Radau, H. Last Chief ...
    trapper. 1962.   3719(0)
Rossiter, H. Twins' birthday
    surprise. 1954.   3894(2)
Roulet, M.F. Our little Alas-
    kan cousin. 1907.   3900(0)
Roy, L. E. Polly in Alaska.
    [c1926]   3906(0)
Sabin, E.L. Klondike partners.
    1929.   3935(7)

JUVENILE - Fiction.   (cont.)

Savage, A.H. Holiday in
  Alaska. 1944.   3982(1)
Savage, A.H. Kulik's first
  seal hunt. [cl948]   3983(5)
Sayler, H.L. Airship Boys due
  North...[cl910]   3988(4)
Schwartzkopf, K.-A. Alaska
  pilot. [cl956]   4017(0)
Shannon, T. Dog team for
  Ongluk. 1962.   4087(5)
Shannon, T. Kidlik's kayak.
  1959.   4088(5)
Shannon, T. Tyee's totem pole.
  1955.   4090(1)
Shiels, A.W. "Tell me a
  'stowry'" n.d.   4119(1)
Shortall, L. Eric in Alaska.
  1967.   4133(0)
Shurtleff, B. Colt Alcan Rd.
  1951.   4139(0)
Shurtleff, B. Escape from ice
  cap. 1952.   4140(4)
Shurtleff, B. Long lash.
  1947.   4141(5)
Shurtleff, B. Two against
  North. 1949.   4142(5)
Smith, L.R. Little Eskimo.
  1931.   4200(4)
Snell, R.J. Eskimo Robinson
  Crusoe. 1917.   4212(8)
Snell, R.J. Arctic stowaways.
  1935.   4213(4)
Snell, R.J. Capt. Kituk.
  1918.   4214(0)
Snell, R.J. Eskimo legends.
  1925.   4215(5)
Snell, R.J. Little White Fox
  Arctic friends. 1916. 4216(4)
Snell, R.J. On Yukon Trail.
  1922.   4217(7)
Snell, R.J. Told beneath
  Northern Lights. 1925.4218(5)
Southwest Operating Co. Chief
  Wholecheeze...coloring...
  [cl966]   4246(1)
Stables, G. Off to Klondike.
  1898.   4274(7)
Stratemeyer, E. To Alaska for
  gold. [cl899]   4361(7)
Strong, C.S. King ram.
  [1961]   4367(2)

Summer Institute of Linguis-
  tics. Unipkaat coloring
  book ...Inupiat.1960.4389(4)
Swenson, M.C. Kayoo, Eskimo
  boy. 1939.   4428(5)
Thompson, A.R. Gold-seeking
  Dalton Trail. 1900. 4504(7)
Thompson, D.S. Loon Lake
  mystery. [cl966]   4505(2)
Tomlinson, E.T. Three boys in
  Alaska. 1928.   4551(0)
True, B. Their first igloo.
  1943.   4581(4)
Turner, M. King bear.
  1968.   4590(8)
Ungermann, K.A. Race to Nome.
  1963.   4609(5)
Uyeda, C. Deer Mountain.
  1959.   4624(0)
Van Loon, D. Papeek.
  1970.   4650(4)
Victor, R. Boy Scouts of
  Yukon. [cl912]   4697(7)
Webb, N.M. Aguk of Alaska.
  1963.   4763(5)
Webster, F.V. Two boy miners...
  1909.   4776(8)
Webster, F.V. Young treasure
  hunters...[cl909]   4777(0)
Wheeler, J.C. Capt. Pete in
  Alaska. 1910.   4807(0)
Whitney, E. Black Fox of Yukon.
  1917.   4844(7)
Whitney, E. Bully of frozen
  north. [cl936]   4845(6)
Whitney, E. King bear of Kodiak
  Island. 1912.   4846(6)
Williamson, T.R. On reindeer
  trail. 1932.   4890(0)
Wilt, R.E. E-Tooka-Shoo, cold
  Eskimo...1941.   4917(5)
Winfield, A.M. Rover Boys in
  Alaska. [cl914]   4920(4)

JUVENILE - Nonfiction -
        Animals, Birds, Fishes.

Beebe, B.F. American bears.
  1965.   465(0)
Berrill, J. Wonders of
  Arctic. 1959.   538(4)
Berry, W.D. Deneki, Alaskan
  moose. 1965.   540(2)

JUVENILE - Nonfiction -
    Animals, Birds, Fishes.
                (cont.)
Bridges, W. Walt Disney's ani-
  mal adventures.1963.   657(4)
Dillon, Wallace. Salmon.
  1962.   1298(0)
Elbert, P.A. Josephine ...
  moose. 1966.   1430(3)
Hader, B. Reindeer trail ...
  1959.   1890(0)
Holzworth, J.M. Twin grizzlies
  Admiralty Isl.1932. 2164(1)
Holzworth, J.M. Woof ...
  bear chaser. 1938.   2166(1)
Jordan, D.S. Matka and Katik.
  1897.   2387(6)
Jordan, D.S. Story of Matka.
  1910.   2389(6)
Lopp, Wm. T. White Sox, story
  reindeer...1924.   2794(5)
Louvain, R. White wilderness.
  1958.   2800(4)
McCracken, H. Toughy; bulldog
  of Arctic. 1948.   2857(4)
Mason, G.F. Bear family.
  1960.   3018(0)
May, Chas. P. Animals of far
  North. 1963.   3038(0)
Mayberry, F. Dachshunds of
  Mama Island. 1963.   3039(1)
O'Brien, E.F. Reindeer round-
  up. 1959.   3373(5)
Price, O. Reindeer Island.
  1960.   3692(0)
Rapaport, S.F. Reindeer rescue.
  1955.   3733(5)
Redding, R.H. Aluk, Alaskan
  caribou. 1967.   3767(3)
Redding, R.H. Mara, the weasel.
  1968.   3768(3)
Reynolds, C. Animal suite of
  Alaska. [c1968]   3797(0)
Riley, J. Little seal with meal
  appeal. 1963.   3825(0)
Savage, A.H. Eben the crane.
  1944.   3980(3)
Savage, A.H. Smoozie, Alaskan
  reindeer fawn. 1941. 3984(2)
Vevers, G. Animals of Arctic.
  1965.   4695(0)
Watson, J.W. Walt Disney's
  seal isl. 1958.   4756(6)

Whitehead, R. First book of
  bears. [c1966]   4842(0)

JUVENILE - Aviation.

Coombs, Chas. Alaska bush
  pilot. 1963.   1063(0)
Coombs, Chas. Bush flying in
  Alaska. 1961.   1064(0)
Helmericks, C. Flight of
  Arctic Tern. 1952. 2029(0)
Herron, E.A. Wings...Carl Ben
  Eielson...1959.   2085(0)
Myers, H. Carl Ben Eielson.
  [c1960]   3264(0)
Potter, J.C. Flying frontiers-
  men. [c1956]   3658(0)
Rolfsrud, E.N. Brother to
  eagle...Eielson.1952.3870(0)

JUVENILE - Biography.

Bell, M.E. Touched with fire
  ...Steller. 1960.   488(6)
Berg, L.S. Velikie russkie...
  1950.   516(0)
Berry, Erick. Mr. Arctic...
  Stefansson. 1966.   539(4)
Borden, Chas. A. He sailed with
  Cook. 1952.   620(2)
Bosco, A. Charles John Seghers
  ... 1960.   623(7)
Calder-Marshall, A. Lone Wolf
  ...Jack London. 1961. 769(2)
Chandler, E.W. Pioneer...skies
  ...Eielson. 1959.   888(0)
Chitty, A.B. Hudson Stuck of
  Alaska. 1962.   918(0)
Coombs, C.J. Alaska bush pilot
  ...Eielson. 1963.   1063(0)
DeLeeuw, A. James Cook ...
  1963.   1250(2)
Faris, J.T. Alaskan pathfinder
  Sheldon Jackson.1913.1525(0)
Franchere, R. Jack London...
  1962.   1628(0)
Garst, D.S. Jack London...
  1944.   1690(0)
Garst, D.S. John Jewitt's
  adventure. 1955.   1691(1)
Garst, D.S. Scotty Allan, king
  dog-team drivers.1946.1692(5)

JUVENILE - Biography.   (cont.)

Grahame, N. Bishop Bompas ...
  1925.   1794(7)
Haig-Brown, R. Capt. *Discovery*
  Vancouver. 1956.   1893(2)
Haines, M. John Muir, protector
  wilds. 1957.   1896(0)
Herron, E.A. Alaska's railroad
  ...Mike Heney. 1960.   2079(1)
Herron, E.A. Dimond of Alaska.
  1957.   2080(1)
Herron, E.A. Dynamite Johnny
  O'Brien...1962.   2081(0)
Herron, E.A. First scientist
  ...W.H.Dall. 1958.   2082(0)
Herron, E.A. Conq. Mt. McKin-
  ley. 1964.[H. Stuck]   2084(2)
Herron, E.A. Wings...Carl Ben
  Eielson. 1959.   2085(0)
Knight, F. Young Capt. Cook.
  1966.   2495(2)
Kugelmass, J.A. Roald Amundsen
  ... 1955.   2569(4)
Lamb, G.F. Franklin...life
  and death. 1956.   2585(4)
Lambert, R.S. Adventure...Sir
  John Franklin.1950.   2587(4)
Lambert, R.S. Franklin of
  Arctic...1949.   2588(4)
Lane, F.A. Greatest adventure
  ...Jack London.1954.   2593(0)
[Ledyard, J.] Adventures
  Yankee...1831.   2664(2)
Merrett, J. Capt. James Cook.
  1957.   3086(2)
Murphy, R. Haunted voyage.
  1961. [V. Bering]   3254(6)
Myers, Hortense. Carl Ben
  Eielson: ... Alaskan pilot.
  [c1960]   3264(0)
Myers, Hortense. Vilhjalmur
  Stefansson. 1966.   3265(4)
Redding, R.H. North to wilder-
  ness. 1970.   3769(3)
Ricker, E.M. Seppala, Alaska
  dog driver. 1930.   3811(5)
Rolfsrud, E.N. Brother to
  eagle...Eielson.1952.   3870(0)
Sarnoff, P. Ice pilot; Bob
  Bartlett. 1966.   3962(4)

Senter, G.E. Kawoo of Alaska.
  [c1964]   4047(1)
Small, Marie. Four fares to
  Juneau. [c1947]   4186(1)
Sperry, A. All about Capt.
  Cook. 1960.   4259(2)
Sutton, A. Steller of North.
  1961.   4407(6)
Sutton, A. Endless quest ...
  Franklin. 1965.   4408(4)
Swift, H.(H.) Edge of April...
  John Burroughs.1957. 4431(0)
Swift, H.H. From eagle's wing
  ...John Muir.1962.   4432(0)
Syme, R. Capt. Cook, Pacific
  explorer. 1960.   4435(2)
Vandercook, J.W. Great sailor
  ...Jas. Cook. 1951. 4645(2)
Voigtländer, O. Drei jahre...
  [190_?]   4713(0)
Whitcombe & Tombs. Capt. Jas.
  Cook. n.d.   4813(2)
Whitcombe & Tombs. Under Cook's
  flag...[19__?]   4814(2)

JUVENILE - Eskimos and Indians.

Bleeker, S. Eskimo...hunters
  & trappers. 1959.   575(4)
Bleeker, S. Sea hunters; In-
  dians...1951.   576(1)
Brewster, B. First book of
  Eskimos. 1952.   655(4)
Brewster, B. First book of
  Indians. 1950.   656(0)
Brindze, R. Story of totem
  pole. 1951.   661(1)
Cameron, E.M. Children of
  tundra. 1963.   786(0)
Copeland, D.A. True book
  little Eskimos. 1953.1069(0)
Dreany, E.J. Life in Arctic.
  1960.   1347(4)
Gillham, C.E. Beyond Clapping
  Mtns. 1943.   1723(5)
Gillham, C.E. Medicine men
  Hooper Bay. 1955.   1724(5)
Glubok, S. Art of Eskimo.
  1964.   1739(0)
Glubok, S. Art North Amer.
  Indian. 1964.   1740(0)
Goetz, Delia. Arctic tundra.
  1958.   1750(4)

706

JUVENILE - Eskimos and Indians.
(cont.)

Haig-Brown, R. Whale people.
1963.   1894(1)

Harris, Christie. Once upon a
totem. 1963.   1959(1)

Harris, Christie. Raven's cry.
1966.   1960(1)

Hofsinde, R. Indian medicine
man. 1966.   2140(1)

Mayberry, G. Eskimo of Little
Diomede. 1961.   3040(5)

Myron, R. Mounds, towns and
totems...1966.   3268(0)

Oliver, E.R. Aleutian boy.
1959.   3402(6)

Oliver, N.N. Alaskan Indian
legends. [c1947]   3403(1)

Osgood, H.K. Yukon River
children. 1944.   3431(3)

Pine, T.S. Eskimos knew.
1957.   3601(0)

Riswold, M. Albert, Eskimo
boy. 1960.   3828(5)

Sickels, D.J. Eskimos, hunters
of Arctic. 1941.   4143(4)

Tucci, J.L. Stone-age people
... [c1959]   4584(0)

Van Loon, D. Papeek.
1970.   4650(4)

Viereck, P. Eskimo Island...
[c1962]   4699(5)

Worthylake, M. Moolack, young
salmon fisherman.1963.4963(1)

Worthylake, M. Nika Illahee
... 1962.   4964(1)

JUVENILE - History & Geography.

Adams, Ben. The last frontier.
[c1961]   10(0)

Agnew, E.J. My Alaska picture
story book. 1948.   17(0)

Bailey, B. Picture book of
Alaska. 1959.   349(0)

Baity, E.C. Americans before
Columbus. 1951.   356(0)

Baldwin, G.C. America's buried
past. 1962.   373(0)

Breetveld, J. Getting to know
Alaska. 1958.   650(0)

Bright, E. Alaska ...
1956.   659(0)

Brindze, R. Story of gold.
1954.   660(0)

Carpenter, A. Alaska; from
past to present.1965. 839(0)

Carpenter, F. Canada and no.
neighbors. 1946.   841(0)

Chapman, J. W. Alaska's great
highway. 1909.   892(0)

Cleveland, L.J. Pacific shores
... 1962.   956(0)

Coe, D. Road to Alaska ...
[c1943]   968(0)

Coe, D. La route de l'Alaska
... 1946.   969(0)

Coe, D. Vägen till Alaska
... 1946.   970(0)

Crichton, C. Frozen-in! ...
1930.   1123(4)

Crump, I. Boy's book Arctic
exploration.1925.   1136(4)

Daniel, H. Bare hands...
[c1929]   1174(6)

Douglas, R.D. In land thunder
mtns.Fr.Hubbard.1932.1337(6)

Dreany, E.J. ...book about
Alaska. 1959.   1346(0)

Dudley, B. Story of Alaska.
[1968]   1361(0)

Ellsberg, E. Cruise of
Jeannette. 1949.   1444(0)

Epstein, S. Real book about
Alaska. 1952.   1483(0)

Fieldhouse, F. Yukon holiday.
1940.   1553(7)

Graber, A.H. East to Alaska.
1960.   1791(6)

Henry, M. Alaska, in stories
and pictures. 1941. 2070(0)

Herron, E.A. Alaska; land of
tomorrow. 1947.   2078(0)

Hewes, A.D. Hundred bridges
to go. 1950.   2092(0)

Ingraham, J. Friendship Road;
...Pan Am. Hy. 1961. 2265(0)

Kinscella, H.G. Flag over
Sitka ... 1947.   2462(1)

Kotzebue, O. ...neue reise...
jugend...1847.   2527(0)

Kotzebue, O. Die neueren ...
reise...Jugend.1848. 2528(0)

Krasilovsky, P. Benny's flag.
1960.   2537(2)

JUVENILE - History & Geography. (cont.)

Kruger, C. Land of tomorrow. 1947. 2548(0)

Lambert, C. Story of Alaska. 1940. 2586(0)

Lindquist, W. Alaska 49th state. 1959. 2714(0)

Lisitzsky, G. Four ways of being human. 1956. 2725(0)

Litchfield, S. Hello Alaska. 1945. 2726(0)

McCracken, H. Story of Alaska. 1956. 2856(0)

McMurray, DeV. All aboard for Alaska! 1941. 2940(0)

McNeer, May. Alaska gold rush. 1960. 2941(0)

Martin, L.A. North to Nome. 1939. 3007(5)

Mudge, Z.A. Arctic heroes. [c1875] 3218(4)

O'Neill, H. Picture story Alaska. 1951. 3412(0)

Peterson, L.J. This is Alaska. 1958. 3549(0)

Rabling, H. Story of Pacific. 1965. 3716(0)

Razin, A. Otkrytie Ameriki ... 1860. 3760(6)

Robarts, V.P. Let's go to Alaska. [c1951] 3829(0)

Robbin, I. Polar regions how and why. 1965. 3831(4)

Rolt-Wheeler, F.W. Boy...U.S. Life-Savers. 1915. 3872(0)

Rolt-Wheeler, F.W. Boy...U.S. Survey. [c1909] 3873(0)

Sanderson, I.T. Continent we live on. 1961. 3956(0)

Savage, A. Forty ninth star. 1959. 3981(0)

Shannon, T. Ride ice down! [c1970] 4089(4)

Smith, A.M. On to Alaska with Buchanan...1937. 4190(0)

Smith, F.C. Men at work in Alaska. 1967. 4196(0)

Smith, F.C. World of Arctic. 1960. 4197(4)

Sperry, A. All about Capt. Cook. 1960. 4259(2)

Sperry, A. All about Arctic & Antarctic. 1957. 4260(4)

Sperry, A. Le Capitaine Cook ... 1965. 4261(2)

Spring, Norma. Alaska, pioneer state. 1967. 4268(0)

Stefansson, E. Here is Alaska. 1943. 4299(0)

Stefansson, E. Within the Circle ... 1945. 4300(4)

Stefansson, V. Northward Ho! 1925. 4309(0)

Stull, Edith. First book of Alaska. 1965. 4375(0)

Sullivan, W. Polar regions ... 1962. 4384(4)

Syme, R. Capt. Cook ... 1960. 4435(2)

Tompkins, S.R. Let's read about Alaska.1949. 4553(0)

Tompkins, S.R. Life in America ...Alaska. 1958. 4554(0)

Voigtländer, O. Drei jahre... [190_?] 4713(0)

Ware, Kay. Let's read about Alaska. 1960. 4739(0)

Warner, O.M.W. Great seamen. 1961. 4744(2)

Whitcombe & Tombs. Capt. Jas. Cook ... n.d. 4813(2)

Whitcombe & Tombs. Under Cook's flag...[19_?]4814(2)

Wolfe, L. Let's go to Klondike goldrush. 1964. 4943(7)

LIBRARIES.

American Library Assoc. ... in Alaska. 1925. 205(1)

Dana, J.C. Far north-west ... 1906. 1171(1)

LINGUISTICS. (See also RELIGION - Translations)

Adelung, J.C. Mithridates ... 1806[-17] 12(0)

Barnum, F. Grammatical ... Inuit ... 1901. 402(5)

Bergsland, K. Grammatical ... Eskimo lang. ...1955. 522(0)

Bergsland, K. Aleut dialects Atka & Attu. 1959. 523(6)

LINGUISTICS. (cont.)

Bergsland, K. Eskimo-Uralic
hypothesis. 1959.   524(0)
Boas, F. Grammatical notes
...Tlinget...1917.   585(1)
Buschmann, J.C.E. Pima-Sprache
...Koloschen. 1857.   750(0)
Buschmann, J.C.E. Spuren...
Norden. 1859.   751(0)
Buschmann, J.C.E. Völker...
brit. Nordamer.1858.   752(0)
Buschmann, J.C.E. ...athapask-
ischen...1860.   753(0)
Buynitzky, S.N. Eng.-Aleut.
vocab. 1871.   760(6)
Carpenter, E.S. Anerca.
1959.   840(0)
Chapman, J. W. Ten'a texts
...Anvik...1914.   894(5)
Davies, G. ...Chinook jargon
... 1888.   1195(0)
Davis, C.B. Songs of totem.
1939.   1198(1)
de La Grasserie, R. Cinq
langues ... 1902.   1239(1)
Dobbs, A. Acct. countries ...
vocabs. ... 1744.   1312(0)
Driver, H.E. Contrib. ...cul-
ture area...1962.   1353(0)
Hale, H.E. Int'l. idiom ...
Chinook...1890.   1899(0)
Hale, H.E. Ethnog. ...
1846.   1900(0)
Hale, H.E. Indians...vocabs.
...1848.   1901(0)
Henry, V. Esquisse ... aleoute
...1879.   2071(6)
Herzog, W. Ueber die...Aleuten
Eskimostamme. 1878.   2086(6)
Hinz, J. Grammar & vocab. ...
Kuskokwim...1944.   2123(5)
Hoijer, H. Studies Athapaskan
1963.   2143(0)
Jenness, D. Comparat. vocab.
w. Eskimo...1928.   2339(5)
Jenness, D. Grammat. notes...
w. Eskimo. 1944.   2344(5)
Jochelson, W. Aleut folk lore,
... n.d.   2357(6)
Jones, N.W. Indian bulletin.
1869.   2386(1)

Krusenstern, A.J. Wörter-
sammlungen...1813.   2567(1)
Marvin, F.R. Yukon overland.
1898.   3015(1)
Milanowski, P.G. Uusii
dinahtt'aa' I. 1965. 3112(3)
Morice, A.G. New methodical
Dèné syllabary.1890. 3191(7)
Petitot, E.F.S.J. Vocab. fran-
çais-esquimau.1876. 3559(4)
Pfizmaier, A. Aufklärungen...
1883.   3565(6)
Pfizmaier, A. Die Sprache der
Aleuten...1884.   3566(6)
Pinart, A.L. ...Dene...A'Tana
Copper River...n.d. 3591(3)
Pinart, A.L. Bibliotheque...
1876.   3592(3)
Platzmann, J. Amerikanisch-
Asiatiche...1871. 3621(0)
Pott, A.F. Die quinare ...
1847.   3655(6)
Rasmussen, K.J.V. Alaskan
Eskimo ... 1941.   3734(0)
Rink, H.J. Eskimo tribes...
1887-91.   3827(0)
Say it in Eskimo. Informal
phonetic...[c1965] 3987(5)
Schérer, J.-B. Recherches...
[1777]   4000(0)
Schmitt, A. Die Alaska-Schrift
... 1951.   4004(5)
Schmitt, A. Untersuchungen...
1900 Alaska. 1940.   4005(5)
Schulenburg, A.C. Die Sprache
Zimshian...1894.   4011(1)
Schultze, A. Brief grammar...
Eskimo...1899.   4013(5)
Schultze, A. Grammar...Kusko-
quim ... 1894.   4014(5)
Summer Inst. Ling. Unipkaat
coloring bk.1960.   4389(4)
Swanton, J.R. Haida...Tsim-
shian ... 1912.   4416(1)
Swanton, J.R. Tlinglt myths
... 1970.   4420(1)
Tate, C.M. Chinook ...
1889.   4460(1)
Tolmie, W.F. Comparat. vocab.
Indian tribes.1884. 4547(1)
Trager, G.L. N.A. Indian lan-
guages. 1958.   4567(0)

LINGUISTICS. (cont.)

Uhlenbeck, C.C. Ontwerp van
eene...eskimo. 1907. 4605(0)
Uhlenbeck, C.C. ...aziatische
Eskimo. 1941.   4606(0)
Vater, J.S. Grammatikin, Lexi-
ken...1847.   4657(0)
Vater, J.S. Linguarum totius...
[1815]   4658(0)
Vdovin, I.S. Istoriia ...
paleoaziat. ... 1954. 4667(0)
Veniaminov, I.E.P. Langues...
Amer. Russe. n.d.   4672(6)
Veniaminov, I.E.P. Opyt gramm.
Aleutsko...1846.   4675(6)
Veniaminov, I.E.P. Zamiecha-
niia...1846.   4681(0)
Voegelin, C.F. Index F. Boas
collection. 1945.   4710(0)
Voegelin, C.F. Languages ...
Amer. fasc. 1.1964. 4711(0)
Washington, J. Eskimaux ...
vocab. ... 1850.   4750(4)
Winkler, H. Uralaltaische
Völker ... 1884.   4921(0)
Yarmolinsky, A. Aleutian ms.
collections. 1944.   4988(6)
Yarmolinsky, A. Kamchadal...
Eskimo ms. ... 1947. 4989(0)
Zibell, W. Unipchaat 1 and 2.
[c1969]   5029-5030(4)
Zibell, W. Unipchaat 3.
[c1970]   5031(4)

MILITARY - World War II.

Bowman, W.G. Bulldozers come
first. 1944.   632(0)
Cherrington, B.M. Theatres of
war ... 1943.   908(0)
Conant, M. Long polar watch.
1962.   999(0)
Donahue, R.J. Ready on right.
1946.   1330(6)
Driscoll, J. War discovers
Alaska. 1943.   1351(0)
Ellsworth, L.R. Guys on ice.
1952.   1447(6)
Ermashev, I.I. "Poliarna
strategica"...1947. 1487(4)
Ford, Corey. Short cut to
Tokyo...1943.   1598(6)

Gilman, Wm. Our hidden front.
1944.   1731(0)
Griffin, D.F. First steps to
Tokyo. 1944.   1857(6)
Hall, G. L. Sometime again...
1945.   1906(6)
Handleman, H. Bridge to
victory. 1943.   1930(6)
Harper, F. Military ski manual
...1943.   1949(0)
Lanks, H.C. Highway to
Alaska. 1944.   2604(0)
Marston, M.R. Men of tundra.
1969.   3001(0)
Morgan, M.C. Bridge to
Russia. 1947.   3181(6)
Morison, S.E. Aleutians, Gil-
berts...1951.   3192(6)
Paneth, P. Alaskan backdoor
to Japan. 1943.   3487(6)
Poor, H.V. Artist sees
Alaska. 1945.   3641(0)
Potter, J.C. Alaska under
arms. 1942.   3657(0)
Read, F.W. G. I. Parson.
1945.   3762(6)
Sillars, R. North Pacific and
Alaska. 1942.   4149(0)
Soldier's souvenir handybook
... [1944?]   4241(0)
Stefansson, V. Blueprint for
...defense. 1941.   4302(0)
Stursberg, P. Journey into
victory. 1944.   4379(0)
Sunderman, J.F. World War II
in air ...[c1962]   4399(6)
Taylor, F.J. High...United
Airlines. [c1951.]   4469(0)

MINING.

Alaska Amalgamated Copper Co.
Reports. 1906.   29(8)
Alaska Bureau. The nation needs
coal. 1917.   39(2)
Alaska Central Railway.Through
...gateway. 1906.   45(2)
Alaska Coal Co. Prospectus.
1871.   46(2)
Alaska Coast Exploration Co.
Six months...1898.   48(0)
Alaska Copper Co. ...office
... [1902?]   55(2)

MINING. (cont.)

Alaska Copper Corp. Report
  Alfred B. Iles. 1913.   56(2)
Alaska Development Co. Coal and
  oil. 1898.   59(1)
Alaska Handy Gold Mining Co. of
  Chichagof Isl. n.d.   64(1)
Alaska Juneau Gold Mining Co.
  Annual report. n.d.   71(1)
Alaska Mexican Gold Mining Co.
  Annual statement. 1894. 85(1)
Alaska Mining & Engr. Soc.
  Constitution. n.d.   86(0)
Alaska Mining & Engr. Soc.Per-
  severance Mine. 1918.   87(1)
Alaska Mining & Engr. Soc.
  Thane meeting. 1918.   88(1)
Alaska Oil & Guano Co. State-
  ment...fisheries.1910. 95(8)
Alaska-Pacific Consolid. Mining
  Co. 6th report. 1940.   98(8)
Alaska Petroleum & Coal Co.
  Prospectus. n.d.   102(2)
Alaska Prospector's Service.
  Gold panning.[ca1958]   104(0)
Alaska Smelting & Development
  Co. Prospectus. n.d.   110(8)
Alaska Tin Mines Co. Few facts
  ... n.d.   130(5)
Alaska Treadwell Gold Mining
  Co. Annual...1892.   134(1)
Alaska United Copper Explorat.
  Co. Annual...1912.   135(2)
Alaska United Copper Explorat.
  Co. Expert...1910.   136(2)
Alaska United Copper Explorat.
  Co. Report...1907.   137(2)
Alaska United Gold Mining Co.
  Annual...1897.   138(8)
Alaska-Yukon-Klondike Gold
  Synd....gold. 1897.   142(7)
Alaska-Yukon-Klondike Gold
  Synd....miners.1897.   143(7)
Alaska-Yukon-Klondike Gold
  Synd. Story...1898.   144(7)
Allen, C.C. Platinum metals.
  1961.   175(0)
Appeal of Yukon miners...
  [1898]   272(7)
Atkinson, T.H. Alaska petrole-
  um directory. 1962.   316(0)

Bartels Tin Mining Co. Tin...
  in Alaska. 1904.   418(5)
Bel, J.-M. Gites auriferes
  Klondike...1905.   474(7)
Bloch, I. Alaska's power re-
  sources ... 1956.   577(0)
Brooks, A.H. Future of Alaska
  coal. 1911.   681(0)
Buddington, A.F. Alaska nickel
  minerals. 1924.   722(0)
Burton, J.E. 24 opinions on
  Alaska tin...1908.   749(0)
Carlson, L.H. Alaskan gold
  mine...9 Above.1951.   834(8)
Chichagof King Mining Co.Great
  ...depression.1934.   914(1)
Christoe, A.H. Treadwell ...
  [1909?]   926(1)
Clark, H.F. Miners' manual...
  1898.   943(0)
Colliery Engr. Co. Placer
  mining ... 1897.   978(7)
Copper River Mining, Trad.&De-
  velop.Co. Guide.1902. 1072(2)
Cordova Daily Times. Coming
  copper port. 1916.   1078(2)
Crane, W.R. Gold and silver...
  1908.   1114(0)
Curle, J.H. Gold mines of
  world. 1902.   1141(0)
Ellis, C.R. Field guide ...
  1939.   1438(0)
Erickson, J. Report Mineral
  Creek claims.1915.   1485(3)
Exploration Co. Annual re-
  ports...1920.   1506(1)
Griffith, Wm. Report Matanuska
  coal field.1905.   1859(2)
Grindall Mining & Smelting Co.
  Copper & gold...1903. 1862(1)
Henning, C.L. Die Erzlager-
  statten ... 1911.   2065(0)
Houston Dredging & Hydraulic
  Co. Facts...n.d.   2195(2)
Independent Petroleum Assoc.
  Oil producing...1961. 2258(0)
Innis, H.A. Settlement and
  mining...1936.   2269(7)
Int'l. Oil Scouts Assoc. ...
  oil and gas...1962.   2283(0)
Joslin, F. Needs of Alaska.
  [1921]   2392(0)

711

MINING. (cont.)

Katalla Publicity League.Hist.
 Bering R. coal.1912   2417(2)
Kennecott Copper Corp. Applica-
 tion stock...1916.   2439(2)
Kennecott Copper Corp. First
 annual...1915.   2440(2)
Kinzie, R.A. Treadwell group
 Douglas Isl. 1903.   2463(1)
Klondike & Boston Gold Min. &
 Mfg. Co. Prosp. 1897. 2487(2)
Knight's Island Alaska Copper
 Co. [1905?]   2496(1)
Lasky, S.G. Transverse faults
 Kennecott...1928.   2632(2)
Lathrop High School. Arctic
 oil ... 1969.   2636(4)
Leehey, M.D. Public land
 policy...1912.   2671(0)
McConnell, R.G. Prelim. report
 Klondike...1900.   2837(7)
McConnell, R.G. Report...Klon-
 dike gravels. 1907.   2839(7)
McConnell, R.G. Report Klon-
 dike...1905.   2840(7)
McDonald, T.P. Why one rule...
 1914.   2886(0)
MacLaren, J.M. Gold; geol.
 ... 1908.   2926(0)
MacLean, T.A. Lode mining ...
 Yukon...1914.   2930(7)
McMillan, A.J. Mineral re-
 sources ... n.d.   2936(7)
Morrow, W.W. "The spoilers."
 1916.   3202(5)
Mother Lode Copper Mines Co.
 Report. n.d.   3208(2)
Ogilvie, W. Information ...
 Yukon...1897.   3391(7)
Ogilvie, W. Lecture Klondike...
 1897.   3392(7)
Ogilvie, W. Lecture Yukon gold
 ...1897.   3393(7)
Ogilvie, W. Klondike official
 guide...1898.   3394(7)
Ogilvie, W. Truths about Klon-
 dike. 1897.   3395(7)
Pacific Tin Mines Co. A few
 facts ... n.d.   3466(8)
Peterson, R.A. Report seismo-
 graph...1949.   3551(4)

Pioneers of Alaska, Igloo 4.
 Gold, mining...1957. 3615(0)
Rampart Hydraulic Mining Co.
 ...Hunter Creek.1904.3729(3)
Rettie, J.C. Problems pipeline
 ... 1944.   3789(0)
Reynolds-Alaska Develop. Co.
 ...statement.1904.   3794(2)
Reynolds-Alaska Develop. Co.
 Annual...1907.   3795(2)
Reynolds-Alaska Develop. Co.
 Industr. dawn.1904. 3796(2)
Rickard, T.A. Romance of
 mining. 1945.   3809(0)
Russell, J.A. Industr. opera-
 tions...weather.1957.3918(4)
Samson, S. Eskimo Princess...
 Cyrus Noble...1941. 3951(5)
Smith, W.D. Northwest Passage
 Manhattan. 1970.   4207(4)
Smyth, N.A. Brief Cunningham
 coal...1912.   4211(3)
Southeastern Alaska Min. Corp.
 ...Jualin...1929.   4245(1)
Stretch, R.H. Placer mines
 origin. 1897.   4363(0)
Sur, F.J. Placer gold mining
 ...1934.   4402(0)
Taylor, R.C. Statistic of coal
 geog. ... 1848.   4472(0)
Trout, P.L. New theory ...
 1901.   4579(5)
Troutman, A. Alaska oil and
 gas ... 1958.   4580(0)
U.S.-Alaska Tin Mining Co.
 Annual...1905.   4621(5)
U.S.-Alaska Tin Mining Co.
 Facts...1904.   4622(5)
Ver Wiebe, W.A. Oil fields...
 N. A. 1949.   4691(0)
von Bernewitz, M.W. Handbook
 prospectors. 1926.   4715(0)
Weed, W.H. Copper mines of
 world. 1907.   4779(0)
Whipple,Jay,Mining Co. Pros-
 pectus. n.d.   4812(8)
Wolff, E. Handbook for Alaskan
 prospector.[c1964]   4944(0)
Young, C.W., & Co. Alaska in-
 formation...1916.   4990(1)
Yukon Basin Gold Dredging Co.
 Prospectus.[ca1908] 5003(3)

MINING. (cont.)

Yukon Gold Co. Abridged hist.
  ... [1911]   5005(0)
Yukon Gold Co. Annual state-
  ment ... [19__]   5006(0)
Yukon Gold Co. Letter from
  president. [1909]   5007(0)
Yukon Trad. Min. & Explor. Co.
  Alaska... [1897?]   5011(8)
Yukon Trad. Min. & Explor. Co.
  Dredging. [1897?]   5012(8)
Yukon Trad. Min. & Explor. Co.
  Facts...1897.   5013(8)
Yukon Trad. Min. & Explor. Co.
  It's gold. [1897?]   5014(8)

MINING - Laws.

Canada. Regulations...Yukon
  R. & tribut. 1897.   811(7)
Charles, S.D. U.S. mining
  laws...1906.   897(0)
Emery, G.D. New mining law
  Alaska...1913.   1454(0)
Heid, J.G. Local mining laws
  Harris ... 1887.   2019(1)
Herbert, C.F. Alaska mining
  law manual. n.d.   2075(0)
Hills, W.J. Klondike; mining
  laws...1897.   2108(7)
Joslin, F. Alaska; proposed
  legislation. 1912. 2391(0)
Leehey, M.D. Mining code use
  miners... [c1900] 2670(0)
Love, W.T. Placer mining laws
  Alaska...1901.   2801(0)
Reynolds, J.W. ...mining laws
  U.S. Canada. 1898. 3798(0)
Roden, H. Alaska mining law.
  1950.   3861(0)
Roden, H. Compiled laws of
  Alaska. [1934?]   3862(0)
Roden, H. Alaska mining law.
  1913.   3863(0)
St. George & Cathcart. Alaska
  mining laws...1915. 3930(0)

MOUNTAIN CLIMBING.

Balch, E.S. Mt. McKinley and
  ... proofs. 1914.   362(2)

Beach, W.N. In shadow of Mt.
  McKinley. 1931.   452(2)
Broke, H.G. With sack and
  stock. 1891.   678(1)
Brooks, A.H. Mountain explora-
  tion in Alaska.1914. 682(0)
Browne, B. Conquest Mt. McKin-
  ley. 1913.   699(2)
Collins, G.A. Mountain climb-
  ing. 1923.   980(0)
Cook, F.A. To top continent
  McKinley...1908.   1012(2)
deFilippi, F. La Spedizione di
  Sua...1900.   1226(1)
deFillippi, F. Ascent Mt. St.
  Elias...1900.   1227(1)
deFilippi, F. Die Forschungs-
  reise...1900.   1228(1)
Dunn, R. Shameless diary...
  explorer. 1907.   1389(2)
Dunn, R. World alive.
  1956.   1391(2)
Farquhar, F.P. List pub.
  mtns. Alaska. 1934. 1528(0)
Freeman, A.A. Case for Dr.
  Cook. 1961.   1646(2)
Gaussen, H. Montagnes.
  1955.   1694(0)
Hall, T.F. Has North Pole
  been disc.? 1917. 1909(2)
Harper, F. Military ski manual
  ... 1943.   1949(0)
Hauser, W.E. 30 hikes in
  Alaska. 1967.   1990(0)
Hazard, J.T. Pacific Crest
  trails...1946.   2009(0)
Hubbard, B.R. Cradle of
  storms. 1935.   2213(6)
Irwin, W.R. Challenge, anthol.
  mtn. 1950.   2301(0)
Mills, J. Airborne to mtns.
  1961.   3137(2)
Moore, T. Mt. McKinley;
  pioneer climbs.1967. 3166(2)
Out of Doors Lib. Mountain
  climbing. 1897.   3441(0)
Pearson, G.H. My life of high
  adventure. [c1962] 3508(2)
Pearson, G.H. Seventy-Mile
  Kid. [c1957]   3509(2)
Pearson, G.H. Taming of
  Denali. 1957.   3510(2)

MOUNTAIN CLIMBING. (cont.)

Robbins, L.H. Mountains and
  men. 1931.   3832(0)
Roberts, D. Deborah ...
  1970.   3833(2)
Roberts, D. Mountain of my
  fear. 1968.   3834(2)
Rost, E.C. Mt. McKinley and
  ...polar...1914.   3896(2)
Stuck, H. Ascent of Denali.
  1914.   4372(2)
Thomas, W.S. Trails and tramps
  Alaska...1913.   4503(0)
Washburn, H.B. Bradford on
  Mt. Fairweather.1930. 4747(1)
Washburn, H.B. Mt. McKinley
  ...bibliog. 1951. 4748(2)

MUSEUMS.

Alaska Hist. Assoc. Descript.
  booklet...1922.   68(0)
Alaska Hist. Assoc. Native
  Alaskan art...1959. 69(0)
Amer. Mus. Nat. Hist. Andrew J.
  Stone explor. 1905. 206(0)
Berlin, Königl. Mus. Amer. ...
  Ergebnisse...1883. 534(1)
Berlin, Königl. Mus. Northwest
  coast. [1883]   535(1)
Berlin, Königl. Mus. Amer. ...
  Neue Folge. 1884. 536(5)
Canada S.S. Lines. Far west,
  catalogue. 1943.   819(0)
Davis, R.T. Native arts ...
  Pac. northwest. 1949. 1209(1)
Fast, E.G. Catalogue antiqui-
  ties...[1869?]   1533(0)
Gunther, E. Art in life north-
  west. 1966.   1883(1)
Gunther, E. Northwest coast
  art...1962.   1884(1)
McCracken, H. God's frozen
  children. 1930.   2844(6)
McGuire, J.A. In Alaska-Yukon
  gameland. 1921.   2899(0)
Museum Amer. Ind. Guide to
  mus. 2d floor.1922. 3259(0)
Natsionalmuseet. Etnog. saml.
  Polarfolk...1960. 3278(5)
Pinart, A.L. Catalogue ...
  Amer. russe. 1872. 3593(0)

Pope, G.D. Eskimo exhibit.
  1941.   3642(0)
Staniukovich, T.V. Kunstkamera
  ... 1953.   4280(0)
Stefansson, V. Stefánsson-
  Anderson Arctic.1919.4323(4)
Stefansson, V. Stef.-Anderson
  Prelim. 1914.   4324(4)

MUSIC, Songbooks. (For Hymnals
  see RELIGION - Translations)

Davis, C.B. Songs of totems.
  1939.   1198(1)
Edgren, A. Jubel Kantat for
  solo...1909.   1411(0)
Groven, E. Eskimomelodier...
  nunamiut. 1956.   1869(5)
Kunst, J. Ethnomusicology.
  1959.   2571(0)
LaVerne's Klondike songster.
  [1898?]   2647(7)
Loyal League. Popular national
  songs...1918.   2804(5)
Presbyterian Church. New Ameri-
  ca in songs. n.d. 2680(0)
Reynolds, C. Animal suite of
  Alaska. [c1968]   3797(0)
Smith, M.W. Tsimshian; arts
  and music. 1951.   4202(1)
Swanton, J. Haida songs.
  1912.   4416(1)

NATIONAL PARKS, Monuments,
             Wildlife Refuges.

Ackerman, R.E. Archaeol. sur-
  vey Glacier Bay. 1964. 1(1)
Albright, H. "Oh Ranger!"
  1928.   165(0)
Bohn, D. Glacier Bay ...
  1967.   595(1)
Brooks, P. Roadless area.
  1964.   686(2)
Butcher, D. Exploring national
  parks...1949.   756(0)
Butcher, D. Exploring our na-
  tional...refuges.1963.757(0)
Butcher, D. Seeing America's
  wildlife...1955.   758(0)
Camp Fire Club. Plea for Mt.
  McKinley. 1916.   797(2)

NATIONAL PARKS, Monuments,
    Wildlife Refuges.(cont.)
Cooper, W.S. Contrib. hist.
    Glacier Bay.1956.   1067(1)
Murie, A. Naturalist in Alaska.
    1961.   3249(0)
Murie, A. Birds of Mt. McKin-
    ley ... [c1963]   3250(2)
Murie, A. Mammals of Mt. McKin-
    ley ... [c1962]   3251(2)
Myers, H.M. Adventures in
    McKinley Pk. 1933.   3262(2)
Myers, H.M. Back trails.
    [1933]   3263(2)
National Geog. Soc. America's
    wonderlands. 1966.   3274(0)
Pearson, G.H. My life of high
    adventure. [c1962]   3508(2)
Pearson, G.H. Seventy Mile
    Kid. [c1957]   3509(2)
Pearson, G.H. Taming of
    Denali. 1957.   3510(2)
Raymond & Whitcomb Co. ...land
    cruises. 1930.   3758(0)
Rolfe, M.A. Our national
    parks. 1928.   3869(2)
Rue, L.L. World of red fox.
    [c1969]   3912(2)
Schiller, E.L. Mammals Katmai
    Nat.Monument.1956.   4001(6)
Udall, S.L. Quiet crisis.
    1963.   4604(0)
Williams, H. Landscapes of
    Alaska. 1958.   4881(0)
Wood, F.E. Mt. Rainier, Mt.
    McKinley...1964.   4951(0)
Yard, R.S. Book of national
    parks. 1919.   4987(0)

NAVIGATION.

Capt. Lillie's B.C. ...s.e.
    ...coast guide.1947.   830(1)
Dawson, W. Coastal cruising.
    1965.   1217(1)
Findlay, A.G. Direct. navig.
    Pac. O. ... 1851.   1556(0)
Gibbs, J.A. Sentinels North
    Pacific. 1955.   1706(0)
G.B.Admiralty.Hydrog.Dept.
    ...tide ... 1959.   1800(0)
G.B.Admiralty.Hydrog.Dept.
    ...pilot...1898.   1801(0)

G.B.Admiralty.Hydrog. Dept....
    Bering...pilot.1941. 1802(0)
G.B.Admiralty.Hydrog. Dept.
    Sailing...1898.   1803(0)
G.B.Admiralty.Hydrog. Dept.S.E.
    pilot...1948.   1804(0)
G.B.Admiralty.Hydrog.Dept.S.E.
    pilot...1959.   1805(0)
G.B.Admiralty.Hydrog.Dept.
    Suppl. no.3...1953.   1806(0)
G.B.Admiralty.Hydrog.Dept.
    Suppl.no.8...1953.   1807(0)
G.B.Admiralty.Hydrog.Dept.
    ...lights.1953.   1808(0)
Hansen, S.E. ...piloting...
    1951 & 1931.   1938-9(0)
Hansen, S.E. Tacoma...
    1917.   1940(0)
Harrington, M.W. Alaskan al-
    manac...1901.   1956(0)
Imray, J. North Pacific pilot.
    1881.   2257(0)
Int'l. Hydrog. Bur. Catalogue
    charts. pt.3. 1935.   2278(0)
Japan, Maritime Safety Bd. ...
    coast pilot. 1932.   2330(1)
Lappo, S.D. Okeanograficheskiĭ
    ... 1940.   2622(0)
Morris, F.L. Marine atlas...
    vol. 2. 1959.   3198(1)
Newell, G.R. SOS North Paci-
    fic. 1955.   3298(0)
Putnam, G.R. Lighthouses and
    lightships. 1917.   3706(0)
Steamship Companies of Puget
    Sd. Appeal...1914.   4290(0)
U.S.S.R.Gidrograf. Upravlenie.
    Lotsiĭa...1938.   4618(0)
Weber, G.A. Coast & Geodetic
    Survey. 1923.   4765(0)
Young, R.B. B.C. pilot.
    1954.   4995(1)

NEWSPAPERS.

Alaska Herald-Free Press.
    1868-1872. 1967.   65(0)
Bankson, R.A. Klondike
    Nugget. 1935.   386(7)
Bell, E. Moberly. Flora Shaw.
    1947.   480(7)
Harrington, J.J. The Esqui-
    meaux. 1867.   1955(4)

NEWSPAPERS. (cont.)

Luciw, W. Ahapius Honcharenko
   Alaska Herald. 1963.   2807(0)
Morrison, H.A. Alaskan news-
   papers checklist.1915.3200(0)
Pacific States newspaper direc-
   tory. 1888.   3463(0)
Thomas, L. Trail of '98.
   [c1962]   4499(7)

NUMISMATICS.

Fernald, K. Rubles to statehood. 1965.   1545(0)
Gould, M.M. Alaska's coinage
   ... 1960.   1787(0)
Taxay, D. Money American Indians. [c1970]   4466(0)

PHILATELY.

Bartley, D.C. Cachets U.S.
   ...*Constitution*. 1934. 422(0)
Couch, J.S. Philately below
   zero. 1957.   1096(0)
Koestler, A.E. Sourdough
   flights. 1941.   2501(0)
Lockley, F. Alaska's first
   free mail. n.d.   2745(0)
Ricks, M.B. Directory Alaska
   postoffices. 1965. 3813(0)

PHOTOGRAPH ALBUMS and Books.

Alaska earthquake ...
   1964.   61(0)
Alaska Mag. Pub. Co. Book of
   animals ... 1940.   80(0)
Alaska Mag. Pub. Co. Book of
   ... frontier. 1941. 81(0)
Alaska Mag. Pub. Co. Book of
   totems...1942.   82(1)
Alaska Mag. Pub. Co. 100 events
   ... 1944.   83(0)
Alaska News Agency. Quake.
   [1964?]   91(0)
Alaska-Yukon-Pac. Exposition.
   Glimpses...1909.   149(0)
Alaska-Yukon-Pac. Exposition.
   150 ...views. 1909. 154(0)
Alaskan Pub. Co. Great Alaska
   earthquake. [1965?] 162(0)

Ameigh, G.C. Alaska's Kodiak
   Island. 1962.   191(6)
American Press. 100 pictures
   Alaska. 1935.   208(6)
Anchorage Daily News. Flood.
   1967.   235(3)
Andrews, R.W. Curtis' western
   Indians. 1962.   259(0)
Andrews, R.W. Indian primi-
   tive. 1960.   261(0)
Artwork of Seattle and Alaska.
   1907.   312(0)
Becker, E.A. Treasury of
   Alaskana. 1969.   462(7)
Becker, E.A. Klondike '98.
   1949.   463(7)
Benedict, N.D. Valdez & Copper
   River trail. 1899. 497(2)
Black, M.L.P. Yukon wild
   flowers. [1940?]   571(7)
Bohn, D. Glacier Bay, land
   & silence. 1967.   595(1)
Cantwell, G.G. Klondike sou-
   venir. [1900]   826(7)
Clum, J.P. Trip to Alaska...
   1899.   961(0)
Cochran, G.M. Indian por-
   traits... 1959.   964(1)
Colby, M.E. Alaska, profile
   with pictures. 1940. 974(0)
Color Art Print. Co. Alaskan
   earthquake pict. 1964.992(0)
Cooke, C. Fascinating Alaska.
   1947.   1059(0)
Crewe, F. Poems Klondyke's
   early days. 1921. 1122(7)
Cromwell, G.R. America scenic
   ...[1894]   1127(0)
Curtis, E.S. North American
   Indian. 1907-15. 1144(0)
Dockstader, F.J. Indian art
   ... 1960.   1315(0)
Eliot, W.A. Birds Pacific
   coast. 1923.   1434(0)
Eskimo life in Alaska ...
   1964.   1494(0)
Fish, Byron. Alaska.
   1965.   1566(0)
Goetze, O.D. Souvenir north-
   west Alaska. n.d. 1751(5)
Greenaway, K.R. Aerial reconn.
   Arctic...1948.   1848(4)

716

PHOTOGRAPH ALBUMS and Books.
(cont.)
Griffith, W. Report Matanuska
coal field. 1905.   1859(2)
Hawthorn, A. Art Kwakiutl
Indians. 1967.   1998(1)
Hegg, Eric A. Souvenir Alaska
... 1900.   2017(0)
Hegg, Eric A. Souvenir Nome
... 1900.   2018(5)
Heller, C.A. Wild flowers...
1966.   2024(0)
Hudson, W.E. Icy Hell...news
reel cameraman.1937. 2217(6)
Island Pub. Co. Kodiak earth-
quake. [ca1964]   2303(6)
Itjen, M. Hist. and scenic
... Skagway. 1933.   2304(1)
Itjen, M. Story tour Skagway
streetcar...1934.   2305(1)
Jesup North Pacific Exped.
Ethnog. album...1900. 2351(5)
Jones, H. Wendy. Man and mtn.
Sydney Laurence. 1962.2379(2)
LaRoche, F. En route to Klon-
dike...1897.   2626(7)
LaRoche, F. En route to Klon-
dike...1898.   2627(7)
McLain, C.M. Gold-rush Nome.
[c1969]   2923(5)
Mac's Photo Service. Alaska
earthquake. 1964.   2949(0)
Morgan, M.C. One man's gold-
rush. 1967.   3183(7)
Prather, J.B. Land of midnight
sun... [c1899]   3673(0)
Prince, B. LeM. Alaska Railroad
in pictures. 1964.   3694(0)
Puhr, C. Modern Alaska.
n. d.   3702(0)
Reat, Lorraine. Alaskan days.
[c1944]   3765(0)
Scenes from land midnight sun.
n.d.   3994(0)
Sprungman, O.I. Photography
afield. 1951.   4272(0)
Thoren, R. Picture atlas of
Arctic. 1969.   4524(4)
Wilson, V. Glimpses of Alaska.
1897.   4914(0)
Wilson, V. Glimpses of Yukon.
1895.   4915(7)

Winter & Pond. Juneau,
Alaska. [c1909]   4925(1)
Winter & Pond. Juneau, gold
belt...1911.   4926(1)
Winter & Pond. Totems of
Alaska. [c1905]   4927(1)
Winter & Pond. Types Alaskan
natives. [c1905]   4928(1)
[Witteman, A.] Picturesque
Alaska. 1888.   4939(0)
Yukon souvenir ...
n. d. . . . . .5009(7)
Zaccarelli, J. ...souvenir...
northland. n.d.   5016(7)

PHYSICAL SCIENCES - General.

Akasofu, S.-I. Polar and mag-
netospheric...[c1968]   24(4)
American Geog. Soc. Problems
...polar...1928.   203(4)
Arctic Institute N.A. Cat.
Library...1968.   300(4)
Black, D.J. Gravity observa-
tions Ice Isl. 1962.   569(4)
Budeler, W. Vortoss ins Unbe-
kannte...1960.   723(4)
Chapman, S. IGY; year of
discovery. 1959.   896(0)
Dozois, L.O.R. Precise le-
veling ... 1951.   1343(7)
Enemark, D.C. Instrumentation
auroral zone...1959. 1468(3)
Forster, J.R. Observations...
phys. geog. 1778.   1613(2)
Innes, M.J.S. Gravity measure-
ments ...1957.   2268(7)
Joesting, H.R. Magnetometer...
1941.   2361(3)
Lenz, H.F.E. Nabliudeniia...
magnitoi...1836.   2678(0)
Libby, W.F. Radiocarbon dating.
1955.   2701(0)
O'Neill, H.E. Auroral drama.
1937.   3411(4)
Pacific Science Congress, 9th.
Abstracts...1957.   3459(0)
Price, E.V. Astronomische...
Kotzebue...1830.   3689(0)
Price, E.V. Astronomicheskii
... 1832.   3690(0)
Shelford, V.E. Ecology N. A.
1963.   4106(0)

PHYSICAL SCIENCES - General.
(cont.)
Thoren, R. Picture atlas of
Arctic. 1969.   4524(4)

PHYSICAL SCIENCES - Geodynamics.

Alaska earthquake ...
1964.   61(0)
Alaska News Agency. Quake.
[1964?]   91(0)
Alaska Publishing Co. Great
...earthquake. [1965?] 162(0)
Båth, M. Ultra-long-period mo-
tions...1958.   429(1)
Color Art Print. Co. Alaskan
earthquake...1964.   992(0)
Engle, E. Earthquake ...
1966.   1474(0)
Erskine, W.F. Katmai.
1962.   1489(6)
Griggs, R.F. Sci. results Kat-
mai exped. ...1920.   1860(6)
Gutenberg, B. Seismicity of
earth. 1949.   1885(0)
Island Pub. Co. Kodiak earth-
quake. [ca1964]   2303(6)
Jaggar, T.A. Volcanoes...
Pacific. 1945.   2321(0)
Karo, H.A. Emergency charting
earthquake. 1964.   2411(0)
Knopoff, L. Analyt. calcul.
faultplane...1961.   2498(1)
Knopoff, L. Statist. ...fault-
plane...1961.   2499(1)
Mac's Photo Service. Alaska
earthquake. 1964.   2949(0)
Nat. Acad. Sci. ...earthquake.
Hydrol. 1968.   3272(0)
National Bd. Fire Underwriters.
...earthquake...1964. 3273(0)
National Geog. Soc. Contrib.
Katmai...1923-29.   3275(6)
Perrey, A. Documents sur trem-
blements...1863.   3538(0)
Perrey, A. Documents...trem-
blements...1866.   3539(6)
Poulter, T.C. Seismic measure-
ments Taku...1949.   3666(1)
Russell, I.C. Volcanoes N.A.
1897.   3917(0)
Seed, H.G. Turnagain Hgts.
landslide...1966.   4038(2)

PHYSICAL SCIENCES - Geology.

American Geog. Soc. 9 glacier
maps...1960.   200(0)
Baird, P.D. Report Snow
Cornice. 1949.   355(1)
Bohn, D. Juneau Ice Field
1958.   596(1)
Bostock, H.S. Physiography n.
55th parallel. 1948. 624(7)
Brooks, A.H. Blazing Alaska's
trails. 1953.   680(0)
Burk, C.A. Geol. Alaska
Peninsula. 1965.   733(6)
Davidson, D.T. Geol. & engr.
...soils. 1959.   1190(0)
Davidson, G. Glaciers...Russ.
charts...1904.   1192(1)
Dawson, G.M. Report...Yukon
... 1898.   1216(7)
Dunbar, C.O. Parafusulina...
Permian ... 1946.   1376(1)
Dutcher, R.R. Petrography...
coals Arctic.[1958?] 1395(4)
Dyson, J.L. World of ice.
1962.   1401(0)
Eichwald, C.E. Geognost.-pal-
eontol. Aleut. 1871. 1424(6)
Frebold, H. Grundzüge ...geol.
1942.   1641(5)
Goldthwait, R.P. Soil develop.
Muir Inlet. 1966.   1761(1)
Greenaway, K.R. Aerial reconn.
Arctic...1948.   1848(4)
Griggs, R.F. Sci. results...
Katmai...1920.   1860(6)
Griggs, R.F. Valley 10,000
Smokes. 1922.   1861(6)
Hansen, H.P. Cycles and geo-
chronology. 1961.   1935(0)
Harriman Alaska Exped. vol. 1.
1910-14.   1950(0)
Harriman Alaska Exped. vol. 3.
1910-14.   1950(0)
Harriman Alaska Exped. vol.4.
1910-14.   1950(0)
Heusser, C.J. Juneau Ice
Field ... 1958.   2090(1)
Holmes, J.F. Project Skijump.
1951.   2158(4)
Hubley, R.C. Progress report
Juneau Ice Field.1955.2216(1)

PHYSICAL SCIENCES - Geology.
                                    (cont.)
Hunting Assoc. Illus. case
   histories...1959.   2239(0)
Hussey, K.M. Environm. ...
   thermal ... 1963.   2241(4)
Hussey, K.M. Foramin. paleo-
   ecol. Gubik...1961.   2242(4)
Hussey, K.M. Tundra relief...
   Barrow. 1961.   2243(4)
Int'l. Assoc. Quaternary Res.
   Guidebook...1965.   2273(0)
Int'l. Geol. Cong.12th. Guide-
   book...1913.   2277(1)
Jaggar, T.A. Journ. Technol.
   Exped. Aleut.Isl.1908.2320(6)
Kerr, M.B. Table elevations
   ... 1895.   2446(0)
LaChappelle, E.R. Snow studies
   Juneau Ice Field.1954.2578(1)
Lord, C.S. Geol. reconn.
   Alaska Hy. ...1944.   2795(7)
Loudon, W.J. Canadian geolo-
   gist. 1930.   2799(7)
MacLaren, J.M. Gold; geol.
   occur. ... 1908.   2926(0)
Matthes, F.E. Variations gla-
   ciers...1939.   3032(0)
Miller, M.M. Juneau Ice Field
   ... 1954.   3124(1)
Miller, M.M. Mechanical core
   drilling Taku. 1954.   3125(1)
Miller, M.M. Prelim. ...Juneau
   Ice Field...1950.   3126(1)
Miller, M.M. Progress...Juneau
   Ice Field...1949.   3127(1)
Miller, M.M. ...Taku-Llewellyn
   Glacier...1954.   3128(1)
Miller, M.M. Sci. obs. Juneau
   Ice Field...1952.   3129(1)
Miller, M.M. Status...Juneau
   Ice Field...1953.   3130(1)
Norford, B.S. Illus. Canad.
   fossils...1962.   3341(1)
Northward, T.D. Depth...Seward
   ice...1948.   3359(5)
Péwé, T.L. Permafrost ...
   [c1966]   3563(0)
Péwé, T.L. Periglacial en-
   vironment...1969.   3564(0)
Porter, S.C. Pleistocene geol.
   Anaktuvuk...1966.   3646(4)

Raasch, G.O. Geol. of Arctic.
   1961.   3715(4)
Reed, J.C. Research geol. &
   geomorphol. ... 1955.3774(0)
Richards, H.G. Annot. bibliog.
   Quaternary...1965.   3803(0)
Russell, I.C. Glaciers N. A.
   1897.   3916(0)
Schmitz, C.A. Festschrift Al-
   fred Bühler. 1965.   4006(0)
Schuchert, C. Atlas paleogeog.
   maps N.A. 1955.   4010(0)
Schultz, G. Glaciers and Ice
   Age...1963.   4012(0)
Seed, H.G. Turnagain Hgts.
   landslide...1966.   4038(2)
Sharp, R.P. Glaciers.
   1960.   4092(0)
Skinner, J.W. Permian fusu-
   linids...1966.   4175(3)
Tarr, R.S. Alaskan glacier
   studies. 1914.   4459(0)
Taylor, L.D. Ice struct. Bur-
   roughs Glacier.1962.   4470(1)
Tedrow, J.C.F. Morphol. evid.
   frost...1962.   4476(4)
Townley, S.D. Descript. cat.
   earthquakes...1939.   4561(0)
Ulrich, E.O. Ozarkian...bra-
   chiopoda. 1938.   4607(0)
Vail, I.N. Alaska, land of
   nugget. 1897.   4629(0)
Vesanen, E. On Alaskan earth-
   quakes. 1947.   4692(0)
Weber, H. Die Entwickelung...
   phys. geog. ...1898. 4766(4)
Wilkerson, A.S. Some frozen
   deposits...1932.   4870(3)
Williams, H. Landscapes of
   Alaska. 1958.   4881(0)
Wolff, F.L. Der Vulkanismus...
   Bd.2:Spec. Teil, Tl. Häfte
   1-2. 1923-29.   4945(0)
Wright, G.F. Ice age in N.A.
   1889.   4969(0)
Wright, G.F. Muir Glacier...
   [1889?]   4970(1)
Wyllie, P.J. Ultramafic and
   related rocks. 1967. 4982(1)
Zubova, Z.N. Aleutskie ostro-
   va fiziko-geograficheskiĭ
   ocherk. 1948.   5039(6)

PHYSICAL SCIENCES - Meteorology.

Anchorage Daily News. Flood.
1967.   235(3)
Batten, E.S. Summertime rever-
sal winds...1959.   430(6)
[Bayly, Wm.] Orig. astronom.
...Cooke...1782.   437(2)
Bent, S. Address ...thermo-
metric...1869.   507(4)
Bent, S. Address ... thermal
paths...1872.   508(4)
Boville, B.W. Atlas strato-
spheric circ. 1959.   627(0)
Canada. Surface water supply...
1955.   815(7)
Corbel, J. Neiges et glaciers.
1962.   1073(0)
Feyerherm, A.M. Probabil. ...
wet & dry days...n.d. 1551(0)
Fofonoff, N.P. Transport com-
putat. ...1963.   1590(6)
Fofonoff, N.P. Transport com-
putat. ...1960.   1591(6)
Fofonoff, N.P. Transport com-
putat. ...1961.   1592(6)
Hagglund, M.G. Formation, pro-
perties sea ice.1955. 1892(4)
Heusser, C.J. Late-Pleistoc.
...changes. 1960.   2091(0)
Jensen, C.A.T. Über grosse
atmosph. ... 1913.   2349(6)
Kupffer, A.T. Observations
meteorologiques.1850. 2572(1)
Macoun, J. Climate and soil...
Yukon. 1903.   2947(7)
Marcus, M.G. Climate-glacier
Juneau Ice Field.1964.2965(1)
Martin, L. Some feat. glaciers
Pr. Wm. Sd. 1913.   3006(2)
Orvig, S. McCall Glacier ...
meteorol. 1961.   3421(4)
Reichelderfer, F.W. Meteorol.
service. 1948.   3776(0)
Rex, R.W. Hydrodynamic ...
lakes...1960.   3792(4)
Robinson, E. Investig. ice fog
...1952.   3846(3)
Robinson, E. Field obs. ...ice
fog ... 1954.   3847(3)
Robinson, E. Some instances...
surf. temp. 1955.   3848(3)

Robinson, E. Wiresonde obs.
... 1954.   3849(3)
Russell, J.A. Industrial
operations...1957. 3918(0)
Ryder, T. Compil. & study ice
thickness...1953.   3930(4)
Smiley, C.H. Atmospheric re-
fract. low alt.1950. 4188(0)
Sverdrup, H.U. Meteorol. pt.2.
1930.   4412(5)
Thuman, W.C. Technique ...
water in air. 1953. 4530(3)
Thuman, W.C. Studies...water
fogs...1955.   4531(3)
Vitvitskiĭ, G.N. Klimaty
Severnoĭ...1953.   4707(0)
Wasowicz, J. Granica śniegu...
1934.   4751(0)
Wells, R.M. Great Circle ...
temps. 1962.   4790(4)
Werenskiold, W. Mean monthly
air transport. 1922. 4796(6)
Wilson, H.P. Comparison...surf.
wind data. 1961.   4911(4)

PHYSICAL SCIENCES -
                 Oceanography.
Aron, W. Distrib. animals ...
1960.   310(0)
Barnes, C.A. Phys. & chem. in-
vestig. Bering...1938.401(0)
Beklemishev, K.V. Distrib.
zooplankton...1959.   473(0)
Canada. Data record...Hecate
...1955.   804(1)
Canada. Phys. & chem. data...
Hecate...1955.   806(1)
Canada. Phys. & chem. data...
Hecate append.1955.   807(1)
Canada. Phys. & chem. data...
Hecate surveys.1958. 808(6)
Canada. Phys. & chem. data...
surveys...1958.   809(6)
Clark, A.H. Arctic...mollusks
...Alpha. 1960.   936(4)
Coachman, L.K. Contrib. Bering
Sea...1961.   962(0)
Dodimead, A.J. Atlas oceanog.
... 1960.   1320(6)
Dodimead, A.J. Oceanog. atlas
... 1961.   1321(0)
Dodimead, A.J. Oceanog. data
... 1960.   1322(0)

PHYSICAL SCIENCES –
            Oceanography. (cont.)
Dodimead, A.J. Oceanog. data
   ... 1961.   1323(0)
Dodimead, A.J. Oceanog. data
   ... 1962.   1324(0)
Dodimead, A.J. Report oceanog.
   ... 1958.   1325(0)
Goodman, J.R. Characteristics
   waters ... 1940.   1775(1)
Goodman, J.R. Phys. & chem. in-
   vestig. ... 1942.   1776(0)
Grier, M. C. Oceanog. ...
   bibliog. 1941.   1855(0)
Hülsemann, K. Radiolaria in
   plankton T-3. 1963.   2225(4)
Int'l. Hydrogr. Bur. Catalogue
   charts. pt. 3. 1935.   2278(0)
Leonov, A.K. Regional'naîa
   okeanog. ... 1960.   2681(0)
McEwen, G.F. Hydrogr. sect.
   ... 1930.   2889(6)
Mears, E.G. Pacific Ocean
   handbook. 1944.   3065(0)
Rex, R.W. Microrelief...sea
   ice...Barrow...1955.   3793(4)
Riehl, H. Ocean analysis...
   1943.   3820(0)
Robinson, M.K. Sea temp. Gulf
   of Alaska. 1957.   3850(0)
Rodahl, K. North ...
   [c1953]   3853(4)
Rodahl, K. T-3, beretningen
   ... 1954.   3857(4)
Rouch, J.A.P. Les mers
   polaires. 1954.   3899(0)
Scripps Inst. Oceanog. Oceanic
   obs. Pac. 1963.   4029(0)
Shepard, F.P. Submarine can-
   yons ... 1966.   4110(0)
Shliamin, B.A. Beringovo
   more. 1958.   4127(0)
Sverdrup, H.U. Dynamics tides
   ... *Maud.* 1926.   4410(4)
Swithinbank, C.W.M. Ice atlas
   Arctic Canada. 1960.   4434(4)
Tanfil'ev, G.I. Moriâ; Kas-
   piîskoe...1931.   4451(0)
Thompson, T.G. Distrib. ...
   oxygen...1934.   4510(0)
Thompson, T.G. Hydrogr. sects.
   ...currents. 1936.   4511(6)

Tokyo Agric. Tech. Res. Soc.
   Inform. oceanog.1954.4543(0)
Tully, J.P. Assessment temp.
   structure ... 1961.   4587(0)
Weeks, T. Ice Island ...
   1965.   4780(4)
Wigan, S.O. Tsunami ...
   1964.   4863(0)
Worthington, L.W. Oceanog. obs.
   ... T-3. 1953.   4962(4)

POETRY.

Alaska League West. Writers.
   Anthol. ... 1956.   73(0)
Alaska Writers Workshop. Alas-
   ka poetry ... n.d.   141(0)
Anderson, J. Boating on Yukon
   River. 1930.   248(0)
Andrews, C.L. Nuggets north-
   land verse. 1935.   253(0)
Andrews, C.L. Pioneers and
   nuggets...1935.   255(0)
Bates, R.S. Man on the dump.
   1909.   428(7)
Best, Eva. Alaska Christmas
   candles. n.d.   550(8)
Bugbee, J.S. Poems on Alaska
   ... 1891.   724(0)
Burrows, E.G. Arctic tern ...
   1957.   746(0)
Camp, F.B. Alaska nuggets.
   1921.   787(0)
Carpenter, E.S. Anerca.
   1959.   840(0)
Cone, Edw. Beyond sky-line...
   1923.   1000(5)
Conkle, E.J. Alaska gold.
   1953.   1002(0)
Craig, M.H. In shadow of
   Pole. 1909.   1111(4)
Crawford, J.W. Souvenir song
   and story. 1898.   1116(8)
Crewe, F. Camp Hades #23...
   1910.   1120(3)
Crewe, F. Log sloop "North"
   Cook's Inlet. 1896.   1121(2)
Crewe, F. Poems Klondyke's
   ... 1921.   1122(7)
Darling, E.B. Up in Alaska.
   1912.   1183(5)
Davis, C.B. Alaska driftwood.
   1953.   1197(1)

POETRY. (cont.)

Dawes, L. I reached for a
star. 1951.   1214(0)
Dunham, S.C. Goldsmith of
Nome ... 1901.   1384(5)
Dunham, S.C. Men who blaze
trail ... 1913.   1385(0)
Elbert, P.A. I love the land.
1963.   1429(3)
Everette, O.P. God has been
Northward...1965.   1504(3)
Fair, A.T. Sourdough's bible.
1910.   1511(8)
Fejes, C. Primeval land.
1959.   1538(0)
Gaines, R. Chilkoot Charlie.
1951.   1671(0)
Gaines, R. Mrs. Maloney.
1955.   1672(0)
Gaines, R. Second book of Chil-
koot Charlie. 1955.   1673(0)
Gilkey, J.A. Heroes of Yukon
... 1932.   1720(7)
Gillham, C.E. Sled dog and
other...1950.   1726(0)
Gilman, I.A. Alaskaland ...
curious...1914.   1730(0)
Gore, L.C. Soul of bearded
seal ... 1967.   1784(5)
Hackett, J.A. Rhymes of
North...1924.   1888(7)
Haines, J. Winter news.
[1966]   1895(3)
Hall, A.B. Songs of sourdough.
1955.   1902(7)
Hanigsman, E. Charming Alaska
verse & picture.1938. 1931(1)
Harriman, A. Wilt thou not
sing? 1912.   1954(0)
Hatt, D.E. Sitka spruce ...
1919.   1986(1)
Higginson, E. Vanishing race...
1911.   2104(0)
Hilton, B. ...book of nursery
rhymes. [1967?]   2112(3)
James, B.W. Alaskana ...
poems. 1892.   2323(0)
James, Sam. Taming Arctic
shrew. 1963.   2328(5)
Johnson, W.E. Alaska ...con-
struction stiff.1956. 2371(0)

[Jones, C.D.] Vagrant verses
by charley. 1962.   2377(5)
June days on Alaska waters...
1887.   2396(8)
Kendrick, S.J. Chilkoot
Pass ... 1926.   2437(0)
Lee, Frank C. Alaska Highway
poems. [c1944]   2667(0)
Lewis, G.E. Yukon lyrics.
1925.   2696(7)
Lockwood, M.J. Writings from
Alaska. [1969?]   2746(0)
McDaniel, E.K. Rainbow to
storms. 1964.   2861(8)
MacKay, A. By trench and trail
... 1918.   2912(7)
MacLennan, E. Songs of
Neukluk. 1912.   2931(5)
Matthews, C.W. Aleutian
interval. 1949.   3033(6)
Maule, F.I. El Dorado "29"
... 1910.   3035(0)
Miller, Inez. This is
Alaska! 1967.   3120(2)
Nelson, G. Blue of Alaska.
[c1936]   3287(0)
Noonan, D.A. Alaska, land
of now. 1921.   3320(0)
Noonan, D.A. Alaska, land of
plenty. 1960.   3321(0)
O'Cotter, P. Rhymes of rough-
neck. 1918.   3379(2)
Officers U.S. Rev. Cutter Serv.
Below zero. 1903.   3382(0)
Ogilvie, D.S. Kandid view
Kiska. 1945.   3387(6)
Paramore, E.E. Ballad of
Yukon Jake. 1928.   3489(7)
Pedersen, H.H.S. Vitus
Berings minde. 1943. 3526(0)
Platinum Bill. Under northern
lights. 1916.   3620(0)
Poetry Soc. of Alaska. 100
years...1966.   3624(0)
Powell, A.M. Echoes from
frontier. 1909.   3667(0)
Reed, E. Kobuk Maiden...
[1933?]   3772(0)
Rosten, N. Big road.
1946.   3897(0)
Royal, C.E. Trail of sourdough
... 1919.   3908(7)

POETRY. (cont.)

Salisbury, H. Alaskan songs
... 1967.   3945(0)
Salisbury, H. Poems of Alaska.
1954.   3946(0)
Salisbury, H. Great land ...
1969.   3947(0)
Scenes from land midnight sun.
n.d.   3994(7)
Service, R.W. Alaska-Yukon
favorites. [1967?]   4048(0)
Service, R.W. Ballads of cheechako. [c1909]   4049(7)
Service, R.W. Bar-room ballads.
1940.   4050(7)
Service, R.W. Collected poems.
1944.   4051(7)
Service, R.W. Collected verse
... [c1930]   4052(7)
Service, R.W. Complete poeti-
cal works. [c1921]   4053(7)
Service, R.W. Rhymes rolling
stone. 1912.   4056(7)
Service, R.W. ...favorites...
[1967?]   4057(7)
Service, R.W. Songs of sour-
dough. [c1907]   4058(7)
Service, R.W. Best of ...
1963.   4059(7)
Service, R.W. Complete poems
... 1933.   4060(7)
Service, R.W. Shooting Dan
McGrew ... 1969.   4061(7)
Service, R.W. Spell of Yukon.
1943.   4062(7)
Service, R.W. Spell of Yukon.
[c1907]   4063(7)
Service, R.W. Yukon poems
... 1967.   4065(7)
Shields, W.C. Ancient ground
... 1918.   4115(5)
Shriever, L.W. Alaskan verses
...native... 1969.   4135(0)
Sutherland, H.V. Bigg's Bar
... 1901.   4405(7)
Sutherland, H.V. Out of North.
1913.   4406(7)
Swerdloff, H.G. Yarns of
Yukon. [c1966]   4430(7)
Taber, R.G. Stray gold ...
1915.   4442(0)

Taylor, S.D. Lure of north-
land...1955.   4473(0)
Thomas, E.L.R. Night in
Sitka. 1948.   4491(1)
Townsend, M.D. Alaska calling.
1938.   4565(1)
Voice of Yukon ...
1930.   4712(7)
Warfel, K. Fow! and other
fingerprints. 1966. 4740(0)
Wiedemann, T. Saga of Alaska.
[c1946]   4862(0)
Wirt, Sherwood. Cracked ice
... [c1937]   4932(0)
Yanert, W. A dab o' sour-
dough. [ca1935?]   4985(3)
Yanert, W. Yukon breezes.
1935(1937)   4986(0)
Yukon Bill. Derby days in
Yukon. [1910]   5004(7)
Z. Q. Alaska; spectacular
Rhino-Russ. 1868.   5015(1)

REFERENCE WORKS.

Alaska almanac.
1905-09.   28(0)
Alaska buyer's guide.
1957.   41(0)
Alaska directory and gazetteer.
1935.   60(0)
Alaska Press Club. Alaska
blue book. 1963.   103(0)
Alaska State Fair. Premium
list & direct.1960.   111(2)
Alaska Weekly. Alaska year
book. 1926.   140(0)
Alcan Pub. Co. Alaskan opportunities. [ca1946]   166(0)
Almanac Pub. Co. Farmer's
almanac. 1966.   188(0)
Atkinson, T.H. Alaska petroleum directory. 1962. 316(0)
Bowen, R.O. Alaska literary
directory. 1964.   620(0)
Bowen, R.O. Alaska dictionary.
1965.   629(0)
Collins, R. Dinak'i Upper Kuskokwim dict. 1966.   984(5)
Daily Alaska Fishing News.
...almanac. 1946.   1152(0)
Davis, E.A. ...encyclopedia
... 1910.   1199(0)

REFERENCE WORKS. (cont.)

Downing & Clarke. Pocket dict.
  Chinook jargon...1898.1342(0)
Dynes, W.M. ...Alaska directory
  buyer's guide. 1920. 1399(0)
Dynes, W.M. ...tours and di-
  rectory s. e. 1921. 1400(1)
Forbes, H.A. Gazetteer No.
  Canada...Alaska.1948. 1597(0)
Freeman, M. Salmon packer's
  directory. 1908. 1647(1)
Harrington, M.W. Alaskan al-
  manac...1901. 1956(0)
[Henry, D.] Tł'eaka Hok'anaga'
  ...Koyukuk...n. d. 2068(5)
Iankievich, F. Straviteljni
  slovar ... 1790-91. 2252(0)
Int'l. North Pac. Fish. Comm.
  Statist. yrbk. 1952. 2282(0)
Lee, C.A. Aleutian Indian and
  Eng. dictionary.1896. 2665(6)
Legal Directories Pub. Co.
  Pac. coast...1961. 2673(0)
Milanowski, P. Dindee Shuu
  Aandeeg. 1961. 3111(3)
Mueller, R.J. Short illus. ...
  dict. Kutchin. 1964. 3220(5)
Naish, C. Eng.-Tlingit dict.
  1963. 3271(1)
No. Pac. Pub. Co. No. Pac.
  almanac...1890. 3348(0)
Pacific States newspaper
  directory. 1888. 3463(0)
Pan American Airways. Panairway
  ...handbook. [1943] 3483(0)
Petitot, E.F.S.J. Dictionnaire
  Dènè...1876. 3557(0)
Polar Bear C.B. Club. Alaska
  C.B.radio direct.1968.3626(0)
Polk, R.L., & Co. ... Alaska-
  Yukon gaz. ...1901. 3628(0)
Polk, R.L., & Co. ...Fairbanks
  city direct. 1959. 3629(3)
Polk, R.L., & Co. Ore., Wash.
  ...gaz. ... 1901. 3630(0)
Radlov, L.F. ...Wörterbuch...
  Kinai-Sprache. 1874. 3723(0)
Research Institute Alaska...
  survey. 1. [c1970] 3784(0)
Research Institute Alaska...
  survey. 2. [c1970] 3785(0)

Snodgrass, J.O. American Indi-
  an painters. 1967. 4224(0)
Soldier's souvenir handy book.
  ... [1944?] 4241(0)
Stefansson, V. Arctic manual.
  1940. 4301(4)
Tanana Directory Co. Directory
  Tanana Valley. 1907. 4447(3)
Terminal Pub. Co. North Pac.
  ports...1914. 4478(0)
Terminal Pub. Co. Terminal
  facilities...1914. 4479(0)
Tewkesbury, W. Alaska business
  directory. [1948] 4480(0)
Tewkesbury, W. Alaska Hy. and
  travel guide.[c1950] 4481(0)
Tewkesbury, W. ...who's who...
  bus. index. [c1947] 4482(0)
Thibert, A. Eng.-Eskimo ...
  dictionary. 1958. 4483(0)
Thomson Statistical Service.
  ...man. finance.1930.4522(0)
Troutman, A. Alaska oil & gas
  handbook. 1958. 4580(0)
Van Winkle, L.E. Juneau-Doug.
  direct. 1915. 4655(1)
Vize, V.I. Russkie poliārnye
  ... 1948. 4709(0)
Walton, W.B. Eskimo or Innuit
  dictionary. 1901. 4736(0)
Webster, D.H. Iñupiat Eskimo
  dictionary. [c1970] 4771(4)
Wood, P. ... 1945 Alaska business direct. [1945] 4953(0)

RELIGION.

Almquist, A. Covenant missions
  in Alaska. 1962. 189(0)
Anatoli, A. Indiane Aliaski
  ... [1907?] 230(0)
Anderson, E.G. Dog-team doc-
  tor. 1940. 243(5)
Archer, F.A. Heroine North
  Charlotte Bompas.1929.275(7)
Arctander, J.W. Apostle ...
  Duncan. [c1909] 276(1)
Baker, J.C. Baptist history
  ... [1912] 359(0)
Barker, E.B. Alaska, hist.
  impersonation. 1912. 399(0)
Barnum, F. Life Alaska mission
  ... 1893. 403(5)

RELIGION. (cont.)

[Barsukov, I.] Innokentiĩa ...
1883.   414(0)
[Barsukov, I.] Life and work
Innocent...1897.   415(0)
[Barsukov, I.] Pis'ma Innoken-
tiĩa. 1897-1901.   416(0)
[Barsukov, I.] Tvoreniĩa
Innokentiĩa...1887.   417(0)
Beattie, W.G. Marsden of
Alaska...1955.   456(1)
Bennett, Mrs. F.S. People
without country. n.d.   500(8)
Bensin, B.M. Hist. Greek Or-
thodox Ch. 1941.   505(0)
Bensin, B.M. Russ. Orthodox
Church. n.d.   506(0)
Bompas, W.C. Diocese Macken-
zie River. 1888.   602(7)
Bompas, W.C. Northern lights
...25 yrs. [18__?]   604(7)
Brady, E.P. Sheldon Jackson,
progressive...1911.   640(0)
Brady, Mrs. J.G. First mis-
sionary Mrs. A. R. Mc-
Farland. 1912.   641(1)
[Calasanctius, Sr.Mary Joseph]
Voice of Alaska.1935.   767(5)
[Calasanctius, Sr. Mary Joseph]
Voix de l'Alaska.1930. 768(5)
Carlson, S.W. Faith...Eastern
Orthodox...1954.   835(0)
Catholic Daughters America.
Alaskan recipes.1960.   870(1)
Chapman, J.W. Camp on Yukon.
1948.   891(3)
Chapman, J.W. Alaska's great
highway. 1909.   892(0)
Chapman, J.W. Our missions in
Alaska. 1894.   893(0)
Chapman, M.N. Animistic be-
liefs Ten'a. 1939.   895(3)
Chitty, A.B. Hudson Stuck of
Alaska. 1952.   918(0)
Church Missionary Soc. Deputa-
tion Metlakatla. n.d.   930(1)
Church Missions Pub. Co. Indian
tribes ... [c1926]   931(0)
Cody, H.A. Apostle of North
W.C.Bompas. 1908.   966(7)
Cody, H.A. On trail and rapid
... 1911.   967(7)

Collison, W.H. In wake of war
canoe. 1915.   988(1)
Colonial Church Chronicle.
Mission Russ. Ch.1849.991(6)
Cox, M. John Driggs among the
Eskimos. 1956.   1103(5)
Cox, M. Peter Trimble Rowe.
1959.   1104(0)
Crosby, T. Up...canoe & mis-
sion ship. [1914]   1128(1)
Cross, J.F. Eskimo adoption.
n.d.   1130(8)
Cross, J.F. Eskimo children.
n.d.   1131(8)
Cross, J.F. The Eskimos. Eski-
mo women. n.d.   1132(8)
Curtis, C.H. Gospel in Alaska.
1946.   1143(0)
Dabovich, S. Holy Orthodox
Church. 1898.   1149(0)
Dabovich, S. Lives of Saints.
1898.   1150(0)
Dashkevich, A. Arkhangels-
Mikhailovskiĭ...1899.1188(1)
Davis, G.T.B. Indian arcadia
Metlakhatla.1904.   1200(1)
Davis, G.T.B. Metlakahtla...
1904.   1201(1)
deBaets, M. ...Seghers...
1896.   1223(8)
DeGarmo, M. Alaska. Questions
...mission. 1912.   1231(0)
Desjardins, J.-A. En Alaska...
1930.   1278(5)
Drebert, F. Brief history...
Bethel...[ca1942]   1348(5)
Drebert, F. Alaska missionary
... 1959.   1349(5)
Dugre, A. Les oblates dans
l'Extreme Nord.1922. 1368(7)
[Duncan, Wm.] Metlahkatlah
...Tsimsheean. 1869.   1382(1)
Duncan, Wm. Metlakahtla & Ch.
Mission Soc. 1887.   1383(1)
Eastman, F. Unfinished business
Presbyt. Ch. 1921.   1403(0)
Eaton, J. Sheldon Jackson...
1898.   1404(0)
[Episcopal Ch.] Alaska...
1883.   1478(0)
Fairbanks Christian Science
Soc. By-laws. 1913.   1514(3)

RELIGION. (cont.)

Fairbanks cook book...Presbyt.
Church. 1913.   1519(3)
Faris, J.T. Alaskan pathfinder
S. Jackson. 1913.   1525(0)
Father Herman, Russ. missionary
... n.d.   1534(6)
Gambell, V.C. Schoolhouse...
St. Lawrence Isl.1910.1677(5)
Gapp, S.H. Kolerat Pitsiulret
Moravian...1936.   1678(5)
Gapp, S.H. Where polar ice...
Moravian... 1928.   1679(5)
Glody, R. Shepherd...W.F.Walsh
... 1934.   1738(0)
Golder, F.A. *Father* Herman...
[191_?]   1756(6)
Grant, D.A.S. Blazing gospel
trail. 1944.   1797(0)
Green, J.S. Journal tour ...
1915.   1846(1)
Guernsey, A.M. Under northern
lights. 1917.   1878(8)
Halcombe, J.J. Stranger than
fiction. 1872.   1897(1)
Hale, C.R. Innocent of Moscow
... 1888.   1898(0)
Hallock, C.M. Forty-eight
plus. 1948.   1915(0)
Hamilton, J.T. Hist. Church
Moravian...1900.   1919(0)
Hamilton, J.T. Hist. missions
Morvanian Church.1901.1920(0)
Hamilton, J.T. Report...
Bishop ... 1906.   1921(0)
Hamilton, J.T. ...Moravian
missions...1890.   1922(0)
Hamilton, K.W. Left on island.
1905.   1923(8)
Harrison, C. Hydah mission, Q.
Charlotte Isl.[1884?] 1968(1)
Hayes, F.S. Land of challenge
... 1941.   2000(0)
Hayes, F.S. Arctic gateway.
1940.   2002(0)
Headley, P.C. Reaper & harvest
E.P.Hammond. 1884.   2012(0)
Hill,E.P. Aaron L. Lindsley,
Presbyt. 1902.   2105(1)
Hubbard, B.R. Mush, you male-
mutes! 1932.   2214(6)

Hulbert, W. Bishop...Sheldon
Jackson. 1948.   2222(0)
Hutton, J.E. Hist. Moravian
missions. 1923.   2248(0)
Jackson, Sheldon. Alaska,
missions...1880.   2311(0)
Jackson, Sheldon. Facts about
Alaska. 1894.   2312(0)
Jackson, Sheldon. Natives
tribes...1883.   2313(0)
Jenkins, T. Man...Peter Trimble
Rowe. 1943.   2338(0)
Johnshoy, W. Apaurak...T. L.
Brevig...1944.   2367(5)
Judge, C.J. Amer. missionary
Wm. H. Judge. 1904. 2394(7)
Kashevarov, A.P. *Father*
Herman ...[1916?]   2413(6)
Kashevaroff, A.P. St. Michael's
Cathedral. n.d.   2415(1)
Knapp, E.J. General convention
...1910.   2492(8)
Kohlstedt, E.D. Glimpse of
Alaska. n.d.   2502(1)
Kohlstedt, E.D. Wm. Duncan
Metlakatla...1957.   2503(1)
LaFortune, B. ...prayers, hymns
Catholic. 1916.   2582(5)
L'Ange-Gardien, M. En
Alaska. 1900.   2597(0)
Lathrop, G.G. Tashekah.
n.d.   2635(1)
Lazell, J.A. Alaskan apostle
Sheldon Jackson.1960.2653(0)
Life *Rev. Mother* Amadeus...
Ursuline...1923.   2709(0)
Lindsley, A.L. Sketches ...
[1879?]   2717(1)
Lopp, W.T. Alaska, a year
alone ... n.d.   2793(5)
McWhinnie, Mrs. Jas. Trip to
Alaska. n.d.   2950(6)
McWhinnie, Mrs. Jas. Hist. Ko-
diak Orphanage. 1912.2951(6)
Mayberry, G. Sheldon Jackson
Jr. College. 1953.   3041(1)
Ménager, F.M. Kingdom of
seal. 1962.   3078(5)
Menzel, B. Dans le toundra
L'Alaska. 1938.   3082(8)
Methodist Alaska Yukon Pac.
Comm.1834-1909. [1909]3089(0)

RELIGION. (cont.)

Metlakahtla ...
1800. . . . . 3090(1)
Metlakatla, Alaska; Church
manual. n.d.   3091(1)
Missionary launch "Princeton"
[ca1925]   3145(1)
Moffett, T.C. American Indian
...gospel. 1914.   3151(0)
Moravian Church in Alaska.
n.d.   3168(0)
Moravian mission among Esquimeaux...1887.   3169(0)
Moravian mission in Alaska.
1895.   3179(0)
Morgan, B.B. Very thought of
thee. 1952.   3177(8)
Morice, A.G. 50 yrs. in
west. Canada. 1930. 3187(7)
Murphy, E.F. Bishop Bompas.
n.d.   3253(7)
Myers, J.L. Great land.
n.d.   3266(0)
Nikolai. ... Orthodox mission
...1894.   3308(0)
Nikolai. Propoviedi ...
1897.   3310(0)
O'Connor, P. Eskimo parish.
[c1947]   3376(5)
Official record Alaska Metho-
dist Episc. ...1904. 3384(0)
Official record Alaska Mission
Methodist...1905.   3385(0)
Oswalt, W.H. Mission of change
Moravian. 1963.   3437(5)
Owens, F.R. Sky pilot of
Alaska. 1949.   3442(0)
Partridge, W.M. Some facts
missions. [1900]   3498(0)
[Piet, J.M.] Land of midnight
sun. 1925.   3585(0)
Pinart, A.L. Eskimaux et
Koloshes...1873.   3594(0)
Pingry, Mrs. J.F. Message of
Alaskan life. 1905. 3602(8)
Presbyt. Ch. Alaska...programs
Jr. meetings. n.d. 3678(0)
Presbyt. Ch. Alaska...poem by
S. H. Young. n.d.   3679(0)
Presbyt. Ch. New America in
songs. n.d.   3680(0)

Presbyt. Ch. Experience of
Chilcat George. 1911.3681(1)
Presbyt. Ch. ...in Alaska...
1886.   3682(0)
Presbyt. Ch. Relation ...
missionary...1900. 3683(0)
Pringle, G.C.F. Adventures in
service. 1929.   3695(7)
Pringle, G.C.F. Tillicums
of trail. [c1922]   3696(7)
Pustinskiĭ, I. Otchet o sost-
vianiĭ...1906.   3704(0)
Radcliffe, J.W. Our northern
possessions. 1894.   3720(0)
Read, F.W. G.I. Parson.
1945.   3762(6)
Reid, W.A. Chips...log"Helen
Gould" YMCA. [1906?] 3779(0)
Ridley, Wm. Senator MacDonald
Metlakatla. 1882.   3816(1)
Ridley, Wm. Snapshots...Bishop
Ridley...1903.   3817(1)
Rodli, A.S. North of heaven.
1963.   3864(5)
Romig, J.H. Annual report...
Moravian...1899.   3877(5)
Ross, Mrs. J.T. Aaron Ladner
Lindsley. [ca1910?] 3886(1)
Rouse, J.J. Pioneer work...
[1935?]   3902(7)
Ryder, C.J. Alaska-history...
n. d.   3929(0)
S., Z. O zhizni...Innokentiĩa
... 1893.   3934(0)
Sabine, B.W. Summer trip...
missions.[ca1910?] 3936(5)
Saint Ann's Academy. ...in B.C.
& Alaska. n.d.   3939(0)
St. Joseph's Hosp. ...recipes
... 1961.   3941(3)
St. Matthew's Episc. Church...
recipes...1944.   3942(3)
St. Matthew's Episc. Church...
cook book. [ca1950?] 3943(3)
Santos, A. Jesuitos...Polo
Norte. 1943.   3958(0)
Savage, A.H. Dogsled apostle.
1942.   3979(0)
Schwalbe, A.B. Dayspring...
Moravian...1951.   4016(5)
Shalamov, T. Po Missii...
1904.   4084(6)

RELIGION. (cont.)

Shalamov, T. Ocherk pokhodnago
zhurnala...1904.   4085(6)
Shenitz, H. ...Father...Russ.
Orthodox ... 1962.   4109(0)
Shiels, A.W. Work of Veniami-
nov. 1947.   4122(0)
Smith, M.P. Alaska.   ]
[1909]-1910.   4203(0)
Stewart, R.L. Sheldon Jackson
... [c1908]   4345(0)
Stuck, H. Alaskan missions...
Episc. Church.1920.   4371(0)
Sturdza, A. Missions de Camt-
chatka...n.d.   4376(0)
Sturdza, A. Oeuvres posthumes
...Russie. 1858.   4377(0)
[Sturdza, A.] Pamiatnik
trudov...1857.   4378(0)
Svenska Missionsförbundet.
Alaska förr...1897.   4409(5)
Thomas, Tay. Cry in wilderness.
[c1967]   4500(0)
Thornton, H.R. Our Alaskan
mission. n.d.   4527(5)
Thornton, H.R. Report Alaska
mission. n.d.   4528(5)
Tosi, P. La missione dell'
Alaska...1893.   4559(0)
Vahl, Jens. Alaska; folket
og missionen. 1872.   4628(0)
Valaam Monastery. K stoliet-
nemu...1894.   4631(0)
[Valaam Monastery] Zhiznj ...
Germana ... 1894.   4632(6)
Veniaminov, I.E.P. Natavlenie
Innokentiĭa. 1899.   4674(0)
Veniaminov, I.E.P. Orthodox
schools. 1905.   4676(0)
Veniaminov, I.E.P. Sostiania
... 1840.   4677(0)
Waid, E.C. Alaska, land of
totem. [1910]   4727(1)
Warner, G.C. Windows into
Alaska. 1928.   4742(0)
Weems, C. Bishop of Arctic.
1912. [P.T.Rowe]   4781(0)
Wellcome, H.S. Story of Met-
lakahtla. 1887.   4785(1)
Wentworth, E. Mission to
Metlakatla. 1968.   4795(1)

Willard, C.M.W. Children of
far north. n.d.   4873(1)
Willard, C.M.W. Kin-da-shon's
wife...[c1892]   4874(1)
Willard, C.M.W. Life in Alaska
letters. 1884.   4875(1)
Winchell, M.E. Home by Bering
Sea. 1951.   4918(6)
Woman's Amer.Baptist Home Mis-
sion.studies.1916.   4947(0)
Woman's Amer.Baptist Home Mis-
sion.Alaska. 1911.   4948(1)
Woman's Soc. Christian Serv.
Come kitchen. [1967]   4949(1)
Woman's Soc. Christian Serv.
Nome cook...[1968?]   4950(5)
Wright, J. McN. Among Alaskans
...[c1883]   4973(8)
Young, S. Hall. Adventures in
Alaska. [c1919]   4996(0)

RELIGION - Translations.

American Bible Soc. God-im
uḵaluŋi. 1946.   193(5)
American Bible Soc. Kanegriarat
ashilret...1929.   194(5)
American Bible Soc. Kanerea-
kakgtak. 1967.   195(5)
American Bible Soc. Tuyurtiŋi
Paulum. 1948.   196(5)
Amerikanskiĭ Pravosl. Viestnik.
Dieĭaniĭa...1902.   211(6)
Bielkov, Z. Molitvy ...
1896.   554(5)
Bompas, Wm. C. Lessons...Ten-
ni or Slavi...1892.   603(7)
Bompas, Wm. C. Western esqui-
maux primer. n.d.   605(7)
Brit. & For. Bible Soc. Acts
Apostles Haida.1898.   664(1)
Brit. & For. Bible Soc. Gospel
St. John Haida. 1899.   665(1)
Brit. & For. Bible Soc. Gospel
St. Luke Haida. 1899.   666(1)
Brit. & For. Bible Soc. Gospel
St. Mark. 1916.   667(1)
Brit. & For. Bible Soc. St.
Mark's kloosh...1912.   668(1)
Campbell, E.O. Pĕ nĕl' lŭ ...
1910.   791(5)
Church of England. Selections.
Tsimshian. n.d.   929(1)

RELIGION - Translations.
(cont.)
Cook Foundation, David C. Ku-
liak̦tuak̦...n.d.   1008(4)
Donskoi, V. Ekuiatle ...
1901.   1332(1)
[Duncan, Wm.] Append. a shimal-
giagum Zimshian.n.d. 1381(1)
[Episcopal Ch.] Book common
prayer Haida. 18991 1479(1)
[Episcopal Ch.] Morning prayer
Eskimo. 1923.   1480(5)
[Episcopal Ch.] Service book...
Indians Tanana. 1908. 1481(3)
[Episcopal Ch.] Tukudh primer
Tinne Indians. n.d.   1482(7)
Harrison, C. Old Testament
Haida. 1893.   1966(1)
Harrison, C. St. Matthew...
Haida. 1891.   1967(1)
Hinz, J. Grammar...Kuskokwim
... 1944.   2123(5)
Hinz, J. Passion week manual.
1915.   2124(5)
Indian Boys' Press. Catholic
prayers...Tinneh.1897.2259(5)
Indian Boys' Press. Tinneh In-
dian catechism. 1897. 2260(5)
Jette, J. Catholic Ch. liturgy
...Tinne...1904.   2352(7)
Keen, J.H. Port. book common
prayer Haida.1899.   2422(1)
Liturgy...Eskimo Kuskokwim...
1945.   2739(5)
Lodochnikov, A. Molitvy ...
1898.   2747(6)
Lonneux, M.J. Catholic manual
Innuit. n.d.   2790(5)
Lonneux, M.J. Mass book ...
Innuit. 1950.   2791(5)
Lonneux, M.J. Graded catechism
Innuit. 1951.   2792(5)
McDonald, R. Book Common Prayer
Takudh. 1873.   2872(7)
McDonald, R. Chiliq Takudh...
1890.   2873(3)
McDonald, R. Cilicu whut ana...
Takudh. 1901.   2874(3)
McDonald, R. David vi Psalmnut
Takudh...1886.   2875(7)
McDonald, R. Ettunetle ...
Takudh...1898.   2876(7)

McDonald, R. 4th & 5th books
Moses...1891.   2877(7)
McDonald, R. Grammar Tukudh...
1911.   2878(7)
McDonald, R. Joshua to 1.
Samuel. 1892.   2879(7)
McDonald, R. Kwunduk nirzi
... 1885.   2880(7)
McDonald, R. Mosis vit ...
ttyig...1890.   2881(7)
[McDonald, R., tr.?] Nuwheh
kukwadhud...1874.   2882(7)
McDonald, R. Ochikthud
ettunetle...1885.   2883(7)
McDonald, R. Tunutrunatli...
1886.   2884(7)
McDonald, R. Zzehkke enjit...
Takudh. 1885.   2885(7)
Metlakahtla ...
1800. . . . .   3090(1)
Nadezhdin, I. Sbornik tserkov-
nykh ... 1896.   3270(1)
Nikolai. Molitvy na koloshin-
skim...1895.   3309(1)
Ostervald, J.F. Ettunetle...
1899.   3434(7)
[Prevost, J.L.] Culic whutana
...1907.   3685(3)
[Prevost, J.L.] Culic whutana
...1915.   3686(3)
Prevost, J.L. Tennatla bu chi-
lichu...1894.   3687(3)
Robau, Fr. Catholic prayers...
Innuit. 1899.   3830(5)
Sbornik tserkovnykh...
1896.   3989(5)
Schultz, A. Liturgy, hymns...
Eskimo. 1902.   4015(5)
Shaiashnikov, I. Kratkoe
pravilo...1902.   4083(6)
Soc. Promot. Christian Knowl.
Kwagutl version.n.d. 4230(1)
Soc. Promot. Christian Knowl.
Am da malshk...1889. 4241(1)
Soc. Promot. Christian Knowl.
Am da malshk...St. Luke.
[1889?]   4232(1)
Soc. Promot. Christian Knowl.
Am da malshk...St. Mark.
[1889?]   4233(1)
Soc. Promot. Christian Knowl.
Am da malshk...St. Matthew.
[1889?]   4234(1)

RELIGION - Translations.
(cont.)
Summer Inst. Linguistics. Or-
der morning...Esk.n.d.4385(5)
Summer Inst. Linguistics. Uk-
piḵtuat...Eskimo.n.d. 4388(5)
Tagarook, P. Jesus kamanaḵtuat
...Eskimo. n.d.
Tikhon, *Bishop*. Sviatoe evangel.
Ioanna. 1902.   4538(6)
Tikhon, *Bishop*. Sviatoe evangel.
Luki...1903.   4539(6)
Tucker, M. Jesus will...[Esk.
pictograph] [ca1967] 4586(5)
Tyzhnov, I. Khrishtianat...
1847.   4602(6)
Tyzhnov, I. ...Ot Matfeīa...
1848.   4603(6)
Veniaminov, I.E.P. Gospoda
... [1840]   4670(6)
Veniaminov, I.E.P. Kratkaīa
...1840.   4671(6)
Veniaminov, I.E.P. Nachatki...
1840.   4673(6)
Veniaminov, I.E.P. Natavlenie
...1899.   4674(6)
Veniaminov, I.E.P. Ukazanie
puti...1901.   4678(6)
Veniaminov, I.E.P. Ukazanie
puti...1840.   4679(6)
Veniaminov, I.E.P. Wegweiser
... 1848.   4680(6)
Wartes, W.C. Utḵiaġvik Iñu-
piat hymn...1959.   4746(4)
Wycliffe Bible Translators.
Jesus nts'aa'...1965. 4978(3)
Wycliffe Bible Translators.
Brass serpent...n.d. 4979(1)
Wycliffe Bible Translators.
Utk'-Uheenee...1963. 4980(1)
Wycliffe Bible Translators.
Ut K'Uheenih.[ca1963?]4981(1)
Zibelī, W. Atuutit Mumiksat.
[1967]   5026(4)

SPORT FISHING. (See HUNTING
          and Sport Fishing)

SPORTS.

Hauser, W.E. Thirty hikes in
Alaska. 1967.   1990(2)

Morgan, L. Woman's guide to
boating...1968.   3179(0)
Palmedo, R. Ski new horizons.
1961.   3477(2)

THESES.

Adler, B.W.K. Der nordasia-
tische Pfeil...1901.   13(0)
Cooley, R.A. Politics and
conservation. 1963. 1061(0)
Martin, L. Some features gla-
ciers...1913.   3006(2)
Müller, M. Koloniale wirt-
schaft...1935.   3236(0)
Oberg, K. Social economy...
Tlingit...1940.   3372(1)
Reid, C.F. Educ. Terr. and
outlying...1940.   3777(0)
Spicer, G.W. Constitutional
status...1927.   4263(0)
Stanton, S.B. Behring Sea
dispute. 1890.   4284(0)
Thomas, B.P. Russo-Amer. re-
lations 1815-67.1930.4489(0)

TELEPATHY.

Wilkins, G.H. Thoughts through
space. 1942.   4872(0)

THEATRE - Playscripts, et al.

Beach, E. The spoilers.
n.d.   447(5)
Conkle, E.P. Two hundred were
chosen. 1937.   1003(2)
Corser, H.P. Mere man ...
1915.   1087(8)
Dobbs' Alaska Moving Picture
Co. Initial ... n.d. 1313(3)
Fairbanks 4th July Celebra-
tion. Off. prog.1909.1521(3)
Kotzebue, A.F.F. Count Benyow-
sky...1798.   2514(0)
Kotzebue, A.F.F. La Peyrouse...
1800.   2515(5)
Vanderbourg. Le Perouse ou le
voyage...1810.   4644(0)
Z., Q. Alaska ...
1868.   5015(1)

TRANSPORTATION - Air.

Fay, Spofford & Thorndike. ...
air terminal Anchorage...
1960.   1535(2)
Fay, Spofford & Thorndike. ...
air terminal Fairbanks...
1960.   1536(3)
Fisher Assoc., L. State of
Alaska air trade...Anchorage
... 1962.   1568(2)
Fisher Assoc., L. State of
Alaska air trade...Fairbanks
...1962.   1569(3)
McKinley, C. U.S.-Canadian...
civil aviation. 1944. 2921(0)
Pan American Airways. Panair
way...[1943]   3483(0)
Weigert, H.W. Compass of
world...1944.   4782(0)
Weigert, H. W. New compass of
world...1949.   4783(0)

TRANSPORTATION - Highways.
     (See also ALASKA HIGHWAY)

Alaska opportunities and hy.
... 1953.   97(0)
Hesse, W.A. Proposed arterial
highway system.1940. 2087(0)
Ingraham, J. Friendship Road
Pan Am. Hy. 1961.   2265(0)
Pan American Hy. System.
1959.   3484(0)
Proposed system of highways...
1945.   3699(0)
Valdez Miner. Alaska, the Ri-
chardson Road. 1922. 3634(0)

TRANSPORTATION - Horses.

Page, E. M. Wild horses and
gold. [c1932]   3469(7)

TRANSPORTATION - Rail.

Alaska Bureau. Alaska tour.
1913.   37(0)
Alaska Central Ry. Map of surveyed route. 1903.   43(2)
Alaska Central R.R. Co. Official prospectus. 1902.   44(2)

Alaska Central Ry. Through...
1906.   45(2)
Alaska-Northwestern R.R.
Prospectus. n.d.   94(2)
Alaska Short Line Ry. & Navi-
gation Co. ... Alaska Short
Line...[1903?]   108(8)
Alaska S.S. Co. Copper R. &
Northwestern Ry. 1914.118(2)
Ballaine, J.E. Strangling
railroad...[1923?]   375(0)
Canadian Nat. R.R. & S.S. Alas-
ka & Yukon...1930.   820(0)
Canadian Pac. Ry. Co. Roads...
1932.   823(0)
Chic. & N.W. Ry. Co. Seattle
[1909?]   912(0)
Coffin, C.C. Seat of empire.
1870.   972(0)
Copper R. & N.W. Ry. Finding
of empire. [1909?]   1070(2)
Council City & Solomon R. R.R.
U.S. mail...1907.   1097(5)
Dawson, C.A. New Northwest.
1947.   1215(0)
Edgar, J.H. Canadian railway
...1933.   1410(0)
Emerson, H. Alaska...projects.
1904.   1451(0)
Emerson, H. Alaskan railway
problem. n.d.   1452(0)
Fish, J. Few facts...Valdez.
1914.   1567(2)
Fitch, E.M. The Alaska Rail-
road. 1967.   1573(0)
Gillette, E. Facts on Alaska
... 1904.   1722(8)
Gilpin, W. Cosmopolitan railway
...1849.   1732(0)
[Graves, S.H.] On "White Pass"
payroll...1908.   1799(1)
Great Northern Ry. Co. Alaska
and ... 1898.   1834(0)
Great Northern Ry. Co. Alaska
land ... n.d.   1035(0)
Great Northern Ry. Co. Alaska
tours...1898.   1836(0)
Great Northern Ry. Co. Golden
sands...1899.   1837(5)
Great Northern Ry. Co. Northern
Pac. tour...[c1888]   1838(0)

TRANSPORTATION - Rail. (cont.)

Herron, E.A. Alaska's Mike
  Heney. 1960.   2079(1)
Howe, R.S. Great Northern
  country. 1902.   2205(0)
Hyde, J. Northern Pacific tours
  ...1889.   2250(0)
Lane, A.W. Letters Franklin K.
  Lane...1922.   2592(0)
Muir, J. Alaska.
  n.d. . . . . 3221(0)
North Pacific Coast country.
  1907.   3344(0)
Northern Pacific R.R. Co.
  Across ...[1890?]   3352(0)
Northern Pacific R.R. Co.
  Alaska...[19__?]   3353(0)
Northern Pacific R.R. Co.
  Puget Sd. ...[19__?] 3354(0)
O'Connor, D.J. Alaska's
  interior...1953.   3375(0)
Pacific Northwest and Alaska
  ... [1915?]   3455(0)
Peattie, E.W. Journey through
  ...1890.
Prince, B. Le M. Alaska Rail-
  road...1964.   3694(0)
Resolution requesting...aid
  r.r. construct.1914. 3786(5)
Russell, J.A. Industrial...
  weather. 1957.   3918(0)
Shiels, A.W. Story two dreams
  ... [c1957]   4121(0)
Syndicat Français du Trans-
  Alaska-Sibérien. Le chemin...
  [1902?]   4436(0)
Tanana Valley R.R. Co. Annual
  report. 1909.   4450(3)
Union Pacific R.R. Co. Sights
  ... 1890.   4612(0)
Union Pacific R.R. Co. Great
  Pacific...[19__?]   4613(0)
Union Pacific R.R. Co. Pacific
  ... 1927.   4614(0)
Western Alaska Construction Co.
  Railroad...[1904?]   4799(5)
Wheeler, O.D. Wonderland '98.
  1898.   4808(0)
White Pass & Yukon Ry. Handbook
  ... [1928?]   4828(0)
White Pass & Yukon Ry. Tour...
  [190_?]   4829(0)

White Pass & Yukon Ry. Alaska
  ... [191_?]   4830(0)
White Pass & Yukon Ry. Alaska
  and ... [19__?]   4831(0)
White Pass & Yukon Ry. Alaska
  and Yukon...1916.   4832(0)
White Pass & Yukon Ry. Alaska,
  Atlin...[1928?]   4833(0)
White Pass & Yukon Ry. Alaska,
  Yukon...[1939]   4834(0)
White Pass & Yukon Ry. Alaska,
  Atlin and...[19__?]   4835(0)
White Pass & Yukon Ry. Incom-
  parable...[1928?]   4836(7)
White Pass & Yukon Ry. White
  Pass...[1901?]   4837(0)
White Pass & Yukon Ry. White
  Pass...1925.   4838(0)
White Pass & Yukon Ry. White
  Pass ... [c1923]   4839(0)
Whiting, F.B. Grit, grief and
  gold. 1933.   4843(1)
Wickersham, J. Address Tanana
  Mines Ry. ... 1905.   4855(3)

TRANSPORTATION - Water.

Alaska Bureau. Alaska tour.
  1913.   37(0)
Alaska Coast Co. Southwestern
  Alaska route. 1907.   47(0)
Alaska Short Line Ry. & Navi-
  gation Co. Ry. [1903?]108(8)
Alaska S.S. Co. Alaska ahead.
  1939.   112(1)
Alaska S.S. Co. Alaska excur-
  sion tours. n.d.   113(1)
Alaska S.S. Co. Alaska glaciers
  ... 1906.   114(1)
Alaska S.S. Co. Alaska Indian
  basketry. 1904.   115(1)
Alaska S.S. Co. An Alaska in-
  terlude. [1939?]   116(1)
Alaska S.S. Co. Alaska
  schedules. 1939.   117(1)
Alaska S.S. Co. Copper River
  & N.W. Ry. 1914.   118(2)
Alaska S.S. Co. Let's go sai-
  laing...[c1948]   119(1)
Alaska S.S. Co. My Alaska
  cruise. [19__?]   120(1)
Alaska S.S. Co. Sailing shel-
  tered...1933.   121(1)

TRANSPORTATION - Water. (cont.)

Alaska S.S. Co. Scenery ahead
... n.d.   122(1)
Alaska S.S. Co. Sportsman's
guide...[ca1952]   123(0)
Alaska S.S. Co. Statement ...
1923.   124(0)
Alaska S.S. Co. This is Alaska.
[c1948]   125(1)
Alaska S.S. Co. Totem poles...
1905.   126(1)
Alaska S.S. Co. Trip to won-
derful ... 1905.   127(1)
Alaska, newest homeland.
1930.   129(0)
Anderson, J. Boating on Yukon.
1930.   248(0)
Anderson, W.R. First under
North Pole. 1959.   251(4)
Anderson, W.R. Nautilus; 90°
north. 1959.   252(4)
Andrews, R.W. This was sea-
faring. 1955.   262(0)
[Bechervaise, J.?] 36 years
seafaring. 1864.   460(0)
Bixby, W. Track of Bear.
1965.   568(0)
Bratrud, O. Beating to wind-
ward. 1961.   648(0)
Calkins, R.H. High tide.
1952.   776(0)
Canada Steamship Lines. Far
west...1943.   819(0)
Canadian National R.R. & S.S.
Alaska...1930.   820(0)
Canadian National S.S. Alaska
via...1958.   821(1)
Canadian Pacific Ry. Co. 1000
miles...1936.   822(1)
Canadian Pacific Ry. Co. Roads
adventure. 1932.   823(0)
Chapelle, H.I. Amer. small
sailing craft. 1951.   890(0)
Chase, W.H. Reminisc. Billie
Moore. [c1947]   900(0)
Crewe, F. Log sloop "North"
Cook's Inlet. 1896.   1121(2)
Cummings, H. Synopsis..."Tusca-
rora"...1874.   1138(0)
Curtin, W.R. Yukon voyage...
Yukoner. 1938.   1142(0)

Ferry to Alaska.
[1967] . . . . . .   1550(1)
Francis, F. War, waves...
Lancashire Witch.18811629(0)
Gleaves, A. Life...Wm. H.
Emory...1923.   1737(0)
Howe, R.S. Great Northern
country. 1902.   2205(0)
Hunt, C.E. Shenandoah ...
1867.   2234(5)
Irvine, T.A. Ice all between.
1959.   2296(4)
Lewis & Dryden's marine hist.
1895.   2695(0)
Longstreth, T.M. Force carries
on. 1954.   2787(4)
McKinley, C. Case ltd. mod. ca-
botage...1944.   2920(0)
McMicken, E.G. Seattle to
Nome. 1900.   2935(5)
Miller, Max. Fog and men on
Bering Sea. 1936.   3122(0)
Mirick, S. Feasib. auto ferry
... 1944.   3142(0)
Mjelde, M.J. Glory of Seas.
1969.   3150(0)
Morgan, M.C. Dixie raider...
Shenandoah. 1948.   3182(4)
Morison, S.E. Maritime hist.
Mass. 1921.   3193(0)
Muir, J. Cruise Corwin.
1917.   3226(4)
Munro, W.H. Tales old sea-
port. 1917.   3243(0)
Newell, G. Pacific steamboats.
1958.   3297(0)
Northern Navigation Co. Alaska
gold fields. n.d.   3351(0)
Northland Transportation Co.
Sea voyage...1941.   3355(1)
Pacific Coast S.S. Co. Alaska
cruises. [1912?]   3444(1)
Pacific Coast S.S. Co. Alaska
excursion. 1915.   3445(1)
Pacific Coast S.S. Co. Alaska
excursions. 1901.   3446(1)
Pacific Coast S.S. Co. Alaska
marvelous...1899.   3447(0)
Pacific Coast S.S. Co. Alaska
via...1906.   3448(1)
Pacific Coast S.S. Co. All
about...1887.   3449(0)

TRANSPORTATION - Water. (cont.)

Pacific Coast S.S. Co. Calif.
  B.C....1904.   3450(0)
Pacific Coast S.S. Co. 4000
  miles...1896.   3451(0)
Pacific Coast S.S. Co. Yukon
  Terr. [1902?]   3453(0)
Pacific S.S. Co. Alaska
  top...1924.   3464(1)
Pacific S.S. Co. Cruising
  ... 1929.   3465(1)
Port Orchard Navigation Co.
  Stikine R. ... 1898. 3644(1)
Shepard, I.S. Cruise "Rush"
  ... 1889.   4111(0)
Shneiderov, V.A.   Phokhod
  "Sibiriakova" 1933.   4129(0)
Steele, G.P. *Seadragon* ...
  1962.   4292(4)
Stephenson, W.S. Collect. pen
  sketches ships.1947. 4337(0)
Sundborg, G. Shipping services
  ... 1944.   4397(0)
Terminal Pub. Co. North Pac.
  ports. 1914.   4478(0)
Terminal Pub. Co. Terminal
  facilities...1914.   4479(0)
Tranter, G.J. Plowing Atlantic
  ... 1944.   4569(0)
Union S.S. Co. Our coastal
  trips. n.d.   4620(0)
Veteran Steamboatmen's Assoc.
  of West. "Eliza Anderson"
  [1940]   4694(0)
Wardman, G. Trip to Alaska...
  1884.   4737(0)
Washington & Alaska S.S. Co.
  Golden ... [1897]   4749(1)
Wead, F.W. Gales, ice and men
  ... *Bear*. 1937.   4761(0)
Whittle, W.C. Cruises ...
  "Shenandoah" 1910.   4847(4)
Wiedemann, T. Cheechako into
  sourdough. [c1942]   4861(0)
Winter, J.M. N.Y. to Alaska
  ..."Dolphin" 1943.   4929(1)

TRAVEL.

Alaska book ... treasureland.
  1960.   33(0)

Alaska Opportunist. Alaska -
  frontier. 1947.   96(0)
Alaska opportunities & hy.
  ... 1953.   97(0)
Alaskans United. Destination
  Juneau. [1964]   163(1)
Anderson, I.W.P. Odd corners.
  1917.   245(8)
[Assher, B.] Nomad in North
  Amer. 1927.   313(8)
Badlam, A. Wonders of Alaska.
  1890.   335(0)
Baedecker, K. Dominion of Ca-
  nada...1894.   336(0)
Baedecker, K. U.S. ... Alaska.
  1909.   337(0)
Ballou, M.M. New Eldorado...
  1889.   376(0)
Barber, O. Meet me in Juneau.
  1960.   397(1)
Bates, E.R. Kaleidoscope.
  1889.   427(0)
Baxter, D.V. On and off Alas-
  kan trails. 1937.   434(0)
Bell, W.H. Quiddities Alaskan
  trip. 1873.   490(1)
Bendel, B. Aus Alaska von
  Sitka...1872.   496(1)
Bergendahl, E. Alaskadage...
  1926.   518(0)
Blount, E.S. North of 53...
  n.d.   580(0)
Bogdanovich, K.I. Ocherki
  Nome. 1901.   594(5)
Boyce, W.D. Alaska and
  Panama. 1914.   633(0)
Boyce, W.D. U.S. colonies...
  1914.   635(0)
Brooks, P. Roadless area.
  1964.   686(2)
Brough, C. Thrill of seeing.
  Alaska. [ca1951]   690(8)
Bundy, H.C. Valdez-Fairbanks
  Trail...1910.   726(0)
Burr, A.R. Alaska...
  1919.   743(0)
Burrall, W.T. Trip to far
  west B.C. 1891.   744(0)
Bush, R.J. Reindeer, dogs...
  1871.   754(5)
Chittenden, N.H. Travels in
  B.C. & Alaska.1882.   917(0)

TRAVEL. (cont.)

Cholnoky, J. Amerika.
1936. 924(0)

Cipolla, A. Norte America ...
Alaska...1929. 934(0)

Clifton, V. Book of Talbot.
1933. 959(0)

Colby, M.E. Alaska, guide
... 1939. 973(0)

Colby, M.E. Alaska, profile
... 1940. 974(0)

Collis, S.M. Woman's trip...
1890. 987(1)

Craig, L.A. Glimpses sunshine
... 1900. 1110(0)

Cromwell, G.R. America scenic
... [1894] 1127(0)

Cross, A.F. Cross roads.
1936. 1129(0)

Dale, J. Round world by doctor's orders. 1894. 1154(1)

Dana, J.C. Far north-west.
1906. 1171(1)

Davis, M.L. We are Alaskans.
1931.

Davis, R.H. Let's go ...
1940. 1208(0)

DeMente, B. Once a fool...
1965. 1262(0)

Denis, F.J. Les Calif. ...
Amér. russe. 1849. 1263(0)

Dennis, J.T. On shores Inland
Sea. 1895. 1271(1)

Descript. cruise Alaska ...
n.d. 1277(1)

DeWindt, H. From Paris to N.Y.
1901. 1284(5)

DeWindt, H. My restless life.
1909. 1285(5)

Dole, N.H. Alaska.
1910. 1328(0)

[Dole, N.H.] Our northern
domain. 1910. 1329(0)

Duncan, S.T. ...Shetland to
B.C.,Alaska. 1911. 1379(0)

Ederer, B.F. Through Alaska's
back...1954. 1409(3)

Edwards, W.S. In to Yukon...
1904. 1415(0)

Eisenlohr, L.H.Memories from
Phila. ... 1918. 1427(5)

Emerson, W.C. Land of midnight
sun. 1956. 1453(0)

Enders-Schichanowsky. A. Im
Wunderland... 1926. 1465(0)

Endreson, F. Alaska Kaller...
1956. 1467(0)

Enock, C.R. Great Pac. coast
... 1909. 1477(0)

Fell, S. Threads of Alaskan
gold. n.d. 1539(0)

Finck, H.T. Pacific coast
scenic...1890. 1554(0)

Francis, F. War, waves & wanderings. 1881. 1629(0)

Franck, H.A. Lure of Alaska.
1939. 1630(0)

Franklin, L.J. Stories and
facts...1921. 1634(0)

Frede, P. Aventures lointaines
Sitka. 1887. 1642(1)

Frede, P. Aventures lointaines
Sitka. 1890. 1643(1)

George, M.M. Little journeys
... 1901. 1697(0)

Gerrish, T. Life in world's
wonderland. n.d. 1698(1)

Gerster, G. Augenschein in
Alaska...1961. 1699(0)

Gillis, C.J. Another summer.
1893. 1727(1)

Goetze, O.D. Souvenir n.w.
Alaska...n.d. 1751(5)

Gordon, R.L. Little journey
...Alaska.1931. 1782(0)

Gorrell, J.R. Trip to Alaska.
1905. 1786(1)

Hall, E.F. Under northern
lights. 1932. 1904(0)

Harrington, R.L. Cinderella
...holiday. [c1937] 1957(0)

Harrison, C.H. Summer outing
... 1891. 1964(8)

[Haselhurst, M.A.] Days forever flown. 1892. 1982(8)

Hazelton, E.C. Alaskan forget
me-nots. 1921. 2010(8)

Herbert, A. Two Dianas in
Alaska. 1909. 2074(8)

Hine, C.C. Trip to Alaska...
1889. 2118(0)

[Holbrook, S.P.] Sketches
by traveller. 1830. 2147(0)

TRAVEL. (cont.)

Holiday Mag.Books. Amer. panorama...1960.   2149(0)
Holiday Pub. Anchorage, crossroads...1962.   2150(0)
Hutchison, I.W. North to rime-
ringed sun. 1934.   2246(0)
Hyde, J. North Pacific tour...
1889.   2250(0)
Irwin, D. Alone across top
world...1935.   2298(4)
Irwin, D. One man against
north. 1940.   2299(4)
Jaques, F.P. As far as Yukon.
1951.   2331(0)
Johann, A.E. Pelzjäger ...
1937.   2362(0)
Johann, A.E. Bolyongások ...
1942.   2363(0)
Johnson, M. Journey of enchant-
ment. 1956.   2370(8)
Keeler, N.E. Trip to Alaska.
1906.   2421(0)
Klaben, H. Hey, I'm alive!
1964.   2484(0)
Kol, E. Tiszaparttól ...
1940.   2504(0)
Krug, W.G. Sprungbrett...
1953.   2547(0)
Large, R.C. Prince Rupert...
1951.   2625(0)
Lesure, T.B. How to see ...
1966.   2692(0)
Lipke, A.C. Under aurora.
1938.   2720(8)
Llorente, S. A. Orillas del
"Kusko" 1951.   2740(5)
Lotz, J.R. Some notes journey
... 1962.   2798(1)
Lukens, M.B. Inland Passage
... 1889.   2809(1)
Lund, M. Inside Passage to
Alaska. 1965.   2812(1)
MacDonald, M. Down North.
1943.   2867(7)
McFarland, J. One mad
scramble. 1940.   2890(1)
McGarvey, L. Along Alaska
trails. 1960.   2893(3)
Machetanz, S. Where else but
Alaska? [c1954]   2908(5)

MacKay, A. By trench and trail
... 1918.   2912(0)
Mallinson, F.L. My travels
... 1914.   2958(8)
Martin, A. Around and about
Alaska. 1959.   3002(0)
Meiji Daigaku. Arasuka chiiki
... 1961.   3069(0)
Mendöl, T. Az Északi-sark...
1939.   3079(0)
Miller, M. Off beaten path.
1970.   3131(0)
Möller, J. Auf nach Alaska.
1897.   3155(0)
Moore, O. Washington illus.
... [1901?]   3164(0)
Morgan, W.G. Trail of a
cheechako. 1928.   3185(8)
Morris, I.D. Pacific coast
vacation. 1901.   3199(1)
Muir, J. Picturesque Calif.
... [c1887-88]   3224(0)
Muir, J. Wilderness world...
1954.   3228(0)
Muir, J. Writings of ...
1915-24.   3229(0)
Muir, J. Travels in Alaska.
1915.   3230(0)
Myers, W. Through wonderland
... 1895.   3267(8)
National Pub. Co. Seattle...
[1907?]   3277(0)
Nome, wonderland of wealth...
1905.   3317(5)
Northwestern Alaska Chamber of
Commerce. Nome.1932. 3358(5)
Page, R.G. This is Kodiak.
1969.   3470(6)
Palmer, A. There's no place
like Nome. 1963.   3478(5)
Pape, R. Poles apart ...
1960.   3488(0)
Parkinson, E.S. Wonderland...
1894.   3494(1)
Parrish, M. Nine pounds of
luggage. 1940.   3496(0)
Perkins, A.V.W. San Diego to
to Sitka. 1902.   3536(1)
Petite, I. Meander to Alaska.
1970.   3556(1)
Phillips, E.L. Alaska summer.
1938.   3571(8)

TRAVEL. (cont.)

Pierrepont, E.W. Fifth Ave. to
Alaska. 1884.   3584(8)
Poor, H.V. Artist sees
Alaska. 1945.   3641(0)
Powell, J.L. Journey to
Alaska. 1891.   3670(8)
Powers, A. Alaska, America's
last...[1921?]   3671(0)
Pyle, E.T. Home country.
[c1947]   3707(0)
Raine, E.C. Here, there ...
[c1959]   3724(0)
Raymond & Whitcomb Co. Series
...tours...1902.   3756(1)
Raymond & Whitcomb Co. Alaska
... 1925.   3757(0)
Raymond & Whitcomb Co. ...
land cruises...1930. 3758(0)
Raymond & Whitcomb Co. Spring
tour. 1906.   3759(1)
Ridger, A.L. Wanderer's trail.
... 1914.   3815(0)
Rogers, L. On and off saddle
... 1894.   3867(0)
Rollins, A.M.W. From palm to
glacier...1892.   3871(1)
Rossiter, H. Alaska calling.
[c1954]   3892(0)
Rossman, E. Black sunlight...
1926.   3895(0)
Ruggieri, V. Du Transvaal a
l'Alaska. 1901.   3913(0)
Rydell, C. Adventures...
seafaring...1924.   3927(0)
Rydell, C. On Pacific fron-
tiers. 1924.   3928(0)
Schneider, A. In beautiful
Alaska. 1909.   4007(2)
Schneider, A. Alaskan trail.
1903.   4008(2)
Schwatka, F. Wonderland...
1886.   4022(1)
Scidmore, E.R. Alaska, sou
thern coast. 1885.   4024(1)
Scidmore, E.R. Journeyings
in Alaska. 1889.   4027(1)
Scott, E.H. Alaska days ...
[c1923]   4028(0)
Seattle Chamber of Commerce.
...tour. 1933.   4035(0)

Selle, R.A. Luck and Alaska.
1932.   4044(0)
Selle, R.A. Lure of gold.
1932.   4045(0)
Senter, G.E. Kawoo of Alaska.
[c1964]   4047(1)
Sessions, F.C. From Yellow-
stone...1890.   4066(1)
Seton-Karr, H.W. Ten yrs.
... 1890.   4069(0)
Sherman, D.F. Alaska caval-
cade. [c1943]   4113(0)
Simoens de Silva, A.C. Viagens
... 1932.   4158(0)
Sloane, H.N. Goodyear guide
state parks. 1967.   4184(0)
Spring, N. Alaska, complete
travel ... [1970]   4269(0)
Stevenson, A.E. From N.Y. to
Alaska. 1893.   ,   4341(0)
Strahorn, C.A. 15,000 miles by
stage...1911.   4357(0)
Stuck, H. Winter circuit
Arctic coast. 1920.   4369(4)
Stuck, H. 10,000 miles dog
sled Interior.1914.   4370(3)
Stuck, H. Voyage Yukon...
1917.   4373(0)
Sunset, edits. Alaska.
1963.   4400(0)
Taylor, C.M. Touring Alaska.
[c1901]   4468(1)
This is Alaska.
1964.   4488(0)
Tichy, H. Alaska; ein Paradies
... 1951.   4532(0)
Tichy, H. Alaszka.
1941.   4533(0)
Viksten, A. Pålsjägarnas
Paradis. 1955.   4701(8)
Villard, H. Journey to Alaska.
1899.   4702(8)
Vyvyan, C.C.(R.) Arctic adven-
ture. 1961.   4718(0)
Wallace, F.T. Alaska, a
dream. n.d.   4734(8)
Watson, W.W. Our Alaskan trip
in letters. 1910.   4757(1)
Webb,W.S. Calif. & Alaska ...
1890.   4764(0)
Weed, A.L. Grandma goes to
Arctic. 1957.   4778(4)

TRAVEL. (cont.)

Wendt, F. Life along Yukon ...
 1936. 4793(0)
Wetherell, J.E. Strange
 corners ... 1927. 4801(0)
White, E.W., Pub. Co. Chips
 & sticks...1886. 4816(0)
Wiley, W.H. Yosemite, Alaska
 ... 1893. 4869(0)
Willoughby, B. Alaska holiday.
 1940. 4893(0)
Wilson, J.A. Bits of Alaska.
 [c1908] 4912(0)
Winslow, K. Alaska bound.
 1960. 4923(0)
[Wittemann, A.] Picturesque
 Alaska. 1888. 4939(0)
Woodcock, G. Ravens & prophets
 ... [c1952] 4956(1)
Woodman, A.J. Picturesque
 Alaska. 1889. 4957(1)

WHALING.

Aldrich, H.L. Arctic Alaska
 and Siberia. 1889. 167(4)
Bering Sea Commercial Co.
 Alaska whaling...n.d. 525(5)
Birkeland, K.B. Whalers of
 Akutan. 1926. 558(6)
Bodfish, H.H. Chasing bowhead.
 1936. 591(4)
Brandt, K. Whale oil ...
 1940. 646(0)
Brandt, K. Whaling and whale
 oil ... 1948. 647(0)
Burns, W.N. Year with a
 whaler. 1913. 740(5)
Colnett, J. Journal...*Argonaut*
 ... 1940. 989(5)
Colnett, J. Voyage So. Atlantic
 ...*Rattler*...1787. 990(5)
Connolly, J.B. Master mariner
 ...Delano. 1943. 1004(5)

Cook, J.A. Pursuing whale.
 1926. 1055(4)
Delano, A. Narrat. voyages...
 1817. 1249(5)
Erskine, W.F. White water.
 1960. 1491(5)
Faber, K. Unter Eskimos Wal-
 fischfängern. 1916. 1509(5)
Holmes, L. Arctic whaleman
 Citizen...1857. 2159(4)
Hunt, C.E. *Shenandoah* ...
 1867. 2234(5)
Jenkens, J.T. Whales and
 modern whaling. 1932.2337(0)
MacDonald, R. Narrat. ... Pac.
 whale ... 1923. 2871(5)
Morgan, M.C. Dixie raider ...
 Shenandoah. 1948. 3182(5)
Munger, J.F. Two yrs. in Pac.
 ... 1852. 3239(4)
Nishimoto, S. Report whale
 marking...1951. 3312(5)
Packard, W. Young ice whalers.
 1903. 3468(4)
Scammon, C.M. Marine mammals
 ... 1874. 3990(0)
Slepŧsov, M.M. Biologiĭa i
 promysel ... 1955. 4180(0)
Starbuck, A. Hist.Amer. whale
 fishery...1878. 4285(0)
Tilton, G.F. Cap'n George
 Fred. 1929. 4541(4)
Van Steensel, M. People of
 light. 1966. 4651(4)
Watson, A.C. Long harpoon...
 1929. 4755(4)
West, E.L. Captain's papers.
 1965. 4798(5)
Whittle, W.C. Cruises ...
 "Shenandoah" ...1910.4847(5)
Williams, H. One whaling
 family. 1964. 4879(0)